Africa 68-69

W9-BPM-343

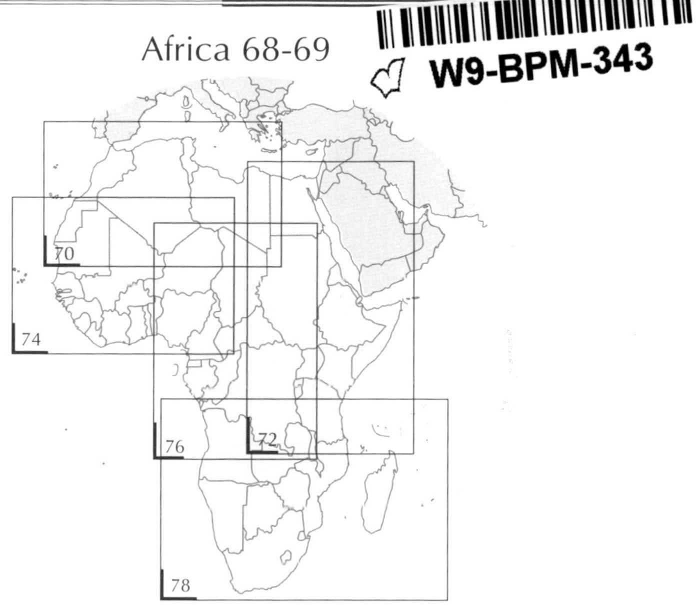

Europe 80-81

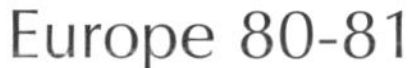

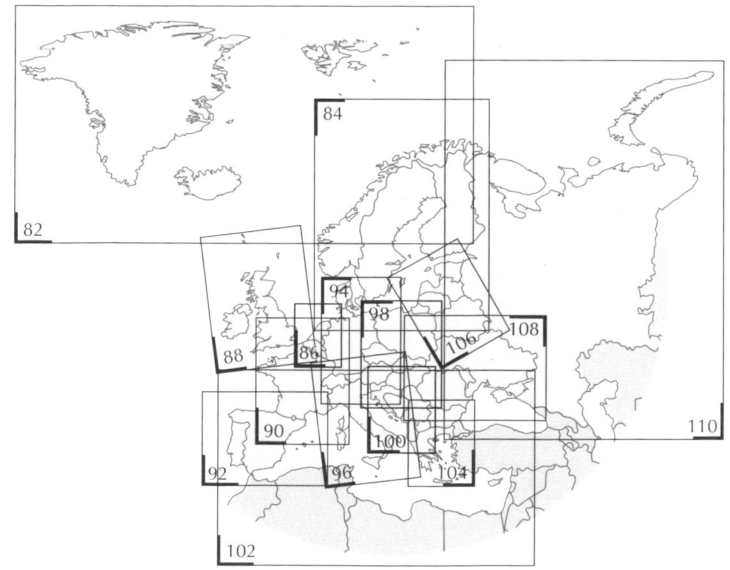

ESSENTIAL
ATLAS
OF THE WORLD

LONDON, NEW YORK, MUNICH, MELBOURNE, DELHI

LONDON, NEW YORK, MELBOURNE, MUNICH, DELHI

FOR THE SIXTH EDITION

PUBLISHING DIRECTOR   Jonathan Metcalf
ART DIRECTOR   Bryn Walls
SENIOR CARTOGRAPHIC MANAGER   David Roberts
SENIOR CARTOGRAPHIC EDITOR   Simon Mumford
PROJECT CARTOGRAPHER   Paul Eames
SYSTEMS COORDINATOR   Philip Rowles
PRODUCTION   Sarah Hewitt

DORLING KINDERSLEY CARTOGRAPHY

PROJECT CARTOGRAPHY AND DESIGN
Julia Lunn, Julie Turner

CARTOGRAPHERS
James Anderson, Roger Bullen, Martin Darlison,
Simon Mumford, John Plumer, Peter Winfield

DESIGN
Katy Wall

INDEX-GAZETTEER
Natalie Clarkson, Ruth Duxbury, Margaret Hynes, Margaret Stevenson

PRODUCTION
Hilary Stephens, David Proffit

EDITORIAL DIRECTION
Andrew Heritage

ART DIRECTION
Chez Picthall

First American edition 1997. Second Edition 1998. Third Edition 2001.
Fourth Edition 2003. Fifth Edition 2005. Sixth Edition 2008.
Previously published as the Concise World Atlas

Published in the United States by Dorling Kindersley Publishing, 375 Hudson Street,
New York, New York 10014
Copyright © 1997, 1998, 2001, 2003, 2005, 2008 Dorling Kindersley Limited, London

A CIP catalog record for this book is available from the Library of Congress

ISBN 978-0-7566-3819-1

Reprographics by Altaimage Ltd, London, UK
Printed and bound by Tien Wah Press, Singapore

See our complete catalog at www.dk.com

Key to map symbols

Physical features

Elevation

- 4000m/13,124ft
- 2000m/6562ft
- 1,000m/3281ft
- 500m/1640ft
- 250m/820ft
- 100m/328ft
- 0
- Below sea level

△	Mountain
▽	Depression
◬	Volcano
)(	Pass/tunnel
▨	Sandy desert

Drainage features

———	Major perennial river
———	Minor perennial river
- - -	Seasonal river
———	Canal
|	Waterfall
⬭	Perennial lake
⬭	Seasonal lake
▨	Wetland

Ice features

▢	Permanent ice cap/ice shelf
▲▲▲	Winter limit of pack ice
▲▲▲	Summer limit of pack ice

Borders

▬▬▬	Full international border
▬ ▬ ▬	Disputed de facto border
• • • •	Territorial claim border
×—×—×	Cease-fire line
▬ ▬ ▪	Undefined boundary
———	Internal administrative boundary

Communications

———	Major road
———	Minor road
———	Rail
✈	International airport

Settlements

◉	Above 500,000
◉	100,000 to 500,000
○	50,000 to 100,000
○	Below 50,000
●	National capital
◉	Internal administrative capital

Miscellaneous features

+	Site of interest
⌐⌐⌐⌐	Ancient wall

Graticule features

———	Line of latitude/longitude/Equator
- - -	Tropic/Polar circle
25°	Degrees of latitude/longitude

Names

Physical features

Andes	
Sahara	Landscape features
Ardennes	
Land's End	Headland
Mont Blanc 4,807m	Elevation/volcano/pass
Blue Nile	River/canal/waterfall
Ross Ice Shelf	Ice feature
PACIFIC OCEAN	
Sulu Sea	Sea features
Palk Strait	
Chile Rise	Undersea feature

Regions

FRANCE	Country
JERSEY (to UK)	Dependent territory
KANSAS	Administrative region
Dordogne	Cultural region

Settlements

PARIS	Capital city
SAN JUAN	Dependent territory capital city
Chicago	
Kettering	Other settlements
Burke	

Inset map symbols

▢	Urban area
⬭	City
▢	Park
▪	Place of interest
▫	Suburb/district

Contents

The World Today

Flags of the World..................................6-7
The Political World................................8-9
The Physical World...............................10-11
Time Zones...12-13
Geology & Structure.............................14-15
World Climate.......................................16-17
Ocean Currents.....................................18-19
Life Zones...20-21
Population...22-23
Languages...24-25
Religion...26-27
The Global Economy..............................28-29
Global Conflict......................................30-31

The World's Regions

North & Central America

North & Central America.......................34-35
Western Canada & Alaska.......................36-37
Eastern Canada.....................................38-39
USA: The Northeast...............................40-41
USA: The Southeast...............................42-43
  Bermuda
USA: Central States...............................44-45
USA: The West......................................46-47
  Los Angeles & Hawai'i

USA: The Southwest...............................48-49
Mexico..50-51
Central America.....................................52-53
The Caribbean.......................................54-55
  Jamaica, St. Lucia, & Barbados

South America

South America.......................................56-57
Northern South America.........................58-59
Western South America..........................60-61
  Galapagos Islands
Brazil..62-63
Southern South America.........................64-65
The Atlantic Ocean................................66-67

Africa

Africa..68-69
Northwest Africa....................................70-71
Northeast Africa.....................................72-73
West Africa..74-75
Central Africa...76-77
  Sao Tome & Principe
Southern Africa......................................78-79

Europe

Europe..80-81
The North Atlantic.................................82-83
Scandinavia & Finland............................84-85
The Low Countries.................................86-87
The British Isles.....................................88-89
  London

continued....

Europe *continued*

France, Andorra, & Monaco 90-91
  Paris, Andorra, & Monaco
Spain & Portugal 92-93
  Azores & Gibraltar
Germany & the Alpine States 94-95
  Liechtenstein
Italy 96-97
  San Marino & Vatican City
Central Europe 98-99
Southeast Europe 100-101
  Bosnia & Herzegovina
The Mediterranean 102-103
  Malta & Cyprus
Bulgaria & Greece 104-105
The Baltic States & Belarus 106-107
Ukraine, Moldova,
  & Romania 108-109
European Russia 110-111

North & West Asia

North & West Asia 112-113
Russia & Kazakhstan 114-115
Turkey & the Caucasus 116-117
The Near East 118-119
  West Bank
The Middle East 120-121
Central Asia 122-123

South & East Asia

South & East Asia 124-125
Western China & Mongolia 126-127

Eastern China & Korea 128-129
  Hong Kong (Xianggang)
Japan 130-131
  Tokyo & Nansei-Shoto
South India & Sri Lanka 132-133
North India, Pakistan,
  & Bangladesh 134-135
Mainland Southeast Asia 136-137
Maritime Southeast Asia 138-139
  Singapore
The Indian Ocean 140-141

Australasia & Oceania

Australasia & Oceania 142-143
The Southwest Pacific 144-145
Western Australia 146-147
Eastern Australia 148-149
  Sydney
New Zealand 150-151
The Pacific Ocean 152-153
Antarctica 154
The Arctic Ocean 155

Index– Gazetteer

Overseas Territories
  & Dependencies 156-159
Glossary of Geographical
  Terms 160-161
Continental Factfiles 162-163
Geographical Comparisons 164-166
Index-Gazetteer of Places
  & Countries 167-256

THE WORLD TODAY
Flags of the World

NORTH & CENTRAL AMERICA

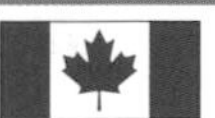

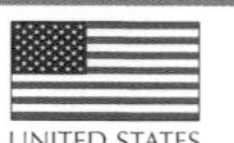

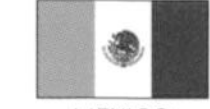

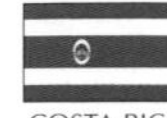

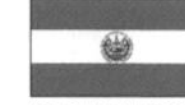

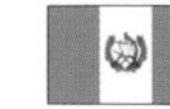

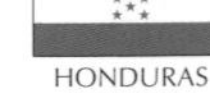

CANADA PAGES 36-39	UNITED STATES OF AMERICA PAGES 40-49	MEXICO PAGES 50-51	BELIZE PAGES 52-53	COSTA RICA PAGES 52-53	EL SALVADOR PAGES 52-53	GUATEMALA PAGES 52-53	HONDURAS PAGES 52-53

SOUTH AMER[I]

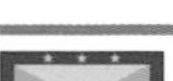

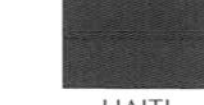

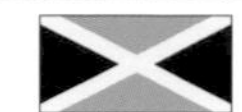

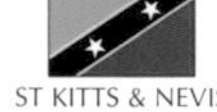

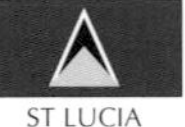

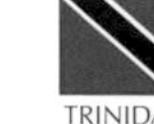

GRENADA PAGES 54-55	HAITI PAGES 54-55	JAMAICA PAGES 54-55	ST KITTS & NEVIS PAGES 54-55	ST LUCIA PAGES 54-55	ST VINCENT & THE GRENADINES PAGES 54-55	TRINIDAD & TOBAGO PAGES 54-55	COLOMBIA PAGES 58-59

AFRICA

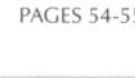

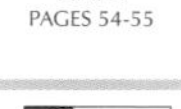

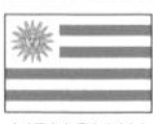

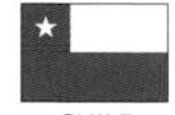

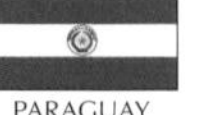

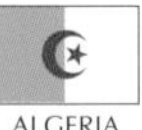

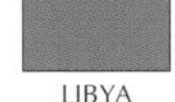

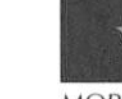

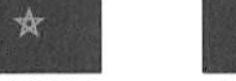

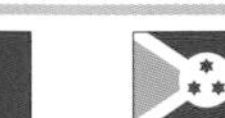

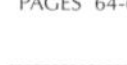

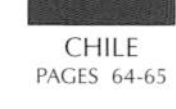

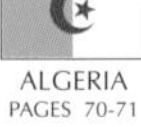

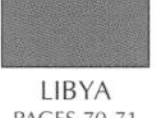

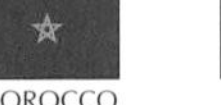

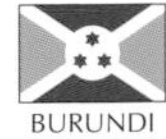

URUGUAY PAGES 64-65	CHILE PAGES 64-65	PARAGUAY PAGES 64-65	ALGERIA PAGES 70-71	LIBYA PAGES 70-71	MOROCCO PAGES 70-71	TUNISIA PAGES 70-71	BURUNDI PAGES 72-73
TANZANIA PAGES 72-73	UGANDA PAGES 72-73	BENIN PAGES 74-75	BURKINA FASO PAGES 74-75	CAPE VERDE PAGES 74-75	CÔTE D'IVOIRE (IVORY COAST) PAGES 74-75	GAMBIA PAGES 74-75	GHANA PAGES 74-75
SIERRA LEONE PAGES 74-75	TOGO PAGES 74-75	CAMEROON PAGES 76-77	CENTRAL AFRICAN REPUBLIC PAGES 76-77	CHAD PAGES 76-77	CONGO PAGES 76-77	DEM. REP. CONGO PAGES 76-77	EQUATORIAL GUINEA PAGES 76-77
MAURITIUS PAGES 78-79	MOZAMBIQUE PAGES 78-79	NAMIBIA PAGES 78-79	SEYCHELLES PAGES 78-79	SOUTH AFRICA PAGES 78-79	SWAZILAND PAGES 78-79	ZAMBIA PAGES 78-79	ZIMBABWE PAGES 78-79
IRELAND PAGES 88-89	UNITED KINGDOM PAGES 88-89	FRANCE PAGES 90-91	MONACO PAGES 90-91	ANDORRA PAGES 90-91	PORTUGAL PAGES 92-93	SPAIN PAGES 92-93	AUSTRIA PAGES 94-95
HUNGARY PAGES 98-99	POLAND PAGES 98-99	SLOVAKIA PAGES 98-99	ALBANIA PAGES 100-101	BOSNIA & HERZEGOVINA PAGES 100-101	CROATIA PAGES 100-101	MACEDONIA PAGES 100-101	MONTENEGRO PAGES 100-101

ASIA

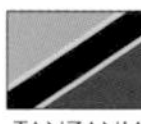

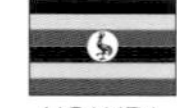

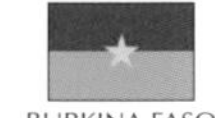

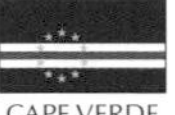

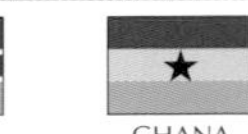

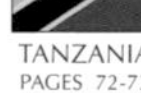

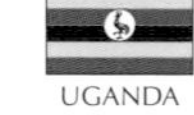

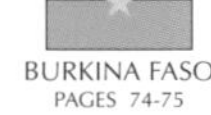

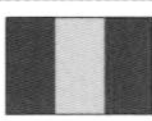

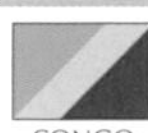

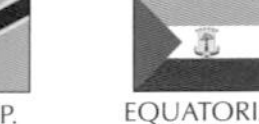

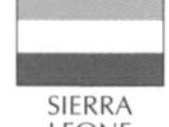

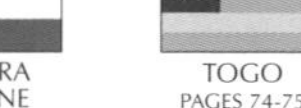

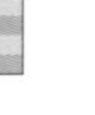

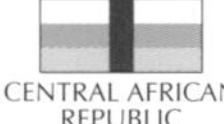

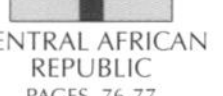

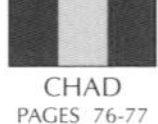

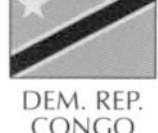

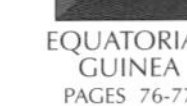

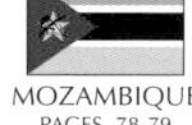

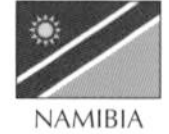

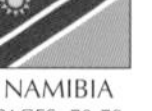

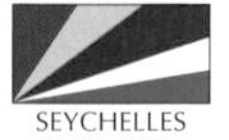

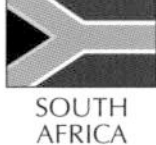

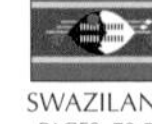

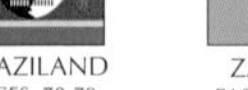

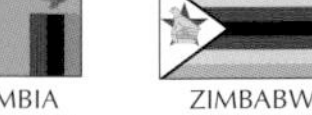

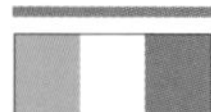

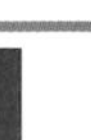

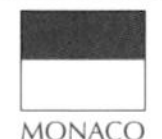

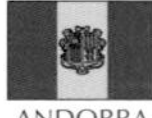

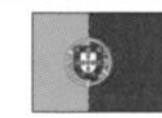

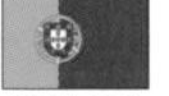

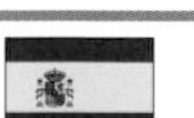

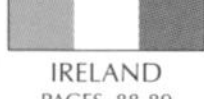

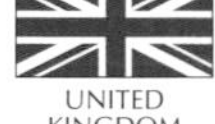

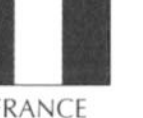

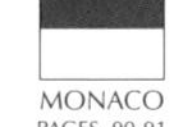

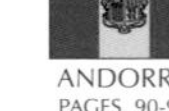

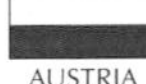

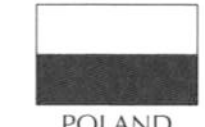

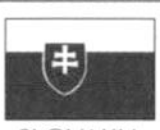

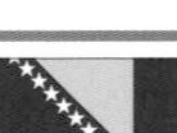

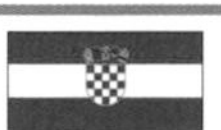

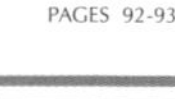

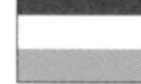

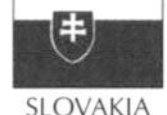

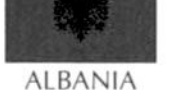

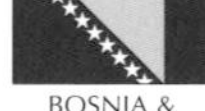

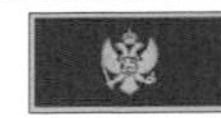

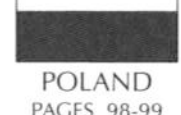

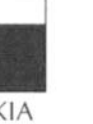

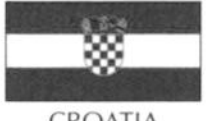

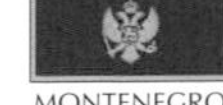

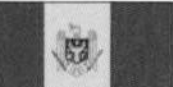

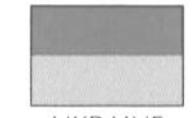

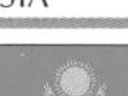

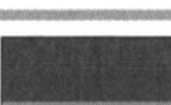

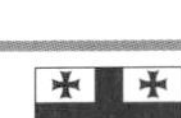

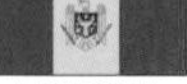

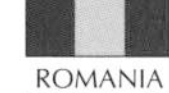

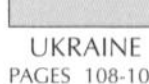

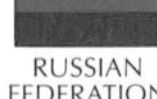

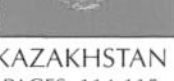

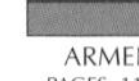

MOLDOVA PAGES 108-109	ROMANIA PAGES 108-109	UKRAINE PAGES 108-109	RUSSIAN FEDERATION PAGES 110-115	KAZAKHSTAN PAGES 114-115	ARMENIA PAGES 116-117	AZERBAIJAN PAGES 116-117	GEORGIA PAGES 116-117
KUWAIT PAGES 120-121	OMAN PAGES 120-121	QATAR PAGES 120-121	SAUDI ARABIA PAGES 120-121	UNITED ARAB EMIRATES PAGES 120-121	YEMEN PAGES 120-121	AFGHANISTAN PAGES 122-123	KYRGYZSTAN PAGES 122-123
JAPAN PAGES 130-131	INDIA PAGES 132-135	SRI LANKA PAGES 132-133	MALDIVES PAGES 132-133	PAKISTAN PAGES 134-135	BANGLADESH PAGES 134-135	BHUTAN PAGES 134-135	NEPAL PAGES 134-135	CAMBODIA PAGES 136-137

AUSTRALASIA & OCEANIA

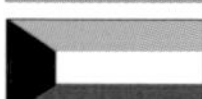

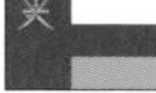

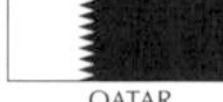

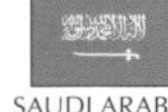

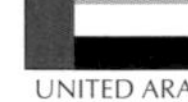

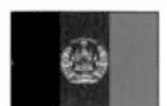

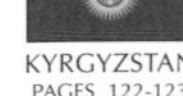

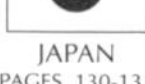

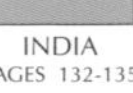

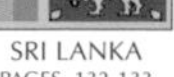

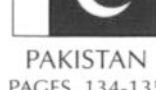

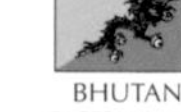

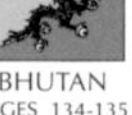

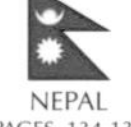

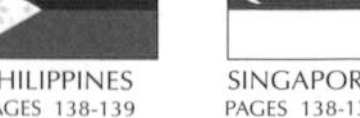

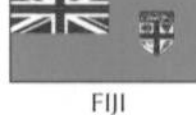

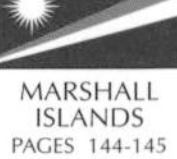

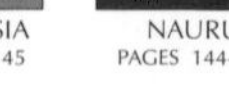

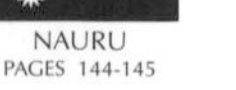

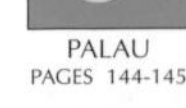

PHILIPPINES PAGES 138-139	SINGAPORE PAGES 138-139	FIJI PAGES 144-145	KIRIBATI PAGES 144-145	MARSHALL ISLANDS PAGES 144-145	MICRONESIA PAGES 144-145	NAURU PAGES 144-145	PALAU PAGES 144-145

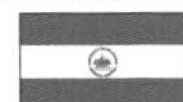

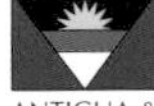

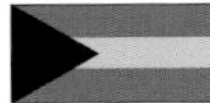

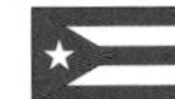

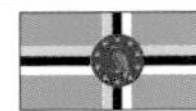

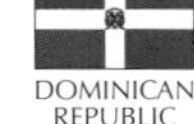

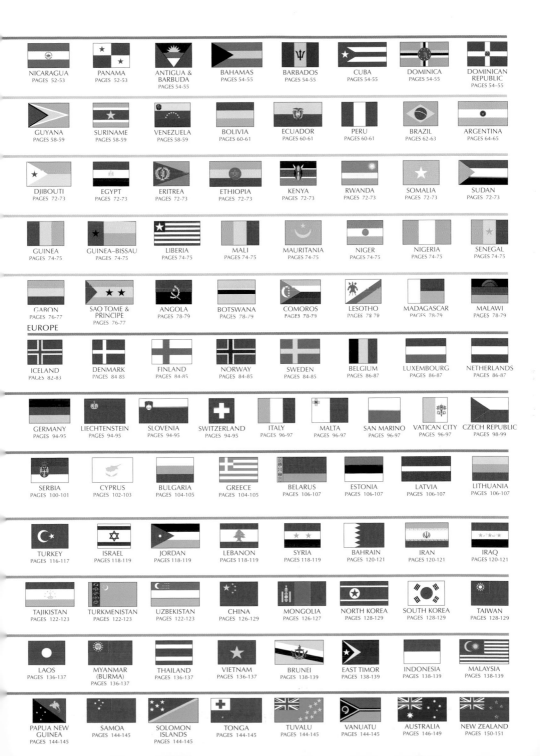

NICARAGUA
PAGES 52-53

PANAMA
PAGES 52-53

**ANTIGUA &
BARBUDA**
PAGES 54-55

BAHAMAS
PAGES 54-55

BARBADOS
PAGES 54-55

CUBA
PAGES 54-55

DOMINICA
PAGES 54-55

**DOMINICAN
REPUBLIC**
PAGES 54–55

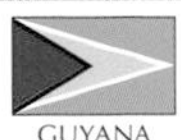

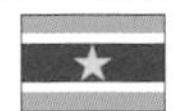

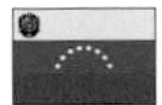

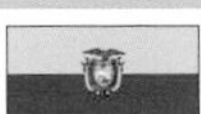

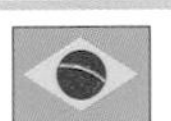

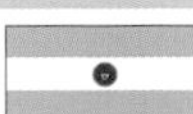

GUYANA
PAGES 58-59

SURINAME
PAGES 58-59

VENEZUELA
PAGES 58-59

BOLIVIA
PAGES 60-61

ECUADOR
PAGES 60-61

PERU
PAGES 60-61

BRAZIL
PAGES 62-63

ARGENTINA
PAGES 64-65

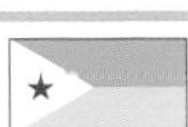

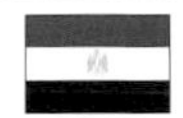

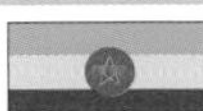

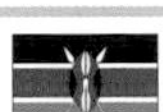

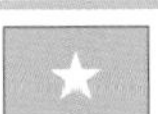

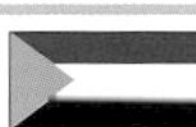

DJIBOUTI
PAGES 72-73

EGYPT
PAGES 72-73

ERITREA
PAGES 72-73

ETHIOPIA
PAGES 72-73

KENYA
PAGES 72-73

RWANDA
PAGES 72-73

SOMALIA
PAGES 72-73

SUDAN
PAGES 72-73

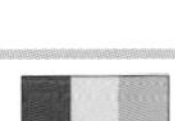

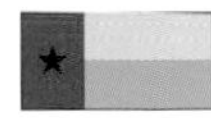

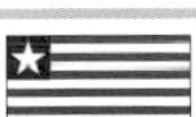

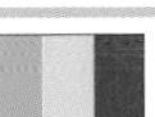

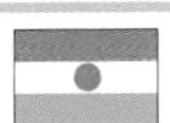

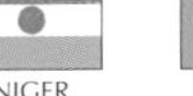

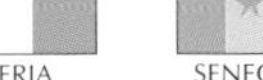

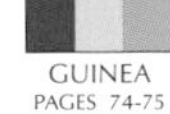

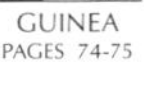

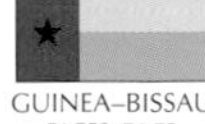

GUINEA
PAGES 74-75

GUINEA–BISSAU
PAGES 74-75

LIBERIA
PAGES 74-75

MALI
PAGES 74-75

MAURITANIA
PAGES 74-75

NIGER
PAGES 74-75

NIGERIA
PAGES 74-75

SENEGAL
PAGES 74-75

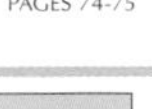

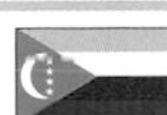

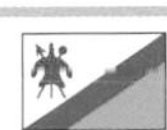

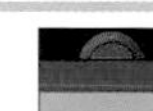

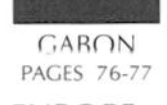

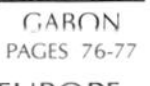

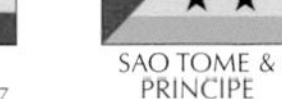

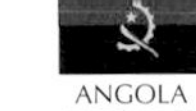

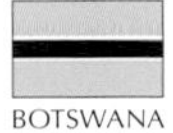

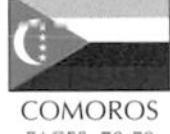

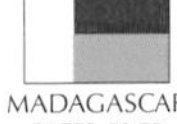

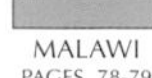

GABON
PAGES 76-77

**SAO TOME &
PRINCIPE**
PAGES 76-77

ANGOLA
PAGES 78-79

BOTSWANA
PAGES 78-79

COMOROS
PAGES 78-79

LESOTHO
PAGES 78-79

MADAGASCAR
PAGES 78-79

MALAWI
PAGES 78-79

EUROPE

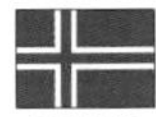

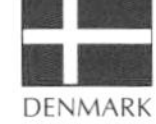

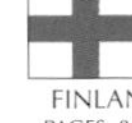

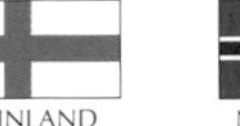

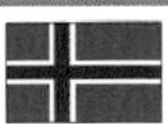

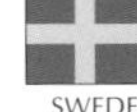

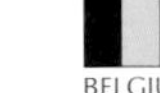

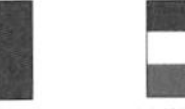

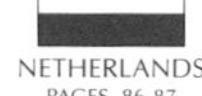

ICELAND
PAGES 82-83

DENMARK
PAGES 84-85

FINLAND
PAGES 84-85

NORWAY
PAGES 84-85

SWEDEN
PAGES 84-85

BELGIUM
PAGES 86-87

LUXEMBOURG
PAGES 86-87

NETHERLANDS
PAGES 86-87

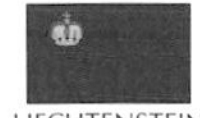

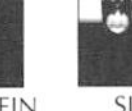

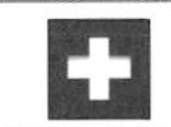

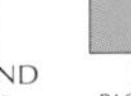

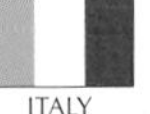

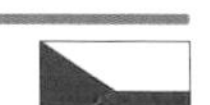

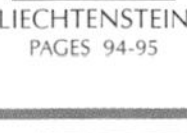

GERMANY
PAGES 94-95

LIECHTENSTEIN
PAGES 94-95

SLOVENIA
PAGES 94-95

SWITZERLAND
PAGES 94-95

ITALY
PAGES 96-97

MALTA
PAGES 96-97

SAN MARINO
PAGES 96-97

VATICAN CITY
PAGES 96-97

CZECH REPUBLIC
PAGES 98-99

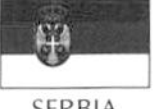

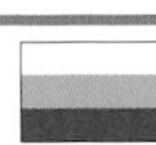

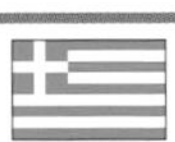

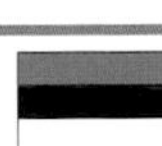

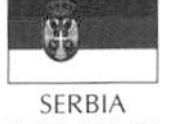

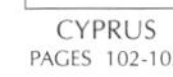

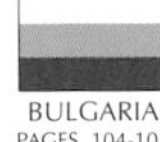

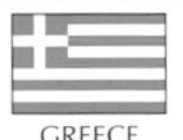

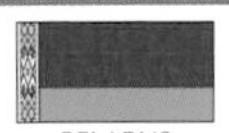

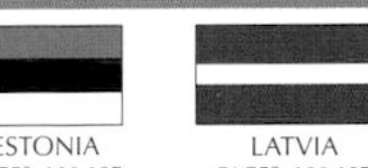

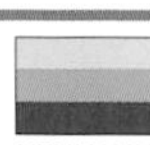

SERBIA
PAGES 100-101

CYPRUS
PAGES 102-103

BULGARIA
PAGES 104-105

GREECE
PAGES 104-105

BELARUS
PAGES 106-107

ESTONIA
PAGES 106-107

LATVIA
PAGES 106-107

LITHUANIA
PAGES 106-107

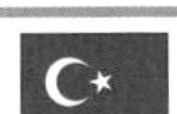

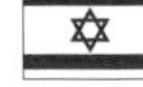

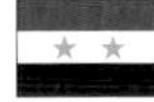

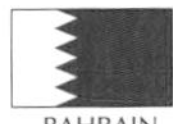

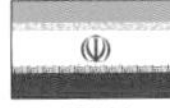

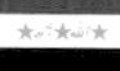

TURKEY
PAGES 116-117

ISRAEL
PAGES 118-119

JORDAN
PAGES 118-119

LEBANON
PAGES 118-119

SYRIA
PAGES 118-119

BAHRAIN
PAGES 120-121

IRAN
PAGES 120-121

IRAQ
PAGES 120-121

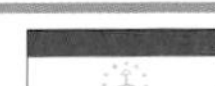

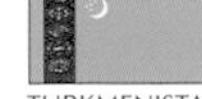

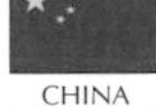

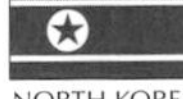

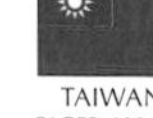

TAJIKISTAN
PAGES 122-123

TURKMENISTAN
PAGES 122-123

UZBEKISTAN
PAGES 122-123

CHINA
PAGES 126-129

MONGOLIA
PAGES 126-127

NORTH KOREA
PAGES 128-129

SOUTH KOREA
PAGES 128-129

TAIWAN
PAGES 128-129

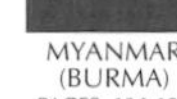

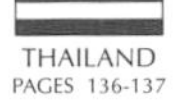

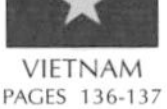

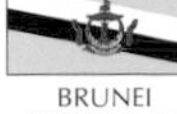

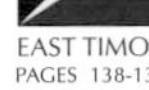

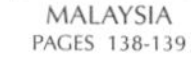

LAOS
PAGES 136-137

**MYANMAR
(BURMA)**
PAGES 136-137

THAILAND
PAGES 136-137

VIETNAM
PAGES 136-137

BRUNEI
PAGES 138-139

EAST TIMOR
PAGES 138-139

INDONESIA
PAGES 138-139

MALAYSIA
PAGES 138-139

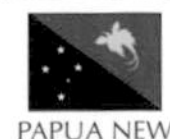

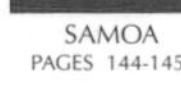

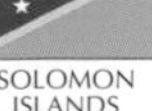

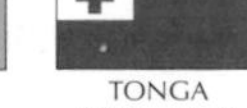

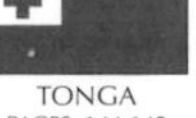

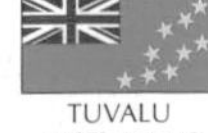

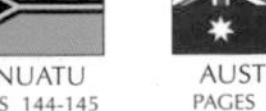

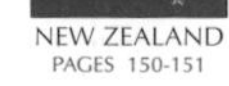

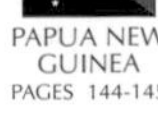

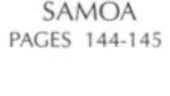

**PAPUA NEW
GUINEA**
PAGES 144-145

SAMOA
PAGES 144-145

**SOLOMON
ISLANDS**
PAGES 144-145

TONGA
PAGES 144-145

TUVALU
PAGES 144-145

VANUATU
PAGES 144-145

AUSTRALIA
PAGES 146-149

NEW ZEALAND
PAGES 150-151

The Political World

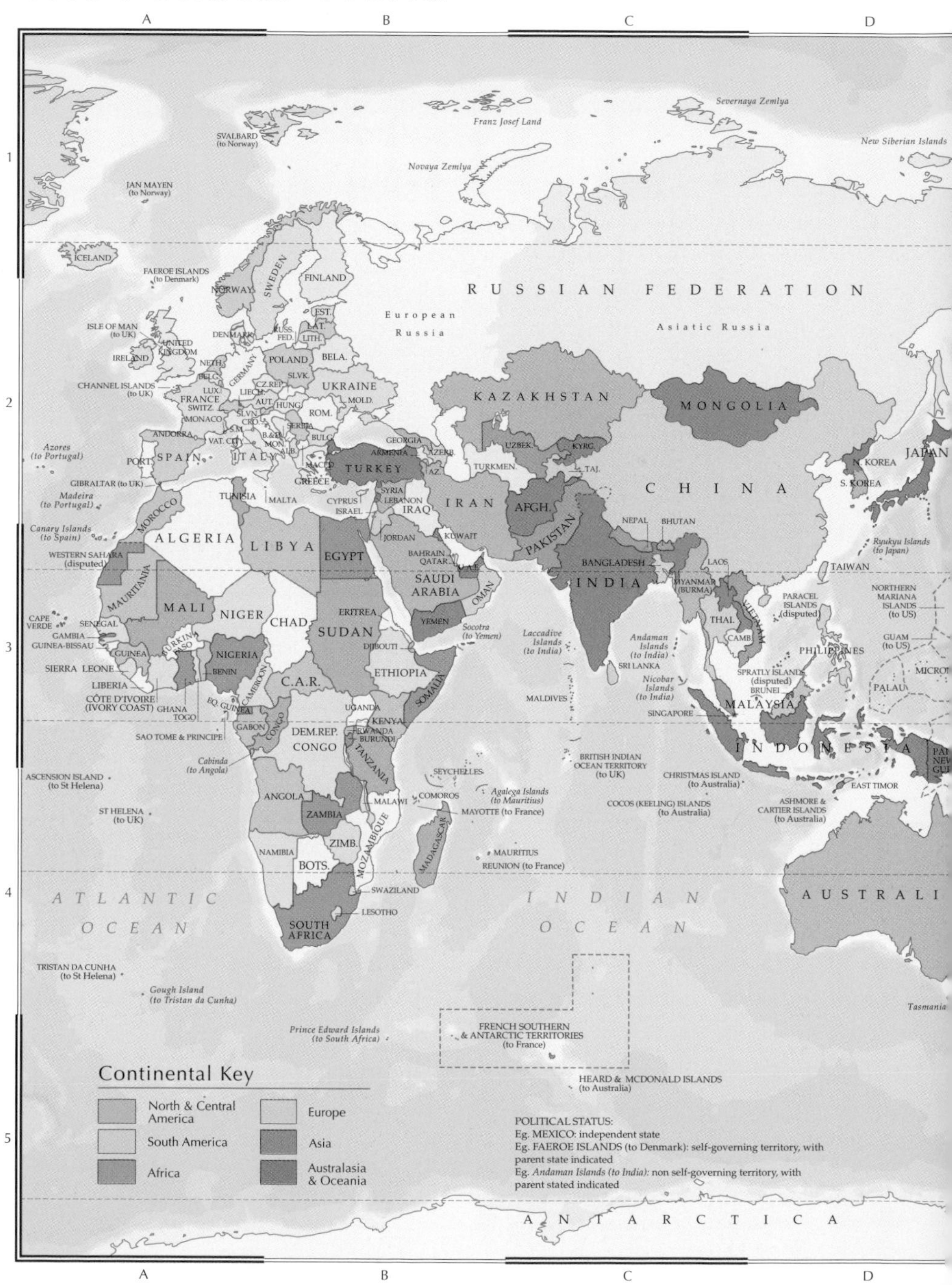

Continental Key

North & Central America	Europe
South America	Asia
Africa	Australasia & Oceania

POLITICAL STATUS:
Eg. MEXICO: independent state
Eg. FAEROE ISLANDS (to Denmark): self-governing territory, with parent state indicated
Eg. *Andaman Islands (to India)*: non self-governing territory, with parent stated indicated

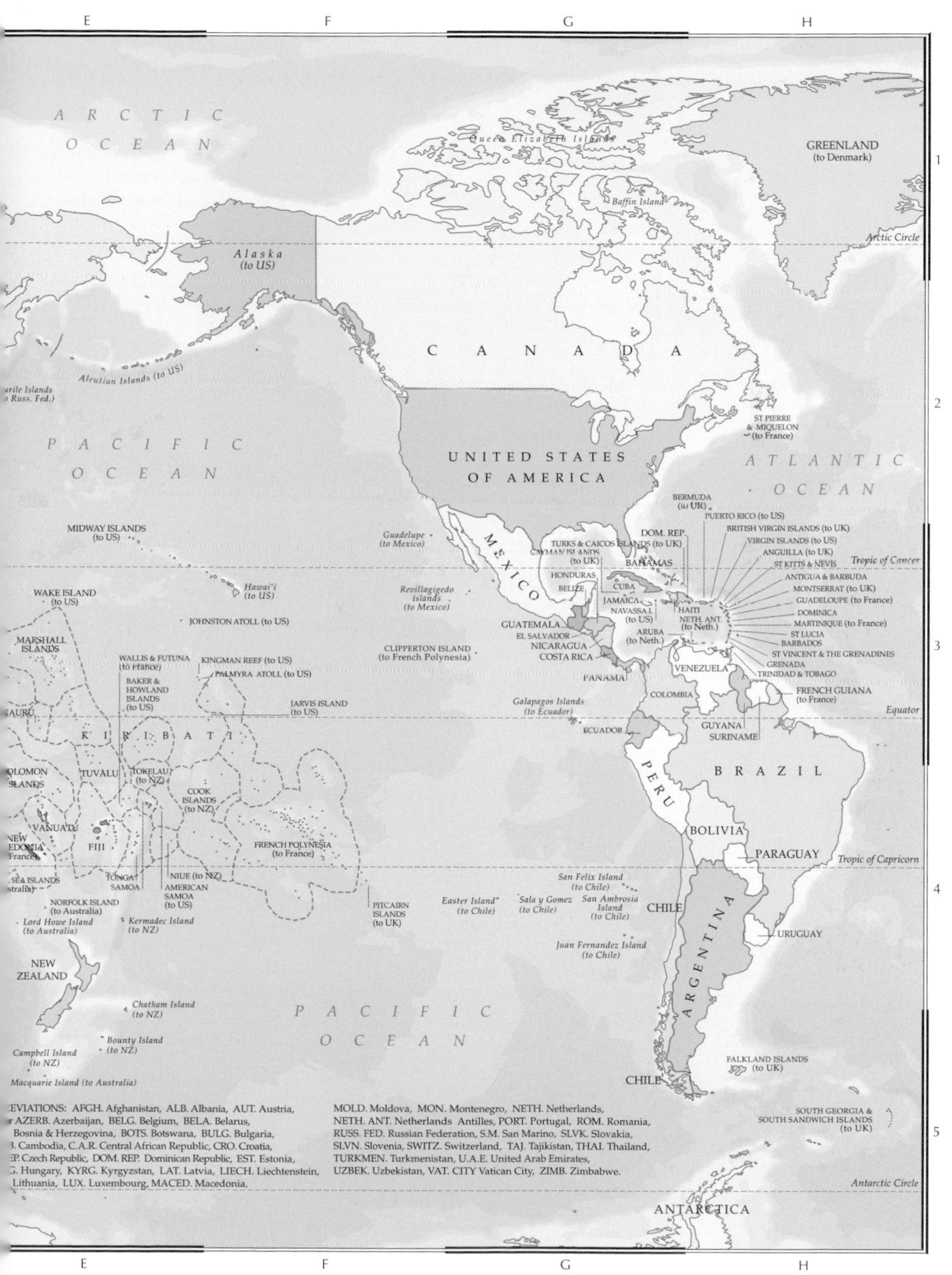

A R C T I C
O C E A N

Queen Elizabeth Islands

GREENLAND
(to Denmark)

1

Baffin Island

Arctic Circle

Alaska
(to US)

C A N A D A

2

*arile Islands
o Russ. Fed.)*

Aleutian Islands (to US)

P A C I F I C

O C E A N

UNITED STATES
OF AMERICA

A T L A N T I C

O C E A N

ST PIERRE
& MIQUELON
(to France)

MIDWAY ISLANDS
(to US)

BERMUDA
(to UK)

PUERTO RICO (to US)
BRITISH VIRGIN ISLANDS (to UK)
VIRGIN ISLANDS (to UK)
ANGUILLA (to UK)
ST KITTS & NEVIS

Tropic of Cancer

WAKE ISLAND
(to US)

Guadalupe
(to Mexico)

DOM. REP.
TURKS & CAICOS ISLANDS (to UK)
CAYMAN ISLANDS
(to UK)

*Revillagigedo
islands
(to Mexico)*

Hawai'i
(to US)

BAHAMAS

HONDURAS
BELIZE

CUBA

ANTIGUA & BARBUDA
MONTSERRAT (to UK)
GUADELOUPE (to France)
DOMINICA
MARTINIQUE (to France)
ST LUCIA
BARBADOS

MARSHALL
ISLANDS

JOHNSTON ATOLL (to US)

JAMAICA
NAVASSA I.
(to US)

HAITI
NETH. ANT.
(to Neth.)

WALLIS & FUTUNA
(to France)

KINGMAN REEF (to US)
PALMYRA ATOLL (to US)

CLIPPERTON ISLAND
(to French Polynesia)

GUATEMALA
EL SALVADOR
NICARAGUA
COSTA RICA

ARUBA
(to Neth.)

ST VINCENT & THE GRENADINES
GRENADA
TRINIDAD & TOBAGO

BAKER &
HOWLAND
ISLANDS
(to US)

AURG.

JARVIS ISLAND
(to US)

PANAMA

VENEZUELA

FRENCH GUIANA
(to France)

K I R I B A T I

*Galapagos Islands
(to Ecuador)*

COLOMBIA

GUYANA
SURINAME

Equator

ECUADOR

OLOMON
SLANDS

TUVALU

TOKELAU
(to NZ)

COOK
ISLANDS
(to NZ)

P
E
R
U

B R A Z I L

VANUATU

NEW
EDONIA
France)

FIJI

FRENCH POLYNESIA
(to France)

BOLIVIA

PARAGUAY

Tropic of Capricorn

SEA ISLANDS
stralia)

TONGA
SAMOA

NIUE (to NZ)
AMERICAN
SAMOA
(to US)

PITCAIRN
ISLANDS
(to UK)

Easter Island
(to Chile)

*San Felix Island
(to Chile)*

*Sala y Gomez
(to Chile)*

*San Ambrosia
Island
(to Chile)*

CHILE

A
R
G
E
N
T
I
N
A

URUGUAY

4

NORFOLK ISLAND
(to Australia)
*Lord Howe Island
(to Australia)*

*Kermadec Island
(to NZ)*

*Juan Fernandez Island
(to Chile)*

NEW
ZEALAND

*Chatham Island
(to NZ)*

P A C I F I C

*Campbell Island
(to NZ)*

*Bounty Island
(to NZ)*

O C E A N

FALKLAND ISLANDS
(to UK)

Macquarie Island (to Australia)

CHILE

SOUTH GEORGIA &
SOUTH SANDWICH ISLANDS
(to UK)

5

Antarctic Circle

ANTARCTICA

The Physical World

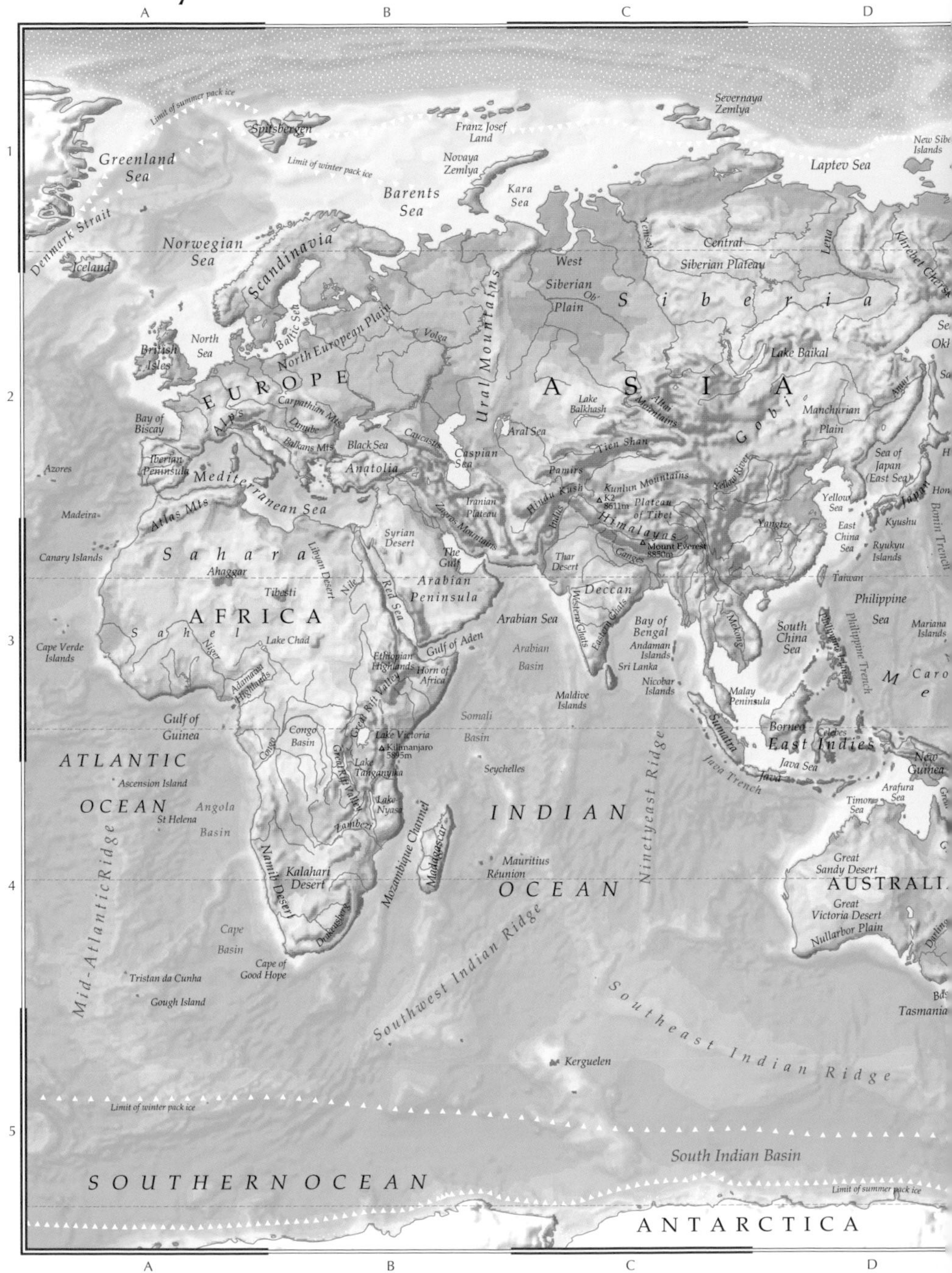

Limit of summer pack ice
Spitsbergen
Greenland Sea
Franz Josef Land
New Siberian Islands
Denmark Strait
Limit of winter pack ice
Novaya Zemlya
Laptev Sea
Barents Sea
Kara Sea
Iceland
Norwegian Sea
Scandinavia
West Siberian Plain
Central Siberian Plateau
S i b e r i a
Sea of Okl
British Isles
North Sea
Baltic Sea
North European Plain
Ural Mountains
Ob
A S I A
Lake Baikal
E U R O P E
Alps
Carpathian Mts.
Danube
Volga
Lake Balkhash
Altai Mountains
Gobi
Manchurian Plain
Sea of Japan (East Sea)
Hon
Bay of Biscay
Balkans Mts.
Black Sea
Caucasus
Aral Sea
Caspian Sea
Tien Shan
Yenisey
Yellow River
Kyushu
Azores
Iberian Peninsula
Anatolia
Pamirs
Kunlun Mountains
Yellow Sea
Ryukyu Islands
Madeira
Atlas Mts.
Mediterranean Sea
Syrian Desert
Iranian Plateau
Hindu Kush
Plateau of Tibet
Himalayas
Yangtze
East China Sea
Bonin Trench
Canary Islands
S a h a r a
Libyan Desert
Zagros Mountains
The Gulf
Mount Everest 8850M
Ganges
Taiwan
Cape Verde Islands
Ahaggar
Tibesti
Nile
Arabian Peninsula
Thar Desert
Deccan
Philippine Sea
Mariana Islands
A F R I C A
S a h e l
Niger
Red Sea
Gulf of Aden
Arabian Sea
Western Ghats
Bay of Bengal
Mekong
South China Sea
M Caro
Lake Chad
Ethiopian Highlands
Arabian Basin
Andaman Islands
Sri Lanka
Philippine Trench
Cape Verde Islands
Horn of Africa
Maldive Islands
Nicobar Islands
Malay Peninsula
Borneo
Celebes
East Indies
Gulf of Guinea
Congo Basin
Kilimanjaro 5895M
Lake Victoria
Somali Basin
Sumatra
Java Sea
New Guinea
ATLANTIC
Congo
Ascension Island
Great Rift Valley
Lake Tanganyika
Seychelles
Java Trench
Java
Timor Sea
Arafura Sea
OCEAN
St Helena
Angola Basin
Lake Nyasa
I N D I A N
Ninetyeast Ridge
Mid-Atlantic Ridge
Zambezi
Mozambique Channel
Madagascar
Mauritius
Réunion
O C E A N
Great Sandy Desert
AUSTRALI
Kalahari Desert
Great Victoria Desert
Namib Desert
Nullarbor Plain
Cape Basin
Orange
Darling
Tristan da Cunha
Cape of Good Hope
Tasmania
Gough Island
Southwest Indian Ridge
Kerguelen
Southeast Indian Ridge
Limit of winter pack ice
South Indian Basin
S O U T H E R N   O C E A N
Limit of summer pack ice
A N T A R C T I C A

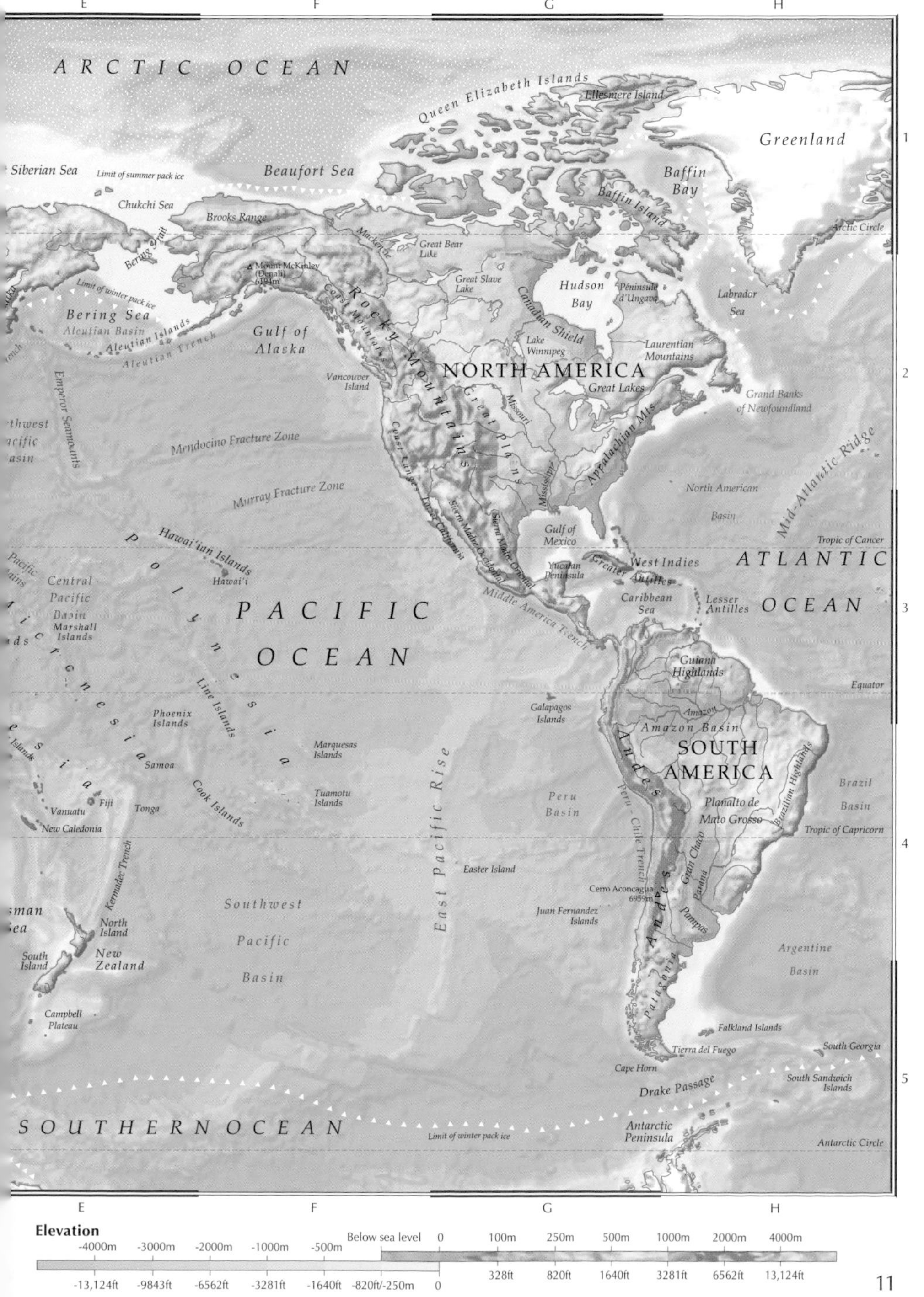

ARCTIC OCEAN

Siberian Sea

Limit of summer pack ice

Chukchi Sea

Beaufort Sea

Queen Elizabeth Islands

Ellesmere Island

Greenland

Baffin Bay

Baffin Island

Arctic Circle

Brooks Range

Mackenzie

Great Bear Lake

Bering Strait

Great Slave Lake

Hudson Bay

Péninsule d'Ungava

Labrador Sea

Limit of winter pack ice

Bering Sea

△ *Mount McKinley (Denali) 6194m*

Rocky Mountains

Canadian Shield

Laurentian Mountains

Grand Banks of Newfoundland

Aleutian Basin

Aleutian Islands

Aleutian Trench

Gulf of Alaska

Vancouver Island

Lake Winnipeg

NORTH AMERICA

Great Lakes

Emperor Seamounts

Northwest Pacific Basin

Mendocino Fracture Zone

Great Plains

Missouri

Mississippi

Appalachian Mts

North American Basin

Mid-Atlantic Ridge

Murray Fracture Zone

Great Basin

Colorado

Gulf of Mexico

Tropic of Cancer

Central Pacific Basin

Hawai'ian Islands

Hawai'i

Sierra Madre Occidental

Yucatan Peninsula

Greater Antilles

West Indies

Lesser Antilles

ATLANTIC OCEAN

Pacific

Marshall Islands

PACIFIC OCEAN

Middle America Trench

Caribbean Sea

P o l y n e s i a

Micronesia

Line Islands

Phoenix Islands

Galapagos Islands

Guiana Highlands

Equator

Samoa

Marquesas Islands

Amazon

Amazon Basin

SOUTH AMERICA

Brazil Basin

Vanuatu

Fiji

Tonga

Cook Islands

Tuamotu Islands

Peru Basin

Andes

Planalto de Mato Grosso

Brazilian Highlands

New Caledonia

Peru Chile Trench

Gran Chaco

Tropic of Capricorn

East Pacific Rise

Easter Island

Cerro Aconcagua 6959m △

Parana

Tasman Sea

Kermadec Trench

North Island

Southwest Pacific Basin

Juan Fernandez Islands

Pampas

Argentine Basin

South Island

New Zealand

Andes

Patagonia

Campbell Plateau

Falkland Islands

South Georgia

Tierra del Fuego

Cape Horn

Drake Passage

South Sandwich Islands

SOUTHERN OCEAN

Limit of winter pack ice

Antarctic Peninsula

Antarctic Circle

Elevation

-4000m	-3000m	-2000m	-1000m	-500m	Below sea level 0	100m	250m	500m	1000m	2000m	4000m
-13,124ft	-9843ft	-6562ft	-3281ft	-1640ft	-820ft/-250m 0	328ft	820ft	1640ft	3281ft	6562ft	13,124ft

Time Zones

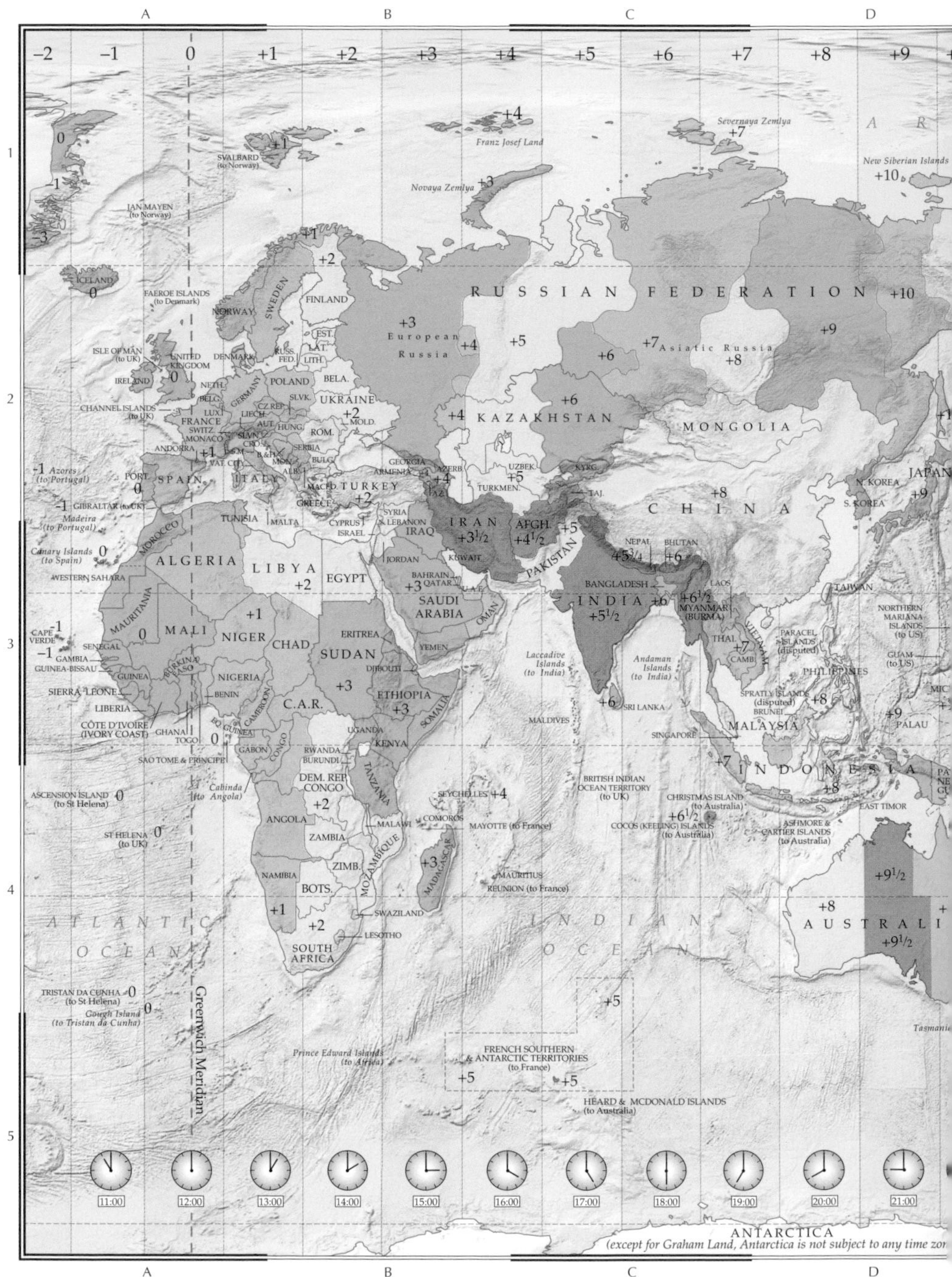

The numbers represented thus; +2/-2, indicate the number of hours each time zone is ahead or behind UCT (Coordinated Universal Time)

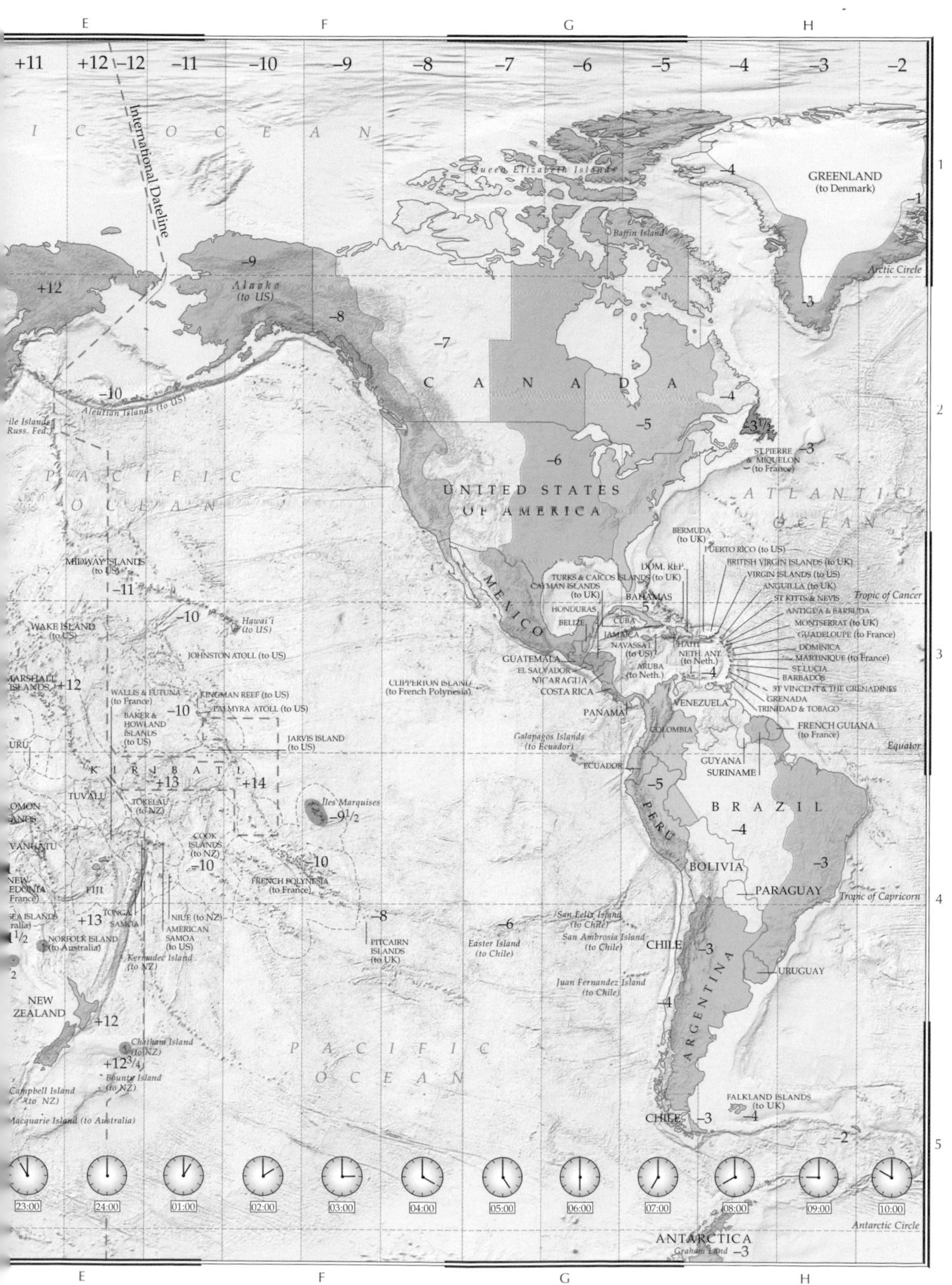

+11 +12 \-12 −11 −10 −9 −8 −7 −6 −5 −4 −3 −2

INTERNATIONAL DATELINE

ARCTIC OCEAN

Queen Elizabeth Islands

GREENLAND
(to Denmark)

−1

Baffin Island

Arctic Circle

−9

Alaska
(to US)

+12

−8

−7

−4

−3

C A N A D A

−5

−4

−10

Aleutian Islands (to US)

Kurile Islands
(to Russ. Fed.)

−6

ST PIERRE
& MIQUELON
(to France)

−3

3½

P A C I F I C

O C E A N

UNITED STATES
OF AMERICA

A T L A N T I C

O C E A N

MIDWAY ISLANDS
(to US)

−11

BERMUDA
(to UK)

PUERTO RICO (to US)

WAKE ISLAND
(to US)

−10

Hawai'i
(to US)

TURKS & CAICOS ISLANDS
(to UK)

CAYMAN ISLANDS
(to UK)

DOM. REP.

BAHAMAS

BRITISH VIRGIN ISLANDS (to UK)

VIRGIN ISLANDS (to US)

ANGUILLA (to UK)

Tropic of Cancer

JOHNSTON ATOLL (to US)

HONDURAS

BELIZE

CUBA

JAMAICA

NAVASSA
(to US)

ST KITTS & NEVIS

ANTIGUA & BARBUDA

MONTSERRAT (to UK)

GUADELOUPE (to France)

MEXICO

5

MARSHALL
ISLANDS +12

WALLIS & FUTUNA
(to France)

KINGMAN REEF (to US)

PALMYRA ATOLL (to US)

−10

GUATEMALA

EL SALVADOR

NICARAGUA

COSTA RICA

CLIPPERTON ISLAND
(to French Polynesia)

HAITI

NETH. ANT.
(to Neth.)

ARUBA
(to Neth.)

−4

DOMINICA

MARTINIQUE (to France)

ST LUCIA

BARBADOS

ST VINCENT & THE GRENADINES

GRENADA

TRINIDAD & TOBAGO

NAURU

BAKER &
HOWLAND
ISLANDS
(to US)

−10

JARVIS ISLAND
(to US)

PANAMA

VENEZUELA

COLOMBIA

FRENCH GUIANA
(to France)

SOLOMON
ISLANDS

TUVALU

K I R I B A T I
+13

+14

Galapagos Islands
(to Ecuador)

Equator

ECUADOR

GUYANA

SURINAME

Iles Marquises
−9½

TOKELAU
(to NZ)

B R A Z I L

VANUATU

COOK
ISLANDS
(to NZ)
−10

FRENCH POLYNESIA
(to France)

−10

P E R U

−5

BOLIVIA

−4

NEW
CALEDONIA
(to France)

FIJI

+13

TONGA

SAMOA

NIUE (to NZ)

AMERICAN
SAMOA
(to US)

−8

PITCAIRN
ISLANDS
(to UK)

San Felix Island
(to Chile)

San Ambrosio Island
(to Chile)

PARAGUAY

−3

Tropic of Capricorn

NORFOLK ISLAND
(to Australia)

Kermadec Island
(to NZ)

−6

Easter Island
(to Chile)

CHILE

−3

URUGUAY

AUSTRALIA
11½

12

Juan Fernandez Island
(to Chile)

−4

A R G E N T I N A

NEW
ZEALAND

+12

Chatham Island
(to NZ)

+12¾

Bounty Island
(to NZ)

P A C I F I C

O C E A N

FALKLAND ISLANDS
(to UK)

Campbell Island
(to NZ)

Macquarie Island (to Australia)

CHILE −3

−2

| 23:00 | 24:00 | 01:00 | 02:00 | 03:00 | 04:00 | 05:00 | 06:00 | 07:00 | 08:00 | 09:00 | 10:00 |

Antarctic Circle

ANTARCTICA
Graham Land −3

E F G H

The clocks and 24-hour times given at the bottom of the map show time in each time zone when it is 12.00 hours noon UCT

Geology & Structure

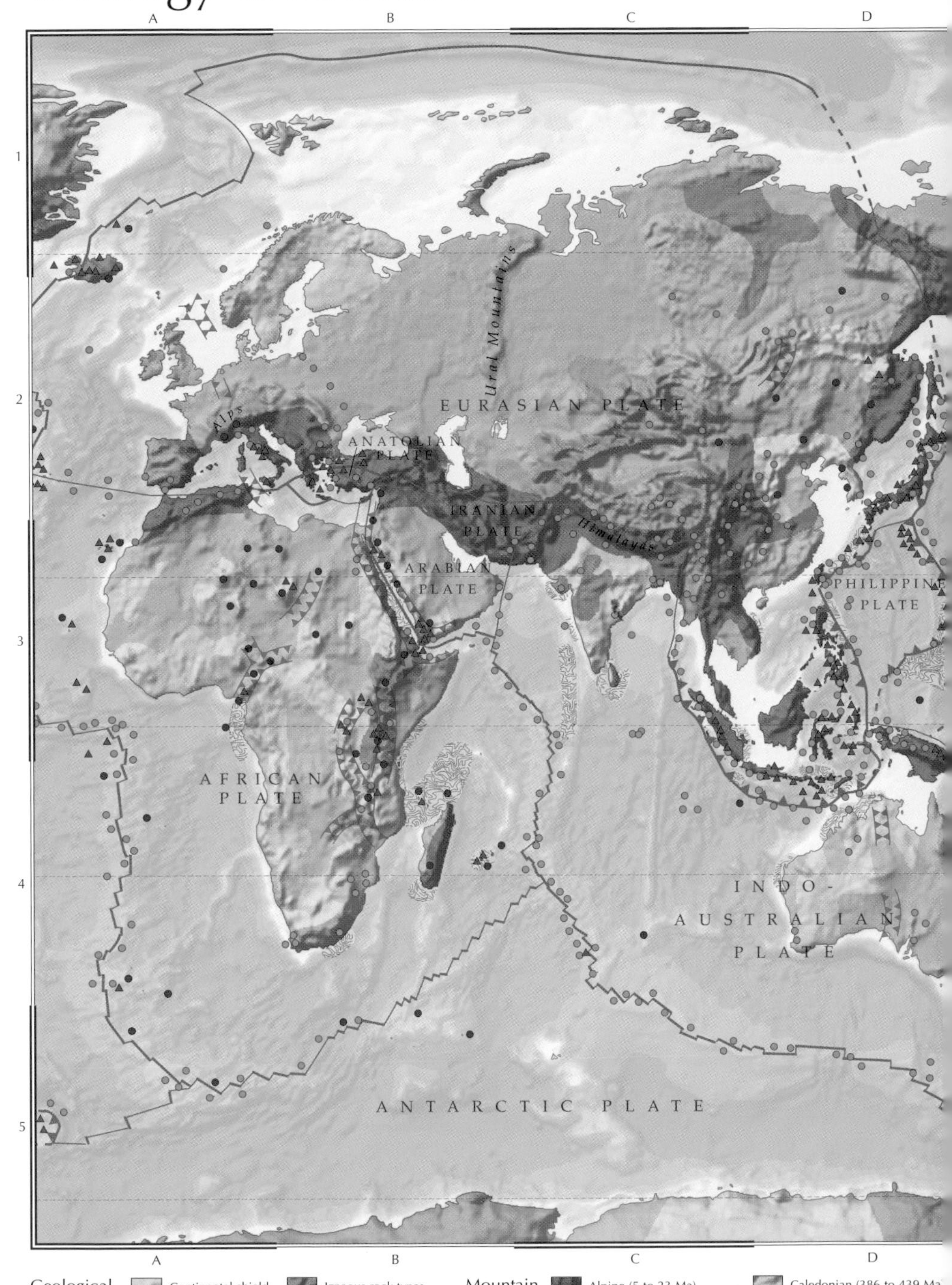

Geological Regions

Continental shield		Igneous rock types
Sedimentary rocks		Coral formation

Mountain Ranges

Alpine (5 to 23 Ma)	Caledonian (386 to 439 Ma)
Hercynian (290 to 362 Ma)	Ma= millions of years ago

14

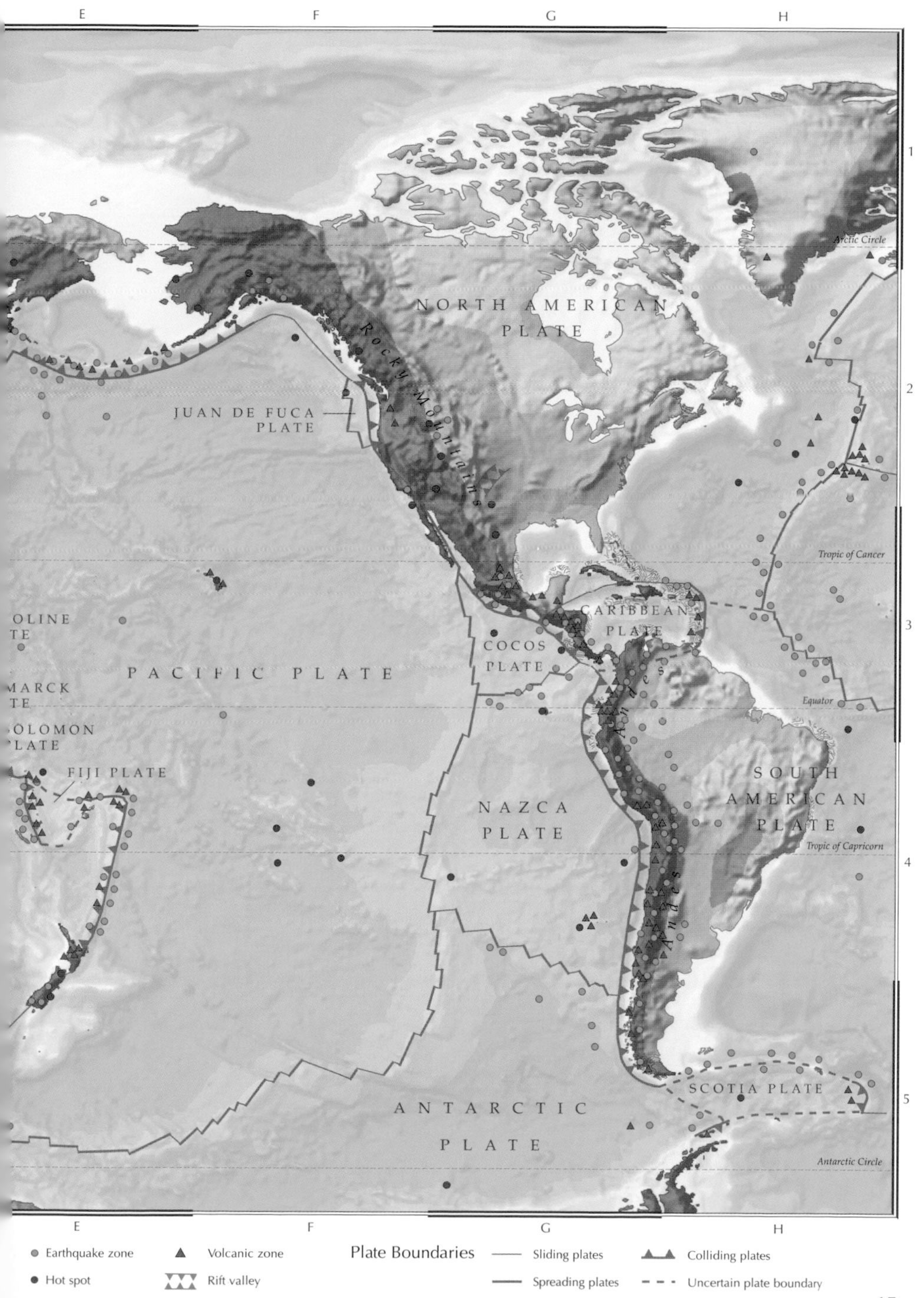

E F G H

1

Arctic Circle

NORTH AMERICAN
PLATE

Rocky Mountains

JUAN DE FUCA
PLATE

2

OLINE
TE

MARCK
TE

OLOMON
LATE

FIJI PLATE

PACIFIC PLATE

Tropic of Cancer

CARIBBEAN
PLATE

COCOS
PLATE

3

Equator

SOUTH
AMERICAN
PLATE

NAZCA
PLATE

Andes

Tropic of Capricorn

4

ANTARCTIC

PLATE

SCOTIA PLATE

5

Antarctic Circle

E F G H

● Earthquake zone   ▲ Volcanic zone   **Plate Boundaries** —— Sliding plates   ▲▲ Colliding plates

● Hot spot   ▲▲▲ Rift valley   —— Spreading plates   - - - Uncertain plate boundary

World Climate

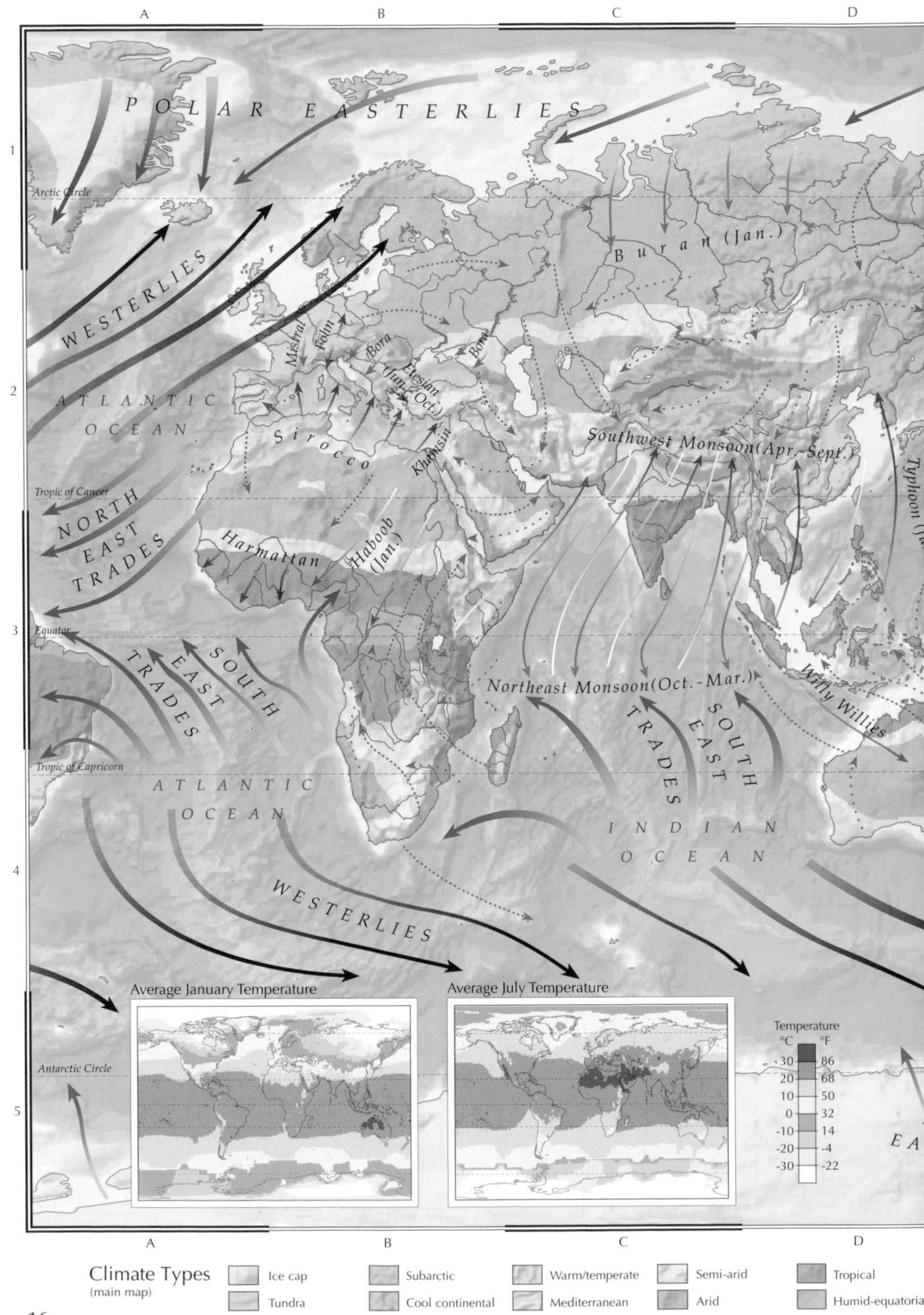

Average January Temperature

Average July Temperature

Temperature	
°C	°F
30	86
20	68
10	50
0	32
-10	14
-20	-4
-30	-22

Climate Types
(main map)

Ice cap	Subarctic	Warm/temperate	Semi-arid	Tropical
Tundra	Cool continental	Mediterranean	Arid	Humid-equatorial

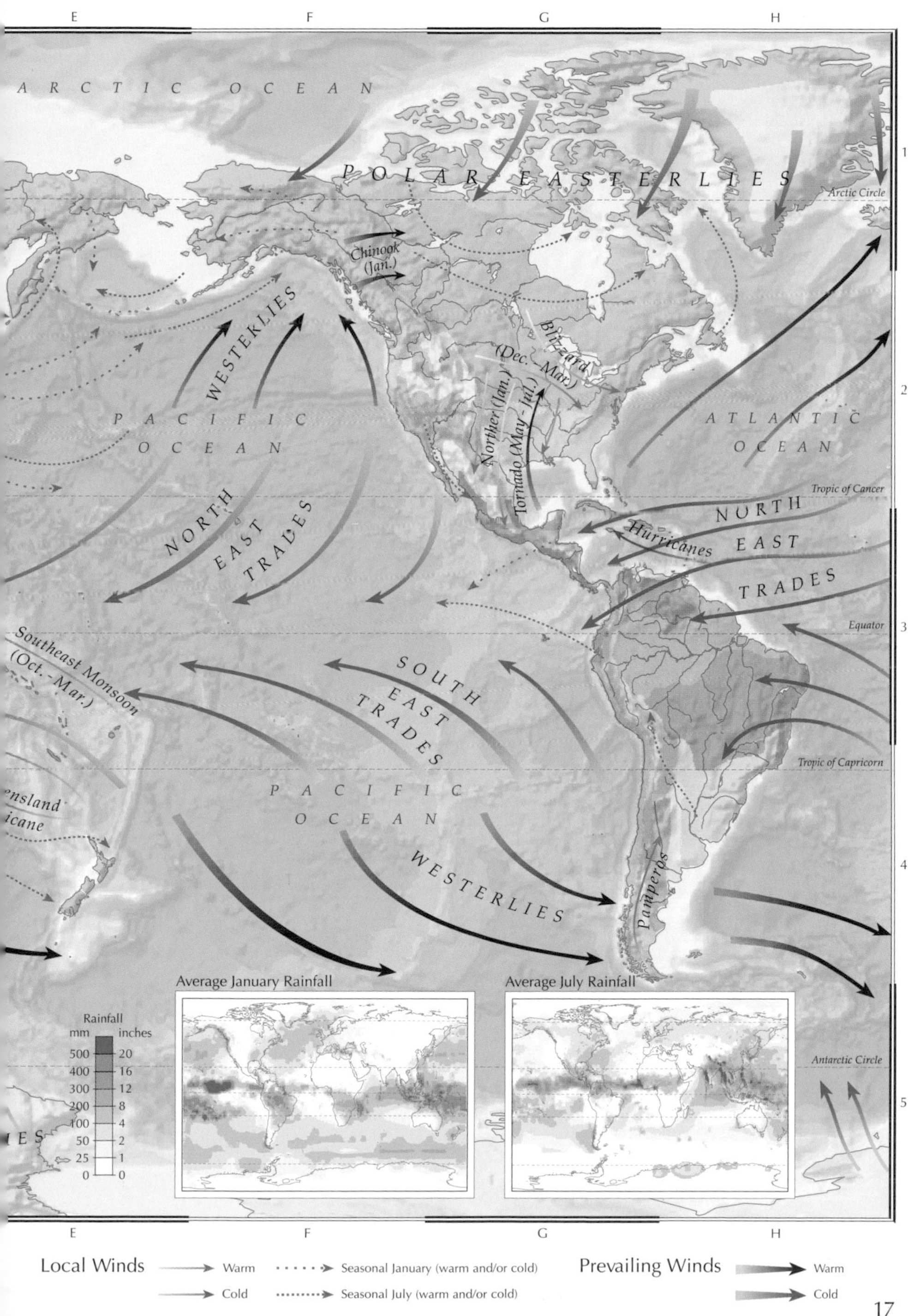

E   F   G   H

ARCTIC OCEAN

POLAR EASTERLIES

1

Arctic Circle

Chinook
(Jan.)

WESTERLIES

Blizzard
(Dec.–Mar.)

Norther (Jan.)

Tornado (May–Jul.)

2

PACIFIC
OCEAN

ATLANTIC
OCEAN

Tropic of Cancer

NORTH
EAST
TRADES

NORTH
EAST

Hurricanes

TRADES

Equator

3

Southeast Monsoon
(Oct.–Mar.)

SOUTH
EAST
TRADES

...nsland
...icane

Tropic of Capricorn

PACIFIC
OCEAN

WESTERLIES

Pamperos

4

...ES

Antarctic Circle

5

Average January Rainfall

Average July Rainfall

Rainfall
mm | inches
500 | 20
400 | 16
300 | 12
200 | 8
100 | 4
50 | 2
25 | 1
0 | 0

E   F   G   H

Local Winds → Warm ·····▷ Seasonal January (warm and/or cold) Prevailing Winds → Warm

       → Cold ········▷ Seasonal July (warm and/or cold)   → Cold

Ocean Currents

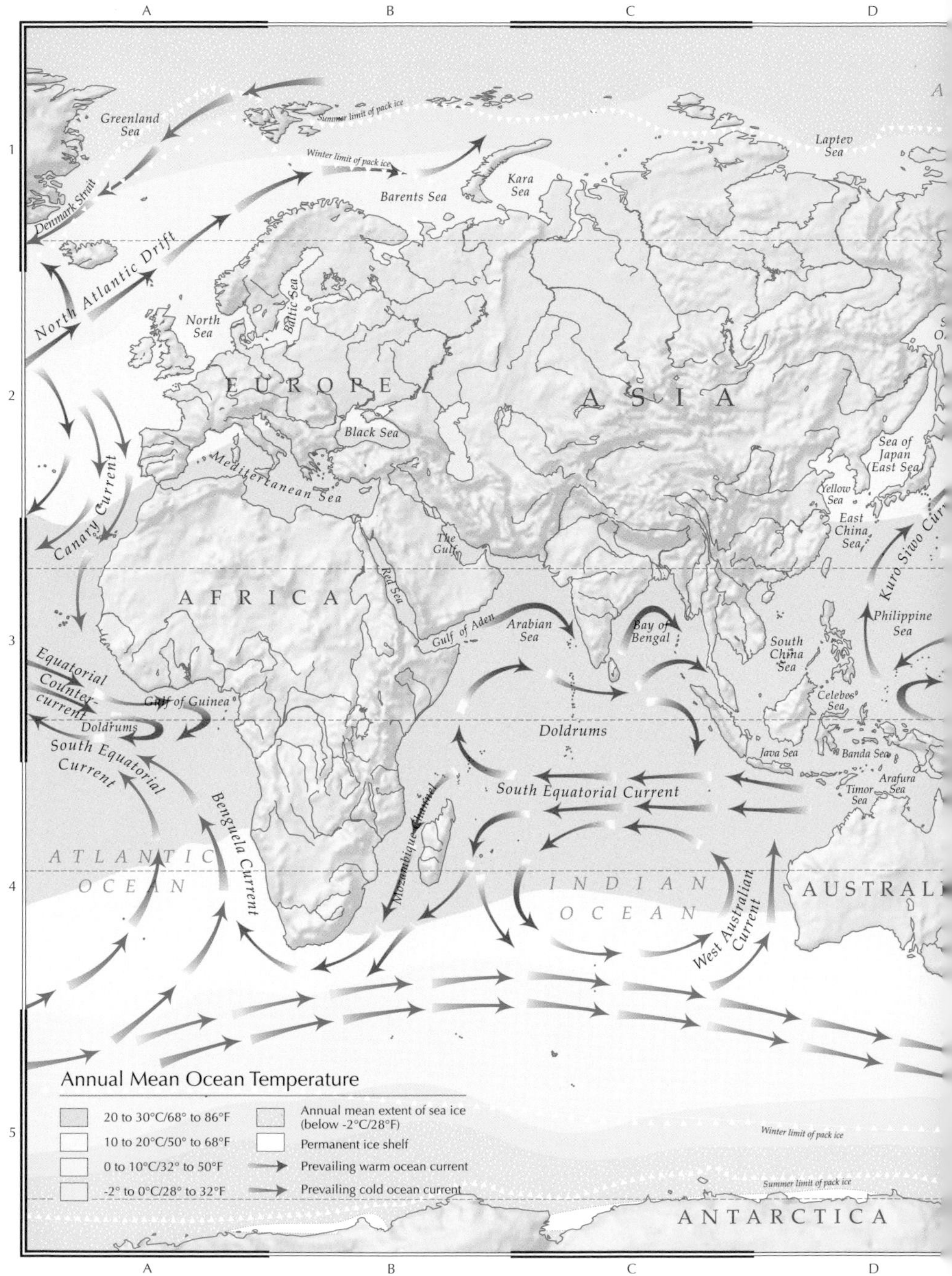

Annual Mean Ocean Temperature

- 20 to 30°C/68° to 86°F
- 10 to 20°C/50° to 68°F
- 0 to 10°C/32° to 50°F
- -2° to 0°C/28° to 32°F
- Annual mean extent of sea ice (below -2°C/28°F)
- Permanent ice shelf
- → Prevailing warm ocean current
- → Prevailing cold ocean current

Greenland Sea, Summer limit of pack ice, Winter limit of pack ice, Barents Sea, Kara Sea, Laptev Sea, Denmark Strait, North Atlantic Drift, North Sea, Baltic Sea, EUROPE, ASIA, Black Sea, Mediterranean Sea, Canary Current, The Gulf, Sea of Japan (East Sea), Yellow Sea, East China Sea, Kuro Siwo Cur., AFRICA, Red Sea, Gulf of Aden, Arabian Sea, Bay of Bengal, South China Sea, Philippine Sea, Equatorial Counter-current, Gulf of Guinea, Doldrums, South Equatorial Current, Celebes Sea, Doldrums, South Equatorial Current, Java Sea, Banda Sea, Timor Sea, Arafura Sea, Benguela Current, Mozambique Current, ATLANTIC OCEAN, INDIAN OCEAN, West Australian Current, AUSTRAL..., Winter limit of pack ice, Summer limit of pack ice, ANTARCTICA

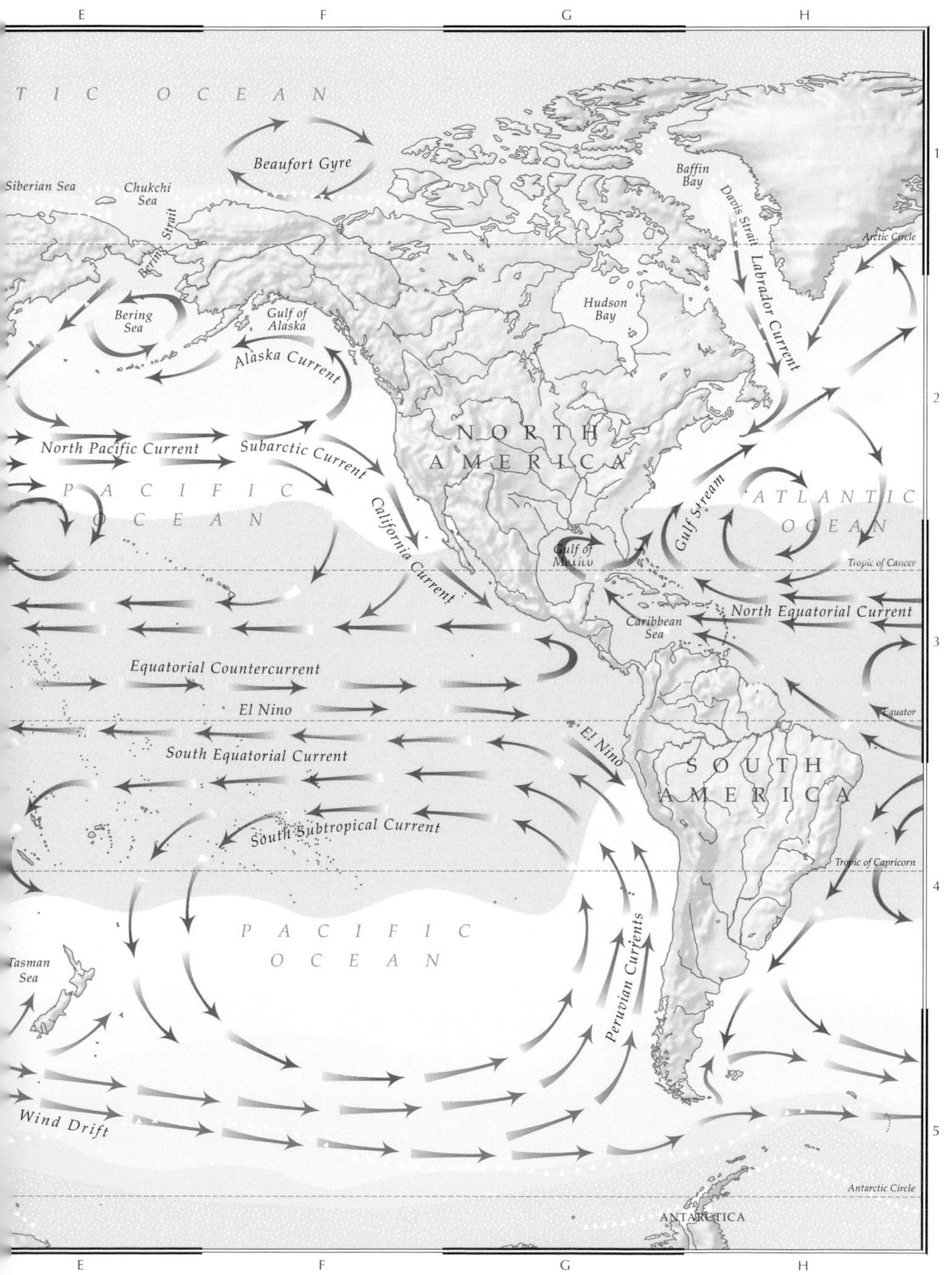
E
F
G
H
TIC OCEAN
Beaufort Gyre
Siberian Sea
Chukchi Sea
Bering Strait
Baffin Bay
Davis Strait
Labrador Current
Arctic Circle
Bering Sea
Gulf of Alaska
Hudson Bay
Alaska Current
NORTH AMERICA
North Pacific Current
Subarctic Current
PACIFIC OCEAN
California Current
Gulf Stream
ATLANTIC OCEAN
Gulf of Mexico
Tropic of Cancer
North Equatorial Current
Caribbean Sea
Equatorial Countercurrent
El Nino
Equator
El Nino
South Equatorial Current
SOUTH AMERICA
South Subtropical Current
Tropic of Capricorn
PACIFIC OCEAN
Peruvian Currents
Tasman Sea
Wind Drift
Antarctic Circle
ANTARCTICA
1
2
3
4
5

Life Zones

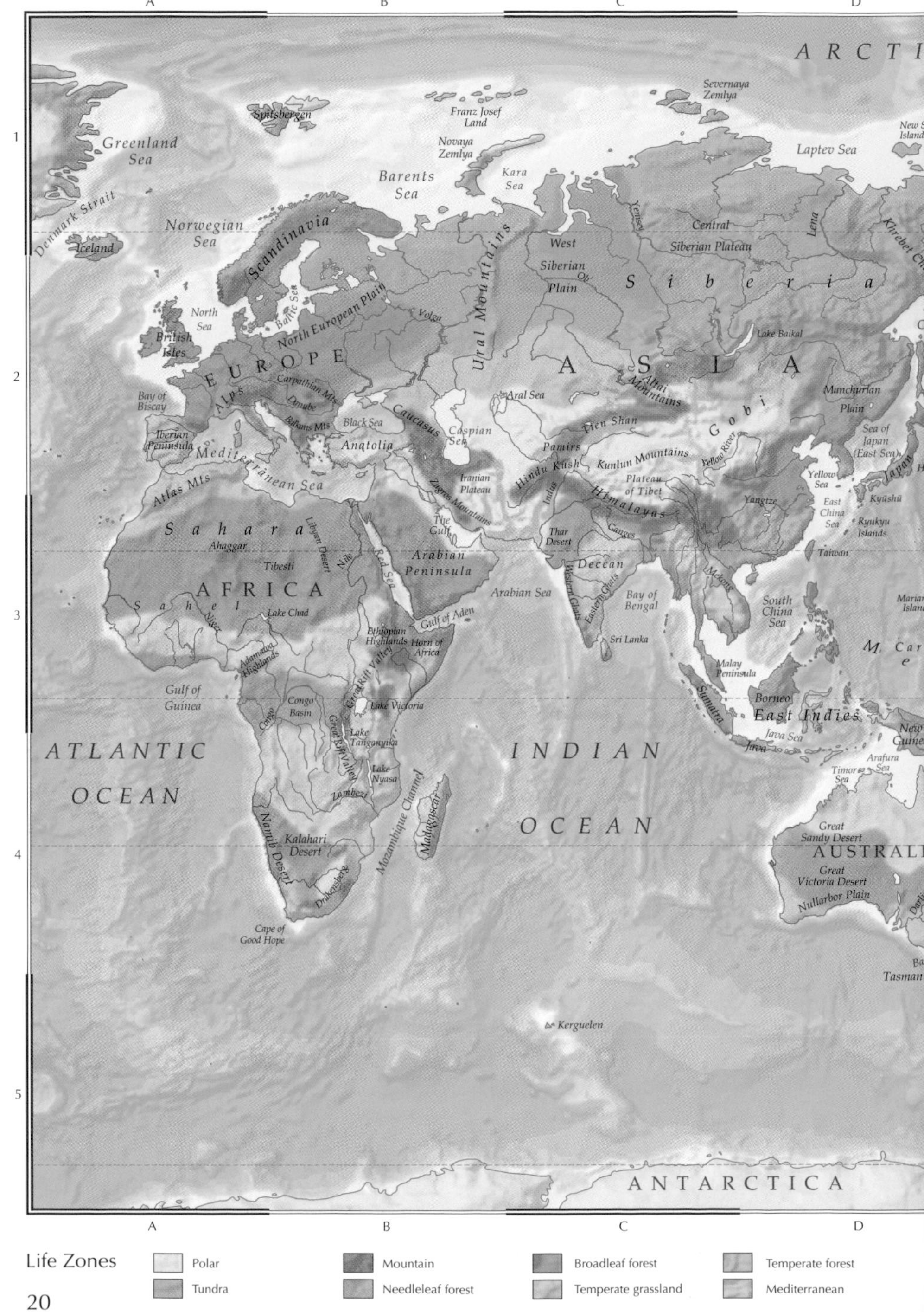

A B C D

ARCTI

Greenland
Sea

Spitsbergen

Franz Josef
Land

Severnaya
Zemlya

New Si
Islands

1

Denmark Strait

Iceland

Norwegian
Sea

Barents
Sea

Novaya
Zemlya

Kara
Sea

Laptev Sea

Khrebet Cher

Scandinavia

West
Siberian
Plain

Central
Siberian Plateau

Siberia

North
Sea

Baltic Sea

North European Plain

Ural Mountains

Ob

Lena

Yenisey

S

British
Isles

EUROPE

Carpathian Mts

Volga

Aral Sea

Altai
Mountains

ASIA

Manchurian
Plain

O

2

Bay of
Biscay

Alps

Danube

Black Sea

Caucasus

Caspian
Sea

Tien Shan

Gobi

Sea of
Japan
(East Sea)

Iberian
Peninsula

Balkans Mts

Anatolia

Mediterranean Sea

Zagros Mountains

Iranian
Plateau

Pamirs

Hindu Kush

Kunlun Mountains

Plateau
of Tibet

Yellow
Sea

Japan

Kyūshū

Atlas Mts

Indus

Himalayas

Yangtze

East
China
Sea

Ryukyu
Islands

Sahara

Ahaggar

Libyan Desert

Tibesti

Nile

The
Gulf

Red Sea

Arabian
Peninsula

Gulf of Aden

Thar
Desert

Ganges

Deccan

Western Ghats

Mekong

Taiwan

3

Sahel

AFRICA

Lake Chad

Ethiopian
Highlands

Horn of
Africa

Arabian Sea

Eastern Ghats

Bay of
Bengal

Sri Lanka

South
China
Sea

M Car

e

Mariana
Islands

Adamawa
Highlands

Great Rift Valley

Gulf of
Guinea

Congo
Basin

Congo

Lake Victoria

Lake
Tanganyika

Malay
Peninsula

Sumatra

Borneo

Java Sea

East Indies

Java

New
Guinea

ATLANTIC

OCEAN

Lake
Nyasa

Zambezi

Mozambique Channel

Madagascar

INDIAN

OCEAN

Timor
Sea

Arafura
Sea

4

Namib Desert

Kalahari
Desert

Drakensberg

Great
Sandy Desert

AUSTRALI

Great
Victoria Desert

Nullarbor Plain

Bar

Cape of
Good Hope

Kerguelen

Tasmani

5

ANTARCTICA

A B C D

Life Zones

Polar

Tundra

Mountain

Needleleaf forest

Broadleaf forest

Temperate grassland

Temperate forest

Mediterranean

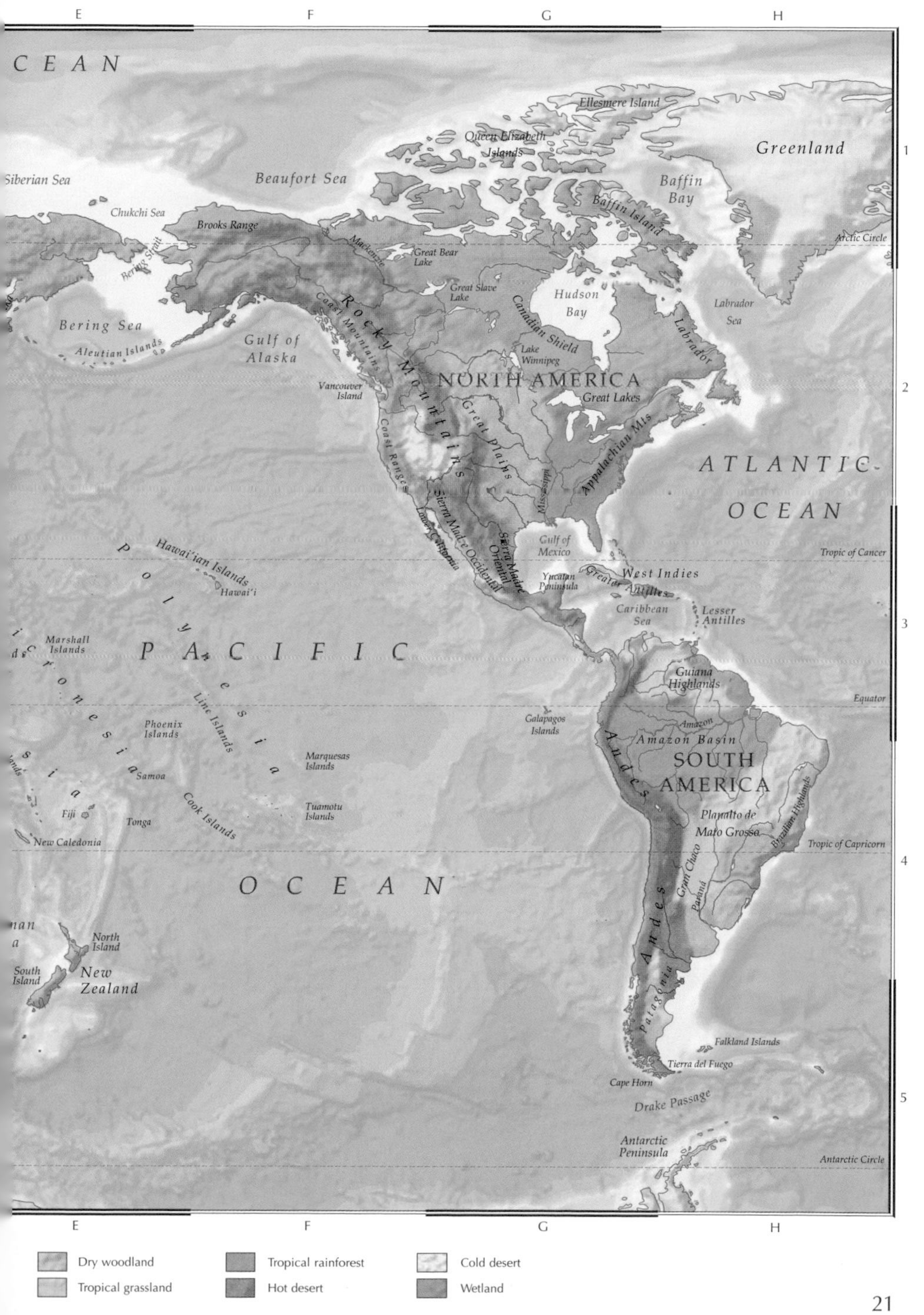

E F G H

OCEAN

Siberian Sea
Chukchi Sea
Bering Sea
Aleutian Islands
Gulf of Alaska

Beaufort Sea
Brooks Range
Mackenzie
Great Bear Lake
Great Slave Lake
Coast Mountains

Ellesmere Island
Queen Elizabeth Islands
Baffin Island
Baffin Bay
Greenland

Arctic Circle

Hudson Bay
Canadian Shield
Labrador Sea

1

2

Vancouver Island
Rocky Mountains
Lake Winnipeg
NORTH AMERICA
Great Plains
Great Lakes
Appalachian Mts.
Mississippi

ATLANTIC OCEAN

Hawaiian Islands
Hawai'i

POLYNESIA

Coast Ranges
Sierra Madre Occidental
Baja California
Sierra Madre Oriental
Gulf of Mexico
Yucatán Peninsula
Greater Antilles
West Indies
Caribbean Sea
Lesser Antilles

Tropic of Cancer

3

PACIFIC

MICRONESIA

Marshall Islands
Phoenix Islands
Line Islands
Marquesas Islands
Samoa
Fiji
Tonga
Cook Islands
Tuamotu Islands
New Caledonia

Galapagos Islands

Guiana Highlands
Amazon
Amazon Basin
SOUTH AMERICA
Andes

Equator

OCEAN

North Island
South Island
New Zealand

Planalto de Mato Grosso
Gran Chaco
Paraná
Brazilian Highlands

Tropic of Capricorn

4

Andes
Patagonia

Falkland Islands
Tierra del Fuego
Cape Horn
Drake Passage

5

Antarctic Peninsula

Antarctic Circle

E F G H

Dry woodland	Tropical rainforest	Cold desert
Tropical grassland	Hot desert	Wetland

Population

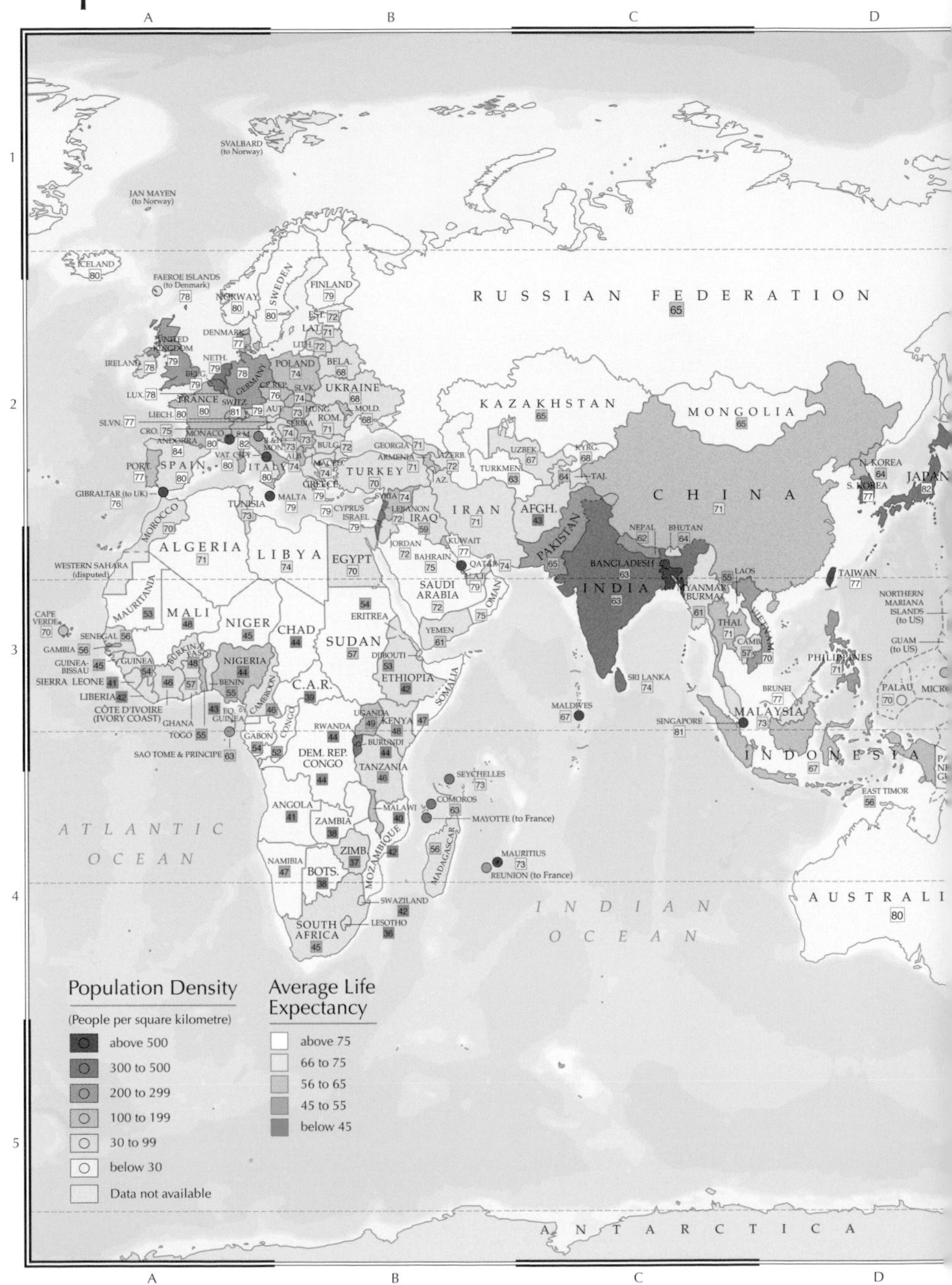

Population Density

(People per square kilometre)

- above 500
- 300 to 500
- 200 to 299
- 100 to 199
- 30 to 99
- below 30
- Data not available

Average Life Expectancy

- above 75
- 66 to 75
- 56 to 65
- 45 to 55
- below 45

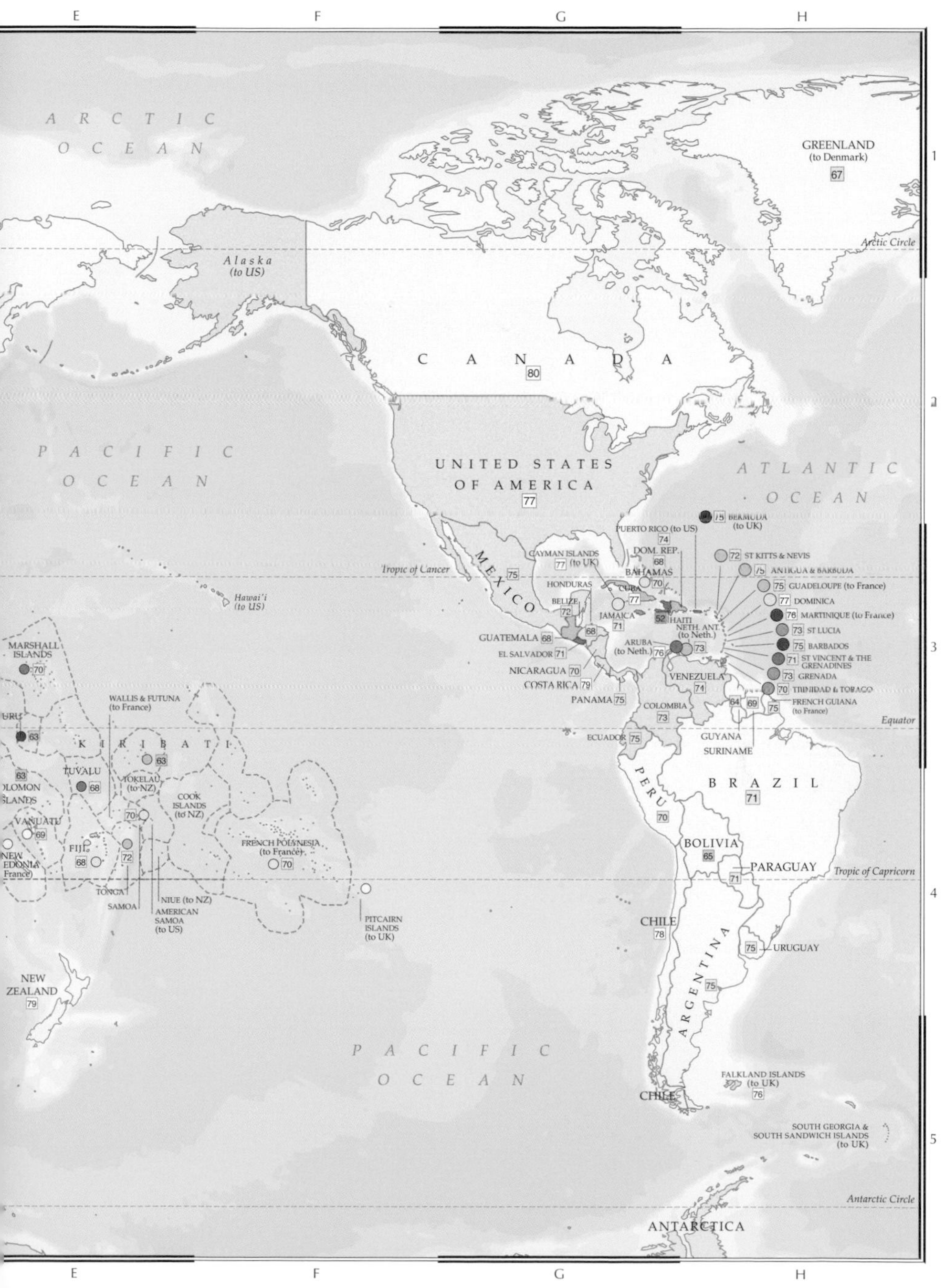

E F G H

1

ARCTIC
OCEAN

GREENLAND
(to Denmark)
67

Arctic Circle

Alaska
(to US)

2

CANADA
80

PACIFIC
OCEAN

UNITED STATES
OF AMERICA
77

ATLANTIC
OCEAN

BERMUDA
75 (to UK)

Tropic of Cancer

Hawai'i
(to US)

MEXICO
75

CAYMAN ISLANDS
(to UK) 77

PUERTO RICO (to US)
74

DOM. REP.
70

BAHAMAS
68

CUBA

ST KITTS & NEVIS
72

ANTIGUA & BARBUDA
75

HONDURAS

BELIZE

JAMAICA
71

CUBA
77

GUADELOUPE (to France)
75

DOMINICA
77

MARTINIQUE (to France)
76

MARSHALL
ISLANDS

70

GUATEMALA 68

EL SALVADOR 71

NICARAGUA 70

COSTA RICA 79

PANAMA 75

68

HAITI
52

NETH. ANT.
(to Neth.)

ARUBA
(to Neth.) 76

VENEZUELA
71

73

ST LUCIA
73

BARBADOS
75

GRENADA
73

ST VINCENT & THE
GRENADINES
71

TRINIDAD & TOBAGO
70

FRENCH GUIANA
(to France)
75

Equator

3

WALLIS & FUTUNA
(to France)

KIRIBATI

63

TUVALU
68

TOKELAU
(to NZ)

COOK
ISLANDS
(to NZ)

VANUATU
69

FIJI
68

72

NEW
CALEDONIA
(to France)

TONGA

SAMOA

NIUE (to NZ)

AMERICAN
SAMOA
(to US)

FRENCH POLYNESIA
(to France)
70

PITCAIRN
ISLANDS
(to UK)

SOLOMON
ISLANDS

63

63

70

COLOMBIA
73

ECUADOR
75

PERU
70

BRAZIL
71

BOLIVIA
85

PARAGUAY
71

Tropic of Capricorn

4

CHILE
78

ARGENTINA
75

URUGUAY
75

NEW
ZEALAND
79

PACIFIC
OCEAN

FALKLAND ISLANDS
(to UK)
76

CHILE

SOUTH GEORGIA &
SOUTH SANDWICH ISLANDS
(to UK)

5

Antarctic Circle

ANTARCTICA

E F G H

Languages

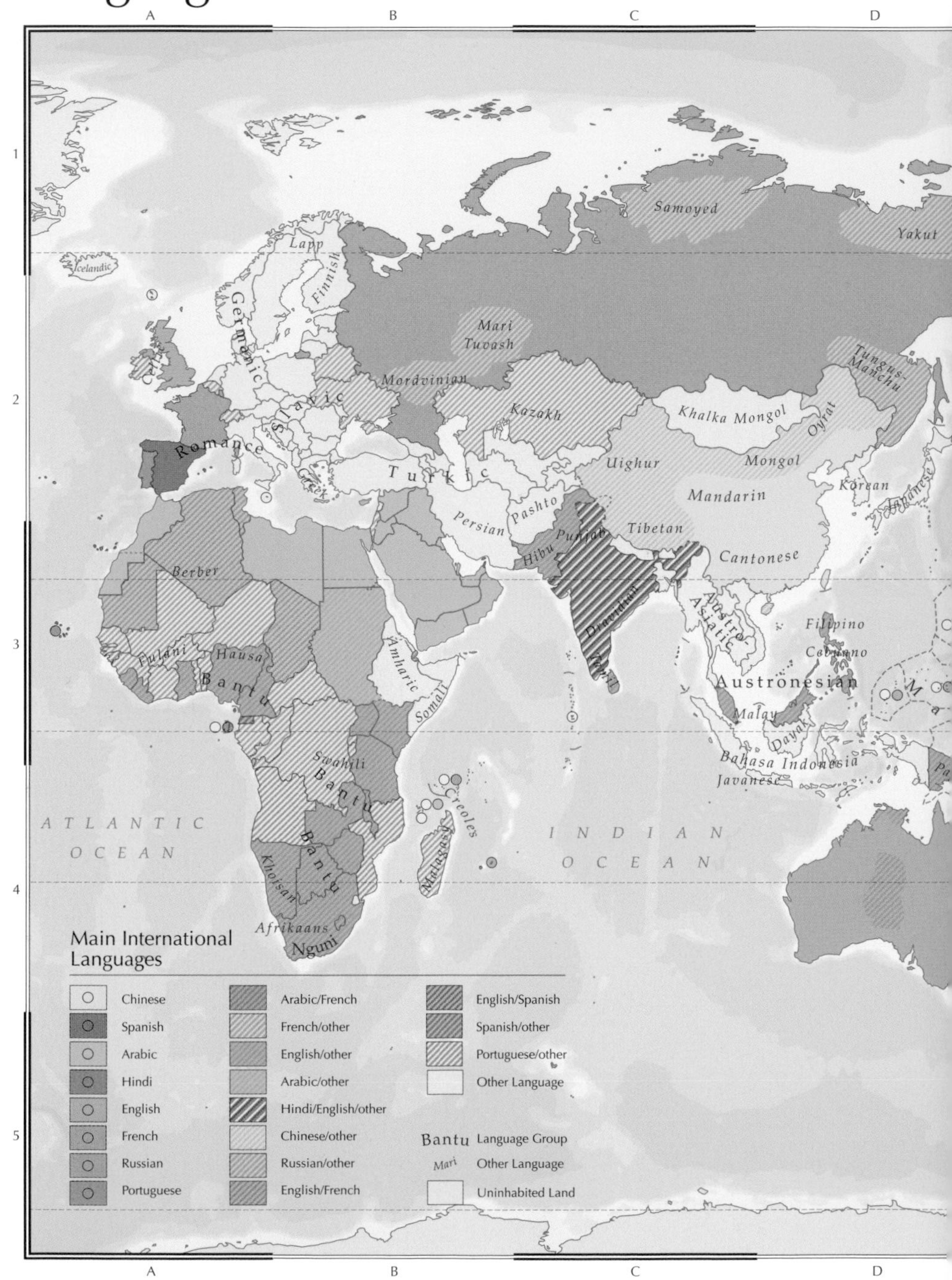

Main International Languages

○ Chinese	Arabic/French	English/Spanish
○ Spanish	French/other	Spanish/other
○ Arabic	English/other	Portuguese/other
○ Hindi	Arabic/other	Other Language
○ English	Hindi/English/other	
○ French	Chinese/other	Bantu Language Group
○ Russian	Russian/other	Mari Other Language
○ Portuguese	English/French	Uninhabited Land

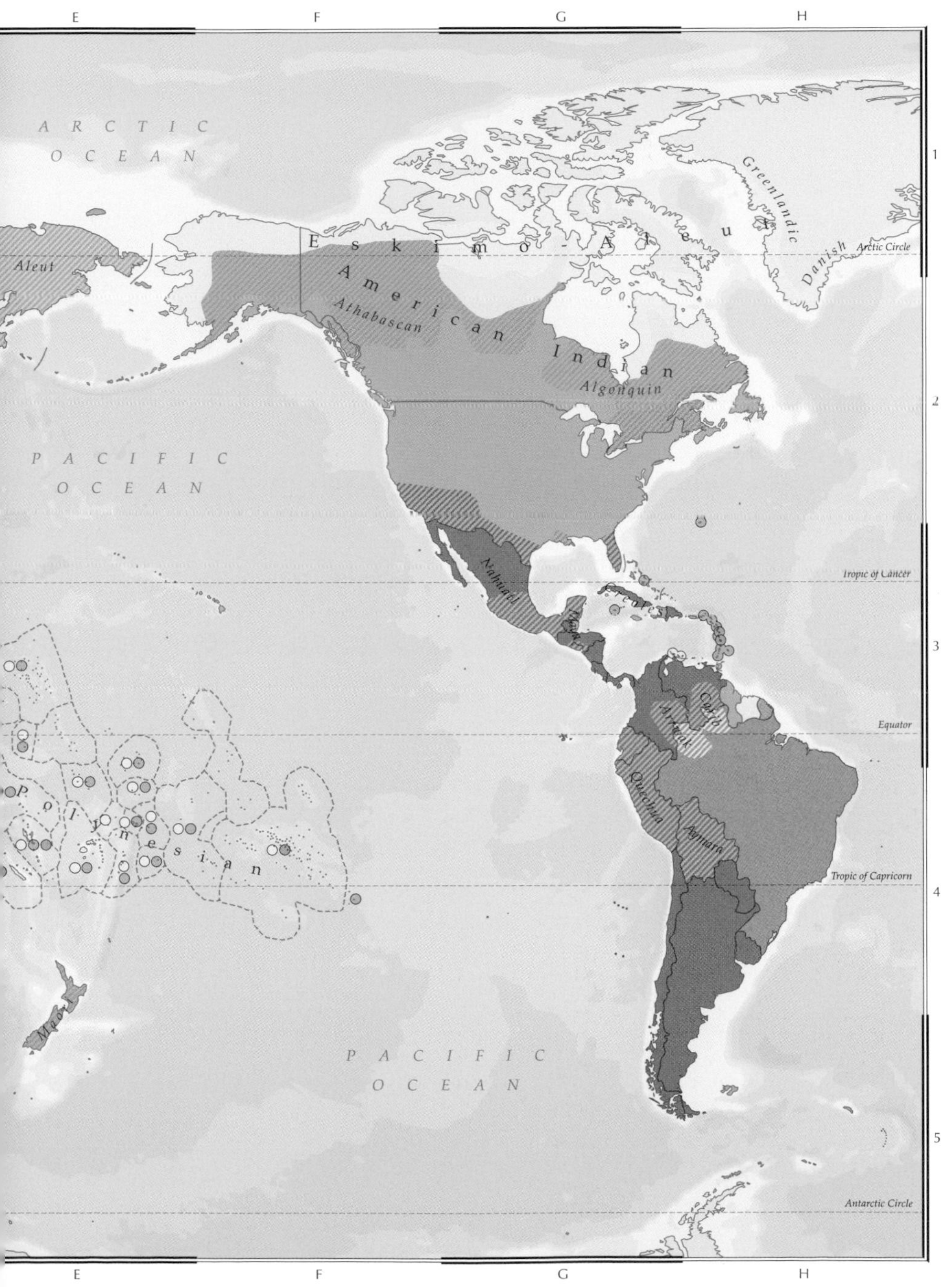

E   F   G   H

ARCTIC
OCEAN

Greenlandic

Danish *Arctic Circle*

Aleut

Eskimo-Aleu

American Indian

Athabascan

Algonquin

PACIFIC
OCEAN

Tropic of Cancer

Nahuatl

Equator

Polynesian

Arawak

Carib

Chibcha

Quechua

Maori

Tropic of Capricorn

PACIFIC
OCEAN

Antarctic Circle

E   F   G   H

Religion

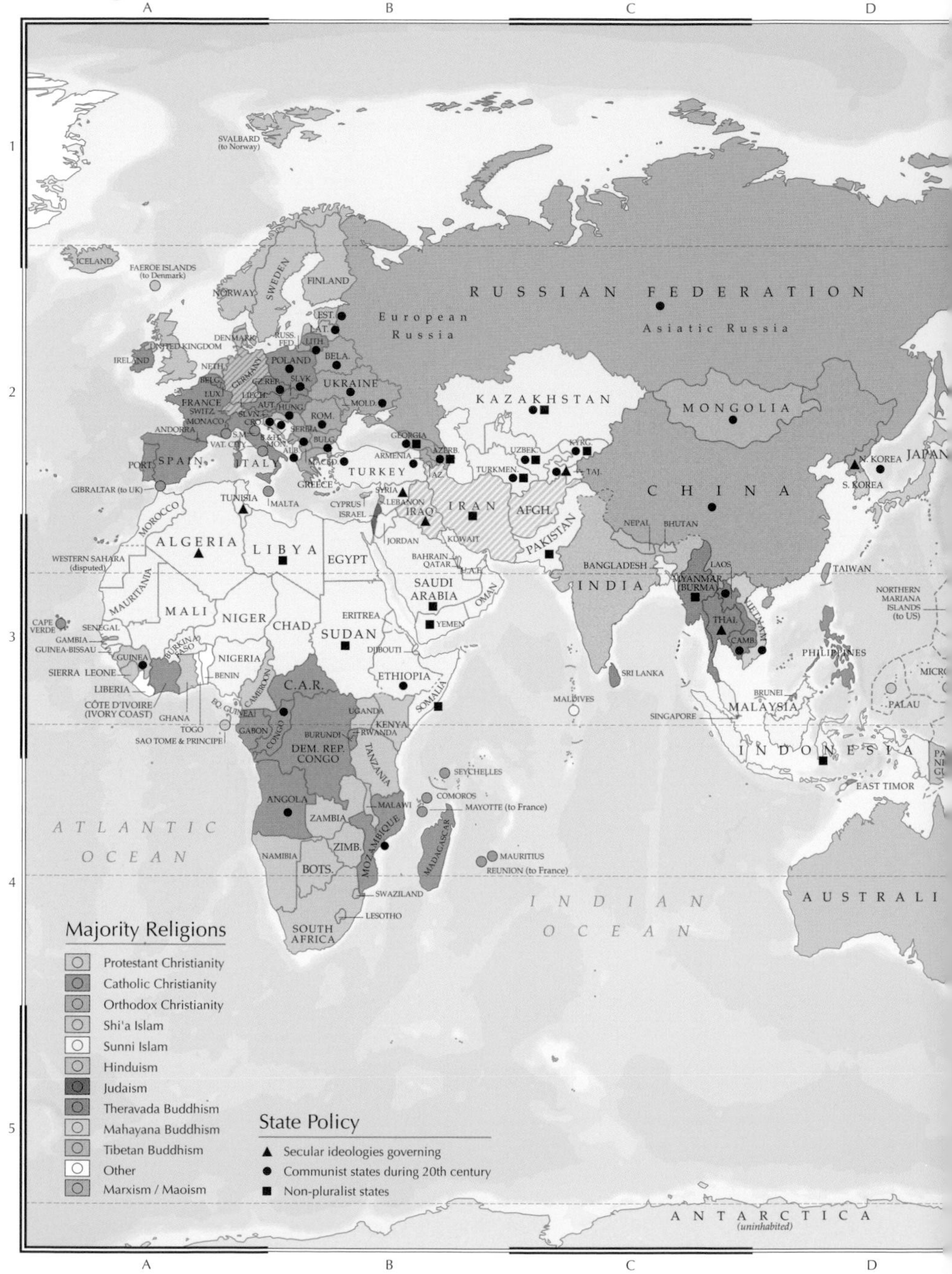

Majority Religions

- Protestant Christianity
- Catholic Christianity
- Orthodox Christianity
- Shi'a Islam
- Sunni Islam
- Hinduism
- Judaism
- Theravada Buddhism
- Mahayana Buddhism
- Tibetan Buddhism
- Other
- Marxism / Maoism

State Policy

- ▲ Secular ideologies governing
- ● Communist states during 20th century
- ■ Non-pluralist states

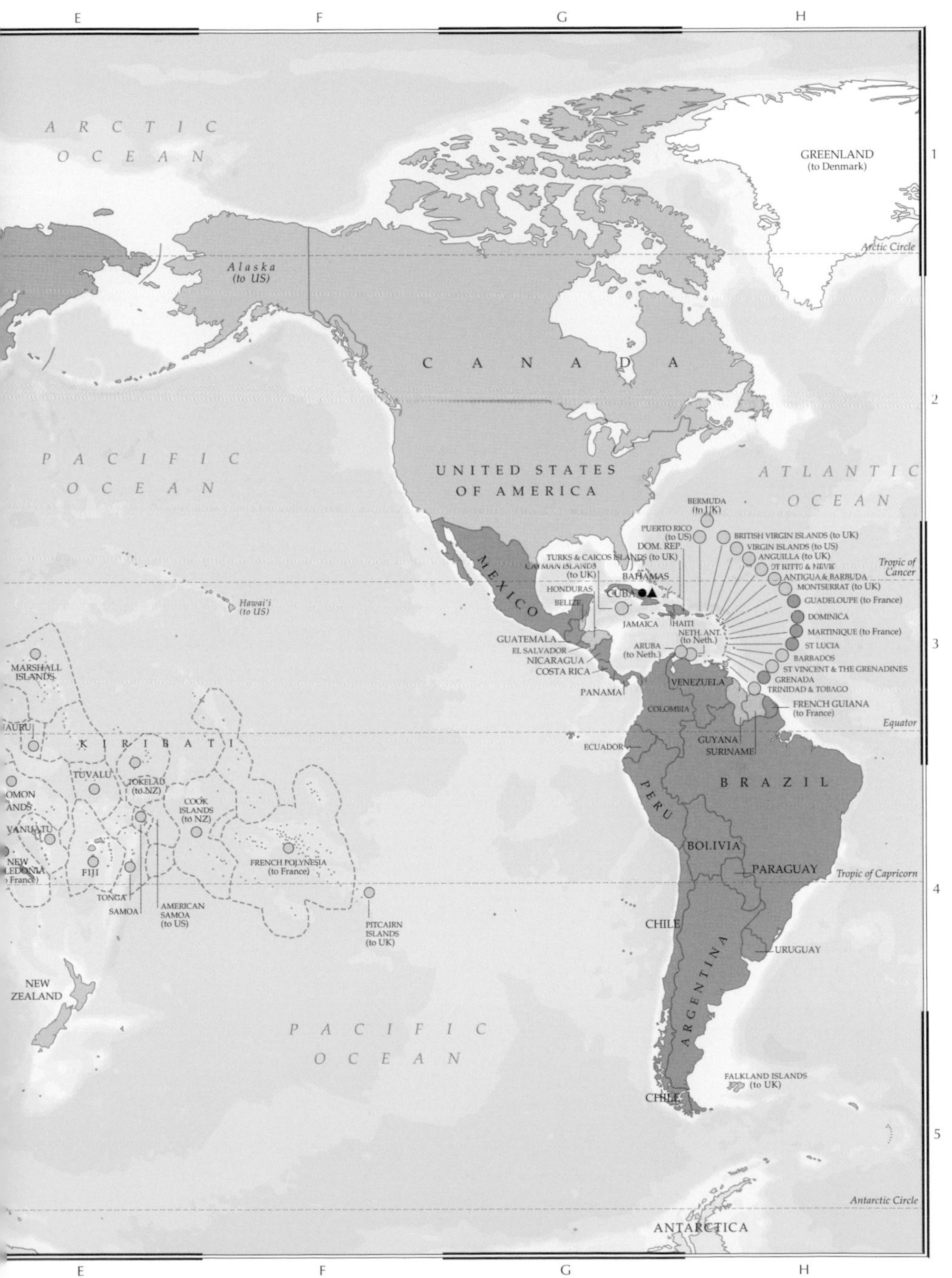

ARCTIC
OCEAN

GREENLAND
(to Denmark)

Arctic Circle

Alaska
(to US)

C A N A D A

PACIFIC
OCEAN

UNITED STATES
OF AMERICA

A T L A N T I C
OCEAN

BERMUDA
(to UK)

PUERTO RICO
(to US)
DOM. REP.

BRITISH VIRGIN ISLANDS (to UK)
VIRGIN ISLANDS (to US)
ANGUILLA (to UK)
ST KITTS & NEVIS
ANTIGUA & BARBUDA
MONTSERRAT (to UK)

Tropic of Cancer

TURKS & CAICOS ISLANDS (to UK)
CAYMAN ISLANDS
(to UK)

M
E
X
I
C
O

Hawai'i
(to US)

BAHAMAS

GUADELOUPE (to France)

HONDURAS
BELIZE
CUBA

MARSHALL
ISLANDS

JAMAICA

DOMINICA

MARTINIQUE (to France)

ST LUCIA

NAURU

GUATEMALA
EL SALVADOR
NICARAGUA
COSTA RICA

HAITI
NETH. ANT.
(to Neth.)
ARUBA
(to Neth.)

BARBADOS
ST VINCENT & THE GRENADINES
GRENADA
TRINIDAD & TOBAGO

K I R I B A T I

PANAMA

VENEZUELA

FRENCH GUIANA
(to France)

Equator

TUVALU

TOKELAU
(to NZ)

COLOMBIA

ECUADOR

GUYANA
SURINAME

SOLOMON
ISLANDS

COOK
ISLANDS
(to NZ)

B R A Z I L

VANUATU

NEW
CALEDONIA
(to France)

FIJI

FRENCH POLYNESIA
(to France)

PERU

TONGA

SAMOA

AMERICAN
SAMOA
(to US)

PITCAIRN
ISLANDS
(to UK)

BOLIVIA

PARAGUAY

Tropic of Capricorn

CHILE

URUGUAY

NEW
ZEALAND

A
R
G
E
N
T
I
N
A

PACIFIC
OCEAN

CHILE

FALKLAND ISLANDS
(to UK)

Antarctic Circle

ANTARCTICA

E   F   G   H

The Global Economy

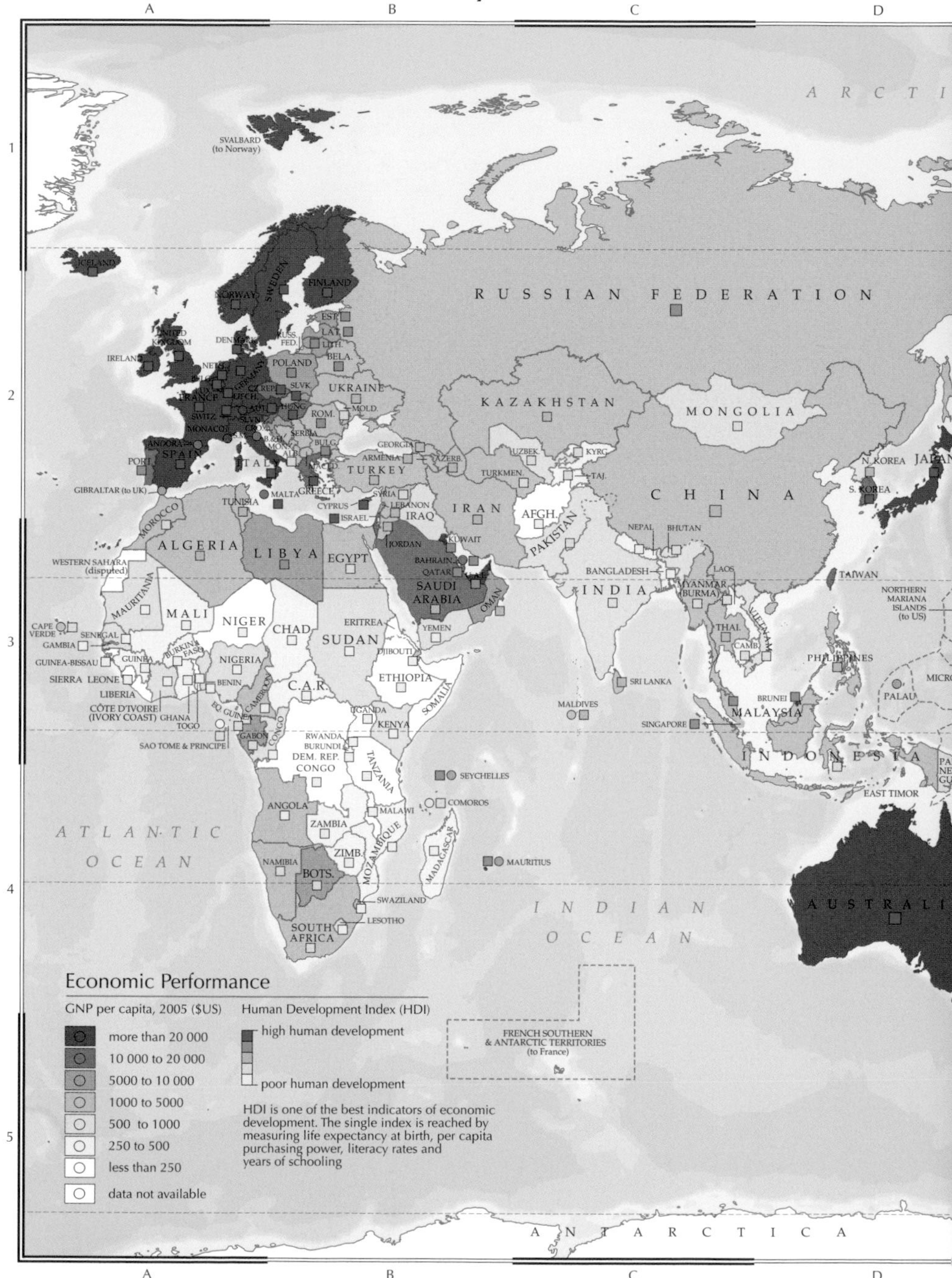

Economic Performance

GNP per capita, 2005 ($US)

- more than 20 000
- 10 000 to 20 000
- 5000 to 10 000
- 1000 to 5000
- 500 to 1000
- 250 to 500
- less than 250
- data not available

Human Development Index (HDI)

- high human development
- poor human development

HDI is one of the best indicators of economic development. The single index is reached by measuring life expectancy at birth, per capita purchasing power, literacy rates and years of schooling

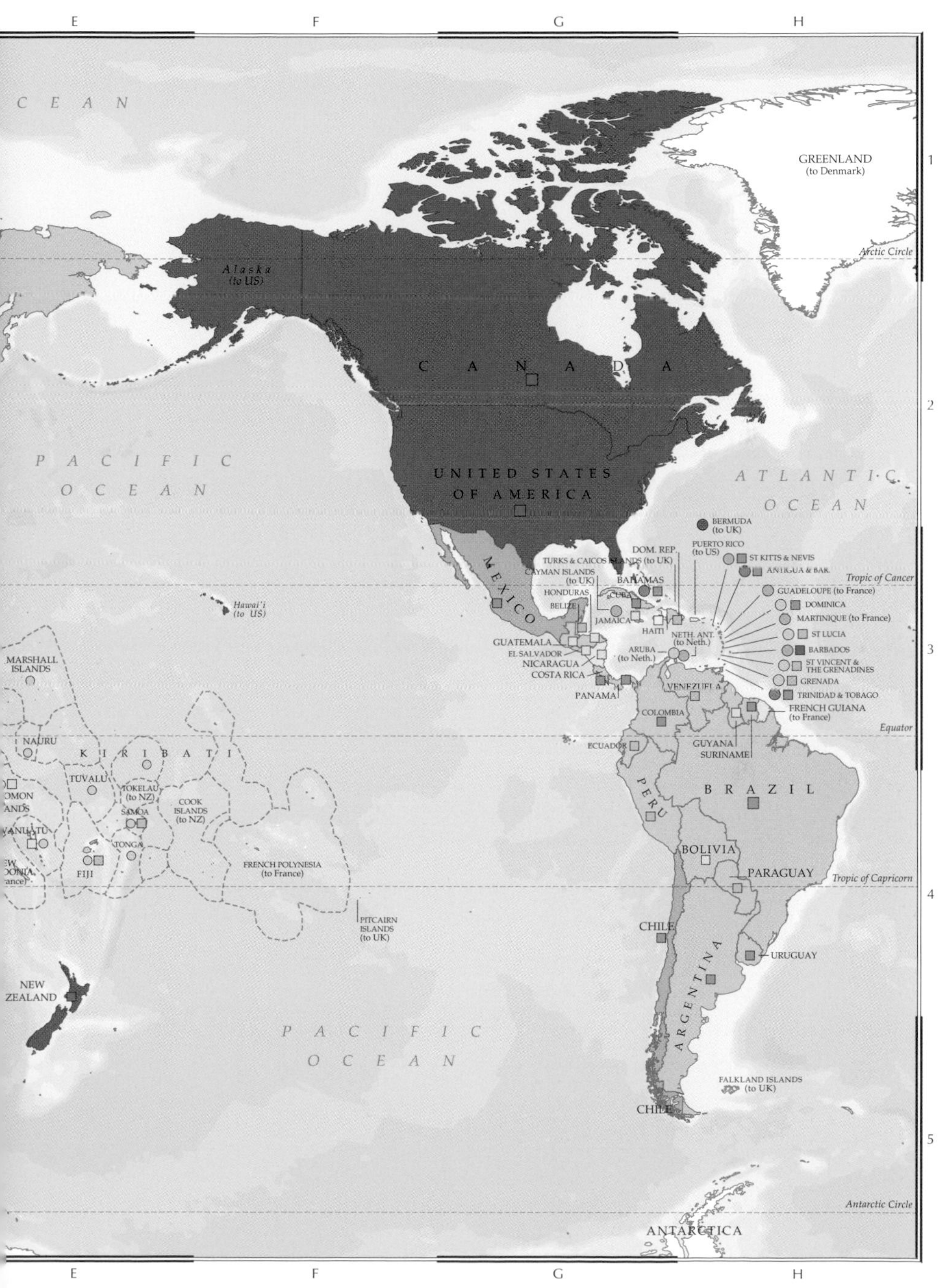
E
F
G
H
1
2
3
4
5
PACIFIC OCEAN
ATLANTIC OCEAN
GREENLAND (to Denmark)
Arctic Circle
Alaska (to US)
CANADA
UNITED STATES OF AMERICA
BERMUDA (to UK)
DOM. REP.
PUERTO RICO (to US)
TURKS & CAICOS ISLANDS (to UK)
ST KITTS & NEVIS
CAYMAN ISLANDS (to UK)
ANTIGUA & BAR.
BAHAMAS
Tropic of Cancer
HONDURAS
GUADELOUPE (to France)
CUBA
BELIZE
DOMINICA
MARTINIQUE (to France)
JAMAICA
HAITI
NETH. ANT. (to Neth.)
ST LUCIA
MEXICO
Hawai'i (to US)
GUATEMALA
EL SALVADOR
NICARAGUA
COSTA RICA
PANAMA
ARUBA (to Neth.)
BARBADOS
ST VINCENT & THE GRENADINES
GRENADA
TRINIDAD & TOBAGO
FRENCH GUIANA (to France)
VENEZUELA
COLOMBIA
Equator
ECUADOR
GUYANA
SURINAME
MARSHALL ISLANDS
NAURU
KIRIBATI
TUVALU
TOKELAU (to NZ)
SAMOA
COOK ISLANDS (to NZ)
TONGA
FIJI
FRENCH POLYNESIA (to France)
PITCAIRN ISLANDS (to UK)
PERU
BRAZIL
BOLIVIA
PARAGUAY
Tropic of Capricorn
CHILE
URUGUAY
ARGENTINA
NEW ZEALAND
FALKLAND ISLANDS (to UK)
Antarctic Circle
ANTARCTICA

Global Conflict

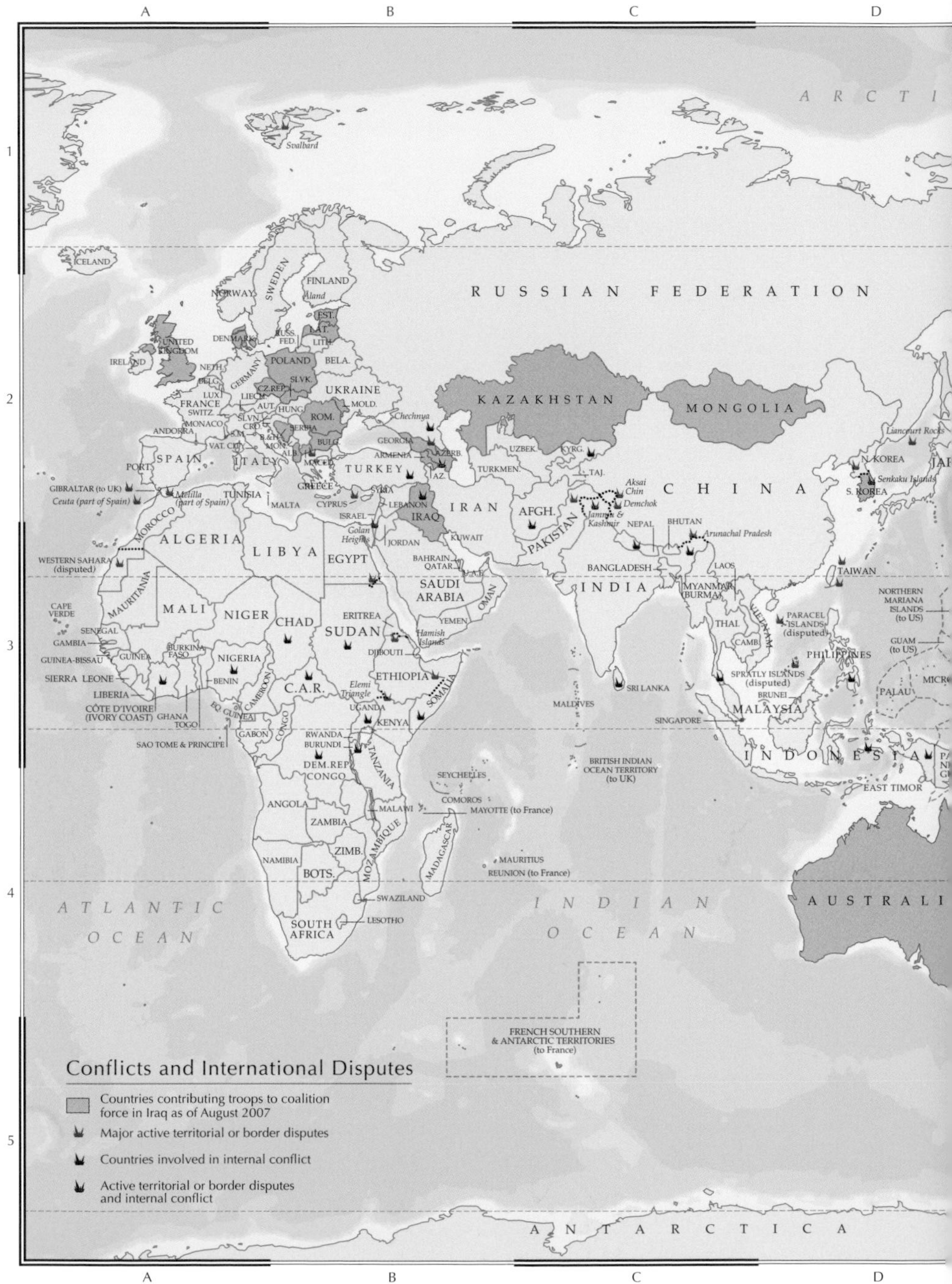

A R C T I

ICELAND

NORWAY SWEDEN FINLAND
Åland
EST.
RUSS. LAT.
FED. LITH.
DENMARK
UNITED IRELAND KINGDOM
NETH.
LUX. GERMANY POLAND BELA.
FRANCE SWITZ. CZ.REP.
MONACO SLVK. UKRAINE
ANDORRA AUT. HUNG. MOLD.
SLVN. SERBIA ROM.
VAT. CITY B.H. BULG. GEORGIA
SPAIN ITALY ALB. ARMENIA AZERB.
MAC.
PORT. TURKEY AZ.
GIBRALTAR (to UK) GREECE TURKMEN.
Ceuta (part of Spain) TUNISIA MALTA CYPRUS SYRIA
Melilla (part of Spain) LEBANON IRAQ IRAN AFGH.
MOROCCO ISRAEL JORDAN
WESTERN SAHARA Golan KUWAIT
(disputed) ALGERIA LIBYA EGYPT Heights BAHRAIN
QATAR. U.A.E.
MAURITANIA SAUDI
CAPE ARABIA OMAN
VERDE MALI NIGER CHAD ERITREA YEMEN
SENEGAL SUDAN Hanish
GAMBIA BURKINA DJIBOUTI Islands
GUINEA-BISSAU GUINEA FASO NIGERIA
SIERRA LEONE BENIN ETHIOPIA
LIBERIA C.A.R. Elemi SOMALIA
CÔTE D'IVOIRE CAMEROON Triangle
(IVORY COAST) GHANA TOGO UGANDA
SAO TOME & PRINCIPE GABON KENYA
RWANDA
DEM. REP. BURUNDI TANZANIA SEYCHELLES
CONGO
ANGOLA COMOROS
ZAMBIA MALAWI MAYOTTE (to France)
NAMIBIA ZIMB. MAURITIUS
BOTS. REUNION (to France)
SWAZILAND
SOUTH LESOTHO
AFRICA

RUSSIAN FEDERATION

KAZAKHSTAN MONGOLIA

Chechnya

UZBEK. KYRG.
TAJ.
Aksai CHINA
Chin
Jammu & Demchok
Kashmir Arunachal Pradesh
PAKISTAN NEPAL BHUTAN
BANGLADESH LAOS
INDIA MYANMAR
(BURMA) THAI.
CAMB.
SRI LANKA
MALDIVES
SINGAPORE

BRITISH INDIAN
OCEAN TERRITORY
(to UK)

N. KOREA JAI
S. KOREA
Senkaku Islands
Liancourt Rocks

TAIWAN
NORTHERN
MARIANA
ISLANDS
(to US)
PARACEL GUAM
ISLANDS (to US)
(disputed)
PHILIPPINES
SPRATLY ISLANDS MICR
(disputed) PALAU
MALAYSIA

BRUNEI
I N D O N E S I A PN
NG
EAST TIMOR

A U S T R A L I

ATLANTIC
OCEAN

I N D I A N
O C E A N

AUSTRALI

FRENCH SOUTHERN
& ANTARCTIC TERRITORIES
(to France)

Svalbard

Conflicts and International Disputes

☐ Countries contributing troops to coalition
force in Iraq as of August 2007

♛ Major active territorial or border disputes

♛ Countries involved in internal conflict

♛ Active territorial or border disputes
and internal conflict

A N T A R C T I C A

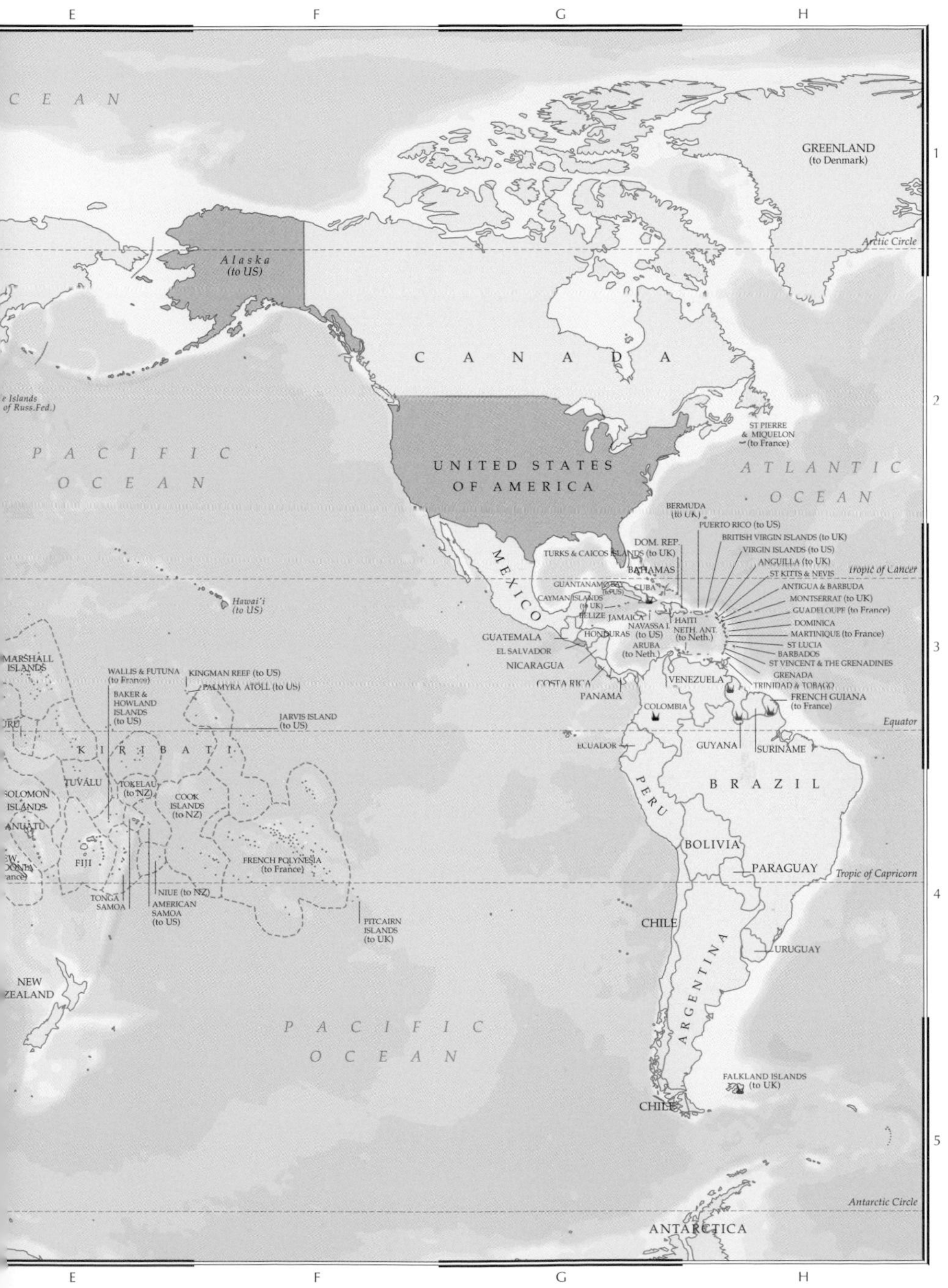

E   F   G   H

O C E A N

GREENLAND
(to Denmark)

1

Arctic Circle

Alaska
(to US)

e Islands
of Russ.Fed.)

2

C A N A D A

P A C I F I C

O C E A N

A T L A N T I C

· O C E A N

UNITED STATES
OF AMERICA

ST PIERRE
& MIQUELON
(to France)

BERMUDA
(to UK)

Hawai'i
(to US)

DOM. REP.
TURKS & CAICOS ISLANDS (to UK)

PUERTO RICO (to US)
BRITISH VIRGIN ISLANDS (to UK)
VIRGIN ISLANDS (to US)
ANGUILLA (to UK)
ST KITTS & NEVIS

MARSHALL
ISLANDS

WALLIS & FUTUNA
(to France)

KINGMAN REEF (to US)

PALMYRA ATOLL (to US)

BAKER &
HOWLAND
ISLANDS
(to US)

JARVIS ISLAND
(to US)

K I R I B A T I

SOLOMON
ISLANDS

ANUATU

TOKELAU
(to NZ)

TUVÁLU

COOK
ISLANDS
(to NZ)

FIJI

W.
OA
ance)

FRENCH POLYNESIA
(to France)

TONGA
SAMOA

NIUE (to NZ)

AMERICAN
SAMOA
(to US)

PITCAIRN
ISLANDS
(to UK)

NEW
ZEALAND

P A C I F I C

O C E A N

Tropic of Cancer

MEXICO

GUANTANAMO

CUBA

CAYMAN ISLANDS
(to UK)

BELIZE
JAMAICA

HAITI

GUATEMALA

EL SALVADOR

HONDURAS

NAVASSA I.
(to US)

NETH. ANT.
(to Neth.)

NICARAGUA

ARUBA
(to Neth.)

COSTA RICA

VENEZUELA

PANAMA

COLOMBIA

ECUADOR

PERU

GUYANA

SURINAME

B R A Z I L

BOLIVIA

ANTIGUA & BARBUDA
MONTSERRAT (to UK)
GUADELOUPE (to France)
DOMINICA
MARTINIQUE (to France)
ST LUCIA
BARBADOS
ST VINCENT & THE GRENADINES
GRENADA
TRINIDAD & TOBAGO
FRENCH GUIANA
(to France)

Equator

BAHAMAS

3

PARAGUAY

Tropic of Capricorn

4

CHILE

URUGUAY

A R G E N T I N A

CHILE

FALKLAND ISLANDS
(to UK)

5

Antarctic Circle

ANTARCTICA

E   F   G   H

The WORLD'S REGIONS

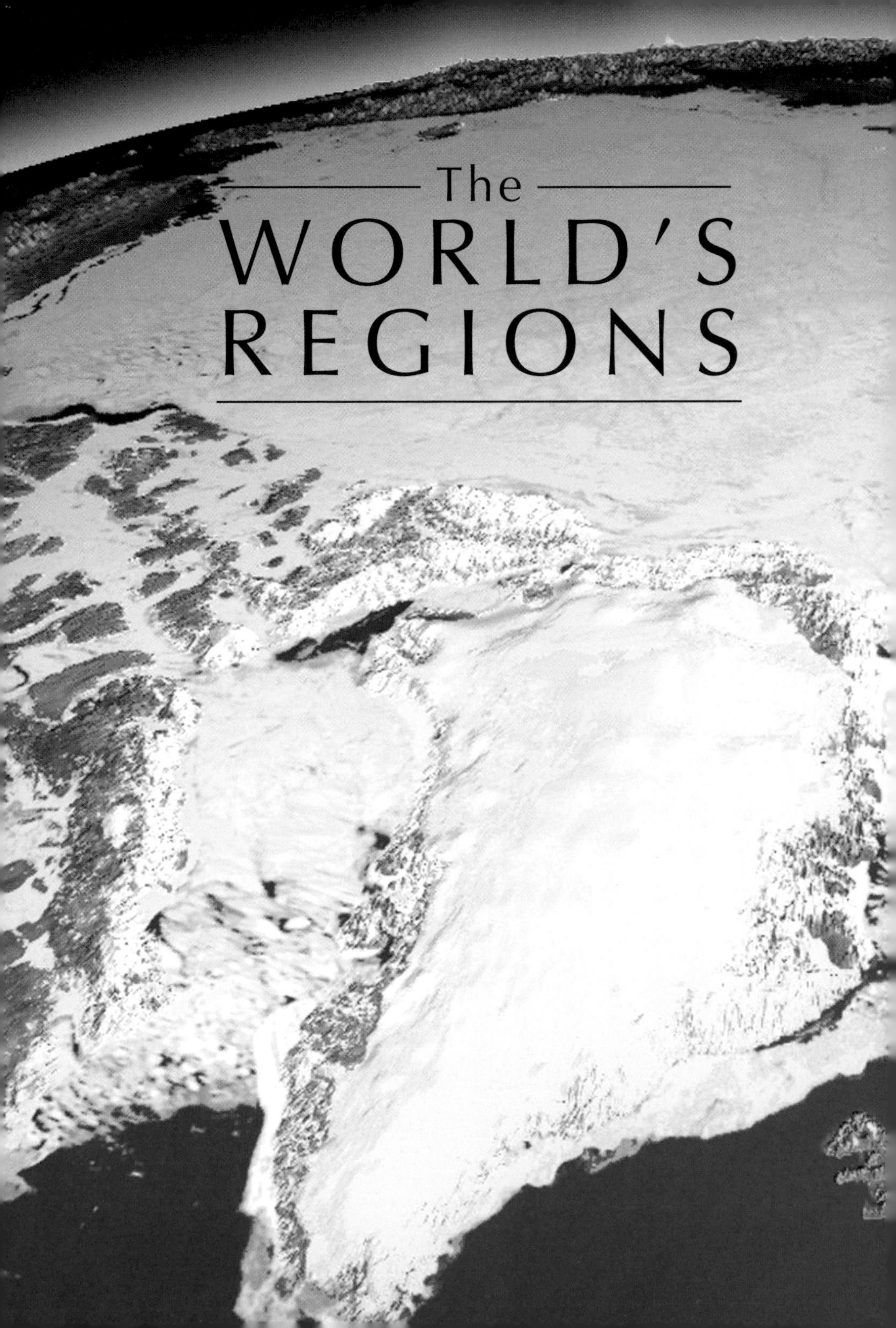

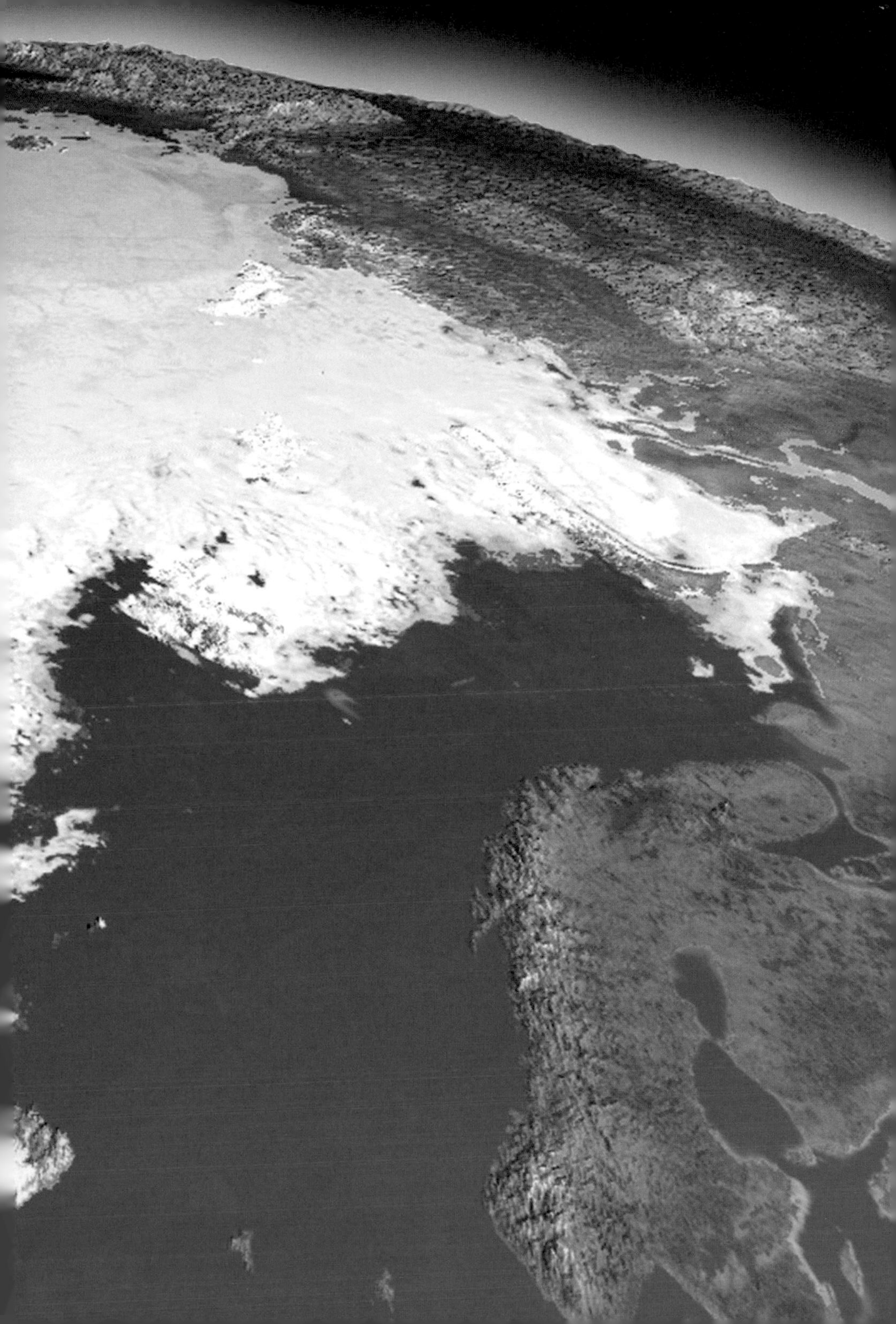

North & Central America

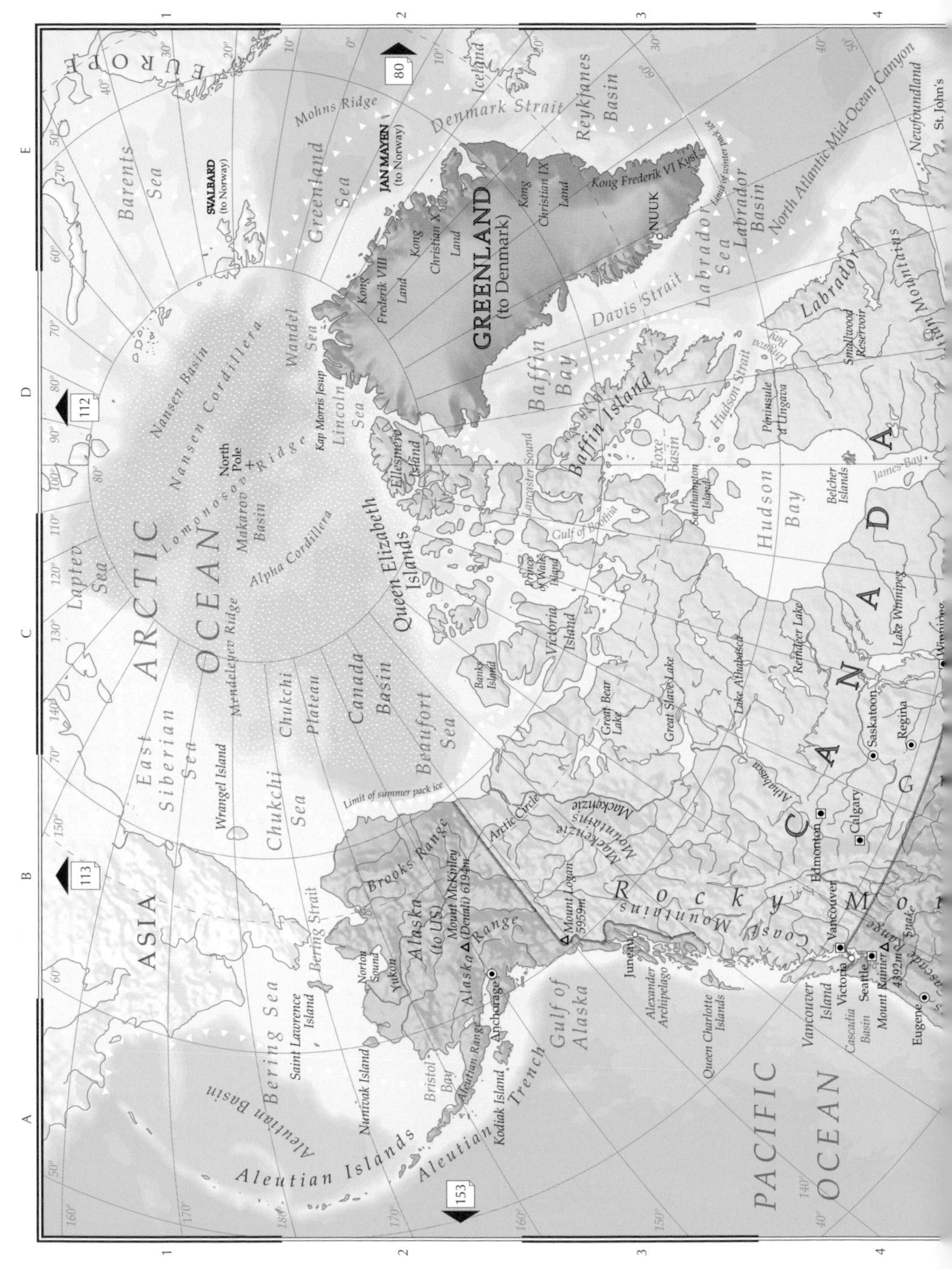

EUROPE

Barents Sea

SVALBARD (to Norway)

Mohns Ridge

JAN MAYEN (to Norway)

Greenland Sea

Denmark Strait

Iceland

Reykjanes Basin

80

Kong Christian IX Land

Kong Frederik VI Kyst

Kong Christian X Land

North Atlantic Mid-Ocean Canyon

Newfoundland

St. John's

GREENLAND (to Denmark)

NUUK

Kong Frederik VIII Land

Kap Morris Jesup

Wandel Sea

Lincoln Sea

Nansen Basin

Nansen Cordillera

Lomonosov Ridge

North Pole

Makarov Basin

Alpha Cordillera

Mendeleyev Ridge

112

Ellesmere Island

Davis Strait

Labrador Sea

Labrador Basin

Baffin Bay

Lancaster Sound

Hudson Strait

Peninsule d'Ungava

Labrador

Smallwood Reservoir

Appalachian Mountains

ARCTIC OCEAN

Queen Elizabeth Islands

Gulf of Boothia

Foxe Basin

Southampton Island

Baffin Island

Hudson Bay

Belcher Islands

James Bay

Reindeer Lake

Lake Winnipeg

Winnipeg

Prince of Wales Island

Victoria Island

Banks Island

Great Bear Lake

Great Slave Lake

Lake Athabasca

Saskatoon

Regina

Laptev Sea

East Siberian Sea

Wrangel Island

Chukchi Sea

Chukchi Plateau

Canada Basin

Beaufort Sea

Limit of summer pack ice

Athabasca

C A N A D A

Calgary

Edmonton

Mackenzie

Mackenzie Mountains

ASIA

Bering Strait

Saint Lawrence Island

Norton Sound

Yukon

Anchorage

Arctic Circle

Brooks Range

Alaska (to US)

Mount McKinley (Denali) 6194m

Alaska Range

Mount Logan 5959m

R o c k y   M o u

Coast

Vancouver

Seattle

Mount Rainier 4392m

Cascadia Basin

Eugene

Juneau

Alexander Archipelago

Vancouver Island

Victoria

Bering Sea

Nunivak Island

Bristol Bay

Aleutian Range

Kodiak Island

Gulf of Alaska

Aleutian Trench

Queen Charlotte Islands

Aleutian Basin

Aleutian Islands

153

PACIFIC OCEAN

113

0 km   1000

0 miles   1000

34

Population

● National capital

○ below 50,000

○ 50,000 to 100,000

◉ 100,000 to 500,000

◙ above 500,000

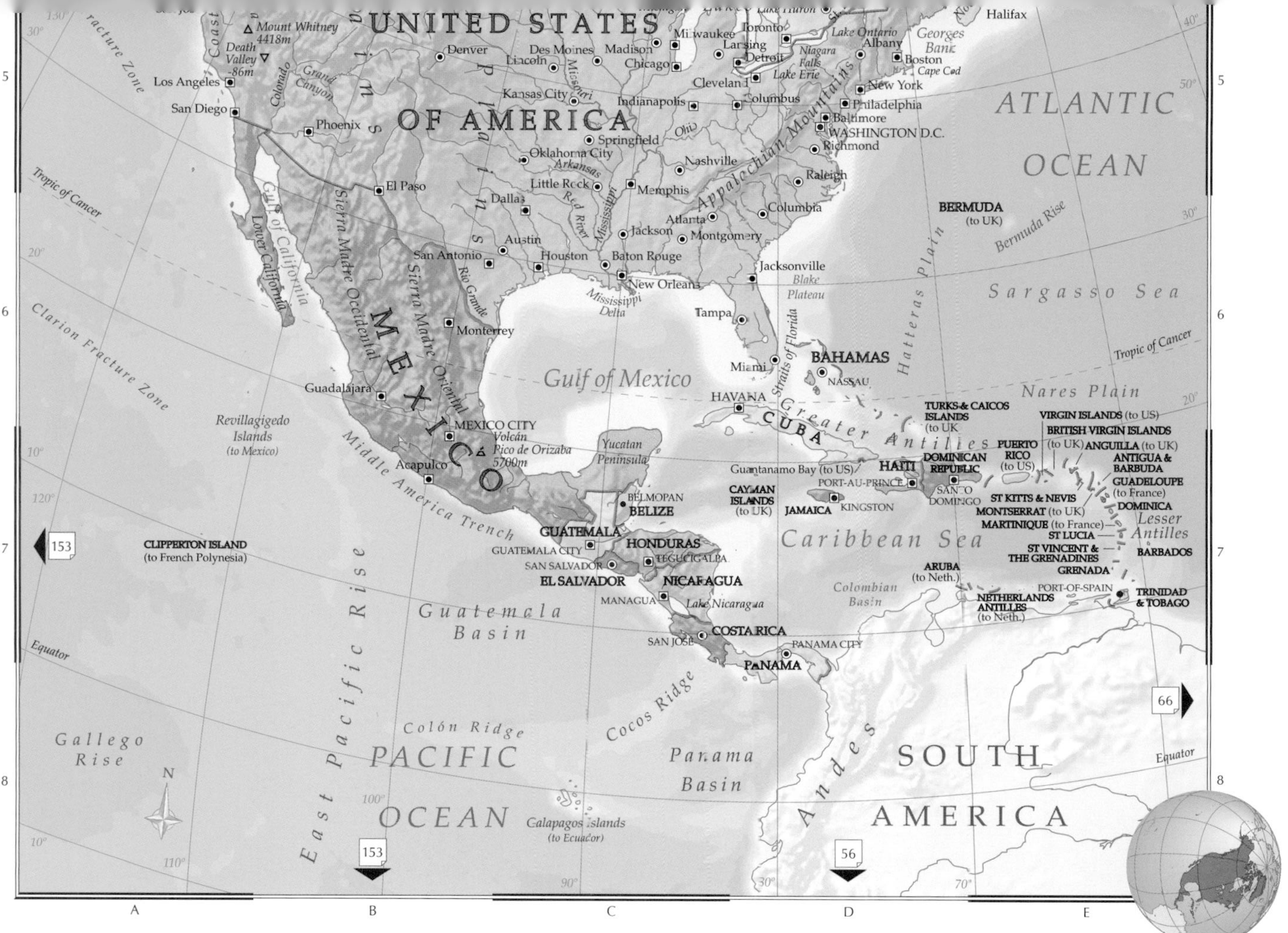

UNITED STATES OF AMERICA
MEXICO
ATLANTIC OCEAN
PACIFIC OCEAN
SOUTH AMERICA
Gulf of Mexico
Caribbean Sea
Sargasso Sea
Gulf of California
Lower California
BAHAMAS
CUBA
HAITI
DOMINICAN REPUBLIC
JAMAICA
BELIZE
GUATEMALA
HONDURAS
EL SALVADOR
NICARAGUA
COSTA RICA
PANAMA
BERMUDA (to UK)
TURKS & CAICOS ISLANDS (to UK
CAYMAN ISLANDS (to UK)
PUERTO RICO (to US)
VIRGIN ISLANDS (to US)
BRITISH VIRGIN ISLANDS (to UK)
ANGUILLA (to UK)
ANTIGUA & BARBUDA
GUADELOUPE (to France)
ST KITTS & NEVIS
MONTSERRAT (to UK)
DOMINICA
MARTINIQUE (to France)
ST LUCIA
ST VINCENT & THE GRENADINES
BARBADOS
GRENADA
TRINIDAD & TOBAGO
ARUBA (to Neth.)
NETHERLANDS ANTILLES (to Neth.)
CLIPPERTON ISLAND (to French Polynesia)
Revillagigedo Islands (to Mexico)
Galapagos Islands (to Ecuador)
WASHINGTON D.C.
MEXICO CITY
HAVANA
NASSAU
PORT-AU-PRINCE
SANTO DOMINGO
KINGSTON
BELMOPAN
GUATEMALA CITY
SAN SALVADOR
TEGUCIGALPA
MANAGUA
SAN JOSÉ
PANAMA CITY
PORT-OF-SPAIN
Halifax
Toronto
Milwaukee
Lansing
Detroit
Lake Ontario
Albany
Georges Bank
Boston
Cape Cod
Niagara Falls
Lake Erie
Denver
Des Moines
Madison
Lincoln
Chicago
Los Angeles
San Diego
Mount Whitney 4418m
Death Valley -86m
Colorado
Grand Canyon
Kansas City
Missouri
Indianapolis
Cleveland
Columbus
New York
Philadelphia
Baltimore
Phoenix
Springfield
Ohio
Richmond
Oklahoma City
Arkansas
Nashville
Appalachian Mountains
El Paso
Little Rock
Memphis
Raleigh
Dallas
Red River
Mississippi
Columbia
Atlanta
Jackson
Montgomery
Austin
San Antonio
Houston
Baton Rouge
Jacksonville
Blake Plateau
New Orleans
Mississippi Delta
Rio Grande
Sierra Madre Occidental
Sierra Madre Oriental
Monterrey
Tampa
Miami
Straits of Florida
Hatteras Plain
Bermuda Rise
Tropic of Cancer
Clarion Fracture Zone
Guadalajara
Nares Plain
Greater Antilles
Lesser Antilles
Volcán Pico de Orizaba 5700m
Yucatan Peninsula
Acapulco
Middle America Trench
Guantanamo Bay (to US)
Colombian Basin
Lake Nicaragua
Guatemala Basin
East Pacific Rise
Equator
Colón Ridge
Cocos Ridge
Panama Basin
Andes
Gallego Rise
N
153
153
56
66

Western Canada & Alaska

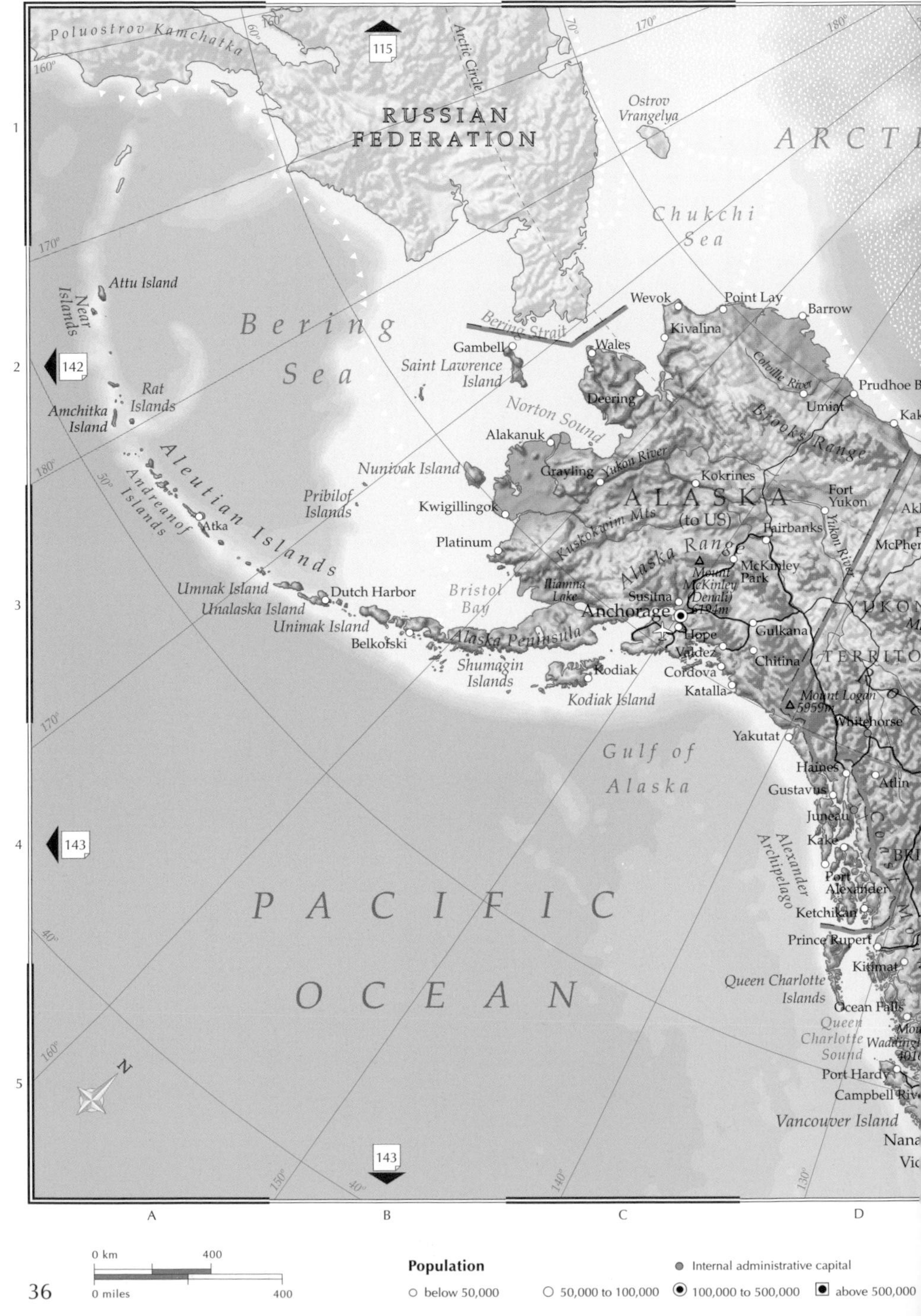

Poluostrov Kamchatka

115

RUSSIAN
FEDERATION

Arctic Circle

Ostrov
Vrangelya

ARCTI

Chukchi
Sea

Near
Islands

Attu Island

142

Bering

Sea

Bering Strait

Wevok

Point Lay

Barrow

Kivalina

Gambell

Wales

Saint Lawrence
Island

Deering

Colville River

Prudhoe
Bay

Kak

Rat
Islands

Norton Sound

Alakanuk

Umiat

Brooks Range

Amchitka
Island

Aleutian Islands

Andreanof
Islands

Atka

Nunivak Island

Grayling

Yukon River

Kokrines

Fort
Yukon

Akl

Pribilof
Islands

Kwigillingok

ALASKA
(to US)

Fairbanks

Yukon River

Kuskokwim Mts.

McPher

F

Platinum

Umnak Island

Unalaska Island

Dutch Harbor

Bristol
Bay

Iliamna
Lake

Alaska Range

Mount
McKinley
(Denali)
6194m

McKinley
Park

YUKON

Unimak Island

Belkofski

Alaska Peninsula

Susitna

Anchorage

Hope

Gulkana

Chitina

TERRITO

M

Shumagin
Islands

Kodiak

Valdez

Cordova

Katalla

Mount Logan
5959m

Kodiak Island

Gulf of
Alaska

Yakutat

Whitehorse

143

PACIFIC

OCEAN

Haines

Gustavus

Juneau

Atlin

Kake

BK

Alexander Archipelago

Port
Alexander

Ketchikan

Prince Rupert

Kitimat

Queen Charlotte
Islands

Ocean Falls

Queen
Charlotte
Sound

Wadding

Mol

401

Port Hardy

Campbell Rive

Vancouver Island

Nana

Vic

143

0 km   400

0 miles   400

Population

○ below 50,000   ○ 50,000 to 100,000   ◉ 100,000 to 500,000   ▣ above 500,000

● Internal administrative capital

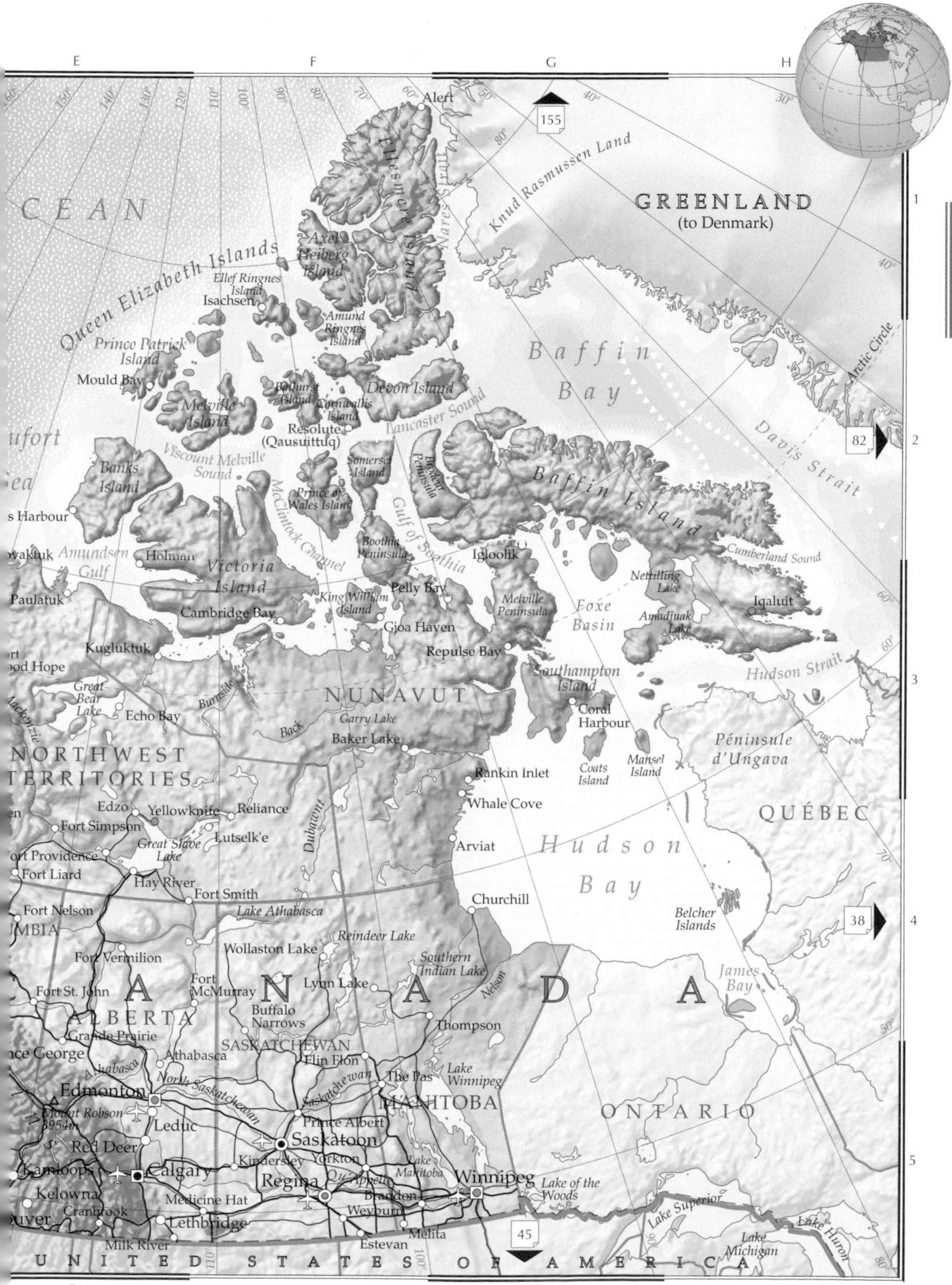
E
F
G
H
155
82
38
45
1
2
3
4
5
GREENLAND
(to Denmark)
Knud Rasmussen Land
Alert
Ellesmere Island
Nares Strait
Axel Heiberg Island
Queen Elizabeth Islands
Ellef Ringnes Island
Isachsen
Amund Ringnes Island
Prince Patrick Island
Mould Bay
Melville Island
Bathurst Island
Cornwallis Island
Devon Island
Resolute
(Qausuittuq)
Lancaster Sound
Baffin Bay
Davis Strait
Arctic Circle
Viscount Melville Sound
Banks Island
Somerset Island
Brodeur Peninsula
Baffin Island
Prince of Wales Island
McClintock Channel
Gulf of Boothia
Boothia Peninsula
Igloolik
Cumberland Sound
Nettilling Lake
Amundsen Gulf
Holman
Victoria Island
Pelly Bay
King William Island
Melville Peninsula
Foxe Basin
Amadjuak Lake
Iqaluit
Paulatuk
Cambridge Bay
Gjoa Haven
Repulse Bay
Kugluktuk
Southampton Island
Hudson Strait
Great Bear Lake
Echo Bay
Burnside
NUNAVUT
Garry Lake
Back
Baker Lake
Coral Harbour
Coats Island
Mansel Island
Péninsule d'Ungava
NORTHWEST TERRITORIES
Rankin Inlet
Whale Cove
QUÉBEC
Edzo
Yellowknife
Reliance
Fort Simpson
Lutselk'e
Great Slave Lake
Dubawnt
Arviat
Hudson Bay
Fort Providence
Fort Liard
Hay River
Fort Smith
Lake Athabasca
Churchill
Fort Nelson
Belcher Islands
Reindeer Lake
Wollaston Lake
Fort Vermilion
Southern Indian Lake
Nelson
James Bay
CANADA
Fort St. John
Fort McMurray
Lynn Lake
ALBERTA
Buffalo Narrows
Thompson
Grande Prairie
SASKATCHEWAN
Athabasca
Flin Flon
The Pas
Lake Winnipeg
Edmonton
North Saskatchewan
Saskatchewan
MANITOBA
ONTARIO
Mount Robson
3954m
Leduc
Prince Albert
Saskatoon
Red Deer
Kindersley
Yorkton
Lake Manitoba
Kamloops
Calgary
Regina
Qu'Appelle
Winnipeg
Lake of the Woods
Kelowna
Medicine Hat
Brandon
Cranbrook
Weyburn
Lake Superior
Lethbridge
Melita
Lake Huron
Milk River
Estevan
Lake Michigan
UNITED STATES OF AMERICA

Elevation

-4000m	-3000m	-2000m	-1000m	-500m	Below sea level	0	100m	250m	500m	1000m	2000m	4000m
-13,124ft	-9843ft	-6562ft	-3281ft	-1640ft	-820ft/-250m	0	328ft	820ft	1640ft	3281ft	6562ft	13,124ft

Eastern Canada

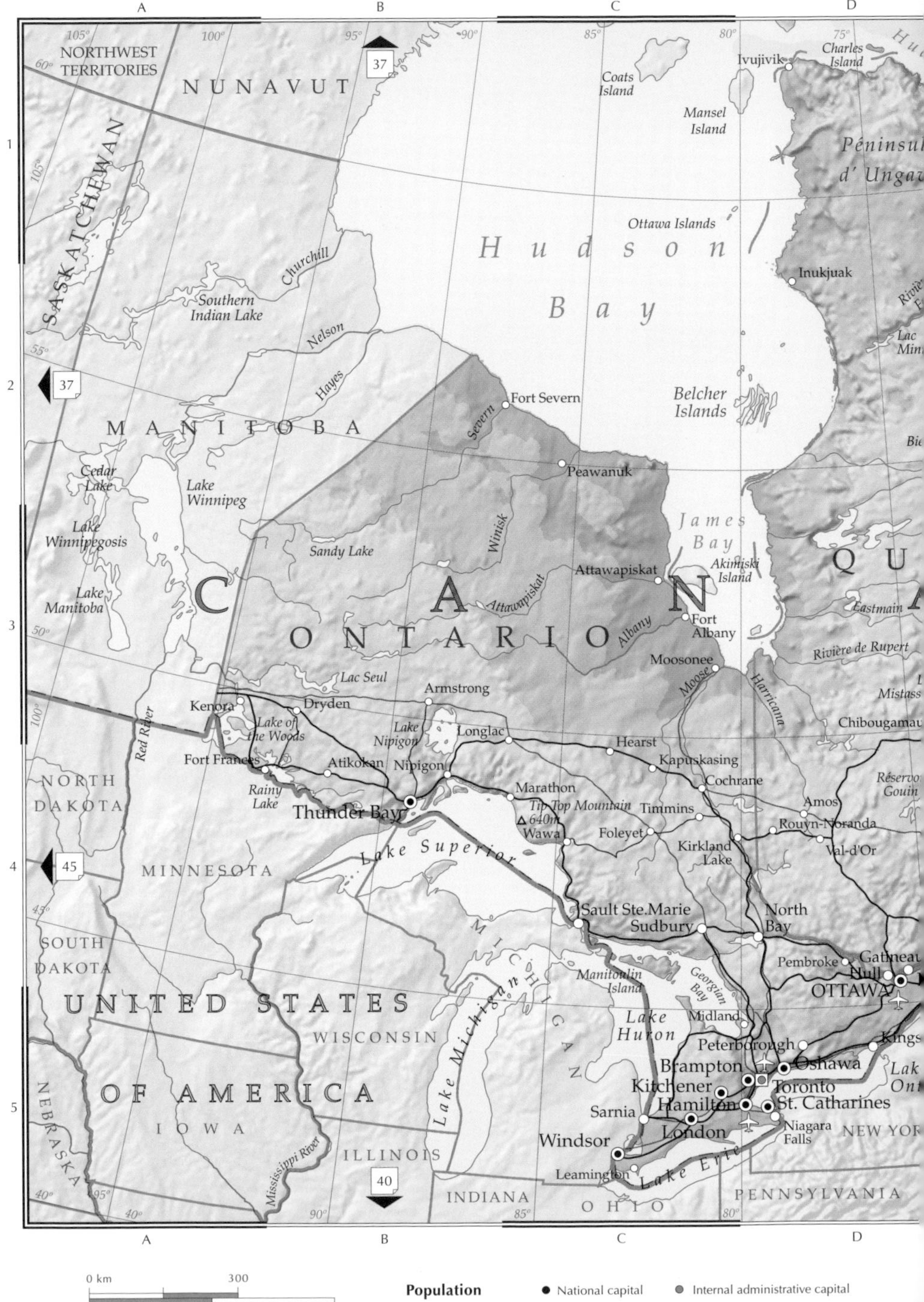

NORTHWEST
TERRITORIES

NUNAVUT

SASKATCHEWAN

Churchill

Southern
Indian Lake

Nelson

M A N I T O B A

Hayes

Severn

Coats
Island

Mansel
Island

Ottawa Islands

H u d s o n

B a y

Ivujivik

Charles
Island

Péninsul
d' Ungav

Inukjuak

Lac
Min

Cedar
Lake

Lake
Winnipeg

Lake
Winnipegosis

Lake
Manitoba

Sandy Lake

C

Winisk

Attawapiskat

Fort Severn

Peawanuk

Belcher
Islands

J a m e s
B a y

Attawapiskat

Akimiski
Island

Bic

QU

Eastmain

Lac Seul

Armstrong

A

N

Albany

Fort
Albany

Moosonee

Moose

Rivière de Rupert

Mistass

O N T A R I O

Kenora

Dryden

Lake of
the Woods

Fort Frances

Atikokan

Lake
Nipigon

Longlac

Nipigon

Hearst

Kapuskasing

Cochrane

Hurricana

Chibougamau

Réservo
Gouin

Red River

Rainy
Lake

Thunder Bay

Marathon

Tip Top Mountain
△ 640m
Wawa

Foleyet

Timmins

Kirkland
Lake

Amos

Rouyn-Noranda

Val-d'Or

NORTH
DAKOTA

MINNESOTA

Lake Superior

Sault Ste.Marie

Sudbury

North
Bay

Pembroke

Gatinea
Hull

OTTAWA

SOUTH
DAKOTA

U N I T E D   S T A T E S

WISCONSIN

Lake Michigan

Manitoulin
Island

Georgian
Bay

Lake
Huron

Midland

Peterborough

Kings

Lak
On

NEBRASKA

O F   A M E R I C A

IOWA

Brampton

Kitchener

Hamilton

Sarnia

London

Oshawa

Toronto

St. Catharines

Niagara
Falls

NEW YOR

Windsor

ILLINOIS

Leamington

Lake Erie

INDIANA

OHIO

PENNSYLVANIA

Mississippi River

0 km   300

0 miles   300

Population

● National capital   ● Internal administrative capital

○ below 50,000   ○ 50,000 to 100,000   ◉ 100,000 to 500,000   ◼ above 500,000

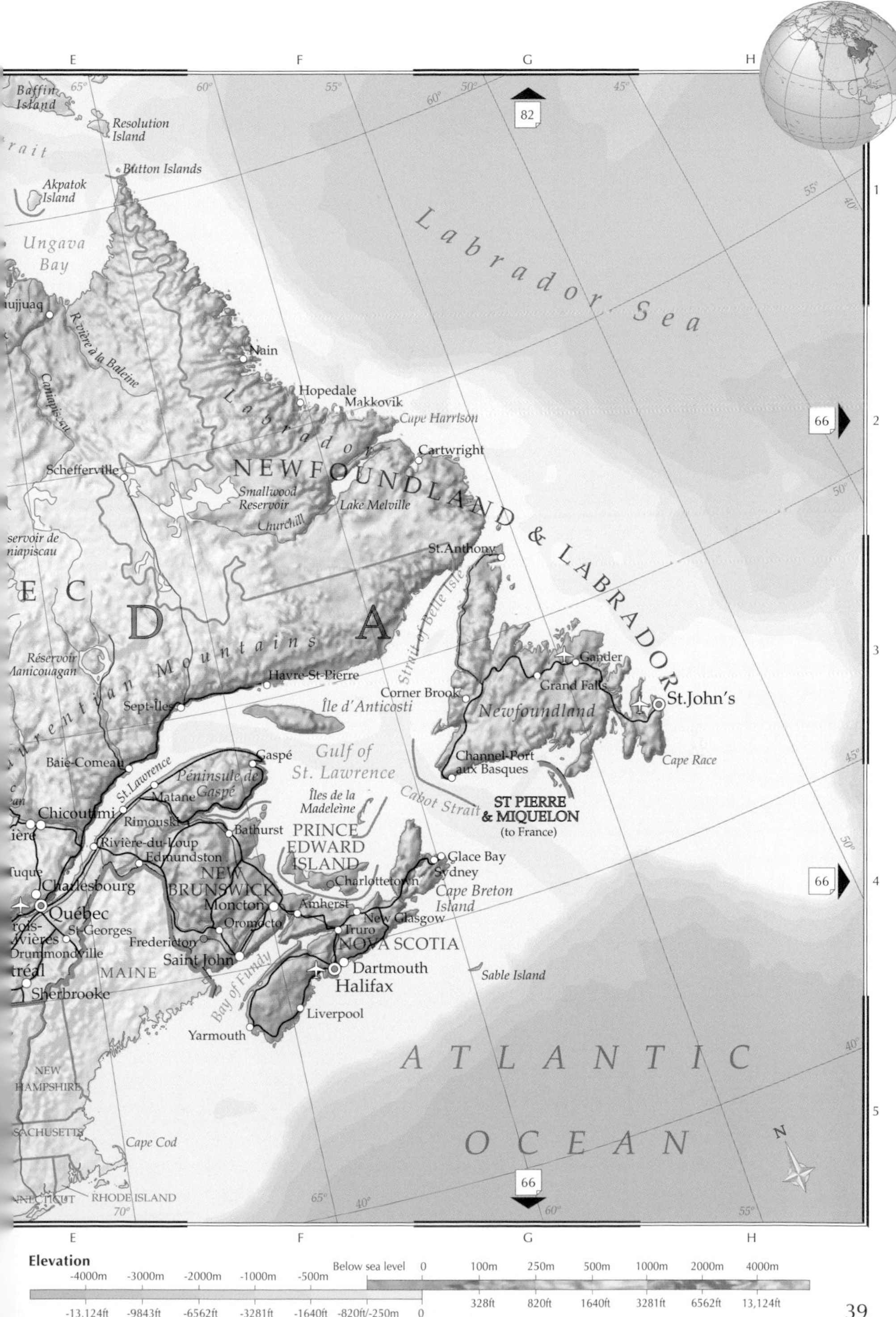

E   F   G   H

65°   60°   55°   50°   45°

82

Baffin Island

Resolution Island

Strait

Button Islands

Akpatok Island

Ungava Bay

uujuaq

Rivière de la Baleine

Nain

Hopedale

Makkovik

Cape Harrison

Cartwright

Scheffeville

NEWFOUNDLAND & LABRADOR

Labrador

L a b r a d o r   S e a

Smallwood Reservoir

Lake Melville

Churchill

St. Anthony

servoir de niapiscau

Réservoir Aanicouagan

E   C

D

Laurentian Mountains

A

Havre-St-Pierre

Sept-Îles

Île d'Anticosti

Strait of Belle Isle

Gander

Corner Brook

Grand Falls

St. John's

Newfoundland

Cape Race

Baie-Comeau

Chicoutimi

St. Lawrence

Gaspé

Péninsule de Gaspé

Matane

Gulf of St. Lawrence

Îles de la Madeleine

Channel-Port aux Basques

Cabot Strait

ST PIERRE & MIQUELON
(to France)

an

iere

Rimouski

Rivière-du-Loup

Bathurst

PRINCE EDWARD ISLAND

uque

Edmundston

NEW BRUNSWICK

Moncton

Charlottetown

Amherst

Glace Bay

Sydney

Cape Breton Island

Charlesbourg

Québec

ois-

St-Georges

Oromocto

New Glasgow

vières

Drummondville

Fredericton

Truro

NOVA SCOTIA

tréal

Saint John

MAINE

Dartmouth

Sherbrooke

Bay of Fundy

Halifax

Sable Island

NEW HAMPSHIRE

Liverpool

Yarmouth

A T L A N T I C

SACHUSETTS

Cape Cod

O C E A N

N

DE ISLAND   RHODE ISLAND

70°   65°   60°   55°

66

66

66

1   2   3   4   5

Elevation

-4000m	-3000m	-2000m	-1000m	-500m	Below sea level	0	100m	250m	500m	1000m	2000m	4000m
-13,124ft	-9843ft	-6562ft	-3281ft	-1640ft	-820ft/-250m	0	328ft	820ft	1640ft	3281ft	6562ft	13,124ft

39

USA: The Northeast

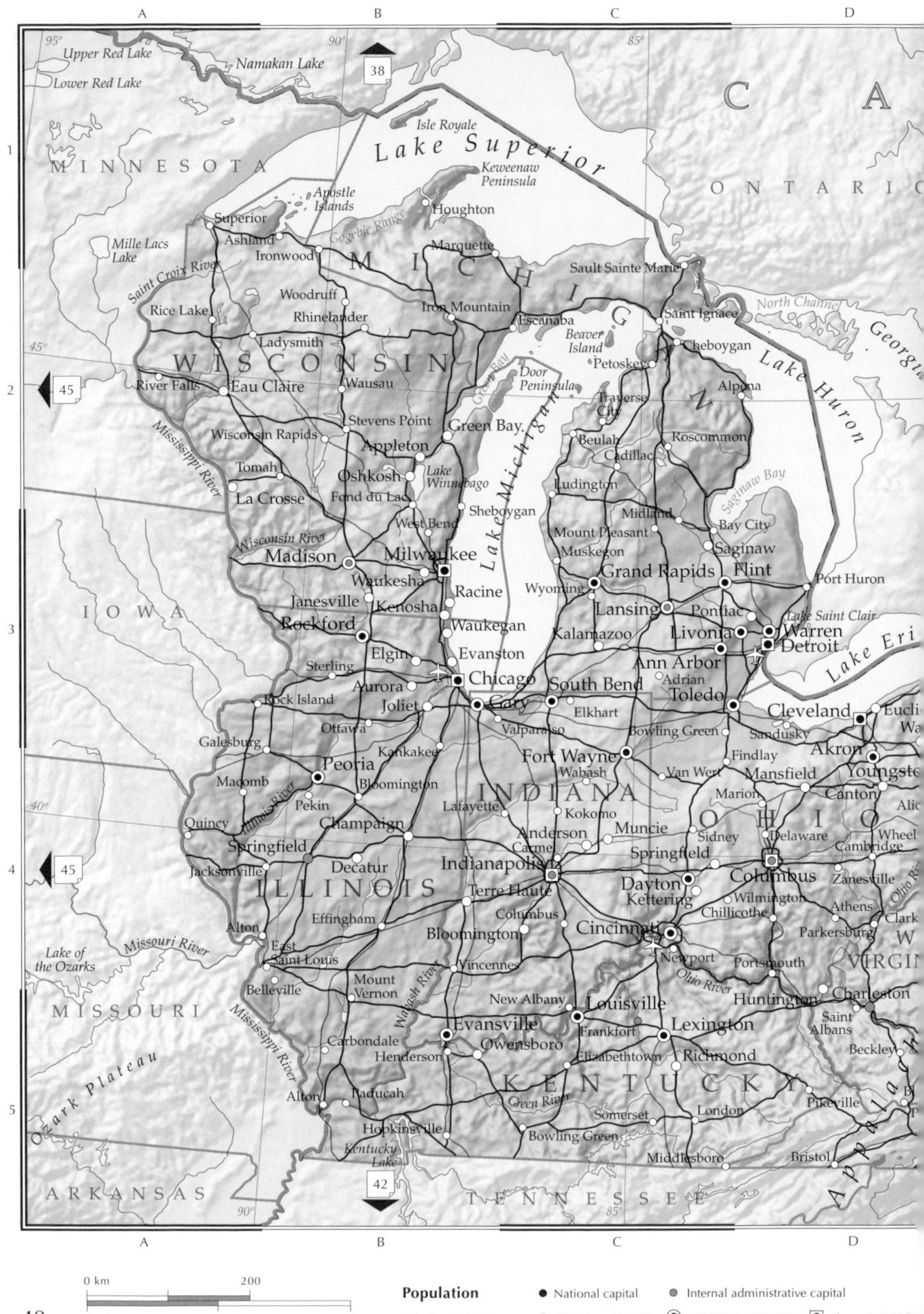

Upper Red Lake
Lower Red Lake
Namakan Lake
38
Isle Royale
Lake Superior
Keweenaw Peninsula
MINNESOTA
ONTARIO
Apostle Islands
Houghton
Superior
Ashland
Mille Lacs Lake
Ironwood
Marquette
MICHIGAN
Sault Sainte Marie
North Channel
Georgia
Woodruff
Rice Lake
Rhinelander
Iron Mountain
Escanaba
Saint Ignace
Cheboygan
Lake Huron
Ladysmith
Beaver Island
Petoskey
River Falls
Eau Claire
WISCONSIN
Wausau
Stevens Point
Door Peninsula
Traverse City
Alpena
Roscommon
Wisconsin Rapids
Appleton
Green Bay
Beulah
Cadillac
Tomah
Oshkosh
Lake Winnebago
Ludington
Midland
Bay City
Saginaw Bay
La Crosse
Fond du Lac
Sheboygan
Mount Pleasant
Muskegon
Saginaw
Flint
Madison
West Bend
Milwaukee
Grand Rapids
Port Huron
Waukesha
Racine
Wyoming
Lansing
Pontiac
Lake Saint Clair
Janesville
Kenosha
Kalamazoo
Livonia
Warren
Detroit
Rockford
Elgin
Waukegan
Ann Arbor
Lake Erie
Sterling
Evanston
Adrian
Toledo
Cleveland
Euclid
Rock Island
Aurora
Chicago
Gary
South Bend
Elkhart
Sandusky
Akron
Wa
Galesburg
Ottawa
Joliet
Valparaiso
Bowling Green
Findlay
Youngstown
Kankakee
Fort Wayne
Van Wert
Mansfield
Canton
Macomb
Peoria
Bloomington
Wabash
Marion
OHIO
Alic
Pekin
Lafayette
Kokomo
INDIANA
Sidney
Delaware
Cambridge
Wheel
Quincy
Champaign
Anderson
Muncie
Springfield
Springfield
Carmel
Columbus
Zanesville
Jacksonville
Decatur
Indianapolis
Dayton
Kettering
Wilmington
Athens
Clark
ILLINOIS
Terre Haute
Chillicothe
Parkersburg
Alton
Effingham
Columbus
Cincinnati
Portsmouth
WEST VIRGINIA
East Saint Louis
Bloomington
Vincennes
Newport
Huntington
Charleston
Belleville
Mount Vernon
New Albany
Louisville
Ohio River
Saint Albans
MISSOURI
Carbondale
Evansville
Owensboro
Frankfort
Lexington
Richmond
Beckley
Henderson
Elizabethtown
Alton
Paducah
Green River
Somerset
London
Pikeville
Bristol
MISSOURI
Lake of the Ozarks
Missouri River
Mississippi River
Ozark Plateau
Hopkinsville
Kentucky Lake
42
Bowling Green
Middlesboro
KENTUCKY
Appalachi
ARKANSAS
TENNESSEE

Population

● National capital   ● Internal administrative capital
○ below 50,000   ◉ 100,000 to 500,000
○ 50,000 to 100,000   ■ above 500,000

0 km   200
0 miles   200

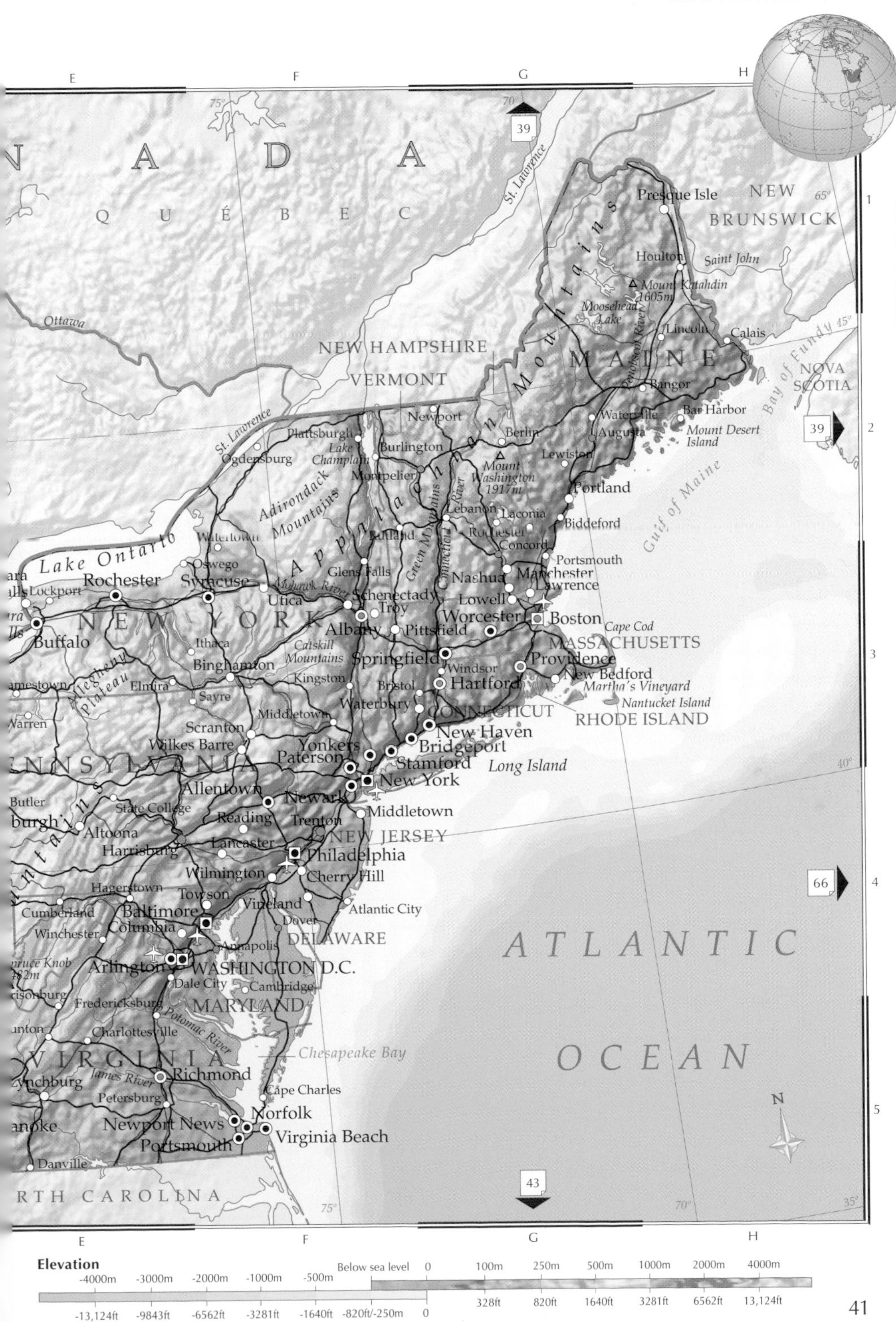

CANADA

QUÉBEC

NEW
BRUNSWICK

Ottawa

St. Lawrence

Presque Isle

Houlton   Saint John

Moosehead
Lake   △ Mount Katahdin
           1605m

Lincoln   Calais

NOVA
SCOTIA

Bay of Fundy

NEW HAMPSHIRE

VERMONT

MAINE

Bangor

Bar Harbor

Newport   Berlin   Waterville   Augusta

Plattsburgh   Lewiston   Mount Desert
Island

Ogdensburg   Burlington   Mount
Washington
1917m   Portland   Gulf of Maine

Lake
Champlain   Montpelier   Laconia

Lebanon   Biddeford

Watertown   Rochester
Rutland   Concord   Portsmouth

Lake Ontario   Oswego   Portland

Rochester   Syracuse   Glens Falls   Nashua   Manchester

Lockport   Utica   Schenectady   Lowell   Lawrence

Buffalo   Ithaca   Troy   Worcester   Boston

NEW YORK   Albany   Pittsfield   Cape Cod

Binghamton   Catskill
Mountains   Springfield   Providence

Jamestown   Elmira   Kingston   Windsor   MASSACHUSETTS

Warren   Sayre   Waterbury   Bristol   Hartford   New Bedford
                                    Martha's Vineyard
Middletown   CONNECTICUT   Nantucket Island

Scranton   New Haven   RHODE ISLAND

PENNSYLVANIA   Wilkes Barre   Yonkers   Bridgeport

Butler   Paterson   Stamford   Long Island

Pittsburgh   State College   Allentown   Newark   New York

Altoona   Reading   Middletown

Harrisburg   Lancaster   Trenton   NEW JERSEY

Hagerstown   Philadelphia

Cumberland   Wilmington   Cherry Hill

Winchester   Towson   Vineland   Atlantic City

Baltimore   Dover   DELAWARE

Columbia   Annapolis   ATLANTIC

Spruce Knob   Arlington   WASHINGTON D.C.

Harrisonburg   Dale City   Cambridge

Fredericksburg   MARYLAND

Charlottesville   Potomac River   OCEAN

VIRGINIA   Chesapeake Bay

Lynchburg   James River   Richmond   Cape Charles

Petersburg   Norfolk

Roanoke   Newport News   Virginia Beach

Danville   Portsmouth

NORTH CAROLINA

Elevation

| -4000m | -3000m | -2000m | -1000m | -500m | Below sea level | 0 | 100m | 250m | 500m | 1000m | 2000m | 4000m |

| -13,124ft | -9843ft | -6562ft | -3281ft | -1640ft | -820ft/-250m | 0 | 328ft | 820ft | 1640ft | 3281ft | 6562ft | 13,124ft |

41

USA: The Southeast

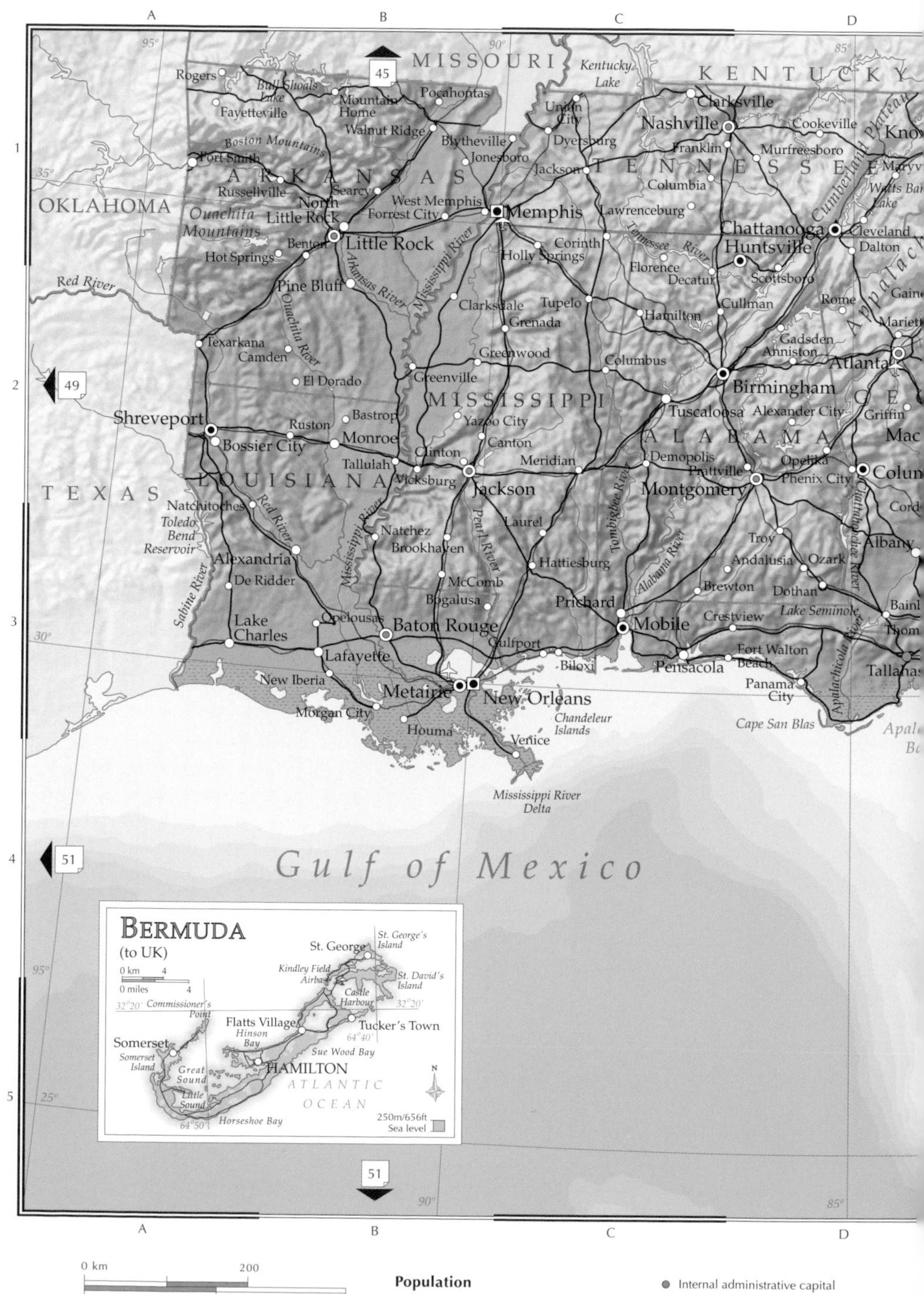

MISSOURI

KENTUCKY

Rogers
Bull Shoals Lake
Fayetteville
Mountain Home
Walnut Ridge
Pocahontas
Clarksville
Nashville
Cookeville
Knox

Fort Smith
Boston Mountains
Blytheville
Jonesboro
Jackson
Franklin
Murfreesboro
Maryv

OKLAHOMA
Russellville
ARKANSAS
Searcy
West Memphis
Memphis
Lawrenceburg
Columbia
Wats Bai
Lake

Little Rock
North Little Rock
Forrest City
Corinth
Florence
Chattanooga
Huntsville
Cleveland
Dalton

Hot Springs
Benton
Little Rock
Holly Springs
Decatur
Scottsboro
Rome
Gain

Pine Bluff
Arkansas River
Clarksdale
Tupelo
Hamilton
Cullman
Gadsden
Anniston
Mariett
Atlanta

Texarkana
Camden
El Dorado
Greenwood
Columbus
Birmingham
Griffin
Mac

Shreveport
Ruston
Bastrop
Monroe
MISSISSIPPI
Tuscaloosa
Alexander City
Col

TEXAS
LOUISIANA
Tallulah
Vicksburg
Clinton
Canton
Meridian
ALABAMA
Demopolis
Prattville
Opelika
Phenix City
Montgomery
Cord

Natchitoches
Toledo Bend Reservoir
Natchez
Brookhaven
Laurel
Troy
Andalusia
Ozark
Albany

Alexandria
De Ridder
McComb
Bogalusa
Hattiesburg
Prichard
Brewton
Dothan
Bainl
Thom

Lake Charles
Opelousas
Baton Rouge
Gulfport
Mobile
Crestview
Lake Seminole

Lafayette
New Iberia
Metairie
New Orleans
Biloxi
Pensacola
Fort Walton Beach
Panama City
Tallahas

Morgan City
Houma
Venice
Chandeleur Islands
Cape San Blas
Apal
Bu

Mississippi River Delta

Gulf of Mexico

BERMUDA
(to UK)

0 km 4
0 miles

St. George
St. George's Island
Kindley Field Airbase
St. David's Island

Commissioner's Point
Castle Harbour
Flatts Village
Hinson Bay
Tucker's Town

Somerset
Somerset Island
Great Sound
HAMILTON
Sue Wood Bay

Little Sound
ATLANTIC OCEAN

Horseshoe Bay
250m/656ft
Sea level

0 km 200
0 miles 200

Population
○ below 50,000   ○ 50,000 to 100,000   ◉ 100,000 to 500,000   ▣ above 500,000
● Internal administrative capital

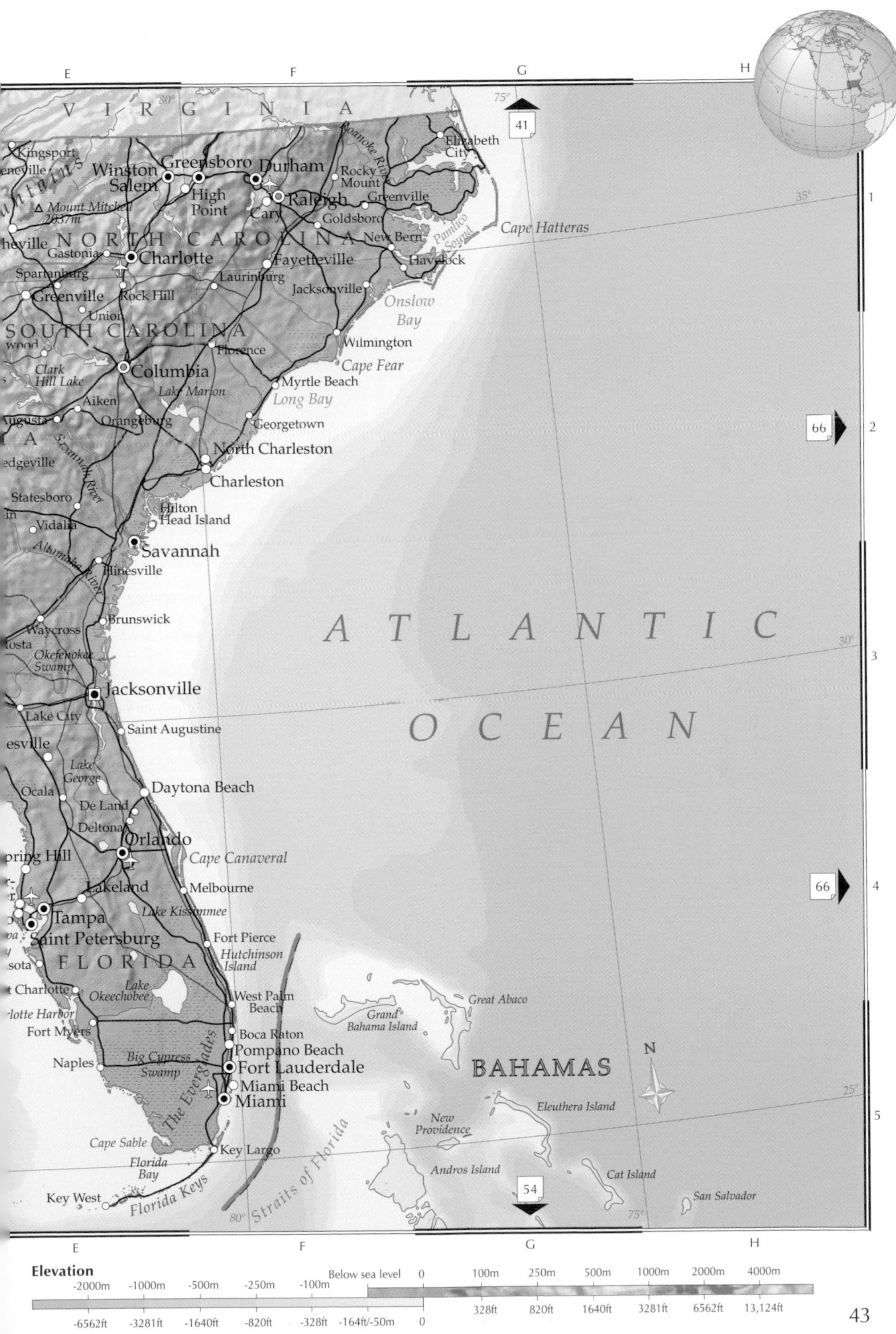

E   F   G   H

41

75°

V I R G I N I A

Kingsport
eneville
Kingsport
Winston Salem
Greensboro
Durham
Rocky Mount
Elizabeth City
High Point
Raleigh
Cary
Greenville
35° 1
Mount Mitchell 2037m
Goldsboro
New Bern
heville
N O R T H   C A R O L I N A
Cape Hatteras
Gastonia
Charlotte
Fayetteville
Havelock
Spartanburg
Laurinburg
Pamlico Sound
Greenville
Rock Hill
Jacksonville
Onslow Bay
Union
S O U T H   C A R O L I N A
wood
Florence
Wilmington

Clark Hill Lake
Columbia
Cape Fear
Aiken
Lake Marion
Myrtle Beach
Orangeburg
Long Bay
Augusta
Georgetown
66 **2**
A
North Charleston
edgeville
Charleston

Statesboro
Hilton Head Island
in
Vidalia

Savannah
Hinesville
A T L A N T I C
Waycross
Brunswick
osta
Okefenokee Swamp
30° **3**
Lake City
Jacksonville

esville
Saint Augustine
O C E A N
Ocala
Lake George
Daytona Beach
De Land
Deltona
pring Hill
Orlando
Cape Canaveral
Lakeland
Melbourne
66 **4**
Lake Kissimmee
Tampa
Fort Pierce
Saint Petersburg
Hutchinson Island
sota
F L O R I D A
Lake Okeechobee
West Palm Beach
Great Abaco
Charlotte
Boca Raton
lotte Harbor
Pompano Beach
Grand Bahama Island
Fort Myers
Big Cypress Swamp
Fort Lauderdale
Naples
Miami Beach
Miami
B A H A M A S
N
Cape Sable
Eleuthera Island
25° **5**
Key Largo
New Providence
Florida Bay
Andros Island
Cat Island
Key West
Florida Keys
San Salvador
Straits of Florida

54

80°   75°

E   F   G   H

Elevation

					Below sea level	0	100m	250m	500m	1000m	2000m	4000m
-2000m	-1000m	-500m	-250m	-100m								
-6562ft	-3281ft	-1640ft	-820ft	-328ft	-164ft/-50m	0	328ft	820ft	1640ft	3281ft	6562ft	13,124ft

USA: Central States

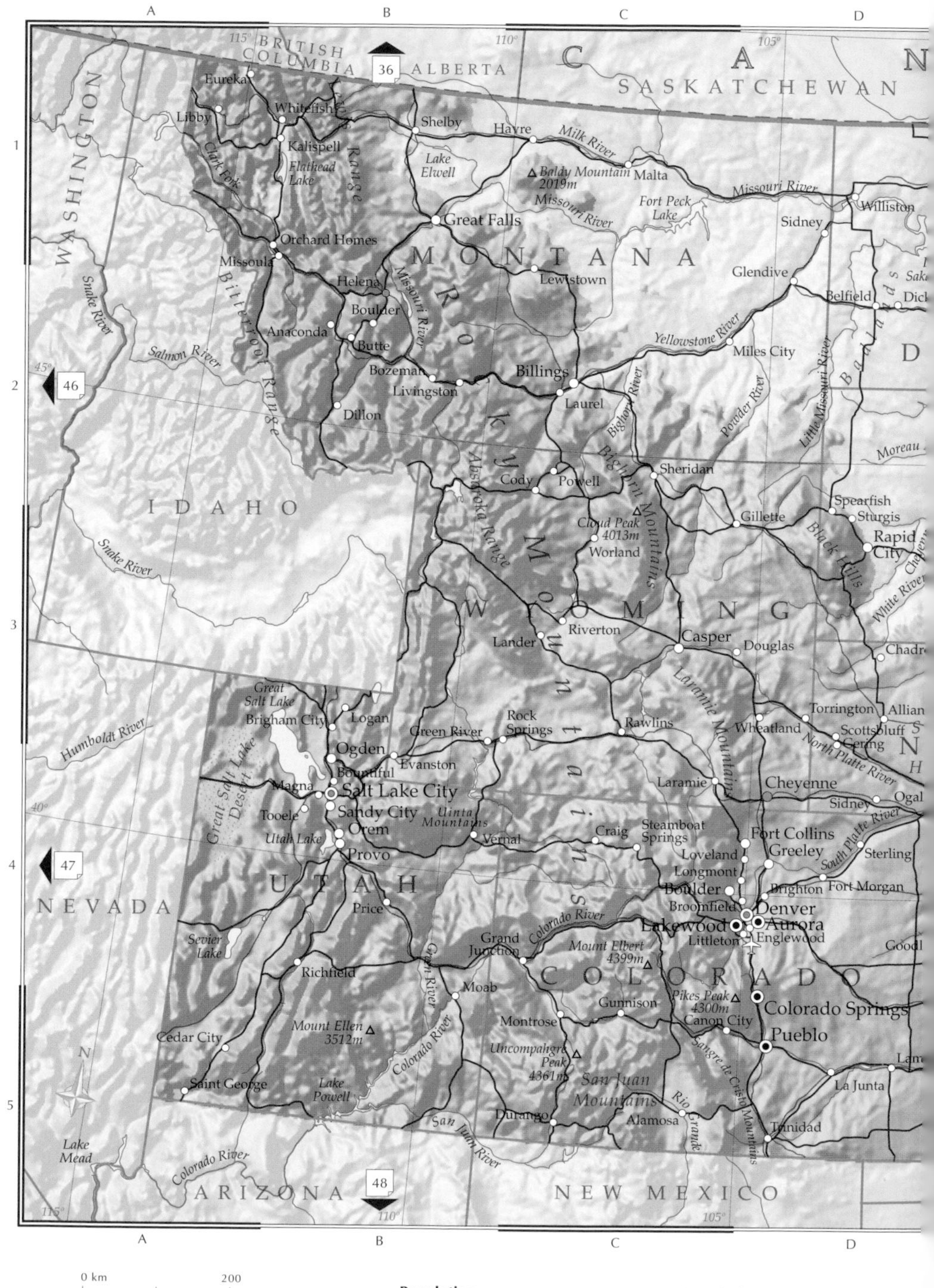

BRITISH COLUMBIA
ALBERTA
SASKATCHEWAN
C A N A D A

Eureka
Libby
Whitefish
Shelby
Havre
Milk River
Malta
Williston
Sidney
Kalispell
Flathead Lake
Lake Elwell
△ Baldy Mountain 2019m
Fort Peck Lake
Missouri River
Missouri River
Orchard Homes
M O N T A N A
Great Falls
Lewistown
Glendive
Belfield
Dick
Missoula
Helena
Boulder
Anaconda
Butte
Bozeman
Livingston
Billings
Laurel
Miles City
Yellowstone River
Powder River
Dillon
Cody
Powell
Sheridan
Moreau
Gillette
Spearfish
Sturgis
Rapid City
Cloud Peak 4013m
Worland
I D A H O
Snake River
W Y O M I N G
Lander
Riverton
Casper
Douglas
Chadr
Green River
Rock Springs
Rawlins
Wheatland
Torrington
Allian
Scottsbluff
Gering
N
Great Salt Lake
Brigham City
Logan
Ogden
Evanston
Laramie
Cheyenne
Sidney
Ogal
Bountiful
Magna
Salt Lake City
Sandy City
Orem
Uinta Mountains
Vernal
Craig
Steamboat Springs
Fort Collins
Greeley
Sterling
Tooele
Utah Lake
Loveland
Longmont
Brighton
Fort Morgan
Provo
Boulder
Broomfield
Denver
Price
U T A H
Lakewood
Aurora
Littleton
Englewood
Goodl
Grand Junction
Colorado River
Mount Elbert 4399m
Richfield
Moab
C O L O R A D O
Pikes Peak △ 4300m
Colorado Springs
Montrose
Gunnison
Canon City
Pueblo
Mount Ellen △ 3512m
Uncompahgre Peak 4361m
San Juan Mountains
La Junta
Cedar City
Saint George
Lake Powell
Colorado River
Durango
Alamosa
Trinidad
Lame
La Junta
Lake Mead
Colorado River
San Juan River
Rio Grande
N E V A D A
Humboldt River
Great Salt Lake Desert
Sevier Lake
Sevier River
WASHINGTON
Libby
Clark Fork
Bitterroot Range
Salmon River
Snake River
Bitterroot Range
Rocky Mountains
Absaroka Range
Bighorn River
Bighorn Mountains
Black Hills
White River
Little Missouri River
Laramie Mountains
North Platte River
South Platte River
Sangre de Cristo Mountains
A R I Z O N A
N E W M E X I C O

Great Salt Lake

Population
○ below 50,000
○ 50,000 to 100,000
◉ 100,000 to 500,000
■ above 500,000
● Internal administrative capital

0 km   200
0 miles   200

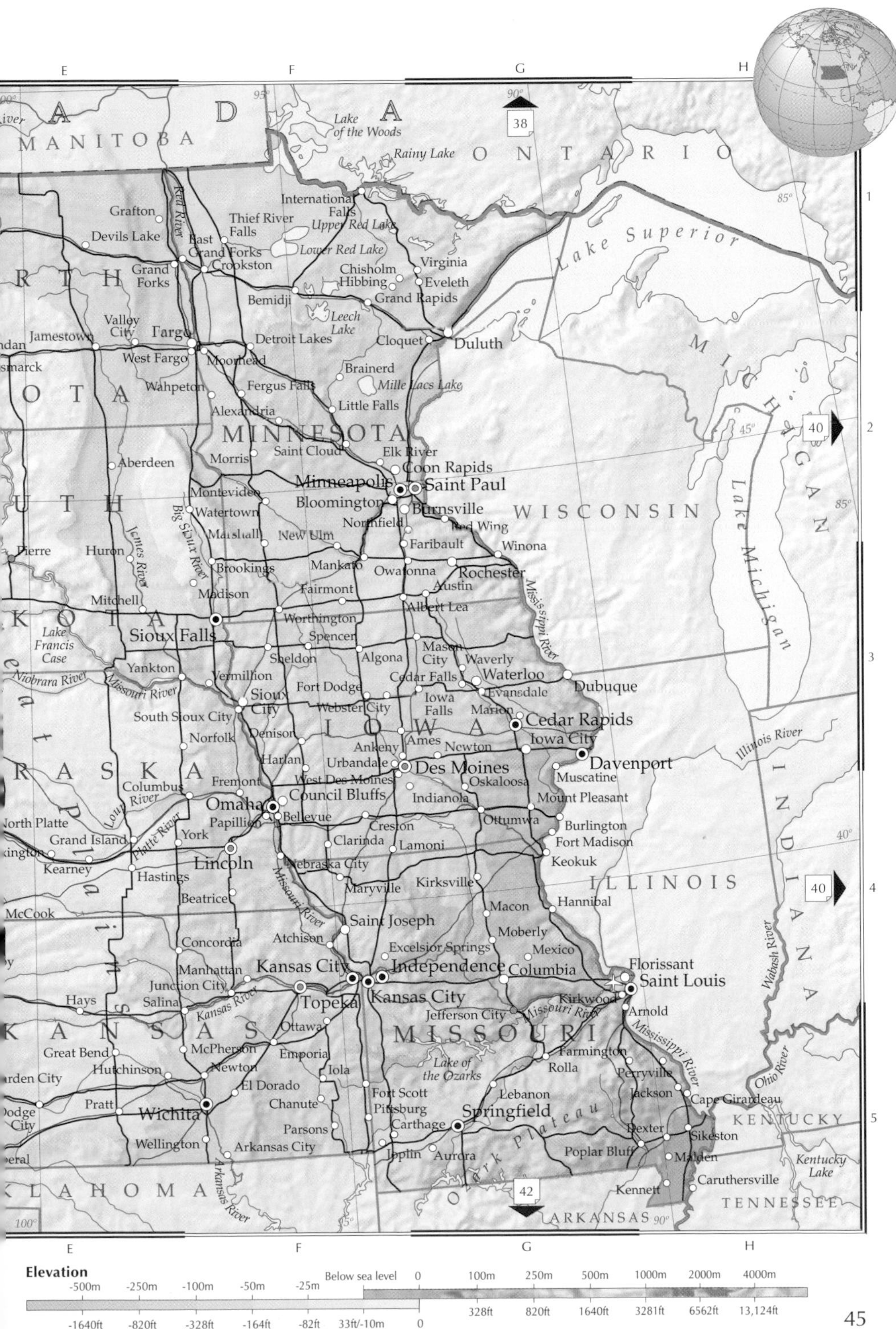

E   F   G   H

MANITOBA

Lake of the Woods
Rainy Lake
ONTARIO
38

CANADA

River

1

Grafton
Devils Lake
East Grand Forks
Crookston
Grand Forks
Jamestown
Valley City
Fargo
West Fargo
Moorhead
Wahpeton
Fergus Falls
Alexandria
Aberdeen
Morris
Saint Cloud
Elk River
Coon Rapids
Minneapolis
Saint Paul
Bloomington
Burnsville
Montevideo
Watertown
Marshall
New Ulm
Northfield
Red Wing
Faribault
Winona

Thief River Falls
International Falls
Upper Red Lake
Lower Red Lake
Chisholm
Hibbing
Virginia
Eveleth
Grand Rapids
Bemidji
Leech Lake
Detroit Lakes
Cloquet
Duluth
Brainerd
Mille Lacs Lake
Little Falls

MINNESOTA

Lake Superior

MICHIGAN

85°
45°
40
2

WISCONSIN

Lake Michigan

85°

NORTH DAKOTA
SOUTH DAKOTA

Bismarck

Pierre
Huron
Mitchell
Sioux Falls
Yankton
Vermillion
Sioux City
South Sioux City
Norfolk

Big Sioux River
James River

Brookings
Madison
Worthington
Spencer
Sheldon
Algona
Mason City
Waverly
Cedar Falls
Waterloo
Evansdale
Dubuque
Fort Dodge
Webster City
Iowa Falls
Marion
Cedar Rapids
Iowa City
Davenport
Muscatine

Lake Francis Case

Niobrara River
Missouri River

NEBRASKA

Brookings
Mankato
Fairmont
Owatonna
Rochester
Austin
Albert Lea

Mississippi River

IOWA

Denison
Ankeny
Ames
Newton
Urbandale
West Des Moines
Des Moines
Indianola
Oskaloosa
Ottumwa
Mount Pleasant
Burlington
Fort Madison
Keokuk

Columbus
Fremont
Omaha
Council Bluffs
Papillion
Bellevue
York
Lincoln
Hastings
Beatrice

North Platte
Grand Island
Kearney
Lexington
McCook

Platte River
Loup River

Harlan

ILLINOIS
INDIANA

Illinois River

40
4

Concordia
Atchison
Maryville
Kirksville
Macon
Hannibal
Excelsior Springs
Mexico
Columbia
Florissant
Saint Louis

Manhattan
Junction City
Kansas City
Independence
Kansas City
Topeka
Ottawa
Jefferson City
Kirkwood
Arnold

Hays
Salina
Saint Joseph
Moberly

KANSAS

Great Bend
McPherson
Newton
El Dorado
Emporia
Iola
Chanute
Parsons
Wichita
Wellington
Arkansas City

MISSOURI

Lake of the Ozarks
Farmington
Rolla
Perryville
Jackson
Cape Girardeau
Lebanon
Springfield
Dexter
Sikeston
Malden

KENTUCKY

Missouri River

Kansas River

Fort Scott
Pittsburg
Carthage
Joplin
Aurora
Poplar Bluff
Kennett
Caruthersville

Ozark Plateau

Mississippi River
Ohio River
Wabash River

Kentucky Lake

TENNESSEE

ARKANSAS
OKLAHOMA

42

5

Elevation

| -500m | -250m | -100m | -50m | -25m | Below sea level | 0 | 100m | 250m | 500m | 1000m | 2000m | 4000m |

| -1640ft | -820ft | -328ft | -164ft | -82ft | 33ft/-10m | 0 | 328ft | 820ft | 1640ft | 3281ft | 6562ft | 13,124ft |

45

USA: The West

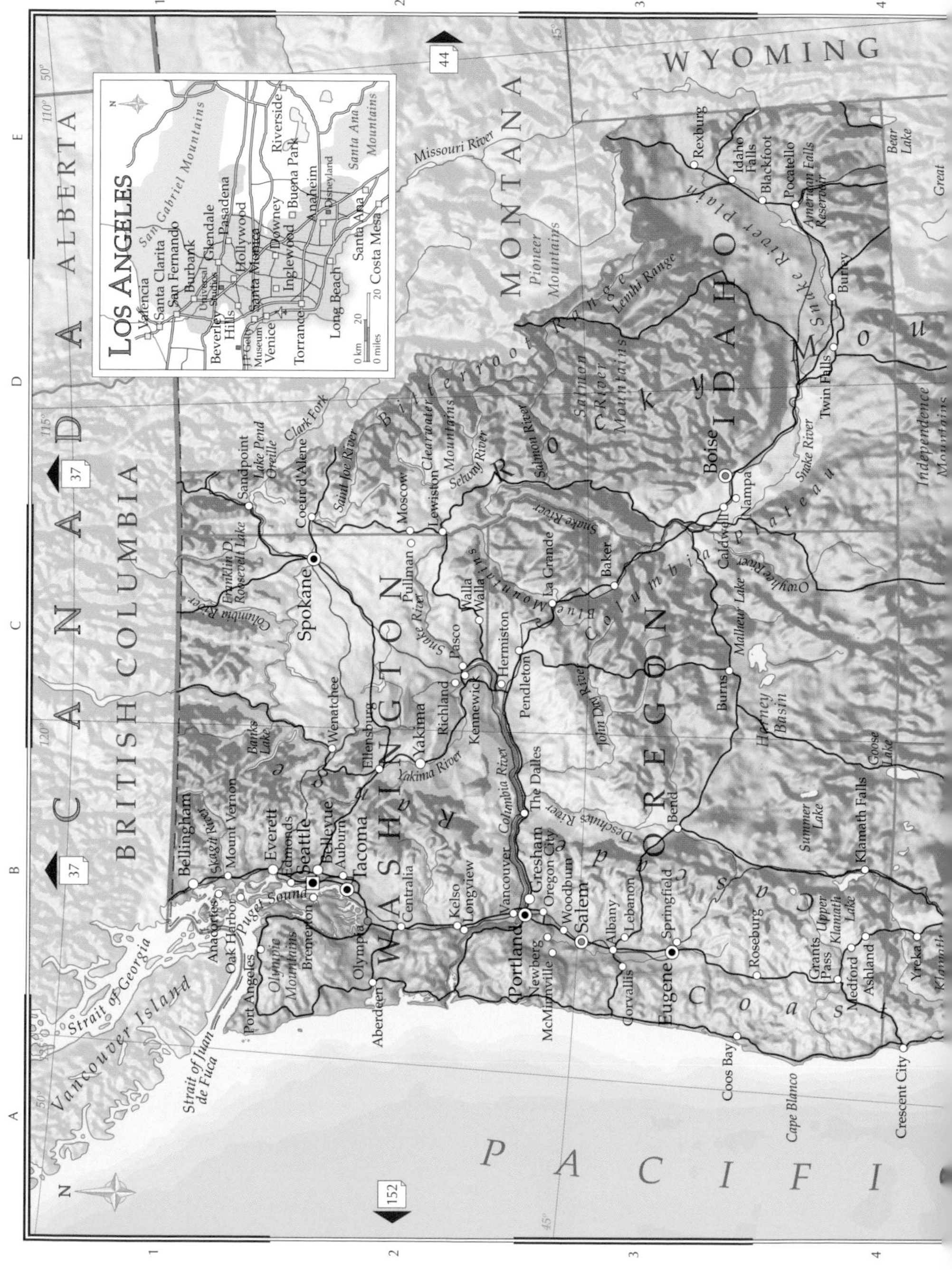

WYOMING

MONTANA

IDAHO

CANADA

ALBERTA

BRITISH COLUMBIA

WASHINGTON

OREGON

PACIFIC

Missouri River

ROCKY Mountains

LOS ANGELES

San Gabriel Mountains

Valencia
Santa Clarita
San Fernando
Burbank
Glendale
Pasadena
Universal Studios
Hollywood
Beverly Hills
Santa Monica
Venice
Torrance
Long Beach
Inglewood
Downey
Buena Park
Anaheim
Disneyland
Santa Ana
Costa Mesa
Riverside
Santa Ana Mountains

Rexburg
Idaho Falls
Blackfoot
Pocatello
American Falls Reservoir
Burley
Bear Lake
Great

Snake River Plain

Sandpoint
Coeur d'Alene
Lake Pend Oreille
Clark Fork
Saint Joe River

Moscow
Lewiston
Clearwater River
Selway River
Salmon River
Lemhi Range
Salmon River
Bitterroot Mountains
Pioneer Mountains

Spokane
Franklin D. Roosevelt Lake
Columbia River

Wenatchee
Banks Lake
Ellensburg
Yakima
Yakima River

Pullman
Snake River
Walla Walla
Pasco
Richland
Kennewick
Hermiston

Boise
Nampa
Caldwell
Columbia Plateau
Payette River
Owyhee River
Malheur Lake
Owyhee River

Independence Mountains

Pendleton
Blue Mountains
La Grande
Baker

Burns
Harney Basin

Bellingham
Anacortes
Oak Harbor
Mount Vernon
Everett
Edmonds
Bremerton
Seattle
Bellevue
Auburn
Tacoma
Olympia
Port Angeles
Aberdeen
Olympic Mountains
Puget Sound
Skagit River

Centralia
Kelso
Longview
Vancouver
Columbia River
Woodburn
Salem
Portland
Gresham
Oregon City
Newberg
McMinnville
Corvallis
Albany
Lebanon
Eugene
Springfield

The Dalles
Deschutes River
Bend
John Day River

Roseburg
Grants Pass
Upper Klamath Lake
Klamath Falls
Summer Lake
Goose Lake
Medford
Ashland
Yreka
Crescent City
Klamath River

Coos Bay
Cape Blanco

Strait of Georgia
Vancouver Island
Strait of Juan de Fuca

Population

○ below 50,000
○ 50,000 to 100,000
◉ 100,000 to 500,000
◼ above 500,000
● Internal administrative capital

0 km 200
0 miles 200

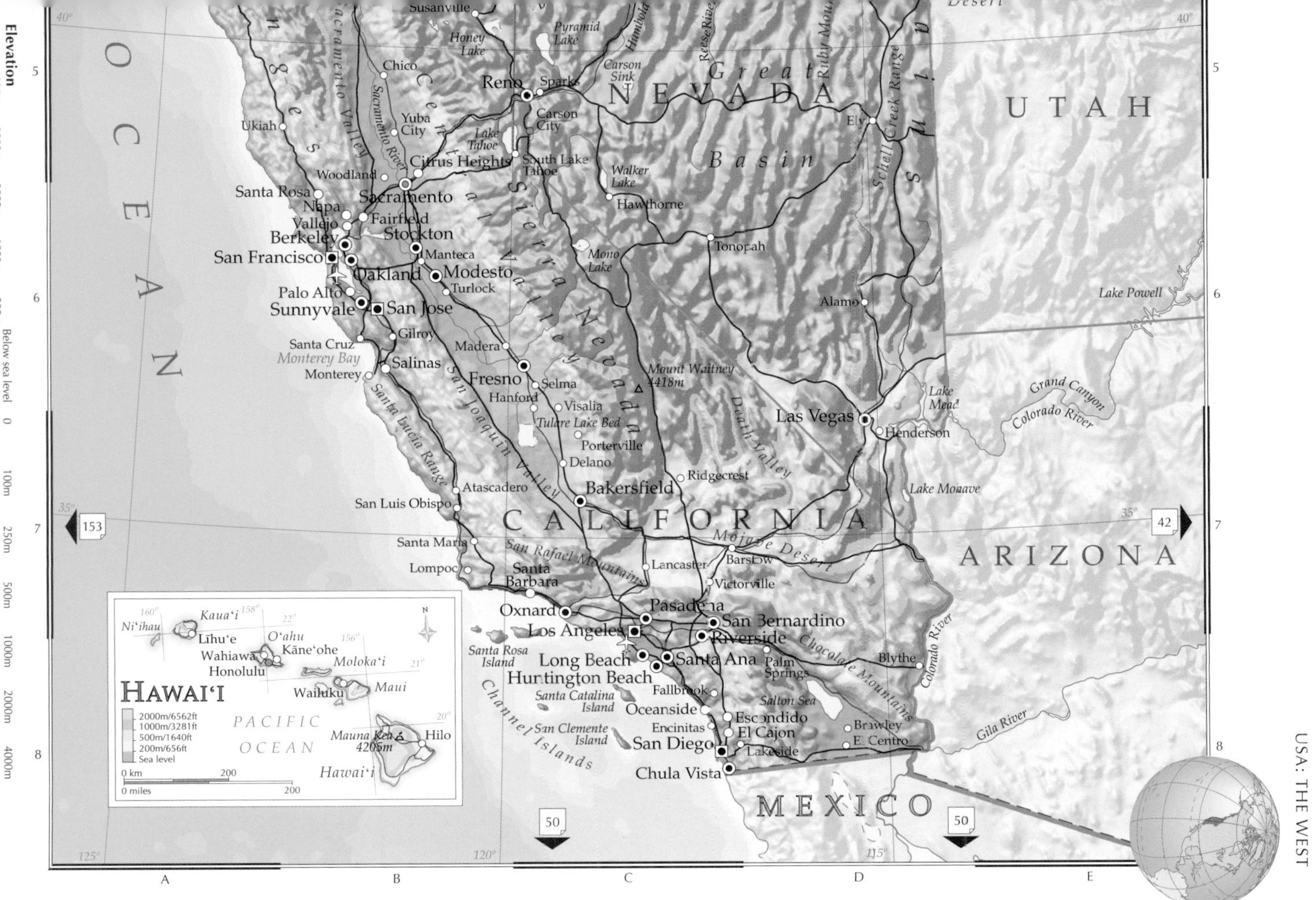

UTAH

ARIZONA

MEXICO

NEVADA

CALIFORNIA

Great Basin

Sierra Nevada

Central Valley

Mojave Desert

Death Valley

Grand Canyon

Colorado River

Lake Powell

Lake Mead

Lake Mohave

Gila River

Schell Creek Range

Ruby Mou.

Reese River

Humboldt

Pyramid Lake

Honey Lake

Carson Sink

Walker Lake

Mono Lake

Smith Lake

Lake Tahoe

Mount Whitney 4418m

Chocolate Mountains

Salton Sea

San Rafael Mountains

Santa Lucia Range

San Joaquin Valley

Sacramento River

Sacramento Valley

Monterey Bay

Channel Islands

Santa Rosa Island

Santa Catalina Island

San Clemente Island

Susanville
Ukiah
Chico
Woodland
Yuba City
Santa Rosa
Napa
Vallejo
Fairfield
Sacramento
Citrus Heights
Stockton
Manteca
Modesto
Turlock
Berkeley
Oakland
San Francisco
Palo Alto
Sunnyvale
San Jose
Santa Cruz
Monterey
Gilroy
Salinas
Madera
Fresno
Hanford
Visalia
Selma
Tulare Lake Bed
Porterville
Delano
Atascadero
San Luis Obispo
Santa Maria
Lompoc
Santa Barbara
Oxnard
Los Angeles
Pasadena
Long Beach
Huntington Beach
Santa Ana
Oceanside
Fallbrook
Encinitas
Escondido
San Diego
Chula Vista
El Cajon
Lakeside
Riverside
San Bernardino
Palm Springs
Victorville
Barstow
Lancaster
Bakersfield
Ridgecrest
Tonopah
Hawthorne
Alamo
Las Vegas
Henderson
Blythe
Brawley
El Centro
Reno
Sparks
Carson City
Sacramento

Reese River

50

42

153

HAWAI'I

PACIFIC OCEAN

Kaua'i
Ni'ihau
Lihu'e
O'ahu
Wahiawā
Kāne'ohe
Honolulu
Moloka'i
Maui
Wailuku
Lāna'i
Hawai'i
Hilo
Mauna Kea 4205m

2000m/6562ft	
1000m/3281ft	
500m/1640ft	
200m/656ft	
Sea level	

0 km 200
0 miles 200

47

USA: The Southwest

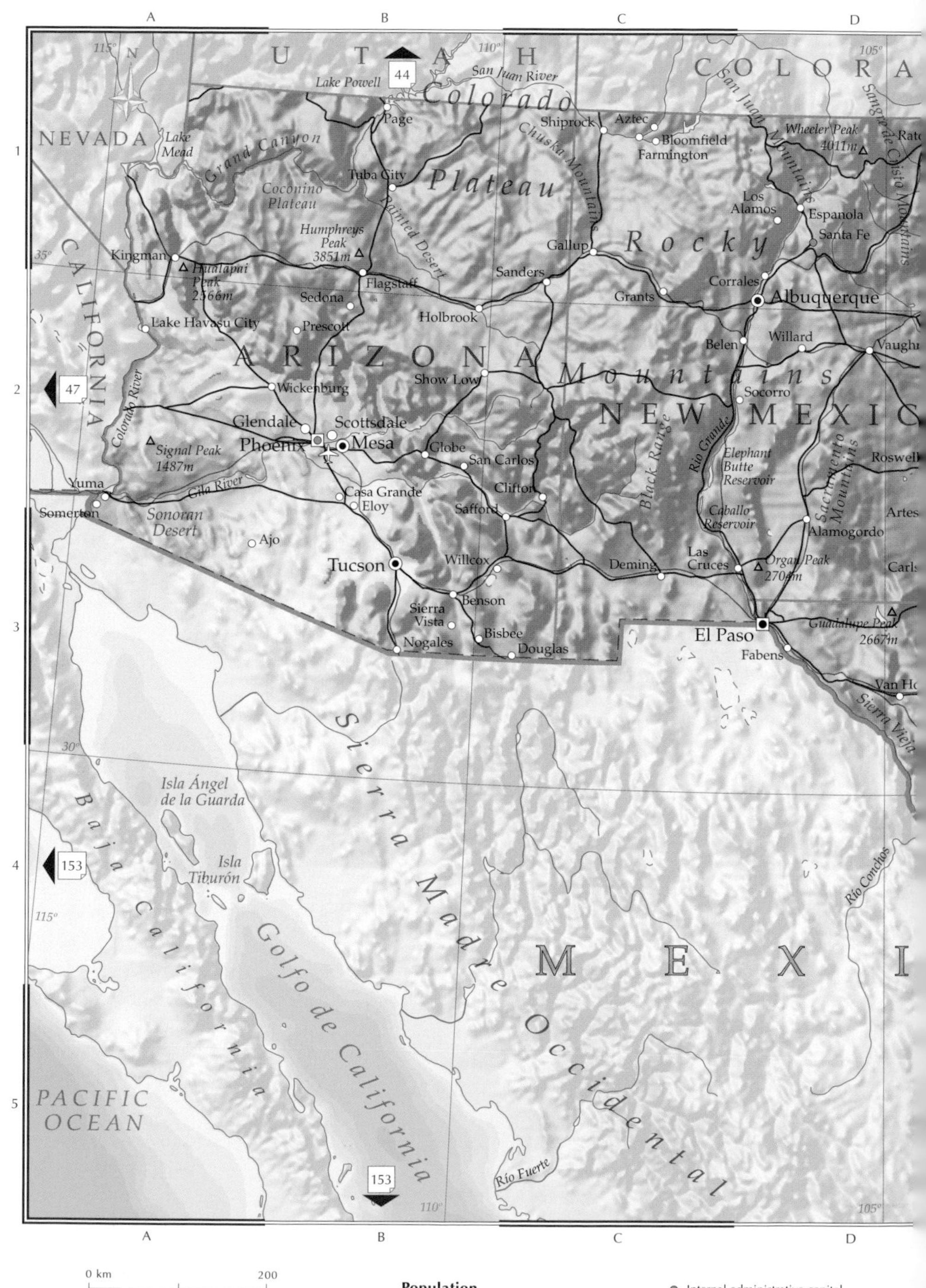

Population

○ below 50,000   ○ 50,000 to 100,000   ◉ 100,000 to 500,000   ■ above 500,000   ● Internal administrative capital

0 km   200

0 miles   200

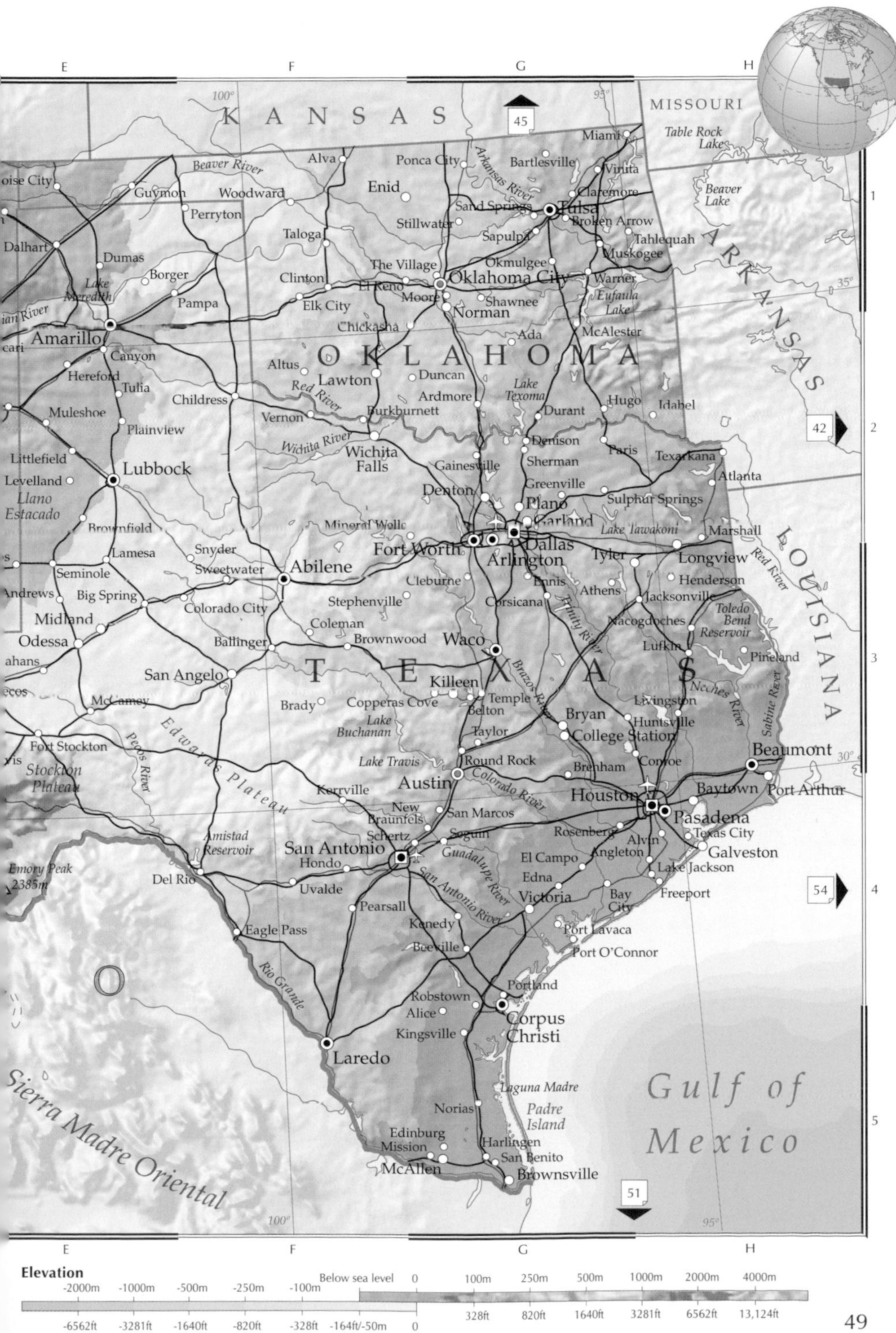

E　　　　F　　　　G　　　　H

KANSAS
MISSOURI
45

oise City
Dalhart
Guymon　Woodward
Perryton
Alva
Ponca City
Enid
Stillwater
Sand Springs
Bartlesville
Miami
Viruta
Claremore　Tulsa
Broken Arrow
Table Rock Lake
Beaver Lake
1

Dumas
Borger
Pampa
Amarillo
Canyon
Hereford
Tulia
Childress
Lake Meredith
ian River
cari
Taloga
Clinton
Elk City
El Reno
Moore
Chickasha
The Village
Oklahoma City
Okmulgee
Sapulpa
Shawnee
Norman
Ada
Warner
Eufaula Lake
Muskogee
Tahlequah
McAlester
35°
ARKANSAS

OKLAHOMA
Altus
Lawton
Duncan
Ardmore
Vernon
Burkburnett
Red River
Wichita River
Muleshoe
Plainview
Littlefield
Levelland
Lubbock
Llano Estacado
Brownfield
Lamesa
Snyder
Sweetwater
Seminole
Andrews
Big Spring
Midland
Odessa
ahans
cos
Wichita Falls
Gainesville
Denton
Plano
Garland
Denison
Sherman
Greenville
Paris
Sulphur Springs
Lake Texoma
Durant
Hugo
Idabel
Texarkana
Atlanta
Marshall
Red River
42
2

Mineral Wells
Fort Worth
Dallas
Arlington
Abilene
Cleburne
Stephenville
Coleman
Brownwood
Waco
Tyler
Longview
Henderson
Jacksonville
Nacogdoches
Athens
Ennis
Corsicana
Lake Tawakoni
Trinity R.
Toledo Bend Reservoir
Lufkin
Pineland
LOUISIANA
3

TEXAS
San Angelo
McCamey
Brady
Copperas Cove
Killeen
Temple
Belton
Taylor
Bryan
College Station
Huntsville
Livingston
Conroe
Brenham
Neches River
Sabine River
Beaumont
30°

Edwards Plateau
Fort Stockton
Stockton Plateau
Emory Peak 2385m
Kerrville
Lake Buchanan
Lake Travis
Austin
Round Rock
San Marcos
New Braunfels
Schertz
Seguin
Houston
Pasadena
Baytown
Port Arthur
Texas City
Galveston
Lake Jackson
54
4

Pecos River
Del Rio
Amistad Reservoir
San Antonio
Hondo
Uvalde
Pearsall
Kenedy
Beeville
El Campo
Edna
Victoria
Angleton
Alvin
Rosenberg
Bay City
Port Lavaca
Port O'Connor
Guadalupe River
San Antonio River

Rio Grande
Eagle Pass
Laredo
Robstown
Alice
Kingsville
Portland
Corpus Christi

Sierra Madre Oriental
Norias
Edinburg
Mission
McAllen
Harlingen
San Benito
Brownsville
Laguna Madre
Padre Island
Gulf of Mexico
51
5

E　　　F　　　G　　　H

Elevation
-2000m -1000m -500m -250m -100m Below sea level 0 100m 250m 500m 1000m 2000m 4000m
-6562ft -3281ft -1640ft -820ft -328ft -164ft/-50m 0 328ft 820ft 1640ft 3281ft 6562ft 13,124ft

49

Mexico

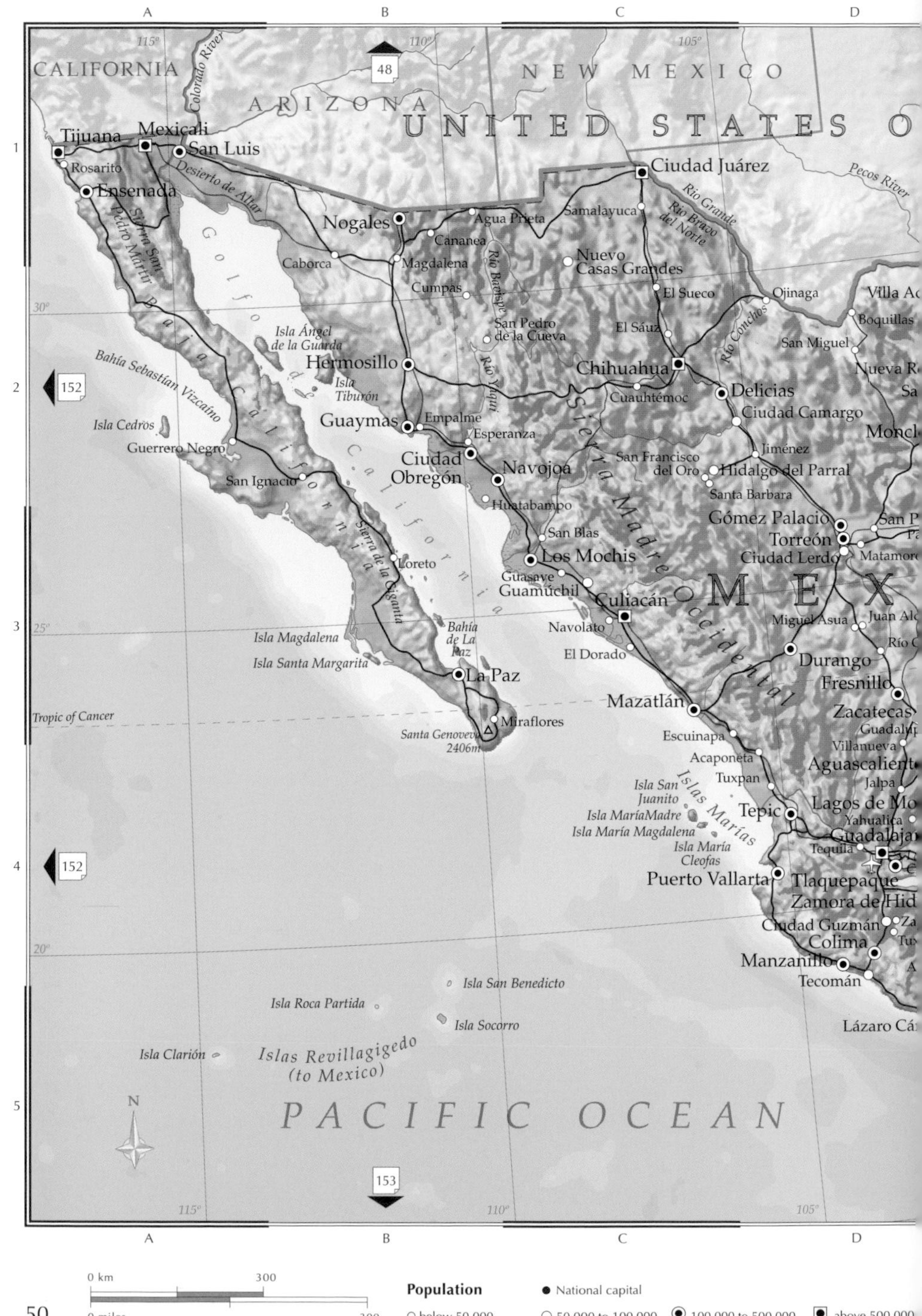

Population   ● National capital

○ below 50,000   ○ 50,000 to 100,000   ◉ 100,000 to 500,000   ◼ above 500,000

0 km   300

0 miles   300

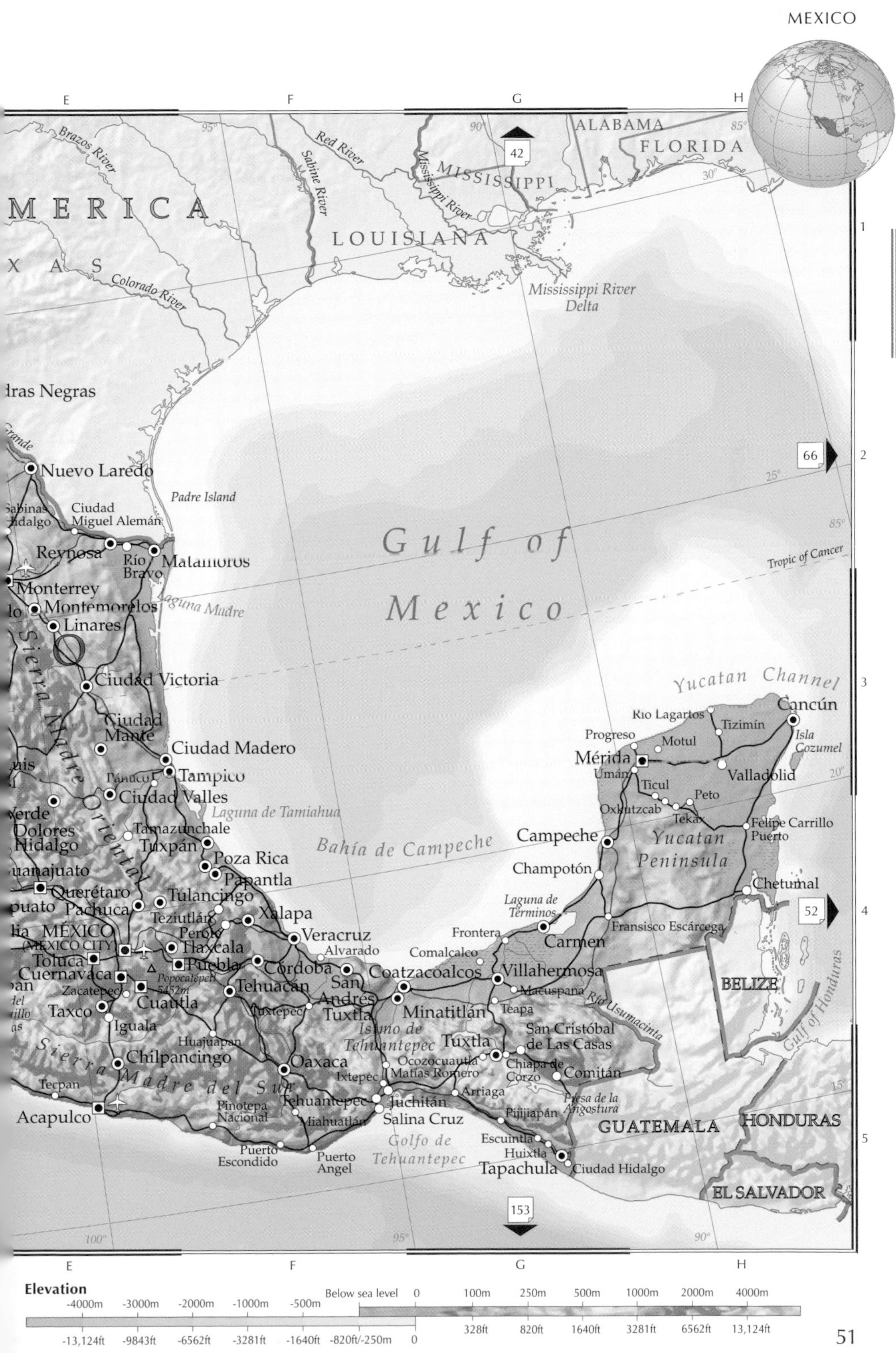

ALABAMA

FLORIDA

42

MISSISSIPPI

30°

LOUISIANA

MERICA

Brazos River

95

Red River

Sabine River

Colorado River

Mississippi River

T X A S

Mississippi River Delta

1

dras Negras

85°

Nuevo Laredo

Padre Island

66

2

85°

Sabinas
Hidalgo

Ciudad
Miguel Alemán

25°

Reynosa

G u l f   o f

Monterrey

Rio
Bravo

Matamoros

Montemorelos

Laguna Madre

M e x i c o

Tropic of Cancer

Linares

Sierra

Ciudad Victoria

Yucatan Channel

3

Ciudad
Mante

Cancún

Rio Lagartos

Ciudad Madero

Progreso

Tizimín

Isla
Cozumel

20°

Madre

Panuco

Tampico

Motul

Mérida

uis

Ciudad Valles

Umán

Valladolid

verde

Tamazunchale

Laguna de Tamiahua

Ticul

Peto

Oriental

Tuxpan

Oxkutzcab

Teka

Dolores
Hidalgo

Bahía de Campeche

Campeche

Felipe Carrillo
Puerto

uanajuato

Poza Rica

Champotón

Yucatan
Peninsula

Querétaro

Papantla

Chetumal

puato

Pachuca

Tulancingo

Laguna de
Términos

52

4

lia

Teziutlán

Xalapa

Fransisco Escárcega

MÉXICO

Perote

Frontera

(MEXICO CITY)

Veracruz

Comalcalco

Carmen

Toluca

Tlaxcala

Alvarado

Villahermosa

BELIZE

Puebla

Córdoba

Coatzacoalcos

San

Cuernavaca

Popocatépetl
5452m

Tehuacán

Andrés

Macuspana

Zacatepec

Cuautla

Ixtepec

Tuxtla

Teapa

Rio Usumacinta

Gulf of Honduras

Taxco

Iguala

Minatitlán

San Cristóbal
de Las Casas

as

Huajuapan

Istmo de
Tehuantepec

Tuxtla

Sierra

Chilpancingo

Oaxaca

Ocozocuautla

Chiapa de
Corzo

Comitán

15°

Madre

del

Sur

Ixtepec

Matías Romero

Tecpan

Tehuantepec

Juchitán

Arriaga

Presa de la
Angostura

Acapulco

Pinotepa
Nacional

Miahuatlán

Salina Cruz

Pijijiapán

GUATEMALA

HONDURAS

Puerto
Escondido

Puerto
Ángel

Golfo de
Tehuantepec

Escuintla

Huixtla

Tapachula

Ciudad Hidalgo

EL SALVADOR

100°

95°

153

90°

Elevation

| -4000m | -3000m | -2000m | -1000m | -500m | Below sea level | 0 | 100m | 250m | 500m | 1000m | 2000m | 4000m |

| -13,124ft | -9843ft | -6562ft | -3281ft | -1640ft | -820ft/-250m | | 328ft | 820ft | 1640ft | 3281ft | 6562ft | 13,124ft |

51

Central America

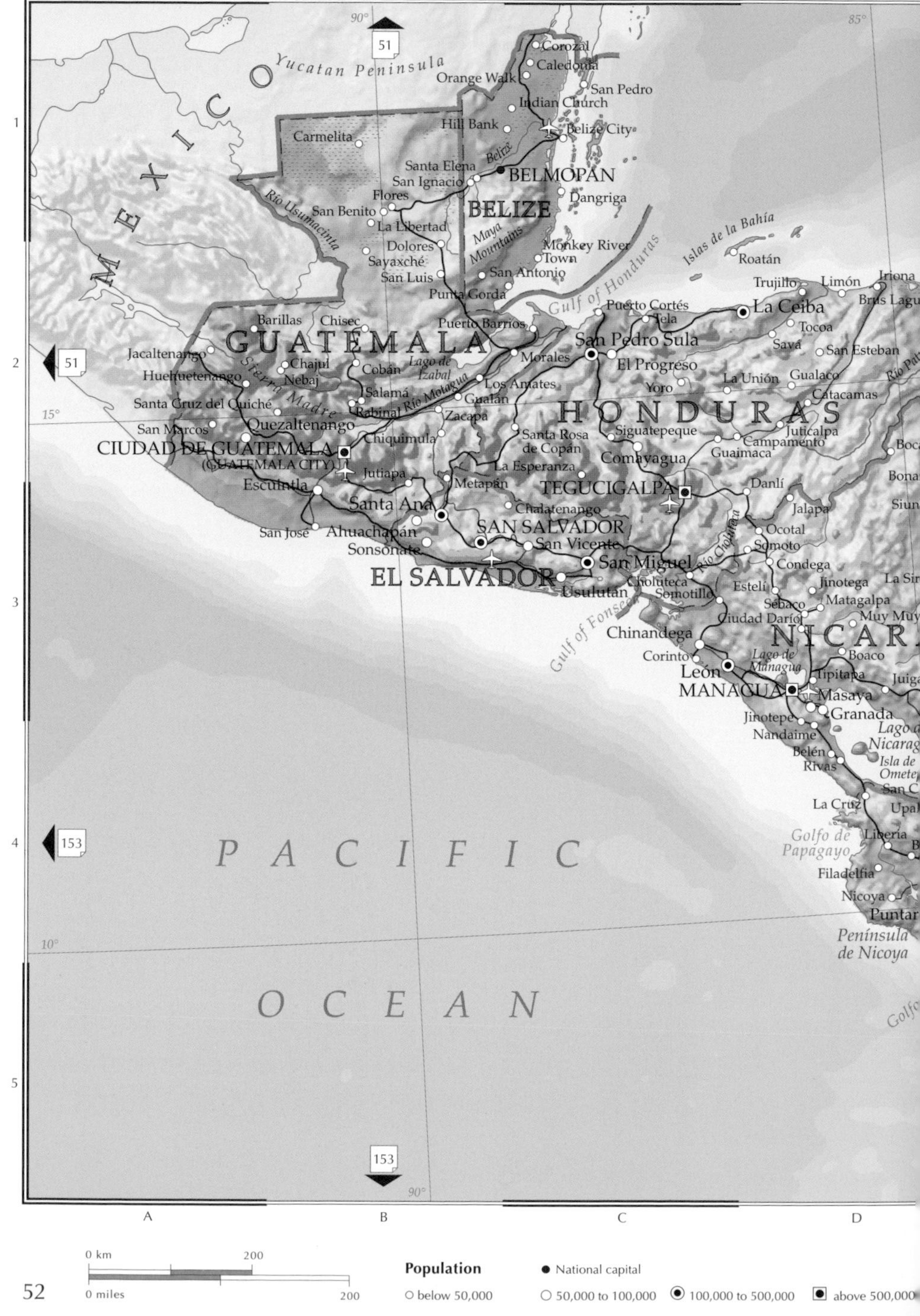

Population

- National capital

○ below 50,000   ○ 50,000 to 100,000   ◉ 100,000 to 500,000   ■ above 500,000

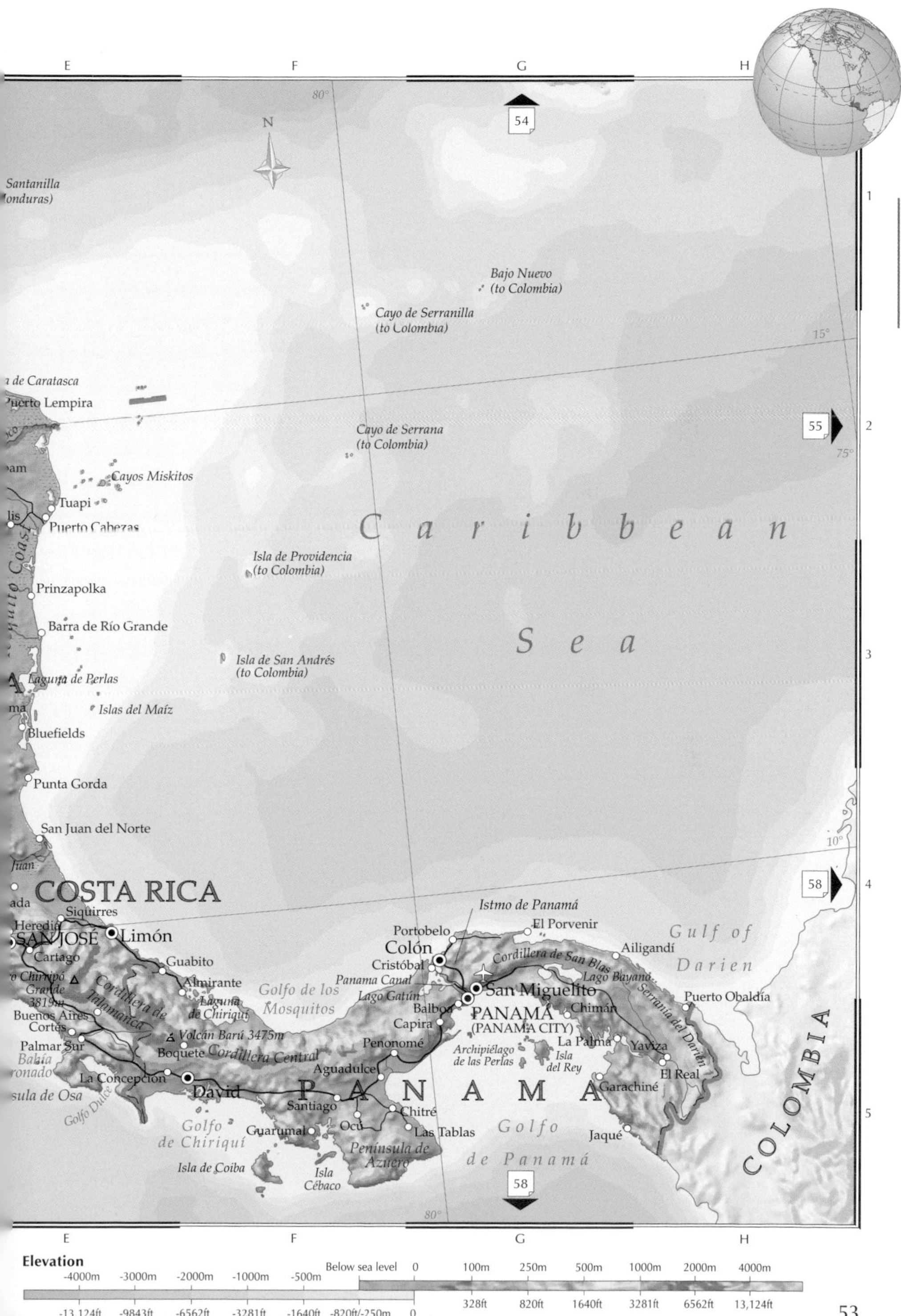

Santanilla
(Honduras)

Bajo Nuevo
(to Colombia)

Cayo de Serranilla
(to Colombia)

15°

Cayo de Serrana
(to Colombia)

55

75°

a de Caratasca
Puerto Lempira

am

Cayos Miskitos

lis
Tuapi
Puerto Cabezas

C   a   r   i   b   b   e   a   n

Prinzapolka

Isla de Providencia
(to Colombia)

S   e   a

Barra de Río Grande

Laguna de Perlas

ma
Islas del Maíz

Isla de San Andrés
(to Colombia)

Bluefields

Punta Gorda

San Juan del Norte

10°

Juan

58

ada

COSTA RICA
Siquirres
Heredia
SAN JOSÉ   Limón
Cartago

Portobelo
Colón
Cristóbal

Istmo de Panamá
El Porvenir
Ailigandí

Gulf of
Darien

Cordillera de San Blas

o Chirripó
3819m
Guabito
Almirante
Laguna
de Chiriquí
Buenos Aires
Cortés
Palmar Sur

Cordillera de
Talamanca

Golfo de los
Mosquitos

Panama Canal
Lago Gatún
Balboa
Capira
Penonomé

San Miguelito
PANAMÁ
(PANAMA CITY)

Lago Bayano
Chimán

Serranía del Darién
Puerto Obaldía

Bahía
ronada
sula de Osa

Volcán Barú 3475m
Boquete   *Cordillera Central*

La Concepción
Golfo Dulce
David

P   A   N   A   M   A

Santiago
Guarumal
Ocú

Aguadulce
Chitré

Archipiélago
de las Perlas
Isla
del Rey
La Palma
Garachiné

Yaviza
El Real

C   O   L   O   M   B   I   A

Golfo
de Chiriquí

Isla de Coiba

Isla
Cébaco

Las Tablas
Península de
Azuero

Golfo
de Panamá

Jaqué

58

80°

Elevation

					Below sea level	0	100m	250m	500m	1000m	2000m	4000m
-4000m	-3000m	-2000m	-1000m	-500m								
-13,124ft	-9843ft	-6562ft	-3281ft	-1640ft	-820ft/-250m	0	328ft	820ft	1640ft	3281ft	6562ft	13,124ft

The Caribbean

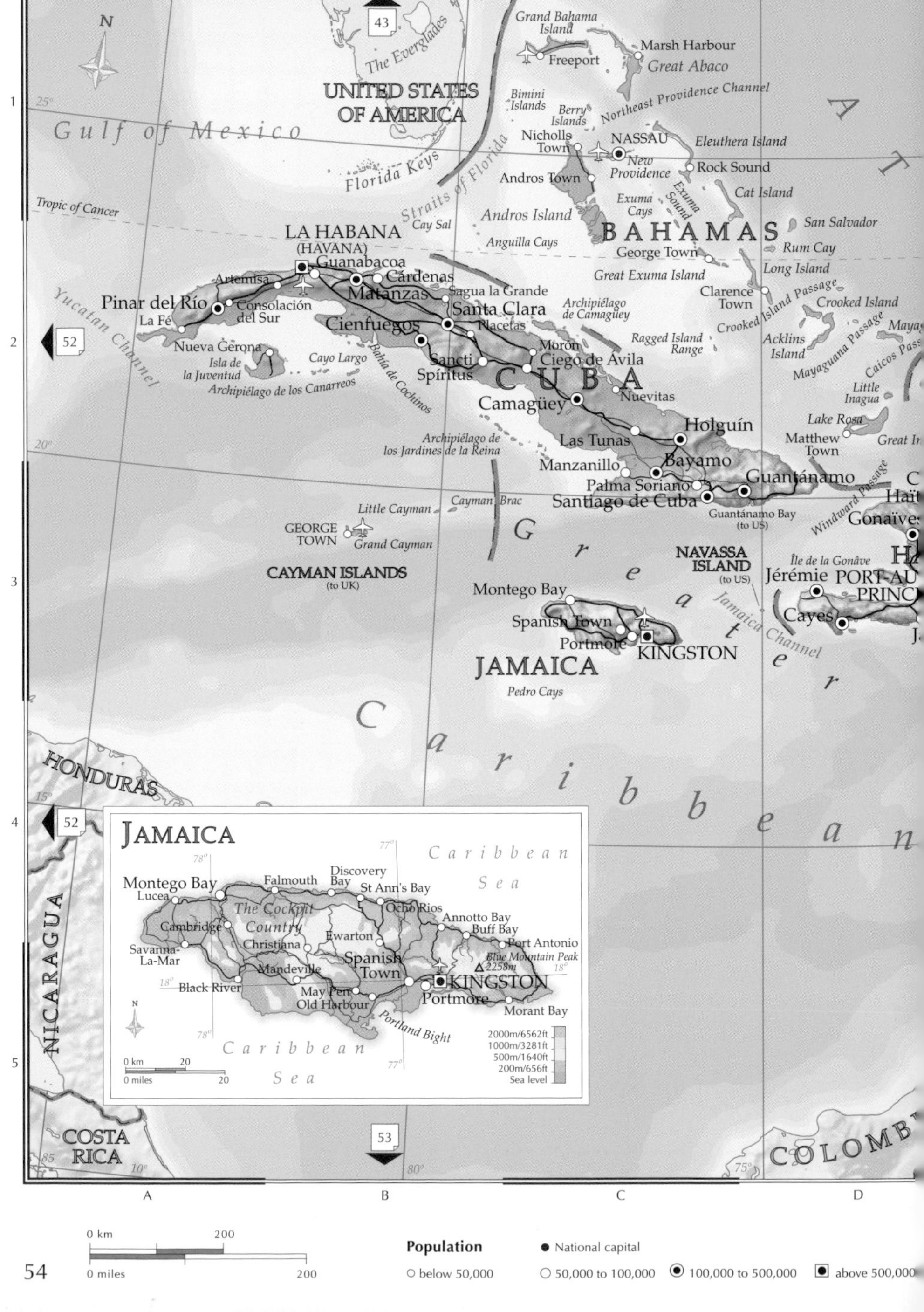

Population   ● National capital

○ below 50,000   ○ 50,000 to 100,000   ◉ 100,000 to 500,000   ◼ above 500,000

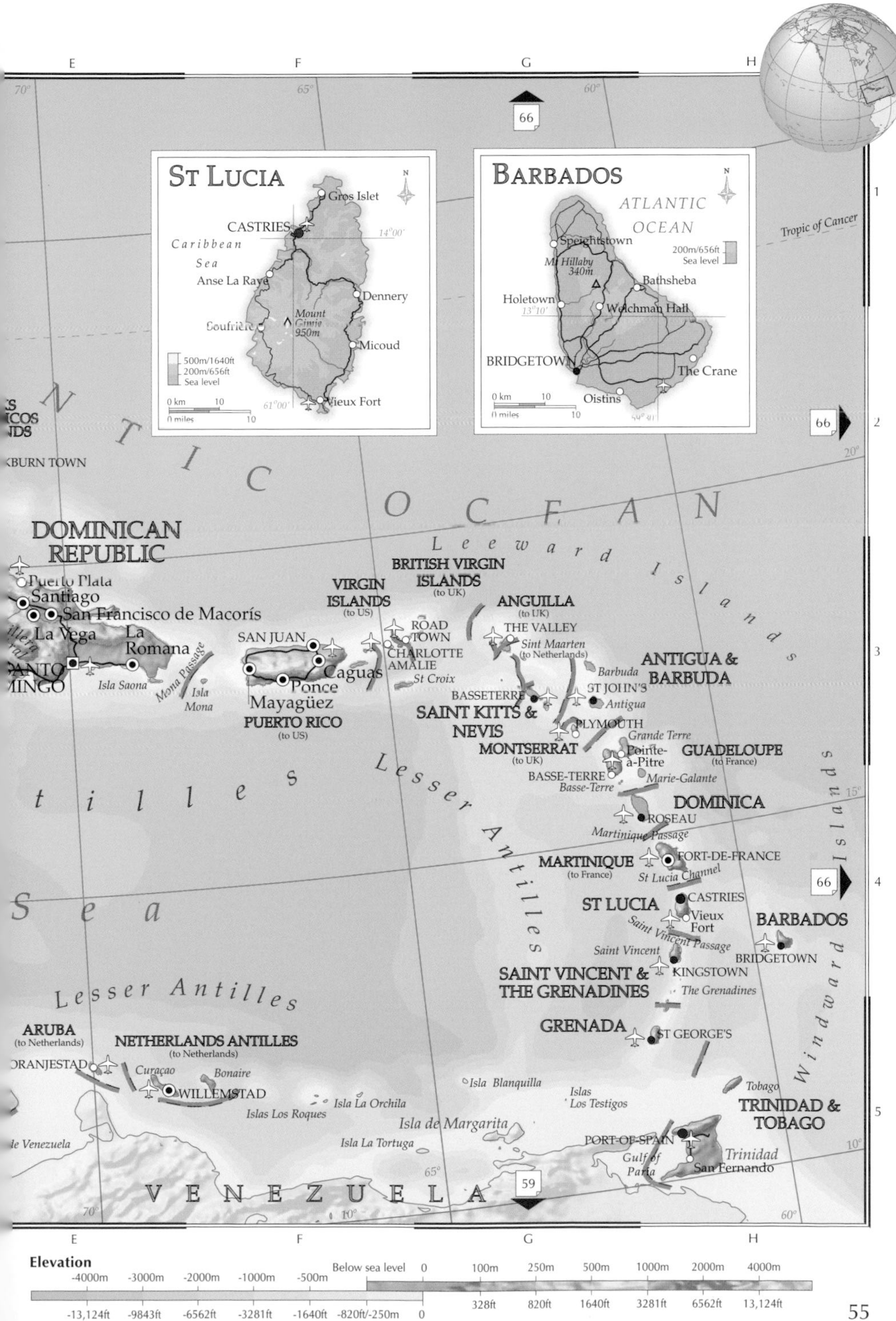

St Lucia

CASTRIES

Gros Islet

Caribbean Sea

Anse La Raye

14°00'

Dennery

Soufrière

Mount Gimie 950m

Micoud

500m/1640ft
200m/656ft
Sea level

0 km   10

0 miles   10

61°00'

Vieux Fort

N

Barbados

ATLANTIC OCEAN

Speightstown

Mt Hillaby 340m

Bathsheba

Holetown

13°10'

Welchman Hall

200m/656ft
Sea level

BRIDGETOWN

The Crane

0 km   10

0 miles   10

Oistins

N

66

66

Tropic of Cancer

20°

A T L A N T I C   O C E A N

KBURN TOWN

S
COS
DS

DOMINICAN REPUBLIC

Puerto Plata
Santiago
San Francisco de Macorís
La Vega
La Romana

SANTO DOMINGO

Isla Saona

Isla Mona

Mona Passage

Leeward Islands

BRITISH VIRGIN ISLANDS
(to UK)

VIRGIN ISLANDS
(to US)

ROAD TOWN

CHARLOTTE AMALIE

St Croix

SAN JUAN

Caguas
Ponce
Mayagüez

PUERTO RICO
(to US)

ANGUILLA
(to UK)

THE VALLEY

Sint Maarten
(to Netherlands)

BASSETERRE

SAINT KITTS & NEVIS

MONTSERRAT
(to UK)

PLYMOUTH

Barbuda

ST JOHN'S

Antigua

ANTIGUA & BARBUDA

Grande Terre

Pointe-à-Pitre

BASSE-TERRE
Basse-Terre

GUADELOUPE
(to France)

Marie-Galante

15°

DOMINICA

ROSEAU

Lesser Antilles

t   i   l   l   e   s

Martinique Passage

MARTINIQUE
(to France)

FORT-DE-FRANCE

St Lucia Channel

ST LUCIA

CASTRIES
Vieux Fort

Saint Vincent

Saint Vincent Passage

SAINT VINCENT & THE GRENADINES

KINGSTOWN

The Grenadines

66

BARBADOS

BRIDGETOWN

Windward Islands

S e a

Lesser Antilles

GRENADA

ST GEORGE'S

ARUBA
(to Netherlands)

ORANJESTAD

NETHERLANDS ANTILLES
(to Netherlands)

Curaçao

Bonaire

WILLEMSTAD

Islas Los Roques

Isla La Orchila

Isla Blanquilla

Islas Los Testigos

Isla de Margarita

Isla La Tortuga

Tobago

TRINIDAD & TOBAGO

PORT-OF-SPAIN

Gulf of Paria

Trinidad

San Fernando

10°

de Venezuela

V E N E Z U E L A

59

70°

65°

60°

Elevation

-4000m	-3000m	-2000m	-1000m	-500m	Below sea level	0	100m	250m	500m	1000m	2000m	4000m
-13,124ft	-9843ft	-6562ft	-3281ft	-1640ft	-820ft/-250m	0	328ft	820ft	1640ft	3281ft	6562ft	13,124ft

South America

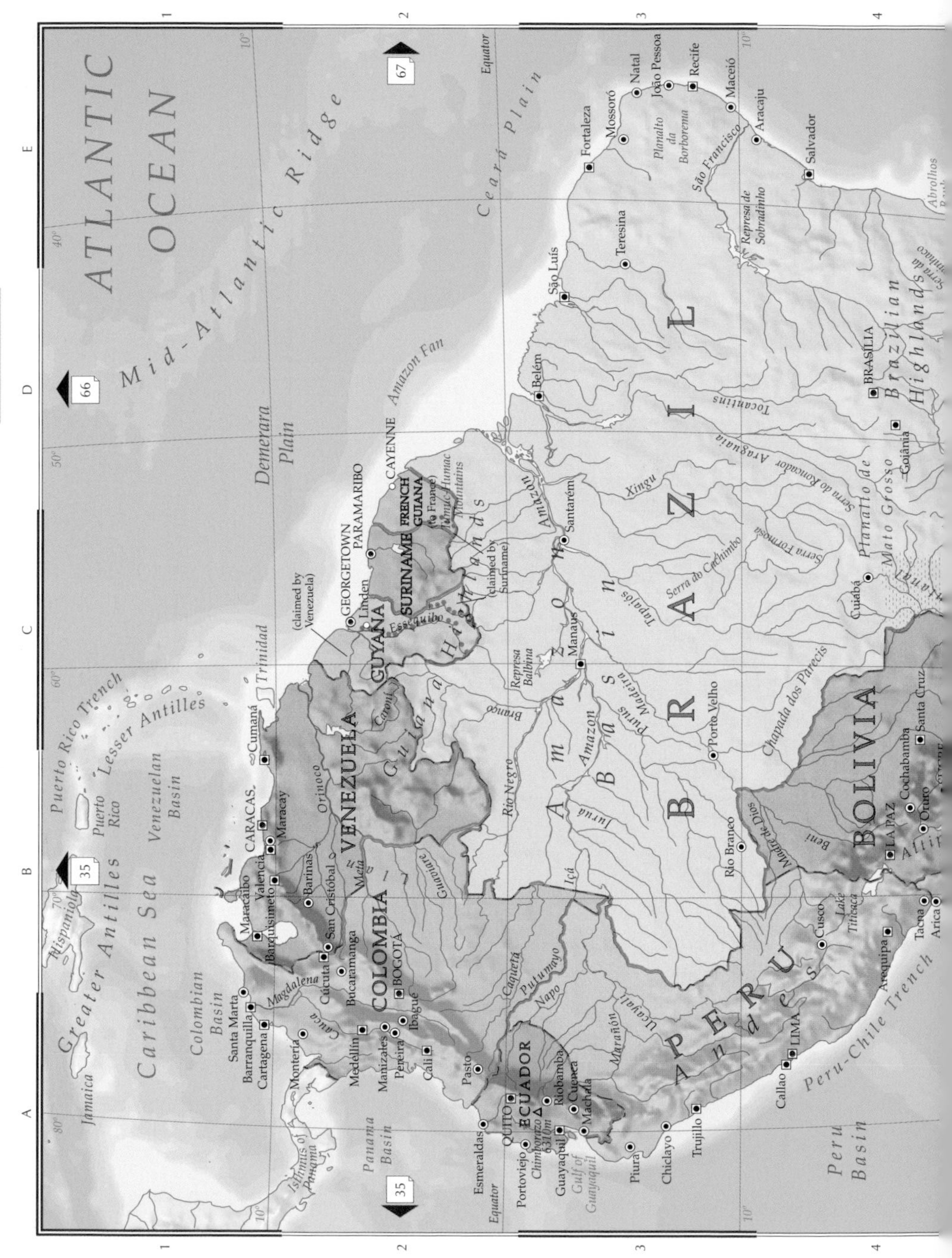

ATLANTIC OCEAN

Mid-Atlantic Ridge

Equator

67

66

35

35

Demerara Plain

Amazon Fan

Ceará Plain

CAYENNE
PARAMARIBO
FRENCH GUIANA
(to France)
SURINAME
GEORGETOWN
(claimed by
Venezuela)
GUYANA

Lethem
Tumuc-Humac
Mountains

(claimed by
Suriname)

Essequibo

Natal
João Pessoa
Recife
Maceió
Aracaju
Mossoró
Fortaleza
Salvador

Planalto
da
Borborema
São Francisco

Represa de
Sobradinho

Abrolhos
Bank

Teresina

São Luís

Belém

BRASÍLIA

Goiânia

Brazilian
Highlands

Tocantins

Araguaia

Serra do Roncador

Planalto de
Mato Grosso

Cuiabá

Chapada dos Parecis

Serra Formosa

Serra do Cachimbo

Santarém

Xingu

Tapajós

Amazon

BRAZIL

Puerto Rico Trench

Greater Antilles

Lesser Antilles

Caribbean Sea

Venezuelan
Basin

Colombian
Basin

Puerto
Rico

Hispaniola

Jamaica

Trinidad

Cumaná

CARACAS
Valencia
Maracay
Barinas
San Cristóbal
Maracaibo
Barquisimeto
Mérida

VENEZUELA

Orinoco

Caroní

Guaviare

Casiquiare

Guiana Highlands

Represa
Balbina

Manaus

Madeira

Porto Velho

Río Branco

BOLIVIA

Santa Cruz

Cochabamba
LA PAZ
Oruro
Lake
Titicaca

Beni

Madre de Dios

Apurímac

COLOMBIA

BOGOTÁ
Cúcuta
Bucaramanga
Medellín
Manizales
Pereira
Ibagué
Cali
Pasto

Magdalena

Cauca

Santa Marta
Barranquilla
Cartagena
Montería

Panama
Basin

Isthmus of
Panama

Esmeraldas
Portoviejo
QUITO
ECUADOR
Chimborazo
Guayaquil
Cuenca
Machala
Gulf of
Guayaquil

Riobamba

Piura

Chiclayo
Trujillo

Callao
LIMA

PERU

Cusco
Arequipa
Tacna
Arica

Peru-Chile Trench

Peru
Basin

Andes

Putumayo
Napo
Caquetá
Içá
Napo
Marañón
Ucayali
Juruá
Purus
Río Negro
Branco
Amazon

Equator

40°

50°

60°

70°

80°

10°

10°

10°

0 km 500
0 miles 500

Population • National capital

○ below 50,000 ⊙ 50,000 to 100,000 ◉ 100,000 to 500,000 ■ above 500,000

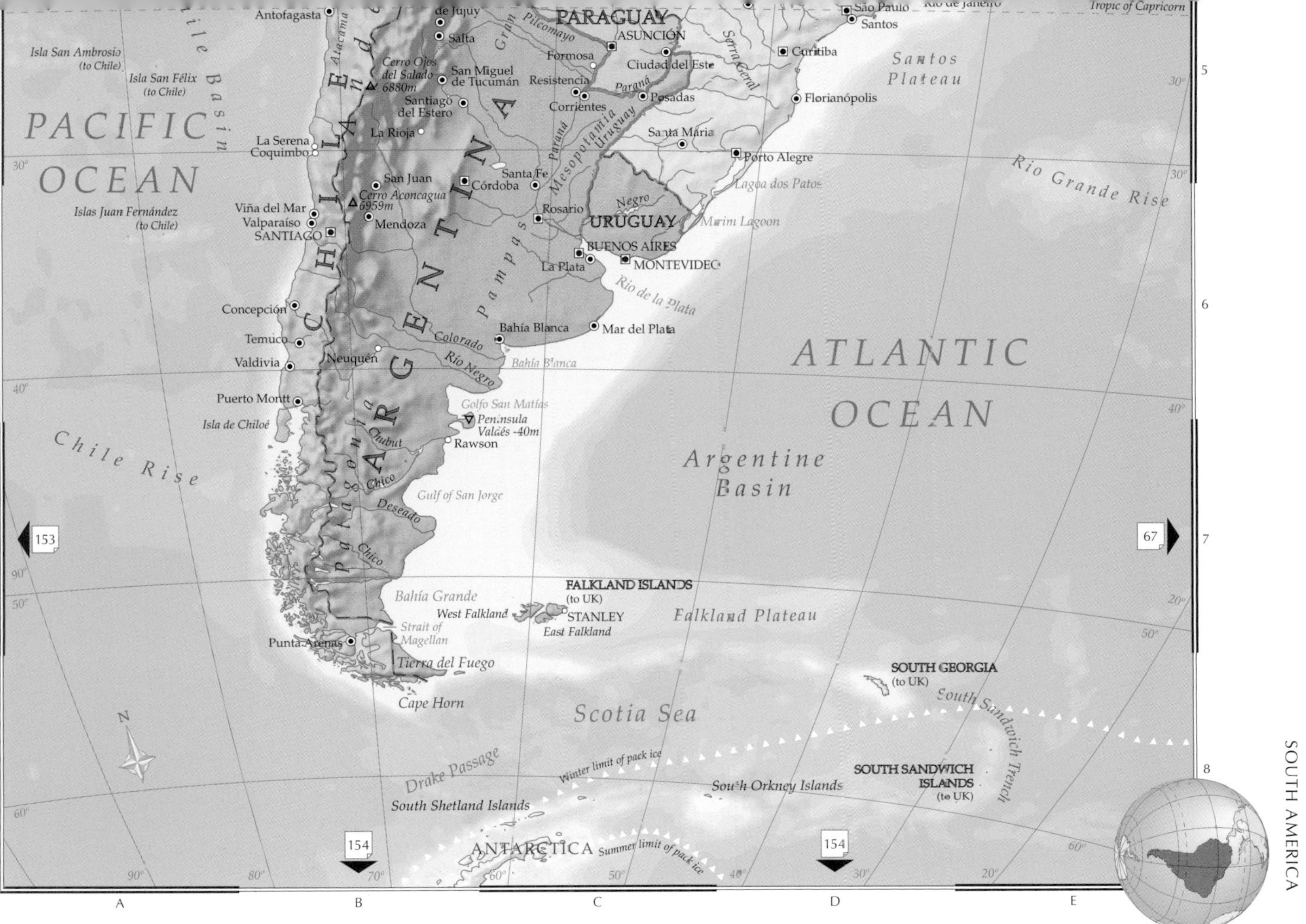
PACIFIC
OCEAN
ATLANTIC
OCEAN
Chile Basin
Chile Rise
Isla San Ambrosio
(to Chile)
Isla San Félix
(to Chile)
Islas Juan Fernández
(to Chile)
Antofagasta
Atacama
de Jujuy
Salta
Cerro Ojos del Salado 6880m
San Miguel de Tucumán
Santiago del Estero
La Rioja
La Serena
Coquimbo
San Juan
Cerro Aconcagua 6959m
Mendoza
Viña del Mar
Valparaíso
SANTIAGO
Córdoba
Santa Fe
Rosario
Concepción
Temuco
Valdivia
Neuquén
Puerto Montt
Isla de Chiloé
Punta Arenas
CHILE
ARGENTINA
ANDES
Patagonia
Pampas
Gran Chaco
Mesopotamia
PARAGUAY
ASUNCIÓN
Pilcomayo
Formosa
Resistencia
Corrientes
Paraná
Uruguay
Posadas
Ciudad del Este
Santa Maria
Serra Geral
Curitiba
São Paulo
Santos
Rio de Janeiro
Florianópolis
Porto Alegre
Lagoa dos Patos
Mirim Lagoon
Negro
URUGUAY
BUENOS AIRES
MONTEVIDEO
La Plata
Río de la Plata
Bahía Blanca
Mar del Plata
Colorado
Río Negro
Golfo San Matías
Península Valdés -40m
Rawson
Chubut
Chico
Deseado
Gulf of San Jorge
Bahía Grande
Strait of Magellan
Tierra del Fuego
Cape Horn
Tropic of Capricorn
Santos Plateau
Rio Grande Rise
Argentine Basin
Falkland Plateau
FALKLAND ISLANDS
(to UK)
West Falkland
STANLEY
East Falkland
Scotia Sea
SOUTH GEORGIA
(to UK)
South Sandwich Trench
SOUTH SANDWICH ISLANDS
(to UK)
South Orkney Islands
Drake Passage
South Shetland Islands
Winter limit of pack ice
Summer limit of pack ice
ANTARCTICA
153
67
154
154
5
6
7
8
A
B
C
D
E

Northern South America

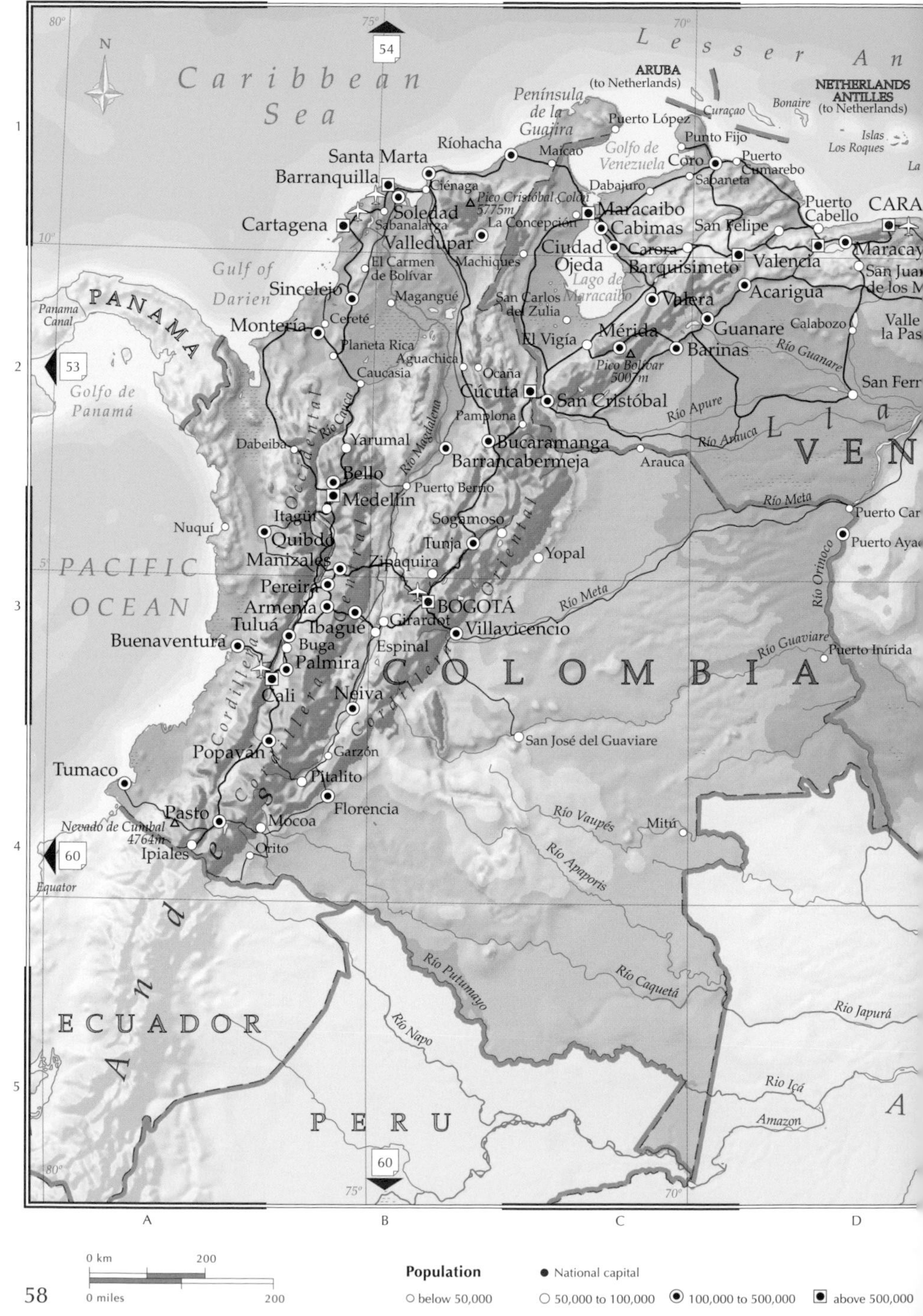

Population

- National capital

○ below 50,000
◐ 50,000 to 100,000
◉ 100,000 to 500,000
▣ above 500,000

0 km   200
0 miles   200

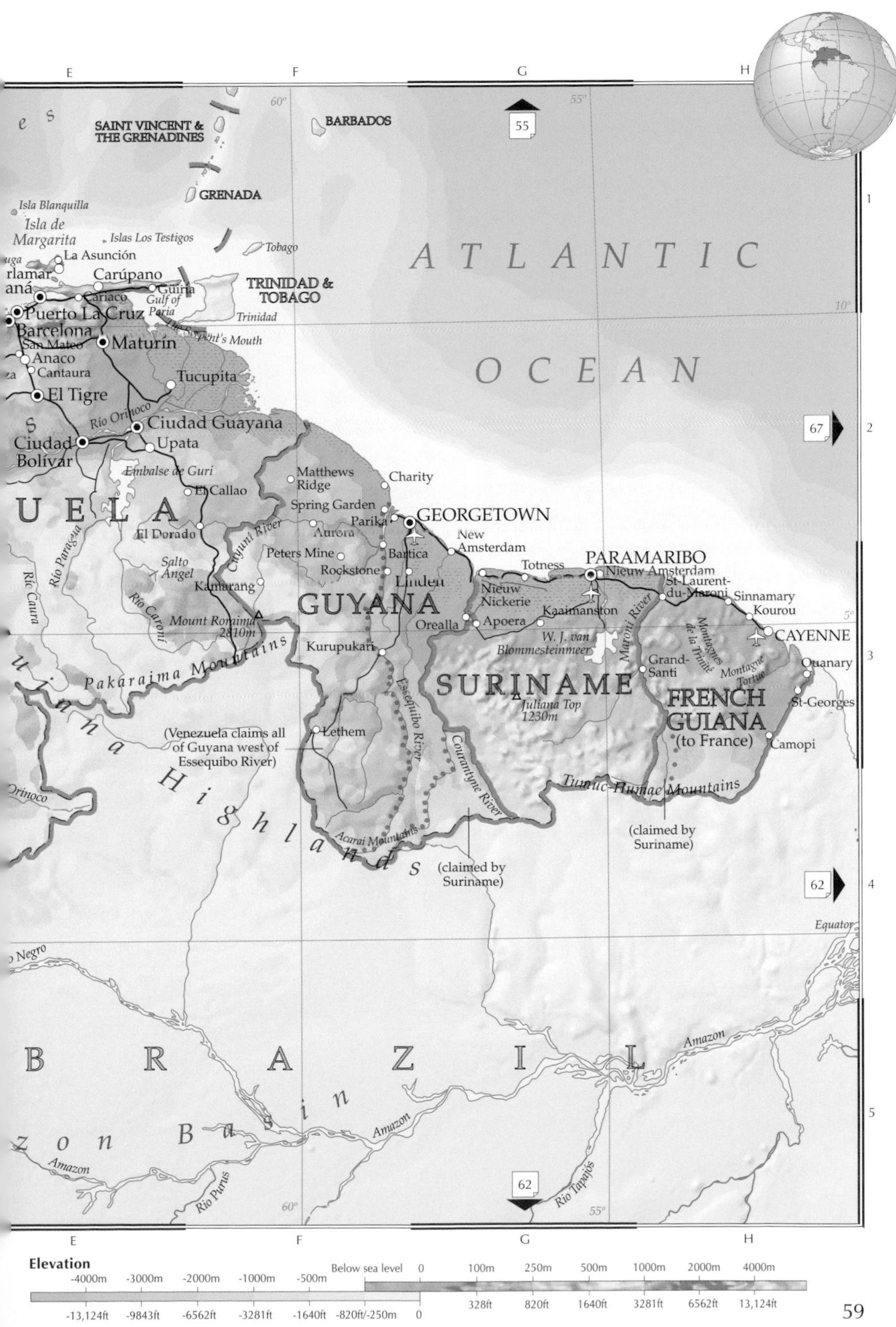

SAINT VINCENT &
THE GRENADINES

BARBADOS

55

Isla Blanquilla

GRENADA

Islas Los Testigos

Isla de
Margarita

Tobago

La Asunción

TRINIDAD &
TOBAGO

1

Carúpano

Cariaco

Güira

Gulf of
Paria

uga

rlamar

aná

Trinidad

Puerto La Cruz

A T L A N T I C

Barcelona

10°

San Mateo

Dragon's Mouth

Anaco

Maturín

za

Cantaura

El Tigre

Tucupita

O C E A N

Río Orinoco

67

2

Ciudad Guayana

Upata

Ciudad
Bolívar

Embalse de Guri

Matthews
Ridge

Charity

El Callao

U E L A

Spring Garden

Cuyuni River

El Dorado

Aurora

Parika

GEORGETOWN

Peters Mine

New
Amsterdam

Salto
Angel

Rockstone

Bartica

Kamarang

Linden

Totness

PARAMARIBO

Río Caura

Río Caroní

Mount Roraima
2810m

GUYANA

Orealla

Nieuw
Nickerie

Nieuw Amsterdam

St-Laurent-
du-Maroni

Sinnamary

Kourou

5°

Apoera

Kaaimanston

Pakáraima Mountains

Kurupukari

W. J. van
Blommesteinmeer

Maroni River

Montagne
de la Trinité

CAYENNE

3

Montagne
Tortue

Ouanary

nh

Rio Negro

Salto
Angel

SURINAME

Juliana Top
1230m

Grand-
Santi

FRENCH
GUIANA

St-Georges

Orinoco

(Venezuela claims all
of Guyana west of
Essequibo River)

Lethem

Essequibo River

Courantyne River

*(to France)

Camopi

H i g h l a

Acarai Mountains

Tumuc-Humac Mountains

(claimed by
Suriname)

(claimed by
Suriname)

62

4

Equator

Rio Negro

B R A Z I L

Amazon

5

z o n B a s i n

Amazon

Amazon

Rio Purús

Amazon

Río Japurá

62

Elevation

-4000m   -3000m   -2000m   -1000m   -500m   Below sea level   0   100m   250m   500m   1000m   2000m   4000m

-13,124ft   -9843ft   -6562ft   -3281ft   -1640ft   -820ft/-250m   0   328ft   820ft   1640ft   3281ft   6562ft   13,124ft

Western South America

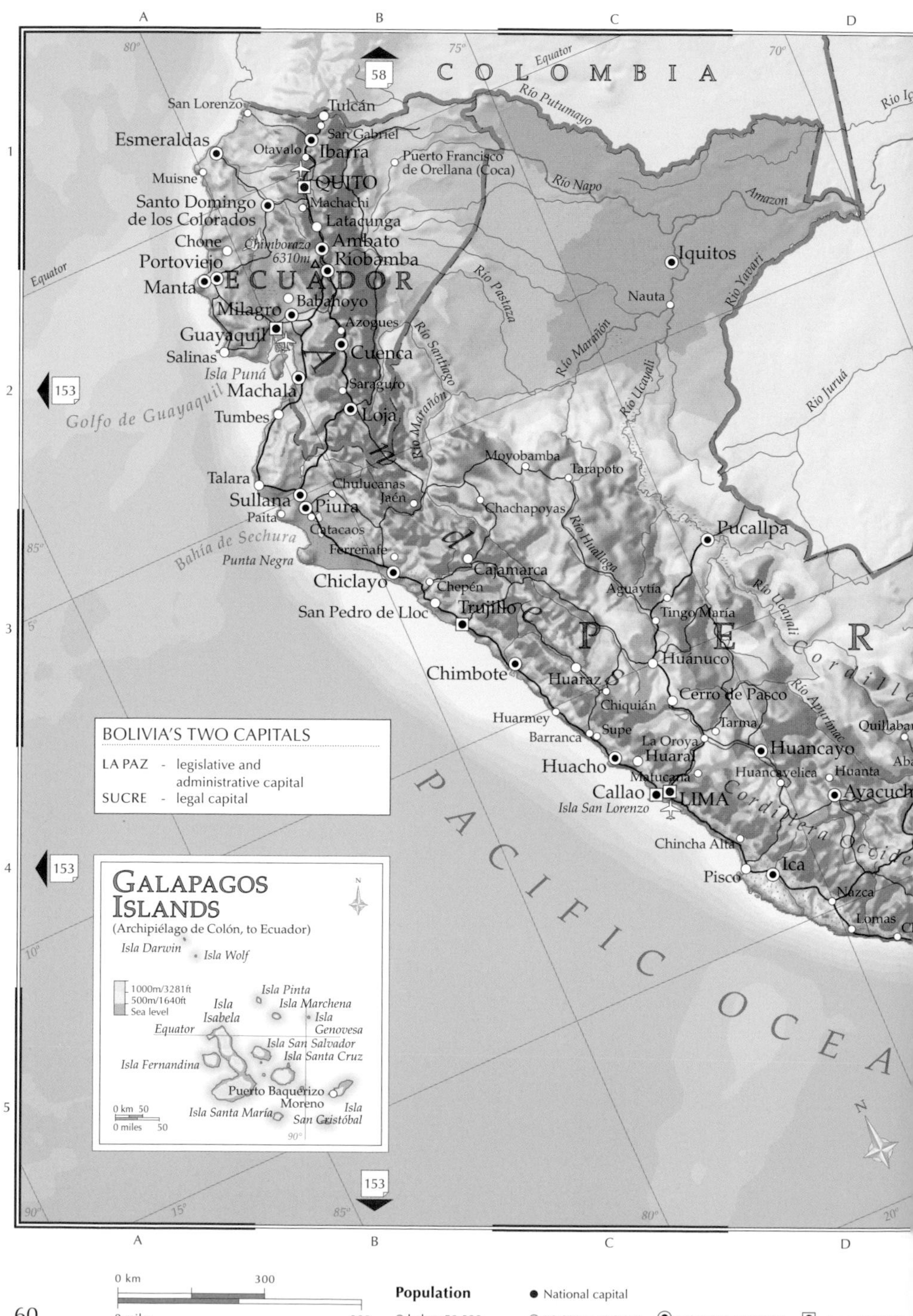

COLOMBIA

80° 75° Equator 70° Río Içá

San Lorenzo
Tulcán
Esmeraldas
San Gabriel
Muisne
Otavalo
Ibarra
Puerto Francisco
de Orellana (Coca)
QUITO
Santo Domingo
de los Colorados
Machachi
Latacunga
Chone
Chimborazo
Ambato
Riobamba
6310m▲
Portoviejo
ECUADOR
Manta
Babahoyo
Milagro
Azogues
Guayaquil
Cuenca
Salinas
Isla Puná
Saraguro
Machala
Loja
Tumbes

Equator
Río Putumayo
Río Napo
Amazon
Iquitos
Río Pastaza
Nauta
Río Marañón
Río Yavarí
Río Santiago
Río Juruá
Río Marañón
Río Ucayali

Golfo de Guayaquil

Talara
Chulucanas
Moyobamba
Tarapoto
Sullana
Jaén
Paita
Piura
Chachapoyas
Catacaos
Ferreñafe
Cajamarca
Punta Negra
Chiclayo
Chepén
San Pedro de Lloc
Trujillo
Aguaytía
Pucallpa
Río Huallaga
Tingo María
Chimbote
Huaraz
Huánuco
Huarmey
Chiquián
Cerro de Pasco
Tarma
Quillabai
Barranca
Supe
La Oroya
Huancayo
Aba
Huancayo
Huacho
Matucana
Huancavelica
Huanta
Callao
LIMA
Ayacuch
Isla San Lorenzo
Chincha Alta
Cordillera Occide
Pisco
Ica
Nazca
Lomas

Bahía de Sechura

85°

Río Apurímac
Cordillera

PERU

PACIFIC OCEA

BOLIVIA'S TWO CAPITALS

LA PAZ — legislative and
administrative capital
SUCRE — legal capital

GALAPAGOS ISLANDS

(Archipiélago de Colón, to Ecuador)

Isla Darwin
Isla Wolf

1000m/3281ft
500m/1640ft
Sea level

Isla Pinta
Isla Marchena
Isla
Isla
Genovesa
Isabela
Equator
Isla San Salvador
Isla Fernandina
Isla Santa Cruz
Puerto Baquerizo
Moreno
Isla
Isla Santa María
San Cristóbal

0 km 50
0 miles 50

90°

58
153
153
153
153

0 km 300
0 miles 300

Population

● National capital

○ below 50,000 ○ 50,000 to 100,000 ◉ 100,000 to 500,000 ◼ above 500,000

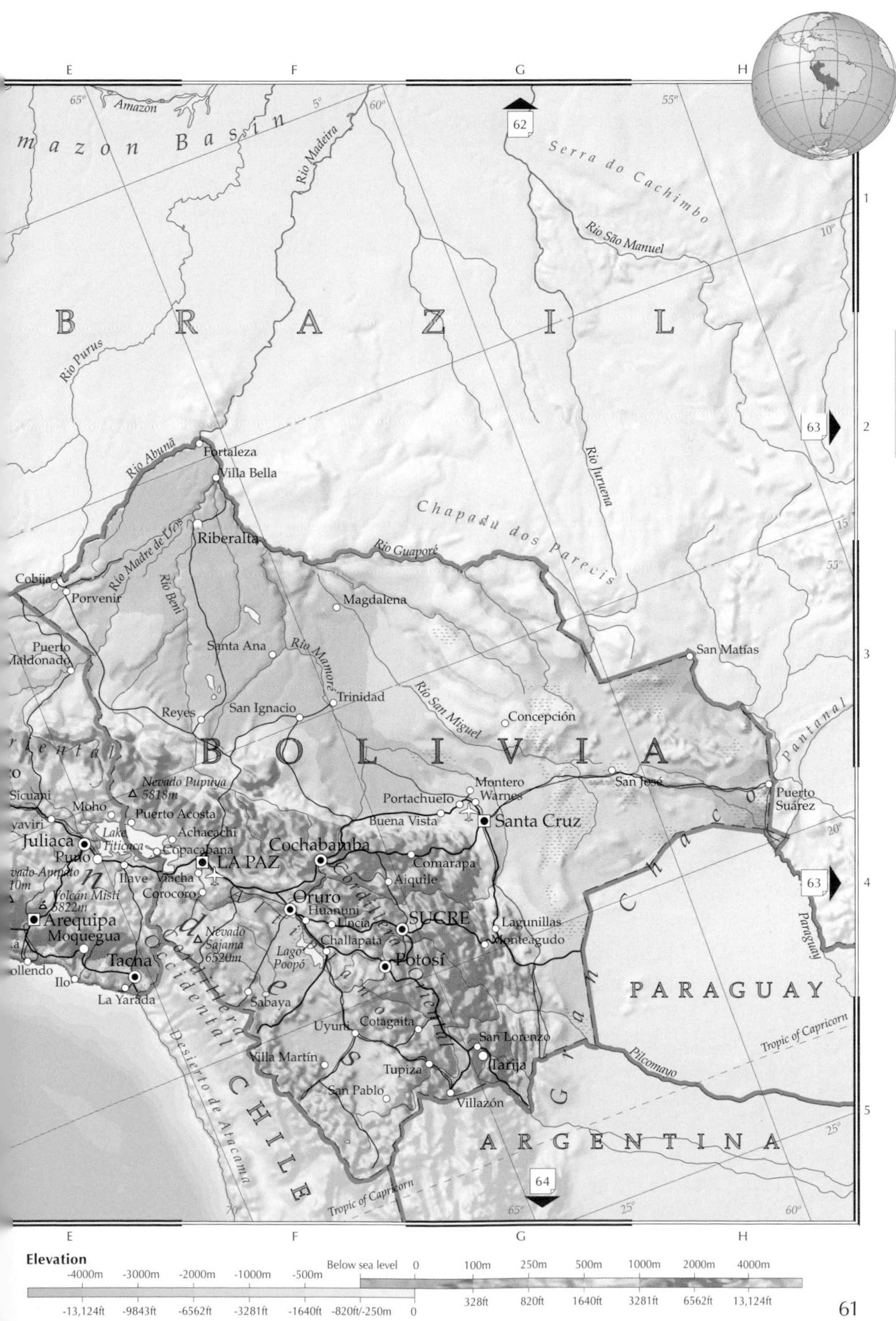

E   F   G   H

1

2

Amazon   65°   5°   60°   55°   10°

m a z o n   B a s i n

Rio Purus

Rio Madeira

Serra do Cachimbo

Rio São Manuel

B   R   A   Z   I   L

15°

55°

Rio Abuná
Fortaleza
Villa Bella

Rio Madre de Dios

Riberalta

Chapada dos Parecis

Rio Guaporé

Rio Juruena

Cobija
Porvenir

Rio Beni

Magdalena

Puerto
Maldonado

Santa Ana   *Rio Mamoré*

San Matías   3

Reyes   San Ignacio   Trinidad   *Rio San Miguel*

Concepción

oriental

o   B   O   L   I   V   I   A

Pantanal

Sicuani   *Nevado Pupuya*
△ 5818m

Portachuelo
Montero
Warnes

San José   Puerto
Suárez

yaviri   Moho   Puerto Acosta   Buena Vista   Santa Cruz   20°

Juliaca   *Lake*
Titicaca   Achacachi   Copacabana   LA PAZ   Cochabamba

Puno   Comarapa
vado Ampato   Aiquile
10m   Ilave   Viacha
△   Corocoro   Oruro   Huanuni   *Gran*   Lagunillas   *Chaco*   63   4

Arequipa   Llica   SUCRE   Monteagudo
Volcán Misti
△ 5822m   Challapata

Moquegua   *Nevado*   Potosí   *Paraguay*
Sajama
△ 6520m

Tacna   *Lago*
Poopó   *oriental*

á   Sabaya   *Cordillera*   PARAGUAY

ollendo   Ilo   Uyuni   Cotagaita

La Yarada   San Lorenzo

Villa Martín   Tupiza   Tarija   *Pilcomayo*   Tropic of Capricorn

San Pablo   *Gran*

Villazón   25°   5

Desierto de Atacama   A   R   G   E   N   T   I   N   A

C   H   I   L   E

70°   65°   60°

Tropic of Capricorn   25°

E   F   G   H

Elevation

| -4000m | -3000m | -2000m | -1000m | -500m | Below sea level | 0 | 100m | 250m | 500m | 1000m | 2000m | 4000m |

| -13,124ft | -9843ft | -6562ft | -3281ft | -1640ft | -820ft/-250m | 0 | 328ft | 820ft | 1640ft | 3281ft | 6562ft | 13,124ft |

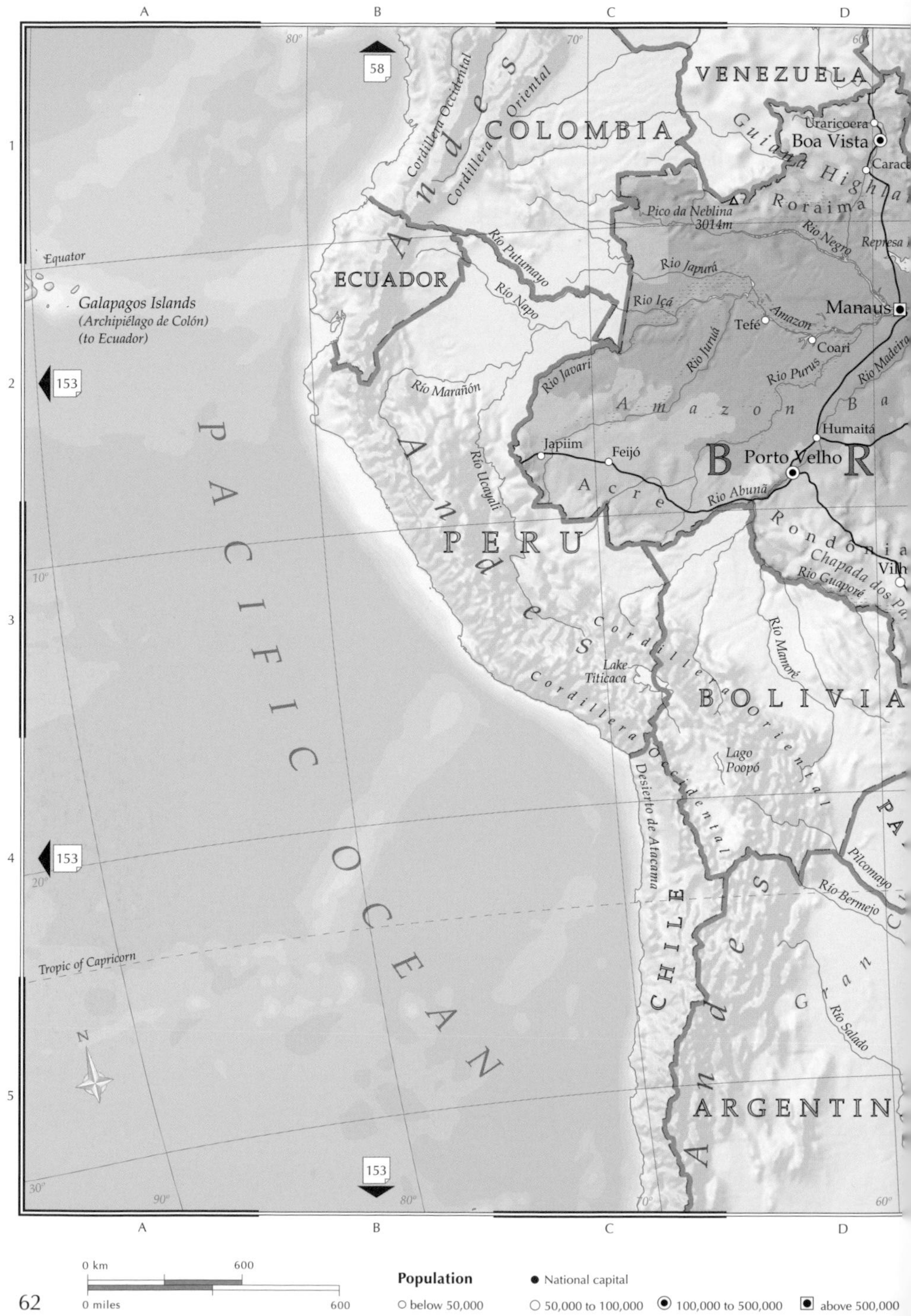

VENEZUELA

COLOMBIA

ECUADOR

Galapagos Islands
(Archipiélago de Colón)
(to Ecuador)

Equator

Cordillera Occidental

Cordillera Oriental

A n d e s

Rio Putumayo

Rio Napo

Rio Marañón

Rio Ucayali

PERU

A n d e s

Lake
Titicaca

Cordillera Occidental

Desierto de Atacama

CHILE

A n d e s

Guiana Highlands

Uraricoera
Boa Vista
Carac

Roraima

Pico da Neblina
3014m

Rio Negro
Represa

Rio Japurá

Rio Içá

Rio Juruá

Tefé

Coari

Amazon

Manaus

Rio Madeira

A m a z o n

B a
R

Rio Purus

Rio Javari

Japiim

Feijó

A c r e

Rio Abunā

B Porto Velho

Humaitá

Rio Napo

Rondonia

Chapada dos Pa
Rio Guaporé

Villa

Rio Mamoré

B O L I V I A

Lago
Poopó

Cordillera Oriental

PA

Pilcomayo

Rio Bermejo

G

Rio Salado

ARGENTIN

P A C I F I C   O C E A N

Tropic of Capricorn

N

58

153

153

153

0 km   600
0 miles   600

Population   ● National capital

○ below 50,000   ◉ 50,000 to 100,000   ◉ 100,000 to 500,000   ■ above 500,000

ATLANTIC OCEAN

FRENCH GUIANA
(to France)

JAME

Tumuc-Humac
Mountains

Amapá

Maçapá

Ilha Caviana de Fora

Mouths of the Amazon

Baía de Marajó

Ilha
de Marajó

Belém

Baía de São Marcos

São Luís

Parnaíba

Camocim

Equator

ruer

Amazon

antarém

Altamira

Itaituba

Rio Xingu

Marabá

Imperatriz

Maranhão

Represa de
Tucuruí

Bacabal

Piripiri

Teresina

Ceará

Fortaleza

Mossoró

Açu

Atol das Rocas

San Fernando de Noronha
(to Brazil)

Cabo de São Roque

Natal

Z I

Pará

Carolina

Florano

Picos

Rio Grande do Norte

Juazeiro do Norte

João Pessoa

Campina Grande

L

Balsas

Piauí

Pará

Paraíba

o Cachimbo

Serra Formosa

Serra dos Gradaus

Rio Tocantins

Palmas do
Tocantins

Represa de Sobradinho

Juazeiro

Pernambuco

Alagoas

Recife

Maceió

Grosso

Rio Araguaia

Goiás

Tocantins

Taguatinga

Rio São Francisco

Chapada
Diamantina

Aracaju

Estância

Bahia

Feira de Santana

Salvador

Cuiabá

Planalto

BRASÍLIA

Central

Janaúba

Salvador

Baía de Todos os Santos

Anápolis

Goiânia

Jataí

Minas

Montes Claros

Araçuai

Gerais

Itabuna

Vitória da Conquista

Canavieiras

Mato Grosso
do Sul

Araguari

Uberlândia

Uberaba

Governador Valadares

Espírito
Santo

onópolis

Campo Grande

dauana

Ribeirão Preto

Marília

São Paulo

Divinópolis

Belo Horizonte

Vitória

Campos

ente Prudente

Londrina

Campinas

Juiz de Fora

Nova
Iguaçu

Rio de Janeiro

Tropic of Capricorn

Maringá

Paraná

São Paulo

Santos

Represa
de Itaipu

Saltos do Rio Iguaçu

Iguaçu

Ponta Grossa

Santa Catarina

Curitiba

Joinville

Blumenau

Florianópolis

Passo Fundo

Rio Grande

Maria

Canoas

Porto Alegre

Lagoa dos Patos

Bagé

Rio Grande

Mirim Lagoon

GUAY

negro

UGUAY

ATLANTIC OCEAN

ATLANTIC OCEAN

50°   40°   30°

66

67

67

67

67

E   F   G   H

1
2
3
4
5

Elevation

-4000m	-3000m	-2000m	-1000m	-500m	Below sea level	0	100m	250m	500m	1000m	2000m	4000m
-13,124ft	-9843ft	-6562ft	-3281ft	-1640ft	-820ft/-250m	0	328ft	820ft	1640ft	3281ft	6562ft	13,124ft

Southern South America

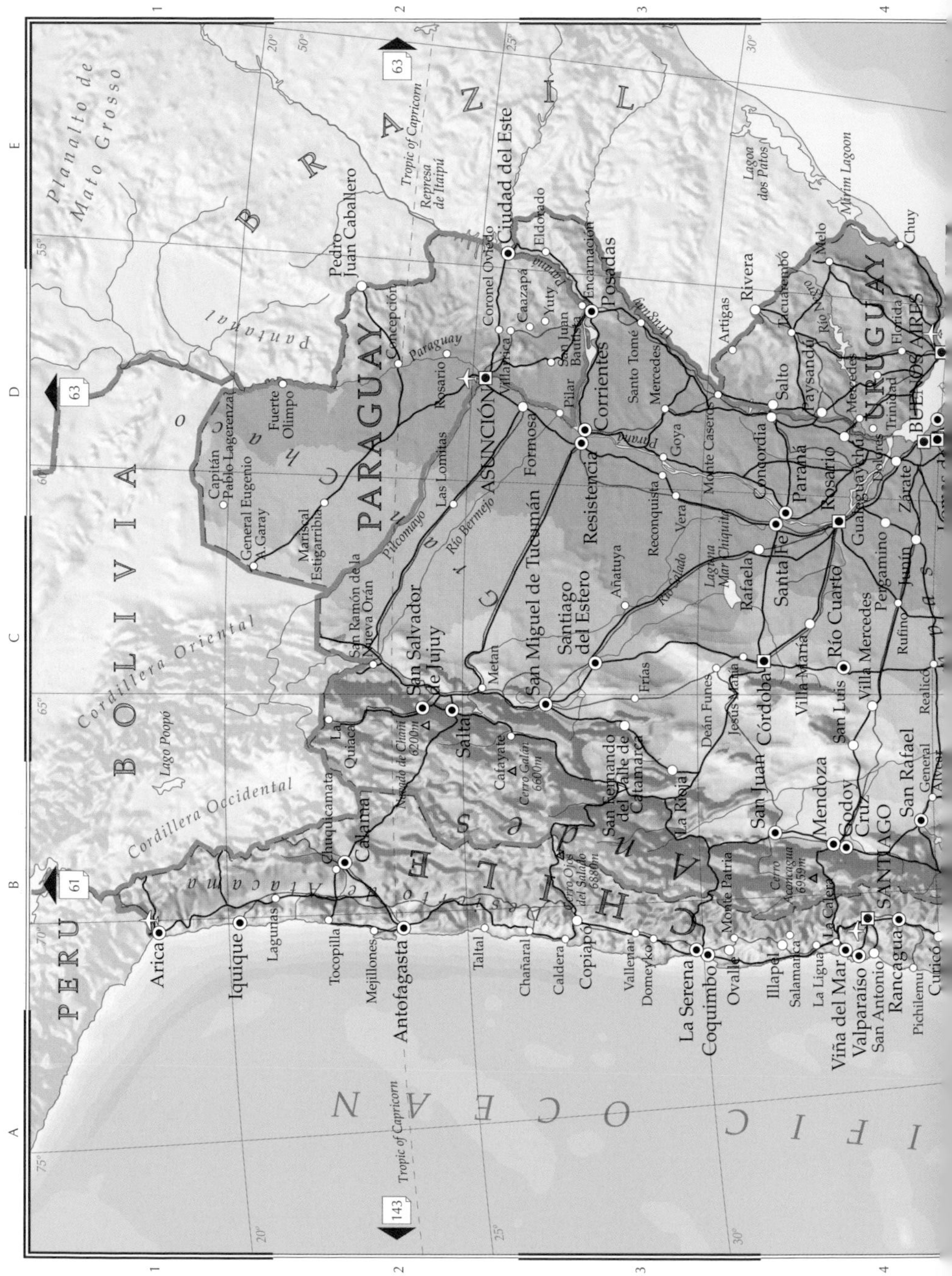

Population   ● National capital

○ below 50,000   ○ 50,000 to 100,000   ◉ 100,000 to 500,000   ◼ above 500,000

0 km   200
0 miles   200

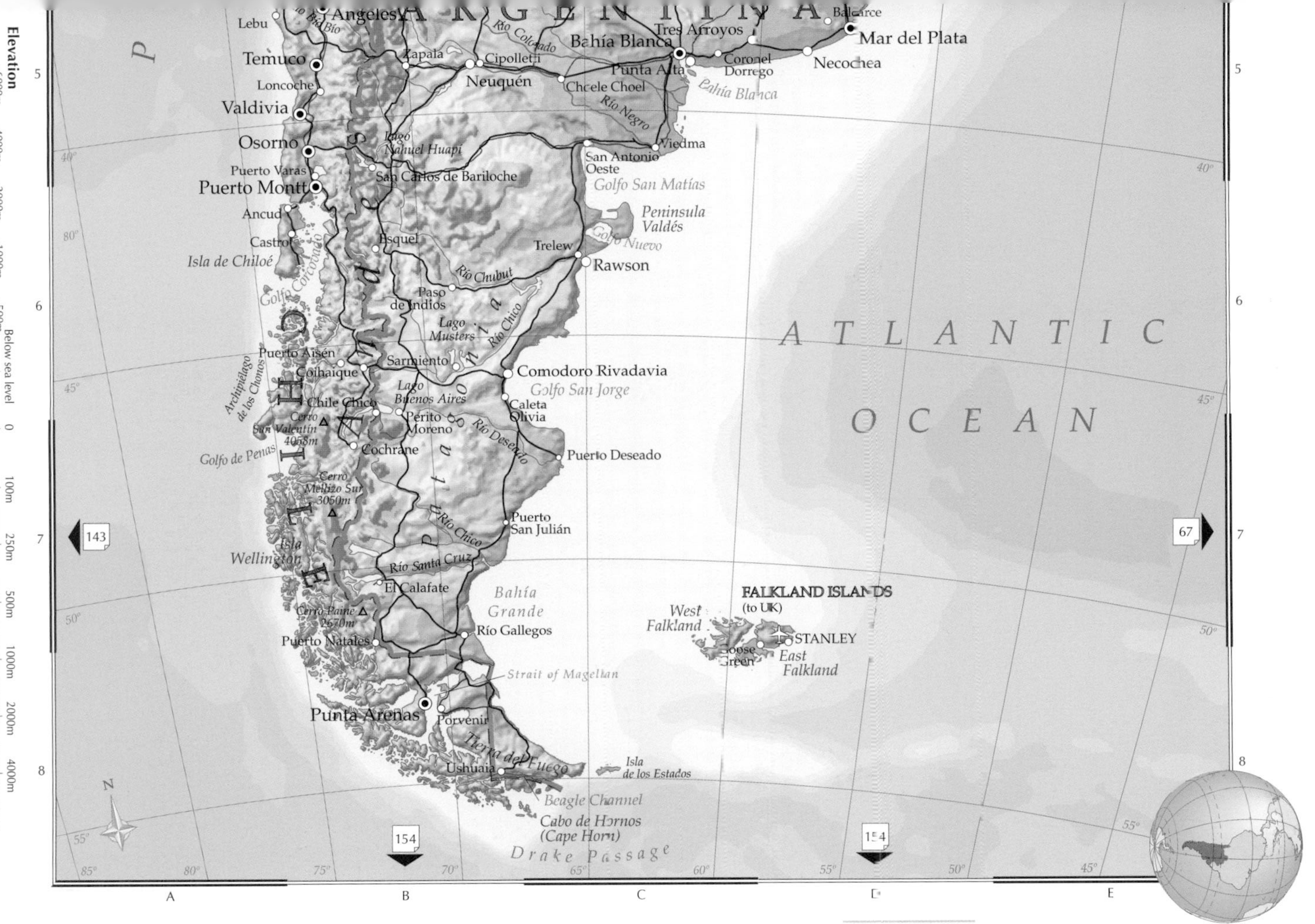

ATLANTIC OCEAN

ARGENTINA

Mar del Plata
Balcarce
Necochea
Coronel Dorrego
Tres Arroyos
Bahía Blanca
Punta Alta
Bahía Blanca
Chele Choel
Río Colorado
Cipolletti
Río Negro
Neuquén
Zapala
Viedma
San Antonio Oeste
Peninsula Valdés
Golfo San Matías
Golfo Nuevo
Rawson
Trelew

FALKLAND ISLANDS
(to UK)
STANLEY
West Falkland
East Falkland
Isla de los Estados

Comodoro Rivadavia
Golfo San Jorge
Caleta Olivia
Puerto Deseado
Río Deseado
Puerto San Julián
Bahía Grande
Río Gallegos

San Carlos de Bariloche
Lago Nahuel Huapi
Esquel
Paso de Indios
Río Chubut
Río Chico
Sarmiento
Lago Musters
Lago Buenos Aires
Perito Moreno
Cochrane
Río Chico
Río Senguerr
El Calafate
Río Santa Cruz

Lebu
Temuco
Loncoche
Valdivia
Río Bío Bío
Osorno
Puerto Varas
Puerto Montt
Ancud
Castro
Isla de Chiloé
Golfo Corcovado
Puerto Aisén
Coihaique
Chile Chico
Cerro San Valentín 4058m
Archipiélago de los Chonos
Golfo de Penas
Isla Wellington
Cerro San Lorenzo 3706m
Puerto Natales

CHILE

Strait of Magellan
Tierra del Fuego
Bahía Channel
Beagle Channel
Cabo de Hornos (Cape Horn)
Drake Passage
Porvenir
Ushuaia
Punta Arenas

N

Elevation

				Below sea level							
-6000m	-4000m	-2000m	-1000m	-500m	0	100m	250m	500m	1000m	2000m	4000m
-19,686ft	-13,124ft	-6562ft	-3281ft	-1640ft	-820ft/-250m	0	328ft	820ft	1640ft	3281ft	6562ft	13,124ft

The Atlantic Ocean

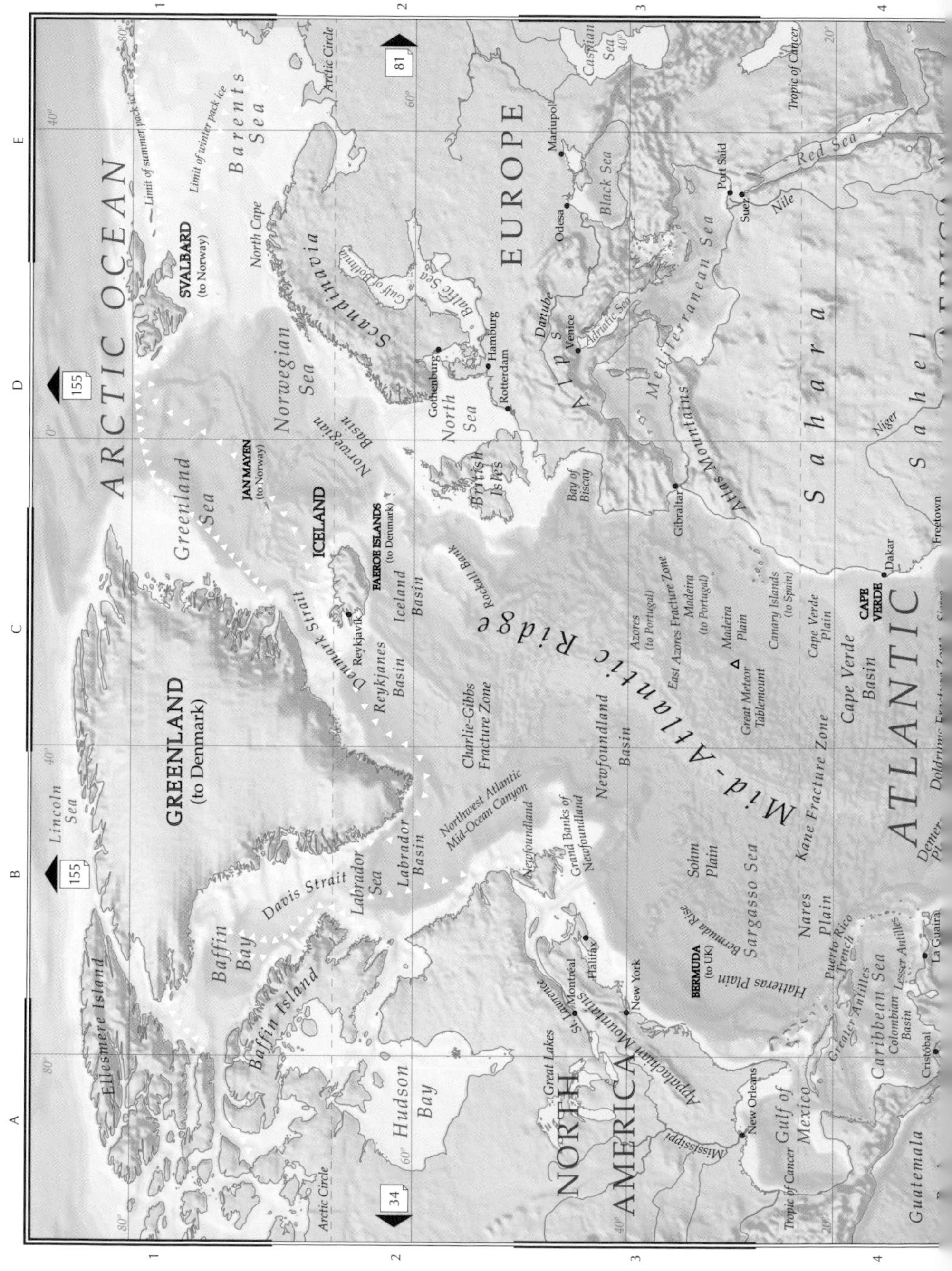

● Major port

0 km   1000

0 miles   1000

INDIAN OCEAN

Southwest Indian Ridge

Mozambique Channel
Madagascar
Lake Nyasa
Lake Tanganyika
Great
Zambezi

Mozambique Plateau

Cape Town
Cape of Good Hope
Orange Fan
Agulhas Plateau
Agulhas Basin

Angola Basin
Lobito

Zaïre Seamount
Walvis Ridge

ASCENSION ISLAND (to UK)
ST HELENA (to UK)

TRISTAN DA CUNHA (to St Helena)
Cape Basin

Gough Island (to Tristan da Cunha)

BOUVET ISLAND (to Norway)

Spiess Seamount

Atlantic-Indian Ridge

Atlantic-Indian Basin

SOUTHERN OCEAN

ANTARCTICA

Enderby Plain

Lazarev Sea

Limit of winter pack ice
Limit of summer pack ice
Antarctic Circle

Mid - Atlantic Ridge

Fernando de Noronha (to Brazil)
Ascension Fracture
Brazil Basin
Recife
Ilha da Trindade (to Brazil)
Vitória Seamount
Rio de Janeiro
Santos Plateau
Rio Grande Rise

Gough Fracture Zone

SOUTH AMERICA

Andes

Paraná
Buenos Aires

Argentine Basin

Zapiola Ridge

Gulf of San Matías
Gulf of San Jorge

FALKLAND ISLANDS (to UK)
Falkland Plateau

SOUTH GEORGIA (to UK)

SOUTH SANDWICH ISLANDS (to UK)
South Sandwich Trench
East Scotia Basin
Scotia Sea
South Orkney Islands

America-Antarctica Ridge

Weddell Plain

Weddell Sea

PACIFIC OCEAN
Peru-Chile Trench
Chile Basin
Peru Basin
Tropic of Capricorn

Chile Rise

Mornington Abyssal Plain

Yaghan Basin
Cape Horn
Drake Passage
South Shetland Islands

Bellingshausen Plain
Bellingshausen Sea
Antarctic Circle

N

141
154
154
153

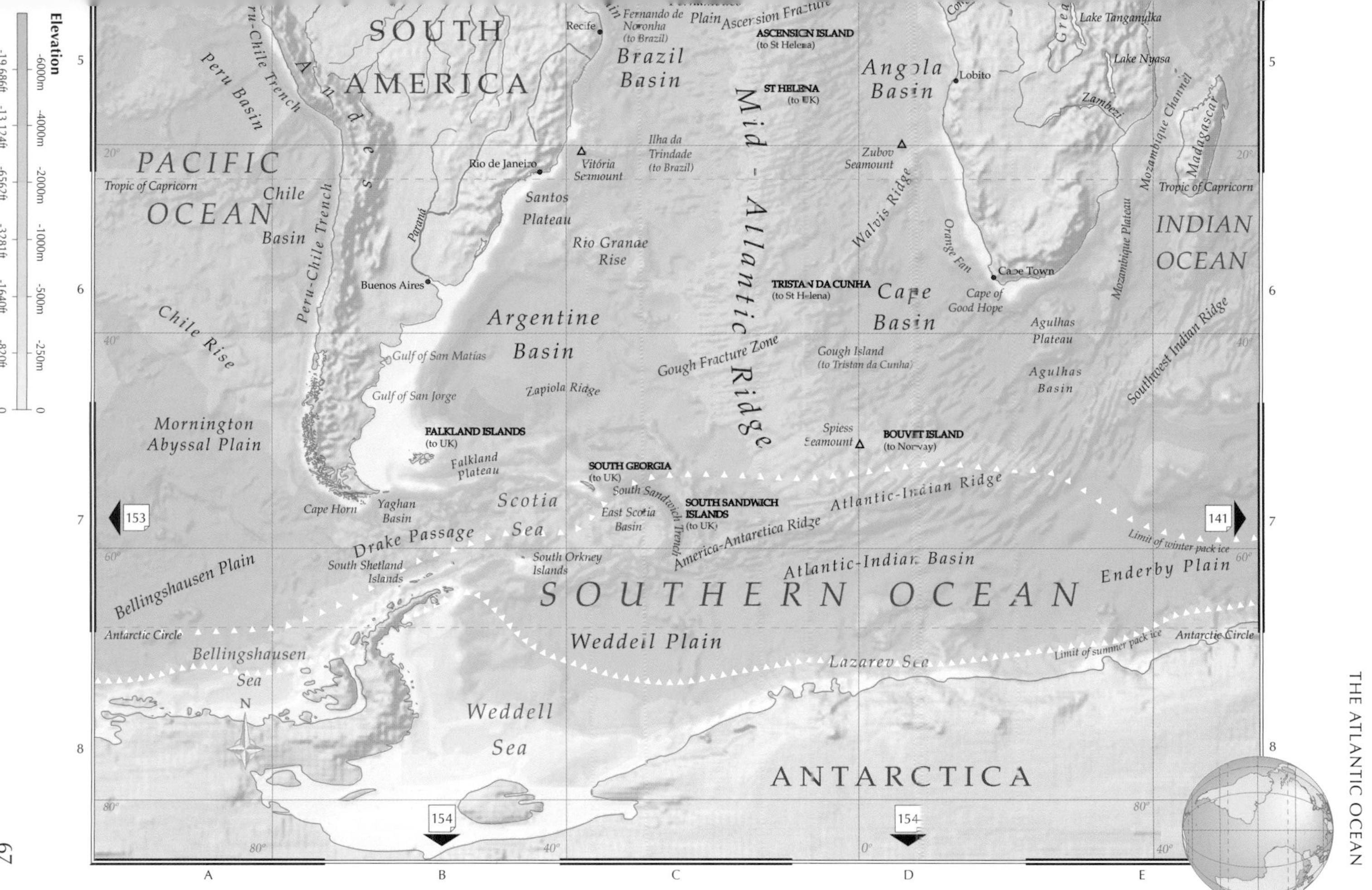

Elevation

-6000m	-4000m	-2000m	-1000m	-500m	-250m	0
-19,686ft	-13,124ft	-6562ft	-3281ft	-1640ft	-820ft	0

67

Africa

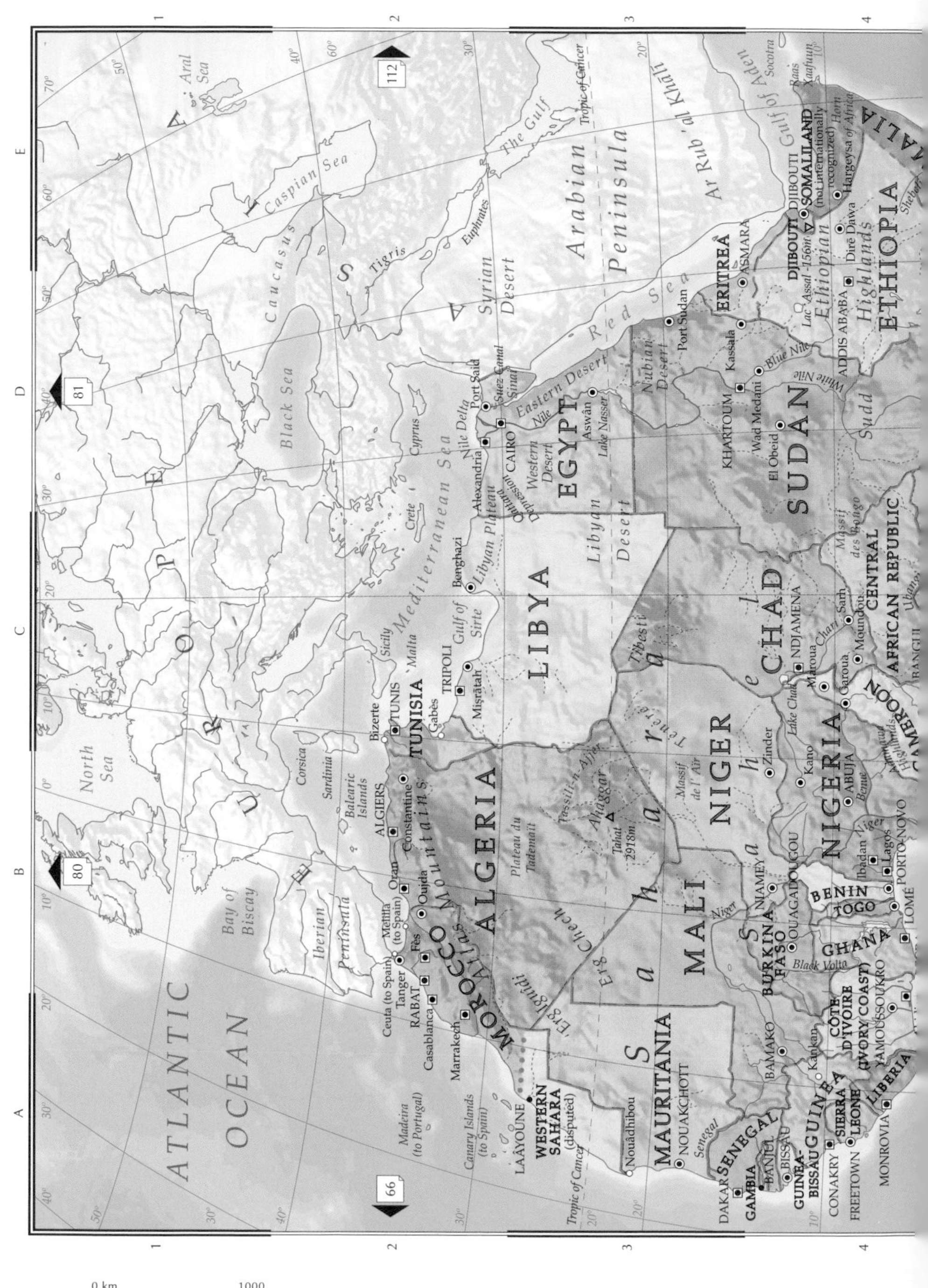

Population

- o below 50,000
- o 50,000 to 100,000
- ◉ 100,000 to 500,000
- ■ above 500,000

● National capital

0 km   1000

0 miles   1000

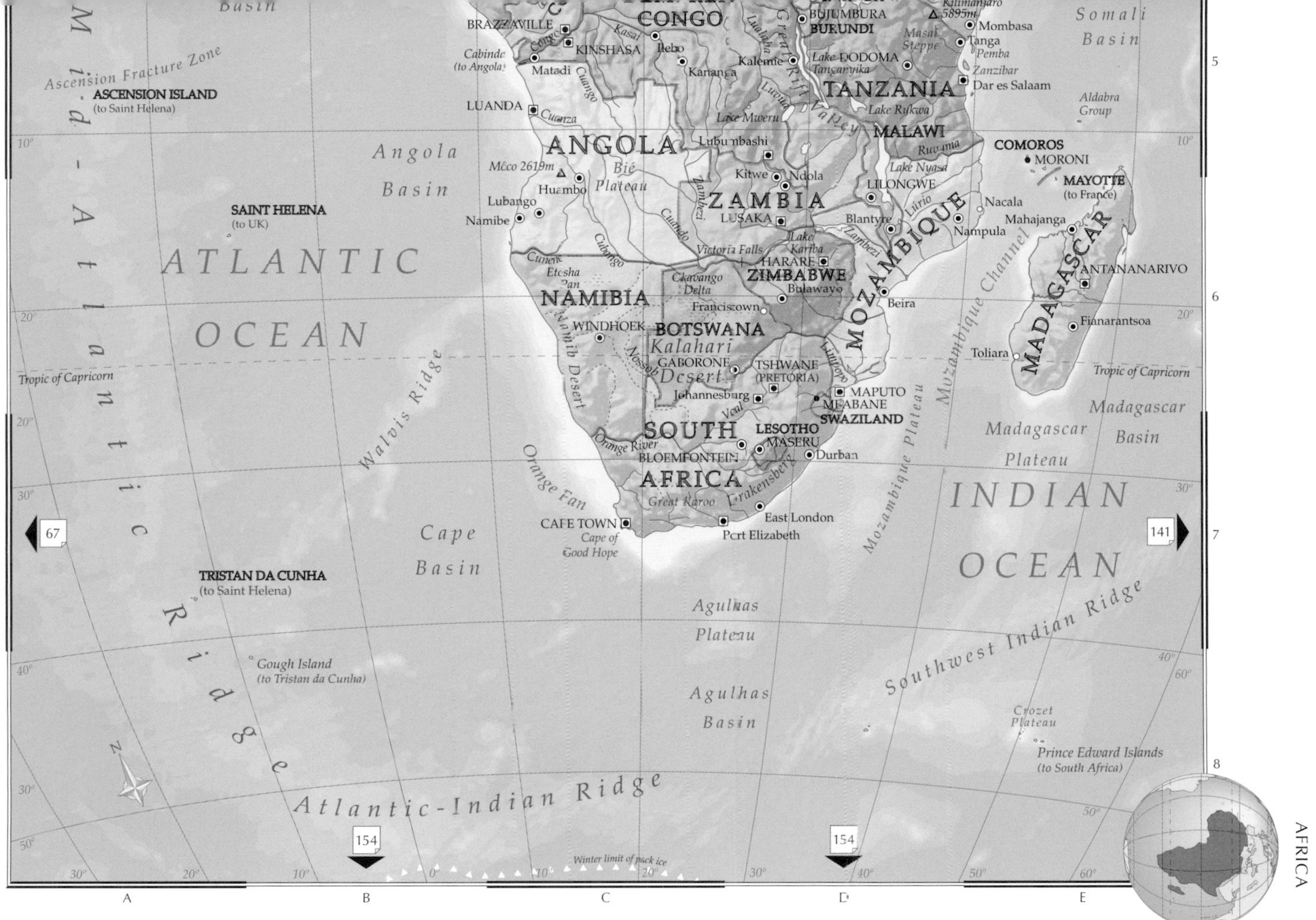
Somali Basin
Aldabra Group
COMOROS
MORONI
MAYOTTE (to France)
MADAGASCAR
ANTANANARIVO
Mahajanga
Fianarantsoa
Toliara
Tropic of Capricorn
Madagascar Basin
Madagascar Plateau
Mozambique Channel
Mozambique Plateau
INDIAN OCEAN
Southwest Indian Ridge
Crozet Plateau
Prince Edward Islands (to South Africa)
Mombasa
Tanga
Pemba
Zanzibar
Dar es Salaam
Kilimanjaro 5895m
Masai Steppe
TANZANIA
DODOMA
Lake Tanganyika
Lake Rukwa
BUJUMBURA
BURUNDI
Great Rift Valley
MALAWI
Lake Nyasa
LILONGWE
Blantyre
Nacala
Nampula
MOZAMBIQUE
Beira
Zambezi
Lurio
Ruvuma
Limpopo
MAPUTO
MBABANE
SWAZILAND
Durban
LESOTHO
MASERU
East London
Port Elizabeth
SOUTH AFRICA
BLOEMFONTEIN
TSHWANE (PRETORIA)
Johannesburg
Vaal
Orange River
Great Karoo
Drakensberg
CAPE TOWN
Cape of Good Hope
GABORONE
BOTSWANA
Kalahari Desert
Nossob
Francistown
Okavango Delta
ZIMBABWE
HARARE
Bulawayo
Lake Kariba
Victoria Falls
ZAMBIA
LUSAKA
Kitwe
Ndola
Lubumbashi
Lake Mweru
Luvua
Kalemie
Kananga
Lualaba
CONGO
KINSHASA
BRAZZAVILLE
Kasai
Ilebo
Matadi
Cuango
Cabinda (to Angola)
LUANDA
Cuanza
ANGOLA
Bié Plateau
Moco 2619m
Huambo
Lubango
Namibe
Cuando
Cubango
Cunene
Etosha Pan
NAMIBIA
WINDHOEK
Namib Desert
Orange Fan
Angola Basin
ATLANTIC OCEAN
Walvis Ridge
Cape Basin
Agulhas Plateau
Agulhas Basin
Mid-Atlantic Ridge
Atlantic-Indian Ridge
Ascension Fracture Zone
ASCENSION ISLAND (to Saint Helena)
SAINT HELENA (to UK)
TRISTAN DA CUNHA (to Saint Helena)
Gough Island (to Tristan da Cunha)
Winter limit of pack ice
67
141
154
154

Northwest Africa

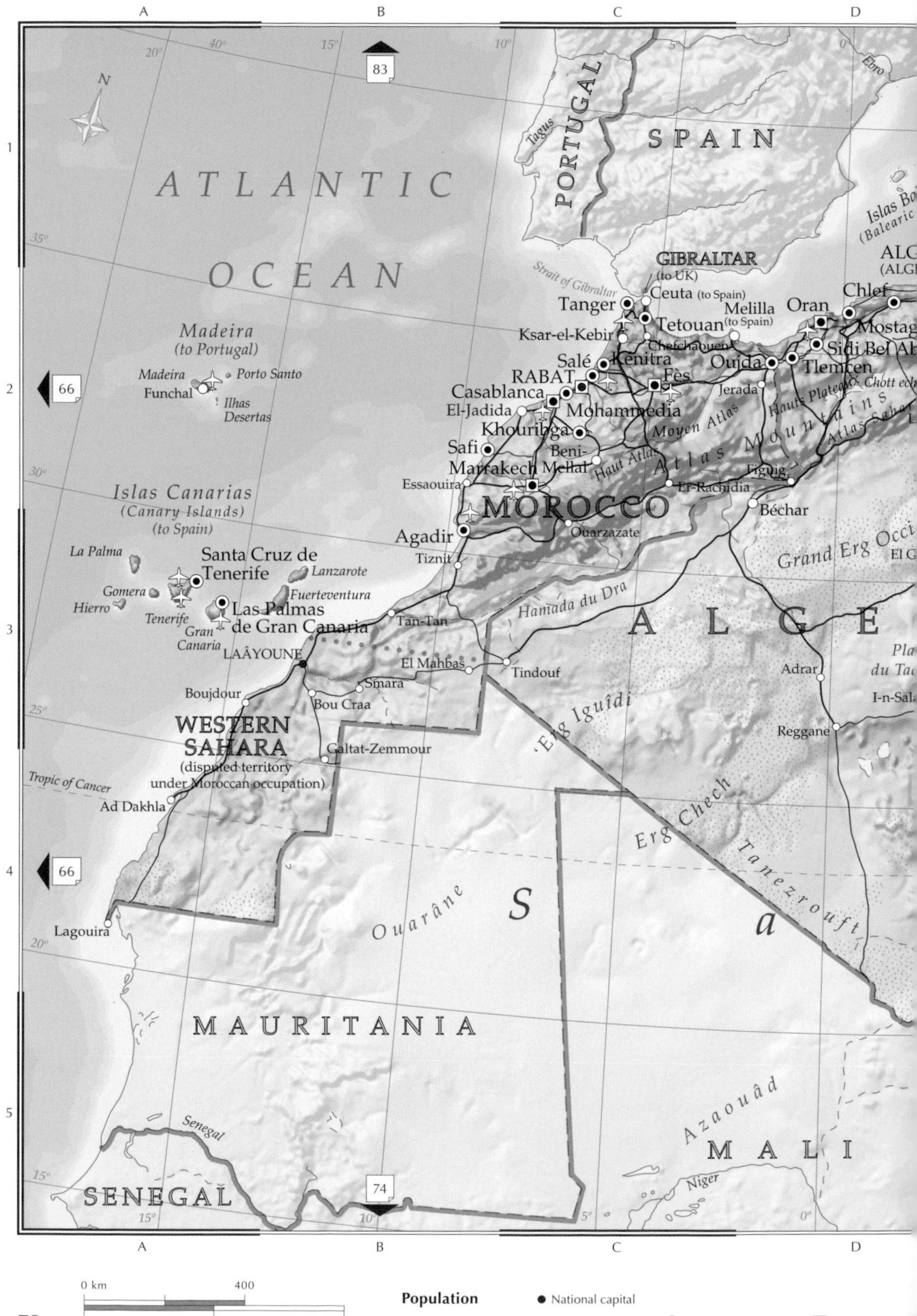

A T L A N T I C

O C E A N

Madeira
(to Portugal)

66

Madeira • Porto Santo
Funchal
Ilhas
Desertas

Islas Canarias
(Canary Islands)
(to Spain)

La Palma
Santa Cruz de
Tenerife • *Lanzarote*
Gomera *Fuerteventura*
Hierro
Las Palmas
Tenerife de Gran Canaria
Gran
Canaria LAÂYOUNE

Boujdour
Smara
Bou Craa

WESTERN
SAHARA
(disputed territory
under Moroccan occupation)

Tropic of Cancer
Ad Dakhla

66

Lagouira

M A U R I T A N I A

Senegal

SENEGAL

74

PORTUGAL

Tagus

S P A I N

GIBRALTAR
(to UK)
Ceuta (to Spain)
Tanger
Tetouan
Melilla
(to Spain)
Ksar-el-Kebir
Chefchaouen
Salé Kenitra Oujda
RABAT Fès
Casablanca Jerada
El-Jadida Mohammedia
Khouribga
Beni
Safi Mellal
Marrakech
Essaouira

Oran Chlef
Mostag
Sidi Bel Ab
Tlemcen
Chott ech

Islas B
(Balearic

ALG
(ALG

MOROCCO

Moyen Atlas
Haut Atlas
Atlas Mountains
Atlas Sahar
El-Rachidia
Figuig

Agadir
Tiznit

Ouarzazate
Béchar

A L G E

Grand Erg Occi
El G

Tan-Tan
Hamada du Dra

El Mahbas
Tindouf

Erg Iguîdi
Adrar
Pla
du Tar
I-n-Sala

Reggane

Galtat-Zemmour

Ouarâne

S

Erg Chech

Tanezrouft

a

Azouâd

M A L I

Niger

Population   ● National capital

○ below 50,000   ○ 50,000 to 100,000   ◉ 100,000 to 500,000   ▣ above 500,000

0 km   400

0 miles   400

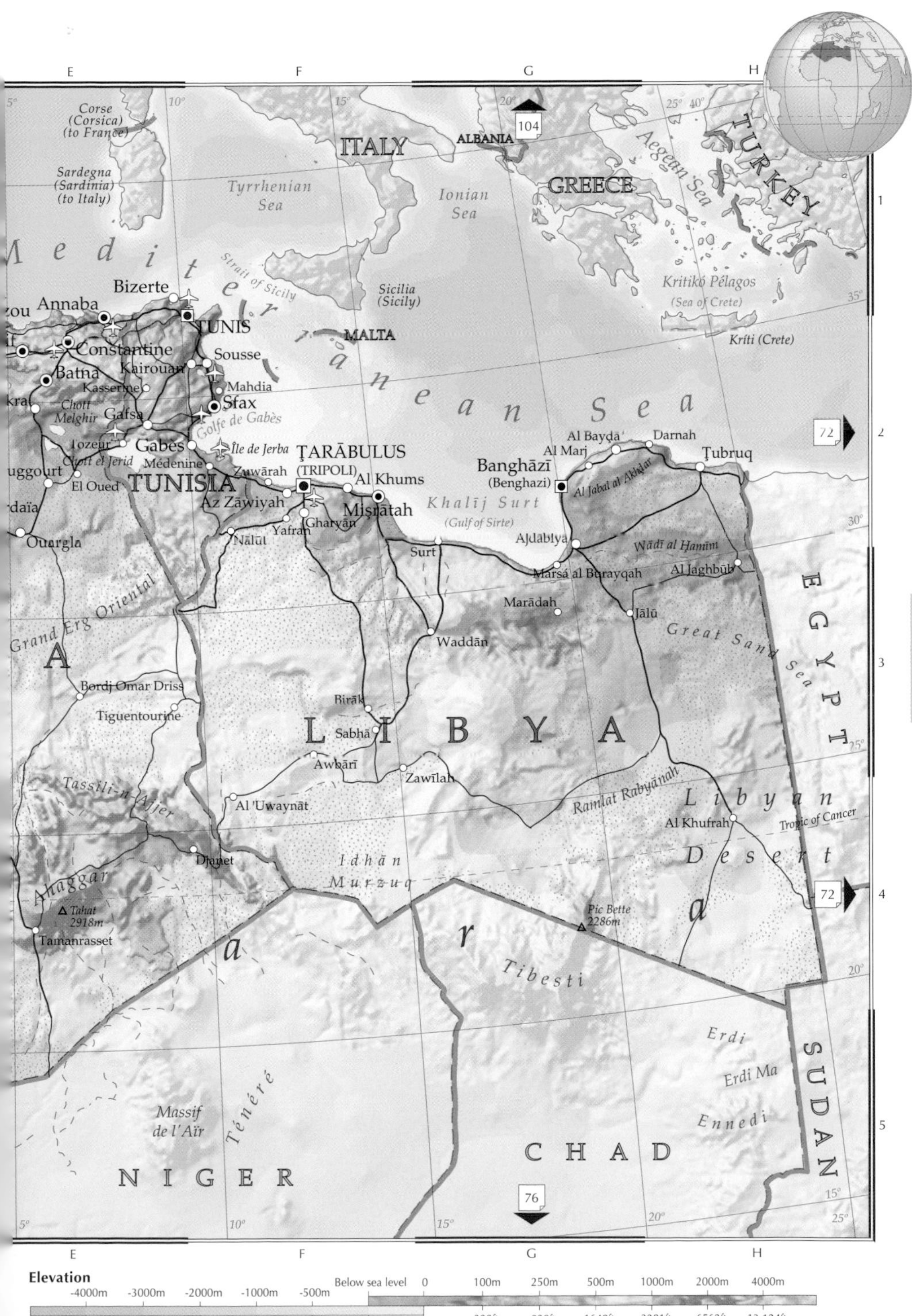

ITALY
ALBANIA
GREECE
TURKEY

Corse
(Corsica)
(to France)

Sardegna
(Sardinia)
(to Italy)

Tyrrhenian
Sea

Ionian
Sea

Aegean
Sea

Kritikó Pélagos
(Sea of Crete)

Kríti (Crete)

M e d i t e r r a n e a n   S e a

Strait of Sicily

Sicilia
(Sicily)

MALTA

72

zou
Annaba
Bizerte
Constantine
Batna
Kasserine
TUNIS
Sousse
Kairouan
Mahdia
Sfax
krat
Chott
Melghir
Gafsa
Golfe de Gabès
Île de Jerba
TARĀBULUS
(TRIPOLI)
Banghāzī
(Benghazi)
Al Bayda'
Al Marj
Darnah
Ţubruq
Tozeur
Gabes
Chott el Jerid
Médenine
Zuwārah
Az Zāwiyah
Al Khums
El Oued
TUNISIA
Yafran
Gharyān
Mişrātah
Al Jabal al Akhdar
Khalīj Surt
(Gulf of Sirte)
Ajdābiyā
Wādī al Ḩamīm
Al Jaghbūb
uggourt
daïa
Ouargla
Nālūt
Surt
Marsá al Burayqah
Jālū

A
Grand Erg Oriental
Bordj Omar Driss
Tiguentourine
Marādah
Waddān

L I B Y A
Birāk
Sabhā
Awbārī
Zawīlah
Ramlat Rabyānah
Al Khufrah
Tropic of Cancer

Tassili n'Ajjer
Al 'Uwaynāt

E G Y P T
Great Sand Sea
L i b y a n   D e s e r t

Ahaggar
Tahat
2918m
Tamanrasset
Djanet

a
I d h ā n   M u r z u q
r
Tibesti
Pic Bette
2286m

Erdi
Erdi Ma
Ennedi

S U D A N

Ténéré
Massif
de l'Aïr

N I G E R
C H A D

76

72

Elevation

					Below sea level	0	100m	250m	500m	1000m	2000m	4000m
-4000m	-3000m	-2000m	-1000m	-500m								
-13,124ft	-9843ft	-6562ft	-3281ft	-1640ft	-820ft/-250m	0	328ft	820ft	1640ft	3281ft	6562ft	13,124ft

71

Northeast Africa

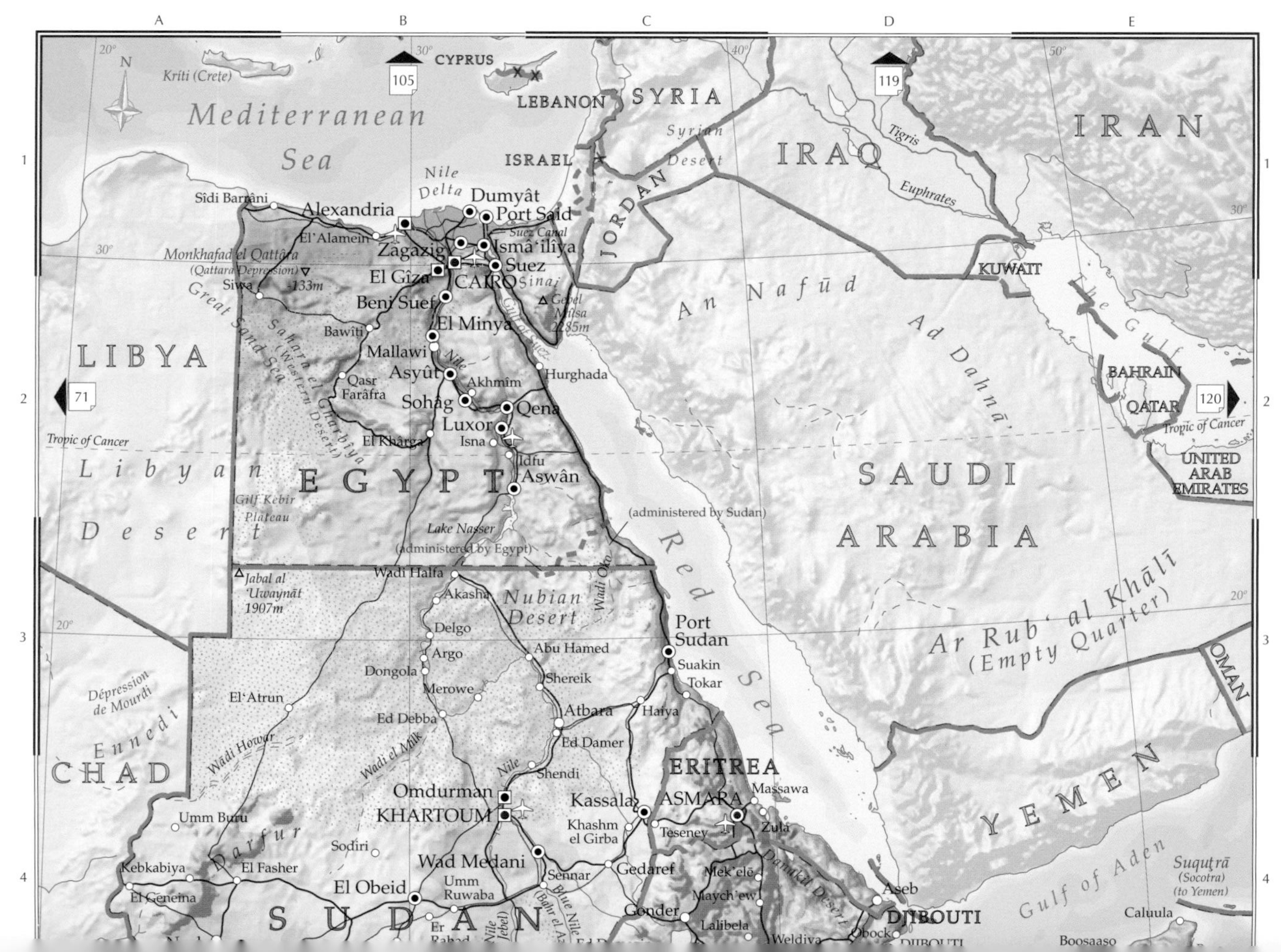

IRAN

IRAQ

SYRIA

LEBANON

CYPRUS

ISRAEL

JORDAN

KUWAIT

BAHRAIN

QATAR

UNITED ARAB EMIRATES

OMAN

SAUDI ARABIA

YEMEN

DJIBOUTI

ERITREA

OMAN

Tigris

Euphrates

Syrian Desert

The Gulf

Ad Dahnā'

An Nafūd

Ar Rub' al Khālī
(Empty Quarter)

Suquṭrā
(Socotra)
(to Yemen)

Gulf of Aden

Caluula

Boosaaso

DJIBOUTI

Djibouti

Aseb

Zula

Massawa

ASMARA

Mek'elē

Maych'ew

Lalibela

Gonder

Gedaref

Teseney

Keren

Danakil Desert

Kassala

Khashm el Girba

Sennar

Blue Nile
(Bahr el Az...

Mediterranean Sea

Kríti (Crete)

Red Sea

Port Sudan

Suakin

Tokar

Hafira

Abu Hamed

Akasha

Wadi Halfa

Nubian Desert

Shereik

Atbara

Ed Damer

Shendi

Omdurman

KHARTOUM

Wād Medani

Umm Ruwaba

Sofiri

El Obeid

El Fasher

El Geneina

Kebkabiya

Umm Buru

Nile

Delgo

Argo

Merowe

Dongola

Ed Debba

Darfur

SUDAN

CHAD

Ennedi

Dépression
de Mourdi

Wādī Howar

El'Atrun

Jabal al
'Uwaynāt
1907m

Lake Nasser
(Administered by Egypt)

Alexandria

El 'Alamein

Sidi Barrani

Dumyāt

Port Said

Zagazig

El Gîza

CAIRO

Benî Suef

El Minya

Mallawi

Asyût

Sohag

Akhmîm

Qena

Luxor

Isna

Idfu

Aswân

El Kharga

Qasr Farâfra

Bawîti

Siwa

Monkhafad el Qattâra
(Qattara Depression)
-133m

Sâhra el Gharbiya
(Western Desert)

Great Sand Sea

Gilf el Kebir
Plateau

Nile
Delta

Ismâ'îliya

Suez

Gulf of Suez

Hurghada

Gebel Katrîna
2637m

Sinai

LIBYA

EGYPT

Libyan Desert

Tropic of Cancer

Wadi Oko

Population

○ below 50,000   ○ 50,000 to 100,000   ◉ 100,000 to 500,000   ▣ above 500,000

● National capital

0 km   400

0 miles   400

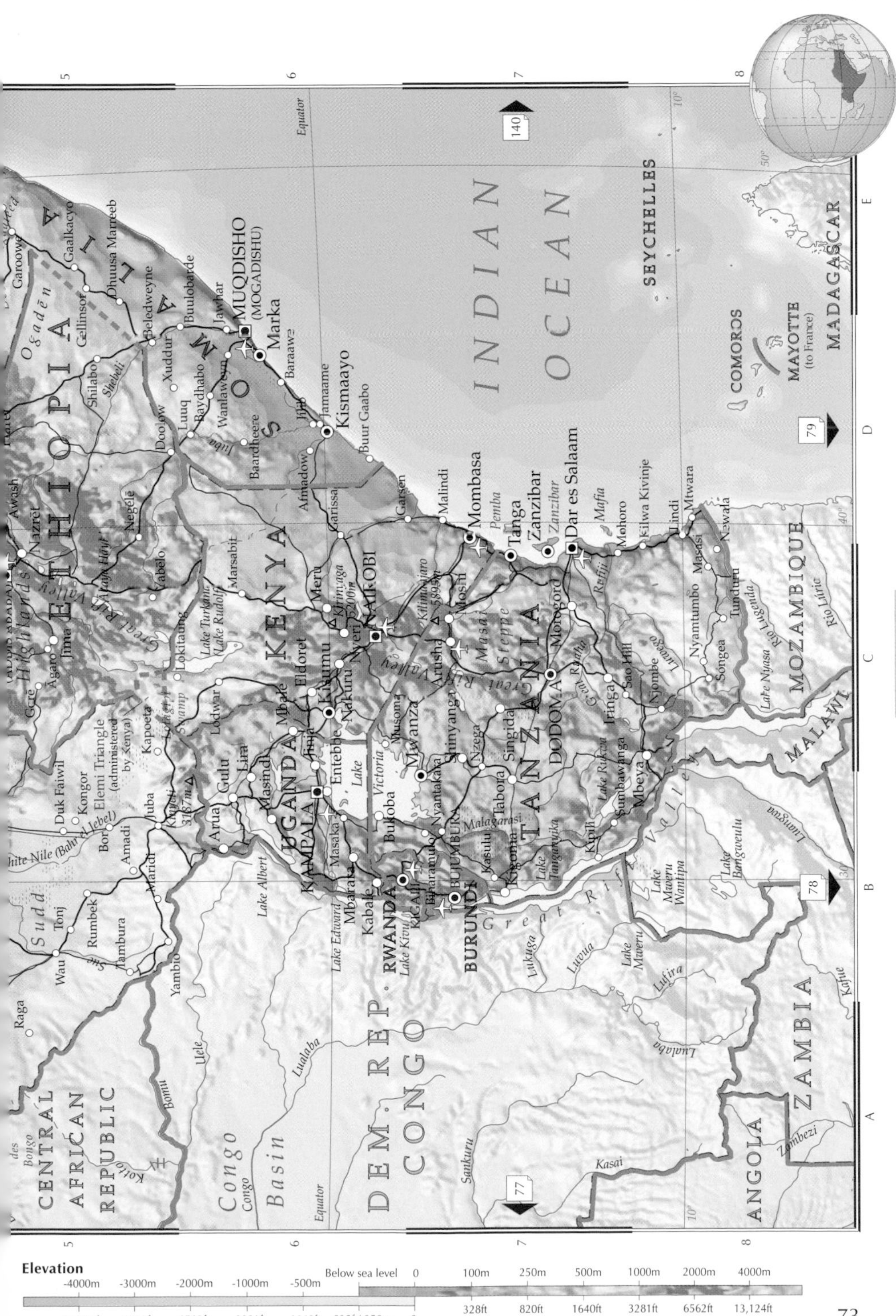

INDIAN OCEAN

SEYCHELLES

COMOROS

MAYOTTE
(to France)

MADAGASCAR

ETHIOPIA

Garoowe
Gaalkacyo
Dhuusa Marreeb

SOMALIA

MUQDISHO
(MOGADISHU)
Marka
Baraawe

Jamaame
Kismaayo
Buur Gaabo

Mombasa
Pemba
Tanga
Zanzibar
Dar es Salaam
Mafia
Kilwa Kivinje
Mtwara

KENYA

NAIROBI

Kilimanjaro
5895m
Moshi
Arusha

Masai Steppe

Morogoro

TANZANIA

DODOMA

Nyombe
Songea

MOZAMBIQUE

MALAWI

UGANDA

KAMPALA

Lake
Victoria

Mwanza

RWANDA

KIGALI

BURUNDI

BUJUMBURA

Lake
Tanganyika

Great Rift Valley

ZAMBIA

ANGOLA

DEM. REP.
CONGO

Congo Basin

CENTRAL
AFRICAN
REPUBLIC

Elevation

-4000m	-3000m	-2000m	-1000m	-500m	Below sea level	0	100m	250m	500m	1000m	2000m	4000m

| -13,124ft | -9843ft | -6562ft | -3281ft | -1640ft | -820ft/-250m | 0 | 328ft | 820ft | 1640ft | 3281ft | 6562ft | 13,124ft |

West Africa

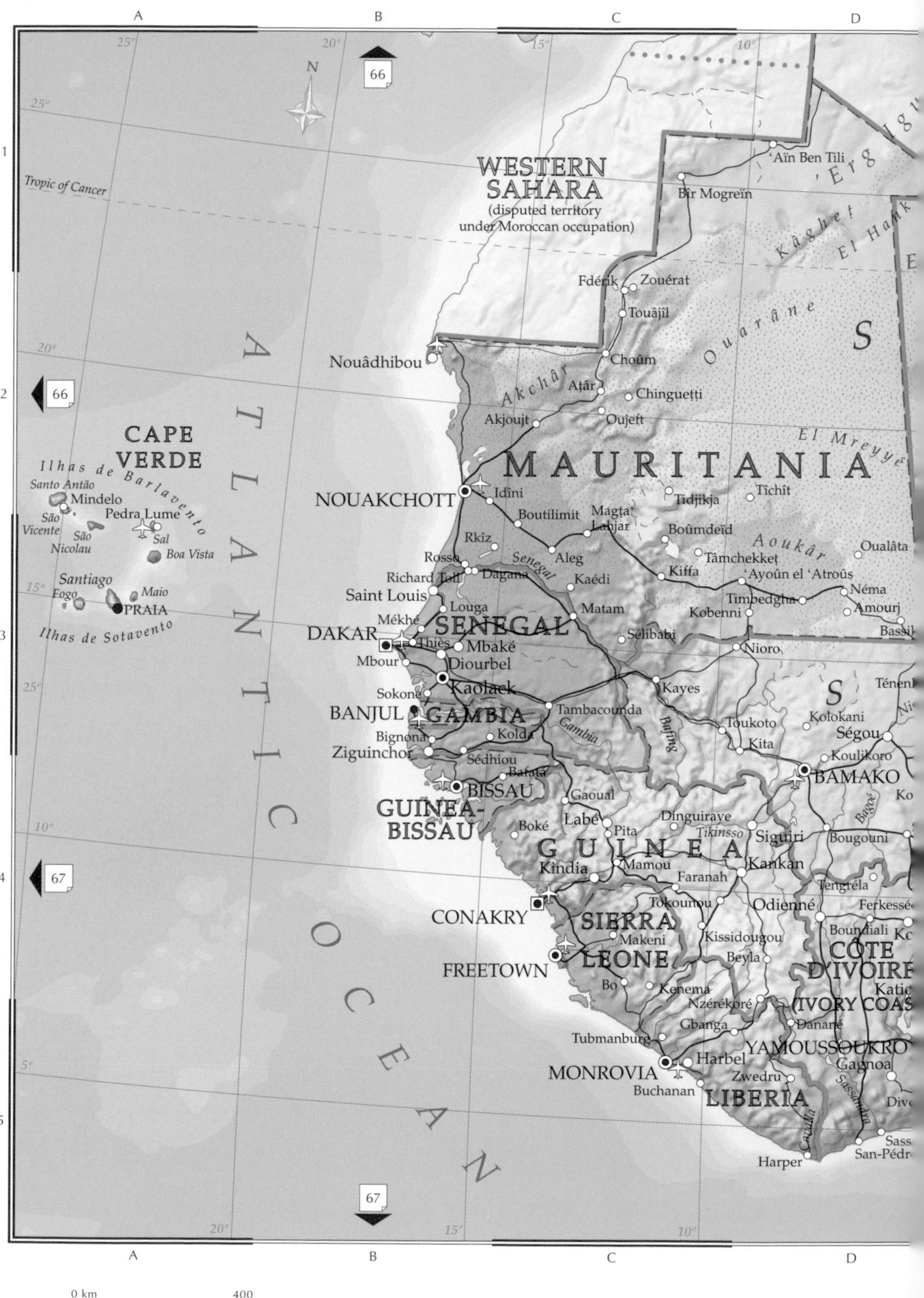

66

N

66

Tropic of Cancer

**WESTERN
SAHARA**
(disputed territory
under Moroccan occupation)

Aïn Ben Tili

Bir Mogreïn

'Erg 18°

Kâghet

El Hank

Fdérik   Zouérat

Touâjil

Ouarâne

S

Nouâdhibou

Choûm

Akchâr

Atâr   Chinguetti

Akjoujt   Oujeft

El Mreyyé

66

**CAPE
VERDE**

Ilhas de Barlavento
Santo Antão
Mindelo
São   Pedra Lume
Vicente São
Nicolau   Sal
        Boa Vista

Santiago   Maio
Fogo
PRAIA

Ilhas de Sotavento

25°

A   T   L   A   N   T   I   C

M A U R I T A N I A

NOUAKCHOTT   Idîni

Boutilimit   Tidjikja   Tîchît

Magta
Lahjar   Boûmdeïd

Rkîz   Aleg   *Aoukâr*

Rosso   Tâmchekket

Richard Toll Dagana   Kaédi   Kiffa   Ayoûn el 'Atroûs   Néma

Saint Louis   *Senegal*   Matam   Timbedgha   Amourj

Louga   Kobenni   Bassi

Mékhé   Sélibabi

DAKAR   Thiès   Nioro

Mbour   Diourbel   S

Sokone   Kaolack   Kayes   Ténen

BANJUL **GAMBIA**   Tambacounda   Toukoto   Kolokani

Bignona Kolda   *Gambia*   Kita   Koulikoro

Ziguinchor   Bafing   Séqou   Ni

Sédhiou   Bafata   BAMAKO

BISSAU   Gaoual   *Bakoy*   Ko

**GUINEA-
BISSAU**   Boké   Labé   Dinguiraye   Siguiri   Bougouni

Pita   Tikinsso

Kindia   Mamou   Faranah   Kankan   Tengréla   Ferkessé

CONAKRY   Tokoumou   Odienné   Boundiali   Ko

FREETOWN   **SIERRA
LEONE**   Makení   Kissidougou   **CÔTE
D'IVOIRE**

Bo   Kenema   Beyla   **IVORY COAST**

Nzérékoré   Danané   Katic

Gbanga   YAMOUSSOUKRO

Tubmanburg   Gagnoa   Div

MONROVIA   Harbel   Zwedru   **LIBERIA**

Buchanan

Harper   Sass   San-Pédr

C E A N

67

Population

O below 50,000

⊙ 50,000 to 100,000

◉ 100,000 to 500,000

■ above 500,000

● National capital

0 km   400
0 miles   400

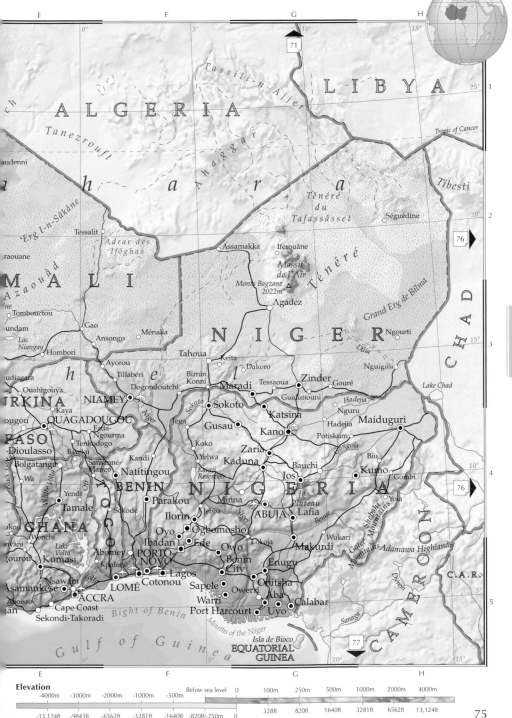

LIBYA

ALGERIA

Tanezrouft

Tassili-n-Ajjer

25° 1

Tropic of Cancer

udenni

Ahaggar

h a a r a

Tibesti

76 ▶ 2

20°

'Erg I-n-Sâkâne

Tessalit

Adrar des Ifôghas

Assamakka

Iferouâne

Ténéré du Tafassâsset

Séguédine

raouane

Massif do l' Aïr

MALI

Azaouâd

Monts Bagzane
2022m △

Ténéré

Grand Erg de Bilma

CHAD

ine

Tombouctou

Agadez

Ngourti

Dirkou

undam

Gao

Ansongo

Ménaka

NIGER

Lake Chad

15° 3

Lac Niangay

Hombori

Ayorou

Tahoua

Keïta

Dakoro

Nguigmi

Nguru

l a

udiagara

Ouahigouya

Tillabéri

Dogondoutchi

Birnin Konni

Maradi

Tessaoua

Zinder

Gouré

ougou

RKINA

Kaya

NIAMEY

Sokoto

Guidimouni

Hadejia

Maiduguri

FASO

OUAGADOUGOU

Fada-Ngourma

Tenkodogo

Jega

Gusau

Katsina

Nguru

Hadejia

Dioulasso

Bawku

Koko

Kano

Potiskum

Biu

Kumo

10° 4

Bolgatanga

Sansanné-Mango

Kandi

Yelwa

Zaria

Bauchi

Gombi

Wa

Yendi

Natitingou

Kainji Reservoir

Kaduna

Jos

76 ▶

Tamale

Sokodé

BENIN

Parakou

Jebba

NIGERIA

Jos Plateau

Yola

Lafia

Shebshi Mountains

Adamawa Highlands

Wenchi

Ilorin

Minna

ABUJA

GHANA

Lake Volta

Oyo

Ogbomosho

Owo

Lokoja

Makurdi

Wukari

C.A.R.

Kumasi

Abomey

Ibadan

Ede

Benin City

Enugu

Kpalimé

PORTO NOVO

Onitsha

5° 5

Nsawam

LOMÉ

Cotonou

Sapele

Owerri

Aba

Calabar

Asamankese

ACCRA

Lagos

Warri

Uyo

CAMEROON

Cape Coast

Bight of Benin

Port Harcourt

Sekondi-Takoradi

Mouths of the Niger

Gulf of Guinea

EQUATORIAL GUINEA

Isla de Bioco

77

Elevation

					Below sea level	0	100m	250m	500m	1000m	2000m	4000m
-4000m	-3000m	-2000m	-1000m	-500m								
-13,124ft	-9843ft	-6562ft	-3281ft	-1640ft	-820ft/-250m		328ft	820ft	1640ft	3281ft	6562ft	13,124ft

Central Africa

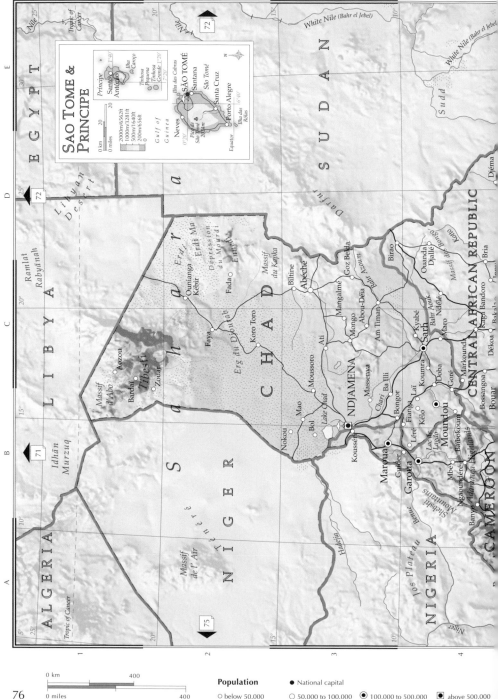

SÃO TOMÉ & PRINCIPE

Principe
Santo
António
Ilha
Caroço

Tinhosa
Pequena
Tinhosa
Grande 1°20'

SÃO TOMÉ
Santana
São Tomé
Santa Cruz

Ilha das Cabras
SÃO TOMÉ (6°40')

Neves
Pico de
São Tomé
2024m

Porto Alegre
Ilha das
Rôlas

Equator

Gulf of Guinea

0 km   20
0 miles   20

2000m/6562ft
1000m/3281ft
500m/1640ft
200m/656ft

N

Population

National capital

○ below 50,000
○ 50,000 to 100,000
◉ 100,000 to 500,000
▣ above 500,000

76

0 km   400
0 miles   400

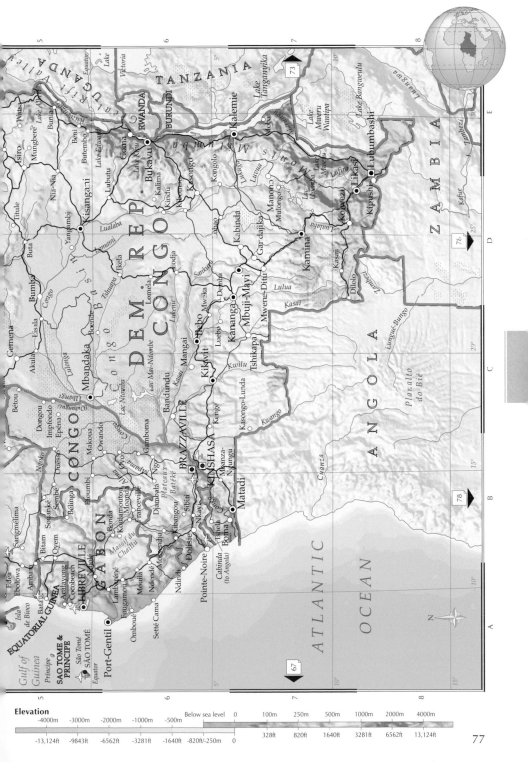

Elevation

					Below sea level	0	100m	250m	500m	1000m	2000m	4000m
-4000m	-3000m	-2000m	-1000m	-500m								
-13,124ft	-9843ft	-6562ft	-3281ft	-1640ft	-820ft/-250m	0	328ft	820ft	1640ft	3281ft	6562ft	13,124ft

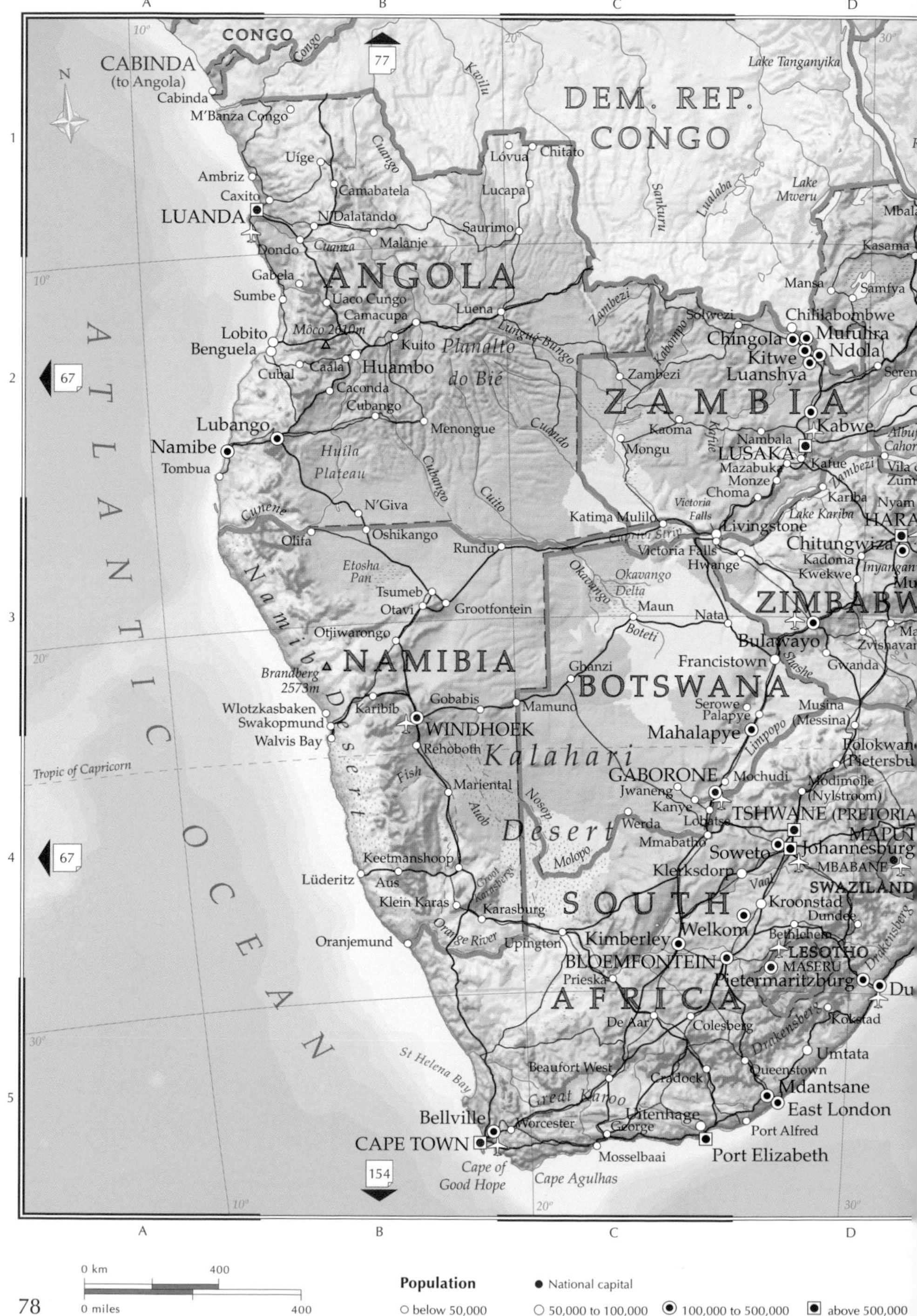

Population

● National capital

○ below 50,000   ○ 50,000 to 100,000   ◉ 100,000 to 500,000   ■ above 500,000

0 km — 400

0 miles — 400

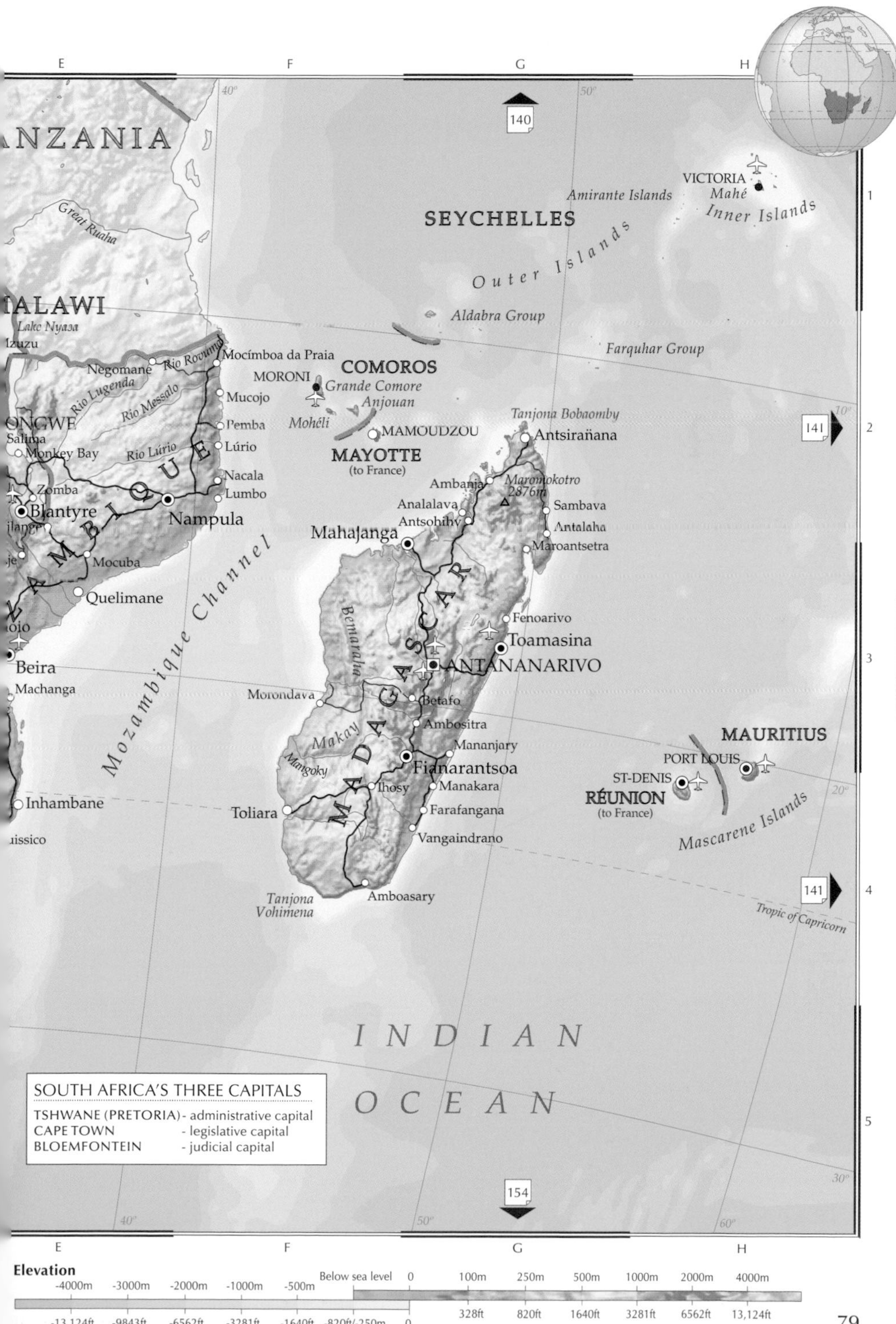

SEYCHELLES

Amirante Islands

VICTORIA
Mahé
Inner Islands

Great Ruaha

TANZANIA

O u t e r   I s l a n d s

MALAWI

Lake Nyasa

Izuzu

Rio Lugenda

Rio Messalo

ONGWE

Salima

Monkey Bay

Zomba

Blantyre

ilanço

je

Mocuba

Rio Rovuma

Negomane

Mocímboa da Praia

Mucojo

Pemba

Rio Lúrio

Lúrio

Nacala

Lumbo

Nampula

Quelimane

MOÇAMBIQUE

Aldabra Group

Farquhar Group

COMOROS

MORONI
Grande Comore
Anjouan
Mohéli

MAMOUDZOU

MAYOTTE
(to France)

Tanjona Bobaomby

Antsirañana

Ambanja

Analalava

Antsohihy

Mahajanga

Maromokotro
2876m

Sambava

Antalaha

Maroantsetra

Bernaraha

MADAGASCAR

Fenoarivo

Toamasina

ANTANANARIVO

Betafo

Ambositra

Mananjary

Manakara

Farafangana

Vangaindrano

Mozambique Channel

Beira

Machanga

Makay

Mangoky

Morondava

Inhambane

Toliara

Ihosy

Fianarantsoa

Tanjona Vohimena

Amboasary

MAURITIUS

PORT LOUIS

ST-DENIS

RÉUNION
(to France)

Mascarene Islands

Tropic of Capricorn

I N D I A N

O C E A N

SOUTH AFRICA'S THREE CAPITALS

TSHWANE (PRETORIA) - administrative capital
CAPE TOWN - legislative capital
BLOEMFONTEIN - judicial capital

Elevation

-4000m	-3000m	-2000m	-1000m	-500m	Below sea level	0	100m	250m	500m	1000m	2000m	4000m
-13,124ft	-9843ft	-6562ft	-3281ft	-1640ft	-820ft/-250m	0	328ft	820ft	1640ft	3281ft	6562ft	13,124ft

Europe

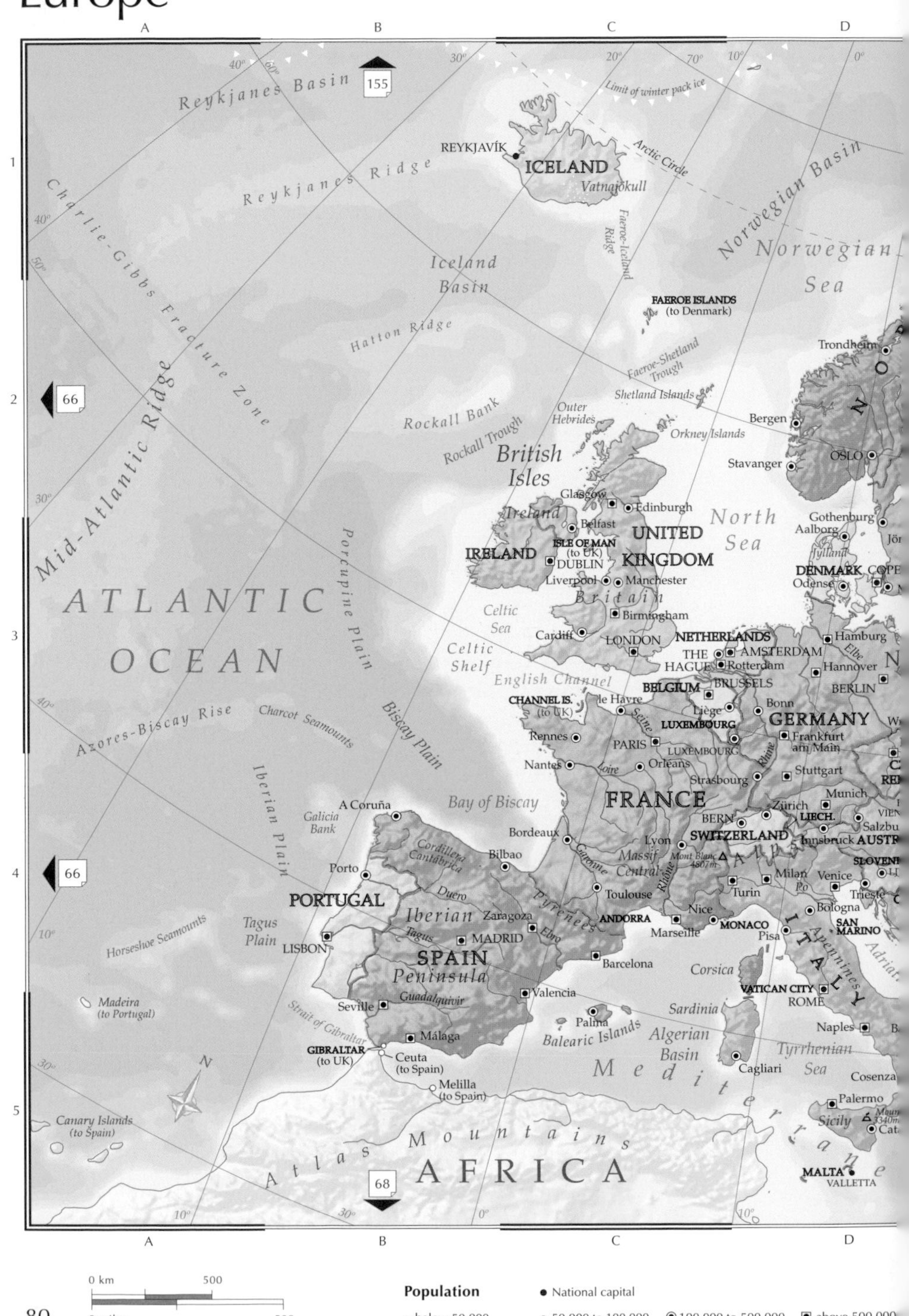

A   B   C   D

155

66

66

68

Reykjanes Basin

Charlie-Gibbs Fracture Zone

Reykjanes Ridge

Limit of winter pack ice

REYKJAVÍK

ICELAND

Vatnajökull

Arctic Circle

Iceland Basin

Hatton Ridge

Faeroe-Iceland Ridge

FAEROE ISLANDS
(to Denmark)

Norwegian Basin

Norwegian Sea

Trondheim

Mid-Atlantic Ridge

Rockall Bank

Rockall Trough

Faeroe-Shetland Trough

Shetland Islands

Outer Hebrides

Orkney Islands

Bergen

Stavanger

OSLO

Gothenburg

Aalborg

Jyllland

Jör

Porcupine Plain

British Isles

Ireland

Glasgow

Edinburgh

Belfast

North Sea

ATLANTIC
OCEAN

IRELAND

ISLE OF MAN
(to UK)

DUBLIN

UNITED
KINGDOM

Liverpool

Manchester

DENMARK

COPE

Odense

Celtic Sea

Britain

Birmingham

Hamburg

Celtic Shelf

Cardiff

LONDON

NETHERLANDS

THE
HAGUE

AMSTERDAM

Rotterdam

Hannover

BERLIN

Elbe

English Channel

CHANNEL IS.
(to UK)

le Havre

BELGIUM

BRUSSELS

Bonn

GERMANY

W

Azores-Biscay Rise

Charcot Seamounts

Biscay Plain

Rennes

Seine

LUXEMBOURG

LUXEMBOURG

Frankfurt
am Main

Iberian Plain

PARIS

Orleans

Strasbourg

Rhine

Stuttgart

RE

Nantes

Loire

FRANCE

Zürich

Munich

VIEN

LIECH.

Salzbu

Bay of Biscay

Bordeaux

Lyon

SWITZERLAND

BERN

Innsbruck

AUST

A Coruña

Galicia Bank

Cordillera Cantábrica

Bilbao

Garonne

Massif Central

Rhône

Mont Blanc
4802m

Milan

Venice

Po

SLOVEN

Porto

PORTUGAL

Duero

Toulouse

Pyrenees

Nice

Turin

Bologna

Trieste

ITALY

Adriat

Iberian Peninsula

Zaragoza

Ebro

ANDORRA

Marseille

MONACO

Pisa

SAN
MARINO

Tagus Plain

Horseshoe Seamounts

LISBON

Tagus

MADRID

SPAIN

Barcelona

Corsica

VATICAN CITY

ROME

Madeira
(to Portugal)

Seville

Guadalquivir

Valencia

Palma

Sardinia

Naples

Málaga

Balearic Islands

Algerian Basin

Tyrrhenian Sea

Cagliari

Cosenza

GIBRALTAR
(to UK)

Ceuta
(to Spain)

Strait of Gibraltar

Melilla
(to Spain)

Mediterra

Palermo

Mount
3340m

Sicily

Canary Islands
(to Spain)

N

Atlas   Mountains

68

AFRICA

MALTA

VALLETTA

A   B   C   D

0 km   500

0 miles   500

Population

● National capital

○ below 50,000

○ 50,000 to 100,000

◉ 100,000 to 500,000

▣ above 500,000

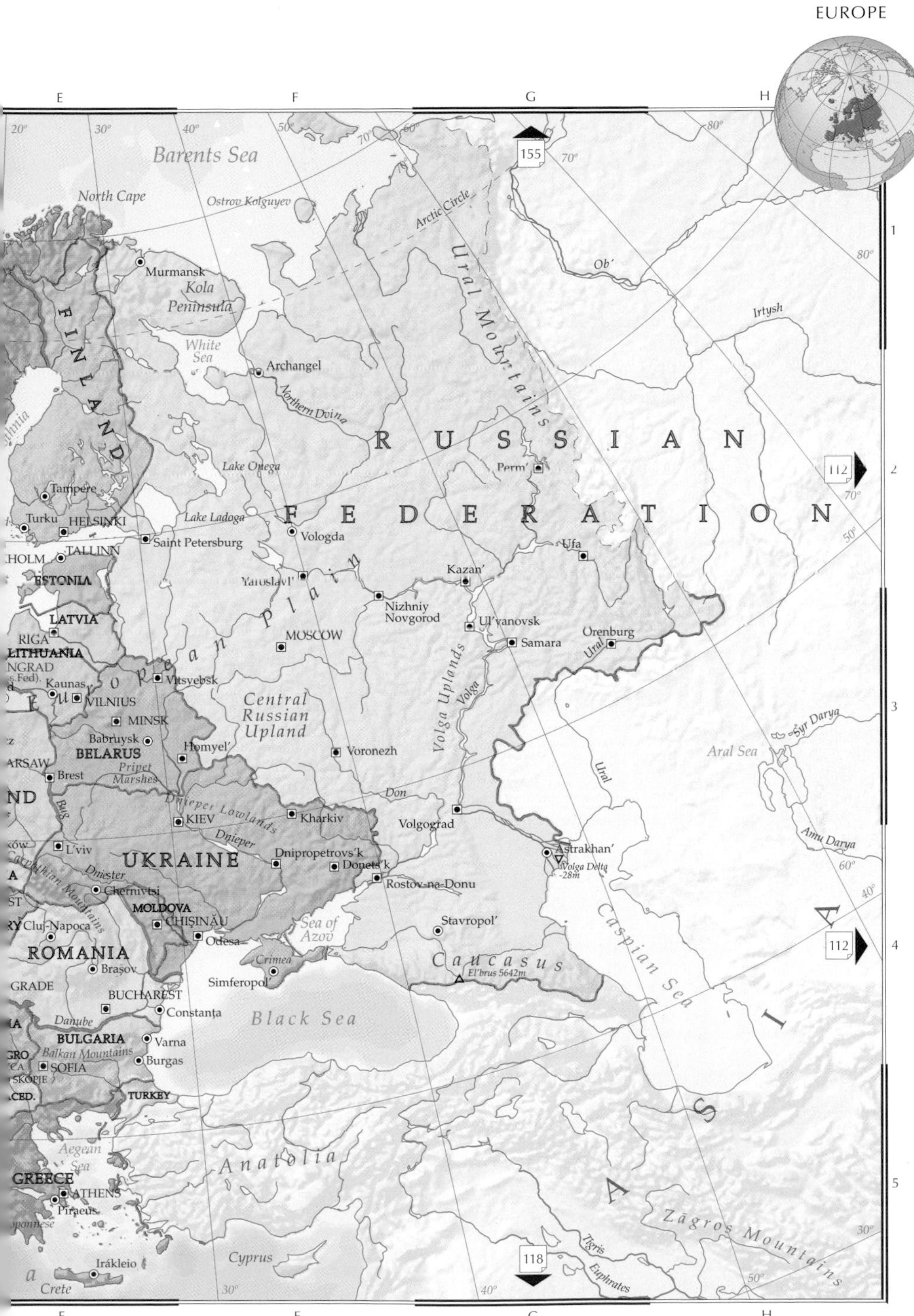

Barents Sea
North Cape
Ostrov Kolguyev
Arctic Circle
Ural Mountains
Ob'
Irtysh
Murmansk
Kola Peninsula
FINLAND
White Sea
Archangel
Northern Dvina
RUSSIAN FEDERATION
Lake Onega
Perm'
Tampere
Turku
HELSINKI
Lake Ladoga
Saint Petersburg
Vologda
Ufa
TALLINN
ESTONIA
Yaroslavl'
Kazan'
Nizhniy Novgorod
LATVIA
RIGA
Ul'yanovsk
Samara
Orenburg
Ural
MOSCOW
LITHUANIA
European Plain
Vitsyebsk
Kaunas
VILNIUS
MINSK
Central Russian Upland
Volga Uplands
Volga
Syr Darya
Aral Sea
Babruysk
BELARUS
Homyel'
Voronezh
Ural
Brest
Pripet Marshes
Don
Dnieper Lowlands
Kharkiv
Bug
KIEV
Volgograd
Dnieper
Amu Darya
L'viv
UKRAINE
Dnipropetrovs'k
Donets'k
Astrakhan'
Volga Delta -28m
Carpathian Mountains
Dniester
Chernivtsi
Rostov-na-Donu
MOLDOVA
CHIŞINĂU
Sea of Azov
Stavropol'
Caspian Sea
Cluj-Napoca
Odesa
ROMANIA
Crimea
Caucasus
El'brus 5642m
Braşov
Simferopol'
BUCHAREST
Constanţa
Black Sea
Danube
BULGARIA
Varna
Balkan Mountains
Burgas
SOFIA
TURKEY
ASIA
Aegean Sea
Anatolia
GREECE
ATHENS
Piraeus
Zāgros Mountains
Tigris
Euphrates
Cyprus
Iráklein
Crete
155
112
112
118
E
F
G
H
1
2
3
4
5
20°
30°
40°
50°
60°
70°
80°

The North Atlantic

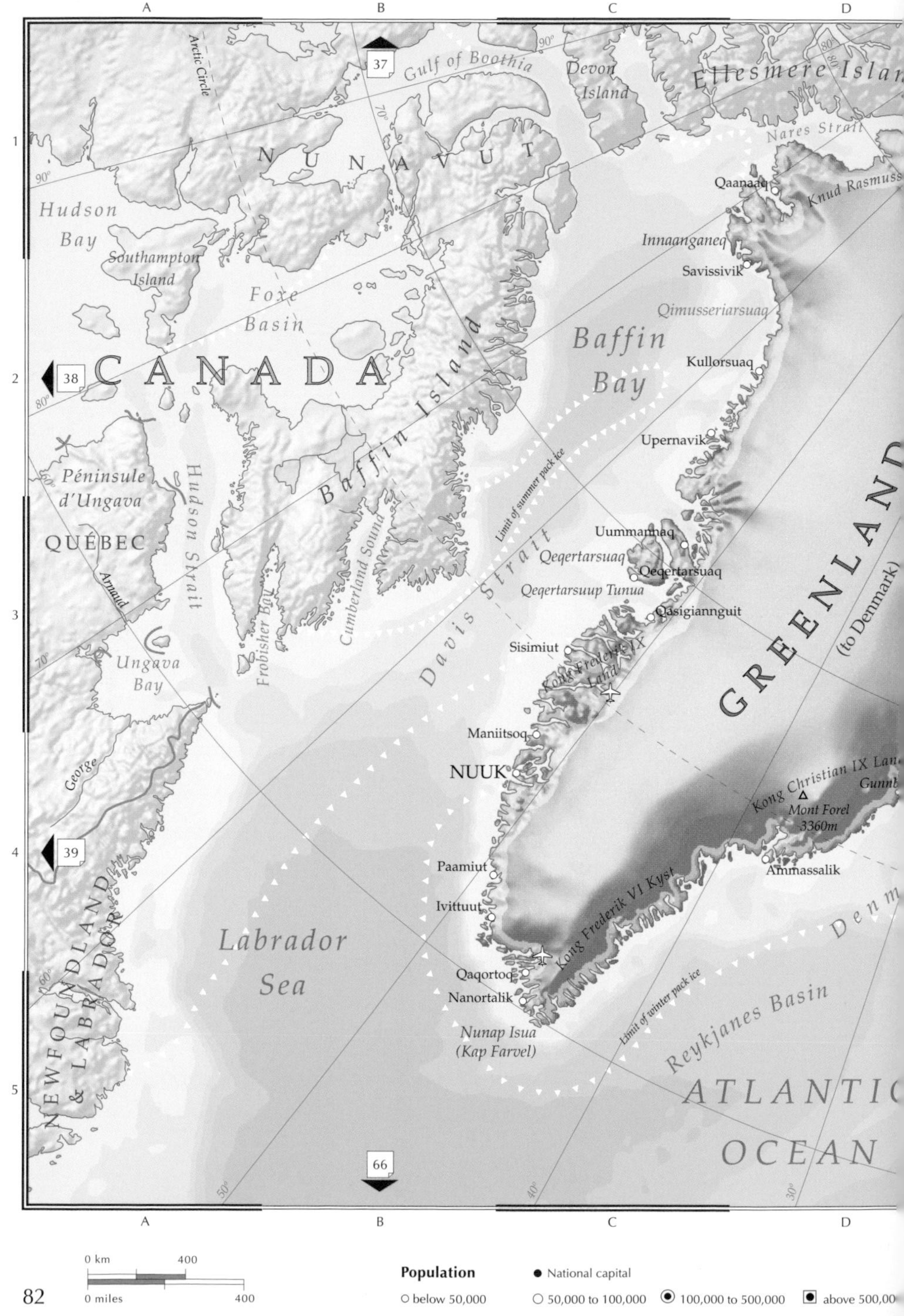

Arctic Circle

37

Gulf of Boothia

Devon Island

Ellesmere Island

Nares Strait

NUNAVUT

Hudson Bay

Southampton Island

Foxe Basin

Qaanaaq

Knud Rasmuss

Innaanganeq

Savissivik

Qimusseriarsuaq

Baffin Bay

Kullorsuaq

38

CANADA

Baffin Island

Upernavik

Péninsule d'Ungava

Uummannaq

Qeqertarsuaq

Qeqertarsuaq

Cumberland Sound

Hudson Strait

QUÉBEC

Qeqertarsuup Tunua

Qasigiannguit

Arnaud

Sisimiut

Kong Frederik IX Land

GREENLAND

(to Denmark)

Frobisher Bay

Davis Strait

Ungava Bay

Maniitsoq

George

NUUK

Kong Christian IX Land

Gunnb

Mont Forel 3360m

Paamiut

Ammassalik

Ivittuut

Labrador Sea

Kong Frederik VI Kyst

Denm

NEWFOUNDLAND & LABRADOR

Qaqortoq

Nanortalik

Nunap Isua (Kap Farvel)

Limit of winter pack ice

Reykjanes Basin

ATLANTIC

39

66

OCEAN

Limit of summer pack ice

0 km 400

0 miles 400

Population ● National capital

○ below 50,000 ○ 50,000 to 100,000 ◉ 100,000 to 500,000 ◘ above 500,00

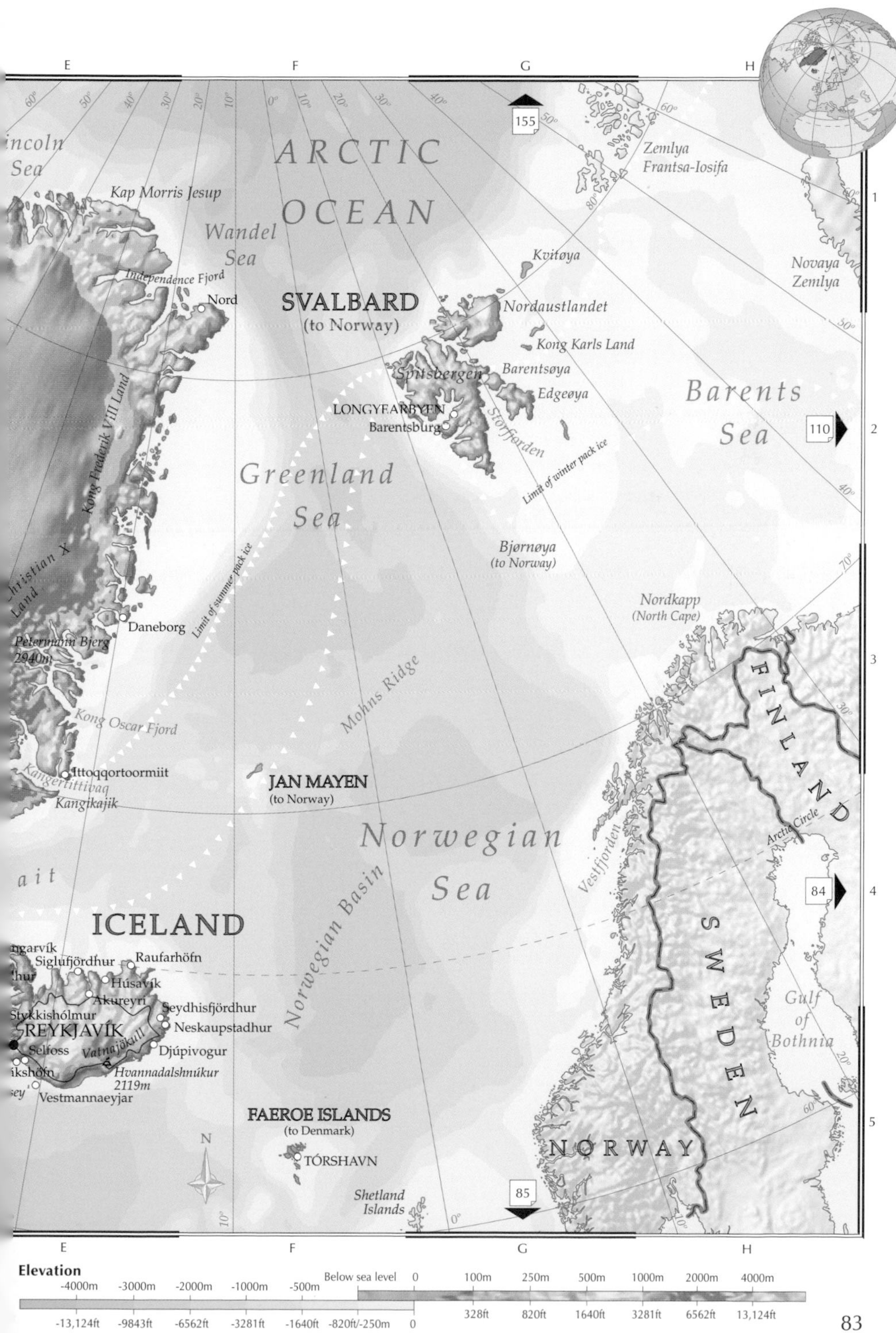

ARCTIC OCEAN

Lincoln Sea

Kap Morris Jesup

Wandel Sea

Zemlya Frantsa-Iosifa

Independence Fjord

Nord

Kviøya

SVALBARD (to Norway)

Nordaustlandet

Novaya Zemlya

Kong Frederik VIII Land

Kong Karls Land

Spitsbergen

Barentsøya

Barents Sea

LONGYEARBYEN
Barentsburg

Edgeøya

Storfjorden

110

Greenland Sea

Christian X Land

Limit of winter pack ice

Bjørnøya (to Norway)

Petermann Bjerg 2940m

Daneborg

Nordkapp (North Cape)

FINLAND

Limit of summer pack ice

Kong Oscar Fjord

Mohns Ridge

Arctic Circle

Ittoqqortoormiit

JAN MAYEN (to Norway)

Kangikajik

Norwegian Basin

Norwegian Sea

Vestfjorden

S W E D E N

ait

ICELAND

Raufarhöfn

Siglufjördhur

Húsavík

gárvík

hur

Akureyri

Seydhisfjördhur

Stykkishólmur

Neskaupstadhur

Vatnajökull

REYKJAVÍK

Selfoss

Djúpivogur

84

iksholm

Hvannadalshnúkur 2119m

Gulf of Bothnia

ey

Vestmannaeyjar

FAEROE ISLANDS (to Denmark)

N

TÓRSHAVN

N O R W A Y

Shetland Islands

85

155

Elevation

-4000m	-3000m	-2000m	-1000m	-500m	Below sea level	0	100m	250m	500m	1000m	2000m	4000m
-13,124ft	-9843ft	-6562ft	-3281ft	-1640ft	-820ft/-250m	0	328ft	820ft	1640ft	3281ft	6562ft	13,124ft

Scandinavia & Finland

RUSSIAN FEDERATION

Barents Sea

Nordkapp
(North Cape)

ARCTIC OCEAN

Norwegian Sea

FINLAND

Oulu

Arctic Circle

Population

- ○ below 50,000
- ○ 50,000 to 100,000
- ◉ 100,000 to 500,000
- ▣ above 500,000

● National capital

0 km   200

0 miles   200

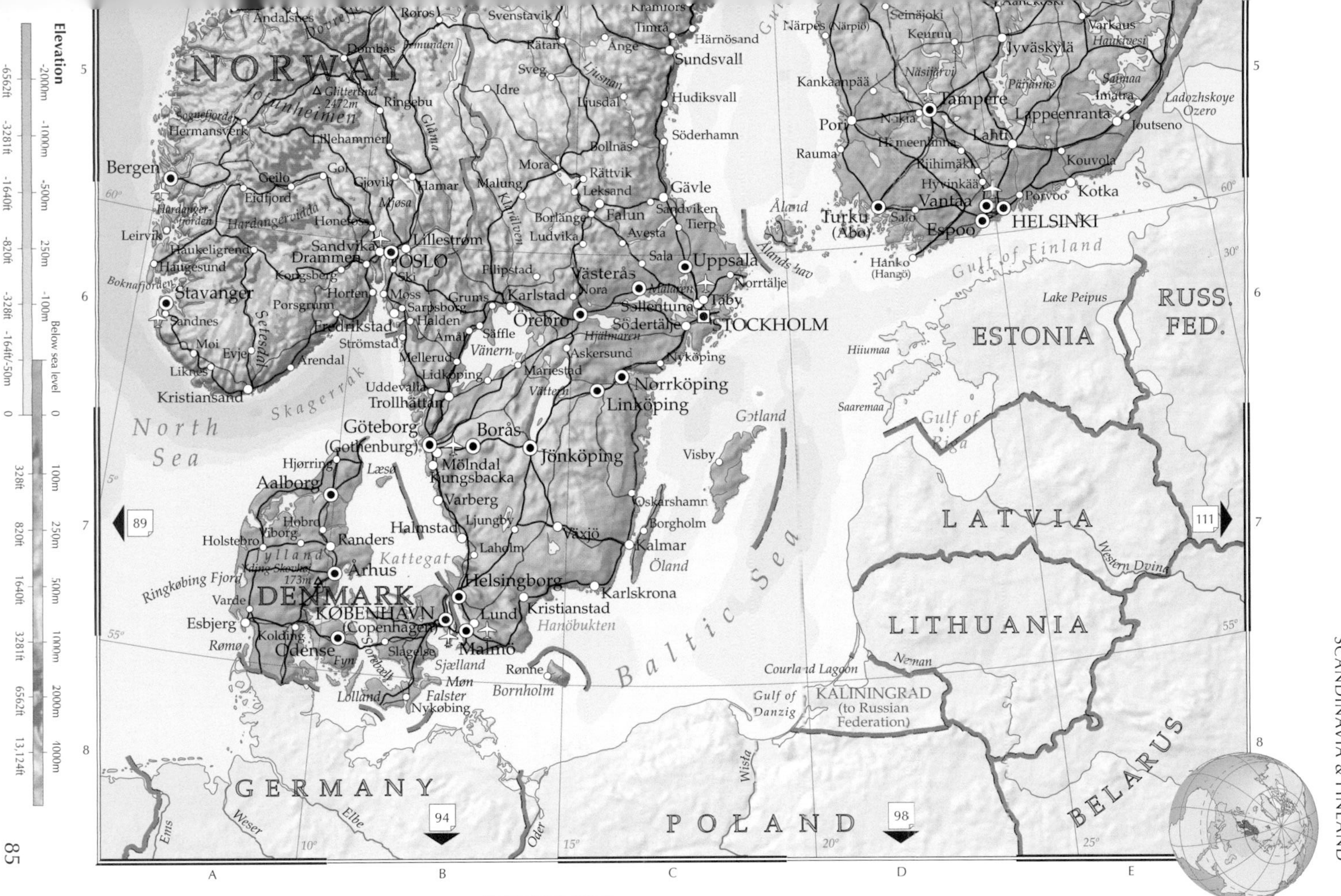

Elevation

-2000m	-1000m	-500m	250m	-100m	Below sea level	0	100m	250m	500m	1000m	2000m	4000m
-6562ft	-3281ft	-1640ft	-820ft	-328ft	-164ft/-50m	0	328ft	820ft	1640ft	3281ft	6562ft	13,124ft

The Low Countries

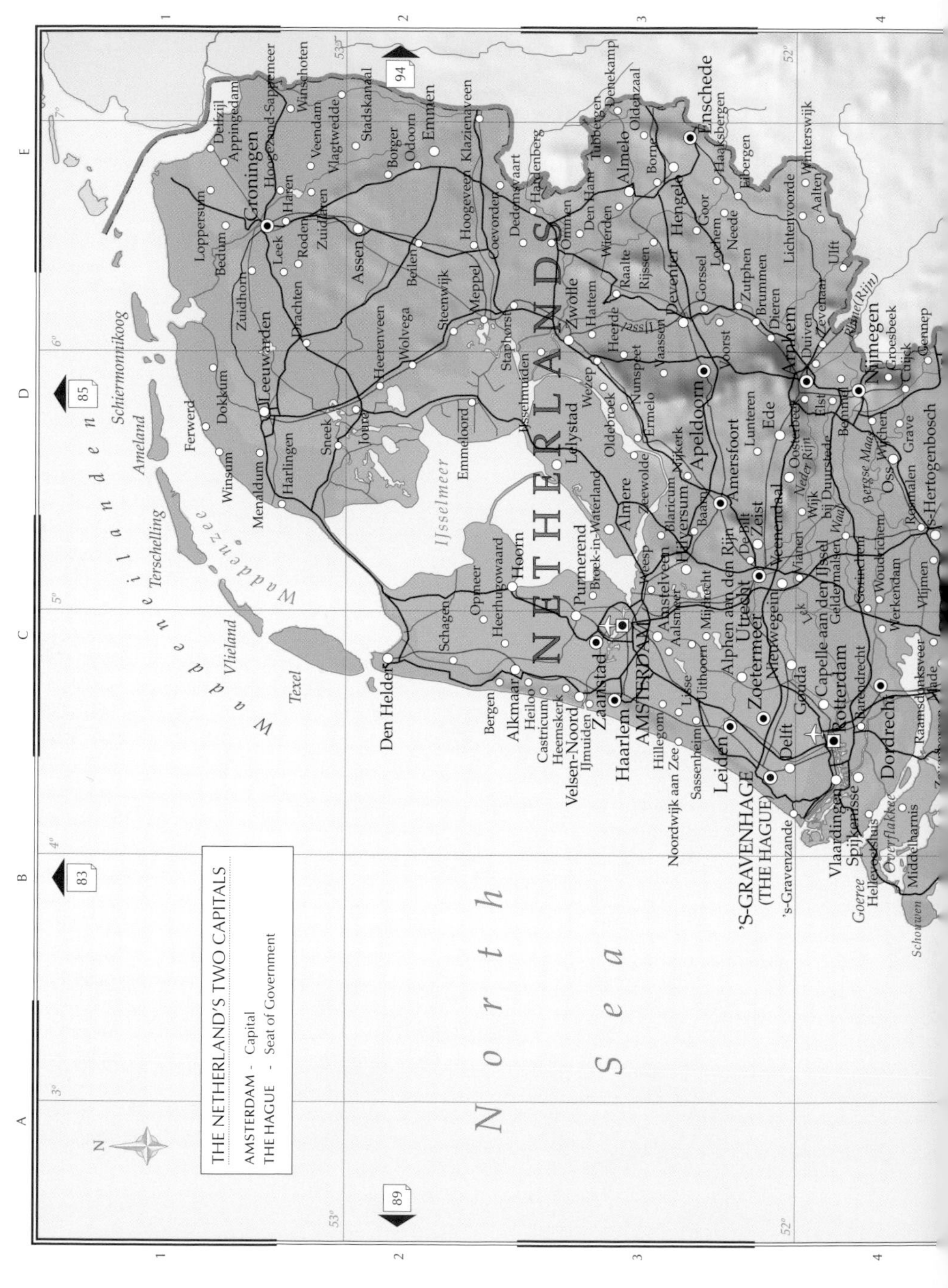

THE NETHERLAND'S TWO CAPITALS

AMSTERDAM - Capital
THE HAGUE - Seat of Government

NETHERLANDS

IJsselmeer

Waddenzee

Waddeneilanden

Schiermonnikoog

Ameland

Terschelling

Vlieland

Texel

Wadden Zee

North Sea

's-GRAVENHAGE
(THE HAGUE)

Den Helder

Groningen

Leeuwarden

Assen

Zwolle

Enschede

Arnhem

Nijmegen

Apeldoorn

Amersfoort

Utrecht

AMSTERDAM

Haarlem

Leiden

Rotterdam

Dordrecht

Gouda

Delft

Zaanstad

Almere

Lelystad

Emmen

N

0 km   50

0 miles   50

Population   ● National capital

○ below 50,000   ◎ 50,000 to 100,000   ◉ 100,000 to 500,000   ◼ above 500,000

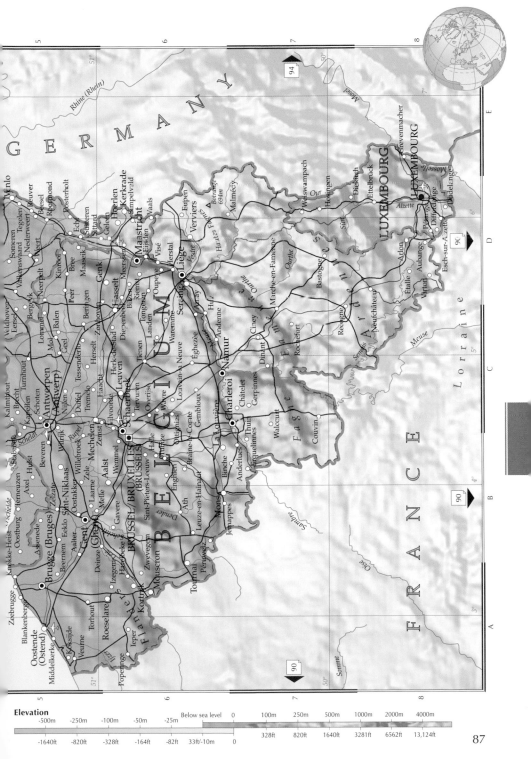

Elevation

					Below sea level	0	100m	250m	500m	1000m	2000m	4000m
-500m	-250m	-100m	-50m	-25m								
-1640ft	-820ft	-328ft	-164ft	-82ft	33ft/-10m	0	328ft	820ft	1640ft	3281ft	6562ft	13,124ft

The British Isles

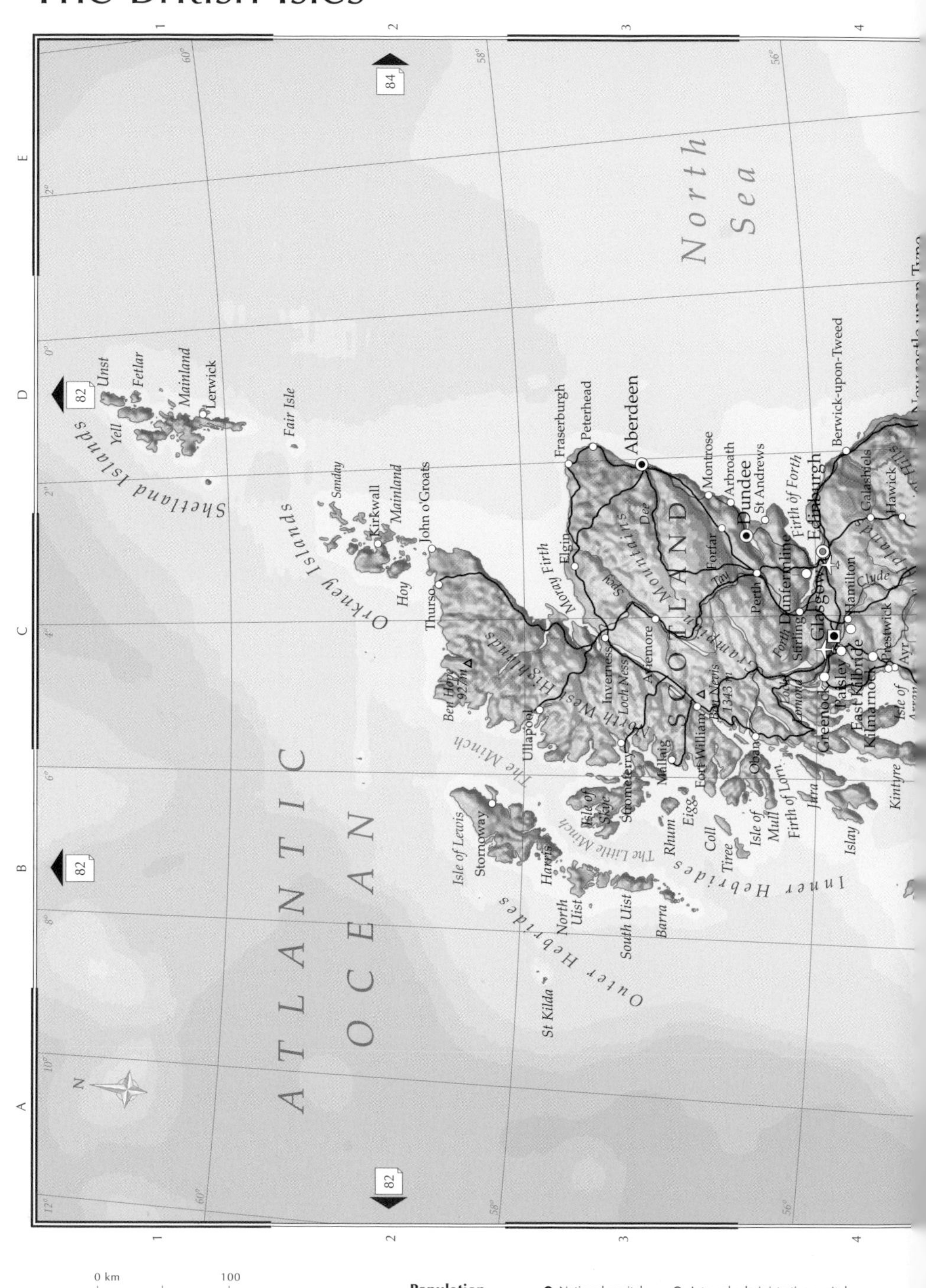

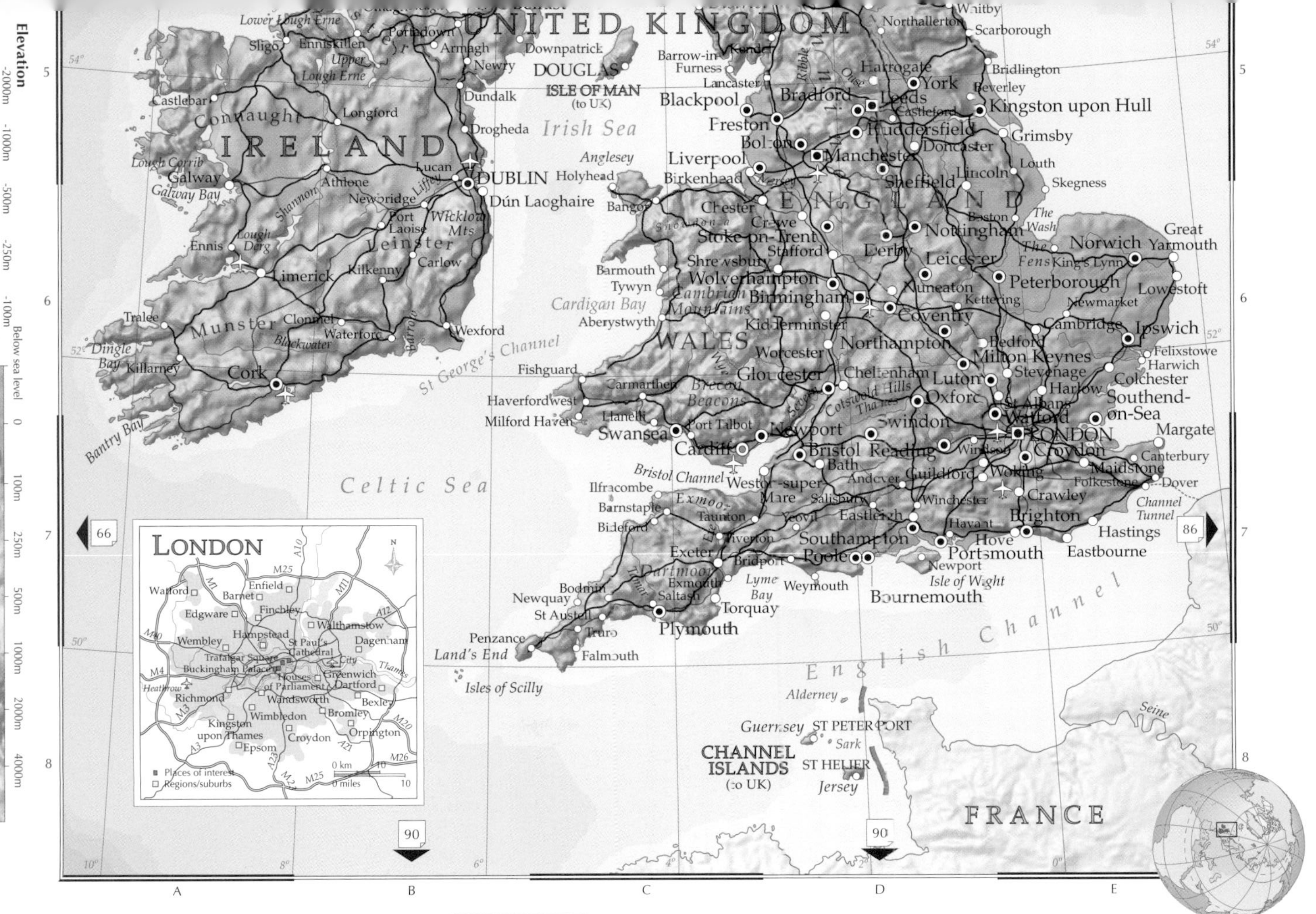

Elevation

				Below sea level	0	100m	250m	500m	1000m	2000m	4000m
-2000m	-1000m	-500m	-250m	-100m							
-6562ft	-3281ft	-1640ft	-820ft	-328ft	-164ft/-50m		328ft	820ft	1640ft	3281ft	6562ft	13,124ft
					0						

France, Andorra & Monaco

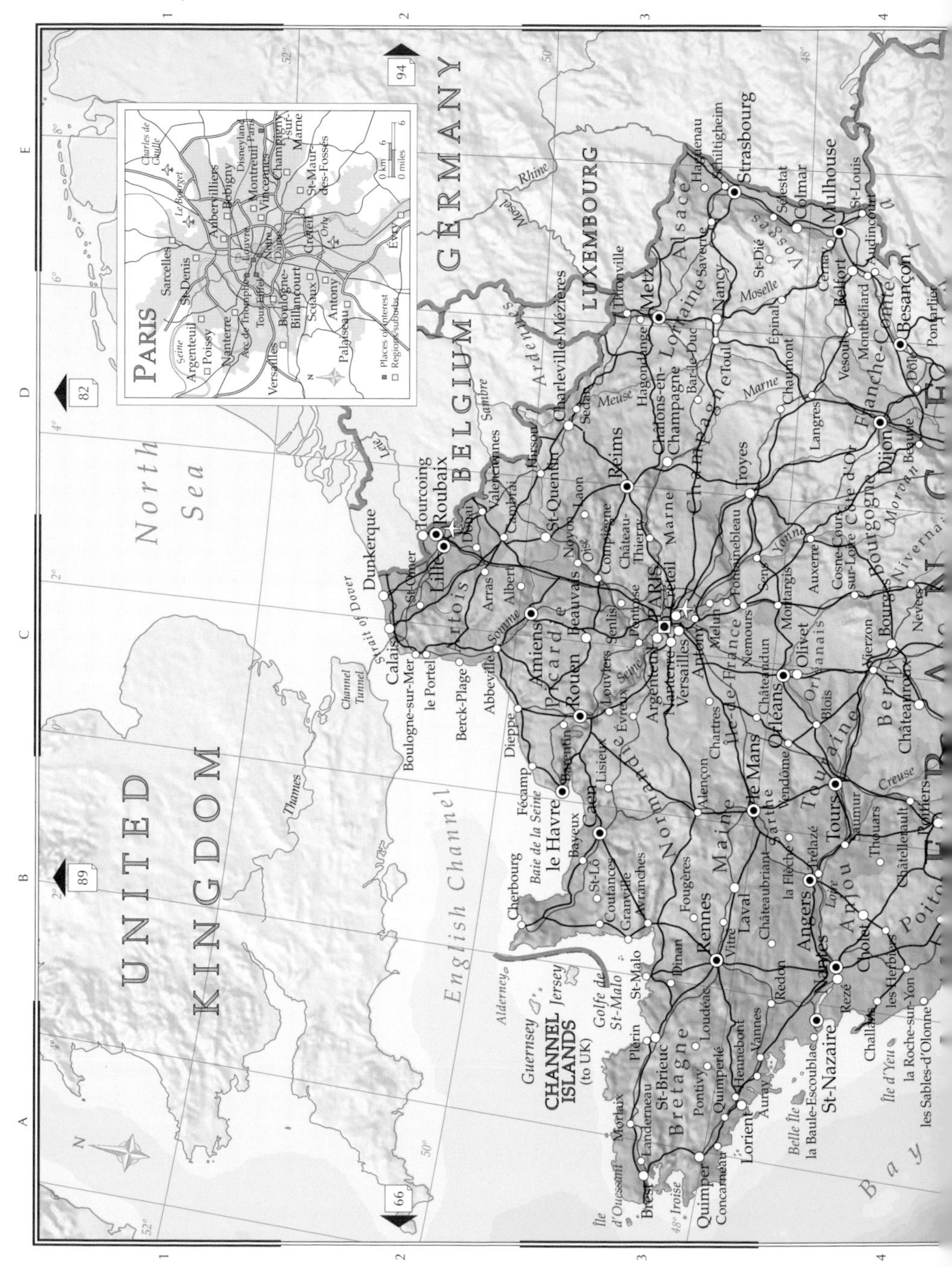

PARIS

Charles de Gaulle
Le Bourget
Sarcelles
St-Denis
Argenteuil □ Poissy
Nanterre
Aubervilliers
Bobigny
Drancy
Noisy-le-Sec
Montreuil Paris
Vincennes
Champigny-sur-Marne
St-Maur-des-Fossés
Versailles
Boulogne-Billancourt
Sèvres
Clamart
Vélizy
Sceaux
Antony
Palaiseau
Orly
Evry
Seine

N

Places of interest
Region/suburbs

GERMANY
BELGIUM
LUXEMBOURG

North Sea
UNITED KINGDOM

Thames

Strait of Dover
Channel Tunnel

Dunkerque
St-Omer
Calais
Lille
Tourcoing
Roubaix
Boulogne-sur-Mer
le Portel
Berck-Plage
Abbeville
Arras
Albert
Somme
Valenciennes
Cambrai
Picardie
Amiens
St-Quentin
Laon
Reims
Charleville-Mézières
Sedan
Meuse
Ardennes
Sambre
Oise
Beauvais
Senlis
Compiègne
Noyon
Château-Thierry
Soissons
Verdun
Metz
Hagondange
Thionville
Ste-Menehould
Châlons-en-Champagne
Bar-le-Duc
Toul
Nancy
Saverne
Haguenau
Bischwiller
Strasbourg
Sélestat
Colmar
Mulhouse
St-Louis
Épinal
St-Dié
Vosges
Alsace
Lorraine
Moselle
Marne
Chaumont
Vesoul
Belfort
Montbéliard
Audincourt
Besançon
Pontarlier
Franche-Comté
Langres
Troyes
Champagne
Fécamp
Dieppe
le Havre
Baie de la Seine
Rouen
Normandie
Pontoise
PARIS
Versailles
Argenteuil
Nanterre
Île-de-France
Melun
Fontainebleau
Nemours
Montargis
Sens
Auxerre
Yonne
Bourgogne
Dijon
Côte-d'Or
Nivernais
Nevers
Bourges
Cosne-sur-Loire
Côte
Morvan
English Channel
Cherbourg
St-Lô
Coutances
Bayeux
Caen
Lisieux
Évreux
Dreux
Chartres
Alençon
le Mans
Sarthe
Orléans
Orléanais
Blois
Vendôme
Tours
Touraine
Berry
Châteauroux
Indre
Vierzon
Châteaudun
Granville
Avranches
Fougères
Vitré
Laval
Maine
Mayenne
Anjou
Angers
la Flèche
Saumur
Creuse
Poitiers
Poitou
Guernsey
Alderney
Jersey
CHANNEL ISLANDS (to UK)
Golfe de St-Malo
St-Malo
Dinan
Dinard
St-Brieuc
Plérin
Morlaix
Landerneau
Île d'Ouessant
Île de Brest
Bretagne
Loudéac
Pontivy
Quimper
Quimperlé
Concarneau
Lorient
Auray
Vannes
Redon
Châteaubriant
Nantes
Rezé
Cholet
Challans
Île d'Yeu
la Roche-sur-Yon
les Herbiers
les Sables-d'Olonne
Belle Île
la Baule-Escoublac
St-Nazaire
Rennes
Loire
Thouars
Châtellerault
Bay

0 km 100
0 miles 100

Population ● National capital

○ below 50,000   ○ 50,000 to 100,000   ◉ 100,000 to 500,000   ■ above 500,000

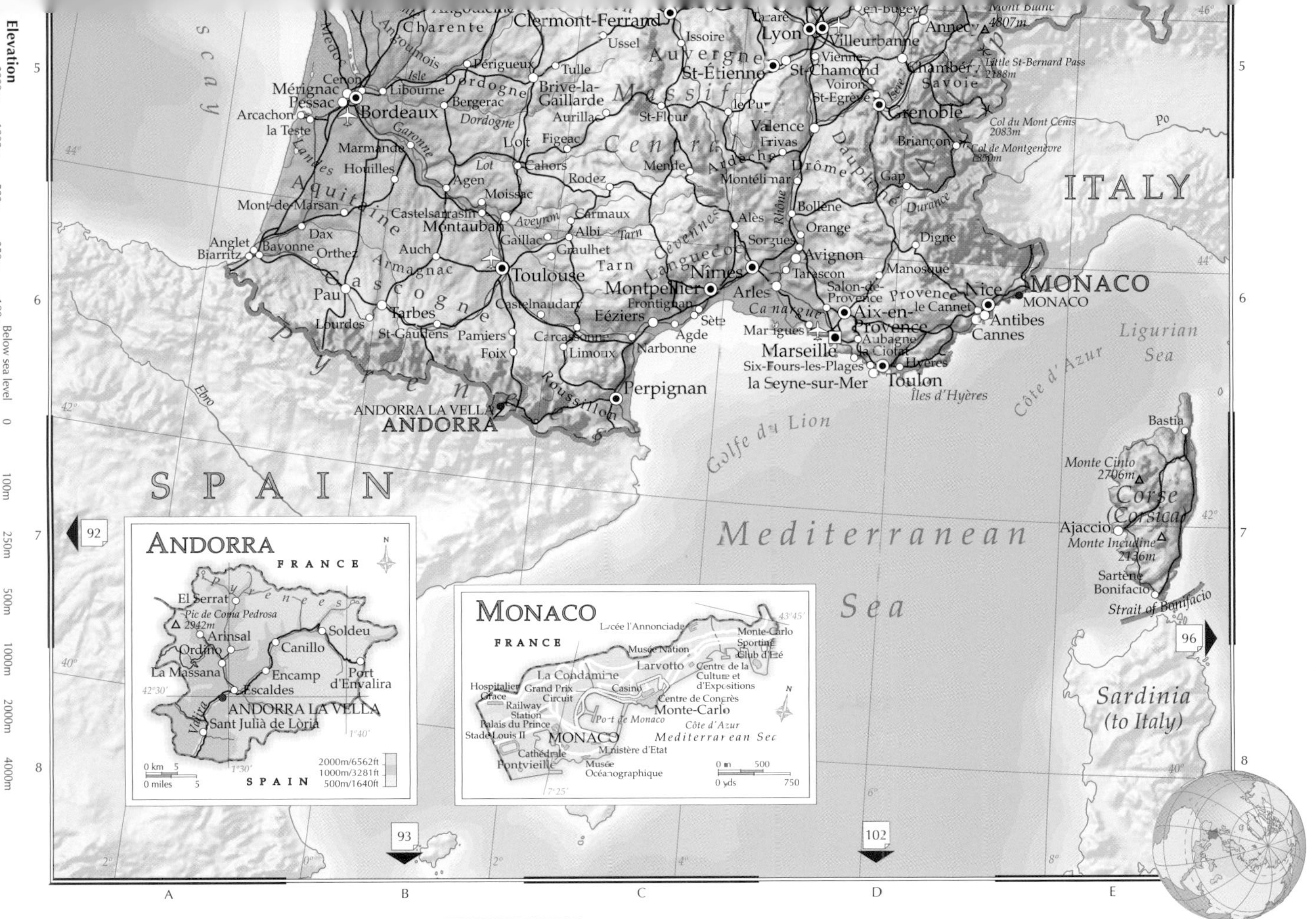

ITALY

MONACO

SPAIN

Mont Blanc
Little St-Bernard Pass
Col du Mont Cenis
Col de Montgenèvre
2083m
Grand-St-Bernard Pass

Ambérieu
Thonon
Annecy
Chambéry
Savoie
Grenoble
Briançon
Digne
Gap

St-Étienne
Vienne
Tillieurbanne
Lyon
Voiron
Dauphiné
Drôme
Manosque
Aix-en-Provence
Salon-de-Provence

Ussel
Issoire
Roanne
St-Chamond
St-Égrève
Valence
Crest
Aubagne
Fréjus
Antibes
Cannes
Nice

Clermont-Ferrand
Auvergne
Aurillac
Le Puy
Privas
Montélimar
Orange
Avignon
Sorgues
Nîmes
Arles
Marseille
Martigues
Six-Fours-les-Plages
la Seyne-sur-Mer
Toulon
Îles d'Hyères

Ligurian
Sea

Côte d'Azur

Mediterranean
Sea

Corte
Monte Cinto
2706m
Corsica
Ajaccio
Monte Incudine
2136m
Bastia
Sartène
Bonifacio
Strait of Bonifacio

Sardinia
(to Italy)

Golfe du Lion

Montpellier
Sète
Agde
Béziers
Narbonne
Perpignan
Roussillon
Languedoc
Cévennes
Tarn

Brive-la-Gaillarde
Tulle
Périgueux
Dordogne
Bergerac
Rodez
Figeac
Cahors
Albi
Gaillac
Montauban
Castres
Castelnaudary
Carcassonne
Limoux
Foix
Pamiers
St-Gaudens

Charente
Angoulême
Libourne
Pessac
Bordeaux
Mérignac
Arcachon
la Teste
Médoc
Marmande
Agen
Moissac
Toulouse
Garonne
Auch
Armagnac
Tarbes
Lourdes
Pau
Dax
Mont-de-Marsan
Lannes
Orthez
Bayonne
Anglet
Biarritz

ANDORRA LA VELLA
ANDORRA
Pyrénées
Gascogne
Aquitaine

scay
Ebro

Elevation

				Below sea level	0	100m	250m	500m	1000m	2000m	4000m
-2000m	-1000m	-500m	-250m	-100m							
-6562ft	-3281ft	-1640ft	-820ft	-328ft	-164ft/-50m	328ft	820ft	1640ft	3281ft	6562ft	13,124ft
					0						

MONACO

FRANCE

Lycée l'Annonciade
Musée National
Larvotto
Sporting
Club d'Été
Monte-Carlo
Centre de la
Culture et
d'Expositions
Centre de Congrès
Monte-Carlo
La Condamine
Casino
Grand Park
Railway
Station
Port de Monaco
Palais du Prince
Ministère d'État
MONACO
Cathédrale
Stade Louis II
Fontvieille
Musée
Océanographique

Côte d'Azur
Mediterranean Sea

ANDORRA

FRANCE

El Serrat
Soldeu
Canillo
Ordino
Arinsal
La Massana
Encamp
les Escaldes
Port
d'Envalira
ANDORRA LA VELLA
Sant Julià de Lòria
Pic de Coma Pedrosa
2942m

SPAIN

	2000m/6562ft
	1000m/3281ft
	500m/1640ft

96
102
93
92

Spain & Portugal

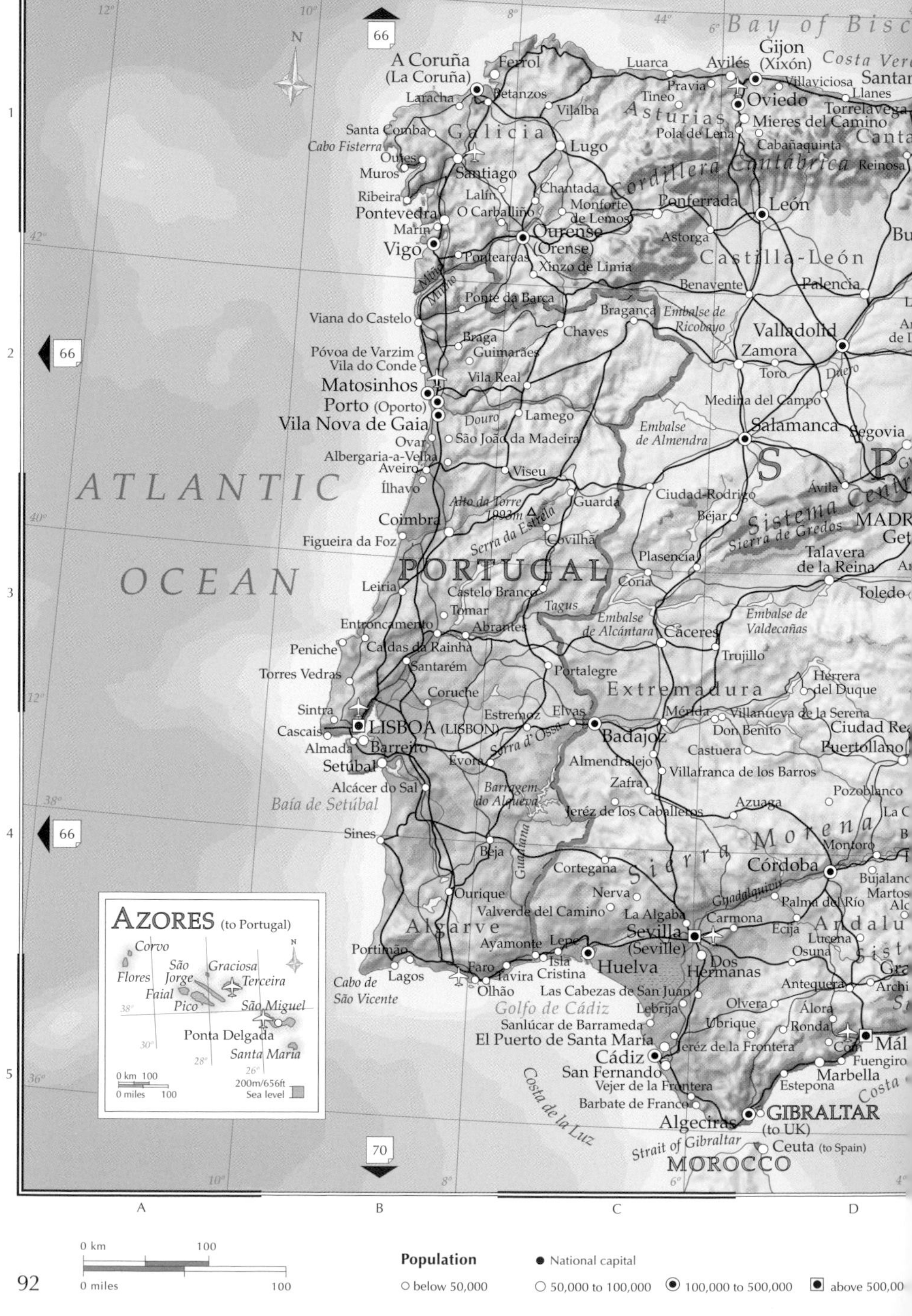

ATLANTIC OCEAN

PORTUGAL

SPAIN

AZORES (to Portugal)

Corvo
Flores
São Jorge   Graciosa
Faial   Terceira
Pico
São Miguel
Ponta Delgada
Santa Maria

0 km 100
0 miles 100
200m/656ft
Sea level

Population

● National capital

○ below 50,000   ○ 50,000 to 100,000   ◉ 100,000 to 500,000   ■ above 500,00

0 km 100
0 miles 100

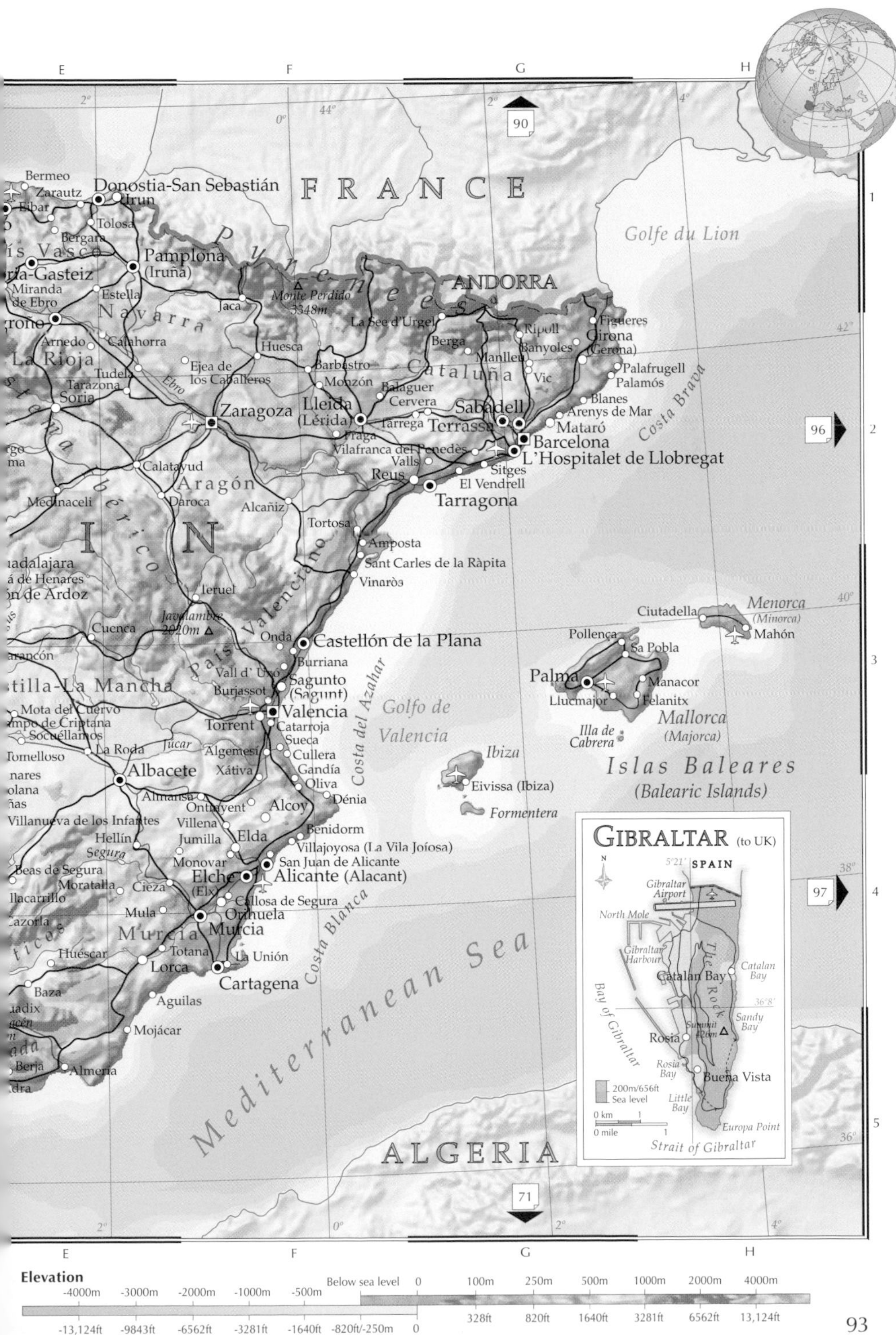

E   F   G   H

2°   0°   44°   2°   4°

90

Bermeo
Zarautz   Donostia-San Sebastián   F R A N C E   *Golfe du Lion*
bar   Irun
is Vasca   Tolosa   Pyrénées
ria-Gasteiz   Bergara   Pamplona
Miranda   (Iruña)   ANDORRA   42°   1
de Ebro   Estella   Jaca   Monte Perdido   La Seo d'Urgel   Ripoll   Figueres
oño   Arnedo   3348m   Berga   Banyoles   Girona   Palafrugell
La Rioja   Calahorra   Navarra   Huesca   Barbastro   (Gerona)   Palamós
Tudela   Ejea de   Monzón   Cataluña   Vic   Blanes
Tarazona   los Caballeros   Balaguer   Cervera   Sabadell   Arenys de Mar   Costa Brava   96   2
Soria   Zaragoza   Lleida   Tàrrega   Terrassa   Mataró
ma   (Lérida)   Fraga   Vilafranca del Penedès   Barcelona
Calatayud   Aragón   Valls   L'Hospitalet de Llobregat
gadalajara   Daroca   Reus   Sitges
á de Henares   Medinaceli   Alcañiz   El Vendrell
in de Ardoz   I   N   Teruel   Tortosa   Tarragona
                    Amposta
rancón   Cuenca   Javalambre   Sant Carles de la Ràpita   40°
                    2020m   Vinaròs
tilla-La Mancha   Onda   Castellón de la Plana   Ciutadella   Menorca   3
Mota del   Vall d'Uxó   Burriana   (Minorca)   Mahón
Cuervo   Sagunto   Pollença   Sa Pobla
npo de Criptana   Burjassot   (Sagunt)   Golfo del Azahar   Palma   Manacor
Socuéllamos   Valencia   Llucmajor   Felanitx
Tomelloso   Torrent   Catarroja   Golfo de   Mallorca
La Roda   Júcar   Algemesí   Sueca   Valencia   Illa de   (Majorca)
nares   Albacete   Xátiva   Cullera   Cabrera
olana   Almansa   Gandía   Ibiza   Islas Baleares
ñas   Hellín   Onteniente   Oliva   Eivissa (Ibiza)   (Balearic Islands)
Villanueva de los Infantes   Villena   Alcoy   Dénia
                    Elda   Formentera
Beas de Segura   Jumilla   Benidorm
Moratalla   Monóvar   Villajoyosa (La Vila Joíosa)
llacarrillo   Cieza   Elche   San Juan de Alicante   38°   97   4
azorla   Mula   (Elx)   Alicante (Alacant)
fico   Totana   Orihuela   Callosa de Segura
Huéscar   Segura   Murcia
Baza   Lorca   La Unión
iadix   Aguilas   Cartagena
ın   Mojácar   Mediterranean Sea
adá
Berja   Almería   36°
ıdra

71

ALGERIA

E   F   G   H

2°   0°   2°

Elevation
-4000m   -3000m   -2000m   -1000m   -500m   Below sea level   0   100m   250m   500m   1000m   2000m   4000m
-13,124ft   -9843ft   -6562ft   -3281ft   -1640ft   -820ft/-250m   0   328ft   820ft   1640ft   3281ft   6562ft   13,124ft

GIBRALTAR (to UK)

SPAIN

5°21'   Gibraltar
                Airport
North Mole   Gibraltar
                Harbour   The Rock   Catalan
Gibraltar   Catalan Bay   Bay
Harbour   Sandy
Bay   Bay
Rosia   Summit   36°8'
Bay   1063
Rosia   Little   Buena Vista
Bay   Bay
200m/656ft   Europa Point
Sea level   Strait of Gibraltar
0 km   1
0 mile   1

93

Germany & the Alpine States

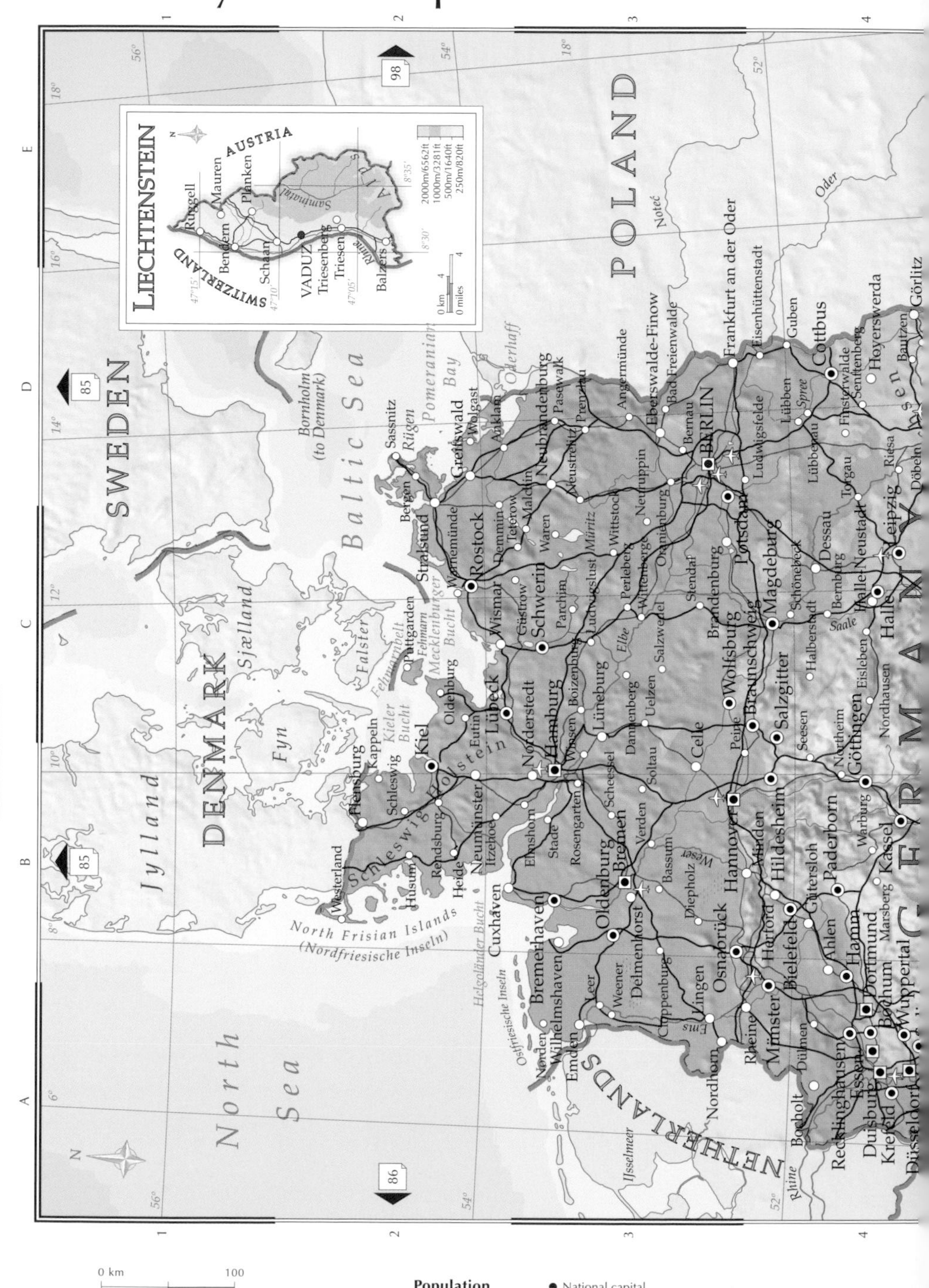

LIECHTENSTEIN

SWITZERLAND

AUSTRIA

Ruggell
Mauren
Planken
Bendern
Eschen
Schaan
VADUZ
Triesenberg
Triesen
Balzers

Saminatal

18°35'

18°30'

47°15'
47°10'
47°05'

2000m/6562ft
1000m/3281ft
500m/1640ft
250m/820ft

0 km   4
0 miles   4

98

85

85

86

SWEDEN

POLAND

18°
56°
54°
18°
52°

Oder

16°
14°

Bornholm
(to Denmark)

Baltic Sea

Pomeraniant Bay

Frankfurt an der Oder

Eisenhüttenstadt

Guben

Cottbus

Hoyerswerda

Görlitz

Noteć

12°
10°

DENMARK

Jylland

Fyn

Falster

Sjælland

Lolland

Femern

Sassnitz
Rügen
Bergen

Greifswald
Wolgast
Usedom
Oderhaff

Angermünde
Eberswalde-Finow
Bad Freienwalde
Bernau
BERLIN
Ludwigsfelde
Lübben
Spree
Finsterwalde
Luckau
Torgau
Senftenberg
Schkeuditz
Leipzig
Riesa
Döbeln
Bautzen

North Frisian Islands
(Nordfriesische Inseln)

Westerland
Flensburg
Kappeln
Schleswig
Rendsburg
Husum
Hede
Heide
Neumünster
Itzehoe

Kiel
Eutin
Oldenburg
Fehmarn
Mecklenburger Bucht
Wismar
Schwerin
Gadebusch
Parchim
Neustrelitz
Stralsund
Rostock
Warnemünde
Demmin
Teterow
Malchin
Waren
Müritz
Wittstock
Neuruppin
Oranienburg
Pasewalk
Prenzlau
Neubrandenburg

North Sea

Ostfriesische Inseln

Norden
Emden
Weener
Leer
Nordhorn

Helgoländer Bucht
Cuxhaven
Bremerhaven
Wilhelmshaven
Delmenhorst
Oldenburg
Cloppenburg
Lingen
Rheine
Münster
Dülmen
Bocholt

Ems

NETHERLANDS

Ijsselmeer

Rhine

Ijssel

Schleswig-Holstein

Norderstedt
Hamburg
Lübeck
Stade
Buxtehude
Scheeßel
Rosengarten
Verden
Bassum
Diepholz
Osnabrück
Bielefeld
Gütersloh
Herford
Ahlen
Hamm
Dortmund
Bochum
Essen
Duisburg
Krefeld
Düsseldorf
Wuppertal
Recklinghausen
Paderborn
Warburg
Kassel
Marsberg
Northeim
Göttingen
Eichsfeld
Nordhausen
Mühlhausen

Elbe

Lüneburg
Boizenburg
Dannenberg
Uelzen
Soltau
Celle
Hannover
Hildesheim
Salzgitter
Seesen

Wolfsburg
Braunschweig
Stendal
Salzwedel
Peine
Magdeburg
Schönebeck
Bernburg
Halberstadt
Eisleben
Halle

Wittenberge
Ludwigslust
Perleberg

Brandenburg
Potsdam

Dessau
Bitterfeld

Saale

Weser

G E R M A N Y

Population   ● National capital

○ below 50,000   ○ 50,000 to 100,000   ◉ 100,000 to 500,000   ◼ above 500,000

0 km   100
0 miles   100

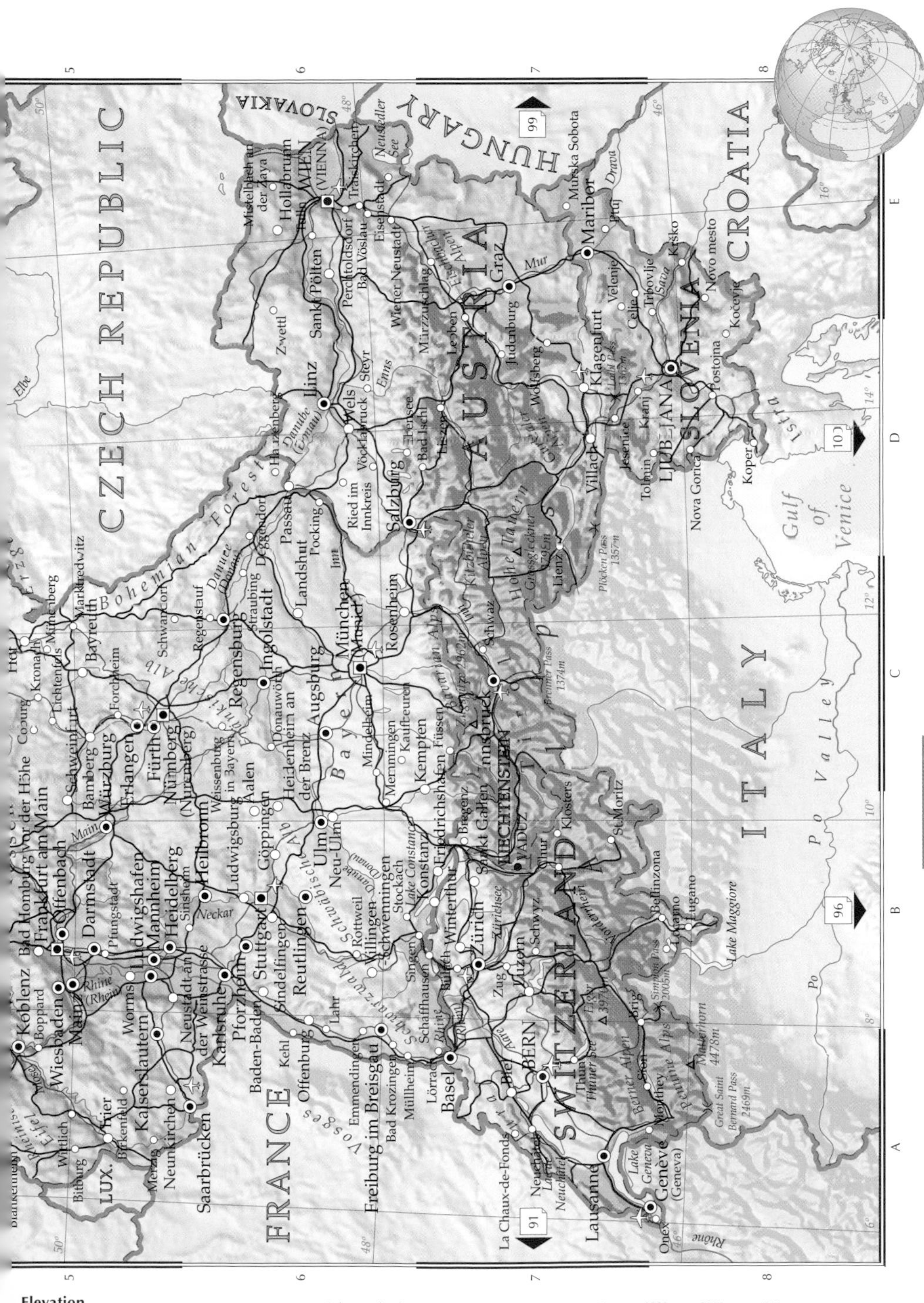

Elevation

-500m	-250m	-100m	-50m	-25m	Below sea level	0	100m	250m	500m	1000m	2000m	4000m
-1640ft	-820ft	-328ft	-164ft	-82ft	33ft/-10m	0	328ft	820ft	1640ft	3281ft	6562ft	13,124ft

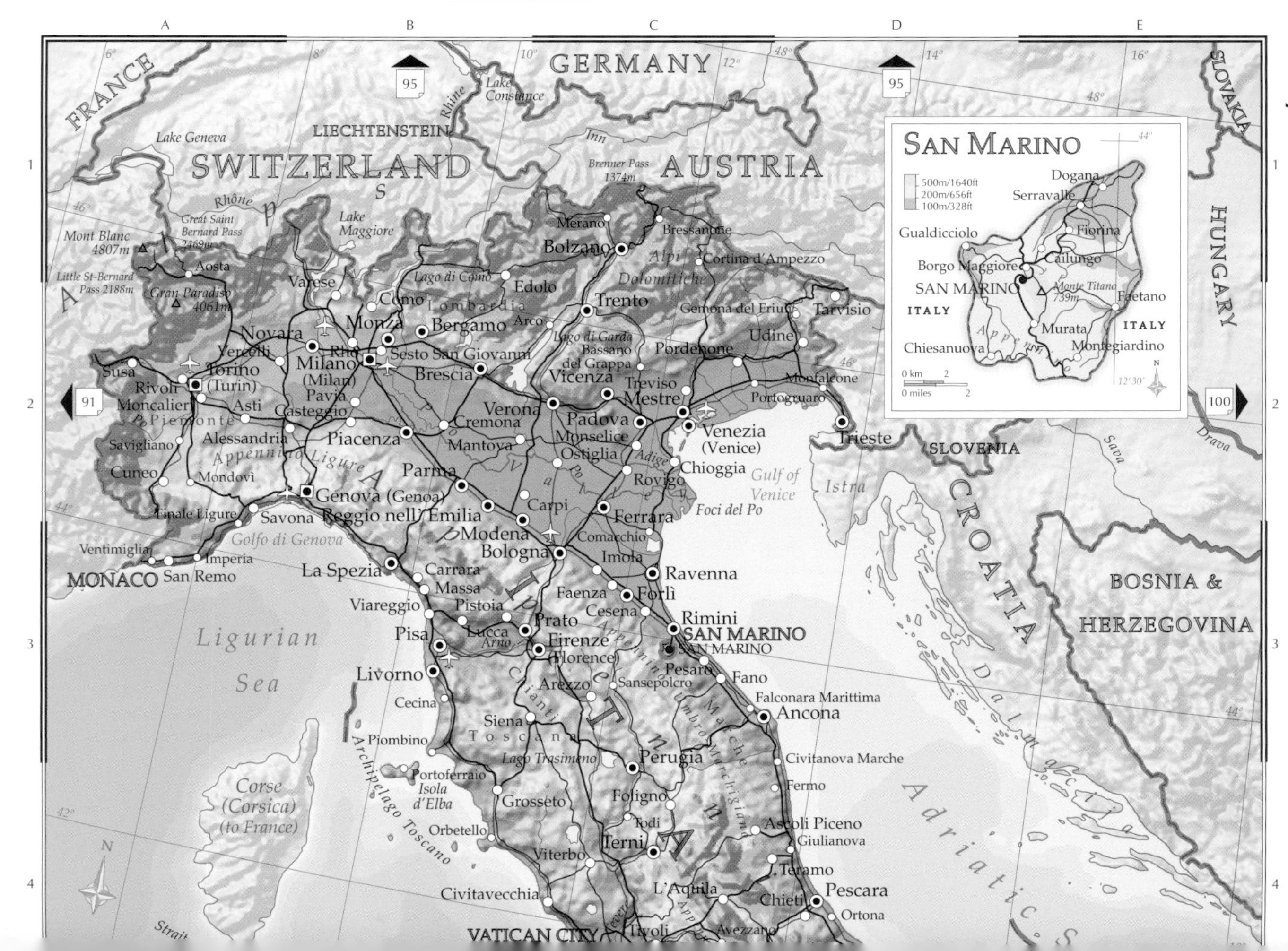

SLOVAKIA
HUNGARY
Drava
Sava

SAN MARINO
Dogana
Serravalle
Fiorina
Falciano
Monte Titano 739m
Acetano
ITALY
Gualdicciolo
Murata
Montegiardino
Borgo Maggiore
SAN MARINO
ITALY
Chiesanuova

500m/1640ft
200m/656ft
100m/328ft
0 km 2
0 miles 2

BOSNIA &
HERZEGOVINA

CROATIA

GERMANY

LIECHTENSTEIN
SWITZERLAND
AUSTRIA

Adriatic Sea

Trieste
Istria
Gulf of
Venice
Udine
Tarvisio
Gemona del Friuli
Portogruaro
Pordenone
Venezia
(Venice)
Chioggia
Foci del Po
Treviso
Mestre
Ravenna
Forlì
Rimini
SAN MARINO
Fano
Falconara Marittima
Ancona
Civitanova Marche
Fermo
Ascoli Piceno
Giulianova
Pescara
Ortona
Chieti

Bressanone
Dolomiti
Cortina d'Ampezzo
Trento
Bolzano
Merano
Edolo
Bergamo
Brescia
Vicenza
Padova
Verona
Mantova
Cremona
Ferrara
Comacchio
Imola
Faenza
Cesena
Bologna
Modena
Carpi
Reggio nell'Emilia
Parma
Piacenza
Perugia
Folignio
Todi
L'Aquila
Terni
Viterbo
Prato
Firenze
(Florence)
Arezzo
Sansepolcro
Siena
Grosseto
Orbetello
Civitavecchia
VATICAN CITY

Lecco
Como
Lago di Como
Monza
Milano
(Milan)
Pavia
Novara
Vercelli
Torino
(Turin)
Asti
Alessandria
Mondovì
Cuneo
Savigliano
Moncalieri
Rivoli
Susa

Mont Blanc
4807m
Little St-Bernard
Pass 2188m
Gran Paradiso
4061m
Grand Saint
Bernard Pass
2469m

La Spezia
Carrara
Massa
Viareggio
Lucca
Pistoia
Pisa
Livorno
Cecina
Piombino
Portoferraio
Isola
d'Elba
Archipelago
Toscano

Genova
(Genoa)
Golfo di Genova
Savona
Imperia
Ventimiglia
San Remo
MONACO

Ligurian
Sea

Corse
(Corsica)
(to France)

FRANCE

0 km 100
0 miles 100

Population
● National capital
○ below 50,000
◎ 50,000 to 100,000
◉ 100,000 to 500,000
▣ above 500,000

Strait of Otranto

Brindisi
Lecce
Maglie
Taranto
Manduria
Gallipoli
Golfo di Taranto
Molfetta
Bari
Bitonto
Barletta
Andria
Cerignola
Foggia
Altamura
Matera
Potenza
Ciro Marino
Crotone
Catanzaro
P u g l i a
B a s i l i c a t a
Rossano
La Sila
Benevento
Avellino
Cassino
Salerno
Napoli
(Naples)
Torre del Greco
Gaeta
Golfo di
Gaeta
Golfo di
Salerno
Isola di Capri
Battipaglia
Agropoli
San Caterina Ionadi
Aspromonte
Calabria
Castrovillari
Cosenza
Amantea
Lamezia
Terme
Palmi
Reggio di Calabria
Siderno
Isola Stromboli
Isola Lipari
Isole Eolie
Isola Vulcano
Messina
Stretto di Messina
Catania
Siracusa
Noto
Monte Etna
3340m
Simeto
Ragusa
Modica
Pozzallo
Vittoria
Gela
Caltanissetta
Enna
Cefalù
Palermo
Alcamo
Castelvetrano
Agrigento
Trapani
Marsala
Isole Egadi
Sicilia
Sicily

Ionian
Sea

Isole Ponziane

Tyrrhenian
Sea

Isola d'Ustica

Isola di
Pantelleria

Strait of Sicily

Mediterranean
Sea

Isole
Pelagie

Malta Channel
Gozo
MALTA
VALLETTA
Malta

7

71

Sardegna
(Sardinia)
Siniscola
Nuoro
Macomer
Oristano
Punta La Marmora
1834m
Villacidro
Iglesias
Carbonia
Cagliari
Quartu Sant'Elena

TUNISIA

VATICAN CITY

N
Main
Entrance
Pigna
Courtyard
Vatican Museums
Vatican
Gardens
Radio
Vaticano
Monte Vaticano
Raphael
Rooms
Sistine
Chapel
Stanza
Papal
Apartments
St Peter's
Square
Saint Peter's
Basilica
Vatican
Railway
Station
Papal
Heliport

R O M E
R O M E

0 m   200
0 yds   250

Elevation

					Below sea level	0	100m	250m	500m	1000m	2000m	4000m
-2000m	-1000m	-500m	-250m	-100m								
-6562ft	-3281ft	-1640ft	-820ft	-328ft	-164ft/-50m	0	328ft	820ft	1640ft	3281ft	6562ft	13,124ft

Central Europe

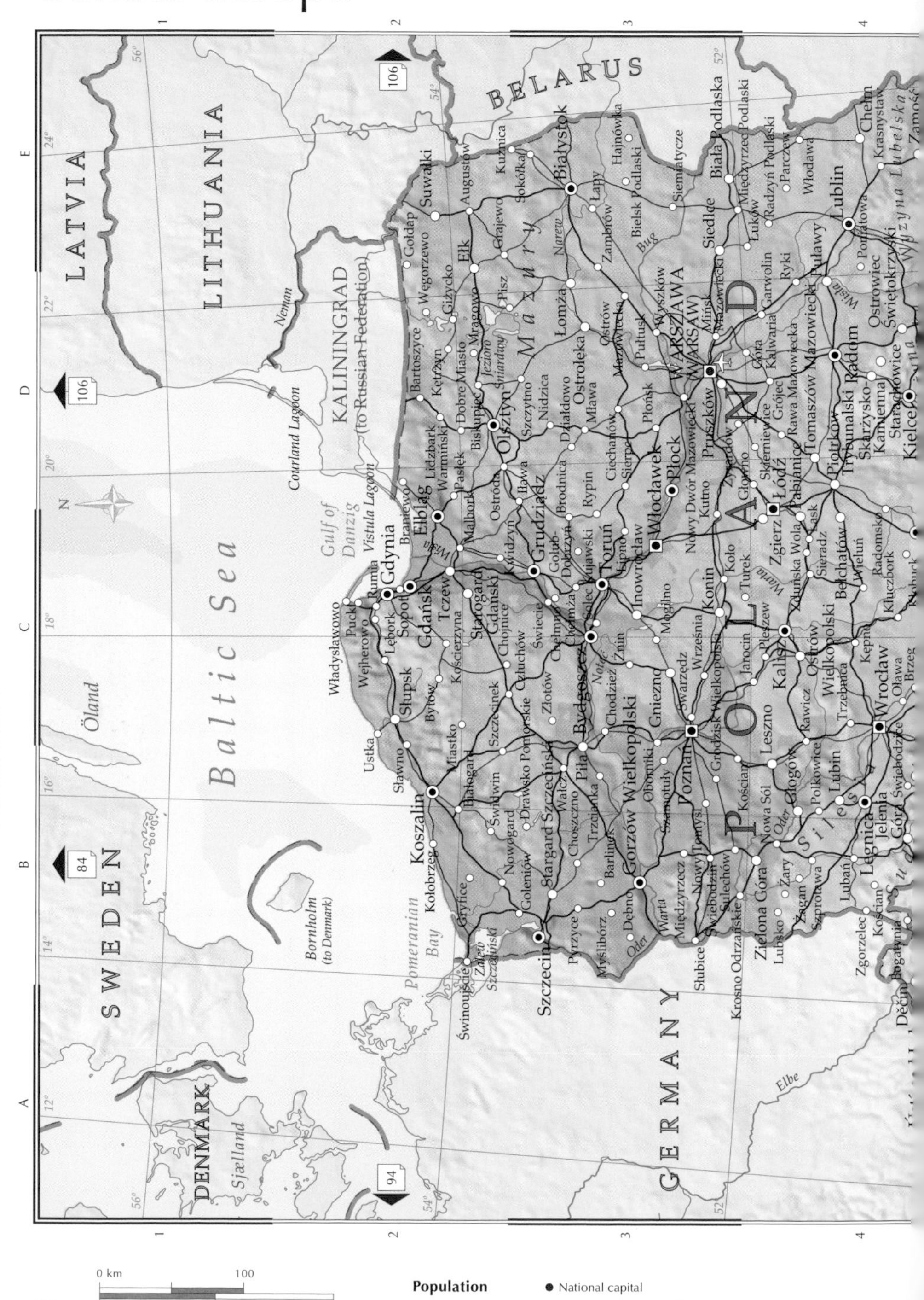

Population   ● National capital

○ below 50,000   ○ 50,000 to 100,000   ◉ 100,000 to 500,000   ▣ above 500,00

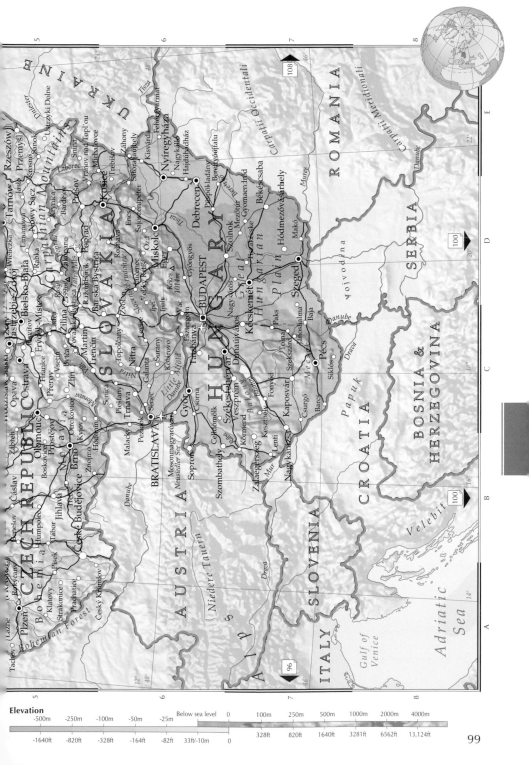

UKRAINE

ROMANIA

SERBIA

BOSNIA & HERZEGOVINA

CROATIA

SLOVENIA

ITALY

AUSTRIA

SLOVAKIA

CZECH REPUBLIC

HUNGARY

Carpathian Mountains

Carpatii Occidentali

Carpatii Meridionali

Vojvodina

Papuk

Velebit

Gulf of Venice

Adriatic Sea

Bohemia

Moravia

Bohemian Forest

Niedere Tauern

Alps

Great Hungarian Plain

Little Alföld

Mecsek

Danube

Drava

Mur

Dráva

Tisza

Mureş

Tisza

Ipel'

108

100

100

96

BUDAPEST

BRATISLAVA

Debrecen

Miskolc

Košice

Nyíregyháza

Szeged

Kecskemét

Pécs

Brno

Ostrava

Plzeň

Zlín

Olomouc

Győr

Szombathely

Székesfehérvár

Veszprém

Nagykanizsa

Kaposvár

Szekszárd

Baja

Hódmezővásárhely

Békéscsaba

Szolnok

Eger

Gyöngyös

Kékes 1014m

Prešov

Žilina

Martin

Trenčín

Nitra

Trnava

Soprón

Sopron

Southeast Europe

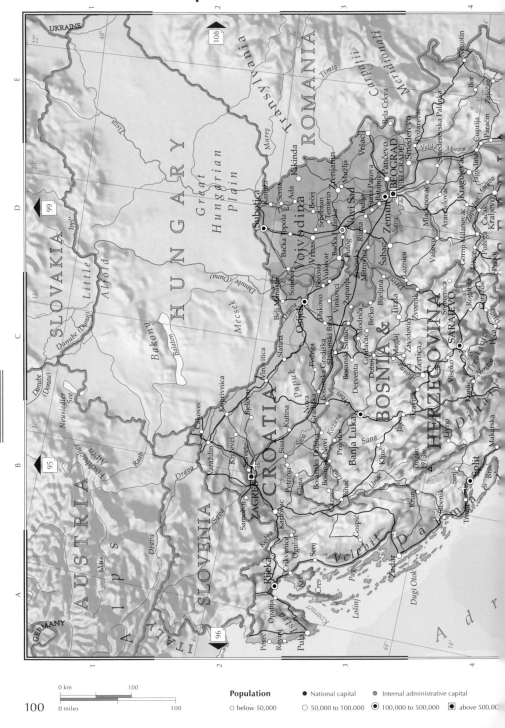

0 km	100
0 miles	100

Population

● National capital   ● Internal administrative capital

○ below 50,000

○ 50,000 to 100,000   ◉ 100,000 to 500,000   ◼ above 500,00

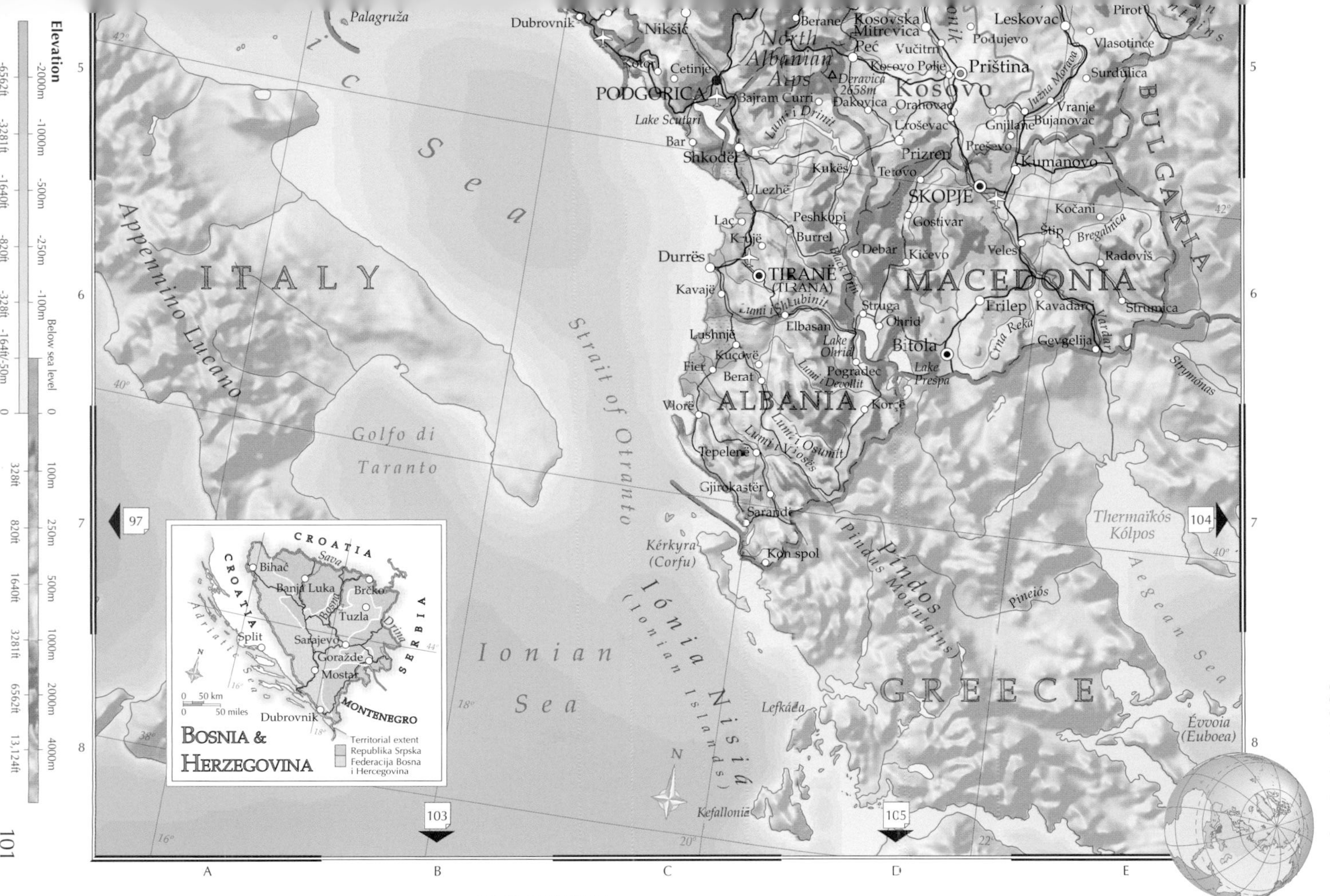

BULGARIA

Pirot
Vlasotince
Vlasina
Surdulica
Leskovac
Podujevo
Priština
KOSOVO
Kosovska
Mitrovica
Peć
Vučitrn
Berane
Rožaj
Dakovica
Gnjilane
Vranje
Bujanovac
Preševo
Kumanovo
Kočani
Štip
Radoviš
Strumica
Bregalnica
Veles
Prilep
Kavadar
Gevgelija
Vardar
Crna
Reka
Resen
Bitola
Prespa
Lake
Prespa
MACEDONIA
Kičevo
Tetovo
Gostivar
Debar
Struga
Ohrid
Lake
Ohrid
Korçë
GREECE
Thermaïkós
Kólpos
Aegean Sea
Strymónas
Pinds
Pinds (Pindus Mountains)
Piniós
Évvoia
(Euboea)
Prizren
Orahovac
Uroševac
Uroševac
Kosovo
Polje
Peshkopi
Dragash
Kukës
Lumi Drini
Black Drin
Burrel
ALBANIA
Elbasan
Lumi Shkumbin
Lake
Devoll
Lumi Devoll
Këlcyrë
Korçë
Lefkáda
Kefalloniá
Ióna Nisiá
(Ionian Islands)
Kótspol
Konspol
Bajram Curri
Lumi i Drinit
Lezhë
Laç
Lumi Mat
Krujë
TIRANË
(TIRANA)
Kavajë
Durrës
Lushnjë
Fier
Berat
Vlorë
Gjirokastër
Tepelenë
Sarandë
Lumi Vjosës
Lumi Osumit
Kérkyra
(Corfu)
Ionian
Sea
Strait of Otranto
Palagruža
Dubrovnik
Kotor
Cetinje
Nikšić
Bar
PODGORICA
Lake Skadar
Shkodër
Berane
North Albanian Alps
Durmitor
2655m
Mati
ITALY
Golfo di
Taranto
Appennino Lucano
Adriatic
Sea

Elevation

-2000m	-1000m	-500m	-250m	-100m	Below sea level	0	100m	250m	500m	1000m	2000m	4000m
-6562ft	-3281ft	-1640ft	-820ft	-328ft	-164ft/-50m	0	328ft	820ft	1640ft	3281ft	6562ft	13,124ft

BOSNIA &
HERZEGOVINA

CROATIA
SERBIA
Sava
Una
Bihać
Banja Luka
Bosna
Brčko
Tuzla
Drina
Goražde
Sarajevo
Mostar
Dubrovnik
Split
CROATIA
MONTENEGRO
Adriatic Sea

Territorial extent
Republika Srpska
Federacija Bosna
i Hercegovina

0   50 km
0   50 miles

The Mediterranean

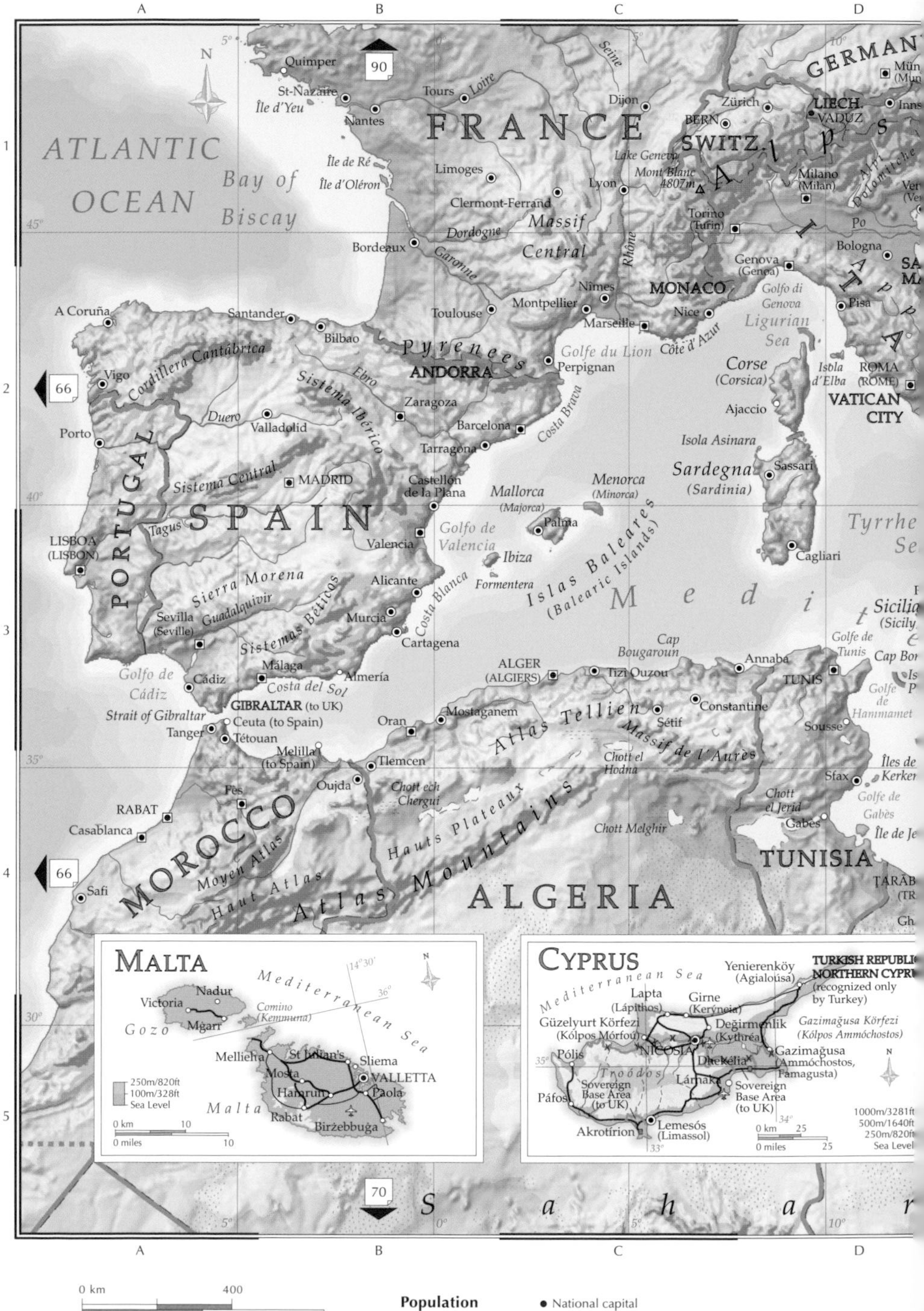

ATLANTIC OCEAN

Bay of Biscay

FRANCE

GERMAN

Quimper
St-Nazaire
Île d'Yeu
Nantes
Tours
Loire
Dijon
Zürich
BERN
SWITZ.
LIECH.
VADUZ
Münn
Inns
Limoges
Clermont-Ferrand
Lyon
Lake Geneva
Mont Blanc
4807m
A L P S
Milano
(Milan)
Ver
Dordogne
Massif
Rhône
Torino
(Turin)
Po
Bologna
Bordeaux
Garonne
Central
Genova
(Genoa)
Pisa
SA
MA
Toulouse
Montpellier
Nîmes
MONACO
Golfo di
Genova
ROMA
(ROME)
A Coruña
Santander
Marseille
Nice
Côte d'Azur
Ligurian
Sea
VATICAN
CITY
Vigo
Bilbao
Pyrenees
ANDORRA
Golfe du Lion
Perpignan
Corse
(Corsica)
Isla
d'Elba
Cordillera Cantábrica
Sistema Ibérico
Ebro
Zaragoza
Costa Brava
Ajaccio
Porto
Duero
Valladolid
Barcelona
Isola Asinara
Sassari
Sardegna
(Sardinia)
Tyrrhe
Se
Tarragona
PORTUGAL
Sistema Central
MADRID
Castellón
de la Plana
Mallorca
(Majorca)
Menorca
(Minorca)
Cagliari
LISBOA
(LISBON)
Tagus
SPAIN
Valencia
Golfo de
Valencia
Palma
M   e   d   i
Sierra Morena
Guadalquivir
Alicante
Ibiza
Islas Baleares
(Balearic Islands)
t
Sicilia
(Sicily)
Sevilla
(Seville)
Sistemas Béticos
Murcia
Costa Blanca
Formentera
Golfo de
Tunis
Cap Bor
Is
Golfo de
Cádiz
Cádiz
Málaga
Almería
Cartagena
ALGER
(ALGIERS)
Cap
Bougaroun
Tizi Ouzou
Annaba
TUNIS
Golfo
de
Hanmamet
Costa del Sol
GIBRALTAR
(to UK)
Oran
Mostaganem
Constantine
Sousse
Strait of Gibraltar
Ceuta (to Spain)
Tanger
Tétouan
Atlas Tellien
Sétif
Massif de l'Aurès
Sfax
Îles de
Kerker
Melilla
(to Spain)
Tlemcen
Chott el
Hodna
Chott
el Jerid
Golfe de
Gabès
RABAT
Fès
Oujda
Chott ech
Chergui
Gabès
Île de Je
Casablanca
MOROCCO
Hauts Plateaux
Chott Melghir
TUNISIA
TARĀB
(TR.
Gh.
Safi
Moyen Atlas
Haut Atlas
Atlas Mountains
ALGERIA

S   a   h   a

MALTA

Mediterranean Sea
Victoria
Nadur
Comino
(Kemmuna)
Gozo
Mġarr
Mellieħa
St Julian's
Mosta
Sliema
VALLETTA
Ħamrun
Paola
Malta
Rabat
Birżebbuġa

250m/820ft
100m/328ft
Sea Level
0 km   10
0 miles   10

CYPRUS

Mediterranean Sea
Yenierenköy
(Agialoúsa)
TURKISH REPUBLI
NORTHERN CYPR
(recognized only
by Turkey)
Lapta
(Lápithos)
Girne
(Kerýneia)
Güzelyurt Körfezi
(Kólpos Mórfou)
Değirmenlik
(Kythréa)
Gazimağusa Körfezi
(Kólpos Ammóchostos)
Pólis
NICOSIA
Gazimağusa
(Ammóchostos,
Famagusta)
Tróödos
Dhekélia
Lárnaka
Sovereign
Base Area
(to UK)
Páfos
Lemesós
(Limassol)
Akrotíri
Sovereign
Base Area
(to UK)

1000m/3281ft
500m/1640ft
250m/820ft
Sea Level
0 km   25
0 miles   25

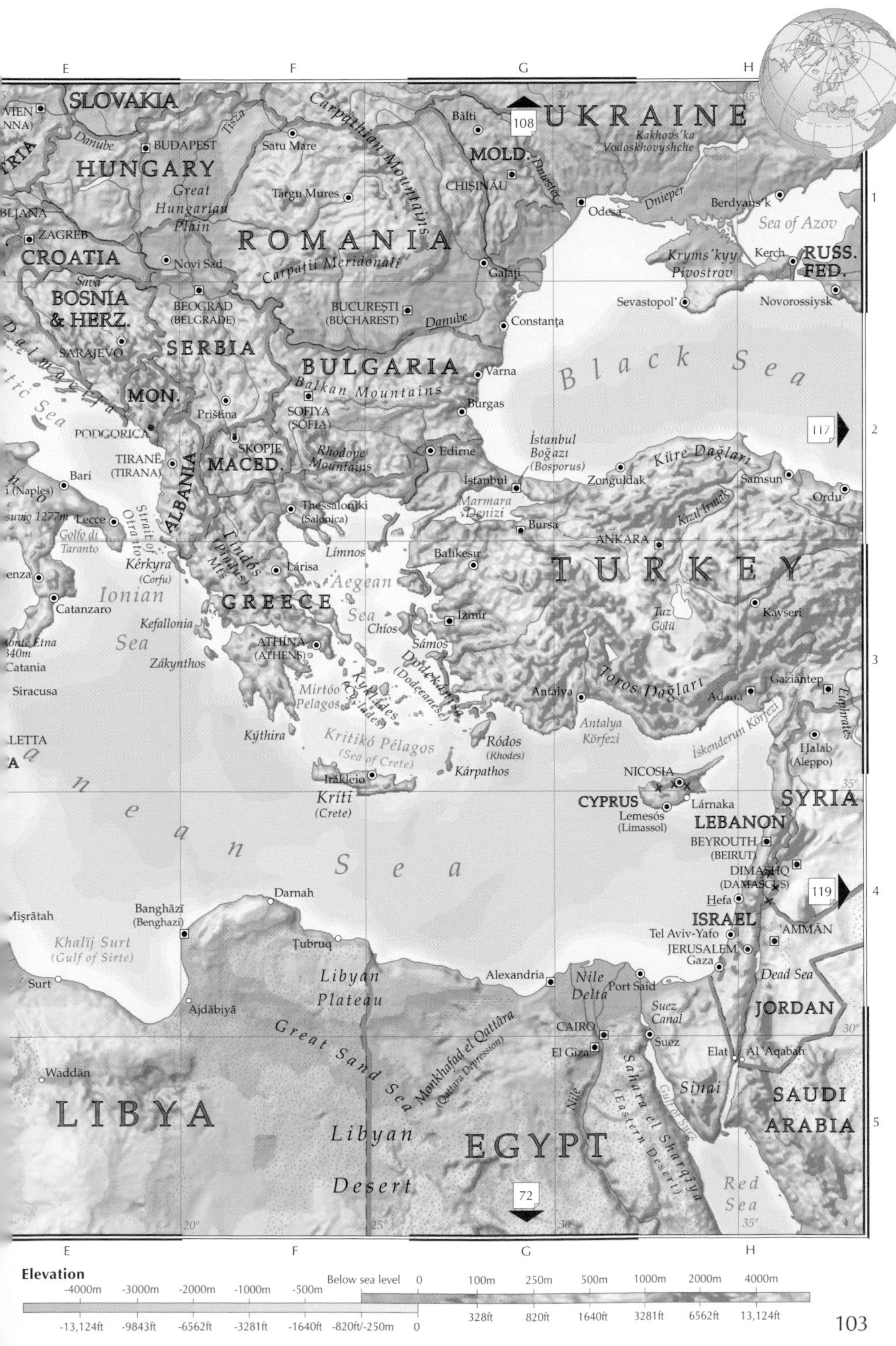

Map of the Mediterranean region, showing parts of southeastern Europe, Turkey, the Black Sea, North Africa, and the Middle East. Countries and features labelled include:

SLOVAKIA, HUNGARY, ROMANIA, CROATIA, BOSNIA & HERZ., SERBIA, MON., BULGARIA, ALBANIA, MACED., GREECE, MOLD., UKRAINE, RUSS. FED., TURKEY, CYPRUS, SYRIA, LEBANON, ISRAEL, JORDAN, SAUDI ARABIA, EGYPT, LIBYA

Cities and places: VIENNA (WIEN), BUDAPEST, Satu Mare, Târgu Mures, Bălti, CHIŞINĂU, Odesa, Berdyans'k, Kerch, Novorossiysk, Sevastopol', Krym'skyy Pivostrov, ZAGREB, Novi Sad, BEOGRAD (BELGRADE), BUCUREŞTI (BUCHAREST), Galaţi, Constanţa, Varna, SARAJEVO, Priština, PODGORICA, TIRANË (TIRANA), SKOPJE, SOFIYA (SOFIA), Edirne, İstanbul Boğazı (Bosporus), İstanbul, Zonguldak, Samsun, Ordu, Bari, Lecce, Thessaloníki (Salónica), Bursa, ANKARA, Kayseri, Catanzaro, Kérkyra (Corfu), Lárisa, Límnos, Balıkesir, İzmir, Tuz Gölü, Gaziantep, Catania, Siracusa, Kefalloniá, ATHÍNA (ATHENS), Chíos, Sámos, Antalya, Adana, I.Jalab (Aleppo), Zákynthos, Kýthira, Irákleio, Kríti (Crete), Ródos (Rhodes), Kárpathos, NICOSIA, Lárnaka, CYPRUS, Lemesós (Limassol), BEYROUTH (BEIRUT), DIMASHQ (DAMASCUS), Hefa, Misrātah, Banghāzī (Benghazi), Darnah, Tubruq, Alexandria, Port Said, Tel Aviv-Yafo, ISRAEL, JERUSALEM, Gaza, 'AMMĀN, Surt, Ajdābiyā, CAIRO, El Giza, Suez, Elat, Al 'Aqabah, Waddān

Water and physical features: Black Sea, Sea of Azov, Marmara Denizi, Aegean Sea, Ionian Sea, Adriatic Sea, Gulf of Taranto (Golfo di Taranto), Strait of Otranto, Kykládes (Cyclades), Dodecanese (Dodekánisa), Kritikó Pélagos (Sea of Crete), Mirtóo Pélagos, Antalya Körfezi, İskenderun Körfezi, Dead Sea, Nile Delta, Suez Canal, Sinai, Gulf of Suez, Red Sea, Khalīj Surt (Gulf of Sirte), Libyan Plateau, Libyan Desert, Great Sand Sea, Munkhafad el Qattâra (Qattara Depression), Sahara el Sharqīya (Eastern Desert), Nile, Danube, Tisza, Sava, Dniester, Dnieper, Carpathian Mountains, Carpaţii Meridionali, Balkan Mountains, Rhodope Mountains, Píndos Mountains, Toros Dağları (Taurus Mountains), Küre Dağları, Kızıl Irmak, Euphrates, Great Hungarian Plain, Kakhovs'ka Vodoskhovyshche, Mte Etna 340m, suvio 1277m

Grid references and page-continuation markers: 108, 117, 119, 72

Elevation

					Below sea level							
-4000m	-3000m	-2000m	-1000m	-500m		0	100m	250m	500m	1000m	2000m	4000m
-13,124ft	-9843ft	-6562ft	-3281ft	-1640ft	-820ft/-250m		328ft	820ft	1640ft	3281ft	6562ft	13,124ft

103

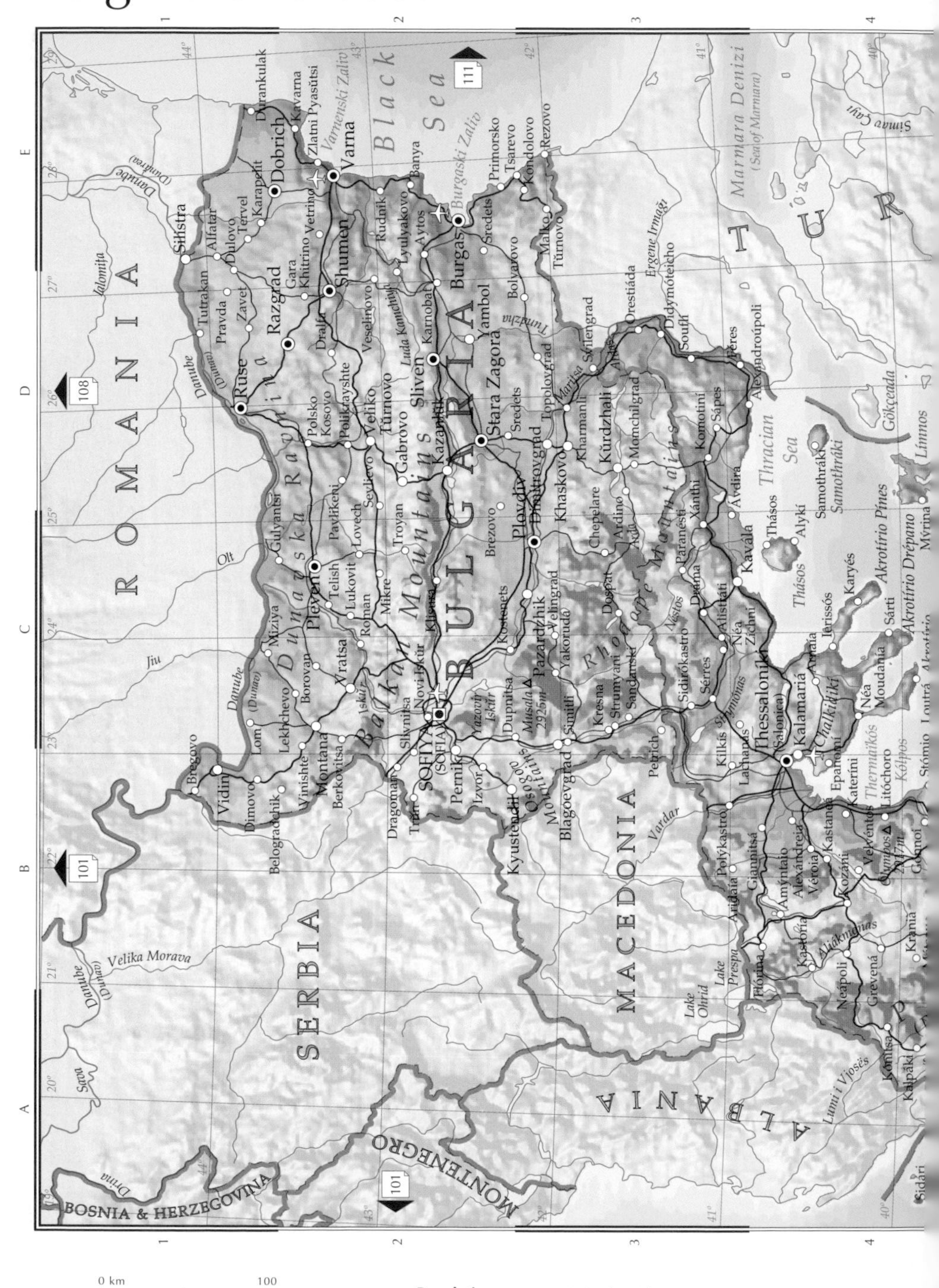

0 km   100

0 miles   100

Population   ● National capital

○ below 50,000   ○ 50,000 to 100,000   ◉ 100,000 to 500,000   ■ above 500,000

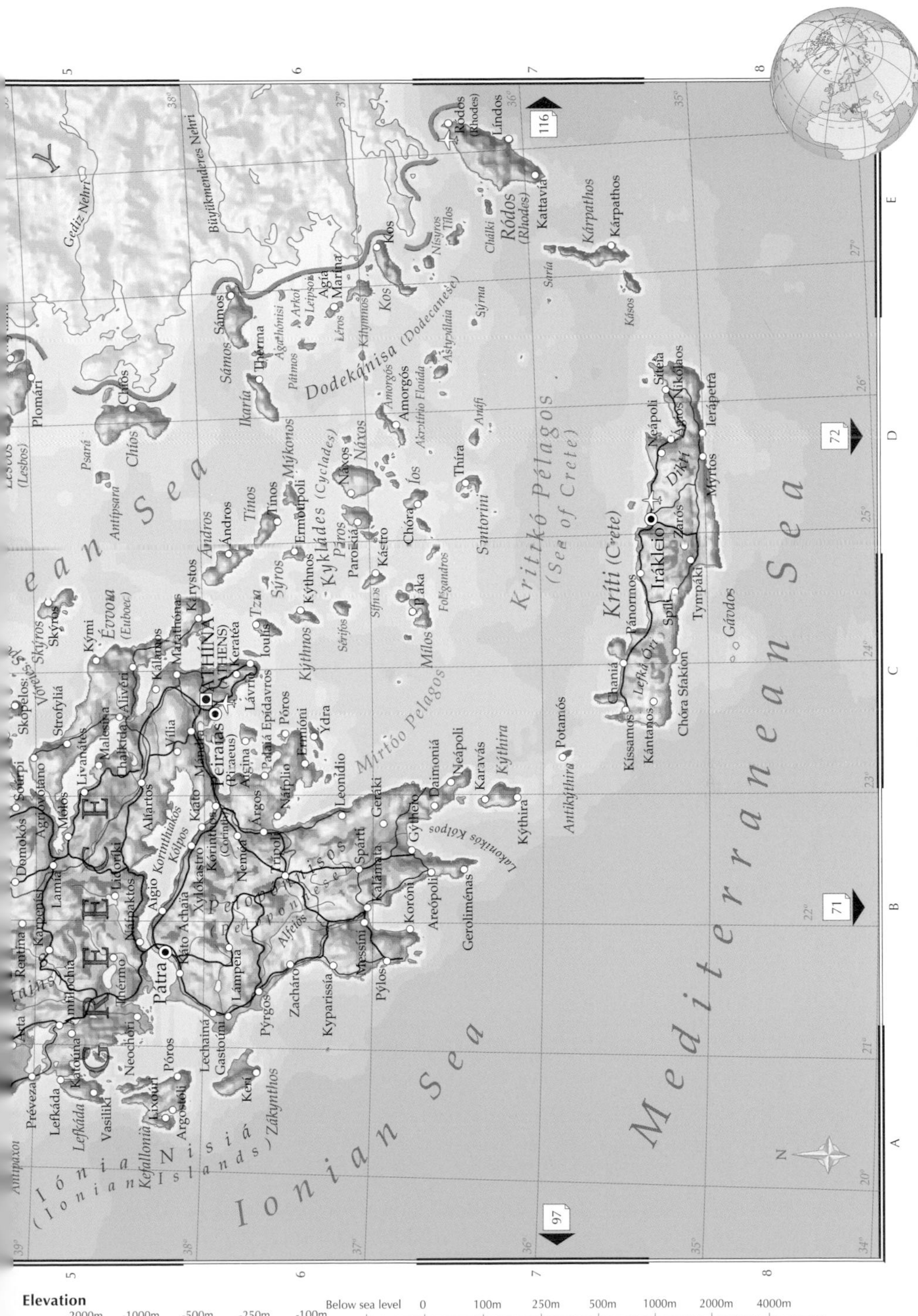

Elevation

-2000m	-1000m	-500m	-250m	-100m	Below sea level	0	100m	250m	500m	1000m	2000m	4000m
-6562ft	-3281ft	-1640ft	-820ft	-328ft/-50m		0	328ft	820ft	1640ft	3281ft	6562ft	13,124ft

The Baltic States & Belarus

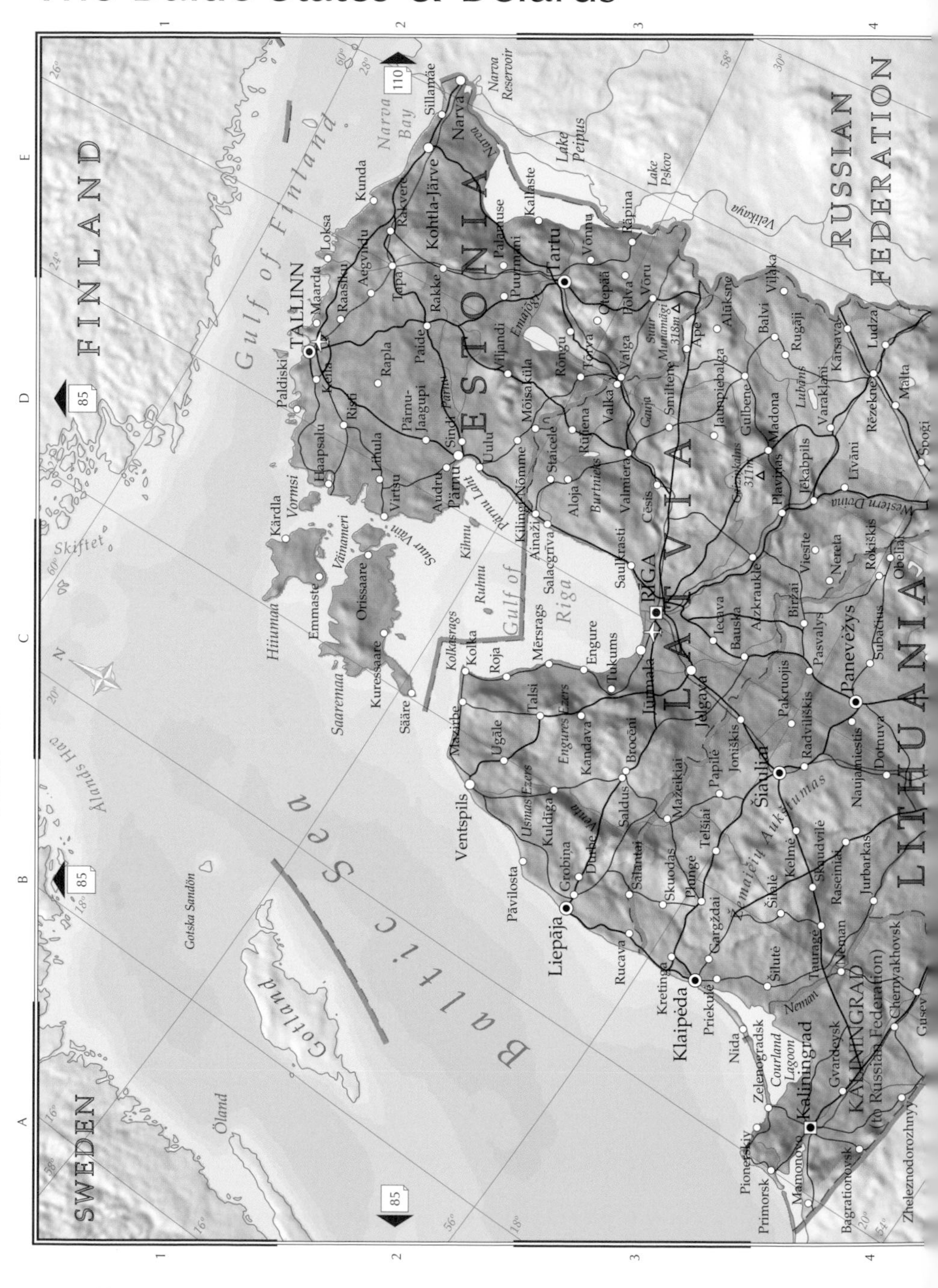

Population

● National capital

○ below 50,000   ◉ 50,000 to 100,000   ◉ 100,000 to 500,000   ■ above 500,000

0 km   100

0 miles   100

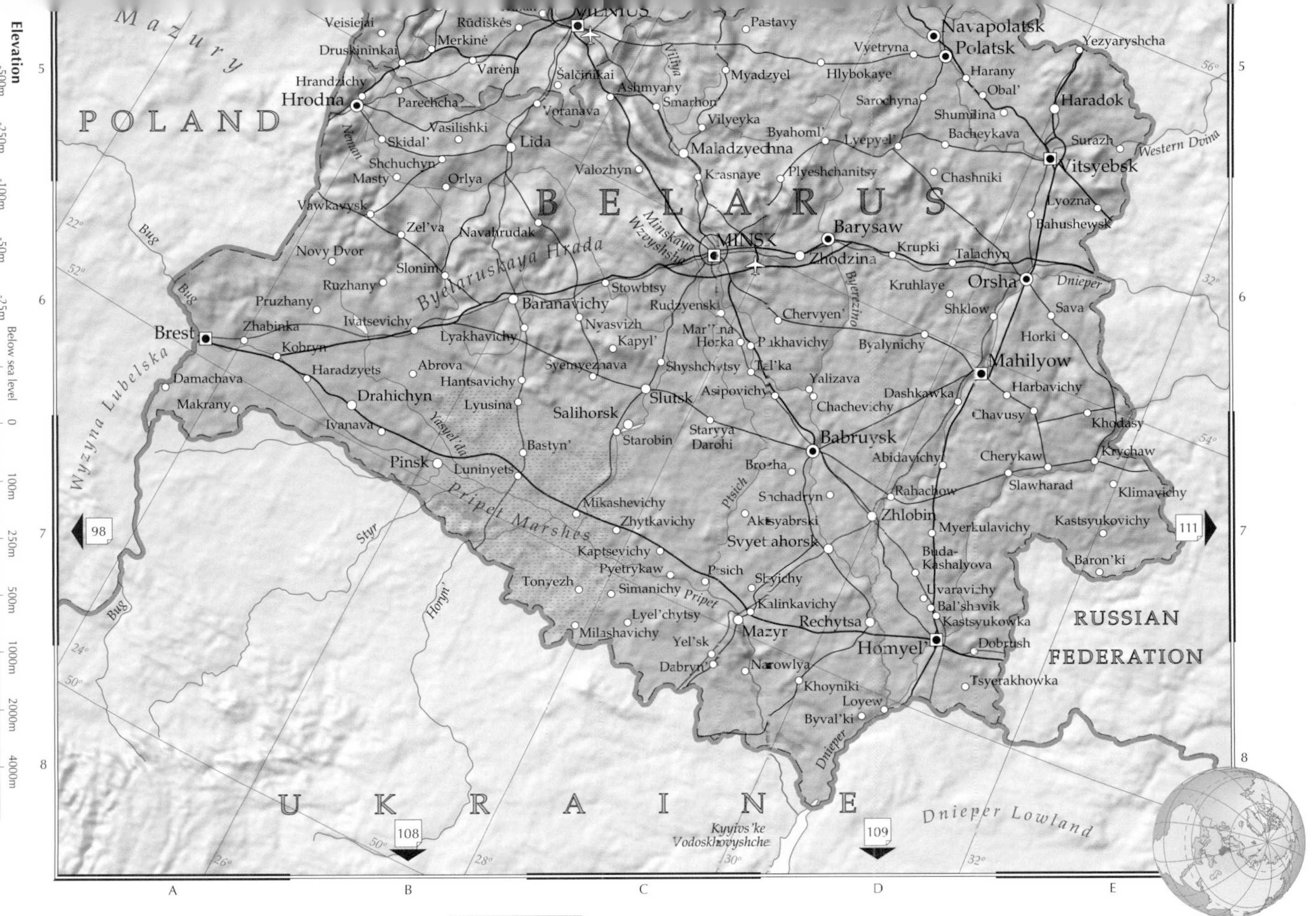

BELARUS
RUSSIAN FEDERATION
UKRAINE
POLAND
Mazury
MINSK
Homyel'
Mahilyow
Vitsyebsk
Hrodna
Brest
Babruysk
Barysaw
Orsha
Pinsk
Mazyr
Baranavichy
Lida
Polatsk
Navapolatsk
Maladzyechna
Salihorsk
Slutsk
Zhlobin
Rechytsa
Svyetlahorsk
Kobryn
Haradok
Drahichyn
Pripet Marshes
Byelaruskaya Hrada
Minskaya Wzvyshsha
Dnieper Lowland
Wyzyna Lubelska
Kyyivs'ke Vodoskhovyshche
Dnieper
Western Dvina
Neman
Pripet
Byerezino
Bug
Horyn'
Styr
Yasyel'da
Viliya
Ptsich
Elevation
Below sea level
-500m
-250m
-100m
-50m
-25m
0
100m
250m
500m
1000m
2000m
4000m
-1640ft
-820ft
-328ft
-164ft
-82ft
33ft/-10m
0
328ft
820ft
1640ft
3281ft
6562ft
13,124ft

Ukraine, Moldova & Romania

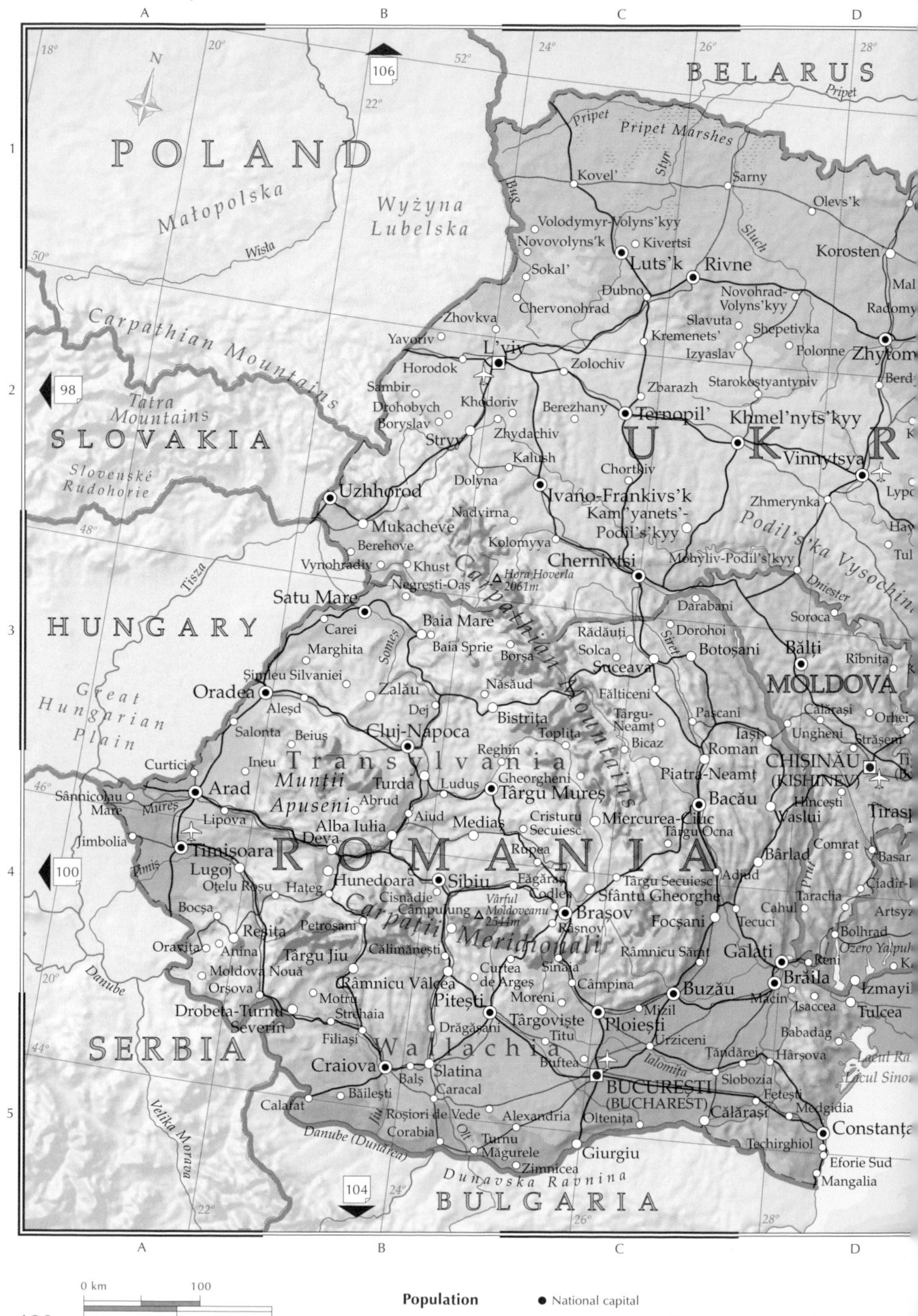

Population ● National capital

○ below 50,000   ◎ 50,000 to 100,000   ◉ 100,000 to 500,000   ■ above 500,00(

0 km   100

0 miles   100

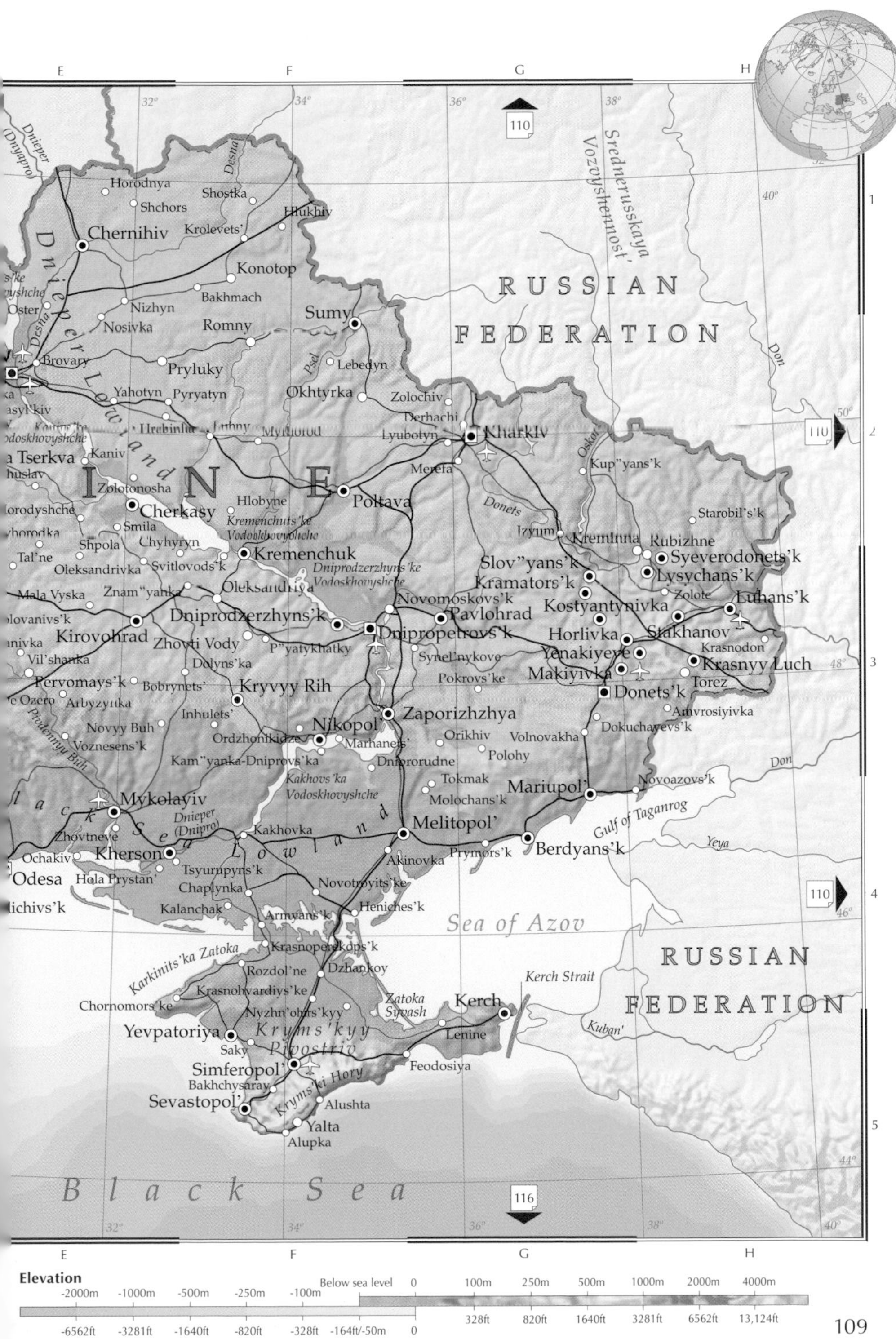

110

E   32°   F   34°   G   36°   38°   H   40°

Dnieper (Dnyapro)

Horodnya
Shchors
Shostka
Hlukhiv
Chernihiv
Krolevets'
Konotop
Nizhyn
Bakhmach
Nosivka
Romny
Sumy
Oster
Brovary
Pryluky
Yahotyn
Pyryatyn
Lebedyn
Psel
Okhtyrka
Zolochiv
Derhachi
Hrebinka
Lubny
Myrhorod
Lyubotyn
Kharkiv
Kup"yans'k

Dnieper Lowland

Tserkva
Kaniv
Zolotonosha
Cherkasy
Hlobyne
Poltava
Donets
Izyum
Kreminna
Starobil's'k
Smila
Chyhyryn
Kremenchuts'ke Vodoskhovyshche
Slov"yans'k
Rubizhne
Syeverodonets'k
Shpola
Svitlovods'k
Kramators'k
Lysychans'k
Znam"yanka
Oleksandriya
Novomoskovs'k
Kostyantynivka
Zolote
Luhans'k
Kirovohrad
Zhovti Vody
Dniprodzerzhyns'k
Pavlohrad
Horlivka
Stakhanov
Vil'shanka
Dolyns'ka
Dnipropetrovs'k
Synel'nykovo
Yenakiyeve
Krasnodon
Pervomays'k
Bobrynets'
Kryvyy Rih
Pokrov's'ke
Makiyivka
Krasnyy Luch
Arbyzynka
Inhulets'
Donets'k
Torez
Novyy Buh
Ordzhonikidze
Marhanets'
Orikhiv
Volnovakha
Dokuchayevs'k
Amvrosiyivka
Voznesens'k
Nikopol
Dniprorudne
Polohy
Novoazovs'k
Kam"yanka-Dniprovs'ka
Zaporizhzhya
Kakhovs'ka Vodoskhovyshche
Tokmak
Mariupol
Gulf of Taganrog
Molochans'k
Dnieper (Dnipro)
Kakhovka
Melitopol'
Mykolayiv
Zhovtneve
Prymors'k
Berdyans'k
Ochakiv
Kherson
Tsyurupyns'k
Akimovka
Odesa
Hola Prystan'
Chaplynka
Novotroyits'ke
Kalanchak
Henichens'k
Armyans'k
Sea of Azov
Krasnoperekops'k
Rozdol'ne
Dzhankoy
Chornomors'ke
Krasnohvardiys'ke
Zatoka Syvash
Nyzhn'ohirs'kyy
Kerch
Kerch Strait
Yevpatoriya
Kryms'kyy Pivostriv
Lenine
Kuban'
Saky
Simferopol'
Feodosiya
Bakhchysaray
Kryms'ki Hory
Sevastopol'
Alushta
Yalta
Alupka

Black Sea

RUSSIAN FEDERATION

Srednerusskaya Vozvyshennost'

Don

RUSSIAN FEDERATION

116

European Russia

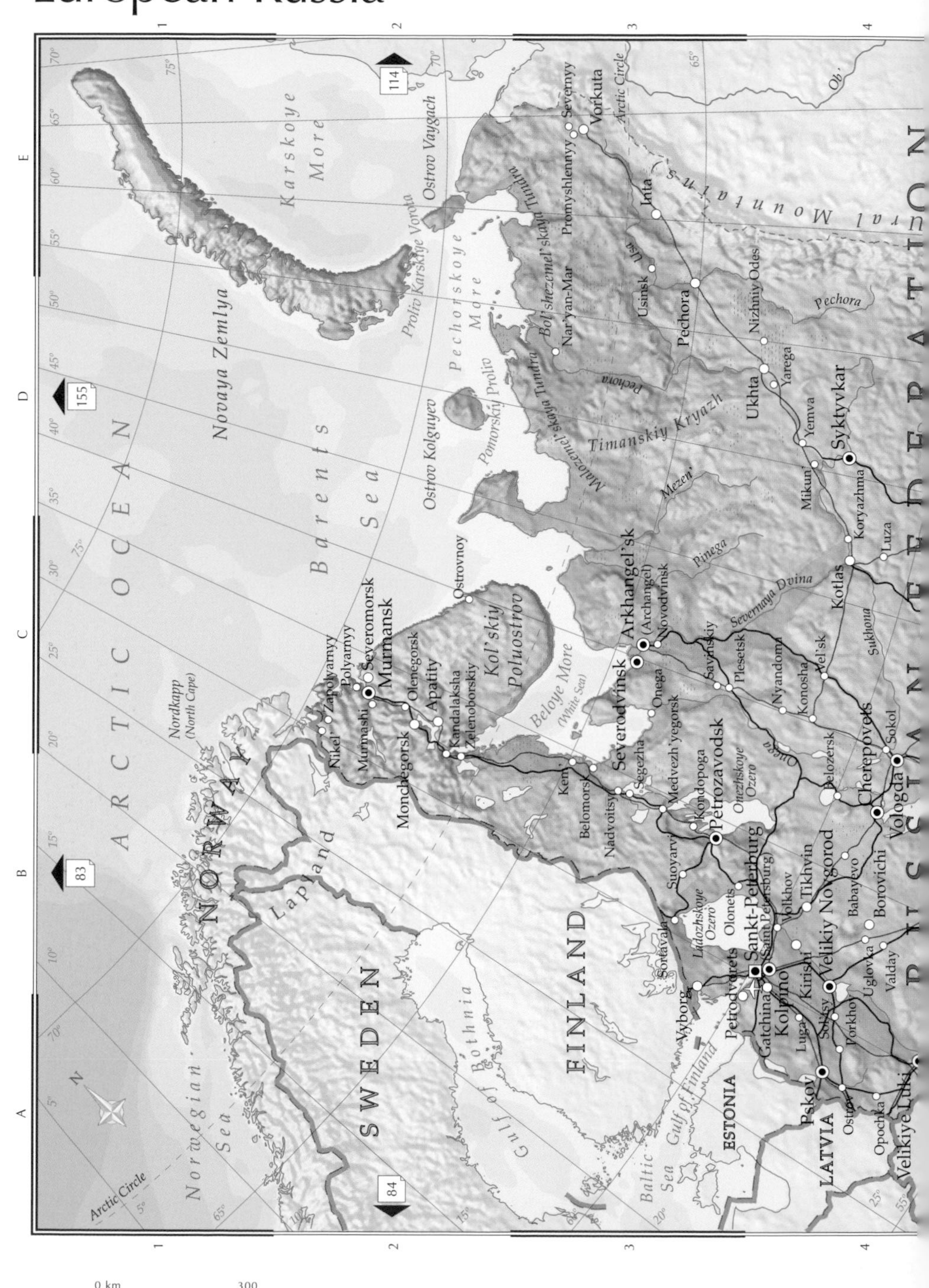

Population

● National capital

○ below 50,000   ◎ 50,000 to 100,000   ◉ 100,000 to 500,000   ◼ above 500,000

0 km   300

0 miles   300

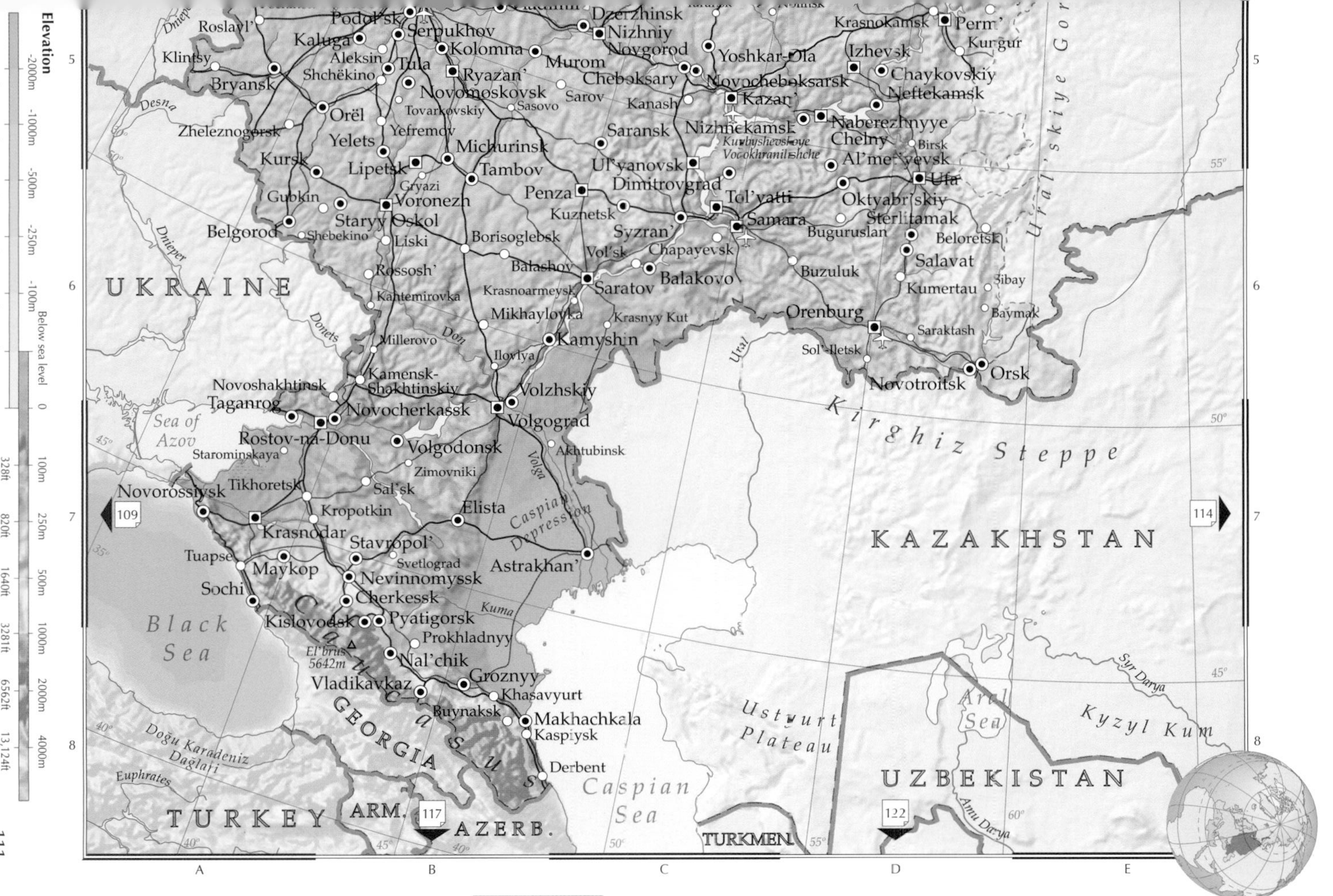

Elevation

-2000m	-1000m	-500m	-250m	-100m	Below sea level	0	100m	250m	500m	1000m	2000m	4000m
-6562ft	-3281ft	-1640ft	-820ft	-328ft	-164ft/-50m	0	328ft	820ft	1640ft	3281ft	6562ft	13,124ft

North & West Asia

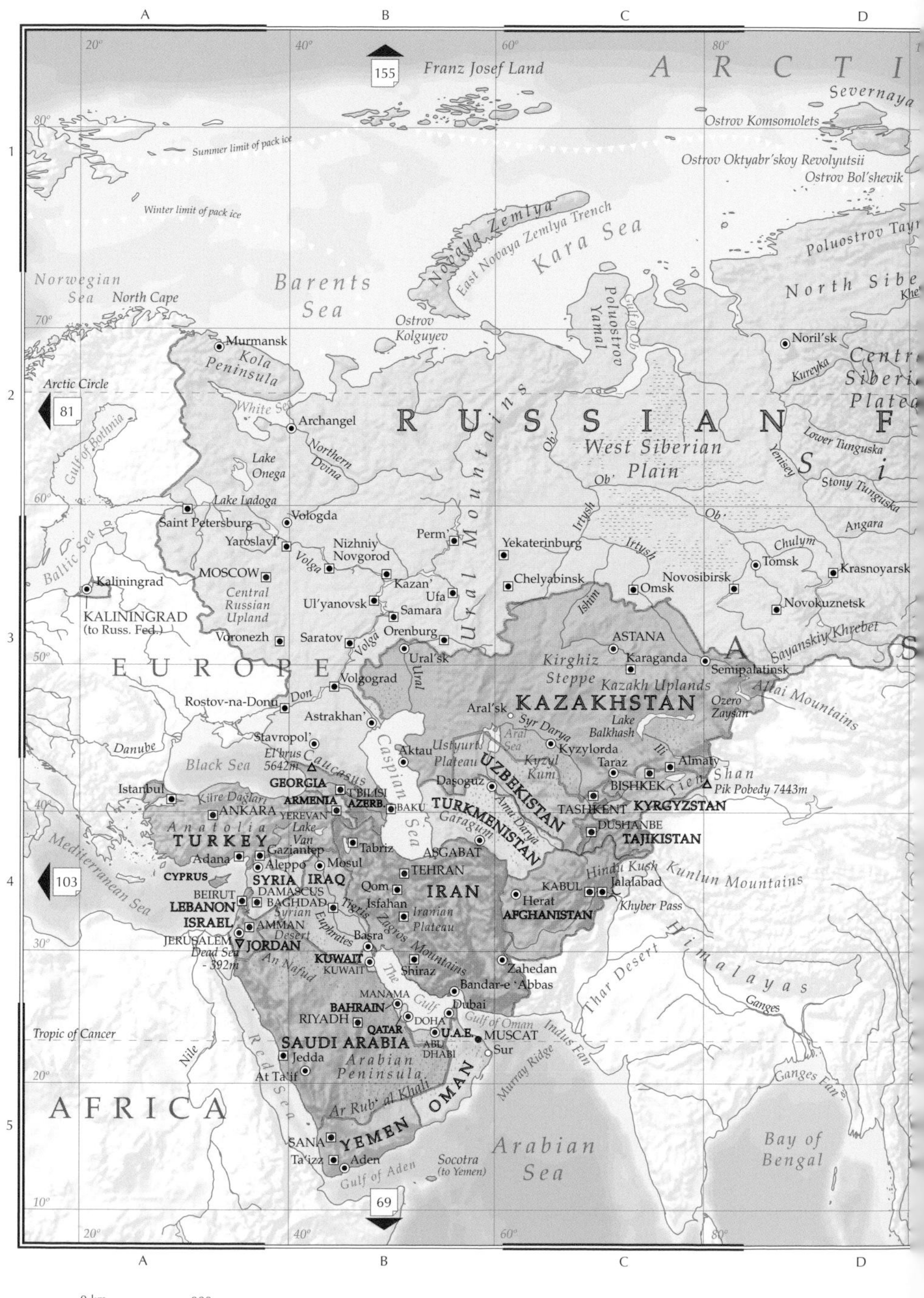

NORTH & WEST ASIA

155

Franz Josef Land

A R C T I

Severnaya

Ostrov Komsomolets

Ostrov Oktyabr'skoy Revolyutsii

Ostrov Bol'shevik

Poluostrov Tayr

Novaya Zemlya

East Nobaya Zemlya Trench

Kara Sea

North Sibe

Khe

Norwegian Sea   *North Cape*

Barents Sea

Ostrov Kolguyev

Noril'sk

Centr

Siberia

Platea

Kureyka

Murmansk

Kola Peninsula

White Sea

Poluostrov Yamal

81

Arctic Circle

Archangel

R U S S I A N   F

West Siberian Plain

S

i

Lower Tunguska

Northern Dvina

Stony Tunguska

Ob'

Angara

Lake Onega

Lake Ladoga

Vologda

Perm

Yekaterinburg

Chulym

Tomsk

Krasnoyarsk

Saint Petersburg

Yaroslavl

Nizhniy Novgorod

Irtysh

Omsk

Novosibirsk

Sayanskiy Khrebet

Novokuznetsk

MOSCOW

Volga

Kazan'

Ufa

Chelyabinsk

Ishim

KALININGRAD

Kaliningrad

Central Russian Upland

Ul'yanovsk

Samara

Orenburg

ASTANA

Karaganda

Semipalatinsk

A

S

(to Russ. Fed.)

Voronezh

Saratov

Ural'sk

Kirghiz Steppe

Kazakh Uplands

Altai Mountains

E U R O P E

Volgograd

Ural

KAZAKHSTAN

Ozero Zaysan

Rostov-na-Donu

Don

Astrakhan'

Aral'sk

Syr Darya

Lake Balkhash

Danube

Stavropol'

El'brus 5642m

Caucasus

Black Sea

Caspian Sea

Aktau

Ustyurt Plateau

Aral Sea

Kyzyl Kum

Kyzylorda

Taraz

Ili

Almaty

Istanbul

Kıbrıs Dağları

GEORGIA

Daşoguz

UZBEKISTAN

Anna Darya

BISHKEK

Shan

Pik Pobedy 7443m

ANKARA

Anatolia

ARMENIA

AZERB.

TBILISI

BAKU

TURKMENISTAN

Garagum

TASHKENT

KYRGYZSTAN

103

TURKEY

Lake Van

Tabriz

AŞGABAT

DUSHANBE

TAJIKISTAN

Adana

Gaziantep

Aleppo

Mosul

CYPRUS

SYRIA

IRAQ

TEHRAN

Hindu Kush

Kunlun Mountains

BEIRUT

LEBANON

DAMASCUS

BAGHDAD

Qom

IRAN

KABUL

Jalalabad

ISRAEL

Syrian Desert

Isfahan

Herat

AFGHANISTAN

Khyber Pass

AMMAN

Euphrates

Tigris

Iranian Plateau

H

JERUSALEM

Dead Sea -392m

JORDAN

Basra

Zahedan

i

m

KUWAIT

Shiraz

Bandar-e 'Abbas

a

KUWAIT

The Gulf

Thar Desert

l

Tropic of Cancer

BAHRAIN

MANAMA

Dubai

a

QATAR

DOHA

U.A.E.

MUSCAT

y

RIYADH

SAUDI ARABIA

ABU DHABI

Sur

OMAN

Gulf of Oman

a

Murray Ridge

Indus Fan

Ganges

Jedda

Arabian Peninsula

Ganges Fan

A F R I C A

Nile

At Ta'if

Ar Rub' al Khali

Arabian Sea

Bay of Bengal

Red Sea

YEMEN

SANA

Ta'izz

Aden

Socotra (to Yemen)

Gulf of Aden

69

Summer limit of pack ice

Winter limit of pack ice

Gulf of Bothnia

Baltic Sea

Kırkheim Dağları

Mediterranean Sea

---

0 km 800

0 miles 800

Population   • National capital

○ below 50,000   ⊙ 50,000 to 100,000   ◉ 100,000 to 500,000   ◼ above 500,000

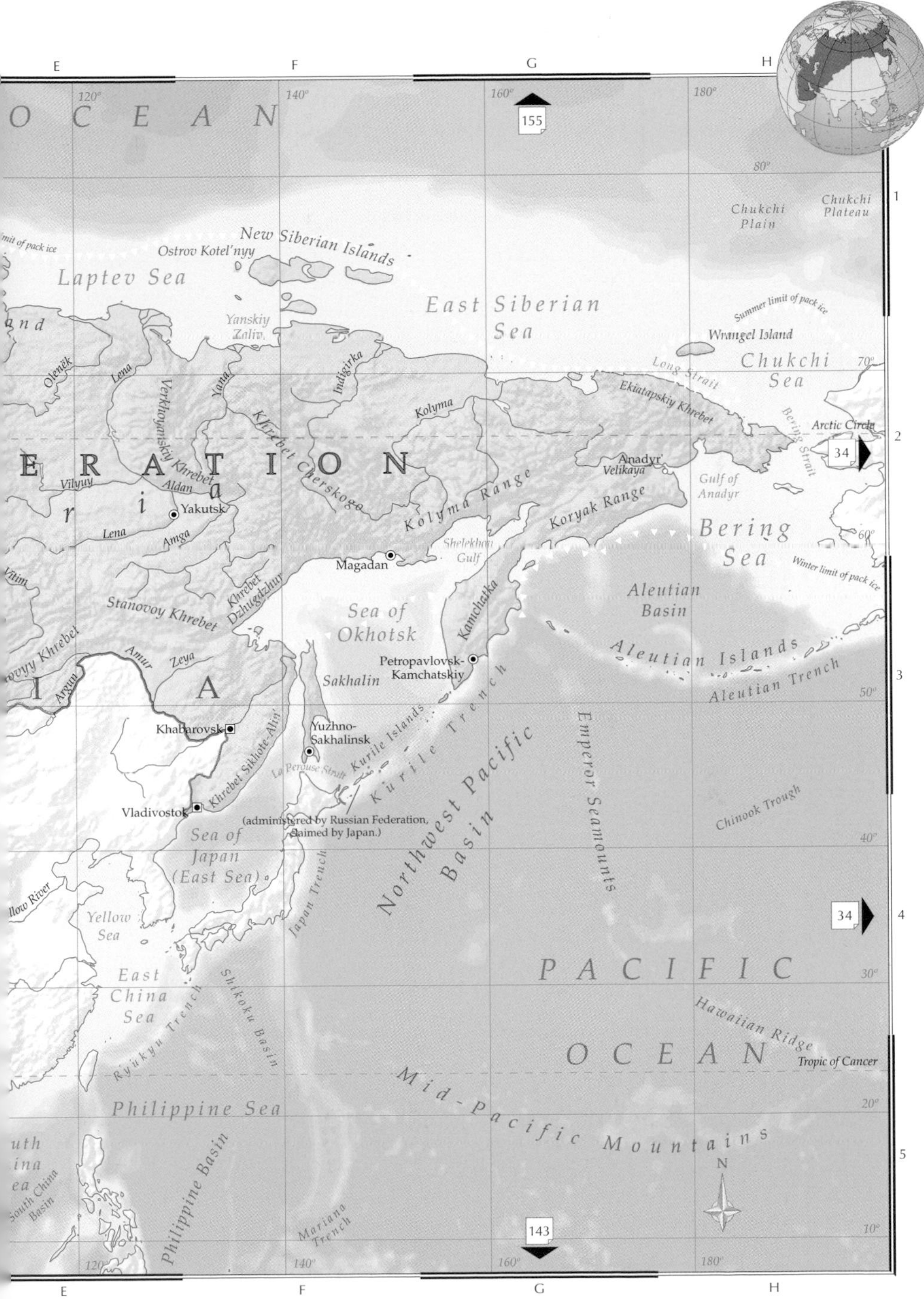

E   F   G   H

120°   140°   160°   180°

O C E A N

155

80°

Chukchi
Plain

Chukchi
Plateau

1

limit of pack ice

New Siberian Islands

Ostrov Kotel'nyy

Laptev Sea

East Siberian
Sea

Yanskiy
Zaliv

Wrangel Island

Summer limit of pack ice

70°

Chukchi
Sea

Indigirka

Long Strait

Olenëk

Lena

Verkhoyanskiy Khrebet

Yana

Kolyma

Ekiatapskiy Khrebet

Bering Strait

Arctic Circle

E R A T I O N

Khrebet Cherskogo

Kolyma Range

Anadyr
Velikaya

34

2

Vilyuy

Aldan

Koryak Range

Gulf of
Anadyr

60°

r i

Yakutsk

Winter limit of pack ice

Lena

Amga

Shelekhov
Gulf

Bering
Sea

Stanovoy Khrebet

Magadan

Kamchatka

Aleutian
Basin

Vtim

Khrebet Dzhugdzhur

Sea of
Okhotsk

Aleutian Islands

3

50°

A

Amur

Zeya

Petropavlovsk-
Kamchatskiy

Aleutian Trench

vvyy Khrebet

Sakhalin

Kurile Trench

Argun

Khabarovsk

Yuzhno-
Sakhalinsk

Khrebet Sikhote-Alin'

Kurile Islands

Northwest Pacific
Basin

Emperor Seamounts

Chinook Trough

40°

Vladivostok

La Perouse Strait

(administered by Russian Federation,
claimed by Japan.)

Japan Trench

34

4

Sea of
Japan
(East Sea)

30°

llow River

Yellow
Sea

PACIFIC

Hawaiian Ridge

Tropic of Cancer

East
China
Sea

Shikoku Basin

O C E A N

Ryukyu Trench

Mid-Pacific Mountains

20°

Philippine Sea

Philippine Basin

N

5

uth
ina
ea

South China
Basin

Mariana
Trench

143

10°

E   F   G   H

Russia & Kazakhstan

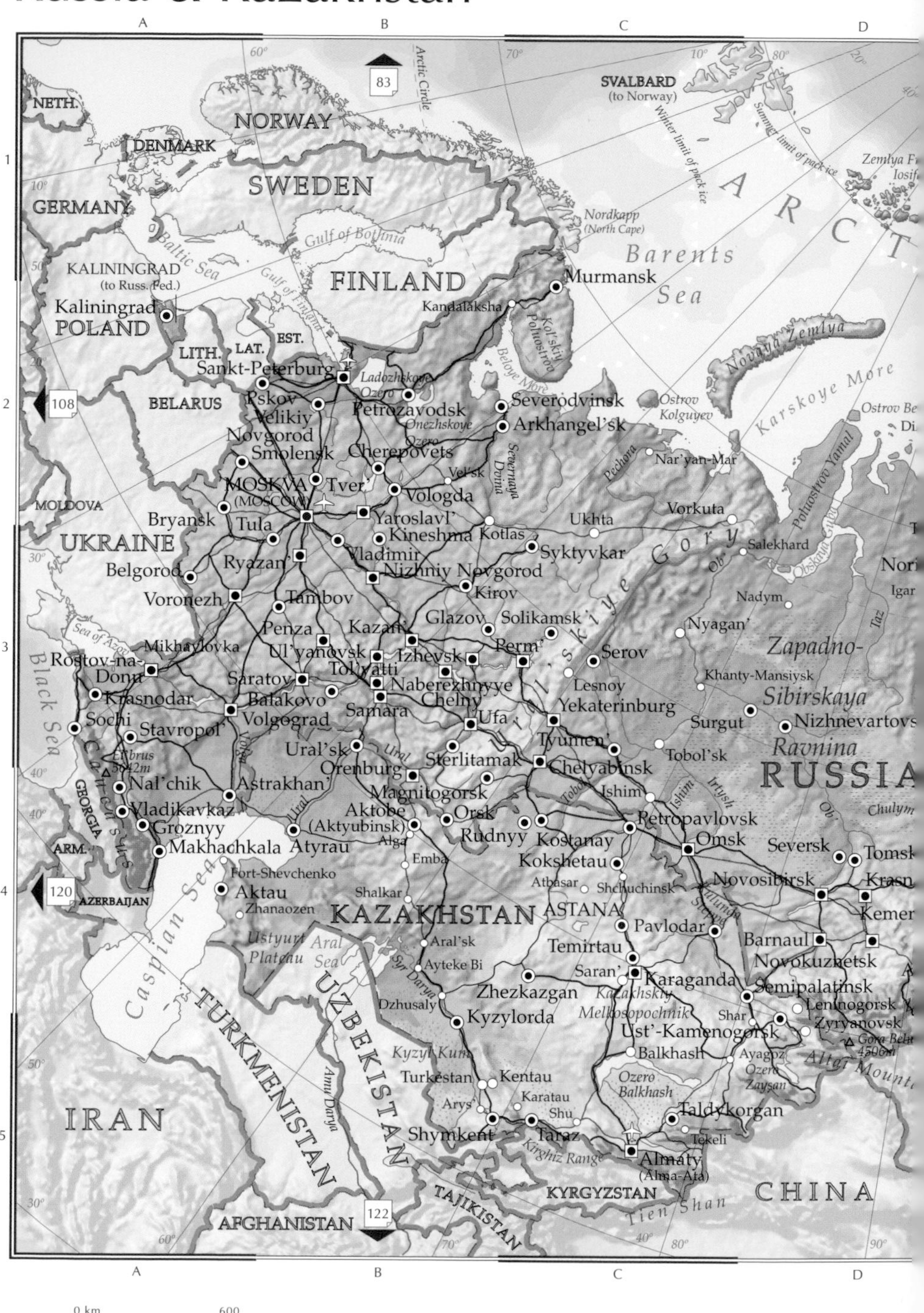

NETH.

DENMARK

NORWAY

SWEDEN

GERMANY

Baltic Sea

KALININGRAD
(to Russ. Fed.)

Kaliningrad
POLAND

LITH. LAT. EST.

BELARUS

Gulf of Bothnia

FINLAND

Gulf of Finland

Sankt-Peterburg

Pskov
Velikiy
Novgorod

Ladozhkoye
Ozero

Smolensk   Cherepovets

MOSKVA   Tver'
(MOSCOW)

Petrozavodsk

Onezhskoye

Vel'sk

Vologda

Murmansk

Kandalaksha

Nordkapp
(North Cape)

Barents
Sea

SVALBARD
(to Norway)

Winter limit of pack ice

Zemlya F
Iosif

Novaya Zemlya

ARCT

Ostrov Be
Di

Karskoye More

Severodvinsk

Arkhangel'sk

Ostrov
Kolguyev

MOLDOVA

UKRAINE

Bryansk   Tula

Belgorod

Voronezh

Ryazan'

Yaroslavl'

Kineshma   Kotlas

Vladimir

Nizhniy Novgorod

Tambov   Kirov

Glazov   Solikamsk

Syktyvkar

Ukhta

Nar'yan-Mar

Pechora

Severnaya Dvina

Beloye More

Kol'skiy
Poluostrov

Vorkuta

Salekhard

Nadym

Nyagan'

Vel'sk

Igar

Nori

Zapadno-

Sibirskaya

Sea of Azov

Black Sea

Rostov-na-
Donu

Krasnodar

Sochi

Mikhaylovka

Penza   Kazan'

Ul'yanovsk   Izhevsk

Tol'yatti

Saratov

Balakovo

Volgograd

Samara

Naberezhnyye
Chelny

Ufa

Perm'

Serov

Lesnoy

Yekaterinburg

Khanty-Mansiysk

Surgut

Nizhnevartovsk

Ravnina

RUSSIA

GEORGIA

Elbrus
5642m

Nal'chik

Vladikavkaz

Groznyy

Makhachkala   Atyrau

Stavropol

Astrakhan'

Ural'sk

Orenburg

Magnitogorsk

Orsk

Aktobe
(Aktyubinsk)

Sterlitamak

Tyumen'

Chelyabinsk

Ishim

Tobol'sk

Petropavlovsk

Omsk

Seversk

Tomsk

Krasn

Kemer

ARM.

AZERBAIJAN

Caspian Sea

Fort-Shevchenko

Aktau

Zhanaozen

Ustyurt
Plateau

Aral
Sea

Shalkar

Emba

Alga

Rudnyy   Kostanay

Kokshetau

Atbasar

Shuchinsk

Astana

Pavlodar

Novosibirsk

Barnaul

Novokuznetsk

Semipalatinsk

Leninogorsk

Zyryanovsk

KAZAKHSTAN

Ayteke Bi

Dzhusaly

Kyzylorda

Syr Darya

Zhezkazgan

Temirtau

Saran'

Karaganda

Kazakhskiy
Melkosopochnik

Shar

Ust'-Kamenogorsk

Balkhash

Ozero
Balkhash

Ayagoz

Ozero
Zaysan

Gora Belu
4506m

Altai Mount-

TURKMENISTAN

UZBEKISTAN

Kyzyl Kum

Amu Darya

Turkestan

Arys'

Kentau

Karatau

Shu

Shymkent   Taraz

Almaty
(Alma-Ata)

Ozero
Balkhash

Taldykorgan

Tekeli

Kirghiz Range

Tien Shan

IRAN

AFGHANISTAN

TAJIKISTAN

KYRGYZSTAN

CHINA

0 km   600

0 miles   600

Population   ● National capital

○ below 50,000   ◉ 50,000 to 100,000   ⦿ 100,000 to 500,000   ■ above 500,00

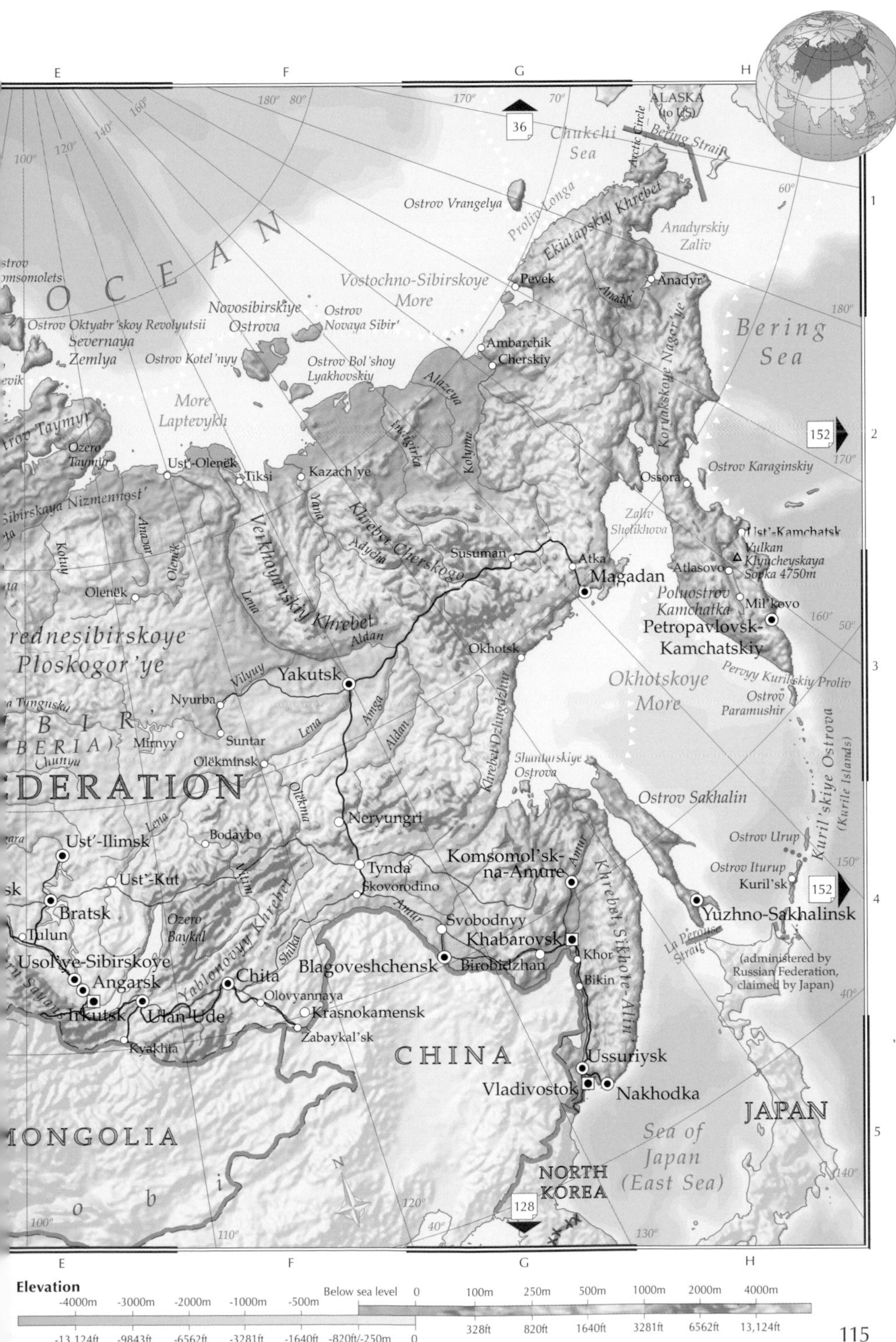

Elevation

-4000m	-3000m	-2000m	-1000m	-500m	Below sea level	0	100m	250m	500m	1000m	2000m	4000m
-13,124ft	-9843ft	-6562ft	-3281ft	-1640ft	-820ft/-250m	0	328ft	820ft	1640ft	3281ft	6562ft	13,124ft

Turkey & the Caucasus

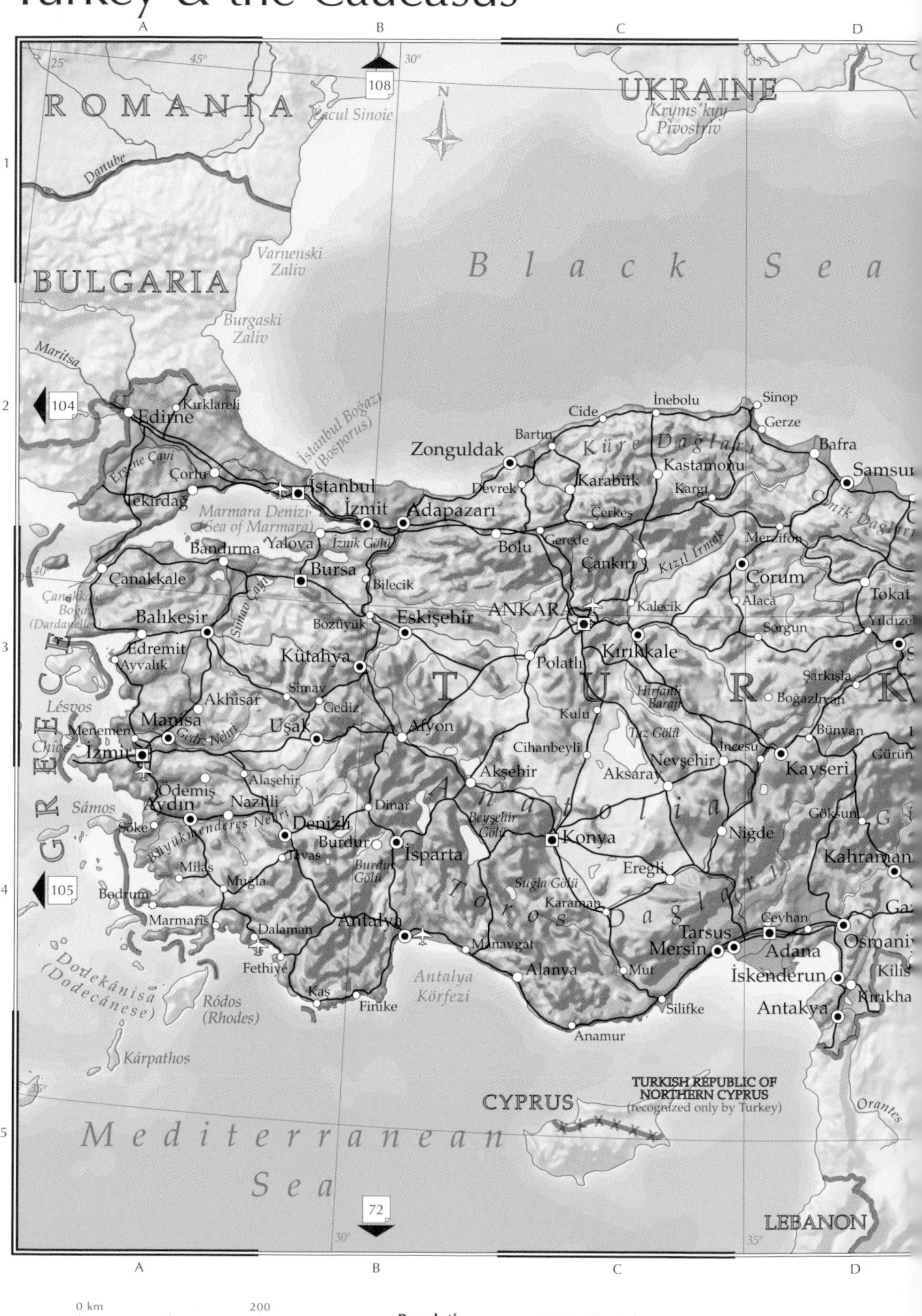

ROMANIA

108

UKRAINE
Krym's'kyy
Pivostriv

BULGARIA

Varnenski
Zaliv

B l a c k   S e a

Burgaski
Zaliv

104
Edirne
Kırklareli

Maritsa

Ergene Çayı
Çorlu
Tekirdağ

İstanbul Boğazı
(Bosporus)

Zonguldak
Cide
İnebolu
Sinop
Gerze
Bartın
Küre Dağları
Kastamonu
Karabük
Kargı
Bafra
Samsun

İstanbul
İzmit
Adapazarı
Devrek
Çerkeş
Merzifon
Canik Dağları

Marmara Denizi
(Sea of Marmara)
Yalova
İznik Gölü
Gerede
Çankırı
Kızıl Irmak
Çorum
Tokat

Çanakkale
Bandırma
Bursa
Bilecik
Bolu
Kalecik
Alaca
Sorgun
Yıldız

Çanakkale
Boğazı
(Dardanelles)

Balıkesir
Bozüyük
Eskişehir
ANKARA
Kırıkkale
Şarkışla
Boğazlıyan

Edremit
Ayvalık
Kütahya
Polatlı
Hirfanlı
Barajı
Bünyan
Gürün

Lésvos
Akhisar
Simav
Gediz
Kulu
Tuz Gölü
Nevşehir
İncesu
Kayseri

Chíos
Menemen
Manisa
Uşak
Afyon
Cihanbeyli
Aksaray
Göksun

İzmir
Alaşehir
Akşehir
Niğde
Kahraman

Ödemiş
Aydın
Nazilli
Dinar
Beyşehir
Gölü
Konya

Sámos
Söke
Büyük Menderes
Denizli
Burdur
Isparta
Ereğli

Milas
Tavas
Burdur
Gölü
Suğla Gölü
Karaman
Tarsus
Ceyhan
Adana
Osmani

Bodrum
Muğla
Antalya
Manavgat
Mut
Mersin
İskenderun
Kilis

Marmaris
Dalaman
Alanya
Silifke
Antakya
Kırıkha

Dodekánisa
(Dodecánese)

Fethiye
Kaş
Finike
Antalya
Körfezi
Anamur

Ródos
(Rhodes)

Kárpathos

TURKISH REPUBLIC OF
NORTHERN CYPRUS
(recognized only by Turkey)

CYPRUS

Orontes

M e d i t e r r a n e a n

S e a

72

LEBANON

Population		National capital
○ below 50,000		●
○ 50,000 to 100,000	◉ 100,000 to 500,000	■ above 500,000

0 km   200
0 miles   200

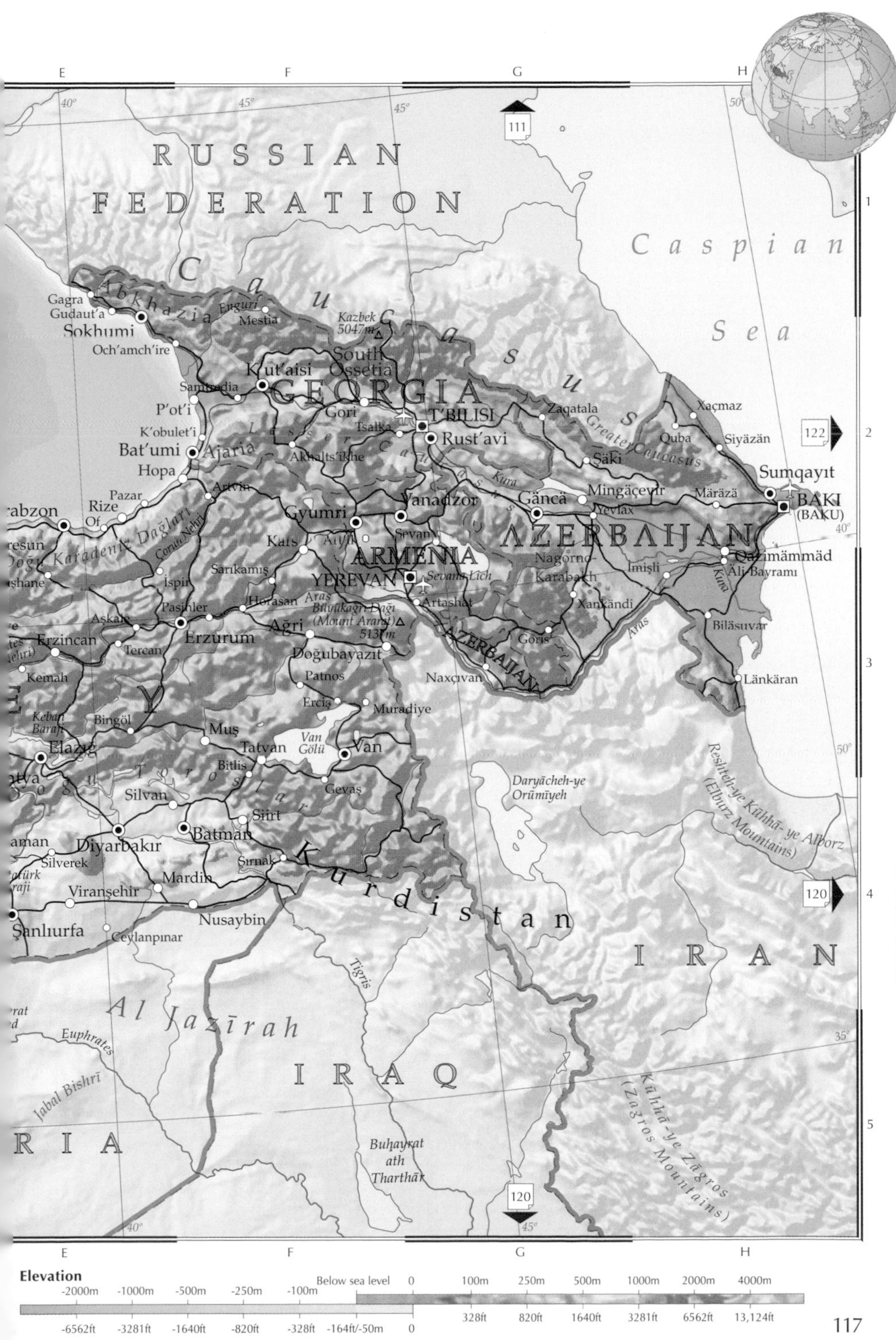

RUSSIAN

FEDERATION

Caspian

Sea

Gagra
Gudaut'a
Sokhumi
Och'amch'ire
Enguri
Mesha
Kazbek
5047m
Kut'aisi
South
Ossetia
Samtredia
C a u c a s u s
Abkhazia
GEORGIA
Gori
Tsalka
T'BILISI
Zaqatala
Xaçmaz
P'ot'i
K'obulet'i
Bat'umi
Ajaria
Hopa
Akhaltsikhe
Rust'avi
Quba
Siyäzän
Greater Caucasus
Säki
Pazar
Rize
Of
Artvin
Gyumri
Vanadzor
Gäncä
Mingäçevir
Märäzä
Sumqayıt
Trabzon
Gümüşhane
Giresun
Doğu Karadeniz Dağları
Çoruh Nehri
İspir
Kars
Ani
Sevan
ARMENIA
YEREVAN
Sevana Lich
Nagorno
Karabakh
İmişli
BAKI
(BAKU)
Qazimämmäd
Äli Bayramı
Sarıkamış
Askale
Pasinler
Horasan
Aras
Büyükağrı Dağı
(Mount Ararat)
5137m
Artashat
Xankändi
Goris
Biläsuvar
Reşteh-ye Kühhā-ye Alborz
(Elburz Mountains)
Erzincan
Tercan
Erzurum
Ağrı
Doğubayazıt
Patnos
Naxçıvan
AZERBAIJAN
Länkäran
Kemah
Kebanı
Barajı
Bingöl
Muş
Erciş
Muradiye
Aras
Elazığ
Silvan
Tatvan
Bitlis
Van
Gölü
Van
Gevaş
Daryācheh-ye
Orūmīyeh
Diyarbakır
Batman
Siirt
Şırnak
Kurdistan
Tigris
IRAN
Silverek
Mardin
Viranşehir
Nusaybin
Ceylanpınar
Şanlıurfa
Al Jazīrah
Euphrates
Jabal Bishrī
IRAQ
Buhayrat
ath
Tharthār
Kūhhā-ye Zāgros
(Zagros Mountains)

120

Elevation

-2000m	-1000m	-500m	-250m	-100m	Below sea level	0	100m	250m	500m	1000m	2000m	4000m
-6562ft	-3281ft	-1640ft	-820ft	-328ft	-164ft/-50m	0	328ft	820ft	1640ft	3281ft	6562ft	13,124ft

The Near East

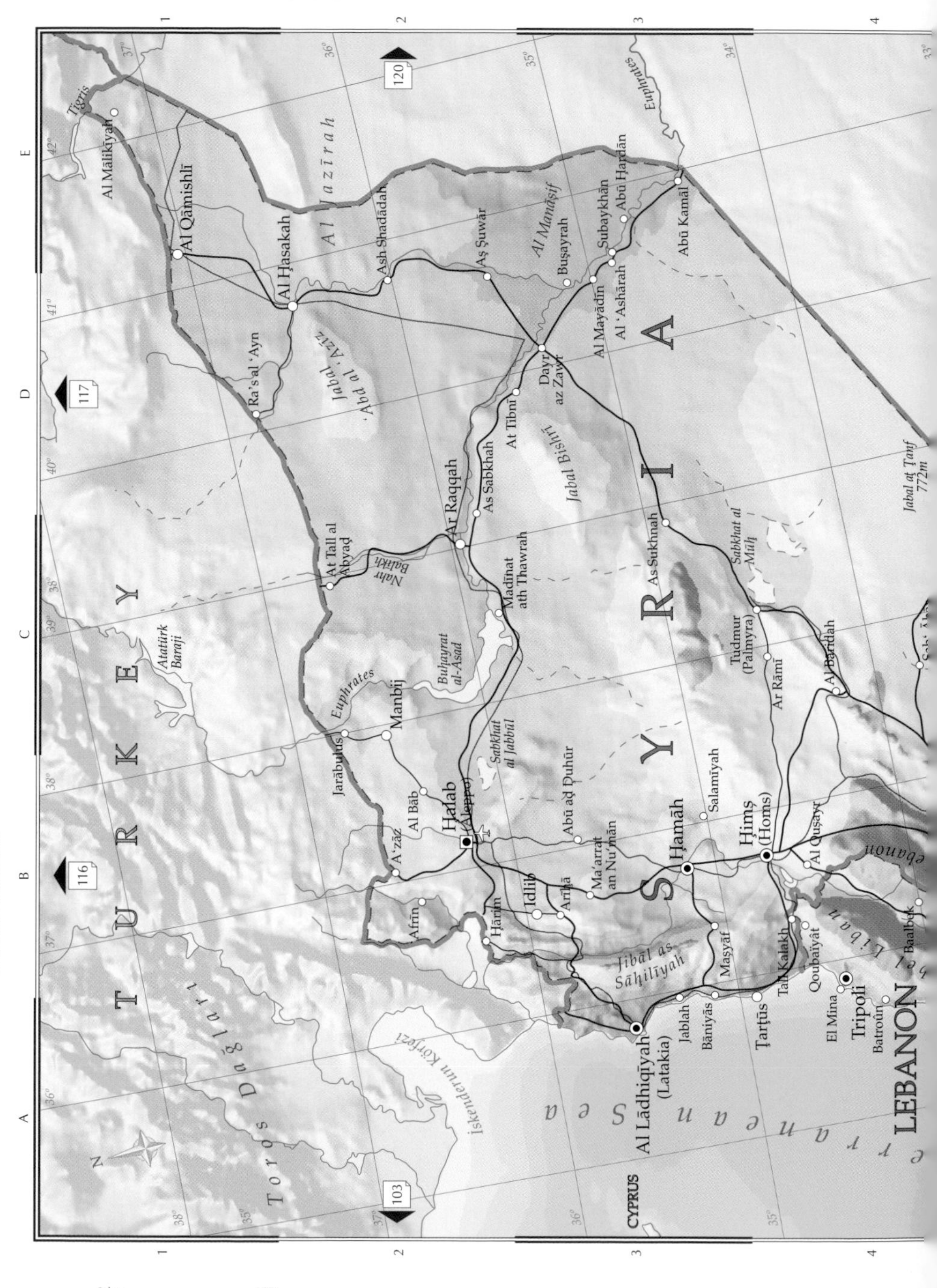

Population

- ● National capital
- ○ below 50,000
- ◎ 50,000 to 100,000
- ◉ 100,000 to 500,000
- ■ above 500,000

0 km   100

0 miles   100

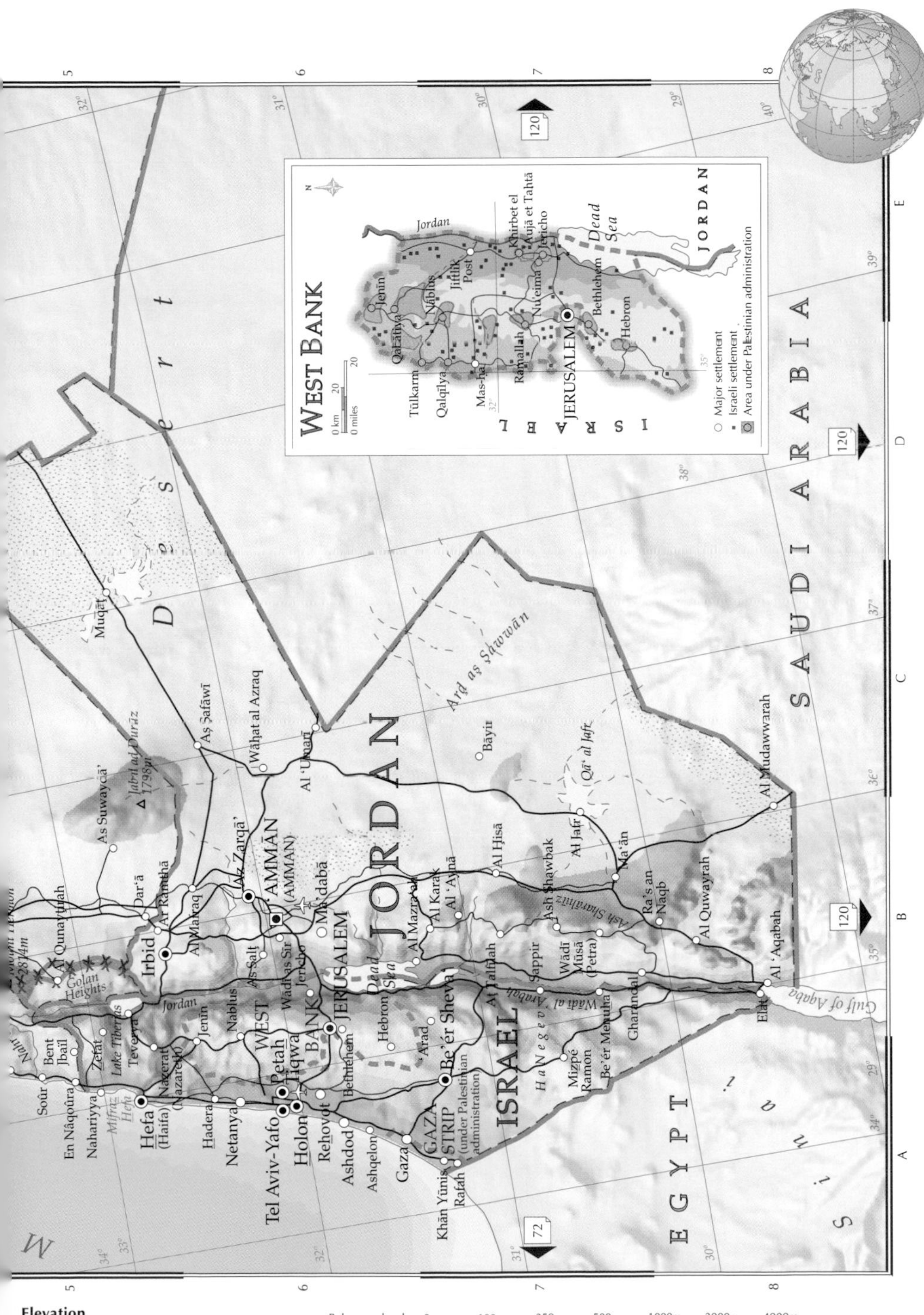

WEST BANK

N

Jordan

Khirbet el 'Aúja et Tahtā
Jenin
Qalqīlya
Nāblus
Jiftlik Post
Nūeima Jericho
Dead Sea
Ramallah
Bethlehem
JERUSALEM
Hebron
Māsha
Tūlkarm
Qalqīlya
Māsha
Nūeima

JORDAN

0 km   20
0 miles   20

ISRAEL

○ Major settlement
■ Israeli settlement
◎ Area under Palestinian administration

JORDAN

ISRAEL

EGYPT

SAUDI ARABIA

Desert

Muqāt

As Şafāwī
Wāhat al Azraq
Al 'Umarī

Jafr al Purāz
△ 1795m

Arḍ as Shawān

Bāyir

Qā' al Jafr

Al Mudawwarah

As Suwaycā'

Darā
Ar Ramthā
Az Zarqā'
AMMĀN
(AMMAN)
Mādabā

Al 'Ubaid
Al Ḥisā
Al Fajr
Maʻān

Irbid
Al Maffraq
As Salt
Wādi's Sir
Jericho
JERUSALEM
Al Mazra'a
Al Karak
Al 'Ajnā
Ash Shawbak
Ash Sharāhit
Ka'ś an Nāqb
Al Quwayrah

Bent
Ibail
At Qunayṭrah
△ 2814m
Golan
Heights
Sappir
Wādi Mūsā
(Petra)
Al 'Aqabah

Soûr
Naharīyya
En Nāqoûra
Zefat
Lake Tiberias
Nazerat
(Nazareth)
Jenin
Nāblus
Tevorya
WEST
BANK
Wādi's Sir
Hebron
At Ṭafīlah
Wādi al 'Arabah
Ghranād
Elat
Gulf of Aqaba

Hefa
(Haifa)
Hadera
Netanya
Petah
Tiqwa
Holon
Rehovot
Ashdod
Ashqelon
Gaza
Khān Yūnis
Rafah
Tel Aviv-Yafo
GAZA
STRIP
(under Palestinian administration)
Bethlehem
Atad
Be'er Sheva'
HaNegev
Mizpé
Ramon
Be'er Menuha

ISRAEL

Sinai

Elevation

-2000m	-1000m	-500m	-250m	-100m	Below sea level 0	100m	250m	500m	1000m	2000m	4000m
-6562ft	-3281ft	-1640ft	-820ft	-328ft	-164ft/-50m 0	328ft	820ft	1640ft	3281ft	6562ft	13,124ft

The Middle East

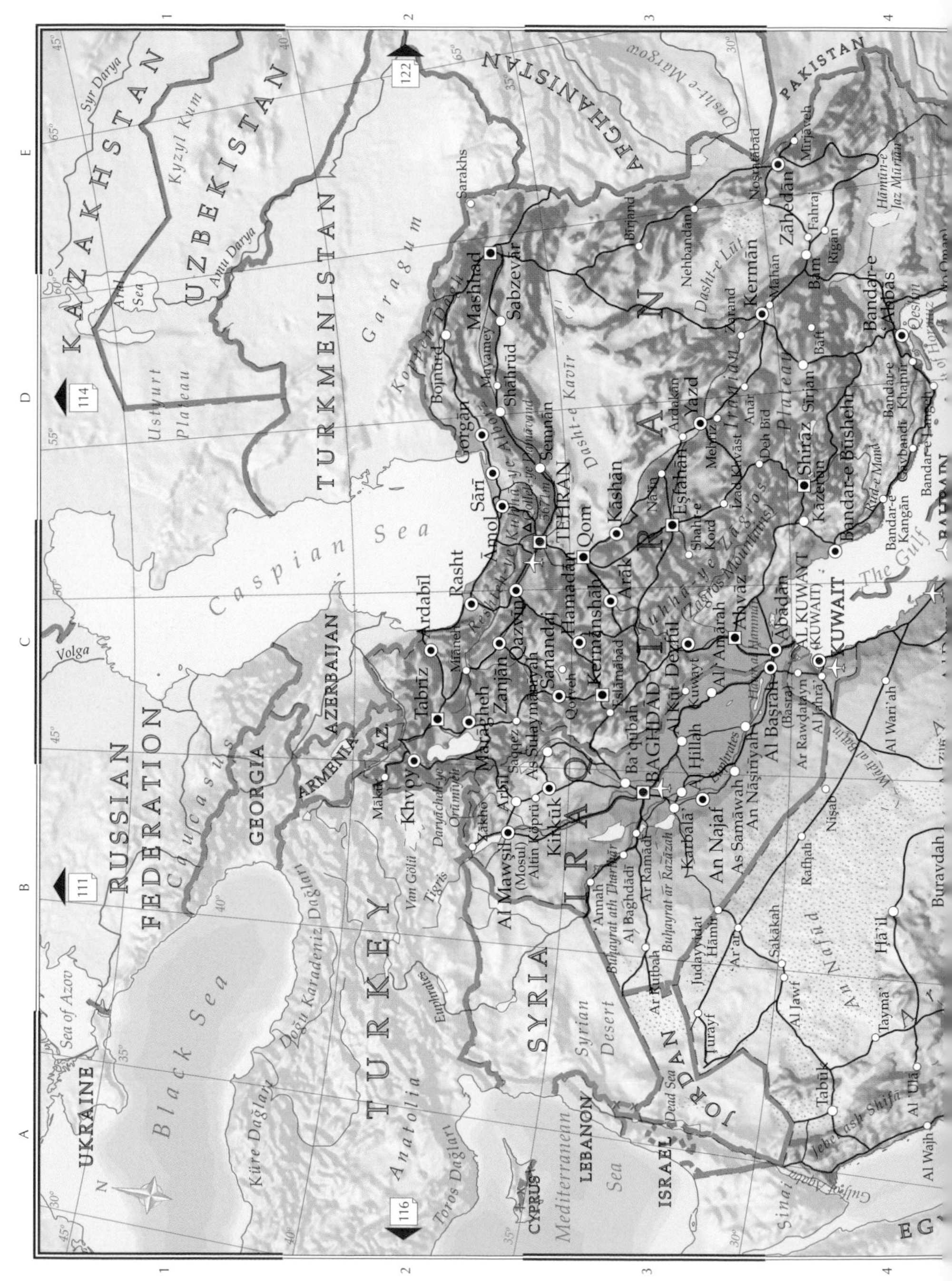

0 km 400

0 miles 400

Population   • National capital

○ below 50,000   ⊙ 50,000 to 100,000   ◉ 100,000 to 500,000   ■ above 500,000

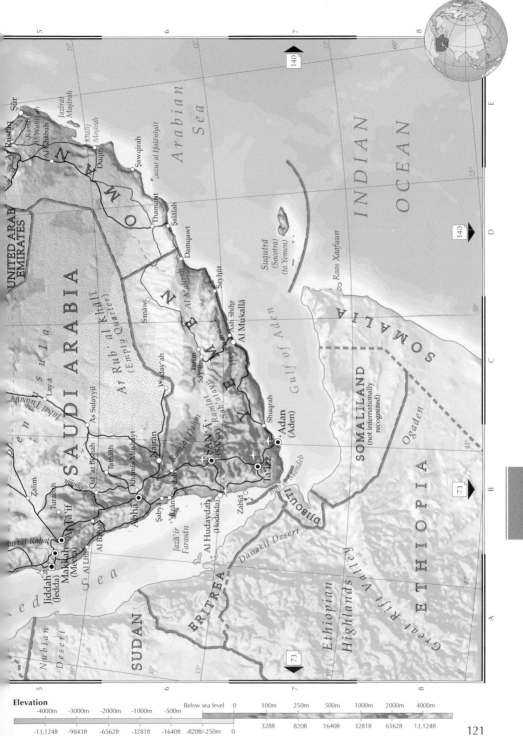

Sūr
Ra's al Ḥadd
Al Kāmil
Al Ashkharah
Jazīrat Maṣīrah
Khalīj Maṣīrah
Ramlat Al Wahībah
Duqm
Ṣawqirah
Jazirat al Ḥalāniyāt
Thamarīt
Salālah
Damqawt
Sayhūt
Smāw
Al Mahrah
Ash Shiḥr
Al Mukallā
Tarīm
Ḥurayḍah
Sayʾūn
Ḥuṣn al ʿAbr
Shuqrah
Zabīd
Adan (Aden)
Taʿizz

Arabian Sea
INDIAN OCEAN
Suqutrā (Socotra) (to Yemen)
Ras Xaafuun
Gulf of Aden
SOMALIA
SOMALILAND (not internationally recognized)
Ogaden

UNITED ARAB EMIRATES
SAUDI ARABIA
O M A N
Y E M E N
Ar Rubʿ al Khālī (Empty Quarter)
Ramlat Dahm
Ramlat as Sabʿatayn

Jabal Tuwayq
Layā
As Sudayyil
As Sulayyil
Najrān
Tathlīth
Khamīs Mushayṭ
Qalʿat Bīshah
Wādī Ḥaḍramawt
Wādīʾah
SANʿĀ (SANA)

Zālim
Turabāh
Aṭ-Ṭāʾif
Ḥarrat Rahat
Makkah (Mecca)
Al Līth
Jiddah (Jedda)
Nubian Desert
Red Sea
Abhā
Al Baḥāʾ
Ṣabyā
 Najrān
ʿAnam Jaydah
Jazāʾir Farasān
Al Hudaydah (Hodeida)

DJIBOUTI
Bāb el-Mandeb
Danakil Desert
ERITREA
SUDAN
ETHIOPIA
Ethiopian Highlands
Great Rift Valley

Elevation

					Below sea level	0	100m	250m	500m	1000m	2000m	4000m
-4000m	-3000m	-2000m	-1000m	-500m								
-13,124ft	-9843ft	-6562ft	-3281ft	-1640ft	-820ft/-250m	0	328ft	820ft	1640ft	3281ft	6562ft	13,124ft

Central Asia

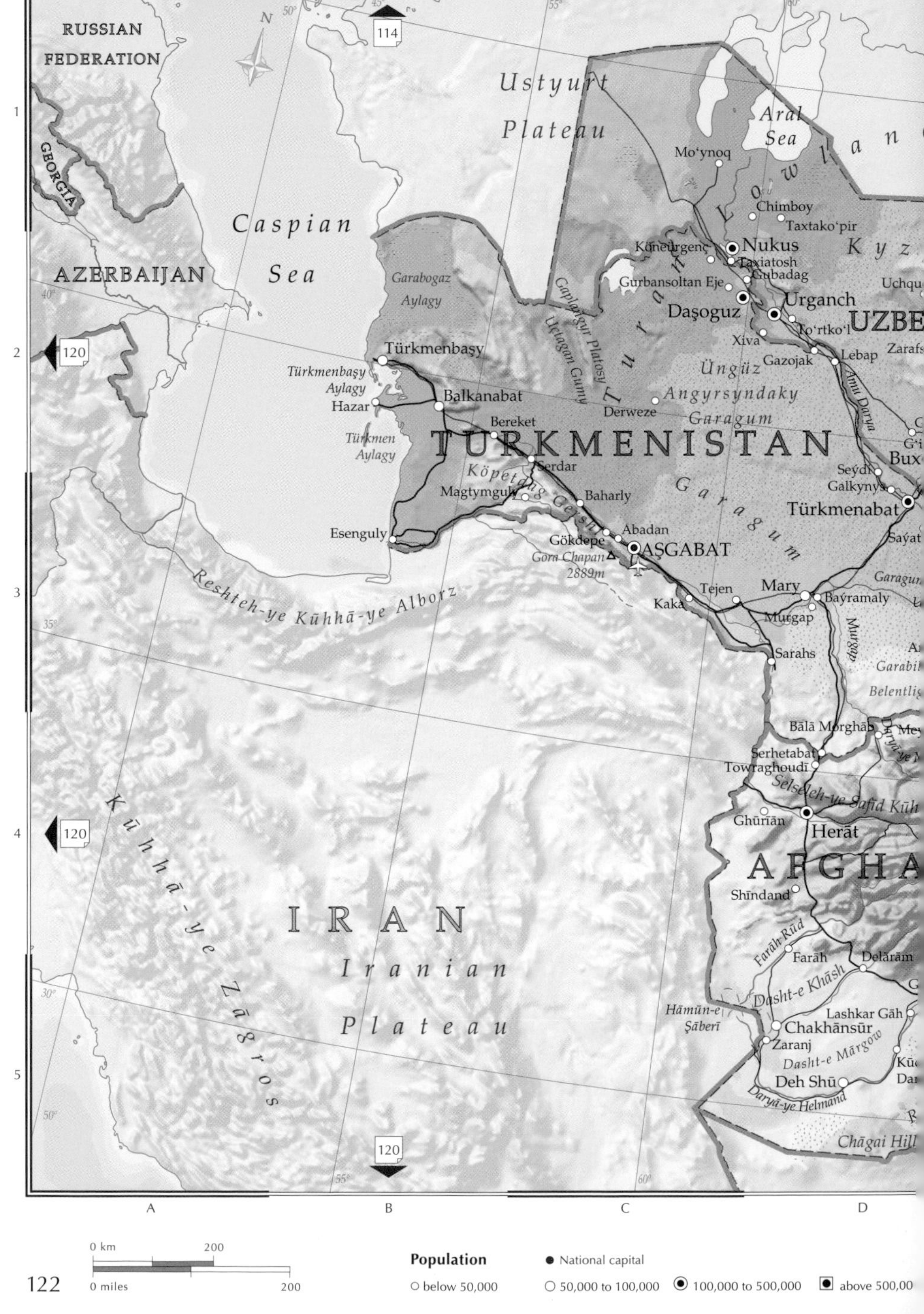

RUSSIAN
FEDERATION

GEORGIA

AZERBAIJAN

Caspian
Sea

*Garabogaz
Aylagy*

Ustyurt
Plateau

Aral
Sea

Mo'ynoq

Chimboy

Taxtako'pir

Küneürgenç

Taxiatosh

Nukus

Gurbansoltan Eje

Cubadag

Urganch

Soltan Eje

Daşoguz

To'rtko'l

UZBE

Xiva

Gazojak

Lebap

Zarafs

Türkmenbaşy

*Türkmenbaşy
Aylagy*

Hazar

Balkanabat

*Türkmen
Aylagy*

Ganlyşor platosy

Uchtagan Gumy

Derweze

*Üngüz
Angyrsyndaky
Garagum*

Amu Darya

Uchqu

C

G'i

Bux

Bereket

Köpet

Serdar

Magtymguly

Baharly

Esenguly

Gökdepe

Abadan

Gora Chapan △
2889m

Kaka

AŞGABAT

Tejen

Mary

Murgap

Sarahs

Garagum

Seýdi

Galkynys

Türkmenabat

Saýat

Garagu

Bäýramaly

Murgap

TURKMENISTAN

Garagum

Reshteh-ye Kūhhā-ye Alborz

Kūhhā-ye Zāgros

I R A N

*Iranian
Plateau*

Bālā Morghāb

Serhetabat

Towraghoudī

Ghūrīān

Shīndand

Herāt

Selseleh-ye Safid Kūh

*Garabil
Belentliş*

Mey

ye

AFGHA

Farāh Rūd

Farah

Delārām

Dasht-e Khash

*Hāmūn-e
Şāberī*

Zaranj

Chakhānsūr

Lashkar Gāh

Dasht-e Mārgow

Deh Shū

Daryā-ye Helmand

Kü

Dar

Chāgai Hill

0 km   200

0 miles   200

Population   ● National capital

○ below 50,000   ○ 50,000 to 100,000   ◉ 100,000 to 500,000   ◪ above 500,00

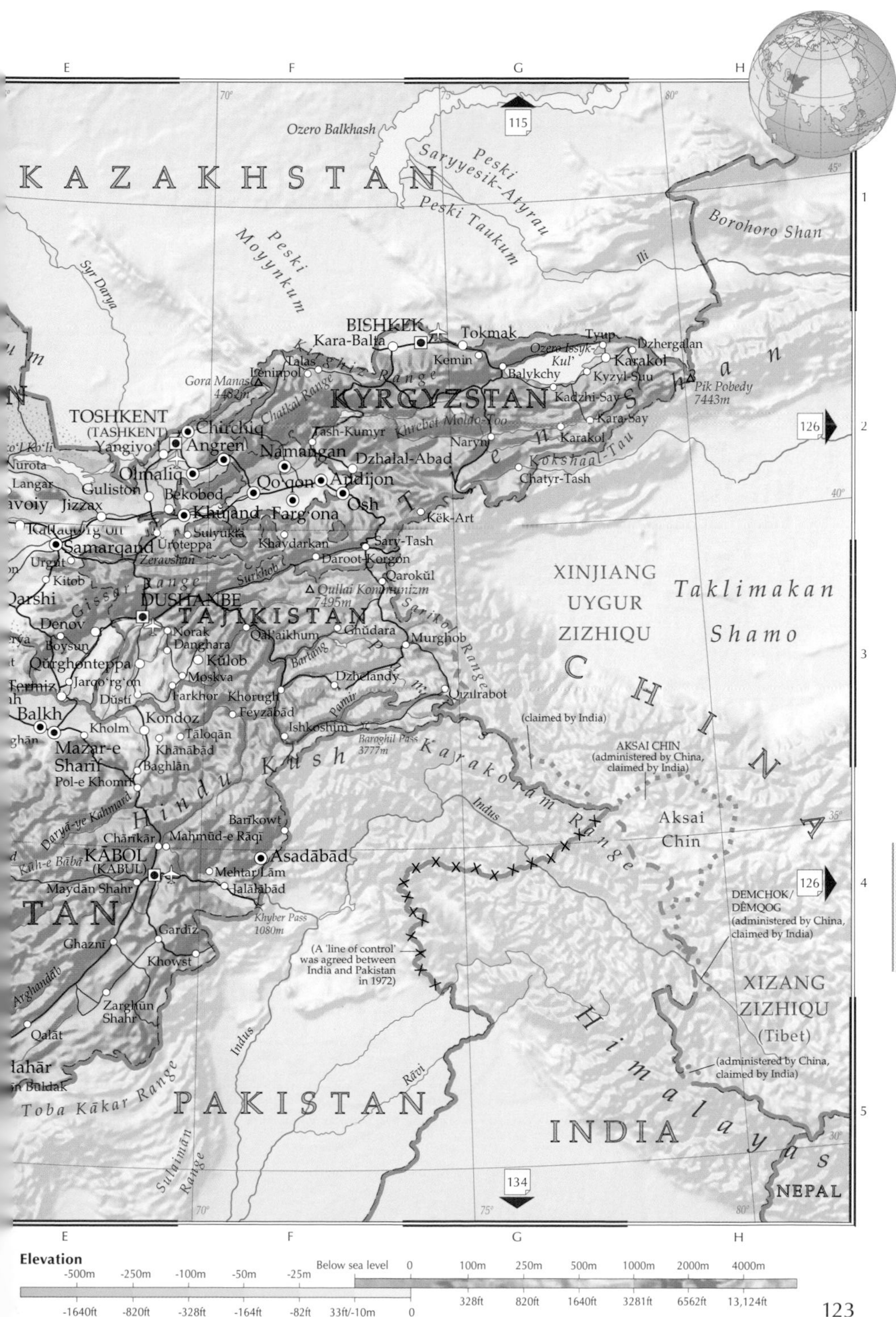

KAZAKHSTAN

Ozero Balkhash

Peski Saryyesik-Atyrau

Peski Taukum

115

Peski Moyynkum

Borohoro Shan

Syr Darya

Ili

BISHKEK

Kara-Balta · Tokmak · Tyup · Dzhergalan

Kara-Balta

126

Gora Manas 4482m

Kemin · Balykchy · Karakol

Izenimpol

Ozero Issyk-Kul'

Kyzyl-Suu

KYRGYZSTAN

Kadzhi-Say

Pik Pobedy 7443m

TOSHKENT
(TASHKENT)

Chirchiq · Kara-Say

Yangiyo'l · Angren

Namangan · Karakol

Kokshaal-Tau

Khrebet Moldo-Too

Olmaliq

Qo'qon · Andijon · Naryn

Bekobod · Osh · Chatyr-Tash

Guliston · Jizzax

Nurota

Langar

Khŭjand · Farg'ona

Samarqand · Uroteppa

Kök-Art

Zeravshan

Khaydarkan

Kitob · Sary-Tash

Daroot-Korgon

XINJIANG
UYGUR
ZIZHIQU

*Taklimakan
Shamo*

DUSHANBE

Qullai Kommunizm 7495m

Qarokŭl

Denov

Gissar Range

TAJIKISTAN

Boysun

Norak · Qakaikhum · Ghŭdara

Danghara

Murghob

Qŭrghonteppa

Kŭlob · Moskva

Dzhelandy

Termiz

Jarqo'rg'on

Qizilrabot

Balkh

Dŭsti · Farkhor · Khorugh

Kondoz · Feyzabad · Ishkoshim

Pamirs

C H I N A

Darya-ye Kŭnduz

Tăloqăn · Khănăbăd

Banghil Pass 3777m

(claimed by India)

AKSAI CHIN
(administered by China,
claimed by India)

Hindu

Mazăr-e
Sharif

Baghlăn

Pol-e Khomri

Kush

Karakoram Range

Indus

Aksai
Chin

126

Barikowt

Chărikăr · Mahmŭd-e Răqi

KABOL
(KABUL)

Asadăbăd

Mehtar Lăm

Maydăn Shahr

Jalălăbăd

DEMCHOK/
DÊMQOG
(administered by China,
claimed by India)

*Khyber Pass
1080m*

TAN

Ghaznĭ

Gardĭz

(A 'line of control'
was agreed between
India and Pakistan
in 1972)

XIZANG
ZIZHIQU
(Tibet)

(administered by China,
claimed by India)

Khowst

Zarghŭn
Shahr

Ayghandăb

Indus

Qalăt

Himalayas

lahăr

n Baldak

Toba Kăkar Range

PAKISTAN

Ravi

INDIA

*Sulaimăn
Range*

134

NEPAL

Elevation

-500m	-250m	-100m	-50m	-25m	Below sea level	0	100m	250m	500m	1000m	2000m	4000m
-1640ft	-820ft	-328ft	-164ft	-82ft	33ft/-10m	0	328ft	820ft	1640ft	3281ft	6562ft	13,124ft

South & East Asia

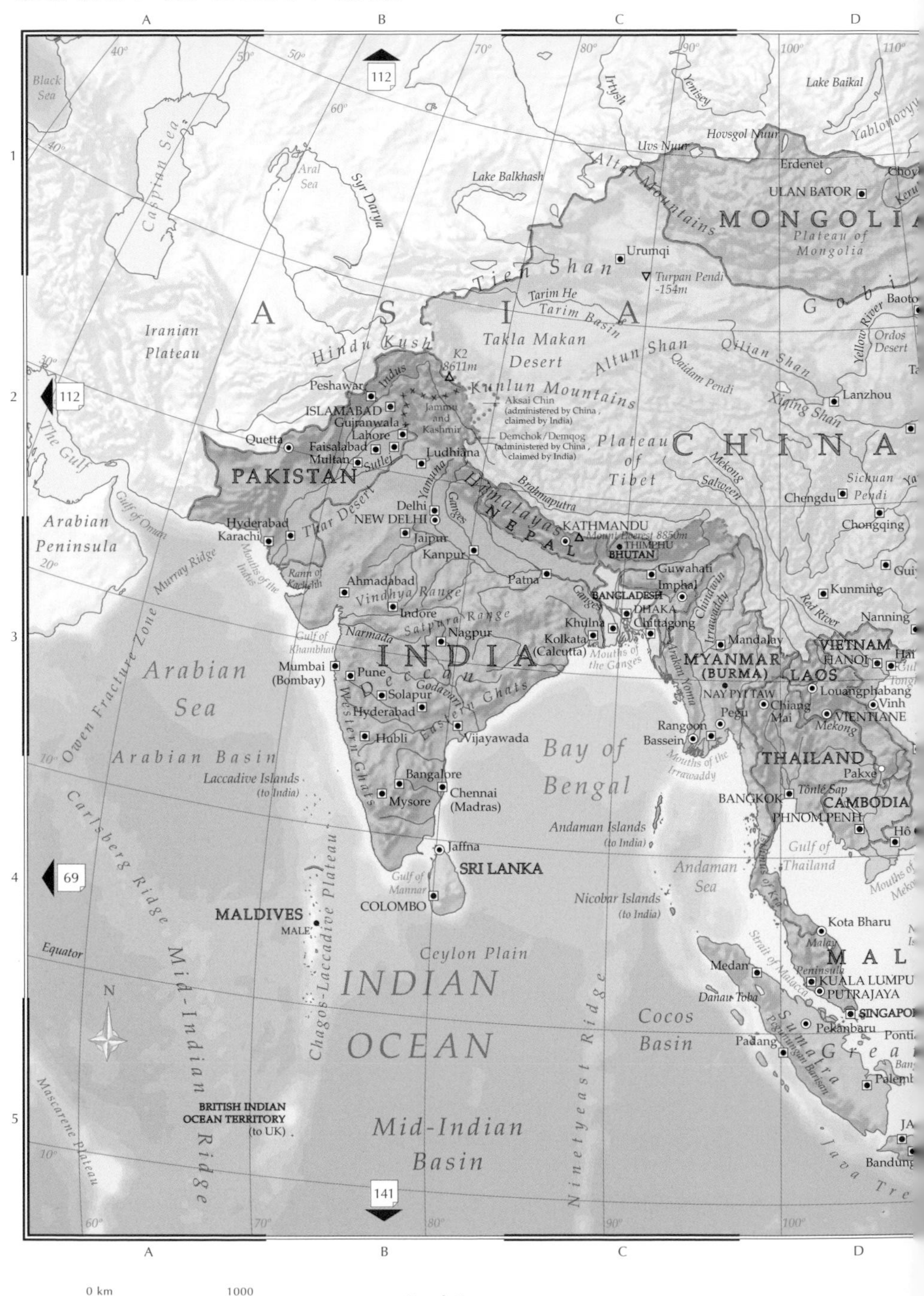

A B C D

Black Sea

40°

50°

70°

80°

90°

100°

110°

60°

Lake Baikal

Irtysh

Yenisey

Yablonovyy

40

Caspian Sea

Aral Sea

Syr Darya

60°

Lake Balkhash

Hovsgol Nuur

Uvs Nuur

Altai Mountains

Erdenet

Choy

ULAN BATOR

1

Iranian Plateau

A   S   I   A

Tien Shan

Urumqi

Plateau of Mongolia

MONGOLIA

Gobi

Baoto

112

Peshawar

Hindu Kush

Tarim He

Tarim Basin

Takla Makan Desert

▽ *Turpan Pendi -154m*

Ordos Desert

Yellow River

Ta

Lanzhou

Xining Shan

K2 8611m

Kunlun Mountains

Altun Shan

Qilian Shan

Chengdu

Sichuan Pendi

2

ISLAMABAD

Gujranwala

Lahore

Quetta

Faisalabad

Multan

Jammu and Kashmir

Aksai Chin (administered by China, claimed by India)

Demchok/Demqog (administered by China, claimed by India)

Qaidam Pendi

Plateau of Tibet

C   H   I   N   A

Chongqing

Indus

Sutlej

PAKISTAN

Ludhiana

Brahmaputra

Mekong

Salween

Gui

Kunming

The Gulf

112

Delhi

Hyderabad

Karachi

NEW DELHI

Jaipur

Ganges

Kanpur

Yamuna

Himalayas

KATHMANDU

NEPAL

Mount Everest 8850m △

THIMPHU

BHUTAN

Guwahati

Imphal

Nanning

VIETNAM

HANOI

Arabian Peninsula

Gulf of Oman

Murray Ridge

Mouths of the Indus

Thar Desert

Rann of Kachchh

Ahmadabad

Vindhya Range

Narmada

Patna

Satpura Range

Ganges

BANGLADESH

DHAKA

Khulna

Chittagong

Kolkata (Calcutta)

Mouths of the Ganges

Mandalay

Chindwin

Irrawaddy

MYANMAR (BURMA)

LAOS

Louangphabang

Vinh

20°

Indore

Nagpur

3

Owen Fracture Zone

Hyderabad

Mumbai (Bombay)

Pune

Solapur

Gulf of Khambhat

Godavari

Deccan

I   N   D   I   A

Western Ghats

Eastern Ghats

Vijayawada

NAY PYI TAW

Pegu

Chiang Mai

VIENTIANE

Mekong

Arabian Sea

Arabian Basin

Hubli

Rangoon

Bassein

Mouths of the Irrawaddy

THAILAND

Pakxe

CAMBODIA

10°

Laccadive Islands (to India)

Bangalore

Mysore

Chennai (Madras)

Bay of Bengal

Andaman Islands (to India)

BANGKOK

PHNOM PENH

Ho

Gulf of

Carlsberg Ridge

Jaffna

Gulf of Mannar

SRI LANKA

Nicobar Islands (to India)

Andaman Sea

Kota Bharu

4

69

MALDIVES

MALE

COLOMBO

Mid-Indian Ridge

Ceylon Plain

INDIAN

OCEAN

Chagos-Laccadive Plateau

Ninetyeast Ridge

Cocos Basin

Medan

Danau Toba

Strait of Malacca

Malay Peninsula

MAL

KUALA LUMPU

PUTRAJAYA

SINGAPOR

Equator

Pekanbaru

Ponti

Gre

Sumatra

N

Macarene Plateau

BRITISH INDIAN OCEAN TERRITORY (to UK)

Mid-Indian Basin

Padang

Barisan

Palemb

Bangi

JA

5

10°

60°

70°

80°

90°

100°

Bandun

Java Tre

A B C D

0 km   1000

0 miles   1000

Population

● National capital

o below 50,000

○ 50,000 to 100,000

◉ 100,000 to 500,000

▪ above 500,000

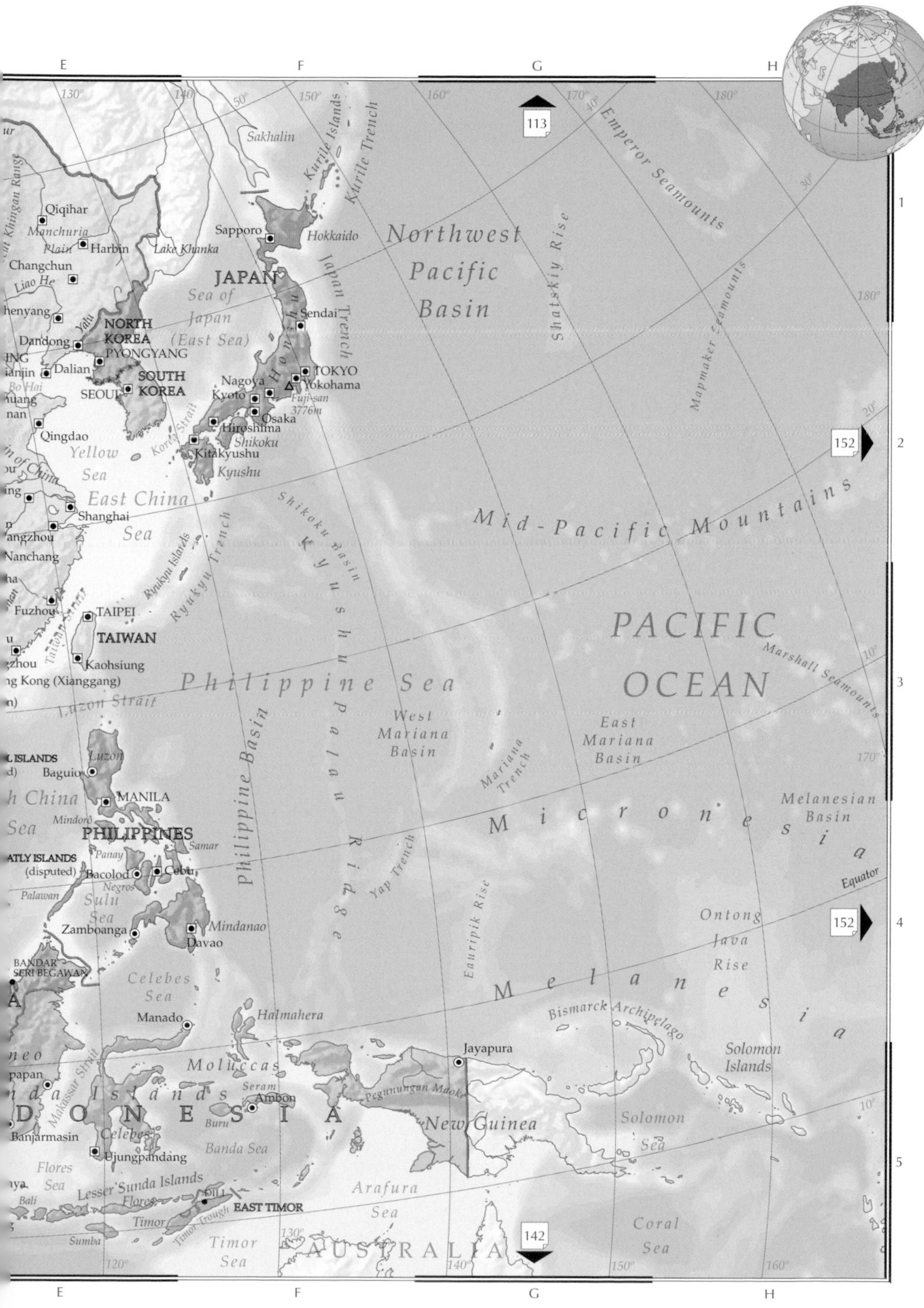

E   F   G   H

130°   140°   50°   150°   160°   40°   170°   180°

Qiqihar
Manchuria   Harbin   Lake Khanka   Sakhalin
Plain
Changchun
Liao He
henyang   NORTH   Hokkaido   *Northwest*
Dandong   KOREA   Sapporo   *Pacific*
NG   PYONGYANG   JAPAN   *Basin*
Dalian   Sea of   Sendai
idnin   SOUTH   Japan
nuan   SEOUL   KOREA   (East Sea)   Kurile Islands
nan   Nagoya   TOKYO   Kurile Trench
Qingdao   Kyoto   Yokohama   Japan Trench
    Osaka   Fujisan   Shatskiy Rise
of   Hiroshima   3776m   Emperor Seamounts
ing   Yellow   Shikoku
    Sea   Kitakyushu
    Kyushu   Honshu
ang hou   Shanghai   East China
Nanchang   Sea   Shikoku Basin   *Mid-Pacific Mountains*
ha   Ryukyu Islands   Mapmaker Seamounts
Fuzhou   TAIPEI   Ryukyu Trench   Kyushu-Palau Ridge   180°
zhou   TAIWAN   *PACIFIC*   20°
ng Kong (Xianggang)   Kaohsiung   *Philippine Sea*   *OCEAN*   Marshall Seamounts
n)   Luzon Strait   10°
L ISLANDS   Luzon   West   East   170°
d)   Baguio   Mariana   Mariana   Melanesian
h China   Basin   Basin   Basin
Sea   MANILA   Mariana Trench
    Mindoro   *Micro n e s*
    PHILIPPINES   Samar   *i a*
ATLY ISLANDS   Panay   Yap Trench   Equator
(disputed)   Bacolod   Cebu   Eauripik Rise
Palawan   Negros
    Sulu   Mindanao   Ontong   152
    Sea   Davao   Java
Zamboanga   Rise
BANDAR
SERI BEGAWAN   Celebes   Halmahera   *M e l a n*
A   Sea   Bismarck Archipelago   *e*
    Manado   Solomon   *s*
neo   Moluccas   Islands   *i*
papan   Islands   Jayapura   *a*
DONESIA   Seram   Solomon
Banjarmasin   Ambon   Pegunungan Maoke   Sea
    Celebes   Buru   *New Guinea*   10°
    Ujungpandang   Banda Sea
Flores   Lesser Sunda Islands
ya   Flores   Arafura
Bali   Timor   Sea   Coral
Sumba   EAST TIMOR   Sea
    Timor Trough   AUSTRALIA
120°   Timor   130°   140°   150°   160°
    Sea

113

152

152

142

E   F   G   H

1

2

3

4

5

Western China & Mongolia

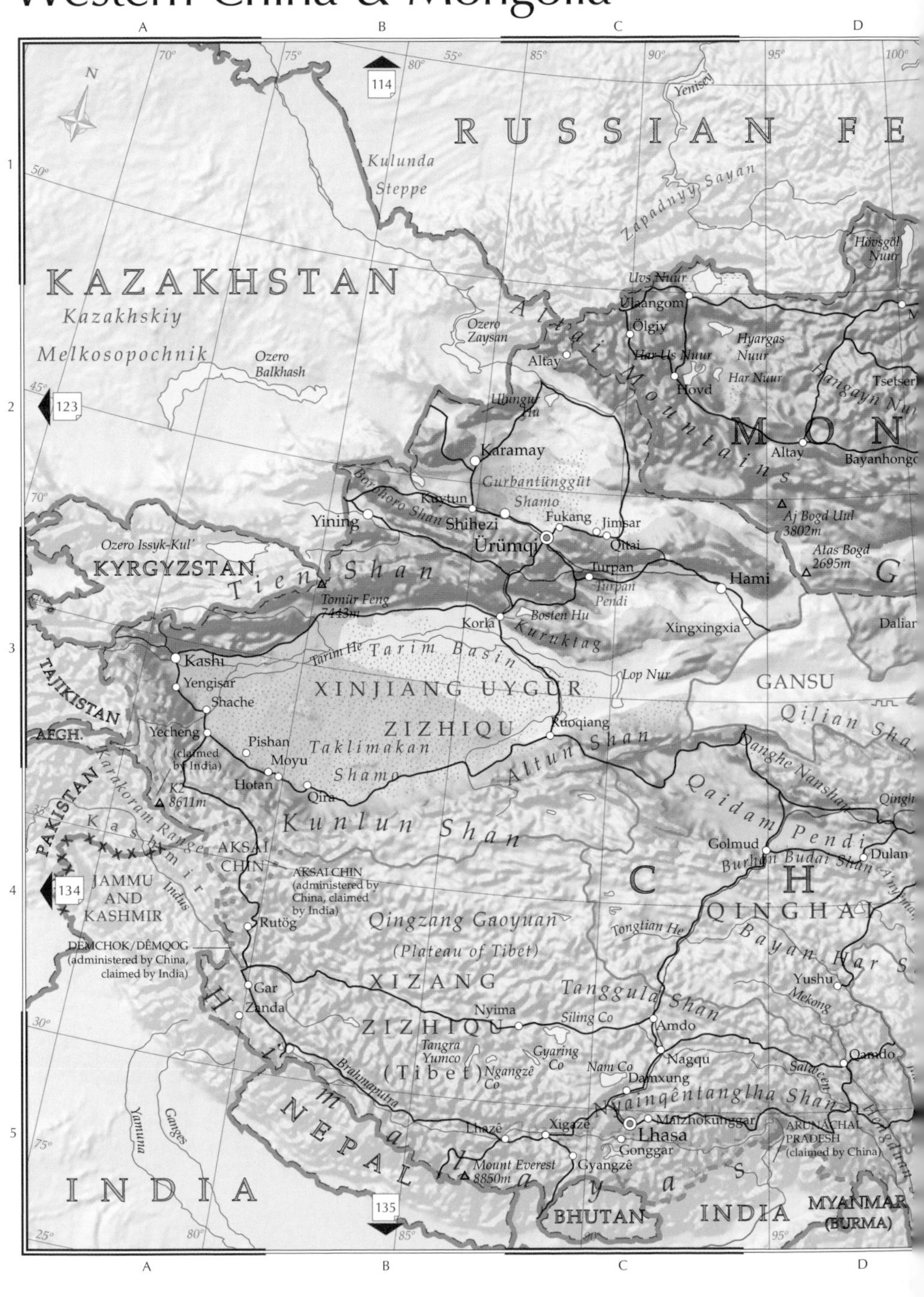

Population

○ below 50,000	
○ 50,000 to 100,000	
◉ 100,000 to 500,000	
◼ above 500,00	

● National capital ● Internal administrative capital

0 km 400
0 miles 400

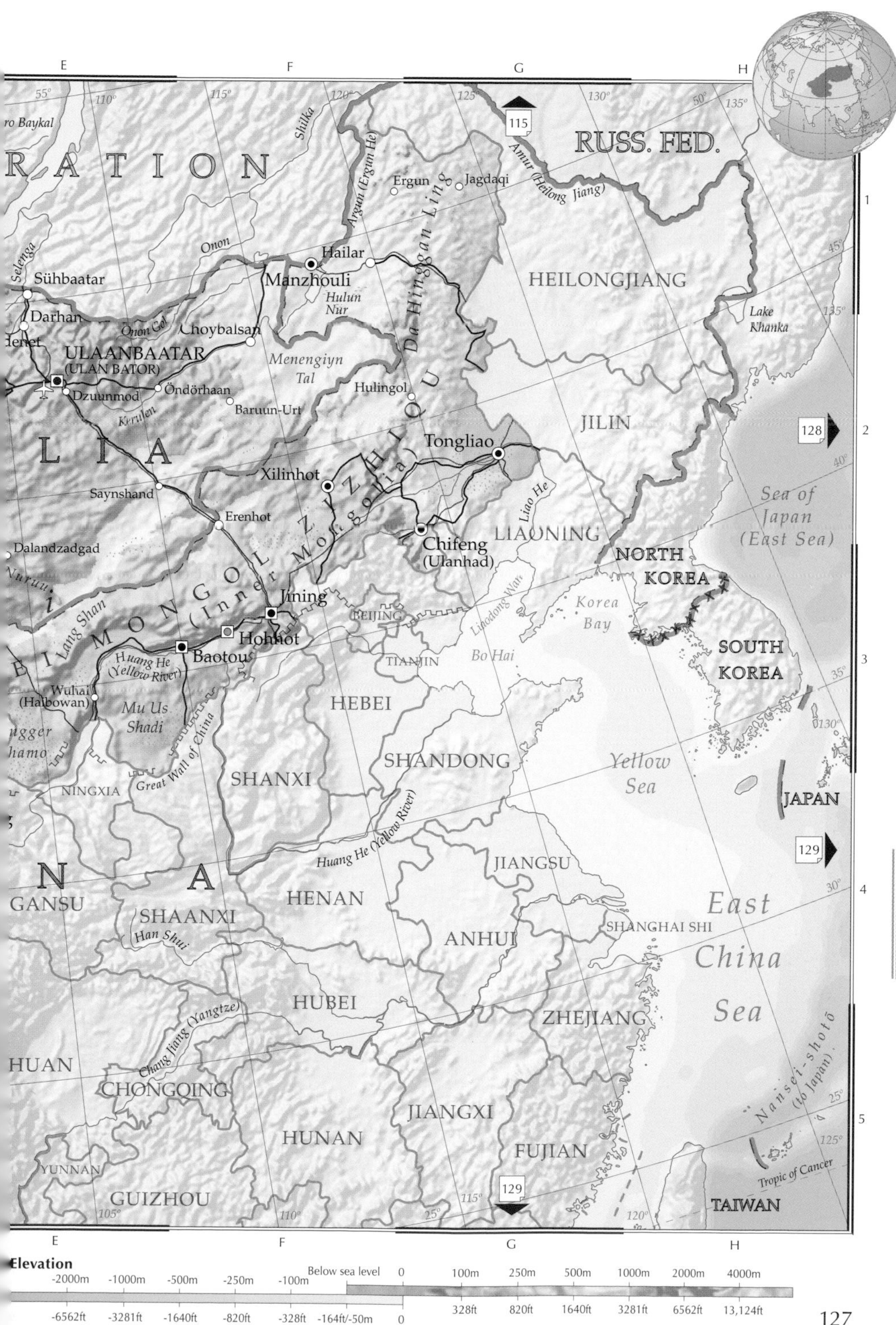

R A T I O N

RUSS. FED.

ro Baykal

55°   110°   115°   120°   125°   130°   50°   135°

115

Ergun   Jagdaqi

Amur (Heilong Jiang)

Selenga

Onon

Sühbaatar   Hailar   HEILONGJIANG

Manzhouli

Darhan   Onon Gol   Choybalsan   Hulun   Lake
                                            Nur   Khanka

ULAANBAATAR   Menengiyn   45°   135°
(ULAN BATOR)   Tal
Dzuunmod   Öndörhaan   Hulingol   JILIN

L I A   Kerulen   Baruun-Urt   128   2

Saynshand   Tongliao   40°

Xilinhot

Dalandzadgad   Erenhot   Chifeng   LIAONING
                              (Ulanhad)

Nuruu   Jining   NORTH   Korea   Sea of
                    BEIJING   KOREA   Bay   Japan
                                                (East Sea)

B I   M O N G O L   Hohhot   Liaodong Wan   SOUTH
Liang Shan   Baotou   TIANJIN   Bo Hai   KOREA   35°

Wuhai   Huang He   HEBEI   Yellow   JAPAN
(Haibowan)   (Yellow River)   Mu Us   Sea
                                  Shadi   SHANDONG   130°

ugger   NINGXIA   Great Wall of China   129
hamo

N   A   Huang He (Yellow River)   JIANGSU   30°   4

GANSU   SHAANXI   HENAN   East
                              ANHUI   China
         Han Shui   SHANGHAI SHI   Sea

HUAN   HUBEI   Nansei-shotō
        Chang Jiang (Yangtze)   ZHEJIANG   (to Japan)
HUAN   CHONGQING   25°   5
                    HUNAN   JIANGXI   125°
YUNNAN   FUJIAN   Tropic of Cancer
        105°   110°   115°   25°   120°   TAIWAN

E   F   G   H

Elevation

-2000m	-1000m	-500m	-250m	-100m	Below sea level	0	100m	250m	500m	1000m	2000m	4000m
-6562ft	-3281ft	-1640ft	-820ft	-328ft	-164ft/-50m	0	328ft	820ft	1640ft	3281ft	6562ft	13,124ft

Eastern China & Korea

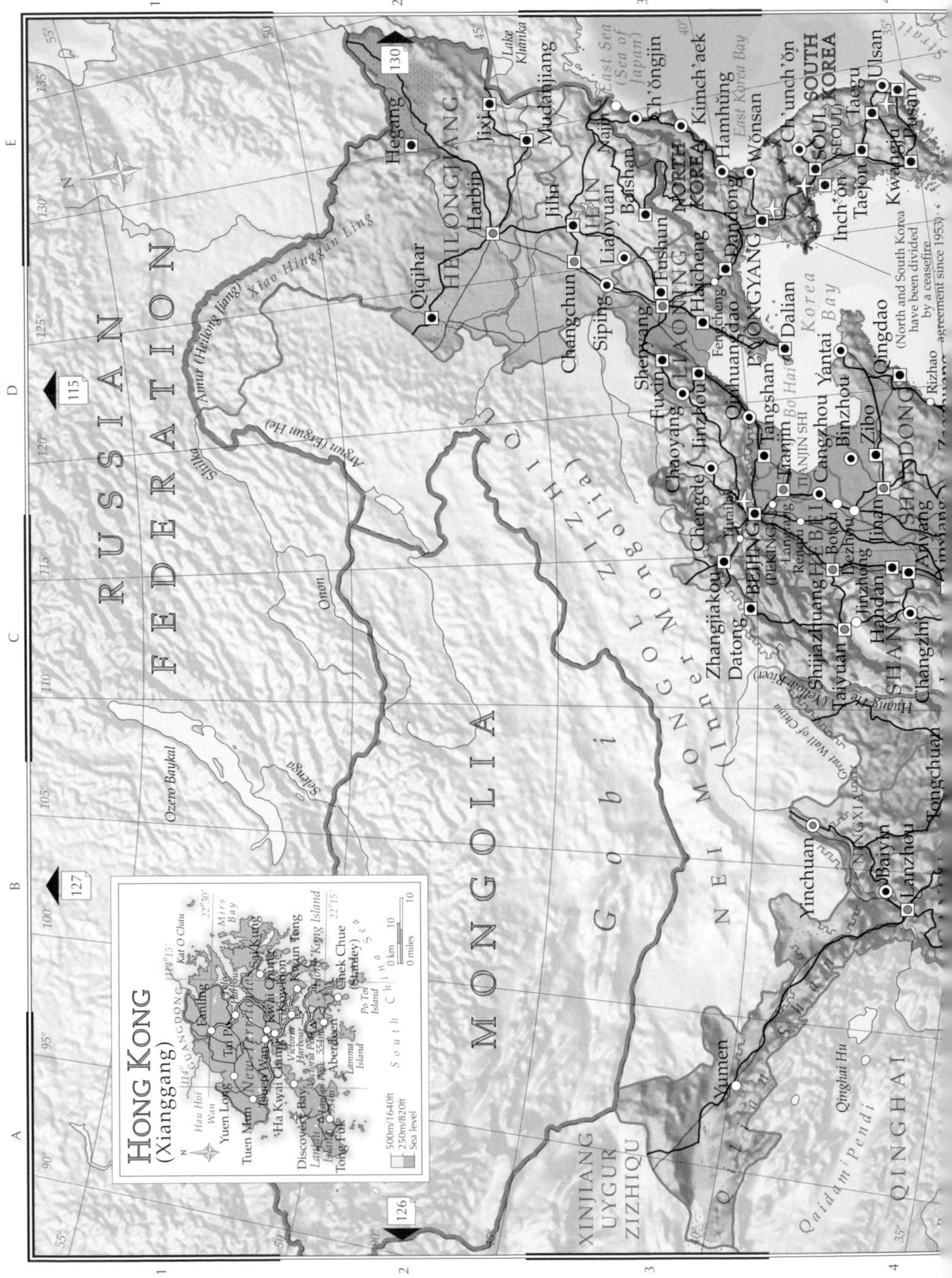

RUSSIAN FEDERATION

MONGOLIA

NEI MONGOL ZIZHIQU

HEILONGJIANG

JILIN

LIAONING

NORTH KOREA

SOUTH KOREA

HEBEI

SHANDONG

SHANXI

NINGXIA

QINGHAI

XINJIANG UYGUR ZIZHIQU

Gobi

Sea of Japan (East Sea)

Lake Khanka

Korea Bay

East Korea Bay

Bo Hai

Yellow River

Great Wall of China

Huang He

Gulf of China

South China Sea

Hegang
Jixi
Mudanjiang
Ch'ŏngjin
Kimch'aek
Harbin
Jilin
Hamhŭng
Wonsan
Qiqihar
Changchun
Siping
Liaoyuan
Fushun
Haicheng
Ch'unch'ŏn
SŎUL
Taegu
Ulsan
Pusan
Taejŏn
Inch'ŏn
Kwangju
Shenyang
Fuxin
Chaoyang
Chengde
Jinzhou
Fengcheng
Qinhuangdao
Dandong
PYONGYANG
Tangshan
Dalian
Yantai
Qingdao
Zhangjiakou
Datong
BEIJING
TIANJIN SHI
Cangzhou
Zibo
Jinan
Binzhou
Rizhao
Shijiazhuang
Baoding
Hengshui
Dezhou
Handan
Jining
Taiyuan
Yinchuan
Bayan
Lanzhou
Yumen
Zhongpuan

Qinghai Hu
Qaidam Pendi

130
115
127
126

HONG KONG (Xianggang)

Kat O Chau
Mirs Bay
Sha Tau Kok
Deep Bay
Kat Ha Hoi
Ping Chau
Tai Po
Sha Tin
Shek Kong
Sai Kung
Tsuen Wan
Sheung Shui
Tuen Mun
Yuen Long
Kowloon
Victoria
Aberdeen
Lamma Island
Lantau Island
Cheung Chau
Ping Teng
Chek Chue (Stanley)
Po Toi Island
Hong Kong Island

GUANGDONG
CHINA

500m/1640ft
250m/820ft
Sea level

0 km 10
0 miles 10

0 km 400
0 miles 400

Population

● National capital   ● Internal administrative capital

○ below 50,000   ○ 50,000 to 100,000   ◉ 100,000 to 500,000   ◼ above 500,0

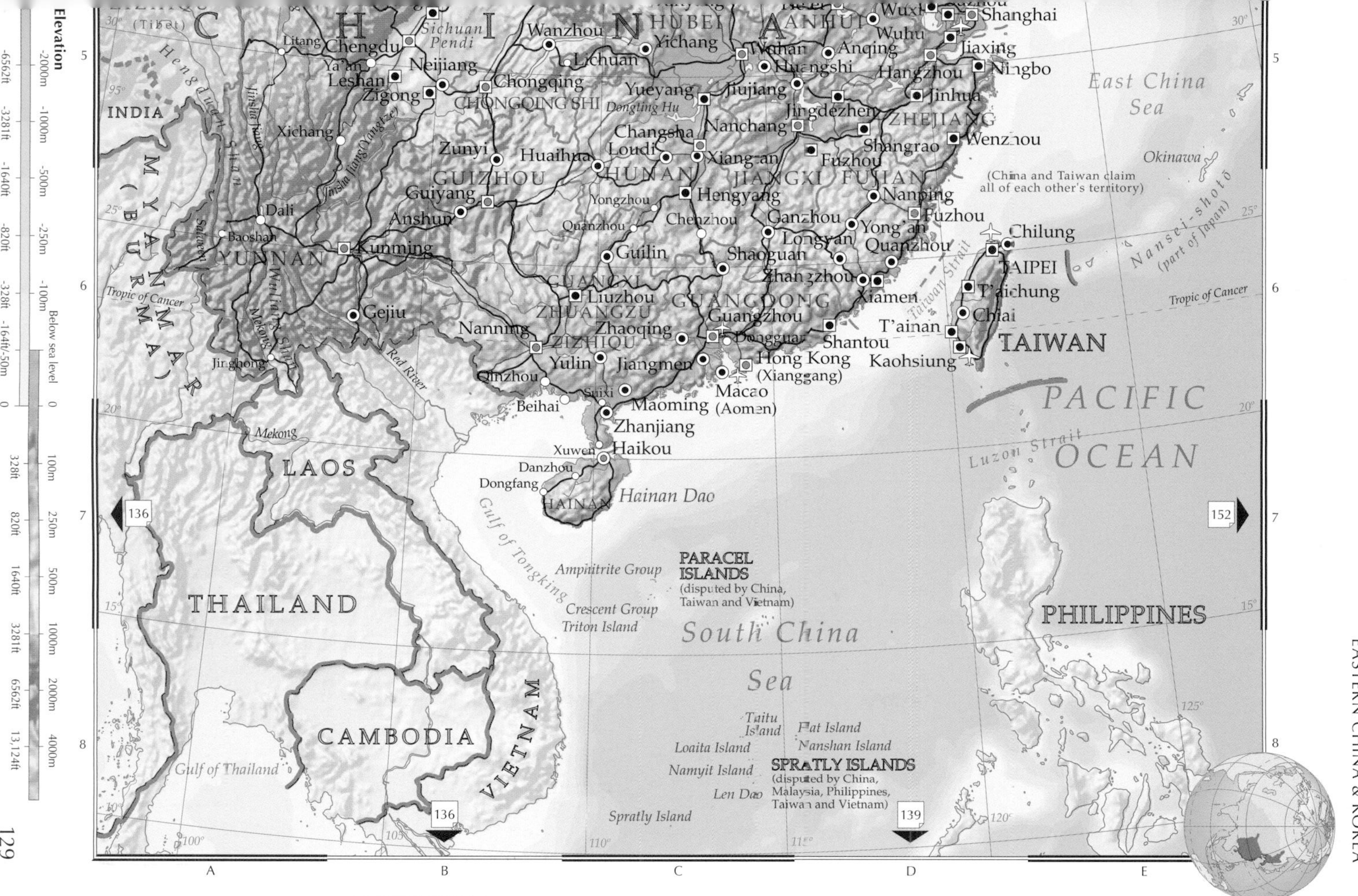

Elevation

-2000m	-1000m	-500m	-250m	-100m	Below sea level	0	100m	250m	500m	1000m	2000m	4000m
-6562ft	-3281ft	-1640ft	-820ft	-328ft	-164ft/-50m	0	328ft	820ft	1640ft	3281ft	6562ft	13,124ft

Japan

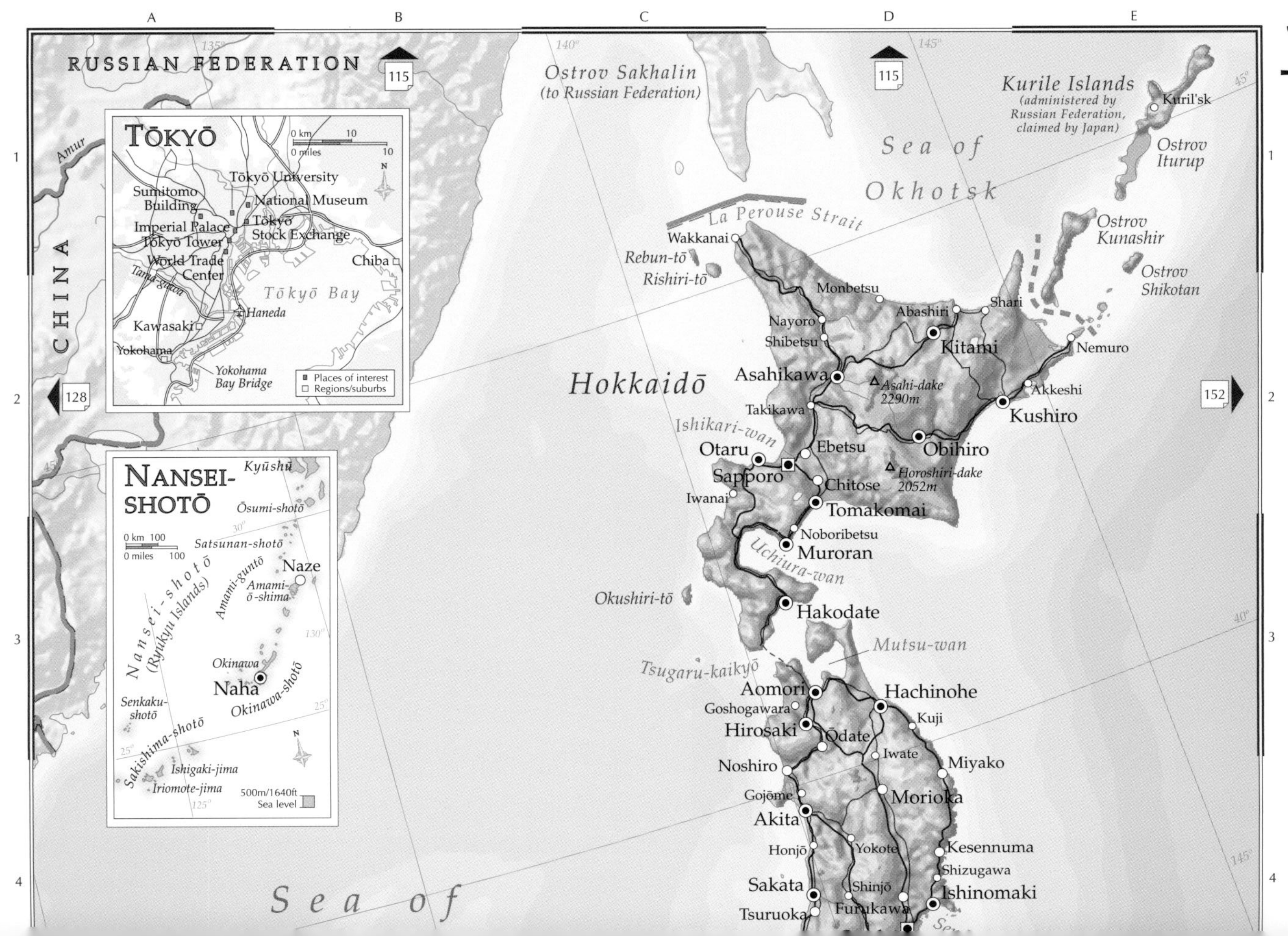

Kuril'sk

Ostrov
Iturup

Ostrov
Shikotan

Ostrov
Kunashir

Kurile Islands
(administered by
Russian Federation,
claimed by Japan)

152

Ostrov Sakhalin
(to Russian Federation)

Sea of
Okhotsk

Nemuro

Akkeshi

Kushiro

Shari

Kitami

Abashiri

Asahi-dake
2290 m

Mombetsu

Nayoro

Shibetsu

Asahikawa

Takikawa

Ebetsu

Obihiro

Horoshiri-dake
2052 m

Chitose

Tomakomai

Noboribetsu

Muroran

Uchiura-wan

Hakodate

Mutsu-wan

Hachinohe

Kuji

Iwate

Miyako

Morioka

Kesennuma

Shizugawa

Ishinomaki

La Perouse Strait

Wakanai

Rebun-tō

Rishiri-tō

Otaru

Iwanai

Sapporo

Ishikari-wan

Hokkaidō

Okushiri-tō

Tsugaru-kaikyō

Aomori

Goshogawara

Hirosaki

Odate

Noshiro

Gojome

Akita

Honjō

Yokote

Shinjō

Sakata

Tsuruoka

Funakawa

115

115

TŌKYŌ

Sumitomo
Building

Imperial Palace

Tōkyō Tower

World Trade
Center

Kawasaki

Yokohama

Tōkyō University

National Museum

Tōkyō
Stock Exchange

Chiba

Tōkyō Bay

Haneda

Yokohama
Bay Bridge

Places of interest
Regions/suburbs

RUSSIAN FEDERATION

Amur

CHINA

128

NANSEI-
SHOTŌ

Kyūshū

Ōsumi-shotō

Satsunan-shotō

Nansei-shotō (Ryūkyū Islands)

Amami-guntō

Naze

Amami-
ō-shima

Tokara-rettō

Okinawa

Naha

Okinawa-shotō

Sakishima-shotō

Ishigaki-jima

Iriomote-jima

Senkaku-
shotō

500m/1640ft
Sea level

Sea of

Sea of

Population

● National capital

○ below 50,000   ○ 50,000 to 100,000   ◉ 100,000 to 500,000   ◼ above 500,0

0 km   200
0 miles   200

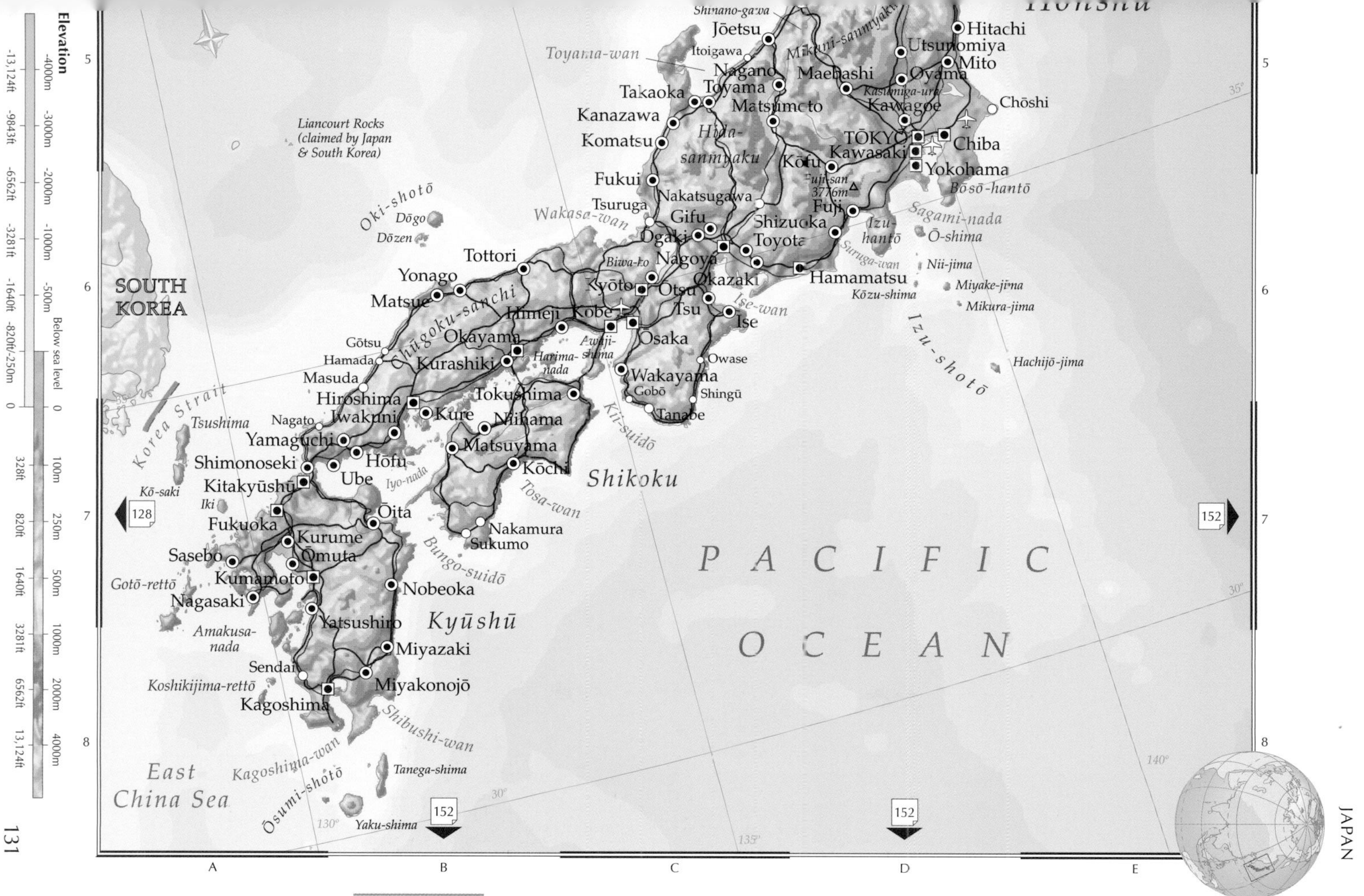

JAPAN

honshu

Hitachi
Utsunomiya
Oyama
Mito
Choshi
Chiba
TOKYO
Kawagoe
Yokohama
Kawasaki
Maebashi
Kashimaze?
Nagano
Matsumoto
Kofu
Fuji
Fujisan 3776m △
Shizuoka
Takaoka
Joetsu
Itoigawa
Toyama
Hida-sammyaku
Nakatsugawa
Toyota
Hamamatsu
Kanazawa
Komatsu
Fukui
Gifu
Ogaki
Nagoya
Tsu
Owase
Shingu
Tsuruga
Okazaki
Tanabe
Osaka
Wakayama
Gobo
Kyoto
Kobe
Fuji-
Biwa-ko
Himeji
Yonago
Tottori
Okayama
Tokushima
Matsue
Kurashiki
Kure
Mihama
Matsuyama
Kochi
Hiroshima
Iwakuni
Hofu
Oita
Nakamura
Sukumo
Nobeoka
Kyūshū
Miyazaki
Masuda
Ube
Miyakonojo
Yamaguchi
Katsushiro
Shimonoseki
Kitakyushu
Kurume
Sendai
Fukuoka
Omuta
Kagoshima
Sasebo
Kumamoto
Nagasaki

SOUTH
KOREA

PACIFIC
OCEAN

Shikoku

East
China Sea

Izu-shotō

Liancourt Rocks
(claimed by Japan
& South Korea)

Oki-shotō

Korea Strait

152
152
152
128

Elevation

PACIFIC OCEAN

131

Southern India & Sri Lanka

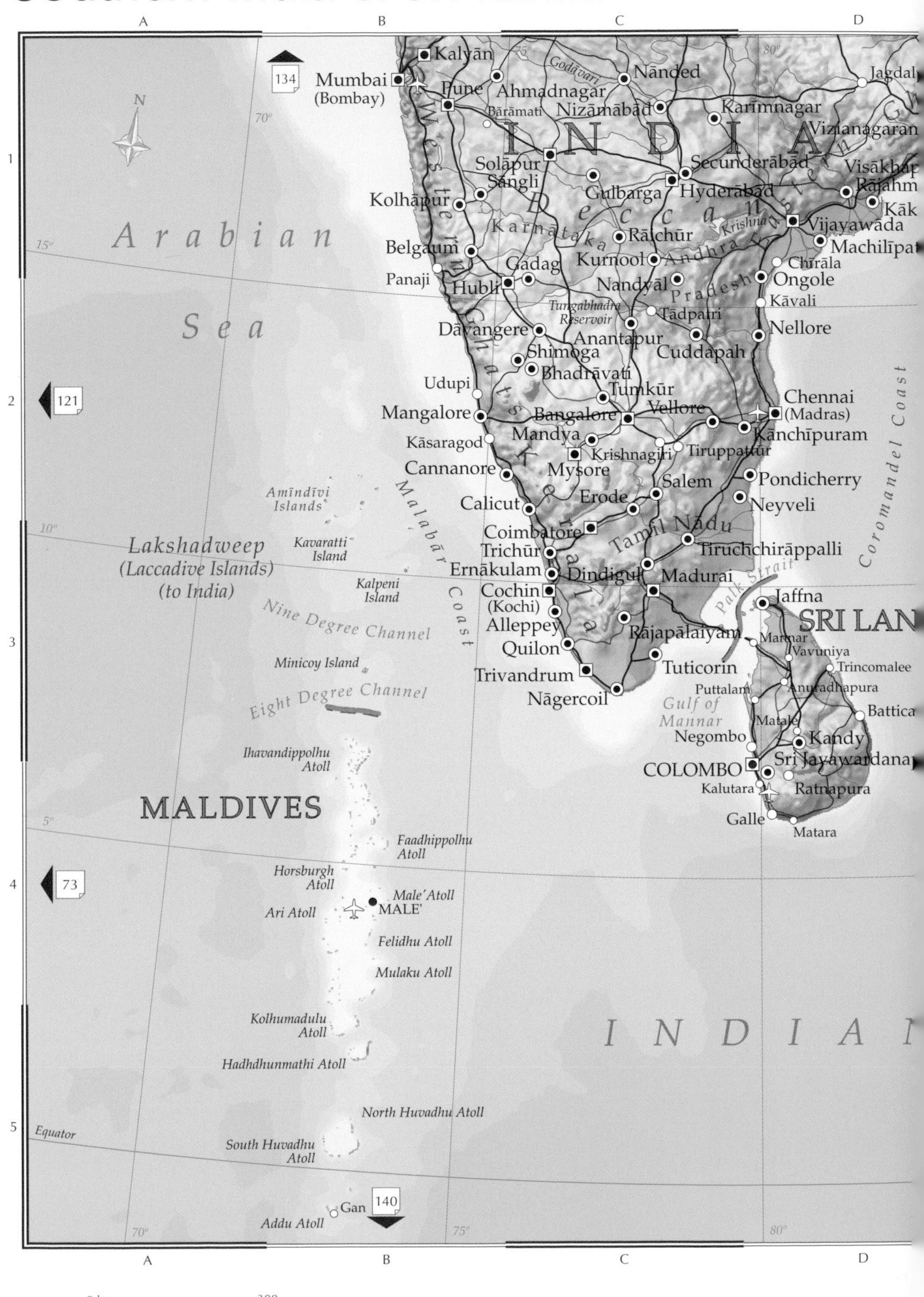

Kalyān
Mumbai (Bombay)
134
Pune
Ahmadnagar
Bāṭāmati
Nizāmābād
Nānded
Jagdal
Karīmnagar
Vizianagaram
INDIA
Secunderābād
Visākhap
Rajahm
Kāk
Solāpur
Sāngli
Gulbarga
Hyderābād
Kolhāpur
Rāichūr
Vijayawāda
Machilīpa
Deccan
Karnātaka
Belgaum
Andhra
Chirāla
Ongole
Kāvali
Panaji
Gadag
Kurnool
Hubli
Nandyāl
Tādpatri
Pradesh
Tungabhadra Reservoir
Davangere
Anantapur
Cuddapah
Nellore
Shimoga
Bhadrāvati
Udupi
Tumkūr
Chennai (Madras)
Mangalore
Bangalore
Vellore
Kāsaragod
Mandya
Krishnagiri
Kānchīpuram
Cannanore
Mysore
Tiruppattur
Calicut
Salem
Pondicherry
Erode
Neyveli
Tamil Nādu
Coimbatore
Tiruchchirāppalli
Trichūr
Ernākulam
Dindigul
Madurai
Cochin (Kochi)
Jaffna
Alleppey
SRI LAN
Rājapālaiyam
Mannar
Quilon
Vavuniya
Trincomalee
Trivandrum
Tuticorin
Anurādhapura
Nāgercoil
Battica
Gulf of Mannar
Matale
Negombo
Kandy
COLOMBO
Sri Jayawardana
Kalutara
Ratnapura
Galle
Matara

Arabian
Sea
121
Malabār Coast
Park Strait
Coromandel Coast

Lakshadweep
(Laccadive Islands)
(to India)
Amīndīvi
Islands
Kavaratti Island
Kalpeni Island
Nine Degree Channel
Minicoy Island
Eight Degree Channel

MALDIVES
Ihavandippolhu Atoll
Faadhippolhu Atoll
Horsburgh Atoll
73
Ari Atoll
Male' Atoll
MALE'
Felidhu Atoll
Mulaku Atoll
Kolhumadulu Atoll
Hadhdhunmathi Atoll
INDIAI
North Huvadhu Atoll
Equator
South Huvadhu Atoll
Gan
140
Addu Atoll

N
70°
15°
10°
5°
Equator
70°
75°
80°

0 km   300
0 miles   300

Population
● National capital
○ below 50,000
○ 50,000 to 100,000
◉ 100,000 to 500,000
◻ above 500,00

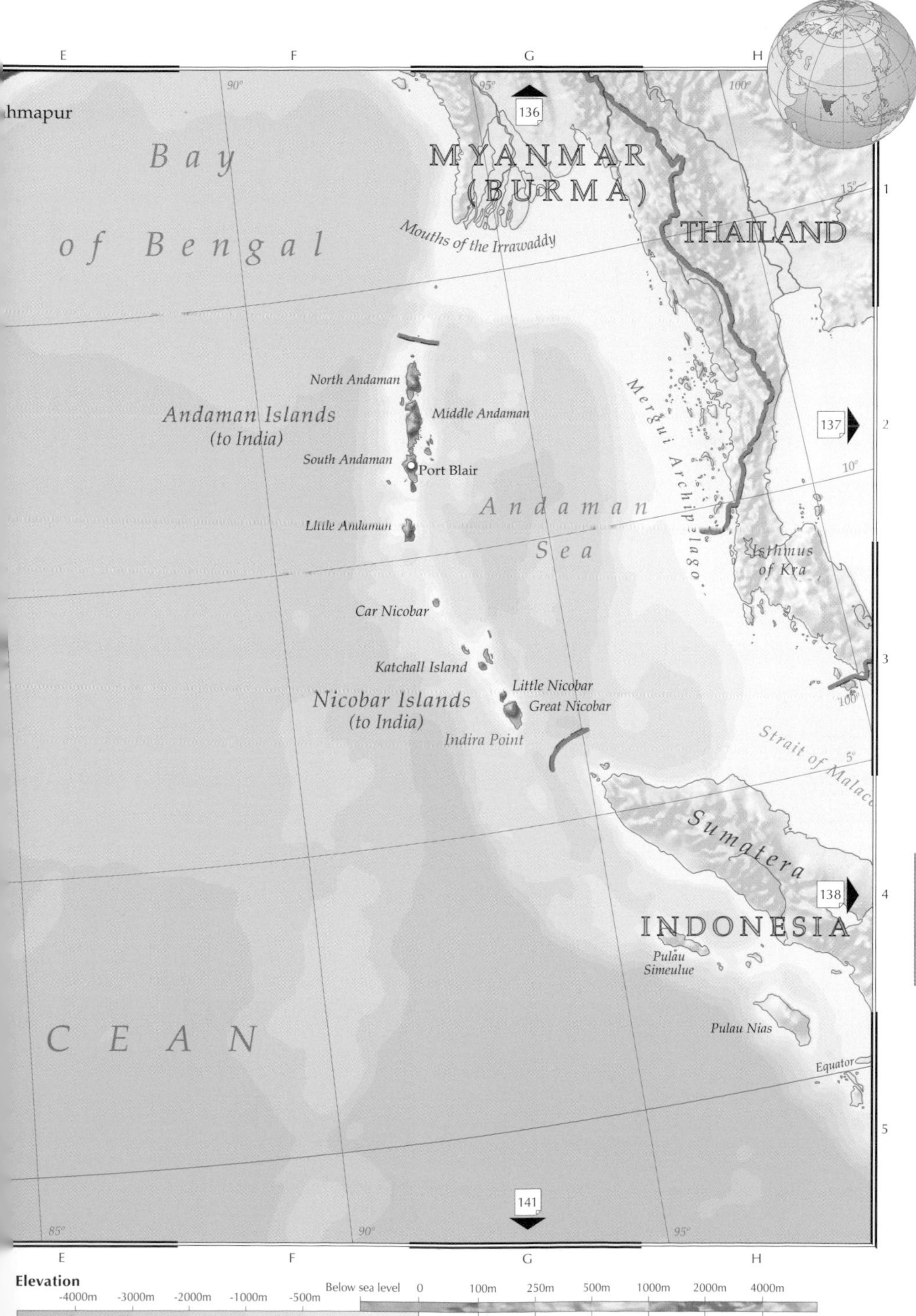

hmapur

Bay

of Bengal

MYANMAR
(BURMA)

THAILAND

Mouths of the Irrawaddy

136

137

North Andaman

Andaman Islands
(to India)

Middle Andaman

South Andaman

Port Blair

Mergui Archipelago

*Isthmus
of Kra*

Little Andaman

A n d a m a n

S e a

Car Nicobar

Katchall Island

Nicobar Islands
(to India)

Little Nicobar
Great Nicobar

Indira Point

Strait of Malacca

S u m a t e r a

138

INDONESIA

Pulau
Simeulue

C E A N

Pulau Nias

Equator

141

Elevation

-4000m	-3000m	-2000m	-1000m	-500m	Below sea level	0	100m	250m	500m	1000m	2000m	4000m
-13,124ft	-9843ft	-6562ft	-3281ft	-1640ft	-820ft/-250m	0	328ft	820ft	1640ft	3281ft	6562ft	13,124ft

133

Northern India, Pakistan & Bangladesh

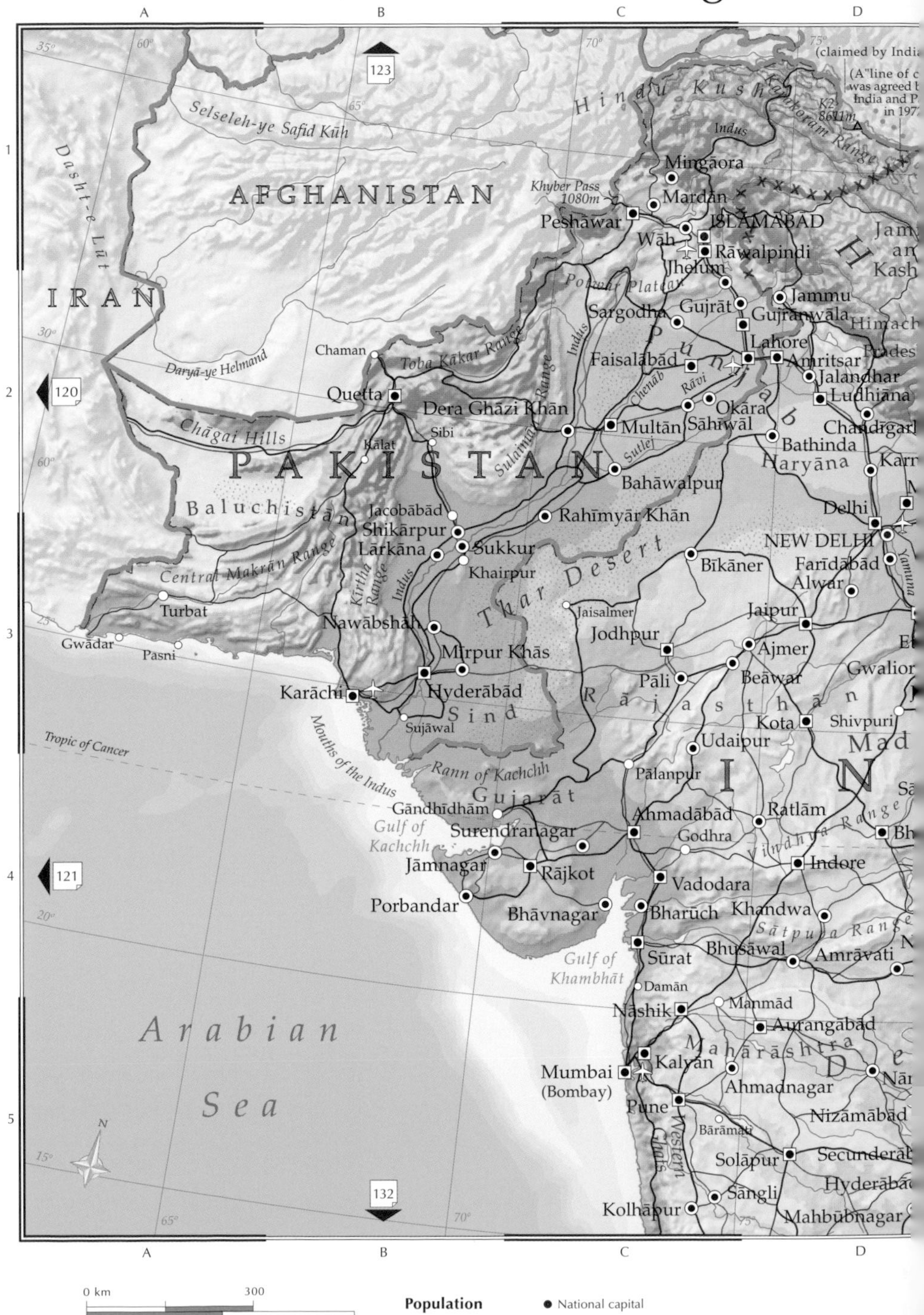

(claimed by Indi

(A"line of c
was agreed b
India and P
in 197

35°

60°

Selseleh-ye Safid Kūh

65°

70°

75°

Hindu Kush

K2
8611m

Karakoram Range

Dasht-e Lūt

AFGHANISTAN

Indus

Mingaora

Jamm

an

Kash

1

Khyber Pass
1080m

Mardan

Peshawar

ISLĀMĀBĀD

IRAN

Pothi Plateau

Wāh

Rāwalpindi

Jhelum

Jammu

Himach

ades

Indus

30°

Sargodha

Gujrāt

Gujranwāla

Daryā-ye Helmand

Chaman

Toba Kakar Range

Faisalābād

Lahore

Amritsar

Jalandhar

Sulaimān Range

P

Chenab

Ludhiāna

Quetta

Dera Ghāzi Khan

Okāra

Sāhiwāl

Chandigar

2

120

Chāgai Hills

Sibi

Kalat

Multān

Ravi

j

b

Bathinda

60°

PAKISTAN

Sutlej

Bahāwalpur

Haryāna

Karr

Delhi

Baluchistan

Jacobābād

Shikārpur

Rahīmyār Khān

Bīkāner

NEW DELHI

Farīdābād

Larkāna

Central Makrān Range

Kirthar Range

Sukkur

Khairpur

Thar Desert

Jaisalmer

Alwar

Turbat

Indus

Jodhpur

Jaipur

Gwalior

25°

Gwādar

Pasni

Nawābshāh

Mīrpur Khās

Pāli

Ajmer

Beāwar

E

3

Karāchi

Hyderābād

Sind

Rājasthān

Kota

Shivpuri

Sujāwal

Udaipur

Mad

Tropic of Cancer

Mouths of the Indus

Rann of Kachchh

Pālanpur

I

N

Gāndhīdhām

Gujarat

Ahmadābād

Ratlām

S

20°

Gulf of Kachchh

Surendranagar

Godhra

Range

Bh

4

121

Jāmnagar

Rājkot

Vadodara

Indore

Porbandar

Bhāvnagar

Bharūch

Khandwa

Vindhya

Satpura Range

Gulf of Khambhāt

Sūrat

Bhusāwal

Amrāvati

Damān

Nāshik

Manmād

Aurangābād

D

A r a b i a n

Kalyān

Mahārāshtra

Nāi

Mumbai
(Bombay)

Ahmadnagar

Nizāmābād

5

S e a

N

Pune

Bārāmati

Secunderā

15°

Western Ghats

Solāpur

Hyderābā

132

Sāngli

Mahbūbnagar

65°

70°

Kolhāpur

75°

A

B

C

D

0 km   300

0 miles   300

Population ● National capital

○ below 50,000   ○ 50,000 to 100,000   ◉ 100,000 to 500,000   ◼ above 500,0

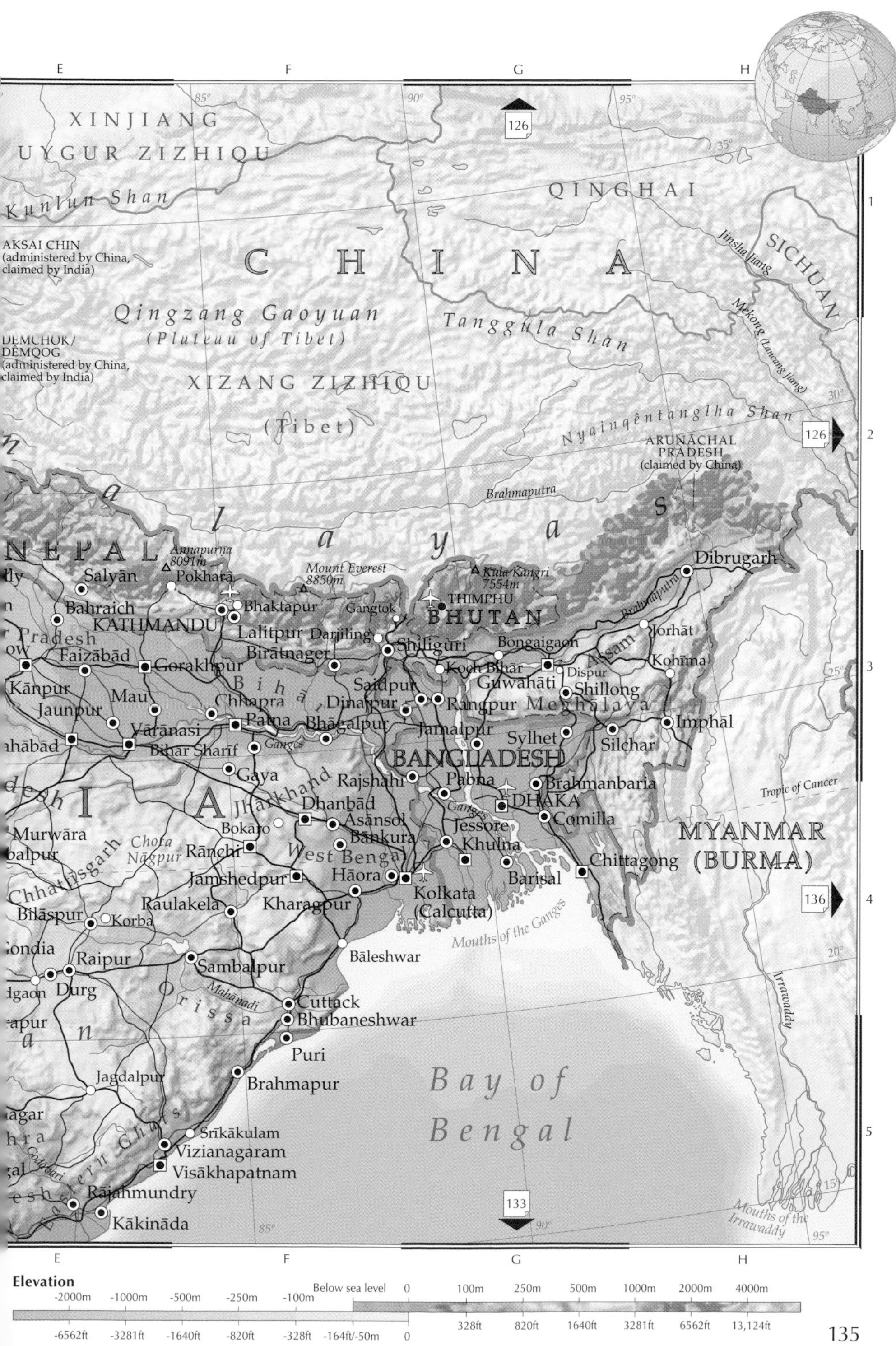

XINJIANG
UYGUR ZIZHIQU

Kunlun Shan

QINGHAI

SICHUAN

Jinsha Jiang

Mekong (Lancang Jiang)

AKSAI CHIN
(administered by China,
claimed by India)

C H I N A

*Qingzang Gaoyuan
(Plateau of Tibet)*

Tanggula Shan

DEMCHOK/
DÊMQOG
(administered by China,
claimed by India)

XIZANG ZIZHIQU

(Tibet)

Nyainqêntanglha Shan

ARUNĀCHAL
PRADESH
(claimed by China)

Brahmaputra

N E P A L

Annapurna
8091m △

Salyān

Pokharā

Mount Everest
8850m △

△ *Kula Kangri*
7554m

Dibrugarh

Bahraich

Bhaktapur

Gangtok

THIMPHU

Jorhat

Faizābād

KATHMANDU

Lalitpur

Darjiling

BHUTAN

Bongaigaon

Kohīma

Gorakhpur

Birātnagar

Shiliguri

Koch Bihar

Guwāhāti

Assam

Pradesh

Kānpur

Jaunpur

Mau

Bihar

Chhapra

Dinājpur

Rangpur

Shillong

Imphāl

Vārānasi

Patna

Saidpur

Jamālpur

Meghalaya

ahābād

Bihar Sharif

Bhāgalpur

Ganges

BANGLADESH

Silchar

Gaya

Rājshāhi

Pabna

Brahmanbaria

Murwāra

Dhanbād

Asānsol

Ganges

DHAKA

Comilla

MYANMAR

alpur

Bokāro

Bankura

Jessore

Khulna

(BURMA)

Bilāspur

*Chota
Nagpur*

Rānchi

West Bengal

Chittagong

Korba

Jamshedpur

Hāora

ondia

Raipur

Raulakela

Kharagpur

Kolkata
(Calcutta)

Barisal

Mouths of the Ganges

Durg

Sambalpur

Bāleshwar

Mahānadi

Orissa

Irrawaddy

Jagdalpur

Cuttack

Bhubaneshwar

*Bay of
Bengal*

Puri

Brahmapur

Srīkākulam

Vizianagaram

Visākhapatnam

Eastern Ghats

Rājahmundry

Kākināda

*Mouths of the
Irrawaddy*

Elevation

-2000m	-1000m	-500m	-250m	-100m	Below sea level	0	100m	250m	500m	1000m	2000m	4000m
-6562ft	-3281ft	-1640ft	-820ft	-328ft	-164ft/-50m	0	328ft	820ft	1640ft	3281ft	6562ft	13,124ft

Mainland Southeast Asia

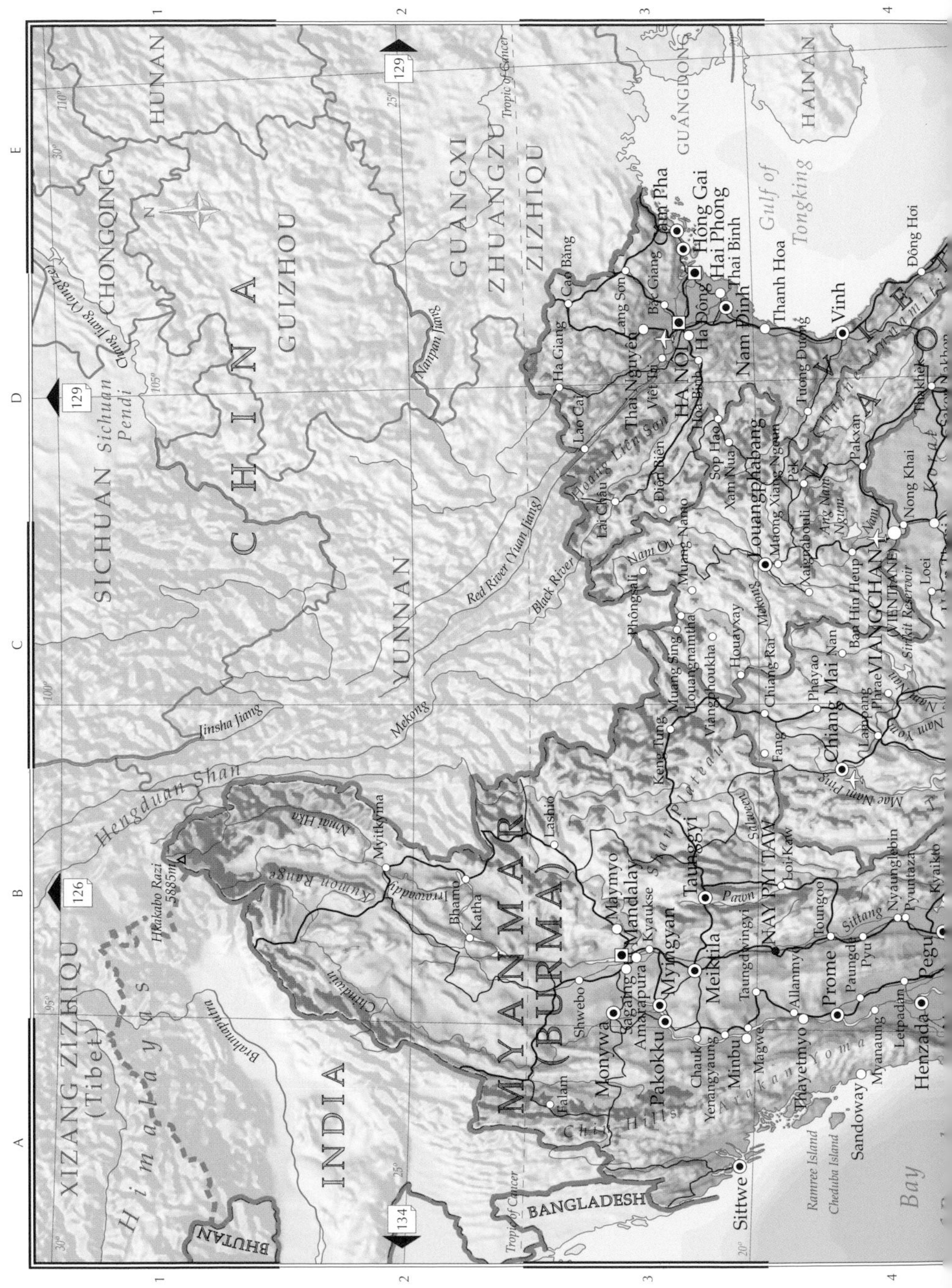

Population
- National capital
- ○ below 50,000
- ○ 50,000 to 100,000
- ◉ 100,000 to 500,000
- ◼ above 500,00

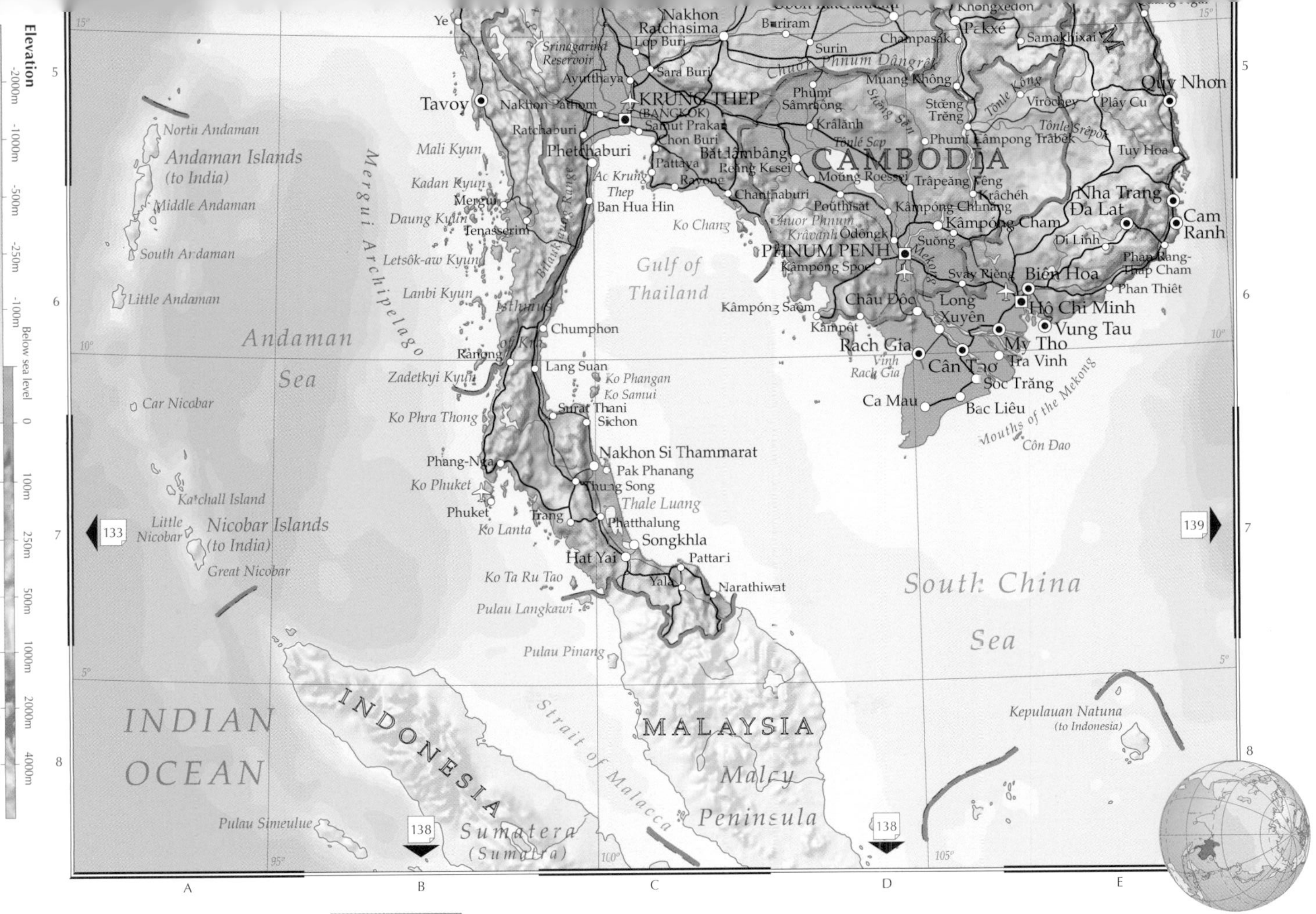

Elevation

Below sea level											
-2000m	-1000m	-500m	-250m	-100m	0	100m	250m	500m	1000m	2000m	4000m
-6562ft	-3281ft	-1640ft	-820ft	-328ft	-164ft/-50m	0	328ft	820ft	1640ft	3281ft	6562ft	13,124ft

Maritime Southeast Asia

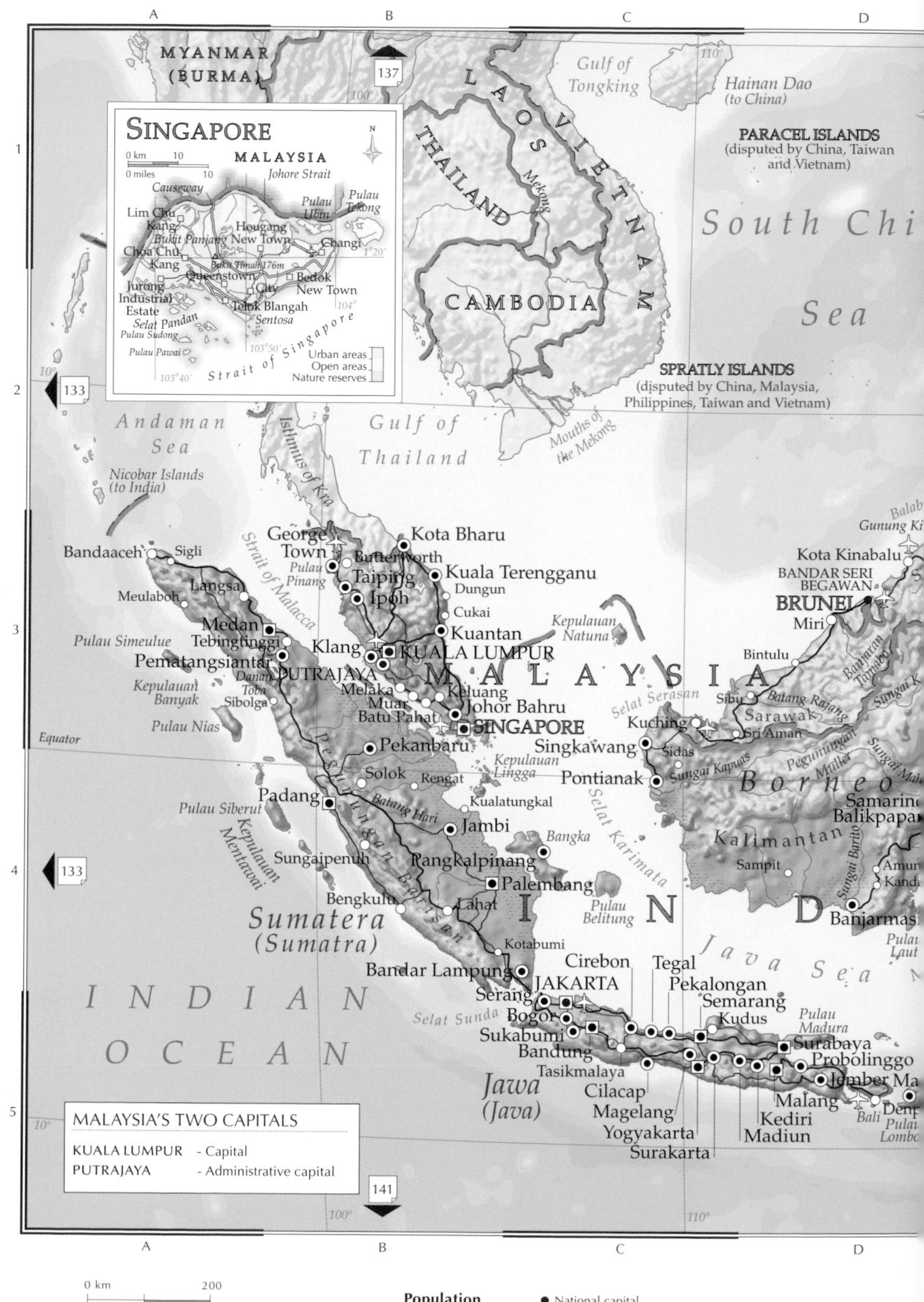

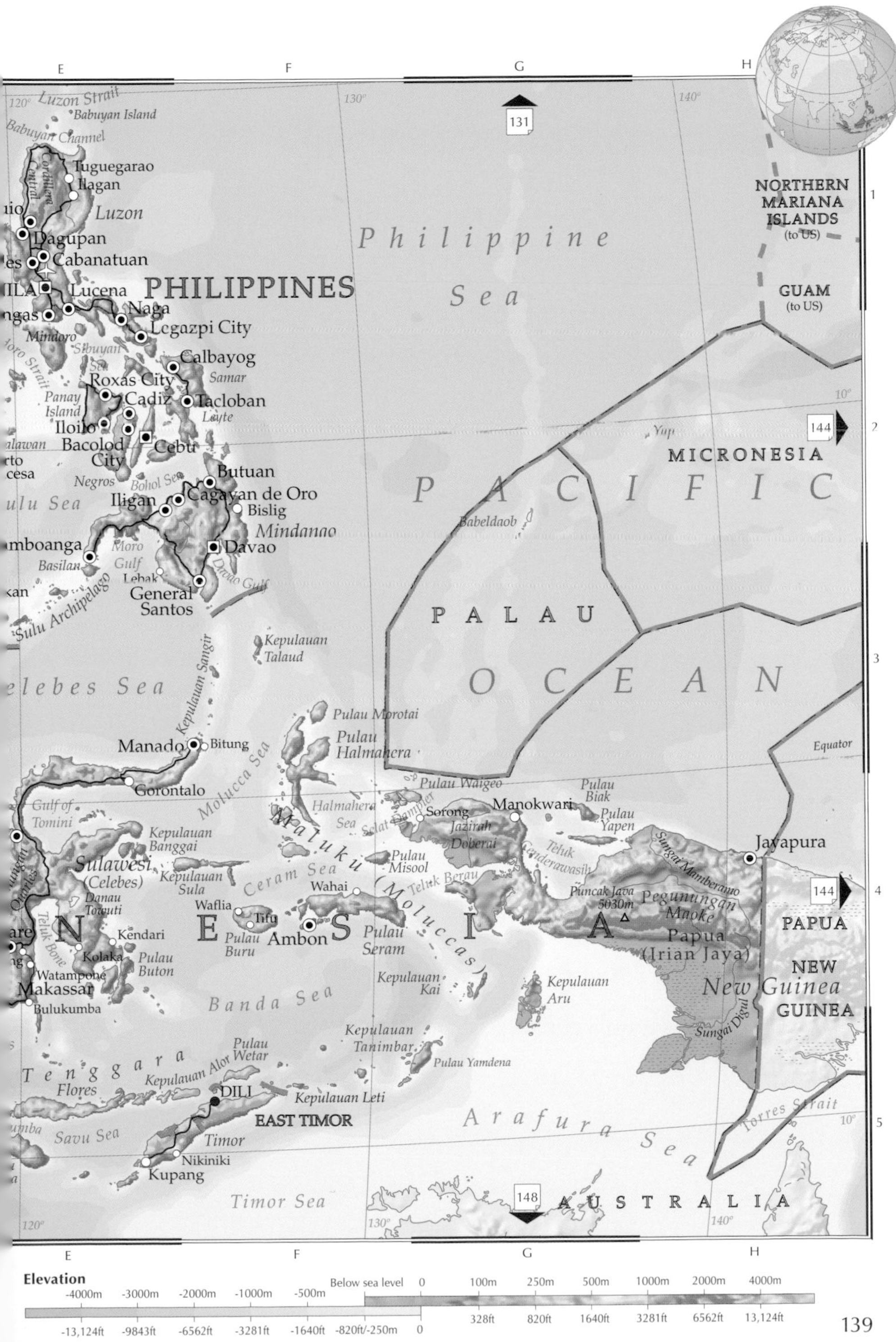

E   F   G   H

Luzon Strait
Babuyan Channel
Babuyan Island

Cordillera Central

131

130°   *140°*

NORTHERN
MARIANA
ISLANDS
(to US)

1

Luzon
Tuguegarao
Ilagan
120°

io•
Dagupan
es•
Cabanatuan
ILA•
Lucena
ngas•

PHILIPPINES

Naga
Legazpi City
Mindoro

P h i l i p p i n e

S e a

GUAM
(to US)

Calbayog
Sibuyan
Samar
Roxas City
Cadiz
Tacloban
Panay
Island
Iloilo
Leyte
Bacolod
City
Cebu

Palawan
cesa
rto

Negros
Bohol Sea
Butuan
Cagayan de Oro
Bislig
Iligan
Mindanao
mboanga•
Basilan
Moro
Gulf
Davao
ulu Sea

10°

144

2

MICRONESIA

P   A   C   I   F   I   C

Babeldaob

kan
Sulu Archipelago
Lebak
General
Santos
Davao Gulf

Kepulauan
Talaud

PALAU

O   C   E   A   N

3

Celebes Sea

Pulau Morotai
Pulau
Halmahera

Equator

Manado
Bitung
Gorontalo
Molucca Sea

Pulau Waigeo
Sorong
Halmahera
Selat Dampier
Manokwari
Pulau
Biak

Javapura

Gulf of
Tomini
Kepulauan
Banggai
Kepulauan
Sula
Ceram Sea
Maluku
(Moluccas)
Jazirah
Doberai
Teluk Berau
Teluk
Cenderawasih
Pulau Yapen
Sungai Mamberamo

144

4

Sulawesi
(Celebes)
Waflia
Danau
Tortuti
Tifu
Pulau
Buru
Ambon
Pulau
Seram
Ceram Sea
(Moluccas)
Pulau
Misool
Puncak Jaya
5030m △
Pegunungan
Maoke
Papua
(Irian Jaya)

PAPUA

NEW
GUINEA

N   E   S   I   A
are•
ng•
Kendari
Kolaka
Pulau
Buton
Watampone
Makassar
Bulukumba

Kepulauan
Kai
Kepulauan
Aru
New Guinea
Sungai Digul

Banda Sea

Kepulauan
Tanimbar
Pulau Yamdena

T   e   n   g   g   a   r   a
Flores
Kepulauan Alor
Pulau
Wetar
Kepulauan Leti
DILI
EAST TIMOR
Torres Strait

10°

5

umba
Savu Sea
Timor
Nikiniki
Kupang
Timor Sea

148
A   U   S   T   R   A   L   I   A

Arafura   Sea

120°   *130°*   *140°*

E   F   G   H

Elevation

					Below sea level	0	100m	250m	500m	1000m	2000m	4000m
-4000m	-3000m	-2000m	-1000m	-500m								
-13,124ft	-9843ft	-6562ft	-3281ft	-1640ft	-820ft/-250m	0	328ft	820ft	1640ft	3281ft	6562ft	13,124ft

The Indian Ocean

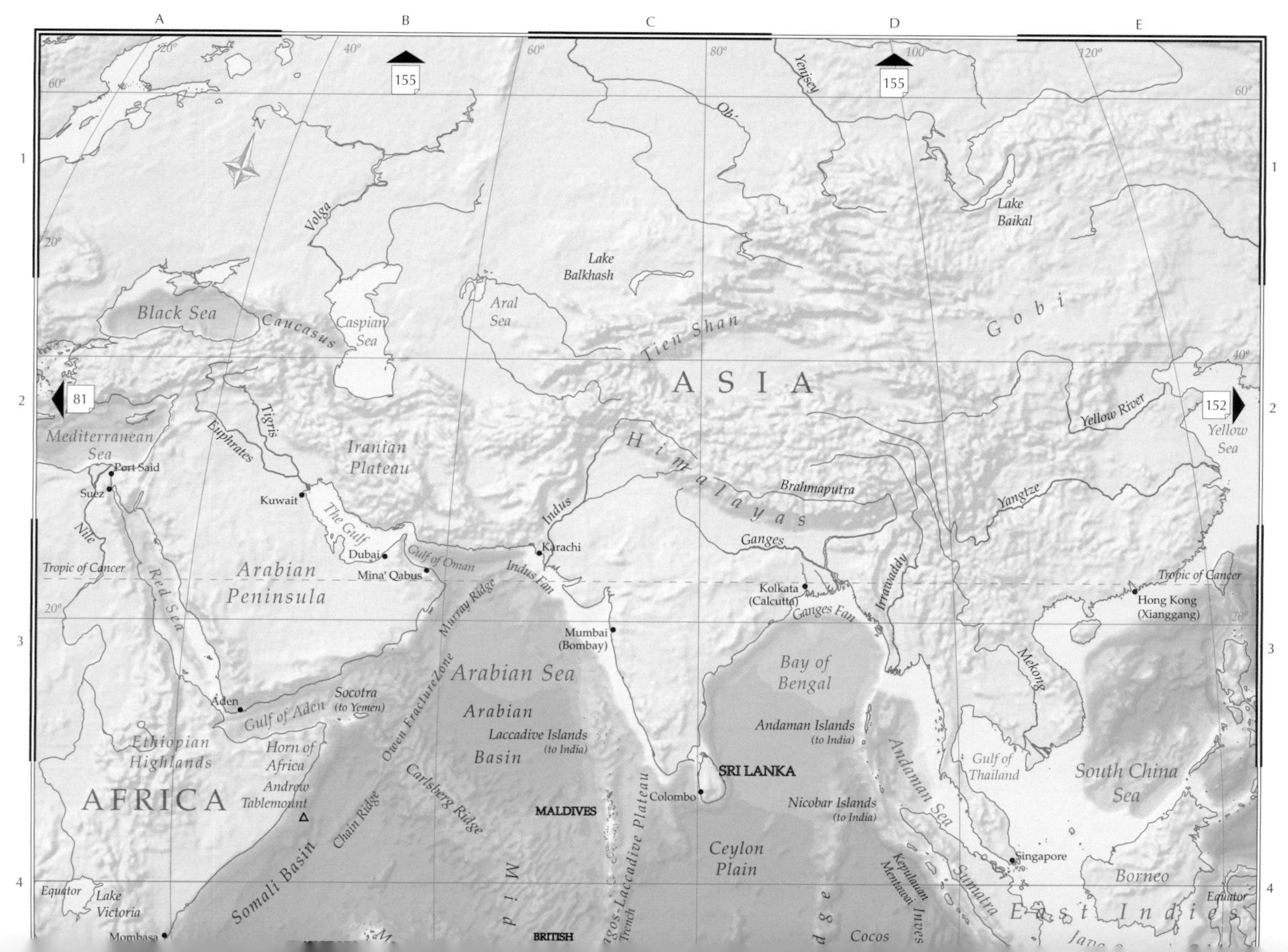

0 km   1500

0 miles   1500

• Major port

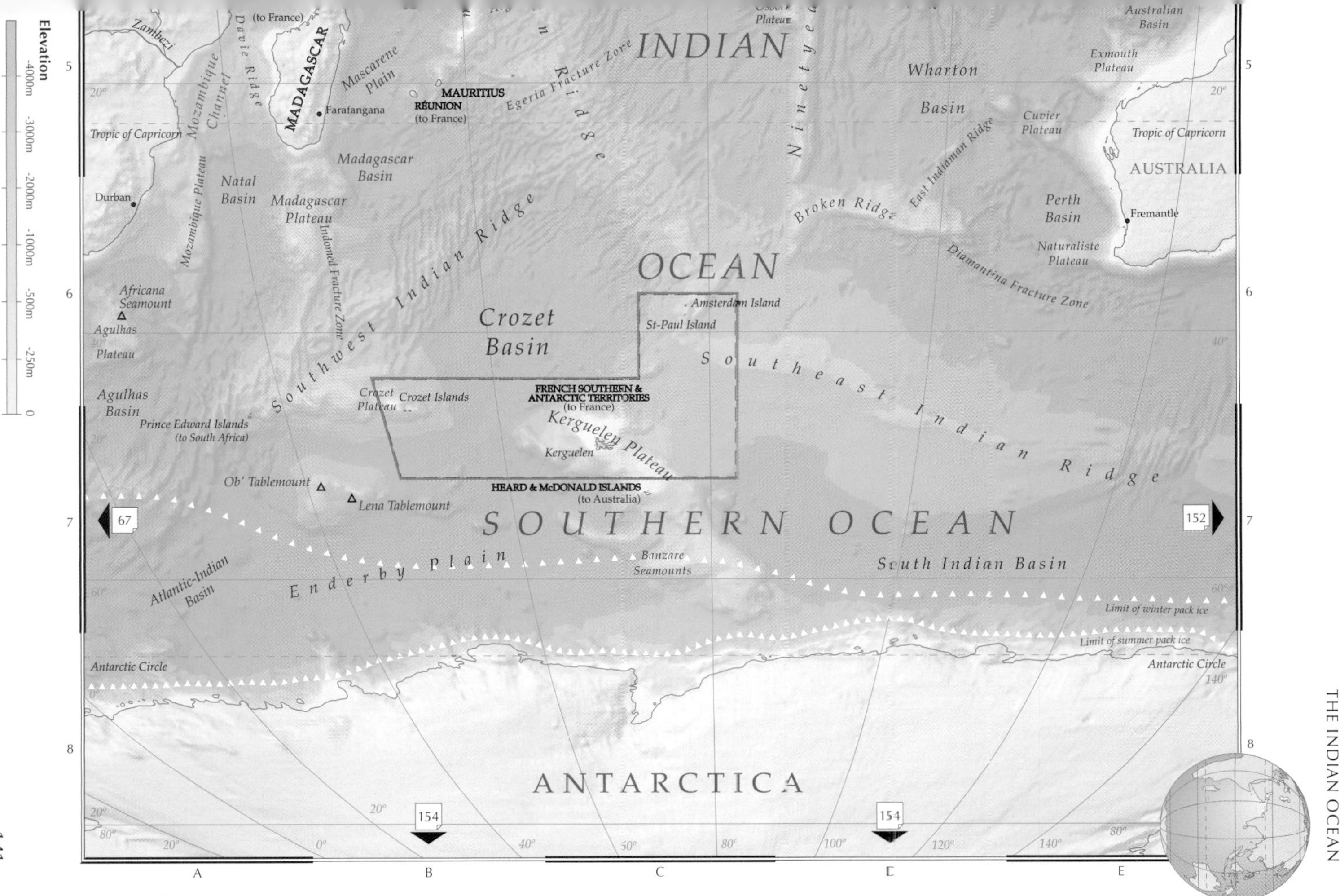

Australian Basin

Exmouth Plateau

Cuvier Plateau

Tropic of Capricorn

AUSTRALIA

Fremantle

Perth Basin

Naturaliste Plateau

Wharton Basin

East Indian Ridge

Diamantina Fracture Zone

Broken Ridge

Ninetyeast Ridge

South east Indian Ridge

152

Limit of winter pack ice

Limit of summer pack ice

Antarctic Circle

South Indian Basin

154

154

INDIAN

OCEAN

SOUTHERN OCEAN

ANTARCTICA

Amsterdam Island

St-Paul Island

Kerguelen Plateau

FRENCH SOUTHERN & ANTARCTIC TERRITORIES
(to France)

Kerguélen

HEARD & McDONALD ISLANDS
(to Australia)

Banzare Seamounts

Enderby Plain

Egeria Fracture Zone

MAURITIUS

RÉUNION
(to France)

Crozet Basin

Crozet Islands

Crozet Plateau

△ Lena Tablemount

Mascarene Plain

Madagascar Basin

Madagascar Plateau

Indomed Fracture Zone

△ Ob' Tablemount

Atlantic-Indian Basin

MADAGASCAR
(to France)

Faralangana

South west Indian Ridge

Prince Edward Islands
(to South Africa)

Davie Ridge

Natal Basin

Mozambique Plateau

Mozambique Channel

Zambezi

Tropic of Capricorn

Durban

Africana Seamount

Agulhas

Agulhas Plateau

Agulhas Basin

Antarctic Circle

67

154

Elevation

-4000m	-3000m	-2000m	-1000m	-500m	-250m	0
-13,124ft	-9843ft	-6562ft	-3281ft	-1640ft	-820ft	0

Australasia & Oceania

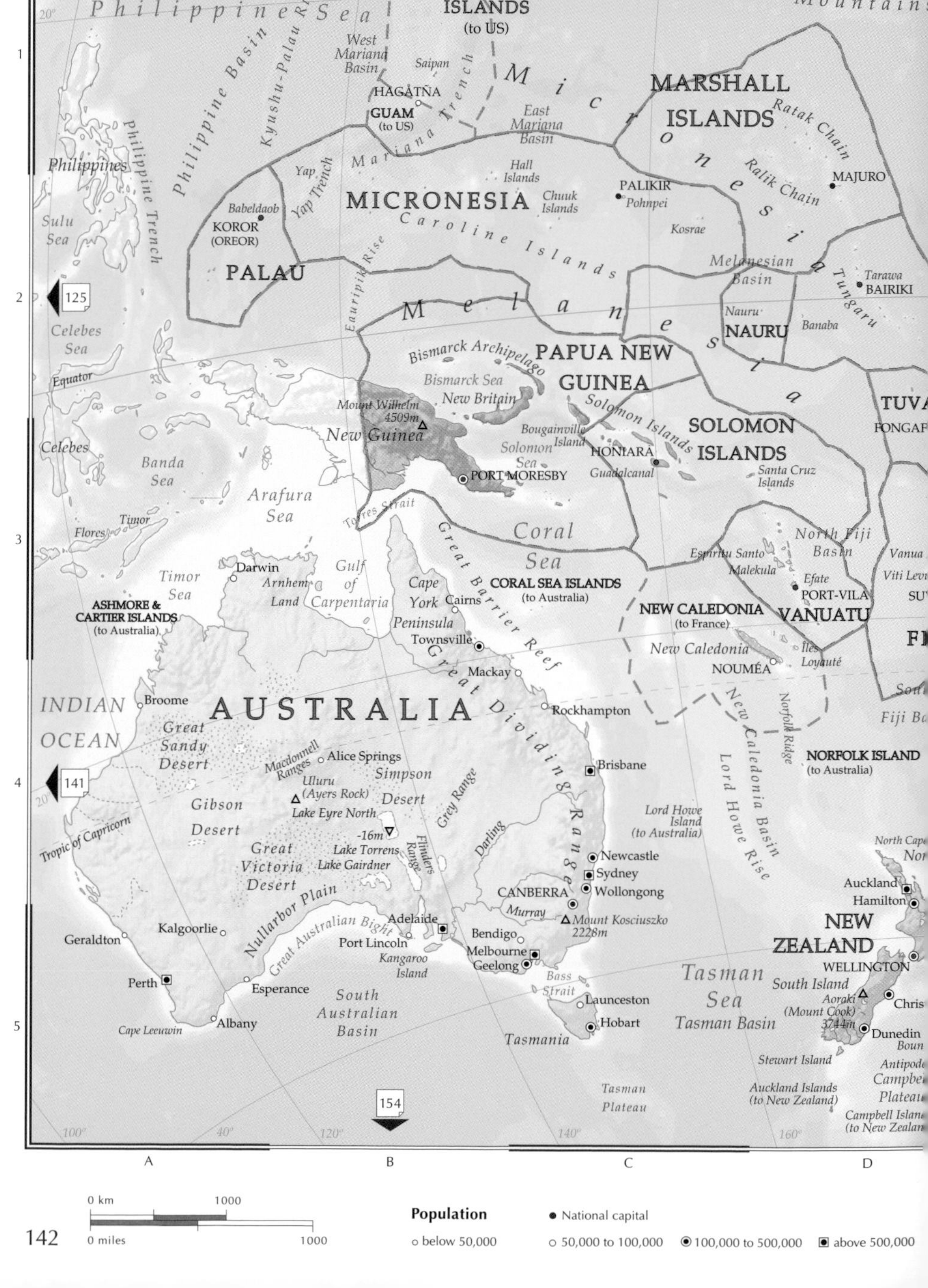

Population ● National capital

o below 50,000 ○ 50,000 to 100,000 ◉ 100,000 to 500,000 ■ above 500,000

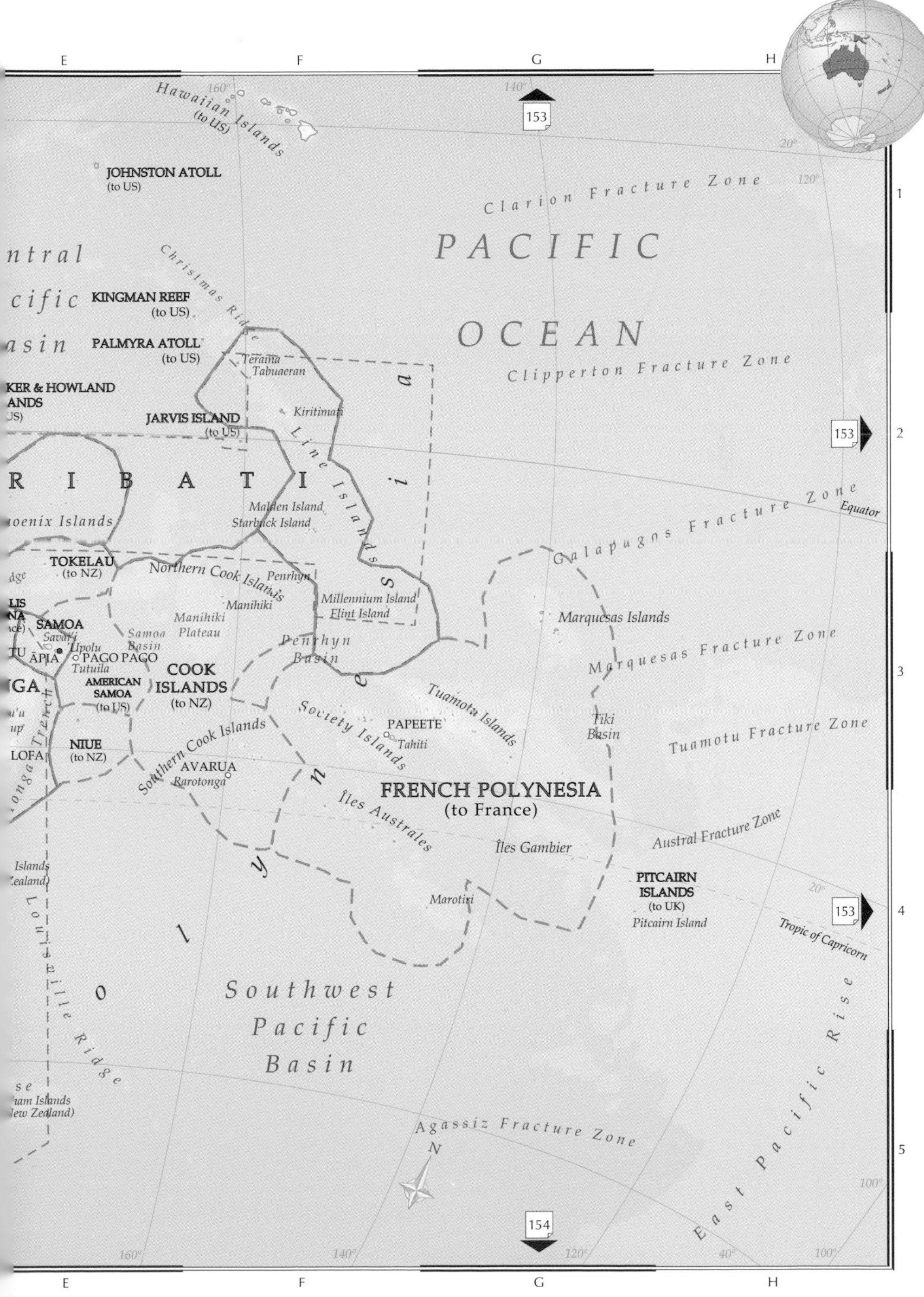

E   F   G   H

153

Hawaiian Islands
(to US)

160°   140°   120°   20°   1

JOHNSTON ATOLL
(to US)

Clarion Fracture Zone

ntral
cific
asin

KINGMAN REEF
(to US)

Christmas Ridge

PALMYRA ATOLL
(to US)

Terama
Tabuaeran

Clipperton Fracture Zone

KER & HOWLAND
ANDS
US)

JARVIS ISLAND
(to US)

Kiritimati

a
i

153 2

Galapagos Fracture Zone   Equator

R I B A T I

Line Islands

oenix Islands

Malden Island
Starbuck Island

TOKELAU
(to NZ)

Northern Cook Islands   *Penrhyn*

Marquesas Islands

LIS
NA
ce)

TU

SAMOA
Savai'i
Upolu
ÁPIA   PAGO PAGO
Tutuila

Manihiki
Samoa
Basin
Manihiki
Plateau

Millennium Island
Flint Island

Marquesas Fracture Zone

Penrhyn
Basin

GA

**AMERICAN
SAMOA**
(to US)

**COOK
ISLANDS**
(to NZ)

Tuamotu Islands

Tiki
Basin

Tuamotu Fracture Zone

a'u
up

NIUE
(to NZ)

Southern Cook Islands

Soviety Islands

PAPEETE
Tahiti

3

LOFA

AVARUA
Rarotonga

y
n

FRENCH POLYNESIA
(to France)

Íles Australes

Austral Fracture Zone

Islands
Zealand)

Íles Gambier

**PITCAIRN
ISLANDS**
(to UK)

Pitcairn Island

20°

153 4

Marotiri

Tropic of Capricorn

100°

o

l

S o u t h w e s t
P a c i f i c
B a s i n

ham Islands
New Zealand)

Agassiz Fracture Zone

N

East Pacific Rise

5

160°   140°   120°   40°   100°

154

E   F   G   H

The Southwest Pacific

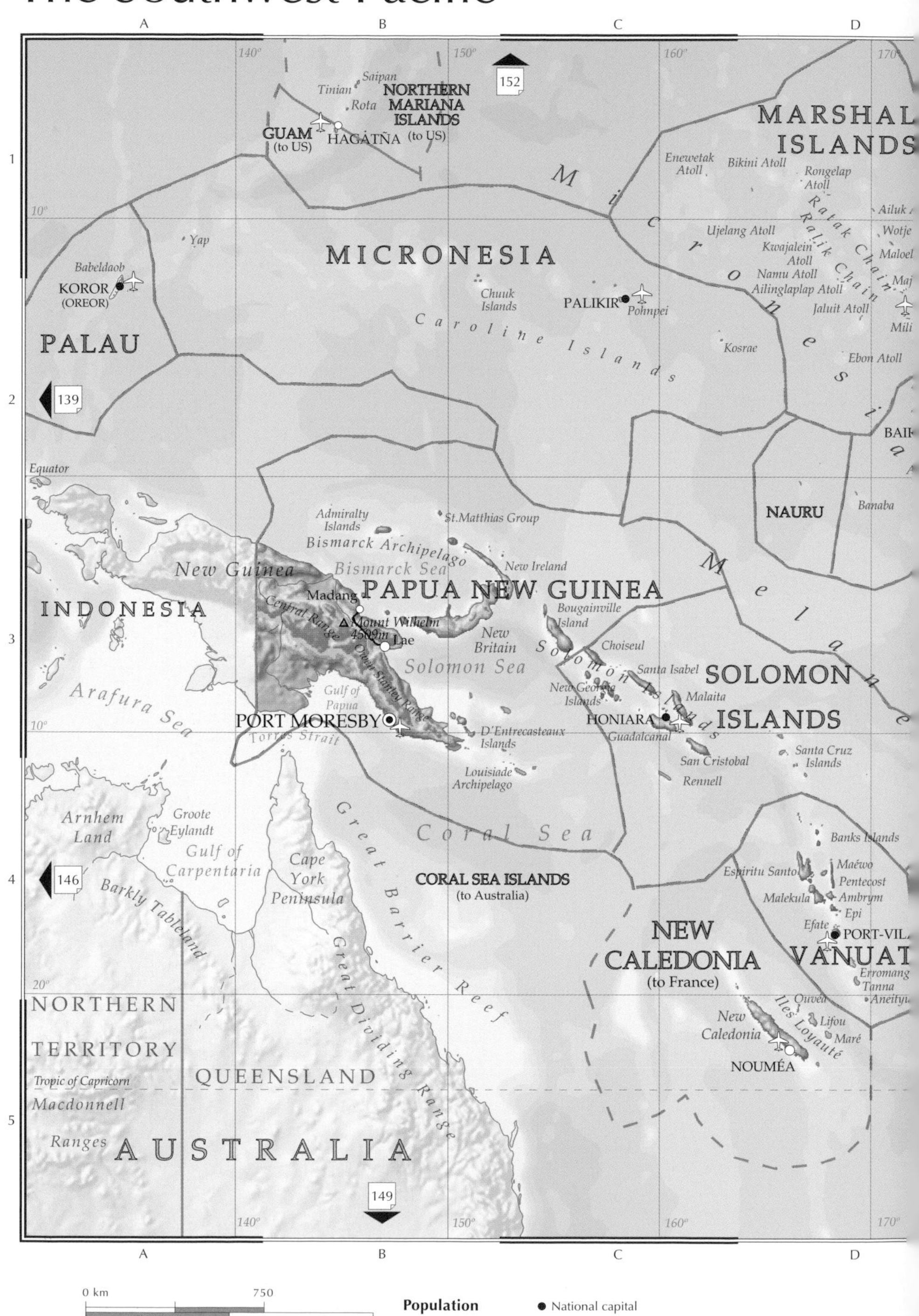

0 km ————————— 750

0 miles ———————— 750

Population ● National capital

○ below 50,000 ○ 50,000 to 100,000 ◉ 100,000 to 500,000 ■ above 500,00

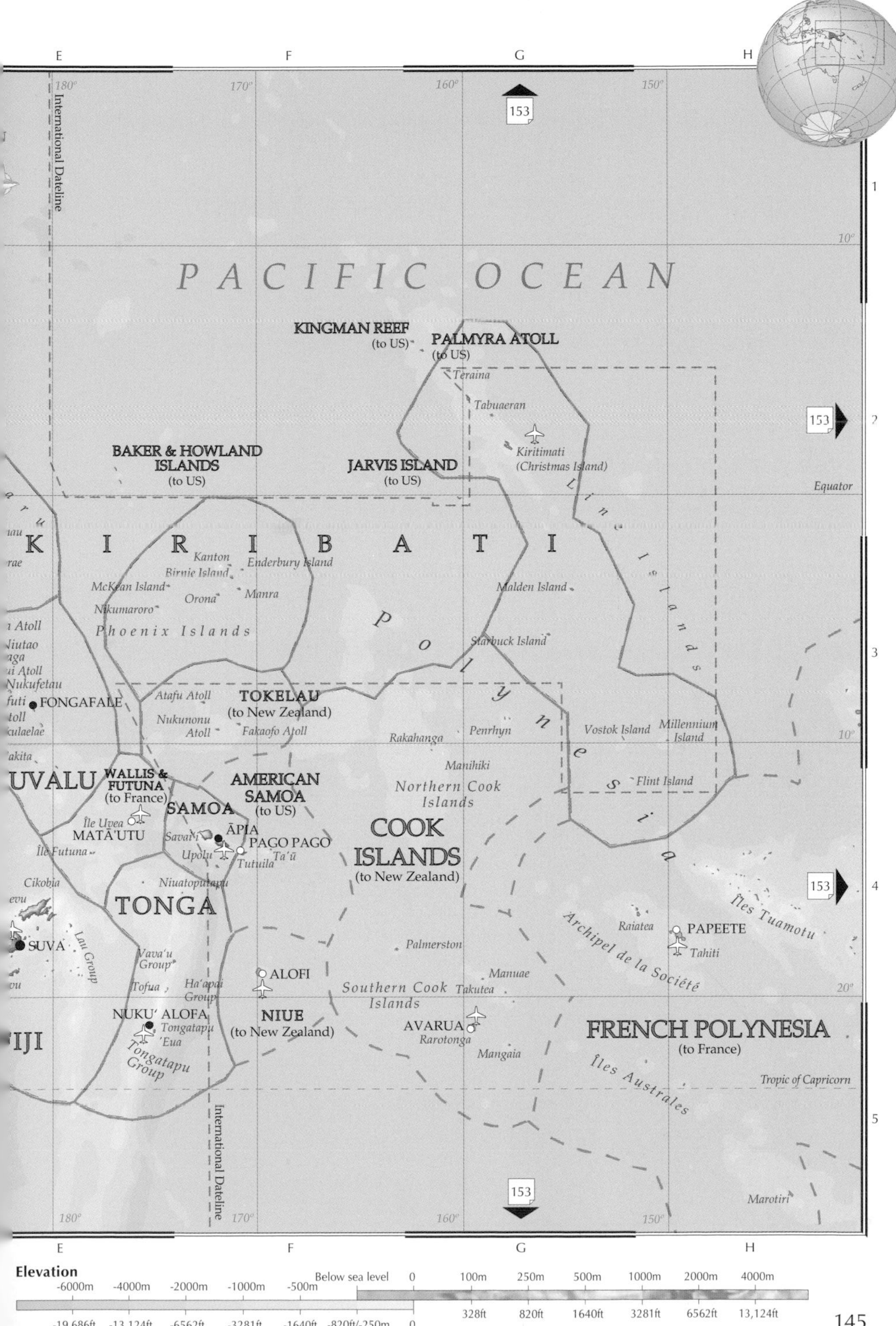

PACIFIC OCEAN

KINGMAN REEF
(to US)

PALMYRA ATOLL
(to US)

Teraina

Tabuaeran

BAKER & HOWLAND
ISLANDS
(to US)

JARVIS ISLAND
(to US)

Kiritimati
(Christmas Island)

Equator

K I R I B A T I

Kanton Enderbury Island

Birnie Island

McKean Island *Manra*

Nikumaroro Orona

Phoenix Islands

Malden Island

Starbuck Island

Atafu Atoll

TOKELAU
(to New Zealand)

Nukunonu
Atoll

Fakaofo Atoll

Rakahanga Penrhyn

Vostok Island Millennium
Island

FONGAFALE

UVALU

WALLIS &
FUTUNA
(to France)

Île Uvea
MATÁ'UTU

Île Futuna

Cikobu

SAMOA

Savaii

Upolu

AMERICAN
SAMOA
(to US)

ÁPIA

PAGO PAGO

Ta'ū

Tutuila

Manihiki

*Northern Cook
Islands*

Flint Island

TONGA

Niuatoputapu

Vava'u
Group

SUVA

Tofua

Lau Group

Ha'apai
Group

NUKU' ALOFA Tongatapu

'Eua

Tongatapu
Group

IJI

NIUE
(to New Zealand)

ALOFI

*Southern Cook
Islands*

Palmerston

Manuae Takutea

AVARUA
Rarotonga

Mangaia

COOK
ISLANDS
(to New Zealand)

Raiatea

PAPEETE

Tahiti

Archipel de la Société

Îles Tuamotu

FRENCH POLYNESIA
(to France)

Îles Australes

Tropic of Capricorn

Marotiri

International Dateline

International Dateline

Lin *Islands*

P o l y n e s i a

Elevation

-6000m	-4000m	-2000m	-1000m	-500m	Below sea level	0	100m	250m	500m	1000m	2000m	4000m
-19,686ft	-13,124ft	-6562ft	-3281ft	-1640ft	-820ft/-250m	0	328ft	820ft	1640ft	3281ft	6562ft	13,124ft

Western Australia

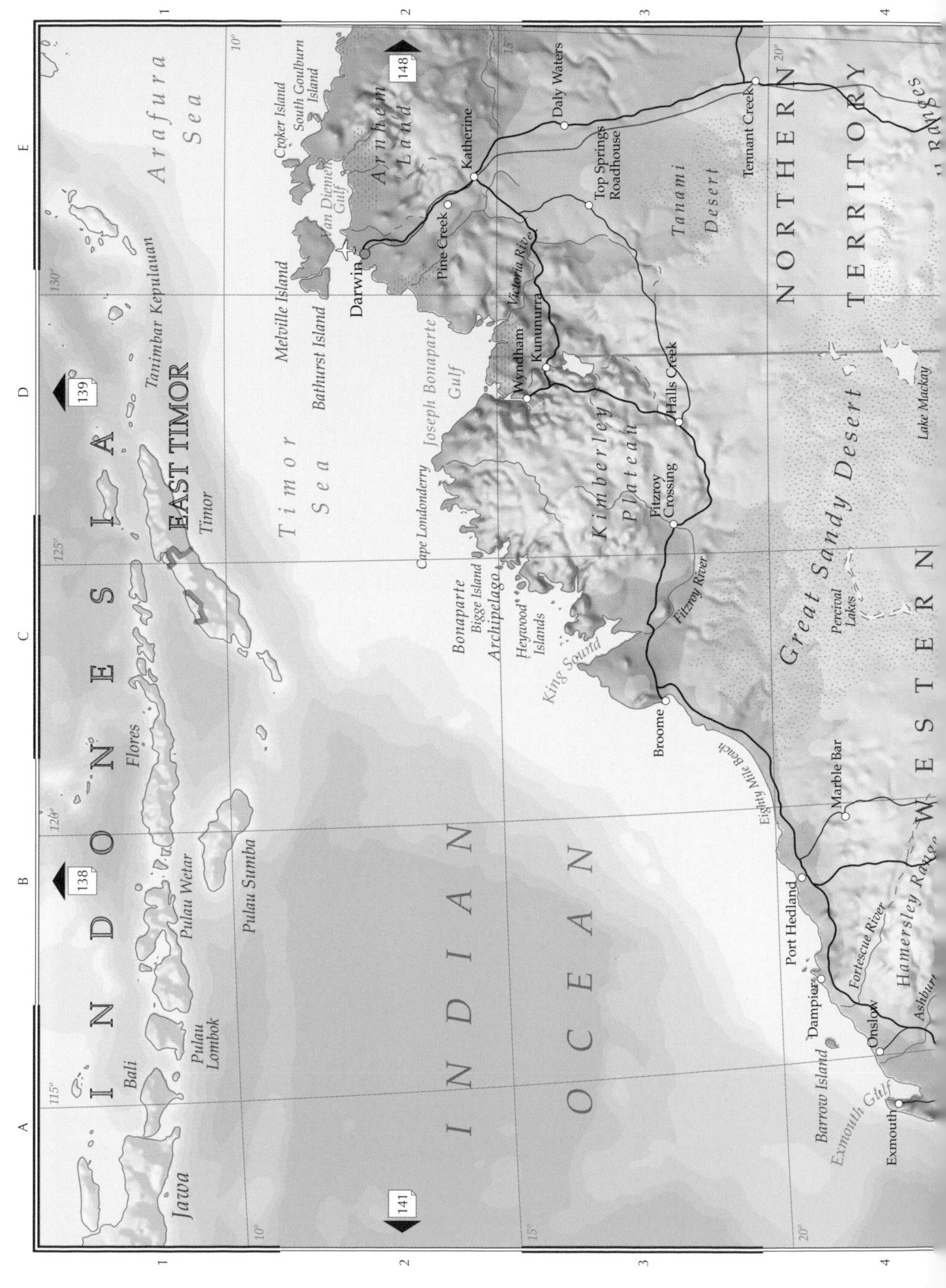

0 km   300
0 miles   300

Population   ● National capital   ● Internal administrative capital

○ below 50,000   ○ 50,000 to 100,000   ◉ 100,000 to 500,000   ◼ above 500,00

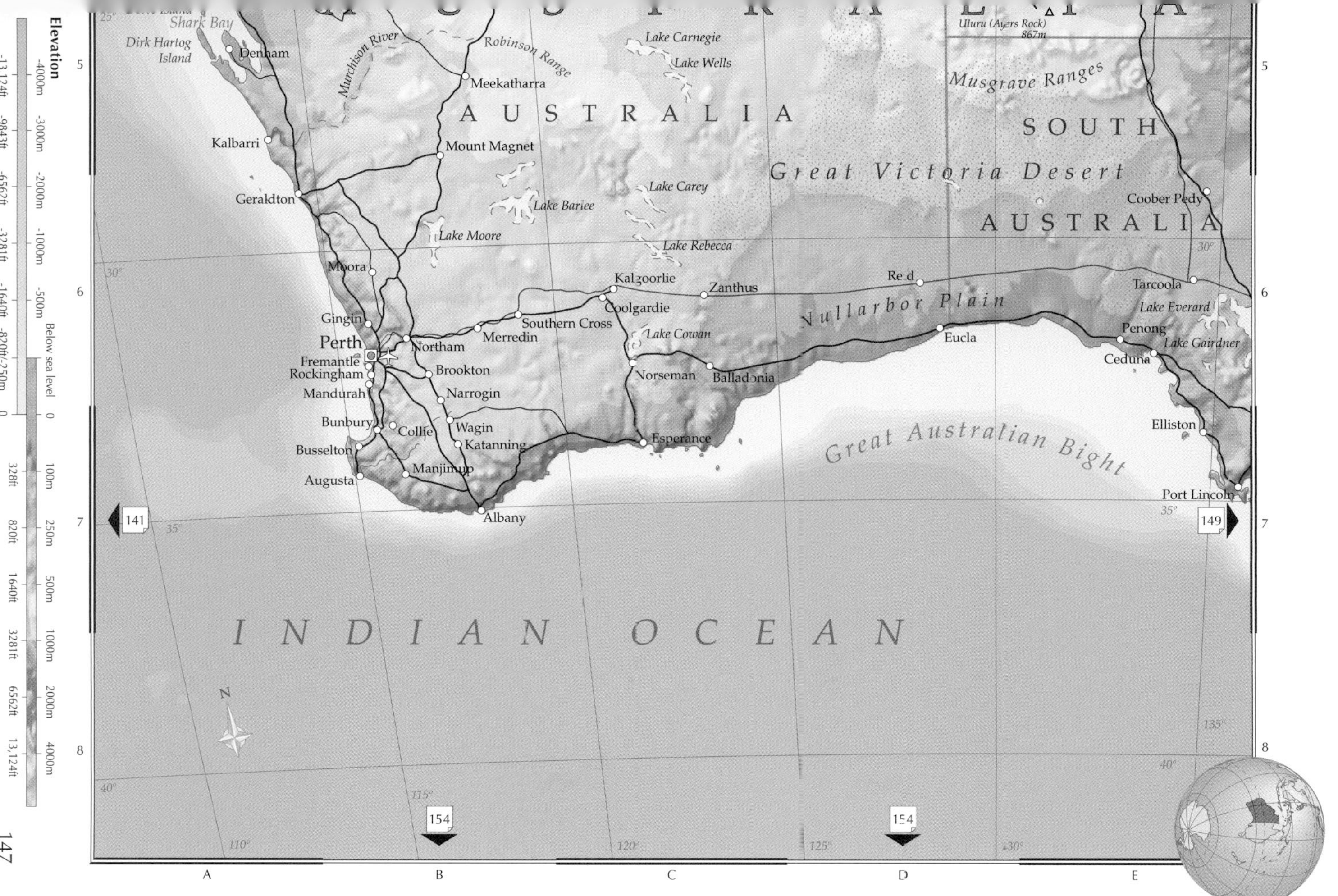

Ularu (Ayers Rock)
862m

Musgrave Ranges

SOUTH

AUSTRALIA

Great Victoria Desert

AUSTRALIA

Coober Pedy
Tarcoola
Lake Everard
Penong
Lake Gairdner
Ceduna
Elliston
Port Lincoln

149

Great Australian Bight

Eucla

Red

Nullarbor Plain

INDIAN OCEAN

154

Zanthus
Lake Cowan
Balladonia
Kalgoorlie
Coolgardie
Norseman
Esperance

Lake Rebecca

Lake Carey

Lake Wells

Lake Carnegie

Robinson Range

Meekatharra

Mount Magnet

Lake Barlee

Lake Moore

Southern Cross
Merredin
Northam
Brookton
Narrogin
Wagin
Katanning
Collie
Manjimup
Albany

154

Murchison River

Moora
Gingin
Perth
Fremantle
Rockingham
Mandurah
Bunbury
Busselton
Augusta

Denham
Shark Bay
Dirk Hartog
Island

Kalbarri

Geraldton

N

141

Elevation

| -4000m | -3000m | -2000m | -1000m | -500m | Below sea level | 0 | 100m | 250m | 500m | 1000m | 2000m | 4000m |

| -13,124ft | -9843ft | -6562ft | -3281ft | -1640ft | -820ft/-250m | 0 | 328ft | 820ft | 1640ft | 3281ft | 6562ft | 13,124ft |

147

Eastern Australia

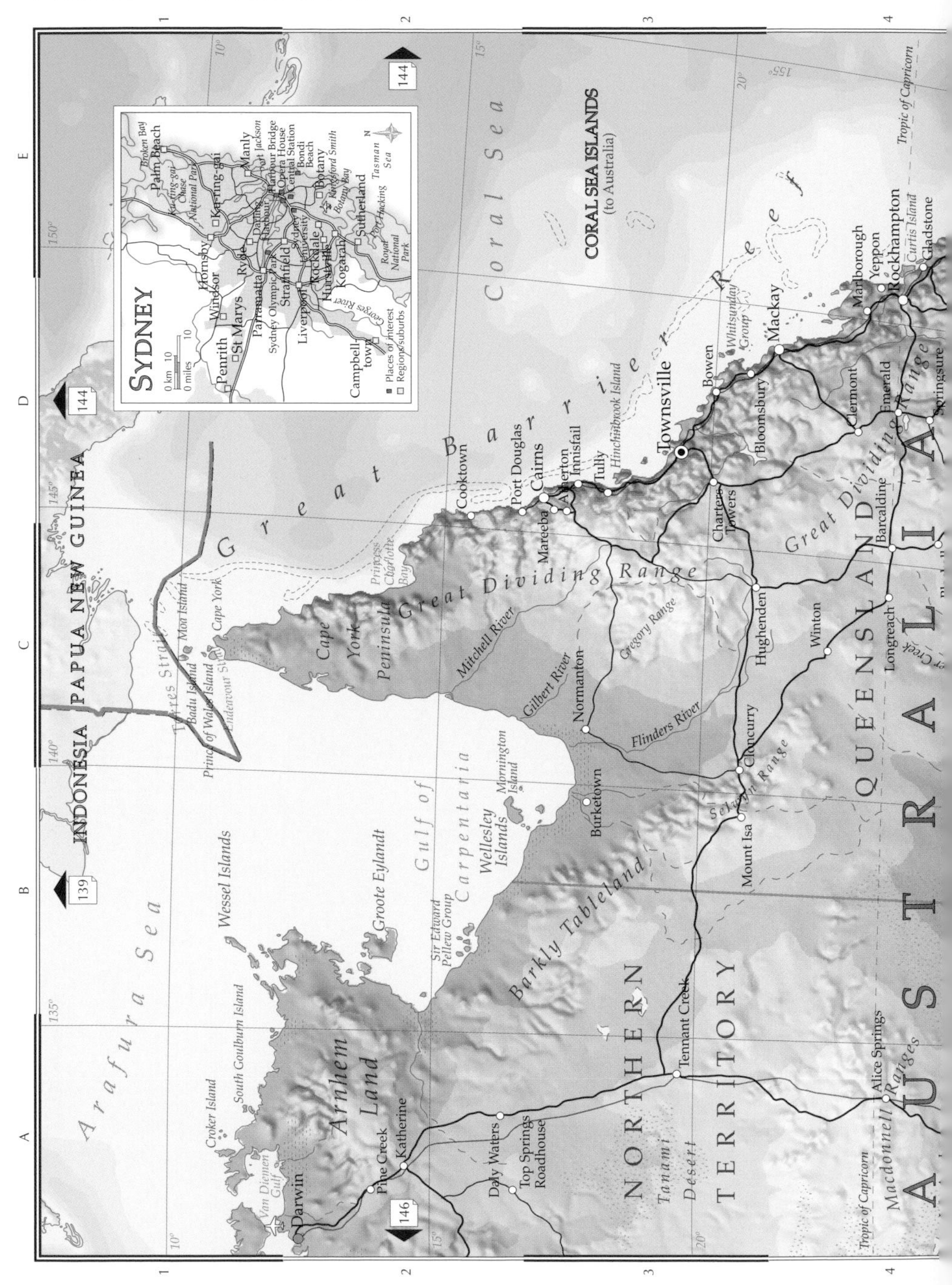

SYDNEY

Token Bay
Palm Beach
Ku-ring-gai
Chase
National Park
Manly
Sydney Harbour Bridge
Port Jackson Opera House
Central Station
Bondi
Beach
Botany
Bay
Tasman
Sea
Hornsby
Ryde
Bankford Smith
Windsor
Parramatta
Strathfield
Sutherland
Botany
Bay
St Marys
Sydney Olympic Park
Auburn
Kogarah
Royal
National
Park
Penrith
Liverpool
Fairfield
George's River
Campbelltown
■ Places of interest
■ Regions/suburbs

0 km   10
0 miles   10

CORAL SEA ISLANDS
(to Australia)

Coral Sea

Great Barrier Reef

PAPUA NEW GUINEA

INDONESIA

Torres Strait

Cape York
Boigu Island
Mer Island
Prince of Wales Island
Endeavour Strait
Cape York

Great Dividing Range

Cooktown
Port Douglas
Cairns
Mareeba
Atherton
Innisfail
Tully
Hinchinbrook Island
Townsville
Bowen
Whitsunday Group
Mackay
Bloomsbury
Marlborough
Yeppoon
Rockhampton
Curtis Island
Gladstone
Springsure

Tropic of Capricorn

Charters Towers

Hughenden
Clermont
Emerald
Barcaldine
Winton
Longreach

QUEENSLAND

Cape
York
Peninsula

Princess
Charlotte
Bay

Mitchell River

Gilbert River

Normanton

Flinders River

Gregory Range

Selwyn Range

Cooper Creek

AUSTRALIA

Great Dividing Range

Gulf of
Carpentaria

Burketown

Mount Isa
Cloncurry

Arafura Sea

Wessel Islands

Groote Eylandt

Sir Edward
Pellew Group
Wellesley
Islands
Mornington
Island

Barkly Tableland

Croker Island
South Goulburn Island

Van Diemen Gulf

Darwin

Arnhem
Land

Pine Creek
Katherine

NORTHERN

TERRITORY

Daly Waters
Top Springs
Roadhouse

Tennant Creek

Tanami Desert

Alice Springs
Macdonnell Ranges

Tropic of Capricorn

0 km   300
0 miles   300

Population

○ below 50,000
○ 50,000 to 100,000
◉ 100,000 to 500,000
◻ above 500,00[0]

● National capital
○ Internal administrative capital

SOUTH AUSTRALIA

NEW SOUTH WALES

VICTORIA

TASMANIA

AUSTRALIAN CAPITAL TERRITORY

Tasman Sea

Great Victoria Desert

Coober Pedy
Lake Eyre North
Lake Eyre South
Marree
Lake Blanche
Lake Callabonna
Lake Frome
Lake Torrens
Lake Gardner
Lake Everard
Tarcoola
Flinders Ranges
Port Augusta
Whyalla
Port Pirie
Eyre Peninsula
Spencer Gulf
Port Lincoln
Elliston
Ceduna
Penong
Kangaroo Island
Investigator Strait
Elizabeth
Adelaide
Gawler
Crystal Brook
Peterborough
Broken Hill
Tailem Bend
Murray River
Keith
Naracoorte
Mount Gambier
Portland
Warrnambool
Ouyen
Mildura
Darling River
Wilcannia
Barrier Range
Grey Range
Cunnamulla
Warrego River
Bourke
Cobar
Ivanhoe
Hay
Murrumbidgee River
Lachlan River
Balonne
Barwon River
Nyngan
Dubbo
Parkes
Cootamundra
Wagga Wagga
Deniliquin
Albury
Wangaratta
Shepparton
Bendigo
Horsham
Ballarat
Geelong
Sunbury
Melbourne
Moe
Traralgon
Sale
Bairnsdale
Australian Alps
Mount Kosciuszko 2228m
Nodonga
Cooma
Bega
Goulburn
CANBERRA
Wollongong
Sydney
Parramatta
Gosford
Newcastle
Lithgow
Bathurst
Orange
Gunnedah
Tamworth
Narrabri
Walgett
Moree
Goondiwindi
St. George
Moonie
Dalby
Toowoomba
Warwick
Stanthorpe
Armidale
Muswellbrook
Taree
Port Macquarie
Coffs Harbour
Grafton
Great Dividing Range
Lismore
Murwillumbah
Surfers Paradise
Gold Coast
Ipswich
Brisbane
Caloundra
Bass Strait
South East Point
King Island
Hunter Island
Flinders Island
Cape Barren Island
Banks Strait
Marrawah
Burnie
Devonport
Launceston
Hobart
Maria Island
South Bruny Island

Elevation

-4000m	-3000m	-2000m	-1000m	-500m	Below sea level	0	100m	250m	500m	1000m	2000m	4000m
-13,124ft	-9843ft	-6562ft	-3281ft	-1640ft	-820ft/-250m	0	328ft	820ft	1640ft	3281ft	6562ft	13,124ft

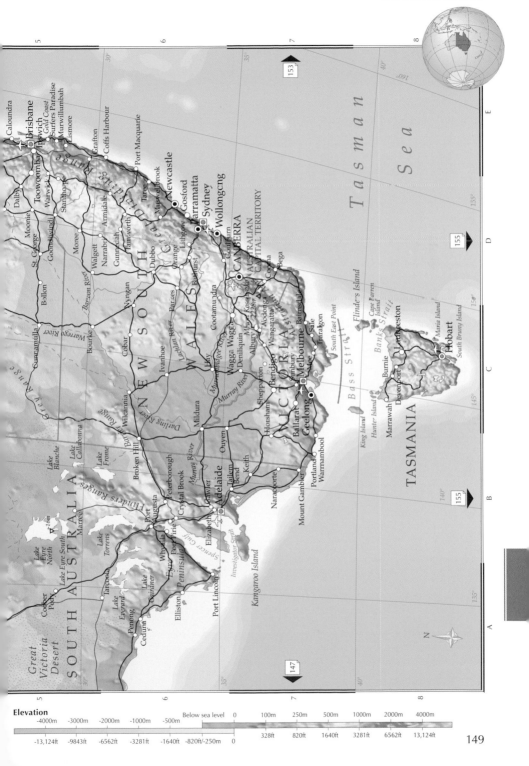

New Zealand

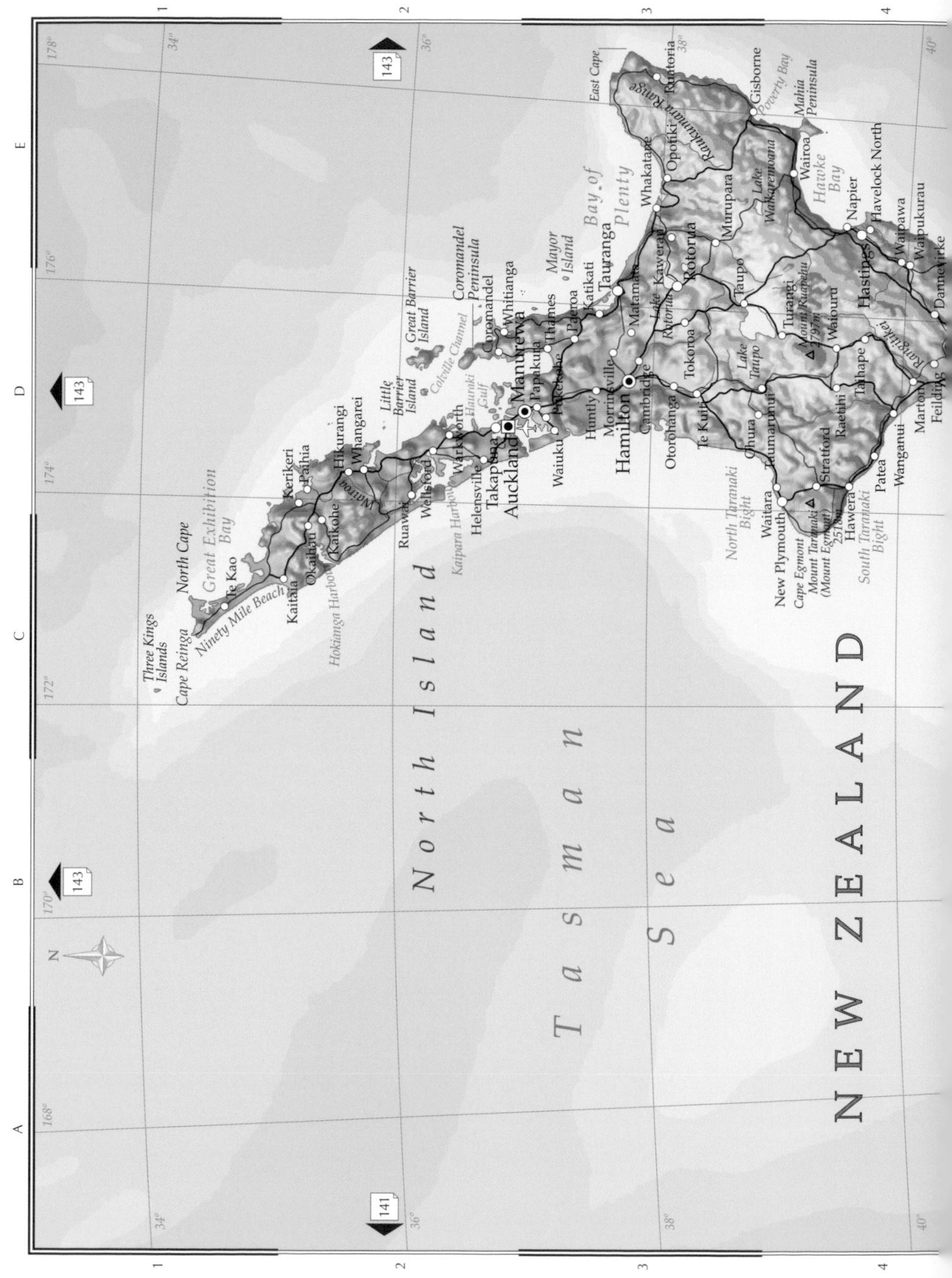

0 km 100

0 miles 100

Population

● National capital

○ below 50,000 ⊙ 50,000 to 100,000 ◉ 100,000 to 500,000 ◼ above 500,000

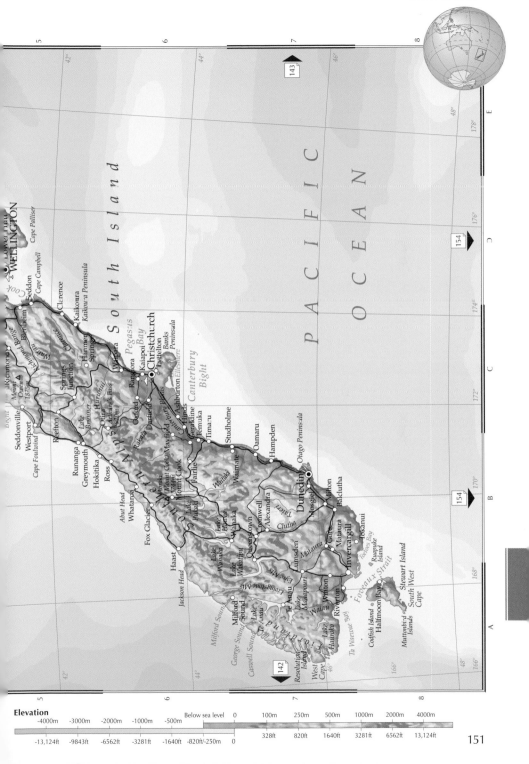

143

154

154

142

WELLINGTON

LOWER HUTT

Cape Palliser

Cape Campbell

Seddon

Cape Clarence

Blenheim

Kaikoura

Richmond

Mount Owen 1875m

Nelson

Kaikoura Peninsula

Hanmer Springs

Springs Junction

Reefton

Murchison

Lake Rotoroa

Lake Brunner

Waiau

Rangiora

Kaiapoi

Christchurch

Lyttelton

Pegasus Bay

Banks Peninsula

Ellesmere

Seddonville

Westport

Cape Foulwind

Runanga

Greymouth

Hokitika

Ross

Abut Head

Whataroa

Fox Glacier

Haast

Jackson Head

Otira

Arthur's Pass 920m

Oxford

Darfield

Sheffield

Rakaia

Mayfield

Ashburton

Geraldine

Temuka

Timaru

Studholme

Oamaru

Hampden

Waimate

Waitaki

Fairlie

Mount Cook

Lake Pukaki

Lake Ohau

Lake Hawea

Wanaka

Lake Wanaka

Lake Wakatipu

Queenstown

Cromwell

Alexandra

Milford Sound

George Sound

Caswell Sound

Te Anau

Lake Te Anau

Lake Manapouri

Lake Hauroko

Resolution Island

West Cape

Manapouri

Waiau

Winton

Riverton

Lumsden

Gore

Mataura

Mataura

Clutha

Taieri

Mosgiel

Milton

Balclutha

Dunedin

Otago Peninsula

Invercargill

Oreti

Bluff

Toetoes Bay

Te Waewae Bay

Codfish Island

Halfmoon Bay

Muttonbird Islands

Ruapuke Island

Stewart Island

South West Cape

Foveaux Strait

Cook Strait

South Island

Southern Alps

Pacific Ocean

Canterbury Bight

Elevation

-4000m	-3000m	-2000m	-1000m	-500m	Below sea level	0	100m	250m	500m	1000m	2000m	4000m
-13,124ft	-9843ft	-6562ft	-3281ft	-1640ft	-820ft/-250m	0	328ft	820ft	1640ft	3281ft	6562ft	13,124ft

The Pacific Ocean

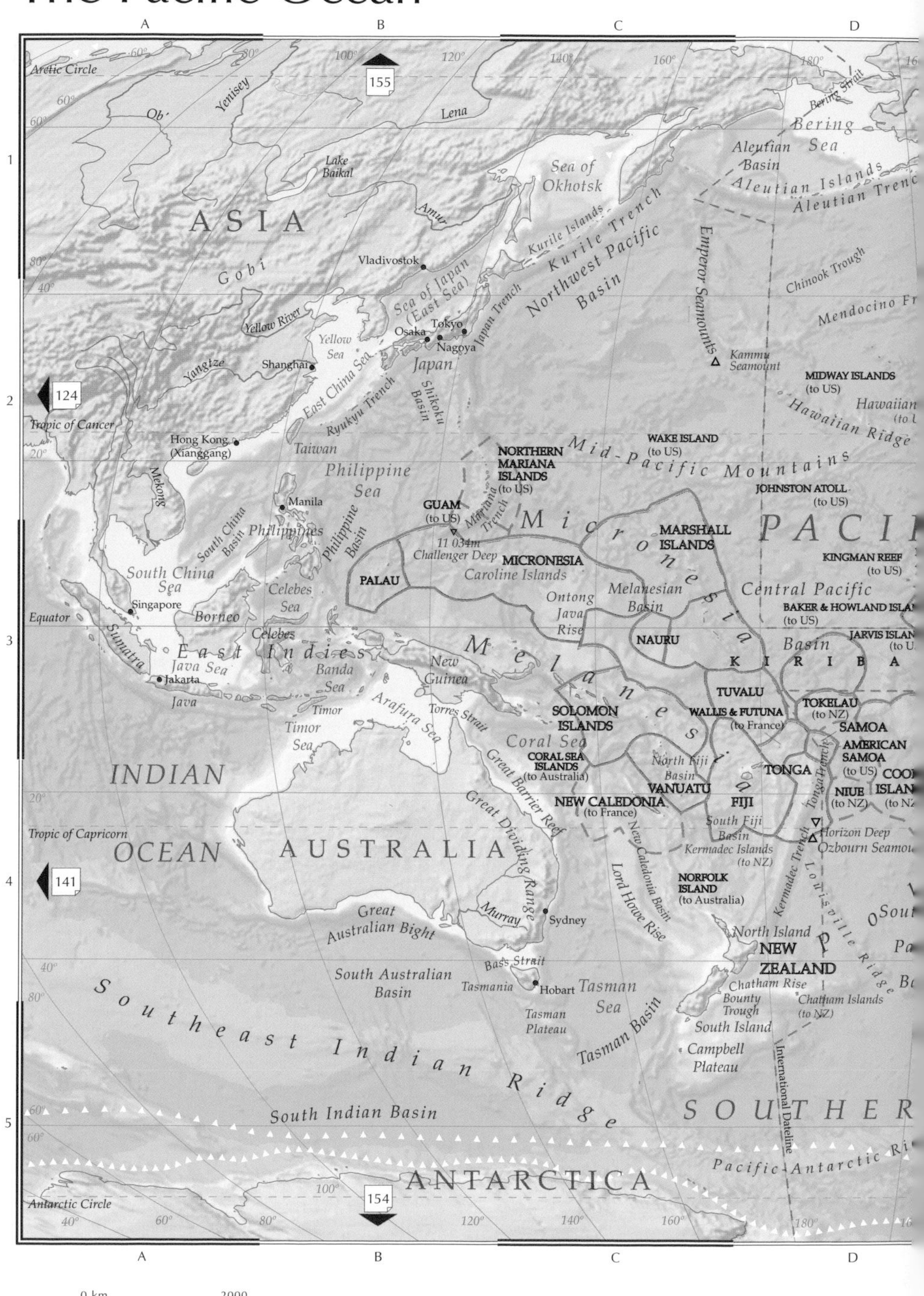

Arctic Circle

Ob'
Yenisey
Lena

155

ASIA

Lake Baikal

Amur

Gobi

Sea of Okhotsk

Bering Sea

Aleutian Basin
Aleutian Islands
Aleutian Trench

Kurile Islands
Kurile Trench
Northwest Pacific Basin

Bering Strait

Chinook Trough

Emperor Seamounts

Mendocino Fr

124

Vladivostok

Yellow River

Yellow Sea

Sea of Japan (East Sea)

Japan Trench

Osaka Tokyo
Nagoya
Japan

Shanghai

Kammu Seamount

MIDWAY ISLANDS (to US)

Hawaiian (to U

Tropic of Cancer

Hong Kong (Xianggang)

Taiwan

East China Sea

Ryukyu Trench

Shikoku Basin

Mid-Pacific Mountains

Hawaiian Ridge

Mekong

Philippine Sea

NORTHERN MARIANA ISLANDS (to US)

Micronesia

PACI

Manila

Philippines

Philippine Basin

GUAM (to US)
11 034m
Challenger Deep

Mariana Trench

MARSHALL ISLANDS

JOHNSTON ATOLL (to US)

South China Basin

MICRONESIA
Caroline Islands

KINGMAN REEF (to US)

South China Sea

PALAU

Celebes Sea

Ontong Java Rise

Melanesian Basin

Central Pacific

BAKER & HOWLAND ISLA (to US)

Singapore

Borneo

NAURU

Basin

JARVIS ISLAN (to U

Equator

Celebes

East Indies

Melanesia

KIRIBA

Java Sea

Banda Sea

New Guinea

TUVALU

WALLIS & FUTUNA (to France)

TOKELAU (to NZ)

Jakarta

Java

Timor

Torres Strait

SOLOMON ISLANDS

SAMOA

Timor Sea

Arafura Sea

Coral Sea

CORAL SEA ISLANDS (to Australia)

North Fiji Basin

TONGA

AMERICAN SAMOA (to US)

NIUE (to NZ)

COO
ISLAN
(to Nz

INDIAN

Great Barrier Reef

NEW CALEDONIA (to France)

VANUATU

FIJI

South Fiji Basin

Horizon Deep
Ozbourn Seamou

Tropic of Capricorn

AUSTRALIA

Great Dividing Range

New Caledonia Basin

Kermadec Islands (to NZ)

141

OCEAN

NORFOLK ISLAND (to Australia)

Lord Howe Rise

Great Australian Bight

Murray

Sydney

North Island

NEW ZEALAND

Sout

Pa

B

South Australian Basin

Bass Strait

Tasmania Hobart

Tasman Sea

Tasman Basin

Chatham Rise

Bounty Trough

Chatham Islands (to NZ)

Southeast Indian Ridge

Tasman Plateau

South Island

Campbell Plateau

SOUTHER

South Indian Basin

Pacific Antarctic Ri

ANTARCTICA

154

Antarctic Circle

0 km   2000
0 miles   2000

● Major port

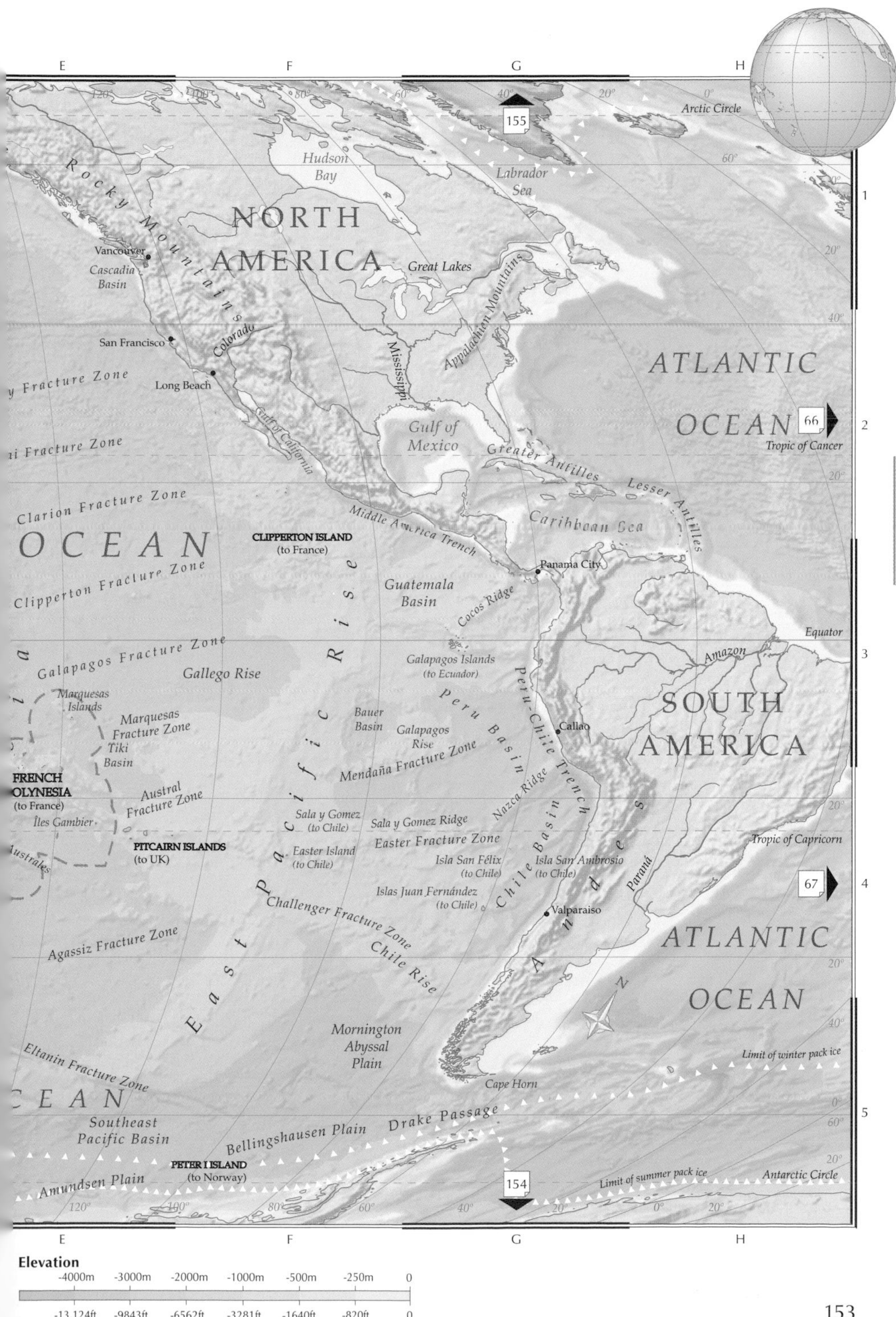

E | F | G | H

Arctic Circle

Hudson Bay

Labrador Sea

155

NORTH AMERICA

Rocky Mountains

Vancouver

Cascadia Basin

Great Lakes

ATLANTIC

San Francisco

Colorado

Appalachian Mountains

Long Beach

Mississippi

OCEAN

66

Tropic of Cancer

y Fracture Zone

Gulf of California

Gulf of Mexico

Greater Antilles

Lesser Antilles

i Fracture Zone

Caribbean Sea

Clarion Fracture Zone

Middle America Trench

OCEAN

Cocos Ridge

Panama City

CLIPPERTON ISLAND
(to France)

Guatemala Basin

Clipperton Fracture Zone

Galapagos Fracture Zone

Gallego Rise

Galapagos Islands
(to Ecuador)

Equator

Amazon

SOUTH

Marquesas Islands

Marquesas Fracture Zone

Tiki Basin

Bauer Basin

Galapagos Rise

Peru Basin

Callao

AMERICA

FRENCH POLYNESIA
(to France)

Austral Fracture Zone

Mendaña Fracture Zone

Nazca Ridge

East Pacific Rise

Peru-Chile Trench

Îles Gambier

Sala y Gomez
(to Chile)

Sala y Gomez Ridge

Chile Basin

Andes

Tropic of Capricorn

Australes

PITCAIRN ISLANDS
(to UK)

Easter Island
(to Chile)

Easter Fracture Zone

Isla San Félix
(to Chile)

Isla San Ambrosio
(to Chile)

Paraná

67

Islas Juan Fernández
(to Chile)

Valparaíso

Challenger Fracture Zone

Chile Rise

ATLANTIC

Agassiz Fracture Zone

N

OCEAN

Eltanin Fracture Zone

Mornington Abyssal Plain

Cape Horn

Limit of winter pack ice

OCEAN

Southeast Pacific Basin

Bellingshausen Plain

Drake Passage

PETER I ISLAND
(to Norway)

Antarctic Circle

Amundsen Plain

154

Limit of summer pack ice

E | F | G | H

Elevation

| -4000m | -3000m | -2000m | -1000m | -500m | -250m | 0 |
| -13,124ft | -9843ft | -6562ft | -3281ft | -1640ft | -820ft | 0 |

Antarctica

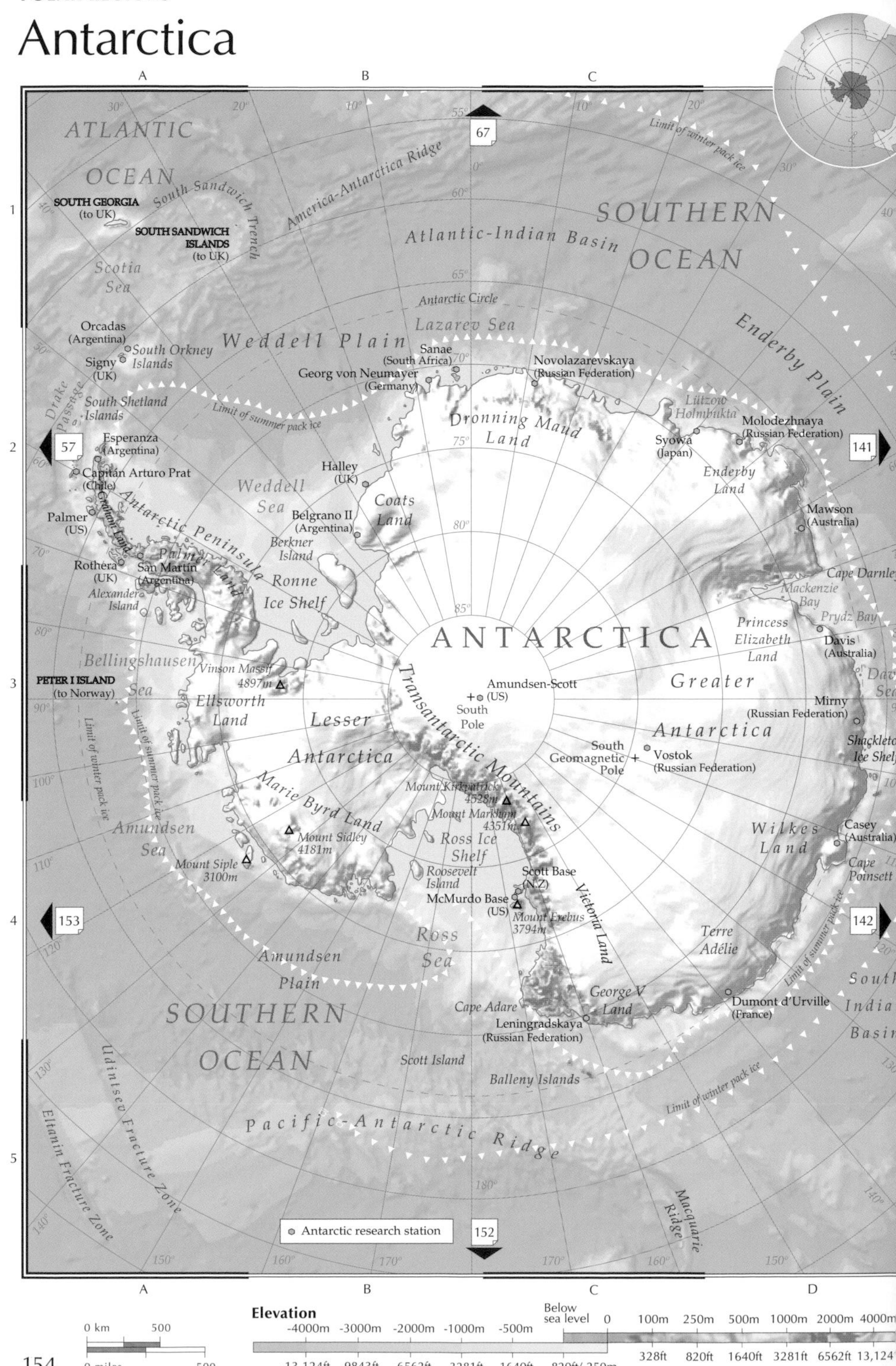

ATLANTIC
OCEAN

SOUTH GEORGIA
(to UK)

SOUTH SANDWICH
ISLANDS
(to UK)

*Scotia
Sea*

South Sandwich Trench

America-Antarctica Ridge

67

SOUTHERN

Atlantic-Indian Basin

OCEAN

Antarctic Circle

Orcadas
(Argentina)

Weddell Plain

Lazarev Sea

Enderby Plain

South Orkney
Islands

Signy
(UK)

South Shetland
Islands

Sanae
(South Africa)

Georg von Neumayer
(Germany)

Novolazarevskaya
(Russian Federation)

Limit of summer pack ice

57

Esperanza
(Argentina)

Capitán Arturo Prat
(Chile)

Palmer
(US)

Halley
(UK)

*Dronning Maud
Land*

Lützow
Holmbukta

Syowa
(Japan)

Molodezhnaya
(Russian Federation)

141

*Weddell
Sea*

Belgrano II
(Argentina)

*Coats
Land*

*Enderby
Land*

Mawson
(Australia)

Rothera
(UK)

San Martín
(Argentina)

Berkner
Island

*Ronne
Ice Shelf*

Cape Darnley

*Mackenzie
Bay*

Prydz Bay

*Alexander
Island*

ANTARCTICA

*Princess
Elizabeth
Land*

Davis
(Australia)

*Day
Sea*

PETER I ISLAND
(to Norway)

*Bellingshausen
Sea*

Vinson Massif
4897m

Amundsen-Scott
(US)

South
Pole

Greater

Mirny
(Russian Federation)

*Shackleto
Ice Shelf*

*Ellsworth
Land*

*Lesser
Antarctica*

South
Geomagnetic
Pole

Vostok
(Russian Federation)

Antarctica

*Amundsen
Sea*

Marie Byrd Land

Mount Sidley
4181m

Mount Kirkpatrick
4528m

Mount Markham
4351m

*Wilkes
Land*

Casey
(Australia)

Cape
Poinsett

Mount Siple
3100m

*Ross Ice
Shelf*

Roosevelt
Island

Scott Base
(NZ)

McMurdo Base
(US)

Mount Erebus
3794m

*Terre
Adélie*

153

*Amundsen
Plain*

*Ross
Sea*

142

SOUTHERN

OCEAN

Cape Adare

Leningradskaya
(Russian Federation)

*George V
Land*

Dumont d'Urville
(France)

*South
India
Basin*

Scott Island

Balleny Islands

Pacific-Antarctic Ridge

*Macquarie
Ridge*

Eltanin Fracture Zone

Udintsev Fracture Zone

⊙ Antarctic research station

152

154

Elevation

-4000m -3000m -2000m -1000m -500m

Below
sea level   0   100m 250m 500m 1000m 2000m 4000m

0 km   500

0 miles   500

-13,124ft -9843ft -6562ft -3281ft -1640ft

-820ft/-250m   328ft 820ft 1640ft 3281ft 6562ft 13,124

Arctic Ocean

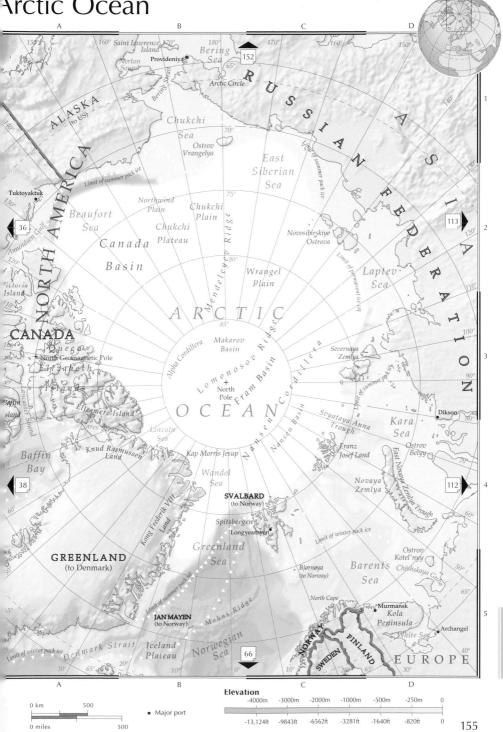

150° Saint Lawrence, 170° 180° 170° 160° 150°
Island
160° Bering
Norton 65° Sea
Sound Provideniya
Arctic Circle

ALASKA
(to USA)
Chukchi
Sea 70°
Ostrov
Vrangelya
East
Siberian
Sea

RUSSIAN FEDERATION

NORTH AMERICA
Tuktoyaktuk
Limit of summer pack ice
Beaufort
Sea
Canada
Basin
Northwind
Plain
Chukchi
Plain
Chukchi
Plateau
75°

Novosibirskiye
Ostrova
Limit of permanent ice cap

Mendeleyev Ridge
80°
Wrangel
Plain

Laptev
Sea

ASIA

CANADA
Victoria
Island
Queen
North Geomagnetic Pole
Elizabeth
Islands
Baffin
Island
Lancaster Sound

Alpha Cordillera
ARCTIC
85°
Makarov
Basin
Lomonosov Ridge
+
North
Pole
Fram Basin

OCEAN

Nansen Cordillera
Severnaya
Zemlya

Ellesmere Island
Nares Strait
Knud Rasmussen
Land
Lincoln
Sea
Kap Morris Jesup

Nansen Basin
Svyataya Anna
Trough

Kara
Sea
Dikson
Ostrov
Belyy

Baffin
Bay
Wandel
Sea
Franz
Josef Land

Novaya
Zemlya
East Novaya Zemlya Trough

GREENLAND
(to Denmark)
Kong Frederik VIII
Land
SVALBARD
(to Norway)
Spitsbergen
Longyearbyen
Greenland
Sea

Limit of winter pack ice
Bjørnøya
(to Norway)

Ostrov
Kotel'nyy
Chëshskaya Guba

Barents
Sea

North Cape

Murmansk
Kola
Peninsula
Archangel

JAN MAYEN
(to Norway)
Iceland
Plateau
Mohns Ridge
Norwegian
Sea
NORWAY
FINLAND
SWEDEN
White Sea
EUROPE

Denmark Strait
Limit of winter pack ice

36
152
113
38
112
66

Elevation
-4000m -3000m -2000m -1000m -500m -250m 0
-13,124ft -9843ft -6562ft -3281ft -1640ft -820ft 0

0 km 500
0 miles 500
• Major port

Overseas territories & dependencies

Despite the rapid process of global decolonization since the Second World War, around 8 million people in more than 50 territories around the world continue to live under the protection of France, Australia, the Netherlands, Denmark, Norway, New Zealand, the UK, or the USA. These remnants of former colonial empires may have persisted for economic, strategic or political reasons and are administered in a variety of ways.

AUSTRALIA

Australia's overseas territories have not been an issue since Papua New Guinea became independent in 1975. Consequently there is no overriding policy toward them. Norfolk Island is inhabited by descendants of the H.M.S Bounty mutineers and more recent Australian migrants.

Ashmore & Cartier Islands
Indian Ocean
Status: External territory
Claimed: 1931
Capital: Not applicable
Population: None
Area: 2 sq miles
(5.2 sq km)

Christmas Island
Indian Ocean
Status: External territory
Claimed: 1958
Capital: The Settlement
Population: 1493
Area: 52 sq miles
(135 sq km)

Cocos Islands
Indian Ocean
Status: External territory
Claimed: 1955
Capital: No official capital
Population: 574
Area: 5.5 sq miles
(14 sq km)

Coral Sea Islands
South Pacific
Status: External territory
Claimed: 1969
Capital: None
Population: 8 (meteorologists)
Area: Less than 1.2 sq miles
(3 sq km)

Heard & McDonald Is.
Indian Ocean
Status: External territory
Claimed: 1947
Capital: Not applicable
Population: None
Area: 161 sq miles
(417 sq km)

Norfolk Island
South Pacific
Status: External territory
Claimed: 1774
Capital: Kingston
Population: 1828
Area: 13 sq miles
(34 sq km)

DENMARK

The Faeroe Islands have been under Danish administration since Queen Margreth I of Denmark inherited Norway in 1380. The Home Rule Act of 1948 gave the Faeroese control over all their internal affairs. Greenland first came under Danish rule in 1380. Today, Denmark is responsible for the island's foreign affairs and defense.

Faeroe Islands
North Atlantic
Status: External territory
Claimed: 1380
Capital: Tórshavn
Population: 47,246
Area: 540 sq miles
(1399 sq km)

Greenland
North Atlantic
Status: External territory
Claimed: 1380
Capital: Nuuk
Population: 56,361
Area: 840,000 sq miles
(2,175,516 sq km)

FRANCE

France has developed economic ties with its *Territoires d'Outre-Mer,* thereby stressing interdependence over independence. Overseas *départements,* officially part of France, have their own governments. Territorial *collectivités* and overseas *territoires* have varying degrees of autonomy.

Clipperton Island
East Pacific
Status: Dependency of French Polynesia
Claimed: 1935
Capital: Not applicable
Population: None
Area: 2.7 sq miles
(7 sq km)

French Guiana
South America
Status: Overseas department
Claimed: 1817
Capital: Cayenne
Population: 199,509
Area: 35,135 sq miles
(90,996 sq km)

French Polynesia
South Pacific
Status: Overseas territory
Claimed: 1843
Capital: Papeete
Population: 260,000
Area: 1608 sq miles
(4165 sq km)

Guadeloupe
West Indies
Status: Overseas department
Claimed: 1635
Capital: Basse-Terre
Population: 452,000
Area: 687 sq miles
(1780 sq km)

Martinique
West Indies
Status: Overseas
department
Claimed: 1635
Capital: Fort-de-France
Population: 397,000
Area: 425 sq miles
(1100 sq km)

Mayotte
Indian Ocean
Status: Territorial
collectivity
Claimed: 1843
Capital: Mamoudzou
Population: 201,234
Area: 144 sq miles
(374 sq km)

New Caledonia
South Pacific
Status: Overseas territory
Claimed: 1853
Capital: Nouméa
Population: 241,000
Area: 7374 sq miles
(19,100 sq km)

Réunion
Indian Ocean
Status: Overseas
department
Claimed: 1638
Capital: Saint-Denis
Population: 796,000
Area: 970 sq miles
(2500 sq km)

St. Pierre & Miquelon
North America
Status: Territorial collectivity
Claimed: 1604
Capital: Saint-Pierre
Population: 7026
Area: 93 sq miles
(242 sq km)

Wallis & Futuna
South Pacific
Status: Overseas territory
Claimed: 1842
Capital: Matá'Utu
Population: 16,025
Area: 106 sq miles
(274 sq km)

NETHERLANDS

The country's two remaining overseas territories were formerly part of the Dutch West Indies. Both are now self-governing, but the Netherlands remains responsible for their defense.

Aruba
West Indies
Status: Autonomous
part of the Netherlands
Claimed: 1643
Capital: Oranjestad
Population: 71,891
Area: 75 sq miles (194 sq km)

Netherlands Antilles
West Indies
Status: Autonomous
part of the Netherlands
Claimed: 1816
Capital: Willemstad
Population: 184,000
Area: 371 sq miles (960 sq km)

NEW ZEALAND

New Zealand's government has no desire to retain any overseas territories. However, the economic weakness of its dependent territory Tokelau and its freely associated states, Niue and the Cook Islands, has forced New Zealand to remain responsible for their foreign policy and defense.

Cook Islands
South Pacific
Status: Associated territory
Claimed: 1901
Capital: Avarua
Population: 21,388
Area: 91 sq miles
(235 sq km)

Niue
South Pacific
Status: Associated territory
Claimed: 1901
Capital: Alofi
Population: 2166
Area: 102 sq miles
(264 sq km)

Tokelau
South Pacific
Status: Dependent territory
Claimed: 1926
Capital: Not applicable
Population: 1392
Area: 4 sq miles (10 sq km)

NORWAY

In 1920, 41 nations signed the Spits-bergen Treaty recognizing Norwegian sovereignty over Svalbard. There is a NATO base on Jan Mayen. Bouvet Island is a nature reserve.

Bouvet Island
South Atlantic
Status: Dependency
Claimed: 1928
Capital: Not applicable
Population: None
Area: 22 sq miles (58 sq km)

Jan Mayen
North Atlantic
Status: Dependency
Claimed: 1929
Capital: Not applicable
Population: None
Area: 147 sq miles
(381 sq km)

Peter I. Island
Southern Ocean
Status: Dependency
Claimed: 1931
Capital: Not applicable
Population: None
Area: 69 sq miles (180 sq km)

Svalbard
Arctic Ocean
Status: Dependency
Claimed: 1920
Capital: Longyearbyen
Population: 2701
Area: 24,289 sq miles
(62,906 sq km)

Continued on p.158

Overseas territories & dependencies

UNITED KINGDOM

The UK still has the largest number of overseas territories. These are locally-governed by a mixture of elected representatives and appointed officials, and they all enjoy a large measure of internal self-government, but certain powers, such as foreign affairs and defense, are reserved for Governors of the British Crown.

Anguilla
West Indies
Status: Dependent territory
Claimed: 1650
Capital: The Valley
Population: 13,477
Area: 37 sq miles (96 sq km)

Ascension Island
South Atlantic
Status: Dependency of St. Helena
Claimed: 1673
Capital: Georgetown
Population: 1177
Area: 34 sq miles (88 sq km)

Bermuda
North Atlantic
Status: Crown colony
Claimed: 1612
Capital: Hamilton
Population: 65,773
Area: 20 sq miles (53 sq km)

British Indian Ocean Territory
Status: Dependent territory
Claimed: 1814
Capital: Diego Garcia
Population: 4000
Area: 23 sq miles (60 sq km)

British Virgin Islands
West Indies
Status: Dependent territory
Claimed: 1672
Capital: Road Town
Population: 23,098
Area: 59 sq miles (153 sq km)

Cayman Islands
West Indies
Status: Dependent territory
Claimed: 1670
Capital: George Town
Population: 45,436
Area: 100 sq miles (259 sq km)

Falkland Islands
South Atlantic
Status: Dependent territory
Claimed: 1832
Capital: Stanley
Population: 2967
Area: 4699 sq miles (12,173 sq km)

Gibraltar
Southwest Europe
Status: Crown colony
Claimed: 1713
Capital: Gibraltar
Population: 27,928
Area: 2.5 sq miles (6.5 sq km)

Guernsey
Channel Islands
Status: Crown dependency
Claimed: 1066
Capital: St. Peter Port
Population: 65,049
Area: 25 sq miles (65 sq km)

Isle of Man
British Isles
Status: Crown dependency
Claimed: 1765
Capital: Douglas
Population: 75,441
Area: 221 sq miles (572 sq km)

Jersey
Channel Islands
Status: Crown dependency
Claimed: 1066
Capital: St. Helier
Population: 90,084
Area: 45 sq miles (116 sq km)

Montserrat
West Indies
Status: Dependent territory
Claimed: 1632
Capital: Plymouth (currently uninhabitable)
Population: 9439
Area: 40 sq miles (102 sq km)

Pitcairn Islands
South Pacific
Status: Dependent territory
Claimed: 1887
Capital: Adamstown
Population: 45
Area: 18 sq miles (47 sq km)

St. Helena
South Atlantic
Status: Dependent territory
Claimed: 1673
Capital: Jamestown
Population: 4299
Area: 47 sq miles (122 sq km)

South Georgia & The South Sandwich Islands
South Atlantic
Status: Dependent territory
Claimed: 1775
Capital: Not applicable
Population: No permanent residents
Area: 1387 sq miles (3592 sq km)

Tristan da Cunha
South Atlantic
Status: Dependency of St. Helena
Claimed: 1612
Capital: Edinburgh
Population: 276
Area: 38 sq miles (98 sq km)

Turks & Caicos Islands
West Indies
Status: Dependent territory
Claimed: 1766
Capital: Cockburn Town
Population: 21,152
Area: 166 sq miles (430 sq km)

UNITED STATES OF AMERICA

America's overseas territories have been seen as strategically useful, if expensive, links with its "backyards." The US has, in most cases, given the local population a say in deciding their own status. A US Commonwealth territory, such as Puerto Rico, has a greater level of independence than that of a US unincorporated or external territory.

American Samoa
South Pacific
Status: Unincorporated territory
Claimed: 1900
Capital: Pago Pago
Population: 57,794
Area: 75 sq miles (195 sq km)

Baker & Howland Islands
South Pacific
Status: Unincorporated territory
Claimed: 1856
Capital: Not applicable
Population: None
Area: 0.5 sq miles (1.4 sq km)

Guam
West Pacific
Status: Unincorporated territory
Claimed: 1898
Capital: Hagåtña
Population: 172,000
Area: 212 sq miles (549 sq km)

Jarvis Island
South Pacific
Status: Unincorporated territory
Claimed: 1856
Capital: Not applicable
Population: None
Area: 1.7 sq miles (4.5 sq km)

Johnston Atoll
Central Pacific
Status: Unincorporated territory
Claimed: 1858
Capital: Not applicable
Population: Not applicable
Area: 1 sq mile (2.8 sq km)

Kingman Reef
Central Pacific
Status: Administered territory
Claimed: 1856
Capital: Not applicable
Population: None
Area: 0.4 sq mile (1 sq km)

Midway Islands
Central Pacific
Status: Administered territory
Claimed: 1867
Capital: Not applicable
Population: None
Area: 2 sq miles (5.2 sq km)

Navassa Island
West Indies
Status: Unincorporated territory
Claimed: 1856
Capital: Not applicable
Population: None
Area: 2 sq miles (5.2 sq km)

Northern Mariana Islands
West Pacific
Status: Commonwealth territory
Claimed: 1947
Capital: Saipan
Population: 82,459
Area: 177 sq miles (457 sq km)

Palmyra Atoll
Central Pacific
Status: Unincorporated territory
Claimed: 1898
Capital: Not applicable
Population: None
Area: 5 sq miles (12 sq km)

Puerto Rico
West Indies
Status: Commonwealth territory
Claimed: 1898
Capital: San Juan
Population: 4.0 million
Area: 3515 sq miles (9104 sq km)

Virgin Islands
West Indies
Status: Unincorporated territory
Claimed: 1917
Capital: Charlotte Amalie
Population: 108,605
Area: 137 sq miles (355 sq km)

Wake Island
Central Pacific
Status: Unincorporated territory
Claimed: 1898
Capital: Not applicable
Population: 200
Area: 2.5 sq miles (6.5 sq km)

Glossary of geographical terms

The following glossary lists all geographical terms occuring on the maps and in the main-entry names in the Index–Gazetteer. These terms may precede, follow or be run together with the proper elements of the name; where they precede it the term is reversed for indexing purposes – thus Poluostov Yamal is indexed as Yamal, Poluostrov.

A

Å *Danish, Norwegian,* River
Alpen *German,* Alps
Altiplanicie *Spanish,* Plateau
Älv(en) *Swedish,* River
Anse *French,* Bay
Archipiélago *Spanish,* Archipelago
Arcipelago *Italian,* Archipelago
Arquipélago *Portuguese,* Archipelago
Aukštuma *Lithuanian,* Upland

B

Bahía *Spanish,* Bay
Baía *Portuguese,* Bay
Baḥr *Arabic,* River
Baie *French,* Bay
Bandao *Chinese,* Peninsula
Banjaran *Malay,* Mountain range
Batang *Malay,* Stream
-berg *Afrikaans, Norwegian,* Mountain
Birket *Arabic,* Lake
Boğazı *Turkish,* Strait
Bucht *German,* Bay
Bugten *Danish,* Bay
Buḥayrat *Arabic,* Lake, reservoir
Buḥeiret *Arabic,* Lake
Bukit *Malay,* Mountain
-bukta *Norwegian,* Bay
bukten *Swedish,* Bay
Burnu *Turkish,* Cape, point
Buuraha *Somali,* Mountains

C

Cabo *Portuguese,* Cape
Cap *French,* Cape
Cascada *Portuguese,* Waterfall
Cerro *Spanish,* Mountain
Chaîne *French,* Mountain range
Chau *Cantonese,* Island
Cháy *Turkish,* Stream
Chhâk *Cambodian,* Bay
Chhu *Tibetan,* River
-chôsuji *Korean,* Reservoir

Chott *Arabic,* Salt lake, depression
Ch'ün-tao *Chinese,* Island group
Cambodian, Mountains
Cordillera *Spanish,* Mountain range
Costa *Spanish,* Coast
Côte *French,* Coast
Cuchilla *Spanish,* Mountains

D

Dağı *Azerbaijani, Turkish,* Mountain
Dağları *Azerbaijani, Turkish,* Mountains
-dake *Japanese,* Peak
Danau *Indonesian,* Lake
Đao *Vietnamese,* Island
Daryá *Persian,* River
Daryácheh *Persian,* Lake
Dasht *Persian,* Plain, desert
Dawḥat *Arabic,* Bay
Dere *Turkish,* Stream
Dili *Azerbaijani,* Spit
-do *Korean,* Island
Dooxo *Somali,* Valley
Düzü *Azerbaijani,* Steppe
-dwíp *Bengali,* Island

E

Embalse *Spanish,* Reservoir
Erg *Arabic,* Dunes
Estany *Catalan,* Lake
Estrecho *Spanish,* Strait
-ey *Icelandic,* Island
Ezero *Bulgarian, Macedonian,* Lake

F

Fjord *Danish,* Fjord
-fjorden *Norwegian,* Fjord
-fjørdhur *Faeroese,* Fjord
Fleuve *French,* River
Fliegu *Maltese,* Channel
-fljór *Icelandic,* River

G

-gang *Korean,* River
Ganga *Nepali, Sinhala,* River
Gaoyuan *Chinese,* Plateau
-gawa *Japanese,* River

Gebel *Arabic,* Mountain
-gebirge *German,* Mountains
Ghubbat *Arabic,* Bay
Gjiri *Albanian,* Bay
Gol *Mongolian,* River
Golfe *French,* Gulf
Golfo *Italian, Spanish,* Gulf
Gora *Russian, Serbian,* Mountain
Gory *Russian,* Mountains
Guba *Russian,* Bay
Gunung *Malay,* Mountain

H

Ḥadd *Arabic,* Spit
-haehyôp *Korean,* Strait
Haff *German,* Lagoon
Hai *Chinese,* Sea, bay
Ḥammádat *Arabic,* Plateau
Hámún *Persian,* Lake
Hawr *Arabic,* Lake
Háyk' *Amharic,* Lake
He *Chinese,* River
Helodrano *Malagasy,* Bay
-hegység *Hungarian,* Mountain range
Hka *Burmese,* River
-ho *Korean,* Lake
Hô *Korean,* Reservoir
/olot *Hebrew,* Dunes
Hora *Belorussian,* Mountain
Hrada *Belorussian,* Mountains, ridge
Hsi *Chinese,* River
Hu *Chinese,* Lake

I

Île(s) *French,* Island(s)
Ilha(s) *Portuguese,* Island(s)
Ilhéu(s) *Portuguese,* Islet(s)
Irmak *Turkish,* River
Isla(s) *Spanish,* Island(s)
Isola (Isole) *Italian,* Island(s)

J

Jabal *Arabic,* Mountain
Jál *Arabic,* Ridge
-järvi *Finnish,* Lake
Jazírat *Arabic,* Island
Jazíreh *Persian,* Island

Jebel *Arabic,* Mountain
Jezero *Serbian/Croatian,* Lake
Jiang *Chinese,* River
-joki *Finnish,* River
-jökull *Icelandic,* Glacier
Juzur *Arabic,* Islands

K

Kaikyó *Japanese,* Strait
-kaise *Lappish,* Mountain
Kali *Nepali,* River
Kalnas *Lithuanian,* Mountain
Kalns *Latvian,* Mountain
Kang *Chinese,* Harbor
Kangri *Tibetan,* Mountain(s)
Kaôh *Cambodian,* Island
Kapp *Norwegian,* Cape
Kavír *Persian,* Desert
K'edi *Georgian,* Mountain range
Kediet *Arabic,* Mountain
Kepulauan *Indonesian, Malay,* Island group
Khalîg, Khalíj *Arabic,* Gulf
Khawr *Arabic,* Inlet
Khola *Nepali,* River
Khrebet *Russian,* Mountain range
Ko *Thai,* Island
Kolpos *Greek,* Bay
-kopf *German,* Peak
Körfäzi *Azerbaijani,* Bay
Körfezi *Turkish,* Bay
Kõrgustik *Estonian,* Upland
Koshi *Nepali,* River
Kowtal *Persian,* Pass
Kúh(há) *Persian,* Mountain(s)
-kundo *Korean,* Island group
-kysten *Norwegian,* Coast
Kyun *Burmese,* Island

L

Laaq *Somali,* Watercourse
Lac *French,* Lake
Lacul *Romanian,* Lake
Lago *Italian, Portuguese, Spanish,* Lake

Laguna *Spanish,* Lagoon, Lake
Laht *Estonian,* Bay
Laut *Indonesian,* Sea
Lembalemba *Malagasy,* Plateau
Lerr *Armenian,* Mountain
Lerrnashght'a *Armenian,* Mountain range
Les *Czech,* Forest
Lich *Armenian,* Lake
Liqeni *Albanian,* Lake
Lumi *Albanian,* River
Lyman *Ukrainian,* Estuary

M

Mae Nam *Thai,* River
-mägi *Estonian,* Hill
Maja *Albanian,* Mountain
-man *Korean,* Bay
Marios *Lithuanian,* Lake
-meer *Dutch,* Lake
Melkosopochnik *Russian,* Plain
-meri *Estonian,* Sea
Mifraz *Hebrew,* Bay
Monkhafad *Arabic,* Depression
Mont(s) *French,* Mountain(s)
Monte *Italian, Portuguese,* Mountain
More *Russian,* Sea
Mörön *Mongolian,* River

N

Nagor'ye *Russian,* Upland
Najal *Hebrew,* River
Nahr *Arabic,* River
Nam *Laotian,* River
Nehri *Turkish,* River
Nevado *Spanish,* Mountain (snow-capped)
Nisoi *Greek,* Islands
Nizmennost' *Russian,* Lowland, plain
Nosy *Malagasy,* Island
Nur *Mongolian,* Lake
Nuruu *Mongolian,* Mountains
Nuur *Mongolian,* Lake
Nyzovyna *Ukrainian,* Lowland, plain

O

Ostrov(a) *Russian,* Island(s)
Oued *Arabic,* Watercourse
-oy *Faeroese,* Island
-øy(a) *Norwegian,* Island
Oya *Sinhala,* River
Ozero *Russian, Ukrainian,* Lake

P

Passo *Italian,* Pass
Pegunungan *Indonesian, Malay,* Mountain range
Pelagos *Greek,* Sea
Penisola *Italian,* Peninsula
Peski *Russian,* Sands
Phanom *Thai,* Mountain
Phou *Laotian,* Mountain
Pic *Catalan,* Peak
Pico *Portuguese, Spanish,* Peak
Pik *Russian,* Peak
Planalto *Portuguese,* Plateau
Planina, Planini *Bulgarian, Macedonian, Serbian, Croatian,* Mountain range
Ploskogor'ye *Russian,* Upland
Poluostrov *Russian,* Peninsula
Potamos *Greek,* River
Proliv *Russian,* Strait
Pulau *Indonesian, Malay,* Island
Pulu *Malay,* Island
Punta *Portuguese, Spanish,* Point

Q

Qá' *Arabic,* Depression
Qolleh *Persian,* Mountain

R

Raas *Somali,* Cape
-rags *Latvian,* Cape
Ramlat *Arabic,* Sands
Ra's *Arabic,* Cape, point, headland
Ravnina *Bulgarian, Russian,* Plain
Récif *French,* Reef
Represa (Rep.) *Spanish, Portuguese,* Reservoir
-rettó *Japanese,* Island chain
Riacho *Spanish,* Stream
Riban' *Malagasy,* Mountains
Rio *Portuguese,* River
Río *Spanish,* River
Riu *Catalan,* River
Rivier *Dutch,* River
Rivière *French,* River
Rowd *Pashtu,* River
Rúd *Persian,* River
Rudohorie *Slovak,* Mountains
Ruisseau *French,* Stream

S

Sabkhat *Arabic,* Salt marsh
Şaḥrá' *Arabic,* Desert
Samudra *Sinhala,* Reservoir
-san *Japanese, Korean,* Mountain
-sanchi *Japanese,* Mountains
-sanmaek *Korean,* Mountains
Sarír *Arabic,* Desert
Sebkha, Sebkhet *Arabic,* Salt marsh, depression
See *German,* Lake
Selat *Indonesian,* Strait
-selkä *Finnish,* Ridge
Selseleh *Persian,* Mountain range
Serra *Portuguese,* Mountain
Serranía *Spanish,* Mountain
Sha'íb *Arabic,* Watercourse
Shamo *Chinese,* Desert
Shan *Chinese,* Mountain(s)
Shan-mo *Chinese,* Mountain range
Shaṭṭ *Arabic,* Distributary
-shima *Japanese,* Island
Shui-tao *Chinese,* Channel
Sierra *Spanish,* Mountains
Sòn *Vietnamese,* Mountain
Sông *Vietnamese,* River
-spitze *German,* Peak
Štít *Slovak,* Peak
Stoeng *Cambodian,* River
Stretto *Italian,* Strait
Su Anbarı *Azerbaijani,* Reservoir
Sungai *Indonesian, Malay,* River
Suu *Turkish,* River

T

Tal *Mongolian,* Plain
Tandavan' *Malagasy,* Mountain range
Tangorombohitr' *Malagasy,* Mountain massif
Tao *Chinese,* Island
Tassili *Berber,* Plateau, mountain
Tau *Russian,* Mountain(s)
Taungdan *Burmese,* Mountain range

Teluk *Indonesian, Malay,* Bay
Terara *Amharic,* Mountain
Tog *Somali,* Valley
Tônlé *Cambodian,* Lake
Top *Dutch,* Peak
-tunturi *Finnish,* Mountain
Tur'at *Arabic,* Channel

V

Väin *Estonian,* Strait
-vatn *Icelandic,* Lake
-vesi *Finnish,* Lake
Vinh *Vietnamese,* Bay
Vodokhranilishche (Vdkhr.) *Russian,* Reservoir
Vodoskhovyshche (Vdskh.) *Ukrainian,* Reservoir
Volcán *Spanish,* Volcano
Vozvyshennost' *Russian,* Upland, plateau
Vrh *Macedonian,* Peak
Vysochyna *Ukrainian,* Upland
Vysočina *Czech,* Upland

W

Waadi *Somali,* Watercourse
Wádí *Arabic,* Watercourse
Wáḥat, Wâhat *Arabic,* Oasis
Wald *German,* Forest
Wan *Chinese,* Bay
Wyżyna *Polish,* Upland

X

Xé *Laotian,* River

Y

Yarımadası *Azerbaijani,* Peninsula
Yazovir *Bulgarian,* Reservoir
Yoma *Burmese,* Mountains
Yü *Chinese,* Island

Z

Zaliv *Bulgarian, Russian,* Bay
Zatoka *Ukrainian,* Bay
Zemlya *Russian,* Land

Continental factfile

North & Central America

Total area:
9,400,000 sq miles
(24,346,000 sq km)

Total number of countries: 23

Total population:
511.3 million

Largest city with population: Mexico City, Mexico 22.8 million

Country with highest population density: Barbados 1627 people per sq mile (628 people per sq km)

Largest country:
Canada 3,855,171 sq miles (9,984,670 sq km)

Smallest country:
St. Kitts & Nevis 101 sq miles (261 sq km)

Largest lake: Lake Superior, Canada/ USA 32,151 sq miles (83,270 sq km)

Longest river: Mississippi-Missouri, USA 3710 miles (5969 km)

Highest point: Mt. McKinley (Denali), Alaska, USA 20,322 ft (6194 m)

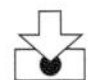

lowest point: Death Valley, California, USA 282 ft (86 m) below sea level

South America

Total area:
6,880,000 sq miles
(17,819,000 sq km)

Total number of countries: 12

Total population:
375.1 million

Largest city with population: São Paulo, Brazil 20.2 million

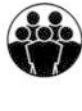

Country with highest population density: Ecuador 123 people per sq mile (48 people per sq km)

Largest country:
Brazil 3,286,470 sq miles (8,511,965 sq km)

Smallest country:
Suriname 63,039 sq miles (163,270 sq km)

Largest lake: Lake Titicaca, Bolivia/Peru 3220 sq miles (8340 sq km)

Longest river: Amazon, Brazil 4049 miles (6516 km)

Highest point: Cerro Aconcagua, Argentina 22,831 ft (6959 m)

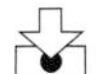

Lowest point: Peninsula Valdés, Argentina 131 ft (40 m) below sea level

Africa

Total area:
11,677,250 sq miles
(30,244,050 sq km)

Total number of countries: 53

Total population:
904.5 million

Largest city with population: Cairo, Egypt 15.6 million

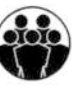

Country with highest population density: Mauritius 1617 people per sq mile (645 people per sq km)

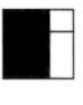

Largest country:
Sudan 967,493 sq miles (2,505,810 sq km)

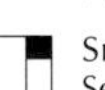

Smallest country:
Seychelles 176 sq miles (455 sq km)

Largest lake: Lake Victoria, Uganda, Kenya, Tanzania 26,828 sq miles (69,484 sq km)

Longest river: Nile, Uganda/Sudan/Egypt 4160 miles (6695 km)

Highest point: Kilimanjaro, Tanzania 19,340 ft (5895 m)

Lowest point: Lac', Assal, Djibouti 512 ft (156 m) below sea level

Europe

Total area:
4,809,200 sq miles
(12,456,000 sq km)

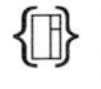

Total number of countries: 45

Total population:
501 million

Largest city with population: Moscow, Euro Russia 13.8 million

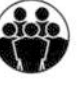

Country with highest population density: Monaco 43,212 people per sq mile (16,620 people per sq km)

Largest country: European Russia 1,527,341 sq miles (3,955,818 sq km)

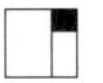

Smallest country:
Vatican City, Italy 0.17 sq miles (0.44 sq km)

Largest lake: Ladoga, European Russia 7100 sq miles (18,390 sq km)

Longest river: Volga, European Russia 2290 miles (3688 km)

Highest point: El'brus, Caucasus Mts, European Russia 18,510 ft (5642 m)

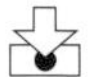

Lowest point: Volga Delta, Caspian Sea, European Russia 92 ft (28 m) below sea level

North & West Asia

Total area:
9,585,500 sq miles
(24,826,600 sq km)

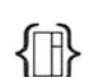

Total number of
countries: 24

Total population:
510 million

Largest city with
population: Tehran, Iran
11.6 million

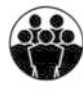

Country with highest
population density: Bahrain
2663 people per sq mile
(1029 people per sq km)

Largest country: Asiatic
Russia 5,065,471 sq miles
(13,119,582 sq km)

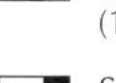

Smallest country:
Bahrain 239 sq miles
(620 sq km)

Largest lake:
Caspian Sea 142,243 sq miles
(371,000 sq km)

Longest river: Ob'-Irtysh,
Asiatic Russia 3461 miles
(5570 km)

Highest point: Pik Pobedy,
Kyrgyzstan/China 24,408 ft
(7439 m)

Lowest point: Dead Sea,
Israel/Jordan 1286 ft
(392 m) below sea level

South & East Asia

Total area:
7,936,200 sq miles
(20,554,700 sq km)

Total number of
countries: 24

Total population:
3550 million

Largest city with
population: Tokyo,
Japan 33.9 million

Country with highest
population density: Singapore
18,220 people per sq mile
(7056 people per sq km)

Largest country:
China 3,705,386 sq miles
(9,596,960 sq km)

Smallest country:
Maldives 116 sq miles
(300 sq km)

Largest lake: Tonle Sap,
Cambodia 1000 sq miles
(2850 sq km)

Longest river: Chang Jiang
(Yangtze) 3965 miles
(6380 km)

Highest point:
Mount Everest, Nepal
29,035 ft (8850 m)

Lowest point: Turpan Hami,
(Turfan basin), China 505 ft
(154 m) below sea level

Australasia & Oceania

Total area:
3,376,700 sq miles
(8,745,750 sq km)

Total number of
countries: 14

Total population:
32.2 million

Largest city with
population: Sydney,
Australia 4.4 million

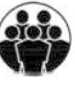

Country with highest
population density: Nauru
1611 people per sq mile
(621 people per sq km)

Largest country:
Australia 2,967,892 sq miles
(7,686,850 sq km)

Smallest country:
Nauru 8 sq miles
(21 sq km)

Largest lake: Lake Eyre,
Australia 3700 sq miles
(9583 sq km)

Longest river: Murray-
Darling, Australia
2330 miles (3750 km)

Highest point: Mt. Wilhelm,
Papua New Guinea 14,795 ft
(4509 m)

Lowest point: Lake Eyre,
Australia 52 ft
(16 m) below sea level

Antarctica

Total area: 5,450,500 sq miles (14,000,000 sq km)
of which approx. 324,300 sq miles
(840,000 sq km) is ice-free.

Total number of countries: The Antarctic Treaty has
30 participating nations and 14 with observer status.
Claims by Australia, France, New Zealand, Norway,
Argentina, Chile, and the UK are not recognized by
other member states.

Total Population: No indigenous population.
74 research stations, (42 are staffed all year-round).
Population varies between about 1000 (winter)
and 4000 (summer).

Total volume of ice:
7,200,000 cu miles (30,000,000 cu km):
contains 90% of Earth's fresh water

Sea ice: 1,158,300 sq miles (3,000,000
sq km) in February. 7,722,000 sq miles
(20,000,000 sq km) in October

Lowest temperature: Vostok station
-89.5°C (-129°F)

Highest point: Vinson Massif
16,072 ft (4897 m)

Lowest Point: Coastline 0ft/m

Geographical comparisons

Largest countries

Russ. Fed. .... 6,592,735 sq miles ....(17,075,200 sq km)
Canada ....3,854,085 sq miles .....(9,984,670 sq km)
USA ....3,717,792 sq miles .... (9,629,091 sq km)
China ....3,705,386 sq miles .....(9,596,960 sq km)
Brazil ....3,286,470 sq miles .....(8,511,965 sq km)
Australia ....2,967,893 sq miles .....(7,686,850 sq km)
India ....1,269,339 sq miles .....(3,287,590 sq km)
Argentina ....1,068,296 sq miles .....(2,766,890 sq km)
Kazakhstan ....1,049,150 sq miles .....(2,717,300 sq km)
Sudan .... 967,493 sq miles .....(2,505,810 sq km)

Smallest countries

Vatican City .... 0.17 sq miles ....(0.44 sq km)
Monaco .... 0.75 sq miles ....(1.95 sq km)
Nauru .... 8 sq miles ....(21 sq km)
Tuvalu .... 10 sq miles ....(26 sq km)
San Marino .... 24 sq miles ....(61 sq km)
Liechtenstein............. 62 sq miles ....(160 sq km)
Marshall Islands......... 70 sq miles ....(181 sq km)
St. Kitts & Nevis .... 101 sq miles ....(261 sq km)
Maldives................... 116 sq miles ....(300 sq km)
Malta........................ 122 sq miles ....(316 sq km)

Largest islands

Greenland...............849,400 sq miles (2,200,000 sq km)
New Guinea ....312,000 sq miles (808,000 sq km)
Borneo ....292,222 sq miles (757,050 sq km)
Madagascar ....229,300 sq miles (594,000 sq km)
Sumatra.....................202,300 sq miles (524,000 sq km)
Baffin Island ....183,800 sq miles (476,000 sq km)
Honshu ....88,800 sq miles (230,000 sq km)
Britain.........................88,700 sq miles (229,800 sq km)
Victoria Island.............81,900 sq miles (212,000 sq km)
Ellesmere Island ....75,700 sq miles (196,000 sq km)

Richest countries (GNI per capita, in US$)

Luxembourg 56,230
Norway...52,030
Liechtenstein.....................................50,000
Switzerland..48,230
USA...41,400
Denmark 40,650
Iceland 38,620
Japan..37,810
Sweden 35,770
Monaco 34,280

Poorest countries (GNI per capita, in US$)

Burundi 90
Ethiopia 110
Liberia 110
Congo, Dem. Rep. 120
Somalia... 120
Guinea-Bissau 160
Malawi 170
Eritrea 180
Sierra Leone 200
Rwanda... 220

Most populous countries

China 1,315,800,000
India 1,103,400,000
USA..298,200,000
Indonesia....................................222,800,000
Brazil 180,400,000
Cameroon 163,000,000
Pakistan......................................157,900,000
Russian Federation.....................143,200,000
Bangladesh 141,800,000
Nigeria..131,500,000

Least populous countries

Vatican City 921
Tuvalu 11,636
Nauru 13,048
Palau...20,303
San Marino 28,880
Monaco 32,409
Liechtenstein...33,717
St. Kitts & Nevis 38,958
Marshall Islands....................................59,071
Antigua & Barbuda...............................68,722

Most densely populated countries

Monaco ....43,212 people per sq mile (16,620 per sq km)
Singapore .... 18,220 people per sq mile (7049 per sq km)
Vatican City.......... 5418 people per sq mile (2090 per sq km)
Malta..................... 3242 people per sq mile (1256 per sq km)
Maldives................ 2836 people per sq mile (1097 per sq km)
Bangladesh .... 2743 people per sq mile (1059 per sq km)
Bahrain................. 2663 people per sq mile (1030 per sq km)
China .... 1838 people per sq mile (710 per sq km)
Mauritius............... 1671 people per sq mile (645 per sq km)
Barbados .... 1627 people per sq mile (628 per sq km)

Most sparsely populated countries

Mongolia.........4 people per sq mile......... (2 per sq km)
Namibia..........6 people per sq mile......... (2 per sq km)
Australia ....7 people per sq mile......... (3 per sq km)
Mauritania ......8 people per sq mile......... (3 per sq km)
Suriname.........8 people per sq mile......... (3 per sq km)
Botswana.........8 people per sq mile......... (3 per sq km)
Iceland ....8 people per sq mile......... (3 per sq km)
Canada ....9 people per sq mile......... (4 per sq km)
Libya ....9 people per sq mile......... (4 per sq km)
Guyana ....10 people per sq mile......... (4 per sq km)

Most widely spoken languages

1. Chinese (Mandarin)   6. Arabic
2. English   7. Bengali
3. Hindi   8. Portuguese
4. Spanish   9. Malay-Indonesian
5. Russian   10. French

Largest conurbations

Tokyo 34,200,000
Mexico City 22,800,000
Seoul 22,300,000
New York 21,900,000
São Paulo 20,200,000
Mumbai 19,850,000
Delhi..19,700,000
Shanghai....................................18,150,000
Los Angeles 18,000,000
Osaka 16,800,000
Jakarta.......................................16,550,000
Kolkata.......................................15,650,000
Cairo..15,600,000
Manila..14,950,000
Karachi.......................................14,300,000
Moscow......................................13,750,000
Buenos Aires 13,450,000
Dacca...13,250,000
Rio de Janeiro............................12,150,000
Beijing 12,100,000
London 12,000,000
Tehran..11,850,000
Istanbul 11,500,000
Lagos 11,100,000
Shenzhen 10,700,000

Longest rivers

Nile (NE Africa) ....4160 miles ...... (6695 km)
Amazon (South America) ....4049 miles ...... (6516 km)
Yangtze (China)...........................3915 miles ...... (6299 km)
Mississippi/Missouri (US) ....3710 miles........ (5969 km)
Ob'-Irtysh (Russ. Fed.) ....3461 miles ...... (5570 km)
Yellow River (China) ....3395 miles ...... (5464 km)
Congo (Central Africa) ....2900 miles ...... (4667 km)
Mekong (Southeast Asia) ....2749 miles ...... (4425 km)
Lena (Russian Federation).........2734 miles...... (4400 km)
Mackenzie (Canada) ....2640 miles...... (4250 km)
Yenisey (Russ. Federation) ......2541 miles ...... (4090 km)

Highest mountains (Height above sea level)

Everest.......................................29,035 ft....... (8850 m)
K2 ....28,253 ft....... (8611 m)
Kanchenjunga I.......................28,210 ft....... (8598 m)
Makalu I ....27,767 ft....... (8463 m)
Cho Oyu ....26,907 ft....... (8201 m)
Dhaulagiri I...............................26,796 ft....... (8167 m)
Manaslu I ....26,783 ft....... (8163 m)
Nanga Parbat I.........................26,661 ft....... (8126 m)
Annapurna I ....26,547 ft....... (8091 m)
Gasherbrum I............................26,471 ft....... (8068 m)

Largest bodies of inland water (Area & depth)

Caspian Sea
143,243 sq miles (371,000 sq km).......3215 ft (980 m)
Lake Superior
32,151 sq miles (83,270 sq km).......1289 ft (393 m)
Lake Victoria
26,560 sq miles (68,880 sq km).........328 ft (100 m)
Lake Huron
23,436 sq miles (60,700 sq km).........751 ft (229 m)
Lake Michigan
22,402 sq miles (58,020 sq km).........922 ft (281 m)
Lake Tanganyika
12,703 sq miles (32,900 sq km).... 4700 ft (1435 m)
Great Bear Lake
12,274 sq miles (31,790 sq km)...... 1047 ft (319 m)
Lake Baikal
11,776 sq miles (30,500 sq km).... 5712 ft (1741 m)
Great Slave Lake
10,981 sq miles (28,440 sq km).........459 ft (140 m)
Lake Erie
9915 sq miles (25,680 sq km)...........197 ft (60 m)

......continued on p.166

Geographical comparisons continued

Deepest ocean features

Challenger Deep, Mariana Trench (Pacific)
36,201 ft .... (11,034 m)
Vityaz III Depth, Tonga Trench (Pacific)
35,704 ft .... (10,882 m)
Vityaz Depth, Kurile-Kamchatka Trench (Pacific)
34,588 ft .... (10,542 m)
Cape Johnson Deep, Philippine Trench (Pacific)
34,441 ft .... (10,497 m)
Kermadec Trench (Pacific)
32,964 ft .... (10,047 m)
Ramapo Deep, Japan Trench (Pacific)
32,758 ft .... (9984 m)
Milwaukee Deep, Puerto Rico Trench (Atlantic)
30,185 ft .... (9200 m)
Argo Deep, Torres Trench (Pacific)
30,070 ft .... (9165 m)
Meteor Depth, South Sandwich Trench (Atlantic)
30,000 ft .... (9144 m)
Planet Deep, New Britain Trench (Pacific)
29,988 ft .... (9140 m)

Greatest waterfalls   (Mean flow of water)

Boyoma (Congo) .... 600,400 cu. ft/sec (17,000 cu.m/sec)
Khône (Laos/Cambodia) ... 410,000 cu. ft/sec (11,600 cu.m/sec)
Niagara (USA/Canada) .... 195,000 cu. ft/sec (5500 cu.m/sec)
Grande (Uruguay) .... 160,000 cu. ft/sec (4500 cu.m/sec)
Paulo Afonso (Brazil) .... 100,000 cu. ft/sec(2800 cu.m/sec)
Urubupunga (Brazil) .... 97,000 cu. ft/sec (2750 cu.m/sec)
Iguaçu (Argentina/Brazil) .... 62,000 cu. ft/sec (1700 cu.m/sec)
Maribondo (Brazil) .... 53,000 cu. ft/sec (1500 cu.m/sec)
Victoria (Zimbabwe) .... 39,000 cu. ft/sec (1100 cu.m/sec)
Kabalega (Uganda) .... 42,000 cu. ft/sec (1200 cu.m/sec)
Churchill (Canada) .... 35,000 cu. ft/sec (1000 cu.m/sec)
Cauvery (India) .... 33,000 cu. ft/sec (900 cu.m/sec)

Highest waterfalls

Angel (Venezuela) .... 3212 ft .... (979 m)
Tugela (South Africa) .... 3110 ft .... (948 m)
Utigard (Norway) .... 2625 ft .... (800 m)
Mongefossen (Norway) .... 2539 ft .... (774 m)
Mtarazi (Zimbabwe) .... 2500 ft .... (762 m)
Yosemite (USA) .... 2425 ft .... (739 m)
Ostre Mardola Foss (Norway) ..... 2156 ft .... (657 m)
Tyssestrengane (Norway) .... 2119 ft .... (646 m)
*Cuquenan (Venezuela) .... 2001 ft .... (610 m)
Sutherland (New Zealand) .... 1903 ft .... (580 m)
*Kjellfossen (Norway) .... 1841 ft .... (561 m)

indicates that the total height is a single leap

Largest deserts

Sahara .... 3,450,000 sq miles (9,065,000 sq km)
Gobi .... 500,000 sq miles (1,295,000 sq km)
Ar Rub al Khali ...... 289,600 sq miles (750,000 sq km)
Great Victorian ..... 249,800 sq miles (647,000 sq km)
Sonoran .... 120,000 sq miles (311,000 sq km)
Kalahari .... 120,000 sq miles (310,800 sq km)
Garagum .... 115,800 sq miles (300,000 sq km)
Takla Makan .... 100,400 sq miles (260,000 sq km)
Namib .... 52,100 sq miles (135,000 sq km)
Thar .... 33,670 sq miles (130,000 sq km)

*NB – Most of Antarctica is a polar desert, with only
2 inches (50 mm) of precipitation annually*

Hottest inhabited places

Djibouti (Djibouti) .... 86.0°F .... (30.0°C)
Timbouctou (Mali) .... 84.7°F .... (29.3°C)
Tirunelveli (India) .... 84.7°F .... (29.3°C)
Tuticorin (India) .... 84.7°F .... (29.3°C)
Nellore (India) .... 84.5°F .... (29.2°C)
Santa Marta (Colombia) .... 84.5°F .... (29.2°C)
Aden (Yemen) .... 84.0°F .... (29.0°C)
Madurai (India) .... 84.0°F .... (29.0°C)
Niamey (Niger) .... 84.0°F .... (29.0°C)

Driest inhabited places

Aswân (Egypt) .... 0.02 in .... (0.5 mm)
Luxor (Egypt) .... 0.03 in .... (0.7 mm)
Arica (Chile) .... 0.04 in .... (1.1 mm)
Ica (Peru) .... 0.10 in .... (2.3 mm)
Antofagasta (Chile) .... 0.20 in .... (4.9 mm)
El Minya (Egypt) .... 0.20 in .... (5.1 mm)
Asyût (Egypt) .... 0.20 in .... (5.2 mm)
Callao (Peru) .... 0.50 in ..... (12.0 mm)
Trujillo (Peru) .... 0.55 in ..... (14.0 mm)
El Faiyûm (Egypt) .... 0.80 in ..... (19.0 mm)

Wettest inhabited places

Buenaventura (Colombia) .... 265 in .... (6743 mm)
Monrovia (Liberia) .... 202 in ... (5131 mm)
Pago Pago (American Samoa) .... 196 in ... (4990 mm)
Moulmein (Myanmar) .... 191 in ... (4852 mm)
Lae (Papua New Guinea) .... 183 in ... (4645 mm)
Baguio (Luzon I., Philippines) ..... 180 in ... (4573 mm)
Sylhet (Bangladesh) .... 176 in ... (4457 mm)
Padang (Sumatra, Indonesia) ...... 166 in ... (4225 mm)
Bogor (Java, Indonesia) .... 166 in ... (4225 mm)
Conakry (Guinea) .... 171 in ...... (4341 mm)

GLOSSARY OF ABBREVIATIONS

This Glossary provides a comprehensive guide to the abbreviations used in this Atlas, and in the Index.

A
abbrev. abbreviated
Afr. Afrikaans
Alb. Albanian
Amh. Amharic
anc. ancient
Ar. Arabic
Arm. Armenian
Az. Azerbaijani

B
Basq. Basque
Bel. Belorussian
Ben. Bengali
Bibl. Biblical
Bret. Breton
Bul. Bulgarian
Bur. Burmese

C
Cam. Cambodian
Cant. Cantonese
Cast. Castilian
Cat. Catalan
Chin. Chinese
Cro. Croat
Cz. Czech

D
Dan. Danish
Dut. Dutch

E
Eng. English
Est. Estonian
est. estimated

F
Faer. Faeroese
Fij. Fijian
Fin. Finnish
Flem. Flemish
Fr. French
Fris. Frisian

G
Geor. Georgian
Ger. German
Gk. Greek
Guj. Gujarati

H
Haw. Hawaiian
Heb. Hebrew
Hind. Hindi
hist. historical
Hung. Hungarian

I
Icel. Icelandic
Ind. Indonesian
In. Inuit
Ir. Irish
It. Italian

J
Jap. Japanese

K
Kaz. Kazakh
Kir. Kirghiz
Kor. Korean
Kurd. Kurdish

L
Lao. Laotian
Lapp. Lappish
Lat. Latin
Latv. Latvian
Lith. Lithanian
Lus. Lusatian

M
Mac. Macedonian
Mal. Malay
Malg. Malagasy
Malt. Maltese
Mon. Montenegro
Mong. Mongolian

N
Nepali. Nepali
Nor. Norwegian

O
off. officially

P
Pash. Pashtu
Per. Persian
Pol. Polish
Port. Portuguese
prev. previously

R
Rmsch. Romansch
Roman. Romanian
Rus. Russian

S
SCr. Serbo - Croatian
Serb. Serbian
Slvk. Slovak
Slvn. Slovene
Som. Somali
Sp. Spanish
Swa. Swahili
Swe. Swedish

T
Taj. Tajik
Th. Thai
Tib. Tibetan
Turk. Turkish
Turkm. Turkmenistan

U
Uigh. Uighur
Ukr. Ukrainian
Uzb. Uzbek

V
var. variant
Vtn. Vietnamese

W
Wel. Welsh

X
Xh. Xhosa

Key to country factboxes within the Index:

Formation
Date of independence

Population
Total population / population density - based on total land area .

Calorie consumption
Average number of calories consumed daily per person.

A

Aa *see* Gauja
Aachen *94 A4 Dut.* Aken, *Fr.* Aix-la-Chapelle; *anc.* Aquae Grani, Aquisgranum. Nordrhein-Westfalen, W Germany
Aaiún *see* Laâyoune
Aalborg *80 D3 var.* Ålborg, Ålborg-Nørresundby; *anc.* Alburgum. Nordjylland, N Denmark
Aalen *95 B6* Baden-Württemberg, S Germany
Aalsmeer *86 C3* Noord-Holland, C Netherlands
Aalst *87 B6 Fr.* Alost. Oost-Vlaanderen, C Belgium
Aalten *86 E4* Gelderland, E Netherlands
Aalter *87 B5* Oost-Vlaanderen, NW Belgium
Aanaarjävri *see* Inarijärvi
Äänekoski *85 D5* Länsi-Soumi, W Finland
Aar *see* Aare
Aare *95 A7 var.* Aar. *river* W Switzerland
Aarhus *see* Århus
Aarlen *see* Arlon
Aat *see* Ath
Aba *77 E5* Orientale, NE Dem. Rep. Congo
Aba *75 G5* Abia, S Nigeria
Abā as Su'ūd *see* Najrān
Abaco Island *see* Great Abaco, Bahamas
Ābādān *120 C4* Khūzestān, SW Iran
Abadan *122 C3 prev.* Bezmein, *Rus.* Büzmeýin. Ahal Welaýaty, C Turkmenistan
Abai *see* Blue Nile
Abakan *114 D4* Respublika Khakasiya, S Russian Federation
Abancay *60 D4* Apurímac, SE Peru
Abariringa *see* Kanton
Abashiri *130 D2 var.* Abasiri. Hokkaidō, NE Japan
Abasiri *see* Abashiri
Ābaya Hāyk' *73 C5 Eng.* Lake Margherita, *It.* Abbaia. *lake* SW Ethiopia
Ābay Wenz *see* Blue Nile
Abbaia *see* Ābaya Hāyk'
Abbatis Villa *see* Abbeville
Abbazia *see* Opatija
Abbeville *90 C2 anc.* Abbatis Villa. Somme, N France
'Abd al 'Azīz, Jabal *118 D2 mountain range* NE Syria
Abéché *76 C3 var.* Abécher, Abeshr. Ouaddaï, SE Chad
Abécher *see* Abéché
Abela *see* Ávila
Abellinum *see* Avellino
Abemama *144 D2 var.* Apamama; *prev.* Roger Simpson Island. *atoll* Tungaru, W Kiribati
Abengourou *75 E5* E Côte d'Ivoire (Ivory Coast)
Aberbrothock *see* Arbroath
Abercorn *see* Mbala
Aberdeen *88 D3 anc.* Devana. NE Scotland, UK
Aberdeen *45 E2* South Dakota, N USA
Aberdeen *46 B2* Washington, NW USA
Abergwaun *see* Fishguard
Abertawe *see* Swansea
Aberystwyth *89 C6* W Wales, UK
Abeshr *see* Abéché
Abhā *121 B6* 'Asīr, SW Saudi Arabia
Abidavichy *107 D7 Rus.* Obidovichi. Mahilyowskaya Voblasts', E Belarus
Abidjan *75 E5* S Côte d'Ivoire (Ivory Coast)
Abilene *49 F3* Texas, SW USA
Abingdon *see* Pinta, Isla
Abkhazia *117 E1 autonomous republic* NW Georgia
Aboisso *75 E5* SE Côte d'Ivoire (Ivory Coast)
Abo, Massif d' *76 B1 mountain range* NW Chad
Abomey *75 F5* S Benin
Abou-Déïa *76 C3* Salamat, SE Chad
Aboudouhour *see* Abū aḍ Ḍuhūr
Abou Kémal *see* Abū Kamāl
Abrantes *92 B3 var.* Abrántes. Santarém, C Portugal
Abrashlare *see* Brezovo
Abrolhos Bank *56 E4 undersea bank* W Atlantic Ocean
Abrova *107 B6 Rus.* Obrovo. Brestskaya Voblasts', SW Belarus
Abrud *108 B4 Ger.* Gross-Schlatten, *Hung.* Abrudbánya. Alba, SW Romania
Abrudbánya *see* Abrud
Abruzzese, Appennino *96 C4 mountain range* C Italy
Absaroka Range *44 B2 mountain range* Montana/Wyoming, NW USA
Abū aḍ Ḍuhūr *118 B3 Fr.* Aboudouhour. Idlib, NW Syria
Abu Dhabi *see* Abū Ẓaby
Abu Hamed *72 C3* River Nile, N Sudan
Abū Ḥardān *118 E3 var.* Hajîne. Dayr az Zawr, E Syria
Abuja *75 G4 country capital* (Nigeria) Federal Capital District, C Nigeria
Abū Kamāl *118 E3 Fr.* Abou Kémal. Dayr az Zawr, E Syria
Abula *see* Ávila
Abunã, Rio *62 C2 var.* Río Abuná. *river* Bolivia/Brazil
Abut Head *151 B6 headland* South Island, New Zealand
Ābuyē Mēda *72 D4 mountain* C Ethiopia
Abū Ẓabī *see* Abū Ẓaby
Abū Ẓaby *121 C5 var.* Abū Ẓabī, *Eng.* Abu Dhabi. *country capital* (United Arab Emirates) Abū Ẓaby, C United Arab Emirates
Abyaḍ, Al Baḥr al *see* White Nile
Abyla *see* Ávila
Abyssinia *see* Ethiopia
Acalayong *77 A5* SW Equatorial Guinea
Acaponeta *50 D4* Nayarit, C Mexico
Acapulco *51 E5 var.* Acapulco de Juárez. Guerrero, S Mexico
Acapulco de Juárez *see* Acapulco
Acarai Mountains *59 F4 Sp.* Serra Acaraí. *mountain range* Brazil/Guyana
Acaraí, Serra *see* Acarai Mountains
Acarigua *58 D2* Portuguesa, N Venezuela
Accra *75 E5 country capital* (Ghana)SE Ghana
Achacachi *61 E4* La Paz, W Bolivia
Acklins Island *54 C2 island* SE Bahamas
Aconcagua, Cerro *64 B4 mountain* W Argentina
Açores/Açores, Arquipélago dos/ Açores, Ilhas dos *see* Azores
A Coruña *92 B1 Cast.* La Coruña, *Eng.* Corunna; *anc.* Caronium. Galicia, NW Spain
Acre *62 C2 off.* Estado do Acre. *state* W Brazil
Acre, Estado do *see* Acre
Açu *63 G2 var.* Assu. Rio Grande do Norte, E Brazil
Acunum Acusio *see* Montélimar
Ada *100 D3* Vojvodina, N Serbia
Ada *49 G2* Oklahoma, C USA
Ada Bazar *see* Adapazarı
Adalia *see* Antalya
Adalia, Gulf of *see* Antalya Körfezi
Adama *see* Nazrēt
'Adan *121 B7 Eng.* Aden. SW Yemen
Adana *116 D4 var.* Seyhan. Adana, S Turkey
Adâncata *see* Horlivka
Adapazarı *116 B2 prev.* Ada Bazar. Sakarya, NW Turkey
Adare, Cape *154 B4 cape* Antarctica
Ad Dahnā' *120 C4 desert* E Saudi Arabia
Ad Dakhla *70 A4 var.* Dakhla. SW Western Sahara
Ad Dalanj *see* Dilling
Ad Damar *see* Ed Damer
Ad Damazīn *see* Ed Damazin
Ad Dāmir *see* Ed Damer
Ad Dammān *120 C4 var.* Dammām. Ash Sharqīyah, NE Saudi Arabia
Ad Dāmūr *see* Damoûr
Ad Dawḥah *120 C4 Eng.* Doha. *country capital* (Qatar) C Qatar
Aḍ Ḍiffah *see* Libyan Plateau
Addis Ababa *see* Ādīs Ābeba
Addu Atoll *132 A5 atoll* S Maldives
Adelaide *149 B6 state capital* South Australia
Adelsberg *see* Postojna
Aden *see* 'Adan
Aden, Gulf of *121 C7 gulf* SW Arabian Sea
Adige *96 C2 Ger.* Etsch. *river* N Italy
Adirondack Mountains *41 F2 mountain range* New York, NE USA

Ādīs Ābeba *73 C5 Eng.* Addis Ababa. *country capital* (Ethiopia) Ādīs Ābeba, C Ethiopia
Adıyaman *117 E4* Adıyaman, SE Turkey
Adjud *108 C4* Vrancea, E Romania
Admiralty Islands *144 B3 island group* N Papua New Guinea
Adra *93 E5* Andalucía, S Spain
Adrar *70 D3* C Algeria
Adrian *40 C3* Michigan, N USA
Adrianople/Adrianopolis *see* Edirne
Adriatico, Mare *see* Adriatic Sea
Adriatic Sea *103 E2 Alb.* Deti Adriatik, *It.* Mare Adriatico, *SCr.* Jadransko More, *Slvn.* Jadransko Morje. *sea* N Mediterranean Sea
Adriatik, Deti *see* Adriatic Sea
Adycha *115 F2 river* NE Russian Federation
Aegean Sea *105 C5 Gk.* Aigaíon Pelagos, Aigaío Pélagos, *Turk.* Ege Denizi. *sea* NE Mediterranean Sea
Aegviidu *106 D2 Ger.* Charlottenhof. Harjumaa, NW Estonia
Aegyptus *see* Egypt
Aelana *see* Al 'Aqabah
Aelok *see* Ailuk Atoll
Aelōnlaplap *see* Ailinglaplap Atoll
Aemona *see* Ljubljana
Aeolian Islands *see* Eolie, Isole
Æsernia *see* Isernia
Afar Depression *see* Danakil Desert
Afars et des Issas, Territoire Français des *see* Djibouti
Afghānestān, Dowlat-e Eslāmī-ye *see* Afghanistan
Afghanistan *122 C4 off.* Islamic State of Afghanistan, *Per.* Dowlat-e Eslāmī-ye Afghānestān; *prev.* Republic of Afghanistan. *country* C Asia

AFGHANISTAN
Central Asia

Official name Islamic State of Afghanistan
Formation 1919 / 1919
Capital Kabul
Population 29.9 million / 119 people per sq mile (46 people per sq km) / 22%
Total area 250,000 sq miles (647,500 sq km)
Languages Pashtu*, Tajik, Dari, Farsi, Uzbek, Turkmen
Religions Sunni Muslim 84%, Shi'a Muslim 15%, Other 1%
Ethnic mix Pashtun 38%, Tajik 25%, Hazara 19%, Uzbek and Turkmen 15%, Other 3%
Government Transitional regime
Currency New afghani = 100 puls
Literacy rate 36%
Calorie consumption 1539 calories

Afghanistan, Islamic State of *see* Afghanistan
Afghanistan, Republic of *see* Afghanistan
Afmadow *73 D6* Jubbada Hoose, S Somalia
Africa *68 continent*
Africa, Horn of *68 E4 physical region* Ethiopia/Somalia
Africana Seamount *141 A6 seamount* SW Indian Ocean
'Afrīn *118 B2* Ḥalab, N Syria
Afyon *116 B3 prev.* Afyonkarahisar. Afyon, W Turkey
Agadès *see* Agadez
Agadez *75 G3 prev.* Agadès. Agadez, C Niger
Agadir *70 B3* SW Morocco
Agana/Agaña *see* Hagåtña
Āgaro *73 C5* Oromo, C Ethiopia
Agassiz Fracture Zone *143 G5 fracture zone* S Pacific Ocean
Agatha *see* Agde
Agathónisi *105 D6 island* Dodekánisa, Greece, Aegean Sea
Agde *91 C6 anc.* Agatha. Hérault, S France
Agedabia *see* Ajdābiyā
Agen *91 B5 anc.* Aginnum. Lot-et-Garonne, SW France
Agendicum *see* Sens
Aghri Dagh *see* Büyükağrı Dağı
Agiá *104 B4 var.* Ayiá. Thessalía, C Greece
Agialoúsa *see* Yenierenköy
Agía Marína *105 E6* Léros, Dodekánisa, Greece, Aegean Sea
Aginnum *see* Agen
Ágios Efstrátios *104 D4 var.* Áyios Evstrátios, Hagios Evstrátios. *island* E Greece
Ágios Nikólaos *105 D8 var.* Áyios Nikólaos. Kríti, Greece, E Mediterranean Sea
Āgra *134 D3* Uttar Pradesh, N India
Agra and Oudh, United Provinces of *see* Uttar Pradesh
Agram *see* Zagreb
Ağrı *117 F3 var.* Karaköse; *prev.* Karakılısse. Ağrı, NE Turkey
Agri Dagi *see* Büyükağrı Dağı
Agrigento *97 C7 Gk.* Akragas; *prev.* Girgenti. Sicilia, Italy, C Mediterranean Sea
Agriovótano *105 C5* Évvoia, C Greece
Agropoli *97 D5* Campania, S Italy
Aguachica *58 B2* Cesar, N Colombia
Aguadulce *53 F5* Coclé, S Panama
Agua Prieta *50 B1* Sonora, NW Mexico
Aguascalientes *50 D4* Aguascalientes, C Mexico
Aguaytía *60 C3* Ucayali, C Peru
Aguilas *93 E4* Murcia, SE Spain
Aguililla *50 D4* Michoacán de Ocampo, SW Mexico
Agulhas Basin *69 D8 undersea basin* SW Indian Ocean
Agulhas, Cape *78 C5 cape* S South Africa
Agulhas Plateau *67 D6 undersea plateau* SW Indian Ocean
Ahaggar *75 F2 high plateau region* SE Algeria
Ahlen *94 B4* Nordrhein-Westfalen, W Germany
Ahmadābād *134 C4 var.* Ahmedabad. Gujarāt, W India
Ahmadnagar *134 C5 var.* Ahmednagar. Mahārāshtra, W India
Ahmedabad *see* Ahmadābād
Ahmednagar *see* Ahmadnagar
Ahuachapán *52 B3* Ahuachapán, W El Salvador
Ahvāz *120 C3 var.* Ahwāz; *prev.* Nāsiri. Khūzestān, SW Iran
Ahvenanmaa *see* Åland
Ahwāz *see* Ahvāz
Aigaíon Pelagos/Aigaío Pélagos *see* Aegean Sea
Aígina *105 C6 var.* Aíyina, Egina. Aígina, C Greece
Aígio *105 B5 var.* Egio; *prev.* Aíyion. Dytikí Ellás, S Greece
Aiken *43 E2* South Carolina, SE USA
Ailigandí *53 G4* San Blas, NE Panama
Ailinglaplap Atoll *144 D2 var.* Aelōnlaplap. *atoll* Ralik Chain, S Marshall Islands
Ailuk Atoll *144 D1 var.* Aelok. *atoll* Ratak Chain, NE Marshall Islands
Ainaži *106 D3 Est.* Heinaste, *Ger.* Hainasch. Limbaži, N Latvia
'Aïn Ben Tili *74 D1* Tiris Zemmour, N Mauritania
Aintab *see* Gaziantep
Aïoun el Atrous/Aïoun el Atroûss *see* 'Ayoûn el 'Atroûs
Aiquile *61 F4* Cochabamba, C Bolivia
Aïr *see* Aïr, Massif de l'
Air du Azbine *see* Aïr, Massif de l'
Aïr, Massif de l' *75 G2 var.* Aïr, Air du Azbine, Asben. *mountain range* NC Niger
Aiud *108 B4 Ger.* Strassburg, *Hung.* Nagyenyed; *prev.* Engeten. Alba, SW Romania
Aix *see* Aix-en-Provence
Aix-en-Provence *91 D6 var.* Aix; *anc.* Aquae Sextiae. Bouches-du-Rhône, SE France
Aix-la-Chapelle *see* Aachen
Aíyina *see* Aígina
Aíyion *see* Aígio
Aizkraukle *106 C4* Aizkraukle, S Latvia
Ajaccio *91 E7* Corse, France, C Mediterranean Sea
Ajaria *117 F2 autonomous republic* SW Georgia
Ajastan *see* Armenia
Aj Bogd Uul *126 D2 mountain* SW Mongolia
Ajdābiyā *71 G2 var.* Agedabia, Ajdābiyah. NE Libya
Ajdābiyah *see* Ajdābiyā
Ajjinena *see* El Geneina
Ajmer *134 D3 var.* Ajmere. Rājasthān, N India
Ajmere *see* Ajmer
Ajo *48 A3* Arizona, SW USA
Akaba *see* Al 'Aqabah
Akamagaseki *see* Shimonoseki
Akasha *72 B3* Northern, N Sudan
Akchâr *74 C2 desert* W Mauritania
Aken *see* Aachen
Akermanceaster *see* Bath
Akhalts'ikhe *117 F2* SW Georgia
Akhisar *116 A3* Manisa, W Turkey
Akhmîm *72 B2 anc.* Panopolis. C Egypt
Akhtubinsk *111 C7* Astrakhanskaya Oblast', SW Russian Federation
Akhtyrka *see* Okhtyrka
Akimiski Island *38 C3 island* Nunavut, C Canada
Akinovka *109 F4* Zaporiz'ka Oblast', S Ukraine
Akita *130 D4* Akita, Honshū, C Japan
Akjoujt *74 C2 prev.* Fort-Repoux. Inchiri, W Mauritania
Akkeshi *130 E2* Hokkaidō, NE Japan
Aklavik *36 D3* Northwest Territories, NW Canada
Akmola *see* Astana
Akmolinsk *see* Astana
Aknavásár *see* Târgu Ocna
Akpatok Island *39 E1 island* Nunavut, E Canada
Akragas *see* Agrigento
Akron *40 D4* Ohio, N USA
Akrotiri *see* Akrotírion
Akrotírion *102 C5 var.* Akrotiri. *UK air base* S Cyprus
Aksai Chin *124 B2 Chin.* Aksayqin. *disputed region* China/India
Aksaray *116 C4* Aksaray, C Turkey
Aksayqin *see* Aksai Chin
Akşehir *116 B4* Konya, W Turkey
Aktash *see* Oqtosh
Aktau *114 A4 Kaz.* Aqtaū; *prev.* Shevchenko. Mangistau, W Kazakhstan
Aktjubinsk/Aktyubinsk *see* Aktobe
Aktobe *114 B4 Kaz.* Aqtöbe; *prev.* Aktjubinsk. Aktyubinsk, NW Kazakhstan
Aktsyabrski *107 C7 Rus.* Oktyabr'skiy; *prev.* Karpilovka. Homyel'skaya Voblasts', SE Belarus
Akula *77 C5* Equateur, NW Dem. Rep. Congo
Akureyri *83 E4* Nordhurland Eystra, N Iceland
Akyab *see* Sittwe
Alabama *51 G1 off.* State of Alabama, *also known as* Camellia State, Heart of Dixie, The Cotton State, Yellowhammer State. *state* S USA
Alabama River *42 C3 river* Alabama, S USA
Alaca *116 C3* Çorum, N Turkey
Alacant *see* Alicante
Alagoas *63 G2 off.* Estado de Alagoas. *state* E Brazil
Alagoas, Estado de *see* Alagoas
Alais *see* Alès
Alajuela *53 E4* Alajuela, C Costa Rica
Alakanuk *36 C2* Alaska, USA
Al 'Alamayn *see* El 'Alamein
Al 'Amārah *120 C3 var.* Amara. E Iraq
Alamo *47 D6* Nevada, W USA
Alamogordo *48 D3* New Mexico, SW USA
Alamosa *44 C5* Colorado, C USA
Åland *85 C6 var.* Aland Islands, *Fin.* Ahvenanmaa. *island group* SW Finland
Aland Islands *see* Åland
Aland Sea *see* Ålands Hav
Ålands Hav *85 C6 var.* Aland Sea. *strait* Baltic Sea/Gulf of Bothnia
Alanya *116 C4* Antalya, S Turkey
Alappuzha *see* Alleppey
Al 'Aqabah *119 B8 var.* Akaba, Aqaba, 'Aqaba; *anc.* Aelana, Elath. Al 'Aqabah, SW Jordan
Al 'Arabīyah as Su'ūdīyah *see* Saudi Arabia
Alasca, Golfo de *see* Alaska, Gulf of
Alaşehir *116 A4* Manisa, W Turkey
Al 'Ashārah *118 E3 var.* Ashara. Dayr az Zawr, E Syria
Alaska *36 C3 off.* State of Alaska, *also known as* Land of the Midnight Sun, The Last Frontier, Seward's Folly; *prev.* Russian America. *state* NW USA
Alaska, Gulf of *36 C4 var.* Golfo de Alasca. *gulf* Canada/USA
Alaska Peninsula *36 C3 peninsula* Alaska, USA
Alaska Range *34 B2 mountain range* Alaska, USA
Al-Asnam *see* Chlef
Alattio *see* Alta
Al Awaynāt *see* Al 'Uwaynāt
Alaykel'/Alay-Kuu *see* Këk-Art
Al 'Aynā *119 B7* Al Karak, W Jordan
Alazeya *115 G2 river* NE Russian Federation
Al Bāb *118 B2* Ḥalab, N Syria
Albacete *93 E3* Castilla-La Mancha, C Spain
Al Baghdādī *120 B3 var.* Khān al Baghdādī. SW Iraq
Al Bāha *see* Al Bāḩah
Al Bāḩah *121 B5 var.* Al Bāha. Al BāḨah, SW Saudi Arabia
Al Baḩrayn *see* Bahrain
Alba Iulia *108 B4 Ger.* Weissenburg, *Hung.* Gyulafehérvár; *prev.* Bălgrad, Karlsburg, Károly-Fehérvár. Alba, W Romania
Albania *101 C7 off.* Republic of Albania, *Alb.* Republika e Shqipqërisë, Shqipëria; *prev.* People's Socialist Republic of Albania. *country* SE Europe

ALBANIA
Southeast Europe

Official name Republic of Albania
Formation 1912 / 1921
Capital Tirana
Population 3.1 million / 293 people per sq mile (113 people per sq km) / 42%
Total area 11,100 sq miles (28,748 sq km)
Languages Albanian*, Greek
Religions Sunni Muslim 70%, Orthodox Christian 20%, Roman Catholic 10%
Ethnic mix Albanian 93%, Greek 5%, Other 2%
Government Parliamentary system
Currency Lek = 100 qindarka (qintars)
Literacy rate 99%
Calorie consumption 2848 calories

Albania *see* Aubagne
Albania, People's Socialist Republic of *see* Albania
Albania, Republic of *see* Albania
Albany *147 B7* Western Australia
Albany *42 D3* Georgia, SE USA
Albany *41 F3 state capital* New York, NE USA
Albany *46 B3* Oregon, NW USA
Albany *38 C3 river* Ontario, S Canada
Alba Regia *see* Székesfehérvár
Al Bāridah *118 C4 var.* Bāridah. Ḥimṣ, C Syria
Al Baṣrah *120 C3 Eng.* Basra, *hist.* Busra, Bussora. SE Iraq
Al Batrūn *see* Batroûn
Al Bayḍā' *71 G2 var.* Beida. NE Libya
Albemarle Island *see* Isabela, Isla
Albemarle Sound *43 G1 inlet* W Atlantic Ocean
Albergaria-a-Velha *92 B2* Aveiro, N Portugal
Albert *90 C3* Somme, N France
Alberta *37 E4 province* SW Canada
Albert Edward Nyanza *see* Edward, Lake
Albert, Lake *73 B6 var.* Albert Nyanza, Lac Mobutu Sese Seko. *lake* Uganda/ Dem. Rep. Congo
Albert Lea *45 F3* Minnesota, N USA
Albert Nyanza *see* Albert, Lake
Albertville *see* Kalemie
Albi *91 C6 anc.* Albiga. Tarn, S France
Albiga *see* Albi
Ålborg *see* Aalborg
Ålborg-Nørresundby *see* Aalborg
Alborz, Reshteh-ye Kūhhā-ye *120 C2 Eng.* Elburz Mountains. *mountain range* N Iran
Albuquerque *48 D2* New Mexico, SW USA
Al Burayqah *see* Marsá al Burayqah
Alburgum *see* Aalborg
Albury *149 C7* New South Wales, SE Australia
Alcácer do Sal *92 B4* Setúbal, W Portugal

Alcalá de Henares *93 E3 Ar.* Alkal'a; *anc.* Complutum. Madrid, C Spain
Alcamo *97 C7* Sicilia, Italy, C Mediterranean Sea
Alcañiz *93 F2* Aragón, NE Spain
Alcántara, Embalse de *92 C3 reservoir* W Spain
Alcaudete *92 D4* Andalucía, S Spain
Alcázar *see* Ksar-el-Kebir
Alcazarquivir *see* Ksar-el-Kebir
Alcoi *see* Alcoy
Alcoy *93 F4 Cat.* Alcoi. País Valenciano, E Spain
Aldabra Group *79 G2 island group* SW Seychelles
Aldan *115 F3 river* NE Russian Federation
al Dar al Baida *see* Rabat
Alderney *90 A2 island* Channel Islands
Aleg *74 C3* Brakna, SW Mauritania
Aleksandriya *see* Oleksandriya
Aleksandropol' *see* Gyumri
Aleksandrovka *see* Oleksandrivka
Aleksandrovsk *see* Zaporizhzhya
Aleksin *111 B5* Tul'skaya Oblast', W Russian Federation
Aleksinac *100 E4* Serbia, SE Serbia
Alençon *90 B3* Orne, N France
Alenquer *63 E2* Pará, NE Brazil
Alep/Aleppo *see* Ḩalab
Alert *37 F1* Ellesmere Island, Nunavut, N Canada
Alès *91 C6 prev.* Alais. Gard, S France
Aleşd *108 B3 Hung.* Élesd. Bihor, SW Romania
Alessandria *96 B2 Fr.* Alexandrie. Piemonte, N Italy
Ålesund *85 A5* Møre og Romsdal, S Norway
Aleutian Basin *113 G3 undersea basin* Bering Sea
Aleutian Islands *36 A3 island group* Alaska, USA
Aleutian Range *34 A2 mountain range* Alaska, USA
Aleutian Trench *113 H3 trench* S Bering Sea
Alexander Archipelago *36 D4 island group* Alaska, USA
Alexander City *42 D2* Alabama, S USA
Alexander Island *154 A3 island* Antarctica
Alexander Range *see* Kirghiz Range
Alexandra *151 B7* Otago, South Island, New Zealand
Alexándreia *104 B4 var.* Alexándria. Kentrikí Makedonía, N Greece
Alexandretta *see* İskenderun
Alexandretta, Gulf of *see* İskenderun Körfezi
Alexandria *72 B1 Ar.* Al Iskandarīyah. N Egypt
Alexandria *108 C5* Teleorman, S Romania
Alexandria *42 B3* Louisiana, S USA
Alexandria *45 F2* Minnesota, N USA
Alexándria *see* Alexándreia
Alexandrie *see* Alessandria
Alexandroúpoli *104 D3 var.* Alexandroúpolis, *Turk.* Dedeagaç, Dedeagach. Anatolikí Makedonía kai Thráki, NE Greece
Alexandroúpolis *see* Alexandroúpoli
Al Fāshir *see* El Fasher
Alfatar *104 E1* Silistra, NE Bulgaria
Alfeiós *105 B6 prev.* Alfiós; *anc.* Alpheius, Alpheus. *river* S Greece
Alfiós *see* Alfeiós
Alföld *see* Great Hungarian Plain
Al-Furāt *see* Euphrates
Alga *114 B4 Kaz.* Algha. Aktyubinsk, NW Kazakhstan
Algarve *92 B4 cultural region* S Portugal
Algeciras *92 C5* Andalucía, SW Spain
Algemesí *93 F3* País Valenciano, E Spain
Al-Genain *see* El Geneina
Alger *71 E1 var.* Algiers, El Djazaïr, Al Jazair. *country capital* (Algeria) N Algeria
Algeria *70 C3 off.* Democratic and Popular Republic of Algeria. *country* N Africa

ALGERIA
North Africa

Official name People's Democratic Republic of Algeria
Formation 1962 / 1962

ALGERIA
(continued)

Capital Algiers
Population 32.9 million / 36 people per sq mile (14 people per sq km) / 60%
Total area 919,590 sq miles (2,381,740 sq km)
Languages Arabic, Tamazight (Kabyle, Shawia, Tamashek), French
Religions Sunni Muslim 99%, Christian and Jewish 1%
Ethnic mix Arab 75%, Berber 24%, European and Jewish 1%
Government Presidential system
Currency Algerian dinar = 100 centimes
Literacy rate 70%
Calorie consumption 3022 calories

Algeria, Democratic and Popular Republic of *see* Algeria
Algerian Basin *80 C5 var.* Balearic Plain. *undersea basin* W Mediterranean Sea
Algha *see* Alga
Al Ghābah *121 E5 var.* Ghaba. C Oman
Alghero *97 A5* Sardegna, Italy, C Mediterranean Sea
Al Ghurdaqah *see* Hurghada
Algiers *see* Alger
Al Golea *see* El Goléa
Algona *45 F3* Iowa, C USA
Al Ḩajār al Gharbī *121 D5 mountain range* N Oman
Al Hamad *see* Syrian Desert
Al Ḩasakah *118 D2 var.* Al Hasijah, El Haseke, *Fr.* Hassetché. Al Ḩasakah, NE Syria
Al Ḩillah *120 B3 var.* Hilla. C Iraq
Al Ḩisā *119 B7* Aţ Ţafīlah, W Jordan
Al Ḩudaydah *121 B6 Eng.* Hodeida. W Yemen
Al Hufūf *120 C4 var.* Hofuf. Ash Sharqīyah, NE Saudi Arabia
Aliákmon *see* Aliákmonas
Aliákmonas *104 B4 prev.* Aliákmon; *anc.* Haliacmon. *river* N Greece
Alíartos *105 C5* Stereá Ellás, C Greece
Alicante *93 F4 Cat.* Alacant, *Lat.* Lucentum. País Valenciano, SE Spain
Alice *49 G5* Texas, SW USA
Alice Springs *148 A4* Northern Territory, C Australia
Aliki *see* Alykí
Alima *77 B6 river* C Congo
Al Imārāt al 'Arabīyahal Muttaḩidah *see* United Arab Emirates
Alindao *76 C4* Basse-Kotto, S Central African Republic
Aliquippa *40 D4* Pennsylvania, NE USA
Al Iskandarīyah *see* Alexandria
Alistráti *104 C3* Kentrikí Makedonía, NE Greece
Alivéri *105 C5 var.* Alivérion. Évvoia, C Greece
Alivérion *see* Alivéri
Al Jabal al Akhḑar *71 G2 mountain range* NE Libya
Al Jafr *119 B7* Ma'ān, S Jordan
Al Jaghbūb *71 H3* NE Libya
Al Jahrā' *120 C4 var.* Al Jahrah, Jahra. C Kuwait
Al Jahrah *see* Al Jahrā'
Al Jamāhīrīyah al 'Arabīyah al Lībīyah ash Sha'bīyah al Ishtirākīy *see* Libya
Al Jawf *120 B4 off.* Jauf. Al Jawf, NW Saudi Arabia
Al Jawlān *see* Golan Heights
Al Jazair *see* Alger
Al Jazīrah *118 E2 physical region* Iraq/Syria
Al Jīzah *see* El Gîza
Al Junaynah *see* El Geneina
Alkal'a *see* Alcalá de Henares
Al Karak *119 B7 var.* El Kerak, Karak, Kerak; *anc.* Kir Moab, Kir of Moab. Al Karak, W Jordan
Al-Kasr al-Kebir *see* Ksar-el-Kebir
Al Khalīl *see* Hebron
Al Khārijah *see* El Khârga
Al Khufrah *71 H4* SE Libya
Al Khums *71 F2 var.* Homs, Khoms, Khums. NW Libya
Alkmaar *86 C2* Noord-Holland, NW Netherlands
Al Kūt *120 C3 var.* Kūt al 'Amārah, Kut al Imara. E Iraq
Al-Kuwait *see* Al Kuwayt
Al Kuwayt *120 C4 var.* Al-Kuwait, *Eng.* Kuwait, Kuwait City; *prev.* Qurein. *country capital* (Kuwait) E Kuwait
Al Lādhiqīyah *see* Lādhiqīyah
Allahābād *135 E3* Uttar Pradesh, N India
Allanmyo *136 B4* Magwe, C Myanmar (Burma)
Allegheny Plateau *41 E3 mountain range* New York/Pennsylvania, NE USA
Allenstein *see* Olsztyn
Allentown *41 F4* Pennsylvania, NE USA
Alleppey *132 C3 var.* Alappuzha; *prev.* Alleppi. Kerala, SW India
Alleppi *see* Alleppey
Alliance *44 D3* Nebraska, C USA
Al Līth *121 B5* Makkah, SW Saudi Arabia
Al Lubnān *see* Lebanon
Alma-Ata *see* Almaty
Almada *92 B4* Setúbal, W Portugal
Al Madīnah *121 A5 Eng.* Medina. Al Madīnah, W Saudi Arabia
Al Mafraq *119 B6 var.* Mafraq. Al Mafraq, N Jordan
Al Mahdīyah *see* Mahdia
Al Mahrah *121 C6 mountain range* E Yemen
Al Majma'ah *120 B4* Ar Riyāḑ, C Saudi Arabia
Al Mālikīyah *118 E1 var.* Malkiye. Al Ḩasakah, N Syria
Almalyk *see* Olmaliq
Al Mamlakah *see* Morocco
Al Mamlaka al Urduniya al Hashemiyah *see* Jordan
Al Manāmah *120 C4 Eng.* Manama. *country capital* (Bahrain) N Bahrain
Al Manāşif *118 E3 mountain range* E Syria
Almansa *93 F4* Castilla-La Mancha, C Spain
Al-Mariyya *see* Almería
Al Marj *71 G2 var.* Barka, *It.* Barce. NE Libya
Almaty *114 C5 var.* Alma-Ata. Almaty, SE Kazakhstan
Al Mawşil *120 B2 Eng.* Mosul. N Iraq
Al Mayādīn *118 D3 var.* Mayadin, *Fr.* Meyadine. Dayr az Zawr, E Syria
Al Mazra' *see* Al Mazra'ah
Al Mazra'ah *119 B6 var.* Al Mazra', Mazra'a. Al Karak, W Jordan
Almelo *86 E3* Overijssel, E Netherlands
Almendra, Embalse de *92 C2 reservoir* Castilla-León, NW Spain
Almendralejo *92 C4* Extremadura, W Spain
Almere *86 C3 var.* Almere-stad. Flevoland, C Netherlands
Almere-stad *see* Almere
Almería *93 E5 Ar.* Al-Mariyya; *anc.* Unci, *Lat.* Portus Magnus. Andalucía, S Spain
Al'met'yevsk *111 D5* Respublika Tatarstan, W Russian Federation
Al Mīnā' *see* El Mina
Al Minyā *see* El Minya
Almirante *53 E4* Bocas del Toro, NW Panama
Al Mudawwarah *119 B8* Ma'ān, SW Jordan
Al Mukallā *121 C6 var.* Mukalla. SE Yemen
Al Obayyid *see* El Obeid
Alofi *145 F4 dependent territory capital* (Niue) W Niue
Aloha State *see* Hawai'i
Aloja *106 D3* Limbaži, N Latvia
Alónnisos *105 C5 island* Vóreioi Sporádes, Greece, Aegean Sea
Álora *92 D5* Andalucía, S Spain
Alor, Kepulauan *139 E5 island group* E Indonesia
Alost *see* Aalst
Al Oued *see* El Oued
Alpen *see* Alps
Alpena *40 D2* Michigan, N USA
Alpes *see* Alps
Alpha Cordillera *155 B3 var.* Alpha Ridge. *seamount range* Arctic Ocean
Alpha Ridge *see* Alpha Cordillera
Alpheius *see* Alfeiós
Alphen *see* Alphen aan den Rijn
Alphen aan den Rijn *86 C3 var.* Alphen. Zuid-Holland, C Netherlands
Alpheus *see* Alfeiós
Alpi *see* Alps
Alpine *49 E4* Texas, SW USA
Alps *102 C1 Fr.* Alpes, *Ger.* Alpen, *It.* Alpi. *mountain range* C Europe
Al Qaḑārif *see* Gedaref
Al Qāhirah *see* Cairo
Al Qāmishlī *118 E1 var.* Kamishli, Qamishly. Al Ḩasakah, NE Syria
Al Qaşrayn *see* Kasserine
Al Qayrawān *see* Kairouan
Al-Qsar al-Kbir *see* Ksar-el-Kebir
Al Qubayyāt *see* Qoubaïyât
Al Quds/Al Quds ash Sharīf *see* Jerusalem
Alqueva, Barragem do *92 C4 reservoir* Portugal/Spain
Al Qunayţirah *119 B5 var.* El Kuneitra, El Quneitra, Kuneitra, Qunaytra. Al Qunayţirah, SW Syria
Al Quşayr *118 B4 var.* El Quseir, Quşayr, *Fr.* Kousseir. Ḩimş, W Syria
Al Quwayrah *119 B8 var.* El Quweira. Al 'Aqabah, SW Jordan
Alsace *90 E3 Ger.* Elsass; *anc.* Alsatia. *cultural region* NE France
Alsace *90 E3 Ger.* Elsass; *anc.* Alsatia. *region* NE France
Alsatia *see* Alsace
Alsdorf *94 A4* Nordrhein-Westfalen, W Germany
Alt *see* Olt
Alta *84 D2 Fin.* Alattio. Finnmark, N Norway
Altai *see* Altai Mountains
Altai Mountains *126 C2 var.* Altai, *Chin.* Altay Shan, *Rus* Altay. *mountain range* Asia/Europe
Altamaha River *43 E3 river* Georgia, SE USA
Altamira *63 E2* Pará, NE Brazil
Altamura *97 E5 anc.* Lupatia. Puglia, SE Italy
Altar, Desierto de *50 A1 var.* Sonoran Desert. *desert* Mexico/USA
Altar, Desierto de *see* Sonoran Desert
Altay *126 C2* Xinjiang Uygur Zizhiqu, NW China
Altay *126 D2 prev.* Yösönbulag. Govĭ-Altay, W Mongolia
Altay Altai Mountains, Asia/Europe
Altay Shan *see* Altai Mountains
Altbetsche *see* Bečej
Altenburg *see* București, Romania
Altin Köprü *120 B3 var.* Altun Kupri. N Iraq
Altiplano *61 F4 physical region* W South America
Altkanischa *see* Kanjiža
Alton *40 B5* Illinois, N USA
Alton *40 B4* Missouri, C USA
Altoona *41 E4* Pennsylvania, NE USA
Alto Paraná *see* Paraná
Altpasua *see* Stara Pazova
Alt-Schwanenburg *see* Gulbene
Altsohl *see* Zvolen
Altun Kupri *see* Altin Köprü
Altun Shan *126 C3 var.* Altyn Tagh. *mountain range* NW China
Altus *49 F2* Oklahoma, C USA
Altyn Tagh *see* Altun Shan
Al Ubayyiḑ *see* El Obeid
Alūksne *106 D3 Ger.* Marienburg. Alūksne, NE Latvia
Al 'Ulā *120 A4* Al Madīnah, NW Saudi Arabia
Al 'Umarī *119 C6* 'Ammān, E Jordan
Alupka *109 F5* Respublika Krym, S Ukraine
Al Uqşur *see* Luxor
Al Urdunn *see* Jordan
Alushta *109 F5* Respublika Krym, S Ukraine
Al 'Uwaynāt *71 F4 var.* Al Awaynāt. SW Libya
Alva *49 F1* Oklahoma, C USA
Alvarado *51 F4* Veracruz-Llave, E Mexico
Alvin *49 H4* Texas, SW USA
Al Wajh *120 A4* Tabūk, NW Saudi Arabia
Alwar *134 D3* Rājasthān, N India
Al Wari'ah *120 C4* Ash Sharqīyah, N Saudi Arabia
Al Yaman *see* Yemen
Alykí *104 C4 var.* Aliki. Thásos, N Greece
Alytus *107 B5 Pol.* Olita. Alytus, S Lithuania

Alzette *87 D8 river* S Luxembourg

Amadeus, Lake *147 D5 seasonal lake* Northern Territory, C Australia

Amadi *73 B5* Western Equatoria, SW Sudan

Amadjuak Lake *37 G3 lake* Baffin Island, Nunavut, N Canada

Amakusa-nada *131 A7 gulf* Kyūshū, SW Japan

Åmål *85 B6* Västra Götaland, S Sweden

Amami-guntō *130 A3 island group* SW Japan

Amami-Ō-shima *130 A3 island* S Japan

Amantea *97 D6* Calabria, SW Italy

Amapá *63 E1* Amapá, NE Brazil

Amara *see* Al ʻAmārah

Amarapura *136 B3* Mandalay, C Myanmar (Burma)

Amarillo *49 E2* Texas, SW USA

Amay *87 C6* Liège, E Belgium

Amazon *63 E1 Sp.* Amazonas. *river* Brazil/Peru

Amazonas *see* Amazon

Amazon Basin *62 D2 basin* N South America

Amazon, Mouths of the *63 F1 delta* NE Brazil

Ambam *77 B5* Sud, S Cameroon

Ambanja *79 G2* Antsirañana, N Madagascar

Ambarchik *115 G2* Respublika Sakha (Yakutiya), NE Russian Federation

Ambato *60 B1* Tungurahua, C Ecuador

Ambérieu-en-Bugey *91 D5* Ain, E France

Ambianum *see* Amiens

Amboasary *79 F4* Toliara, S Madagascar

Amboina *see* Ambon

Ambon *139 F4 prev.* Amboina, Amboyna. Pulau Ambon, E Indonesia

Ambositra *79 G3* Fianarantsoa, SE Madagascar

Amboyna *see* Ambon

Ambracia *see* Árta

Ambre, Cap d' *see* Bobaomby, Tanjona

Ambrim *see* Ambrym

Ambriz *78 A1* Bengo, NW Angola

Ambrym *144 D4 var.* Ambrim. *island* C Vanuatu

Amchitka Island *36 A2 island* Aleutian Islands, Alaska, USA

Amdo *126 C5* Xizang Zizhiqu, W China

Ameland *86 D1 Fris.* It Amelân. *island* Waddeneilanden, N Netherlands

Amelân, It *see* Ameland

America *see* United States of America

America-Antarctica Ridge *67 C7 undersea ridge* S Atlantic Ocean

America in Miniature *see* Maryland

American Falls Reservoir *46 E4 reservoir* Idaho, NW USA

American Samoa *145 E4 US unincorporated territory* W Polynesia

Amersfoort *86 D3* Utrecht, C Netherlands

Ames *45 F3* Iowa, C USA

Amfilochía *105 A5 var.* Amfilokhía. Dytikí Ellás, C Greece

Amfilokhía *see* Amfilochía

Amga *115 F3 river* NE Russian Federation

Amherst *39 F4* Nova Scotia, SE Canada

Amherst *see* Kyaikkami

Amida *see* Diyarbakır

Amiens *90 C3 anc.* Ambianum, Samarobriva. Somme, N France

Amíndaion/Amindeo *see* Amýntaio

Amīndīvi Islands *132 A2 island group* Lakshadweep, India, N Indian Ocean

Amirante Islands *79 G1 var.* Amirantes Group. *island group* C Seychelles

Amirantes Group *see* Amirante Islands

Amistad, Presa de la *see* Amistad Reservoir

Amistad Reservoir *49 F4 var.* Presa de la Amistad. *reservoir* Mexico/USA

Amisus *see* Samsun

Ammaia *see* Portalegre

ʻAmmān *119 B6 var.* Amman; *anc.* Philadelphia, *Bibl.* Rabbah Ammon, Rabbath Ammon. *country capital* (Jordan) ʻAmmān, NW Jordan

Ammassalik *82 D4 var.* Angmagssalik. Tunu, S Greenland

Ammóchostos *see* Gazimağusa

Ammóchostos, Kólpos *see* Gazimağusa Körfezi

Amnok-kang *see* Yalu

Amoea *see* Portalegre

Amoentai *see* Amuntai

Āmol *120 D2 var.* Amul. Māzandarān, N Iran

Amorgós *105 D6* Amorgós, Kykládes, Greece, Aegean Sea

Amorgós *105 D6 island* Kykládes, Greece, Aegean Sea

Amos *38 D4* Québec, SE Canada

Amourj *74 D3* Hodh ech Chargui, SE Mauritania

Amoy *see* Xiamen

Ampato, Nevado *61 E4 mountain* S Peru

Amposta *93 F2* Cataluña, NE Spain

Amraoti *see* Amrāvati

Amrāvati *134 D4 prev.* Amraoti. Mahārāshtra, C India

Amritsar *134 D2* Punjab, N India

Amstelveen *86 C3* Noord-Holland, C Netherlands

Amsterdam *86 C3 country capital* (Netherlands) Noord-Holland, C Netherlands

Amsterdam Island *141 C6 island* NE French Southern and Antarctic Territories

Am Timan *76 C3* Salamat, SE Chad

Amu Darya *122 D2 Rus.* Amudar'ya, *Taj.* Dar"yoi Amu, *Turkm.* Amyderya, *Uzb.* Amudaryo; *anc.* Oxus. *river* C Asia

Amu-Dar'ya *see* Amyderya

Amudar'ya/Amudaryo/Amu, Dar"yoi *see* Amu Darya

Amul *see* Āmol

Amund Ringnes Island *37 F2 Island* Nunavut, N Canada

Amundsen Basin *see* Fram Basin

Amundsen Gulf *37 E2 gulf* Northwest Territories, N Canada

Amundsen Plain *154 A4 abyssal plain* S Pacific Ocean

Amundsen-Scott *154 B3 US research station* Antarctica

Amundsen Sea *154 A4 sea* S Pacific Ocean

Amuntai *138 D4 prev.* Amoentai. Borneo, C Indonesia

Amur *115 G4 Chin.* Heilong Jiang. *river* China/Russian Federation

Amvrosiyevka *see* Amvrosiyivka

Amvrosiyivka *109 H3 Rus.* Amvrosiyevka. Donets'ka Oblast', SE Ukraine

Amyderya *123 E3 Rus.* Amu-Dar'ya. Lebap Welaýaty, NE Turkmenistan

Amyderya *see* Amu Darya

Amýntaio *104 B4 var.* Amindeo; *prev.* Amíndaion. Dytikí Makedonía, N Greece

Anabar *115 E2 river* NE Russian Federation

An Abhainn Mhór *see* Blackwater

Anaco *59 E2* Anzoátegui, NE Venezuela

Anaconda *44 B2* Montana, NW USA

Anacortes *46 B1* Washington, NW USA

Anadolu Dağlari *see* Doğu Karadeniz Dağları

Anadyr' *115 H1* Chukotskiy Avtonomnyy Okrug, NE Russian Federation

Anadyr' *115 G1 river* NE Russian Federation

Anadyr, Gulf of *see* Anadyrskiy Zaliv

Anadyrskiy Zaliv *115 H1 Eng.* Gulf of Anadyr. *gulf* NE Russian Federation

Anáfi *105 D7 anc.* Anaphe. *island* Kykládes, Greece, Aegean Sea

ʻĀnah *see* ʻAnnah

Anaheim *46 E2* California, W USA

Anaiza *see* ʻUnayzah

Analalava *79 G2* Mahajanga, NW Madagascar

Anamur *116 C5* Mersin, S Turkey

Anantapur *132 C2* Andhra Pradesh, S India

Anaphe *see* Anáfi

Anápolis *63 F3* Goiás, C Brazil

Anār *120 D3* Kermān, C Iran

Anatolia *116 C4 plateau* C Turkey

Anatom *see* Aneityum

Añatuya *64 C3* Santiago del Estero, N Argentina

An Bhearú *see* Barrow

Anchorage *36 C3* Alaska, USA

Ancona *96 C3* Marche, C Italy

Ancud *65 B6 prev.* San Carlos de Ancud. Los Lagos, S Chile

Ancyra *see* Ankara

Åndalsnes *85 A5* Møre og Romsdal, S Norway

Andalucía *92 D4 cultural region* S Spain Europe

Andalusia *42 C3* Alabama, S USA

Andaman Islands *124 B4 island group* India, NE Indian Ocean

Andaman Sea *124 C4 sea* NE Indian Ocean

Andenne *87 C6* Namur, SE Belgium

Anderlues *87 B7* Hainaut, S Belgium

Anderson *40 C4* Indiana, N USA

Andes *64 B3 mountain range* W South America

Andhra Pradesh *135 E5 state* E India

Andhra Pradesh *135 E5 cultural region* E India

Andijon *123 F2 Rus.* Andizhan. Andijon Viloyati, E Uzbekistan

Andikíthira *see* Antikýthira

Andipaxi *see* Antípaxoi

Andípsara *see* Antípsara

Ándissa *see* Ántissa

Andizhan *see* Andijon

Andkhvoy *122 D3* Fāryāb, N Afghanistan

Andorra *91 A7 off.* Principality of Andorra, *Cat.* Valls d'Andorra, *Fr.* Vallée d'Andorre. *country* SW Europe

ANDORRA

Southwest Europe

Official name Principality of Andorra
Formation 1278 / 1278
Capital Andorra la Vella
Population 70,549 / 392 people per sq mile (152 people per sq km) / 63%
Total area 181 sq miles (468 sq km)
Languages Spanish, Catalan, French, Portuguese
Religions Roman Catholic 94%, Other 6%
Ethnic mix Spanish 46%, Andorran 28%, Other 18%, French 8%
Government Parliamentary system
Currency Euro = 100 cents
Literacy rate 99%
Calorie consumption Not available

Andorra *see* Andorra la Vella

Andorra la Vella *91 A8 var.* Andorra, *Fr.* Andorre la Vielle, *Sp.* Andorra la Vieja. *country capital* (Andorra) C Andorra

Andorra la Vieja *see* Andorra la Vella

Andorra, Principality of *see* Andorra

Andorra, Valls d'/Andorra, Vallée d' *see* Andorra

Andorre la Vielle *see* Andorra la Vella

Andover *89 D7* S England, UK

Andøya *84 C2 island* C Norway

Andreanof Islands *36 A3 island group* Aleutian Islands, Alaska, USA

Andrews *49 E3* Texas, SW USA

Andrew Tablemount *140 A4 var.* Gora Andryu. *seamount* W Indian Ocean

Andria *97 D5* Puglia, SE Italy

An Droichead Nua *see* Newbridge

Andropov *see* Rybinsk

Ándros *105 D6* Ándros, Kykládes, Greece, Aegean Sea

Ándros *105 C6 island* Kykládes, Greece, Aegean Sea

Andros Island *54 B2 island* NW Bahamas

Andros Town *54 C1* Andros Island, NW Bahamas

Andryu, Gora *see* Andrew Tablemount

Aneityum *144 D5 var.* Anatom; *prev.* Kéamu. *island* S Vanuatu

Änewetak *see* Enewetak Atoll

Angara *115 E4 river* C Russian Federation

Angarsk *115 E4* Irkutskaya Oblast', S Russian Federation

Ånge *85 C5* Västernorrland, C Sweden

Ángel de la Guarda, Isla *50 B2 island* NW Mexico

Angeles *139 E1 off.* Angeles City. Luzon, N Philippines

Angeles City *see* Angeles

Angel Falls *see* Ángel, Salto

Ángel, Salto *59 E3 Eng.* Angel Falls. *waterfall* E Venezuela

Angerburg *see* Węgorzewo

Ångermanälven *84 C4 river* N Sweden

Angermünde *94 D3* Brandenburg, NE Germany

Angers *90 B4 anc.* Juliomagus. Maine-et-Loire, NW France

Anglesey *89 C5 island* NW Wales, UK

Anglet *91 A6* Pyrénées-Atlantiques, SW France

Angleton *49 H4* Texas, SW USA

Anglia *see* England

Anglo-Egyptian Sudan *see* Sudan

Angmagssalik *see* Ammassalik

Ang Nam Ngum *136 C4 lake* C Laos

Angola *78 B2 off.* Republic of Angola; *prev.* People's Republic of Angola, Portuguese West Africa. *country* SW Africa

ANGOLA

Southern Africa

Official name Republic of Angola
Formation 1975 / 1975
Capital Luanda
Population 15.9 million / 33 people per sq mile (13 people per sq km) / 34%
Total area 481,351 sq miles (1,246,700 sq km)
Languages Portuguese*, Umbundu, Kimbundu, Kikongo
Religions Roman Catholic 50%, Other 30%, Protestant 20%
Ethnic mix Ovimbundu 37%, Other 25%, Kimbundu 25%, Bakongo 13%
Government Presidential system
Currency Readjusted kwanza = 100 lwei
Literacy rate 67%
Calorie consumption 2083 calories

Angola Basin *69 B5 undersea basin* E Atlantic Ocean

Angola, People's Republic of *see* Angola

Angola, Republic of *see* Angola

Angora *see* Ankara

Angostura *see* Ciudad Bolívar

Angostura, Presa de la *51 G5 reservoir* SE Mexico

Angoulême *91 B5 anc.* Iculisma. Charente, W France

Angoumois *91 B5 cultural region* W France

Angra Pequena *see* Lüderitz

Angren *123 F2* Toshkent Viloyati, E Uzbekistan

Anguilla *55 G3 UK dependent territory* E West Indies

Anguilla Cays *54 B2 islets* SW Bahamas

Anhui *128 C5 var.* Anhui Sheng, Anhwei, Wan. *province* E China

AnhuiSheng/Anhwei Wan *see* Anhui

Anicium *see* le Puy

Anina *108 A4 Ger.* Steierdorf, *Hung.* Stájerlakanina; *prev.* Ştaierdorf-Anina, Steierdorf-Anina, Steyerlak-Anina. Caraş-Severin, SW Romania

Anjou *90 B4 cultural region* NW France

Anjouan *79 F2 var.* Nzwani, Johanna Island. *island* SE Comoros

Ankara *116 C3 prev.* Angora; *anc.* Ancyra. *country capital* (Turkey) Ankara, C Turkey

Ankeny *45 F3* Iowa, C USA

Anklam *94 D2* Mecklenburg-Vorpommern, NE Germany

An Mhuir Cheilteach *see* Celtic Sea

Annaba *71 E1 prev.* Bône. NE Algeria

An Nafūd *120 B4 desert* NW Saudi Arabia

ʻAnnah *120 B3 var.* ʻĀnah. NW Iraq

An Najaf *120 B3 var.* Najaf. S Iraq

Annamitique, Chaîne *136 D4 mountain range* C Laos

Annapolis *41 F4 state capital* Maryland, NE USA

Annapurṇa *135 E3 mountain* C Nepal

An Nāqūrah *see* En Nâqoûra

Ann Arbor *40 C3* Michigan, N USA

An Nāṣirīyah *120 C3 var.* Nasiriya. SE Iraq

Anneciacum *see* Annecy

Annecy *91 D5 anc.* Anneciacum. Haute Savoie, E France

An Nīl al Abyaḍ *see* White Nile

An Nīl al Azraq *see* Blue Nile

Anniston *42 D2* Alabama, S USA

Annotto Bay *54 B4* C Jamaica
An Ómaigh *see* Omagh
Anqing *128 D5* Anhui, E China
Anse La Raye *55 F1* NW Saint Lucia
Anshun *128 B6* Guizhou, S China
Ansongo *75 E3* Gao, E Mali
An Srath Bán *see* Strabane
Antakya *116 D4* *anc.* Antioch, Antiochia. Hatay, S Turkey
Antalaha *79 G2* Antsirañana, NE Madagascar
Antalya *116 B4* *prev.* Adalia; *anc.* Attaleia, *Bibl.* Attalia. Antalya, SW Turkey
Antalya, Gulf of *see* Antalya Körfezi
Antalya Körfezi *116 B4* *var.* Gulf of Adalia, *Eng.* Gulf of Antalya. *gulf* SW Turkey
Antananarivo *79 G3* *prev.* Tananarive. *country capital* (Madagascar) Antananarivo, C Madagascar
Antarctica *154 B3* *continent*
Antarctic Peninsula *154 A2* *peninsula* Antarctica
Antep *see* Gaziantep
Antequera *92 D5* *anc.* Anticaria, Antiquaria. Andalucía, S Spain
Antequera *see* Oaxaca
Antibes *91 D6* *anc.* Antipolis. Alpes-Maritimes, SE France
Anticaria *see* Antequera
Anticosti, Île d' *39 F3* *Eng.* Anticosti Island. *island* Québec, E Canada
Anticosti Island *see* Anticosti, Île d'
Antigua *55 G3* *island* S Antigua and Barbuda, Leeward Islands
Antigua and Barbuda *55 G3* *country* E West Indies

ANTIGUA & BARBUDA
West Indies

Official name Antigua and Barbuda
Formation 1981 / 1981
Capital St. John's
Population 68,722 / 404 people per sq mile (156 people per sq km) / 37%
Total area 170 sq miles (442 sq km)
Languages English, English patois
Religions Anglican 45%, Other Protestant 42%, Roman Catholic 10%, Other 2%, Rastafarian 1%
Ethnic mix Black African 95%, Other 5%
Government Parliamentary system
Currency Eastern Caribbean dollar = 100 cents
Literacy rate 86%
Calorie consumption 2349 calories

Antikýthira *105 B7* *var.* Andikíthira. *island* S Greece
Anti-Lebanon *118 B4* *var.* Jebel esh Sharqi, *Ar.* Al Jabal ash Sharqī, *Fr.* Anti-Liban. *mountain range* Lebanon/Syria
Anti-Liban *see* Anti-Lebanon
Antioch *see* Antakya
Antiochia *see* Antakya
Antípaxoi *105 A5* *var.* Andipaxi. *island* Iónioi Nísoi, Greece, C Mediterranean Sea
Antipodes Islands *142 D5* *island group* S New Zealand
Antipolis *see* Antibes
Antípsara *105 D5* *var.* Andípsara. *island* E Greece
Antiquaria *see* Antequera
Ántissa *105 D5* *var.* Ándissa. Lésvos, E Greece
An tIúr *see* Newry
Antivari *see* Bar
Antofagasta *64 B2* Antofagasta, N Chile
Antony *90 E2* Hauts-de-Seine, N France
An tSionainn *see* Shannon
Antsirañana *79 G2* *province* N Madagascar
Antsohihy *79 G2* Mahajanga, NW Madagascar
An-tung *see* Dandong
Antwerpen *87 C5* *Eng.* Antwerp, *Fr.* Anvers. Antwerpen, N Belgium
Anuradhapura *132 D3* North Central Province, C Sri Lanka
Anvers *see* Antwerpen
Anyang *128 C4* Henan, C China
A'nyêmaqên Shan *126 D4* *mountain range* C China
Anykščiai *106 C4* Utena, E Lithuania
Anzio *97 C5* Lazio, C Italy
Aomen *see* Macao
Aomori *130 D3* Aomori, Honshū, C Japan
Aóos *see* Vjosës, Lumi i
Aoraki *151 B6* *prev.* Aorangi, Mount Cook. *mountain* South Island, New Zealand
Aorangi *see* Aoraki
Aosta *96 A1* *anc.* Augusta Praetoria. Valle d'Aosta, NW Italy
Aoukâr *74 D3* *var.* Aouker. *plateau* C Mauritania
Aouk, Bahr *76 C4* *river* Central African Republic/Chad
Aouker *see* Aoukâr
Aozou *76 C1* Borkou-Ennedi-Tibesti, N Chad
Apalachee Bay *42 D3* *bay* Florida, SE USA
Apalachicola River *42 D3* *river* Florida, SE USA
Apamama *see* Abemama
Apaporis, Río *58 C4* *river* Brazil/Colombia
Apatity *110 C2* Murmanskaya Oblast', NW Russian Federation
Ape *106 D3* Alūksne, NE Latvia
Apeldoorn *86 D3* Gelderland, E Netherlands
Apennines *see* Appennino
Āpia *145 F4* *country capital* (Samoa) Upolu, SE Samoa
Apoera *59 G3* Sipaliwini, NW Suriname
Apostle Islands *40 B1* *island group* Wisconsin, N USA
Appalachian Mountains *35 D5* *mountain range* E USA
Appennino *96 E2* *Eng.* Apennines. *mountain range* Italy/San Marino
Appingedam *86 E1* Groningen, NE Netherlands
Appleton *40 B2* Wisconsin, N USA
Apulia *see* Puglia
Apure, Río *58 C2* *river* W Venezuela
Apurímac, Río *60 D3* *river* S Peru
Apuseni, Munții *108 A4* *mountain range* W Romania
Aqaba/'Aqaba *see* Al 'Aqabah
Aqaba, Gulf of *120 A4* *var.* Gulf of Elat, *Ar.* Khalīj al 'Aqabah; *anc.* Sinus Aelaniticus. *gulf* NE Red Sea
'Aqabah, Khalīj al *see* Aqaba, Gulf of
Āqchah *123 E3* *var.* Āqcheh. Jowzjān, N Afghanistan
Āqcheh *see* Āqchah
Aqmola *see* Astana
Aqtöbe *see* Aktobe
Aquae Augustae *see* Dax
Aquae Calidae *see* Bath
Aquae Flaviae *see* Chaves
Aquae Grani *see* Aachen
Aquae Sextiae *see* Aix-en-Provence
Aquae Solis *see* Bath
Aquae Tarbelicae *see* Dax
Aquidauana *63 E4* Mato Grosso do Sul, S Brazil
Aquila/Aquila degli Abruzzi *see* L'Aquila
Aquisgranum *see* Aachen
Aquitaine *91 B6* *region* SW France
Aquitaine *91 B6* *cultural region* SW France
'Arabah, Wādī al *135 B7* *Heb.* Ha'Arava. *dry watercourse* Israel/Jordan
Arabian Basin *124 A4* *undersea basin* N Arabian Sea
Arabian Desert *see* Sahara el Sharqîya
Arabian Peninsula *121 B5* *peninsula* SW Asia
Arabian Sea *124 A3* *sea* NW Indian Ocean
Arabicus, Sinus *see* Red Sea
Khalīj al 'Arabī *see* Gulf, The
'Arabīyah as Su'ūdīyah, Al Mamlakah al *see* Saudi Arabia
'Arabīyah Jumhūrīyah, Mişr al *see* Egypt
Arab Republic of Egypt *see* Egypt
Aracaju *63 G3* *state capital* Sergipe, E Brazil
Araçuai *63 F3* Minas Gerais, SE Brazil
'Arad *119 B7* Southern, S Israel
Arad *108 A4* Arad, W Romania
Arafura Sea *142 A3* *Ind.* Laut Arafuru. *sea* W Pacific Ocean
Arafuru, Laut *see* Arafura Sea
Aragón *93 E2* *autonomous community* E Spain
Araguaia, Río *63 E3* *var.* Araguaya. *river* C Brazil
Araguari *63 F3* Minas Gerais, SE Brazil
Araguaya *see* Araguaia, Río
Ara Jovis *see* Aranjuez
Arāk *120 C3* *prev.* Sultānābād. Markazī, W Iran
Arakan Yoma *136 A3* *mountain range* W Myanmar (Burma)
Araks/Arak's *see* Aras
Aral *see* Aralsk, Kazakhstan
Aral Sea *122 C1* *Kaz.* Aral Tengizi, *Rus.* Aral'skoye More, *Uzb.* Orol Dengizi. *inland sea* Kazakhstan/Uzbekistan
Aral'sk *114 B4* *Kaz.* Aral. Kzylorda, SW Kazakhstan
Aral'skoye More/Aral Tengizi *see* Aral Sea
Aranda de Duero *92 D2* Castilla-León, N Spain
Aranđelovac *100 D4* *prev.* Arandjelovac. Serbia, C Serbia
Arandjelovac *see* Aranđelovac
Aranjuez *92 D3* *anc.* Ara Jovis. Madrid, C Spain
Araouane *75 E2* Tombouctou, N Mali
'Ar'ar *120 B3* Al Ḩudūd ash Shamālīyah, NW Saudi Arabia
Ararat, Mount *see* Büyükağrı Dağı
Aras *117 G3* *Arm.* Arak's, *Az.* Araz Nehri, *Per.* Rūd-e Aras, *Rus.* Araks; *prev.* Araxes. *river* SW Asia
Aras, Rūd-e *see* Aras
Arauca *58 C2* Arauca, NE Colombia
Arauca, Río *58 C2* *river* Colombia/Venezuela
Arausio *see* Orange
Araxes *see* Aras
Araz Nehri *see* Aras
Arbela *see* Arbīl
Arbīl *120 B2* *var.* Erbil, Irbil, *Kurd.* Hawlēr; *anc.* Arbela. N Iraq
Arbroath *88 D3* *anc.* Aberbrothock. E Scotland, UK
Arbuzinka *see* Arbyzynka
Arbyzynka *109 E3* *Rus.* Arbuzinka. Mykolayivs'ka Oblast', S Ukraine
Arcachon *91 B5* Gironde, SW France
Arcae Remorum *see* Châlons-en-Champagne
Arcata *46 A4* California, W USA
Archangel *see* Arkhangel'sk
Archangel Bay *see* Chēshskaya Guba
Archidona *92 D5* Andalucía, S Spain
Arco *96 C2* Trentino-Alto Adige, N Italy
Arctic Mid Oceanic Ridge *see* Nansen Cordillera
Arctic Ocean *172 B3* *ocean*
Arda *104 C3* *var.* Ardhas, *Gk.* Ardas. *river* Bulgaria/Greece
Arda *see* Ardas
Ardabīl *120 C2* *var.* Ardebil. Ardabīl, NW Iran
Ardakān *120 D3* Yazd, C Iran
Ardas *104 D3* *var.* Ardhas, *Bul.* Arda. *river* Bulgaria/Greece
Ardas *see* Arda
Ard aş Şawwān *119 C7* *var.* Ardh es Suwwān. *plain* S Jordan
Ardeal *see* Transylvania
Ardebil *see* Ardabīl
Ardèche *91 C5* *cultural region* E France
Ardèche *91 C5* *department* E France
Ardennes *87 C8* *physical region* Belgium/France
Ardhas *see* Arda/Ardas
Ardh es Suwwān *see* Ard aş Şawwān
Ardino *104 D3* Kŭrdzhali, S Bulgaria
Ard Mhacha *see* Armagh
Ardmore *49 G2* Oklahoma, C USA
Arel *see* Arlon
Arelas/Arelate *see* Arles
Arendal *85 A6* Aust-Agder, S Norway
Arensburg *see* Kuressaare
Arenys de Mar *93 G2* Cataluña, NE Spain
Areópoli *105 B7* *prev.* Areópolis. Pelopónnisos, S Greece
Areópolis *see* Areópoli
Arequipa *61 E4* Arequipa, SE Peru
Arezzo *96 C3* *anc.* Arretium. Toscana, C Italy
Argalastí *105 C5* Thessalía, C Greece
Argenteuil *90 D1* Val-d'Oise, N France
Argentina *65 B5* *off.* Republic of Argentina. *country* S South America

ARGENTINA
South America

Official name Republic of Argentina
Formation 1816 / 1816
Capital Buenos Aires
Population 38.7 million / 37 people per sq mile (14 people per sq km) / 90%
Total area 1,068,296 sq miles (2,766,890 sq km)
Languages Spanish*, Italian, Amerindian languages
Religions Roman Catholic 90%, Other 6%, Protestant 2%, Jewish 2%
Ethnic mix Indo-European 83%, Mestizo 14%, Jewish 2%, Amerindian 1%
Government Presidential system
Currency new Argentine peso = 100 centavos
Literacy rate 97%
Calorie consumption 2992 calories

Argentina Basin *see* Argentine Basin
Argentina, Republic of *see* Argentina
Argentine Basin *57 C7* *var.* Argentina Basin. *undersea basin* SW Atlantic Ocean
Argentine Rise *see* Falkland Plateau
Argentoratum *see* Strasbourg
Arghandāb, Daryā-ye *123 E5* *river* SE Afghanistan
Argirocastro *see* Gjirokastër
Argo *72 B3* Northern, N Sudan
Argo Fracture Zone *141 C5* *tectonic Feature* C Indian Ocean
Árgos *105 B6* Pelopónnisos, S Greece
Argostóli *105 A5* *var.* Argostólion. Kefallonía, Iónia Nísiá, Greece, C Mediterranean Sea
Argostólion *see* Argostóli
Argun *125 E1* *Chin.* Ergun He, *Rus.* Argun'. *river* China/Russian Federation
Argyrokastron *see* Gjirokastër
Århus *85 B7* *var.* Aarhus. Århus, C Denmark
Aria *see* Herāt
Ari Atoll *132 A4* *atoll* C Maldives
Arica *64 B1* *hist.* San Marcos de Arica. Tarapacá, N Chile
Aridaía *104 B3* *var.* Aridea, Aridhaía. Dytikí Makedonía, N Greece
Aridea *see* Aridaía
Aridhaía *see* Aridaía
Arīhā *118 B3* Al Karak, W Jordan
Arīḩā *see* Jericho
Ariminum *see* Rimini
Arinsal *91 A7* NW Andorra Europe
Arizona *48 A2* *off.* State of Arizona, *also known as* Copper State, Grand Canyon State. *state* SW USA
Arkansas *42 A1* *off.* State of Arkansas, *also known as* The Land of Opportunity. *state* S USA
Arkansas City *45 F5* Kansas, C USA
Arkansas River *49 G1* *river* C USA
Arkhangel'sk *114 B2* *Eng.* Archangel. Arkhangel'skaya Oblast', NW Russian Federation
Arkoí *105 E6* *island* Dodekánisa, Greece, Aegean Sea
Arles *91 D6* *var.* Arles-sur-Rhône; *anc.* Arelas, Arelate. Bouches-du-Rhône, SE France
Arles-sur-Rhône *see* Arles
Arlington *49 G2* Texas, SW USA
Arlington *41 E4* Virginia, NE USA
Arlon *87 D8* *Dut.* Aarlen, *Ger.* Arel, *Lat.* Orolaunum. Luxembourg, SE Belgium
Armagh *89 B5* *Ir.* Ard Mhacha. S Northern Ireland, UK
Armagnac *91 B6* *cultural region* S France
Armenia *58 B3* Quindío, W Colombia
Armenia *117 F3* *off.* Republic of Armenia, *var.* Ajastan, *Arm.* Hayastani Hanrapetut'yun; *prev.* Armenian Soviet Socialist Republic. *country* SW Asia

ARMENIA
Southwest Asia

Official name Republic of Armenia
Formation 1991 / 1991
Capital Yerevan

ARMENIA
(continued)

Population 3 million / 261 people per sq mile (101 people per sq km) / 70%
Total area 11,506 sq miles (29,800 sq km)
Languages Armenian*, Azeri, Russian
Religions Armenian Apostolic Church (Orthodox) 94%, Other 6%
Ethnic mix Armenian 93%, Azeri 3%, Other 2%, Russian 2%
Government Presidential system
Currency Dram = 100 luma
Literacy rate 99%
Calorie consumption 2268 calories

Armenian Soviet Socialist Republic *see* Armenia
Armenia, Republic of *see* Armenia
Armidale *149 D6* New South Wales, SE Australia
Armstrong *38 B3* Ontario, S Canada
Armyans'k *109 F4 Rus.* Armyansk. Respublika Krym, S Ukraine
Arnaía *104 C4 Cont.* Arnea. Kentrikí Makedonía, N Greece
Arnaud *82 A3 river* Québec, E Canada
Arnea *see* Arnaía
Arnedo *93 E2* La Rioja, N Spain
Arnhem *86 D4* Gelderland, SE Netherlands
Arnhem Land *148 A2 physical region* Northern Territory, N Australia
Arno *96 B3 river* C Italy
Arnold *45 G4* Missouri, C USA
Arnswalde *see* Choszczno
Aroe Islands *see* Aru, Kepulauan
Arorae *145 E3 atoll* Tungaru, W Kiribati
Arrabona *see* Győr
Ar Rahad *see* Er Rahad
Ar Ramādī *120 B3 var.* Ramadi, Rumadiya. SW Iraq
Ar Rāmī *118 C4* Ḥimṣ, C Syria
Ar Ramthā *119 B5 var.* Ramtha. Irbid, N Jordan
Arran, Isle of *88 C4 island* SW Scotland, UK
Ar Raqqah *118 C2 var.* Rakka; *anc.* Nicephorium. Ar Raqqah, N Syria
Arras *90 C2 anc.* Nemetocenna. Pas-de-Calais, N France
Ar Rawḍatayn *120 C4 var.* Raudhatain. N Kuwait
Arretium *see* Arezzo
Arriaca *see* Guadalajara
Arriaga *51 G5* Chiapas, SE Mexico
Ar Riyāḍ *121 C5 Eng.* Riyadh. *country capital* (Saudi Arabia) Ar Riyāḍ, C Saudi Arabia
Ar Rub 'al Khālī *121 C6 Eng.* Empty Quarter, Great Sandy Desert. *desert* SW Asia
Ar Rustāq *121 E5 var.* Rostak, Rustaq. N Oman
Ar Ruṭbah *120 B3 var.* Rutba. SW Iraq
Árta *105 A5 anc.* Ambracia. Ípeiros, W Greece
Artashat *117 F3* S Armenia
Artemisa *54 B2* La Habana, W Cuba
Artesia *48 D3* New Mexico, SW USA
Arthur's Pass *151 C6 pass* South Island, New Zealand
Artigas *64 D3 prev.* San Eugenio, San Eugenio del Cuareim. Artigas, N Uruguay
Art'ik *117 F2* W Armenia
Artois *90 C2 cultural region* N France
Artsiz *see* Artsyz
Artsyz *108 D4 Rus.* Artsiz. Odes'ka Oblast', SW Ukraine
Artvin *117 F2* Artvin, NE Turkey
Arua *73 B6* NW Uganda
Aruba *58 C1 var.* Oruba. *Dutch autonomous region* S West Indies
Aru Islands *see* Aru, Kepulauan
Aru, Kepulauan *139 G4 Eng.* Aru Islands; *prev.* Aroe Islands. *island group* E Indonesia
Arunāchal Pradesh *135 G3 prev.* North East Frontier Agency, North East Frontier Agency of Assam. *state* NE India
Arunāchal Pradesh *135 G3 prev.* North East Frontier Agency, North East Frontier Agency of Assam. *cultural region* NE India
Arusha *73 C7* Arusha, N Tanzania
Arviat *37 G4 prev.* Eskimo Point. Nunavut, C Canada
Arvidsjaur *84 C4* Norrbotten, N Sweden
Arys' *114 B5 Kaz.* Arys. Yuzhnyy Kazakhstan, S Kazakhstan
Arys *see* Arys'
Asadābād *123 F4 var.* Asadābād; *prev.* Chaghasarāy. Konar, E Afghanistan
Asadābād *see* Asadābād
Asad, Buḥayrat al *134 C2 lake* N Syria
Asahi-dake *130 D2 mountain* Hokkaidō, N Japan
Asahikawa *130 D2* Hokkaidō, N Japan
Asamankese *75 E5* SE Ghana
Āsānsol *135 F4* West Bengal, NE India
Asben *see* Aïr, Massif de l'
Ascension Fracture Zone *69 A5 tectonic Feature* C Atlantic Ocean
Ascension Island *85 A5 dependency of St.Helena* C Atlantic Ocean
Ascoli Piceno *96 C4 anc.* Asculum Picenum. Marche, C Italy
Asculum Picenum *see* Ascoli Piceno
Aseb *72 D4 var.* Assab, *Amh.* Āseb. SE Eritrea
Aşgabat *122 C3 prev.* Ashgabat, Ashkhabad, Poltoratsk. *country capital* (Turkmenistan) Ahal Welaýaty, C Turkmenistan
Ashara *see* Al 'Ashārah
Ashburton *151 C6* Canterbury, South Island, New Zealand
Ashburton River *146 A4 river* Western Australia
Ashdod *119 A6 anc.* Azotos, *Lat.* Azotus. Central, W Israel
Asheville *43 E1* North Carolina, SE USA
Ashgabat *see* Aşgabat
Ashkelon *see* Ashqelon
Ashkhabad *see* Aşgabat
Ashland *46 B4* Oregon, NW USA
Ashland *40 B1* Wisconsin, N USA
Ashmore and Cartier Islands *142 A3 Australian external territory* E Indian Ocean
Ashmyany *107 C5 Rus.* Oshmyany. Hrodzyenskaya Voblasts', W Belarus
Ashqelon *119 A6 var.* Ashkelon. Southern, C Israel
Ash Shadādah *118 D2 var.* Ash Shaddādah, Jisr ash Shadadi, Shaddādī, Shedadi, Tell Shedadi. Al Ḥasakah, NE Syria
Ash Shaddādah *see* Ash Shadādah
Ash Shām *see* Dimashq
Ash Sharāh *119 B7 var.* Esh Sharā. *mountain range* W Jordan
Ash Shāriqah *120 D4 Eng.* Sharjah. Ash Shāriqah, NE United Arab Emirates
Ash Shawbak *119 B7* Ma'ān, W Jordan
Ash Shiḥr *121 C6* SE Yemen
Asia *25 C2 continent*
Asinara, Isola *96 A4 island* W Italy
Asipovichy *107 D6 Rus.* Osipovichi. Mahilyowskaya Voblasts', C Belarus
Aşkale *117 E3* Erzurum, NE Turkey
Askersund *85 C6* Örebro, C Sweden
Asmara *72 C4 Amh.* Āsmera. *country capital* (Eritrea) C Eritrea
Āsmera *see* Asmara
Aspadana *see* Eşfahān
Asphaltites, Lacus *see* Dead Sea
Aspinwall *see* Colón
Assab *see* Aseb
As Sabkhah *118 D2 var.* Sabkha. Ar Raqqah, NE Syria
Aş Şafāwī *119 C6* Al Mafraq, N Jordan
Aş Şaḥrā' al Gharbīyah *see* Sahara el Gharbîya
Aş Şaḥrā' ash Sharqīyah *see* Sahara el Sharqîya
As Salamīyah *see* Salamīyah
'Assal, Lac *68 E4 lake* C Djibouti
As Salṭ *119 B6 var.* Salt. Al Balqā', NW Jordan
Assamaka *see* Assamakka
Assamakka *75 F2 var.* Assamaka. Agadez, NW Niger
As Samāwah *120 B3 var.* Samawa. S Iraq
Assen *86 E2* Drenthe, NE Netherlands
Assenede *87 B5* Oost-Vlaanderen, NW Belgium
Assiout *see* Asyût
Assiut *see* Asyût
Assling *see* Jesenice
Assouan *see* Aswân
Assu *see* Açu
Assuan *see* Aswân
As Sukhnah *118 C3 var.* Sukhne, *Fr.* Soukhné. Ḥimṣ, C Syria
As Sulaymānīyah *120 C3 var.* Sulaimaniya, *Kurd.* Slēmānī. NE Iraq
As Sulayyil *121 B5* Ar Riyāḍ, S Saudi Arabia
Aş Şuwār *118 D2 var.* Şuwār. Dayr az Zawr, E Syria
As Suwaydā' *119 B5 var.* El Suweida, Es Suweida, Suweida, *Fr.* Soueida. As Suwaydā', SW Syria
As Suways *see* Suez
Asta Colonia *see* Asti
Astacus *see* İzmit
Astana *114 C4 prev.* Akmola, Akmolinsk, Tselinograd, Aqmola. *country capital* (Kazakhstan) Akmola, N Kazakhstan
Asta Pompeia *see* Asti
Astarabad *see* Gorgān
Asterābād *see* Gorgān
Asti *96 A2 anc.* Asta Colonia, Asta Pompeia, Hasta Colonia, Hasta Pompeia. Piemonte, NW Italy
Astigi *see* Ecija
Astipálaia *see* Astypálaia
Astorga *92 C1 anc.* Asturica Augusta. Castilla-León, N Spain
Astrabad *see* Gorgān
Astrakhan' *111 C7* Astrakhanskaya Oblast', SW Russian Federation
Asturias *92 C1 autonomous community* NW Spain
Asturias *see* Oviedo
Asturica Augusta *see* Astorga
Astypálaia *105 D7 var.* Astipálaia, *It.* Stampalia. *island* Kykládes, Greece, Aegean Sea
Asunción *64 D2 country capital* (Paraguay) Central, S Paraguay
Aswân *72 B2 var.* Assouan, Assuan; *anc.* Syene. SE Egypt
Asyût *72 B2 var.* Assiout, Assiut, Siut; *anc.* Lycopolis. C Egypt
Atacama Desert *see* Atacama, Desierto de
Atacama, Desierto de *64 B2 Eng.* Atacama Desert. *desert* N Chile
Atafu Atoll *145 E3 island* NW Tokelau
Atamyrat *122 D3 prev.* Kerki. Lebap Welaýaty, E Turkmenistan
Aţâr *74 C2* Adrar, W Mauritania
Atas Bogd *126 D3 mountain* SW Mongolia
Atascadero *47 B7* California, W USA
Atatürk Barajī *117 E4 reservoir* S Turkey
Atbara *72 C3 var.* 'Aṭbārah. River Nile, NE Sudan
'Aṭbārah/'Aṭbarah, Nahr *see* Atbara
Atbasar *114 C4* Akmola, N Kazakhstan
Atchison *45 F4* Kansas, C USA
Aternum *see* Pescara
Ath *87 B6 var.* Aat. Hainaut, SW Belgium
Athabasca *37 E5* Alberta, SW Canada
Athabasca *37 E5 var.* Athabaska. *river* Alberta, SW Canada
Athabasca, Lake *37 F4 lake* Alberta/ Saskatchewan, SW Canada
Athabaska *see* Athabasca
Athenae *see* Athína
Athens *43 E2* Georgia, SE USA
Athens *40 D4* Ohio, N USA
Athens *49 G3* Texas, SW USA
Athens *see* Athína
Atherton *148 D3* Queensland, NE Australia
Athína *105 C6 Eng.* Athens, *prev.* Athínai; *anc.* Athenae. *country capital* (Greece) Attikí, C Greece
Athínai *see* Athína
Athlone *89 B5 Ir.* Baile Átha Luain. C Ireland
Ath Thawrah *see* Madīnat ath Thawrah
Ati *76 C3* Batha, C Chad
Atikokan *38 B4* Ontario, S Canada
Atka *115 G3* Magadanskaya Oblast', E Russian Federation
Atka *36 A3* Atka Island, Alaska, USA
Atlanta *42 D2 state capital* Georgia, SE USA
Atlanta *49 H2* Texas, SW USA
Atlantic City *41 F4* New Jersey, NE USA
Atlantic-Indian Basin *67 D7 undersea basin* SW Indian Ocean
Atlantic-Indian Ridge *69 B8 undersea ridge* SW Indian Ocean
Atlantic Ocean *66 B4 ocean*
Atlas Mountains *70 C2 mountain range* NW Africa
Atlasovo *115 H3* Kamchatskaya Oblast', E Russian Federation
Atlas Saharien *70 D2 var.* Saharan Atlas. *mountain range* Algeria/Morocco
Atlas, Tell *see* Atlas Tellien
Atlas Tellien *102 C3 Eng.* Tell Atlas. *mountain range* N Algeria
Atlin *36 D4* British Columbia, W Canada
Aṭ Ṭafīlah *119 B7 var.* Et Tafila, Tafila. Aṭ Ṭafīlah, W Jordan
Aṭ Ṭā'if *121 B5* Makkah, W Saudi Arabia
Attaleia/Attalia *see* Antalya
At Tall al Abyaḍ *118 C2 var.* Tall al Abyaḍ, Tell Abyad, *Fr.* Tell Abiad. Ar Raqqah, N Syria
Aṭ Ṭanf *118 D4* Ḥimṣ, S Syria
Attapu *see* Samakhixai
Attawapiskat *38 C3* Ontario, C Canada
Attawapiskat *38 C3 river* Ontario, S Canada
At Tibnī *118 D2 var.* Tibnī. Dayr az Zawr, NE Syria
Attopeu *see* Samakhixai
Attu Island *36 A2 island* Aleutian Islands, Alaska, USA
Atyrau *114 B4 prev.* Gur'yev. Atyrau, W Kazakhstan
Aubagne *91 D6 anc.* Albania. Bouches-du-Rhône, SE France
Aubange *87 D8* Luxembourg, SE Belgium
Aubervilliers *90 E1* Seine-St-Denis, Île-de-France, N France Europe
Auburn *46 B2* Washington, NW USA
Auch *91 B6 Lat.* Augusta Auscorum, Elimberrum. Gers, S France
Auckland *150 D2* Auckland, North Island, New Zealand
Auckland Islands *142 C5 island group* S New Zealand
Audern *see* Audru
Audincourt *90 E4* Doubs, E France
Audru *106 D2 Ger.* Audern. Pärnumaa, SW Estonia
Augathella *149 D5* Queensland, E Australia
Augsbourg *see* Augsburg
Augsburg *95 C6 Fr.* Augsbourg; *anc.* Augusta Vindelicorum. Bayern, S Germany
Augusta *147 A7* Western Australia
Augusta *43 E2* Georgia, SE USA
Augusta *41 G2 state capital* Maine, NE USA
Augusta *see* London
Augusta Auscorum *see* Auch
Augusta Emerita *see* Mérida
Augusta Praetoria *see* Aosta
Augusta Trajana *see* Stara Zagora
Augusta Treverorum *see* Trier
Augusta Vangionum *see* Worms
Augusta Vindelicorum *see* Augsburg
Augustobona Tricassium *see* Troyes
Augustodurum *see* Bayeux
Augustoritum Lemovicensium *see* Limoges
Augustów *98 E2 Rus.* Avgustov. Podlaskie, NE Poland
Aulie Ata/Auliye-Ata *see* Taraz
Auob *78 B4 var.* Oup. *river* Namibia/ South Africa
Aurangābād *134 D5* Mahārāshtra, C India
Auray *90 A3* Morbihan, NW France
Aurelia Aquensis *see* Baden-Baden
Aurelianum *see* Orléans
Aurès, Massif de l' *102 C4 mountain range* NE Algeria
Aurillac *91 C5* Cantal, C France
Aurium *see* Ourense
Aurora *59 F2* NW Guyana
Aurora *44 D4* Colorado, C USA
Aurora *40 B3* Illinois, N USA
Aurora *45 G5* Missouri, C USA
Aurora *see* Maéwo, Vanuatu
Aus *78 B4* Karas, SW Namibia
Ausa *see* Vic
Aussig *see* Ústí nad Labem
Austin *45 G3* Minnesota, N USA
Austin *49 G3 state capital* Texas, SW USA
Australes, Archipel des *see* Australes, Île
Australes et Antarctiques Françaises, Terres *see* French Southern and Antarctic Territories

Australes, Îles *143 F4 var.* Archipel des
  Australes, Îles Tubuai, Tubuai Islands,
  Eng. Austral Islands. *island group*
  SW French Polynesia
Austral Fracture Zone *143 H4 tectonic
  feature* S Pacific Ocean
Australia *142 A4 off.* Commonwealth of
  Australia. *country*

AUSTRALIA
Australasia & Oceania

Official name Commonwealth of
  Australia
Formation 1901 / 1901
Capital Canberra
Population 20.2 million / 7 people per
  sq mile (3 people per sq km) / 85%
Total area 2,967,893 sq miles (7,686,850
  sq km)
Languages English*, Italian, Cantonese,
  Greek, Arabic, Vietnamese, Aboriginal
  languages
Religions Roman Catholic 26%,
  Anglican 24%, Other 23%,
  Nonreligious 13%, United Church 8%,
  Other Protestant 6%
Ethnic mix European 92%, Asian 5%,
  Aboriginal and other 3%
Government Parliamentary system
Currency Australian dollar = 100 cents
Literacy rate 99%
Calorie consumption 3054 calories

Australia, Commonwealth of *see*
  Australia
Australian Alps *149 C7 mountain range*
  SE Australia
Australian Capital Territory *149 D7
  prev.* Federal Capital Territory. *territory*
  SE Australia
Australie, Bassin Nord de l' *see* North
  Australian Basin
Austria *95 D7 off.* Republic of Austria,
  Ger. Österreich. *country* C Europe

AUSTRIA
Central Europe

Official name Republic of Austria
Formation 1918 / 1919
Capital Vienna
Population 8.2 million / 257 people per
  sq mile (99 people per sq km) / 65%
Total area 32,378 sq miles (83,858 sq km)
Languages German*, Croatian, Slovenian,
  Hungarian (Magyar)
Religions Roman Catholic 78%,
  Nonreligious 9%, Other (including
  Jewish and Muslim) 8%, Protestant 5%
Ethnic mix Austrian 93%, Croat, Slovene,
  and Hungarian 6%, Other 1%
Government Parliamentary system
Currency Euro = 100 cents
Literacy rate 99%
Calorie consumption 3673 calories

Austria, Republic of *see* Austria
Autesiodorum *see* Auxerre
Autissiodorum *see* Auxerre
Autricum *see* Chartres
Auvergne *91 C5 region* C France
Auvergne *91 C5 cultural region*
  C France
Auxerre *90 C4 anc.* Autesiodorum,
  Autissiodorum. Yonne, C France
Avaricum *see* Bourges
Avarua *145 G5 dependent territory
  capital* (Cook Islands) Rarotonga,
  S Cook Islands
Avasfelsőfalu *see* Negreşti-Oaş
Ávdira *104 C3* Anatolikí Makedonía kai
  Thráki, NE Greece
Aveiro *92 B2 anc.* Talabriga. Aveiro,
  W Portugal
Avela *see* Ávila
Avellino *97 D5 anc.* Abellinum.
  Campania, S Italy
Avenio *see* Avignon
Avesta *85 C6* Dalarna, C Sweden
Aveyron *91 C6 river* S France
Avezzano *96 C4* Abruzzo,
  C Italy
Avgustov *see* Augustów
Aviemore *88 C3* N Scotland, UK
Avignon *91 D6 anc.* Avenio. Vaucluse,
  SE France

Ávila *92 D3 var.* Avila; *anc.* Abela,
  Abula, Abyla, Avela. Castilla-León,
  C Spain
Avilés *92 C1* Asturias, NW Spain
Avranches *90 B3* Manche, N France
Avveel *see* Ivalo
Avvil *see* Ivalo
Awaji-shima *131 C6 island* SW Japan
Āwash *73 D5 var.* Hawash. *river*
  C Ethiopia
Awbārī *71 F3* SW Libya
Ax *see* Dax
Axel *87 B5* Zeeland, SW Netherlands
Axel Heiberg Island *37 E1 var.* Axel
  Heiburg. *island* Nunavut, N Canada
Axel Heiburg *see* Axel Heiberg Island
Axiós *see* Vardar
Ayacucho *60 D4* Ayacucho, S Peru
Ayagoz *130 C5 var.* Ayaguz, *Kaz.*
  Ayakoz. *river* E Kazakhstan
Ayakoz *see* Ayagoz
Ayamonte *92 C4* Andalucía,
  S Spain
Ayaviri *61 E4* Puno, S Peru
Aydarko'l Ko'li *123 E2 Rus.* Ozero
  Aydarkul'. *lake* C Uzbekistan
Aydarkul', Ozero *see* Aydarko'l Ko'li
Aydın *116 A4 var.* Aïdin; *anc.* Tralles
  Aydın. Aydın, SW Turkey
Ayers Rock *see* Uluru
Ayeyarwady *see* Irrawaddy
Ayiá *see* Agiá
Áyios Evstrátios *see* Ágios Efstrátios
Áyios Nikólaos *see* Ágios Nikólaos
Ayorou *75 E3* Tillabéri, W Niger
'Ayoûn el 'Atroûs *74 D3 var.* Aïoun el
  Atrous, Aïoun el Atroûss. Hodh el
  Gharbi, SE Mauritania
Ayr *88 C4* W Scotland, UK
Ayteke Bi *130 B4 Kaz.* Zhangaqazaly;
  prev. Novokazalinsk. Kzylorda,
  SW Kazakhstan
Aytos *104 E2* Burgas, E Bulgaria
Ayutthaya *137 C5 var.* Phra Nakhon Si
  Ayutthaya. Phra Nakhon Si Ayutthaya,
  C Thailand
Ayvalik *116 A3* Balıkesir, W Turkey
Azahar, Costa del *93 F3 coastal region*
  E Spain
Azaouâd *75 E3 desert* C Mali
Azärbaycan/Azärbaycan Respublikasï
  see Azerbaijan
A'zāz *118 B2* Ḥalab, NW Syria
Azerbaijan *117 G2 off.* Azerbaijani
  Republic, *Az.* Azärbaycan, Azärbaycan
  Respublikasï; *prev.* Azerbaijan SSR.
  country SE Asia

AZERBAIJAN
Southwest Asia

Official name Republic of Azerbaijan
Formation 1991 / 1991
Capital Baku
Population 8.4 million / 251 people per
  sq mile (97 people per sq km) / 57%
Total area 33,436 sq miles (86,600 sq km)
Languages Azeri, Russian
Religions Shi'a Muslim 68%, Sunni
  Muslim 26%, Russian Orthodox 3%,
  Armenian Apostolic Church
  (Orthodox) 2%, Other 1%
Ethnic mix Azeri 90%, Dagestani 3%,
  Russian 3%, Other 2%, Armenian 2%
Government Presidential system
Currency Manat = 100 gopik
Literacy rate 99%
Calorie consumption 2575 calories

Azerbaijani Republic *see* Azerbaijan
Azerbaijan SSR *see* Azerbaijan
Azimabad *see* Patna
Azizie *see* Telish
Azogues *60 B2* Cañar, S Ecuador
Azores *92 A4
  var.* Açores, Ilhas dos Açores, *Port.*
  Arquipélago dos Açores. *island group*
  Portugal, NE Atlantic Ocean
Azores-Biscay Rise *80 A3 undersea rise*
  E Atlantic Ocean
Azotos/Azotus *see* Ashdod
Azoum, Bahr *76 C3 seasonal river*
  SE Chad
Azov, Sea of *103 H1 Rus.* Azovskoye
  More, *Ukr.* Azovs'ke More. *sea*
  NE Black Sea
Azovs'ke More/Azovskoye More *see*
  Azov, Sea of

Azraq, Wāḥat al *135 C6 oasis* N Jordan
Aztec *48 C1* New Mexico, SW USA
Azuaga *92 C4* Extremadura, W Spain
Azuero, Península de *53 F5 peninsula*
  S Panama
Azul *65 D5* Buenos Aires, E Argentina
Azur, Côte d' *107 E6 coastal region*
  SE France
'Azza *see* Gaza
Az Zaqāziq *see* Zagazig
Az Zarqā' *119 B6 var.* Zarqa. Az Zarqā',
  NW Jordan
Az Zāwiyah *71 F2 var.* Zawia. NW Libya
Az Zilfī *120 B4* Ar Riyāḍ, N Saudi Arabia

B

Ba *100 D3 prev.* Mba. Viti Levu, W Fiji
Baalbek *118 B4 var.* Ba'labakk; *anc.*
  Heliopolis. E Lebanon
Baardheere *73 D6 var.* Bardere, *It.*
  Bardera. Gedo, SW Somalia
Baarle-Hertog *87 C5* Antwerpen,
  N Belgium
Baarn *86 C3* Utrecht, C Netherlands
Babadag *108 D5* Tulcea, SE Romania
Babahoyo *60 B2 prev.* Bodegas. Los
  Ríos, C Ecuador
Bābā, Kūh-e *123 E4 mountain range*
  C Afghanistan
Babayevo *110 B4* Vologodskaya Oblast',
  NW Russian Federation
Babeldaob *144 A1 var.* Babeldaop,
  Babelthuap. *island* N Palau
Babeldaop *see* Babeldaob
Bab el Mandeb *121 B7 strait* Gulf of
  Aden/Red Sea
Babelthuap *see* Babeldaob
Babian Jiang *see* Black River
Babruysk *107 D7 Rus.* Bobruysk.
  Mahilyowskaya Voblasts', E Belarus
Babuyan Channel *139 E1 channel*
  N Philippines
Babuyan Island *139 E1 island*
  N Philippines
Bacabal *63 F2* Maranhão, E Brazil
Bacău *108 C4 Hung.* Bákó. Bacău,
  NE Romania
Băc Bô, Vinh *see* Tongking, Gulf of
Băc Giang *136 D3* Ha Băc, N Vietnam
Bacheykava *107 D5 Rus.* Bocheykovo.
  Vitsyebskaya Voblasts', N Belarus
Back *37 F3 river* Nunavut, N Canada
Bačka Palanka *100 D3 prev.* Palanka.
  Serbia, NW Serbia
Bačka Topola *100 D3 Hung.* Topolya;
  prev. Hung. Bácstopola. Vojvodina,
  N Serbia
Bac Liêu *137 D6 var.* Vinh Loi. Minh
  Hai, S Vietnam
Bacolod *125 E4 off.* Bacolod City.
  Negros, C Philippines
Bacolod City *see* Bacolod
Bácstopolya *see* Bačka Topola
Bactra *see* Balkh
Badajoz *92 C4 anc.* Pax Augusta.
  Extremadura, W Spain
Baden-Baden *95 B6 anc.* Aurelia
  Aquensis. Baden-Württemberg,
  SW Germany
Bad Freienwalde *94 D3* Brandenburg,
  NE Germany
Badger State *see* Wisconsin
Bad Hersfeld *94 B4* Hessen, C Germany
Bad Homburg *see* Bad Homburg vor
  der Höhe
Bad Homburg vor der Höhe *95 B5 var.*
  Bad Homburg. W Germany
Bad Ischl *95 D7* Oberösterreich,
  N Austria
Bad Krozingen *95 A6* Baden-
  Württemberg, SW Germany
Badlands *44 D2 physical region* North
  Dakota, N USA
Badu Island *148 C1 island* Queensland,
  NE Australia
Bad Vöslau *95 E6* Niederösterreich,
  NE Austria
Baeterrae/Baeterrae Septimanorum
  see Béziers
Baetic Cordillera/Baetic Mountains
  see Béticos, Sistemas
Bafatá *74 C4* C Guinea-Bissau
Baffin Bay *35 G2 bay* Canada/Greenland
Baffin Island *37 G2 island* Nunavut,
  NE Canada
Bafing *74 C3 river* W Africa

Bafoussam *76 A4* Ouest, W Cameroon
Bafra *116 D2* Samsun, N Turkey
Bäft *120 D4* Kermān, S Iran
Bagaces *52 D4* Guanacaste,
  NW Costa Rica
Bagdad *see* Baghdād
Bagé *63 E5* Rio Grande do Sul, S Brazil
Baghdād *120 B3 var.* Bagdad, *Eng.*
  Baghdad. *country capital* (Iraq) C Iraq
Baghdad *see* Baghdād
Baghlān *123 E3* Baghlān, NE Afghanistan
Bago *see* Pegu
Bagoé *74 D4 river* Côte d'Ivoire
  (Ivory Coast)/Mali
Bagrationovsk *106 A4 Ger.* Preussisch
  Eylau. Kaliningradskaya Oblast',
  W Russian Federation
Bagrax Hu *see* Bosten Hu
Baguio *139 E1 off.* Baguio City. Luzon,
  N Philippines
Baguio City *see* Baguio
Bagzane, Monts *75 F3 mountain*
  N Niger
Bahama Islands *see* Bahamas
Bahamas *54 C2 off.* Commonwealth of
  the Bahamas. *country* N West Indies

BAHAMAS
West Indies

Official name Commonwealth of the
  Bahamas
Formation 1973 / 1973
Capital Nassau
Population 323,000 / 84 people per
  sq mile
  (32 people per sq km) / 89%
Total area 5382 sq miles (13,940 sq km)
Languages English*, English Creole,
  French Creole
Religions Baptist 32%, Anglican 20%,
  Roman Catholic 19%, Other 17%,
  Methodist 6%, Church of God 6%
Ethnic mix black African 85%,
  Other 15%
Government Parliamentary system
Currency Bahamian dollar = 100 cents
Literacy rate 96%
Calorie consumption 2755 calories

Bahamas *35 D6 var.* Bahama Islands.
  island group N West Indies
Bahamas, Commonwealth of the *see*
  Bahamas
Baharly *122 C3 var.* Bäherden, *Rus.*
  Bakharden; *prev.* Bakherden. Ahal
  Welayaty, C Turkmenistan
Bahāwalpur *134 C2* Punjab, E Pakistan
Bäherden *see* Baharly
Bahia *63 F3 off.* Estado da Bahia. *state*
  E Brazil
Bahía Blanca *65 C5* Buenos Aires,
  E Argentina
Bahia, Estado da *see* Bahia
Bahía, Islas de la *52 C1 Eng.* Bay Islands.
  island group N Honduras
Bahir Dar *72 C4 var.* Bahir Dar, Bahrdar
  Giyorgis. Amhara, N Ethiopia
Bahraich *135 E3* Uttar Pradesh, N India
Bahrain *120 C4 off.* State of Bahrain,
  Dawlat al Bahrayn, *Ar.* Al Baḥrayn,
  prev. Bahrein; *anc.* Tylos, Tyros.
  country SW Asia

BAHRAIN
Southwest Asia

Official name Kingdom of Bahrain
Formation 1971 / 1971
Capital Manama
Population 727,000 / 2663 people per
  sq mile (1030 people per sq km) / 97%
Total area 239 sq miles (620 sq km)
Languages Arabic*
Religions Muslim (mainly Shi'a) 99%,
  Other 1%
Ethnic mix Bahraini 70%, Iranian, Indian,
  and Pakistani 24%, Other Arab 4%,
  European 2%
Government Monarchy
Currency Bahraini dinar = 1000 fils
Literacy rate 88%
Calorie consumption Not available

Bahrain, State of *see* Bahrain
Bahrayn, Dawlat al *see* Bahrain
Bahr Dar/Bahrdar Giyorgis *see*
  Bahir Dar

Bahrein see Bahrain
Bahr el, Azraq see Blue Nile
Bahr Tabariya, Sea of see Tiberias, Lake
Bahushewsk 107 E6 *Rus.* Bogushëvsk. Vitsyebskaya Voblasts', NE Belarus
Baia Mare 108 B3 *Ger.* Frauenbach, *Hung.* Nagybánya; *prev.* Neustadt. Maramureş, NW Romania
Baia Sprie 108 B3 *Ger.* Mittelstadt, *Hung.* Felsőbánya. Maramureş, NW Romania
Baïbokoum 76 B4 Logone-Oriental, SW Chad
Baidoa see Baydhabo
Baie-Comeau 39 E3 Québec, SE Canada
Baikal, Lake see Baykal, Ozero
Baile Átha Cliath see Dublin
Baile Átha Luain see Athlone
Bailén 92 D4 Andalucía, S Spain
Baile na Mainistreach see Newtownabbey
Băileşti 108 B5 Dolj, SW Romania
Ba Illi 76 B3 Chari-Baguirmi, SW Chad
Bainbridge 42 D3 Georgia, SE USA
Bā'ir see Bāyir
Baireuth see Bayreuth
Bairiki 144 D2 *country capital* (Kiribati) Tarawa, NW Kiribati
Bairnsdale 149 C7 Victoria, SE Australia
Baishan 128 E3 *prev.* Hunjiang. Jilin, NE China
Baiyin 128 B4 Gansu, C China
Baja 99 C7 Bács-Kiskun, S Hungary
Baja California 50 B2 *state* NW Mexico
Baja California 48 A4 *Eng.* Lower California. *peninsula* NW Mexico
Bajo Boquete see Boquete
Bajram Curri 101 D5 Kukës, N Albania
Bakala 76 C4 Ouaka, C Central African Republic
Bakan see Shimonoseki
Baker 46 C3 Oregon, NW USA
Baker and Howland Islands 145 E2 *US unincorporated territory* W Polynesia
Baker Lake 37 F3 Nunavut, N Canada
Bakersfield 47 C7 California, W USA
Bakharden see Baharly
Bakhchisaray see Bakhchysaray
Bakhchysaray 109 F5 *Rus.* Bakhchisaray. Respublika Krym, S Ukraine
Bakherden see Baharly
Bakhmach 109 F1 Chernihivs'ka Oblast', N Ukraine
Bäkhtarän see Kermänshäh
Bakı 117 H2 *Eng.* Baku. *country capital* (Azerbaijan) E Azerbaijan
Bákó see Bacău
Bakony 99 C7 *Eng.* Bakony Mountains, *Ger.* Bakonywald. *mountain range* W Hungary
Bakony Mountains/Bakonywald see Bakony
Baku see Bakı
Bakwanga see Mbuji-Mayi
Balabac Island 129 C8 *island* W Philippines
Balabac, Selat see Balabac Strait
Balabac Strait 138 D2 *var.* Selat Balabac. *strait* Malaysia/Philippines
Ba'labakk see Baalbek
Balaguer 93 F2 Cataluña, NE Spain
Balakovo 111 C6 Saratovskaya Oblast', W Russian Federation
Bālā Morghāb 122 D4 Laghmān, NW Afghanistan
Balashov 111 B6 Saratovskaya Oblast', W Russian Federation
Balasore see Bāleshwar
Balaton 99 C7 *var.* Lake Balaton, *Ger.* Plattensee. *lake* W Hungary
Balaton, Lake see Balaton
Balbina, Represa 62 D1 *reservoir* NW Brazil
Balboa 53 G4 Panamá, C Panama
Balcarce 65 D5 Buenos Aires, E Argentina
Balclutha 151 B7 Otago, South Island, New Zealand
Baldy Mountain 44 C1 *mountain* Montana, NW USA
Bâle see Basel
Balearic Plain see Algerian Basin
Baleares, Islas 93 G3 *Eng.* Balearic Islands. *island group* Spain, W Mediterranean Sea
Baleares Major see Mallorca
Balearic Islands see Baleares, Islas
Balearis Minor see Menorca

Baleine, Rivière à la 39 E2 *river* Québec, E Canada
Balen 87 C5 Antwerpen, N Belgium
Bāleshwar 135 F4 *prev.* Balasore. Orissa, E India
Bălgrad see Alba Iulia
Bali 138 D5 *island* C Indonesia
Balıkesir 116 A3 Balıkesir, W Turkey
Balikh, Nahr 118 C2 *river* N Syria
Balikpapan 138 D4 Borneo, C Indonesia
Balkanabat 122 B2 *Rus.* Nebitdag.
Balkan Welaýaty, W Turkmenistan
Balkan Mountains 104 C2 *Bul./SCr.* Stara Planina. *mountain range* Bulgaria/Serbia
Balkh 123 E3 *anc.* Bactra. Balkh, N Afghanistan
Balkhash 114 C5 *Kaz.* Balqash. Karaganda, SE Kazakhstan
Balkhash, Lake see Balkhash, Ozero
Balkhash, Ozero 114 C5 *Eng.* Lake Balkhash, *Kaz.* Balqash. *lake* SE Kazakhstan
Balladonia 147 C6 Western Australia
Ballarat 149 C7 Victoria, SE Australia
Balleny Islands 154 B5 *island group* Antarctica
Ballinger 49 F3 Texas, SW USA
Balochistān see Baluchistān
Balqash see Balkhash, Ozero
Balqash see Balkhash
Bals 108 B5 Olt, S Romania
Balsas 63 F2 Maranhão, E Brazil
Balsas, Río 51 E5 *var.* Río Mexcala. *river* S Mexico
Bal'shavik 107 D7 *Rus.* Bol'shevik. Homyel'skaya Voblasts', SE Belarus
Balta 108 D3 Odes'ka Oblast', SW Ukraine
Bălţi 108 D3 *Rus.* Bel'tsy. N Moldova
Baltic Port see Paldiski
Baltic Sea 85 C7 *Ger.* Ostee, *Rus.* Baltiskoye More.. *sea* N Europe
Baltimore 41 F4 Maryland, NE USA
Baltischport/Baltiski see Paldiski
Baltiskoye More see Baltic Sea
Baltkrievija see Belarus
Baluchistān 134 B3 *var.* Balochistān, Beluchistan. *province* SW Pakistan
Balvi 106 D4 Balvi, NE Latvia
Balykchy 123 G2 *Kir.* Ysyk-Köl; *prev.* Issyk-Kul', Rybach'ye. Issyk-Kul'skaya Oblast', NE Kyrgyzstan
Balzers 94 E2 S Liechtenstein
Bam 120 E4 Kermān, SE Iran
Bamako 74 D4 *country capital* (Mali) Capital District, SW Mali
Bambari 76 C4 Ouaka, C Central African Republic
Bamberg 95 C5 Bayern, SE Germany
Bamenda 76 A4 Nord-Ouest, W Cameroon
Banaba 144 D2 *var.* Ocean Island. *island* Tungaru, W Kiribati
Banaras see Vārānasi
Bandaaceh 138 A3 *var.* Banda Atjeh; *prev.* Koetaradja, Kutaradja, Kutaraja. Sumatera, W Indonesia
Banda Atjeh see Bandaaceh
Banda, Laut see Banda Sea
Bandama 74 D5 *var.* Bandama Fleuve. *river* S Côte d'Ivoire (Ivory Coast)
Bandama Fleuve see Bandama
Bandar 'Abbās see Bandar-e 'Abbās
Bandarbeyla 73 E5 *var.* Bender Beila, Bender Beyla. Bari, NE Somalia
Bandar-e 'Abbās 120 D4 *var.* Bandar 'Abbās; *prev.* Gombroon. Hormozgān, S Iran
Bandar-e Büshehr 120 C4 *var.* Büsehr, *Eng.* Bushire. Büshehr, S Iran
Bandar-e Kangān 120 D4 Büshehr, S Iran
Bandar-e Khamïr 120 D4 Hormozgän, S Iran
Bandar-e Langeh 120 D4 *var.* Bandar-e Lengeh, Lingeh. Hormozgän, S Iran
Bandar-e Lengeh see Bandar-e Langeh
Bandar Kassim see Boosaaso
Bandar Lampung 138 C4 *var.* Bandarlampung, Tanjungkarang-Telukbetung; *prev.* Tandjoengkarang, Tanjungkarang, Teloekbetoeng, Telukbetung. Sumatera, W Indonesia
Bandarlampung see Bandar Lampung
Bandar Maharani see Muar
Bandar Masulipatnam see Machilipatnam

Bandar Penggaram see Batu Pahat
Bandar Seri Begawan 138 D3 *prev.* Brunei Town. *country capital* (Brunei) N Brunei
Banda Sea 139 F5 *var.* Laut Banda. *sea* E Indonesia
Bandiagara 75 E3 Mopti, C Mali
Bandırma 116 A3 *var.* Penderma. Balıkesir, NW Turkey
Bandjarmasin see Banjarmasin
Bandoeng see Bandung
Bandundu 77 C6 *prev.* Banningville. Bandundu, W Dem. Rep. Congo
Bandung 138 C5 *prev.* Bandoeng. Jawa, C Indonesia
Bangalore 132 C2 *state capital* Karnātaka, S India
Bangassou 76 D4 Mbomou, SE Central African Republic
Banggai, Kepulauan 139 E4 *island group* C Indonesia
Banghāzī 71 G2 *Eng.* Bengazi, Benghazi, *It.* Bengasi. NE Libya
Bangka, Pulau 138 C4 *island* W Indonesia
Bangkok see Krung Thep
Bangkok, Bight of see Krung Thep, Ao
Bangladesh 135 G3 *off.* People's Republic of Bangladesh; *prev.* East Pakistan. *country* S Asia

BANGLADESH
South Asia

Official name People's Republic of Bangladesh
Formation 1971 / 1971
Capital Dhaka
Population 142 million / 2743 people per sq mile (1059 people per sq km) / 25%
Total area 55,598 sq miles (144,000 sq km)
Languages Bengali*, Urdu, Chakma, Marma (Magh), Garo, Khasi, Santhali, Tripuri, Mro
Religions Muslim (mainly Sunni) 87%, Hindu 12%, Other 1%
Ethnic mix Bengali 98%, Other 2%
Government Parliamentary system
Currency Taka = 100 poisha
Literacy rate 41%
Calorie consumption 2205 calories

Bangladesh, People's Republic of see Bangladesh
Bangor 89 C6 NW Wales, UK
Bangor 89 B5 *Ir.* Beannchar. E Northern Ireland, UK
Bangor 41 G2 Maine, NE USA
Bang Pla Soi see Chon Buri
Bangui 77 B5 *country capital* (Central African Republic) Ombella-Mpoko, SW Central African Republic
Bangweulu, Lake 73 B8 *var.* Lake Bengwelu. *lake* N Zambia
Ban Hat Yai see Hat Yai
Ban Hin Heup 136 C4 Viangchan, C Laos
Ban Houayxay/Ban Houei Sai see Houayxay
Ban Hua Hin 137 C6 *var.* Hua Hin. Prachuap Khiri Khan, SW Thailand
Bani 74 D3 *river* S Mali
Banias see Bāniyās
Banī Suwayf see Beni Suef
Bāniyās 118 B3 *var.* Banias, Baniyas, Paneas. Ţarţūs, W Syria
Banjak, Kepulauan see Banyak, Kepulauan
Banja Luka 100 B3 Republika Srpska, NW Bosnia and Herzegovina
Banjarmasin 138 D4 *prev.* Bandjarmasin. Borneo, C Indonesia
Banjul 74 B3 *prev.* Bathurst. *country capital* (Gambia) W Gambia
Banks, Îles see Banks Islands
Banks Island 37 E2 *island* Banks Island, Northwest Territories, NW Canada
Banks Islands 144 D4 *Fr.* Îles Banks. *island group* N Vanuatu
Banks Lake 46 B1 *reservoir* Washington, NW USA
Banks Peninsula 151 C6 *peninsula* South Island, New Zealand
Banks Strait 149 C8 *strait* SW Tasman Sea
Bänkura 135 F4 West Bengal, NE India

Ban Mak Khaeng see Udon Thani
Banmo see Bhamo
Banningville see Bandundu
Bañolas see Banyoles
Ban Pak Phanang see Pak Phanang
Ban Sichon see Sichon
Banská Bystrica 99 C6 *Ger.* Neusohl, *Hung.* Besztercebánya. Banskobystrický Kraj, C Slovakia
Bantry Bay 89 A7 *Ir.* Bá Bheanntraí. *bay* SW Ireland
Banya 104 E2 Burgas, E Bulgaria
Banyak, Kepulauan 138 A3 *prev.* Kepulauan Banjak. *island group* NW Indonesia
Banyo 76 B4 Adamaoua, NW Cameroon
Banyoles 93 G2 *var.* Bañolas. Cataluña, NE Spain
Banzare Seamounts 141 C7 *seamount range* S Indian Ocean
Banzart see Bizerte
Baoji 128 B4 *var.* Pao-chi, Paoki. Shaanxi, C China
Baoro 76 B4 Nana-Mambéré, W Central African Republic
Baoshan 128 A6 *var.* Pao-shan. Yunnan, SW China
Baotou 127 F3 *var.* Pao-t'ou, Paotow. Nei Mongol Zizhiqu, N China
Ba'qübah 120 B3 *var.* Qubba. C Iraq
Baquerizo Moreno see Puerto Baquerizo Moreno
Bar 101 C5 *It.* Antivari. S Montenegro
Baraawe 73 D6 *It.* Brava. Shabeellaha Hoose, S Somalia
Bärämati 134 C5 Mahärāshtra, W India
Baranavichy 107 B6 *Pol.* Baranowicze, *Rus.* Baranovichi. Brestskaya Voblasts', SW Belarus
Baranovichi/Baranowicze see Baranavichy
Barbados 55 G1 *country* SE West Indies

BARBADOS
West Indies

Official name Barbados
Formation 1966 / 1966
Capital Bridgetown
Population 270,000 / 1627 people per sq mile (628 people per sq km) / 50%
Total area 166 sq miles (430 sq km)
Languages English*, Bajan (Barbadian English)
Religions Anglican 40%, Other 24%, Nonreligious 17%, Pentecostal 8%, Methodist 7%, Roman Catholic 4%
Ethnic mix Black African 90%, Other 10%
Government Parliamentary system
Currency Barbados dollar = 100 cents
Literacy rate 99%
Calorie consumption 3091 calories

Barbastro 93 F2 Aragón, NE Spain
Barbate de Franco 92 C5 Andalucía, S Spain
Barbuda 55 G3 *island* N Antigua and Barbuda
Barcaldine 148 C4 Queensland, E Australia
Barcarozsnyó see Râşnov
Barcău see Berettyó
Barce see Al Marj
Barcelona 93 G2 *anc.* Barcino, Barcinona. Cataluña, E Spain
Barcelona 59 E2 Anzoátegui, NE Venezuela
Barcino/Barcinona see Barcelona
Barcoo see Cooper Creek
Barcs 99 C7 Somogy, SW Hungary
Bardaï 76 C1 Borkou-Ennedi-Tibesti, N Chad
Bardejov 99 D5 *Ger.* Bartfeld, *Hung.* Bártfa. Presovský Kraj, E Slovakia
Bardera/Bardere see Baardheere
Barduli see Barletta
Bareilly 135 E3 *var.* Bareli. Uttar Pradesh, N India
Bareli see Bareilly
Barendrecht 86 C4 Zuid-Holland, SW Netherlands
Barentin 90 C3 Seine-Maritime, N France
Barentsburg 83 G2 Spitsbergen, W Svalbard
Barentsevo More/Barents Havet see Barents Sea

Barentsøya *83 G2 island* E Svalbard
Barents Sea *110 C2 Nor.* Barents Havet, *Rus.* Barentsevo More. *sea* Arctic Ocean
Barents Trough *81 E1 trough* SW Barents Sea
Bar Harbor *41 H2* Mount Desert Island, Maine, NE USA
Bari *97 E5 var.* Bari delle Puglie; *anc.* Barium. Puglia, SE Italy
Bārīdah *see* Al Bārīdah
Bari delle Puglie *see* Bari
Barikot *see* Barīkowṯ
Barīkowṯ *123 F4 var.* Barikot. Konar, NE Afghanistan
Barillas *52 A2 var.* Santa Cruz Barillas. Huehuetenango, NW Guatemala
Barinas *58 C2* Barinas, W Venezuela
Barisal *135 G4* Barisal, S Bangladesh
Barisan, Pegunungan *138 B4 mountain range* Sumatera, W Indonesia
Barito, Sungai *138 D4 river* Borneo, C Indonesia
Barium *see* Bari
Barka *see* Al Marj
Barkly Tableland *148 B3 plateau* Northern Territory/Queensland, N Australia
Bârlad *108 D4 prev.* Bîrlad. Vaslui, E Romania
Barlavento, Ilhas de *74 A2 var.* Windward Islands. *island group* N Cape Verde
Bar-le-Duc *90 D3 var.* Bar-sur-Ornain. Meuse, NE France
Barlee, Lake *147 B6 lake* Western Australia
Barlee Range *146 A4 mountain range* Western Australia
Barletta *97 D5 anc.* Barduli. Puglia, SE Italy
Barlinek *98 B3 Ger.* Berlinchen. Zachodnio-pomorskie, NW Poland
Barmen-Elberfeld *see* Wuppertal
Barmouth *89 C6* NW Wales, UK
Barnaul *114 D4* Altayskiy Kray, C Russian Federation
Barnet *89 A7* UK
Barnstaple *89 C7* SW England, UK
Baroda *see* Vadodara
Baroghil Pass *123 F3 var.* Kowtal-e Barowghīl. *pass* Afghanistan/Pakistan
Baron'ki *107 E7 Rus.* Boron'ki. Mahilyowskaya Voblasts', E Belarus
Barowghīl, Kowtal-e *see* Baroghil Pass
Barquisimeto *58 C2* Lara, NW Venezuela
Barra *88 B3 island* NW Scotland, UK
Barra de Río Grande *53 E3* Región Autónoma Atlántico Sur, E Nicaragua
Barranca *60 C3* Lima, W Peru
Barrancabermeja *58 B2* Santander, N Colombia
Barranquilla *58 B1* Atlántico, N Colombia
Barreiro *92 B4* Setúbal, W Portugal
Barrier Range *149 C6 hill range* New South Wales, SE Australia
Barrow *36 D2* Alaska, USA
Barrow *89 B6 Ir.* An Bhearú. *river* SE Ireland
Barrow-in-Furness *89 C5* NW England, UK
Barrow Island *146 A4 island* Western Australia
Barstow *47 C7* California, W USA
Bar-sur-Ornain *see* Bar-le-Duc
Bartang *123 F3 river* SE Tajikistan
Bartenstein *see* Bartoszyce
Bártfa/Bartfeld *see* Bardejov
Bartica *59 F3* N Guyana
Bartın *116 C2* Bartın, NW Turkey
Bartlesville *49 G1* Oklahoma, C USA
Bartoszyce *98 D2 Ger.* Bartenstein. Warmińsko-mazurskie, NE Poland
Baruun-Urt *127 F2* Sühbaatar, E Mongolia
Barú, Volcán *53 E5 var.* Volcán de Chiriquí. *volcano* W Panama
Barwon River *149 D5 river* New South Wales, SE Australia
Barysaw *107 D6 Rus.* Borisov. Minskaya Voblasts', NE Belarus
Basarabeasca *108 D4 Rus.* Bessarabka. SE Moldova
Basel *95 A7 Eng.* Basle, *Fr.* Bâle. Basel-Stadt, NW Switzerland
Basilan *139 E3 island* Mindanao, SW Philippines Asia Celebes Sea/Sulu Sea Pacific Ocean
Basle *see* Basel
Basra *see* Al Başrah
Bassano del Grappa *96 C2* Veneto, NE Italy
Bassein *136 A4 var.* Pathein. Irrawaddy, SW Myanmar (Burma)
Basseterre *55 G4 country capital* (Saint Kitts and Nevis) Saint Kitts, Saint Kitts and Nevis
Basse-Terre *55 G3 dependent territory capital* (Guadeloupe) Basse Terre, SW Guadeloupe
Basse Terre *55 G4 island* W Guadeloupe
Bassikounou *74 D3* Hodh ech Chargui, SE Mauritania
Bass, Îlots de *see* Marotiri
Bass Strait *149 C7 strait* SE Australia
Bassum *94 B3* Niedersachsen, NW Germany
Bastia *91 E7* Corse, France, C Mediterranean Sea
Bastogne *87 D7* Luxembourg, SE Belgium
Bastrop *42 B2* Louisiana, S USA
Bastyn' *107 B7 Rus.* Bostyn'. Brestskaya Voblasts', SW Belarus
Basuo *see* Dongfang
Basutoland *see* Lesotho
Bata *77 A5* NW Equatorial Guinea
Batae Coritanorum *see* Leicester
Batajnica *100 D3* Vojvodina, N Serbia
Batangas *139 E2 off.* Batangas City. Luzon, N Philippines
Batangas City *see* Batangas
Batavia *see* Jakarta
Bătdâmbâng *137 C5 prev.* Battambang. Bătdâmbâng, NW Cambodia
Batéké, Plateaux *77 B6 plateau* S Congo
Bath *89 D7 hist.* Akermanceaster; *anc.* Aquae Calidae, Aquae Solis. SW England, UK
Bathinda *134 D2* Punjab, NW India
Bathsheba *55 G1* E Barbados
Bathurst *149 D6* New South Wales, SE Australia
Bathurst *39 F4* New Brunswick, SE Canada
Bathurst *see* Banjul
Bathurst Island *146 D2 island* Northern Territory, N Australia
Bathurst Island *37 F2 island* Parry Islands, Nunavut, N Canada
Bāṭin, Wādī al *136 C4 dry watercourse* SW Asia
Batman *117 E4 var.* İluh. Batman, SE Turkey
Batna *71 E2* NE Algeria
Baton Rouge *42 B3 state capital* Louisiana, S USA
Batroûn *118 A4 var.* Al Batrūn. N Lebanon
Battambang *see* Bătdâmbâng
Batticaloa *132 D3* Eastern Province, E Sri Lanka
Battipaglia *97 D5* Campania, S Italy
Battle Born State *see* Nevada
Bat'umi *117 F2* W Georgia
Batu Pahat *138 B3 prev.* Bandar Penggaram. Johor, Peninsular Malaysia
Bauchi *75 G4* Bauchi, NE Nigeria
Bauer Basin *153 F3 undersea basin* E Pacific Ocean
Bauska *106 C3 Ger.* Bauske. Bauska, S Latvia
Bauske *see* Bauska
Bautzen *94 D4 Lus.* Budyšin. Sachsen, E Germany
Bauzanum *see* Bolzano
Bavaria *see* Bayern
Bavarian Alps *95 C7 Ger.* Bayrische Alpen. *mountain range* Austria/Germany
Bavière *see* Bayern
Bavispe, Río *50 C2 river* NW Mexico
Bawîṭi *72 B2* N Egypt
Bawku *75 E4* N Ghana
Bayamo *54 C3* Granma, E Cuba
Bayan Har Shan *126 D4 var.* Bayan Khar. *mountain range* C China
Bayanhongor *126 D2* Bayanhongor, C Mongolia
Bayan Khar *see* Bayan Har Shan
Bayano, Lago *53 G4 lake* E Panama
Bay City *40 C3* Michigan, N USA
Bay City *49 G4* Texas, SW USA
Baydhabo *73 D6 var.* Baydhowa, Isha Baydhabo, *It.* Baidoa. Bay, SW Somalia
Baydhowa *see* Baydhabo
Bayern *95 C6 Eng.* Bavaria, *Fr.* Bavière. *state* SE Germany
Bayeux *90 B3 anc.* Augustodurum. Calvados, N France
Bāyir *119 C7 var.* Bā'ir. Ma'ān, S Jordan
Bay Islands *see* Bahía, Islas de la
Baykal, Ozero *115 E4 Eng.* Lake Baikal. *lake* S Russian Federation
Baymak *111 D6* Respublika Bashkortostan, W Russian Federation
Bayonne *91 A6 anc.* Lapurdum. Pyrénées-Atlantiques, SW France
Bayou State *see* Mississippi
Bayram-Ali *see* Baýramaly
Baýramaly *122 D3 var.* Bayramaly; *prev.* Bayram-Ali. Mary Welaýaty, S Turkmenistan
Bayreuth *95 C5 var.* Baireuth. Bayern, SE Germany
Bayrische Alpen *see* Bavarian Alps
Bayrūt *see* Beyrouth
Bay State *see* Massachusetts
Baysun *see* Boysun
Bayt Laḥm *see* Bethlehem
Baytown *49 H4* Texas, SW USA
Baza *93 E4* Andalucía, S Spain
Bazargic *see* Dobrich
Bazin *see* Pezinok
Beagle Channel *65 C8 channel* Argentina/Chile
Béal Feirste *see* Belfast
Beannchar *see* Bangor, Northern Ireland, UK
Bear Island *see* Bjørnøya
Bear Lake *46 E4 lake* Idaho/Utah, NW USA
Beas de Segura *93 E4* Andalucía, S Spain
Beata, Isla *55 E3 island* SW Dominican Republic
Beatrice *45 F4* Nebraska, C USA
Beaufort Sea *36 D2 sea* Arctic Ocean
Beaufort-Wes *see* Beaufort West
Beaufort West *78 C5 Afr.* Beaufort-Wes. Western Cape, SW South Africa
Beaumont *49 H3* Texas, SW USA
Beaune *90 D4* Côte d'Or, C France
Beauvais *90 C3 anc.* Bellovacum, Caesaromagus. Oise, N France
Beaver Island *40 C2 island* Michigan, N USA
Beaver Lake *49 H1 reservoir* Arkansas, C USA
Beaver River *49 F1 river* Oklahoma, C USA
Beaver State *see* Oregon
Beāwar *134 C3* Rājasthān, N India
Bečej *100 D3 Ger.* Altbetsche, *Hung.* Óbecse, Rácz-Becse; *prev.* Magyar-Becse, Stari Bečej. Vojvodina, N Serbia
Béchar *70 D2 prev.* Colomb-Béchar. W Algeria
Beckley *40 D5* West Virginia, NE USA
Bécs *see* Wien
Bedford *89 D6* E England, UK
Bedum *86 E1* Groningen, NE Netherlands
Beehive State *see* Utah
Be'ér Menuḫa *119 B7 var* Be'er Menukha. Southern, S Israel
Be'erMenukha *see* Be'ér Menuḫa
Beernem *87 A5* West-Vlaanderen, NW Belgium
Beersheba *see* Be'ér Sheva'
Be'ér Sheva' *119 A7 var.* Beersheba, *Ar.* Bir es Saba. Southern, S Israel
Beesel *87 D5* Limburg, SE Netherlands
Beeville *49 G4* Texas, SW USA
Bega *149 D7* New South Wales, SE Australia
Begoml' *see* Byahoml'
Begovat *see* Bekobod
Behagle *see* Laï
Behar *see* Bihār
Beibu Wan *see* Tongking, Gulf of
Beida *see* Al Bayḍā'
Beihai *128 B6* Guangxi Zhuangzu Zizhiqu, S China
Beijing *128 C3 var.* Pei-ching, *Eng.* Peking; *prev.* Pei-p'ing. *country capital* (China) Beijing Shi, E China
Beilen *86 E2* Drenthe, NE Netherlands
Beira *79 E3* Sofala, C Mozambique
Beirut *see* Beyrouth
Beiuş *108 B3 Hung.* Belényes. Bihor, NW Romania
Beja *92 B4 anc.* Pax Julia. Beja, SE Portugal
Béjar *92 C3* Castilla-León, N Spain
Bejraburi *see* Phetchaburi
Bekabad *see* Bekobod
Békás *see* Bicaz
Bek-Budi *see* Qarshi
Békéscsaba *99 D7 Rom.* Bichiş-Ciaba. Békés, SE Hungary
Bekobod *123 E2 Rus.* Bekabad; *prev.* Begovat. Toshkent Viloyati, E Uzbekistan
Bela Crkva *100 E3 Ger.* Weisskirchen, *Hung.* Fehértemplom. Vojvodina, W Serbia
Belarus *107 B6 off.* Republic of Belarus, *var.* Belorussia, *Latv.* Baltkrievija; *prev.* Belorussian SSR, *Rus.* Belorusskaya SSR. *country* E Europe

BELARUS
Eastern Europe

Official name Republic of Belarus
Formation 1991 / 1991
Capital Minsk
Population 9.8 million / 122 people per sq mile (47 people per sq km) / 71%
Total area 80,154 sq miles (207,600 sq km)
Languages Belarussian*, Russian
Religions Orthodox Christian 60%, Other 32%, Roman Catholic 8%
Ethnic mix Belarussian 78%, Russian 13%, Polish 4%, Ukrainian 3%, Other 2%
Government Presidential system
Currency Belarussian rouble = 100 kopeks
Literacy rate 99%
Calorie consumption 3000 calories

Belarus, Republic of *see* Belarus
Belau *see* Palau
Belaya Tserkov' *see* Bila Tserkva
Bełchatów *98 C4 var.* Belchatow. Łódzski, C Poland
Belchatow *see* Bełchatów
Belcher, Îles *see* Belcher Islands
Belcher Islands *38 C2 Fr.* Îles Belcher. *island group* Nunavut, SE Canada
Beledweyne *73 D5 var.* Belet Huen, *It.* Belet Uen. Hiiraan, C Somalia
Belém *63 F1 var.* Pará. *state capital* Pará, N Brazil
Belén *52 D4* Rivas, SW Nicaragua
Belen *48 D2* New Mexico, SW USA
Belényes *see* Beiuş
Belet Huen/Belet Uen *see* Beledweyne
Belfast *89 B5 Ir.* Béal Feirste. *national capital* E Northern Ireland, UK
Belfield *44 D2* North Dakota, N USA
Belfort *90 E4* Territoire-de-Belfort, E France
Belgard *see* Białogard
Belgaum *132 B1* Karnātaka, W India
Belgian Congo *see* Congo (Democratic Republic of)
België/Belgique *see* Belgium
Belgium *87 B6 off.* Kingdom of Belgium, *Dut.* België, *Fr.* Belgique. *country* NW Europe

BELGIUM
Northwest Europe

Official name Kingdom of Belgium
Formation 1830 / 1919
Capital Brussels
Population 10.4 million / 821 people per sq mile (317 people per sq km) / 97%
Total area 11,780 sq miles (30,510 sq km)
Languages Dutch*, French*, German
Religions Roman Catholic 88%, Other 10%, Muslim 2%
Ethnic mix Fleming 58%, Walloon 33%, Other 6%, Italian 2%, Moroccan 1%
Government Parliamentary system
Currency Euro = 100 cents
Literacy rate 99%
Calorie consumption 3584 calories

Belgium, Kingdom of *see* Belgium
Belgorod *111 A6* Belgorodskaya Oblast', W Russian Federation
Belgrano II *154 A2 Argentinian research station* Antarctica
Belice *see* Belize/Belize City
Beligrad *see* Berat

Beli Manastir 100 C3 *Hung.*
Pélmonostor; *prev.* Monostor. Osijek-
Baranja, NE Croatia
Bélinga 77 B5 Ogooué-Ivindo, NE Gabon
Belitung, Pulau 138 C4 *island*
W Indonesia
Belize 52 B1 *Sp.* Belice; *prev.* British
Honduras, Colony of Belize. *country*
Central America

BELIZE
Central America

Official name Belize
Formation 1981 / 1981
Capital Belmopan
Population 270,000 / 31 people per
sq mile
(12 people per sq km) / 54%
Total area 8867 sq miles (22,966 sq km)
Languages English*, English Creole,
Spanish, Mayan, Garifuna (Carib)
Religions Roman Catholic 62%,
Other 13%, Anglican 12%, Methodist 6%,
Mennonite 4%, Seventh-day
Adventist 3%
Ethnic mix Mestizo 44%, Creole 30%,
Maya 11%, Garifuna 7%, Other 4%, Asian
Indian 4%
Government Parliamentary system
Currency Belizean dollar = 100 cents
Literacy rate 77%
Calorie consumption 2869 calories

Belize 52 B1 *river* Belize/Guatemala
Belize *see* Belize City
Belize City 52 C1 *var.* Belize, *Sp.* Belice.
Belize, NE Belize
Belize, Colony of *see* Belize
Beljak *see* Villach
Belkofski 36 B3 Alaska, USA
Belle Île 90 A4 *island* NW France
Belle Isle, Strait of 39 G3 *strait*
Newfoundland and Labrador, E Canada
Bellenz *see* Bellinzona
Belleville 40 B4 Illinois, N USA
Bellevue 45 F4 Iowa, C USA
Bellevue 46 B2 Washington, NW USA
Bellingham 46 B1 Washington, NW USA
Belling Hausen Mulde *see* Southeast
Pacific Basin
Bellingshausen Abyssal Plain *see*
Bellingshausen Plain
Bellingshausen Plain 153 F5 *var.*
Bellingshausen Abyssal Plain. *abyssal
plain* SE Pacific Ocean
Bellingshausen Sea 154 A3 *sea*
Antarctica
Bellinzona 95 B8 *Ger.* Bellenz. Ticino,
S Switzerland
Bello 58 B2 Antioquia, W Colombia
Bello Horizonte *see* Belo Horizonte
Bellovacum *see* Beauvais
Bellville 78 B5 Western Cape, SW South
Africa
Belmopan 52 C1 *country capital* (Belize)
Cayo, C Belize
Belogradchik 104 B1 Vidin,
NW Bulgaria
Belo Horizonte 63 F4 *prev.* Bello
Horizonte. *state capital* Minas Gerais,
SE Brazil
Belomorsk 110 B3 Respublika Kareliya,
NW Russian Federation
Beloretsk 111 D6 Respublika
Bashkortostan, W Russian Federation
Belorussia/Belorussian SSR *see* Belarus
Belorusskaya Gryada *see* Byelaruskaya
Hrada
Belorusskaya SSR *see* Belarus
Beloshchel'ye *see* Nar'yan-Mar
Belostok *see* Białystok
Belovár *see* Bjelovar
Beloye More 110 C3 *Eng.* White Sea. *sea*
NW Russian Federation
Belozërsk 110 B4 Vologodskaya Oblast',
NW Russian Federation
Belton 49 G3 Texas, SW USA
Bel'tsy *see* Bălţi
Beluchistan *see* Baluchistān
Belukha, Gora 114 D5 *mountain*
Kazakhstan/Russian Federation
Belynichi *see* Byalynichy
Belyy, Ostrov 114 D2 *island* N Russian
Federation
Bemaraha 79 F3 *var.* Plateau du
Bemaraha. *mountain range*
W Madagascar

Bemaraha, Plateau du *see* Bemaraha
Bemidji 45 F1 Minnesota, N USA
Bemmel 86 D4 Gelderland,
SE Netherlands
Benaco *see* Garda, Lago di
Benares *see* Vārānasi
Benavente 92 D2 Castilla-León, N Spain
Bend 46 B3 Oregon, NW USA
Bender *see* Tighina
Bender Beila/Bender Beyla *see*
Bandarbeyla
Bender Cassim *see* Bender Cassim/
Bender Qaasim
Bendern 94 E1 NW Liechtenstein Europe
Bendery *see* Tighina
Bendigo 149 C7 Victoria, SE Australia
Beneschau *see* Benešov
Beneški Zaliv *see* Venice, Gulf of
Benešov 99 B5 *Ger.* Beneschau.
Středočeský Kraj, W Czech Republic
Benevento 97 D5 *anc.* Beneventum,
Malventum. Campania, S Italy
Beneventum *see* Benevento
Bengal, Bay of 124 C4 *bay* N Indian
Ocean
Bengasi *see* Banghāzī
Bengazi *see* Banghāzī
Bengbu 128 D5 *var.* Peng-pu. Anhui,
E China
Benghazi *see* Banghāzī
Bengkoeloe *see* Bengkulu
Bengkulu 138 B4 *prev.* Bengkoeloe,
Benkoelen, Benkulen. Sumatera,
W Indonesia
Benguela 78 A2 *var.* Benguella.
Benguela, W Angola
Benguella *see* Benguela
Bengweulu, Lake *see* Bangweulu, Lake
Ben Hope 88 B2 *mountain* N Scotland,
UK
Beni 77 E5 Nord Kivu, NE Dem. Rep.
Congo
Beni 56 B4 *var.* El Beni. *department*
N Bolivia
Benidorm 93 F4 País Valenciano,
SE Spain
Beni-Mellal 70 C2 C Morocco
Benin 75 F4 *off.* Republic of Benin; *prev.*
Dahomey. *country* W Africa

BENIN
West Africa

Official name Republic of Benin
Formation 1960 / 1960
Capital Porto-Novo
Population 8.4 million / 197 people per
sq mile (76 people per sq km) / 42%
Total area 43,483 sq miles
(112,620 sq km)
Languages French*, Fon, Bariba, Yoruba,
Adja, Houeda, Somba
Religions Voodoo 50%, Muslim 30%,
Christian 20%
Ethnic mix Fon 40%, Other 31%, Adja 12%,
Bariba 10%
Government Presidential system
Currency CFA franc = 100 centimes
Literacy rate 34%
Calorie consumption 2548 calories

Benin, Bight of 75 F5 *gulf* W Africa
Benin City 75 F5 Edo, SW Nigeria
Benin, Republic of *see* Benin
Beni, Río 61 E3 *river* N Bolivia
Beni Suef 72 B2 *var.* Banī Suwayf.
N Egypt
Benkoelen *see* Bengkulu
Ben Nevis 88 C3 *mountain* N Scotland,
UK
Bénoué *see* Benue
Benson 48 B3 Arizona, SW USA
Bent Jbaïl 119 A5 *var.* Bint Jubayl.
S Lebanon
Benton 42 B1 Arkansas, C USA
Benue 75 G4 *state* SE Nigeria
Benue 76 B4 *Fr.* Bénoué. *river*
Cameroon/Nigeria
Beograd 100 D3 *Eng.* Belgrade. Serbia,
N Serbia
Berane 101 D5 *prev.* Ivangrad.
E Montenegro
Berat 101 C6 *var.* Berati, *SCr.* Beligrad.
Berat, C Albania
Berātau *see* Berettyó
Berati *see* Berat
Berau, Teluk 139 G4 *var.* MacCluer Gulf.
bay Papua, E Indonesia

Berbera 72 D4 Sahil, NW Somalia
Berbérati 77 B5 Mambéré-Kadéï,
SW Central African Republic
Berck-Plage 90 C2 Pas-de-Calais,
N France
Berdichev *see* Berdychiv
Berdyans'k 109 G4 *Rus.* Berdyansk;
prev. Osipenko. Zaporiz'ka Oblast',
SE Ukraine
Berdychiv 108 D2 *Rus.* Berdichev.
Zhytomyrs'ka Oblast', N Ukraine
Beregovo/Beregszász *see* Berehove
Berehove 108 B3 *Cz.* Berehovo,
Hung. Beregszász, *Rus.* Beregovo.
Zakarpats'ka Oblast', W Ukraine
Berehovo *see* Berehove
Bereket 122 B2 *prev. Rus.* Gazandzhyk,
Kazandzhik, *Turkm.* Gazanjyk. Balkan
Welaýaty, W Turkmenistan
Beretäu *see* Berettyó
Berettyó 99 D7 *Rom.* Barcău;
prev. Berătău, Beretău. *river*
Hungary/Romania
Berettyóújfalu 99 D6 Hajdú-Bihar,
E Hungary
Berezhany 108 C2 *Pol.* Brzeżany.
Ternopil's'ka Oblast', W Ukraine
Berezina *see* Byerezino
Berezniki 111 D5 Permskaya Oblast',
NW Russian Federation
Berga 93 G2 Cataluña, NE Spain
Bergamo 96 B2 *anc.* Bergomum.
Lombardia, N Italy
Bergara 93 E1 País Vasco, N Spain
Bergen 94 D2 Mecklenburg-
Vorpommern, NE Germany
Bergen 86 C2 Noord-Holland,
NW Netherlands
Bergen 85 A5 Hordaland, S Norway
Bergen *see* Mons
Bergerac 91 B5 Dordogne, SW France
Bergeyk 87 C5 Noord-Brabant,
S Netherlands
Bergomum *see* Bergamo
Bergse Maas 86 C4 *river* S Netherlands
Beringen 87 C5 Limburg, NE Belgium
Beringov Proliv *see* Bering Strait
Bering Sea 36 A2 *sea* N Pacific Ocean
Bering Strait 14 *var.* Rus. Beringov Proliv.
strait Bering Sea/Chukchi Sea
Berja 93 E5 Andalucía, S Spain
Berkeley 47 B6 California, W USA
Berkner Island 154 A2 *island* Antarctica
Berkovitsa 104 C2 Montana,
NW Bulgaria
Berlin 94 D3 *country capital* (Germany)
Berlin, NE Germany
Berlin 41 G2 New Hampshire,
NE USA
Berlinchen *see* Barlinek
Bermejo, Río 64 C2 *river* N Argentina
Bermeo 93 E1 País Vasco, N Spain
Bermuda 35 D6 *var.* Bermuda Islands,
Bermudas; *prev.* Somers Islands. *UK
crown colony* NW Atlantic Ocean
Bermuda Islands *see* Bermuda
Bermuda Rise 33 E6 *undersea rise*
C Sargasso Sea
Bermudas *see* Bermuda
Bern 95 A7 *Fr.* Berne. *country capital*
(Switzerland) Bern, W Switzerland
Bernau 94 D3 Brandenburg,
NE Germany
Bernburg 94 C4 Sachsen-Anhalt,
C Germany
Berne *see* Bern
Berner Alpen 95 A7 *var.* Berner
Oberland, *Eng.* Bernese Oberland.
mountain range SW Switzerland
Berner Oberland/Bernese Oberland *see*
Berner Alpen
Bernier Island 147 A5 *island* Western
Australia
Beroea *see* Ḥalab
Berry 90 C4 *cultural region* C France
Berry Islands 54 C1 *island group*
N Bahamas
Bertoua 77 B5 Est, E Cameroon
Beru 145 F2 *var.* Peru. *atoll* Tungaru,
W Kiribati
Berwick-upon-Tweed 88 D4 N England,
UK
Berytus *see* Beyrouth
Besançon 90 D4 *anc.* Besontium,
Vesontio. Doubs, E France
Beskra *see* Biskra
Besontium *see* Besançon
Bessarabka *see* Basarabeasca

Beszterce *see* Bistriţa
Besztercebánya *see* Banská Bystrica
Betafo 79 G3 Antananarivo,
C Madagascar
Betanzos 92 B1 Galicia, NW Spain
Bethlehem 78 D4 Free State, C South
Africa
Bethlehem 119 B6 *Ar.* Bayt Laḥm, *Heb.*
Bet Leḥem. C West Bank
Bet Leḥem *see* Bethlehem
Béticos, Sistemas 92 D4 *var.* Sistema
Penibético, *Eng.* Baetic Cordillera,
Baetic Mountains. *mountain range*
S Spain
Bétou 77 C5 La Likouala, N Congo
Bette, Pic 71 G4 *var.* Bikkū Bīttī, *It.* Picco
Bette. *mountain* S Libya
Bette, Picco *see* Bette, Pic
Beulah 40 C2 Michigan, N USA
Beuthen *see* Bytom
Beveren 87 B5 Oost-Vlaanderen,
N Belgium
Beverley 89 D5 E England, UK
Bexley 89 B8 Bexley, SE England, UK
Beyla 74 D4 SE Guinea
Beyrouth 118 A4 *var.* Beyrūt, *Eng.*
Beirut; *anc.* Berytus. *country capital*
(Lebanon) W Lebanon
Beyşehir 116 B4 Konya, SW Turkey
Beyşehir Gölü 116 B4 *lake* C Turkey
Béziers 91 C6 *anc.* Baeterrae, Baeterrae
Septimanorum, Julia Beterrae. Héraul
S France
Bezmein *see* Abadan
Bezwada *see* Vijayawāda
Bhadrāvati 132 C2 Karnātaka, SW India
Bhāgalpur 135 F3 Bihār, NE India
Bhaktapur 135 F3 Central, C Nepal
Bhamo 136 B2 *var.* Banmo. Kachin
State, N Myanmar (Burma)
Bhārat *see* India
Bharūch 134 C4 Gujarāt, W India
Bhaunagar *see* Bhāvnagar
Bhāvnagar 134 C4 *prev.* Bhaunagar.
Gujarāt, W India
Bheanntraí, Bá *see* Bantry Bay
Bhopāl 134 D4 *state capital* Madhya
Pradesh, C India
Bhubaneshwar 135 F5 *prev.*
Bhubaneswar, Bhuvaneshwar. *state
capital* Orissa, E India
Bhubaneswar *see* Bhubaneshwar
Bhuket *see* Phuket
Bhusaval *see* Bhusāwal
Bhusāwal 134 D4 *prev.* Bhusaval.
Mahārāshtra, C India
Bhutan 135 G3 *off.* Kingdom of Bhutan,
var. Druk-yul. *country* S Asia

BHUTAN
Southeast Asia

Official name Kingdom of Bhutan
Formation 1656 / 1865
Capital Thimphu
Population 2.2 million / 121 people per
sq mile (47 people per sq km) / 7%
Total area 18,147 sq miles
(47,000 sq km)
Languages Dzongkha*, Nepali,
Assamese
Religions Mahayana Buddhist 70%,
Hindu 24%, Other 6%
Ethnic mix Bhute 50%, Other 25%,
Nepalese 25%
Government Monarchy
Currency Ngultrum = 100 chetrum
Literacy rate 47%
Calorie consumption Not available

Bhutan, Kingdom of *see* Bhutan
Bhuvaneshwar *see* Bhubaneshwar
Biak, Pulau 139 G4 *island* E Indonesia
Biała Podlaska 98 E3 Lubelskie Polan
Białograd 98 B2 Ger. Belgard.
Zachodnio-pomorskie, NW Poland
Białystok 98 E3 Rus. Belostok, Bielosto
Podlaskie, NE Poland
Bianco, Monte *see* Blanc, Mont
Biarritz 91 A6 Pyrénées-Atlantiques,
SW France
Bicaz 108 C3 *Hung.* Békás. Neamţ,
NE Romania
Bichis-Ciaba *see* Békéscsaba
Biddeford 41 G2 Maine, NE USA
Bideford 89 C7 SW England, UK
Biel 95 A7 *Fr.* Bienne. Bern,
W Switzerland

Bielefeld 94 B4 Nordrhein-Westfalen, NW Germany
Bielitz/Bielitz-Biala *see* Bielsko-Biała
Bielostok *see* Białystok
Bielsko-Biała 99 C5 *Ger.* Bielitz, Bielitz-Biala. Śląskie, S Poland
Bielsk Podlaski 98 E3 Białystok, E Poland
Bien Bien *see* Điện Biên
Biên Đông *see* South China Sea
Biên Hoa 137 E6 Đông Nai, S Vietnam
Bienne *see* Biel
Bienville, Lac 38 D2 *lake* Québec, C Canada
Bié, Planalto do 78 B2 *var.* Bié Plateau. *plateau* C Angola
Bié Plateau *see* Bié, Planalto do
Big Cypress Swamp 43 E5 *wetland* Florida, SE USA
Bigge Island 146 C2 *island* Western Australia
Bighorn Mountains 44 C2 *mountain range* Wyoming, C USA
Bighorn River 44 C2 *river* Montana/Wyoming, NW USA
Bignona 74 B3 SW Senegal
Bigorra *see* Tarbes
Bigosovo *see* Bihosava
Big Sioux River 45 E2 *river* Iowa/South Dakota, N USA
Big Spring 49 E3 Texas, SW USA
Bihać 100 B3 NW Bosnia and Herzegovina
Bihār 135 F3 *prev.* Behar. *cultural region* N India
Bihār 135 F3 *prev.* Behar. *state* N India
Bihār *see* Bihār Sharīf
Biharamulo 73 B7 Kagera, NW Tanzania
Bihār Sharīf 135 F3 *var.* Bihār. Bihār, N India
Bihosava 107 D5 *Rus.* Bigosovo. Vitsyebskaya Voblasts', NW Belarus
Bijeljina 100 C3 Republika Srpska, NE Bosnia and Herzegovina
Bijelo Polje 101 D5 E Montenegro
Bīkāner 134 C3 Rājasthān, NW India
Bikin 115 G4 Khabarovskiy Kray, SE Russian Federation
Bikini Atoll 144 C1 *var.* Pikinni. *atoll* Ralik Chain, NW Marshall Islands
Bīkkū Bīttī *see* Bette, Pic
Bilāspur 135 E4 Chhattīsgarh, C India
Biläsuvar 117 H3 *Rus.* Bilyasuvar; *prev.* Pushkino. SE Azerbaijan
Bila Tserkva 109 E2 *Rus.* Belaya Tserkov'. Kyyivs'ka Oblast', N Ukraine
Bilauktaung Range 137 C6 *var.* Thanintari Taungdan. *mountain range* Myanmar (Burma)/Thailand
Bilbao 93 E1 *Basq.* Bilbo. País Vasco, N Spain
Bilbo *see* Bilbao
Bilecik 116 B3 Bilecik, NW Turkey
Billings 44 C2 Montana, NW USA
Bilma, Grand Erg de 75 H3 *desert* NE Niger
Biloela 148 D4 Queensland, E Australia
Biloxi 42 C3 Mississippi, S USA
Biltine 76 C3 Biltine, E Chad
Bilwi *see* Puerto Cabezas
Bilyasuvar *see* Biläsuvar
Bilzen 87 D6 Limburg, NE Belgium
Bimini Islands 54 C1 *island group* W Bahamas
Binche 87 B7 Hainaut, S Belgium
Bindloe Island *see* Marchena, Isla
Bin Ghalfān, Jazā'ir *see* Ḩalāniyāt, Juzur al
Binghamton 41 F3 New York, NE USA
Bingöl 117 E3 Bingöl, E Turkey
Bint Jubayl *see* Bent Jbaïl
Bintulu 138 D3 Sarawak, East Malaysia
Binzhou 128 D4 Shandong, E China
Bío Bío, Río 65 B5 *river* C Chile
Bioco, Isla de 77 A5 *var.* Bioko, *Eng.* Fernando Po, *Sp.* Fernando Póo; *prev.* Macías Nguema Biyogo. *island* NW Equatorial Guinea
Bioko *see* Bioco, Isla de
Birāk 71 F3 *var.* Brak. C Libya
Birao 76 D3 Vakaga, NE Central African Republic
Birātnagar 135 F3 Eastern, SE Nepal
Bir es Saba *see* Be'ér Sheva'
Bīrjand 120 E3 Khorāsān-e Janūbī, E Iran
Birkenfeld 95 A5 Rheinland-Pfalz, SW Germany
Birkenhead 89 C5 NW England, UK
Bîrlad *see* Bârlad
Birmingham 89 C6 C England, UK
Birmingham 42 C2 Alabama, S USA
Bir Moghrein *see* Bîr Mogreïn
Bîr Mogreïn 74 C1 *var.* Bir Moghrein; *prev.* Fort-Trinquet. Tiris Zemmour, N Mauritania
Birnie Island 145 E3 *atoll* Phoenix Islands, C Kiribati
Birnin Konni 75 F3 *var.* Birni-Nkonni. Tahoua, SW Niger
Birni-Nkonni *see* Birnin Konni
Birobidzhan 115 G4 Yevreyskaya Avtonomnaya Oblast', SE Russian Federation
Birsen *see* Biržai
Birsk 111 D5 Respublika Bashkortostan, W Russian Federation
Biržai 106 C4 *Ger.* Birsen. Panevėžys, NE Lithuania
Birżebbuġa 102 B5 SE Malta
Bisanthe *see* Tekirdağ
Bisbee 48 B3 Arizona, SW USA
Biscaia, Baía de *see* Biscay, Bay of
Biscay, Bay of 80 B4 *Sp.* Golfo de Vizcaya, *Port.* Baía de Biscaia. *bay* France/Spain
Biscay Plain 80 B3 *abyssal plain* SE Bay of Biscay
Bischofsburg *see* Biskupiec
Bīshah, Wādī 121 B5 *dry watercourse* C Saudi Arabia
Bishkek 123 G2 *var.* Pishpek; *prev.* Frunze. *country capital* (Kyrgyzstan) Chuyskaya Oblast', N Kyrgyzstan
Bishop's Lynn *see* King's Lynn
Bishrī, Jabal 118 D3 *mountain range* E Syria
Biskara *see* Biskra
Biskra 71 E2 *var.* Beskra, Biskara. NE Algeria
Biskupiec 98 D2 *Ger.* Bischofsburg. Warmińsko-Mazurskie, NE Poland
Bislig 139 F2 Mindanao, S Philippines
Bismarck 45 E2 *state capital* North Dakota, N USA
Bismarck Archipelago 144 B3 *island group* NE Papua New Guinea
Bismarck Sea 144 B3 *sea* W Pacific Ocean
Bisnulok *see* Phitsanulok
Bissau 74 B4 *country capital* (Guinea-Bissau) W Guinea-Bissau
Bistriţa 108 B3 *Ger.* Bistritz, *Hung.* Beszterce; *prev.* Nösen. Bistriţa-Năsăud, N Romania
Bistritz *see* Bistriţa
Bitam 77 B5 Woleu-Ntem, N Gabon
Bitburg 95 A5 Rheinland-Pfalz, SW Germany
Bitlis 117 F3 Bitlis, SE Turkey
Bitoeng *see* Bitung
Bitola 101 D6 *Turk.* Monastir; *prev.* Bitolj. S FYR Macedonia
Bitolj *see* Bitola
Bitonto 97 D5 *anc.* Butuntum. Puglia, SE Italy
Bitterroot Range 46 D2 *mountain range* Idaho/Montana, NW USA
Bitung 139 F3 *prev.* Bitoeng. Sulawesi, C Indonesia
Biu 75 H4 Borno, E Nigeria
Biwa-ko 131 C6 *lake* Honshū, SW Japan
Bizerta *see* Bizerte
Bizerte 71 E1 *Ar.* Banzart, *Eng.* Bizerta. N Tunisia
Bjelovar 100 B2 *Hung.* Belovár. Bjelovar-Bilogora, N Croatia
Bjeshkët e Namuna *see* North Albanian Alps
Björneborg *see* Pori
Bjørnøya 83 F3 *Eng.* Bear Island. *island* N Norway
Blackall 148 C4 Queensland, E Australia
Black Drin 101 D6 *Alb.* Lumi i Drinit të Zi, *SCr.* Crni Drim. *river* Albania/FYR Macedonia
Blackfoot 46 E4 Idaho, NW USA
Black Forest *see* Schwarzwald
Black Hills 44 D3 *mountain range* South Dakota/Wyoming, N USA
Blackpool 89 C5 NW England, UK
Black Range 48 C2 *mountain range* New Mexico, SW USA
Black River 54 A5 W Jamaica
Black River 136 C3 *Chin.* Babian Jiang, Lixian Jiang, *Fr.* Rivière Noire, *Vtn.* Sông Đa. *river* China/Vietnam
Black Rock Desert 47 C5 *desert* Nevada, W USA
Black Sand Desert *see* Garagum
Black Sea 116 B1 *var.* Euxine Sea, *Bul.* Cherno More, *Rom.* Marea Neagră, *Rus.* Chernoye More, *Turk.* Karadeniz, *Ukr.* Chorne More. *sea* Asia/Europe
Black Sea Lowland 109 E4 *Ukr.* Prychornomor'ska Nyzovyna. *depression* SE Europe
Black Volta 75 E4 *var.* Borongo, Mouhoun, Moun Hou, *Fr.* Volta Noire. *river* W Africa
Blackwater 89 A6 *Ir.* An Abhainn Mhór. *river* S Ireland
Blackwater State *see* Nebraska
Blagoevgrad 104 C3 *prev.* Gorna Dzhumaya. Blagoevgrad, W Bulgaria
Blagoveshchensk 115 G4 Amurskaya Oblast', SE Russian Federation
Blake Plateau 35 D6 *var.* Blake Terrace. *undersea plateau* W Atlantic Ocean
Blake Terrace *see* Blake Plateau
Blanca, Bahía 65 C5 *bay* E Argentina
Blanca, Costa 93 F4 *physical region* SE Spain
Blanche, Lake 149 B5 *lake* South Australia
Blanc, Mont 91 D5 *It.* Monte Bianco. *mountain* France/Italy
Blanco, Cape 46 A4 *headland* Oregon, NW USA
Blanes 93 G2 Cataluña, NE Spain
Blankenberge 87 A5 West-Vlaanderen, NW Belgium
Blankenheim 95 A5 Nordrhein-Westfalen, W Germany
Blanquilla, Isla 59 E1 *var.* La Blanquilla. *island* N Venezuela
Blanquilla, La *see* Blanquilla, Isla
Blantyre 79 E2 *var.* Blantyre-Limbe. Southern, S Malawi
Blantyre-Limbe *see* Blantyre
Blaricum 86 C3 Noord-Holland, C Netherlands
Blatnitsa *see* Durankulak
Blenheim 151 C5 Marlborough, South Island, New Zealand
Blesae *see* Blois
Blida 70 D2 *var.* El Boulaida, El Boulaïda. N Algeria
Bloemfontein 78 C4 *var.* Mangaung. *country capital* (South Africa-judicial capital) Free State, C South Africa
Blois 90 C4 *anc.* Blesae. Loir-et-Cher, C France
Bloomfield 48 C1 New Mexico, SW USA
Bloomington 40 B4 Illinois, N USA
Bloomington 40 C4 Indiana, N USA
Bloomington 45 F2 Minnesota, N USA
Bloomsbury 148 D3 Queensland, NE Australia
Bluefield 40 D5 West Virginia, NE USA
Bluefields 53 E3 Región Autónoma Atlántico Sur, SE Nicaragua
Bluegrass State *see* Kentucky
Blue Hen State *see* Delaware
Blue Law State *see* Connecticut
Blue Mountain Peak 54 B5 *mountain* E Jamaica
Blue Mountains 46 C3 *mountain range* Oregon/Washington, NW USA
Blue Nile 72 C4 *state* E Sudan
Blue Nile 68 D4 *var.* Abai, Bahr el, Azraq, *Amh.* Ābay Wenz, *Ar.* An Nīl al Azraq. *river* Ethiopia/Sudan
Blumenau 63 E5 Santa Catarina, S Brazil
Blythe 47 D8 California, W USA
Blytheville 42 C1 Arkansas, C USA
Bo 74 C4 S Sierra Leone
Boaco 52 D3 Boaco, S Nicaragua
Boa Vista 62 D1 *state capital* Roraima, NW Brazil
Boa Vista 74 A3 *island* Ilhas de Barlavento, E Cape Verde
Bobaomby, Tanjona 79 G2 *Fr.* Cap d'Ambre. *headland* N Madagascar
Bobigny 90 E1 Seine-St-Denis, N France
Bobo-Dioulasso 74 D4 SW Burkina Faso
Bobrinets *see* Bobrynets'
Bobruysk *see* Babruysk
Bobrynets' 109 E3 *Rus.* Bobrinets. Kirovohrads'ka Oblast', C Ukraine
Boca Raton 43 F5 Florida, SE USA
Bocay 52 D2 Jinotega, N Nicaragua
Bocheykovo *see* Bacheykava
Bocholt 94 A4 Nordrhein-Westfalen, W Germany
Bochum 94 A4 Nordrhein-Westfalen, W Germany
Bocşa 108 A4 *Ger.* Bokschen, *Hung.* Boksánbánya. Caraş-Severin, SW Romania
Bodaybo 115 F4 Irkutskaya Oblast', E Russian Federation
Bodegas *see* Babahoyo
Boden 84 D4 Norrbotten, N Sweden
Bodensee *see* Constance, Lake, C Europe
Bodmin 89 C7 SW England, UK
Bodø 84 C3 Nordland, C Norway
Bodrum 116 A4 Muğla, SW Turkey
Boeloekoemba *see* Bulukumba
Boende 77 C5 Equateur, C Dem. Rep. Congo
Boeroe *see* Buru, Pulau
Boetoeng *see* Buton, Pulau
Bogale 136 B4 Irrawaddy, SW Myanmar (Burma)
Bogalusa 42 B3 Louisiana, S USA
Bogatynia 98 B4 *Ger.* Reichenau. Dolnośląskie, SW Poland
Boğazlıyan 116 D3 Yozgat, C Turkey
Bogendorf *see* Łuków
Bogor 138 C5 *Dut.* Buitenzorg. Jawa, C Indonesia
Bogotá 58 B3 *prev.* Santa Fe, Santa Fe de Bogotá. *country capital* (Colombia) Cundinamarca, C Colombia
Bogushëvsk *see* Bahushewsk
Boguslav *see* Bohuslav
Bo Hai 128 D4 *var.* Gulf of Chihli. *gulf* NE China
Bohemia 99 A5 *Cz.* Čechy, *Ger.* Böhmen. *cultural and historical region* W Czech Republic
Bohemian Forest 95 C5 *Cz.* Ceský Les, Sumava, *Ger.* Böhmerwald. *mountain range* C Europe
Böhmen *see* Bohemia
Böhmerwald *see* Bohemian Forest
Böhmisch-Krumau *see* Český Krumlov
Bohol Sea 139 E2 *var.* Mindanao Sea. *sea* S Philippines
Bohuslav 109 E2 *Rus.* Boguslav. Kyyivs'ka Oblast', N Ukraine
Boise 46 D3 *var.* Boise City. *state capital* Idaho, NW USA
Boise City 49 E1 Oklahoma, C USA
Boise City *see* Boise
Bois, Lac des *see* Woods, Lake of the
Bois-le-Duc *see* 's-Hertogenbosch
Boizenburg 94 C3 Mecklenburg-Vorpommern, N Germany
Bojador *see* Boujdour
Bojnūrd 120 D2 *var.* Bujnurd. Khorāsān-e Shemālī, N Iran
Bokāro 135 F4 Jhārkhand, N India
Boké 74 C4 W Guinea
Bokhara *see* Buxoro
Boknafjorden 85 A6 *fjord* S Norway
Boksánbánya/Bokschen *see* Bocşa
Bol 76 B3 Lac, W Chad
Bolgatanga 75 E4 N Ghana
Bolgrad *see* Bolhrad
Bolhrad 108 D4 *Rus.* Bolgrad. Odes'ka Oblast', SW Ukraine
Bolívar, Pico 58 C2 *mountain* W Venezuela
Bolivia 61 F3 *off.* Republic of Bolivia. *country* W South America

BOLIVIA
South America

Official name Republic of Bolivia
Formation 1825 / 1938
Capital La Paz (administrative); Sucre (judicial)
Population 9.2 million / 22 people per sq mile (8 people per sq km) / 63%
Total area 424,162 sq miles (1,098,580 sq km)
Languages Aymara*, Quechua*, Spanish*
Religions Roman Catholic 93%, Other 7%
Ethnic mix Quechua 37%, Aymara 32%, Mixed race 13%, European 10%, Other 8%
Government Presidential system
Currency Boliviano = 100 centavos

BOLIVIA
(continued)

Literacy rate 87%
Calorie consumption 2235 calories

Bolivia, Republic of *see* Bolivia
Bollène *91 D6* Vaucluse, SE France
Bollnäs *85 C5* Gävleborg, C Sweden
Bollon *149 D5* Queensland, C Australia
Bologna *96 C3* Emilia-Romagna, N Italy
Bol'shevik *see* Bal'shavik
Bol'shevik, Ostrov *115 E2 island* Severnaya Zemlya, N Russian Federation
Bol'shezemel'skaya Tundra *110 E3 physical region* NW Russian Federation
Bol'shoy Lyakhovskiy, Ostrov *115 F2 island* NE Russian Federation
Bolton *89 D5 prev.* Bolton-le-Moors. NW England, UK
Bolton-le-Moors *see* Bolton
Bolu *116 B3* Bolu, NW Turkey
Bolungarvík *83 E4* Vestfirdhir, NW Iceland
Bolyarovo *104 D3 prev.* Pashkeni. Yambol, E Bulgaria
Bolzano *96 C1 Ger.* Bozen; *anc.* Bauzanum. Trentino-Alto Adige, N Italy
Boma *77 B6* Bas-Congo, W Dem. Rep. Congo
Bombay *see* Mumbai
Bomu *76 D4 var.* Mbomou, Mbomu, M'Bomu. *river* Central African Republic/Dem. Rep. Congo
Bonaire *55 F5 island* E Netherlands Antilles
Bonanza *52 D2* Región Autónoma Atlántico Norte, NE Nicaragua
Bonaparte Archipelago *146 C2 island group* Western Australia
Bon, Cap *102 D3 headland* N Tunisia
Bonda *77 B6* Ogooué-Lolo, C Gabon
Bondoukou *75 E4* E Côte d'Ivoire (Ivory Coast)
Bône *see* Annaba
Bone *see* Watampone
Bone, Teluk *139 E4 bay* Sulawesi, C Indonesia
Bongaigaon *135 G3* Assam, NE India
Bongo, Massif des *76 D4 var.* Chaîne des Mongos. *mountain range* NE Central African Republic
Bongor *76 B3* Mayo-Kébbi, SW Chad
Bonifacio *91 E7* Corse, France, C Mediterranean Sea
Bonifacio, Bocche de/Bonifacio, Bouches de *see* Bonifacio, Strait of
Bonifacio, Strait of *96 A4 Fr.* Bouches de Bonifacio, *It.* Bocche di Bonifacio. *strait* C Mediterranean Sea
Bonn *95 A5* Nordrhein-Westfalen, W Germany
Bononia *see* Vidin, Bulgaria
Bononia *see* Boulogne-sur-Mer, France
Boosaaso *72 E4 var.* Bandar Kassim, Bender Qaasim, Bosaso, *It.* Bender Cassim. Bari, N Somalia
Boothia Felix *see* Boothia Peninsula
Boothia, Gulf of *37 F2 gulf* Nunavut, NE Canada
Boothia Peninsula *37 F2 prev.* Boothia Felix. *peninsula* Nunavut, NE Canada
Boppard *95 A5* Rheinland-Pfalz, W Germany
Boquete *53 E5 var.* Bajo Boquete. Chiriquí, W Panama
Boquillas *50 D2 var.* Boquillas del Carmen. Coahuila de Zaragoza, NE Mexico
Boquillas del Carmen *see* Boquillas
Bor *100 E4* Serbia, E Serbia
Bor *73 B5* Jonglei, S Sudan
Borås *85 B7* Västra Götaland, S Sweden
Borbetomagus *see* Worms
Borborema, Planalto da *56 E3 plateau* NE Brazil
Bordeaux *91 B5 anc.* Burdigala. Gironde, SW France
Bordj Omar Driss *71 E3* E Algeria
Borgå *see* Porvoo
Børgefjelt *84 C4 mountain range* C Norway
Borger *86 E2* Drenthe, NE Netherlands
Borger *49 E1* Texas, SW USA
Borgholm *85 C7* Kalmar, S Sweden
Borgo Maggiore *96 E1* NW San Marino
Borislav *see* Boryslav
Borisoglebsk *111 B6* Voronezhskaya Oblast', W Russian Federation
Borisov *see* Barysaw
Borlänge *85 C6* Dalarna, C Sweden
Borne *86 E3* Overijssel, E Netherlands
Borneo *138 C4 island* Brunei/Indonesia/Malaysia
Bornholm *85 B8 island* E Denmark
Borohoro Shan *126 B2 mountain range* NW China
Borongo *see* Black Volta
Boron'ki *see* Baron'ki
Borosjenő *see* Ineu
Borovan *104 C2* Vratsa, NW Bulgaria
Borovichi *110 B4* Novgorodskaya Oblast', W Russian Federation
Borovo *100 C3* Vukovar-Srijem, NE Croatia
Borşa *108 C3 Hung.* Borsa. Maramureş, N Romania
Boryslav *108 B2 Pol.* Borysław, *Rus.* Borislav. L'vivs'ka Oblast', NW Ukraine
Borysław *see* Boryslav
Bosanska Dubica *100 B3 var.* Kozarska Dubica. Republika Srpska, NW Bosnia and Herzegovina
Bosanska Gradiška *100 B3 var.* Gradiška. Republika Srpska, N Bosnia and Herzegovina
Bosanski Novi *100 B3 var.* Novi Grad. Republika Srpska, NW Bosnia and Herzegovina
Bosanski Šamac *100 C3 var.* Šamac. Republika Srpska, N Bosnia and Herzegovina
Bosaso *see* Boosaaso
Bösing *see* Pezinok
Boskovice *99 B5 Ger.* Boskowitz. Jihomoravský Kraj, SE Czech Republic
Boskowitz *see* Boskovice
Bosna *100 C4 river* N Bosnia and Herzegovina
Bosnia and Herzegovina *100 B3 off.* Republic of Bosnia and Herzegovina. *country* SE Europe

BOSNIA & HERZEGOVINA
Southeast Europe

Official name Bosnia and Herzegovina
Formation 1992 / 1992
Capital Sarajevo
Population 3.9 million / 198 people per sq mile (76 people per sq km) / 43%
Total area 19,741 sq miles (51,129 sq km)
Languages Serbo-Croat*
Religions Muslim (mainly Sunni) 40%, Orthodox Christian 31%, Roman Catholic 15%, Other 10%, Protestant 4%
Ethnic mix Bosniak 48%, Serb 38%, Croat 14%
Government Parliamentary system
Currency Marka = 100 pfeninga
Literacy rate 95%
Calorie consumption 2894 calories

Bosnia and Herzegovina, Republic of *see* Bosnia and Herzegovina
Bōsō-hantō *131 D6 peninsula* Honshū, S Japan
Bosphorus/Bosporus *see* İstanbul Boğazı
Bosporus Cimmerius *see* Kerch Strait
Bosporus Thracius *see* İstanbul Boğazı
Bossangoa *76 C4* Ouham, C Central African Republic
Bossembélé *76 C4* Ombella-Mpoko, C Central African Republic
Bossier City *42 A2* Louisiana, S USA
Bosten Hu *126 C3 var.* Bagrax Hu. *lake* NW China
Boston *89 E6 prev.* St.Botolph's Town. E England, UK
Boston *41 G3 state capital* Massachusetts, NE USA
Boston Mountains *42 B1 mountain range* Arkansas, C USA
Bostyn' *see* Bastyn'
Botany *148 E2* New South Wales, E Australia
Botany Bay *148 E2 inlet* New South Wales, SE Australia
Boteti *78 C3 var.* Botletle. *river* N Botswana
Bothnia, Gulf of *85 D5 Fin.* Pohjanlahti, *Swe.* Bottniska Viken. *gulf* N Baltic Sea
Botletle *see* Boteti
Botoşani *108 C3 Hung.* Botosány. Botoşani, NE Romania
Botosány *see* Botoşani
Botou *128 C4 prev.* Bozhen. Hebei, E China
Botrange *87 D6 mountain* E Belgium
Botswana *78 C3 off.* Republic of Botswana. *country* S Africa

BOTSWANA
Southern Africa

Official name Republic of Botswana
Formation 1966 / 1966
Capital Gaborone
Population 1.8 million / 8 people per sq mile (3 people per sq km) / 50%
Total area 231,803 sq miles (600,370 sq km)
Languages English*, Setswana, Shona, San, Khoikhoi, isiNdebele
Religions Traditional beliefs 50%, Christian (mainly Protestant) 30%, Other (including Muslim) 20%
Ethnic mix Tswana 98%, Other 2%
Government Presidential system
Currency Pula = 100 thebe
Literacy rate 79%
Calorie consumption 2151 calories

Botswana, Republic of *see* Botswana
Bottniska Viken *see* Bothnia, Gulf of
Bouar *76 B4* Nana-Mambéré, W Central African Republic
Bou Craa *70 B3 var.* Bu Craa. NW Western Sahara
Bougainville Island *142 B3 island* NE Papua New Guinea
Bougaroun, Cap *102 C3 headland* NE Algeria
Bougouni *74 D4* Sikasso, SW Mali
Boujdour *70 A3 var.* Bojador. W Western Sahara
Boulder *44 C4* Colorado, C USA
Boulder *44 B2* Montana, NW USA
Boulogne *see* Boulogne-sur-Mer
Boulogne-Billancourt *90 D1* Hauts-de-Seine, Île-de-France, N France Europe
Boulogne-sur-Mer *90 C2 var.* Boulogne; *anc.* Bononia, Gesoriacum, Gessoriacum. Pas-de-Calais, N France
Boûmdeïd *74 C3 var.* Boumdeït. Assaba, S Mauritania
Boumdeït *see* Boûmdeïd
Boundiali *74 D4* N Côte d'Ivoire (Ivory Coast)
Bountiful *44 B4* Utah, W USA
Bounty Basin *see* Bounty Trough
Bounty Islands *142 D5 island group* S New Zealand
Bounty Trough *152 C5 var.* Bounty Basin. *trough* S Pacific Ocean
Bourbonnais *90 C4* Illinois, N USA
Bourbon Vendée *see* la Roche-sur-Yon
Bourg *see* Bourg-en-Bresse
Bourgas *see* Burgas
Bourge-en-Bresse *see* Bourg-en-Bresse
Bourg-en-Bresse *91 D5 var.* Bourg, Bourge-en-Bresse. Ain, E France
Bourges *90 C4 anc.* Avaricum. Cher, C France
Bourgogne *90 C4 Eng.* Burgundy. *region* E France
Bourgogne *90 C4 Eng.* Burgundy. *cultural region* E France
Bourke *149 C5* New South Wales, SE Australia
Bournemouth *89 D7* S England, UK
Boutilimit *74 C3* Trarza, SW Mauritania
Bouvet Island *67 D7 Norwegian dependency* S Atlantic Ocean
Bowen *148 D3* Queensland, NE Australia
Bowling Green *40 B5* Kentucky, S USA
Bowling Green *40 C3* Ohio, N USA
Boxmeer *86 D4* Noord-Brabant, SE Netherlands
Boyarka *109 E2* Kyyivs'ka Oblast', N Ukraine
Boysun *123 E3 Rus.* Baysun. Surkhondaryo Viloyati, S Uzbekistan
Bozeman *44 B2* Montana, NW USA
Bozen *see* Bolzano
Bozhen *see* Botou
Bozüyük *116 B3* Bilecik, NW Turkey
Brač *100 B4 var.* Brach, *It.* Brazza; *anc.* Brattia. *island* S Croatia
Bracara Augusta *see* Braga
Brach *see* Brač
Bradford *89 D5* N England, UK
Brady *49 F3* Texas, SW USA
Braga *92 B2 anc.* Bracara Augusta. Braga, NW Portugal
Bragança *92 C2 Eng.* Braganza; *anc.* Julic Briga. Bragança, NE Portugal
Braganza *see* Bragança
Brahestad *see* Raahe
Brahmanbaria *135 G4* Chittagong, E Bangladesh
Brahmapur *135 F5* Orissa, E India
Brahmaputra *135 H3 var.* Padma, Tsangpo, *Ben.* Jamuna, *Chin.* Yarlung Zangbo Jiang, *Ind.* Bramaputra, Dihang, Siang. *river* S Asia
Brăila *108 D4* Brăila, E Romania
Braine-le-Comte *87 B6* Hainaut, SW Belgium
Brainerd *45 F2* Minnesota, N USA
Brak *see* Birāk
Bramaputra *see* Brahmaputra
Brampton *38 D5* Ontario, S Canada
Branco, Rio *56 C3 river* N Brazil
Brandberg *78 A3 mountain* NW Namibia
Brandenburg *94 C3 var.* Brandenburg an der Havel. Brandenburg, NE Germany
Brandenburg an der Havel *see* Brandenburg
Brandon *37 F5* Manitoba, S Canada
Braniewo *98 D2 Ger.* Braunsberg. Warmińsko-mazurskie, N Poland
Brasil *see* Brazil
Brasília *63 F3 country capital* (Brazil) Distrito Federal, C Brazil
Brasil, Repùblica Federativa do *see* Brazil
Braşov *108 C4 Ger.* Kronstadt, *Hung.* Brassó; *prev.* Oraşul Stalin. Braşov, C Romania
Brassó *see* Braşov
Bratislava *99 C6 Ger.* Pressburg, *Hung.* Pozsony. *country capital* (Slovakia) Bratislavský Kraj, W Slovakia
Bratsk *115 E4* Irkutskaya Oblast', C Russian Federation
Brattia *see* Brač
Braunsberg *see* Braniewo
Braunschweig *94 C4 Eng./Fr.* Brunswick. Niedersachsen, N Germany
Brava *see* Baraawe
Brava, Costa *93 H2 coastal region* NE Spain
Bravo del Norte, Río/Bravo, Río *see* Grande, Rio
Bravo, Río *50 C1 river* Mexico/USA North America
Brawley *47 D8* California, W USA
Brazil *62 C2 off.* Federative Republic of Brazil, *Port.* Repùblica Federativa do Brasil, *Sp.* Brasil; *prev.* United States of Brazil. *country* South America

BRAZIL
South America

Official name Federative Republic of Brazil
Formation 1822 / 1828
Capital Brasília
Population 186 million / 57 people per sq mile (22 people per sq km) / 81%
Total area 3,286,470 sq miles (8,511,965 sq km)
Languages Portuguese*, German, Italian, Spanish, Polish, Japanese, Amerindian languages
Religions Roman Catholic 74%, Protestant 15%, Atheist 7%, Other 4%
Ethnic mix Black 53%, Mixed race 40%, White 6%, Other 1%
Government Presidential system
Currency Real = 100 centavos
Literacy rate 88%
Calorie consumption 3049 calories

Brazil Basin *67 C5 var.* Brazilian Basin, Brazil'skaya Kotlovina. *undersea basin* W Atlantic Ocean
Brazil, Federative Republic of *see* Brazil
Brazilian Basin *see* Brazil Basin
Brazilian Highlands *see* Central, Planalto
Brazil'skaya Kotlovina *see* Brazil Basin
Brazil, United States of *see* Brazil
Brazos River *49 G3 river* Texas, SW USA
Brazza *see* Brač

Brazzaville *77 B6 country capital* (Congo) Capital District, S Congo
Brčko *100 C3* Republika Srpska, NE Bosnia and Herzegovina
Brecht *87 C5* Antwerpen, N Belgium
Brecon Beacons *89 C6 mountain range* S Wales, UK
Breda *86 C4* Noord-Brabant, S Netherlands
Bree *87 D5* Limburg, NE Belgium
Bregalnica *101 E6 river* E FYR Macedonia
Bregenz *57 B7 anc.* Brigantium. Vorarlberg, W Austria
Bregovo *104 B1* Vidin, NW Bulgaria
Bremen *94 B3 Fr.* Brême. Bremen, NW Germany
Bremerhaven *94 B3* Bremen, NW Germany
Bremerton *46 B2* Washington, NW USA
Brenham *49 G3* Texas, SW USA
Brenner, Col du/Brennero, Passo del *see* Brenner Pass
Brenner Pass *96 C1 var.* Brenner Sattel, *Fr.* Col du Brenner, *Ger.* Brennerpass, *It.* Passo del Brennero. *pass* Austria/Italy
Brennerpass *see* Brenner Pass
Brenner Sattel *see* Brenner Pass
Brescia *96 B2 anc.* Brixia. Lombardia, N Italy
Breslau *see* Wrocław
Bressanone *96 C1 Ger.* Brixen. Trentino-Alto Adige, N Italy
Brest *107 A6 Pol.* Brześć nad Bugiem, *Rus.* Brest-Litovsk; *prev.* Brześć Litewski. Brestskaya Voblasts', SW Belarus
Brest *90 A3* Finistère, NW France
Brest-Litovsk *see* Brest
Bretagne *90 A3 Eng.* Brittany, *Lat.* Britannia Minor. *region* NW France
Bretagne *90 A3 Eng.* Brittany, *Lat.* Britannia Minor. *cultural region* NW France
Brewster, Kap *see* Kangikajik
Brewton *42 C3* Alabama, S USA
Brezhnev *see* Naberezhnyye Chelny
Brezovo *104 D2 prev.* Abrashlare. Plovdiv, C Bulgaria
Bria *76 D4* Haute-Kotto, C Central African Republic
Briançon *91 D5 anc.* Brigantio. Hautes-Alpes, SE France
Bricgstow *see* Bristol
Bridgeport *41 F3* Connecticut, NE USA
Bridgetown *55 G2 country capital* (Barbados) SW Barbados
Bridlington *89 D5* E England, UK
Bridport *89 D7* S England, UK
Brieg *see* Brzeg
Brig *95 A7 Fr.* Brigue, *It.* Briga. Valais, SW Switzerland
Briga *see* Brig
Brigantio *see* Briançon
Brigantium *see* Bregenz
Brigham City *44 B3* Utah, W USA
Brighton *89 E7* SE England, UK
Brighton *44 D4* Colorado, C USA
Brigue *see* Brig
Brindisi *97 E5 anc.* Brundisium, Brundusium. Puglia, SE Italy
Briovera *see* St-Lô
Brisbane *149 E5 state capital* Queensland, E Australia
Bristol *89 D7 anc.* Bricgstow. SW England, UK
Bristol *41 F3* Connecticut, NE USA
Bristol *40 D5* Tennessee, S USA
Bristol Bay *36 B3 bay* Alaska, USA
Bristol Channel *89 C7 inlet* England/ Wales, UK
Britain *80 C3 var.* Great Britain. *island* UK
Britannia Minor *see* Bretagne
British Columbia *36 D4 Fr.* Colombie-Britannique. *province* SW Canada
British Guiana *see* Guyana
British Honduras *see* Belize
British Indian Ocean Territory *141 B5 UK dependent territory* C Indian Ocean
British Isles *89 island group* NW Europe
British North Borneo *see* Sabah
British Solomon Islands Protectorate *see* Solomon Islands
British Virgin Islands *55 F3 var.* Virgin Islands. *UK dependent territory* E West Indies
Brittany *see* Bretagne
Briva Curretia *see* Brive-la-Gaillarde
Briva Isarae *see* Pontoise
Brive *see* Brive-la-Gaillarde
Brive-la-Gaillarde *91 C5 prev.* Brive; *anc.* Briva Curretia. Corrèze, C France
Brixen *see* Bressanone
Brixia *see* Brescia
Brno *99 B5 Ger.* Brünn. Jihomoravský Kraj, SE Czech Republic
Broceni *106 B3* Saldus, SW Latvia
Brod/Bród *see* Slavonski Brod
Brodeur Peninsula *37 F2 peninsula* Baffin Island, Nunavut, NE Canada
Brod na Savi *see* Slavonski Brod
Brodnica *98 C3 Ger.* Buddenbrock. Kujawski-pomorskie, C Poland
Broek-in-Waterland *86 C3* Noord-Holland, C Netherlands
Broken Arrow *49 G1* Oklahoma, C USA
Broken Bay *148 E1 bay* New South Wales, SE Australia
Broken Hill *149 B6* New South Wales, SE Australia
Broken Ridge *141 D6 undersea plateau* S Indian Ocean
Bromberg *see* Bydgoszcz
Bromley *89 B8* UK
Brookhaven *42 B3* Mississippi, S USA
Brookings *45 F3* South Dakota, N USA
Brooks Range *36 D2 mountain range* Alaska, USA
Brookton *147 B6* Western Australia
Broome *146 B3* Western Australia
Broomfield *44 D4* Colorado, C USA
Broucsella *see* Brussel/Bruxelles
Brovary *109 E2* Kyyivs'ka Oblast', N Ukraine
Brownfield *49 E2* Texas, SW USA
Brownsville *49 G5* Texas, SW USA
Brownwood *49 F3* Texas, SW USA
Brozha *107 D7* Mahilyowskaya Voblasts', E Belarus
Bruges *see* Brugge
Brugge *87 A5 Fr.* Bruges. West-Vlaanderen, NW Belgium
Brummen *86 D3* Gelderland, E Netherlands
Brundisium/Brundusium *see* Brindisi
Brunei *138 D3 off.* Sultanate of Brunei, *Mal.* Negara Brunei Darussalam. *country* SE Asia

BRUNEI
Southeast Asia

Official name Sultanate of Brunei
Formation 1984 / 1984
Capital Bandar Seri Begawan
Population 374,000 / 184 people per sq mile (71 people per sq km) / 72%
Total area 2228 sq miles (5770 sq km)
Languages Malay*, English, Chinese
Religions Muslim (mainly Sunni) 66%, Buddhist 14%, Other 10%, Christian 10%
Ethnic mix Malay 67%, Chinese 16%, Other 11%, Indigenous 6%
Government Monarchy
Currency Brunei dollar = 100 cents
Literacy rate 93%
Calorie consumption 2855 calories

Brunei, Sultanate of *see* Brunei
Brunei Town *see* Bandar Seri Begawan
Brünn *see* Brno
Brunner, Lake *151 C5 lake* South Island, New Zealand
Brunswick *43 E3* Georgia, SE USA
Brunswick *see* Braunschweig
Brusa *see* Bursa
Brus Laguna *52 D2* Gracias a Dios, E Honduras
Brussa *see* Bursa
Brussel *87 C6 var.* Brussels, *Fr.* Bruxelles, *Ger.* Brüssel; *anc.* Broucsella. *country capital* (Belgium) Brussels, C Belgium
Brüssel/Brussels *see* Brussel/Bruxelles
Brussels Brussel/Bruxelles
Brüx *see* Most
Bruxelles *see* Brussel
Bryan *49 G3* Texas, SW USA
Bryansk *111 A5* Bryanskaya Oblast', W Russian Federation
Brzeg *98 C4 Ger.* Brieg; *anc.* Civitas Altae Ripae. Opolskie, S Poland
Brześć Litewski/Brześć nad Bugiem *see* Brest
Brzeżany *see* Berezhany
Bucaramanga *58 B2* Santander, N Colombia
Buchanan *74 C5 prev.* Grand Bassa. SW Liberia
Buchanan, Lake *49 F3 reservoir* Texas, SW USA
Bucharest *see* București
Buckeye State *see* Ohio
Bu Craa *see* Bou Craa
București *108 C5 Eng.* Bucharest, *Ger.* Bukarest, *prev.* Altenburg; *anc.* Cetatea Damboviței. *country capital* (Romania) București, S Romania
Buda-Kashalyova *107 D7 Rus.* Buda-Koshelëvo. Homyel'skaya Voblasts', SE Belarus
Buda-Koshelëvo *see* Buda-Kashalyova
Budapest *99 C6 off.* Budapest Főváros, *SCr.* Budimpešta. *country capital* (Hungary) Pest, N Hungary
Budapest Főváros *see* Budapest
Budaun *134 D3* Uttar Pradesh, N India
Buddenbrock *see* Brodnica
Budimpešta *see* Budapest
Budweis *see* České Budějovice
Budyšin *see* Bautzen
Buena Park *46 E2* California, W USA North America
Buenaventura *58 A3* Valle del Cauca, W Colombia
Buena Vista *61 G4* Santa Cruz, C Bolivia
Buena Vista *93 H5* S Gibraltar Europe
Buenavista *93 H5* Baja California Sur, W Mexico
Buenavista *93 H5* Sonora, NW Mexico North America
Buena Vista *93 H5* Cerro Largo, Uruguay
Buena Vista *93 H5* Colorado, C USA
Buena Vista *93 H5* Georgia, SE USA
Buena Vista *93 H5* Virginia, NE USA
Buenos Aires *64 D4 hist.* Santa Maria del Buen Aire. *country capital* (Argentina) Buenos Aires, E Argentina
Buenos Aires *53 E5* Puntarenas, SE Costa Rica
Buenos Aires, Lago *65 B6 var.* Lago General Carrera. *lake* Argentina/Chile
Buffalo *41 E3* New York, NE USA
Buffalo Narrows *37 F4* Saskatchewan, C Canada
Buff Bay *54 B5* E Jamaica
Buftea *108 C5* Ilfov, S Romania
Bug *81 E3 Bel.* Zakhodni Buh, *Eng.* Western Bug, *Rus.* Zapadnyy Bug, *Ukr.* Zakhidnyy Buh. *river* E Europe
Buga *58 B3* Valle del Cauca, W Colombia
Bughotu *see* Santa Isabel
Buguruslan *111 D6* Orenburgskaya Oblast', W Russian Federation
Buitenzorg *see* Bogor
Bujalance *92 D4* Andalucía, S Spain
Bujanovac *101 E5* Kosovo, SE Serbia
Bujnurd *see* Bojnūrd
Bujumbura *73 B7 prev.* Usumbura. *country capital* (Burundi) W Burundi
Bukarest *see* București
Bukavu *77 E6 prev.* Costermansville. Sud Kivu, E Dem. Rep. Congo
Bukhara *see* Buxoro
Bukoba *73 B6* Kagera, NW Tanzania
Bülach *95 B7* Zürich, NW Switzerland
Bulawayo *78 D3* Matabeleland North, SW Zimbabwe
Bulgan *127 E2* Bulgan, N Mongolia
Bulgaria *104 C2 off.* Republic of Bulgaria, *Bul.* Bŭlgariya; *prev.* People's Republic of Bulgaria. *country* SE Europe
Bulgaria, People's Republic of *see* Bulgaria

BULGARIA
Southeast Europe

Official name Republic of Bulgaria
Formation 1908 / 1947
Capital Sofia
Population 7.7 million / 180 people per sq mile (70 people per sq km) / 70%
Total area 42,822 sq miles (110,910 sq km)

BULGARIA
(continued)

Languages Bulgarian*, Turkish, Romani
Religions Orthodox Christian 83%, Muslim 12%, Other 4%, Roman Catholic 1%
Ethnic mix Bulgarian 84%, Turkish 9%, Roma 5%, Other 2%
Government Parliamentary system
Currency Lev = 100 stotinki
Literacy rate 98%
Calorie consumption 2848 calories

Bulgaria, Republic of *see* Bulgaria
Bŭlgariya *see* Bulgaria
Bullion State *see* Missouri
Bull Shoals Lake *42 B1 reservoir* Arkansas/Missouri, C USA
Bulukumba *139 E4 prev.* Boeloekoemba. Sulawesi, C Indonesia
Bumba *77 D5* Equateur, N Dem. Rep. Congo
Bunbury *147 A7* Western Australia
Bundaberg *148 E4* Queensland, E Australia
Bungo-suidō *131 B7 strait* SW Japan
Bunia *77 E5* Orientale, NE Dem. Rep. Congo
Bünyan *116 D3* Kayseri, C Turkey
Buraida *see* Buraydah
Buraydah *120 B4 var.* Buraida. Al Qaṣīm, N Saudi Arabia
Burdigala *see* Bordeaux
Burdur *116 B4 var.* Buldur. Burdur, SW Turkey
Burdur Gölü *116 B4 salt lake* SW Turkey
Burē *72 C4* Amhara, N Ethiopia
Burgas *104 E2 var.* Bourgas. Burgas, E Bulgaria
Burgaski Zaliv *104 E2 gulf* E Bulgaria
Burgos *92 D2* Castilla-León, N Spain
Burgundy *see* Bourgogne
Burhan Budai Shan *126 D4 mountain range* C China
Buriram *137 D5 var.* Buri Ram, Puriramya. Buri Ram, E Thailand
Buri Ram *see* Buriram
Burjassot *93 F3* País Valenciano, E Spain
Burkburnett *49 F2* Texas, SW USA
Burketown *148 B3* Queensland, NE Australia
Burkina *see* Burkina Faso
Burkina Faso *75 E4 var.* Burkina; *prev.* Upper Volta. *country* W Africa

BURKINA FASO
West Africa

Official name Burkina Faso
Formation 1960 / 1960
Capital Ouagadougou
Population 13.2 million / 125 people per sq mile (48 people per sq km) / 19%
Total area 105,869 sq miles (274,200 sq km)
Languages French*, Mossi, Fulani, Tuareg, Dyula, Songhai
Religions Muslim 55%, Traditional beliefs 35%, Roman Catholic 9%, Other Christian 1%
Ethnic mix Other 50%, Mossi 50%
Government Presidential system
Currency CFA franc = 100 centimes
Literacy rate 13%
Calorie consumption 2462 calories

Burley *46 D4* Idaho, NW USA
Burlington *45 G4* Iowa, C USA
Burlington *41 F2* Vermont, NE USA
Burma *see* Myanmar
Burnie *149 C8* Tasmania, SE Australia
Burns *46 C3* Oregon, NW USA
Burnside *37 F3 river* Nunavut, NW Canada
Burnsville *45 F2* Minnesota, N USA
Burrel *101 D6 var.* Burreli. Dibër, C Albania
Burreli *see* Burrel
Burriana *93 F3* País Valenciano, E Spain
Bursa *116 B3 var.* Brussa, *prev.* Brusa; *anc.* Prusa. Bursa, NW Turkey

Būr Sa'īd *see* Port Said
Burtnieks *106 C3 var.* Burtnieks Ezers. *lake* N Latvia
Burtnieks Ezers *see* Burtnieks
Burundi *73 B7 off.* Republic of Burundi; *prev.* Kingdom of Burundi, Urundi. *country* C Africa

BURUNDI
Central Africa

Official name Republic of Burundi
Formation 1962 / 1962
Capital Bujumbura
Population 7.5 million / 757 people per sq mile (292 people per sq km) / 9%
Total area 10,745 sq miles (27,830 sq km)
Languages Kirundi*, French*, Kiswahili
Religions Christian 60%, Traditional beliefs 39%, Muslim 1%
Ethnic mix Hutu 85%, Tutsi 14%, Twa 1%
Government Presidential system
Currency Burundi franc = 100 centimes
Literacy rate 59%
Calorie consumption 1649 calories

Burundi, Kingdom of *see* Burundi
Burundi, Republic of *see* Burundi
Buru, Pulau *139 F4 prev.* Boeroe. *island* E Indonesia
Busan *see* Pusan
Buşayrah *118 D3* Dayr az Zawr, E Syria
Būshehr/Bushire *see* Bandar-e Būshehr
Busra *see* Al Başrah, Iraq
Busselton *147 A7* Western Australia
Bussora *see* Al Başrah
Buta *77 D5* Orientale, N Dem. Rep. Congo
Butembo *77 E5* Nord Kivu, NE Dem. Rep. Congo
Butler *41 E4* Pennsylvania, NE USA
Buton, Pulau *139 E4 var.* Pulau Butung; *prev.* Boetoeng. *island* C Indonesia
Bütow *see* Bytów
Butte *44 B2* Montana, NW USA
Butterworth *138 B3* Pinang, Peninsular Malaysia
Button Islands *39 E1 island group* Nunavut, NE Canada
Butuan *139 F2 off.* Butuan City. Mindanao, S Philippines
Butuan City *see* Butuan
Butung, Pulau *see* Buton, Pulau
Butuntum *see* Bitonto
Buulobarde *73 D5 var.* Buulo Berde. Hiiraan, C Somalia Africa
Buulo Berde *see* Buulobarde
Buur Gaabo *73 D6* Jubbada Hoose, S Somalia
Buxoro *122 D2 var.* Bokhara, *Rus.* Bukhara. Buxoro Viloyati, C Uzbekistan
Buynaksk *111 B8* Respublika Dagestan, SW Russian Federation
Büyükağrı Dağı *117 F3 var.* Aghri Dagh, Agri Dagi, Koh I Noh, Masis, *Eng.* Great Ararat, Mount Ararat. *mountain* E Turkey
Büyükmenderes Nehri *116 A4 river* SW Turkey
Buzău *108 C4* Buzău, SE Romania
Buzuluk *111 D6* Akmola, C Kazakhstan
Byahoml' *107 D5 Rus.* Begoml'. Vitsyebskaya Voblasts', N Belarus
Byalynichy *107 D6 Rus.* Belynichi. Mahilyowskaya Voblasts', E Belarus
Byan Tumen *see* Choybalsan
Bydgoszcz *98 C3 Ger.* Bromberg. Kujawski-pomorskie, C Poland
Byelaruskaya Hrada *107 B6 Rus.* Belorusskaya Gryada. *ridge* N Belarus
Byerezino *107 D6 Rus.* Berezina. *river* C Belarus
Byron Island *see* Nikunau
Bystrovka *see* Kemin
Bytča *99 C5* Žilinský Kraj, N Slovakia
Bytom *99 C5 Ger.* Beuthen. Śląskie, S Poland
Bytów *98 C2 Ger.* Bütow. Pomorskie, N Poland
Byuzmeyin *see* Abadan
Byval'ki *107 D8* Homyel'skaya Voblasts', SE Belarus
Byzantium *see* İstanbul

C

Caála *78 B2 var.* Kaala, Robert Williams, *Port.* Vila Robert Williams. Huambo, C Angola
Caazapá *64 D3* Caazapá, S Paraguay
Caballo Reservoir *48 C3 reservoir* New Mexico, SW USA
Cabañaquinta *92 D1* Asturias, N Spain
Cabanatuan *139 E1 off.* Cabanatuan City. Luzon, N Philippines
Cabanatuan City *see* Cabanatuan
Cabillonum *see* Chalon-sur-Saône
Cabimas *58 C1* Zulia, NW Venezuela
Cabinda *78 A1 var.* Kabinda. Cabinda, NW Angola
Cabinda *78 A1 var.* Kabinda. *province* NW Angola
Cabora Bassa, Lake *see* Cahora Bassa, Albufeira de
Caborca *50 B1* Sonora, NW Mexico
Cabot Strait *39 G4 strait* E Canada
Cabo Verde, Ilhas do *see* Cape Verde
Cabras, Ilha das *76 E2 island* S Sao Tome and Principe, Africa, E Atlantic Ocean
Cabrera *93 G3 river* NW Spain
Cabrera, Illa de *93 G4 island* Islas Baleares, Spain, W Mediterranean Sea
Cáceres *92 C3 Ar.* Qazris. Extremadura, W Spain
Cachimbo, Serra do *63 E2 mountain range* C Brazil
Caconda *78 B2* Huíla, C Angola
Čadca *99 C5 Hung.* Csaca. Žilinský Kraj, N Slovakia
Cadillac *40 C2* Michigan, N USA
Cadiz *139 E2 off.* Cadiz City. Negros, C Philippines
Cádiz *92 C5 anc.* Gades, Gadier, Gadir, Gadire. Andalucía, SW Spain
Cadiz City *see* Cadiz
Cádiz, Golfo de *92 B5 Eng.* Gulf of Cadiz. *gulf* Portugal/Spain
Cadiz, Gulf of *see* Cádiz, Golfo de
Cadurcum *see* Cahors
Caen *90 B3* Calvados, N France
Caene/Caenepolis *see* Qena
Caerdydd *see* Cardiff
Caer Glou *see* Gloucester
Caer Gybi *see* Holyhead
Caerleon *see* Chester
Caer Luel *see* Carlisle
Caesaraugusta *see* Zaragoza
Caesarea Mazaca *see* Kayseri
Caesarobriga *see* Talavera de la Reina
Caesarodunum *see* Tours
Caesaromagus *see* Beauvais
Caesena *see* Cesena
Cafayate *64 C2* Salta, N Argentina
Cagayan de Oro *139 E2 off.* Cagayan de Oro City. Mindanao, S Philippines
Cagayan de Oro City *see* Cagayan de Oro
Cagliari *97 A6 anc.* Caralis. Sardegna, Italy, C Mediterranean Sea
Caguas *55 F3* E Puerto Rico
Cahora Bassa, Albufeira de *78 D2 var.* Lake Cabora Bassa. *reservoir* NW Mozambique
Cahors *91 C5 anc.* Cadurcum. Lot, S France
Cahul *108 D4 Rus.* Kagul. S Moldova
Caicos Passage *54 D2 strait* Bahamas/ Turks and Caicos Islands
Caiffa *see* Hefa
Cailungo *96 E1* N San Marino
Caiphas *see* Hefa
Cairns *148 D3* Queensland, NE Australia
Cairo *72 B2 Ar.* Al Qāhirah, *var.* El Qâhira. *country capital* (Egypt) N Egypt
Caisleán an Bharraigh *see* Castlebar
Cajamarca *60 B3 prev.* Caxamarca. Cajamarca, NW Peru
Čakovec *100 B2 Ger.* Csakathurn, *Hung.* Csáktornya; *prev. Ger.* Tschakathurn. Medimurje, N Croatia
Calabar *75 G5* Cross River, S Nigeria
Calabozo *58 D2* Guárico, C Venezuela
Calafat *108 B5* Dolj, SW Romania
Calafate *see* El Calafate
Calahorra *93 E2* La Rioja, N Spain
Calais *90 C2* Pas-de-Calais, N France
Calais *41 H2* Maine, NE USA
Calais, Pas de *see* Dover, Strait of
Calama *64 B2* Antofagasta, N Chile
Calamianes *see* Calamian Group
Calamian Group *129 C7 var.* Calamianes. *island group* W Philippines
Călăras *see* Călăraşi
Călăraşi *108 D3 var.* Călăras, *Rus.* Kalarash. C Moldova
Călăraşi *108 C5* Călăraşi, SE Romania
Calatayud *93 E2* Aragón, NE Spain
Calbayog *139 E2 off.* Calbayog City. Samar, C Philippines
Calbayog City *see* Calbayog
Calcutta *see* Kolkata
Caldas da Rainha *92 B3* Leiria, W Portugal
Caldera *64 B3* Atacama, N Chile
Caldwell *46 C3* Idaho, NW USA
Caledonia *52 C1* Corozal, N Belize
Caleta Olivia *65 B6* Santa Cruz, SE Argentina
Calgary *37 E5* Alberta, SW Canada
Cali *58 B3* Valle del Cauca, W Colombia
Calicut *132 C2 var.* Kozhikode. Kerala, SW India
California *47 B7 off.* State of California, *also known as* El Dorado, The Golden State. *state* W USA
California, Golfo de *50 B2 Eng.* Gulf of California; *prev.* Sea of Cortez. *gulf* W Mexico
California, Gulf of *see* California, Golfo de
Călimăneşti *108 B4* Vâlcea, SW Romania
Calisia *see* Kalisz
Callabonna, Lake *149 B5 lake* South Australia
Callao *60 C4* Callao, W Peru
Callatis *see* Mangalia
Callosa de Segura *93 F4* País Valenciano, E Spain
Calmar *see* Kalmar
Caloundra *149 E5* Queensland, E Australia
Caltanissetta *97 C7* Sicilia, Italy, C Mediterranean Sea
Caluula *72 E4* Bari, NE Somalia
Camabatela *78 B1* Cuanza Norte, NW Angola
Camacupa *78 B2 var.* General Machado, *Port.* Vila General Machado. Bié, C Angola
Camagüey *54 C2 prev.* Puerto Príncipe. Camagüey, C Cuba
Camagüey, Archipiélago de *54 C2 island group* C Cuba
Camana *61 E4 var.* Camaná. Arequipa, SW Peru
Camargue *91 D6 physical region* SE France
Ca Mau *137 D6 var.* Quan Long. Minh Hai, S Vietnam
Cambay, Gulf of *see* Khambhāt, Gulf of
Camberia *see* Chambéry
Cambodia *137 D5 off.* Kingdom of Cambodia, *var.* Democratic Kampuchea, Roat Kampuchea, *Cam.* Kampuchea; *prev.* People's Democratic Republic of Kampuchea. *country* SE Asia

CAMBODIA
Southeast Asia

Official name Kingdom of Cambodia
Formation 1953 / 1953
Capital Phnom Penh
Population 14.1 million / 207 people per sq mile (80 people per sq km) / 16%
Total area 69,900 sq miles (181,040 sq km)
Languages Khmer*, French, Chinese, Vietnamese, Cham
Religions Buddhist 93%, Muslim 6%, Christian 1%
Ethnic mix Khmer 90%, Other 5%, Vietnamese 4%, Chinese 1%
Government Parliamentary system
Currency Riel = 100 sen
Literacy rate 74%
Calorie consumption 2046 calories

Cambodia, Kingdom of *see* Cambodia
Cambrai *90 C2 Flem.* Kambryk, *prev.* Cambray; *anc.* Cameracum. Nord, N France
Cambray *see* Cambrai
Cambrian Mountains *89 C6 mountain range* C Wales, UK
Cambridge *54 A4* W Jamaica
Cambridge *150 D3* Waikato, North Island, New Zealand
Cambridge *89 E6 Lat.* Cantabrigia. E England, UK
Cambridge *41 F4* Maryland, NE USA
Cambridge *40 D4* Ohio, NE USA
Cambridge Bay *37 F3* Victoria Island, Nunavut, NW Canada
Camden *42 B2* Arkansas, C USA
Camellia State *see* Alabama
Cameracum *see* Cambrai
Cameroon *76 A4 off.* Republic of Cameroon, *Fr.* Cameroun. *country* W Africa

CAMEROON
Central Africa

Official name Republic of Cameroon
Formation 1960 / 1961
Capital Yaoundé
Population 16.3 million / 907 people per sq mile (350 people per sq km) / 49%
Total area 183,567 sq miles (475,400 sq km)
Languages English*, French*, Bamileke, Fang, Fulani
Religions Roman Catholic 35%, Traditional beliefs 25%, Muslim 22%, Protestant 18%
Ethnic mix Cameroon highlanders 31%, Other 21%, Equatorial Bantu 19%, Kirdi 11%, Fulani 10%, Northwestern Bantu 8%
Government Presidential system
Currency CFA franc = 100 centimes
Literacy rate 68%
Calorie consumption 2273 calories

Cameroon, Republic of *see* Cameroon
Cameroun *see* Cameroon
Camocim *63 F2* Ceará, E Brazil
Camopi *59 H3* E French Guiana
Campamento *52 C2* Olancho, C Hondura
Campania *97 D5 Eng.* Champagne. *region* S Italy
Campbell, Cape *151 D5 headland* South Island, New Zealand
Campbell Island *142 D5 island* S New Zealand
Campbell Plateau *142 D5 undersea plateau* SW Pacific Ocean
Campbell River *36 D5* Vancouver Island, British Columbia, SW Canada
Campeche *51 G4* Campeche, SE Mexico
Campeche, Bahía de *51 F4 Eng.* Bay of Campeche. *bay* E Mexico
Campeche, Bay of *see* Campeche, Bahía de
Câm Pha *136 E3* Quang Ninh, N Vietnam
Câmpina *108 C4 prev.* Cîmpina. Prahova, SE Romania
Campina Grande *63 G2* Paraíba, E Brazil
Campinas *63 F4* São Paulo, S Brazil
Campobasso *97 D5* Molise, C Italy
Campo Criptana *see* Campo de Criptana
Campo de Criptana *93 E3 var.* Campo Criptana. Castilla-La Mancha, C Spain
Campo dos Goitacazes *see* Campos
Campo Grande *63 E4 state capital* Mato Grosso do Sul, SW Brazil
Campos *63 F4 var.* Campo dos Goitacazes. Rio de Janeiro, SE Brazil
Câmpulung *108 B4 prev.* Câmpulung-Muşcel, Cîmpulung. Argeş, S Romani
Câmpulung-Muşcel *see* Câmpulung
Campus Stellae *see* Santiago
Cam Ranh *137 E6* Khanh Hoa, S Vietnam
Canada *34 B4 country* N North America

CANADA
North America

Official name Canada
Formation 1867 / 1949
Capital Ottawa
Population 32.3 million / 9 people per sq mile (4 people per sq km) / 77%
Total area 3,854,085 sq miles (9,984,670 sq km)
Languages English*, French*, Chinese, Italian, German, Ukrainian, Inuktitut, Cre
Religions Roman Catholic 44%, Canada Protestant 29%, Other and nonreligious 27%

CANADA
(continued)

Ethnic mix British origin 44%, French origin 25%, Other European 20%, Other 11%.
Government Parliamentary system
Currency Canadian dollar = 100 cents
Literacy rate 99%
Calorie consumption 3589 calories

Canada Basin *34 C2 undersea basin* Arctic Ocean
Canadian River *49 E2 river* SW USA
Çanakkale *116 A3 var.* Dardanelli; *prev.* Chanak, Kale Sultanie. Çanakkale, W Turkey
Çanakkale Boğazı *116 A2 Eng.* Dardanelles. *strait* NW Turkey
Cananea *50 B1* Sonora, NW Mexico
Canarias, Islas *70 A2 Eng.* Canary Islands. *island group* Islas Canarias, SW Spain Europe E Atlantic Ocean
Canarreos, Archipiélago de los *54 B2 island group* W Cuba
Canary Islands *see* Canarias, Islas
Cañas *52 D4* Guanacaste, NW Costa Rica
Canaveral, Cape *43 E4 headland* Florida, SE USA
Canavieiras *63 G3* Bahia, E Brazil
Canberra *142 C4 country capital* (Australia) Australian Capital Territory, SE Australia
Cancún *51 H3* Quintana Roo, SE Mexico
Candia *see* Irákleio
Canea *see* Chaniá
Cangzhou *128 D4* Hebei, E China
Caniapiscau *39 E2 river* Québec, E Canada
Caniapiscau, Réservoir de *38 D3 reservoir* Québec, C Canada
Canik Dağları *116 D2 mountain range* N Turkey
Canillo *91 A7* Canillo, C Andorra Europe
Çankırı *116 C3 var.* Chankiri; *anc.* Gangra, Germanicopolis. Çankın, N Turkey
Cannanore *132 B2 var.* Kananur, Kannur. Kerala, SW India
Cannes *91 D6* Alpes-Maritimes, SE France
Canoas *63 E5* Rio Grande do Sul, S Brazil
Canon City *44 C5* Colorado, C USA
Cantabria *92 D1 autonomous community* N Spain
Cantábrica, Cordillera *92 C1 mountain range* N Spain
Cantabrigia *see* Cambridge
Cantaura *59 E2* Anzoátegui, NE Venezuela
Canterbury *89 E7 hist.* Cantwaraburh; *anc.* Durovernum, *Lat.* Cantuaria. SE England, UK
Canterbury Bight *151 C6 bight* South Island, New Zealand
Canterbury Plains *151 C6 plain* South Island, New Zealand
Cân Thơ *137 E6* Cân Thơ, S Vietnam
Canton *42 B2* Mississippi, S USA
Canton *40 D4* Ohio, N USA
Canton *see* Guangzhou
Canton Island *see* Kanton
Cantuaria/Cantwaraburh *see* Canterbury
Canyon *49 E2* Texas, SW USA
Cao Băng *136 D3 var.* Caobang. Cao Băng, N Vietnam
Caobang *see* Cao Băng
Cap-Breton, Île du *see* Cape Breton Island
Cape Barren Island *149 C8 island* Furneaux Group, Tasmania, SE Australia
Cape Basin *69 B7 undersea basin* S Atlantic Ocean
Cape Breton Island *39 G4 Fr.* Île du Cap-Breton. *island* Nova Scotia, SE Canada
Cape Charles *41 F5* Virginia, NE USA
Cape Coast *75 E5 prev.* Cape Coast Castle. S Ghana
Cape Coast Castle *see* Cape Coast
Cape Girardeau *45 H5* Missouri, C USA
Capelle aan den IJssel *86 C4* Zuid-Holland, SW Netherlands
Cape Palmas *see* Harper
Cape Saint Jacques *see* Vung Tau
Cape Town *78 B5 var.* Ekapa, *Afr.* Kaapstad, Kapstad. *country capital* (South Africa-legislative capital) Western Cape, SW South Africa
Cape Verde *74 A2 off.* Republic of Cape Verde, *Port.* Cabo Verde, Ilhas do Cabo Verde. *country* E Atlantic Ocean

CAPE VERDE
Atlantic Ocean

Official name Republic of Cape Verde
Formation 1975
Capital Praia
Population 507,000 / 326 people per sq mile (126 people per sq km) / 62%
Total area 1557 sq miles (4033 sq km)
Languages Portuguese*, Portuguese Creole
Religions Roman Catholic 97%, Other 2%, Protestant (Church of the Nazarene) 1%
Ethnic mix Mestiço 60%, African 30%, Other 10%
Government Mixed presidential–parliamentary system
Currency Cape Verde escudo = 100 centavos
Literacy rate 76%
Calorie consumption 3243 calories

Cape Verde Basin *66 C4 undersea basin* E Atlantic Ocean
Cape Verde Plain *66 C4 abyssal plain* E Atlantic Ocean
Cape Verde, Republic of *see* Cape Verde
Cape York Peninsula *148 C2 peninsula* Queensland, N Australia
Cap-Haïtien *54 D3 var.* Le Cap. N Haiti
Capira *53 G5* Panamá, C Panama
Capitán Arturo Prat *154 A2 Chilean research station* South Shetland Islands, Antarctica
Capitán Pablo Lagerenza *64 D1 var.* Mayor Pablo Lagerenza. Chaco, N Paraguay
Capodistria *see* Koper
Capri, Isola di *97 C5 island* S Italy
Caprivi Concession *see* Caprivi Strip
Caprivi Strip *78 C3 Ger.* Caprivizipfel; *prev.* Caprivi Concession. *cultural region* NE Namibia
Caprivizipfel *see* Caprivi Strip
Cap Saint-Jacques *see* Vung Tau
Caquetá *56 B3 off.* Departamanto del Caquetá. *province* S Colombia
Caquetá, Departamanto del *see* Caquetá
Caquetá, Río *58 C5 var.* Rio Japurá, Yapurá. *river* Brazil/Colombia
Caquetá, Río *see* Japurá, Rio
CAR *see* Central African Republic
Caracal *108 B5* Olt, S Romania
Caracaraí *62 D1* Rondônia, W Brazil
Caracas *58 D1 country capital* (Venezuela) Distrito Federal, N Venezuela
Caralis *see* Cagliari
Caratasca, Laguna de *53 E2 lagoon* NE Honduras
Carballiño *see* O Carballiño
Carbondale *40 B5* Illinois, N USA
Carbonia *97 A6 var.* Carbonia Centro. Sardegna, Italy, C Mediterranean Sea
Carbonia Centro *see* Carbonia
Carcaso *see* Carcassonne
Carcassonne *91 C6 anc.* Carcaso. Aude, S France
Cardamomes, Chaîne des *see* Krâvanh, Chuŏr Phnum
Cardamom Mountains *see* Krâvanh, Chuŏr Phnum
Cárdenas *54 B2* Matanzas, W Cuba
Cardiff *89 C7 Wel.* Caerdydd. *national capital* S Wales, UK
Cardigan Bay *89 C6 bay* W Wales, UK
Carei *108 B3 Ger.* Gross-Karol, Karol, *Hung.* Nagykároly; *prev.* Careii-Mari. Satu Mare, NW Romania
Careii-Mari *see* Carei
Carey, Lake *147 B6 lake* Western Australia
Cariaco *59 E1* Sucre, NE Venezuela
Caribbean Sea *54 C4 sea* W Atlantic Ocean
Caribrod *see* Dimitrovgrad
Carlisle *88 C4 anc.* Caer Luel, Luguvallium, Luguvallum. NW England, UK
Carlow *89 B6 Ir.* Ceatharlach. SE Ireland
Carlsbad *48 D3* New Mexico, SW USA
Carlsbad *see* Karlovy Vary
Carlsberg Ridge *140 B4 undersea ridge* S Arabian Sea
Carlsruhe *see* Karlsruhe
Carmana/Carmania *see* Kermān
Carmarthen *89 C6* SW Wales, UK
Carmaux *91 C6* Tarn, S France
Carmel *40 C4* Indiana, N USA
Carmelita *52 B1* Petén, N Guatemala
Carmen *51 G4 var.* Ciudad del Carmen. Campeche, SE Mexico
Carmona *92 C4* Andalucía, S Spain
Carmona *see* Uíge
Carnaro *see* Kvarner
Carnarvon *147 A5* Western Australia
Carnegie, Lake *147 B5 salt lake* Western Australia
Car Nicobar *133 F3 island* Nicobar Islands, India, NE Indian Ocean
Caroąo, Ilha *76 E1 island* N Sao Tome and Principe, Africa, E Atlantic Ocean
Carolina *63 F2* Maranhão, E Brazil
Caroline Island *see* Millennium Island
Caroline Islands *106 C2 island group* C Micronesia
Carolopois *see* Châlons-en-Champagne
Caroní, Río *59 E3 river* E Venezuela
Caronium *see* A Coruña
Carora *58 C1* Lara, N Venezuela
Carpathian Mountains *81 E4 var.* Carpathians, *Cz./Pol.* Karpaty, *Ger.* Karpaten. *mountain range* E Europe
Carpathians *see* Carpathian Mountains
Carpathos/Carpathus *see* Kárpathos
Carpații Meridionali *108 B4 var.* Alpi Transilvaniei, Carpații Sudici, *Eng.* South Carpathians, Transylvanian Alps, *Ger.* Südkarpaten, Transsylvanische Alpen, *Hung.* Déli-Kárpátok, Erdélyi-Havasok. *mountain range* C Romania
Carpații Occidentali *99 E7 mountain range* W Romania Europe
Carpații Sudici *see* Carpații Meridionali
Carpentaria, Gulf of *148 B2 gulf* N Australia
Carpi *96 C2* Emilia-Romagna, N Italy
Carrara *96 B3* Toscana, C Italy
Carson City *47 C5 state capital* Nevada, W USA
Carson Sink *47 C5 salt flat* Nevada, W USA
Carstensz, Puntjak *see* Jaya, Puncak
Cartagena *58 B1 var.* Cartagena de los Indes. Bolívar, NW Colombia
Cartagena *93 F4 anc.* Carthago Nova. Murcia, SE Spain
Cartagena de los Indes *see* Cartagena
Cartago *53 E4* Cartago, C Costa Rica
Carthage *45 F5* Missouri, C USA
Carthago Nova *see* Cartagena
Cartwright *39 F2* Newfoundland and Labrador, E Canada
Carúpano *59 E1* Sucre, NE Venezuela
Carusbur *see* Cherbourg
Caruthersville *45 H5* Missouri, C USA
Cary *43 F1* North Carolina, SE USA
Casablanca *70 C2 Ar.* Dar-el-Beida. NW Morocco
Casa Grande *48 B2* Arizona, SW USA
Cascade Range *46 B3 mountain range* Oregon/Washington, NW USA
Cascadia Basin *34 A4 undersea basin* NE Pacific Ocean
Cascais *92 B4* Lisboa, C Portugal
Caserta *97 D5* Campania, S Italy
Casey *154 D4 Australian research station* Antarctica
Casino *91 C8* New South Wales, SE Australia
Čáslav *99 B5 Ger.* Tschaslau. Střední Čechy, C Czech Republic
Casper *44 C3* Wyoming, C USA
Caspian Depression *111 B7 Kaz.* Kaspīy Mangy Oypaty, *Rus.* Prikaspiyskaya Nizmennost'. *depression* Kazakhstan/Russian Federation
Caspian Sea *114 A4 Az.* Xäzär Dänizi, *Kaz.* Kaspiy Tengizi, *Per.* Baḩr-e Khazar, Daryā-ye Khazar, *Rus.* Kaspiyskoye More. *inland sea* Asia/Europe
Cassai *see* Kasai
Cassel *see* Kassel
Castamoni *see* Kastamonu
Casteggio *96 B2* Lombardia, N Italy
Castelló de la Plana *see* Castellón de la Plana
Castellón *see* Castellón de la Plana
Castellón de la Plana *93 F3 Cat.* Castelló de la Plana, Castellón. País Valenciano, E Spain
Castelnaudary *91 C6* Aude, S France
Castelo Branco *92 C3* Castelo Branco, C Portugal
Castelsarrasin *91 B6* Tarn-et-Garonne, S France
Castelvetrano *97 C7* Sicilia, Italy, C Mediterranean Sea
Castilla-La Mancha *93 E3 autonomous community* NE Spain
Castilla-León *92 C2 var.* Castillia y Leon. *autonomous community* NW Spain
Castillia y Leon *see* Castilla-León
Castlebar *89 A5 Ir.* Caisleán an Bharraigh. W Ireland
Castleford *89 D5* N England, UK
Castle Harbour *42 B5 inlet* Bermuda, NW Atlantic Ocean
Castra Regina *see* Regensburg
Castricum *86 C3* Noord-Holland, W Netherlands
Castries *55 F1 country capital* (Saint Lucia) N Saint Lucia
Castro *65 B6* Los Lagos, W Chile
Castrovillari *97 D6* Calabria, SW Italy
Castuera *92 D4* Extremadura, W Spain
Caswell Sound *151 A7 sound* South Island, New Zealand
Catacamas *52 D2* Olancho, C Honduras
Catacaos *60 B3* Piura, NW Peru
Catalan Bay *93 H4 bay* E Gibraltar Europe Mediterranean Sea Atlantic Ocean
Cataluña *93 G2 cultural region* N Spain Europe
Catamarca *see* San Fernando del Valle de Catamarca
Catania *97 D7* Sicilia, Italy, C Mediterranean Sea
Catanzaro *97 D6* Calabria, SW Italy
Catarroja *93 F3* País Valenciano, E Spain
Cat Island *54 C1 island* C Bahamas
Catskill Mountains *41 F3 mountain range* New York, NE USA
Cattaro *see* Kotor
Cauca, Río *58 B2 river* N Colombia
Caucasia *58 B2* Antioquia, NW Colombia
Caucasus *81 G4 Rus.* Kavkaz. *mountain range* Georgia/Russian Federation
Caura, Río *59 E3 river* C Venezuela
Cavaia *see* Kavajë
Cavalla *74 D5 var.* Cavally, Cavally Fleuve. *river* Côte d'Ivoire (Ivory Coast)/Liberia
Cavally/Cavally Fleuve *see* Cavalla
Caviana de Fora, Ilha *63 E1 var.* Ilha Caviana. *island* N Brazil
Caviana, Ilha *see* Caviana de Fora, Ilha
Cawnpore *see* Kānpur
Caxamarca *see* Cajamarca
Caxito *78 B1* Bengo, NW Angola
Cayenne *59 H3 dependent territory/arrondissement capital* (French Guiana) NE French Guiana
Cayes *54 D3 var.* Les Cayes. SW Haiti
Cayman Brac *54 B3 island* E Cayman Islands
Cayman Islands *54 B3 UK dependent territory* W West Indies
Cayo *see* San Ignacio
Cay Sal *54 B2 islet* SW Bahamas
Cazin *100 B3* Federacija Bosna I Hercegovina, NW Bosnia and Herzegovina
Cazorla *93 E4* Andalucía, S Spain
Ceadâr-Lunga *see* Ciadîr-Lunga
Ceará *63 F2 off.* Estado do Ceará. *state* C Brazil
Ceará *see* Fortaleza
Ceara Abyssal Plain *see* Ceará Plain
Ceará, Estado do *see* Ceará
Ceará Plain *56 E3 var.* Ceara Abyssal Plain. *abyssal plain* W Atlantic Ocean
Ceatharlach *see* Carlow
Cébaco, Isla *53 F5 island* SW Panama
Cebu *139 E2 off.* Cebu City. Cebu, C Philippines
Cebu City *see* Cebu
Čechy *see* Bohemia
Cecina *96 B3* Toscana, C Italy

Cedar City *44 A5* Utah, W USA
Cedar Falls *45 G3* Iowa, C USA
Cedar Lake *38 A2 lake* Manitoba, C Canada
Cedar Rapids *45 G3* Iowa, C USA
Cedros, Isla *50 A2 island* W Mexico
Ceduna *149 A6* South Australia
Cefalù *97 C7 anc.* Cephaloedium. Sicilia, Italy, C Mediterranean Sea
Celebes *see* Sulawesi
Celebes Sea *139 E3 Ind.* Laut Sulawesi. *sea* Indonesia/Philippines
Celje *95 E7 Ger.* Cilli. C Slovenia
Celldömölk *99 C6* Vas, W Hungary
Celle *94 B3 var.* Zelle. Niedersachsen, N Germany
Celovec *see* Klagenfurt
Celtic Sea *89 B7 Ir.* An Mhuir Cheilteach. *sea* SW British Isles
Celtic Shelf *80 B3 continental shelf* E Atlantic Ocean
Cenderawasih, Teluk *139 G4 var.* Teluk Irian, Teluk Sarera. *bay* W Pacific Ocean
Cenon *91 B5* Gironde, SW France
Centennial State *see* Colorado
Centrafricaine, République *see* Central African Republic
Central African Republic *76 C4 var.* République Centrafricaine, *abbrev.* CAR; *prev.* Ubangi-Shari, Oubangui-Chari, Territoire de l'Oubangui-Chari. *country* C Africa

CENTRAL AFRICAN REPUBLIC
Central Africa

Official name Central African Republic
Formation 1960 / 1960
Capital Bangui
Population 4 million / 17 people per sq mile (6 people per sq km) / 41%
Total area 240,534 sq miles (622,984 sq km)
Languages Sango, Banda, Gbaya, French
Religions Traditional beliefs 60%, Christian (mainly Roman Catholic) 35%, Muslim 5%
Ethnic mix Baya 34%, Banda 27%, Mandjia 21%, Sara 10%, Other 8%
Government Presidential system
Currency CFA franc = 100 centimes
Literacy rate 49%
Calorie consumption 1980 calories

Central, Cordillera *58 B3 mountain range* W Colombia
Central, Cordillera *55 E3 mountain range* C Dominican Republic
Central, Cordillera *53 F5 mountain range* C Panama
Central, Cordillera *139 E1 mountain range* Luzon, N Philippines
Central Group *see* Inner Islands
Centralia *46 B2* Washington, NW USA
Central Indian Ridge *see* Mid-Indian Ridge
Central Makrān Range *134 A3 mountain range* W Pakistan
Central Pacific Basin *142 D1 undersea basin* C Pacific Ocean
Central, Planalto *63 F3 var.* Brazilian Highlands. *mountain range* E Brazil
Central Provinces and Berar *see* Madhya Pradesh
Central Range *144 B3 mountain range* NW Papua New Guinea
Central Russian Upland *see* Srednerusskaya Vozvyshennost'
Central Siberian Plateau/Central Siberian Uplands *see* Srednesibirskoye Ploskogor'ye
Central, Sistema *92 D3 mountain range* C Spain
Central Valley *47 B6 valley* California, W USA
Centum Cellae *see* Civitavecchia
Ceos *see* Tziá
Cephaloedium *see* Cefalù
Ceram *see* Seram, Pulau
Ceram Sea *139 F4 Ind.* Laut Seram. *sea* E Indonesia
Cerasus *see* Giresun
Ceretê *58 B2* Córdoba, NW Colombia
Cergy-Pontoise *see* Pontoise
Cerignola *97 D5* Puglia, SE Italy
Çerkes *116 C2* Çankırı, N Turkey
Cernăuţi *see* Chernivtsi
Cernay *90 E4* Haut-Rhin, NE France
Cerro de Pasco *60 C3* Pasco, C Peru
Cervera *93 F2* Cataluña, NE Spain
Cervino, Monte *see* Matterhorn
Cesena *96 C3 anc.* Caesena. Emilia-Romagna, N Italy
Cēsis *106 D3 Ger.* Wenden. Cēsis, C Latvia
Česká Republika *see* Czech Republic
České Budějovice *99 B5 Ger.* Budweis. Jihočeský Kraj, S Czech Republic
Český Krumlov *99 A5 var.* Böhmisch-Krumau, *Ger.* Krummau. Jihočeský Kraj, S Czech Republic
Ceský Les *see* Bohemian Forest
Cetatea Damboviţei *see* Bucureşti
Cetinje *101 C5 It.* Cettigne. S Montenegro
Cette *see* Sète
Cettigne *see* Cetinje
Ceuta *70 C2 enclave* Spain, N Africa
Cévennes *91 C6 mountain range* S France
Ceyhan *116 D4* Adana, S Turkey
Ceylanpinar *117 E4* Şanlıurfa, SE Turkey
Ceylon *see* Sri Lanka
Ceylon Plain *124 B4 abyssal plain* N Indian Ocean
Ceyre to the Caribs *see* Marie-Galante
Chachapoyas *60 B2* Amazonas, NW Peru
Chachevichy *107 D6 Rus.* Chechevichi. Mahilyowskaya Voblasts', E Belarus
Chaco *see* Gran Chaco
Chad *76 C3 off.* Republic of Chad, *Fr.* Tchad. *country* C Africa

CHAD
Central Africa

Official name Republic of Chad
Formation 1960 / 1960
Capital N'Djamena
Population 9.7 million / 20 people per sq mile (8 people per sq km) / 24%
Total area 495,752 sq miles (1,284,000 sq km)
Languages French, Sara, Arabic, Maba
Religions Muslim 55%, Traditional beliefs 35%, Christian 10%
Ethnic mix Nomads (Tuareg and Toubou) 38%, Sara 30%, Other 17%, Arab 15%
Government Presidential system
Currency CFA franc = 100 centimes
Literacy rate 26%
Calorie consumption 2114 calories

Chad, Lake *76 B3 Fr.* Lac Tchad. *lake* C Africa
Chad, Republic of *see* Chad
Chadron *44 D3* Nebraska, C USA
Chadyr-Lunga *see* Ciadîr-Lunga
Chāgai Hills *134 A2 var.* Chāh Gay. *mountain range* Afghanistan/Pakistan
Chaghasarāy *see* Asadābād
Chagos-Laccadive Plateau *124 B4 undersea plateau* N Indian Ocean
Chagos Trench *141 C5 trench* N Indian Ocean
Chāh Gay *see* Chāgai Hills
Chaillu, Massif du *77 B6 mountain range* C Gabon
Chain Ridge *140 B4 undersea ridge* W Indian Ocean
Chajul *52 B2* Quiché, W Guatemala
Chakhānsūr *122 D5* Nīmrūz, SW Afghanistan
Chala *60 D4* Arequipa, SW Peru
Chalatenango *52 C3* Chalatenango, N El Salvador
Chalcidice *see* Chalkidikí
Chalcis *see* Chalkída
Chálki *105 E7 island* Dodekánisa, Greece, Aegean Sea
Chalkída *105 C5 var.* Halkida, *prev.* Khalkís; *anc.* Chalcis. Evvoia, E Greece
Chalkidikí *104 C4 var.* Khalkidhikí; *anc.* Chalcidice. *peninsula* NE Greece
Challans *90 B4* Vendée, NW France
Challapata *61 F4* Oruro, SW Bolivia
Challenger Deep *152 B3 trench* W Pacific Ocean
Challenger Deep *see* Mariana Trench
Challenger Fracture Zone *153 F4 tectonic feature* SE Pacific Ocean
Châlons-en-Champagne *90 D3 prev.* Châlons-sur-Marne, *hist.* Arcae Remorum; *anc.* Carolopois. Marne, NE France
Châlons-sur-Marne *see* Châlons-en-Champagne
Chalon-sur-Saône *90 D4 anc.* Cabillonum. Saône-et-Loire, C France
Cha Mai *see* Thung Song
Chaman *134 B2* Baluchistān, SW Pakistan
Chambéry *91 D5 anc.* Camberia. Savoie, E France
Champagne *90 D3* Yukon Territory, W Canada
Champagne *see* Campania
Champaign *40 B4* Illinois, N USA
Champasak *137 D5* Champasak, S Laos
Champlain, Lake *41 F2 lake* Canada/USA
Champotón *51 G4* Campeche, SE Mexico
Chanak *see* Çanakkale
Chañaral *64 B3* Atacama, N Chile
Chan-chiang/Chanchiang *see* Zhanjiang
Chandeleur Islands *42 C3 island group* Louisiana, S USA
Chandīgarh *134 D2 state capital* Punjab, N India
Chandrapur *135 E5* Mahārāshtra, C India
Changan *see* Xi'an
Changane *79 E3 river* S Mozambique
Changchun *128 D3 var.* Ch'angch'un, Ch'ang-ch'un; *prev.* Hsinking. *province capital* Jilin, NE China
Ch'angch'un/Ch'ang-ch'un *see* Changchun
Chang Jiang *128 B5 var.* Yangtze Kiang, *Eng.* Yangtze. *river* C China
Changkiakow *see* Zhangjiakou
Chang, Ko *137 C6 island* S Thailand
Changsha *128 C5 var.* Ch'angsha, Ch'ang-sha. *province capital* Hunan, S China
Ch'angsha/Ch'ang-sha *see* Changsha
Changzhi *128 C4* Shanxi, C China
Chaniá *105 C7 var.* Hania, Khaniá, *Eng.* Canea; *anc.* Cydonia. Kríti, Greece, E Mediterranean Sea
Chañi, Nevado de *64 B2 mountain* NW Argentina
Chankiri *see* Çankırı
Channel Islands *89 C8 Fr.* Iles Normandes. *island group* S English Channel
Channel Islands *47 B8 island group* California, W USA
Channel-Port aux Basques *39 G4* Newfoundland, Newfoundland and Labrador, SE Canada
Channel, The *see* English Channel
Channel Tunnel *90 C2 tunnel* France/UK
Chantabun/Chantaburi *see* Chanthaburi
Chantada *92 C1* Galicia, NW Spain
Chanthaburi *137 C6 var.* Chantabun, Chantaburi. Chantaburi, S Thailand
Chanute *45 F5* Kansas, C USA
Chaouèn *see* Chefchaouen
Chaoyang *128 D3* Liaoning, NE China
Chapala, Lago de *50 D4 lake* C Mexico
Chapan, Gora *122 B3 mountain* C Turkmenistan
Chapayevsk *111 C6* Samarskaya Oblast', W Russian Federation
Chaplynka *109 F4* Khersons'ka Oblast', S Ukraine
Chapra *see* Chhapra
Charcot Seamounts *80 B3 seamount range* E Atlantic Ocean
Chardzhev *see* Türkmenabat
Chardzhou/Chardzhui *see* Türkmenabat
Charente *91 B5 department* W France
Charente *91 B5 cultural region* W France
Charente *91 B5 river* W France
Chari *76 B3 var.* Shari. *river* Central African Republic/Chad
Chārīkār *123 E4* Parvān, NE Afghanistan
Charity *59 F2* NW Guyana
Chärjew *see* Türkmenabat
Charkhlik/Charkhliq *see* Ruoqiang
Charleroi *87 C7* Hainaut, S Belgium
Charlesbourg *39 E4* Québec, SE Canada
Charles de Gaulle *90 E1* (Paris) Seine-et-Marne, N France
Charles Island *38 D1 island* Nunavut, NE Canada
Charles Island *see* Santa María, Isla
Charleston *43 F2* South Carolina, SE USA
Charleston *40 D5 state capital* West Virginia, NE USA
Charleville *149 D5* Queensland, E Australia
Charleville-Mézières *90 D3* Ardennes, N France
Charlie-Gibbs Fracture Zone *66 C2 tectonic feature* N Atlantic Ocean
Charlotte *43 E1* North Carolina, SE USA
Charlotte Amalie *55 F3 prev.* Saint Thomas. *dependent territory capital* (Virgin Islands (US)) Saint Thomas, N Virgin Islands (US)
Charlotte Harbor *43 E5 inlet* Florida, SE USA
Charlottenhof *see* Aegviidu
Charlottesville *41 E5* Virginia, NE USA
Charlottetown *39 F4 province capital* Prince Edward Island, Prince Edward Island, SE Canada
Charlotte Town *see* Roseau
Charsk *see* Shar
Charters Towers *148 D3* Queensland, NE Australia
Chartres *90 C3 anc.* Autricum, Civitas Carnutum. Eure-et-Loir, C France
Chashniki *107 D5 Rus.* Chashniki. Vitsyebskaya Voblasts', N Belarus
Châteaubriant *90 B4* Loire-Atlantique, NW France
Châteaudun *90 C3* Eure-et-Loir, C France
Châteauroux *90 C4 prev.* Indreville. Indre, C France
Château-Thierry *90 C3* Aisne, N France
Châtelet *87 C7* Hainaut, S Belgium
Châtelherault *see* Châtellerault
Châtellerault *90 B4 var.* Châtelherault. Vienne, W France
Chatham Island *see* San Cristóbal, Isla
Chatham Island Rise *see* Chatham Rise
Chatham Islands *143 E5 island group* New Zealand, SW Pacific Ocean
Chatham Rise *142 D5 var.* Chatham Island Rise. *undersea rise* S Pacific Ocean
Chatkal Range *123 F2 Rus.* Chatkal'skiy Khrebet. *mountain range* Kyrgyzstan/Uzbekistan
Chatkal'skiy Khrebet *see* Chatkal Range
Chāttagām *see* Chittagong
Chattahoochee River *42 D3 river* SE USA
Chattanooga *42 D1* Tennessee, S USA
Chatyr-Tash *123 G2* Narynskaya Oblast C Kyrgyzstan
Châu Đốc *137 D6 var.* Chauphu, Chau Phu. An Giang, S Vietnam
Chauk *136 A3* Magwe, W Myanmar (Burma)
Chaumont *90 D4 prev.* Chaumont-en-Bassigny. Haute-Marne, N France
Chaumont-en-Bassigny *see* Chaumont
Chau Phu *see* Châu Đốc
Chausy *see* Chavusy
Chaves *92 C2 anc.* Aquae Flaviae. Vila Real, N Portugal
Chávez, Isla *see* Santa Cruz, Isla
Chavusy *107 E6 Rus.* Chausy. Mahilyowskaya Voblasts', E Belarus
Chaykovskiy *111 D5* Permskaya Oblast NW Russian Federation
Cheb *99 A5 Ger.* Eger. Karlovarský Kraj W Czech Republic
Cheboksary *111 C5* Chavash Respubliki W Russian Federation
Cheboygan *40 C2* Michigan, N USA
Chechaouèn *see* Chefchaouen
Chech, Erg *74 D1 desert* Algeria/Mali
Chechevichi *see* Chachevichy
Che-chiang *see* Zhejiang
Cheduba Island *136 A4 island* W Myanmar (Burma)
Chefchaouen *70 C2 var.* Chaouèn, Chechaouèn, *Sp.* Xauen. N Morocco
Chefoo *see* Yantai
Cheju-do *129 E4 Jap.* Saishū; *prev.* Quelpart. *island* S South Korea
Cheju-haehyŏp *129 E4 strait* S South Korea
Chekiang *see* Zhejiang
Cheleken *see* Hazar
Chelkar *see* Shalkar
Chełm *98 E4 Rus.* Kholm. Lubelskie, SE Poland

Chełmno 98 C3 *Ger.* Culm, Kulm.
Kujawski-pomorskie, C Poland

Chełmża 98 C3 *Ger.* Culmsee, Kulmsee.
Kujawski-pomorskie, C Poland

Cheltenham 89 D6 C England, UK

Chelyabinsk 114 C3 Chelyabinskaya
Oblast', C Russian Federation

Chemnitz 94 D4 *prev.* Karl-Marx-Stadt.
Sachsen, E Germany

Chemulpo *see* Inch'ŏn

Chenāb 134 C2 *river* India/Pakistan

Chengchiatun *see* Liaoyuan

Chengde 128 D3 *var.* Jehol. Hebei,
E China

Chengdu 128 B5 *var.* Chengtu,
Ch'eng-tu. *province capital* Sichuan,
C China

Chenghsien *see* Zhengzhou

Chengtu/Ch'eng-tu *see* Chengdu

Chennai 132 D2 *prev.* Madras. *state
capital* Tamil Nādu, S India

Chenstokhov *see* Częstochowa

Chen Xian/Chenxian/Chen Xiang *see*
Chenzhou

Chenzhou 128 C6 *var.* Chenxian, Chen
Xian, Chen Xiang. Hunan, S China

Chepelare 104 C3 Smolyan, S Bulgaria

Chepén 60 B3 La Libertad, C Peru

Cher 90 C4 *river* C France

Cherbourg 90 B3 *anc.* Carusbur.
Manche, N France

Cherepovets 110 B4 Vologodskaya
Oblast', NW Russian Federation

Chergui, Chott ech 70 D2 *salt lake*
NW Algeria

Cherikov *see* Cherykaw

Cherkasy *see* Cherkasy

Cherkassy 109 E2 *Rus.* Cherkassy.
Cherkas'ka Oblast', C Ukraine

Cherkessk 111 B7 Karachayevo-
Cherkesskaya Respublika, SW Russian
Federation

Chernigov *see* Chernihiv

Chernihiv 109 E1 *Rus.* Chernigov.
Chernihivs'ka Oblast', NE Ukraine

Chernivtsi 108 C3 *Ger.* Czernowitz,
Rom. Cernăuţi, *Rus.* Chernovtsy.
Chernivets'ka Oblast', W Ukraine

Cherno More *see* Black Sea

Chernomorskoye *see* Chornomors'ke

Chernovtsy *see* Chernivtsi

Chernoye More *see* Black Sea

Chernyakhovsk 106 A4 *Ger.* Insterburg.
Kaliningradskaya Oblast', W Russian
Federation

Cherry Hill 41 F4 New Jersey, NE USA

Cherski Range *see* Cherskogo, Khrebet

Cherskiy 115 G2 Respublika Sakha
(Yakutiya), NE Russian Federation

Cherskogo, Khrebet 115 F2 *var.* Cherski
Range. *mountain range* NE Russian
Federation

Cherso *see* Cres

Cherven' *see* Chervyen'

Chervonograd 108 C2 *Rus.*
Chervonograd. L'vivs'ka Oblast',
NW Ukraine

Chervyen' 107 D6 *Rus.* Cherven'.
Minskaya Voblasts', C Belarus

Cherykaw 107 E7 *Rus.* Cherikov.
Mahilyowskaya Voblasts', E Belarus

Chesapeake Bay 41 F5 *inlet* NE USA

Chesha Bay *see* Cheshskaya Guba

Chëshskaya Guba 172 D5 *var.*
Archangel Bay, Chesha Bay, Dvina
Bay. *bay* NW Russian Federation

Chester 89 C6 *Wel.* Caerleon, *hist.*
Legaceaster, *Lat.* Deva, Devana Castra.
C England, UK

Chetumal 51 H4 *var.* Payo Obispo.
Quintana Roo, SE Mexico

Cheviot Hills 88 D4 *hill range* England/
Scotland, UK

Cheyenne 44 D4 *state capital* Wyoming,
C USA

Cheyenne River 44 D3 *river* South
Dakota/Wyoming, N USA

Chezdi-Oşorheiu *see* Târgu Secuiesc

Chhapra 135 F3 *prev.* Chapra. Bihār,
N India

Chhattisgarh 135 E4 E India

Chhattisgarh 135 E4 *cultural region*
E India

Chiai 128 D6 *var.* Chia-i, Chiayi, Kiayi,
Jiayi, *Jap.* Kagi. C Taiwan

Chia-i *see* Chiai

Chiang-hsi *see* Jiangxi

Chiang Mai 136 B4 *var.* Chiangmai,
Chiengmai, Kiangmai. Chiang Mai,
NW Thailand

Chiangmai *see* Chiang Mai

Chiang Rai 136 C3 *var.* Chianpai,
Chienrai, Muang Chiang Rai. Chiang
Rai, NW Thailand

Chiang-su *see* Jiangsu

Chianning/Chian-ning *see* Nanjing

Chianpai *see* Chiang Rai

Chianti 96 C3 *cultural region* C Italy

Chiapa *see* Chiapa de Corzo

Chiapa de Corzo 51 G5 *var.* Chiapa.
Chiapas, SE Mexico

Chiayi *see* Chiai

Chiba 130 B1 *var.* Tiba. Chiba, Honshū,
S Japan

Chibougamau 38 D3 Québec,
SE Canada

Chicago 40 B3 Illinois, N USA

Ch'i-ch'i-ha-erh *see* Qiqihar

Chickasha 49 G2 Oklahoma, C USA

Chiclayo 60 B3 Lambayeque, NW Peru

Chico 47 B5 California, W USA

Chico, Río 65 B7 *river* SE Argentina

Chico, Río 65 B6 *river* S Argentina

Chicoutimi 39 E4 Québec, SE Canada

Chiengmai *see* Chiang Mai

Chienrai *see* Chiang Rai

Chietí 96 D4 *var.* Teate. Abruzzo,
C Italy

Chifeng 127 G2 *var.* Ulanhad. Nei
Mongol Zizhiqu, N China

Chigirin *see* Chyhyryn

Chih-fu *see* Yantai

Chihli *see* Hebei

Chihli, Gulf of *see* Bo Hai

Chihuahua 50 C2 Chihuahua,
NW Mexico

Childress 49 F2 Texas, SW USA

Chile 64 B3 *off.* Republic of Chile.
country SW South America

Chile Basin 57 A5 *undersea basin*
E Pacific Ocean

Chile Chico 65 B6 Aisén, W Chile

Chile, Republic of *see* Chile

Chile Rise 57 A7 *undersea rise* SE Pacific
Ocean

Chilia-Nouă *see* Kiliya

Chililabombwe 78 D2 Copperbelt,
C Zambia

Chi-lin *see* Jilin

Chillán 65 B5 Bío Bío, C Chile

Chillicothe 40 D4 Ohio, N USA

Chill Mhantáin, Sléibhte *see* Wicklow
Mountains

Chiloé, Isla de *var.* Isla Grande de
Chiloé. *island* W Chile

Chilpancingo 51 E5 *var.* Chilpancingo
de los Bravos. Guerrero, S Mexico

Chilpancingo de los Bravos *see*
Chilpancingo

Chilung 128 D6 *var.* Keelung, *Jap.* Kirun,
Kirun', *prev. Sp.* Santissima Trinidad.
N Taiwan

Chimán 53 G5 Panamá, E Panama

Chimbay *see* Chimboy

Chimborazo 60 A1 *volcano* C Ecuador

Chimbote 60 C3 Ancash, W Peru

Chimboy 122 D1 *Rus.* Chimbay.
Qoraqalpog'iston Respublikasi,
NW Uzbekistan

Chimkent *see* Shymkent

Chimoio 79 E3 Manica, C Mozambique

China 124 C2 *off.* People's Republic
of China, *Chin.* Chung-hua Jen-min
Kung-ho-kuo, Zhonghua Renmin
Gongheguo; *prev.* Chinese Empire.
country E Asia

CHINA
East Asia

Official name People's Republic of China
Formation 960 / 1999
Capital Beijing
Population 1.3 billion / 365 people per
sq mile (141 people per sq km) / 32%
Total area 3,705,386 sq miles
(9,596,960 sq km)
Languages Mandarin*, Wu, Cantonese,
Hsiang, Min, Hakka, Kan
Religions Nonreligious 59%, Traditional
beliefs 20%, Other 13%, Buddhist 6%,
Muslim 2%
Ethnic mix Han 92%, Other 6%, Hui 1%,
Zhuang 1%
Government One-party state
Currency Renminbi (known as yuan)
= 10 jiao
Literacy rate 91%
Calorie consumption 2951 calories

Chi-nan/Chinan *see* Jinan

Chinandega 52 C3 Chinandega,
NW Nicaragua

China, People's Republic of *see* China

China, Republic of *see* Taiwan

Chincha Alta 60 D4 Ica, SW Peru

Chin-chiang *see* Quanzhou

Chin-chou/Chinchow *see* Jinzhou

Chindwin 136 B2 *river*
N Myanmar (Burma)

Chinese Empire *see* China

Chinghai *see* Qinghai, China

Ch'ing Hai *see* Qinghai Hu, China

Chingola 78 D2 Copperbelt, C Zambia

Ching-Tao/Ch'ing-tao *see* Qingdao

Chinguetti 74 C2 *var.* Chinguetti. Adrar,
C Mauritania

Chin Hills 136 A3 *mountain range*
W Myanmar (Burma)

Chinhsien *see* Jinzhou

Chinnereth *see* Tiberias, Lake

Chinook Trough 113 H4 *trough*
N Pacific Ocean

Chioggia 96 C2 *anc.* Fossa Claudia.
Veneto, NE Italy

Chíos 105 D5 *var.* Hios, Khíos, *It.* Scio,
Turk. Sakiz-Adasi. Chíos, E Greece

Chíos 105 D5 *var.* Khíos. *island*
E Greece

Chipata 78 D2 *prev.* Fort Jameson.
Eastern, E Zambia

Chiquián 60 C3 Ancash, W Peru

Chiquimula 52 B2 Chiquimula,
SE Guatemala

Chīrāla 132 D1 Andhra Pradesh,
E India

Chirchik *see* Chirchiq

Chirchiq 123 E2 *Rus.* Chirchik.
Toshkent Viloyati, E Uzbekistan

Chiriquí, Golfo de 53 E5 *Eng.* Chiriqui
Gulf. *gulf* SW Panama

Chiriquí Gulf *see* Chiriquí, Golfo de

Chiriquí, Laguna de 53 E5 *lagoon*
NW Panama

Chiriquí, Volcán de *see* Barú, Volcán

Chirripó, Cerro *see* Chirripó Grande,
Cerro

Chirripó Grande, Cerro 52 D4 *var.*
Cerro Chirripó. *mountain* SE Costa
Rica

Chisec 52 B2 Alta Verapaz, C Guatemala

Chisholm 45 F1 Minnesota, N USA

Chisimaio/Chisimayu *see* Kismaayo

Chişinău 108 D4 *Rus.* Kishinev.
country capital (Moldova) C Moldova

Chita 115 F4 Chitinskaya Oblast',
S Russian Federation

Chitangwiza *see* Chitungwiza

Chitato 78 C1 Lunda Norte, NE Angola

Chitina 36 D3 Alaska, USA

Chitose 130 D2 *var.* Titose. Hokkaidō,
NE Japan

Chitré 53 F5 Herrera, S Panama

Chittagong 135 G4 *Ben.* Chāttagām.
Chittagong, SE Bangladesh

Chitungwiza 78 D3 *prev.* Chitangwiza.
Mashonaland East, NE Zimbabwe

Chkalov *see* Orenburg

Chlef 70 D2 *var.* Ech Cheliff, Ech
Chleff; *prev.* Al-Asnam, El Asnam,
Orléansville. NW Algeria

Chocolate Mountains 47 D8 *mountain
range* California, W USA

Chodorów *see* Khodoriv

Chodzież 98 C3 Wielkopolskie, C Poland

Choele Choel 65 C5 Río Negro,
C Argentina

Choiseul 144 C3 *var.* Lauru. *island*
NW Solomon Islands

Chojnice 98 C2 *Ger.* Konitz. Pomorskie,
N Poland

Ch'ok'ē 72 C4 *var.* Choke Mountains.
mountain range NW Ethiopia

Choke Mountains *see* Ch'ok'ē

Cholet 90 B4 Maine-et-Loire,
NW France

Choluteca 52 C3 Choluteca, S Honduras

Choluteca, Río 52 C3 *river* SW Honduras

Choma 78 D2 Southern, S Zambia

Chomutov 98 A4 *Ger.* Komotau.
Ústecký Kraj, NW Czech Republic

Chona 113 E2 *river* C Russian Federation

Chon Buri 137 C5 *prev.* Bang Pla Soi.
Chon Buri, S Thailand

Chone 60 A1 Manabí, W Ecuador

Ch'ŏngjin 129 E3 NE North Korea

Chongqing 128 B5 *var.* Ch'ung-ching,
Ch'ung-ch'ing, Chungking, Pahsien,
Tch'ongking, Yuzhou. Chongqing
Shi, C China

Chongqing Shi 128 B5 *province* C China

Chonnacht *see* Connaught

Chonos, Archipiélago de los 65 A6
island group S Chile

Chóra 105 D6 *prev.* Íos. Kykládes, Greece,
Aegean Sea

Chóra Sfakíon 105 C8 *var.* Sfákia. Kríti,
Greece, E Mediterranean Sea

Chorne More *see* Black Sea

Chornomors'ke 109 E4 *Rus.*
Chernomorskoye. Respublika Krym,
S Ukraine

Chorokh/Chorokhi *see* Çoruh Nehri

Chortkiv 108 C2 *Rus.* Chortkov.
Ternopil's'ka Oblast', W Ukraine

Chortkov *see* Chortkiv

Chorzów 99 C5 *Ger.* Königshütte; *prev.*
Królewska Huta. Śląskie, S Poland

Chośebuz *see* Cottbus

Chōsen-kaikyō *see* Korea Strait

Chōshi 131 D5 *var.* Tyōsi. Chiba,
Honshū, S Japan

Chosŏn-minjujuŭi-inmin-kanghwaguk
see North Korea

Choszczno 98 B3 *Ger.* Arnswalde.
Zachodnio-pomorskie, NW Poland

Chota Nāgpur 135 E4 *plateau* N India

Choûm 74 C2 Adrar, C Mauritania

Choybalsan 127 F2 *prev.* Byan Tumen.
Dornod, E Mongolia

Christchurch 151 C6 Canterbury, South
Island, New Zealand

Christiana 54 B5 C Jamaica

Christiania *see* Oslo

Christiansand *see* Kristiansand

Christianshåb *see* Qasigiannguit

Christiansund *see* Kristiansund

Christmas Island 141 D5 *Australian
external territory* E Indian Ocean

Christmas Island *see* Kiritimati

Christmas Ridge 143 E1 *undersea ridge*
C Pacific Ocean

Chuan *see* Sichuan

Ch'uan-chou *see* Quanzhou

Chubek *see* Moskva

Chubut 57 B7 *off.* Provincia de Chubut.
province S Argentina

Chubut, Provincia de *see* Chubut

Chubut, Río 65 B6 *river* SE Argentina

Chu-chiang *see* Shaoguan

Chudskoye Ozero *see* Peipus, Lake

Chūgoku-sanchi 131 B6 *mountain range*
Honshū, SW Japan

Chui *see* Chuy

Chukai *see* Cukai

Chukchi Plain 155 B2 *abyssal plain*
Arctic Ocean

Chukchi Plateau 34 C2 *undersea plateau*
Arctic Ocean

Chukchi Sea 34 B2 *Rus.* Chukotskoye
More. *sea* Arctic Ocean

Chukotskoye More *see* Chukchi Sea

Chula Vista 47 C8 California, W USA

Chulucanas 60 B2 Piura, NW Peru

Chulym 114 D4 *river* C Russian
Federation

Chumphon 137 C6 var. Jumporn.
Chumphon, SW Thailand
Ch'unch'ŏn 129 E4 Jap. Shunsen.
N South Korea
Ch'ung-ch'ing/Ch'ung-ching see
Chongqing
Chung-hua Jen-min Kung-ho-kuo
see China
Chungking see Chongqing
Chunya 115 E3 river C Russian
Federation
Chuquicamata 64 B2 Antofagasta,
N Chile
Chuquisaca see Sucre
Chur 95 B7 Fr. Coire, It. Coira, Rmsch.
Cuera, Quera; anc. Curia Rhaetorum.
Graubünden, E Switzerland
Churchill 37 G4 Manitoba, C Canada
Churchill 38 B2 river Manitoba/
Saskatchewan, C Canada
Churchill 39 F2 river Newfoundland and
Labrador, E Canada
Chuska Mountains 48 C1 mountain
range Arizona/New Mexico, SW USA
Chusovoy 111 D5 Permskaya Oblast',
NW Russian Federation
Chust see Khust
Chuuk Islands 144 B2 var. Hogoley
Islands; prev. Truk Islands. island
group Caroline Islands, C Micronesia
Chuy 64 E4 var. Chuí. Rocha, E Uruguay
Chyhyryn 109 E2 Rus. Chigirin.
Cherkas'ka Oblast', N Ukraine
Ciadir-Lunga 108 D4 var. Ceadâr-
Lunga, Rus. Chadyr-Lunga. S Moldova
Cide 116 C2 Kastamonu, N Turkey
Ciechanów 98 D3 prev. Zichenau.
Mazowieckie, C Poland
Ciego de Ávila 54 C2 Ciego de Ávila,
C Cuba
Ciénaga 58 B1 Magdalena, N Colombia
Cienfuegos 54 B2 Cienfuegos, C Cuba
Cieza 93 E4 Murcia, SE Spain
Cihanbeyli 116 C3 Konya, C Turkey
Cikobia 145 E4 prev. Thikombia.
island N Fiji
Cilacap 138 C5 prev. Tjilatjap. Jawa,
C Indonesia
Cill Airne see Killarney
Cill Chainnigh see Kilkenny
Cilli see Celje
Cill Mhantáin see Wicklow
Cimpina see Câmpina
Cimpulung see Câmpulung
Cina Selatan, Laut see South China Sea
Cincinnati 40 C4 Ohio, N USA
Ciney 87 C7 Namur, SE Belgium
Cinto, Monte 91 E7 mountain Corse,
France, C Mediterranean Sea
Cintra see Sintra
Cipolletti 65 B5 Río Negro, C Argentina
Cirebon 138 C4 prev. Tjirebon. Jawa,
S Indonesia
Cirkvenica see Crikvenica
Cirò Marina 97 E6 Calabria, S Italy
Cirquenizza see Crikvenica
Cisnădie 108 B4 Ger. Heltau, Hung.
Nagydisznód. Sibiu, SW Romania
Citharista see la Ciotat
Citlaltépetl see Orizaba, Volcán Pico de
Citrus Heights 47 B5 California, W USA
Ciudad Acuña see Villa Acuña
Ciudad Bolívar 59 E2 prev. Angostura.
Bolívar, E Venezuela
Ciudad Camargo 50 D2 Chihuahua,
N Mexico
Ciudad Cortés see Cortés
Ciudad Darío 52 D3 var. Dario.
Matagalpa, W Nicaragua
Ciudad de Dolores Hidalgo see Dolores
Hidalgo
Ciudad de Guatemala 52 B2
Eng. Guatemala City; prev. Santiago
de los Caballeros. country capital
(Guatemala) Guatemala, C Guatemala
Ciudad del Carmen see Carmen
Ciudad del Este 64 E2 prev. Ciudad
Presidente Stroessner, Presidente
Stroessner, Puerto Presidente
Stroessner. Alto Paraná, SE Paraguay
Ciudad Delicias see Delicias
Ciudad de México see México
Ciudad de Panamá see Panamá
Ciudad Guayana 59 E2 prev. San Tomé
de Guayana, Santo Tomé de Guayana.
Bolívar, NE Venezuela
Ciudad Guzmán 50 D4 Jalisco,
SW Mexico

Ciudad Hidalgo 51 G5 Chiapas,
SE Mexico
Ciudad Juárez 50 C1 Chihuahua,
N Mexico
Ciudad Lerdo 50 D3 Durango,
C Mexico
Ciudad Madero 51 E3 var. Villa Cecilia.
Tamaulipas, C Mexico
Ciudad Mante 51 E3 Tamaulipas,
C Mexico
Ciudad Miguel Alemán 51 E2
Tamaulipas, C Mexico
Ciudad Obregón 50 B2 Sonora,
NW Mexico
Ciudad Ojeda 58 C1 Zulia,
NW Venezuela
Ciudad Porfirio Díaz see Piedras Negras
Ciudad Quesada see Quesada
Ciudad Real 92 D3 Castilla-La Mancha,
C Spain
Ciudad-Rodrigo 92 C3 Castilla-León,
N Spain
Ciudad Trujillo see Santo Domingo
Ciudad Valles 51 E3 San Luis Potosí,
C Mexico
Ciudad Victoria 51 E3 Tamaulipas,
C Mexico
Ciutadella 93 H3 var. Ciutadella
de Menorca. Menorca, Spain,
W Mediterranean Sea
Ciutadella Ciutadella de Menorca see
Ciutadella
Civitanova Marche 96 D3 Marche,
C Italy
Civitas Altae Ripae see Brzeg
Civitas Carnutum see Chartres
Civitas Eburovicum see Évreux
Civitavecchia 96 C4 anc. Centum Cellae,
Trajani Portus. Lazio, C Italy
Claremore 49 G1 Oklahoma, C USA
Clarence 151 C5 Canterbury, South
Island, New Zealand
Clarence 151 C5 river South Island,
New Zealand
Clarence Town 54 D2 Long Island,
C Bahamas
Clarinda 45 F4 Iowa, C USA
Clarion Fracture Zone 153 E2 tectonic
feature NE Pacific Ocean
Clarión, Isla 50 A5 island W Mexico
Clark Fork 44 A1 river Idaho/Montana,
NW USA
Clark Hill Lake 43 E2 var. J.Storm
Thurmond Reservoir. reservoir
Georgia/South Carolina, SE USA
Clarksburg 40 D4 West Virginia,
NE USA
Clarksdale 42 B2 Mississippi, S USA
Clarksville 42 C1 Tennessee, S USA
Clausentum see Southampton
Clayton 49 E1 New Mexico, SW USA
Clearwater 43 E4 Florida, SE USA
Clearwater Mountains 46 D2 mountain
range Idaho, NW USA
Cleburne 49 G3 Texas, SW USA
Clermont 148 D4 Queensland,
E Australia
Clermont-Ferrand 91 C5 Puy-de-Dôme,
C France
Cleveland 40 D3 Ohio, N USA
Cleveland 42 D1 Tennessee, S USA
Clifton 48 C2 Arizona, SW USA
Clinton 42 B2 Mississippi, S USA
Clinton 49 F1 Oklahoma, C USA
Clipperton Fracture Zone 153 E3
tectonic feature E Pacific Ocean
Clipperton Island 35 A7 French
dependency of French Polynesia
E Pacific Ocean
Cloncurry 148 B3 Queensland,
C Australia
Clonmel 89 B6 Ir. Cluain Meala.
S Ireland
Cloppenburg 94 B3 Niedersachsen,
NW Germany
Cloquet 45 G2 Minnesota, N USA
Cloud Peak 44 C3 mountain Wyoming,
C USA
Clovis 49 E2 New Mexico, SW USA
Cluain Meala see Clonmel
Cluj see Cluj-Napoca
Cluj-Napoca 108 B3 Ger. Klausenburg,
Hung. Kolozsvár; prev. Cluj. Cluj,
NW Romania
Clutha 151 B7 river South Island, New
Zealand
Clyde 88 C4 river W Scotland, UK
Coari 62 D2 Amazonas, N Brazil

Coast Mountains 36 D4 Fr. Chaîne
Côtière. mountain range Canada/USA
Coast Ranges 46 A4 mountain range
W USA
Coats Island 37 G3 island Nunavut,
NE Canada
Coats Land 154 B2 physical region
Antarctica
Coatzacoalcos 51 G4 var. Quetzalcoalco;
prev. Puerto México. Veracruz-Llave,
E Mexico
Cobán 52 B2 Alta Verapaz, C Guatemala
Cobar 149 C6 New South Wales,
SE Australia
Cobija 61 E3 Pando, NW Bolivia
Coblence/Coblenz see Koblenz
Coburg 95 C5 Bayern, SE Germany
Coca see Puerto Francisco de Orellana
Cocanada see Kākināda
Cochabamba 61 F4 hist. Oropeza.
Cochabamba, C Bolivia
Cochin 132 C3 var. Kochi. Kerala,
SW India
Cochinos, Bahía de 54 B2 Eng. Bay of
Pigs. bay SE Cuba
Cochrane 38 C4 Ontario, S Canada
Cochrane 65 B7 Aisén, S Chile
Cocibolca see Nicaragua, Lago de
Cockade State see Maryland
Cockburn Town 55 E2 San Salvador,
E Bahamas
Cockpit Country, The 54 A4 physical
region W Jamaica
Cocobeach 77 A5 Estuaire, NW Gabon
Coconino Plateau 48 B1 plain Arizona,
SW USA
Coco, Río 53 E2 var. Río
Wanki, Segoviao Wangkí. river
Honduras/Nicaragua
Cocos Basin 124 C5 undersea basin
E Indian Ocean
Cocos Island Ridge see Cocos Ridge
Cocos Islands 141 D5 island group
E Indian Ocean
Cocos Ridge 35 C8 var. Cocos Island
Ridge. undersea feature E Pacific Ocean
Cod, Cape 41 G3 headland
Massachusetts, NE USA
Codfish Island 151 A8 island SW New
Zealand
Codlea 108 C4 Ger. Zeiden, Hung.
Feketehalom. Brașov, C Romania
Cody 44 C2 Wyoming, C USA
Coeur d'Alene 46 C2 Idaho, NW USA
Coevorden 86 E2 Drenthe,
NE Netherlands
Coffs Harbour 149 E6 New South Wales,
SE Australia
Cognac 91 B5 anc. Compniacum.
Charente, W France
Cohalm see Rupea
Coiba, Isla de 53 E5 island SW Panama
Coihaique 65 B6 var. Coyhaique. Aisén,
S Chile
Coimbatore 132 C3 Tamil Nādu, S India
Coimbra 92 B3 anc. Conimbria,
Conimbriga. Coimbra, W Portugal
Coín 92 D5 Andalucía, S Spain
Coira/Coire see Chur
Coirib, Loch see Corrib, Lough
Colby 45 E4 Kansas, C USA
Colchester 89 E6 Connecticut, NE USA
Coleman 49 F3 Texas, SW USA
Coleraine 88 B4 Ir. Cúil Raithin.
N Northern Ireland, UK
Colesberg 78 C5 Northern Cape,
C South Africa
Colima 50 D4 Colima, S Mexico
Coll 88 B3 island W Scotland, UK
College Station 49 G3 Texas, SW USA
Collie 147 A7 Western Australia
Collipo see Leiria
Colmar 90 E4 Ger. Kolmar. Haut-Rhin,
NE France
Cöln see Köln
Cologne see Köln
Colomb-Béchar see Béchar
Colombia 58 B3 off. Republic of
Colombia. country N South America

COLOMBIA
(continued)

Total area 439,733 sq miles
(1,138,910 sq km)
Languages Spanish*, Wayuu, Páez, and
other Amerindian languages
Religions Roman Catholic 95%,
Other 5%
Ethnic mix Mestizo 58%, White 20%,
European–African 14%, African 4%,
African–Amerindian 3%, Amerindian 1%
Government Presidential system
Currency Colombian peso =
100 centavos
Literacy rate 94%
Calorie consumption 2585 calories

Colombian Basin 56 A1 undersea basin
SW Caribbean Sea
Colombia, Republic of see Colombia
Colombie-Britannique see British
Columbia
Colombo 132 C4 country capital
(Sri Lanka) Western Province,
W Sri Lanka
Colón 53 G4 prev. Aspinwall. Colón,
C Panama
Colón, Archipiélago de 153 F3 var.
Islas de los Galápagos, Eng. Galapagos
Islands, Tortoise Islands. island group
Ecuador, E Pacific Ocean
Colonia Agrippina see Köln
Colón Ridge 35 B8 undersea ridge
E Pacific Ocean
Colorado 44 C4 off. State of Colorado,
also known as Centennial State, Silver
State. state C USA
Colorado City 49 F3 Texas, SW USA
Colorado Plateau 48 B1 plateau
W USA
Colorado, Rio 65 C5 river E Argentina
Colorado, Río see Colorado River
Colorado River 35 B5 var. Río Colorado.
river Mexico/USA
Colorado River 49 G4 river Texas,
SW USA
Colorado Springs 44 D5 Colorado,
C USA
Columbia 41 E4 Maryland, NE USA
Columbia 45 G4 Missouri, C USA
Columbia 43 E2 state capital South
Carolina, SE USA
Columbia 42 C1 Tennessee, S USA
Columbia 46 B3 river Canada/USA
Columbia Plateau 46 C3 plateau
Idaho/Oregon, NW USA
Columbus 42 D2 Georgia, SE USA
Columbus 40 C4 Indiana, N USA
Columbus 42 C2 Mississippi,
S USA
Columbus 45 F4 Nebraska, C USA
Columbus 40 D4 state capital Ohio,
N USA
Colville Channel 150 D2 channel North
Island, New Zealand
Colville River 36 D2 river Alaska, USA
Comacchio 96 C3 var. Commachio; anc.
Comactium. Emilia-Romagna, N Italy
Comactium see Comacchio
Comalcalco 51 G4 Tabasco, SE Mexico
Coma Pedrosa, Pic de 91 A7 mountain
NW Andorra
Comarapa 61 F4 Santa Cruz, C Bolivia
Comayagua 52 C2 Comayagua,
W Honduras
Comer See see Como, Lago di
Comilla 135 G4 Ben. Kumillā.
Chittagong, E Bangladesh
Comino 102 A5 Malt. Kemmuna. island
C Malta
Comitán 51 G5 var. Comitán de
Domínguez. Chiapas, SE Mexico
Comitán de Domínguez see Comitán
Commachio see Comacchio
Commissioner's Point 42 A5 headland
W Bermuda
Como 96 B2 anc. Comum. Lombardia,
N Italy
Comodoro Rivadavia 65 B6 Chubut,
SE Argentina
Como, Lago di 96 B2 var. Lario, Eng.
Lake Como, Ger. Comer See. lake
N Italy
Como, Lake see Como, Lago di
**Comores, République Fédérale
Islamique des** see Comoros

Comoros *79 F2 off.* Federal Islamic Republic of the Comoros, *Fr.* République Fédérale Islamique des Comores. *country* W Indian Ocean

COMOROS
Indian Ocean

Official name Union of the Comoros
Formation 1975 / 1975
Capital Moroni
Population 798,000 / 927 people per sq mile (358 people per sq km) / 33%
Total area 838 sq miles (2170 sq km)
Languages Arabic*, Comoran, French
Religions Muslim (mainly Sunni) 98%, Other 1%, Roman Catholic 1%
Ethnic mix Comoran 97%, Other 3%
Government Presidential system
Currency Comoros franc = 100 centimes
Literacy rate 56%
Calorie consumption 1754 calories

Comoros, Federal Islamic Republic of the *see* Comoros
Compiègne *90 C3* Oise, N France
Complutum *see* Alcalá de Henares
Compniacum *see* Cognac
Compostella *see* Santiago
Comrat *108 D4 Rus.* Komrat. S Moldova
Comum *see* Como
Conakry *74 C4 country capital* (Guinea) SW Guinea
Conca *see* Cuenca
Concarneau *90 A3* Finistère, NW France
Concepción *61 G3* Santa Cruz, E Bolivia
Concepción *65 B5* Bío Bío, C Chile
Concepción *64 D2 var.* Villa Concepción. Concepción, C Paraguay
Concepción *see* La Concepción
Concepción de la Vega *see* La Vega
Conchos, Río *48 D4 river* NW Mexico
Conchos, Río *50 D2 river* C Mexico
Concord *41 G3 state capital* New Hampshire, NE USA
Concordia *64 D4* Entre Ríos, E Argentina
Concordia *45 E4* Kansas, C USA
Côn Đao *137 E7 var.* Con Son. *island* S Vietnam
Condate *see* Rennes, Ille-et-Vilaine, France
Condate *see* St-Claude, Jura, France
Condega *52 D3* Estelí, NW Nicaragua
Condivincum *see* Nantes
Confluentes *see* Koblenz
Công Hoa Xa Hôi Chu Nghia Viêt Nam *see* Vietnam
Congo *77 D5 off.* Republic of the Congo, *Fr.* Moyen-Congo; *prev.* Middle Congo. *country* C Africa

CONGO
Central Africa

Official name Republic of the Congo
Formation 1960 / 1960
Capital Brazzaville
Population 4 million / 30 people per sq mile (12 people per sq km) / 63%
Total area 132,046 sq miles (342,000 sq km)
Languages French*, Kongo, Teke, Lingala
Religions Traditional beliefs 50%, Roman Catholic 25%, Protestant 23%, Muslim 2%
Ethnic mix Bakongo 48%, Sangha 20%, Teke 17%, Mbochi 12%, Other 3%
Government Presidential system
Currency CFA franc = 100 centimes
Literacy rate 83%
Calorie consumption 2162 calories

Congo *77 C6 off.* Democratic Republic of Congo; *prev.* Zaire, Belgian Congo, Congo (Kinshasa). *country* C Africa

CONGO, DEM. REP.
Central Africa

Official name Democratic Republic of the Congo
Formation 1960 / 1960
Capital Kinshasa
Population 57.5 million / 66 people per sq mile (25 people per sq km) / 30%

CONGO, DEM. REP.
(continued)

Total area 905,563 sq miles (2,345,410 sq km)
Languages French*, Kiswahili, Tshiluba, Kikongo, Lingala
Religions Roman Catholic 50%, Protestant 20%, Traditional beliefs and other 10%, Muslim 10%, Kimbanguist 10%
Ethnic mix Other 55%, Bantu and Hamitic 45%
Government Transitional regime
Currency Congolese franc = 100 centimes
Literacy rate 65%
Calorie consumption 1599 calories

Congo *77 C6 var.* Kongo, *Fr.* Zaire. *river* C Africa
Congo Basin *77 C6 drainage basin* W Dem. Rep. Congo
Congo/Congo (Kinshasa) *see* Congo (Democratic Republic of)
Coni *see* Cuneo
Conimbria/Conimbriga *see* Coimbra
Conjeeveram *see* Kānchīpuram
Connacht *see* Connaught
Connaught *89 A5 var.* Connacht, *Ir.* Chonnacht, Cúige. *province* W Ireland
Connecticut *41 F3 off.* State of Connecticut, *also known as* Blue Law State, Constitution State, Land of Steady Habits, Nutmeg State. *state* NE USA
Connecticut *41 G3 river* Canada/USA
Conroe *49 G3* Texas, SW USA
Consentia *see* Cosenza
Consolación del Sur *54 A2* Pinar del Río, W Cuba
Con Son *see* Côn Đao
Constance *see* Konstanz
Constance, Lake *95 B7 Ger.* Bodensee. *lake* C Europe
Constanţa *108 D5 var.* Küstendje, *Eng.* Constanza, *Ger.* Konstanza, *Turk.* Küstence. Constanţa, SE Romania
Constantia *see* Coutances
Constantia *see* Konstanz
Constantine *71 E2 var.* Qacentina, *Ar.* Qoussantîna. NE Algeria
Constantinople *see* İstanbul
Constantiola *see* Olteniţa
Constanz *see* Konstanz
Constanza *see* Constanţa
Constitution State *see* Connecticut
Coo *see* Kos
Coober Pedy *149 A5* South Australia
Cookeville *42 D1* Tennessee, S USA
Cook Islands *145 F4 territory in free association with New Zealand* S Pacific Ocean
Cook, Mount *see* Aoraki
Cook Strait *151 D5 var.* Raukawa. *strait* New Zealand
Cooktown *148 D2* Queensland, NE Australia
Coolgardie *147 B6* Western Australia
Cooma *149 D7* New South Wales, SE Australia
Coomassie *see* Kumasi
Coon Rapids *45 F2* Minnesota, N USA
Cooper Creek *148 C4 var.* Barcoo, Cooper's Creek. *seasonal river* Queensland/South Australia
Cooper's Creek *see* Cooper Creek
Coos Bay *46 A3* Oregon, NW USA
Cootamundra *149 D6* New South Wales, SE Australia
Copacabana *61 E4* La Paz, W Bolivia
Copenhagen *see* København
Copiapó *64 B3* Atacama, N Chile
Copperas Cove *49 G3* Texas, SW USA
Coppermine *see* Kugluktuk
Copper State *see* Arizona
Coquilhatville *see* Mbandaka
Coquimbo *64 B3* Coquimbo, N Chile
Corabia *108 B5* Olt, S Romania
Coral Harbour *37 G3* Southampton Island, Northwest Territories, NE Canada
Coral Sea *142 B3 sea* SW Pacific Ocean
Coral Sea Islands *144 B4 Australian external territory* SW Pacific Ocean
Corantijn Rivier *see* Courantyne River
Corcovado, Golfo *65 B6 gulf* S Chile
Corcyra Nigra *see* Korčula
Cordele *42 D3* Georgia, SE USA
Córdoba *64 C3* Córdoba, C Argentina
Córdoba *51 F4* Veracruz-Llave, E Mexico
Córdoba *92 D4 var.* Cordoba, *Eng.* Cordova; *anc.* Corduba. Andalucía, SW Spain
Cordova *36 C3* Alaska, USA
Cordova/Cordoba *see* Córdoba
Corduba *see* Córdoba
Corentyne River *see* Courantyne River
Coria *92 C3* Extremadura, W Spain
Corinth *42 C1* Mississippi, S USA
Corinth *see* Kórinthos
Corinth, Gulf of/Corinthiacus Sinus *see* Korinthiakós Kólpos
Corinthus *see* Kórinthos
Corinto *52 C3* Chinandega, NW Nicaragua
Cork *89 A6 Ir.* Corcaigh. S Ireland
Çorlu *116 A2* Tekirdağ, NW Turkey
Corner Brook *39 G3* Newfoundland, Newfoundland and Labrador, E Canada
Cornhusker State *see* Nebraska
Corn Islands *see* Maíz, Islas del
Cornwallis Island *37 F2 Island* Nunavut, N Canada
Coro *58 C1 prev.* Santa Ana de Coro. Falcón, NW Venezuela
Corocoro *61 F4* La Paz, W Bolivia
Coromandel *150 D2* Waikato, North Island, New Zealand
Coromandel Coast *132 D2 coast* E India
Coromandel Peninsula *150 D2 peninsula* North Island, New Zealand
Coronado, Bahía de *52 D5 bay* S Costa Rica
Coronel Dorrego *65 C5* Buenos Aires, E Argentina
Coronel Oviedo *64 D2* Caaguazú, SE Paraguay
Corozal *52 C1* Corozal, N Belize
Corpus Christi *49 G4* Texas, SW USA
Corrales *48 D2* New Mexico, SW USA
Corrib, Lough *89 A5 Ir.* Loch Coirib. *lake* W Ireland
Corrientes *64 D3* Corrientes, NE Argentina
Corriza *see* Korçë
Corse *91 E7 Eng.* Corsica. *island* France, C Mediterranean Sea
Corsica *see* Corse
Corsicana *49 G3* Texas, SW USA
Cortegana *92 C4* Andalucía, S Spain
Cortés *53 E5 var.* Ciudad Cortés. Puntarenas, SE Costa Rica
Cortez, Sea of *see* California, Golfo de
Cortina d'Ampezzo *96 C1* Veneto, NE Italy
Coruche *92 B3* Santarém, C Portugal
Çoruh Nehri *117 E3 Geor.* Chorokh, *Rus.* Chorokhi. *river* Georgia/Turkey
Çorum *116 D3 var.* Chorum. Çorum, N Turkey
Corunna *see* A Coruña
Corvallis *46 B3* Oregon, NW USA
Corvo *92 A5 var.* Ilha do Corvo. *island* Azores, Portugal, NE Atlantic Ocean
Corvo, Ilha do *see* Corvo
Cos *see* Kos
Cosenza *97 D6 anc.* Consentia. Calabria, SW Italy
Cosne-Cours-sur-Loire *90 C4* Nièvre, Bourgogne, C France Europe
Costa Mesa *46 D2* California, W USA North America
Costa Rica *53 E4 off.* Republic of Costa Rica. *country* Central America

COSTA RICA
Central America

Official name Republic of Costa Rica
Formation 1838 / 1838
Capital San José
Population 4.3 million / 218 people per sq mile (84 people per sq km) / 52%
Total area 19,730 sq miles (51,100 sq km)
Languages Spanish*, English Creole, Bribri, Cabecar
Religions Roman Catholic 76%, Other (including Protestant) 24%
Ethnic mix Mestizo and European 96%, Black 2%, Chinese 1%, Amerindian 1%
Government Presidential system

COSTA RICA
(continued)

Currency Costa Rican colón = 100 centimos
Literacy rate 96%
Calorie consumption 2876 calories

Costa Rica, Republic of *see* Costa Rica
Costermansville *see* Bukavu
Cotagaita *61 F5* Potosí, S Bolivia
Côte d'Ivoire *74 D4 off.* Republic of Côte d'Ivoire, *Eng.* Ivory Coast, *Fr.* République de la Côte d'Ivoire. *country* W Africa

COTE D'IVOIRE (IVORY COAST)
West Africa

Official name Republic of Côte d'Ivoire
Formation 1960 / 1960
Capital Yamoussoukro
Population 18.2 million / 148 people per sq mile (57 people per sq km) / 46%
Total area 124,502 sq miles (322,460 sq km)
Languages French*, Akan, Kru, Voltaic
Religions Muslim 38%, Traditional beliefs 25%, Roman Catholic 25%, Protestant 6%, Other 6%
Ethnic mix Baoule 23%, Other 19%, Bété 18%, Senufo 15%, Agni-Ashanti 14%, Mandinka 11%
Government Presidential system
Currency CFA franc = 100 centimes
Literacy rate 48%
Calorie consumption 2631 calories

Côte d'Ivoire, République de la *see* Côte d'Ivoire
Côte d'Or *90 D4 cultural region* C France
Côte Française des Somalis *see* Djibouti
Côtière, Chaîne *see* Coast Mountains
Cotonou *75 F5 var.* Kotonu. S Benin
Cotrone *see* Crotone
Cotswold Hills *89 D6 var.* Cotswolds. *hill range* S England, UK
Cotswolds *see* Cotswold Hills
Cottbus *94 D4 Lus.* Chośebuz; *prev.* Kottbus. Brandenburg, E Germany
Cotton State, The *see* Alabama
Cotyora *see* Ordu
Couentrey *see* Coventry
Council Bluffs *45 F4* Iowa, C USA
Courantyne River *59 G4 var.* Corantijn Rivier, Corentyne River. *river* Guyana/Suriname
Courland Lagoon *106 A4 Ger.* Kurisches Haff, *Rus.* Kurskiy Zaliv. *lagoon* Lithuania/Russian Federation
Courtrai *see* Kortrijk
Coutances *90 B3 anc.* Constantia. Manche, N France
Couvin *87 C7* Namur, S Belgium
Coventry *89 D6 anc.* Couentrey. C England, UK
Covilhã *92 C3* Castelo Branco, E Portugal
Cowan, Lake *147 B6 lake* Western Australia
Coxen Hole *see* Roatán
Coxin Hole *see* Roatán
Coyhaique *see* Coihaique
Coyote State, The *see* South Dakota
Cozumel, Isla *51 H3 island* SE Mexico
Cracovia/Cracow *see* Kraków
Cradock *78 C5* Eastern Cape, S South Africa
Craig *44 C4* Colorado, C USA
Craiova *108 B5* Dolj, SW Romania
Cranbrook *37 E5* British Columbia, SW Canada
Crane *see* The Crane
Cranz *see* Zelenogradsk
Crawley *89 E7* SE England, UK
Cremona *96 B2* Lombardia, N Italy
Creole State *see* Louisiana
Cres *100 A3 It.* Cherso; *anc.* Crexa. *island* W Croatia
Crescent City *46 A4* California, W USA
Crescent Group *128 C7 island group* C Paracel Islands
Creston *45 F4* Iowa, C USA
Crestview *42 D3* Florida, SE USA
Créteil *90 E2* Val-de-Marne, N France
Crete, Sea of/Creticum, Mare *see* Kritikó Pélagos
Creuse *90 B4 river* C France
Crewe *89 D6* C England, UK

Crexa see Cres
Crikvenica 100 A3 It. Cirquenizza; prev. Cirkvenica, Crjkvenica. Primorje-Gorski Kotar, NW Croatia
Cristóbal 53 G4 Colón, C Panama
Cristóbal Colón, Pico 58 B1 mountain N Colombia
Cristur/Cristuru Săcuiesc see Cristuru Secuiesc
Cristuru Secuiesc 108 C4 prev. Cristur, Cristuru Săcuiesc, Sitaş Cristuru, Ger. Kreutz, Hung. Székelykeresztúr, Szitás-Keresztúr. Harghita, C Romania
Crjkvenica see Crikvenica
Crna Gora see Montenegro
Crna Reka 101 D6 river S FYR Macedonia
Crni Drim see Black Drin
Croatia 100 B3 off. Republic of Croatia, Ger. Kroatien, SCr. Hrvatska. country SE Europe

CROATIA
Southeast Europe

Official name Republic of Croatia
Formation 1991 / 1991
Capital Zagreb
Population 4.6 million / 211 people per sq mile (81 people per sq km) / 58%
Total area 21,831 sq miles (56,542 sq km)
Languages Croatian*
Religions Roman Catholic 88%, Other 7%, Orthodox Christian 4%, Muslim 1%
Ethnic mix Croat 90%, Other 5%, Serb 4%, Bosniak 1%
Government Parliamentary system
Currency Kuna = 100 lipas
Literacy rate 98%
Calorie consumption 2799 calories

Croatia, Republic of see Croatia
Crocodile see Limpopo
Croia see Krujë
Croker Island 146 E2 island Northern Territory, N Australia
Cromwell 151 B7 Otago, South Island, New Zealand
Crooked Island 54 D2 island SE Bahamas
Crooked Island Passage 54 D2 channel SE Bahamas
Crookston 45 F1 Minnesota, N USA
Crossen see Krosno Odrzańskie
Croton/Crotona see Crotone
Crotone 97 E6 var. Cotrone; anc. Croton, Crotona. Calabria, SW Italy
Croydon 89 A8 SE England, UK
Crozet Basin 141 B6 undersea basin S Indian Ocean
Crozet Islands 141 B7 island group French Southern and Antarctic Territories
Crozet Plateau 141 B7 var. Crozet Plateaus. undersea plateau SW Indian Ocean
Crozet Plateaus see Crozet Plateau
Crystal Brook 149 B6 South Australia
Csaca see Čadca
Csakathurn/Csáktornya see Čakovec
Csíkszereda see Miercurea-Ciuc
Csorna 99 C6 Győr-Moson-Sopron, NW Hungary
Csurgó 99 C7 Somogy, SW Hungary
Cuando 78 C2 var. Kwando. river S Africa
Cuango 78 B1 var. Kwango. river Angola/Dem. Rep. Congo
Cuango see Kwango
Cuanza 78 B1 var. Kwanza. river C Angola
Cuauhtémoc 50 C2 Chihuahua, N Mexico
Cuautla 51 E4 Morelos, S Mexico
Cuba 54 B2 off. Republic of Cuba. country W West Indies

CUBA
West Indies

Official name Republic of Cuba
Formation 1902 / 1902
Capital Havana
Population 11.3 million / 264 people per sq mile (102 people per sq km) / 75%

CUBA
(continued)

Total area 42,803 sq miles (110,860 sq km)
Languages Spanish*
Religions Nonreligious 49%, Roman Catholic 40%, Atheist 6%, Other 4%, Protestant 1%
Ethnic mix White 66%, European–African 22%, Black 12%
Government One-party state
Currency Cuban peso = 100 centavos
Literacy rate 97%
Calorie consumption 3152 calories

Cubal 78 B2 Benguela, W Angola
Cubango 78 B2 var. Kuvango, Port. Vila Artur de Paiva, Vila da Ponte. Huíla, SW Angola
Cubango 78 B2 var. Kavango, Kavengo, Kubango, Okavango, Okavanggo. river S Africa
Cuba, Republic of see Cuba
Cúcuta 58 C2 var. San José de Cúcuta. Norte de Santander, N Colombia
Cuddapah 132 C2 Andhra Pradesh, S India
Cuenca 60 B2 Azuay, S Ecuador
Cuenca 93 E3 anc. Conca. Castilla-La Mancha, C Spain
Cuera see Chur
Cuernavaca 51 E4 Morelos, S Mexico
Cuiabá 63 E3 prev. Cuyabá. state capital Mato Grosso, SW Brazil
Cuidad Presidente Stroessner see Ciudad del Este
Cúige see Connaught
Cúige Laighean see Leinster
Cúige Mumhan see Munster
Cuijck 86 D4 Noord-Brabant, SE Netherlands
Cúil Raithin see Coleraine
Cuito 78 B2 var. Kwito. river SE Angola
Cukai 138 B3 var. Chukai, Kemaman. Terengganu, Peninsular Malaysia
Cularo see Grenoble
Culiacán 50 C3 var. Culiacán Rosales, Culiacán-Rosales. Sinaloa, C Mexico
Culiacán-Rosales/Culiacán Rosales see Culiacán
Cullera 93 F3 País Valenciano, E Spain
Cullman 42 C2 Alabama, S USA
Culm see Chełmno
Culmsee see Chełmża
Cumaná 59 E1 Sucre, NE Venezuela
Cumbal, Nevado de 58 A4 elevation S Colombia
Cumberland 41 E4 Maryland, NE USA
Cumberland Plateau 42 D1 plateau E USA
Cumberland Sound 37 H3 inlet Baffin Island, Nunavut, NE Canada
Cumpas 50 B2 Sonora, NW Mexico
Cunene 78 A3 province S Angola
Cunene 69 C6 var. Kunene. river Angola/Namibia
Cuneo 96 A2 Fr. Coni. Piemonte, NW Italy
Cunnamulla 149 C5 Queensland, E Australia
Ćuprija 100 E4 Serbia, E Serbia
Curaçao 55 E5 island Netherlands Antilles
Curia Rhaetorum see Chur
Curicó 64 B4 Maule, C Chile
Curieta see Krk
Curitiba 63 E4 prev. Curytiba. state capital Paraná, S Brazil
Curtbunar see Tervel
Curtea de Argeş 108 C4 var. Curtea-de-Argeş. Argeş, S Romania
Curtea-de-Arges see Curtea de Argeş
Curtici 108 A4 Ger. Kurtitsch, Hung. Kürtös. Arad, W Romania
Curtis Island 148 E4 island Queensland, SE Australia
Curytiba see Curitiba
Curzola see Korčula
Cusco 61 E4 var. Cuzco. Cusco, C Peru
Cusset 91 C5 Allier, C France
Cutch, Gulf of see Kachchh, Gulf of
Cuttack 135 F4 Orissa, E India
Cuvier Plateau 141 E6 undersea plateau E Indian Ocean
Cuxhaven 94 B2 Niedersachsen, NW Germany
Cuyabá see Cuiabá
Cuyuni, Río see Cuyuni River
Cuyuni River 59 F3 var. Río Cuyuni. river Guyana/Venezuela
Cuzco see Cusco
Cyclades see Kykládes
Cydonia see Chaniá
Cymru see Wales
Cyprus 102 C4 off. Republic of Cyprus, Gk. Kypros, Turk. Kıbrıs, Kıbrıs Cumhuriyeti. country E Mediterranean Sea

CYPRUS
Southeast Europe

Official name Republic of Cyprus
Formation 1960 / 1960
Capital Nicosia
Population 835,000 / 234 people per sq mile (90 people per sq km) / 57%
Total area 3571 sq miles (9250 sq km)
Languages Greek, Turkish
Religions Orthodox Christian 78%, Muslim 18%, Other 4%
Ethnic mix Greek 85%, Turkish 12%, Other 3%
Government Presidential system
Currency Cyprus pound (Turkish lira in TRNC) = 100 cents (Cyprus pound); 100 kurus (Turkish lira)
Literacy rate 97%
Calorie consumption 3255 calories

Cyprus, Republic of see Cyprus
Cythnos see Kýthnos
Czech Republic 99 A5 Cz. Česká Republika. country C Europe

CZECH REPUBLIC
Central Europe

Official name Czech Republic
Formation 1993 / 1993
Capital Prague
Population 10.2 million / 335 people per sq mile (129 people per sq km) / 75%
Total area 30,450 sq miles (78,866 sq km)
Languages Czech*, Slovak, Hungarian (Magyar)
Religions Roman Catholic 39%, Atheist 38%, Other 18%, Protestant 3%, Hussite 2%
Ethnic mix Czech 81%, Moravian 13%, Slovak 6%
Government Parliamentary system
Currency Czech koruna = 100 haleru
Literacy rate 99%
Calorie consumption 3171 calories

Czenstochau see Częstochowa
Czernowitz see Chernivtsi
Częstochowa 98 C4 Ger. Czenstochau, Tschenstochau, Rus. Chenstokhov. Śląskie, S Poland
Człuchów 98 C3 Ger. Schlochau. Pomorskie, NW Poland

D

Dabajuro 58 C1 Falcón, NW Venezuela
Dabeiba 58 B2 Antioquia, NW Colombia
Dąbrowa Tarnowska 99 D5 Małopolskie, S Poland
Dabryn' 107 C8 Rus. Dobryn'. Homyel'skaya Voblasts', SE Belarus
Dacca see Dhaka
Daegu see Taegu
Dagana 74 B3 N Senegal
Dagda 106 D4 Krāslava, SE Latvia
Dagden see Hiiumaa
Dagenham 89 B8 UK
Dağliq Quarabağ see Nagorno-Karabakh
Dagö see Hiiumaa
Dagupan 139 E1 off. Dagupan City. Luzon, N Philippines
Dagupan City see Dagupan
Da Hinggan Ling 127 G1 Eng. Great Khingan Range. mountain range NE China
Dahm, Ramlat 121 B6 desert NW Yemen
Dahomey see Benin
Daihoku see T'aipei
Daimiel 92 D3 Castilla-La Mancha, C Spain
Daimoniá 105 B7 Pelopónnisos, S Greece
Dainan see T'ainan
Daingin, Bá an see Dingle Bay
Dairen see Dalian
Dakar 74 B3 country capital (Senegal) W Senegal
Dakhla see Ad Dakhla
Dakoro 75 G3 Maradi, S Niger
Đakovica 101 D5 var. Djakovica, Alb. Gjakovë. Kosovo, S Serbia
Đakovo 100 C3 var. Djakovo, Hung. Diakovár. Osijek-Baranja, E Croatia
Dakshin see Deccan
Dalain Hob 126 D3 var. Ejin Qi. Nei Mongol Zizhiqu, N China
Dalai Nor see Hulun Nur
Dalaman 116 A4 Muğla, SW Turkey
Dalandzadgad 127 E3 Ömnögovĭ, S Mongolia
Đa Lat 137 E6 Lâm Đông, S Vietnam
Dalby 149 D5 Queensland, E Australia
Dale City 41 E4 Virginia, NE USA
Dalhart 49 E1 Texas, SW USA
Dali 128 A6 var. Xiaguan. Yunnan, SW China
Dalian 128 D4 var. Dairen, Dalien, Lüda, Ta-lien, Rus. Dalny. Liaoning, NE China
Dalien see Dalian
Dallas 49 G2 Texas, SW USA
Dalmacija 100 B4 Eng. Dalmatia, Ger. Dalmatien, It. Dalmazia. cultural region S Croatia
Dalmatia/Dalmatien/Dalmazia see Dalmacija
Dalmatien see Dalmacija
Dalny see Dalian
Dalton 42 D1 Georgia, SE USA
Dálvvadis see Jokkmokk
Daly Waters 148 A2 Northern Territory, N Australia
Damachava 107 A6 var. Damachova, Pol. Domaczewo, Rus. Domachëvo. Brestskaya Voblasts', SW Belarus
Damachova see Damachava
Damān 134 C4 Damān and Diu, W India
Damara 76 C4 Ombella-Mpoko, S Central African Republic
Damas see Dimashq
Damasco see Dimashq
Damascus see Dimashq
Damāvand, Qolleh-ye 120 D3 mountain N Iran
Damietta see Dumyāt
Dammām see Ad Dammān
Damoûr 119 A5 var. Ad Dāmūr. W Lebanon
Dampier 146 A4 Western Australia
Dampier, Selat 139 F4 strait Papua, E Indonesia
Damqawt 121 D6 var. Damqut. E Yemen
Damqut see Damqawt
Damxung 126 C5 var. Gongtang. Xizang Zizhiqu, W China
Danakil Desert 72 D4 var. Afar Depression, Danakil Plain. desert E Africa
Danakil Plain see Danakil Desert
Danané 74 D5 W Côte d'Ivoire (Ivory Coast)
Đă Năng 137 E5 prev. Tourane. Quang Nam-Đa Năng, C Vietnam
Danborg see Daneborg
Dandong 128 D3 var. Tan-tung; prev. An-tung. Liaoning, NE China
Daneborg 83 E3 var. Danborg. Tunu, N Greenland
Dänew see Galkynyş
Dangara see Danghara
Dangerous Archipelago see Tuamotu, Îles
Danghara 123 E3 Rus. Dangara. SW Tajikistan
Danghe Nanshan 126 D3 mountain range W China
Dang Raek, Phanom/Dangrek, Chaîne des see Dângrêk, Chuŏr Phnum
Dângrêk, Chuŏr Phnum 137 D5 var. Phanom Dang Raek, Phanom Dong Rak, Fr. Chaîne des Dangrek. mountain range Cambodia/Thailand
Dangriga 52 C1 prev. Stann Creek. Stann Creek, E Belize
Danish West Indies see Virgin Islands (US)
Danlí 52 D2 El Paraíso, S Honduras

Danmark see Denmark
Danmarksstraedet see Denmark Strait
Dannenberg 94 C3 Niedersachsen, N Germany
Dannevirke 150 D4 Manawatu-Wanganui, North Island, New Zealand
Dantzig see Gdańsk
Danube 81 E4 Bul. Dunav, Cz. Dunaj, Ger. Donau, Hung. Duna, Rom. Dunărea. river C Europe
Danubian Plain see Dunavska Ravnina
Danum see Doncaster
Danville 41 E5 Virginia, NE USA
Danxian/Dan Xian see Danzhou
Danzhou 128 C7 prev. Danxian, Dan Xian, Nada. Hainan, S China
Danzig see Gdańsk
Danziger Bucht see Danzig, Gulf of
Danzig, Gulf of 98 C2 var. Gulf of Gdańsk, Ger. Danziger Bucht, Pol. Zakota Gdańska, Rus. Gdan'skaya Bukhta. gulf N Poland
Daqm see Duqm
Darʿā 119 B5 var. Derʿa, Fr. Déraa. Darʿā, SW Syria
Darabani 108 C3 Botoşani, NW Romania
Daraut-Kurgan see Daroot-Korgon
Dardanelles see Çanakkale Boğazı
Dardanelli see Çanakkale
Dar-el-Beida see Casablanca
Dar es Salaam 73 C7 Dar es Salaam, E Tanzania
Darfield 151 C6 Canterbury, South Island, New Zealand
Darfur 72 A4 var. Darfur Massif. cultural region W Sudan
Darfur Massif see Darfur
Darhan 127 E2 Darhan Uul, N Mongolia
Darien, Golfo del see Darién, Gulf of
Darien, Gulf of 58 A2 Sp. Golfo del Darién. gulf S Caribbean Sea
Darien, Isthmus of see Panama, Istmo de
Darién, Serranía del 53 H5 mountain range Colombia/Panama
Dario see Ciudad Darío
Dariorigum see Vannes
Darjeeling see Darjiling
Darjiling 135 F3 prev. Darjeeling. West Bengal, NE India
Darling River 149 C6 river New South Wales, SE Australia
Darlington 89 D5 N England, UK
Darmstadt 95 B5 Hessen, SW Germany
Darnah 71 G2 var. Derna. NE Libya
Darnley, Cape 154 D2 cape Antarctica
Daroca 91 E2 Aragón, NE Spain
Daroot-Korgon 123 F3 var. Daraut-Kurgan. Oshskaya Oblast', SW Kyrgyzstan
Dartford 89 B8 SE England, UK
Dartmoor 89 C7 moorland SW England, UK
Dartmouth 39 F4 Nova Scotia, SE Canada
Darvaza see Derweze, Turkmenistan
Darwin 146 D2 prev. Palmerston, Port Darwin. territory capital Northern Territory, N Australia
Darwin, Isla 60 A4 island Galápagos, Galapagos Islands, W Ecuador
Dashhowuz see Daşoguz
Dashkawka 107 D6 Rus. Dashkovka. Mahilyowskaya Voblasts', E Belarus
Dashkovka see Dashkawka
Daşoguz 122 C2 Rus. Dashkhovuz, Turkm. Dashhowuz; prev. Tashauz. Daşoguz Welaýaty, N Turkmenistan
Đa, Sông see Black River
Datong 128 C3 var. Tatung, Ta-t'ung. Shanxi, C China
Daugava see Western Dvina
Daugavpils 106 D4 Ger. Dünaburg; prev. Rus. Dvinsk. Daugvapils, SE Latvia
Daung Kyun 137 B6 island S Myanmar (Burma)
Dauphiné 91 D5 cultural region E France
Dävangere 132 C1 Karnātaka, W India
Davao 139 F3 off. Davao City. Mindanao, S Philippines
Davao City see Davao
Davao Gulf 139 F3 gulf Mindanao, S Philippines
Davenport 45 G3 Iowa, C USA
David 53 E5 Chiriquí, W Panama
Davie Ridge 141 A5 undersea ridge W Indian Ocean

Davis 154 D3 Australian research station Antarctica
Davis Sea 154 D3 sea Antarctica
Davis Strait 82 B3 strait Baffin Bay/Labrador Sea
Dawei see Tavoy
Dawlat Qaṭar see Qatar
Dax 91 B6 var. Ax; anc. Aquae Augustae, Aquae Tarbelicae. Landes, SW France
Dayr az Zawr 118 D3 var. Deir ez Zor. Dayr az Zawr, E Syria
Dayton 40 C4 Ohio, N USA
Daytona Beach 43 E4 Florida, SE USA
De Aar 78 C5 Northern Cape, C South Africa
Dead Sea 119 B6 var. Bahret Lut, Lacus Asphaltites, Ar. Al Baḥr al Mayyit, Baḥrat Lūṭ, Heb. Yam HaMelaḥ. salt lake Israel/Jordan
Deán Funes 64 C3 Córdoba, C Argentina
Death Valley 47 C7 valley California, W USA
Deatnu 84 D2 Fin. Tenojoki, Nor. Tana. river Finland/Norway
Debar 101 D6 Ger. Dibra, Turk. Debre. W FYR Macedonia
De Behagle see Laï
Dębica 99 D5 Podkarpackie, SE Poland
De Bildt see De Bilt
De Bilt 86 C3 var. De Bildt. Utrecht, C Netherlands
Dębno 98 B3 Zachodnio-pomorskie, NW Poland
Debre see Debar
Debrecen 99 D6 Ger. Debreczin, Rom. Debreţin; prev. Debreczen. Hajdú-Bihar, E Hungary
Debreczen/Debreczin see Debrecen
Debreţin see Debrecen
Decatur 42 C1 Alabama, S USA
Decatur 40 B4 Illinois, N USA
Deccan 134 D5 Hind. Dakshin. plateau C India
Děčín 98 B4 Ger. Tetschen. Ústecký Kraj, NW Czech Republic
Dedeagaç/Dedeagach see Alexandroúpoli
Dedemsvaart 86 E3 Overijssel, E Netherlands
Dee 88 C3 river NE Scotland, UK
Deering 36 C2 Alaska, USA
Deés see Dej
Deggendorf 95 D6 Bayern, SE Germany
Değirmenlik 102 C5 Gk. Kythrea. N Cyprus
Deh Bīd 120 D3 Fārs, C Iran
Dehli see Delhi
Deh Shū 122 D5 var. Deshu. Helmand, S Afghanistan
Deinze 87 B5 Oost-Vlaanderen, NW Belgium
Deir ez Zor see Dayr az Zawr
Deirgeirt, Loch see Derg, Lough
Dej 108 B3 Hung. Dés; prev. Deés. Cluj, NW Romania
De Jouwer see Joure
Dekéleia see Dhekéleia
Dékoa 76 C4 Kémo, C Central African Republic
De Land 43 E4 Florida, SE USA
Delano 47 C7 California, W USA
Delārām 122 D5 Nīmrūz, SW Afghanistan
Delaware 40 D4 Ohio, N USA
Delaware 41 F4 off. State of Delaware, also known as Blue Hen State, Diamond State, First State. state NE USA
Delft 86 B4 Zuid-Holland, W Netherlands
Delfzijl 86 E1 Groningen, NE Netherlands
Delgo 72 B3 Northern, N Sudan
Delhi 134 D3 var. Dehli, Hind. Dilli, hist. Shahjahanabad. union territory capital Delhi, N India
Delicias 50 D2 var. Ciudad Delicias. Chihuahua, N Mexico
Déli-Kárpátok see Carpaţii Meridionali
Delmenhorst 94 B3 Niedersachsen, NW Germany
Del Rio 49 F4 Texas, SW USA
Deltona 43 F4 Florida, SE USA
Demba 77 D6 Kasai Occidental, C Dem. Rep. Congo
Dembia 76 D4 Mbomou, SE Central African Republic
Demchok 126 A4 China/India
Demchok 126 A5 var. Dêmqog. disputed region China/India

Demchok see Dêmqog
Demerara Plain 56 C2 abyssal plain W Atlantic Ocean
Deming 48 C3 New Mexico, SW USA
Demmin 94 C2 Mecklenburg-Vorpommern, NE Germany
Demopolis 42 C2 Alabama, S USA
Dêmqog 126 A5 var. Demchok. China/India
Dêmqog see Demchok
Dêmqog see Demchok
Denali see McKinley, Mount
Denau see Denow
Dender 87 B6 Fr. Dendre. river W Belgium
Dendre see Dender
Denekamp 86 E3 Overijssel, E Netherlands
Den Haag see 's-Gravenhage
Denham 147 A5 Western Australia
Den Ham 86 E3 Overijssel, E Netherlands
Den Helder 86 C2 Noord-Holland, NW Netherlands
Dénia 93 F4 País Valenciano, E Spain
Deniliquin 149 C7 New South Wales, SE Australia
Denison 45 F3 Iowa, C USA
Denison 49 G2 Texas, SW USA
Denizli 116 B4 Denizli, SW Turkey
Denmark 85 A7 off. Kingdom of Denmark, Dan. Danmark; anc. Hafnia. country N Europe

DENMARK
Northern Europe

Official name Kingdom of Denmark
Formation AD 950 / 1945
Capital Copenhagen
Population 5.4 million / 330 people per sq mile (127 people per sq km) / 85%
Total area 16,639 sq miles (43,094 sq km)
Languages Danish*
Religions Evangelical Lutheran 89%, Other 10%, Roman Catholic 1%
Ethnic mix Danish 96%, Other (including Scandinavian and Turkish) 3%, Faeroese and Inuit 1%
Government Parliamentary system
Currency Danish krone = 100 øre
Literacy rate 99%
Calorie consumption 3439 calories

Denmark, Kingdom of see Denmark
Denmark Strait 82 D4 var. Danmarksstraedet. strait Greenland/Iceland
Dennery 55 F1 E Saint Lucia
Denow 123 E3 Rus. Denau. Surkhondaryo Viloyati, S Uzbekistan
Denpasar 138 D5 prev. Paloe. Bali, C Indonesia
Denton 49 G2 Texas, SW USA
D'Entrecasteaux Islands 144 B3 island group SE Papua New Guinea
Denver 44 D4 state capital Colorado, C USA
Déraa see Dar'ā
Der'a/Dar'ā/Déraa see Dar'ā
Dera Ghāzi Khān 134 C2 var. Dera Ghāzīkhān. Punjab, C Pakistan
Dera Ghāzīkhān see Dera Ghāzi Khān
Đeravica 101 D5 mountain S Serbia
Derbent 111 B8 Respublika Dagestan, SW Russian Federation
Derby 89 D6 C England, UK
Dereli see Gónnoi
Dergachi see Derhachi
Derg, Lough 89 A6 Ir. Loch Deirgeirt. lake W Ireland
Derhachi 109 G2 Rus. Dergachi. Kharkivs'ka Oblast', E Ukraine
De Ridder 42 A3 Louisiana, S USA
Dérna see Darnah
Derry see Londonderry
Dertosa see Tortosa
Derventa 100 B3 Republika Srpska, N Bosnia and Herzegovina
Derweze 122 C2 Rus. Darvaza. Ahal Welaýaty, C Turkmenistan
Dés see Dej
Deschutes River 46 B3 river Oregon, NW USA
Desē 72 C4 var. Dese, It. Dessie. Amhara, N Ethiopia
Deseado, Río 65 B7 river S Argentina

Desertas, Ilhas 70 A2 island group Madeira, Portugal, NE Atlantic Ocean
Deshu see Deh Shū
Des Moines 45 F3 state capital Iowa, C USA
Desna 109 E2 river Russian Federation/Ukraine
Dessau 94 C4 Sachsen-Anhalt, E Germany
Desse see Desē
Dessie see Desē
Destêrro see Florianópolis
Detroit 40 D3 Michigan, N USA
Detroit Lakes 45 F2 Minnesota, N USA
Deurne 87 D5 Noord-Brabant, SE Netherlands
Deutschendorf see Poprad
Deutsch-Eylau see Iława
Deutsch Krone see Wałcz
Deutschland/Deutschland, Bundesrepublik see Germany
Deutsch-Südwestafrika see Namibia
Deva 108 B4 Ger. Diemrich, Hung. Déva. Hunedoara, W Romania
Déva see Deva
Deva see Chester
Devana see Aberdeen
Devana Castra see Chester
Đevđelija see Gevgelija
Deventer 86 D3 Overijssel, E Netherlands
Devils Lake 45 E1 North Dakota, N USA
Devoll see Devollit, Lumi i
Devollit, Lumi i 101 D6 var. Devoll. river SE Albania
Devon Island 37 F2 prev. North Devon Island. island Parry Islands, Nunavut, NE Canada
Devonport 149 C8 Tasmania, SE Australia
Devrek 116 C2 Zonguldak, N Turkey
Dexter 45 H5 Missouri, C USA
Deynau see Galkynyş
Dezfūl 120 C3 var. Dizful. Khūzestān, SW Iran
Dezhou 128 D4 Shandong, E China
Dhaka 135 G4 prev. Dacca. country capital (Bangladesh) Dhaka, C Bangladesh
Dhanbād 135 F4 Jhārkhand, NE India
Dhekélia 102 C5 Eng. Dhekelia, Gk. Dekéleia. UK air base SE Cyprus
Dhidhimóteicho see Didymóteicho
Dhikti Ori see Díkti
Dhodhekánisos see Dodekánisa
Dhomókós see Domokós
Dhráma see Dráma
Dhrepanon, Akrotírio see Drépano, Akrotírio
Dhún na nGall, Bá see Donegal Bay
Dhuusa Marreeb 73 E5 var. Dusa Marreb, It. Dusa Mareb. Galguduud, C Somalia
Diakovár see Đakovo
Diamantina, Chapada 63 F3 mountain range E Brazil
Diamantina Fracture Zone 141 E6 tectonic feature E Indian Ocean
Diamond State see Delaware
Diarbekr see Diyarbakır
Dibio see Dijon
Dibra see Debar
Dibrugarh 135 H3 Assam, NE India
Dickinson 44 D2 North Dakota, N USA
Dicle see Tigris
Didimotiho see Didymóteicho
Didymóteicho 104 D3 var. Dhidhimótikhon, Didimotiho. Anatolikí Makedonía kai Thráki, NE Greece
Diedenhofen see Thionville
Diekirch 87 D7 Diekirch, C Luxembourg
Diemrich see Deva
Điện Biên 136 C3 var. Bien Bien, Dien Bien Phu. Lai Châu, N Vietnam
Dien Bien Phu see Điện Biên
Diepenbeek 87 D6 Limburg, NE Belgium
Diepholz 94 B3 Niedersachsen, NW Germany
Dieppe 90 C2 Seine-Maritime, N France
Dieren 86 D4 Gelderland, E Netherlands
Differdange 87 D8 Luxembourg, SW Luxembourg
Digne 91 D6 var. Digne-les-Bains. Alpes-de-Haute-Provence, SE France
Digne-les-Bains see Digne

Digoel see Digul, Sungai
Digoin 90 C4 Saône-et-Loire, C France
Digul, Sungai 139 H5 prev. Digoel. river
  Papua, E Indonesia
Dihang see Brahmaputra
Dijlah see Tigris
Dijon 90 D4 anc. Dibio. Côte d'Or,
  C France
Dikhil 72 D4 SW Djibouti
Dikson 114 D2 Taymyrskiy
  (Dolgano-Nenetskiy) Avtonomnyy
  Okrug, N Russian Federation
Díkti 105 D8 var. Dhíkti Ori.
  mountain range Kríti, Greece,
  E Mediterranean Sea
Dili 139 F5 var. Dilli, Dilly. country
  capital (East Timor) N East Timor
Dilia 75 G3 var. Dilli. river SE Niger
Di Linh 137 E6 Lâm Đông, S Vietnam
Dilli see Dili, East Timor
Dilli see Delhi, India
Dillia see Dilia
Dilling 72 B4 var. Ad Dalanj. Southern
  Kordofan, C Sudan
Dillon 44 B2 Montana, NW USA
Dilly see Dili
Dilolo 77 D7 Katanga,
  S Dem. Rep. Congo
Dimashq 119 B5 var. Ash Shām, Esh
  Sham, Eng. Damascus, Fr. Damas,
  It. Damasco. country capital (Syria)
  Dimashq, SW Syria
Dimitrovgrad 104 D3 Khaskovo,
  S Bulgaria
Dimitrovgrad 111 C6 prev. Caribrod.
  Serbia, SE Serbia
Dimitrovo see Pernik
Dimovo 104 B1 Vidin, NW Bulgaria
Dinajpur 135 F3 Rajshahi,
  NW Bangladesh
Dinan 90 B3 Côtes d'Armor, NW France
Dinant 87 C7 Namur, S Belgium
Dinar 116 B4 Afyon, SW Turkey
Dinara see Dinaric Alps
Dinaric Alps 100 C4 var. Dinara.
  mountain range Bosnia and
  Herzegovina/Croatia
Dindigul 132 C3 Tamil Nādu, SE India
Dingle Bay 89 A6 Ir. Bá an Daingin. bay
  SW Ireland
Dinguiraye 74 C4 N Guinea
Diourbel 74 B3 W Senegal
Dirê Dawa 73 D5 Dirê Dawa, E Ethiopia
Dirk Hartog Island 147 A5 island
  Western Australia
Dirschau see Tczew
Disappointment, Lake 146 C4 salt lake
  Western Australia
Discovery Bay 54 B4 Middlesex,
  Jamaica, Greater Antilles, C Jamaica
  Caribbean Sea
Disko Bugt see Qeqertarsuup Tunua
Dispur 135 G3 state capital Assam,
  NE India
Divinópolis 63 F4 Minas Gerais,
  SE Brazil
Divo 74 D5 S Côte d'Ivoire (Ivory Coast)
Divodurum Mediomatricum see Metz
Diyarbakır 117 E4 var. Diarbekr; anc.
  Amida. Diyarbakır, SE Turkey
Dizful see Dezfūl
Djailolo see Halmahera, Pulau
Djajapura see Jayapura
Djakarta see Jakarta
Djakovica see Đakovica
Djakovo see Đakovo
Djambala 77 B6 Plateaux, C Congo
Djambi see Jambi
Djambi see Hari, Batang
Djanet 71 E4 prev. Fort Charlet.
  SE Algeria
Djéblé see Jablah
Djelfa 70 D2 var. El Djelfa. N Algeria
Djéma 76 D4 Haut-Mbomou,
  E Central African Republic
Djember see Jember
Djérablous see Jarābulus
Djerba see Jerba, Île de
Djérem 76 B4 river C Cameroon
Djevdjelija see Gevgelija
Djibouti 72 D4 var. Jibuti. country
  capital (Djibouti) E Djibouti
Djibouti 72 D4 off. Republic of Djibouti,
  var. Jibuti; prev. French Somaliland,
  French Territory of the Afars and
  Issas, Côte Française des Somalis, Fr.
  Territoire Français des Afars et des
  Issas. country E Africa

DJIBOUTI
East Africa

Official name Republic of Djibouti
Formation 1977 / 1977
Capital Djibouti
Population 793,000 / 89 people per
  sq mile (34 people per sq km) / 83%
Total area 8494 sq miles (22,000 sq km)
Languages French*, Arabic*, Somali,
  Afar
Religions Muslim (mainly Sunni) 94%,
  Christian 6%
Ethnic mix Issa 60%, Afar 35%, Other 5%
Government Presidential system
Currency Djibouti franc = 100 centimes
Literacy rate 66%
Calorie consumption 2220 calories

Djibouti, Republic of see Djibouti
Djokjakarta see Yogyakarta
Djourab, Erg du 76 C2 desert N Chad
Djúpivogur 83 E5 Austurland,
  SE Iceland
Dmitriyevsk see Makiyivka
Dnepr see Dnieper
Dneprodzerzhinsk see
  Dniprodzerzhyns'k
Dneprodzerzhinskoye
  Vodokhranilishche see
  Dniprodzerzhyns'ke Vodoskhovyshche
Dnepropetrovsk see Dnipropetrovs'k
Dneprorudnoye see Dniprorudne
Dnestr see Dniester
Dnieper 81 F4 Bel. Dnyapro, Rus. Dnepr,
  Ukr. Dnipro. river E Europe
Dnieper Lowland 109 E2 Bel.
  Prydnyaprowskaya Nizina, Ukr.
  Prydniprovs'ka Nyzovyna. lowlands
  Belarus/Ukraine
Dniester 81 E4 Rom. Nistru, Rus.
  Dnestr, Ukr. Dnister; anc. Tyras. river
  Moldova/Ukraine
Dnipro see Dnieper
Dniprodzerzhyns'k 109 F3 Rus.
  Dneprodzerzhinsk; prev. Kamenskoye.
  Dnipropetrovs'ka Oblast', E Ukraine
Dniprodzerzhyns'ke Vodoskhovyshche
  109 F3 Rus. Dneprodzerzhinskoye
  Vodokhranilishche. reservoir
  C Ukraine
Dnipropetrovs'k 109 F3 Rus.
  Dnepropetrovsk; prev. Yekaterinoslav.
  Dnipropetrovs'ka Oblast', E Ukraine
Dniprorudne 109 F3 Rus.
  Dneprorudnoye. Zaporiz'ka Oblast',
  SE Ukraine
Dnister see Dniester
Dnyapro see Dnieper
Doba 76 C4 Logone-Oriental,
  S Chad
Döbeln 94 D4 Sachsen, E Germany
Doberai, Jazirah 139 G4 Dut. Vogelkop.
  peninsula Papua, E Indonesia
Doboj 100 C3 Republika Srpska,
  N Bosnia and Herzegovina
Dobre Miasto 98 D2 Ger. Guttstadt.
  Warmińsko-mazurskie, NE Poland
Dobrich 104 E1 Rom. Bazargic; prev.
  Tolbukhin. Dobrich, NE Bulgaria
Dobrush 107 D7 Homyel'skaya
  Voblasts', SE Belarus
Dobryn' see Dabryn'
Dodecanese see Dodekánisa
Dodekánisa 105 D6 var. Nóties
  Sporádes, Eng. Dodecanese; prev.
  Dhodhekánisos, Dodekanisos. island
  group SE Greece
Dodekanisos see Dodekánisa
Dodge City 45 E5 Kansas,
  C USA
Dodoma 69 D5 country capital
  (Tanzania) Dodoma, C Tanzania
Dodoma 73 C7 region C Tanzania
Dogana 96 E1 NE San Marino Europe
Dōgo 131 B6 island Oki-shotō,
  SW Japan
Dogondoutchi 75 F3 Dosso,
  SW Niger
Dogrular see Pravda
Doğubayazıt 117 F3 Ağrı, E Turkey
Doğu Karadeniz Dağları 117 E3 var.
  Anadolu Dağları. mountain range
  NE Turkey
Doha see Ad Dawḥah
Doire see Londonderry
Dokkum 86 D1 Friesland, N Netherlands

Dokuchayevs'k 109 G3 var.
  Dokuchayevsk. Donets'ka Oblast',
  SE Ukraine
Dokuchayevsk see Dokuchayevs'k
Doldrums Fracture Zone 66 C4 fracture
  zone W Atlantic Ocean
Dôle 90 D4 Jura, E France
Dolina see Dolyna
Dolinskaya see Dolyns'ka
Dolisie 77 B6 prev. Loubomo. Le Niari,
  S Congo
Dolomites/Dolomiti see Dolomitiche,
  Alpi
Dolomitiche, Alpi 96 C1 var. Dolomiti,
  Eng. Dolomites. mountain range
  NE Italy
Dolores 64 D4 Buenos Aires, E Argentina
Dolores 52 B1 Petén, N Guatemala
Dolores 64 D4 Soriano, SW Uruguay
Dolores Hidalgo 51 E4 var. Ciudad
  de Dolores Hidalgo. Guanajuato,
  C Mexico
Dolyna 108 B2 Rus. Dolina. Ivano-
  Frankivs'ka Oblast', W Ukraine
Dolyns'ka 109 F3 Rus. Dolinskaya.
  Kirovohrads'ka Oblast', S Ukraine
Domachëvo/Domaczewo see Damachava
Dombås 85 B5 Oppland, S Norway
Domel Island see Letsôk-aw Kyun
Domesnes, Cape see Kolkasrags
Domeyko 64 B3 Atacama, N Chile
Dominica 55 H4 off. Commonwealth of
  Dominica. country E West Indies

DOMINICA
West Indies

Official name Commonwealth of
  Dominica
Formation 1978 / 1978
Capital Roseau
Population 69,029 / 238 people per
  sq mile
  (92 people per sq km) / 71%
Total area 291 sq miles (754 sq km)
Languages English*, French Creole
Religions Roman Catholic 77%,
  Protestant 15%, Other 8%
Ethnic mix Black 91%, Mixed race 6%,
  Carib 2%, Other 1%
Government Parliamentary system
Currency Eastern Caribbean dollar =
  100 cents
Literacy rate 88%
Calorie consumption 2763 calories

Dominica Channel see Martinique
  Passage
Dominica, Commonwealth of see
  Dominica
Dominican Republic 55 E2 country
  C West Indies

DOMINICAN REPUBLIC
West Indies

Official name Dominican Republic
Formation 1865 / 1865
Capital Santo Domingo
Population 8.9 million / 476 people per
  sq mile (184 people per sq km) / 65%
Total area 18,679 sq miles (48,380 sq km)
Languages Spanish*, French Creole
Religions Roman Catholic 92%,
  Other and nonreligious 8%
Ethnic mix Mixed race 75%, White 15%,
  Black 10%
Government Presidential system
Currency Dominican Republic peso =
  100 centavos
Literacy rate 88%
Calorie consumption 2347 calories

Domokós 105 B5 var. Dhomokós. Stereá
  Ellás, C Greece
Don 111 B6 var. Duna, Tanais. river
  SW Russian Federation
Donau see Danube
Donauwörth 95 C6 Bayern, S Germany
Don Benito 92 C3 Extremadura,
  W Spain
Doncaster 89 D5 anc. Danum. N
  England, UK
Dondo 78 B1 Cuanza Norte, NW Angola
Donegal 89 B5 Ir. Dún na nGall.
  Donegal, NW Ireland
Donegal Bay 89 A5 Ir. Bá Dhún na nGall.
  bay NW Ireland

Donets 109 G2 river Russian
  Federation/Ukraine
Donets'k 109 G3 Rus. Donetsk; prev.
  Stalino. Donets'ka Oblast', E Ukraine
Dongfang 128 B7 var. Basuo. Hainan,
  S China
Dongguan 128 C6 Guangdong, S China
Đông Hai see East China Sea
Đông Hới 136 D4 Quang Binh,
  C Vietnam
Dongliao see Liaoyuan
Dongola 72 B3 var. Donqola, Dunqulah.
  Northern, N Sudan
Dongou 77 C5 La Likouala, NE Congo
Dong Rak, Phanom see Dângrêk, Chuŏr
  Phnum
Dongting Hu 128 C5 var. Tung-t'ing
  Hu. lake S China
Donostia-San Sebastián 93 E1 País
  Vasco, N Spain
Donqola see Dongola
Doolow 73 D5 Somali, E Ethiopia
Doornik see Tournai
Door Peninsula 40 C2 peninsula
  Wisconsin, N USA
Dooxo Nugaaleed 73 E5 var. Nogal
  Valley. valley E Somalia
Dordogne 91 B5 department SW France
Dordogne 91 B5 cultural region
  SW France
Dordogne 91 B5 river W France
Dordrecht 86 C4 var. Dordt, Dort.
  Zuid-Holland, SW Netherlands
Dordt see Dordrecht
Dorohoi 108 C3 Botoşani, NE Romania
Dorotea 84 C4 Västerbotten, N Sweden
Dorpat see Tartu
Dorre Island 147 A5 island Western
  Australia
Dort see Dordrecht
Dortmund 94 A4 Nordrhein-Westfalen,
  W Germany
Dos Hermanas 92 C4 Andalucía, S Spain
Dospad Dagh see Rhodope Mountains
Dospat 104 C3 Smolyan, S Bulgaria
Dothan 42 D3 Alabama, S USA
Dotnuva 106 B4 Kaunas, C Lithuania
Douai 90 C2 prev. Douay; anc. Duacum.
  Nord, N France
Douala 77 A5 var. Duala. Littoral,
  W Cameroon
Douay see Douai
Douglas 89 C5 dependent territory
  capital (Isle of Man) E Isle of Man
Douglas 48 C3 Arizona, SW USA
Douglas 44 D3 Wyoming, C USA
Douma see Dūmā
Douro 92 B2 Port. Duero. river
  Portugal/Spain
Douro see Duero
Douvres see Dover
Dover 89 E7 Fr. Douvres, Lat. Dubris
  Portus. SE England, UK
Dover 41 F4 state capital Delaware,
  NE USA
Dover, Strait of 90 C2 var. Straits of
  Dover, Fr. Pas de Calais. strait England,
  UK/France
Dover, Straits of see Dover, Strait of
Dovrefjell 85 B5 plateau S Norway
Downpatrick 89 B5 Ir. Dún Pádraig.
  SE Northern Ireland, UK
Dōzen 131 B6 island Oki-shotō,
  SW Japan
Drãa, Hammada du see Dra, Hamada du
Drač/Draç see Durrës
Drachten 86 D2 N Netherlands
Drăgăşani 108 B5 Vâlcea, SW Romania
Dragoman 104 B2 Sofiya, W Bulgaria
Dra, Hamada du 70 C3 var. Hammada
  du Drâa, Haut Plateau du Dra. plateau
  W Algeria
Dra, Haut Plateau du see Dra, Hamada
  du
Drahichyn 107 B6 Pol. Drohiczyn
  Poleski, Rus. Drogichin. Brestskaya
  Voblasts', SW Belarus
Drakensberg 78 D5 mountain range
  Lesotho/South Africa
Drake Passage 57 B8 passage Atlantic
  Ocean/Pacific Ocean
Dralfa 104 D2 Tŭrgovishte, N Bulgaria
Dráma 104 C3 var. Dhráma. Anatolikí
  Makedonía kai Thráki, NE Greece
Dramburg see Drawsko Pomorskie
Drammen 85 B6 Buskerud, S Norway

Drau *see* Drava
Drava *100 C3 var.* Drau, *Eng.* Drave, *Hung.* Dráva. *river* C Europe
Dráva/Drave *see* Drau/Drava
Drawsko Pomorskie *98 B3 Ger.* Dramburg. Zachodnio-pomorskie, NW Poland
Drépano, Akrotírio *104 C4 var.* Akrotírio Dhrepanon. *cape* N Greece
Drepanum *see* Trapani
Dresden *94 D4* Sachsen, E Germany
Drin *see* Drinit, Lumi
Drina *100 C3 river* Bosnia and Herzegovina/Serbia
Drinit, Lumi *101 D5 var.* Drin. *river* NW Albania
Drinit të Zi, Lumi i *see* Black Drin
Drissa *see* Drysa
Drobeta-Turnu Severin *108 B5 prev.* Turnu Severin. Mehedinți, SW Romania
Drogheda *89 B5 Ir.* Droichead Átha. NE Ireland
Drogichin *see* Drahichyn
Drogobych *see* Drohobych
Drohiczyn Poleski *see* Drahichyn
Drohobych *108 B2 Pol.* Drohobycz, *Rus.* Drogobych. L'vivs'ka Oblast', NW Ukraine
Drohobycz *see* Drohobych
Droichead Átha *see* Drogheda
Drôme *91 D5 cultural region* E France
Drôme *91 D5 department* E France
Dronning Maud Land *154 B2 physical region* Antarctica
Drontheim *see* Trondheim
Drug *see* Durg
Druk-yul *see* Bhutan
Drummondville *39 F4* Québec, SE Canada
Druskienniki *see* Druskininkai
Druskininkai *107 B5 Pol.* Druskienniki. Alytus, S Lithuania
Dryden *38 B3* Ontario, C Canada
Drysa *107 D5 Rus.* Drissa. *river* N Belarus
Duacum *see* Douai
Duala *see* Douala
Dubai *see* Dubayy
Dubăsari *108 D3 Rus.* Dubossary. NE Moldova
Dubawnt *37 F4 river* Nunavut, NW Canada
Dubayy *120 D4 Eng.* Dubai. Dubayy, NE United Arab Emirates
Dubbo *149 D6* New South Wales, SE Australia
Dublin *89 B5 Ir.* Baile Átha Cliath; *anc.* Eblana. *country capital* (Ireland) Dublin, E Ireland
Dublin *43 E2* Georgia, SE USA
Dubno *108 C2* Rivnens'ka Oblast', NW Ukraine
Dubossary *see* Dubăsari
Dubris Portus *see* Dover
Dubrovnik *101 B5 It.* Ragusa. Dubrovnik-Neretva, SE Croatia
Dubuque *45 G3* Iowa, C USA
Dudelange *87 D8 var.* Forge du Sud, *Ger.* Dudelingen. Luxembourg, S Luxembourg
Dudelingen *see* Dudelange
Duero *92 D2 Port.* Douro. *river* Portugal/Spain
Duero *see* Douro
Duesseldorf *see* Düsseldorf
Duffel *87 C5* Antwerpen, C Belgium
Dugi Otok *100 A4 var.* Isola Grossa, *It.* Isola Lunga. *island* W Croatia
Duinekerke *see* Dunkerque
Duisburg *94 A4 prev.* Duisburg-Hamborn. Nordrhein-Westfalen, W Germany
Duisburg-Hamborn *see* Duisburg
Duiven *86 D4* Gelderland, E Netherlands
Duk Faiwil *73 B5* Jonglei, SE Sudan
Dulan *126 D4 var.* Qagan Us. Qinghai, C China
Dulce, Golfo *53 E5 gulf* S Costa Rica
Dulce, Golfo *see* Izabal, Lago de
Dülmen *94 A4* Nordrhein-Westfalen, W Germany
Dulovo *104 E1* Silistra, NE Bulgaria
Duluth *45 G2* Minnesota, N USA
Dūmā *119 B5 Fr.* Douma. Dimashq, SW Syria
Dumas *49 E1* Texas, SW USA
Dumfries *88 C4* S Scotland, UK
Dumont d'Urville *154 C4 French research station* Antarctica
Dumyât *72 B1 Eng.* Damietta. N Egypt
Duna *see* Danube, C Europe
Düna *see* Western Dvina
Duna *see* Don, Russian Federation
Dünaburg *see* Daugavpils
Dunaj *see* Wien, Austria
Dunaj *see* Danube, C Europe
Dunapentele *see* Dunaújváros
Dunărea *see* Danube
Dunaújváros *99 C7 prev.* Dunapentele, Sztálinváros. Fejér, C Hungary
Dunav *see* Danube
Dunavska Ravnina *104 C2 Eng.* Danubian Plain. *lowlands* N Bulgaria
Duncan *49 G2* Oklahoma, C USA
Dundalk *89 B5 Ir.* Dún Dealgan. Louth, NE Ireland
Dún Dealgan *see* Dundalk
Dundee *78 D4* KwaZulu/Natal, E South Africa
Dundee *88 C4* E Scotland, UK
Dunedin *151 B7* Otago, South Island, New Zealand
Dunfermline *88 C4* C Scotland, UK
Dungu *77 E5* Orientale, NE Dem. Rep. Congo
Dungun *138 B3 var.* Kuala Dungun. Terengganu, Peninsular Malaysia
Dunholme *see* Durham
Dunkerque *90 C2 Eng.* Dunkirk, *Flem.* Duinekerke; *prev.* Dunquerque. Nord, N France
Dunkirk *see* Dunkerque
Dún Laoghaire *89 B6 Eng.* Dunleary; *prev.* Kingstown. E Ireland
Dunleary *see* Dún Laoghaire
Dún Pádraig *see* Downpatrick
Dunquerque *see* Dunkerque
Dunqulah *see* Dongola
Dupnitsa *104 C2 prev.* Marek, Stanke Dimitrov. Kyustendil, W Bulgaria
Duqm *121 E5 var.* Daqm. E Oman
Durance *91 D6 river* SE France
Durango *50 D3 var.* Victoria de Durango. Durango, W Mexico
Durango *44 C5* Colorado, C USA
Durankulak *104 E1 Rom.* Răcari; *prev.* Blatnitsa, Duranulac. Dobrich, NE Bulgaria
Durant *49 G2* Oklahoma, C USA
Duranulac *see* Durankulak
Durazzo *see* Durrës
Durban *78 D4 var.* Port Natal. KwaZulu/Natal, E South Africa
Durbe *106 B3 Ger.* Durben. Liepāja, W Latvia
Durben *see* Durbe
Durg *135 E4 prev.* Drug. Chhattīsgarh, C India
Durham *89 D5 hist.* Dunholme. N England, UK
Durham *43 F1* North Carolina, SE USA
Durocortorum *see* Reims
Durostorum *see* Silistra
Durovernum *see* Canterbury
Durrës *101 C6 var.* Durrësi, Dursi, *It.* Durazzo, *SCr.* Drač, *Turk.* Draç. Durrës, W Albania
Durrësi *see* Durrës
Dursi *see* Durrës
Durūz, Jabal ad *119 C5 mountain* SW Syria
D'Urville Island *150 C4 island* C New Zealand
Dusa Mareb/Dusa Marreb *see* Dhuusa Marreeb
Dushanbe *123 E3 var.* Dyushambe; *prev.* Stalinabad, *Taj.* Stalinobod. *country capital* (Tajikistan) W Tajikistan
Düsseldorf *94 A4 var.* Duesseldorf. Nordrhein-Westfalen, W Germany
Dŭstí *123 E3 Rus.* Dusti. SW Tajikistan
Dutch East Indies *see* Indonesia
Dutch Guiana *see* Surinam
Dutch Harbor *36 B3* Unalaska Island, Alaska, USA
Dutch New Guinea *see* Papua
Dutch West Indies *see* Netherlands Antilles
Duzdab *see* Zāhedān
Dvina Bay *see* Chëshskaya Guba
Dvinsk *see* Daugavpils
Dyanev *see* Galkynyş
Dyersburg *42 C1* Tennessee, S USA
Dyushambe *see* Dushanbe
Dza Chu *see* Mekong
Dzaudzhikau *see* Vladikavkaz
Dzerzhinsk *111 C5* Nizhegorodskaya Oblast', W Russian Federation
Dzerzhinskiy *see* Nar'yan-Mar
Dzhalal-Abad *123 F2 Kir.* Jalal-Abad. Dzhalal-Abadskaya Oblast', W Kyrgyzstan
Dzhankoy *109 F4* Respublika Krym, S Ukraine
Dzharkurgan *see* Jarqo'rg'on
Dzhelandy *123 F3* SE Tajikistan
Dzhergalan *123 G2 Kir.* Jyrgalan. Issyk-Kul'skaya Oblast', NE Kyrgyzstan
Dzhezkazgan *see* Zhezkazgan
Dzhizak *see* Jizzax
Dzhugdzhur, Khrebet *115 G3 mountain range* E Russian Federation
Dzhusaly *114 B4 Kaz.* Zholsaly. Kzylorda, SW Kazakhstan
Działdowo *98 D3* Warmińsko-Mazurskie, C Poland
Dzuunmod *127 E2* Töv, C Mongolia
Dzüün Soyonï Nuruu *see* Eastern Sayans
Dzvina *see* Western Dvina

E

E *see* Hubei
Eagle Pass *49 F4* Texas, SW USA
East Açores Fracture Zone *see* East Azores Fracture Zone
East Antarctica *see* Greater Antarctica
East Australian Basin *see* Tasman Basin
East Azores Fracture Zone *66 C3 var.* East Açores Fracture Zone. *tectonic feature* E Atlantic Ocean
Eastbourne *89 E7* SE England, UK
East Cape *150 E3 headland* North Island, New Zealand
East China Sea *125 E2 Chin.* Dong Hai. *sea* W Pacific Ocean
Easter Fracture Zone *153 G4 tectonic feature* E Pacific Ocean
Easter Island *see* Pascua, Isla de
Eastern Desert *see* Sahara el Sharqîya
Eastern Ghats *124 B3 mountain range* SE India
Eastern Sayans *115 E4 Mong.* Dzüün Soyonï Nuruu, *Rus.* Vostochnyy Sayan. *mountain range* Mongolia/Russian Federation
Eastern Sierra Madre *see* Sierra Madre Oriental
East Falkland *65 D8 var.* Isla Soledad. *island* E Falkland Islands
East Frisian Islands *see* Ostfriesische Inseln
East Grand Forks *45 E1* Minnesota, N USA
East Indiaman Ridge *141 D6 undersea ridge* E Indian Ocean
East Indies *152 A3 island group* SE Asia
East Kilbride *88 C4* S Scotland, UK
East Korea Bay *129 E3 bay* E North Korea Pacific Ocean Sea of Japan
Eastleigh *89 D7* S England, UK
East London *78 D5 Afr.* Oos-Londen; *prev.* Emonti, Port Rex. Eastern Cape, S South Africa
Eastmain *38 D3 river* Québec, C Canada
East Mariana Basin *142 B1 undersea basin* W Pacific Ocean
East Novaya Zemlya Trough *112 C1 var.* Novaya Zemlya Trough. *trough* W Kara Sea
East Pacific Rise *153 F4 undersea rise* E Pacific Ocean
East Pakistan *see* Bangladesh
East Saint Louis *40 B4* Illinois, N USA
East Scotia Basin *67 C7 undersea basin* SE Scotia Sea
East Sea *130 A4 var.* Sea of Japan, *Rus.* Yapanskoye More. *Sea* NW Pacific Ocean
East Siberian Sea *see* Vostochno-Sibirskoye More
East Timor *139 F5 var.* Loro Sae; *prev.* Portuguese Timor, Timor Timur. *country* S Indonesia

EAST TIMOR
Southeast Asia

Official name Democratic Republic of Timor-Leste
Formation 2002 / 2002
Capital Dili

EAST TIMOR
(continued)

Population 947,000 / 168 people per sq mile (65 people per sq km) / 8%
Total area 5756 sq miles (14,874 sq km)
Languages Tetum (Portuguese/Austronesian), Bahasa Indonesia, and Portuguese
Religions Roman Catholic 95%, Other (including Muslim and Protestant) 5%
Ethnic mix Papuan groups approx 85%, Indonesian approx 13%, Chinese 2%
Government Parliamentary system
Currency US dollar = 100 cents
Literacy rate 59%
Calorie consumption 2806 calories

Eau Claire *40 A2* Wisconsin, N USA
Eau Claire, Lac à L' *see* St. Clair, Lake
Eauripik Rise *142 B2 undersea rise* W Pacific Ocean
Ebensee *95 D6* Oberösterreich, N Austria
Eberswalde-Finow *94 D3* Brandenburg, E Germany
Ebetsu *130 D2 var.* Ebetu. Hokkaidō, NE Japan
Ebetu *see* Ebetsu
Eblana *see* Dublin
Ebolowa *77 A5* Sud, S Cameroon
Ebon Atoll *144 D2 var.* Epoon. *atoll* Ralik Chain, S Marshall Islands
Ebora *see* Évora
Eboracum *see* York
Ebro *93 E2 river* NE Spain
Eburacum *see* York
Ebusus *see* Eivissa
Ebusus *see* Eivissa
Ebusus *see* Eivissa
Ecbatana *see* Hamadān
Ech Cheliff/Ech Chleff *see* Chlef
Echo Bay *37 E3* Northwest Territories, NW Canada
Echt *87 D5* Limburg, SE Netherlands
Ecija *92 D4 anc.* Astigi. Andalucía, SW Spain
Eckengraf *see* Viesīte
Ecuador *60 B1 off.* Republic of Ecuador. *country* NW South America

ECUADOR
South America

Official name Republic of Ecuador
Formation 1830 / 1941
Capital Quito
Population 13.2 million / 123 people per sq mile (48 people per sq km) / 65%
Total area 109,483 sq miles (283,560 sq km)
Languages Spanish*, Quechua*, other Amerindian languages
Religions Roman Catholic 93%, Protestant, Jewish, and other 7%
Ethnic mix Mestizo 55%, Amerindian 25%, White 10%, Black 10%
Government Presidential system
Currency US dollar = 100 cents
Literacy rate 91%
Calorie consumption 2754 calories

Ecuador, Republic of *see* Ecuador
Ed Da'ein *72 A4* Southern Darfur, W Sudan
Ed Damazin *72 C4 var.* Ad Damazīn. Blue Nile, E Sudan
Ed Damer *72 C3 var.* Ad Dāmir, Ad Damar. River Nile, NE Sudan
Ed Debba *72 B3* Northern, N Sudan
Ede *86 D4* Gelderland, C Netherlands
Ede *75 F5* Osun, SW Nigeria
Edéa *77 A5* Littoral, SW Cameroon
Edessa *see* Şanlıurfa
Edfu *see* Idfu
Edgeøya *83 G2 island* S Svalbard
Edgware *89 A7* Harrow, SE England, UK
Edinburg *49 G5* Texas, SW USA
Edinburgh *88 C4 national capital* S Scotland, UK
Edingen *see* Enghien
Edirne *116 A2 Eng.* Adrianople, *anc* Adrianopolis, Hadrianopolis. Edirne, NW Turkey
Edmonds *46 B2* Washington, NW USA

Edmonton *37 E5 province capital* Alberta, SW Canada
Edmundston *39 E4* New Brunswick, SE Canada
Edna *49 G4* Texas, SW USA
Edolo *96 B1* Lombardia, N Italy
Edremit *116 A3* Balıkesir, NW Turkey
Edward, Lake *77 E5 var.* Albert Edward Nyanza, Edward Nyanza, Lac Idi Amin, Lake Rutanzige. *lake* Uganda/Dem. Rep. Congo
Edward Nyanza *see* Edward, Lake
Edwards Plateau *49 F3 plain* Texas, SW USA
Edzo *53 E4 prev.* Rae-Edzo. Northwest Territories, NW Canada
Eeklo *87 B5 var.* Eekloo. Oost-Vlaanderen, NW Belgium
Eekloo *see* Eeklo
Eems *see* Ems
Eersel *87 C5* Noord-Brabant, S Netherlands
Eesti Vabariik *see* Estonia
Éfaté *144 D4 var.* Efate, *Fr.* Vaté; *prev.* Sandwich Island. *island* C Vanuatu
Efate *see* Éfaté
Effingham *40 B4* Illinois, N USA
Eforie Sud *108 D5* Constanţa, E Romania
Egadi, Isole *97 B7 island group* S Italy
Ege Denizi *see* Aegean Sea
Eger *99 D6 Ger.* Erlau. Heves, NE Hungary
Eger *see* Cheb
Egeria Fracture Zone *141 C5 tectonic feature* W Indian Ocean
Éghezèe *87 C6* Namur, C Belgium
Egina *see* Aígina
Egio *see* Aígio
Egmont *see* Taranaki, Mount
Egmont, Cape *150 C4 cape* North Island, New Zealand
Egoli *see* Johannesburg
Egypt *72 B2 off.* Arab Republic of Egypt, *Ar.* Jumhūrīyah Mişr al 'Arabīyah, *prev.* United Arab Republic; *anc.* Aegyptus. *country* NE Africa

EGYPT
North Africa

Official name Arab Republic of Egypt
Formation 1936 / 1982
Capital Cairo
Population 74 million / 193 people per sq mile (74 people per sq km) / 45%
Total area 386,660 sq miles (1,001,450 sq km)
Languages Arabic*, French, English, Berber
Religions Muslim (mainly Sunni) 94%, Coptic Christian and other 6%
Ethnic mix Eastern Hamitic 90%, Nubian, Armenian, and Greek 10%
Government Presidential system
Currency Egyptian pound = 100 piastres
Literacy rate 56%
Calorie consumption 3338 calories

Eibar *93 E1* País Vasco, N Spain
Eibergen *86 E3* Gelderland, E Netherlands
Eidfjord *85 A5* Hordaland, S Norway
Eier-Berg *see* Suur Munamägi
Eifel *95 A5 plateau* W Germany
Eiger *95 B7 mountain* C Switzerland
Eigg *88 B3 island* W Scotland, UK
Eight Degree Channel *132 B3 channel* India/Maldives
Eighty Mile Beach *146 B4 beach* Western Australia
Eijsden *87 D6* Limburg, SE Netherlands
Eilat *see* Elat
Eindhoven *87 D5* Noord-Brabant, S Netherlands
Eipel *see* Ipel'
Éire *see* Ireland
Éireann, Muir *see* Irish Sea
Eisenhüttenstadt *94 D4* Brandenburg, E Germany
Eisenmarkt *see* Hunedoara
Eisenstadt *95 E6* Burgenland, E Austria
Eisleben *94 C4* Sachsen-Anhalt, C Germany
Eivissa *93 G3 var.* Iviza, *Cast.* Ibiza; *anc.* Ebusus. Ibiza, Spain, W Mediterranean Sea
Ejea de los Caballeros *93 E2* Aragón, NE Spain
Ejin Qi *see* Dalain Hob
Ekapa *see* Cape Town
Ekaterinodar *see* Krasnodar
Ekiatapskiy Khrebet *115 G1 mountain range* NE Russian Federation
El 'Alamein *72 B1 var.* Al 'Alamayn. N Egypt
El Asnam *see* Chlef
Elat *119 B8 var.* Eilat, Elath. Southern, S Israel
Elat, Gulf of *see* Aqaba, Gulf of
Elath *see* Elat, Israel
Elath *see* Al 'Aqabah, Jordan
El'Atrun *72 B3* Northern Darfur, NW Sudan
Elâzīğ *117 E3 var.* Elâzig, Elâziz. Elâzıǧ, E Turkey
Elba, Isola d' *96 B4 island* Archipelago Toscano, C Italy
Elbasan *101 D6 var.* Elbasani. Elbasan, C Albania
Elbasani *see* Elbasan
Elbe *80 D3 Cz.* Labe. *river* Czech Republic/Germany
El Beni *see* Beni
Elbert, Mount *44 C4 mountain* Colorado, C USA
Elbing *see* Elbląg
Elbląg *98 C2 var.* Elblag, *Ger.* Elbing. Warmińsko-Mazurskie, NE Poland
El Boulaida/El Boulaïda *see* Blida
El'brus *111 A8 var.* Gora El'brus. *mountain* SW Russian Federation
El'brus, Gora *see* El'brus
El Burgo de Osma *93 E2* Castilla-León, C Spain
Elburz Mountains *see* Alborz, Reshteh-ye Kūhhā-ye
El Cajon *47 C8* California, W USA
El Calafate *65 B7 var.* Calafate. Santa Cruz, S Argentina
El Callao *59 E2* Bolívar, E Venezuela
El Campo *49 G4* Texas, SW USA
El Carmen de Bolívar *58 B2* Bolívar, NW Colombia
El Cayo *see* San Ignacio
El Centro *47 D8* California, W USA
Elche *93 F4 Cat.* Elx; *anc.* Ilici, *Lat.* Illicis. País Valenciano, E Spain
Elda *93 F4* País Valenciano, E Spain
El Djazaïr *see* Alger
El Djelfa *see* Djelfa
Eldorado *64 E3* Misiones, NE Argentina
El Dorado *50 C3* Sinaloa, C Mexico
El Dorado *42 B2* Arkansas, C USA
El Dorado *45 F5* Kansas, C USA
El Dorado *59 F2* Bolívar, E Venezuela
El Dorado *see* California
Eldoret *73 C6* Rift Valley, W Kenya
Elektrostal' *111 B5* Moskovskaya Oblast', W Russian Federation
Elemi Triangle *73 B5 disputed region* Kenya/Sudan
Elephant Butte Reservoir *48 C2 reservoir* New Mexico, SW USA
Élesd *see* Aleşd
Eleuthera Island *54 C1 island* N Bahamas
El Fasher *72 A4 var.* Al Fāshir. Northern Darfur, W Sudan
El Ferrol/El Ferrol del Caudillo *see* Ferrol
El Gedaref *see* Gedaref
El Geneina *72 A4 var.* Ajjinena, Al-Genain, Al Junaynah. Western Darfur, W Sudan
Elgin *88 C3* NE Scotland, UK
Elgin *40 B3* Illinois, N USA
El Gîza *72 B1 var.* Al Jīzah, Gîza, Gizeh. N Egypt
El Goléa *70 D3 var.* Al Golea. C Algeria
El Ḩank *74 D1 cliff* N Mauritania
El Haseke *see* Al Ḩasakah
Elimberrum *see* Auch
Eliocroca *see* Lorca
Élisabethville *see* Lubumbashi
Elista *111 B7* Respublika Kalmykiya, SW Russian Federation
Elizabeth *149 B6* South Australia
Elizabeth City *43 G1* North Carolina, SE USA
Elizabethtown *40 C5* Kentucky, S USA
El-Jadida *70 C2 prev.* Mazagan. W Morocco
Ełk *98 E2 Ger.* Lyck. Warmińsko-mazurskie, NE Poland
Elk City *49 F1* Oklahoma, C USA
El Khalil *see* Hebron
El Khârga *72 B2 var.* Al Khārijah. C Egypt
Elkhart *40 C3* Indiana, N USA
El Khartûm *see* Khartoum
Elk River *45 F2* Minnesota, N USA
El Kuneitra *see* Al Qunayţirah
Ellás *see* Greece
Ellef Ringnes Island *37 E1 island* Nunavut, N Canada
Ellen, Mount *44 B5 mountain* Utah, W USA
Ellensburg *46 B2* Washington, NW USA
Ellesmere Island *37 F1 island* Queen Elizabeth Islands, Nunavut, N Canada
Ellesmere, Lake *151 C6 lake* South Island, New Zealand
Ellice Islands *see* Tuvalu
Elliston *149 A6* South Australia
Ellsworth Land *154 A3 physical region* Antarctica
El Mahbas *70 B3 var.* Mahbés. SW Western Sahara
El Mina *118 B4 var.* Al Mīnā'. N Lebanon
El Minya *72 B2 var.* Al Minyā, Minya. C Egypt
Elmira *41 E3* New York, NE USA
El Mreyyé *74 D2 desert* E Mauritania
Elmshorn *94 B3* Schleswig-Holstein, N Germany
El Muglad *72 B4* Western Kordofan, C Sudan
El Obeid *72 B4 var.* Al Obayyid, Al Ubayyiḑ. Northern Kordofan, C Sudan
El Ouâdi *see* El Oued
El Oued *71 E2 var.* Al Oued, El Ouâdi, El Wad. NE Algeria
Eloy *48 B2* Arizona, SW USA
El Paso *48 D3* Texas, SW USA
El Porvenir *53 G4* San Blas, N Panama
El Progreso *52 C2* Yoro, NW Honduras
El Puerto de Santa María *92 C5* Andalucía, S Spain
El Qâhira *see* Cairo
El Quneitra *see* Al Qunayţirah
El Quseir *see* Al Quşayr
El Quweira *see* Al Quwayrah
El Rama *53 E3* Región Autónoma Atlántico Sur, SE Nicaragua
El Real *53 H5 var.* El Real de Santa María. Darién, SE Panama
El Real de Santa María *see* El Real
El Reno *49 F1* Oklahoma, C USA
El Salvador *52 B3 off.* Republica de El Salvador. *country* Central America

EL SALVADOR
Central America

Official name Republic of El Salvador
Formation 1841 / 1841
Capital San Salvador
Population 6.9 million / 862 people per sq mile (333 people per sq km) / 47%
Total area 8124 sq miles (21,040 sq km)
Languages Spanish*
Religions Roman Catholic 80%, Evangelical 18%, Other 2%
Ethnic mix Mestizo 94%, Amerindian 5%, White 1%
Government Presidential system
Currency Salvadorean colón & US dollar = 100 centavos (colón); 100 cents (US dollar)
Literacy rate 80%
Calorie consumption 2584 calories

El Salvador, Republica de *see* El Salvador
Elsass *see* Alsace
El Sáuz *50 C2* Chihuahua, N Mexico
El Serrat *91 A7* N Andorra Europe
Elst *86 D4* Gelderland, E Netherlands
El Sueco *50 C2* Chihuahua, N Mexico
El Suweida *see* As Suwaydā'
El Suweis *see* Suez
Eltanin Fracture Zone *153 E5 tectonic feature* SE Pacific Ocean
El Tigre *59 E2* Anzoátegui, NE Venezuela
Elvas *92 C4* Portalegre, C Portugal
El Vendrell *93 G2* Cataluña, NE Spain
El Vigía *58 C2* Mérida, NW Venezuela
El Wad *see* El Oued
Elwell, Lake *44 B1 reservoir* Montana, NW USA
Elx *see* Elche
Ely *47 D5* Nevada, W USA
El Yopal *see* Yopal
Emajõgi *106 D3 Ger.* Embach. *river* SE Estonia
Emāmrūd *see* Shāhrūd
Emāmshahr *see* Shāhrūd
Emba *114 B4 Kaz.* Embi. Aktyubinsk, W Kazakhstan
Embach *see* Emajõgi
Embi *see* Emba
Emden *94 A3* Niedersachsen, NW Germany
Emerald *148 D4* Queensland, E Australia
Emerald Isle *see* Montserrat
Emesa *see* Ḩimş
Emmaste *106 C2* Hiiumaa, W Estonia
Emmeloord *86 D2* Flevoland, N Netherlands
Emmen *86 E2* Drenthe, NE Netherlands
Emmendingen *95 A6* Baden-Württemberg, SW Germany
Emona *see* Ljubljana
Emonti *see* East London
Emory Peak *49 E4 mountain* Texas, SW USA
Empalme *50 B2* Sonora, NW Mexico
Emperor Seamounts *113 G3 seamount range* NW Pacific Ocean
Empire State of the South *see* Georgia
Emporia *45 F5* Kansas, C USA
Empty Quarter *see* Ar Rub 'al Khālī
Ems *94 A3 Dut.* Eems. *river* NW Germany
Enaretrāsk *see* Inarijärvi
Encamp *91 A8* Encamp, C Andorra Europe
Encarnación *64 D3* Itapúa, S Paraguay
Encinitas *47 C8* California, W USA
Encs *99 D6* Borsod-Abaúj-Zemplén, NE Hungary
Endeavour Strait *148 C1 strait* Queensland, NE Australia
Enderbury Island *145 F3 atoll* Phoenix Islands, C Kiribati
Enderby Land *154 C2 physical region* Antarctica
Enderby Plain *154 D2 abyssal plain* S Indian Ocean
Endersdorf *see* Jędrzejów
Enewetak Atoll *144 C1 var.* Ānewetak, Eniwetok. *atoll* Ralik Chain, W Marshall Islands
Enfield *89 A7* UK
Engeten *see* Aiud
Enghien *87 B6 Dut.* Edingen. Hainaut, SW Belgium
England *89 D5 Lat.* Anglia. *cultural region* England, UK
England *89 D5 Lat.* Anglia. *national region* England, UK
Englewood *44 D4* Colorado, C USA
English Channel *89 D8 var.* The Channel, *Fr.* la Manche. *channel* NW Europe
Engure *106 C3* Tukums, W Latvia
Engures Ezers *106 B3 lake* NW Latvia
Enguri *117 F1 Rus.* Inguri. *river* NW Georgia
Enid *49 F1* Oklahoma, C USA
Enikale Strait *see* Kerch Strait
Eniwetok *see* Enewetak Atoll
En Nâqoûra *119 A5 var.* An Nāqūrah. SW Lebanon
En Nazira *see* Naẕerat
Ennedi *76 D2 plateau* E Chad
Ennis *89 A6 Ir.* Inis. Clare, W Ireland
Ennis *49 G3* Texas, SW USA
Enniskillen *89 B5 var.* Inniskilling, *Ir.* Inis Ceithleann. SW Northern Ireland, UK
Enns *95 D6 river* C Austria
Enschede *86 E3* Overijssel, E Netherlands
Ensenada *50 A1* Baja California, NW Mexico
Entebbe *73 B6* S Uganda
Entroncamento *92 B3* Santarém, C Portugal
Enugu *75 G5* Enugu, S Nigeria
Eolie, Isole *97 C6 var.* Isole Lipari, *Eng.* Aeolian Islands, Lipari Islands. *island group* S Italy
Epanomí *104 B4* Kentrikí Makedonía, N Greece

Epéna *77 B5* La Likouala, NE Congo
Eperies/Eperjes *see* Prešov
Epi *144 D4 var.* Épi. *island* C Vanuatu
Épi *see* Epi
Épinal *90 D4* Vosges, NE France
Epiphania *see* Ḩamāh
Epitoli *see* Tshwane
Epoon *see* Ebon Atoll
Epsom *89 A8* UK
Equality State *see* Wyoming
Equatorial Guinea *77 A5 off.* Equatorial Guinea, Republic of. *country* C Africa

EQUATORIAL GUINEA
Central Africa

Official name Republic of Equatorial Guinea
Formation 1968 / 1968
Capital Malabo
Population 504,000 / 47 people per sq mile (18 people per sq km) / 48%
Total area 10,830 sq miles (28,051 sq km)
Languages Spanish*, Fang, Bubi
Religions Roman Catholic 90%, Other 10%
Ethnic mix Fang 85%, Other 11%, Bubi 4%
Government Presidential system
Currency CFA franc = 100 centimes
Literacy rate 84%
Calorie consumption Not available

Equatorial Guinea, Republic of *see* Equatorial Guinea
Erautini *see* Johannesburg
Erbil *see* Arbīl
Erciş *117 F3* Van, E Turkey
Erdély *see* Transylvania
Erdélyi-Havasok *see* Carpaţii Meridionali
Erdenet *127 E2* Orhon, N Mongolia
Erdi *76 C2 plateau* NE Chad
Erdi Ma *76 D2 desert* NE Chad
Erebus, Mount *154 B4 volcano* Ross Island, Antarctica
Ereğli *116 C4* Konya, S Turkey
Erenhot *127 F2 var.* Erlian. Nei Mongol Zizhiqu, NE China
Erfurt *94 C4* Thüringen, C Germany
Ergene Çayi *116 A2 var.* Ergene Irmaği. *river* NW Turkey
Ergene Irmaği *see* Ergene Çayi
Ergun *127 F1 var.* Labudalin; *prev.* Ergun Youqi. Nei Mongol Zizhiqu, N China
Ergun He *see* Argun
Ergun Youqi *see* Ergun
Erie *40 D3* Pennsylvania, NE USA
Érié, Lac *see* Erie, Lake
Erie, Lake *40 D3 Fr.* Lac Érié. *lake* Canada/USA
Eritrea *72 C4 off.* State of Eritrea, Ērtra. *country* E Africa

ERITREA
East Africa

Official name State of Eritrea
Formation 1993 / 2002
Capital Asmara
Population 4.4 million / 97 people per sq mile (37 people per sq km) / 19%
Total area 46,842 sq miles (121,320 sq km)
Languages Arabic*, Tigrinya*, English, Tigre, Afar, Bilen, Kunama, Nara, Saho, Hadareb
Religions Christian 45%, Muslim 45%, Other 10%
Ethnic mix Tigray 50%, Tigray and Kunama 40%, Afar 4%, Other 3%, Saho 3%
Government Transitional regime
Currency Nakfa = 100 cents
Literacy rate 57%
Calorie consumption 1513 calories

ritrea, State of *see* Eritrea
rivan *see* Yerevan
rlangen *95 C5* Bayern, S Germany
rlau *see* Eger
rlian *see* Erenhot
rmelo *86 D3* Gelderland, C Netherlands
rmióni *105 C6* Pelopónnisos, S Greece
Ermoúpoli *105 D6 var.* Hermoupolis; *prev.* Ermoúpolis. Sýyros, Kykládes, Greece, Aegean Sea
Ermoúpolis *see* Ermoúpoli
Ernākulam *132 C3* Kerala, SW India
Erode *132 C2* Tamil Nādu, SE India
Erquelinnes *87 B7* Hainaut, S Belgium
Er-Rachidia *70 C2 var.* Ksar al Soule. E Morocco
Er Rahad *72 B4 var.* Ar Rahad. Northern Kordofan, C Sudan
Erromango *144 D4 island* S Vanuatu
Ertis *see* Irtysh, C Asia
Ērtra *see* Eritrea
Erzerum *see* Erzurum
Erzgebirge *95 C5 Cz.* Krušné Hory, *Eng.* Ore Mountains. *mountain range* Czech Republic/Germany
Erzincan *117 E3 var.* Erzinjan. Erzincan, E Turkey
Erzinjan *see* Erzincan
Erzurum *117 E3 prev.* Erzerum. Erzurum, NE Turkey
Esbjerg *85 A7* Ribe, W Denmark
Esbo *see* Espoo
Escaldes *91 A8* Escaldes Engordany, C Andorra Europe
Escanaba *40 C2* Michigan, N USA
Escaut *see* Scheldt
Esch-sur-Alzette *87 D8* Luxembourg, S Luxembourg
Esclaves, Grand Lac des *see* Great Slave Lake
Escondido *47 C8* California, W USA
Escuinapa *50 D3 var.* Escuinapa de Hidalgo. Sinaloa, C Mexico
Escuinapa de Hidalgo *see* Escuinapa
Escuintla *52 B2* Escuintla, S Guatemala
Escuintla *51 G5* Chiapas, SE Mexico
Eşenguly *122 B3 Rus.* Gasan-Kuli. Balkan Welaýaty, W Turkmenistan
Eşfahān *120 C3 Eng.* Isfahan; *anc.* Aspadana. Eşfahān, C Iran
Esh Sharā *see* Ash Sharāh
Esil *see* Ishim, Kazakhstan/Russian Federation
Eskimo Point *see* Arviat
Eskişehir *116 B3 var.* Eskishehr. Eskişehir, W Turkey
Eskishehr *see* Eskişehir
Eslāmābād *120 C3 var.* Eslāmābād-e Gharb; *prev.* Harunabad, Shāhābād. Kermānshāhān, W Iran
Eslāmābād-e Gharb *see* Eslāmābād
Esmeraldas *60 A1* Esmeraldas, N Ecuador
Esna *see* Isna
España *see* Spain
Espanola *48 D1* New Mexico, SW USA
Esperance *147 B7* Western Australia
Esperanza *50 B2* Sonora, NW Mexico
Esperanza *154 A2 Argentinian research station* Antarctica
Espinal *58 B3* Tolima, C Colombia
Espinhaço, Serra do *56 D4 mountain range* SE Brazil
Espírito Santo *63 F4 off.* Estado do Espírito Santo. *state* E Brazil
Espírito Santo, Estado do *see* Espírito Santo
Espiritu Santo *144 C4 var.* Santo. *island* W Vanuatu
Espoo *85 D6 Swe.* Esbo. Etelä-Suomi, S Finland
Esquel *65 B6* Chubut, SW Argentina
Essaouira *70 B2 prev.* Mogador. W Morocco
Esseg *see* Osijek
Es Semara *see* Smara
Essen *87 C5* Antwerpen, N Belgium
Essen *94 A4 var.* Essen an der Ruhr. Nordrhein-Westfalen, W Germany
Essen an der Ruhr *see* Essen
Essequibo River *59 F3 river* C Guyana
Es Suweida *see* As Suwaydā'
Estacado, Llano *49 E2 plain* New Mexico/Texas, SW USA
Estados, Isla de los *65 C8 prev. Eng.* Staten Island. *island* S Argentina
Estância *63 G3* Sergipe, E Brazil
Estelí *52 D3* Estelí, NW Nicaragua
Estella *93 E1 Bas.* Lizarra. Navarra, N Spain
Estepona *92 D5* Andalucía, S Spain
Estevan *37 F5* Saskatchewan, S Canada
Estland *see* Estonia
Estonia *106 D2 off.* Republic of Estonia, *Est.* Eesti Vabariik, *Ger.* Estland, *Latv.* Igaunija; *prev.* Estonian SSR, *Rus.* Estonskaya SSR. *country* NE Europe

ESTONIA
Northeast Europe

Official name Republic of Estonia
Formation 1991 / 1991
Capital Tallinn
Population 1.3 million / 75 people per sq mile (29 people per sq km) / 69%
Total area 17,462 sq miles (45,226 sq km)
Languages Estonian*, Russian
Religions Evangelical Lutheran 56%, Orthodox Christian 25%, Other 19%
Ethnic mix Estonian 62%, Russian 30%, Other 8%
Government Parliamentary system
Currency Kroon = 100 senti
Literacy rate 99%
Calorie consumption 3002 calories

Estonian SSR *see* Estonia
Estonia, Republic of *see* Estonia
Estonskaya SSR *see* Estonia
Estrela, Serra da *92 C3 mountain range* C Portugal
Estremadura *see* Extremadura
Estremoz *92 C4* Évora, S Portugal
Eszék *see* Osijek
Esztergom *99 C6 Ger.* Gran; *anc.* Strigonium. Komárom-Esztergom, N Hungary
Étalle *87 D8* Luxembourg, SE Belgium
Etāwah *134 D3* Uttar Pradesh, N India
Ethiopia *73 C5 off.* Federal Democratic Republic of Ethiopia; *prev.* Abyssinia, People's Democratic Republic of Ethiopia. *country* E Africa

ETHIOPIA
East Africa

Official name Federal Democratic Republic of Ethiopia
Formation 1896 / 2002
Capital Addis Ababa
Population 77.4 million / 181 people per sq mile (70 people per sq km) / 18%
Total area 435,184 sq miles (1,127,127 sq km)
Languages Amharic*, Tigrinya, Galla, Sidamo, Somali, English, Arabic
Religions Orthodox Christian 40%, Muslim 40%, Traditional beliefs 15%, Other 5%
Ethnic mix Oromo 40%, Amhara 25%, Other 14%, Sidamo 9%, Berta 6%, Somali 6%
Government Parliamentary system
Currency Ethiopian birr = 100 cents
Literacy rate 42%
Calorie consumption 1857 calories

Ethiopia, Federal Democratic Republic of *see* Ethiopia
Ethiopian Highlands *73 C5 var.* Ethiopian Plateau. *plateau* N Ethiopia
Ethiopian Plateau *see* Ethiopian Highlands
Ethiopia, People's Democratic Republic of *see* Ethiopia
Etna, Monte *97 C7 Eng.* Mount Etna. *volcano* Sicilia, Italy, C Mediterranean Sea
Etna, Mount *see* Etna, Monte
Etosha Pan *78 B3 salt lake* N Namibia
Etoumbi *77 B5* Cuvette Ouest, NW Congo
Etsch *see* Adige
Et Tafila *see* Aţ Ţafīlah
Ettelbrück *87 D8* Diekirch, C Luxembourg
'Eua *145 E5 prev.* Middleburg Island. *island* Tongatapu Group, SE Tonga
Euboea *see* Évvoia
Eucla *147 D6* Western Australia
Euclid *40 D3* Ohio, N USA
Eufaula Lake *49 G1 var.* Eufaula Reservoir. *reservoir* Oklahoma, C USA
Eufaula Reservoir *see* Eufaula Lake
Eugene *46 B3* Oregon, NW USA
Eumolpias *see* Plovdiv
Eupen *87 D6* Liège, E Belgium
Euphrates *112 B4 Ar.* Al-Furāt, *Turk.* Firat Nehri. *river* SW Asia
Eureka *47 A5* California, W USA
Eureka *44 A1* Montana, NW USA
Europa Point *93 H5 headland* S Gibraltar
Europe *34 E1 continent*
Eutin *94 C2* Schleswig-Holstein, N Germany
Euxine Sea *see* Black Sea
Evansdale *45 G3* Iowa, C USA
Evanston *40 B3* Illinois, N USA
Evanston *44 B4* Wyoming, C USA
Evansville *40 B5* Indiana, N USA
Eveleth *45 G1* Minnesota, N USA
Everard, Lake *149 A6 salt lake* South Australia
Everest, Mount *126 B5 Chin.* Qomolangma Feng, *Nep.* Sagarmāthā. *mountain* China/Nepal
Everett *46 B2* Washington, NW USA
Everglades, The *43 F5 wetland* Florida, SE USA
Evje *85 A6* Aust-Agder, S Norway
Evmolpia *see* Plovdiv
Évora *92 B4 anc.* Ebora, *Lat.* Liberalitas Julia. Évora, C Portugal
Évreux *90 C3 anc.* Civitas Eburovicum. Eure, N France
Évros *see* Maritsa
Évry *90 E2* Essonne, N France
Évvoia *101 E8 Lat.* Euboea. *island* C Greece
Ewarton *54 B5* C Jamaica
Excelsior Springs *45 F4* Missouri, C USA
Exe *89 C7 river* SW England, UK
Exeter *89 C7 anc.* Isca Damnoniorum. SW England, UK
Exmoor *89 C7 moorland* SW England, UK
Exmouth *146 A4* Western Australia
Exmouth *89 C7* SW England, UK
Exmouth Gulf *146 A4 gulf* Western Australia
Exmouth Plateau *141 E5 undersea plateau* E Indian Ocean
Extremadura *92 C3 var.* Estremadura. *autonomous community* W Spain
Exuma Cays *54 C1 islets* C Bahamas
Exuma Sound *54 C1 sound* C Bahamas
Eyre Mountains *151 A7 mountain range* South Island, New Zealand
Eyre North, Lake *149 A5 salt lake* South Australia
Eyre Peninsula *149 A6 peninsula* South Australia
Eyre South, Lake *149 A5 salt lake* South Australia
Ezo *see* Hokkaidō

F

Faadhippolhu Atoll *132 B4 var.* Fadiffolu, Lhaviyani Atoll. *atoll* N Maldives
Fabens *48 D3* Texas, SW USA
Fada *76 C2* Borkou-Ennedi-Tibesti, E Chad
Fada-Ngourma *75 E4* E Burkina Faso
Fadiffolu *see* Faadhippolhu Atoll
Faenza *96 C3 anc.* Faventia. Emilia-Romagna, N Italy
Faeroe-Iceland Ridge *80 C1 undersea ridge* NW Norwegian Sea
Faeroe Islands *83 E5 Dan.* Færøerne, *Faer.* Føroyar. *Danish external territory* N Atlantic Ocean
Færøerne *see* Faeroe Islands
Faeroe-Shetland Trough *80 C2 trough* NE Atlantic Ocean
Faetano *96 E2* E San Marino
Făgăraş *108 C4 Ger.* Fogarasch, *Hung.* Fogaras. Braşov, C Romania
Fagibina, Lake *see* Faguibine, Lac
Fagne *87 C7 hill range* S Belgium
Faguibine, Lac *75 E3 var.* Lake Fagibina. *lake* NW Mali
Fahlun *see* Falun
Fahraj *120 E4* Kermān, SE Iran
Faial *92 A5 var.* Ilha do Faial. *island* Azores, Portugal, NE Atlantic Ocean

Faial, Ilha do *see* Faial
Faifo *see* Hôi An
Fairbanks 36 D3 Alaska, USA
Fairfield 47 B6 California, W USA
Fair Isle 88 D2 *island* NE Scotland, UK
Fairlie 151 B6 Canterbury, South Island, New Zealand
Fairmont 45 F3 Minnesota, N USA
Faisalābād 134 C2 *prev.* Lyallpur. Punjab, NE Pakistan
Faizābād 135 E3 Uttar Pradesh, N India
Faizabad/Faizābād *see* Feyẓābād
Fakaofo Atoll 145 F3 *island* SE Tokelau
Falam 136 A3 Chin State, W Myanmar (Burma)
Falconara Marittima 96 C3 Marche, C Italy
Falkenau an der Eger *see* Sokolov
Falkland Islands 65 D7 *var.* Falklands, Islas Malvinas. *UK dependent territory* SW Atlantic Ocean
Falkland Plateau 57 D7 *var.* Argentine Rise. *undersea feature* SW Atlantic Ocean
Falklands *see* Falkland Islands
Falknov nad Ohří *see* Sokolov
Fallbrook 47 C8 California, W USA
Falmouth 54 A4 W Jamaica
Falmouth 89 C7 SW England, UK
Falster 85 B8 *island* SE Denmark
Fălticeni 108 C3 *Hung.* Falticsén. Suceava, NE Romania
Falticsén *see* Fălticeni
Falun 85 C6 *var.* Fahlun. Kopparberg, C Sweden
Famagusta *see* Gazimağusa
Famagusta Bay *see* Gazimağusa Körfezi
Famenne 87 C7 *physical region* SE Belgium
Fang 136 C3 Chiang Mai, NW Thailand
Fanning Island *see* Tabuaeran
Fanø 96 C3 *island* W Denmark
Farafangana 79 G4 Fianarantsoa, SE Madagascar
Farāh 122 D4 *var.* Farah, Fararud.
Farāh, W Afghanistan
Farāh Rūd 122 D4 *river* W Afghanistan
Faranah 74 C4 Haute-Guinée, S Guinea
Fararud *see* Farāh
Farasān, Jazā'ir 121 A6 *island group* SW Saudi Arabia
Farewell, Cape 150 C4 *headland* South Island, New Zealand
Farewell, Cape *see* Nunap Isua
Fargo 45 F2 North Dakota, N USA
Farg'ona 123 F2 *Rus.* Fergana; *prev.* Novyy Margilan. Farg'ona Viloyati, E Uzbekistan
Faribault 45 F2 Minnesota, N USA
Farīdābād 134 D3 Haryāna, N India Asia
Farkhor 123 E3 *Rus.* Parkhar. SW Tajikistan
Farmington 45 G5 Missouri, C USA
Farmington 48 C1 New Mexico, SW USA
Faro 92 B5 Faro, S Portugal
Farquhar Group 79 G2 *island group* S Seychelles
Farvel, Kap *see* Nunap Isua
Fastiv 109 E2 *Rus.* Fastov. Kyyivs'ka Oblast', NW Ukraine
Fastov *see* Fastiv
Fauske 84 C3 Nordland, C Norway
Faventia *see* Faenza
Faxa Bay *see* Faxaflói
Faxaflói 82 D5 *Eng.* Faxa Bay. *bay* W Iceland
Faya 76 C2 *prev.* Faya-Largeau, Largeau. Borkou-Ennedi-Tibesti, N Chad
Faya-Largeau *see* Faya
Fayetteville 42 A1 Arkansas, C USA
Fayetteville 43 F1 North Carolina, SE USA
Fdérick *see* Fdérik
Fdérik 74 C2 *var.* Fdérick, *Fr.* Fort Gouraud. Tiris Zemmour, NW Mauritania
Fear, Cape 43 F2 *headland* Bald Head Island, North Carolina, SE USA
Fécamp 90 B3 Seine-Maritime, N France
Fédala *see* Mohammedia
Federal Capital Territory *see* Australian Capital Territory
Fehérgyarmat 99 E6 Szabolcs-Szatmár-Bereg, E Hungary
Fehértemplom *see* Bela Crkva
Fehmarn 94 C2 *island* N Germany

Fehmarn Belt 94 C2 *Dan.* Femern Bælt, *Ger.* Fehmarnbelt. *strait* Denmark /Germany
Fehmarnbelt Fehmarn Belt/Femer Bælt
Feijó 62 C2 Acre, W Brazil
Feilding 150 D4 Manawatu-Wanganui, North Island, New Zealand
Feira *see* Feira de Santana
Feira de Santana 63 G3 *var.* Feira. Bahia, E Brazil
Feketehalom *see* Codlea
Felanitx 93 G3 Mallorca, Spain, W Mediterranean Sea
Felicitas Julia *see* Lisboa
Felidhu Atoll 132 B4 *atoll* C Maldives
Felipe Carrillo Puerto 51 H4 Quintana Roo, SE Mexico
Felixstowe 89 E6 E England, UK
Fellin *see* Viljandi
Felsőbánya *see* Baia Sprie
Felsőmuzslya *see* Mužlja
Femern Bælt *see* Fehmarn Belt
Femunden 85 B5 *lake* S Norway
Fengcheng 128 D3 *var.* Feng-cheng, Fenghwangcheng. Liaoning, NE China
Feng-cheng *see* Fengcheng
Fenghwangcheng *see* Fengcheng
Fengtien *see* Liaoning, China
Fengtien *see* Shenyang, China
Fenoarivo 79 G3 Toamasina, E Madagascar
Fens, The 89 E6 *wetland* E England, UK
Feodosiya 109 F5 *var.* Kefe, It. Kaffa; *anc.* Theodosia. Respublika Krym, S Ukraine
Ferdinand *see* Montana, Bulgaria
Ferdinandsberg *see* Oțelu Roșu
Féres 104 D3 Anatolikí Makedonía kai Thráki, NE Greece
Fergana *see* Farg'ona
Fergus Falls 45 F2 Minnesota, N USA
Ferizaj *see* Uroševac
Ferkessédougou 74 D4 N Côte d'Ivoire (Ivory Coast)
Fermo 96 C4 *anc.* Firmum Picenum. Marche, C Italy
Fernandina, Isla 60 A5 *var.* Narborough Island. *island* Galapagos Islands, Ecuador, E Pacific Ocean
Fernando de Noronha 63 H2 *island* E Brazil
Fernando Po/Fernando Póo *see* Bioco, Isla de
Ferrara 96 C2 *anc.* Forum Alieni. Emilia-Romagna, N Italy
Ferreñafe 60 B3 Lambayeque, W Peru
Ferro *see* Hierro
Ferrol 92 B1 *var.* El Ferrol; *prev.* El Ferrol del Caudillo. Galicia, NW Spain
Fertő *see* Neusiedler See
Ferwerd 86 D1 *Fris.* Ferwert. Friesland, N Netherlands
Ferwert *see* Ferwerd
Fès 70 C2 *Eng.* Fez. N Morocco
Fetești 108 D5 Ialomița, SE Romania
Fethiye 116 B4 Muğla, SW Turkey
Fetlar 88 D1 *island* NE Scotland, UK
Feuilles, Rivière aux 38 D2 *river* Québec, E Canada
Feyzābād 123 F3 *var.* Faizabad, Faizābād, Feyẓābād, Fyzabad. Badakhshān, NE Afghanistan
Feyẓābād *see* Feyzābād
Fez *see* Fès
Fianarantsoa 79 F3 Fianarantsoa, C Madagascar
Fianga 76 B4 Mayo-Kébbi, SW Chad
Fier 101 C6 *var.* Fieri. Fier, SW Albania
Fieri *see* Fier
Figeac 91 C5 Lot, S France
Figig *see* Figuig
Figueira da Foz 92 B3 Coimbra, W Portugal
Figueres 93 G2 Cataluña, E Spain
Figuig 70 D2 *var.* Figig. E Morocco
Fiji 145 E5 *off.* Sovereign Democratic Republic of Fiji, *Fij.* Viti. *country* SW Pacific Ocean

FIJI
Australasia & Oceania

Official name Republic of the Fiji Islands
Formation 1970 / 1970
Capital Suva
Population 848,000 / 120 people per sq mile (46 people per sq km) / 49%

FIJI
(continued)

Total area 7054 sq miles (18,270 sq km)
Languages English*, Fijian*, Hindi, Urdu, Tamil, Telugu
Religions Hindu 38%, Methodist 37%, Roman Catholic 9%, Other 8%, Muslim 8%
Ethnic mix Melanesian 48%, Indian 46%, Other 6%
Government Parliamentary system
Currency Fiji dollar = 100 cents
Literacy rate 93%
Calorie consumption 2894 calories

Fiji, Sovereign Democratic Republic of *see* Fiji
Filadelfia 52 D4 Guanacaste, W Costa Rica
Filiași 108 B5 Dolj, SW Romania
Filipstad 85 B6 Värmland, C Sweden
Finale Ligure 96 A3 Liguria, NW Italy
Finchley 89 A7 UK
Findlay 40 C4 Ohio, N USA
Finike 116 B4 Antalya, SW Turkey
Finland 84 D4 *off.* Republic of Finland, *Fin.* Suomen Tasavalta, Suomi. *country* N Europe

FINLAND
Northern Europe

Official name Republic of Finland
Formation 1917 / 1947
Capital Helsinki
Population 5.2 million / 44 people per sq mile (17 people per sq km) / 67%
Total area 130,127 sq miles (337,030 sq km)
Languages Finnish*, Swedish*, Sámi
Religions Evangelical Lutheran 89%, Orthodox Christian 1%, Roman Catholic 1%, Other 9%
Ethnic mix Finnish 93%, Other (including Sámi) 7%
Government Parliamentary system
Currency Euro = 100 cents
Literacy rate 99%
Calorie consumption 3100 calories

Finland, Gulf of 85 D6 *Est.* Soome Laht, *Fin.* Suomenlahti, *Ger.* Finnischer Meerbusen, *Rus.* Finskiy Zaliv, *Swe.* Finska Viken. *gulf* E Baltic Sea
Finland, Republic of *see* Finland
Finnischer Meerbusen *see* Finland, Gulf of
Finnmarksvidda 84 D2 *physical region* N Norway
Finska Viken/Finskiy Zaliv *see* Finland, Gulf of
Finsterwalde 94 D4 Brandenburg, E Germany
Fiordland 151 A7 *physical region* South Island, New Zealand
Fiorina 96 E1 NE San Marino
Firat Nehri *see* Euphrates
Firenze 96 C3 *Eng.* Florence; *anc.* Florentia. Toscana, C Italy
Firmum Picenum *see* Fermo
First State *see* Delaware
Fischbacher Alpen 95 E7 *mountain range* E Austria
Fischhausen *see* Primorsk
Fish 78 B4 *var.* Vis. *river* S Namibia
Fishguard 89 C6 *Wel.* Abergwaun. SW Wales, UK
Fisterra, Cabo 92 B1 *cape* NW Spain
Fitzroy Crossing 146 C3 Western Australia
Fitzroy River 146 C3 *river* Western Australia
Fiume *see* Rijeka
Flagstaff 48 B2 Arizona, SW USA
Flanders 87 A6 *Dut.* Vlaanderen, *Fr.* Flandre. *cultural region* Belgium/France
Flandre *see* Flanders
Flathead Lake 44 B1 *lake* Montana, NW USA
Flat Island 128 C8 *island* NE Spratly Islands
Flatts Village 42 B5 *var.* The Flatts Village. C Bermuda
Flensburg 94 B2 Schleswig-Holstein, N Germany

Flessingue *see* Vlissingen
Flickertail State *see* North Dakota
Flinders Island 149 C8 *island* Furneaux Group, Tasmania, SE Australia
Flinders Ranges 149 B6 *mountain range* South Australia
Flinders River 148 C3 *river* Queensland, NE Australia
Flin Flon 37 F5 Manitoba, C Canada
Flint 40 C3 Michigan, N USA
Flint Island 145 G4 *island* Line Islands, E Kiribati
Floreana, Isla *see* Santa María, Isla
Florence 42 C1 Alabama, S USA
Florence 43 F2 South Carolina, SE USA
Florence *see* Firenze
Florencia 58 B4 Caquetá, S Colombia
Florentia *see* Firenze
Flores 52 B1 Petén, N Guatemala
Flores 139 E5 *island* Nusa Tenggara, C Indonesia
Flores 92 A5 *island* Azores, Portugal, NE Atlantic Ocean
Flores, Laut *see* Flores Sea
Flores Sea 138 D5 *Ind.* Laut Flores. *sea* C Indonesia
Floriano 63 F2 Piauí, E Brazil
Florianópolis 63 F5 *prev.* Destêrro. *state capital* Santa Catarina, S Brazil
Florida 64 D4 Florida, S Uruguay
Florida 43 E4 *off.* State of Florida, *also known as* Peninsular State, Sunshine State. *state* SE USA
Florida Bay 43 E5 *bay* Florida, SE USA
Florida Keys 43 E5 *island group* Florida, SE USA
Florida, Straits of 54 B1 *strait* Atlantic Ocean/Gulf of Mexico
Flórina 104 B4 *var.* Phlórina. Dytikí Makedonía, N Greece
Florissant 45 G4 Missouri, C USA
Floúda, Akrotírio 105 D7 *cape* Astypálaia, Kykládes, Greece, Aegean Sea
Flushing *see* Vlissingen
Flylân *see* Vlieland
Foča 100 C4 SE Bosnia and Herzegovina
Focșani 108 C4 Vrancea, E Romania
Fogaras/Fogarasch *see* Făgăraș
Foggia 97 D5 Puglia, SE Italy
Fogo 74 A3 *island* Ilhas de Sotavento, SW Cape Verde
Foix 91 B6 Ariège, S France
Folégandros 105 C7 *island* Kykládes, Greece, Aegean Sea
Foleyet 38 C4 Ontario, S Canada
Foligno 96 C4 Umbria, C Italy
Folkestone 89 E7 SE England, UK
Fond du Lac 40 B2 Wisconsin, N USA
Fongafale 145 E3 *var.* Funafuti. *country capital* (Tuvalu) Funafuti Atoll, SE Tuvalu
Fonseca, Golfo de *see* Fonseca, Gulf of
Fonseca, Gulf of 52 C3 *Sp.* Golfo de Fonseca. *gulf* C Central America
Fontainebleau 90 C3 Seine-et-Marne, N France
Fontenay-le-Comte 90 B4 Vendée, NW France
Fontvieille 91 B8 SW Monaco Europe
Fonyód 99 C7 Somogy, W Hungary
Foochow *see* Fuzhou
Foochow *see* Fuzhou
Forchheim 95 C5 Bayern, SE Germany
Forel, Mont 82 D4 *mountain* SE Greenland
Forfar 88 C3 E Scotland, UK
Forge du Sud *see* Dudelange
Forlì 96 C3 *anc.* Forum Livii. Emilia-Romagna, N Italy
Formentera 93 G4 *anc.* Ophiusa, Lat. Frumentum. *island* Islas Baleares, Spain, W Mediterranean Sea
Formosa 64 D2 Formosa, NE Argentina
Formosa/Formo'sa *see* Taiwan
Formosa, Serra 63 F3 *mountain range* C Brazil
Formosa Strait *see* Taiwan Strait
Føroyar *see* Faeroe Islands
Forrest City 42 B1 Arkansas, C USA
Fort Albany 38 C3 Ontario, C Canada
Fortaleza 61 F2 Pando, N Bolivia

Fortaleza *63 G2 prev.* Ceará. *state capital* Ceará, NE Brazil
Fort-Archambault *see* Sarh
Fort-Bayard *see* Zhanjiang
Fort-Cappolani *see* Tidjikja
Fort Charlet *see* Djanet
Fort-Chimo *see* Kuujjuaq
Fort Collins *44 D4* Colorado, C USA
Fort-Crampel *see* Kaga Bandoro
Fort Davis *49 E3* Texas, SW USA
Fort-de-France *55 H4 prev.* Fort-Royal. *dependent territory capital* (Martinique) W Martinique
Fort Dodge *45 F3* Iowa, C USA
Fortescue River *146 A4 river* Western Australia
Fort-Foureau *see* Kousséri
Fort Frances *38 B4* Ontario, S Canada
Fort Good Hope *37 E3 var.* Good Hope. Northwest Territories, NW Canada
Fort Gouraud *see* Fdérik
Forth *88 C4 river* C Scotland, UK
Forth, Firth of *88 C4 estuary* E Scotland, UK
Fortín General Eugenio Garay *see* General Eugenio A. Garay
Fort Jameson *see* Chipata
Fort-Lamy *see* Ndjamena
Fort Lauderdale *43 F5* Florida, SE USA
Fort Liard *37 E4 var.* Liard. Northwest Territories, W Canada
Fort Madison *45 G4* Iowa, C USA
Fort McMurray *37 E4* Alberta, C Canada
Fort McPherson *36 D3 var.* McPherson. Northwest Territories, NW Canada
Fort Morgan *44 D4* Colorado, C USA
Fort Myers *43 E5* Florida, SE USA
Fort Nelson *37 E4* British Columbia, W Canada
Fort Peck Lake *44 C1 reservoir* Montana, NW USA
Fort Pierce *43 F4* Florida, SE USA
Fort Providence *37 E4 var.* Providence. Northwest Territories, W Canada
Fort-Repoux *see* Akjoujt
Fort Rosebery *see* Mansa
Fort Rousset *see* Owando
Fort-Royal *see* Fort-de-France
Fort St. John *37 E4* British Columbia, W Canada
Fort Scott *45 F5* Kansas, C USA
Fort Severn *38 C2* Ontario, C Canada
Fort-Shevchenko *114 A4* Mangistau, W Kazakhstan
Fort-Sibut *see* Sibut
Fort Simpson *37 E4 var.* Simpson. Northwest Territories, W Canada
Fort Smith *37 E4* Northwest Territories, W Canada
Fort Smith *42 B1* Arkansas, C USA
Fort Stockton *49 E3* Texas, SW USA
Fort-Trinquet *see* Bîr Mogreïn
Fort Vermilion *37 E4* Alberta, W Canada
Fort Victoria *see* Masvingo
Fort Walton Beach *42 C3* Florida, SE USA
Fort Wayne *40 C4* Indiana, N USA
Fort William *88 C3* N Scotland, UK
Fort Worth *49 G2* Texas, SW USA
Fort Yukon *36 D3* Alaska, USA
Forum Alieni *see* Ferrara
Forum Livii *see* Forlì
Fossa Claudia *see* Chioggia
Fougamou *77 A6* Ngounié, C Gabon
Fougères *90 B3* Ille-et-Vilaine, NW France
Fou-hsin *see* Fuxin
Foulwind, Cape *151 B5 headland* South Island, New Zealand
Foumban *76 A4* Ouest, NW Cameroon
Fou-shan *see* Fushun
oveaux Strait *151 A8 strait* S New Zealand
oxe Basin *37 G3 sea* Nunavut, N Canada
ox Glacier *151 B6* West Coast, South Island, New Zealand
raga *93 F2* Aragón, NE Spain
ram Basin *155 C3 var.* Amundsen Basin. *undersea basin* Arctic Ocean
rance *90 B4 off.* French Republic, *It./Sp.* Francia; *prev.* Gaul, Gaule, *Lat.* Gallia. *country* W Europe

FRANCE
Western Europe

Official name French Republic
Formation 987 / 1919
Capital Paris
Population 60.5 million / 285 people per sq mile (110 people per sq km) / 76%
Total area 211,208 sq miles (547,030 sq km)
Languages French*, Provençal, German, Breton, Catalan, Basque
Religions Roman Catholic 88%, Muslim 8%, Protestant 2%, Buddhist 1%, Jewish 1%
Ethnic mix French 90%, North African (mainly Algerian) 6%, German (Alsace) 2%, Breton 1%, Other (including Corsicans) 1%
Government Mixed presidential–parliamentary system
Currency Euro = 100 cents
Literacy rate 99%
Calorie consumption 3654 calories

Franceville *77 B6 var.* Massoukou, Masuku. Haut-Ogooué, E Gabon
Francfort *see* Frankfurt am Main
Franche-Comté *90 D4 region* E France
Franche-Comté *90 D4 cultural region* E France
Francia *see* France
Francis Case, Lake *45 E3 reservoir* South Dakota, N USA
Francisco Escárcega *51 G4* Campeche, SE Mexico
Francistown *78 D3* North East, NE Botswana
Franconian Jura *see* Fränkische Alb
Frankenalb *see* Fränkische Alb
Frankenstein/Frankenstein in Schlesien *see* Ząbkowice Śląskie
Frankfort *40 C5 state capital* Kentucky, S USA
Frankfort on the Main *see* Frankfurt am Main
Frankfurt *see* Frankfurt am Main, Germany
Frankfurt *see* Słubice, Poland
Frankfurt am Main *95 B5 var.* Frankfurt, *Fr.* Francfort; *prev. Eng.* Frankfort on the Main. Hessen, SW Germany
Frankfurt an der Oder *94 D3* Brandenburg, E Germany
Fränkische Alb *95 C6 var.* Frankenalb, *Eng.* Franconian Jura. *mountain range* S Germany
Franklin *42 C1* Tennessee, S USA
Franklin D. Roosevelt Lake *46 C1 reservoir* Washington, NW USA
Frantsa-Iosifa, Zemlya *114 D1 Eng.* Franz Josef Land. *island group* N Russian Federation
Franz Josef Land *see* Frantsa-Iosifa, Zemlya
Fraserburgh *88 D3* NE Scotland, UK
Fraser Island *148 E4 var.* Great Sandy Island. *island* Queensland, E Australia
Frauenbach *see* Baia Mare
Frauenburg *see* Saldus, Latvia
Fredericksburg *41 E5* Virginia, NE USA
Fredericton *39 F4 province capital* New Brunswick, SE Canada
Frederikshåb *see* Paamiut
Fredrikshald *see* Halden
Fredrikstad *85 B6* Østfold, S Norway
Freeport *54 C1* Grand Bahama Island, N Bahamas
Freeport *49 H4* Texas, SW USA
Free State *see* Maryland
Freetown *74 C4 country capital* (Sierra Leone) W Sierra Leone
Freiburg *see* Freiburg im Breisgau, Germany
Freiburg im Breisgau *95 A6 var.* Freiburg, *Fr.* Fribourg-en-Brisgau. Baden-Württemberg, SW Germany
Freiburg in Schlesien *see* Świebodzice
Fremantle *147 A6* Western Australia
Fremont *45 F4* Nebraska, C USA
French Guiana *59 H3 var.* Guiana, Guyane. *French overseas department* N South America
French Guinea *see* Guinea
French Polynesia *143 F4 French overseas territory* C Polynesia
French Republic *see* France
French Somaliland *see* Djibouti
French Southern and Antarctic Territories *141 B7 Fr.* Terres Australes et Antarctiques Françaises. *French overseas territory* S Indian Ocean
French Sudan *see* Mali
French Territory of the Afars and Issas *see* Djibouti
French Togoland *see* Togo
Fresnillo *50 D3* Zacatecas, C Mexico
Fresnillo de González Echeverría *see* Fresnillo
Fresno *47 C6* California, W USA
Frías *64 C3* Catamarca, N Argentina
Fribourg-en-Brisgau *see* Freiburg im Breisgau
Friedek-Mistek *see* Frýdek-Místek
Friedrichshafen *95 B7* Baden-Württemberg, S Germany
Friendly Islands *see* Tonga
Frisches Haff *see* Vistula Lagoon
Frobisher Bay *82 B3 inlet* Baffin Island, Nunavut, NE Canada
Frobisher Bay *see* Iqaluit
Frohavet *84 B4 sound* C Norway
Frome, Lake *149 B6 salt lake* South Australia
Frontera *51 G4* Tabasco, SE Mexico
Frontignan *91 C6* Hérault, S France
Frostviken *see* Kvarnbergsvattnet
Frøya *84 A4 island* W Norway
Frumentum *see* Formentera
Frunze *see* Bishkek
Frýdek-Místek *99 C5 Ger.* Friedek-Mistek. Moravskoslezský Kraj, E Czech Republic
Fu-chien *see* Fujian
Fu-chou *see* Fuzhou
Fu-chou *see* Fuzhou
Fuengirola *92 D5* Andalucía, S Spain
Fuerte Olimpo *64 D2 var.* Olimpo. Alto Paraguay, NE Paraguay
Fuerte, Río *48 C5 river* C Mexico
Fuerteventura *70 B3 island* Islas Canarias, Spain, NE Atlantic Ocean
Fuhkien *see* Fujian
Fu-hsin *see* Fuxin
Fuji *131 D6 var.* Huzi. Shizuoka, Honshū, S Japan
Fujian *128 D6 var.* Fu-chien, Fuhkien, Fukien, Min, Fujian Sheng. *province* SE China
Fujian Sheng *see* Fujian
Fuji, Mount/Fujiyama *see* Fuji-san
Fuji-san *131 C6 var.* Fujiyama, *Eng.* Mount Fuji. *mountain* Honshū, SE Japan
Fukang *126 C2* Xinjiang Uygur Zizhiqu, W China
Fukien *see* Fujian
Fukui *131 C6 var.* Hukui. Fukui, Honshū, SW Japan
Fukuoka *131 A7 var.* Hukuoka, *hist.* Najima. Fukuoka, Kyūshū, SW Japan
Fukushima *130 D4 var.* Hukusima. Fukushima, Honshū, C Japan
Fulda *95 B5* Hessen, C Germany
Funafuti *see* Fongafale
Funafuti Atoll *145 E3 atoll* C Tuvalu
Funchal *70 A2* Madeira, Portugal, NE Atlantic Ocean
Fundy, Bay of *39 F5 bay* Canada/USA
Fünen *see* Fyn
Fünfkirchen *see* Pécs
Furnes *see* Veurne
Fürth *95 C5* Bayern, S Germany
Furukawa *130 D4 var.* Hurukawa. Miyagi, Honshū, C Japan
Fusan *see* Pusan
Fushun *128 D3 var.* Fou-shan, Fu-shun. Liaoning, NE China
Fu-shun *see* Fushun
Fusin *see* Fuxin
Füssen *95 C7* Bayern, S Germany
Futog *100 D3* Vojvodina, NW Serbia
Futuna, Île *145 E4 island* S Wallis and Futuna
Fuxin *128 D3 var.* Fou-hsin, Fu-hsin, Fusin. Liaoning, NE China
Fuzhou *128 D6 var.* Foochow, Fu-chou. *province capital* Fujian, SE China
Fyn *85 B8 Ger.* Fünen. *island* C Denmark
FYR Macedonia/FYROM *see* Macedonia, FYR
Fyzabad *see* Feyẕābād

G

Gaafu Alifu Atoll *see* North Huvadhu Atoll
Gaalkacyo *73 E5 var.* Galka'yo, *It.* Galcaio. Mudug, C Somalia
Gabela *78 B2* Cuanza Sul, W Angola
Gaberones *see* Gaborone
Gabès *71 E2 var.* Qābis. E Tunisia
Gabès, Golfe de *71 F2 Ar.* Khalīj Qābis. *gulf* E Tunisia
Gabon *77 B6 off.* Gabonese Republic. *country* C Africa

GABON
Central Africa

Official name Gabonese Republic
Formation 1960 / 1960
Capital Libreville
Population 1.4 million / 14 people per sq mile (5 people per sq km) / 81%
Total area 103,346 sq miles (267,667 sq km)
Languages French*, Fang, Punu, Sira, Nzebi, Mpongwe
Religions Christian (mainly Roman Catholic) 55%, Traditional beliefs 40%, Other 4%, Muslim 1%
Ethnic mix Fang 35%, Other Bantu 29%, Eshira 25%, European and other African 9%, French 2%
Government Presidential system
Currency CFA franc = 100 centimes
Literacy rate 71%
Calorie consumption 2637 calories

Gabonese Republic *see* Gabon
Gaborone *78 C4 prev.* Gaberones. *country capital* (Botswana) South East, SE Botswana
Gabrovo *104 D2* Gabrovo, N Bulgaria
Gadag *132 C1* Karnātaka, W India
Gades/Gadier/Gadir/Gadire *see* Cádiz
Gadsden *42 D2* Alabama, S USA
Gaeta *97 C5* Lazio, C Italy
Gaeta, Golfo di *97 C5 var.* Gulf of Gaeta. *gulf* C Italy
Gaeta, Gulf of *see* Gaeta, Golfo di
Gäfle *see* Gävle
Gafsa *71 E2 var.* Qafṣah. W Tunisia
Gagnoa *74 D5* C Côte d'Ivoire (Ivory Coast)
Gagra *117 E1* NW Georgia
Gaillac *91 C6 var.* Gaillac-sur-Tarn. Tarn, S France
Gaillac-sur-Tarn *see* Gaillac
Gaillimh *see* Galway
Gaillimhe, Cuan na *see* Galway Bay
Gainesville *43 E3* Florida, SE USA
Gainesville *42 D2* Georgia, SE USA
Gainesville *49 G2* Texas, SW USA
Gairdner, Lake *149 A6 salt lake* South Australia
Gaizina Kalns *see* Gaiziņakalns
Gaiziņakalns *106 C3 var.* Gaizina Kalns. *mountain* E Latvia
Galán, Cerro *64 B3 mountain* NW Argentina
Galanta *99 C6 Hung.* Galánta. Trnavský Kraj, W Slovakia
Galapagos Fracture Zone *153 E3 tectonic feature* E Pacific Ocean
Galapagos Islands *see* Colón, Archipiélago de
Galápagos, Islas de los *see* Colón, Archipiélago de
Galapagos Rise *153 F3 undersea rise* E Pacific Ocean
Galashiels *88 C4* SE Scotland, UK
Galați *108 D4 Ger.* Galatz. Galați, E Romania
Galatz *see* Galați
Galcaio *see* Gaalkacyo
Galesburg *40 B3* Illinois, N USA
Galicia *92 B1 anc.* Gallaecia. *autonomous community* NW Spain
Galicia Bank *80 B4 undersea bank* E Atlantic Ocean
Galilee, Sea of *see* Tiberias, Lake
Galka'yo *see* Gaalkacyo

Galkynyş *122 D3 prev. Rus.* Deynau, Dyanev, *Turkm.* Dänew. Lebap Welaýaty, NE Turkmenistan
Gallaecia *see* Galicia
Galle *132 D4 prev.* Point de Galle. Southern Province, SW Sri Lanka
Gallego Rise *153 F3 undersea rise* E Pacific Ocean
Gallegos *see* Río Gallegos
Gallia *see* France
Gallipoli *97 E6* Puglia, SE Italy
Gällivare *84 C3 Lapp.* Váhtjer. Norrbotten, N Sweden
Gallup *48 C1* New Mexico, SW USA
Galtat-Zemmour *70 B3* C Western Sahara
Galveston *49 H4* Texas, SW USA
Galway *89 A5 Ir.* Gaillimh. Galway, W Ireland
Galway Bay *89 A6 Ir.* Cuan na Gaillimhe. *bay* W Ireland
Gámas *see* Kaamanen
Gambell *36 C2* Saint Lawrence Island, Alaska, USA
Gambia *74 B3 off.* Republic of The Gambia, The Gambia. *country* W Africa

GAMBIA
West Africa

Official name Republic of the Gambia
Formation 1965 / 1965
Capital Banjul
Population 1.5 million / 389 people per sq mile (150 people per sq km) / 33%
Total area 4363 sq miles (11,300 sq km)
Languages English*, Mandinka, Fulani, Wolof, Jola, Soninke
Religions Sunni Muslim 90%, Christian 9%, Traditional beliefs 1%
Ethnic mix Mandinka 42%, Fulani 18%, Wolof 16%, Jola 10%, Serahuli 9%, Other 5%
Government Presidential system
Currency Dalasi = 100 butut
Literacy rate 38%
Calorie consumption 2273 calories

Gambia *74 C3 Fr.* Gambie. *river* W Africa
Gambia, Republic of The *see* Gambia
Gambia, The *see* Gambia
Gambie *see* Gambia
Gambier, Îles *143 G4 island group* E French Polynesia
Gamboma *77 B6* Plateaux, E Congo
Gamlakarleby *see* Kokkola
Gan *132 B5* Addu Atoll, C Maldives
Gan *see* Gansu
Gan *see* Jiangxi
Ganaane *see* Juba
Gäncä *117 G2 Rus.* Gyandzha; *prev.* Kirovabad, Yelisavetpol. W Azerbaijan
Gand *see* Gent
Gandajika *77 D7* Kasai Oriental, S Dem. Rep. Congo
Gander *39 G3* Newfoundland, Newfoundland and Labrador, SE Canada
Gāndhīdhām *134 C4* Gujarāt, W India
Gandía *93 F3* País Valenciano, E Spain
Ganges *135 F3 Ben.* Padma. *river* Bangladesh/India
Ganges Cone *see* Ganges Fan
Ganges Fan *140 D3 var.* Ganges Cone. *undersea fan* N Bay of Bengal
Ganges, Mouths of the *135 G4 delta* Bangladesh/India
Gangra *see* Çankırı
Gangtok *135 F3 state capital* Sikkim, N India
Gansos, Lago dos *see* Goose Lake
Gansu *128 B4 var.* Gan, Gansu Sheng, Kansu. *province* N China
Gansu Sheng *see* Gansu
Gantsevichi *see* Hantsavichy
Ganzhou *128 D6* Jiangxi, S China
Gao *75 E3* Gao, E Mali
Gaocheng *see* Litang
Gaoual *74 C4* N Guinea
Gaoxiong *see* Kaohsiung
Gap *91 D5 anc.* Vapincum. Hautes-Alpes, SE France
Gaplaňgyr Platosy *122 C2 Rus.* Plato Kaplangky. *ridge* Turkmenistan/Uzbekistan
Gar *126 A4 var.* Gar Xincun. Xizang Zizhiqu, W China
Garabil Belentligi *122 D3 Rus.* Vozvyshennost' Karabil'. *mountain range* S Turkmenistan
Garabogaz Aylagy *122 B2 Rus.* Zaliv Kara-Bogaz-Gol. *bay* NW Turkmenistan
Garachiné *53 G5* Darién, SE Panama
Garagum *122 C3 var.* Garagumy, Qara Qum, *Eng.* Black Sand Desert, Kara Kum; *prev.* Peski Karakumy. *desert* C Turkmenistan
Garagum Kanaly *122 D3 var.* Kara Kum Canal, *Rus.* Karagumskiy Kanal, Karakumskiy Kanal. *canal* C Turkmenistan
Garagumy *see* Garagum
Gara Khitrino *104 D2* Shumen, NE Bulgaria
Gárassavon *see* Kaaresuvanto
Garda, Lago di *96 C2 var.* Benaco, *Eng.* Lake Garda, *Ger.* Gardasee. *lake* NE Italy
Garda, Lake *see* Garda, Lago di
Gardasee *see* Garda, Lago di
Garden City *45 E5* Kansas, C USA
Garden State, The *see* New Jersey
Gardeyz *see* Gardīz
Gardēz *see* Gardīz
Gardīz *123 E4 var.* Gardeyz, Gardēz, Gordiaz. Paktīā, E Afghanistan
Gardner Island *see* Nikumaroro
Garegegasnjárga *see* Karigasniemi
Gargždai *106 B3* Klaipėda, W Lithuania
Garissa *73 D6* Coast, E Kenya
Garland *49 G2* Texas, SW USA
Garoe *see* Garoowe
Garonne *91 B5 anc.* Garumna. *river* S France
Garoowe *73 E5 var.* Garoe. Nugaal, N Somalia
Garoua *76 B4 var.* Garua. Nord, N Cameroon
Garrygala *see* Magtymguly
Garry Lake *37 F3 lake* Nunavut, N Canada
Garsen *73 D6* Coast, S Kenya
Garua *see* Garoua
Garumna *see* Garonne
Garwolin *98 D4* Mazowieckie, E Poland
Gar Xincun *see* Gar
Gary *40 B3* Indiana, N USA
Garzón *58 B4* Huila, S Colombia
Gasan-Kuli *see* Esenguly
Gascogne *91 B6 Eng.* Gascony. *cultural region* S France
Gascony *see* Gascogne
Gascoyne River *147 A5 river* Western Australia
Gaspé *39 F3* Québec, SE Canada
Gaspé, Péninsule de *39 E4 var.* Péninsule de la Gaspésie. *peninsula* Québec, SE Canada
Gaspésie, Péninsule de la *see* Gaspé, Péninsule de
Gastonia *43 E1* North Carolina, SE USA
Gastoúni *105 B6* Dytikí Ellás, S Greece
Gatchina *110 B4* Leningradskaya Oblast', NW Russian Federation
Gatineau *38 D4* Québec, SE Canada
Gatooma *see* Kadoma
Gatún, Lago *53 F4 reservoir* C Panama
Gauhāti *see* Guwāhāti
Gauja *106 D3 Ger.* Aa. *river* Estonia/Latvia
Gaul/Gaule *see* France
Gauteng *see* Johannesburg, South Africa
Gāvbandī *120 D4* Hormozgān, S Iran
Gávdos *105 C8 island* SE Greece
Gavere *87 B6* Oost-Vlaanderen, NW Belgium
Gävle *85 C6 var.* Gäfle; *prev.* Gefle. Gävleborg, C Sweden
Gawler *149 B6* South Australia
Gaya *135 F3* Bihār, N India
Gaya *see* Kyjov
Gayndah *149 E5* Queensland, E Australia
Gaysin *see* Haysyn
Gaza *119 A6 Ar.* Ghazzah, *Heb.* 'Azza. NE Gaza Strip
Gaz-Achak *see* Gazojak
Gazandzhyk/Gazanjyk *see* Bereket
Gaza Strip *119 A7 Ar.* Qita Ghazzah. *disputed region* SW Asia
Gaziantep *116 D4 var.* Gazi Antep; *prev.* Aintab, Antep. Gaziantep, S Turkey
Gazi Antep *see* Gaziantep
Gazimağusa *102 D5 var.* Famagusta, *Gk.* Ammóchostos. E Cyprus
Gazimağusa Körfezi *102 C5 var.* Famagusta Bay, *Gk.* Kólpos Ammóchostos. *bay* E Cyprus
Gazli *122 D2* Buxoro Viloyati, C Uzbekistan
Gazojak *122 D2 Rus.* Gaz-Achak. Lebap Welaýaty, NE Turkmenistan
Gbanga *74 D5 var.* Gbarnga. N Liberia
Gbarnga *see* Gbanga
Gdańsk *98 C2 Fr.* Dantzig, *Ger.* Danzig. Pomorskie, N Poland
Gdan'skaya Bukhta/Gdańsk, Gulf of *see* Danzig, Gulf of
Gdańska, Zakota *see* Danzig, Gulf of
Gdingen *see* Gdynia
Gdynia *98 C2 Ger.* Gdingen. Pomorskie, N Poland
Gedaref *72 C4 var.* Al Qaḍārif, El Gedaref. Gedaref, E Sudan
Gediz *116 B3* Kütahya, W Turkey
Gediz Nehri *116 A3 river* W Turkey
Geel *87 C5 var.* Gheel. Antwerpen, N Belgium
Geelong *149 C7* Victoria, SE Australia
Ge'e'mu *see* Golmud
Gefle *see* Gävle
Geilo *85 A5* Buskerud, S Norway
Gejiu *128 B6 var.* Kochiu. Yunnan, S China
Gëkdepe *see* Gökdepe
Gela *97 C7 prev.* Terranova di Sicilia. Sicilia, Italy, C Mediterranean Sea
Geldermalsen *86 C4* Gelderland, C Netherlands
Geleen *87 D6* Limburg, SE Netherlands
Gelib *see* Jilib
Gellinsor *73 E5* Mudug, C Somalia
Gembloux *87 C6* Namur, Belgium
Gemena *77 C5* Equateur, NW Dem. Rep. Congo
Gem of the Mountains *see* Idaho
Gemona del Friuli *96 D2* Friuli-Venezia Giulia, NE Italy
Gem State *see* Idaho
Genalē Wenz *see* Juba
Genck *see* Genk
General Alvear *64 B4* Mendoza, W Argentina
General Carrera, Lago *see* Buenos Aires, Lago
General Eugenio A. Garay *64 C1 var.* Fortín General Eugenio Garay; *prev.* Yrendagüé. Nueva Asunción, NW Paraguay
General José F.Uriburu *see* Zárate
General Machado *see* Camacupa
General Santos *139 F3 off.* General Santos City. Mindanao, S Philippines
General Santos City *see* General Santos
Gênes *see* Genova
Geneva *see* Genève
Geneva, Lake *95 A7 Fr.* Lac de Genève, Lac Léman, *var.* le Léman, *Ger.* Genfer See. *lake* France/Switzerland
Genève *95 A7 Eng.* Geneva, *Ger.* Genf, *It.* Ginevra. Genève, SW Switzerland
Genève, Lac de *see* Geneva, Lake
Genf *see* Genève
Genfer See *see* Geneva, Lake
Genichesk *see* Heniches'k
Genk *87 D6 var.* Genck. Limburg, NE Belgium
Gennep *86 D4* Limburg, SE Netherlands
Genoa *see* Genova
Genoa, Gulf of *see* Genova, Golfo di
Genova *102 D1 Eng.* Genoa; *anc.* Genua, *Fr.* Gênes. Liguria, NW Italy
Genova, Golfo di *96 A3 Eng.* Gulf of Genoa. *gulf* NW Italy
Genovesa, Isla *60 B5 var.* Tower Island. *island* Galapagos Islands, Ecuador, E Pacific Ocean
Gent *87 B5 Eng.* Ghent, *Fr.* Gand. Oost-Vlaanderen, NW Belgium
Genua *see* Genova
Geok-Tepe *see* Gökdepe
George *78 C5* Western Cape, S South Africa
George *82 A4 river* Newfoundland and Labrador/Québec, E Canada
George, Lake *43 E3 lake* Florida, SE USA
Georgenburg *see* Jurbarkas
Georges Bank *35 D5 undersea bank* W Atlantic Ocean
George Sound *151 A7 sound* South Island, New Zealand
Georges River *148 D2 river* New South Wales, E Australia
Georgetown *59 F2 country capital* (Guyana) N Guyana
George Town *54 C2* Great Exuma Island, C Bahamas
George Town *54 B3 var.* Georgetown. *dependent territory capital* (Cayman Islands) Grand Cayman, SW Cayman Islands
George Town *138 B3 var.* Penang, Pinang. Pinang, Peninsular Malaysia
Georgetown *43 F2* South Carolina, SE USA
Georgetown *see* George Town
George V Land *154 C4 physical region* Antarctica
Georgia *117 F2 off.* Republic of Georgia, *Geor.* Sak'art'velo, *Rus.* Gruzinskaya SSR, Gruziya. *country* SW Asia

GEORGIA
Southwest Asia

Official name Georgia
Formation 1991 / 1991
Capital Tbilisi
Population 4.5 million / 167 people per sq mile (65 people per sq km) / 61%
Total area 26,911 sq miles (69,700 sq km)
Languages Georgian*, Russian, Azeri, Armenian, Mingrelian, Ossetian, Abkhazian
Religions Georgian Orthodox 65%, Muslim 11%, Russian Orthodox 10%, Armenian Orthodox 8%, Other 6%
Ethnic mix Georgian 70%, Armenian 8%, Russian 6%, Azeri 6%, Ossetian 3%, Other 7%
Government Presidential system
Currency Lari = 100 tetri
Literacy rate 99%
Calorie consumption 2354 calories

Georgia *42 D2 off.* State of Georgia, *also known as* Empire State of the South, Peach State. *state* SE USA
Georgian Bay *40 D2 lake bay* Ontario, S Canada
Georgia, Republic of *see* Georgia
Georgia, Strait of *46 A1 strait* British Columbia, W Canada
Georgi Dimitrov *see* Kostenets
Georgiu-Dezh *see* Liski
Georg von Neumayer *154 A2 German research station* Antarctica
Gera *94 C4* Thüringen, E Germany
Geráki *105 B6* Pelopónnisos, S Greece
Geraldine *151 B6* Canterbury, South Island, New Zealand
Geraldton *147 A6* Western Australia
Geral, Serra *57 D5 mountain range* S Brazil
Gerede *116 C2* Bolu, N Turkey
Gereshk *122 D5* Helmand, SW Afghanistan
Gering *44 D3* Nebraska, C USA
German East Africa *see* Tanzania
Germanicopolis *see* Çankırı
Germanicum, Mare/German Ocean *see* North Sea
German Southwest Africa *see* Namibia
Germany *94 B4 off.* Federal Republic of Germany, Bundesrepublik Deutschland, *Ger.* Deutschland. *country* N Europe

GERMANY
Northern Europe

Official name Federal Republic of Germany
Formation 1871 / 1990
Capital Berlin
Population 82.7 million / 613 people per sq mile (237 people per sq km) / 88%
Total area 137,846 sq miles (357,021 sq km)
Languages German*, Turkish
Religions Protestant 34%, Roman Catholic 33%, Other 30%, Muslim 3%
Ethnic mix German 92%, Other 3%, Other European 3%, Turkish 2%

GERMANY
(continued)

Government Parliamentary system
Currency Euro = 100 cents
Literacy rate 99%
Calorie consumption 3496 calories

Germany, Federal Republic of *see* Germany
Geroliménas *105 B7* Pelopónnisos, S Greece
Gerona *see* Girona
Gerpinnes *87 C7* Hainaut, S Belgium
Gerunda *see* Girona
Gerze *116 D2* Sinop, N Turkey
Gesoriacum *see* Boulogne-sur-Mer
Gessoriacum *see* Boulogne-sur-Mer
Getafe *92 D3* Madrid, C Spain
Gevaş *117 F3* Van, SE Turkey
Gevgeli *see* Gevgelija
Gevgelija *101 E6* *var.* Đevđelija, Djevdjelija, *Turk.* Gevgeli. SE Macedonia
Ghaba *see* Al Ghābah
Ghana *75 E5* *off.* Republic of Ghana. *country* W Africa

GHANA
West Africa

Official name Republic of Ghana
Formation 1957 / 1957
Capital Accra
Population 22.1 million / 249 people per sq mile (96 people per sq km) / 38%
Total area 92,100 sq miles (238,540 sq km)
Languages Twi, Fanti, Ewe, Ga, Adangbe, Gurma, Dagomba (Dagbani)
Religions Christian 69%, Muslim 16%, Traditional beliefs 9%, Other 6%
Ethnic mix Ashanti and Fanti 52%, Moshi-Dagomba 16%, Ewe 12%, Other 11%, Ga and Ga-adanbe 8%, Yoruba 1%
Government Presidential system
Currency Cedi = 100 psewas
Literacy rate 54%
Calorie consumption 2667 calories

Ghanzi *78 C3* *var.* Khanzi. Ghanzi, W Botswana
Gharandal *119 B7* Al'Aqabah, SW Jordan
Gharbt, Jabal al *see* Liban, Jebel
Ghardaïa *70 D2* N Algeria
Gharvān *see* Gharyān
Gharyān *71 F2* *var.* Gharvān. NW Libya
Ghawdex *see* Gozo
Ghaznī *123 E4* *var.* Ghazni. Ghaznī, E Afghanistan
Ghazzah *see* Gaza
Gheel *see* Geel
Ghent *see* Gent
Gheorgheni *108 C4* *prev.* Gheorghieni, Sîn-Miclăuş, *Ger.* Niklasmarkt, *Hung.* Gyergyószentmiklós. Harghita, C Romania
Gheorghieni *see* Gheorgheni
Ghŭdara *123 F3* *var.* Gudara, *Rus.* Kudara. SE Tajikistan
Ghurdaqah *see* Hurghada
Ghūrīān *122 D4* Herāt, W Afghanistan
Giamame *see* Jamaame
Giannitsá *104 B4* *var.* Yiannitsá. Kentrikí Makedonía, N Greece
Gibraltar *93 G4* *UK dependent territory* SW Europe
Gibraltar, Bay of *93 G5* *bay* Gibraltar/Spain Europe Mediterranean Sea Atlantic Ocean
Gibraltar, Détroit de/Gibraltar, Estrecho de *see* Gibraltar, Strait of
Gibraltar, Strait of *92 C5* *Fr.* Détroit de Gibraltar, *Sp.* Estrecho de Gibraltar. *strait* Atlantic Ocean/Mediterranean Sea
Gibson Desert *147 B5* *desert* Western Australia
Giedraičiai *107 C5* Utena, E Lithuania
Giessen *95 B5* Hessen, W Germany
Gifu *131 C6* *var.* Gihu. Gifu, Honshū, SW Japan
Giganta, Sierra de la *50 B3* *mountain range* W Mexico
Gihu *see* Gifu
G'ijduvon *122 D2* *Rus.* Gizhduvon. Buxoro Viloyati, C Uzbekistan
Gijón *92 D1* *var.* Xixón. Asturias, NW Spain
Gilani *see* Gnjilane
Gila River *48 A2* *river* Arizona, SW USA
Gilbert Islands *see* Tungaru
Gilbert River *148 C3* *river* Queensland, NE Australia
Gilf Kebir Plateau *72 A2* *Ar.* Haḍabat al Jilf al Kabīr. *plateau* SW Egypt
Gillette *44 D3* Wyoming, C USA
Gilolo *see* Halmahera, Pulau
Gilroy *47 B6* California, W USA
Gimie, Mount *55 F1* *mountain* C Saint Lucia
Gimma *see* Jīma
Ginevra *see* Genève
Gingin *147 A6* Western Australia
Giohar *see* Jawhar
Gipeswic *see* Ipswich
Girardot *58 B3* Cundinamarca, C Colombia
Giresun *117 E2* *var.* Kerasunt; *anc.* Cerasus, Pharnacia. Giresun, NE Turkey
Girgenti *see* Agrigento
Girin *see* Jilin
Girne *102 C5* *Gk.* Kerýneia, Kyrenia. N Cyprus
Giron *see* Kiruna
Girona *93 G2* *var.* Gerona; *anc.* Gerunda. Cataluña, NE Spain
Gisborne *150 E3* Gisborne, North Island, New Zealand
Gissar Range *123 E3* *Rus.* Gissarskiy Khrebet. *mountain range* Tajikistan/Uzbekistan
Gissarskiy Khrebet *see* Gissar Range
Githio *see* Gýtheio
Giulianova *96 D4* Abruzzi, C Italy
Giumri *see* Gyumri
Giurgiu *108 C5* Giurgiu, S Romania
Gîza/Gizeh *see* El Gîza
Gizhduvon *see* G'ijduvon
Giżycko *98 D2* Warmińsko-Mazurskie, NE Poland
Gjakovë *see* Đakovica
Gjilan *see* Gnjilane
Gjinokastër *see* Gjirokastër
Gjirokastër *101 C7* *var.* Gjirokastra; *prev.* Gjinokastër, *Gk.* Argyrokastron, *It.* Argirocastro. Gjirokastër, S Albania
Gjirokastra *see* Gjirokastër
Gjoa Haven *37 F3* King William Island, Nunavut, NW Canada
Gjøvik *85 B5* Oppland, S Norway
Glace Bay *39 G4* Cape Breton Island, Nova Scotia, SE Canada
Gladstone *148 E4* Queensland, E Australia
Glåma *85 B5* *var.* Glommen. *river* S Norway
Glasgow *88 C4* S Scotland, UK
Glavn'a Morava *see* Velika Morava
Glazov *111 D5* Udmurtskaya Respublika, NW Russian Federation
Gleiwitz *see* Gliwice
Glendale *48 B2* Arizona, SW USA
Glendive *44 D2* Montana, NW USA
Glens Falls *41 F3* New York, NE USA
Glevum *see* Gloucester
Glina *100 B3* Sisak-Moslavina, NE Croatia
Glittertind *85 A5* *mountain* S Norway
Gliwice *99 C5* *Ger.* Gleiwitz. Śląskie, S Poland
Globe *48 B2* Arizona, SW USA
Globino *see* Hlobyne
Glogau *see* Głogów
Głogów *98 B4* *Ger.* Glogau, Glogow. Dolnośląskie, SW Poland
Glogow *see* Głogów
Glomma *see* Glåma
Glommen *see* Glåma
Gloucester *89 D6* *hist.* Caer Glou, *Lat.* Glevum. C England, UK
Głowno *98 D4* Łódź, C Poland
Glubokoye *see* Hlybokaye
Glukhov *see* Hlukhiv
Gnesen *see* Gniezno
Gniezno *98 C3* *Ger.* Gnesen. Weilkopolskie, C Poland
Gnjilane *101 D5* *var.* Gilani, *Alb.* Gjilan. Kosovo, S Serbia
Gobabis *78 B3* Omaheke, E Namibia
Gobi *126 D3* *desert* China/Mongolia
Gobō *131 C6* Wakayama, Honshū, SW Japan
Godāvari *124 B3* *var.* Godavari. *river* C India
Godavari *see* Godāvari
Godhavn *see* Qeqertarsuaq
Godhra *134 C4* Gujarāt, W India
Göding *see* Hodonín
Godoy Cruz *64 B4* Mendoza, W Argentina
Godthaab/Godthåb *see* Nuuk
Godwin Austen, Mount *see* K2
Goede Hoop, Kaap de *see* Good Hope, Cape of
Goeie Hoop, Kaap die *see* Good Hope, Cape of
Goeree *86 B4* *island* SW Netherlands
Goes *87 B5* Zeeland, SW Netherlands
Goettingen *see* Göttingen
Gogebic Range *40 B1* *hill range* Michigan/Wisconsin, N USA
Goiânia *63 E3* *prev.* Goyania. *state capital* Goiás, C Brazil
Goiás *63 E3* Goiás, C Brazil
Gojōme *130 D4* Akita, Honshū, NW Japan
Gökçeada *104 D4* *var.* Imroz Adasī, *Gk.* Imbros. *island* NW Turkey
Gökdepe *122 C3* *Rus.* Gëkdepe, Geok-Tepe. Ahal Welaýaty, C Turkmenistan
Göksun *116 D4* Kahramanmaraş, C Turkey
Gol *85 A5* Buskerud, S Norway
Golan Heights *119 B5* *Ar.* Al Jawlān, *Heb.* HaGolan. *mountain range* SW Syria
Golaya Pristan *see* Hola Prystan'
Gołdap *98 E2* *Ger.* Goldap. Warmińsko-Mazurskie, NE Poland
Gold Coast *149 E5* *cultural region* Queensland, E Australia
Golden Bay *150 C4* *bay* South Island, New Zealand
Golden State, The *see* California
Goldingen *see* Kuldīga
Goldsboro *43 F1* North Carolina, SE USA
Goleniów *98 B3* *Ger.* Gollnow. Zachodnio-pomorskie, NW Poland
Gollnow *see* Goleniów
Golmo *see* Golmud
Golmud *126 D4* *var.* Ge'e'mu, Golmo, *Chin.* Ko-erh-mu. Qinghai, C China
Golovanevsk *see* Holovanivs'k
Golub-Dobrzyń *98 C3* Kujawski-pomorskie, C Poland
Goma *77 E6* Nord Kivu, NE Dem. Rep. Congo
Gombi *75 H4* Adamawa, E Nigeria
Gombroon *see* Bandar-e 'Abbās
Gomel' *see* Homyel'
Gomera *70 A3* *island* Islas Canarias, Spain, NE Atlantic Ocean
Gómez Palacio *50 D3* Durango, C Mexico
Gonaïves *54 D3* *var.* Les Gonaïves. N Haiti
Gonâve, Île de la *54 D3* *island* C Haiti
Gondar *see* Gonder
Gonder *72 C4* *var.* Gondar. NW Ethiopia
Gondia *135 E4* Mahārāshtra, C India
Gonggar *126 C5* *var.* Gyixong. Xizang Zizhiqu, W China
Gongola *75 G4* *river* E Nigeria
Gongtang *see* Damxung
Gonni/Gónnos *see* Gónnoi
Gónnoi *104 B4* *var.* Gonni, Gónnos; *prev.* Derelí. Thessalía, C Greece
Good Hope *see* Fort Good Hope
Good Hope, Cape of *78 B5* *Afr.* Kaap de Goede Hoop, Kaap die Goeie Hoop. *cape* SW South Africa
Goodland *44 D4* Kansas, C USA
Goondiwindi *149 D5* Queensland, E Australia
Goor *86 E3* Overijssel, E Netherlands
Goose Green *65 D7* *var* Prado del Ganso. East Falkland, Falkland Islands
Goose Lake *46 B4* *var.* Lago dos Gansos. *lake* California/Oregon, W USA
Gopher State *see* Minnesota
Göppingen *95 B6* Baden-Württemberg, SW Germany
Góra Kalwaria *114 D4* Mazowieckie, C Poland
Gorakhpur *135 E3* Uttar Pradesh, N India
Gorany *see* Harany
Goražde *100 C4* Federacija Bosna I Hercegovina, SE Bosnia and Herzegovina
Gorbovichi *see* Harbavichy
Gordiaz *see* Gardīz
Goré *76 C4* Logone-Oriental, S Chad
Gorē *73 C5* Oromo, C Ethiopia
Gore *151 B7* Southland, South Island, New Zealand
Gorgān *120 D2* *var.* Astarabad, Astrabad, Gurgan, *prev.* Asterābād; *anc.* Hyrcania. Golestán, N Iran
Gori *117 F2* C Georgia
Gorinchem *86 C4* *var.* Gorkum. Zuid-Holland, C Netherlands
Goris *117 G3* SE Armenia
Gorki *see* Horki
Gor'kiy *see* Nizhniy Novgorod
Gorkum *see* Gorinchem
Görlitz *94 D4* Sachsen, E Germany
Görlitz *see* Zgorzelec
Gorlovka *see* Horlivka
Gorna Dzhumaya *see* Blagoevgrad
Gornja Mužlja *see* Mužlja
Gornji Milanovac *100 C4* Serbia, C Serbia
Gorodets *see* Haradzyets
Gorodishche *see* Horodyshche
Gorodnya *see* Horodnya
Gorodok *see* Haradok
Gorodok/Gorodok Yagellonski *see* Horodok
Gorontalo *139 E4* Sulawesi, C Indonesia
Gorontalo, Teluk *see* Tomini, Gulf of
Gorssel *86 D3* Gelderland, E Netherlands
Goryn *see* Horyn'
Gorzów Wielkopolski *98 B3* *Ger.* Landsberg, Landsberg an der Warthe Lubuskie, W Poland
Gosford *149 D6* New South Wales, SE Australia
Goshogawara *130 D3* *var.* Gosyogawara. Aomori, Honshū, C Japan
Gospić *100 A3* Lika-Senj, C Croatia
Gostivar *101 D6* W FYR Macedonia
Gosyogawara *see* Goshogawara
Göteborg *85 B7* *Eng.* Gothenburg. Västra Götaland, S Sweden
Gotel Mountains *75 G5* *mountain range* E Nigeria
Gotha *94 C4* Thüringen, C Germany
Gothenburg *80 D3* Nebraska, C USA
Gothenburg *see* Göteborg
Gotland *85 C7* *island* SE Sweden
Gotō-rettō *131 A7* *island group* SW Japan
Gotska Sandön *106 B1* *island* SE Sweden
Gōtsu *131 B6* *var.* Gôtu. Shimane, Honshū, SW Japan
Göttingen *94 B4* *var.* Goettingen. Niedersachsen, C Germany
Gottschee *see* Kočevje
Gottwaldov *see* Zlín
Gôtu *see* Gōtsu
Gouda *86 C4* Zuid-Holland, C Netherlands
Gough Fracture Zone *67 C6* *tectonic feature* S Atlantic Ocean
Gough Island *69 B8* *island* Tristan da Cunha, S Atlantic Ocean
Gouin, Réservoir *38 D4* *reservoir* Québec, SE Canada
Goulburn *149 D6* New South Wales, SE Australia
Goundam *75 E3* Tombouctou, NW Mali
Gouré *75 G3* Zinder, SE Niger
Goverla, Gora *see* Hoverla, Hora
Governador Valadares *63 F4* Minas Gerais, SE Brazil
Govĭ Altayn Nuruu *127 E3* *mountain range* S Mongolia
Goya *64 D3* Corrientes, NE Argentina
Goyania *see* Goiânia
Goz Beïda *76 C3* Ouaddaï, SE Chad
Gozo *97 C8* *var.* Ghawdex. *island* N Malta
Graciosa *92 A5* *var.* Ilha Graciosa. *island* Azores, Portugal, NE Atlantic Ocean
Graciosa, Ilha *see* Graciosa
Gradačac *100 C3* Federacija Bosna I Hercegovina, N Bosnia and Herzegovina

Gradaús, Serra dos *63 E3 mountain range* C Brazil
Gradiška *see* Bosanska Gradiška
Grafton *149 E5* New South Wales, SE Australia
Grafton *45 E1* North Dakota, N USA
Graham Land *154 A2 physical region* Antarctica
Grajewo *98 E3* Podlaskie, NE Poland
Grampian Mountains *88 C3 mountain range* C Scotland, UK
Gran *see* Esztergom
Granada *52 D3* Granada, SW Nicaragua
Granada *92 D5* Andalucía, S Spain
Gran Canaria *70 A3 var.* Grand Canary. *island* Islas Canarias, Spain, NE Atlantic Ocean
Gran Chaco *64 D2 var.* Chaco. *lowland plain* South America
Grand Bahama Island *54 B1 island* N Bahamas
Grand Banks of Newfoundland *34 E4 undersea basin* NW Atlantic Ocean
Grand Bassa *see* Buchanan
Grand Canary *see* Gran Canaria
Grand Canyon *48 A1 canyon* Arizona, SW USA
Grand Canyon State *see* Arizona
Grand Cayman *54 B3 island* SW Cayman Islands
Grand Duchy of Luxembourg *see* Luxembourg
Grande, Bahía *65 B7 bay* S Argentina
Grande Comore *79 F2 var.* Njazidja, Great Comoro. *island* NW Comoros
Grande de Chiloé, Isla *see* Chiloé, Isla de
Grande Prairie *37 E4* Alberta, W Canada
Grand Erg Occidental *70 D3 desert* W Algeria
Grand Erg Oriental *71 E3 desert* Algeria/Tunisia
Grande, Rio *51 E2 var.* Río Bravo, Sp. Río Bravo del Norte, Bravo del Norte. *river* Mexico/USA
Grande Terre *55 G3 island* E West Indies
Grand Falls *39 G3* Newfoundland, Newfoundland and Labrador, SE Canada
Grand Forks *45 E1* North Dakota, N USA
Grandichi *see* Hrandzichy
Grand Island *45 E4* Nebraska, C USA
Grand Junction *44 C4* Colorado, C USA
Grand Paradis *see* Gran Paradiso
Grand Rapids *40 C3* Michigan, N USA
Grand Rapids *45 F1* Minnesota, N USA
Grand-Saint-Bernard, Col du *see* Great Saint Bernard Pass
Grand-Santi *59 G3* W French Guiana
Granite State *see* New Hampshire
Gran Lago *see* Nicaragua, Lago de
Gran Malvina *see* West Falkland
Gran Paradiso *96 A2 Fr.* Grand Paradis. *mountain* NW Italy
Gran San Bernardo, Passo di *see* Great Saint Bernard Pass
Gran Santiago *see* Santiago
Grants *48 C2* New Mexico, SW USA
Grants Pass *46 B4* Oregon, NW USA
Granville *90 B3* Manche, N France
Gratianopolis *see* Grenoble
Gratz *see* Graz
Graudenz *see* Grudziądz
Graulhet *91 C6* Tarn, S France
Grave *86 D4* Noord-Brabant, SE Netherlands
Grayling *36 C2* Alaska, USA
Graz *95 E7 prev.* Gratz. Steiermark, SE Austria
Great Abaco *54 C1 var.* Abaco Island. *island* N Bahamas
Great Alfold *see* Great Hungarian Plain
Great Ararat *see* Büyükağrı Dağ
Great Australian Bight *147 D7 bight* S Australia
Great Barrier Island *150 D2 island* N New Zealand
Great Barrier Reef *148 D2 reef* Queensland, NE Australia
Great Basin *47 C5 basin* W USA
Great Bear Lake *37 E3 Fr.* Grand Lac de l'Ours. *lake* Northwest Territories, NW Canada
Great Belt *see* Storebælt

Great Bend *45 E5* Kansas, C USA
Great Britain *see* Britain
Great Comoro *see* Grande Comore
Great Dividing Range *148 D4 mountain range* NE Australia
Greater Antarctica *154 C3 var.* East Antarctica. *physical region* Antarctica
Greater Antilles *54 D3 island group* West Indies
Greater Caucasus *117 G2 mountain range* Azerbaijan/Georgia/Russian Federation Asia/Europe
Greater Sunda Islands *124 D5 var.* Sunda Islands. *island group* Indonesia
Great Exhibition Bay *150 C1 inlet* North Island, New Zealand
Great Exuma Island *54 C2 island* C Bahamas
Great Falls *44 B1* Montana, NW USA
Great Grimsby *see* Grimsby
Great Hungarian Plain *99 C7 var.* Great Alfold, Plain of Hungary, Hung. Alföld. *plain* SE Europe
Great Inagua *54 D2 var.* Inagua Islands. *island* S Bahamas
Great Indian Desert *see* Thar Desert
Great Khingan Range *see* Da Hinggan Ling
Great Lake *see* Tônlé Sap
Great Lakes *35 C5 lakes* Ontario, Canada/USA
Great Lakes State *see* Michigan
Great Meteor Seamount *see* Great Meteor Tablemount
Great Meteor Tablemount *66 B3 var.* Great Meteor Seamount. *seamount* E Atlantic Ocean
Great Nicobar *133 G3 island* Nicobar Islands, India, NE Indian Ocean
Great Plain of China *125 E2 plain* E China
Great Plains *44 D3 var.* High Plains. *plains* Canada/USA
Great Rift Valley *73 C5 var.* Rift Valley. *depression* Asia/Africa
Great Ruaha *73 C7 river* S Tanzania
Great Saint Bernard Pass *96 A1 Fr.* Col du Grand-Saint-Bernard, *It.* Passo del Gran San Bernardo. *pass* Italy/Switzerland
Great Salt Desert *see* Kavīr, Dasht-e
Great Salt Lake *44 A3 salt lake* Utah, W USA
Great Salt Lake Desert *44 A4 plain* Utah, W USA
Great Sand Sea *71 H3 desert* Egypt/Libya
Great Sandy Desert *146 C4 desert* Western Australia
Great Sandy Desert *see* Ar Rub 'al Khālī
Great Sandy Island *see* Fraser Island
Great Slave Lake *37 E4 Fr.* Grand Lac des Esclaves. *lake* Northwest Territories, NW Canada
Great Sound *42 A5 sound* Bermuda, NW Atlantic Ocean
Great Victoria Desert *147 C5 desert* South Australia/Western Australia
Great Wall of China *128 C4 ancient monument* N China Asia
Great Yarmouth *89 E6 var.* Yarmouth. E England, UK
Grebenka *see* Hrebinka
Gredos, Sierra de *92 D3 mountain range* W Spain
Greece *81 E5* New York, NE USA
Greece *105 A5 off.* Hellenic Republic, *Gk.* Ellás; *anc.* Hellas. *country* SE Europe

GREECE
Southeast Europe

Official name Hellenic Republic
Formation 1829 / 1947
Capital Athens
Population 11.1 million / 220 people per sq mile (85 people per sq km) / 60%
Total area 50,942 sq miles (131,940 sq km)
Languages Greek*, Turkish, Macedonian, Albanian
Religions Orthodox Christian 98%, Other 1%, Muslim 1%
Ethnic mix Greek 98%, Other 2%
Government Parliamentary system
Currency Euro = 100 cents
Literacy rate 91%
Calorie consumption 3721 calories

Greeley *44 D4* Colorado, C USA
Green Bay *40 B2* Wisconsin, N USA
Green Bay *40 B2 lake bay* Michigan/Wisconsin, N USA
Greeneville *43 E1* Tennessee, S USA
Greenland *82 D3 Dan.* Grønland, *Inuit* Kalaallit Nunaat. *Danish external territory* NE North America
Greenland Sea *83 F2 sea* Arctic Ocean
Green Mountains *41 G2 mountain range* Vermont, NE USA
Green Mountain State *see* Vermont
Greenock *88 C4* W Scotland, UK
Green River *44 B4 river* Wyoming, C USA
Green River *40 C5 river* Kentucky, C USA
Green River *44 B4 river* Utah, W USA
Greensboro *43 F1* North Carolina, SE USA
Greenville *42 B2* Mississippi, S USA
Greenville *43 F1* North Carolina, SE USA
Greenville *43 E1* South Carolina, SE USA
Greenville *49 G2* Texas, SW USA
Greenwich *89 B8* UK
Greenwood *42 B2* Mississippi, S USA
Greenwood *43 E2* South Carolina, SE USA
Gregory Range *148 C3 mountain range* Queensland, E Australia
Greifenberg/Greifenberg in Pommern *see* Gryfice
Greifswald *94 D2* Mecklenburg-Vorpommern, NE Germany
Grenada *42 C2* Mississippi, S USA
Grenada *55 G5 country* SE West Indies

GRENADA
West Indies

Official name Grenada
Formation 1974 / 1974
Capital St. George's
Population 89,502 / 683 people per sq mile (263 people per sq km) / 38%
Total area 131 sq miles (340 sq km)
Languages English*, English Creole
Religions Roman Catholic 68%, Anglican 17%, Other 15%
Ethnic mix Black African 82%, Mulatto (mixed race) 13%, East Indian 3%, Other 2%
Government Parliamentary system
Currency Eastern Caribbean dollar = 100 cents
Literacy rate 96%
Calorie consumption 2932 calories

Grenadines, The *55 H4 island group* Grenada/St Vincent and the Grenadines
Grenoble *91 D5 anc.* Cularo, Gratianopolis. Isère, E France
Gresham *46 B3* Oregon, NW USA
Grevená *104 B4* Dytikí Makedonía, N Greece
Grevenmacher *87 E8* Grevenmacher, E Luxembourg
Greymouth *151 B5* West Coast, South Island, New Zealand
Grey Range *149 C5 mountain range* New South Wales/Queensland, E Australia
Greytown *see* San Juan del Norte
Griffin *42 D2* Georgia, SE USA
Grimari *76 C4* Ouaka, C Central African Republic
Grimsby *89 E5 prev.* Great Grimsby. E England, UK
Grobin *see* Grobiņa
Grobiņa *106 B3 Ger.* Grobin. Liepāja, W Latvia
Gródek Jagielloński *see* Horodok
Grodno *see* Hrodna
Grodzisk Wielkopolski *98 B3* Weilkopolskie, C Poland
Groesbeek *86 D4* Gelderland, SE Netherlands
Grójec *98 D4* Mazowieckie, C Poland
Groningen *86 E1* Groningen, NE Netherlands
Grønland *see* Greenland
Groote Eylandt *148 B2 island* Northern Territory, N Australia

Grootfontein *78 B3* Otjozondjupa, N Namibia
Groot Karasberge *78 B4 mountain range* S Namibia
Gros Islet *55 F1* N Saint Lucia
Grossa, Isola *see* Dugi Otok
Grossbetschkerek *see* Zrenjanin
Grosse Morava *see* Velika Morava
Grosser Sund *see* Suur Väin
Grosseto *96 B4* Toscana, C Italy
Grossglockner *95 C7 mountain* W Austria
Grosskanizsa *see* Nagykanizsa
Gross-Karol *see* Carei
Grosskikinda *see* Kikinda
Grossmichel *see* Michalovce
Gross-Schlatten *see* Abrud
Grosswardein *see* Oradea
Grozny *111 B8* Chechenskaya Respublika, SW Russian Federation
Grudovo *see* Sredets
Grudziądz *98 D3 Ger.* Graudenz. Kujawsko-pomorskie, C Poland
Grums *85 B6* Värmland, C Sweden
Grünberg/Grünberg in Schlesien *see* Zielona Góra
Grüneberg *see* Zielona Góra
Gruzinskaya SSR/Gruziya *see* Georgia
Gryazi *111 B6* Lipetskaya Oblast', W Russian Federation
Gryfice *98 B2 Ger.* Greifenberg, Greifenberg in Pommern. Zachodnio-pomorskie, NW Poland
Guabito *53 E4* Bocas del Toro, NW Panama
Guadalajara *50 D4* Jalisco, C Mexico
Guadalajara *93 E3 Ar.* Wad Al-Hajarah; *anc.* Arriaca. Castilla-La Mancha, C Spain
Guadalcanal *144 C3 island* C Solomon Islands
Guadalquivir *92 D4 river* W Spain
Guadalupe *50 D3* Zacatecas, C Mexico
Guadalupe Peak *48 D3 mountain* Texas, SW USA
Guadalupe River *49 G4 river* SW USA
Guadarrama, Sierra de *93 E2 mountain range* C Spain
Guadeloupe *55 H3 French overseas department* E West Indies
Guadiana *92 C4 river* Portugal/Spain
Guadix *93 E4* Andalucía, S Spain
Guaimaca *52 C2* Francisco Morazán, C Honduras
Guajira, Península de la *58 B1 peninsula* N Colombia
Gualaco *52 D2* Olancho, C Honduras
Gualán *52 B2* Zacapa, C Guatemala
Gualdicciolo *96 D1* NW San Marino
Gualeguaychú *64 D4* Entre Ríos, E Argentina
Guam *144 B1* US *unincorporated territory* W Pacific Ocean
Guamúchil *50 C3* Sinaloa, C Mexico
Guanabacoa *54 B2* La Habana, W Cuba
Guanajuato *51 E4* Guanajuato, C Mexico
Guanare *58 C2* Portuguesa, N Venezuela
Guanare, Río *58 D2 river* W Venezuela
Guangdong *128 C6 var.* Guangdong Sheng, Kuang-tung, Kwangtung, Yue. *province* S China
Guangdong Sheng *see* Guangdong
Guangju *see* Kwangju
Guangxi *see* Guangxi Zhuangzu Zizhiqu
Guangxi Zhuangzu Zizhiqu *128 C6 var.* Guangxi, Gui, Kuang-hsi, Kwangsi, *Eng.* Kwangsi Chuang Autonomous Region. *autonomous region* S China
Guangyuan *128 B5 var.* Kuang-yuan, Kwangyuan. Sichuan, C China
Guangzhou *128 C6, var.* Kwangchow, *Eng.* Canton. *province capital* Guangdong, S China
Guantánamo *54 D3* Guantánamo, SE Cuba
Guantánamo, Bahía de *54 D3 Eng.* Guantanamo Bay. *US military base* SE Cuba
Guantanamo Bay *see* Guantánamo, Bahía de
Guaporé, Rio *62 D3 var.* Río Iténez. *river* Bolivia/Brazil
Guarda *92 C3* Guarda, N Portugal
Guarumal *53 F5* Veraguas, S Panama
Guasave *50 C3* Sinaloa, C Mexico

Guatemala *52 A2 off.* Republic of Guatemala. *country* Central America

GUATEMALA
Central America

Official name Republic of Guatemala
Formation 1838 / 1838
Capital Guatemala City
Population 12.6 million / 301 people per sq mile (116 people per sq km) / 40%
Total area 42,042 sq miles (108,890 sq km)
Languages Spanish*, Quiché, Mam, Cakchiquel, Kekchí
Religions Roman Catholic 65%, Protestant 33%, Other and nonreligious 2%
Ethnic mix Amerindian 60%, Mestizo 30%, Other 10%
Government Presidential system
Currency Quetzal = 100 centavos
Literacy rate 69%
Calorie consumption 2219 calories

Guatemala Basin *35 B7 undersea basin* E Pacific Ocean
Guatemala City *see* Ciudad de Guatemala
Guatemala, Republic of *see* Guatemala
Guaviare *56 B2 off.* Comisaría Guaviare. *province* S Colombia
Guaviare, Comisaría *see* Guaviare
Guaviare, Río *58 D3 river* E Colombia
Guayanas, Macizo de las *see* Guiana Highlands
Guayaquil *60 A2 var.* Santiago de Guayaquil. Guayas, SW Ecuador
Guayaquil, Golfo de *60 A2 var.* Gulf of Guayaquil. *gulf* SW Ecuador
Guayaquil, Gulf of *see* Guayaquil, Golfo de
Guaymas *50 B2* Sonora, NW Mexico
Gubadag *122 C2 Turkm.* Tel'man; *prev.* Tel'mansk. Daşoguz Welaýaty, N Turkmenistan
Guben *94 D4 var.* Wilhelm-Pieck-Stadt. Brandenburg, E Germany
Gudara *see* Ghŭdara
Gudaut'a *117 E1* NW Georgia
Guéret *90 C4* Creuse, C France
Guernsey *89 D8 island* Channel Islands, NW Europe
Guerrero Negro *50 A2* Baja California Sur, NW Mexico
Gui *see* Guangxi Zhuangzu Zizhiqu
Guiana *see* French Guiana
Guiana Highlands *62 D1 var.* Macizo de las Guayanas. *mountain range* N South America
Guiba *see* Juba
Guidder *see* Guider
Guider *76 B4 var.* Guidder. Nord, N Cameroon
Guidimouni *75 G3* Zinder, S Niger
Guildford *89 D7* SE England, UK
Guilin *128 C6 var.* Kuei-lin, Kweilin. Guangxi Zhuangzu Zizhiqu, S China
Guimarães *92 B2 var.* Guimaráes. Braga, N Portugal
Guimaráes *see* Guimarães
Guinea *74 C4 off.* Republic of Guinea, *var.* Guinée; *prev.* French Guinea, People's Revolutionary Republic of Guinea. *country* W Africa

GUINEA
West Africa

Official name Republic of Guinea
Formation 1958 / 1958
Capital Conakry
Population 9.4 million / 99 people per sq mile (38 people per sq km) / 33%
Total area 94,925 sq miles (245,857 sq km)
Languages French*, Fulani, Malinke, Soussou
Religions Muslim 65%, Traditional beliefs 33%, Christian 2%
Ethnic mix Fulani 30%, Malinke 30%, Soussou 15%, Kissi 10%, Other tribes 10%, Other 5%
Government Presidential system
Currency Guinea franc = 100 centimes
Literacy rate 41%
Calorie consumption 2409 calories

Guinea Basin *69 A5 undersea basin* E Atlantic Ocean
Guinea-Bissau *74 B4 off.* Republic of Guinea-Bissau, *Fr.* Guinée-Bissau, *Port.* Guiné-Bissau; *prev.* Portuguese Guinea. *country* W Africa

GUINEA-BISSAU
West Africa

Official name Republic of Guinea-Bissau
Formation 1974 / 1974
Capital Bissau
Population 1.6 million / 147 people per sq mile (57 people per sq km) / 24%
Total area 13,946 sq miles (36,120 sq km)
Languages Portuguese*, Balante, Fulani, Malinke, Portuguese Creole
Religions Traditional beliefs 52%, Muslim 40%, Christian 8%
Ethnic mix Other tribes 31%, Balante 25%, Fula 20%, Mandinka 12%, Mandyako 11%, Other 1%
Government Presidential system
Currency CFA franc = 100 centimes
Literacy rate 40%
Calorie consumption 2024 calories

Guinea-Bissau, Republic of *see* Guinea-Bissau
Guinea, Gulf of *68 B4 Fr.* Golfe de Guinée. *gulf* E Atlantic Ocean
Guinea, People's Revolutionary Republic of *see* Guinea
Guinea, Republic of *see* Guinea
Guiné-Bissau *see* Guinea-Bissau
Guinée *see* Guinea
Guinée-Bissau *see* Guinea-Bissau
Guinée, Golfe de *see* Guinea, Gulf of
Güiria *59 E1* Sucre, NE Venezuela
Guiyang *128 B6 var.* Kuei-Yang, Kuei-yang, Kueyang, Kweiyang; *prev.* Kweichu. *province capital* Guizhou, S China
Guizhou *128 B6* China
Gujarāt *134 C4 var.* Gujerat. *cultural region* W India
Gujarāt *134 C4 var.* Gujerat. *state* W India
Gujerat *see* Gujarāt
Gujrānwāla *134 D2* Punjab, NE Pakistan
Gujrāt *134 D2* Punjab, E Pakistan
Gulbarga *132 C1* Karnātaka, C India
Gulbene *106 D3 Ger.* Alt-Schwanenburg. Gulbene, NE Latvia
Gulf of Liaotung *see* Liaodong Wan
Gulfport *42 C3* Mississippi, S USA
Gulf, The *120 C4 var.* Persian Gulf, *Ar.* Khalīj al 'Arabī, *Per.* Khalīj-e Fars. *Gulf* SW Asia
Gulistan *see* Guliston
Guliston *123 E2 Rus.* Gulistan. Sirdaryo Viloyati, E Uzbekistan
Gulja *see* Yining
Gulkana *36 D3* Alaska, USA
Gulu *73 B6* N Uganda
Gulyantsi *104 C1* Pleven, N Bulgaria
Guma *see* Pishan
Gumbinnen *see* Gusev
Gumpolds *see* Humpolec
Gümülcine/Gümüljina *see* Komotiní
Gümüşane *see* Gümüşhane
Gümüşhane *117 E3 var.* Gümüşane, Gumushkhane. Gümüşhane, NE Turkey
Gumushkhane *see* Gümüşhane
Güney Doğu Toroslar *117 E4 mountain range* SE Turkey
Gunnbjørn Fjeld *82 D4 var.* Gunnbjörns Bjerge. *mountain* C Greenland
Gunnbjörns Bjerge *see* Gunnbjørn Fjeld
Gunnedah *149 D6* New South Wales, SE Australia
Gunnison *44 C5* Colorado, C USA
Gurbansoltan Eje *122 C2 Prev.* Ýylanly, *Rus.* Il'yaly. Daşoguz Welaýaty, N Turkmenistan
Gurbantünggüt Shamo *126 B2 desert* W China
Gurgan *see* Gorgān
Guri, Embalse de *59 E2 reservoir* E Venezuela
Gurkfeld *see* Krško
Gurktaler Alpen *95 D7 mountain range* S Austria
Gürün *116 D3* Sivas, C Turkey
Gur'yev/Gur'yevskaya Oblast' *see* Atyrau
Gusau *75 G4* Zamfara, NW Nigeria
Gusev *106 B4 Ger.* Gumbinnen. Kaliningradskaya Oblast', W Russian Federation
Gushgy *see* Serhetabat
Gustavus *36 D4* Alaska, USA
Güstrow *94 C3* Mecklenburg-Vorpommern, NE Germany
Guta/Gúta *see* Kolárovo
Gütersloh *94 B4* Nordrhein-Westfalen, W Germany
Gutta *see* Kolárovo
Guttstadt *see* Dobre Miasto
Guwāhāti *135 G3 prev.* Gauhāti. Assam, NE India
Guyana *59 F3 off.* Cooperative Republic of Guyana; *prev.* British Guiana. *country* N South America

GUYANA
South America

Official name Cooperative Republic of Guyana
Formation 1966 / 1966
Capital Georgetown
Population 751,000 / 10 people per sq mile (4 people per sq km) / 38%
Total area 83,000 sq miles (214,970 sq km)
Languages English*, Hindi, Tamil, Amerindian languages, English Creole
Religions Christian 57%, Hindu 33%, Muslim 9%, Other 1%
Ethnic mix East Indian 52%, Black African 38%, Other 4%, Amerindian 4%, European and Chinese 2%
Government Presidential system
Currency Guyanese dollar = 100 cents
Literacy rate 97%
Calorie consumption 2692 calories

Guyana, Cooperative Republic of *see* Guyana
Guyane *see* French Guiana
Guymon *49 E1* Oklahoma, C USA
Güzelyurt Körfezi *102 C5 Gk.* Kólpos Mórfu, Mórfou, Morphou. W Cyprus
Gvardeysk *106 A4 Ger.* Tapaiu. Kaliningradskaya Oblast', W Russian Federation
Gwādar *134 A3 var.* Gwadur. Baluchistān, SW Pakistan
Gwadur *see* Gwādar
Gwalior *134 D3* Madhya Pradesh, C India
Gwanda *78 D3* Matabeleland South, SW Zimbabwe
Gwy *see* Wye
Gyandzha *see* Gäncä
Gyangzê *126 C5* Xizang Zizhiqu, W China
Gyaring Co *126 C5 lake* W China
Gyêgu *see* Yushu
Gyergyószentmiklós *see* Gheorgheni
Gyixong *see* Gonggar
Gympie *149 E5* Queensland, E Australia
Gyomaendrőd *99 D7* Békés, SE Hungary
Gyöngyös *99 D6* Heves, NE Hungary
Győr *99 C6 Ger.* Raab, *Lat.* Arrabona. Győr-Moson-Sopron, NW Hungary
Gýtheio *105 B6 var.* Githio; *prev.* Yíthion. Pelopónnisos, S Greece
Gyulafehérvár *see* Alba Iulia
Gyumri *117 F2 var.* Giumri, *Rus.* Kumayri; *prev.* Aleksandropol', Leninakan. W Armenia
Gyzyrlabat *see* Serdar

H

Haabai *see* Ha'apai Group
Haacht *87 C6* Vlaams Brabant, C Belgium
Haaksbergen *86 E3* Overijssel, E Netherlands
Ha'apai Group *145 F4 var.* Haabai. *island group* C Tonga
Haapsalu *106 D2 Ger.* Hapsal. Läänemaa, W Estonia
Ha'Arava *see* 'Arabah, Wādī al
Haarlem *86 C3 prev.* Harlem. Noord-Holland, W Netherlands
Haast *151 B6* West Coast, South Island, New Zealand
Hachijō-jima *131 D6 island* Izu-shotō, SE Japan
Hachinohe *130 D3* Aomori, Honshū, C Japan
Hadama *see* Nazrēt
Hadejia *75 G4* Jigawa, N Nigeria
Hadejia *75 G3 river* N Nigeria
Hadera *119 A6 var.* Khadera. Haifa, C Israel
Hadhdhunmathi Atoll *132 A5 atoll* S Maldives
Hadhramaut *see* Ḥaḍramawt
Ha Đông *136 D3 var.* Hadong. Ha Tây, N Vietnam
Hadong *see* Ha Đông
Ḥaḍramawt *121 C6 Eng.* Hadhramaut. *mountain range* S Yemen
Hadrianopolis *see* Edirne
Haerbin/Haerhpin/Ha-erh-pin *see* Harbin
Hafnia *see* Denmark
Hafnia *see* København
Hafren *see* Severn
Hafun, Ras *see* Xaafuun, Raas
Hagåtña *160 B1 var.* Agana, *var.* Agaña. *dependent territory capital* (Guam) NW Guam
Hagerstown *41 E4* Maryland, NE USA
Ha Giang *136 D3* Ha Giang, N Vietnam
Hagios Evstrátios *see* Ágios Efstrátios
HaGolan *see* Golan Heights
Hagondange *90 D3* Moselle, NE France
Haguenau *90 E3* Bas-Rhin, NE France
Haibowan *see* Wuhai
Haicheng *128 D3* Liaoning, NE China
Haidarabad *see* Hyderabad
Haifa *see* Hefa
Haifa, Bay of *see* Hefa, Mifraz
Haifong *see* Hai Phong
Haikou *128 C7 var.* Hai-k'ou, Hoihow, *Fr.* Hoï-Hao. *province capital* Hainan, S China
Hai-k'ou *see* Haikou
Ḥā'il *120 B4* Ḥā'il, NW Saudi Arabia
Hai-la-erh *see* Hailar
Hailar *127 F1 var.* Hai-la-erh; *prev.* Hulun. Nei Mongol Zizhiqu, N China
Hailuoto *84 D4 Swe.* Karlö. *island* W Finland
Hainan *128 B7 var.* Hainan Sheng, Qiong. *province* S China
Hainan Dao *128 C7 island* S China
Hainan Sheng *see* Hainan
Hainasch *see* Ainaži
Haines *36 D4* Alaska, USA
Hainichen *94 D4* Sachsen, E Germany
Hai Phong *136 D3 var.* Haifong, Haiphong. N Vietnam
Haiphong *see* Hai Phong
Haiti *54 D3 off.* Republic of Haiti. *country* C West Indies

HAITI
West Indies

Official name Republic of Haiti
Formation 1804 / 1844
Capital Port-au-Prince
Population 8.5 million / 799 people per sq mile (308 people per sq km) / 36%
Total area 10,714 sq miles (27,750 sq km)
Languages French Creole*, French*
Religions Roman Catholic 80%, Protestant 16%, Other (including Voodoo) 3%, Nonreligious 1%
Ethnic mix Black African 95%, Mulatto (mixed race) and European 5%
Government Transitional regime
Currency Gourde = 100 centimes
Literacy rate 52%
Calorie consumption 2086 calories

Haiti, Republic of *see* Haiti
Haiya *72 C3* Red Sea, NE Sudan
Hajdúhadház *99 D6* Hajdú-Bihar, E Hungary
Hajîne *see* Abū Ḥardān
Hajnówka *98 E3 Ger.* Hermhausen. Podlaskie, NE Poland
Hakodate *130 D3* Hokkaidō, NE Japan
Hal *see* Halle
Ḥalab *118 B2 Eng.* Aleppo, *Fr.* Alep; *anc.* Beroea. Ḥalab, NW Syria

Ḥalāniyāt, Juzur almu 137 D6 var.
 Jazā'ir Bin Ghalfān, Eng. Kuria Muria
 Islands. island group S Oman
Halberstadt 94 C4 Sachsen-Anhalt,
 C Germany
Halden 85 B6 prev. Fredrikshald.
 Østfold, S Norway
Halfmoon Bay 151 A8 var. Oban.
 Stewart Island, Southland, New Zealand
Haliacmon see Aliákmonas
Halifax 39 F4 province capital Nova
 Scotia, SE Canada
Halkida see Chalkída
Halle 87 B6 Fr. Hal. Vlaams Brabant,
 C Belgium
Halle 94 C4 var. Halle an der Saale.
 Sachsen-Anhalt, C Germany
Halle an der Saale see Halle
Halle-Neustadt 94 C4 Sachsen-Anhalt,
 C Germany
Halley 154 B2 UK research station
 Antarctica
Hall Islands 142 B2 island group
 C Micronesia
Halls Creek 146 C3 Western Australia
Halmahera, Laut see Halmahera Sea
Halmahera, Pulau 139 F3 prev. Djailolo,
 Gilolo, Jailolo. island E Indonesia
Halmahera Sea 139 F4 Ind. Laut
 Halmahera. sea E Indonesia
Halmstad 85 B7 Halland, S Sweden
Hälsingborg see Helsingborg
Hamada 131 B6 Shimane, Honshū,
 SW Japan
Hamadān 120 C3 anc. Ecbatana.
 Hamadān, W Iran
Ḥamāh 118 B3 var. Hama; anc.
 Epiphania, Bibl. Hamath. Ḥamāh,
 W Syria
Hamamatsu 131 D6 var. Hamamatu.
 Shizuoka, Honshū, S Japan
Hamamatu see Hamamatsu
Hamar 85 B5 prev. Storhammer.
 Hedmark, S Norway
Hamath see Ḥamāh
Hamburg 94 B3 Hamburg, N Germany
Ḥamḍ, Wādī al 136 A4 dry watercourse
 W Saudi Arabia
Hämeenlinna 85 D5 Swe. Tavastehus.
 Etelä-Suomi, S Finland
HaMela h, Yam see Dead Sea
Hamersley Range 146 A4 mountain
 range Western Australia
Hamhŭng 129 E3 C North Korea
Hami 126 C3 var. Ha-mi, Uigh. Kumul,
 Qomul. Xinjiang Uygur Zizhiqu,
 NW China
Ha-mi see Hami
Hamilton 42 A5 dependent territory
 capital (Bermuda) C Bermuda
Hamilton 38 D5 Ontario, S Canada
Hamilton 150 D3 Waikato, North Island,
 New Zealand
Hamilton 88 C4 S Scotland, UK
Hamilton 42 C2 Alabama, S USA
Ḥamīm, Wādī al 87 G2 river NE Libya
Hamïs Musait see Khamïs Mushayt
Hamm 94 B4 var. Hamm in Westfalen.
 Nordrhein-Westfalen, W Germany
Ḥammāmāt, Khalij al see Hammamet,
 Golfe de
Hammamet, Golfe de 102 D3 Ar. Khalij
 al Ḥammāmāt. gulf NE Tunisia
Ḥammār, Hawr al 136 C3 lake SE Iraq
Hamm in Westfalen see Hamm
Hampden 151 B7 Otago, South Island,
 New Zealand
Hampstead 89 A7 Maryland, USA
Hamrun 102 B5 C Malta
Hāmūn, Daryācheh-ye Ṣāberī,
 Hāmūn-e/Sīstān, Daryācheh-ye
Hamwih see Southampton
Hânceşti see Hînceşti
Hancewicze see Hantsavichy
Handan 128 C4 var. Han-tan. Hebei,
 E China
Haneda 130 A2 (Tōkyō) Tōkyō, Honshū,
 S Japan
HaNegev 119 A7 Eng. Negev. desert
 S Israel
Hanford 47 C6 California, W USA
Hangayn Nuruu 126 D2 mountain
 range C Mongolia
Hang-chou/Hangchow see Hangzhou
Hangö see Hanko
Hangzhou 128 D5 var. Hang-chou,
 Hangchow. province capital Zhejiang,
 SE China

Hania see Chaniá
Hanka, Lake see Khanka, Lake
Hanko 85 D6 Swe. Hangö. Etelä-Suomi,
 SW Finland
Han-kou/Han-k'ou/Hankow see Wuhan
Hanmer Springs 151 C5 Canterbury,
 South Island, New Zealand
Hannibal 45 G4 Missouri, C USA
Hannover 94 B3 Eng. Hanover.
 Niedersachsen, NW Germany
Hanöbukten 85 B7 bay S Sweden
Ha Nôi 136 D3 Eng. Hanoi,
 Fr. Hanoï. country capital (Vietnam)
 N Vietnam
Hanover see Hannover
Han Shui 127 E4 river C China
Han-tan see Handan
Hantsavichy 107 B6 Pol. Hancewicze,
 Rus. Gantsevichi. Brestskaya Voblasts',
 SW Belarus
Hanyang see Wuhan
Hanzhong 128 B5 Shaanxi, C China
Hāora 135 F4 prev. Howrah. West
 Bengal, NE India
Haparanda 84 D4 Norrbotten, N Sweden
Hapsal see Haapsalu
Haradok 107 E5 Rus. Gorodok.
 Vitsyebskaya Voblasts', N Belarus
Haradzyets 107 B6 Rus. Gorodets.
 Brestskaya Voblasts', SW Belarus
Haramachi 130 D4 Fukushima, Honshū,
 E Japan
Harany 107 D5 Rus. Gorany.
 Vitsyebskaya Voblasts', N Belarus
Harare 78 D3 prev. Salisbury. country
 capital (Zimbabwe) Mashonaland East,
 NE Zimbabwe
Harbavichy 107 E6 Rus. Gorbovichi.
 Mahilyowskaya Voblasts', E Belarus
Harbel 74 C5 W Liberia
Harbin 129 E2 var. Haerbin, Ha-
 erh-pin, Kharbin; prev. Haerhpin,
 Pingkiang, Pinkiang. province capital
 Heilongjiang, NE China
Hardangerfjorden 85 A6 fjord S Norway
Hardangervidda 85 A6 plateau
 S Norway
Hardenberg 86 E3 Overijssel,
 E Netherlands
Harelbeke 87 A6 var. Harlebeke. West-
 Vlaanderen, W Belgium
Haren 86 E2 Groningen, NE Netherlands
Härer 73 D5 E Ethiopia
Hargeisa see Hargeysa
Hargeysa 73 D5 var. Hargeisa. Woqooyi
 Galbeed, NW Somalia
Hariana see Haryāna
Hari, Batang 138 B4 prev. Djambi. river
 Sumatera, W Indonesia
Ḥārim 118 B2 var. Harem. Idlib, W Syria
Harima-nada 131 B6 sea S Japan
Harīrūd 123 E4 var. Tedzhen, Turkm.
 Tejen. river Afghanistan/Iran
Harlan 45 F3 Iowa, C USA
Harlebeke see Harelbeke
Harlem see Haarlem
Harlingen 86 D2 Fris. Harns. Friesland,
 N Netherlands
Harlingen 49 G5 Texas, SW USA
Harlow 89 F7 E England, UK
Harney Basin 46 B4 basin Oregon,
 NW USA
Härnösand 85 C5 var. Hernösand.
 Västernorrland, C Sweden
Harns see Harlingen
Harper 74 D5 var. Cape Palmas.
 NE Liberia
Harricana 38 D3 river Québec,
 SE Canada
Harris 88 B3 physical region
 NW Scotland, UK
Harrisburg 41 F4 state capital
 Pennsylvania, NE USA
Harrisonburg 41 E4 Virginia, NE USA
Harrison, Cape 39 F2 cape
 Newfoundland and Labrador, E Canada
Harris Ridge see Lomonosov Ridge
Harrogate 89 D5 N England, UK
Hârşova 108 D5 prev. Hîrşova.
 Constanţa, SE Romania
Harstad 84 C2 Troms, N Norway
Hartford 41 G3 state capital Connecticut,
 NE USA
Hartlepool 89 D5 N England, UK
Harunabad see Eslāmābād
Har Us Nuur 126 C2 lake NW Mongolia
Harwich 89 E6 E England, UK

Haryāna 134 D2 var. Hariana. cultural
 region N India
Haryāna 134 D2 var. Hariana. state
 N India
Hashemite Kingdom of Jordan see
 Jordan
Hasselt 87 C6 Limburg, NE Belgium
Hassetché see Al Ḥasakah
Hasta Colonia/Hasta Pompeia see Asti
Hastings 150 E4 Hawke's Bay, North
 Island, New Zealand
Hastings 89 E7 SE England, UK
Hastings 45 E4 Nebraska, C USA
Haţeg 108 B4 Ger. Wallenthal, Hung.
 Hátszeg; prev. Hatzeg, Hötzing.
 Hunedoara, SW Romania
Hátszeg see Haţeg
Hattem 86 D3 Gelderland, E Netherlands
Hatteras, Cape 43 G1 headland North
 Carolina, SE USA
Hatteras Plain 35 D6 abyssal plain
 W Atlantic Ocean
Hattiesburg 42 C3 Mississippi, S USA
Hatton Bank see Hatton Ridge
Hatton Ridge 80 B2 var. Hatton Bank.
 undersea ridge N Atlantic Ocean
Hat Yai 137 C7 var. Ban Hat Yai.
 Songkhla, SW Thailand
Hatzeg see Haţeg
Hatzfeld see Jimbolia
Haugesund 85 A6 Rogaland,
 S Norway
Haukeligrend 85 A6 Telemark,
 S Norway
Haukivesi 85 E5 lake SE Finland
Hauraki Gulf 150 D2 gulf North Island,
 N New Zealand
Hauroko, Lake 151 A7 lake South
 Island, New Zealand
Haut Atlas 70 C2 Eng. High Atlas.
 mountain range C Morocco
Hautes Fagnes 87 D6 Ger. Hohes Venn.
 mountain range E Belgium
Hauts Plateaux 70 D2 plateau
 Algeria/Morocco
Hauzenberg 95 D6 Bayern, SE Germany
Havana 35 D6 Illinois, N USA
Havana see La Habana
Havant 89 D7 S England, UK
Havelock 43 F1 North Carolina, SE USA
Havelock North 150 E4 Hawke's Bay,
 North Island, New Zealand
Haverfordwest 89 C6 SW Wales, UK
Havířov 99 C5 Moravskoslezský Kraj,
 E Czech Republic
Havre 44 C1 Montana, NW USA
Havre see le Havre
Havre-St-Pierre 39 F3 Québec,
 E Canada
Hawai'i 47 A8 off. State of Hawai'i,
 also known as Aloha State, Paradise
 of the Pacific, var. Hawaii. state USA,
 C Pacific Ocean
Hawai'i 47 B8 var. Hawaii. island
 Hawaiian Islands, USA, C Pacific Ocean
Hawaiian Islands 152 D2 prev.
 Sandwich Islands. island group
 Hawaii, USA
Hawaiian Ridge 113 H4 undersea ridge
 N Pacific Ocean
Hawash see Āwash
Hawea, Lake 151 B6 lake South Island,
 New Zealand
Hawera 150 D4 Taranaki, North Island,
 New Zealand
Hawick 88 C4 SE Scotland, UK
Hawke Bay 150 E4 bay North Island,
 New Zealand
Hawkeye State see Iowa
Hawlêr see Arbil
Hawthorne 47 C6 Nevada, W USA
Hay 149 C6 New South Wales,
 SE Australia
HaYarden see Jordan
Hayastani Hanrapetut'yun see Armenia
Hayes 38 B2 river Manitoba, C Canada
Hay River 37 E4 Northwest Territories,
 W Canada
Hays 45 E5 Kansas, C USA
Haysyn 108 D3 Rus. Gaysin. Vinnyts'ka
 Oblast', C Ukraine
Hazar 122 B2 prev. Rus. Cheleken.
 Balkan Welaýaty, W Turkmenistan
Heard and McDonald Islands 141 B7
 Australian external territory S Indian
 Ocean
Hearst 38 C4 Ontario, S Canada
Heart of Dixie see Alabama

Heathrow 89 A8 (London) SE England,
 UK
Hebei 128 C4 var. Hebei Sheng, Hopeh,
 Hopei, Ji; prev. Chihli. province
 E China
Hebei Sheng see Hebei
Hebron 119 A6 var. Al Khalïl, El Khalïl,
 Heb. Hevron; anc. Kiriath-Arba.
 S West Bank
Heemskerk 86 C3 Noord-Holland,
 W Netherlands
Heerde 86 D3 Gelderland, E Netherlands
Heerenveen 86 D2 Fris. It Hearrenfean.
 Friesland, N Netherlands
Heerhugowaard 86 C2 Noord-Holland,
 NW Netherlands
Heerlen 87 D6 Limburg, SE Netherlands
Heerwegen see Polkowice
Hefa 119 A5 var. Haifa, hist. Caiffa,
 Caiphas; anc. Sycaminum. Haifa,
 N Israel
Hefa, Mifraz 119 A5 Eng. Bay of Haifa.
 bay N Israel
Hefei 128 D5 var. Hofei, hist. Luchow.
 province capital Anhui, E China
Hegang 129 E2 Heilongjiang, NE China
Hei see Heilongjiang
Heide 94 B2 Schleswig-Holstein,
 N Germany
Heidelberg 95 B5 Baden-Württemberg,
 SW Germany
Heidenheim see Heidenheim an der
 Brenz
Heidenheim an der Brenz 95 B6 var.
 Heidenheim. Baden-Württemberg,
 S Germany
Hei-ho see Nagqu
Heilbronn 95 B6 Baden-Württemberg,
 SW Germany
Heiligenbeil see Mamonovo
Heilongjiang 128 D2 var. Hei,
 Heilongjiang Sheng, Hei-lung-chiang,
 Heilungkiang. province NE China
Heilong Jiang see Amur
Heilongjiang Sheng see Heilongjiang
Heiloo 86 C3 Noord-Holland,
 NW Netherlands
Heilsberg see Lidzbark Warmiński
Hei-lung-chiang/Heilungkiang see
 Heilongjiang
Heimdal 85 B5 Sør-Trøndelag, S Norway
Heinaste see Ainaži
Hekimhan 116 D3 Malatya, C Turkey
Helena 44 B2 state capital Montana,
 NW USA
Helensville 150 D2 Auckland, North
 Island, New Zealand
Helgoland Bay see Helgoländer Bucht
Helgoländer Bucht 94 A2 var.
 Helgoland Bay, Heligoland Bight. bay
 NW Germany
Heligoland Bight see Helgoländer Bucht
Heliopolis see Baalbek
Hellas see Greece
Hellenic Republic see Greece
Hellevoetsluis 86 B4 Zuid-Holland,
 SW Netherlands
Hellín 93 E4 Castilla-La Mancha, C Spain
Helmand, Daryā-ye 122 D5 var. Rūd-e
 Hirmand. river Afghanistan/Iran
Helmantica see Salamanca
Helmond 87 D5 Noord-Brabant,
 S Netherlands
Helsingborg 85 B7 prev. Hälsingborg.
 Skåne, S Sweden
Helsingfors see Helsinki
Helsinki 85 D6 Swe. Helsingfors.
 country capital (Finland) Etelä-Suomi,
 S Finland
Heltau see Cisnădie
Helvetia see Switzerland
Henan 128 C5 var. Henan Sheng,
 Honan, Yu. province C China
Henderson 40 B5 Kentucky, S USA
Henderson 47 D7 Nevada, W USA
Henderson 49 H3 Texas, SW USA
Hendü Kosh see Hindu Kush
Hengchow see Hengyang
Hengduan Shan 128 A5 mountain range
 SW China
Hengelo 86 E3 Overijssel, E Netherlands
Hengnan see Hengyang
Hengyang 128 C6 var. Hengnan, Heng-
 yang; prev. Hengchow. Hunan, S China
Heng-yang see Hengyang
Heniches'k 109 F4 Rus. Genichesk.
 Khersons'ka Oblast', S Ukraine
Hennebont 90 A3 Morbihan, NW France

Henrique de Carvalho *see* Saurimo
Henzada *136 B4* Irrawaddy, SW Myanmar (Burma)
Herakleion *see* Irákleio
Herāt *122 D4 var.* Herat; *anc.* Aria. Herāt, W Afghanistan
Heredia *53 E4* Heredia, C Costa Rica
Hereford *49 E2* Texas, SW USA
Herford *94 B4* Nordrhein-Westfalen, NW Germany
Héristal *see* Herstal
Herk-de-Stad *87 C6* Limburg, NE Belgium
Herlen Gol/Herlen He *see* Kerulen
Hermannstadt *see* Sibiu
Hermansverk *85 A5* Sogn Og Fjordane, S Norway
Hermhausen *see* Hajnówka
Hermiston *46 C2* Oregon, NW USA
Hermon, Mount *119 B5 Ar.* Jabal ash Shaykh. *mountain* S Syria
Hermosillo *50 B2* Sonora, NW Mexico
Hermoupolis *see* Ermoúpoli
Hernösand *see* Härnösand
Herrera del Duque *92 D3* Extremadura, W Spain
Herselt *87 C5* Antwerpen, C Belgium
Herstal *87 D6 Fr.* Héristal. Liège, E Belgium
Herzogenbusch *see* 's-Hertogenbosch
Hesse *see* Hessen
Hessen *95 B5 Eng./Fr.* Hesse. *state* C Germany
Hevron *see* Hebron
Heydebrech *see* Kędzierzyn-Kozle
Heydekrug *see* Šilutė
Heywood Islands *146 C3 island group* Western Australia
Hibbing *43 F1* Minnesota, N USA
Hibernia *see* Ireland
Hidalgo del Parral *50 C2 var.* Parral. Chihuahua, N Mexico
Hida-sanmyaku *131 C5 mountain range* Honshū, S Japan
Hierosolyma *see* Jerusalem
Hierro *70 A3 var.* Ferro. *island* Islas Canarias, Spain, NE Atlantic Ocean
High Atlas *see* Haut Atlas
High Plains *see* Great Plains
High Point *43 E1* North Carolina, SE USA
Hiiumaa *106 C2 Ger.* Dagden, *Swe.* Dagö. *island* W Estonia
Hikurangi *150 D2* Northland, North Island, New Zealand
Hildesheim *94 B4* Niedersachsen, N Germany
Hilla *see* Al Ḩillah
Hillaby, Mount *55 G1 mountain* N Barbados
Hill Bank *52 C1* Orange Walk, N Belize
Hillegom *86 C3* Zuid-Holland, W Netherlands
Hilo *47 B8* Hawai'i, USA, C Pacific Ocean
Hilton Head Island *43 E2* South Carolina, SE USA
Hilversum *86 C3* Noord-Holland, C Netherlands
Himalaya/Himalaya Shan *see* Himalayas
Himalayas *135 E2 var.* Himalaya, *Chin.* Himalaya Shan. *mountain range* S Asia
Himeji *131 C6 var.* Himezi. Hyōgo, Honshū, SW Japan
Himezi *see* Himeji
Ḩimş *118 B4 var.* Homs; *anc.* Emesa. Ḩimş, C Syria
Hîncești *108 D4 var.* Hâncești; *prev.* Kotovsk. C Moldova
Hinchinbrook Island *148 D3 island* Queensland, NE Australia
Hinds *151 C6* Canterbury, South Island, New Zealand
Hindu Kush *123 F4 Per.* Hendū Kosh. *mountain range* Afghanistan/Pakistan
Hinesville *43 E3* Georgia, SE USA
Hinnøya *84 C3 Lapp.* Iinnasuolu. *island* C Norway
Hinson Bay *42 A5 bay* W Bermuda W Atlantic Ocean
Hios *see* Chíos
Hirfanlı Barajı *116 C3 reservoir* C Turkey
Hīrmand, Rūd-e *see* Helmand, Daryā-ye
Hirosaki *130 D3* Aomori, Honshū, C Japan
Hiroshima *131 B6 var.* Hirosima. Hiroshima, Honshū, SW Japan
Hirschberg/Hirschberg im Riesengebirge/Hirschberg in Schlesien *see* Jelenia Góra
Hirson *90 D3* Aisne, N France
Hîrșova *see* Hârșova
Hispalis *see* Sevilla
Hispana/Hispania *see* Spain
Hispaniola *56 B1 island* Dominion Republic/Haiti
Hitachi *131 D5 var.* Hitati. Ibaraki, Honshū, S Japan
Hitati *see* Hitachi
Hitra *84 A4 prev.* Hitteren. *island* S Norway
Hitteren *see* Hitra
Hjälmaren *85 C6 Eng.* Lake Hjalmar. *lake* C Sweden
Hjalmar, Lake *see* Hjälmaren
Hjørring *85 B7* Nordjylland, N Denmark
Hkakabo Razi *136 B1 mountain* Myanmar (Burma)/China
Hlobyne *109 F2 Rus.* Globino. Poltavs'ka Oblast', NE Ukraine
Hlukhiv *109 F1 Rus.* Glukhov. Sums'ka Oblast', NE Ukraine
Hlybokaye *107 D5 Rus.* Glubokoye. Vitsyebskaya Voblasts', N Belarus
Hoa Binh *136 D3* Hoa Binh, N Vietnam
Hoang Liên Sơn *136 D3 mountain range* N Vietnam
Hobart *149 C8 prev.* Hobarton, Hobart Town. *state capital* Tasmania, SE Australia
Hobarton/Hobart Town *see* Hobart
Hobbs *49 E3* New Mexico, SW USA
Hobro *85 A7* Nordjylland, N Denmark
Hô Chi Minh *137 E6 var.* Ho Chi Minh City; *prev.* Saigon. S Vietnam
Ho Chi Minh City *see* Hô Chi Minh
Hodeida *see* Al Ḩudaydah
Hódmezővásárhely *99 D7* Csongrád, SE Hungary
Hodna, Chott El *118 C4 var.* Chott el-Hodna, *Ar.* Shatt al-Hodna. *salt lake* N Algeria
Hodna, Chott el-/Hodna, Shatt al- *see* Hodna, Chott El
Hodonín *99 C5 Ger.* Göding. Jihomoravský Kraj, SE Czech Republic
Hoei *see* Huy
Hoey *see* Huy
Hof *95 C5* Bayern, SE Germany
Hofei *see* Hefei
Hōfu *131 B7* Yamaguchi, Honshū, SW Japan
Hofuf *see* Al Hufūf
Hogoley Islands *see* Chuuk Islands
Hohensalza *see* Inowrocław
Hohenstadt *see* Zábřeh
Hohes Venn *see* Hautes Fagnes
Hohe Tauern *95 C7 mountain range* W Austria
Hohhot *127 F3 var.* Huhehot, Huhohaote, *Mong.* Kukukhoto; *prev.* Kweisui, Kwesui. Nei Mongol Zizhiqu, N China
Hôi An *137 E5 prev.* Faifo. Quang Nam-Đa Năng, C Vietnam
Hoï-Hao/Hoihow *see* Haikou
Hokianga Harbour *150 C2 inlet* SE Tasman Sea
Hokitika *151 B5* West Coast, South Island, New Zealand
Hokkaidō *130 C2 prev.* Ezo, Yeso, Yezo. *island* NE Japan
Hola Prystan' *109 E4 Rus.* Golaya Pristan. Khersons'ka Oblast', S Ukraine
Holbrook *48 B2* Arizona, SW USA
Holetown *55 G1 prev.* Jamestown. W Barbados
Holguín *54 C2* Holguín, SE Cuba
Hollabrunn *95 E6* Niederösterreich, NE Austria
Holland *see* Netherlands
Hollandia *see* Jayapura
Holly Springs *42 C1* Mississippi, S USA
Holman *37 E3* Victoria Island, Northwest Territories, N Canada
Holmsund *84 D4* Västerbotten, N Sweden
Holon *119 A6 var* Kholon. Tel Aviv, C Israel
Holovanivs'k *109 E3 Rus.* Golovanevsk. Kirovohrads'ka Oblast', C Ukraine
Holstebro *85 A7* Ringkøbing, W Denmark
Holsteinborg/Holsteinsborg/Holstenborg/Holstensborg *see* Sisimiut
Holyhead *89 C5 Wel.* Caer Gybi. NW Wales, UK
Hombori *75 E3* Mopti, S Mali
Homs *see* Al Khums, Libya
Homs *see* Ḩimş
Homyel' *107 D7 Rus.* Gomel'. Homyel'skaya Voblasts', SE Belarus
Honan *see* Luoyang, China
Honan *see* Henan, China
Hondo *49 F4* Texas, SW USA
Hondo *see* Honshū
Honduras *52 C2 off.* Republic of Honduras. *country* Central America

HONDURAS
Central America

Official name Republic of Honduras
Formation 1838 / 1838
Capital Tegucigalpa
Population 7.2 million / 167 people per sq mile (64 people per sq km) / 53%
Total area 43,278 sq miles (112,090 sq km)
Languages Spanish*, Garífuna (Carib), English Creole
Religions Roman Catholic 97%, Protestant 3%
Ethnic mix Mestizo 90%, Black African 5%, Amerindian 4%, White 1%
Government Presidential system
Currency Lempira = 100 centavos
Literacy rate 80%
Calorie consumption 2356 calories

Honduras, Golfo de *see* Honduras, Gulf of
Honduras, Gulf of *52 C2 Sp.* Golfo de Honduras. *gulf* W Caribbean Sea
Honduras, Republic of *see* Honduras
Hønefoss *85 B6* Buskerud, S Norway
Honey Lake *47 B5 lake* California, W USA
Hon Gai *see* Hông Gai
Hongay *see* Hông Gai
Hông Gai *136 E3 var.* Hon Gai, Hongay. Quang Ninh, N Vietnam
Hông Hà, Sông *see* Red River
Hong Kong *128 A1 Chin.* Xianggang. Hong Kong, S China
Hong Kong Island *128 B2 island* S China Asia
Honiara *144 C3 country capital* (Solomon Islands) Guadalcanal, C Solomon Islands
Honjō *130 D4 var.* Honzyô. Akita, Honshū, C Japan
Honolulu *47 A8 state capital* O'ahu, Hawai'i, USA
Honshū *131 E5 var.* Hondo, Honsyû. *island* SW Japan
Honsyû *see* Honshū
Honte *see* Westerschelde
Honzyô *see* Honjō
Hoogeveen *86 E2* Drenthe, NE Netherlands
Hoogezand-Sappemeer *86 E2* Groningen, NE Netherlands
Hoorn *86 C2* Noord-Holland, NW Netherlands
Hoosier State *see* Indiana
Hopa *117 E2* Artvin, NE Turkey
Hope *36 C3* British Columbia, SW Canada
Hopedale *39 F2* Newfoundland and Labrador, NE Canada
Hopeh/Hopei *see* Hebei
Hopkinsville *40 B5* Kentucky, S USA
Horasan *117 F3* Erzurum, NE Turkey
Horizon Deep *152 D4 trench* W Pacific Ocean
Horki *107 E6 Rus.* Gorki. Mahilyowskaya Voblasts', E Belarus
Horlivka *109 G3 Rom.* Adâncata, *Rus.* Gorlovka. Donets'ka Oblast', E Ukraine
Hormoz, Tangeh-ye *see* Hormuz, Strait of
Hormuz, Strait of *120 D4 var.* Strait of Ormuz, *Per.* Tangeh-ye Hormoz. *strait* Iran/Oman
Horn, Cape *see* Hornos, Cabo de
Hornos, Cabo de *65 C8 Eng.* Cape Horn. *cape* S Chile
Hornsby *148 E1* New South Wales, SE Australia
Horodnya *109 E1 Rus.* Gorodnya. Chernihivs'ka Oblast', NE Ukraine
Horodok *108 B2 Pol.* Gródek Jagielloński, *Rus.* Gorodok, Gorodok Yagellonski. L'vivs'ka Oblast', NW Ukraine
Horodyshche *109 E2 Rus.* Gorodishche. Cherkas'ka Oblast', C Ukraine
Horoshiri-dake *130 D2 var.* Horosiri Dake. *mountain* Hokkaidō, N Japan
Horosiri Dake *see* Horoshiri-dake
Horsburgh Atoll *132 A4 atoll* N Maldives
Horseshoe Bay *42 A5 bay* W Bermuda W Atlantic Ocean
Horseshoe Seamounts *80 A4 seamount range* E Atlantic Ocean
Horsham *149 B7* Victoria, SE Australia
Horst *87 D5* Limburg, SE Netherlands
Horten *85 B6* Vestfold, S Norway
Horyn' *107 B7 Rus.* Goryn. *river* NW Ukraine
Hosingen *87 D7* Diekirch, NE Luxembourg
Hospitalet *see* L'Hospitalet de Llobregat
Hotan *126 B4 var.* Khotan, *Chin.* Ho-t'ien. Xinjiang Uygur Zizhiqu, NW China
Ho-t'ien *see* Hotan
Hoting *84 C4* Jämtland, C Sweden
Hot Springs *42 B1* Arkansas, C USA
Hötzing *see* Hațeg
Houayxay *136 C3 var.* Ban Houayxay. Bokèo, N Laos
Houghton *40 B1* Michigan, N USA
Houilles *91 B5* Yvelines, Île-de-France, N France Europe
Houlton *41 H1* Maine, NE USA
Houma *42 B3* Louisiana, S USA
Houston *49 H4* Texas, SW USA
Hovd *126 C2 var.* Khovd, Kobdo; *prev.* Jirgalanta. Hovd, W Mongolia
Hove *89 E7* SE England, UK
Hoverla, Hora *108 C3 Rus.* Gora Goverla. *mountain* W Ukraine
Hovsgol, Lake *see* Hövsgöl Nuur
Hövsgöl Nuur *126 D1 var.* Lake Hovsgol. *lake* N Mongolia
Howa, Ouadi *see* Howar, Wādi
Howar, Wādi *72 A3 var.* Ouadi Howa. *river* Chad/Sudan
Howrah *see* Hāora
Hoy *88 C2 island* N Scotland, UK
Hoyerswerda *94 D4 Lus.* Wojerecy. Sachsen, E Germany
Hradec Králové *99 B5 Ger.* Königgrätz. Královéhradecký Kraj, N Czech Republic
Hrandzichy *107 B5 Rus.* Grandichi. Hrodzyenskaya Voblasts', W Belarus
Hranice *99 C5 Ger.* Mährisch-Weisskirchen. Olomoucký Kraj, E Czech Republic
Hrebinka *109 E2 Rus.* Grebenka. Poltavs'ka Oblast', NE Ukraine
Hrodna *107 B5 Pol.* Grodno. Hrodzyenskaya Voblasts', W Belarus
Hrvatska *see* Croatia
Hsia-men *see* Xiamen
Hsiang-t'an *see* Xiangtan
Hsi Chiang *see* Xi Jiang
Hsing-K'ai Hu *see* Khanka, Lake
Hsi-ning/Hsining *see* Xining
Hsinking *see* Changchun
Hsin-yang *see* Xinyang
Hsu-chou *see* Xuzhou
Hu *see* Shanghai Shi
Huacho *60 C4* Lima, W Peru
Hua Hin *see* Ban Hua Hin
Huaihua *128 C5* Hunan, S China
Huailai *128 C3 var.* Shacheng. Hebei, E China
Huainan *128 D5 var.* Huai-nan, Hwainan. Anhui, E China
Huai-nan *see* Huainan
Huajuapan *51 F5 var.* Huajuapan de León. Oaxaca, SE Mexico
Huajuapan de León *see* Huajuapan
Hualapai Peak *48 A2 mountain* Arizona, SW USA
Huallaga, Río *60 C3 river* N Peru
Huambo *78 B2 Port.* Nova Lisboa. Huambo, C Angola
Huancavelica *60 D4* Huancavelica, SW Peru
Huancayo *60 D3* Junín, C Peru
Huang Hai *see* Yellow Sea
Huang He *128 C4 var.* Yellow River. *river* C China
Huangshi *128 C5 var.* Huang-shih, Hwangshih. Hubei, C China

Huang-shih *see* Huangshi
Huanta *60 D4* Ayacucho, C Peru
Huánuco *60 C3* Huánuco, C Peru
Huanuni *61 F4* Oruro, W Bolivia
Huaral *60 C4* Lima, W Peru
Huarás *see* Huaraz
Huaraz *60 C3 var.* Huarás. Ancash, W Peru
Huarmey *60 C3* Ancash, W Peru
Huatabampo *50 C2* Sonora, NW Mexico
Hubei *129 C5 var.* E, Hubei Sheng, Hupeh, Hupei. *province* C China
Hubei Sheng *see* Hubei
Hubli *124 B3* Karnātaka, SW India
Huddersfield *89 D5* N England, UK
Hudiksvall *85 C5* Gävleborg, C Sweden
Hudson Bay *37 G4 bay* NE Canada
Hudson, Détroit d' *see* Hudson Strait
Hudson Strait *37 H3 Fr.* Détroit d'Hudson. *strait* Northwest Territories/ Québec, NE Canada
Hudur *see* Xuddur
Huê *136 E4* Th,a Thiên-Huê, C Vietnam
Huehuetenango *52 A2* Huehuetenango, W Guatemala
Huelva *92 C4 anc.* Onuba. Andalucía, SW Spain
Huesca *93 F2 anc.* Osca. Aragón, NE Spain
Huéscar *93 E4* Andalucía, S Spain
Hughenden *148 C3* Queensland, NE Australia
Hugo *49 G2* Oklahoma, C USA
Huhehot/Huhohaote *see* Hohhot
Huíla Plateau *78 B2 plateau* S Angola
Huixtla *51 G5* Chiapas, SE Mexico
Hulingol *127 G2 prev.* Huolin Gol. Nei Mongol Zizhiqu, N China
Hull *38 D4* Québec, SE Canada
Hull *see* Kingston upon Hull
Hull Island *see* Orona
Hulst *87 B5* Zeeland, SW Netherlands
Hulun *see* Hailar
Hu-lun Ch'ih *see* Hulun Nur
Hulun Nur *127 F1 var.* Hu-lun Ch'ih; *prev.* Dalai Nor. *lake* NE China
Humaitá *62 D2* Amazonas, N Brazil
Humboldt River *47 C5 river* Nevada, W USA
Humphreys Peak *48 B1 mountain* Arizona, SW USA
Humpolec *99 B5 Ger.* Gumpolds, Humpoletz. Vysočina, C Czech Republic
Humpoletz *see* Humpolec
Hunan *128 C6 var.* Hunan Sheng, Xiang. *province* S China
Hunan Sheng *see* Hunan
Hunedoara *108 B4 Ger.* Eisenmarkt, *Hung.* Vajdahunyad. Hunedoara, SW Romania
Hünfeld *95 B5* Hessen, C Germany
Hungarian People's Republic *see* Hungary
Hungary *99 C6 off.* Republic of Hungary, *Ger.* Ungarn, *Hung.* Magyarország, *Rom.* Ungaria, *SCr.* Mađarska, *Ukr.* Uhorshchyna; *prev.* Hungarian People's Republic. *country* C Europe
Hungary, Plain of *see* Great Hungarian Plain

HUNGARY
Central Europe

Official name Republic of Hungary
Formation 1918 / 1947
Capital Budapest
Population 10.1 million / 283 people per sq mile (109 people per sq km) / 64%
Total area 35,919 sq miles (93,030 sq km)
Languages Hungarian (Magyar)*
Religions Roman Catholic 52%, Calvinist 16%, Other 15%, Nonreligious 14%, Lutheran 3%
Ethnic mix Magyar 90%, Other 7%, Roma 2%, German 1%
Government Parliamentary system
Currency Forint = 100 fillér
Literacy rate 99%
Calorie consumption 3483 calories

Hungary, Republic of *see* Hungary
Hunjiang *see* Baishan
Hunter Island *149 B8 island* Tasmania, SE Australia
Huntington *40 D4* West Virginia, NE USA
Huntington Beach *47 B8* California, W USA
Huntly *150 D3* Waikato, North Island, New Zealand
Huntsville *42 D1* Alabama, S USA
Huntsville *49 G3* Texas, SW USA
Huolin Gol *see* Hulingol
Hupeh *see* Hubei
Hupei *see* Hubei
Hurghada *72 C2 var.* Al Ghurdaqah, Ghurdaqah. E Egypt
Huron *45 E3* South Dakota, N USA
Huron, Lake *40 D2 lake* Canada/USA
Hurukawa *see* Furukawa
Hurunui *151 C5 river* South Island, New Zealand
Húsavík *83 E4* Nordhurland Eystra, NE Iceland
Husté *see* Khust
Husum *94 B2* Schleswig-Holstein, N Germany
Huszt *see* Khust
Hutchinson *45 E5* Kansas, C USA
Hutchinson Island *43 F4 island* Florida, SE USA
Huy *87 C6 Dut.* Hoei, Hoey. Liège, E Belgium
Huzi *see* Fuji
Hvannadalshnúkur *83 E5 volcano* S Iceland
Hvar *100 B4 It.* Lesina; *anc.* Pharus. *island* S Croatia
Hwainan *see* Huainan
Hwange *78 D3 prev.* Wankie. Matabeleland North, W Zimbabwe
Hwang-Hae *see* Yellow Sea
Hwangshih *see* Huangshi
Hyargas Nuur *126 C2 lake* NW Mongolia
Hyderābād *134 D5 var.* Haidarabad. *state capital* Andhra Pradesh, C India
Hyderābād *134 B3 var.* Haidarabad. Sind, SE Pakistan
Hyères *91 D6* Var, SE France
Hyères, Îles d' *91 D6 island group* S France
Hypanis *see* Kuban'
Hyrcania *see* Gorgān
Hyvinge *see* Hyvinkää
Hyvinkää *85 D5 Swe.* Hyvinge. Uusimaa, S Finland

I

Iader *see* Zadar
Ialomiţa *108 C5 river* SE Romania
Iaşi *108 D3 Ger.* Jassy. Iaşi, NE Romania
Ibadan *75 F5* Oyo, SW Nigeria
Ibagué *58 B3* Tolima, C Colombia
Ibar *100 D4 Alb.* Ibër. *river* C Serbia
Ibarra *60 B1 var.* San Miguel de Ibarra. Imbabura, N Ecuador
Ibër *see* Ibar
Iberia *see* Spain
Iberian Mountains *see* Ibérico, Sistema
Iberian Peninsula *80 B4 physical region* Portugal/Spain
Iberian Plain *80 B4 abyssal plain* E Atlantic Ocean
Ibérica, Cordillera *see* Ibérico, Sistema
Ibérico, Sistema *93 E2 var.* Cordillera Ibérica, *Eng.* Iberian Mountains. *mountain range* NE Spain
Ibiza *93 G3 island* Spain, W Mediterranean Sea
Ibiza *see* Eivissa
Ibo *see* Sassandra
Ica *60 D4* Ica, SW Peru
Icaria *see* Ikaría
Içá, Rio *62 C2 var.* Río Putumayo. *river* NW South America
Içá, Rio *see* Putumayo, Río
Iceland *83 E4 off.* Republic of Iceland, *Dan.* Island, *Icel.* Ísland. *country* N Atlantic Ocean

ICELAND
Northwest Europe

Official name Republic of Iceland
Formation 1944 / 1944
Capital Reykjavík
Population 295,000 / 8 people per sq mile (3 people per sq km) / 93%
Total area 39,768 sq miles (103,000 sq km)

ICELAND
(continued)

Languages Icelandic*
Religions Evangelical Lutheran 93%, Nonreligious 6%, Other (mostly Christian) 1%
Ethnic mix Icelandic 94%, Other 5%, Danish 1%
Government Parliamentary system
Currency Icelandic króna = 100 aurar
Literacy rate 99%
Calorie consumption 3249 calories

Iceland Basin *80 B1 undersea basin* N Atlantic Ocean
Icelandic Plateau *see* Iceland Plateau
Iceland Plateau *172 B5 var.* Icelandic Plateau. *undersea plateau* S Greenland Sea
Iceland, Republic of *see* Iceland
Iconium *see* Konya
Iculisma *see* Angoulême
Idabel *49 H2* Oklahoma, C USA
Idaho *46 D3 off.* State of Idaho, *also known as* Gem of the Mountains, Gem State. *state* NW USA
Idaho Falls *46 E3* Idaho, NW USA
Idensalmi *see* Iisalmi
Idfu *72 B2 var.* Edfu. SE Egypt
Idi Amin, Lac *see* Edward, Lake
Idîni *74 B2* Trarza, W Mauritania
Idlib *118 B3* Idlib, NW Syria
Idre *85 B5* Dalarna, C Sweden
Iecava *106 C3* Bauska, S Latvia
Ieper *87 A6 Fr.* Ypres. West-Vlaanderen, W Belgium
Ierápetra *105 D8* Kríti, Greece, E Mediterranean Sea
Ierisós *see* Ierissós
Ierissós *104 C4 var.* Ierisós. Kentrikí Makedonía, N Greece
Iferouâne *75 G2* Agadez, N Niger
Ifôghas, Adrar des *75 E2 var.* Adrar des Iforas. *mountain range* NE Mali
Iforas, Adrar des *see* Ifôghas, Adrar des
Igarka *114 D3* Krasnoyarskiy Kray, N Russian Federation
Igaunija *see* Estonia
Iglau/Iglawa/Igława *see* Jihlava
Iglesias *97 A5* Sardegna, Italy, C Mediterranean Sea
Igloolik *37 G2* Nunavut, N Canada
Igoumenítsa *104 A4* Ípeiros, W Greece
Iguaçu, Rio *63 E4 Sp.* Río Iguazú. *river* Argentina/Brazil
Iguaçu, Saltos do *63 E4 Sp.* Cataratas del Iguazú; *prev.* Victoria Falls. *waterfall* Argentina/Brazil
Iguala *51 E4 var.* Iguala de la Independencia. Guerrero, S Mexico
Iguala de la Independencia *see* Iguala
Iguazú, Cataratas del *see* Iguaçu, Saltos do
Iguazú, Río *see* Iguaçu, Rio
Iguid, Erg *see* Iguîdi, 'Erg
Iguîdi, 'Erg *70 C3 var.* Erg Iguid. *desert* Algeria/Mauritania
Ihavandippolhu Atoll *132 A3 atoll* N Maldives
Ihosy *79 F4* Fianarantsoa, S Madagascar
Iinnasuolu *see* Hinnøya
Iisalmi *84 E4 var.* Idensalmi. Isä-Suomi, C Finland
IJmuiden *86 C3* Noord-Holland, W Netherlands
IJssel *86 D3 var.* Yssel. *river* Netherlands
IJsselmeer *86 C2 prev.* Zuider Zee. *lake* N Netherlands
IJsselmuiden *86 D3* Overijssel, E Netherlands
Ijzer *87 A6 river* W Belgium
Ikaría *105 D6 var.* Kariot, Nicaria, Nikaria; *anc.* Icaria. *island* Dodekánisa, Greece, Aegean Sea
Ikela *77 D6* Equateur, C Dem. Rep. Congo
Iki *131 A7 island* SW Japan
Ilagan *139 E1* Luzon, N Philippines
Ilave *61 E4* Puno, S Peru
Iława *98 D3 Ger.* Deutsch-Eylau. Warmińsko-Mazurskie, NE Poland
Ilebo *77 C6 prev.* Port-Francqui. Kasai Occidental, W Dem. Rep. Congo
Île-de-France *90 C3 region* N France
Île-de-France *90 C3 cultural region* N France
Ilerda *see* Lleida
Ilfracombe *89 C7* SW England, UK
Ílhavo *92 B2* Aveiro, N Portugal
Iliamna Lake *36 C3 lake* Alaska, USA
Il'ichevsk *see* Illichivs'k
Ilici *see* Elche
Iligan *139 E2 off.* Iligan City. Mindanao, S Philippines
Iligan City *see* Iligan
Illapel *64 B4* Coquimbo, C Chile
Illichivs'k *109 E4 Rus.* Il'ichevsk. Odes'ka Oblast', SW Ukraine
Illicis *see* Elche
Illinois *40 A4 off.* State of Illinois, *also known as* Prairie State, Sucker State. *state* C USA
Illinois River *40 B4 river* Illinois, N USA
Illurco *see* Lorca
Illuro *see* Mataró
Ilo *61 E4* Moquegua, SW Peru
Iloilo *139 E2 off.* Iloilo City. Panay Island, C Philippines
Iloilo City *see* Iloilo
Ilorin *75 F4* Kwara, W Nigeria
Ilovlya *111 B6* Volgogradskaya Oblast', SW Russian Federation
İluh *see* Batman
Il'yaly *see* Gurbansoltan Eje
Imatra *85 E5* Kymi, SE Finland
Imbros *see* Gökçeada
Imishli *see* İmişli
İmişli *117 H3 Rus.* Imishli. C Azerbaijan
Imola *96 C3* Emilia-Romagna, N Italy
Imperatriz *63 F2* Maranhão, NE Brazil
Imperia *96 A3* Liguria, NW Italy
Impfondo *77 C5* La Likouala, NE Congo
Imphāl *135 H3 state capital* Manipur, NE India
Imroz Adası *see* Gökçeada
Inagua Islands *see* Great Inagua
Inagua Islands *see* Little Inagua
Inarijärvi *84 D2 Lapp.* Aanaarjävri, *Swe.* Enareträsk. *lake* N Finland
Inău *see* Ineu
Inawashiro-ko *131 D5 var.* Inawasiro Ko. *lake* Honshū, C Japan
Inawasiro Ko *see* Inawashiro-ko
İncesu *116 D3* Kayseri, Turkey Asia
Inch'ŏn *129 E4 off.* Inch'ŏn-gwangyŏksi, *Jap.* Jinsen; *prev.* Chemulpo. NW South Korea
Inch'ŏn-gwangyŏksi *see* Inch'ŏn
Incudine, Monte *91 E7 mountain* Corse, France, C Mediterranean Sea
Indefatigable Island *see* Santa Cruz, Isla
Independence *45 F4* Missouri, C USA
Independence Fjord *83 E1 fjord* N Greenland
Independence Island *see* Malden Island
Independence Mountains *46 C4 mountain range* Nevada, W USA
India *124 B3 off.* Republic of India, *var.* Indian Union, Union of India, *Hind.* Bhārat. *country* S Asia

INDIA
South Asia

Official name Republic of India
Formation 1947 / 1947
Capital New Delhi
Population 1.1 billion / 961 people per sq mile (371 people per sq km) / 28%
Total area 1,269,338 sq miles (3,287,590 sq km)
Languages Hindi*, English*, Bengali, Marathi, Telugu, Tamil, Bihari, Gujarati, Kanarese, Urdu
Religions Hindu 83%, Muslim 11%, Christian 2%, Sikh 2%, Other 1%, Buddhist 1%
Ethnic mix Indo-Aryan 72%, Dravidian 25%, Mongoloid and other 3%
Government Parliamentary system
Currency Indian rupee = 100 paise
Literacy rate 61%
Calorie consumption 2459 calories

India *see* Indija
Indiana *40 B4 off.* State of Indiana, *also known as* Hoosier State. *state* N USA
Indianapolis *40 C4 state capital* Indiana, N USA

Indian Church *52 C1* Orange Walk, N Belize
Indian Desert *see* Thar Desert
Indianola *45 F4* Iowa, C USA
Indian Union *see* India
India, Republic of *see* India
India, Union of *see* India
Indigirka *115 F2 river* NE Russian Federation
Inđija *100 D3 Hung.* India; *prev.* Indjija. Vojvodina, N Serbia
Indira Point *132 G3 headland* Andaman and Nicobar Island, India, NE Indian Ocean
Indjija *see* Inđija
Indomed Fracture Zone *141 B6 tectonic feature* SW Indian Ocean
Indonesia *138 B4 off.* Republic of Indonesia, *Ind.* Republik Indonesia; *prev.* Dutch East Indies, Netherlands East Indies, United States of Indonesia. *country* SE Asia

INDONESIA
Southeast Asia

Official name Republic of Indonesia
Formation 1949 / 1999
Capital Jakarta
Population 223 million / 321 people per sq mile (124 people per sq km) / 41%
Total area 741,096 sq miles (1,919,440 sq km)
Languages Bahasa Indonesia*, Javanese, Sundanese, Madurese, Dutch
Religions Sunni Muslim 87%, Protestant 6%, Roman Catholic 3%, Hindu 2%, Other 1%, Buddhist 1%
Ethnic mix Javanese 45%, Sundanese 14%, Coastal Malays 8%, Madurese 8%, Other 25%
Government Presidential system
Currency Rupiah = 100 sen
Literacy rate 88%
Calorie consumption 2904 calories

Indonesian Borneo *see* Kalimantan
Indonesia, Republic of *see* Indonesia
Indonesia, Republik *see* Indonesia
Indonesia, United States of *see* Indonesia
Indore *134 D4* Madhya Pradesh, C India
Indreville *see* Châteauroux
Indus *134 C2 Chin.* Yindu He; *prev.* Yin-tu Ho. *river* S Asia
Indus Cone *see* Indus Fan
Indus Fan *112 C5 var.* Indus Cone. *undersea fan* N Arabian Sea
Indus, Mouths of the *134 B4 delta* S Pakistan
İnebolu *116 C2* Kastamonu, N Turkey
Ineu *108 A4 Hung.* Borosjenő; *prev.* Inău. Arad, W Romania
Infiernillo, Presa del *51 E4 reservoir* S Mexico
Inglewood *46 D2* California, W USA
Ingolstadt *95 C6* Bayern, S Germany
Ingulets *see* Inhulets'
Inguri *see* Enguri
Inhambane *79 E4* Inhambane, SE Mozambique
Inhulets' *109 F3 Rus.* Ingulets. Dnipropetrovs'ka Oblast', E Ukraine
I-ning *see* Yining
Inis *see* Ennis
Inis Ceithleann *see* Enniskillen
Inn *95 C6 river* C Europe
Innaanganeq *82 C1 var.* Kap York. *headland* NW Greenland
Inner Hebrides *88 B4 island group* W Scotland, UK
Inner Islands *79 H1 var.* Central Group. *island group* NE Seychelles
Innisfail *148 D3* Queensland, NE Australia
nniskilling *see* Enniskillen
nnsbruch *see* Innsbruck
nnsbruck *95 C7 var.* Innsbruch. Tirol, W Austria
noucdjouac *see* Inukjuak
nowrazlaw *see* Inowrocław
nowrocław *98 C3 Ger.* Hohensalza; *prev.* Inowrazlaw. Kujawski-pomorskie, C Poland
I-n-Salah *70 D3 var.* In Salah. C Algeria
Insterburg *see* Chernyakhovsk
Insula *see* Lille
Inta *110 E3* Respublika Komi, NW Russian Federation
Interamna *see* Teramo
Interamna Nahars *see* Terni
International Falls *45 F1* Minnesota, N USA
Inukjuak *38 D2 var.* Inoucdjouac; *prev.* Port Harrison. Québec, NE Canada
Inuuvik *see* Inuvik
Inuvik *36 D3 var.* Inuuvik. Northwest Territories, NW Canada
Invercargill *151 A7* Southland, South Island, New Zealand
Inverness *88 C3* N Scotland, UK
Investigator Ridge *141 D5 undersea ridge* E Indian Ocean
Investigator Strait *149 B7 strait* South Australia
Inyangani *78 D3 mountain* NE Zimbabwe
Ioánnina *104 A4 var.* Janina, Yannina. Ípeiros, W Greece
Iola *45 F5* Kansas, C USA
Ionia Basin *see* Ionian Basin
Ionian Basin *80 D5 var.* Ionia Basin. *undersea basin* Ionian Sea, C Mediterranean Sea
Iónia Nisiá *105 A5 Eng.* Ionian Islands. *region* W Greece
Ionian Sea *103 E3 Gk.* Iónio Pélagos, *It.* Mar Ionio. *sea* C Mediterranean Sea
Ionio, Mar/Iónio Pélagos *see* Ionian Sea
Íos *105 D6 var.* Nio. *island* Kykládes, Greece, Aegean Sea
Íos *see* Chóra
Ioulís *105 C6 prev.* Kéa. Tziá, Kykládes, Greece, Aegean Sea
Iowa *45 F3 off.* State of Iowa, *also known as* Hawkeye State. *state* C USA
Iowa City *45 G3* Iowa, C USA
Iowa Falls *45 G3* Iowa, C USA
Ipek *see* Peć
Ipel' *99 C6 var.* Ipoly, *Ger.* Eipel. *river* Hungary/Slovakia
Ipiales *58 A4* Nariño, SW Colombia
Ipoh *138 B3* Perak, Peninsular Malaysia
Ipoly *see* Ipel'
Ippy *76 C4* Ouaka, C Central African Republic
Ipswich *149 E5* Queensland, E Australia
Ipswich *89 E6 hist.* Gipeswic. E England, UK
Iqaluit *37 H3 prev.* Frobisher Bay. *province capital* Baffin Island, Nunavut, NE Canada
Iquique *64 B1* Tarapacá, N Chile
Iquitos *60 C1* Loreto, N Peru
Irákleio *105 D7 var.* Herakleion, *Eng.* Candia; *prev.* Iráklion. Kríti, Greece, E Mediterranean Sea
Iráklion *see* Irákleio
Iran *120 C3 off.* Islamic Republic of Iran; *prev.* Persia. *country* SW Asia

IRAN
Southwest Asia

Official name Islamic Republic of Iran
Formation 1502 / 1990
Capital Tehran
Population 69.5 million / 110 people per sq mile (42 people per sq km) / 62%
Total area 636,293 sq miles (1,648,000 sq km)
Languages Farsi*, Azeri, Luri, Gilaki, Mazanderani, Kurdish, Turkmen, Arabic, Baluchi
Religions Shi'a Muslim 93%, Sunni Muslim 6%, Other 1%
Ethnic mix Persian 50%, Azari 24%, Other 10%, Kurdish 8%, Lur and Bakhtiari 8%
Government Islamic theocracy
Currency Iranian rial = 100 dinars
Literacy rate 77%
Calorie consumption 3085 calories

Iranian Plateau *120 D3 var.* Plateau of Iran. *plateau* N Iran
Iran, Islamic Republic of *see* Iran
Iran, Plateau of *see* Iranian Plateau
Irapuato *51 E4* Guanajuato, C Mexico
Iraq *120 B3 off.* Republic of Iraq, *Ar.* 'Irāq. *country* SW Asia

IRAQ
Southwest Asia

Official name Republic of Iraq
Formation 1932 / 1990
Capital Baghdad
Population 28.8 million / 171 people per sq mile (66 people per sq km) / 77%
Total area 168,753 sq miles (437,072 sq km)
Languages Arabic*, Kurdish, Turkic languages, Armenian, Assyrian
Religions Shi'a Muslim 60%, Sunni Muslim 35%, Other (including Christian) 5%
Ethnic mix Arab 80%, Kurdish 15%, Turkmen 3%, Other 2%
Government Transitional regime
Currency New Iraqi dinar = 1000 fils
Literacy rate 40%
Calorie consumption 2197 calories

'Irāq *see* Iraq
Iraq, Republic of *see* Iraq
Irbid *119 B5* Irbid, N Jordan
Irbīl *see* Arbīl
Ireland *89 A5 off.* Republic of Ireland, *Ir.* Éire. *country* NW Europe
Ireland *80 C3 Lat.* Hibernia. *island* Ireland/UK

IRELAND
Northwest Europe

Official name Ireland
Formation 1922 / 1922
Capital Dublin
Population 4.1 million / 154 people per sq mile (60 people per sq km) / 59%
Total area 27,135 sq miles (70,280 sq km)
Languages English*, Irish Gaelic*
Religions Roman Catholic 88%, Other and nonreligious 9%, Anglican 3%
Ethnic mix Irish 93%, Other 4%, British 3%
Government Parliamentary system
Currency Euro = 100 cents
Literacy rate 99%
Calorie consumption 3656 calories

Ireland, Republic of *see* Ireland
Irian *see* New Guinea
Irian Barat *see* Papua
Irian Jaya *see* Papua
Iringa *73 C7* Iringa, C Tanzania
Iriomote-jima *130 A4 island* Sakishima-shotō, SW Japan
Iriona *52 D2* Colón, NE Honduras
Irish Sea *89 C5 Ir.* Muir Éireann. *sea* C British Isles
Irkutsk *115 E4* Irkutskaya Oblast', S Russian Federation
Irminger Basin *see* Reykjanes Basin
Iroise *90 A3 sea* NW France
Iron Mountain *40 B2* Michigan, N USA
Ironwood *40 B1* Michigan, N USA
Irrawaddy *136 B2 var.* Ayeyarwady. *river* W Myanmar (Burma)
Irrawaddy, Mouths of the *137 A5 delta* SW Myanmar (Burma)
Irtish *see* Irtysh
Irtysh *114 C4 var.* Irtish, *Kaz.* Ertis. *river* C Asia
Irun *93 E1* País Vasco, N Spain
Iruña *see* Pamplona
Isabela, Isla *60 A5 var.* Albemarle Island. *island* Galapagos Islands, Ecuador, E Pacific Ocean
Isaccea *108 D4* Tulcea, E Romania
Isachsen *37 F1* Northwest Territories, Ellef Ringnes Island, N Canada North America
Ísafjördhur *83 E4* Vestfirdhir, NW Iceland
Isbarta *see* Isparta
Isca Damnoniorum *see* Exeter
Ise *131 C6* Mie, Honshū, SW Japan
Iseghem *see* Izegem
Isère *91 D5 river* E France
Isernia *97 D5 var.* Æsernia. Molise, C Italy
Ise-wan *131 C6 bay* S Japan
Isfahan *see* Eşfahān
Isha Baydhabo *see* Baydhabo
Ishigaki-jima *130 A4 island* Sakishima-shotō, SW Japan
Ishikari-wan *130 C2 bay* Hokkaidō, NE Japan
Ishim *114 C4* Tyumenskaya Oblast', C Russian Federation
Ishim *114 C4 Kaz.* Esil. *river* Kazakhstan/Russian Federation
Ishinomaki *130 D4 var.* Isinomaki. Miyagi, Honshū, C Japan
Ishkashim *see* Ishkoshim
Ishkoshim *123 F3 Rus.* Ishkashim. S Tajikistan
Isinomaki *see* Ishinomaki
Isiro *77 E5* Orientale, NE Dem. Rep. Congo
Iskăr *see* Iskŭr
İskenderun *116 D4 Eng.* Alexandretta. Hatay, S Turkey
İskenderun Körfezi *118 A2 Eng.* Gulf of Alexandretta. *gulf* S Turkey
Iskŭr *104 C2 var.* Iskăr. *river* NW Bulgaria
Iskŭr, Yazovir *104 B2 prev.* Yazovir Stalin. *reservoir* W Bulgaria
Isla Cristina *92 C4* Andalucía, S Spain
Isla de León *see* San Fernando
Islāmābād *134 C1 country capital* (Pakistan) Federal Capital Territory Islāmābād, NE Pakistan
Island/Ísland *see* Iceland
I-n-Sâkâne, 'Erg *75 E2 desert* N Mali
Islay *88 B4 island* SW Scotland, UK
Isle *91 B5 river* W France
Isle of Man *89 B5 UK crown dependency* NW Europe
Ismailia *see* Ismâ'ilîya
Ismâ'ilîya *72 B1 var.* Ismailia. N Egypt
Ismid *see* İzmit
Isna *72 B2 var.* Esna. SE Egypt
Isoka *78 D1* Northern, NE Zambia
Isparta *116 B4 var.* Isbarta. Isparta, SW Turkey
İspir *117 E3* Erzurum, NE Turkey
Israel *119 A7 off.* State of Israel, *var.* Medinat Israel, *Heb.* Yisrael, Yisra'el. *country* SW Asia

ISRAEL
Southwest Asia

Official name State of Israel
Formation 1948 / 1994
Capital Jerusalem (not internationally recognized)
Population 6.7 million / 854 people per sq mile (330 people per sq km) / 91%
Total area 8019 sq miles (20,770 sq km)
Languages Hebrew*, Arabic, Yiddish, German, Russian, Polish, Romanian, Persian
Religions Jewish 80%, Muslim (mainly Sunni) 16%, Druze and other 2%, Christian 2%
Ethnic mix Jewish 80%, Other (mostly Arab) 20%
Government Parliamentary system
Currency Shekel = 100 agorot
Literacy rate 97%
Calorie consumption 3666 calories

Israel, State of *see* Israel
Issa *see* Vis
Issiq Köl *see* Issyk-Kul', Ozero
Issoire *91 C5* Puy-de-Dôme, C France
Issyk-Kul' *see* Balykchy
Issyk-Kul', Ozero *123 G2 var.* Issiq Köl, *Kir.* Ysyk-Köl. *lake* E Kyrgyzstan
İstanbul *116 B2 Bul.* Tsarigrad, *Eng.* Istanbul, *prev.* Constantinople; *anc.* Byzantium. Istanbul, NW Turkey
İstanbul Boğazı *116 B2 var.* Bosporus Thracius, *Eng.* Bosphorus, Bosporus, *Turk.* Karadeniz Boğazi. *strait* NW Turkey
Istarska Županija *see* Istra
Istra *100 A3 off.* Istarska Županija. *province* NW Croatia
Istra *100 A3 Eng.* Istria, *Ger.* Istrien. *cultural region* NW Croatia
Istria/Istrien *see* Istra
Itabuna *63 G3* Bahia, E Brazil

Itagüí 58 B3 Antioquia,
W Colombia
Itaipú, Represa de 63 E4 *reservoir*
Brazil/Paraguay
Itaituba 63 E2 Pará, NE Brazil
Italia/Italiana, Republica/Italian
Republic, The *see* Italy
Italian Somaliland *see* Somalia
Italy 80 D4 Texas, SW USA
Italy 96 C3 *off.* The Italian Republic, *It.*
Italia, Repubblica Italiana. *country*
S Europe

ITALY
Southern Europe

Official name Italian Republic
Formation 1861 / 1947
Capital Rome
Population 58.1 million / 512 people per
sq mile (198 people per sq km) / 67%
Total area 116,305 sq miles
(301,230 sq km)
Languages Italian*, German, French,
Rhaeto-Romanic, Sardinian
Religions Roman Catholic 85%, Other
and nonreligious 13%, Muslim 2%
Ethnic mix Italian 94%, Other 4%,
Sardinian 2%
Government Parliamentary system
Currency Euro = 100 cents
Literacy rate 99%
Calorie consumption 3671 calories

Iténez, Río *see* Guaporé, Rio
Ithaca 41 E3 New York, NE USA
It Hearrenfean *see* Heerenveen
Itoigawa 131 C5 Niigata, Honshū,
C Japan
Itseqqortoormiit *see* Ittoqqortoormiit
Ittoqqortoormiit 83 E3 *var.*
Itseqqortoormiit, *Dan.* Scoresbysund,
Eng. Scoresby Sound. Tunu,
C Greenland
Iturup, Ostrov 130 E1 *island* Kuril'skiye
Ostrova, SE Russian Federation
Itzehoe 94 B2 Schleswig-Holstein,
N Germany
Ivalo 84 D2 Lapp. Avveel, Avvil. Lappi,
N Finland
Ivanava 107 B7 *Pol.* Janów, Janów
Poleski, *Rus.* Ivanovo. Brestskaya
Voblasts', SW Belarus
Ivangrad *see* Berane
Ivanhoe 149 C6 New South Wales,
SE Australia
Ivano-Frankivs'k 108 C2
Ger. Stanislau, *Pol.* Stanisławów, *Rus.*
Ivano-Frankovsk; *prev.* Stanislav.
Ivano-Frankivs'ka Oblast', W Ukraine
Ivano-Frankovsk *see* Ivano-Frankivs'k
Ivanovo 111 B5 Ivanovskaya Oblast',
W Russian Federation
Ivanovo *see* Ivanava
Ivantsevichi/Ivantsevichi *see* Ivatsevichy
Ivatsevichy 107 B6 *Pol.* Iwacewicze,
Rus. Ivantsevichi, Ivatsevichi.
Brestskaya Voblasts', SW Belarus
Ivigtut *see* Ivittuut
Ivittuut 82 B4 *var.* Ivigtut. Kitaa,
S Greenland
Iviza *see* Eivissa
Iviza *see* Eivissa
Iviza *see* Eivissa
Ivory Coast *see* Côte d'Ivoire
Ivory Coast, Republic of the *see* Côte
d'Ivoire
Ivujivik 38 D1 Québec, NE Canada
Iwacewicze *see* Ivatsevichy
Iwaki 131 D5 Fukushima, Honshū,
N Japan
Iwakuni 131 B7 Yamaguchi, Honshū,
SW Japan
Iwanai 130 C2 Hokkaidō, NE Japan
Iwate 130 D3 Iwate, Honshū,
N Japan
Ixtapa 51 E5 Guerrero, S Mexico
Ixtepec 51 F5 Oaxaca, SE Mexico
Iyo-nada 131 B7 *sea* S Japan
Izabal, Lago de 52 B2 *prev.* Golfo Dulce.
lake E Guatemala
Izad Khvāst 120 D3 Fārs, C Iran
Izegem 87 A6 *prev.* Iseghem.
West-Vlaanderen, W Belgium
Izhevsk 111 D5 *prev.* Ustinov.
Udmurtskaya Respublika,
NW Russian Federation
Izmail *see* Izmayil

Izmayil 108 D4 *Rus.* Izmail. Odes'ka
Oblast', SW Ukraine
Izmir 116 A3 *prev.* Smyrna. İzmir,
W Turkey
İzmit 116 B2 *var.* Ismid; *anc.* Astacus.
Kocaeli, NW Turkey
İznik Gölü 116 B3 *lake* NW Turkey
Izu-hantō 131 D6 *peninsula* Honshū,
S Japan
Izu Shichito *see* Izu-shotō
Izu-shotō 131 D6 *var.* Izu Shichito.
island group S Japan
Izvor 104 B2 Pernik, W Bulgaria
Izyaslav 108 C2 Khmel'nyts'ka Oblast',
W Ukraine
Izyum 109 G2 Kharkivs'ka Oblast',
E Ukraine

J

Jabal ash Shifā 120 A4 *desert*
NW Saudi Arabia
Jabalpur 135 E4 *prev.* Jubbulpore.
Madhya Pradesh, C India
Jabbūl, Sabkhat al 134 B2 *sabkha*
NW Syria
Jablah 118 A3 *var.* Jeble, *Fr.* Djéblé.
Al Lādhiqīyah, W Syria
Jaca 93 F1 Aragón, NE Spain
Jacaltenango 52 A2 Huehuetenango,
W Guatemala
Jackson 42 B2 *state capital* Mississippi,
S USA
Jackson 45 H5 Missouri, C USA
Jackson 42 C1 Tennessee, S USA
Jackson Head 151 A6 *headland* South
Island, New Zealand
Jacksonville 43 E3 Florida, SE USA
Jacksonville 40 B4 Illinois, N USA
Jacksonville 43 F1 North Carolina,
SE USA
Jacksonville 49 G3 Texas, SW USA
Jacmel 54 D3 *var.* Jaquemel. S Haiti
Jacob *see* Nkayi
Jacobābād 134 B3 Sind, SE Pakistan
Jadotville *see* Likasi
Jadransko More/Jadransko Morje *see*
Adriatic Sea
Jaén 60 B2 Cajamarca, N Peru
Jaén 92 D4 Andalucía, SW Spain
Jaffna 132 D3 Northern Province,
N Sri Lanka
Jagannath *see* Puri
Jagdalpur 135 E5 Chhattīsgarh,
C India
Jagdaqi 127 G1 Nei Mongol Zizhiqu,
N China
Jagodina 100 D4 *prev.* Svetozarevo.
Serbia, C Serbia
Jahra *see* Al Jahrā'
Jailolo *see* Halmahera, Pulau
Jaipur 134 D3 *prev.* Jeypore. *state capital*
Rājasthān, N India
Jaisalmer 134 C3 Rājasthān,
NW India
Jajce 100 B3 Federacija Bosna
I Hercegovina, W Bosnia and
Herzegovina
Jakarta 138 C5 *prev.* Djakarta, *Dut.*
Batavia. *country capital* (Indonesia)
Jawa, C Indonesia
Jakobstad 84 D4 *Fin.* Pietarsaari. Länsi-
Suomi, W Finland
Jakobstadt *see* Jēkabpils
Jalālābād 123 F4 *var.* Jalalabad,
Jelalabad. Nangarhār, E Afghanistan
Jalal-Abad *see* Dzhalal-Abad
Jalandhar 134 D2 *prev.* Jullundur.
Punjab, N India
Jalapa 52 D3 Nueva Segovia,
NW Nicaragua
Jalpa 50 D4 Zacatecas, C Mexico
Jālū 71 G3 *var.* Jūlā. NE Libya
Jaluit Atoll 144 D2 *var.* Jālwōj. *atoll*
Ralik Chain, S Marshall Islands
Jālwōj *see* Jaluit Atoll
Jamaame 73 D6 *It.* Giamame;
prev. Margherita. Jubbada Hoose,
S Somalia
Jamaica 54 A4 *country* W West Indies

JAMAICA
West Indies

Official name Jamaica
Formation 1962 / 1962
Capital Kingston

JAMAICA
(continued)

Population 2.7 million / 646 people per
sq mile (249 people per sq km) / 56%
Total area 4243 sq miles (10,990 sq km)
Languages English*, English Creole
Religions Other and nonreligious 45%,
Other Protestant 20%, Church of
God 18%, Baptist 10%, Anglican 7%
Ethnic mix Black African 75%, Mulatto
(mixed race) 13%, European and
Chinese 11%, East Indian 1%
Government Parliamentary system
Currency Jamaican dollar = 100 cents
Literacy rate 88%
Calorie consumption 2685 calories

Jamaica 56 A1 *island* W West Indies
Jamaica Channel 54 D3 *channel*
Haiti/Jamaica
Jamālpur 135 F3 Bihār, NE India
Jambi 138 B4 *var.* Telanaipura; *prev.*
Djambi. Sumatera, W Indonesia
Jamdena *see* Yamdena, Pulau
James Bay 38 C3 *bay* Ontario/Québec,
E Canada
James River 45 E2 *river* North Dakota/
South Dakota, N USA
James River 41 E5 *river* Virginia,
NE USA
Jamestown 41 E3 New York, NE USA
Jamestown 45 E2 North Dakota, N USA
Jamestown *see* Holetown
Jammu 134 D2 *prev.* Jummoo. *state
capital* Jammu and Kashmir, NW India
Jammu and Kashmir 134 D1 *disputed
region* India/Pakistan
Jāmnagar 134 C4 *prev.* Navanagar.
Gujarāt, W India
Jamshedpur 135 F4 Jhārkhand, NE India
Jamuna *see* Brahmaputra
Janaúba 63 F3 Minas Gerais, SE Brazil
Janesville 40 B3 Wisconsin, N USA
Janina *see* Ioánnina
Janischken *see* Joniškis
Jankovac *see* Jánoshalma
Jan Mayen 83 F4 *Norwegian dependency*
N Atlantic Ocean
Jánoshalma 99 C7 *SCr.* Jankovac. Bács-
Kiskun, S Hungary
Janów *see* Ivanava, Belarus
Janów/Janów *see* Jonava, Lithuania
Janów Poleski *see* Ivanava
Japan 130 C4 *var.* Nippon, *Jap.* Nihon.
country E Asia

JAPAN
East Asia

Official name Japan
Formation 1590 / 1972
Capital Tokyo
Population 128 million / 881 people per
sq mile (340 people per sq km) / 79%
Total area 145,882 sq miles
(377,835 sq km)
Languages Japanese, Korean, Chinese
Religions Shinto and Buddhist 76%,
Buddhist 16%, Other (including
Christian) 8%
Ethnic mix Japanese 99%,
Other (mainly Korean) 1%
Government Parliamentary system
Currency Yen = 100 sen
Literacy rate 99%
Calorie consumption 2761 calories

Japan, Sea of 130 A4 *var.* East Sea, *Rus.*
Yaponskoye More. *sea* NW Pacific
Ocean
Japan Trench 125 F1 *trench* NW Pacific
Ocean
Japen *see* Yapen, Pulau
Japiim 62 C2 *var.* Máncio Lima. Acre,
W Brazil
Japurá, Rio 62 C2 *var.* Río Caquetá,
Yapurá. *river* Brazil/Colombia
Japurá, Rio *see* Caquetá, Río
Jaqué 53 G5 Darién, SE Panama
Jaquemel *see* Jacmel
Jarablos *see* Jarābulus
Jarābulus 118 C2 *var.* Jarablos, Jerablus,
Fr. Djérablous. Ḥalab, N Syria
Jarbah, Jazīrat *see* Jerba, Île de
**Jardines de la Reina, Archipiélago de
los** 54 B2 *island group* C Cuba

Jarid, Shaṭṭ al *see* Jerid, Chott el
Jarocin 98 C4 Wielkopolskie,
C Poland
Jaroslau *see* Jarosław
Jarosław 99 E5 *Ger.* Jaroslau, *Rus.*
Yaroslav. Podkarpackie,
SE Poland
Jarqo'rg'on 123 E3 *Rus.* Dzharkurgan.
Surkhondaryo Viloyati, S Uzbekistan
Jarvis Island 145 G2 *US unincorporated
territory* C Pacific Ocean
Jasło 99 D5 Podkarpackie, SE Poland
Jastrzębie-Zdrój 99 C5 Śląskie,
S Poland
Jataí 63 E3 Goiás, C Brazil
Jativa *see* Xátiva
Jauf *see* Al Jawf
Jaunpiebalga 106 D3 Gulbene,
NE Latvia
Jaunpur 135 E3 Uttar Pradesh,
N India
Java 152 A3 South Dakota, N USA
Javalambre 93 E3 *mountain* E Spain
Javari, Rio 62 C2 *var.* Yavarí. *river*
Brazil/Peru
Java Sea 138 D4 *Ind.* Laut Jawa. *sea*
W Indonesia
Java Trench 124 D5 *var.* Sunda Trench.
trench E Indian Ocean
Jawa, Laut *see* Java Sea
Jawhar 73 D6 *var.* Jowhar, *It.* Giohar.
Shabeellaha Dhexe, S Somalia
Jaworów *see* Yavoriv
Jaya, Puncak 139 G4 *prev.* Puntjak
Carstensz, Puntjak Sukarno. *mountain*
Papua, E Indonesia
Jayapura 139 H4 *var.* Djajapura,
Dut. Hollandia; *prev.* Kotabaru,
Sukarnapura. Papua, E Indonesia
Jayhawker State *see* Kansas
Jaz Mūrīān, Hāmūn-e 120 E4 *lake*
SE Iran
Jebba 75 F4 Kwara, W Nigeria
Jebel, Bahr el *see* White Nile
Jeble *see* Jablah
Jedda *see* Jiddah
Jędrzejów 98 D4 *Ger.* Endersdorf.
Świętokrzyskie, C Poland
Jefferson City 45 G5 *state capital*
Missouri, C USA
Jega 75 F4 Kebbi, NW Nigeria
Jehol *see* Chengde
Jēkabpils 106 D4 *Ger.* Jakobstadt.
Jēkabpils, S Latvia
Jelalabad *see* Jalālābād
Jelenia Góra 98 B4 *Ger.* Hirschberg,
Hirschberg im Riesengebirge,
Hirschberg in Riesengebirge,
Hirschberg in Schlesien. Dolnośląskie,
SW Poland
Jelgava 106 C3 *Ger.* Mitau. Jelgava,
C Latvia
Jemappes 87 B6 Hainaut, S Belgium
Jember 138 D5 *prev.* Djember. Jawa,
C Indonesia
Jena 94 C4 Thüringen, C Germany
Jenin 119 A6 N West Bank
Jerablus *see* Jarābulus
Jerada 70 D2 NE Morocco
Jerba, Île de 71 F2 *var.* Djerba, Jazīrat
Jarbah. *island* E Tunisia
Jérémie 54 D3 SW Haiti
Jerez *see* Jeréz de la Frontera, Spain
Jeréz de la Frontera 92 C5 *var.* Jerez;
prev. Xeres. Andalucía, SW Spain
Jeréz de los Caballeros 92 C4
Extremadura, W Spain
Jericho 119 B6 *Ar.* Arīḥā, *Heb.* Yeriḥo.
E West Bank
Jerid, Chott el 87 E2 *var.* Shaṭṭ al Jarīd.
salt lake W Tunisia
Jersey 89 D8 *UK crown dependency*
Channel Islands, Jersey NW Europe
Jerusalem 103 H4 *Ar.* Al Quds, Al Quds
ash Sharīf, *Heb.* Yerushalayim; *anc.*
Hierosolyma. *country capital* (Israel)
Jerusalem, NE Israel
Jerusalem 112 A4 *district* E Israel
Jesenice 95 D7 *Ger.* Assling.
NW Slovenia
Jesselton *see* Kota Kinabalu
Jessore 135 G4 Khulna, W Bangladesh
Jesús María 64 C3 Córdoba,
C Argentina
Jeypore *see* Jaipur, Rājasthān, India
Jhānsi 134 D3 Uttar Pradesh, N India
Jhārkhand 135 F4 *cultural region*
NE India

Jhārkhand *135 F4 state* NE India
Jhelum *134 C2* Punjab, NE Pakistan
Ji *see* Hebei, China
Ji *see* Jilin, China
Jiangmen *128 C6* Guangdong, S China
Jiangsu *128 D4 var.* Chiang-su, Jiangsu Sheng, Kiangsu, Su. *province* E China
Jiangsu *see* Nanjing
Jiangsu Sheng *see* Jiangsu
Jiangxi *128 C6 var.* Chiang-hsi, Gan, Jiangxi Sheng, Kiangsi. *province* S China
Jiangxi Sheng *see* Jiangxi
Jiaxing *128 D5* Zhejiang, SE China
Jiayi *see* Chiai
Jibuti *see* Djibouti
Jiddah *121 A5 Eng.* Jedda. Makkah, W Saudi Arabia
Jih-k'a-tse *see* Xigazê
Jihlava *99 B5 Ger.* Iglau, *Pol.* Igława. Vysočina, E Czech Republic
Jilf al Kabīr, Haḑabat al *see* Gilf Kebir Plateau
Jilib *73 D6 It.* Gelib. Jubbada Dhexe, S Somalia
Jilin *128 E3 var.* Chi-lin, Girin, Kirin; *prev.* Yungki, Yunki. Jilin, NE China
Jilin *128 E3 var.* Chi-lin, Girin, Ji, Jilin Sheng, Kirin. *province* NE China
Jilin Sheng *see* Jilin
Jīma *73 C5 var.* Jimma, *It.* Gimma. Oromo, C Ethiopia
Jimbolia *108 A4 Ger.* Hatzfeld, *Hung.* Zsombolya. Timiş, W Romania
Jiménez *50 D2* Chihuahua, N Mexico
Jimma *see* Jīma
Jimsar *126 C3* Xinjiang Uygur Zizhiqu, NW China
Jin *see* Shanxi
Jin *see* Tianjin Shi
Jinan *128 C4 var.* Chinan, Chi-nan, Tsinan. *province capital* Shandong, E China
Jingdezhen *128 C5* Jiangxi, S China
Jinghong *128 A6 var.* Yunjinghong. Yunnan, SW China
Jinhua *128 D5* Zhejiang, SE China
Jining *127 F3* Shandong, E China
Jinja *73 C6* S Uganda
Jinotega *52 D3* Jinotega, NW Nicaragua
Jinotepe *52 D3* Carazo, SW Nicaragua
Jinsen *see* Inch'ŏn
Jinsha Jiang *128 A5 Eng* Yangtze. *river* SW China
Jinzhong *128 C4 var.* Yuci. Shanxi, C China
Jinzhou *128 D3 var.* Chin-chou, Chinchow; *prev.* Chinhsien. Liaoning, NE China
Jirgalanta *see* Hovd
Jisr ash Shadadi *see* Ash Shadādah
Jiu *108 B5 Ger.* Schil, Schyl, *Hung.* Zsil, Zsily. *river* S Romania
Jiujiang *128 C5* Jiangxi, S China
Jixi *129 E2* Heilongjiang, NE China
Jīzān *121 B6 var.* Qīzān. Jīzān, SW Saudi Arabia
Jizzax *123 E2 Rus.* Dzhizak. Jizzax Viloyati, C Uzbekistan
João Belo *see* Xai-Xai
João Pessoa *63 G2 prev.* Paraíba. *state capital* Paraíba, E Brazil
Joazeiro *see* Juazeiro
Job'urg *see* Johannesburg
Jo-ch'iang *see* Ruoqiang
Jodhpur *134 C3* Rājasthān, NW India
Joensuu *85 E5* Itä-Suomi, SE Finland
Jōetsu *131 C5 var.* Zyôetu. Niigata, Honshū, C Japan
Jogjakarta *see* Yogyakarta
Johanna Island *see* Anjouan
Johannesburg *78 D4 var.* Egoli, Erautini, Gauteng, *abbrev.* Job'urg. Gauteng, NE South Africa
Johannisburg *see* Pisz
John Day River *46 C3 river* Oregon, NW USA
John o'Groats *88 C2* N Scotland, UK
Johnston Atoll *143 E1 US unincorporated territory* C Pacific Ocean
Johor Baharu *see* Johor Bahru
Johor Bahru *138 B3 var.* Johor Baharu, Johore Bahru. Johor, Peninsular Malaysia
Johore Bahru *see* Johor Bahru
Johore Strait *138 A1 strait* Johor, Peninsular Malaysia, Malaysia/ Singapore Asia Andaman Sea/South China Sea
Joinvile *see* Joinville
Joinville *63 E4 var.* Joinvile. Santa Catarina, S Brazil
Jokkmokk *84 C3 Lapp.* Dálvvadis. Norrbotten, N Sweden
Jokyakarta *see* Yogyakarta
Joliet *40 B3* Illinois, N USA
Jonava *106 B4 Ger.* Janow, *Pol.* Janów. Kaunas, C Lithuania
Jonesboro *42 B1* Arkansas, C USA
Joniškis *106 C3 Ger.* Janischken. Šiaulai, N Lithuania
Jönköping *85 B7* Jönköping, S Sweden
Jonquière *39 E4* Québec, SE Canada
Joplin *45 F5* Missouri, C USA
Jordan *119 B6 off.* Hashemite Kingdom of Jordan, *Ar.* Al Mamlaka al Urduniya al Hashemiyah, Al Urdunn; *prev.* Transjordan. *country* SW Asia

JORDAN
Southwest Asia

Official name Hashemite Kingdom of Jordan
Formation 1946 / 1967
Capital Amman
Population 5.6 million / 163 people per sq mile (63 people per sq km) / 74%
Total area 35,637 sq miles (92,300 sq km)
Languages Arabic*
Religions Muslim (mainly Sunni) 92%, Other (mostly Christian) 8%
Ethnic mix Arab 98%, Circassian 1%, Armenian 1%
Government Monarchy
Currency Jordanian dinar = 1000 fils
Literacy rate 90%
Calorie consumption 2673 calories

Jordan *119 B5 Ar.* Urdunn, *Heb.* HaYarden. *river* SW Asia
Jorhāt *135 H3* Assam, NE India
Jos *75 G4* Plateau, C Nigeria
Joseph Bonaparte Gulf *146 D2 gulf* N Australia
Jos Plateau *75 G4 plateau* C Nigeria
Jotunheimen *85 A5 mountain range* S Norway
Joûnié *118 A4 var.* Juniyah. W Lebanon
Joure *86 D2 Fris.* De Jouwer. Friesland, N Netherlands
Joutseno *85 E5* Etelä-Suomi, SE Finland
Jowhar *see* Jawhar
J.Storm Thurmond Reservoir *see* Clark Hill Lake
Juan Aldama *50 D3* Zacatecas, C Mexico
Juan de Fuca, Strait of *46 A1 strait* Canada/USA
Juan Fernandez Islands *see* Juan Fernández, Islas
Juan Fernández, Islas *57 A6 Eng.* Juan Fernandez Islands. *island group* W Chile
Juazeiro *63 G2 prev.* Joazeiro. Bahia, E Brazil
Juazeiro do Norte *63 G2* Ceará, E Brazil
Juba *73 B5 var.* Jūbā. Bahr el Gabel, S Sudan
Juba *73 D6 Amh.* Genalē Wenz, *It.* Guiba, *Som.* Ganaane, Webi Jubba. *river* Ethiopia/Somalia
Jubba, Webi *see* Juba
Jubbulpore *see* Jabalpur
Júcar *93 E3 var.* Jucar. *river* C Spain
Juchitán *51 F5 var.* Juchitán de Zaragosa. Oaxaca, SE Mexico
Juchitán de Zaragosa *see* Juchitán
Judayyidat Hāmir *120 B3* S Iraq
Judenburg *95 D7* Steiermark, C Austria
Jugoslavija *see* Serbia
Juigalpa *52 D3* Chontales, S Nicaragua
Juiz de Fora *63 F4* Minas Gerais, SE Brazil
Jujuy *see* San Salvador de Jujuy
Jūlā *see* Jālū, Libya
Julia Beterrae *see* Béziers
Juliaca *61 E4* Puno, SE Peru
Juliana Top *59 G3 mountain* C Suriname
Julianehåb *see* Qaqortoq
Julio Briga *see* Bragança
Juliobriga *see* Logroño
Juliomagus *see* Angers
Jullundur *see* Jalandhar
Jumilla *93 E4* Murcia, SE Spain
Jummoo *see* Jammu
Jumna *see* Yamuna
Jumporn *see* Chumphon
Junction City *45 F4* Kansas, C USA
Juneau *36 D4 state capital* Alaska, USA
Junín *64 C4* Buenos Aires, E Argentina
Junīyah *see* Joûnié
Junkseylon *see* Phuket
Jur *73 B5 river* C Sudan
Jura *90 D4 cultural region* E France
Jura *90 D4 department* E France
Jura *95 A7 var.* Jura Mountains. *mountain range* France/Switzerland
Jura *88 B4 island* SW Scotland, UK
Jura Mountains *see* Jura
Jurbarkas *106 B4 Ger.* Georgenburg, Jurburg. Tauragė, W Lithuania
Jurburg *see* Jurbarkas
Jūrmala *106 C3* Rīga, C Latvia
Juruá, Rio *62 C2 var.* Río Yuruá. *river* Brazil/Peru
Juruena, Rio *62 D3 river* W Brazil
Jutiapa *52 B2* Jutiapa, S Guatemala
Juticalpa *52 D2* Olancho, C Honduras
Jutland *see* Jylland
Juvavum *see* Salzburg
Juventud, Isla de la *54 A2 var.* Isla de Pinos, *Eng.* Isle of Youth; *prev.* The Isle of the Pines. *island* W Cuba
Južna Morava *101 E5 Ger.* Südliche Morava. *river* SE Serbia
Jwaneng *78 C4* Southern, S Botswana Africa
Jylland *85 A7 Eng.* Jutland. *peninsula* W Denmark
Jyrgalan *see* Dzhergalan
Jyväskylä *85 D5* Länsi-Soumi, C Finland

K

K2 *126 A4 Chin.* Qogir Feng, *Eng.* Mount Godwin Austen. *mountain* China/Pakistan
Kaafu Atoll *see* Male' Atoll
Kaaimanston *59 G3* Sipaliwini, N Suriname
Kaakhka *see* Kaka
Kaala *see* Caála
Kaamanen *84 D2 Lapp.* Gámas. Lappi, N Finland
Kaapstad *see* Cape Town
Kaaresuvanto *84 C3 Lapp.* Gárassavon. Lappi, N Finland
Kabale *73 B6* SW Uganda
Kabinda *77 D7* Kasai Oriental, SE Dem. Rep. Congo
Kabinda *see* Cabinda
Kabompo *78 C2 river* W Zambia
Kābol *123 E4 var.* Kabul, *pash.* Kābul. *country capital* (Afghanistan) Kabol, E Afghanistan
Kabul *123 E4 var.* Daryā-ye Kābul. *river* Afghanistan/Pakistan
Kabul *see* Kābol
Kābul, Daryā-ye *see* Kabul
Kabwe *78 D2* Central, C Zambia
Kachchh, Gulf of *134 B4 var.* Gulf of Cutch, Gulf of Kutch. *gulf* W India
Kachchh, Rann of *134 B4 var.* Rann of Kachh, Rann of Kutch. *salt marsh* India/Pakistan
Kachh, Rann of *see* Kachchh, Rann of
Kadan Kyun *137 B5 prev.* King Island. *island* Mergui Archipelago, S Myanmar (Burma)
Kadavu *145 E4 prev.* Kandavu. *island* S Fiji
Kadoma *78 D3 prev.* Gatooma. Mashonaland West, C Zimbabwe
Kadugli *72 B4* Southern Kordofan, S Sudan
Kaduna *75 G4* Kaduna, C Nigeria
Kadzhi-Say *123 G2 Kir.* Kajisay. Issyk-Kul'skaya Oblast', NE Kyrgyzstan
Kaédi *74 C3* Gorgol, S Mauritania
Kaffa *see* Feodosiya
Kafue *78 D2* Lusaka, SE Zambia
Kafue *78 C2 river* C Zambia
Kaga Bandoro *76 C4 prev.* Fort-Crampel. Nana-Grébizi, C Central African Republic
Kagan *see* Kogon
Kâgheț *74 D1 var.* Karet. *physical region* N Mauritania
Kagi *see* Chiai
Kagoshima *131 B8 var.* Kagosima. Kagoshima, Kyūshū, SW Japan
Kagoshima-wan *131 A8 bay* SW Japan
Kagosima *see* Kagoshima
Kagul *see* Cahul
Kahmard, Daryā-ye *123 E4 prev.* Darya-i-surkhab. *river* NE Afghanistan
Kahramanmaraş *116 D4 var.* Kahraman Maraş, Maraş, Marash. Kahramanmaraş, S Turkey
Kaiapoi *151 C6* Canterbury, South Island, New Zealand
Kaifeng *128 C4* Henan, C China
Kai, Kepulauan *139 F4 prev.* Kei Islands. *island group* Maluku, SE Indonesia
Kaikohe *150 C2* Northland, North Island, New Zealand
Kaikoura *151 C5* Canterbury, South Island, New Zealand
Kaikoura Peninsula *151 C5 peninsula* South Island, New Zealand
Kainji Lake *see* Kainji Reservoir
Kainji Reservoir *75 F4 var.* Kainji Lake. *reservoir* W Nigeria
Kaipara Harbour *150 C2 harbour* North Island, New Zealand
Kairouan *71 E2 var.* Al Qayrawān. E Tunisia
Kaisaria *see* Kayseri
Kaiserslautern *95 A5* Rheinland-Pfalz, SW Germany
Kaišiadorys *107 B5* Kaunas, S Lithuania
Kaitaia *150 C2* Northland, North Island, New Zealand
Kajaani *84 E4 Swe.* Kajana. Oulu, C Finland
Kajan *see* Kayan, Sungai
Kajana *see* Kajaani
Kajisay *see* Kadzhi Say
Kaka *122 C2 Rus.* Kaakhka. Ahal Welaýaty, S Turkmenistan
Kake *36 D4* Kupreanof Island, Alaska, USA
Kakhovka *109 F4* Khersons'ka Oblast', S Ukraine
Kakhovs'ke Vodoskhovyshche *109 F4 Rus.* Kakhovskoye Vodokhranilishche. *reservoir* SE Ukraine
Kakhovskoye Vodokhranilishche *see* Kakhovs'ke Vodoskhovyshche
Kākināda *132 D1 prev.* Cocanada. Andhra Pradesh, E India
Kakshaal-Too, Khrebet *see* Kokshaal-Tau
Kaktovik *36 D2* Alaska, USA
Kalaallit Nunaat *see* Greenland
Kalahari Desert *78 B4 desert* Southern Africa
Kalaikhum *see* Qal'aikhum
Kalámai *see* Kalámata
Kalamariá *104 B4* Kentrikí Makedonía, N Greece
Kalamás *104 A4 var.* Thiamis, *prev* Thýamis. *river* W Greece
Kalámata *105 B6 prev.* Kalámai. Pelopónnisos, S Greece
Kalamazoo *40 C3* Michigan, N USA
Kalambaka *see* Kalampáka
Kálamos *105 C5* Attikí, C Greece
Kalampáka *104 B4 var.* Kalambaka. Thessalía, C Greece
Kalanchak *109 F4* Khersons'ka Oblast', S Ukraine
Kalarash *see* Călăraşi
Kalasin *136 D4 var.* Muang Kalasin. Kalasin, E Thailand
Kalāt *134 B2 var.* Kelat, Khelat. Baluchistān, SW Pakistan

Kalāt *see* Qalāt
Kalbarri *147 A5* Western Australia
Kalecik *116 C3* Ankara, N Turkey
Kalemie *77 E6 prev.* Albertville. Katanga, SE Dem. Rep. Congo
Kale Sultanie *see* Çanakkale
Kalgan *see* Zhangjiakou
Kalgoorlie *147 B6* Western Australia
Kalima *77 D6* Maniema, E Dem. Rep. Congo
Kalimantan *138 D4 Eng.* Indonesian Borneo. *geopolitcal region* Borneo, C Indonesia
Kalinin *see* Tver'
Kaliningrad *106 A4* Kaliningradskaya Oblast', W Russian Federation
Kaliningrad *see* Kaliningradskaya Oblast'
Kaliningradskaya Oblast' *106 B4 var.* Kaliningrad. *province and enclave* W Russian Federation
Kalinkavichy *107 C7 Rus.* Kalinkovichi. Homyel'skaya Voblasts', SE Belarus
Kalinkovichi *see* Kalinkavichy
Kalisch/Kalish *see* Kalisz
Kalispell *44 B1* Montana, NW USA
Kalisz *98 C4 Ger.* Kalisch, *Rus.* Kalish; *anc.* Calisia. Wielkopolskie, C Poland
Kalix *84 D4* Norrbotten, N Sweden
Kalixälven *84 D3 river* N Sweden
Kallaste *106 E3 Ger.* Krasnogor. Tartumaa, SE Estonia
Kallavesi *85 E5 lake* SE Finland
Kalloní *105 D5* Lésvos, E Greece
Kalmar *85 C7 var.* Calmar. Kalmar, S Sweden
Kalmthout *87 C5* Antwerpen, N Belgium
Kalpáki *104 A4* Ípeiros, W Greece
Kalpeni Island *132 B3 island* Lakshadweep, India, N Indian Ocean
Kaltdorf *see* Pruszków
Kaluga *111 B5* Kaluzhskaya Oblast', W Russian Federation
Kalush *108 C2 Pol.* Kałusz. Ivano-Frankivs'ka Oblast', W Ukraine
Kałusz *see* Kalush
Kalutara *132 D4* Western Province, SW Sri Lanka
Kalvarija *107 B5 Pol.* Kalwaria. Marijampol·e, S Lithuania
Kalwaria *see* Kalvarija
Kalyān *134 C5* Mahārāshtra, W India
Kálymnos *105 D6 var.* Kálimnos. *island* Dodekánisa, Greece, Aegean Sea
Kama *110 D4 river* NW Russian Federation
Kamarang *59 F3* W Guyana
Kambryk *see* Cambrai
Kamchatka *see* Kamchatka, Poluostrov
Kamchatka, Poluostrov *115 G3 Eng.* Kamchatka. *peninsula* E Russian Federation
Kamenets-Podol'skiy *see* Kam"yanets'-Podil's'kyy
Kamenka Dneprovskaya *see* Kam"yanka-Dniprovs'ka
Kamenskoye *see* Dniprodzerzhyns'k
Kamensk-Shakhtinskiy *111 B6* Rostovskaya Oblast', SW Russian Federation
Kamina *77 D7* Shaba, S Dem. Rep. Congo
Kamishli *see* Al Qāmishlī
Kamloops *37 E5* British Columbia, SW Canada
Kammu Seamount *152 C2 guyot* N Pacific Ocean
Kampala *73 B6 country capital* (Uganda) S Uganda
Kâmpóng Cham *137 D6 prev.* Kompong Cham. Kâmpóng Cham, C Cambodia
Kâmpóng Chhnăng *137 D6 prev.* Kompong. Kâmpóng Chhnăng, C Cambodia
Kâmpóng Saôm *137 D6 prev.* Kompong Som, Sihanoukville. Kâmpóng Saôm, SW Cambodia
Kâmpóng Spoe *137 D6 prev.* Kompong Speu. Kâmpóng Spœ, S Cambodia
Kâmpôt *137 D6* Kâmpôt, SW Cambodia
Kampuchea *see* Cambodia
Kampuchea, Democratic *see* Cambodia
Kampuchea, People's Democratic Republic of *see* Cambodia
Kam"yanets'-Podil's'kyy *108 C3 Rus.* Kamenets-Podol'skiy. Khmel'nyts'ka Oblast', W Ukraine
Kam"yanka-Dniprovs'ka *109 F3 Rus.* Kamenka Dneprovskaya. Zaporiz'ka Oblast', SE Ukraine
Kamyshin *111 B6* Volgogradskaya Oblast', SW Russian Federation
Kanaky *see* New Caledonia
Kananga *77 D6 prev.* Luluabourg. Kasai Occidental, S Dem. Rep. Congo
Kananur *see* Cannanore
Kanara *see* Karnātaka
Kanash *111 C5* Chuvashskaya Respublika, W Russian Federation
Kanazawa *131 C5* Ishikawa, Honshū, SW Japan
Kanbe *136 B4* Yangon, SW Myanmar (Burma)
Kānchīpuram *132 C2 prev.* Conjeeveram. Tamil Nādu, SE India
Kandahār *123 E5 Per.* Qandahār. Kandahār, S Afghanistan
Kandalakša *see* Kandalaksha
Kandalaksha *110 B2 var.* Kandalakša, *Fin.* Kantalahti. Murmanskaya Oblast', NW Russian Federation
Kandangan *138 D4* Borneo, C Indonesia
Kandau *see* Kandava
Kandava *106 C3 Ger.* Kandau. Tukums, W Latvia
Kandavu *see* Kadavu
Kandi *75 F4* N Benin
Kandy *132 D3* Central Province, C Sri Lanka
Kane Fracture Zone *66 B4 fracture zone* NW Atlantic Ocean
Kāne'ohe *47 A8 var.* Kaneohe. O'ahu, Hawai'i, USA
Kanestron, Akra *see* Palioúri, Ákrotírio
Kanëv *see* Kaniv
Kanevskoye Vodokhranilishche *see* Kanivs'ke Vodoskhovyshche
Kangaroo Island *149 A7 island* South Australia
Kangertittivaq *83 E4 Dan.* Scoresby Sund. *fjord* E Greenland
Kangikajik *83 E4 var.* Kap Brewster. *headland* E Greenland
Kaniv *109 E2 Rus.* Kanëv. Cherkas'ka Oblast', C Ukraine
Kanivs'ke Vodoskhovyshche *109 E2 Rus.* Kanevskoye Vodokhranilishche. *reservoir* C Ukraine
Kanjiža *100 D2 Ger.* Altkanischa, *Hung.* Magyarkanizsa, Ókanizsa; *prev.* Stara Kanjiža. Vojvodina, N Serbia
Kankaanpää *85 D5* Länsi-Soumi, SW Finland
Kankakee *40 B3* Illinois, N USA
Kankan *74 D4* Haute-Guinée, E Guinea
Kannur *see* Cannanore
Kano *75 G4* Kano, N Nigeria
Kānpur *135 E3 Eng.* Cawnpore. Uttar Pradesh, N India
Kansas *45 F5 off.* State of Kansas, *also known as* Jayhawker State, Sunflower State. *state* C USA
Kansas City *45 F4* Kansas, C USA
Kansas City *45 F4* Missouri, C USA
Kansas River *45 F5 river* Kansas, C USA
Kansk *115 E4* Krasnoyarskiy Kray, S Russian Federation
Kansu *see* Gansu
Kantalahti *see* Kandalaksha
Kántanos *105 C7* Kríti, Greece, E Mediterranean Sea
Kantemirovka *111 B6* Voronezhskaya Oblast', W Russian Federation
Kantipur *see* Kathmandu
Kanton *145 F3 var.* Abariringa, Canton Island; *prev.* Mary Island. *atoll* Phoenix Islands, C Kiribati
Kanye *78 C4* Southern, SE Botswana
Kaohsiung *128 D6 var.* Gaoxiong, *Jap.* Takao, Takow. S Taiwan
Kaolack *74 B3 var.* Kaolak. W Senegal
Kaolak *see* Kaolack
Kaolan *see* Lanzhou
Kaoma *78 C2* Western, W Zambia
Kapelle *87 B5* Zeeland, SW Netherlands
Kapellen *87 C5* Antwerpen, N Belgium
Kapka, Massif du *76 C2 mountain range* E Chad
Kaplangky, Plato *see* Gaplaňgyr Platosy
Kapoeas *see* Kapuas, Sungai
Kapoeta *73 C5* Eastern Equatoria, SE Sudan
Kaposvár *99 C7* Somogy, SW Hungary
Kappeln *94 B2* Schleswig-Holstein, N Germany
Kaproncza *see* Koprivnica
Kapstad *see* Cape Town
Kapsukas *see* Marijampolė
Kaptsevichy *107 C7 Rus.* Koptsevichi. Homyel'skaya Voblasts', SE Belarus
Kapuas, Sungai *138 C4 prev.* Kapoeas. *river* Borneo, C Indonesia
Kapuskasing *38 C4* Ontario, S Canada
Kapyl' *107 C6 Rus.* Kopyl'. Minskaya Voblasts', C Belarus
Kara-Balta *123 F2* Chuyskaya Oblast', N Kyrgyzstan
Karabil', Vozvyshennost' *see* Garabil Belentligi
Kara-Bogaz-Gol, Zaliv *see* Garabogaz Aylagy
Karabük *116 C2* Karabük, NW Turkey
Karāchi *134 B3* Sind, SE Pakistan
Karácsonkő *see* Piatra-Neamţ
Karadeniz *see* Black Sea
Karadeniz Boğazi *see* İstanbul Boğazı
Karaferiye *see* Véroia
Karaganda *114 C4 Kaz.* Qaraghandy. Karaganda, C Kazakhstan
Karaginskiy, Ostrov *115 H2 island* E Russian Federation
Karagumskiy Kanal *see* Garagum Kanaly
Karak *see* Al Karak
Kara-Kala *see* Magtymguly
Karakax *see* Moyu
Karakılısse *see* Ağrı
Karakol *123 G2 var.* Karakolka. Issyk-Kul'skaya Oblast', NE Kyrgyzstan
Karakol *123 G2 prev.* Przheval'sk. Issyk-Kul'skaya Oblast', NE Kyrgyzstan
Karakolka *see* Karakol
Karakoram Range *134 D1 mountain range* C Asia
Karaköse *see* Ağrı
Karakul' *see* Qarokŭl
Kara Kum *see* Garagum
Kara Kum Canal/Karakumskiy Kanal *see* Garagum Kanaly
Karakumy, Peski *see* Garagum
Karamai *see* Karamay
Karaman *116 C4* Karaman, S Turkey
Karamay *126 B2 var.* Karamai, Kelamayi; *prev. Chin.* K'o-la-ma-i. Xinjiang Uygur Zizhiqu, NW China
Karamea Bight *151 B5 gulf* South Island, New Zealand
Karapelit *104 E1 Rom.* Stejarul. Dobrich, NE Bulgaria
Kara-Say *123 G2* Issyk-Kul'skaya Oblast', NE Kyrgyzstan
Karasburg *78 B4* Karas, S Namibia
Kara Sea *see* Karskoye More
Kara Strait *see* Karskiye Vorota, Proliv
Karatau *114 C5 Kaz.* Qarataū. Zhambyl, S Kazakhstan
Karavás *105 B7* Kýthira, S Greece
Karbalā' *120 B3 var.* Kerbala, Kerbela. S Iraq
Kardeljevo *see* Ploče
Kardhítsa *see* Kardítsa
Kardítsa *105 B5 var.* Kardhítsa. Thessalía, C Greece
Kärdla *106 C2 Ger.* Kertel. Hiiumaa, W Estonia
Kărdžali *see* Kŭrdzhali
Karet *see* Kâghet
Kargı *116 C2* Çorum, N Turkey
Kargilik *see* Yecheng
Kariba *78 D2* Mashonaland West, N Zimbabwe
Kariba, Lake *78 D3 reservoir* Zambia/Zimbabwe
Karibib *78 B3* Erongo, C Namibia
Karies *see* Karyés
Karigasniemi *84 D2 Lapp.* Garegegasnjárga. Lappi, N Finland
Karimata, Selat *138 C4 strait* W Indonesia
Karīmnagar *134 D5* Andhra Pradesh, C India
Karin *72 D4* Woqooyi Galbeed, N Somalia
Kariot *see* Ikaría
Káristos *see* Kárystos
Karkinits'ka Zatoka *109 E4 Rus.* Karkinitskiy Zaliv. *gulf* S Ukraine
Karkinitskiy Zaliv *see* Karkinits'ka Zatoka
Karkūk *see* Kirkūk
Karleby *see* Kokkola
Karl-Marx-Stadt *see* Chemnitz
Karlö *see* Hailuoto
Karlovac *100 B3 Ger.* Karlstadt, *Hung.* Károlyváros. Karlovac, C Croatia
Karlovy Vary *99 A5 Ger.* Karlsbad; *prev. Eng.* Carlsbad. Karlovarský Kraj, W Czech Republic
Karlsbad *see* Karlovy Vary
Karlsburg *see* Alba Iulia
Karlskrona *85 C7* Blekinge, S Sweden
Karlsruhe *95 B6 var.* Carlsruhe. Baden-Württemberg, SW Germany
Karlstad *85 B6* Värmland, C Sweden
Karlstadt *see* Karlovac
Karnāl *134 D2* Haryāna, N India
Karnātaka *132 C1 var.* Kanara; *prev.* Maisur, Mysore. *cultural region* W India
Karnātaka *132 C1 var.* Kanara; *prev.* Maisur, Mysore. *state* W India
Karnobat *104 D2* Burgas, E Bulgaria
Karnul *see* Kurnool
Karol *see* Carei
Károly-Fehérvár *see* Alba Iulia
Károlyváros *see* Karlovac
Karpaten *see* Carpathian Mountains
Kárpathos *105 E7* Kárpathos, SE Greece
Kárpathos *105 E7 It.* Scarpanto; *anc.* Carpathos, Carpathus. *island* SE Greece
Karpaty *see* Carpathian Mountains
Karpenísi *105 B5 prev.* Karpenísion. Stereá Ellás, C Greece
Karpenísion *see* Karpenísi
Karpilovka *see* Aktsyabrski
Kars *117 F2 var.* Qars. Kars, NE Turkey
Karsau *see* Kārsava
Kārsava *106 D4 Ger.* Karsau; *prev. Rus.* Korsovka. Ludza, E Latvia
Karshi *see* Qarshi, Uzbekistan
Karskiye Vorota, Proliv *110 E2 Eng.* Kara Strait. *strait* N Russian Federation
Karskoye More *114 D2 Eng.* Kara Sea. *sea* Arctic Ocean
Karyés *104 C4 var.* Karies. Ágion Óros, N Greece
Kárystos *105 C6 var.* Káristos. Évvoia, C Greece
Kasai *77 C6 var.* Cassai, Kassai. *river* Angola/Dem. Rep. Congo
Kasaji *77 D7* Katanga, S Dem. Rep. Congo
Kasama *78 D1* Northern, N Zambia
Kasan *see* Koson
Kāsaragod *132 B2* Kerala, SW India
Kaschau *see* Košice
Kāshān *120 C3* Eşfahān, C Iran
Kashgar *see* Kashi
Kashi *126 A3 Chin.* Kaxgar, K'o-shih, *Uigh.* Kashgar. Xinjiang Uygur Zizhiqu NW China
Kasi *see* Vārānasi
Kasongo *77 D6* Maniema, E Dem. Rep. Congo
Kasongo-Lunda *77 C7* Bandundu, SW Dem. Rep. Congo
Kásos *105 D7 island* S Greece
Kaspīy Mangy Oypaty *see* Caspian Depression
Kaspiysk *111 B8* Respublika Dagestan, SW Russian Federation
Kaspiyskoye More/Kaspiy Tengizi *see* Caspian Sea
Kassa *see* Košice
Kassai *see* Kasai
Kassala *72 C4* Kassala, E Sudan
Kassel *94 B4 prev.* Cassel. Hessen, C Germany
Kasserine *71 E2 var.* Al Qaşrayn. W Tunisia
Kastamonu *116 C2 var.* Castamoni, Kastamuni. Kastamonu, N Turkey
Kastamuni *see* Kastamonu
Kastaneá *104 B4* Kentrikí Makedonía, N Greece
Kastélli *see* Kíssamos
Kastoría *104 B4* Dytikí Makedonía, N Greece
Kástro *105 C6* Sífnos, Kykládes, Greece, Aegean Sea
Kastsyukovichy *107 E7 Rus.* Kostyukovichi. Mahilyowskaya Voblasts', E Belarus

Kastsyukowka *107 D7 Rus.* Kostyukovka. Homyel'skaya Voblasts', SE Belarus
Kasulu *73 B7* Kigoma, W Tanzania
Kasumiga-ura *131 D5 lake* Honshū, S Japan
Katahdin, Mount *41 G1 mountain* Maine, NE USA
Katalla *36 C3* Alaska, USA
Katana *see* Qaṭanā
Katanning *147 B7* Western Australia
Katawaz *see* Zarghūn Shahr
Katchall Island *133 F3 island* Nicobar Islands, India, NE Indian Ocean
Kateríni *104 B4* Kentrikí Makedonía, N Greece
Katha *136 B2* Sagaing, N Myanmar (Burma)
Katherine *148 A2* Northern Territory, N Australia
Kathmandu *124 C3 prev.* Kantipur. *country capital* (Nepal) Central, C Nepal
Katikati *150 D3* Bay of Plenty, North Island, New Zealand
Katima Mulilo *78 C3* Caprivi, NE Namibia
Katiola *74 D4* C Côte d'Ivoire (Ivory Coast)
Káto Achaïa *105 B5 var.* Kato Ahaia, Káto Akhaía. Dytikí Ellás, S Greece
Kato Ahaia/Káto Akhaía *see* Káto Achaïa
Katoúna *105 A5* Dytikí Ellás, C Greece
Katowice *99 C5 Ger.* Kattowitz. Śląskie, S Poland
Katsina *75 G3* Katsina, N Nigeria
Kattakurgan *see* Kattaqo'rg'on
Kattaqo'rg'on *123 E2 Rus.* Kattakurgan. Samarqand Viloyati, C Uzbekistan
Kattavía *105 E7* Ródos, Dodekánisa, Greece, Aegean Sea
Kattegat *85 B7 Dan.* Kattegatt. *strait* N Europe
Kattegatt *see* Kattegat
Kattowitz *see* Katowice
Kaua'i *47 A7 var.* Kauai. *island* Hawaiian Islands, Hawai'i, USA, C PacificOcean
Kauai *see* Kaua'i
Kauen *see* Kaunas
Kaufbeuren *95 C6* Bayern, S Germany
Kaunas *106 B4 Ger.* Kauen, *Pol.* Kowno; *prev. Rus.* Kovno. Kaunas, C Lithuania
Kavadar *see* Kavadarci
Kavadarci *101 E6 Turk.* Kavadar. C Macedonia
Kavaja *see* Kavajë
Kavajë *101 C6 It.* Cavaia, Kavaja. Tiranë, W Albania
Kavakli *see* Topolovgrad
Kavála *104 C3 prev.* Kavála. Anatolikí Makedonía kai Thráki, NE Greece
Kāvali *132 D2* Andhra Pradesh, E India
Kavála *see* Kavála
Kavango *see* Cubango/Okavango
Kavaratti Island *132 A3 island* Lakshadweep, Lakshadweep, SW India Asia N Indian Ocean
Kavarna *104 E2* Dobrich, NE Bulgaria
Kavengo *see* Cubango/Okavango
Kavīr, Dasht-e *120 D3 var.* Great Salt Desert. *salt pan* N Iran
Kavkaz *see* Caucasus
Kawagoe *131 D5* Saitama, Honshū, S Japan
Kawasaki *130 A2* Kanagawa, Honshū, S Japan
Kawerau *150 E3* Bay of Plenty, North Island, New Zealand
Kaxgar *see* Kashi
Kaya *75 E3* C Burkina Faso
Kayan *136 B4* Yangon, SW Myanmar (Burma)
Kayan, Sungai *138 D3 prev.* Kajan. *river* Borneo, C Indonesia
Kayes *74 C3* Kayes, W Mali
Kayseri *116 D3 var.* Kaisaria; *anc.* Caesarea Mazaca, Mazaca. Kayseri, C Turkey
Kazach'ye *115 F2* Respublika Sakha (Yakutiya), NE Russian Federation
Kazakhskaya SSR/Kazakh Soviet Socialist Republic *see* Kazakhstan
Kazakhskiy Melkosopochnik *114 C4 Eng.* Kazakh Uplands, Kirghiz Steppe, *Kaz.* Saryarqa. *uplands* C Kazakhstan
Kazakhstan *114 B4 off.* Republic of Kazakhstan, *var.* Kazakstan, *Kaz.* Qazaqstan, Qazaqstan Respublikasy; *prev.* Kazakh Soviet Socialist Republic, *Rus.* Kazakhskaya SSR. *country* C Asia

KAZAKHSTAN
Central Asia

Official name Republic of Kazakhstan
Formation 1991 / 1991
Capital Astana
Population 14.8 million / 14 people per sq mile (5 people per sq km) / 56%
Total area 1,049,150 sq miles (2,717,300 sq km)
Languages Kazakh*, Russian*, Ukrainian, Tatar, German, Uzbek, Uighur
Religions Muslim (mainly Sunni) 47%, Orthodox Christian 44%, Other 9%
Ethnic mix Kazakh 53%, Russian 30%, Other 9%, Ukrainian 4%, Tatar 2%, German 2%
Government Presidential system
Currency Tenge = 100 tiyn
Literacy rate 99%
Calorie consumption 2677 calories

Kazakhstan, Republic of *see* Kazakhstan
Kazakh Uplands *see* Kazakhskiy Melkosopochnik
Kazakstan *see* Kazakhstan
Kazan' *111 C5* Respublika Tatarstan, W Russian Federation
Kazandzhik *see* Bereket
Kazanlik *see* Kazanlŭk
Kazanlŭk *104 D2 prev.* Kazanlik. Stara Zagorat, C Bulgaria
Kazatin *see* Kozyatyn
Kazbegi *see* Kazbek
Kazbek *117 F1 var.* Kazbegi, *Geor.* Mqinvartsveri. *mountain* N Georgia
Kāzerūn *120 D4* Fārs, S Iran
Kazi Magomed *see* Qazimämmäd
Kazvin *see* Qazvīn
Kéa *see* Tziá
Kéa *see* Ioulís
Kea, Mauna *47 B8 mountain* Hawaii, USA
Kéamu *see* Aneityum
Kearney *45 E4* Nebraska, C USA
Keban Barajı *117 E3 reservoir* C Turkey
Kebkabiya *72 A4* Northern Darfur, W Sudan
Kebnekaise *84 C3 mountain* N Sweden
Kecskemét *99 D7* Bács-Kiskun, C Hungary
Kediri *138 D5* Jawa, C Indonesia
Kędzierzyn-Kozle *99 C5 Ger.* Heydebrech. Opolskie, S Poland
Keelung *see* Chilung
Keetmanshoop *78 B4* Karas, S Namibia
Kefallinía *see* Kefalloniá
Kefalloniá *105 A5 var.* Kefallinía. *island* Iónioi Nísoi, Greece, C Mediterranean Sea
Kefe *see* Feodosiya
Kegel *see* Keila
Kehl *95 A6* Baden-Württemberg, SW Germany
Kei Islands *see* Kai, Kepulauan
Keijō *see* Sŏul
Keila *106 D2 Ger.* Kegel. Harjumaa, NW Estonia
Keïta *75 F3* Tahoua, C Niger
Keitele *84 D4 lake* C Finland
Keith *149 B7* South Australia
Këk-Art *123 G2 prev.* Alaykel', Alay-Kuu. Oshskaya Oblast', SW Kyrgyzstan
Kékes *99 C6 mountain* N Hungary
Kelamayi *see* Karamay
Kelang *see* Klang
Kelat *see* Kalāt
Kelifskiy Uzboy *see* Kelifskiy Uzboýy
Kelifskiy Uzboýy *122 D3 Rus.* Kelifskiy Uzboy. *salt marsh* Lebap Welaýaty, E Turkmenistan
Kelkit Çayı *117 E3 river* N Turkey
Kelmė *106 B4* Šiaulai, C Lithuania
Kélo *76 B4* Tandjilé, SW Chad
Kelowna *37 E5* British Columbia, SW Canada
Kelso *46 B2* Washington, NW USA
Keltsy *see* Kielce
Keluang *138 B3 var.* Kluang. Johor, Peninsular Malaysia
Kem' *110 B3* Respublika Kareliya, NW Russian Federation
Kemah *117 E3* Erzincan, E Turkey
Kemaman *see* Cukai
Kemerovo *114 D4 prev.* Shcheglovsk. Kemerovskaya Oblast', C Russian Federation
Kemi *84 D4* Lappi, NW Finland
Kemijärvi *84 D3 Swe.* Kemiträsk. Lappi, N Finland
Kemijoki *84 D3 river* NW Finland
Kemin *123 G2 prev.* Bystrovka. Chuyskaya Oblast', N Kyrgyzstan
Kemins Island *see* Nikumaroro
Kemiträsk *see* Kemijärvi
Kemmuna *see* Comino
Kempele *84 D4* Oulu, C Finland
Kempten *95 B7* Bayern, S Germany
Kendal *89 D5* NW England, UK
Kendari *139 E4* Sulawesi, C Indonesia
Kenedy *49 G4* Texas, SW USA
Kenema *74 C4* SE Sierra Leone
Këneurgench *see* Köneürgench
Kenge *77 C6* Bandundu, SW Dem. Rep. Congo
Keng Tung *136 C3 var.* Kentung. Shan State, E Myanmar (Burma)
Kénitra *70 C2 prev.* Port-Lyautey. NW Morocco
Kennett *45 H5* Missouri, C USA
Kennewick *46 C2* Washington, NW USA
Kenora *38 A3* Ontario, S Canada
Kenosha *40 B3* Wisconsin, N USA
Kentau *114 B5* Yuzhnyy Kazakhstan, S Kazakhstan
Kentucky *40 C5 off.* Commonwealth of Kentucky, *also known as* Bluegrass State. *state* C USA
Kentucky Lake *40 B5 reservoir* Kentucky/Tennessee, S USA
Kentung *see* Keng Tung
Kenya *73 C6 off.* Republic of Kenya. *country* E Africa

KENYA
East Africa

Official name Republic of Kenya
Formation 1963 / 1963
Capital Nairobi
Population 34.3 million / 157 people per sq mile (60 people per sq km) / 33%
Total area 224,961 sq miles (582,650 sq km)
Languages Kiswahili*, English*, Kikuyu, Luo, Kalenjin, Kamba
Religions Christian 60%, Traditional beliefs 25%, Other 9%, Muslim 6%
Ethnic mix Other 30%, Kikuyu 21%, Luhya 14%, Luo 13%, Kalenjin 11%, Kamba 11%
Government Presidential system
Currency Kenya shilling = 100 cents
Literacy rate 74%
Calorie consumption 2090 calories

Kenya, Mount *see* Kirinyaga
Kenya, Republic of *see* Kenya
Keokuk *45 G4* Iowa, C USA
Kéos *see* Tziá
Kępno *98 C4* Wielkopolskie, C Poland
Keppel Island *see* Niuatoputapu
Kerak *see* Al Karak
Kerala *132 C2 cultural region* S India
Kerala *132 C2 state* S India
Kerasunt *see* Giresun
Keratéa *105 C6 var.* Keratea. Attikí, C Greece
Keratea *see* Keratéa
Kerbala/Kerbela *see* Karbalā'
Kerch *109 G5 Rus.* Kerch'. Respublika Krym, SE Ukraine
Kerch' *see* Kerch
Kerchens'ka Protska/Kerchenskiy Proliv *see* Kerch Strait
Kerch Strait *109 G4 var.* Bosporus Cimmerius, Enikale Strait, *Rus.* Kerchenskiy Proliv, *Ukr.* Kerchens'ka Protska. *strait* Black Sea/Sea of Azov
Keremitlik *see* Lyulyakovo
Kerguelen *141 C7 island* C French Southern and Antarctic Territories
Kerguelen Plateau *141 C7 undersea plateau* S Indian Ocean
Kerí *105 A6* Zákynthos, Iónioi Nísoi, Greece, C Mediterranean Sea
Kerikeri *150 D2* Northland, North Island, New Zealand
Kerkenah, Îles de *102 D4 var.* Kerkenna Islands, *Ar.* Juzur Qarqannah. *island group* E Tunisia
Kerkenna Islands *see* Kerkenah, Îles de
Kerki *see* Atamyrat
Kerkrade *87 D6* Limburg, SE Netherlands
Kerkuk *see* Kirkūk
Kérkyra *104 A4 var.* Kérkira, *Eng.* Corfu. *island* Iónioi Nísoi, Greece, C Mediterranean Sea
Kermadec Islands *152 C4 island group* New Zealand, SW Pacific Ocean
Kermadec Trench *143 E4 trench* SW Pacific Ocean
Kermān *120 D3 var.* Kirman; *anc.* Carmana. Kermān, C Iran
Kermānshāh *120 C3 var.* Qahremānshahr; *prev.* Bākhtarān. Kermānshāhān, W Iran
Kerrville *49 F4* Texas, SW USA
Kertel *see* Kärdla
Kerulen *127 E2 Chin.* Herlen He, *Mong.* Herlen Gol. *river* China/Mongolia
Kerýneia *see* Girne
Kesennuma *130 D4* Miyagi, Honshū, C Japan
Keszthely *99 C7* Zala, SW Hungary
Ketchikan *36 D4* Revillagigedo Island, Alaska, USA
Kętrzyn *98 D2 Ger.* Rastenburg. Warmińsko-Mazurskie, NE Poland
Kettering *89 D6* C England, UK
Kettering *40 C4* Ohio, N USA
Keupriya *see* Primorsko
Keuruu *85 D5* Länsi-Soumi, C Finland
Keweenaw Peninsula *40 B1 peninsula* Michigan, N USA
Key Largo *43 F5* Key Largo, Florida, SE USA
Keystone State *see* Pennsylvania
Key West *43 E5* Florida Keys, Florida, SE USA
Kezdivásárhely *see* Târgu Secuiesc
Khabarovsk *115 G4* Khabarovskiy Kray, SE Russian Federation
Khachmas *see* Xaçmaz
Khadera *see* Hadera
Khairpur *134 B3* Sind, SE Pakistan
Khalīj-e Fars *see* Gulf, The
Khalkidikí *see* Chalkidikí
Khalkís *see* Chalkída
Khambhāt, Gulf of *134 C4 Eng.* Gulf of Cambay. *gulf* W India
Khamīs Mushayt *121 B6 var.* Hamīs Musait. 'Asīr, SW Saudi Arabia
Khānābād *123 E3* Kunduz, NE Afghanistan
Khān al Baghdādī *see* Al Baghdādī
Khandwa *134 D4* Madhya Pradesh, C India
Khanh Hung *see* Soc Trăng
Khaniá *see* Chaniá
Khanka, Lake *129 E2 var.* Hsing-K'ai Hu, Lake Hanka, *Chin.* Xingkai Hu, *Rus.* Ozero Khanka. *lake* China/ Russian Federation
Khanka, Ozero *see* Khanka, Lake
Khankendi *see* Xankändi
Khanthabouli *136 D4 var.* Savannakhét. S Laos
Khanty-Mansiysk *114 C3 prev.* Ostyako-Voguls'k. Khanty-Mansiyskiy Avtonomnyy Okrug, C Russian Federation
Khān Yūnis *119 A7 var.* Khān Yūnus. S Gaza Strip
Khān Yūnus *see* Khān Yūnis
Khanzi *see* Ghanzi
Kharagpur *135 F4* West Bengal, NE India
Kharbin *see* Harbin
Kharkiv *109 G2 Rus.* Khar'kov. Kharkivs'ka Oblast', NE Ukraine
Khar'kov *see* Kharkiv
Kharmanli *104 D3* Khaskovo, S Bulgaria
Khartoum *72 B4 var.* El Khartûm, Khartum. *country capital* (Sudan) Khartoum, C Sudan

Khartum see Khartoum
Khasavyurt *111 B8* Respublika Dagestan, SW Russian Federation
Khāsh, Dasht-e *122 D5 Eng.* Khash Desert. *desert* SW Afghanistan
Khash Desert see Khāsh, Dasht-e
Khashim Al Qirba/Khashm al Qirbah see Khashm el Girba
Khashm el Girba *72 C4 var.* Khashim Al Qirba, Khashm al Qirbah. Kassala, E Sudan
Khaskovo *104 D3* Khaskovo, S Bulgaria
Khaybar, Kowtal-e see Khyber Pass
Khaydarkan *123 F2 var.* Khaydarken. Batkenskaya Oblast', SW Kyrgyzstan
Khaydarken see Khaydarkan
Khazar, Baḥr-e/Khazar, Daryā-ye see Caspian Sea
Khelat see Kalāt
Kherson *109 E4* Khersons'ka Oblast', S Ukraine
Kheta *115 E2 river* N Russian Federation
Khíos see Chíos
Khirbet el 'Aujā et Taḥtā *119 E7* E West Bank Asia
Khiva/Khiwa see Xiva
Khmel'nitskiy see Khmel 'nyts'kyy
Khmel 'nyts'kyy *108 C2 Rus.* Khmel'nitskiy; *prev.* Proskurov. Khmel'nyts'ka Oblast', W Ukraine
Khodasy *107 E6 Rus.* Khodosy. Mahilyowskaya Voblasts', E Belarus
Khodoriv *108 C2 Pol.* Chodorów, *Rus.* Khodorov. L'vivs'ka Oblast', NW Ukraine
Khodorov see Khodoriv
Khodosy see Khodasy
Khodzhent see Khŭjand
Khoi see Khvoy
Khojend see Khŭjand
Khokand see Qo'qon
Kholm *123 E3 var.* Tashqurghan, *Pash.* Khulm. Balkh, N Afghanistan
Kholm see Chelm
Kholon see Ḥolon
Khoms see Al Khums
Khong Sedone see Muang Khôngxédôn
Khon Kaen *136 D4 var.* Muang Khon Kaen. Khon Kaen, E Thailand
Khor *115 G4* Khabarovskiy Kray, SE Russian Federation
Khorat see Nakhon Ratchasima
Khorog see Khorugh
Khorugh *123 F3 Rus.* Khorog. S Tajikistan
Khotan see Hotan
Khouribga *70 B2* C Morocco
Khovd see Hovd
Khowst *123 F4* Khowst, E Afghanistan
Khoy see Khvoy
Khoyniki *107 D8 Rus.* Khoyniki. Homyel'skaya Voblasts', SE Belarus
Khudzhand see Khŭjand
Khŭjand *123 E2 var.* Khodzhent, Khojend, *Rus.* Khudzhand; *prev.* Leninabad, *Taj.* Leninobod. N Tajikistan
Khulm see Kholm
Khulna *135 G4* Khulna, SW Bangladesh
Khums see Al Khums
Khust *108 B3 Cz.* Chust, *var.* Husté, *Hung.* Huszt. Zakarpats'ka Oblast', W Ukraine
Khvoy *120 C2 var.* Khoi, Khoy. Āzarbāyjān-e Bākhtari, NW Iran
Khyber Pass *134 C1 var.* Kowtal-e Khaybar. *pass* Afghanistan/Pakistan
Kiangmai see Chiang Mai
Kiang-ning see Nanjing
Kiangsi see Jiangxi
Kiangsu see Jiangsu
Kiáto *105 B6 prev.* Kiáton. Pelopónnisos, S Greece
Kiáton see Kiáto
Kiayi see Chiai
Kibangou *77 B6* Le Niari, SW Congo
Kibombo *77 D6* Maniema, E Dem. Rep. Congo
Kıbrıs/Kıbrıs Cumhuriyeti see Cyprus
Kičevo *101 D6* SW FYR Macedonia
Kidderminster *89 D6* C England, UK
Kiel *94 B2* Schleswig-Holstein, N Germany
Kielce *98 D4 Rus.* Keltsy. Świętokrzyskie, C Poland

Kieler Bucht *94 B2 bay* N Germany
Kiev see Kyyiv
Kiev Reservoir see Kyyivs'ke Vodoskhovyshche
Kiffa *74 C3* Assaba, S Mauritania
Kigali *73 B8 country capital* (Rwanda) C Rwanda
Kigoma *73 B7* Kigoma, W Tanzania
Kihnu *106 C2 var.* Kihnu Saar, *Ger.* Kühnö. *island* SW Estonia
Kihnu Saar see Kihnu
Kii-suidō *131 C7 strait* S Japan
Kikinda *100 D3 Ger.* Grosskikinda, *Hung.* Nagykikinda; *prev.* Velika Kikinda. Vojvodina, N Serbia
Kikládhes see Kykládes
Kikwit *77 C6* Bandundu, W Dem. Rep. Congo
Kilien Mountains see Qilian Shan
Kilimane see Quelimane
Kilimanjaro *69 E5 region* E Tanzania
Kilimanjaro *73 C7 var.* Uhuru Peak. *volcano* NE Tanzania
Kilingi-Nõmme *106 D3 Ger.* Kurkund. Pärnumaa, SW Estonia
Kilis *116 D4* Kilis, S Turkey
Kiliya *108 D4 Rom.* Chilia-Nouă. Odes'ka Oblast', SW Ukraine
Kilkenny *89 B6 Ir.* Cill Chainnigh. Kilkenny, S Ireland
Kilkís *104 B3* Kentrikí Makedonía, N Greece
Killarney *89 A6 Ir.* Cill Airne. Kerry, SW Ireland
Killeen *49 G3* Texas, SW USA
Kilmain see Quelimane
Kilmarnock *88 C4* W Scotland, UK
Kilwa see Kilwa Kivinje
Kilwa Kivinje *73 C7 var.* Kilwa. Lindi, SE Tanzania
Kimberley *78 C4* Northern Cape, C South Africa
Kimberley Plateau *146 C3 plateau* Western Australia
Kimch'aek *129 E3 prev.* Sŏngjin. E North Korea
Kinabalu, Gunung *138 D3 mountain* East Malaysia
Kindersley *37 F5* Saskatchewan, S Canada
Kindia *74 C4* Guinée-Maritime, SW Guinea
Kindley Field *42 A4 air base* E Bermuda
Kindu *77 D6 prev.* Kindu-Port-Empain. Maniema, C Dem. Rep. Congo
Kindu-Port-Empain see Kindu
Kineshma *111 C5* Ivanovskaya Oblast', W Russian Federation
King Charles Islands see Kong Karls Land
King Christian IX Land see Kong Christian IX Land
King Frederik VI Coast see Kong Frederik VI Kyst
King Frederik VIII Land see Kong Frederik VIII Land
King Island *149 B8 island* Tasmania, SE Australia
King Island see Kadan Kyun
Kingissepp see Kuressaare
Kingman *48 A1* Arizona, SW USA
Kingman Reef *145 E2 US territory* C Pacific Ocean
Kingsford Smith *148 E2* (Sydney) New South Wales, SE Australia
King's Lynn *89 E6 var.* Bishop's Lynn, Kings Lynn, Lynn, Lynn Regis. E England, UK
Kings Lynn see King's Lynn
King Sound *146 B3 sound* Western Australia
Kingsport *43 E1* Tennessee, S USA
Kingston *54 B5 country capital* (Jamaica) E Jamaica
Kingston *38 D5* Ontario, SE Canada
Kingston *41 F3* New York, NE USA
Kingston upon Hull *89 D5 var.* Hull. E England, UK
Kingston upon Thames *89 A8* SE England, UK
Kingstown *55 H4 country capital* (Saint Vincent and the Grenadines) Saint Vincent, Saint Vincent and the Grenadines

Kingstown see Dún Laoghaire
Kingsville *49 G5* Texas, SW USA
King William Island *37 F3 island* Nunavut, N Canada Arctic Ocean
Kinneret, Yam see Tiberias, Lake
Kinrooi *87 D5* Limburg, NE Belgium
Kinshasa *77 B6 prev.* Léopoldville. *country capital* (Dem. Rep. Congo) Kinshasa, W Dem. Rep. Congo
Kintyre *88 B4 peninsula* W Scotland, UK
Kinyeti *73 B5 mountain* S Sudan
Kiparissía see Kyparissía
Kipili *73 B7* Rukwa, W Tanzania
Kipushi *77 D8* Katanga, SE Dem. Rep. Congo
Kirdzhali see Kŭrdzhali
Kirghizia see Kyrgyzstan
Kirghiz Range *123 F2 Rus.* Kirgizskiy Khrebet; *prev.* Alexander Range. *mountain range* Kazakhstan/Kyrgyzstan
Kirghiz SSR see Kyrgyzstan
Kirghiz Steppe see Kazakhskiy Melkosopochnik
Kirgizskaya SSR see Kyrgyzstan
Kirgizskiy Khrebet see Kirghiz Range
Kiriath-Arba see Hebron
Kiribati *145 F2 off.* Republic of Kiribati. *country* C Pacific Ocean

---

KIRIBATI
Australasia & Oceania

Official name Republic of Kiribati
Formation 1979 / 1979
Capital Bairiki (Tarawa Atoll)
Population 103,092 / 376 people per sq mile (145 people per sq km) / 36%
Total area 277 sq miles (717 sq km)
Languages English*, Kiribati
Religions Roman Catholic 53%, Kiribati Protestant Church 39%, Other 8%
Ethnic mix Micronesian 96%, Other 4%
Government Nonparty system
Currency Australian dollar = 100 cents
Literacy rate 99%
Calorie consumption 2859 calories

Kiribati, Republic of see Kiribati
Kırıkhan *116 D4* Hatay, S Turkey
Kırıkkale *116 C3 province* C Turkey
Kirin see Jilin
Kirinyaga *73 C6 prev.* Mount Kenya. *volcano* C Kenya
Kirishi *110 B4 var.* Kirisi. Leningradskaya Oblast', NW Russian Federation
Kirisi see Kirishi
Kiritimati *145 G2 prev.* Christmas Island. *atoll* Line Islands, E Kiribati
Kirkenes *84 E2 Fin.* Kirkkoniemi. Finnmark, N Norway
Kirk-Kilissa see Kırklareli
Kirkkoniemi see Kirkenes
Kirkland Lake *38 D4* Ontario, S Canada
Kırklareli *116 A2 prev.* Kirk-Kilissa. Kırklareli, NW Turkey
Kirkpatrick, Mount *154 B3 mountain* Antarctica
Kirksville *45 G4* Missouri, C USA
Kirkūk *120 B3 var.* Karkūk, Kerkuk. N Iraq
Kirkwall *88 C2* NE Scotland, UK
Kirkwood *45 G4* Missouri, C USA
Kir Moab see Al Karak
Kir of Moab see Al Karak
Kirov *111 C5 prev.* Vyatka. Kirovskaya Oblast', NW Russian Federation
Kirovabad see Gäncä
Kirovakan see Vanadzor
Kirovo-Chepetsk *111 D5* Kirovskaya Oblast', NW Russian Federation
Kirovograd *109 E3 Rus.* Kirovograd; *prev.* Kirovo, Yelizavetgrad, Zinov'yevsk. Kirovohrads'ka Oblast', C Ukraine
Kirovo/Kirovograd see Kirovohrad
Kirthar Range *134 B3 mountain range* S Pakistan
Kiruna *84 C3 Lapp.* Giron. Norrbotten, N Sweden
Kirun/Kirun' see Chilung

Kisalföld see Little Alföld
Kisangani *77 D5 prev.* Stanleyville. Orientale, NE Dem. Rep. Congo
Kishinev see Chişinău
Kislovodsk *111 B7* Stavropol'skiy Kray, SW Russian Federation
Kismaayo *73 D6 var.* Chisimayu, Kismayu, *It.* Chisimaio. Jubbada Hoose, S Somalia
Kismayu see Kismaayo
Kissámos *105 C7 prev* Kastélli. Kríti, Greece, E Mediterranean Sea
Kissidougou *74 C4* Guinée-Forestière, S Guinea
Kissimmee, Lake *43 E4 lake* Florida, SE USA
Kistna see Krishna
Kisumu *73 C6 prev.* Port Florence. Nyanza, W Kenya
Kisvárda *99 E6 Ger.* Kleinwardein. Szabolcs-Szatmár-Bereg, E Hungary
Kita *74 G3* Kayes, W Mali
Kitab see Kitob
Kitakyūshū *131 A7 var.* Kitakyūsyū. Fukuoka, Kyūshū, SW Japan
Kitakyūsyū see Kitakyūshū
Kitami *130 D2* Hokkaidō, NE Japan
Kitchener *38 C5* Ontario, S Canada
Kíthnos see Kýthnos
Kitimat *36 D4* British Columbia, SW Canada
Kitinen *84 D3 river* N Finland
Kitob *123 E3 Rus.* Kitab. Qashqadaryo Viloyati, S Uzbekistan
Kitwe *78 D2 var.* Kitwe-Nkana. Copperbelt, C Zambia
Kitwe-Nkana see Kitwe
Kitzbüheler Alpen *95 C7 mountain range* W Austria
Kivalina *36 C2* Alaska, USA
Kivalo *84 D3 ridge* C Finland
Kivertsi *108 C1 Pol.* Kiwerce, *Rus.* Kivertsy. Volyns'ka Oblast', NW Ukraine
Kivertsy see Kivertsi
Kivu, Lac see Kivu, Lake
Kivu, Lake *77 E6 Fr.* Lac Kivu. *lake* Rwanda/Dem. Rep. Congo
Kiwerce see Kivertsi
Kiyev see Kyyiv
Kiyevskoye Vodokhranilishche see Kyyivs'ke Vodoskhovyshche
Kızıl Irmak *116 C3 river* C Turkey
Kizil Kum see Kyzyl Kum
Kizyl-Arvat see Serdar
Kladno *99 A5* Střední Čechy, NW Czech Republic
Klagenfurt *95 D7 Slvn.* Celovec. Kärnten, S Austria
Klaipėda *106 B3 Ger.* Memel. Klaipėda, NW Lithuania
Klamath Falls *46 B4* Oregon, NW USA
Klamath Mountains *46 A4 mountain range* California/Oregon, W USA
Klang *138 B3 var.* Kelang; *prev.* Port Swettenham. Selangor, Peninsular Malaysia
Klarälven *85 B6 river* Norway/Sweden
Klatovy *99 A5 Ger.* Klattau. Plzeňský Kraj, W Czech Republic
Klattau see Klatovy
Klausenburg see Cluj-Napoca
Klazienaveen *86 E2* Drenthe, NE Netherlands
Kleines Ungarisches Tiefland see Little Alföld
Klein Karas *78 B4* Karas, S Namibia
Kleinwardein see Kisvárda
Kleisoúra *105 A5* Ípeiros, W Greece
Klerksdorp *78 D4* North-West, N South Africa
Klimavichy *107 E7 Rus.* Klimovichi. Mahilyowskaya Voblasts', E Belarus
Klimovichi see Klimavichy
Klintsy *111 A5* Bryanskaya Oblast', W Russian Federation
Klisura *104 C2* Plovdiv, C Bulgaria
Ključ *100 B3* Federacija Bosna I Hercegovina, NW Bosnia and Herzegovina
Klobuck *98 C4* Śląskie, S Poland
Klosters *95 B7* Graubünden, SE Switzerland

INDEX - GAZETTEER: **Kluang – Kowno**

Kluang *see* Keluang
Kluczbork *98 C4 Ger.* Kreuzburg, Kreuzburg in Oberschlesien. Opolskie, S Poland
Klyuchevskaya Sopka, Vulkan *115 H3 volcano* E Russian Federation
Knin *100 B4* Šibenik-Knin, S Croatia
Knjaževac *100 E4* Serbia, E Serbia
Knokke-Heist *87 A5* West-Vlaanderen, NW Belgium
Knoxville *42 D1* Tennessee, S USA
Knud Rasmussen Land *82 D1 physical region* N Greenland
Kobdo *see* Hovd
Kōbe *131 C6* Hyōgo, Honshū, SW Japan
København *85 B7 Eng.* Copenhagen; *anc.* Hafnia. *country capital* (Denmark) Sjælland, København, E Denmark
Kobenni *74 D3* Hodh el Gharbi, S Mauritania
Koblenz *95 A5 prev.* Coblenz, *Fr.* Coblence; *anc.* Confluentes. Rheinland-Pfalz, W Germany
Kobrin *see* Kobryn
Kobryn *107 A6 Pol.* Kobryn, *Rus.* Kobrin. Brestskaya Voblasts', SW Belarus
K'obulet'i *117 F2* W Georgia
Kočani *101 E6* NE FYR Macedonia
Kočevje *95 D8 Ger.* Gottschee. S Slovenia
Koch Bihār *135 G3* West Bengal, NE India
Kōchi *131 B7 var.* Kôti. Kōchi, Shikoku, SW Japan
Kochi *see* Cochin
Kochiu *see* Gejiu
Kodiak *36 C3* Kodiak Island, Alaska, USA
Kodiak Island *36 C3 island* Alaska, USA
Koedoes *see* Kudus
Koeln *see* Köln
Koepang *see* Kupang
Ko-erh-mu *see* Golmud
Koetai *see* Mahakam, Sungai
Koetaradja *see* Bandaaceh
Kōfu *131 D5 var.* Kôhu. Yamanashi, Honshū, S Japan
Kogarah *148 E2* New South Wales, E Australia
Kogon *122 D2 Rus.* Kagan. Buxoro Viloyati, C Uzbekistan
Kőhalom *see* Rupea
Kohīma *135 H3 state capital* Nāgāland, E India
Koh I Noh *see* Büyükağrı Dağı
Kohtla-Järve *106 E2* Ida-Virumaa, NE Estonia
Kôhu *see* Kōfu
Kokand *see* Qo'qon
Kokchetav *see* Kokshetau
Kokkola *84 D4 Swe.* Karleby; *prev. Swe.* Gamlakarleby. Länsi-Soumi, W Finland
Koko *75 F4* Kebbi, W Nigeria
Kokomo *40 C4* Indiana, N USA
Koko Nor *see* Qinghai, China
Koko Nor *see* Qinghai Hu, China
Kokrines *36 C2* Alaska, USA
Kokshaal-Tau *123 G2 Rus.* Khrebet Kakshaal-Too. *mountain range* China/Kyrgyzstan
Kokshetau *114 C4 Kaz.* Kökshetaū; *prev.* Kokchetav. Kokshetau, N Kazakhstan
Kökshetaū *see* Kokshetau
Koksijde *87 A5* West-Vlaanderen, W Belgium
Koksoak *39 E2 river* Québec, E Canada
Kokstad *78 D5* KwaZulu/Natal, E South Africa
Kolaka *139 E4* Sulawesi, C Indonesia
Kolam *see* Quilon
K'o-la-ma-i *see* Karamay
Kola Peninsula *see* Kol'skiy Poluostrov
Kolari *84 D3* Lappi, NW Finland
Kolárovo *99 C6 Ger.* Gutta; *prev.* Guta, *Hung.* Gúta. Nitriansky Kraj, SW Slovakia
Kolberg *see* Kołobrzeg
Kolda *74 C3* S Senegal
Kolding *85 A7* Vejle, C Denmark
Kölen *81 E1 mountain range* Norway/Sweden
Kolguyev, Ostrov *110 C2 island* NW Russian Federation
Kolhāpur *132 B1* Mahārāshtra, SW India
Kolhumadulu Atoll *132 A5 atoll* S Maldives
Kolín *99 B5 Ger.* Kolin. Střední Čechy, C Czech Republic
Kolka *106 C2* Talsi, NW Latvia
Kolkasrags *106 C2 prev. Eng.* Cape Domesnes. *cape* NW Latvia
Kolkata *135 G4 prev.* Calcutta. West Bengal, N India
Kollam *see* Quilon
Kolmar *see* Colmar
Köln *94 A4 var.* Koeln, *Eng./Fr.* Cologne, *prev.* Cöln; *anc.* Colonia Agrippina, Oppidum Ubiorum. Nordrhein-Westfalen, W Germany
Koło *98 C3* Wielkopolskie, C Poland
Kołobrzeg *98 B2 Ger.* Kolberg. Zachodnio-pomorskie, NW Poland
Kolokani *74 D3* Koulikoro, W Mali
Kolomea *see* Kolomyya
Kolomna *111 B5* Moskovskaya Oblast', W Russian Federation
Kolomyya *108 C3 Ger.* Kolomea. Ivano-Frankivs'ka Oblast', W Ukraine
Kolozsvár *see* Cluj-Napoca
Kolpa *100 A2 Ger.* Kulpa, *SCr.* Kupa. *river* Croatia/Slovenia
Kolpino *110 B4* Leningradskaya Oblast', NW Russian Federation
Kol'skiy Poluostrov *110 C2 Eng.* Kola Peninsula. *peninsula* NW Russian Federation
Kolwezi *77 D7* Katanga, S Dem. Rep. Congo
Kolyma *115 G2 river* NE Russian Federation
Komatsu *131 C5 var.* Komatu. Ishikawa, Honshū, SW Japan
Komatu *see* Komatsu
Kommunizm, Qullai *123 F3 mountain* E Tajikistan
Komoé *75 E4 var.* Komoé Fleuve. *river* E Côte d'Ivoire (Ivory Coast)
Komoé Fleuve *see* Komoé
Komotau *see* Chomutov
Komotiní *104 D3 var.* Gümüljina, *Turk.* Gümülcine. Anatolikí Makedonía kai Thráki, NE Greece
Kompong *see* Kâmpóng Chhnăng
Kompong Cham *see* Kâmpóng Cham
Kompong Som *see* Kâmpóng Saôm
Kompong Speu *see* Kâmpóng Spoe
Komrat *see* Comrat
Komsomolets, Ostrov *115 E1 island* Severnaya Zemlya, N Russian Federation
Komsomol'sk-na-Amure *115 G4* Khabarovskiy Kray, SE Russian Federation
Kondolovo *104 E3* Burgas, E Bulgaria
Kondopoga *110 B3* Respublika Kareliya, NW Russian Federation
Kondoz *123 E3 Pash.* Kunduz. *province* NE Afghanistan
Këneurgench *122 C2 var.* Köneürgench, *Rus.* Këneurgench; *prev.* Kunya-Urgench. Daşoguz Welaýaty, N Turkmenistan
Köneürgench *see* Këneurgench
Kong Christian IX Land *82 D4 Eng.* King Christian IX Land. *physical region* SE Greenland
Kong Frederik IX Land *82 C3 physical region* SW Greenland
Kong Frederik VIII Land *83 E2 Eng.* King Frederik VIII Land. *physical region* NE Greenland
Kong Frederik VI Kyst *82 C4 Eng.* King Frederik VI Coast. *physical region* SE Greenland
Kong Karls Land *83 G2 Eng.* King Charles Islands. *island group* SE Svalbard
Kongo *see* Congo (river)
Kongolo *77 D6* Katanga, E Dem. Rep. Congo
Kongor *73 B5* Jonglei, SE Sudan
Kong Oscar Fjord *83 E3 fjord* E Greenland
Kongsberg *85 B6* Buskerud, S Norway
Kông, Tônle *137 E5 var.* Xê Kong. *river* Cambodia/Laos
Kong, Xê *see* Kông, Tônle
Königgrätz *see* Hradec Králové
Königshütte *see* Chorzów
Konin *98 C3 Ger.* Kuhnau. Weilkopolskie, C Poland
Koninkrijk der Nederlanden *see* Netherlands
Konispol *101 C7 var.* Konispoli. Vlorë, S Albania
Konispoli *see* Konispol
Kónitsa *104 A4* Ípeiros, W Greece
Konitz *see* Chojnice
Konjic *100 C4* Federacija Bosna I Hercegovina, S Bosnia and Herzegovina
Konosha *110 C4* Arkhangel'skaya Oblast', NW Russian Federation
Konotop *109 F1* Sums'ka Oblast', NE Ukraine
Konstantinovka *see* Kostyantynivka
Konstanz *95 B7 var.* Constanz, *Eng.* Constance, *hist.* Kostnitz; *anc.* Constantia. Baden-Württemberg, S Germany
Konstanza *see* Constanța
Konya *116 C4 var.* Konieh, *prev.* Konia; *anc.* Iconium. Konya, C Turkey
Kopaonik *101 D5 mountain range* S Serbia
Kopar *see* Koper
Koper *95 D8 It.* Capodistria; *prev.* Kopar. SW Slovenia
Köpetdag Gershi *122 C3 mountain range* Iran/Turkmenistan
Köpetdag Gershi/Kopetdag, Khrebet *see* Koppeh Dāgh
Koppeh Dāgh *120 D2 Rus.* Khrebet Kopetdag, *Turkm.* Köpetdag Gershi. *mountain range* Iran/Turkmenistan
Kopreinitz *see* Koprivnica
Koprivnica *100 B2 Ger.* Kopreinitz, *Hung.* Kaproncza. Koprivnica-Kri»zevci, N Croatia
Köprülü *see* Veles
Koptsevichi *see* Kaptsevichy
Kopyl' *see* Kapyl'
Korat *see* Nakhon Ratchasima
Korat Plateau *136 D4 plateau* E Thailand
Korba *135 E4* Chhattīsgarh, C India
Korça *see* Korçë
Korçë *101 D6 var.* Korça, *Gk.* Korytsa, *It.* Corriza; *prev.* Koritsa. Korçë, SE Albania
Korčula *100 B4 It.* Curzola; *anc.* Corcyra Nigra. *island* S Croatia
Korea Bay *127 G3 bay* China/North Korea
Korea, Democratic People's Republic of *see* North Korea
Korea, Republic of *see* South Korea
Korea Strait *131 A7 Jap.* Chōsen-kaikyō, *Kor.* Taehan-haehyŏp. *channel* Japan/South Korea
Korhogo *74 D4* N Côte d'Ivoire (Ivory Coast)
Korinthiakós Kólpos *105 B5 Eng.* Gulf of Corinth; *anc.* Corinthiacus Sinus. *gulf* C Greece
Kórinthos *105 B6 anc.* Corinthus *Eng.* Corinth. Pelopónnisos, S Greece
Koritsa *see* Korçë
Kōriyama *131 D5* Fukushima, Honshū, C Japan
Korla *126 C3 Chin.* K'u-erh-lo. Xinjiang Uygur Zizhiqu, NW China
Körmend *99 B7* Vas, W Hungary
Koróni *105 B6* Pelopónnisos, S Greece
Koror *144 A2 var.* Oreor. *country capital* (Palau) Oreor, N Palau
Kőrös *see* Križevci
Korosten' *108 D1* Zhytomyrs'ka Oblast', NW Ukraine
Koro Toro *76 C2* Borkou-Ennedi-Tibesti, N Chad
Korsovka *see* Kārsava
Kortrijk *87 A6 Fr.* Courtrai. West-Vlaanderen, W Belgium
Koryak Range *see* Koryakskoye Nagor'ye
Koryakskiy Khrebet *see* Koryakskoye Nagor'ye
Koryakskoye Nagor'ye *115 H2 var.* Koryakskiy Khrebet, *Eng.* Koryak Range. *mountain range* NE Russian Federation
Koryazhma *110 C4* Arkhangel'skaya Oblast', NW Russian Federation
Korytsa *see* Korçë
Kos *105 E6* Kos, Dodekánisa, Greece, Aegean Sea
Kos *105 E6 It.* Coo; *anc.* Cos. *island* Dodekánisa, Greece, Aegean Sea
Kō-saki *131 A7 headland* Nagasaki, Tsushima, SW Japan
Kościan *98 B4 Ger.* Kosten. Wielkopolskie, C Poland
Kościerzyna *98 C2* Pomorskie, NW Poland
Kosciusko, Mount *see* Kosciuszko, Mount
Kosciuszko, Mount *149 C7 prev.* Mount Kosciusko. *mountain* New South Wales, SE Australia
K'o-shih *see* Kashi
Koshikijima-rettō *131 A8 var.* Kosikizima Rettô. *island group* SW Japan
Kōshū *see* Kwangju
Košice *99 D6 Ger.* Kaschau, *Hung.* Kassa. Košický Kraj, E Slovakia
Kosikizima Rettô *see* Koshikijima-rettō
Köslin *see* Koszalin
Koson *123 E3 Rus.* Kasan. Qashqadaryo Viloyati, S Uzbekistan
Kosovo *101 D5 prev.* Autonomous Province of Kosovo and Metohija. *province* S Serbia
Kosovo and Metohija, Autonomous Province of *see* Kosovo
Kosovo Polje *101 D5* Kosovo, S Serbia
Kosovska Mitrovica *101 D5 Alb.* Mitrovicë; *prev.* Mitrovica, Titova Mitrovica. Kosovo, S Serbia
Kosrae *144 C2 prev.* Kusaie. *island* Caroline Islands, E Micronesia
Kossou, Lac de *74 D5 lake* C Côte d'Ivoire (Ivory Coast)
Kostanay *130 C4 var.* Kustanay, *Kaz.* Qostanay. Kustanay, N Kazakhstan
Kosten *see* Kościan
Kostenets *104 C2 prev.* Georgi Dimitrov. Sofiya, W Bulgaria
Kostnitz *see* Konstanz
Kostroma *110 B4* Kostromskaya Oblast', NW Russian Federation
Kostyantynivka *109 G3 Rus.* Konstantinovka. Donets'ka Oblast', SE Ukraine
Kostyukovichi *see* Kastsyukovichy
Kostyukovka *see* Kastsyukowka
Koszalin *98 B2 Ger.* Köslin. Zachodnio-pomorskie, NW Poland
Kota *134 D3 prev.* Kotah. Rājasthān, N India
Kota Baharu *see* Kota Bharu
Kota Bahru *see* Kota Bharu
Kotabaru *see* Jayapura
Kota Bharu *138 B3 var.* Kota Baharu, Kota Bahru. Kelantan, Peninsular Malaysia
Kotaboemi *see* Kotabumi
Kotabumi *138 B4 prev.* Kotaboemi. Sumatera, W Indonesia
Kotah *see* Kota
Kota Kinabalu *138 D3 prev.* Jesselton. Sabah, East Malaysia
Kotel'nyy, Ostrov *115 E2 island* Novosibirskiye Ostrova, N Russian Federation
Kotka *85 E5* Kymi, S Finland
Kotlas *110 C4* Arkhangel'skaya Oblast', NW Russian Federation
Kotonu *see* Cotonou
Kotor *101 C5 It.* Cattaro. SW Montenegro
Kotovs'k *108 D3 Rus.* Kotovsk. Odes'ka Oblast', SW Ukraine
Kotovsk *see* Hîncești
Kottbus *see* Cottbus
Kotte *see* Sri Jayawardanapura
Kotto *76 D4 river* Central African Republic/Dem. Rep. Congo
Kotuy *115 E2 river* N Russian Federation
Koudougou *75 E4* C Burkina Faso
Koulamoutou *77 B6* Ogooué-Lolo, C Gabon
Koulikoro *74 D3* Koulikoro, SW Mali
Koumra *76 C4* Moyen-Chari, S Chad
Kourou *59 H3* N French Guiana
Kousseir *see* Al Quşayr
Kousséri *76 B3 prev.* Fort-Foureau. Extrême-Nord, NE Cameroon
Koutiala *74 D4* Sikasso, S Mali
Kouvola *85 E5* Kymi, S Finland
Kovel' *108 C1 Pol.* Kowel. Volyns'ka Oblast', NW Ukraine
Kovno *see* Kaunas
Koweit *see* Kuwait
Kowel *see* Kovel'
Kowloon *128 A2* Hong Kong, S China
Kowno *see* Kaunas

Kozáni *104 B4* Dytikí Makedonía,
N Greece
Kozara *100 B3 mountain range*
NW Bosnia and Herzegovina
Kozarska Dubica *see* Bosanska Dubica
Kozhikode *see* Calicut
Kōzu-shima *131 D6 island* E Japan
Kozyatyn *108 D2. Rus.* Kazatin.
Vinnyts'ka Oblast', C Ukraine
Kpalimé *75 E5 var.* Palimé.
SW Togo
Krächéh *137 D6 prev.* Kratie. Krächéh,
E Cambodia
Kragujevac *100 D4* Serbia, C Serbia
Krainburg *see* Kranj
Kra, Isthmus of *137 B6 isthmus*
Malaysia/Thailand
Krakau *see* Kraków
Kraków *99 D5 Eng.* Cracow, *Ger.*
Krakau; *anc.* Cracovia.
S Poland
Králánh *137 D5* Siêmréab,
NW Cambodia
Kraljevo *100 D4 prev.* Rankovićevo.
Serbia, C Serbia
Kramators'k *109 G3 Rus.* Kramatorsk.
Donets'ka Oblast', SE Ukraine
Kramatorsk *see* Kramators'k
Kramfors *85 C5* Västernorrland,
C Sweden
Kranéa *see* Kraniá
Kraniá *104 B4 var* Kranéa. Dytikí
Makedonía, N Greece
Kranj *95 D7 Ger.* Krainburg.
NW Slovenia
Kranz *see* Zelenogradsk
Kräslava *106 D4* Krāslava, SE Latvia
Krasnaye *107 C5 Rus.* Krasnoye.
Minskaya Voblasts', C Belarus
Krasnoarmeysk *111 C6* Saratovskaya
Oblast', W Russian Federation
Krasnodar *111 A7 prev.* Ekaterinodar,
Yekaterinodar. Krasnodarskiy Kray,
SW Russian Federation
Krasnodon *109 H3* Luhans'ka Oblast',
E Ukraine
Krasnogor *see* Kallaste
Krasnogvardeyskoye *see*
Krasnohvardiys'ke
Krasnohvardiys'ke *109 F4 Rus.*
Krasnogvardeyskoye. Respublika
Krym, S Ukraine
Krasnokamensk *115 F4* Chitinskaya
Oblast', S Russian Federation
Krasnokamsk *111 D5* Permskaya
Oblast', W Russian Federation
Krasnoperekops'k *109 F4 Rus.*
Krasnoperekopsk. Respublika Krym,
S Ukraine
Krasnoperekopsk *see* Krasnoperekops'k
Krasnostav *see* Krasnystaw
Krasnovodsk *see* Türkmenbaşy
Krasnovodskiy Zaliv *see* Türkmenbasy
Aylagy
Krasnowodsk Aylagy *see* Türkmenbasy
Aylagy
Krasnoyarsk *114 D4* Krasnoyarskiy
Kray, S Russian Federation
Krasnoye *see* Krasnaye
Krasnystaw *98 E4 Rus.* Krasnostav.
Lubelskie, SE Poland
Krasnyy Kut *111 C6* Saratovskaya
Oblast', W Russian Federation
Krasnyy Luch *109 H3 prev.*
Krindachevka. Luhans'ka Oblast',
E Ukraine
Kratie *see* Krächéh
Krävanh, Chuŏr Phnum *137 C6 Eng.*
Cardamom Mountains, *Fr.* Chaîne
des Cardamomes. *mountain range*
W Cambodia
Krefeld *94 A4* Nordrhein-Westfalen,
W Germany
Kreisstadt *see* Krosno Odrzańskie
Kremenchug *see* Kremenchuk
**Kremenchugskoye Vodokhranilishche/
Kremenchuk Reservoir** *see*
Kremenchuts'ke Vodokhovyshche
Kremenchuk *109 F2 Rus.* Kremenchug.
Poltavs'ka Oblast', NE Ukraine
Kremenchuts'ke Vodoskhovyshche *109*
F2 Eng. Kremenchuk Reservoir, *Rus.*
Kremenchugskoye Vodokhranilishche.
reservoir C Ukraine
Kremenets' *108 C2 Pol.* Krzemieniec,
Rus. Kremenets. Ternopil's'ka Oblast',
W Ukraine
Kremennaya *see* Kreminna

Kreminna *109 G2 Rus.* Kremennaya.
Luhans'ka Oblast', E Ukraine
Kresena *see* Kresna
Kresna *104 C3 var.* Kresena.
Blagoevgrad, SW Bulgaria
Kretikon Delagos *see* Kritikó Pélagos
Kretinga *106 B3 Ger.* Krottingen.
Klaipėda, NW Lithuania
Kreutz *see* Cristuru Secuiesc
Kreuz *see* Risti
**Kreuzburg/Kreuzburg in
Oberschlesien** *see* Kluczbork
Krichëv *see* Krychaw
Krievija *see* Russian Federation
Krindachevka *see* Krasnyy Luch
Krishna *132 C1 prev.* Kistna. *river*
C India
Krishnagiri *132 C2* Tamil Nādu,
SE India
Kristiania *see* Oslo
Kristiansand *85 A6 var.* Christiansand.
Vest-Agder, S Norway
Kristianstad *85 B7* Skåne, S Sweden
Kristiansund *84 A4 var.* Christiansund.
Møre og Romsdal, S Norway
Kriti *105 C7 Eng.* Crete. *island* Greece,
Aegean Sea
Kritikó Pélagos *105 D7 var.* Kretikon
Delagos, *Eng.* Sea of Crete;
anc. Mare Creticum. *sea* Greece,
Aegean Sea
Krivoy Rog *see* Kryvyy Rih
Križevci *100 B2 Ger.* Kreuz, *Hung.*
Kőrös. Varaždin, NE Croatia
Krk *100 A3 It.* Veglia; *anc.* Curieta.
island NW Croatia
Kroatien *see* Croatia
Krolevets' *109 F1 Rus.* Krolevets.
Sums'ka Oblast', NE Ukraine
Krolevets *see* Krolevets'
Królewska Huta *see* Chorzów
Kronach *95 C5* Bayern, E Germany
Kronstadt *see* Braşov
Kroonstad *78 D4* Free State, C South
Africa
Kropotkin *111 A7* Krasnodarskiy Kray,
SW Russian Federation
Krosno *99 D5 Ger.* Krossen.
Podkarpackie, SE Poland
Krosno Odrzańskie *98 B3*
Ger. Crossen, Kreisstadt.
Lubuskie, W Poland
Krossen *see* Krosno
Krottingen *see* Kretinga
Krško *95 E8 Ger.* Gurkfeld;
prev. Videm-Krško. E Slovenia
Krugloye *see* Kruhlaye
Kruhlaye *107 D6 Rus.* Krugloye.
Mahilyowskaya Voblasts', E Belarus
Kruja *see* Krujë
Krujë *101 C6 var.* Kruja, *It.* Croia.
Durrës, C Albania
Krummau *see* Český Krumlov
Krung Thep *137 C5 var.* Krung Thep
Mahanakhon, *Eng.* Bangkok. *country
capital* (Thailand) Bangkok,
C Thailand
Krung Thep, Ao *137 C5 var.* Bight of
Bangkok. *bay* S Thailand
Krung Thep Mahanakhon *see* Krung
Thep
Krupki *107 D6 Rus.* Krupki. Minskaya
Voblasts', C Belarus
Krušné Hory *see* Erzgebirge
Krychaw *107 E7 Rus.* Krichëv.
Mahilyowskaya Voblasts', E Belarus
Krym *81 F4 peninsula* SE Ukraine
Europe
Kryms'ki Hory *109 F5 mountain range*
S Ukraine
Kryms'kyy Pivostriv *109 F5 peninsula*
S Ukraine
Krynica *99 D5 Ger.* Tannenhof.
Małopolskie, S Poland
Kryve Ozero *109 E3* Odes'ka Oblast',
SW Ukraine
Kryvyy Rih *109 F3 Rus.* Krivoy Rog.
Dnipropetrovs'ka Oblast', SE Ukraine
Krzemieniec *see* Kremenets'
Ksar al Kabir *see* Ksar-el-Kebir
Ksar al Soule *see* Er-Rachidia
Ksar-el-Kebir *70 C2 var.* Alcázar,
Ksar al Kabir, Ksar-el-Kébir, *Ar.*
Al-Kasr al-Kebir, Al-Qsar al-Kbir, *Sp.*
Alcazarquivir. NW Morocco
Ksar-el-Kébir *see* Ksar-el-Kebir
Kuala Dungun *see* Dungun

Kuala Lumpur *138 B3 country capital*
(Malaysia) Kuala Lumpur, Peninsular
Malaysia
Kuala Terengganu *138 B3 var.* Kuala
Trengganu. Terengganu, Peninsular
Malaysia
Kualatungkal *138 B4* Sumatera,
W Indonesia
Kuang-chou *see* Guangzhou
Kuang-hsi *see* Guangxi Zhuangzu Zizhiqu
Kuang-tung *see* Guangdong
Kuang-yuan *see* Guangyuan
Kuantan *138 B3* Pahang, Peninsular
Malaysia
Kuba *see* Quba
Kuban' *109 G5 var.* Hypanis. *river*
SW Russian Federation
Kubango *see* Cubango/Okavango
Kuching *138 C3 prev.* Sarawak. Sarawak,
East Malaysia
Küchnay Darweyshān *122 D5* Helmand,
S Afghanistan
Kuçova *see* Kuçovë
Kuçovë *101 C6 var.* Kuçova; *prev.* Qyteti
Stalin. Berat, C Albania
Kudara *see* Ghūdara
Kudus *138 C5 prev.* Koedoes. Jawa,
C Indonesia
Kuei-lin *see* Guilin
Kuei-Yang/Kuei-yang *see* Guiyang
K'u-erh-lo *see* Korla
Kueyang *see* Guiyang
Kugluktuk *53 E3 var.* Qurlurtuuq;
prev. Coppermine. Nunavut,
NW Canada
Kuhmo *84 E4* Oulu, E Finland
Kuhnau *see* Konin
Kühnö *see* Kihnu
Kuibyshev *see* Kuybyshevskoye
Vodokhranilishche
Kuito *78 B2 Port.* Silva Porto. Bié,
C Angola
Kuji *130 D3 var.* Kuzi. Iwate, Honshū,
C Japan
Kukës *101 D5 var.* Kukësi. Kukës,
NE Albania
Kukësi *see* Kukës
Kukong *see* Shaoguan
Kukukhoto *see* Hohhot
Kula Kangri *135 G3 var.* Kulhakangri.
mountain Bhutan/China
Kuldiga *106 B3 Ger.* Goldingen. Kuldiga,
W Latvia
Kuldja *see* Yining
Kulhakangri *see* Kula Kangri
Kullorsuaq *82 D2 var.* Kuvdlorssuak.
Kitaa, C Greenland
Kulm *see* Chełmno
Kulmsee *see* Chełmża
Külob *123 F3 Rus.* Kulyab.
SW Tajikistan
Kulpa *see* Kolpa
Kulu *116 C3* Konya, W Turkey
Kulunda Steppe *114 C4 Kaz.* Qulyndy
Zhazyghy, *Rus.* Kulundinskaya
Ravnina. *grassland* Kazakhstan/
Russian Federation
Kulundinskaya Ravnina *see* Kulunda
Steppe
Kulyab *see* Külob
Kum *see* Qom
Kuma *111 B7 river* SW Russian
Federation
Kumamoto *131 A7* Kumamoto,
Kyūshū, SW Japan
Kumanova *see* Kumanovo
Kumanovo *101 E5 Turk.* Kumanova.
N Macedonia
Kumasi *75 E5 prev.* Coomassie.
C Ghana
Kumayri *see* Gyumri
Kumba *77 A5* Sud-Ouest,
W Cameroon
Kumertau *111 D6* Respublika
Bashkortostan, W Russian Federation
Kumillä *see* Comilla
Kumo *75 G4* Gombi, E Nigeria
Kumon Range *136 B2 mountain range*
N Myanmar (Burma)
Kumul *see* Hami
Kunashiri *see* Kunashir, Ostrov
Kunashir, Ostrov *130 I1*
var. Kunashiri. *island* Kuril'skiye
Ostrova, SE Russian Federation
Kunda *106 E2* Lääne-Virumaa,
NE Estonia
Kunduz *see* Kondoz
Kunene *see* Cunene

Kungsbacka *85 B7* Halland, S Sweden
Kungur *111 D5* Permskaya Oblast',
NW Russian Federation
Kunlun Mountains *see* Kunlun Shan
Kunlun Shan *126 B4 Eng.* Kunlun
Mountains. *mountain range* NW China
Kunming *128 B6 var.* K'un-ming; *prev.*
Yunnan. *province capital* Yunnan,
SW China
K'un-ming *see* Kunming
Kununurra *146 D3* Western Australia
Kunya-Urgench *see* Köneurgench
Kuopio *85 E5* Kuopio, C Finland
Kupa *see* Kolpa
Kupang *139 E5 prev.* Koepang. Timor,
C Indonesia
Kup"yans'k *109 G2 Rus.* Kupyansk.
Kharkivs'ka Oblast', E Ukraine
Kupyansk *see* Kup"yans'k
Kür *see* Kura
Kura *117 H3 Az.* Kür, *Geor.* Mtkvari,
Turk. Kura Nehri. *river* SW Asia
Kura Nehri *see* Kura
Kurashiki *131 B6 var.* Kurasiki.
Okayama, Honshū, SW Japan
Kurasiki *see* Kurashiki
Kurdistan *117 F4 cultural region* SW Asia
Kürdzhali *104 D3 var.* Kirdzhali,
Kărdžali. Kürdzhali, S Bulgaria
Kure *131 B7* Hiroshima, Honshū,
SW Japan
Küre Dağları *116 C2 mountain range*
N Turkey
Kuressaare *106 C2 Ger.* Arensburg; *prev.*
Kingissepp. Saaremaa, W Estonia
Kureyka *112 D2 river* N Russian
Federation
Kurgan-Tyube *see* Qŭrghonteppa
Kuria Muria Islands *see* Ḩalāniyāt,
Juzur al
Kurile Islands *see* Kuril'skiye Ostrova
Kurile-Kamchatka Depression *see*
Kurile Trench
Kurile Trench *113 F3 var.* Kurile-
Kamchatka Depression. *trench*
NW Pacific Ocean
Kuril'sk *130 E1* Kuril'skiye Ostrova,
Sakhalinskaya Oblasts', SE Russian
Federation
Kuril'skiye Ostrova *115 H4 Eng.* Kurile
Islands. *island group* SE Russian
Federation
Ku-ring-gai *148 E1* New South Wales,
E Australia
Kurisches Haff *see* Courland Lagoon
Kurkund *see* Kilingi-Nõmme
Kurnool *132 C1 var.* Karnul. Andhra
Pradesh, S India
Kursk *111 A6* Kurskaya Oblast',
W Russian Federation
Kurskiy Zaliv *see* Courland Lagoon
Kuršumlija *101 D5* Serbia, S Serbia
Kurtbunar *see* Tervel
Kurtitsch/Kürtös *see* Curtici
Kuruktag *126 C3 mountain range*
NW China
Kurume *131 A7* Fukuoka, Kyūshū,
SW Japan
Kurupukari *59 F3* C Guyana
Kusaie *see* Kosrae
Kushiro *130 D2 var.* Kusiro. Hokkaidō,
NE Japan
Kushka *see* Serhetabat
Kusiro *see* Kushiro
Kuskokwim Mountains *36 C3*
mountain range Alaska, USA
Kustanay *see* Kostanay
Küstence/Küstendje *see* Constanţa
Kütahya *116 B3 prev.* Kutaia. Kütahya,
W Turkey
Kutai *see* Mahakam, Sungai
Kut'aisi *117 F2* W Georgia
Kut al 'Amārah *see* Al Kūt
Kut al Imara *see* Al Kūt
Kutaradja/Kutaraja *see* Bandaaceh
Kutch, Gulf of *see* Kachchh, Gulf of
Kutch, Rann of *see* Kachchh, Rann of
Kutina *100 B3* Sisak-Moslavina,
NE Croatia
Kutno *98 D3* Łódzkie, C Poland
Kuujjuaq *39 E2 prev.* Fort-Chimo.
Québec, E Canada
Kuusamo *84 E3* Oulu, E Finland
Kuvango *see* Cubango
Kuvdlorssuak *see* Kullorsuaq
Kuwait *120 C4 off.* State of Kuwait, *var.*
Dawlat al Kuwait, Koweit, Kuwet.
country SW Asia

KUWAIT
Southwest Asia

Official name State of Kuwait
Formation 1961 / 1961
Capital Kuwait City
Population 2.7 million / 392 people per sq mile (152 people per sq km) / 98%
Total area 6880 sq miles (17,820 sq km)
Languages Arabic*, English
Religions Sunni Muslim 45%, Shi'a Muslim 40%, Christian, Hindu, and other 15%
Ethnic mix Kuwaiti 45%, Other Arab 35%, South Asian 9%, Other 7%, Iranian 4%
Government Monarchy
Currency Kuwaiti dinar = 1000 fils
Literacy rate 83%
Calorie consumption 3010 calories

Kuwait *see* Al Kuwayt
Kuwait City *see* Al Kuwayt
Kuwait, Dawlat al *see* Kuwait
Kuwait, State of *see* Kuwait
Kuwajleen *see* Kwajalein Atoll
Kuwayt *120 C3* E Iraq
Kuweit *see* Kuwait
Kuybyshev *see* Samara
Kuybyshev Reservoir *see* Kuybyshevskoye Vodokhranilishche
Kuybyshevskoye Vodokhranilishche *111 C5 var.* Kuibyshev, *Eng.* Kuybyshev Reservoir. *reservoir* W Russian Federation
Kuytun *126 B2* Xinjiang Uygur Zizhiqu, NW China
Kuzi *see* Kuji
Kuznetsk *111 B6* Penzenskaya Oblast', W Russian Federation
Kuźnica *98 E2* Białystok, NE Poland
Kvaløya *84 C2 island* N Norway
Kvarnbergsvattnet *84 B4 var.* Frostviken. *lake* N Sweden
Kvarner *100 A3 var.* Carnaro, *It.* Quarnero. *gulf* W Croatia
Kvitøya *83 G1 island* NE Svalbard
Kwajalein Atoll *144 C1 var.* Kuwajleen. *atoll* Ralik Chain, C Marshall Islands
Kwando *see* Cuando
Kwangchow *see* Guangzhou
Kwangchu *see* Kwangju
Kwangju *129 E4 off.* Kwangju-gwangyŏksi, *var.* Guangju, Kwangchu, *Jap.* Kōshū. SW South Korea
Kwangju-gwangyŏksi *see* Kwangju
Kwango *77 C7 Port.* Cuango. *river* Angola/Dem. Rep. Congo
Kwango *see* Cuango
Kwangsi/Kwangsi Chuang Autonomous Region *see* Guangxi Zhuangzu Zizhiqu
Kwangtung *see* Guangdong
Kwangyuan *see* Guangyuan
Kwanza *see* Cuanza
Kweichu *see* Guiyang
Kweilin *see* Guilin
Kweisui *see* Hohhot
Kweiyang *see* Guiyang
Kwekwe *78 D3 prev.* Que Que. Midlands, C Zimbabwe
Kwesui *see* Hohhot
Kwidzyń *98 C2 Ger.* Marienwerder. Pomorskie, N Poland
Kwigillingok *36 C3* Alaska, USA
Kwilu *77 C6 river* W Dem. Rep. Congo
Kwito *see* Cuito
Kyabé *76 C4* Moyen-Chari, S Chad
Kyaikkami *137 B5 prev.* Amherst. Mon State, S Myanmar (Burma)
Kyaiklat *136 B4* Irrawaddy, SW Myanmar (Burma)
Kyaikto *136 B4* Mon State, S Myanmar (Burma)
Kyakhta *115 E5* Respublika Buryatiya, S Russian Federation
Kyaukse *136 B3* Mandalay, C Myanmar (Burma)
Kyjov *99 C5 Ger.* Gaya. Jihomoravský Kraj, SE Czech Republic
Kykládes *105 D6 var.* Kikládhes, *Eng.* Cyclades. *island group* SE Greece
Kými *105 C5* Évvoia, C Greece
Kyŏngsŏng *see* Sŏul
Kyōto *131 C6* Kyōto, Honshū, SW Japan
Kyparissía *105 B6 var.* Kiparissía. Pelopónnisos, S Greece
Kypros *see* Cyprus
Kyrá Panagía *105 C5 island* Vóreies Sporádes, Greece, Aegean Sea
Kyrenia *see* Girne
Kyrgyz Republic *see* Kyrgyzstan
Kyrgyzstan *123 F2 off.* Kyrgyz Republic, *var.* Kirghizia; *prev.* Kirgizskaya SSR, Kirghiz SSR, Republic of Kyrgyzstan. *country* C Asia

KYRGYZSTAN
Central Asia

Official name Kyrgyz Republic
Formation 1991 / 1991
Capital Bishkek
Population 5.3 million / 69 people per sq mile (27 people per sq km) / 33%
Total area 76,641 sq miles (198,500 sq km)
Languages Kyrgyz*, Russian*, Uzbek, Tatar, Ukrainian
Religions Muslim (mainly Sunni) 70%, Orthodox Christian 30%
Ethnic mix Kyrgyz 57%, Russian 19%, Uzbek 13%, Other 7%, Tatar 2%, Ukrainian 2%
Government Presidential system
Currency Som = 100 tyyn
Literacy rate 99%
Calorie consumption 2999 calories

Kyrgyzstan, Republic of *see* Kyrgyzstan
Kýthira *105 C7 var.* Kíthira, *It.* Cerigo, *Lat.* Cythera. *island* S Greece
Kýthnos *105 C6* Kńythnos, Kykládes, Greece, Aegean Sea
Kýthnos *105 C6 var.* Kíthnos, Thermiá, *It.* Termia; *anc.* Cythnos. *island* Kykládes, Greece, Aegean Sea
Kythréa *see* Değirmenlik
Kyūshū *131 B7 var.* Kyûsyû. *island* SW Japan
Kyushu-Palau Ridge *125 F3 var.* Kyusyu-Palau Ridge. *undersea ridge* W Pacific Ocean
Kyustendil *104 B2 anc.* Pautalia. Kyustendil, W Bulgaria
Kyûsyû *see* Kyūshū
Kyusyu-Palau Ridge *see* Kyushu-Palau Ridge
Kyyiv *109 E2 Eng.* Kiev, *Rus.* Kiyev. *country capital* (Ukraine) Kyyivs'ka Oblast', N Ukraine
Kyyivs'ke Vodoskhovyshche *109 E1 Eng.* Kiev Reservoir, *Rus.* Kiyevskoye Vodokhranilishche. *reservoir* N Ukraine
Kyzyl *114 D4* Respublika Tyva, C Russian Federation
Kyzyl Kum *122 D2 var.* Kizil Kum, Qizil Qum, *Uzb.* Qizilqum. *desert* Kazakhstan/Uzbekistan
Kyzylorda *114 B5 var.* Kzyl-Orda, Qizil Orda, Qyzylorda; *prev.* Perovsk. Kyzylorda, S Kazakhstan
Kyzylrabot *see* Qizilrabot
Kyzyl-Suu *123 G2 prev.* Pokrovka. Issyk-Kul'skaya Oblast', NE Kyrgyzstan
Kzyl-Orda *see* Kyzylorda

L

Laaland *see* Lolland
La Algaba *92 C4* Andalucía, S Spain
Laarne *87 B5* Oost-Vlaanderen, NW Belgium
La Asunción *59 E1* Nueva Esparta, NE Venezuela
Laatokka *see* Ladozhskoye, Ozero
Laâyoune *70 B3 var.* Aaiún. *country capital* (Western Sahara) NW Western Sahara
La Banda Oriental *see* Uruguay
la Baule-Escoublac *90 A4* Loire-Atlantique, NW France
Labé *74 C4* NW Guinea
Labe *see* Elbe
Laborca *see* Laborec
Laborec *99 E5 Hung.* Laborca. *river* E Slovakia
Labrador *39 F2 cultural region* Newfoundland and Labrador, SW Canada
Labrador Basin *34 E3 var.* Labrador Sea Basin. *undersea basin* Labrador Sea
Labrador Sea *82 A4 sea* NW Atlantic Ocean
Labrador Sea Basin *see* Labrador Basin
Labudalin *see* Ergun
Labutta *137 A5* Irrawaddy, SW Myanmar (Burma)
Laç *101 C6 var.* Laci. Lezhë, C Albania
La Calera *64 B4* Valparaíso, C Chile
La Carolina *92 D4* Andalucía, S Spain
Laccadive Islands/Laccadive Minicoy and Amindivi Islands, the *see* Lakshadweep
La Ceiba *52 D2* Atlántida, N Honduras
Lachanás *104 B3* Kentrikí Makedonía, N Greece
La Chaux-de-Fonds *95 A7* Neuchâtel, W Switzerland
Lachlan River *149 C6 river* New South Wales, SE Australia
Laci *see* Laç
la Ciotat *91 D6 anc.* Citharista. Bouches-du-Rhône, SE France
Lacobriga *see* Lagos
La Concepción *53 E5 var.* Concepción. Chiriquí, W Panama
La Concepción *58 C1* Zulia, NW Venezuela
La Condamine *91 C8* W Monaco
Laconia *41 G2* New Hampshire, NE USA
La Crosse *40 A2* Wisconsin, N USA
La Cruz *52 D4* Guanacaste, NW Costa Rica
Lādhiqīyah *118 A3 Eng.* Latakia, *Fr.* Lattaquié, *var.* Al Lādhiqīyah; *anc.* Laodicea, Laodicea ad Mare. Al Lādhiqīyah, W Syria
Ladoga, Lake *see* Ladozhskoye, Ozero
Ladozhskoye, Ozero *110 B3 Eng.* Lake Ladoga, *Fin.* Laatokka. *lake* NW Russian Federation
Ladysmith *40 B2* Wisconsin, N USA
Lae *144 B3* Morobe, W Papua New Guinea
Læsø *85 B7 island* N Denmark
La Esperanza *52 C2* Intibucá, SW Honduras
Lafayette *40 C4* Indiana, N USA
Lafayette *42 B3* Louisiana, S USA
La Fé *54 A2* Pinar del Río, W Cuba
Lafia *75 G4* Nassarawa, C Nigeria
la Flèche *90 B4* Sarthe, NW France
Lagdo, Lac de *76 B4 lake* N Cameroon
Laghouat *70 D2* N Algeria
Lagos *75 F5* Lagos, SW Nigeria
Lagos *92 B5 anc.* Lacobriga. Faro, S Portugal
Lagos de Moreno *51 E4* Jalisco, SW Mexico
Lagouira *70 A4* SW Western Sahara
La Grande *46 C3* Oregon, NW USA
La Guaira *66 B4* Distrito Federal, N Venezuela
Lagunas *64 B1* Tarapacá, N Chile
Lagunillas *61 G4* Santa Cruz, SE Bolivia
La Habana *54 B2 var.* Havana. *country capital* (Cuba) Ciudad de La Habana, W Cuba
Lahat *138 B4* Sumatera, W Indonesia
La Haye *see* 's-Gravenhage
Laholm *85 B7* Halland, S Sweden
Lahore *134 D2* Punjab, NE Pakistan
Lahr *95 A6* Baden-Württemberg, S Germany
Lahti *85 D5 Swe.* Lahtis. Etelä-Suomi, S Finland
Lahtis *see* Lahti
Laï *76 B4 prev.* Behagle, De Behagle. Tandjilé, S Chad
Laibach *see* Ljubljana
Lai Châu *136 D3* Lai Châu, N Vietnam
Laila *see* Laylā
La Junta *44 D5* Colorado, C USA
Lake Charles *42 A3* Louisiana, S USA
Lake City *43 E3* Florida, SE USA
Lake District *89 C5 physical region* NW England, UK
Lake Havasu City *48 A2* Arizona, SW USA
Lake Jackson *49 H4* Texas, SW USA
Lakeland *43 E4* Florida, SE USA
Lakeside *47 C8* California, W USA
Lake State *see* Michigan
Lakewood *44 D4* Colorado, C USA
Lakhnau *see* Lucknow
Lakonikós Kólpos *105 B7 gulf* S Greece
Lakselv *84 D2 Lapp.* Leavdnja. Finnmark, N Norway
Lakshadweep *132 A3 Eng.* Laccadive Islands. *island group* India, N Indian Ocean
la Laon *see* Laon
Lalibela *72 C4* Amhara, Ethiopia
La Libertad *52 B1* Petén, N Guatemala
La Ligua *64 B4* Valparaíso, C Chile
Lalín *92 C1* Galicia, NW Spain
Lalitpur *135 F3* Central, C Nepal
La Louvière *87 B6* Hainaut, S Belgium
la Maddalena *96 A4* Sardegna, Italy, C Mediterranean Sea
la Manche *see* English Channel
Lamar *44 D5* Colorado, C USA
La Marmora, Punta *97 A5 mountain* Sardegna, Italy, C Mediterranean Sea
La Massana *91 A8* La Massana, W Andorra Europe
Lambaréné *77 A6* Moyen-Ogooué, W Gabon
Lamego *92 C2* Viseu, N Portugal
Lamesa *49 E3* Texas, SW USA
Lamezia Terme *97 D6* Calabria, SE Italy
Lamía *105 B5* Stereá Ellás, C Greece
Lamoni *45 F4* Iowa, C USA
La Mosquitia *53 E3 var.* Miskito Coast, *Eng.* Mosquito Coast. *coastal region* E Nicaragua
Lampang *136 C4 var.* Muang Lampang. Lampang, NW Thailand
Lámpeia *105 B6* Dytikí Ellás, S Greece
Lanbi Kyun *137 B6 prev.* Sullivan Island. *island* Mergui Archipelago, S Myanmar (Burma)
Lancang Jiang *see* Mekong
Lancaster *89 D5* NW England, UK
Lancaster *47 C7* California, W USA
Lancaster *41 F4* Pennsylvania, NE USA
Lancaster Sound *37 F2 sound* Nunavut, N Canada
Lan-chou/Lan-chow/Lanchow *see* Lanzhou
Landao *see* Lantau Island
Landen *87 C6* Vlaams Brabant, C Belgium
Lander *44 C3* Wyoming, C USA
Landerneau *90 A3* Finistère, NW France
Landes *91 B5 cultural region* SW France
Landes *91 B5 department* SW France
Land of Enchantment *see* New Mexico
The Land of Opportunity *see* Arkansas
Land of Steady Habits *see* Connecticut
Land of the Midnight Sun *see* Alaska
Landsberg *see* Gorzów Wielkopolski, Lubuskie, Poland
Landsberg an der Warthe *see* Gorzów Wielkopolski
Land's End *89 B8 headland* SW England, UK
Landshut *95 C6* Bayern, SE Germany
Langar *123 E2 Rus.* Lyangar. Navoiy Viloyati, C Uzbekistan
Langfang *128 D4* Hebei, E China
Langkawi, Pulau *137 B7 island* Peninsular Malaysia
Langres *90 D4* Haute-Marne, N France
Langsa *138 A3* Sumatera, W Indonesia
Lang Shan *127 E3 mountain range* N China
Lang Sơn *136 D3 var.* Langson. Lang Sơn, N Vietnam
Langson *see* Lang Sơn
Lang Suan *137 B6* Chumphon, SW Thailand
Languedoc *91 C6 cultural region* S France
Länkäran *117 H3 Rus.* Lenkoran'. S Azerbaijan
Lansing *40 C3 state capital* Michigan, N USA
Lanta, Ko *137 B7 island* S Thailand
Lantau Island *128 A2 Cant.* Tai Yue Shan, *Chin.* Landao. *island* Hong Kong, S China
Lan-ts'ang Chiang *see* Mekong
Lantung, Gulf of *see* Liaodong Wan
Lanzarote *70 B3 island* Islas Canarias, Spain, NE Atlantic Ocean
Lanzhou *128 B4 var.* Lan-chou, Lanchow, Lan-chow; *prev.* Kaolan. *province capital* Gansu, C China
Lao Cai *136 D3* Lao Cai, N Vietnam
Laodicea/Laodicea ad Mare *see* Lādhiqīyah
Laoet *see* Laut, Pulau
Laojunmiao *see* Yumen
Laon *90 D3 var.* la Laon; *anc.* Laudunum. Aisne, N France

Lao People's Democratic Republic
see Laos
La Orchila, Isla *58 D1 island*
N Venezuela
La Oroya *60 C3* Junín, C Peru
Laos *136 D4 off.* Lao People's Democratic
Republic. *country* SE Asia

LAOS
Southeast Asia

Official name Lao People's Democratic
Republic
Formation 1953 / 1953
Capital Vientiane
Population 5.9 million / 66 people per
sq mile (26 people per sq km) / 24%
Total area 91,428 sq miles
(236,800 sq km)
Languages Lao*, Mon-Khmer, Yao,
Vietnamese, Chinese, French
Religions Buddhist 85%, Other (including
animist) 15%
Ethnic mix Lao Loum 66%, Lao
Theung 30%, Other 2%, Lao Soung 2%
Government One-party state
Currency New kip = 100 at
Literacy rate 69%
Calorie consumption 2312 calories

La Palma *53 G5* Darién, SE Panama
La Palma *70 A3 island* Islas Canarias,
Spain, NE Atlantic Ocean
La Paz *61 F4 var.* La Paz de Ayacucho.
country capital (Bolivia-legislative
and administrative capital) La Paz,
W Bolivia
La Paz *50 B3* Baja California Sur,
NW Mexico
La Paz, Bahía de *50 B3 bay*
W Mexico
La Paz de Ayacucho *see* La Paz
La Perouse Strait *130 D1 Jap.* Sōya-
kaikyō, *Rus.* Proliv Laperuza. *strait*
Japan/Russian Federation
Laperuza, Proliv *see* La Perouse Strait
Lápithos *see* Lapta
Lapland *84 D3 Fin.* Lappi, *Swe.*
Lappland. *cultural region* N Europe
La Plata *64 D4* Buenos Aires, E Argentina
La Plata *see* Sucre
Lappeenranta *85 E5 Swe.* Villmanstrand.
Etelä-Suomi, SE Finland
Lappi/Lappland *see* Lapland
Lappo *see* Lapua
Lapta *102 C5 Gk.* Lápithos.
NW Cyprus
Laptev Sea *see* Laptevykh, More
Laptevykh, More *115 E2 Eng.* Laptev
Sea. *sea* Arctic Ocean
Lapua *85 D5 Swe.* Lappo. Länsi-Soumi,
W Finland
Lapurdum *see* Bayonne
Łapy *98 E3* Podlaskie, NE Poland
La Quiaca *64 C2* Jujuy, N Argentina
L'Aquila *96 C4 var.* Aquila, Aquila degli
Abruzzi. Abruzzo, C Italy
Laracha *92 B1* Galicia, NW Spain
Laramie *44 C4* Wyoming, C USA
Laramie Mountains *44 C3 mountain
range* Wyoming, C USA
Laredo *93 E1* Cantabria, N Spain
Laredo *49 F5* Texas, SW USA
La Réunion *see* Réunion
Largeau *see* Faya
Largo *43 E4* Florida, SE USA
Largo, Cayo *54 B2 island* W Cuba
Lario *see* Como, Lago di
La Rioja *93 E2* La Rioja, NW Argentina
Lárisa *104 B4 var.* Larissa. Thessalía,
C Greece
Larissa *see* Lárisa
Lärkäna *134 B3 var.* Larkhana.
Sind, SE Pakistan
Larkhana *see* Lärkäna
Larnaca *see* Lárnaka
Lárnaka *102 C5 var.* Larnaca, Larnax.
SE Cyprus
Larnax *see* Lárnaka
la Rochelle *90 B4 anc.* Rupella.
Charente-Maritime, W France
la Roche-sur-Yon *90 B4*
prev. Bourbon Vendée, Napoléon-
Vendée. Vendée, NW France
La Roda *93 E3* Castilla-La Mancha,
C Spain
La Romana *55 E3* E Dominican Republic
Larvotto *91 C8* N Monaco Europe

La-sa *see* Lhasa
Las Cabezas de San Juan *92 C5*
Andalucía, S Spain
Las Cruces *48 D3* New Mexico, SW USA
La See d'Urgel *93 G1 var.* La Seu
d'Urgell, Seo de Urgel. Cataluña,
NE Spain
La Serena *64 B3* Coquimbo, C Chile
La Seu d'Urgell *see* La See d'Urgel
la Seyne-sur-Mer *91 D6* Var, SE France
Lashio *136 B3* Shan State,
E Myanmar (Burma)
Lashkar Gäh *122 D5 var.* Lash-Kar-Gar'.
Helmand, S Afghanistan
Lash-Kar-Gar' *see* Lashkar Gäh
La Sila *97 D6 mountain range* SW Italy
La Sirena *52 D3* Región Autónoma
Atlántico Sur, E Nicaragua
Łask *98 C4* Łódzkie, C Poland
Las Lomitas *64 D2* Formosa,
N Argentina
La Solana *93 E4* Castilla-La Mancha,
C Spain
Las Palmas *70 A3 var.* Las Palmas de
Gran Canaria. Gran Canaria, Islas
Canarias, Spain, NE Atlantic Ocean
Las Palmas de Gran Canaria *see* Las
Palmas
La Spezia *96 B3* Liguria, NW Italy
Lassa *see* Lhasa
Las Tablas *53 F5* Los Santos, S Panama
Last Frontier, The *see* Alaska
Las Tunas *54 C2 var.* Victoria de las
Tunas. Las Tunas, E Cuba
La Suisse *see* Switzerland
Las Vegas *47 D7* Nevada, W USA
Latacunga *60 B1* Cotopaxi, C Ecuador
la Teste *91 B5* Gironde, SW France
Latina *97 C5 prev.* Littoria. Lazio, C Italy
La Tortuga, Isla *59 E1 var.* Isla Tortuga.
island N Venezuela
La Tuque *39 E4* Québec, SE Canada
Latvia *106 C3 off.* Republic of Latvia,
Ger. Lettland, *Latv.* Latvija, Latvijas
Republika; *prev.* Latvian SSR, *Rus.*
Latviyskaya SSR. *country* NE Europe

LATVIA
Northeast Europe

Official name Republic of Latvia
Formation 1991 / 1991
Capital Riga
Population 2.3 million / 92 people per
sq mile (36 people per sq km) / 69%
Total area 24,938 sq miles
(64,589 sq km)
Languages Latvian*, Russian
Religions Lutheran 55%, Roman
Catholic 24%, Other 12%, Orthodox
Christian 9%
Ethnic mix Latvian 57%, Russian 32%,
Belarussian 4%, Ukrainian 3%, Polish 2%,
Other 2%
Government Parliamentary system
Currency Lats = 100 santims
Literacy rate 99%
Calorie consumption 2938 calories

Latvian SSR/Latvija/Latvijas
Republika/Latviyskaya SSR *see* Latvia
Latvia, Republic of *see* Latvia
Laudunum *see* Laon
Laudus *see* St-Lô
Lauenburg/Lauenburg in Pommern
see Lębork
Lau Group *145 E4 island group* E Fiji
Lauis *see* Lugano
Launceston *149 C8* Tasmania,
SE Australia
La Unión *52 C2* Olancho, C Honduras
La Unión *93 F4* Murcia, SE Spain
Laurel *42 C3* Mississippi, S USA
Laurel *44 C2* Montana, NW USA
Laurentian Highlands *see* Laurentian
Mountains
Laurentian Mountains *39 E3 var.*
Laurentian Highlands, *Fr.* Les
Laurentides. *plateau* Newfoundland
and Labrador/Québec, Canada
Laurentides, Les *see* Laurentian
Mountains
Lauria *97 D6* Basilicata, S Italy
Laurinburg *43 F1* North Carolina,
SE USA
Lauru *see* Choiseul
Lausanne *95 A7 It.* Losanna. Vaud,
SW Switzerland

Laut, Pulau *138 D4 prev.* Laoet. *island*
Borneo, C Indonesia
Laval *38 D4* Québec, SE Canada
Laval *90 B3* Mayenne, NW France
La Vall D'Uixó *93 F3 var.* Vall D'Uxó.
País Valenciano, E Spain
La Vega *55 E3 var.* Concepción de la
Vega. C Dominican Republic
La Vila Joiosa *see* Villajoyosa
Lávrio *105 C6 prev.* Lávrion. Attikí,
C Greece
Lávrion *see* Lávrio
Lawrence *41 G3* Massachusetts, NE USA
Lawrenceburg *42 C1* Tennessee, S USA
Lawton *49 F2* Oklahoma, C USA
La Yarada *61 E4* Tacna, SW Peru
Laylä *121 C5 var.* Laila. Ar Riyäḍ,
C Saudi Arabia
Lazarev *154 B1 sea* Antarctica
Lázaro Cárdenas *51 E5* Michoacán de
Ocampo, SW Mexico
Leal *see* Lihula
Leamhcán *see* Lucan
Leamington *38 C5* Ontario, S Canada
Leavdnja *see* Lakselv
Lebak *139 E3* Mindanao, S Philippines
Lebanon *45 G5* Missouri, C USA
Lebanon *41 G2* New Hampshire,
NE USA
Lebanon *46 B3* Oregon, NW USA
Lebanon *118 A4 off.* Republic of
Lebanon, *Ar.* Al Lubnän, *Fr.* Liban.
country SW Asia

LEBANON
Southwest Asia

Official name Republic of Lebanon
Formation 1941 / 1941
Capital Beirut
Population 3.6 million / 911 people per
sq mile (352 people per sq km) / 90%
Total area 4015 sq miles
(10,400 sq km)
Languages Arabic*, French, Armenian,
Assyrian
Religions Muslim 70%, Christian 30%
Ethnic mix Arab 94%, Armenian 4%,
Other 2%
Government Parliamentary system
Currency Lebanese pound = 100 piastres
Literacy rate 87%
Calorie consumption 3196 calories

Lebanon, Mount *see* Liban, Jebel
Lebanon, Republic of *see* Lebanon
Lebap *122 D2* Lebapskiy Velayat,
NE Turkmenistan
Lebedin *see* Lebedyn
Lebedyn *109 F2 Rus.* Lebedin. Sums'ka
Oblast', NE Ukraine
Lębork *98 C2 var.* Lębórk, *Ger.*
Lauenburg, Lauenburg in Pommern.
Pomorskie, N Poland
Lebrija *92 C5* Andalucía, S Spain
Lebu *65 A5* Bío Bío, C Chile
le Cannet *91 D6* Alpes-Maritimes,
SE France
Le Cap *see* Cap-Haïtien
Lecce *97 E6* Puglia, SE Italy
Lechaina *105 B6 var.* Lehena, Lekhainá.
Dytiki Elláis, S Greece
Ledo Salinarius *see* Lons-le-Saunier
Leduc *37 E5* Alberta, SW Canada
Leech Lake *45 F1* lake Minnesota, N USA
Leeds *89 D5* N England, UK
Leek *86 E2* Groningen, NE Netherlands
Leer *94 A3* Niedersachsen, NW Germany
Leeuwarden *86 D1 Fris.* Ljouwert.
Friesland, N Netherlands
Leeuwin, Cape *142 A5 headland*
Western Australia
Leeward Islands *55 G3 island group*
E West Indies
Leeward Islands Sotavento, Ilhas de
Lefkáda *105 A5 prev.* Levkás.
Lefkáda, Iónioi Nísoi, Greece,
C Mediterranean Sea
Lefkáda *105 A5 It.* Santa Maura, *prev.*
Levkás; *anc.* Leucas. *island* Lefkáda,
Iónioi Nísoi, Greece, C Mediterranean
Sea
Lefká Óri *105 C7 mountain range* Kriti,
Greece, E Mediterranean Sea
Lefkímmi *105 A5 var.* Levkímmi.
Kérkyra, Iónia Nisiá, Greece,
C Mediterranean Sea
Lefkosía/Lefkoşa *see* Nicosia
Legaceaster *see* Chester

Legaspi *see* Legazpi City
Legazpi City *139 E1 var.* Legaspi. Luzon,
N Philippines
Leghorn *see* Livorno
Legnica *98 B4 Ger.* Liegnitz.
Dolnośląskie, SW Poland
le Havre *90 B3 Eng.* Havre; *prev.* le
Havre-de-Gráce. Seine-Maritime,
N France
le Havre-de-Gráce *see* le Havre
Lehena *see* Lechainá
Leicester *89 D6 Lat.* Batae Coritanorum.
C England, UK
Leiden *86 B3 prev.* Leyden; *anc.*
Lugdunum Batavorum. Zuid-Holland,
W Netherlands
Leie *90 D2 Fr.* Lys. *river*
Belgium/France
Leinster *89 B6 Ir.* Cúige Laighean.
cultural region E Ireland
Leipsic *see* Leipzig
Leipsoí *105 E6 island* Dodekánisa,
Greece, Aegean Sea
Leipzig *94 C4 Pol.* Lipsk, *hist.* Leipsic;
anc. Lipsia. Sachsen, E Germany
Leiria *92 B3 anc.* Collipo. Leiria,
C Portugal
Leirvik *85 A6* Hordaland, S Norway
Lek *86 C4 river* SW Netherlands
Lekhainá *see* Lechainá
Lekhchevo *104 C2* Montana,
NW Bulgaria
Leksand *85 C5* Dalarna, C Sweden
Lel'chitsy *see* Lyel'chytsy
le Léman *see* Geneva, Lake
Lelystad *86 D3* Flevoland,
C Netherlands
Léman, Lac *see* Geneva, Lake
le Mans *90 B3* Sarthe, NW France
Lemberg *see* L'viv
Lemesós *102 C5 var.* Limassol.
SW Cyprus
Lemhi Range *46 D3 mountain range*
Idaho, C USA North America
Lemnos *see* Límnos
Lemovices *see* Limoges
Lena *115 F3 river* NE Russian Federation
Lena Tablemount *141 B7 seamount*
S Indian Ocean
Len Dao *128 C8 island* S Spratly Islands
Lengshuitan *see* Yongzhou
Leninabad *see* Khüjand
Leninakan *see* Gyumri
Lenine *109 G5 Rus.* Lenino. Respublika
Krym, S Ukraine
Leningor *see* Leninogorsk
Leningrad *see* Sankt-Peterburg
Leningradskaya *154 B4 Russian research*
station Antarctica
Lenino *see* Lenine
Leninobod *see* Khüjand
Leninogorsk *114 D4 Kaz.* Leningor.
Vostochnyy Kazakhstan, E Kazakhstan
Leninpol' *123 F2* Talasskaya Oblast',
NW Kyrgyzstan
Lenin-Turkmenski *see* Türkmenabat
Lenkoran' *see* Länkäran
Lenti *99 B7* Zala, SW Hungary
Lentia *see* Linz
Leoben *95 E7* Steiermark, C Austria
León *51 E4 var.* León de los Aldamas.
Guanajuato, C Mexico
León *52 C3* León, NW Nicaragua
León *92 D1* Castilla-León, NW Spain
León de los Aldamas *see* León
Leonídio *105 B6 var.* Leonídi.
Peloponnisos, S Greece
Leonídi *see* Leonídio
Léopold II, Lac *see* Mai-Ndombe, Lac
Léopoldville *see* Kinshasa
Lepe *92 C4* Andalucía, S Spain
Lepel' *see* Lyepyel'
le Portel *90 C2* Pas-de-Calais, N France
Le Puglie *see* Puglia
le Puy *91 C5 prev.* le Puy-en-Velay,
hist. Anicium, Podium Anicensis.
Haute-Loire, C France
le Puy-en-Velay *see* le Puy
Léré *76 B4* Mayo-Kébbi, SW Chad
Lérida *see* Lleida
Lerma *92 D2* Castilla-León, N Spain
Léros *105 D6 island* Dodekánisa, Greece,
Aegean Sea
Lerrnayin Gharabakh *see*
Nagorno-Karabakh
Lerwick *88 D1* NE Scotland, UK
Lesbos *see* Lésvos
Les Cayes *see* Cayes

Les Gonaïves *see* Gonaïves
Leshan *128 B5* Sichuan, C China
les Herbiers *90 B4* Vendée, NW France
Lesh/Leshi *see* Lezhë
Lesina *see* Hvar
Leskovac *101 E5* Serbia, SE Serbia
Lesnoy *114 C3* Sverdlovskaya Oblast', C Russian Federation
Lesotho *78 D4* *off.* Kingdom of Lesotho; *prev.* Basutoland. *country* S Africa

LESOTHO
Southern Africa

Official name Kingdom of Lesotho
Formation 1966 / 1966
Capital Maseru
Population 1.8 million / 154 people per sq mile (59 people per sq km) / 28%
Total area 11,720 sq miles (30,355 sq km)
Languages English*, Sesotho*, isiZulu
Religions Christian 90%, Traditional beliefs 10%
Ethnic mix Sotho 97%, European and Asian 3%
Government Parliamentary system
Currency Loti = 100 lisente
Literacy rate 81%
Calorie consumption 2638 calories

Lesotho, Kingdom of *see* Lesotho
les Sables-d'Olonne *90 B4* Vendée, NW France
Lesser Antarctica *154 A3* *var.* West Antarctica. *physical region* Antarctica
Lesser Antilles *55 G4* *island group* E West Indies
Lesser Caucasus *117 F2* *Rus.* Malyy Kavkaz. *mountain range* SW Asia
Lesser Khingan Range *see* Xiao Hinggan Ling
Lesser Sunda Islands *see* Nusa Tenggara
Lésvos *116 A3* *anc.* Lesbos. *island* E Greece
Leszno *98 B4* *Ger.* Lissa. Wielkopolskie, C Poland
Lethbridge *37 E5* Alberta, SW Canada
Lethem *59 F3* S Guyana
Leti, Kepulauan *139 F5* *island group* E Indonesia
Letpadan *136 B4* Pegu, SW Myanmar (Burma)
Letsôk-aw Kyun *137 B6* *var.* Letsutan Island; *prev.* Domel Island. *island* Mergui Archipelago, S Myanmar (Burma)
Letsutan Island *see* Letsôk-aw Kyun
Lettland *see* Latvia
Lëtzebuerg *see* Luxembourg
Leucas *see* Lefkáda
Leuven *87 C6* *Fr.* Louvain, *Ger.* Löwen. Vlaams Brabant, C Belgium
Leuze *see* Leuze-en-Hainaut
Leuze-en-Hainaut *87 B6* *var.* Leuze. Hainaut, SW Belgium
Léva *see* Levice
Levanger *84 B4* Nord-Trøndelag, C Norway
Levelland *49 E2* Texas, SW USA
Leverkusen *94 A4* Nordrhein-Westfalen, W Germany
Levice *99 C6* *Ger.* Lewentz, *Hung.* Léva, Lewenz. Nitriansky Kraj, SW Slovakia
Levin *150 D4* Manawatu-Wanganui, North Island, New Zealand
Levkás *see* Lefkáda
Levkímmi *see* Lefkímmi
Lewentz/Lewenz *see* Levice
Lewis, Isle of *88 B2* *island* NW Scotland, UK
Lewis Range *44 B1* *mountain range* Montana, NW USA
Lewiston *46 C2* Idaho, NW USA
Lewiston *41 G2* Maine, NE USA
Lewistown *44 C1* Montana, NW USA
Lexington *40 C5* Kentucky, S USA
Lexington *45 E4* Nebraska, C USA
Leyden *see* Leiden
Leyte *139 F2* *island* C Philippines
Leżajsk *99 E5* Podkarpackie, SE Poland
Lezha *see* Lezhë
Lezhë *101 C6* *var.* Lezha; *prev.* Lesh, Leshi. Lezhë, NW Albania
Lhasa *126 C5* *var.* La-sa, Lassa. Xizang Zizhiqu, W China
Lhaviyani Atoll *see* Faadhippolhu Atoll
Lhazê *126 C5* *var.* Quxar. Xizang Zizhiqu, China E Asia
L'Hospitalet de Llobregat *93 G2* *var.* Hospitalet. Cataluña, NE Spain
Liancourt Rocks *131 A5* *island group* Japan/South Korea Asia Sea of Japan
Lianyungang *128 D4* *var.* Xinpu. Jiangsu, E China
Liao *see* Liaoning
Liaodong Wan *127 G3* *Eng.* Gulf of Lantung, Gulf of Liaotung. *gulf* NE China
Liao He *125 E1* *river* NE China
Liaoning *128 D3* *var.* Liao, Liaoning Sheng, Shengking, *hist.* Fengtien, Shenking. *province* NE China
Liaoning Sheng *see* Liaoning
Liaoyuan *129 E3* *var.* Dongliao, Shuang-liao, *Jap.* Chengchiatun. Jilin, NE China
Liard *see* Fort Liard
Liban *see* Lebanon
Liban, Jebel *118 B4* *Ar.* Jabal al Gharbt, Jabal Lubnān, *Eng.* Mount Lebanon. *mountain range* C Lebanon
Libau *see* Liepāja
Libby *44 A1* Montana, NW USA
Liberal *45 E5* Kansas, C USA
Liberalitas Julia *see* Évora
Liberec *98 B4* *Ger.* Reichenberg. Liberecký Kraj, N Czech Republic
Liberia *52 D4* Guanacaste, NW Costa Rica
Liberia *74 C5* *off.* Republic of Liberia. *country* W Africa

LIBERIA
West Africa

Official name Republic of Liberia
Formation 1847 / 1847
Capital Monrovia
Population 3.3 million / 89 people per sq mile (34 people per sq km) / 45%
Total area 43,000 sq miles (111,370 sq km)
Languages English*, Kpelle, Vai, Bassa, Kru, Grebo, Kissi, Gola, Loma
Religions Christian 68%, Traditional beliefs 18%, Muslim 14%
Ethnic mix Indigenous tribes (16 main groups) 95%, Americo-Liberians 5%
Government Transitional regime
Currency Liberian dollar = 100 cents
Literacy rate 58%
Calorie consumption 1900 calories

Liberia, Republic of *see* Liberia
Libian Desert *see* Libyan Desert
Lībīyah, Aş Şahrā' al *see* Libyan Desert
Libourne *91 B5* Gironde, SW France
Libreville *77 A5* *country capital* (Gabon) Estuaire, NW Gabon
Libya *71 F3* *off.* Socialist People's Libyan Arab Jamahiriya, *Ar.* Al Jamāhīrīyah al 'Arabīyah al Lībīyah ash Sha'bīyah al Ishtirākīy; *prev.* Libyan Arab Republic. *country* N Africa

LIBYA
North Africa

Official name Great Socialist People's Libyan Arab Jamahariyah
Formation 1951 / 1951
Capital Tripoli
Population 5.9 million / 9 people per sq mile (3 people per sq km) / 88%
Total area 679,358 sq miles (1,759,540 sq km)
Languages Arabic*, Tuareg
Religions Muslim (mainly Sunni) 97%, Other 3%
Ethnic mix Arab and Berber 95%, Other 5%
Government One-party state
Currency Libyan dinar = 1000 dirhams
Literacy rate 82%
Calorie consumption 3320 calories

Libyan Arab Republic *see* Libya
Libyan Desert *71 H4* *var.* Libian Desert, *Ar.* Aş Şahrā' al Lībīyah. *desert* N Africa
Libyan Plateau *103 F4* *var.* Aḍ Ḍiffah. *plateau* Egypt/Libya
Lichtenfels *95 C5* Bayern, SE Germany
Lichtenvoorde *86 E4* Gelderland, E Netherlands
Lichuan *128 C5* Hubei, C China
Lida *107 B5* *Rus.* Lida. Hrodzyenskaya Voblasts', W Belarus
Lidhorikíon *see* Lidoríki
Lidköping *85 B6* Västra Götaland, S Sweden
Lidokhorikion *see* Lidoríki
Lidoríki *105 B5* *prev.* Lidhorikíon, Lidokhorikion. Stereá Ellás, C Greece
Lidzbark Warmiński *98 D2* *Ger.* Heilsberg. Olsztyn, N Poland
Liechtenstein *94 D1* *off.* Principality of Liechtenstein. *country* C Europe

LIECHTENSTEIN
Central Europe

Official name Principality of Liechtenstein
Formation 1719 / 1719
Capital Vaduz
Population 33,717 / 544 people per sq mile (211 people per sq km) / 21%
Total area 62 sq miles (160 sq km)
Languages German*, Alemannish dialect, Italian
Religions Roman Catholic 81%, Other 12%, Protestant 7%
Ethnic mix Liechtensteiner 62%, Foreign residents 38%
Government Parliamentary system
Currency Swiss franc = 100 rappen/centimes
Literacy rate 99%
Calorie consumption Not available

Liechtenstein, Principality of *see* Liechtenstein
Liège *87 D6* *Dut.* Luik, *Ger.* Lüttich. Liège, E Belgium
Liegnitz *see* Legnica
Lienz *95 D7* Tirol, W Austria
Liepāja *106 B3* *Ger.* Libau. Liepāja, W Latvia
Lietuva *see* Lithuania
Lievenhof *see* Līvāni
Liezen *95 D7* Steiermark, C Austria
Liffey *89 B6* *river* Ireland
Lifou *144 D5* *island* Îles Loyauté, E New Caledonia
Liger *see* Loire
Ligure, Appennino *96 A2* *Eng.* Ligurian Mountains. *mountain range* NW Italy
Ligure, Mar *see* Ligurian Sea
Ligurian Mountains *see* Ligure, Appennino
Ligurian Sea *96 A3* *Fr.* Mer Ligurienne, *It.* Mar Ligure. *sea* N Mediterranean Sea
Ligurienne, Mer *see* Ligurian Sea
Lihu'e *47 A7* *var.* Lihue. Kaua'i, Hawai'i, USA North America
Lihue *see* Līhu'e
Lihula *106 D2* *Ger.* Leal. Läänemaa, W Estonia
Liivi Laht *see* Riga, Gulf of
Likasi *77 D7* *prev.* Jadotville. Shaba, SE Dem. Rep. Congo
Liknes *85 A6* Vest-Agder, S Norway
Lille *90 C2* *var.* l'Isle, *Dut.* Rijssel, *Flem.* Ryssel, *prev.* Lisle; *anc.* Insula. Nord, N France
Lillehammer *85 B5* Oppland, S Norway
Lillestrøm *85 B6* Akershus, S Norway
Lilongwe *79 E2* *country capital* (Malawi) Central , W Malawi
Lilybaeum *see* Marsala
Lima *60 C4* *country capital* (Peru) Lima, W Peru
Limanowa *99 D5* Małopolskie, S Poland
Limassol *see* Lemesós
Limerick *89 A6* *Ir.* Luimneach. Limerick, SW Ireland
Limín Vathéos *see* Sámos
Límnos *103 F3* *anc.* Lemnos. *island* E Greece
Limoges *91 C5* *anc.* Augustoritum Lemovicensium, Lemovices. Haute-Vienne, C France
Limón *53 E4* *var.* Puerto Limón. Limón, E Costa Rica
Limón *52 D2* Colón, NE Honduras
Limonum *see* Poitiers
Limousin *91 C5* *region* C France
Limousin *91 C5* *cultural region* C France
Limoux *91 C6* Aude, S France
Limpopo *78 D3* *var.* Crocodile. *river* S Africa
Linares *64 B4* Maule, C Chile
Linares *51 E3* Nuevo León, NE Mexico
Linares *92 D4* Andalucía, S Spain
Lincoln *89 D5* *anc.* Lindum, Lindum Colonia. E England, UK
Lincoln *41 H2* Maine, NE USA
Lincoln *45 F4* *state capital* Nebraska, C USA
Lincoln Sea *34 D2* *sea* Arctic Ocean
Linden *59 F3* E Guyana
Líndhos *see* Líndos
Lindi *73 D8* Lindi, SE Tanzania
Líndos *105 E7* *var.* Líndhos. Ródos, Dodekánisa, Greece, Aegean Sea
Lindum/Lindum Colonia *see* Lincoln
Line Islands *145 G3* *island group* E Kiribati
Lingeh *see* Bandar-e Langeh
Lingen *94 A3* *var.* Lingen an der Ems. Niedersachsen, NW Germany
Lingen an der Ems *see* Lingen
Lingga, Kepulauan *138 B4* *island group* W Indonesia
Linköping *85 C6* Östergötland, S Sweden
Linz *95 D6* *anc.* Lentia. Oberösterreich, N Austria
Lion, Golfe du *91 C7* *Eng.* Gulf of Lion, Gulf of Lions; *anc.* Sinus Gallicus. *gulf* S France
Lion, Gulf of/Lions, Gulf of *see* Lion, Golfe du
Liozno *see* Lyozna
Lipari Islands/Lipari, Isole *see* Eolie, Isole
Lipari, Isola *97 D6* *island* Isole Eolie, S Italy
Lipetsk *111 B5* Lipetskaya Oblast', W Russian Federation
Lipno *98 C3* Kujawsko-pomorskie, C Poland
Lipova *108 A4* *Hung.* Lippa. Arad, W Romania
Lipovets *see* Lypovets'
Lippa *see* Lipova
Lipsia/Lipsk *see* Leipzig
Lira *73 B6* N Uganda
Lisala *77 C5* Equateur, N Dem. Rep. Congo
Lisboa *92 B4* *Eng.* Lisbon; *anc.* Felicitas Julia, Olisipo. *country capital* (Portugal) Lisboa, W Portugal
Lisbon *see* Lisboa
Lisichansk *see* Lysychans'k
Lisieux *90 B3* *anc.* Noviomagus. Calvados, N France
Liski *111 B6* *prev.* Georgiu-Dezh. Voronezhskaya Oblast', W Russian Federation
Lisle/l'Isle *see* Lille
Lismore *149 E5* Victoria, SE Australia
Lissa *see* Vis
Lissa *see* Leszno
Lisse *86 C3* Zuid-Holland, W Netherlands
Litang *128 A5* *var.* Gaocheng. Sichuan, C China
Lītani, Nahr el *135 B5* *var.* Nahr al Litant. *river* C Lebanon
Litant, Nahr al *see* Lītani, Nahr el
Litauen *see* Lithuania
Lithgow *149 D6* New South Wales, SE Australia
Lithuania *106 B4* *off.* Republic of Lithuania, *Ger.* Litauen, *Lith.* Lietuva, *Pol.* Litwa, *Rus.* Litva; *prev.* Lithuanian SSR, *Rus.* Litovskaya SSR. *country* NE Europe

LITHUANIA
Northeast Europe

Official name Republic of Lithuania
Formation 1991 / 1991
Capital Vilnius
Population 3.4 million / 135 people per sq mile (52 people per sq km) / 68%
Total area 25,174 sq miles (65,200 sq km)
Languages Lithuanian*, Russian
Religions Roman Catholic 83%, Other 12%, Protestant 5%
Ethnic mix Lithuanian 80%, Russian 9%, Polish 7%, Other 2%, Belarussian 2%
Government Parliamentary system
Currency Litas (euro is also legal tender) = 100 centu
Literacy rate 99%
Calorie consumption 3324 calories

Lithuanian SSR see Lithuania
Lithuania, Republic of see Lithuania
Litóchoro 104 B4 var. Litohoro,
  Litókhoron. Kentrikí Makedonía,
  N Greece
Litohoro/Litókhoron see Litóchoro
Litovskaya SSR see Lithuania
Little Alföld 99 C6 Ger. Kleines
  Ungarisches Tiefland, Hung. Kisalföld,
  Slvk. Podunajská Rovina. plain
  Hungary/Slovakia
Little Andaman 133 F2 island Andaman
  Islands, India, NE Indian Ocean
Little Barrier Island 150 D2 island
  N New Zealand
Little Bay 93 H5 bay S Gibraltar,
  Europe, Alboran Sea,
  Mediterranean Sea, Atlantic Ocean
Little Cayman 54 B3 island E Cayman
  Islands
Little Falls 45 F2 Minnesota, N USA
Littlefield 49 E2 Texas, SW USA
Little Inagua 54 D2 var. Inagua Islands.
  island S Bahamas
Little Minch, The 88 B3 strait
  NW Scotland, UK
Little Missouri River 44 D2 river
  NW USA
Little Nicobar 133 G3 island Nicobar
  Islands, India, NE Indian Ocean
Little Rhody see Rhode Island
Little Rock 42 B1 state capital Arkansas,
  C USA
Little Saint Bernard Pass 91 D5 Fr. Col
  du Petit St-Bernard, It. Colle del Piccolo
  San Bernardo. pass France/Italy
Little Sound 24 A5 bay Bermuda,
  NW Atlantic Ocean
Littleton 44 D4 Colorado, C USA
Littoria see Latina
Litva/Litwa see Lithuania
Liuzhou 128 C6 var. Liu-chou, Liuchow.
  Guangxi Zhuangzu Zizhiqu, S China
Livanátai see Livanátes
Livanátes 105 B5 prev. Livanátai. Stereá
  Ellás, C Greece
Livāni 106 D4 Ger. Lievenhof. Preiļi,
  SE Latvia
Liverpool 39 F5 Nova Scotia,
  SE Canada
Liverpool 89 C5 NW England, UK
Livingston 44 B2 Montana, NW USA
Livingston 49 H3 Texas, SW USA
Livingstone 78 C3 var. Maramba.
  Southern, S Zambia
Livingstone Mountains 151 A7
  mountain range South Island, New
  Zealand
Livno 100 B4 Federicija Bosna
  I Hercegovina, SW Bosnia and
  Herzegovina
Livojoki 84 D4 river C Finland
Livonia 40 D3 Michigan, N USA
Livorno 96 B3 Eng. Leghorn. Toscana,
  C Italy
Lixian Jiang see Black River
Lixoúri 105 A5 prev. Lixoúrion.
  Kefallinía, Iónia Nisiá, Greece,
  C Mediterranean Sea
Lixoúrion see Lixoúri
Lizarra see Estella
Ljouwert see Leeuwarden
Ljubelj see Loibl Pass
Ljubljana 95 D7 Ger. Laibach, It.
  Lubiana; anc. Aemona, Emona.
  country capital (Slovenia) C Slovenia
Ljungby 85 B7 Kronoberg, S Sweden
Ljusdal 85 C5 Gävleborg, C Sweden
Ljusnan 85 C5 river C Sweden
Llanelli 89 C6 prev. Llanelly.
  SW Wales, UK
Llanelly see Llanelli
Llanes 92 D1 Asturias, N Spain
Llanos 58 D2 physical region
  Colombia/Venezuela
Lleida 93 F2 Cast. Lérida; anc. Ilerda.
  Cataluña, NE Spain
Llucmajor 93 G3 Mallorca, Spain,
  W Mediterranean Sea
Loaita Island 128 C8 island
  W Spratly Islands
Loanda see Luanda
Lobatse 78 C4 var. Lobatsi. Kgatleng,
  SE Botswana
Lobatsi see Lobatse
Löbau 94 D4 Sachsen, E Germany
Lobito 78 B2 Benguela, W Angola

Lob Nor see Lop Nur
Lobositz see Lovosice
Loburi see Lop Buri
Locarno 95 B8 Ger. Luggarus. Ticino,
  S Switzerland
Lochem 86 E3 Gelderland, E Netherlands
Lockport 41 E3 New York, NE USA
Lodja 77 D6 Kasai Oriental, C Dem.
  Rep. Congo
Lodwar 73 C6 Rift Valley, NW Kenya
Łódź 98 D4 Rus. Lodz. Łódzkie,
  C Poland
Loei 136 C4 var. Loey, Muang Loei.
  Loei, C Thailand
Loey see Loei
Lofoten 84 B3 var. Lofoten Islands.
  island group C Norway
Lofoten Islands see Lofoten
Logan 44 B3 Utah, W USA
Logan, Mount 36 D3 mountain Yukon
  Territory, W Canada
Logroño 93 E1 anc. Vareia, Lat.
  Juliobriga. La Rioja, N Spain
Loibl Pass 95 D7 Ger. Loiblpass, Slvn.
  Ljubelj. pass Austria/Slovenia
Loiblpass see Loibl Pass
Loi-Kaw 136 B4 Kayah State,
  C Myanmar (Burma)
Loire 90 B4 var. Liger. river C France
Loja 60 B2 Loja, S Ecuador
Lokitaung 73 C5 Rift Valley, NW Kenya
Lokoja 75 G4 Kogi, C Nigeria
Loksa 106 E2 Ger. Loxa. Harjumaa,
  NW Estonia
Lolland 85 B8 prev. Laaland. island
  S Denmark
Lom 104 C1 prev. Lom-Palanka.
  Montana, NW Bulgaria
Lomami 77 D6 river C Dem. Rep. Congo
Lomas 60 D4 Arequipa, SW Peru
Lomas de Zamora 60 D4 Buenos Aires,
  E Argentina
Lombardia 96 B2 Eng. Lombardy.
  region N Italy
Lombardy see Lombardia
Lombok, Pulau 138 D5 island Nusa
  Tenggara, C Indonesia
Lomé 75 F5 country capital (Togo)
  S Togo
Lomela 77 D6 Kasai Oriental, C Dem.
  Rep. Congo
Lommel 87 C5 Limburg, N Belgium
Lomond, Loch 88 B4 lake C Scotland, UK
Lomonosov Ridge 155 B3 var. Harris
  Ridge, Rus. Khrebet Homonsova.
  undersea ridge Arctic Ocean
Lomonsova, Khrebet see Lomonosov
  Ridge
Lom-Palanka see Lom
Lompoc 47 B7 California, W USA
Lom Sak 136 C4 var. Muang Lom Sak.
  Phetchabun, C Thailand
Łomża 98 D3 Rus. Lomzha. Podlaskie,
  NE Poland
Lomzha see Łomża
Loncoche 65 B5 Araucanía, C Chile
Londinium see London
London 89 A7 anc. Augusta, Lat.
  Londinium. country capital
  (United Kingdom) SE England, UK
London 38 C5 Ontario, S Canada
London 40 C5 Kentucky, S USA
Londonderry 88 B4 var. Derry,
  Ir. Doire. NW Northern Ireland, UK
Londonderry, Cape 146 C2 cape
  Western Australia
Londrina 63 E4 Paraná, S Brazil
Lone Star State see Texas
Longa, Proliv 115 G1 Eng. Long Strait.
  strait NE Russian Federation
Long Bay 43 F2 bay W Jamaica
Long Beach 47 C7 California, W USA
Longford 89 B5 Ir. An Longfort.
  Longford, C Ireland
Long Island 54 D2 island C Bahamas
Long Island 41 G4 island New York,
  NE USA
Longlac 38 C3 Ontario, S Canada
Longmont 44 D4 Colorado,
  C USA
Longreach 148 C4 Queensland,
  E Australia
Long Strait see Longa, Proliv
Longview 49 H3 Texas, SW USA
Longview 46 B2 Washington,
  NW USA
Long Xuyên 137 D6 var. Longxuyen.
  An Giang, S Vietnam

Longxuyen see Long Xuyên
Longyan 128 D6 Fujian, SE China
Longyearbyen 83 G2 dependent
  territory capital (Svalbard) Spitsbergen,
  W Svalbard
Lons-le-Saunier 90 D4 anc. Ledo
  Salinarius. Jura, E France
Lop Buri 137 C5 var. Loburi. Lop Buri,
  C Thailand
Lop Nor see Lop Nur
Lop Nur 126 C3 var. Lob Nor, Lop Nor,
  Lo-pu Po. seasonal lake NW China
Loppersum 86 E1 Groningen,
  NE Netherlands
Lo-pu Po see Lop Nur
Lorca 93 E4 Ar. Lurka; anc. Eliocroca,
  Lat. Illurco. Murcia, S Spain
Lord Howe Island 142 C4 island
  E Australia
Lord Howe Rise 142 C4 undersea rise
  SW Pacific Ocean
Loreto 50 B3 Baja California Sur,
  W Mexico
Lorient 90 A3 prev. l'Orient. Morbihan,
  NW France
l'Orient see Lorient
Lorn, Firth of 88 B4 inlet W Scotland,
  UK
Loro Sae see East Timor
Lörrach 95 A7 Baden-Württemberg,
  S Germany
Lorraine 90 D3 region NE France
Lorraine 90 D3 cultural region
  NE France
Los Alamos 48 C1 New Mexico, SW USA
Los Amates 52 B2 Izabal, E Guatemala
Los Ángeles 65 B5 Bío Bío, C Chile
Los Angeles 47 C7 California, W USA
Losanna see Lausanne
Lošinj 100 A3 Ger. Lussin, It. Lussino.
  island W Croatia
Loslau see Wodzisław Śląski
Los Mochis 50 C3 Sinaloa, C Mexico
Losonc/Losontz see Lučenec
Los Roques, Islas 58 D1 island group
  N Venezuela
Lot 91 B5 department S France
Lot 91 B5 cultural region S France
Lot 91 B5 river S France
Lotagipi Swamp 73 C5 wetland
  Kenya/Sudan
Loualaba see Lualaba
Louangnamtha 136 C3 var. Luong Nam
  Tha. Louang Namtha, N Laos
Louangphabang 124 D3 var.
  Louangphrabang, Luang Prabang,
  Louanghabang, N Laos
Louangphrabang see Louangphabang
Loubomo see Dolisie
Loudéac 90 A3 Côtes d'Armor,
  NW France
Loudi 128 C5 Hunan, S China
Louga 74 B3 NW Senegal
Louisiade Archipelago 144 B4 island
  group SE Papua New Guinea
Louisiana 42 A2 off. State of Louisiana,
  also known as Creole State, Pelican
  State. state S USA
Louisville 40 C5 Kentucky, S USA
Louisville Ridge 143 E4 undersea ridge
  S Pacific Ocean
Loup River 45 E4 river Nebraska, C USA
Lourdes 91 B6 Hautes-Pyrénées, S France
Lourenço Marques see Maputo
Louth 89 E5 E England, UK
Loutrá 104 C4 Kentrikí Makedonía,
  N Greece
Louvain see Leuven
Louvain-la Neuve 87 C6 Walloon
  Brabant, C Belgium
Louviers 90 C3 Eure, N France
Lovech 104 C2 Lovech, N Bulgaria
Loveland 44 D4 Colorado, C USA
Lovosice 99 A4 Ger. Lobositz. Ústecký
  Kraj, NW Czech Republic
Lóvua 78 D1 Moxico, E Angola
Lowell 41 G3 Massachusetts, NE USA
Löwen see Leuven
Lower California see Baja California
Lower Hutt 151 D5 Wellington, North
  Island, New Zealand
Lower Lough Erne 89 A5 lake
  SW Northern Ireland, UK
Lower Red Lake 45 F1 lake Minnesota,
  N USA
Lower Rhine see Neder Rijn
Lower Tunguska see Nizhnyaya
  Tunguska

Lowestoft 89 E6 E England, UK
Loxa see Loksa
Lo-yang see Luoyang
Loyauté, Îles 144 D5 island group S New
  Caledonia
Loyev see Loyew
Loyew 107 D8 Rus. Loyev. Homyel'skaya
  Voblasts', SE Belarus
Loznica 100 C3 Serbia, W Serbia
Lu see Shandong
Lualaba 77 D6 Fr. Loualaba. river
  SE Dem. Rep. Congo
Luanda 78 A1 var. Loanda, Port. São
  Paulo de Loanda. country capital
  (Angola) Luanda, NW Angola
Luang Prabang see Louangphabang
Luang, Thale 137 C7 lagoon S Thailand
Luangua, Rio see Luangwa
Luangwa 73 B8 var. Rio Luangua. river
  Mozambique/Zambia
Luanshya 78 D2 Copperbelt, C Zambia
Luarca 92 C1 Asturias, N Spain
Lubaczów 99 E5 var. Lúbaczów.
  Podkarpackie, SE Poland
L'uban' 98 B4 Leningradskaya Oblast',
  Russian Federation
Lubānas Ezers see Lubāns
Lubango 78 B2 Port. Sá da Bandeira.
  Huíla, SW Angola
Lubāns 106 D4 var. Lubānas Ezers.
  lake E Latvia
Lubao 77 D6 Kasai Oriental, C Dem.
  Rep. Congo
Lübben 94 D4 Brandenburg, E Germany
Lübbenau 94 D4 Brandenburg,
  E Germany
Lubbock 49 E2 Texas, SW USA
Lübeck 94 C2 Schleswig-Holstein,
  N Germany
Lubelska, Wyżyna 98 E4 plateau
  SE Poland
Lüben see Lubin
Lubiana see Ljubljana
Lubin 98 B4 Ger. Lüben. Dolnośląskie,
  SW Poland
Lublin 98 E4 Rus. Lyublin. Lubelskie,
  E Poland
Lubliniec 98 C4 Śląskie, S Poland
Lubnán, Jabal see Liban, Jebel
Lubny 109 F2 Poltavs'ka Oblast',
  NE Ukraine
Lubsko 98 B4 Ger. Sommerfeld.
  Lubuskie, W Poland
Lubumbashi 77 E8 prev. Élisabethville.
  Shaba, SE Dem. Rep. Congo
Lubutu 77 D6 Maniema,
  E Dem. Rep. Congo
Luca see Lucca
Lucan 89 B5 Ir. Leamhcán. Dublin,
  E Ireland
Lucanian Mountains see Lucano,
  Appennino
Lucano, Appennino 97 D5
  Eng. Lucanian Mountains.
  mountain range S Italy
Lucapa 78 C1 var. Lukapa.
  Lunda Norte, NE Angola
Lucca 96 B3 anc. Luca. Toscana,
  C Italy
Lucea 54 A4 W Jamaica
Lucena 139 E1 off. Lucena City. Luzon,
  N Philippines
Lucena 92 D4 Andalucía, S Spain
Lucena City see Lucena
Lučenec 99 D6 Ger. Losontz, Hung.
  Losonc. Banskobystrický Kraj,
  C Slovakia
Lucentum see Alicante
Lucerna/Lucerne see Luzern
Luchow see Hefei
Łuck see Luts'k
Lucknow 135 E3 var. Lakhnau. state
  capital Uttar Pradesh, N India
Lüda see Dalian
Luda Kamchiya 104 D2 river E Bulgaria
Ludasch see Luduş
Lüderitz 78 B4 prev. Angra Pequena.
  Karas, SW Namibia
Ludhiāna 134 D2 Punjab, N India
Ludington 40 C2 Michigan, N USA
Ludsan see Ludza
Luduş 108 B4 Ger. Ludasch, Hung.
  Marosludas. Mureş, C Romania
Ludvika 85 C6 Dalarna, C Sweden
Ludwigsburg 95 B6 Baden-
  Württemberg, SW Germany
Lüdwigsfelde 94 D3 Brandenburg,
  NE Germany

Ludwigshafen *95 B5 var.* Ludwigshafen am Rhein. Rheinland-Pfalz, W Germany
Ludwigshafen am Rhein *see* Ludwigshafen
Ludwigslust *94 C3* Mecklenburg-Vorpommern, N Germany
Ludza *106 D4 Ger.* Ludsan. Ludza, E Latvia
Luebo *77 C6* Kasai Occidental, SW Dem. Rep. Congo
Luena *78 C2 var.* Lwena, *Port.* Luso. Moxico, E Angola
Lufira *77 E7 river* SE Dem. Rep. Congo
Lufkin *49 H3* Texas, SW USA
Luga *110 A4* Leningradskaya Oblast', NW Russian Federation
Lugano *95 B8 Ger.* Lauis. Ticino, S Switzerland
Lugansk *see* Luhans'k
Lugdunum *see* Lyon
Lugdunum Batavorum *see* Leiden
Lugenda, Rio *79 E2 river* N Mozambique
Luggarus *see* Locarno
Lugh Ganana *see* Luuq
Lugo *92 C1 anc.* Lugus Augusti. Galicia, NW Spain
Lugoj *108 A4 Ger.* Lugosch, *Hung.* Lugos. Timiş, W Romania
Lugos/Lugosch *see* Lugoj
Lugus Augusti *see* Lugo
Luguvallium/Luguvallum *see* Carlisle
Luhans'k *109 H3 Rus.* Lugansk; *prev.* Voroshilovgrad. Luhans'ka Oblast', E Ukraine
Luimneach *see* Limerick
Lukapa *see* Lucapa
Lukenie *77 C6 river* C Dem. Rep. Congo
Lukovit *104 C2* Lovech, N Bulgaria
Łuków *98 E4 Ger.* Bogendorf. Lubelskie, E Poland
Lukuga *77 D7 river* SE Dem. Rep. Congo
Luleå *84 D4* Norrbotten, N Sweden
Luleälven *84 C3 river* N Sweden
Lulonga *77 C5 river* NW Dem. Rep. Congo
Lulua *77 D7 river* S Dem. Rep. Congo
Luluabourg *see* Kananga
Lumber State *see* Maine
Lumbo *79 F2* Nampula, NE Mozambique
Lumsden *151 A7* Southland, South Island, New Zealand
Lund *85 B7* Skåne, S Sweden
Lüneburg *94 C3* Niedersachsen, N Germany
Lunga, Isola *see* Dugi Otok
Lungkiang *see* Qiqihar
Lungué-Bungo *78 C2 var.* Lungwebungu. *river* Angola/Zambia
Lungwebungu *see* Lungué-Bungo
Luninets *see* Luninyets
Łuniniec *see* Luninyets
Luninyets *107 B7 Pol.* Łuniniec, *Rus.* Luninets. Brestskaya Voblasts', SW Belarus
Lunteren *86 D4* Gelderland, C Netherlands
Luong Nam Tha *see* Louangnamtha
Luoyang *128 C4 var.* Honan, Lo-yang. Henan, C China
Lupatia *see* Altamura
Lúrio *79 F2* Nampula, NE Mozambique
Lúrio, Rio *79 E2 river* NE Mozambique
Lurka *see* Lorca
Lusaka *78 D2 country capital* (Zambia) Lusaka, SE Zambia
Lushnja *see* Lushnjë
Lushnjë *101 C6 var.* Lushnja. Fier, C Albania
Luso *see* Luena
Lussin/Lussino *see* Lošinj
Lut, Bahrat/Lut, Bahret *see* Dead Sea
Lut, Dasht e *120 D3 var.* Kavīr-e Lūt. *desert* E Iran
Lutetia/Lutetia Parisiorum *see* Paris
Lūt, Kavīr-e *see* Lut, Dasht-e
Luton *89 D6* E England, UK
Lutselk'e *37 F4 prev.* Snowdrift. Northwest Territories, W Canada
Luts'k *108 C1 Pol.* Łuck, *Rus.* Lutsk. Volyns'ka Oblast', NW Ukraine
Lutsk *see* Luts'k
Lüttich *see* Liège
Lützow-Holm Bay *see* Lützow Holmbukta
Lützow Holmbukta *154 C2 var.* Lutzow-Holm Bay. *bay* Antarctica

Luuq *73 D6 It.* Lugh Ganana. Gedo, SW Somalia
Luvua *77 D7 river* SE Dem. Rep. Congo
Luwego *73 C8 river* S Tanzania
Luxembourg *87 D8 country capital* (Luxembourg) Luxembourg, S Luxembourg
Luxembourg *87 D8 off.* Grand Duchy of Luxembourg, *var.* Lëtzebuerg, Luxembourg. *country* NW Europe

LUXEMBOURG
Northwest Europe

Official name Grand Duchy of Luxembourg
Formation 1867 / 1867
Capital Luxembourg-Ville
Population 465,000 / 466 people per sq mile (180 people per sq km)
Total area 998 sq miles (2586 sq km)
Languages Luxembourgish*, German*, French*
Religions Roman Catholic 97%, Protestant, Orthodox Christian, and Jewish 3%
Ethnic mix Luxembourger 73%, Foreign residents 27%
Government Parliamentary system
Currency Euro = 100 cents
Literacy rate 99%
Calorie consumption 3701 calories

Luxembourg *see* Luxembourg
Luxor *72 B2 Ar.* Al Uqsur. E Egypt
Luza *110 C4* Kirovskaya Oblast', NW Russian Federation
Luz, Costa de la *92 C5 coastal region* SW Spain
Luzern *95 B7 Fr.* Lucerne, *It.* Lucerna. Luzern, C Switzerland
Luzon *139 E1 island* N Philippines
Luzon Strait *125 E3 strait* Philippines/Taiwan
L'viv *108 B2 Ger.* Lemberg, *Pol.* Lwów, *Rus.* L'vov. L'vivs'ka Oblast', W Ukraine
L'vov *see* L'viv
Lwena *see* Luena
Lwów *see* L'viv
Lyakhavichy *107 B6 Rus.* Lyakhovichi. Brestskaya Voblasts', SW Belarus
Lyakhovichi *see* Lyakhavichy
Lyallpur *see* Faisalābād
Lyangar *see* Langar
Lyck *see* Ełk
Lycksele *84 C4* Västerbotten, N Sweden
Lycopolis *see* Asyūt
Lyel'chytsy *107 C7 Rus.* Lel'chitsy. Homyel'skaya Voblasts', SE Belarus
Lyepyel' *107 D5 Rus.* Lepel'. Vitsyebskaya Voblasts', N Belarus
Lyme Bay *89 C7 bay* S England, UK
Lynchburg *41 E5* Virginia, NE USA
Lynn *see* King's Lynn
Lynn Lake *37 F4* Manitoba, C Canada
Lynn Regis *see* King's Lynn
Lyon *91 D5 Eng.* Lyons; *anc.* Lugdunum. Rhône, E France
Lyons *see* Lyon
Lyozna *107 E6 Rus.* Liozno. Vitsyebskaya Voblasts', NE Belarus
Lypovets' *108 D2 Rus.* Lipovets. Vinnyts'ka Oblast', C Ukraine
Lys *see* Leie
Lysychans'k *109 H3 Rus.* Lisichansk. Luhans'ka Oblast', E Ukraine
Lyttelton *151 C6* Canterbury, South Island, New Zealand
Lyublin *see* Lublin
Lyubotin *see* Lyubotyn
Lyubotyn *109 G2 Rus.* Lyubotin. Kharkivs'ka Oblast', E Ukraine
Lyulyakovo *104 E2 prev.* Keremitlik. Burgas, E Bulgaria
Lyusina *107 B6 Rus.* Lyusino. Brestskaya Voblasts', SW Belarus
Lyusino *see* Lyusina

M

Maale *see* Male'
Ma'ān *119 B7* Ma'ān, SW Jordan
Maardu *106 D2 Ger.* Maart. Harjumaa, NW Estonia
Ma'aret-en-Nu'man *see* Ma'arrat an Nu'mān

Ma'arrat an Nu'mān *118 B3 var.* Ma'aret-en-Nu'man, *Fr.* Maarret enn Naamâne. Idlib, NW Syria
Maarret enn Naamâne *see* Ma'arrat an Nu'mān
Maart *see* Maardu
Maas *see* Meuse
Maaseik *87 D5 prev.* Maeseyck. Limburg, NE Belgium
Maastricht *87 D6 var.* Maestricht; *anc.* Traiectum ad Mosam, Traiectum Tungorum. Limburg, SE Netherlands
Macao *129 C6 Chin.* Aomen, *Port.* Macau. E Asia
Macapá *63 E1 state capital* Amapá, N Brazil
Macarsca *see* Makarska
Macassar *see* Makassar
Macău *see* Makó, Hungary
Macau *see* Macao
MacCluer Gulf *see* Berau, Teluk
Macdonnell Ranges *146 D4 mountain range* Northern Territory, C Australia
Macedonia *see* Macedonia, FYR
Macedonia, FYR *101 D6 off.* the Former Yugoslav Republic of Macedonia, *var.* Macedonia, *Mac.* Makedonija, *abbrev.* FYR Macedonia. *country* SE Europe

MACEDONIA
Southeast Europe

Official name Republic of Macedonia
Formation 1991 / 1991
Capital Skopje
Population 2 million / 201 people per sq mile (78 people per sq km) / 62%
Total area 9781 sq miles (25,333 sq km)
Languages Macedonian, Albanian, Serbo-Croat
Religions Orthodox Christian 59%, Muslim 26%, Other 10%, Roman Catholic 4%, Protestant 1%
Ethnic mix Macedonian 64%, Albanian 25%, Turkish 4%, Roma 3%, Other 2%, Serb 2%
Government Mixed presidential–parliamentary system
Currency Macedonian denar = 100 deni
Literacy rate 96%
Calorie consumption 2655 calories

Macedonia, the Former Yugoslav Republic of *see* Macedonia, FYR
Maceió *63 G3 state capital* Alagoas, E Brazil
Machachi *60 B1* Pichincha, C Ecuador
Machala *60 B2* El Oro, SW Ecuador
Machanga *79 E3* Sofala, E Mozambique
Machilipatnam *132 D1 var.* Bandar Masulipatnam. Andhra Pradesh, E India
Machiques *58 C2* Zulia, NW Venezuela
Macías Nguema Biyogo *see* Bioco, Isla de
Măcin *108 D5* Tulcea, SE Romania
Mackay *148 D4* Queensland, NE Australia
Mackay, Lake *146 C4 salt lake* Northern Territory/Western Australia
Mackenzie *37 E3 river* Northwest Territories, NW Canada
Mackenzie Bay *154 D3 bay* Antarctica
Mackenzie Mountains *36 D3 mountain range* Northwest Territories, NW Canada
Macleod, Lake *146 A4 lake* Western Australia
Macomb *40 A4* Illinois, N USA
Macomer *97 A5* Sardegna, Italy, C Mediterranean Sea
Mâcon *91 D5 anc.* Matisco, Matisco Ædourum. Saône-et-Loire, C France
Macon *42 D2* Georgia, SE USA
Macon *45 G4* Missouri, C USA
Macquarie Ridge *154 C5 undersea ridge* SW Pacific Ocean
Macuspana *51 G4* Tabasco, SE Mexico
Ma'dabā *119 B6 var.* Mādabā, Madeba; *anc.* Medeba, *Hebr.* Mādabā, NW Jordan
Mādabā *see* Ma'dabā
Madagascar *79 F3 off.* Democratic Republic of Madagascar, *Malg.* Madagasikara; *prev.* Malagasy Republic. *country* W Indian Ocean

MADAGASCAR
Indian Ocean

Official name Republic of Madagascar
Formation 1960 / 1960
Capital Antananarivo
Population 18.6 million / 83 people per sq mile (32 people per sq km) / 30%
Total area 226,656 sq miles (587,040 sq km)
Languages Malagasy*, French*
Religions Traditional beliefs 52%, Christian (mainly Roman Catholic) 41%, Muslim 7%
Ethnic mix Other Malay 46%, Merina 26%, Betsimisaraka 15%, Betsileo 12%, Other 1%
Government Presidential system
Currency Ariary = 5 iraimbilanja
Literacy rate 71%
Calorie consumption 2005 calories

Madagascar *79 F3 island* W Indian Ocean
Madagascar Basin *69 E7 undersea basin* W Indian Ocean
Madagascar, Democratic Republic of *see* Madagascar
Madagascar Plateau *69 E7 var.* Madagascar Ridge, Madagascar Rise, *Rus.* Madagaskarskiy Khrebet. *undersea plateau* W Indian Ocean
Madagascar Rise/Madagascar Ridge *see* Madagascar Plateau
Madagasikara *see* Madagascar
Madagaskarskiy Khrebet *see* Madagascar Plateau
Madang *144 B3* Madang, N Papua New Guinea
Madanīyīn *see* Médenine
Madarska *see* Hungary
Made *86 C4* Noord-Brabant, S Netherlands
Madeira *70 A2 var.* Ilha de Madeira. *island* Madeira, Portugal, NE Atlantic Ocean
Madeira, Ilha de *see* Madeira
Madeira Plain *66 C3 abyssal plain* E Atlantic Ocean
Madeira, Rio *62 D2 var.* Río Madera. *river* Bolivia/Brazil
Madeleine, Îles de la *39 F4 Eng.* Magdalen Islands. *island group* Québec, E Canada
Madera *47 B6* California, W USA
Madera, Río *see* Madeira, Rio
Madhya Pradesh *135 E4 prev.* Central Provinces and Berar. *state* C India
Madhya Pradesh *135 E4 prev.* Central Provinces and Berar. *cultural region* C India
Madinat ath Thawrah *118 C2 var.* Ath Thawrah. Ar Raqqah, N Syria Asia
Madioen *see* Madiun
Madison *45 F3* South Dakota, N USA
Madison *40 B3 state capital* Wisconsin, N USA
Madiun *138 D5 prev.* Madioen. Jawa, C Indonesia
Madoera *see* Madura, Pulau
Madona *106 D4 Ger.* Modohn. Madona, E Latvia
Madras *see* Chennai
Madras *see* Tamil Nādu
Madre de Dios *56 B4 off.* Departamento de Madre de Dios. *department* E Peru
Madre de Dios, Departamento de *see* Madre de Dios
Madre de Dios, Río *61 E3 river* Bolivia/Peru
Madre, Laguna *51 F3 lagoon* NE Mexico
Madre, Laguna *49 G5 lagoon* Texas, SW USA
Madrid *92 D3 country capital* (Spain) Madrid, C Spain
Madura *see* Madurai
Madurai *132 C3 prev.* Madura, Mathurai. Tamil Nādu, S India
Madura, Pulau *138 D5 prev.* Madoera. *island* C Indonesia
Maebashi *131 D5 var.* Maebasi, Mayebashi. Gunma, Honshū, S Japan
Maebasi *see* Maebashi
Mae Nam Khong *see* Mekong

Mae Nam Nan *136 C4 river* NW Thailand
Mae Nam Yom *136 C4 river* W Thailand
Maeseyck *see* Maaseik
Maestricht *see* Maastricht
Maéwo *144 D4 prev.* Aurora. *island* C Vanuatu
Mafia *73 D7 island* E Tanzania
Mafraq/Muḩāfaẓat al Mafraq *see* Al Mafraq
Magadan *115 G3* Magadanskaya Oblast', E Russian Federation
Magallanes *see* Punta Arenas
Magallanes, Estrecho de *see* Magellan, Strait of
Magangué *58 B2* Bolívar, N Colombia
Magdalena *61 F3* Beni, N Bolivia
Magdalena *50 B1* Sonora, NW Mexico
Magdalena *56 A2 off.* Departamento del Magdalena. *province* N Colombia
Magdalena, Departamento del *see* Magdalena
Magdalena, Isla *50 B3 island* W Mexico
Magdalena, Río *58 B2 river* C Colombia
Magdalen Islands *see* Madeleine, Îles de la
Magdeburg *94 C4* Sachsen-Anhalt, C Germany
Magelang *138 C5* Jawa, C Indonesia
Magellan, Strait of *65 B8 Sp.* Estrecho de Magallanes. *strait* Argentina/Chile
Magerøy *see* Magerøya
Magerøya *84 D1 var.* Magerøy, *Lapp.* Máhkarávju. *island* N Norway
Maggiore, Lago *see* Maggiore, Lake
Maggiore, Lake *96 B1 It.* Lago Maggiore. *lake* Italy/Switzerland
Maglaj *100 C3* Federacija Bosna I Hercegovina, N Bosnia and Herzegovina
Maglie *97 E6* Puglia, SE Italy
Magna *44 B4* Utah, W USA
Magnesia *see* Manisa
Magnitogorsk *114 B4* Chelyabinskaya Oblast', C Russian Federation
Magnolia State *see* Mississippi
Magta' Lahjar *74 C3 var.* Magta Lahjar, Magta' Lahjar, Magtá Lahjar. Brakna, SW Mauritania
Magtymguly *122 B3 prev.* Garrygala, *Rus.* Kara-Kala. *island* N Norway
Magwe *136 A3 var.* Magway. Magwe, W Myanmar (Burma)
Magyar-Becse *see* Bečej
Magyarkanizsa *see* Kanjiža
Magyarország *see* Hungary
Mahajanga *79 F2 var.* Majunga. Mahajanga, NW Madagascar
Mahakam, Sungai *138 D4 var.* Koetai, Kutai. *river* Borneo, C Indonesia
Mahalapye *78 D3 var.* Mahalatswe. Central, SE Botswana
Mahalatswe *see* Mahalapye
Māhān *120 D3* Kermān, E Iran
Mahanādi *135 F4 river* E India
Mahārāshtra *134 D5 state* W India
Mahārāshtra *134 D5 cultural region* W India
Mahbés *see* El Mahbas
Mahbūbnagar *134 D5* Andhra Pradesh, C India
Mahdia *71 F2 var.* Al Mahdīyah, Mehdia. NE Tunisia
Mahé *79 H1 island* Inner Islands, NE Seychelles
Mahia Peninsula *150 E4 peninsula* North Island, New Zealand
Mahilyow *107 D6 Rus.* Mogilëv. Mahilyowskaya Voblasts', E Belarus
Máhkarávju *see* Magerøya
Mahmūd-e 'Erāqī *see* Maḩmūd-e Rāqī
Maḩmūd-e Rāqī *123 E4 var.* Mahmūd-e 'Erāqī. Kāpīsā, NE Afghanistan
Mahón *93 H3 Cat.* Maó, *Eng.* Port Mahon; *anc.* Portus Magonis. Menorca, Spain, W Mediterranean Sea
Mährisch-Weisskirchen *see* Hranice
Maicao *58 C1* La Guajira, N Colombia
Mai Ceu/Mai Chio *see* Maych'ew
Maidstone *89 E7* SE England, UK
Maiduguri *75 H4* Borno, NE Nigeria
Mailand *see* Milano
Maimāna *see* Meymaneh
Main *95 B5 river* C Germany
Mai-Ndombe, Lac *77 C6 prev.* Lac Léopold II. *lake* W Dem. Rep. Congo
Maine *41 G2 off.* State of Maine, *also known as* Lumber State, Pine Tree State. *state* NE USA
Maine *90 B3 cultural region* NW France
Maine, Gulf of *41 H2 gulf* NE USA
Mainland *88 C2 island* N Scotland, UK
Mainland *88 D1 island* NE Scotland, UK
Mainz *95 B5 Fr.* Mayence. Rheinland-Pfalz, SW Germany
Maio *74 A3 var.* Mayo. *island* Ilhas de Sotavento, SE Cape Verde
Maisur *see* Mysore, India
Maisur *see* Karnātaka, India
Maizhokunggar *126 C5* Xizang Zizhiqu, W China
Maíz, Islas del *53 E3 var.* Corn Islands. *island group* SE Nicaragua
Majorca *see* Mallorca
Mājro *see* Majuro Atoll
Majunga *see* Mahajanga
Majuro Atoll *144 D2 var.* Mājro. *atoll* Ratak Chain, SE Marshall Islands
Makale *see* Mek'elē
Makarov Basin *155 B3 undersea basin* Arctic Ocean
Makarska *100 B4 It.* Macarsca. Split-Dalmacija, SE Croatia
Makasar *see* Makassar
Makasar, Selat *see* Makassar Straits
Makassar *139 E4 var.* Macassar, Makasar; *prev.* Ujungpandang. Sulawesi, C Indonesia
Makassar Straits *138 D4 Ind.* Makasar Selat. *strait* C Indonesia
Makay *79 F3 var.* Massif du Makay. *mountain range* SW Madagascar
Makay, Massif du *see* Makay
Makedonija *see* Macedonia, FYR
Makeni *74 C4* C Sierra Leone
Makeyevka *see* Makiyivka
Makhachkala *114 A4 prev.* Petrovsk-Port. Respublika Dagestan, SW Russian Federation
Makin *144 D2 prev.* Pitt Island. *atoll* Tungaru, W Kiribati
Makira *see* San Cristobal
Makiyivka *109 G3 Rus.* Makeyevka; *prev.* Dmitriyevsk. Donets'ka Oblast', E Ukraine
Makkah *121 A5 Eng.* Mecca. Makkah, W Saudi Arabia
Makkovik *39 F2* Newfoundland and Labrador, NE Canada
Makó *99 D7 Rom.* Macău. Csongrád, SE Hungary
Makoua *77 B5* Cuvette, C Congo
Makran Coast *120 E4 coastal region* SE Iran
Makrany *107 A6 Rus.* Mokrany. Brestskaya Voblasts', SW Belarus
Mākū *120 B2* Āzarbāyjān-e Gharbī, NW Iran
Makurdi *75 G4* Benue, C Nigeria
Mala *see* Malaita, Solomon Islands
Malabār Coast *132 B3 coast* SW India
Malabo *77 A5 prev.* Santa Isabel. *country capital* (Equatorial Guinea) Isla de Bioco, NW Equatorial Guinea
Malaca *see* Málaga
Malacca, Strait of *138 B3 Ind.* Selat Malaka. *strait* Indonesia/Malaysia
Malacka *see* Malacky
Malacky *99 C6 Hung.* Malacka. Bratislavský Kraj, W Slovakia
Maladzyechna *107 C5 Pol.* Molodeczno, *Rus.* Molodechno. Minskaya Voblasts', C Belarus
Málaga *92 D5 anc.* Malaca. Andalucía, S Spain
Malagarasi River *73 B7 river* W Tanzania Africa
Malagasy Republic *see* Madagascar
Malaita *144 C3 var.* Mala. *island* N Solomon Islands
Malakal *73 B5* Upper Nile, S Sudan
Malakula *see* Malekula
Malang *138 D5* Jawa, C Indonesia
Malange *see* Malanje
Malanje *78 B1 var.* Malange. Malanje, NW Angola
Mälaren *85 C6 lake* C Sweden
Malatya *117 E4 anc.* Melitene. Malatya, SE Turkey
Mala Vyska *109 E3 Rus.* Malaya Viska. Kirovohrads'ka Oblast', S Ukraine
Malawi *79 E1 off.* Republic of Malaŵi; *prev.* Nyasaland, Nyasaland Protectorate. *country* S Africa

MALAWI
Southern Africa

Official name Republic of Malawi
Formation 1964 / 1964
Capital Lilongwe
Population 12.9 million / 355 people per sq mile (137 people per sq km) / 25%
Total area 45,745 sq miles (118,480 sq km)
Languages English*, Chewa*, Lomwe, Yao, Ngoni
Religions Protestant 55%, Roman Catholic 20%, Muslim 20%, Traditional beliefs 5%
Ethnic mix Bantu 99%, Other 1%
Government Presidential system
Currency Malawi kwacha = 100 tambala
Literacy rate 64%
Calorie consumption 2155 calories

Malawi, Lake *see* Nyasa, Lake
Malaŵi, Republic of *see* Malawi
Malaya Viska *see* Mala Vyska
Malay Peninsula *124 D4 peninsula* Malaysia/Thailand
Malaysia *138 B3 var.* Federation of Malaysia; *prev.* the separate territories of Federation of Malaya, Sarawak and Sabah (North Borneo) and Singapore. *country* SE Asia

MALAYSIA
Southeast Asia

Official name Federation of Malaysia
Formation 1963 / 1965
Capital Kuala Lumpur; Putrajaya (administrative)
Population 25.3 million / 199 people per sq mile (77 people per sq km) / 57%
Total area 127,316 sq miles (329,750 sq km)
Languages Malay*, Chinese*, Bahasa Malaysia, Tamil, English
Religions Muslim (mainly Sunni) 53%, Buddhist 19%, Chinese faiths 12%, Other 7%, Christian 7%, Traditional beliefs 2%
Ethnic mix Malay 48%, Chinese 29%, Indigenous tribes 12%, Indian 6%, Other 5%
Government Parliamentary system
Currency Ringgit = 100 sen
Literacy rate 89%
Calorie consumption 2881 calories

Malaysia, Federation of *see* Malaysia
Malbork *98 C2 Ger.* Marienburg, Marienburg in Westpreussen. Pomorskie, N Poland
Malchin *94 C3* Mecklenburg-Vorpommern, N Germany
Malden *45 H5* Missouri, C USA
Malden Island *145 G3 prev.* Independence Island. *atoll* E Kiribati
Maldives *132 A4 off.* Maldivian Divehi, Republic of Maldives. *country* N Indian Ocean

MALDIVES
Indian Ocean

Official name Republic of Maldives
Formation 1965 / 1965
Capital Male'
Population 329,000 / 2836 people per sq mile (1097 people per sq km) / 30%
Total area 116 sq miles (300 sq km)
Languages Dhivehi (Maldivian)*, Sinhala, Tamil, Arabic
Religions Sunni Muslim 100%
Ethnic mix Arab–Sinhalese–Malay 100%
Government Nonparty system
Currency Rufiyaa = 100 lari
Literacy rate 97%
Calorie consumption 2548 calories

Maldives, Republic of *see* Maldives
Maldivian Divehi *see* Maldives
Male' *132 B4 Div.* Maale. *country capital* (Maldives) Male' Atoll, C Maldives
Male' Atoll *132 B4 var.* Kaafu Atoll. *atoll* C Maldives
Malekula *144 D4 var.* Malakula; *prev.* Mallicolo. *island* W Vanuatu
Malesína *105 C5* Stereá Ellás, E Greece
Malheur Lake *46 C3 lake* Oregon, NW USA
Mali *75 E3 off.* Republic of Mali, *Fr.* République du Mali; *prev.* French Sudan, Sudanese Republic. *country* W Africa

MALI
West Africa

Official name Republic of Mali
Formation 1960 / 1960
Capital Bamako
Population 13.5 million / 29 people per sq mile (11 people per sq km) / 30%
Total area 478,764 sq miles (1,240,000 sq km)
Languages French*, Bambara, Fulani, Senufo, Soninke
Religions Muslim (mainly Sunni) 80%, Traditional beliefs 18%, Christian 1%, Other 1%
Ethnic mix Bambara 32%, Other 26%, Fulani 14%, Senufu 12%, Soninka 9%, Tuareg 7%
Government Presidential system
Currency CFA franc = 100 centimes
Literacy rate 19%
Calorie consumption 2174 calories

Malik, Wadi al *see* Milk, Wadi el
Mali Kyun *137 B5 var.* Tavoy Island. *island* Mergui Archipelago, S Myanmar (Burma)
Malin *see* Malyn
Malindi *73 D7* Coast, SE Kenya
Malines *see* Mechelen
Mali, Republic of *see* Mali
Mali, République du *see* Mali
Malkiye *see* Al Mālikīyah
Malko Tŭrnovo *104 E3* Burgas, E Bulgaria
Mallaig *88 B3* N Scotland, UK
Mallawi *72 B2* C Egypt
Mallicolo *see* Malekula
Mallorca *93 G3 Eng.* Majorca; *anc.* Baleares Major. *island* Islas Baleares, Spain, W Mediterranean Sea
Malmberget *84 C3 Lapp.* Malmivaara. Norrbotten, N Sweden
Malmédy *87 D6* Liège, E Belgium
Malmivaara *see* Malmberget
Malmö *85 B7* Skåne, S Sweden
Maļoeļap *see* Maloelap Atoll
Maloelap Atoll *144 D1 var.* Maļoeļap. *atoll* E Marshall Islands
Małopolska, Wyżyna *98 D4 plateau* S Poland
Malozemel'skaya Tundra *110 D3 physical region* NW Russian Federation
Malta *106 D4* Rēzekne, SE Latvia
Malta *44 C1* Montana, NW USA
Malta *97 C8 off.* Republic of Malta. *country* C Mediterranean Sea

MALTA
Southern Europe

Official name Republic of Malta
Formation 1964 / 1964
Capital Valletta
Population 402,000 / 3242 people per sq mile (1256 people per sq km) / 91%
Total area 122 sq miles (316 sq km)
Languages Maltese*, English
Religions Roman Catholic 98%, Other and nonreligious 2%
Ethnic mix Maltese 96%, Other 4%
Government Parliamentary system
Currency Maltese lira = 100 cents
Literacy rate 88%
Calorie consumption 3587 calories

Malta *97 C8 island* Malta, C Mediterrnean Sea
Malta, Canale di *see* Malta Channel
Malta Channel *97 C8 It.* Canale di Malta. *strait* Italy/Malta
Malta, Republic of *see* Malta
Maluku *139 F4 Dut.* Molukken, *Eng.* Moluccas; *prev.* Spice Islands. *island group* E Indonesia
Maluku, Laut *see* Molucca Sea
Malung *85 B6* Dalarna, C Sweden

Malventum *see* Benevento
Malvinas, Islas *see* Falkland Islands
Malyn *108 D2* *Rus.* Malin. Zhytomyrs'ka Oblast', N Ukraine
Malyy Kavkaz *see* Lesser Caucasus
Mamberamo, Sungai *139 H4* *river* Papua, E Indonesia
Mambij *see* Manbij
Mamonovo *106 A4* *Ger.* Heiligenbeil. Kaliningradskaya Oblast', W Russian Federation
Mamoré, Rio *61 F3* *river* Bolivia/Brazil
Mamou *74 C4* W Guinea
Mamoudzou *79 F2* *dependent territory capital* (Mayotte) C Mayotte
Mamuno *78 C3* Ghanzi, W Botswana
Manacor *93 G3* Mallorca, Spain, W Mediterranean Sea
Manado *139 F3* *prev.* Menado. Sulawesi, C Indonesia
Managua *52 D3* *country capital* (Nicaragua) Managua, W Nicaragua
Managua, Lago de *52 C3* *var.* Xolotlán. *lake* W Nicaragua
Manakara *79 G4* Fianarantsoa, SE Madagascar
Manama *see* Al Manāmah
Mananjary *79 G3* Fianarantsoa, SE Madagascar
Manáos *see* Manaus
Manapouri, Lake *151 A7* *lake* South Island, New Zealand
Manar *see* Mannar
Manas, Gora *123 E2* *mountain* Kyrgyzstan/Uzbekistan
Manaus *62 D2* *prev.* Manáos. *state capital* Amazonas, NW Brazil
Manavgat *116 B4* Antalya, SW Turkey
Manbij *118 C2* *var.* Mambij, *Fr.* Membidj. Ḥalab, N Syria
Manchester *89 D5* *Lat.* Mancunium. NW England, UK
Manchester *41 G3* New Hampshire, NE USA
Man-chou-li *see* Manzhouli
Manchurian Plain *125 E1* *plain* NE China
Máncio Lima *see* Japiim
Mancunium *see* Manchester
Mand *see* Mand, Rūd-e
Mandalay *136 B3* Mandalay, C Myanmar (Burma)
Mandan *45 E2* North Dakota, N USA
Mandeville *54 B5* C Jamaica
Mándra *105 C6* Attikí, C Greece
Mand, Rūd-e *120 D4* *var.* Mand. *river* S Iran
Mandurah *147 A6* Western Australia
Manduria *97 E5* Puglia, SE Italy
Mandya *132 C2* Karnātaka, C India
Manfredonia *97 D5* Puglia, SE Italy
Mangai *77 C6* Bandundu, W Dem. Rep. Congo
Mangaia *145 G5* *island group* S Cook Islands
Mangalia *108 D5* *anc.* Callatis. Constanța, SE Romania
Mangalmé *76 C3* Guéra, SE Chad
Mangalore *132 B2* Karnātaka, W India
Mangaung *see* Bloemfontein
Mango *see* Sansanné-Mango, Togo
Mangoky *79 F3* *river* W Madagascar
Manhattan *45 F4* Kansas, C USA
Manicouagan, Réservoir *38 D3* *lake* Québec, E Canada
Manihiki *145 G4* *atoll* N Cook Islands
Manihiki Plateau *143 E3* *undersea plateau* C Pacific Ocean
Maniitsoq *82 C3* *var.* Manîtsoq, *Dan.* Sukkertoppen. Kitaa, S Greenland
Manila *139 E1* *off.* City of Manila. *country capital* (Philippines) Luzon, N Philippines
Manila, City of *see* Manila
Manisa *116 A3* *var.* Manissa, *prev.* Saruhan; *anc.* Magnesia. Manisa, W Turkey
Manissa *see* Manisa
Manitoba *37 F5* *province* S Canada
Manitoba, Lake *37 F5* *lake* Manitoba, S Canada
Manitoulin Island *38 C4* *island* Ontario, S Canada
Manîtsoq *see* Maniitsoq
Manizales *58 B3* Caldas, W Colombia
Manjimup *147 A7* Western Australia
Mankato *45 F3* Minnesota, N USA
Manlleu *93 G2* Cataluña, NE Spain
Manly *148 E1* Iowa, C USA
Manmād *134 C5* Mahārāshtra, W India
Mannar *132 C3* *var.* Manar. Northern Province, NW Sri Lanka
Mannar, Gulf of *132 C3* *gulf* India/Sri Lanka
Mannheim *95 B5* Baden-Württemberg, SW Germany
Manokwari *139 G4* Papua, E Indonesia
Manono *77 E7* Shabo, SE Dem. Rep. Congo
Manosque *91 D6* Alpes-de-Haute-Provence, SE France
Manra *145 F3* *prev.* Sydney Island. *atoll* Phoenix Islands, C Kiribati
Mansa *78 D2* *prev.* Fort Rosebery. Luapula, N Zambia
Mansel Island *37 G3* *island* Nunavut, NE Canada
Mansfield *40 D4* Ohio, N USA
Manta *60 A2* Manabí, W Ecuador
Manteca *47 B6* California, W USA
Mantoue *see* Mantova
Mantova *96 B2* *Eng.* Mantua, *Fr.* Mantoue. Lombardia, NW Italy
Mantua *see* Mantova
Manuae *145 G4* *island* S Cook Islands
Manukau *see* Manurewa
Manurewa *150 D3* *var.* Manukau. Auckland, North Island, New Zealand
Manzanares *93 E3* Castilla-La Mancha, C Spain
Manzanillo *54 C3* Granma, E Cuba
Manzanillo *50 D4* Colima, SW Mexico
Manzhouli *127 F1* *var.* Man-chou-li. Nei Mongol Zizhiqu, N China
Mao *76 B3* Kanem, W Chad
Maó *see* Mahón
Maoke, Pegunungan *139 H4* *Dut.* Sneeuw-gebergte, *Eng.* Snow Mountains. *mountain range* Papua, E Indonesia
Maoming *128 C6* Guangdong, S China
Mapmaker Seamounts *125 H2* *seamount range* N Pacific Ocean
Maputo *78 D4* *prev.* Lourenço Marques. *country capital* (Mozambique) Maputo, S Mozambique
Marabá *63 F2* Pará, NE Brazil
Maracaibo *58 C1* Zulia, NW Venezuela
Maracaibo, Gulf of *see* Venezuela, Golfo de
Maracaibo, Lago de *58 C2* *var.* Lake Maracaibo. *inlet* NW Venezuela
Maracaibo, Lake *see* Maracaibo, Lago de
Maracay *58 D2* Aragua, N Venezuela
Marada *see* Marādah
Marādah *71 G3* *var.* Marada. N Libya
Maradi *75 G3* Maradi, S Niger
Maragha *see* Marāgheh
Marāgheh *120 C2* *var.* Maragha. Āžarbāyjān-e Khāvarī, NW Iran
Marajó, Baía de *63 F1* *bay* N Brazil
Marajó, Ilha de *63 E1* *island* N Brazil
Marakesh *see* Marrakech
Maramba *see* Livingstone
Maramba *see* Livingstone
Maranhão *63 F2* *off.* Estado do Maranhão. *state* E Brazil
Maranhão, Estado do *see* Maranhão
Marañón, Río *60 B2* *river* N Peru
Marathon *38 C4* Ontario, S Canada
Marathón *see* Marathónas
Marathónas *105 C5* *prev.* Marathón. Attikí, C Greece
Märäzä *117 H2* *Rus.* Maraza. E Azerbaijan
Maraza *see* Märäzä
Marbella *92 D5* Andalucía, S Spain
Marble Bar *146 B4* Western Australia
Marburg *see* Marburg an der Lahn
Marburg *see* Maribor
Marburg an der Lahn *94 B4* *hist.* Marburg. Hessen, W Germany
March *see* Morava
Marche *96 C3* *Eng.* Marches. *region* C Italy
Marche *91 C5* *cultural region* C France
Marche-en-Famenne *87 C7* Luxembourg, SE Belgium
Marchena, Isla *60 B5* *var.* Bindloe Island. *island* Galapagos Islands, Ecuador, E Pacific Ocean
Marches *see* Marche
Mar Chiquita, Laguna *64 C3* *lake* C Argentina
Marcounda *see* Markounda
Mardān *134 C1* North-West Frontier Province, N Pakistan
Mar del Plata *65 D5* Buenos Aires, E Argentina
Mardin *117 E4* Mardin, SE Turkey
Maré *144 D5* *island* Îles Loyauté, E New Caledonia
Marea Neagră *see* Black Sea
Mareeba *148 D3* Queensland, NE Australia
Marek *see* Dupnitsa
Marganets *see* Marhanets'
Margarita, Isla de *59 E1* *island* N Venezuela
Margate *89 E7* *prev.* Mergate. SE England, UK
Margherita *see* Jamaame
Margherita, Lake *see* Ābaya Hāyk'
Marghita *108 B3* *Hung.* Margitta. Bihor, NW Romania
Margitta *see* Marghita
Marhanets' *109 F3* *Rus.* Marganets. Dnipropetrovs'ka Oblast', E Ukraine
María Cleofas, Isla *50 C4* *island* C Mexico
Maria Island *149 C8* *island* Tasmania, SE Australia
María Madre, Isla *50 C4* *island* C Mexico
María Magdalena, Isla *50 C4* *island* C Mexico
Mariana Trench *125 G4* *var.* Challenger Deep. *trench* W Pacific Ocean
Mariánské Lázně *99 A5* *Ger.* Marienbad. Karlovarský Kraj, W Czech Republic
Marías, Islas *50 C4* *island group* C Mexico North America
Maria-Theresiopel *see* Subotica
Maribor *95 E7* *Ger.* Marburg. NE Slovenia
Maridi *73 B5* Western Equatoria, SW Sudan
Marie Byrd Land *154 A3* *physical region* Antarctica
Marie-Galante *55 G4* *var.* Ceyre to the Caribs. *island* SE Guadeloupe
Marienbad *see* Mariánské Lázně
Marienburg *see* Alūksne, Latvia
Marienburg *see* Malbork, Poland
Marienburg in Westpreussen *see* Malbork
Marienhausen *see* Viļaka
Mariental *78 B4* Hardap, SW Namibia
Marienwerder *see* Kwidzyń
Mariestad *85 B6* Västra Götaland, S Sweden
Marietta *42 D2* Georgia, SE USA
Marijampolė *106 B4* *prev.* Kapsukas. Marijampole, S Lithuania
Marília *63 E4* São Paulo, S Brazil
Marín *92 B1* Galicia, NW Spain
Mar'ina Gorka *see* Mar"ina Horka
Mar"ina Horka *107 C6* *Rus.* Mar'ina Gorka. Minskaya Voblasts', C Belarus
Maringá *63 E4* Paraná, S Brazil
Marion *45 G3* Iowa, C USA
Marion *40 D4* Ohio, N USA
Marion, Lake *43 E2* *reservoir* South Carolina, SE USA
Mariscal Estigarribia *64 D2* Boquerón, NW Paraguay
Maritsa *104 D3* *var.* Marica, *Gk.* Évros, *Turk.* Meriç; *anc.* Hebrus. *river* SW Europe
Maritzburg *see* Pietermaritzburg
Mariupol' *109 G4* *prev.* Zhdanov. Donets'ka Oblast', SE Ukraine
Marka *73 D6* *var.* Merca. Shabeellaha Hoose, S Somalia
Markham, Mount *154 B4* *mountain* Antarctica
Markounda *76 C4* *var.* Marcounda. Ouham, NW Central African Republic
Marktredwitz *95 C5* Bayern, E Germany
Marlborough *148 D4* Queensland, E Australia
Marmanda *see* Marmande
Marmande *91 B5* *anc.* Marmanda. Lot-et-Garonne, SW France
Marmara Denizi *116 A2* *Eng.* Sea of Marmara. *sea* NW Turkey
Marmara, Sea of *see* Marmara Denizi
Marmaris *116 A4* Muğla, SW Turkey
Marne *90 C3* *department* N France
Marne *90 C3* *cultural region* N France
Marne *90 D3* *river* N France
Maro *76 C4* Moyen-Chari, S Chad
Maroantsetra *79 G2* Toamasina, NE Madagascar
Maromokotro *79 G2* *mountain* N Madagascar
Maroni *59 G3* *Dut.* Marowijne. *river* French Guiana/Suriname
Maroshevíz *see* Toplița
Marosludas *see* Luduș
Marosvásárhely *see* Târgu Mureș
Marotiri *143 F4* *var.* Îlots de Bass, Morotiri. *island group* Îles Australes, SW French Polynesia
Maroua *76 B3* Extrême-Nord, N Cameroon
Marowijne *see* Maroni
Marquesas Fracture Zone *153 E3* *fracture zone* E Pacific Ocean
Marquette *40 B1* Michigan, N USA
Marrakech *70 C2* *var.* Marakesh, *Eng.* Marrakesh; *prev.* Morocco. W Morocco
Marrakesh *see* Marrakech
Marrawah *149 C8* Tasmania, SE Australia
Marree *149 B5* South Australia
Marsá al Burayqah *71 G3* *var.* Al Burayqah. N Libya
Marsabit *73 C6* Eastern, N Kenya
Marsala *97 B7* *anc.* Lilybaeum. Sicilia, Italy, C Mediterranean Sea
Marsberg *94 B4* Nordrhein-Westfalen, W Germany
Marseille *91 D6* *Eng.* Marseilles; *anc.* Massilia. Bouches-du-Rhône, SE France
Marseilles *see* Marseille
Marshall *45 F2* Minnesota, N USA
Marshall *49 H2* Texas, SW USA
Marshall Islands *144 C1* *off.* Republic of the Marshall Islands. *country* W Pacific Ocean

MARSHALL ISLANDS
Australasia & Oceania

Official name Republic of the Marshall Islands
Formation 1986 / 1986
Capital Majuro
Population 59,071 / 844 people per sq mile (326 people per sq km) / 69%
Total area 70 sq miles (181 sq km)
Languages Marshallese*, English*, Japanese, German
Religions Protestant 90%, Roman Catholic 8%, Other 2%
Ethnic mix Micronesian 97%, Other 3%
Government Presidential system
Currency US dollar = 100 cents
Literacy rate 91%
Calorie consumption Not available

Marshall Islands, Republic of the *see* Marshall Islands
Marshall Seamounts *125 H3* *seamount range* SW Pacific Ocean
Marsh Harbour *54 C1* Great Abaco, W Bahamas
Martaban *136 B4* *var.* Moktama. Mon State, S Myanmar (Burma)
Martha's Vineyard *41 G3* *island* Massachusetts, NE USA
Martigues *91 D6* Bouches-du-Rhône, SE France
Martin *99 C5* *Ger.* Sankt Martin, *Hung.* Turócszentmárton; *prev.* Turčiansky Svätý Martin. Žilinský Kraj, N Slovakia
Martinique *55 G4* *French overseas department* E West Indies
Martinique Channel *see* Martinique Passage
Martinique Passage *55 G4* *var.* Dominica Channel, Martinique Channel. *channel* Dominica/Martinique
Marton *150 D4* Manawatu-Wanganui, North Island, New Zealand
Martos *92 D4* Andalucía, S Spain
Marungu *77 E7* *mountain range* SE Dem. Rep. Congo
Mary *122 D3* *prev.* Merv. Mary Welaýaty, S Turkmenistan
Maryborough *149 D4* Queensland, E Australia
Maryborough *see* Port Laoise
Mary Island *see* Kanton
Maryland *41 E5* *off.* State of Maryland, *also known as* America in Miniature, Cockade State, Free State, Old Line State. *state* NE USA

Maryland, State of see Maryland
Maryville 45 F4 Missouri, C USA
Maryville 42 D1 Tennessee, S USA
Masai Steppe 73 C7 grassland
NW Tanzania
Masaka 73 B6 SW Uganda
Masallı 117 H3 Rus. Masally.
S Azerbaijan
Masally see Masallı
Masasi 73 C8 Mtwara, SE Tanzania
Masawa see Massawa
Masaya 52 D3 Masaya, W Nicaragua
Mascarene Basin 141 B5 undersea basin
W Indian Ocean
Mascarene Islands 79 H4 island group
W Indian Ocean
Mascarene Plain 141 B5 abyssal plain
W Indian Ocean
Mascarene Plateau 141 B5 undersea
plateau W Indian Ocean
Maseru 78 D4 country capital (Lesotho)
W Lesotho
Mas-ha 119 D7 W West Bank Asia
Mashhad 120 E2 var. Meshed.
Khorāsān-Razavī, NE Iran
Masindi 73 C6 W Uganda
Masira see Maṣīrah, Jazīrat
Masira, Gulf of see Maṣīrah, Khalīj
Maṣīrah, Jazīrat 121 E5 var. Masīra.
island E Oman
Maṣīrah, Khalīj 121 E5 var. Gulf of
Masira. bay E Oman
Masis see Büyükağrı Dağı
Maskat see Masqaṭ
Mason City 45 F3 Iowa, C USA
Masqaṭ 121 E5 var. Maskat, Eng. Muscat.
country capital (Oman) NE Oman
Massa 96 B3 Toscana, C Italy
Massachusetts 41 G3 off.
Commonwealth of Massachusetts, also
known as Bay State, Old Bay State, Old
Colony State. state NE USA
Massawa 72 C4 var. Masawa, Amh.
Mits'iwa. E Eritrea
Massenya 76 B3 Chari-Baguirmi,
SW Chad
Massif Central 91 C5 plateau C France
Massilia see Marseille
Massoukou see Franceville
Mastanli see Momchilgrad
Masterton 151 D5 Wellington, North
Island, New Zealand
Masty 107 B5 Rus. Mosty.
Hrodzyenskaya Voblasts', W Belarus
Masuda 131 A6 Shimane, Honshū,
SW Japan
Masuku see Franceville
Masvingo 78 D3 prev. Fort Victoria,
Nyanda, Víctoria. Masvingo,
SE Zimbabwe
Maṣyāf 118 B3 Fr. Misiaf. Ḥamāh,
C Syria
Matadi 77 B6 Bas-Congo, W Dem.
Rep. Congo
Matagalpa 52 D3 Matagalpa,
C Nicaragua
Matale 132 D3 Central Province,
C Sri Lanka
Matam 74 C3 NE Senegal
Matamata 150 D3 Waikato, North
Island, New Zealand
Matamoros 50 D3 Coahuila de Zaragoza,
NE Mexico
Matamoros 51 E2 Tamaulipas, C Mexico
Matane 39 E4 Québec, SE Canada
Matanzas 54 B2 Matanzas, NW Cuba
Matara 132 D4 Southern Province,
S Sri Lanka
Mataram 138 D5 Pulau Lombok,
C Indonesia
Mataró 93 G2 anc. Illuro. Cataluña,
E Spain
Mataura 151 B7 Southland, South Island,
New Zealand
Mataura 151 B7 river South Island,
New Zealand
Mata Uta see Matâ'utu
Matâ'utu 145 E4 var. Mata Uta.
dependent territory capital (Wallis and
Futuna) Île Uvea, Wallis and Futuna
Matera 97 E5 Basilicata, S Italy
Mathurai see Madurai
Matías Romero 51 F5 Oaxaca,
SE Mexico
Matisco/Matisco Ædourum see Mâcon
Mato Grosso 63 E4 prev. Vila Bela da
Santissima Trindade. Mato Grosso,
W Brazil

Mato Grosso do Sul 63 E4
off. Estado de Mato Grosso do Sul.
state S Brazil
Mato Grosso do Sul, Estado de see Mato
Grosso do Sul
Mato Grosso, Planalto de 56 C4 plateau
C Brazil
Matosinhos 92 B2 prev. Matozinhos.
Porto, NW Portugal
Matozinhos see Matosinhos
Matsue 131 B6 var. Matsuye, Matue.
Shimane, Honshū, SW Japan
Matsumoto 131 C5 var. Matumoto.
Nagano, Honshū, S Japan
Matsuyama 131 B7 var. Matuyama.
Ehime, Shikoku, SW Japan
Matsuye see Matsue
Matterhorn 95 A8 It. Monte Cervino.
mountain Italy/Switzerland
Matthews Ridge 59 F2 N Guyana
Matthew Town 54 D2 Great Inagua,
S Bahamas
Matucana 60 C4 Lima, W Peru
Matue see Matsue
Matumoto see Matsumoto
Maturín 59 E2 Monagas,
NE Venezuela
Matuyama see Matsuyama
Mau 135 E3 var. Maunāth Bhanjan.
Uttar Pradesh, N India
Maui 47 B8 island Hawai'i, USA,
C Pacific Ocean
Maulmain see Moulmein
Maun 78 C3 North-West, C Botswana
Maunāth Bhanjan see Mau
Mauren 94 E1 NE Liechtenstein Europe
Maurice see Mauritius
Mauritania 74 C2 off. Islamic Republic
of Mauritania, Ar. Mūrītānīyah.
country W Africa

MAURITANIA
West Africa

Official name Islamic Republic of
Mauritania
Formation 1960 / 1960
Capital Nouakchott
Population 3.1 million / 8 people per
sq mile (3 people per sq km) / 58%
Total area 397,953 sq miles
(1,030,700 sq km)
Languages French*, Hassaniyah Arabic,
Wolof
Religions Sunni Muslim 100%
Ethnic mix Maure 81%, Wolof 7%,
Tukolor 5%, Other 4%, Soninka 3%
Government Transitional regime
Currency Ouguiya = 5 khoums
Literacy rate 51%
Calorie consumption 2772 calories

Mauritania, Islamic Republic of see
Mauritania
Mauritius 79 H3 off. Republic of
Mauritius, Fr. Maurice. country
W Indian Ocean

MAURITIUS
Indian Ocean

Official name Republic of Mauritius
Formation 1968 / 1968
Capital Port Louis
Population 1.2 million / 1671 people per
sq mile (645 people per sq km) / 41%
Total area 718 sq miles
(1860 sq km)
Languages English*, French Creole,
Hindi, Urdu, Tamil, Chinese, French
Religions Hindu 52%, Roman
Catholic 26%, Muslim 17%, Other 3%,
Protestant 2%
Ethnic mix Indo-Mauritian 68%,
Creole 27%, Sino-Mauritian 3%,
Franco-Mauritian 2%
Government Parliamentary system
Currency Mauritian rupee = 100 cents
Literacy rate 84%
Calorie consumption 2955 calories

Mauritius 141 B5 island W Indian Ocean
Mauritius, Republic of see Mauritius
Mawlamyine see Moulmein
Mawson 154 D2 Australian research
station Antarctica
Maya 52 B1 river E Russian Federation
Mayadin see Al Mayādīn

Mayaguana 54 D2 island SE Bahamas
Mayaguana Passage 54 D2 passage
SE Bahamas
Mayagüez 55 F3 W Puerto Rico
Mayamey 120 D2 Semnān, N Iran
Maya Mountains 52 B2 Sp.
Montañas Mayas. mountain range
Belize/Guatemala
Mayas, Montañas see Maya Mountains
Maych'ew 72 C4 var. Mai Chio, It. Mai
Ceu. Tigray, N Ethiopia
Maydān Shahr see Meydān Shahr
Mayebashi see Maebashi
Mayence see Mainz
Mayfield 151 B6 Canterbury, South
Island, New Zealand
Maykop 111 A7 Respublika Adygeya,
SW Russian Federation
Maymana see Meymaneh
Maymyo 136 B3 Mandalay,
C Myanmar (Burma)
Mayo see Maio
Mayor Island 150 D3 island NE New
Zealand
Mayor Pablo Lagerenza see Capitán
Pablo Lagerenza
Mayotte 79 F2 French territorial
collectivity E Africa
May Pen 54 B5 C Jamaica
Mayyit, Al Baḥr al see Dead Sea
Mazabuka 78 D2 Southern, S Zambia
Mazaca see Kayseri
Mazagan see El-Jadida
Mazár-e Sharīf 123 E3 var. Mazár-i
Sharif. Balkh, N Afghanistan
Mazár-i Sharif see Mazár-e Sharīf
Mazatlán 50 C3 Sinaloa, C Mexico
Mažeikiai 106 B3 Telšiai, NW Lithuania
Mazirbe 106 C2 Talsi, NW Latvia
Mazra'a see Al Mazra'ah
Mazury 98 D3 physical region NE Poland
Mazyr 107 C7 Rus. Mozyr'.
Homyel'skaya Voblasts', SE Belarus
Mba see Ba
Mbabane 78 D4 country capital
(Swaziland) NW Swaziland
Mbacké see Mbaké
Mbaïki 77 C5 var. M'Baiki. Lobaye,
SW Central African Republic
M'Baiki see Mbaïki
Mbaké 74 B3 var. Mbacké. W Senegal
Mbala 78 D1 prev. Abercorn. Northern,
NE Zambia
Mbale 73 C6 E Uganda
Mbandaka 77 C5 prev. Coquilhatville.
Equateur, NW Dem. Rep. Congo
M'Banza Congo 78 B1 var. Mbanza
Congo; prev. São Salvador, São
Salvador do Congo. Dem. Rep. Congo,
NW Angola
Mbanza-Ngungu 77 B6 Bas-Congo,
W Dem. Rep. Congo
Mbarara 73 B6 SW Uganda
Mbé 76 B4 Nord, N Cameroon
Mbeya 73 C7 Mbeya, SW Tanzania
Mbomou/M'Bomu/Mbomu see Bomu
Mbour 74 B3 W Senegal
Mbuji-Mayi 77 D7 prev. Bakwanga.
Kasai Oriental, S Dem. Rep. Congo
McAlester 49 G2 Oklahoma, C USA
McAllen 49 F5 Texas, SW USA
McCamey 49 E3 Texas, SW USA
McClintock Channel 37 F2 channel
Nunavut, N Canada
McComb 42 B3 Mississippi, S USA
McCook 45 E4 Nebraska, C USA
McKean Island 145 E3 island Phoenix
Islands, C Kiribati
McKinley, Mount 36 C3 var. Denali.
mountain Alaska, USA
McKinley Park 36 C3 Alaska, USA
McMinnville 46 B3 Oregon, NW USA
McMurdo 154 B4 US research station
Antarctica
McPherson 45 E5 Kansas, C USA
McPherson see Fort McPherson
Mdantsane 78 D5 Eastern Cape,
SE South Africa
Mead, Lake 47 D6 reservoir Arizona/
Nevada, W USA
Mecca see Makkah
Mechelen 87 C5 Eng. Mechlin, Fr.
Malines. Antwerpen, C Belgium
Mechlin see Mechelen
Mecklenburger Bucht 94 C2 bay
N Germany
Mecsek 99 C7 mountain range
SW Hungary

Medan 138 B3 Sumatera, E Indonesia
Medeba see Ma'dabā
Medellín 58 B3 Antioquia,
NW Colombia
Médenine 71 F2 var. Madanīyīn.
SE Tunisia
Medeshamstede see Peterborough
Medford 46 B4 Oregon, NW USA
Medgidia 108 D5 Constanţa,
SE Romania
Medgyes see Mediaş
Mediaş 108 B4 Ger. Mediasch, Hung.
Medgyes. Sibiu, C Romania
Mediasch see Mediaş
Medicine Hat 37 F5 Alberta, SW Canada
Medina see Al Madīnah
Medinaceli 93 E2 Castilla-León, N Spain
Medina del Campo 92 D2 Castilla-León,
N Spain
Medinat Israel see Israel
Mediolanum see Saintes, France
Mediolanum see Milano, Italy
Mediomatrica see Metz
Mediterranean Sea 102 D3 Fr. Mer
Méditerranée. sea Africa/Asia/Europe
Méditerranée, Mer see Mediterranean
Sea
Médoc 91 B5 cultural region SW France
Medvezh'yegorsk 110 B3 Respublika
Kareliya, NW Russian Federation
Meekatharra 147 B5 Western Australia
Meemu Atoll see Mulaku Atoll
Meerssen 87 D6 var. Mersen. Limburg,
SE Netherlands
Meerut 134 D2 Uttar Pradesh, N India
Megáli Préspa, Límni see Prespa, Lake
Meghálaya 113 G3 state NE India
Meghálaya 113 G3 cultural region
NE India
Mehdia see Mahdia
Meheso see Mi'ēso
Me Hka see Nmai Hka
Mehrīz 120 D3 Yazd, C Iran
Mehtar Lām 123 F4 var. Mehtarlām,
Meterlam, Metharlam, Metharlam.
Laghmān, E Afghanistan
Mehtarlām see Mehtar Lām
Meiktila 136 B3 Mandalay,
C Myanmar (Burma)
Méjico see Mexico
Mejillones 64 B2 Antofagasta, N Chile
Mek'elē 72 C4 var. Makale. Tigray,
N Ethiopia
Mékhé 74 B3 NW Senegal
Mekong 124 D3 var. Lan-ts'ang Chiang,
' Cam. Mékôngk, Chin. Lancang Jiang,
Lao. Mènam Khong, Th. Mae Nam
Khong, Tib. Dza Chu, Vtn. Sông Tiên
Giang. river SE Asia
Mékôngk see Mekong
Mekong, Mouths of the 137 E6 delta
S Vietnam
Melaka 138 B3 var. Malacca. Melaka,
Peninsular Malaysia
Melaka, Selat see Malacca, Strait of
Melanesia 144 D3 island group W Pacific
Ocean
Melanesian Basin 142 C2 undersea
basin W Pacific Ocean
Melbourne 149 C7 state capital Victoria,
SE Australia
Melbourne 43 E4 Florida, SE USA
Meleda see Mljet
Melghir, Chott 71 E2 var. Chott Melrhir.
salt lake E Algeria
Melilla 80 B5 anc. Rusaddir, Russadir.
Melilla, Spain, N Africa
Melilla 70 D2 enclave Spain, N Africa
Melita 37 F5 Manitoba, S Canada
Melita see Mljet
Melitene see Malatya
Melitopol' 109 F4 Zaporiz'ka Oblast',
SE Ukraine
Melle 87 B5 Oost-Vlaanderen,
NW Belgium
Mellerud 85 B6 Västra Götaland,
S Sweden
Mellieha 102 B5 E Malta
Mellizo Sur, Cerro 65 A7 mountain
S Chile
Melo 64 E4 Cerro Largo, NE Uruguay
Melodunum see Melun
Melrhir, Chott see Melghir, Chott
Melsungen 94 B4 Hessen, C Germany
Melun 90 C3 anc. Melodunum. Seine-et-
Marne, N France
Melville Bay/Melville Bugt see
Qimusseriarsuaq

Melville Island *146 D2 island* Northern Territory, N Australia
Melville Island *37 E2 island* Parry Islands, Northwest Territories, NW Canada
Melville, Lake *39 F2 lake* Newfoundland and Labrador, E Canada
Melville Peninsula *37 G3 peninsula* Nunavut, NE Canada
Melville Sound *see* Viscount Melville Sound
Membidj *see* Manbij
Memel *see* Neman, NE Europe
Memel *see* Klaipeda, Lithuania
Memmingen *95 B6* Bayern, S Germany
Memphis *42 C1* Tennessee, S USA
Menaam *see* Menaldum
Menado *see* Manado
Ménaka *75 F3* Goa, E Mali
Menaldum *86 D1 Fris.* Menaam. Friesland, N Netherlands
Mènam Khong *see* Mekong
Mendaña Fracture Zone *153 F4 fracture zone* E Pacific Ocean
Mende *91 C5 anc.* Mimatum. Lozère, S France
Mendeleyev Ridge *155 B2 undersea ridge* Arctic Ocean
Mendocino Fracture Zone *152 D2 fracture zone* NE Pacific Ocean
Mendoza *64 B4* Mendoza, W Argentina
Menemen *116 A3* 4Izmır, W Turkey
Menengiyn Tal *127 F2 plain* E Mongolia
Menongue *78 B2 var.* Vila Serpa Pinto, *Port.* Serpa Pinto. Cuando Cubango, C Angola
Menorca *93 H3 Eng.* Minorca; *anc.* Balearis Minor. *island* Islas Baleares, Spain, W Mediterranean Sea
Mentawai, Kepulauan *138 A4 island group* W Indonesia
Meppel *86 D2* Drenthe, NE Netherlands
Meran *see* Merano
Merano *96 C1 Ger.* Meran. Trentino-Alto Adige, N Italy
Merca *see* Marka
Mercedes *64 D3* Corrientes, NE Argentina
Mercedes *64 D4* Soriano, SW Uruguay
Meredith, Lake *49 E1 reservoir* Texas, SW USA
Merefa *109 G2* Kharkivs'ka Oblast', E Ukraine
Mergate *see* Margate
Mergui *137 B6* Tenasserim, S Myanmar (Burma)
Mergui Archipelago *137 B6 island group* S Myanmar (Burma)
Mérida *51 H3* Yucatán, SW Mexico
Mérida *92 C4 anc.* Augusta Emerita. Extremadura, W Spain
Mérida *58 C2* Mérida, W Venezuela
Meridian *42 C2* Mississippi, S USA
Mérignac *91 B5* Gironde, SW France
Merín, Laguna *see* Mirim Lagoon
Merkulovichi *see* Myerkulavichy
Merowe *72 B3* Northern, N Sudan
Merredin *147 B6* Western Australia
Mersen *see* Meerssen
Mersey *89 D5 river* NW England, U K
Mersin *116 C4* Mersin, S Turkey
Mērsrags *106 C3* Talsi, NW Latvia
Meru *73 C6* Eastern, C Kenya
Merv *see* Mary
Merzifon *116 D2* Amasya, N Turkey
Merzig *95 A5* Saarland, SW Germany
Mesa *48 B2* Arizona, SW USA
Meseritz *see* Międzyrzecz
Meshed *see* Mashhad
Mesopotamia *57 C5 var.* Mesopotamia Argentina. *physical region* NE Argentina
Mesopotamia Argentina *see* Mesopotamia
Messalo, Rio *79 E2 var.* Mualo. *river* NE Mozambique
Messana/Messene *see* Messina
Messina *97 D7 var.* Messana, Messene; *anc.* Zancle. Sicilia, Italy, C Mediterranean Sea
Messina *see* Musina
Messina, Strait of *see* Messina, Stretto di
Messina, Stretto di *97 D7 Eng.* Strait of Messina. *strait* SW Italy
Messíni *105 B6* Pelopónnisos, S Greece
Mesta *see* Néstos
Mestghanem *see* Mostaganem
Mestia *117 F1 var.* Mestiya. N Georgia
Mestiya *see* Mestia
Mestre *96 C2* Veneto, NE Italy
Meta *56 B2 off.* Departamento del Meta. *province* C Colombia
Meta, Departamento del *see* Meta
Metairie *42 B3* Louisiana, S USA
Metán *64 C2* Salta, N Argentina
Metapán *52 B2* Santa Ana, NW El Salvador
Meta, Río *58 D3 river* Colombia/Venezuela
Meterlam *see* Mehtar Lām
Methariam/Metharlam *see* Mehtar Lām
Metis *see* Metz
Metković *100 B4* Dubrovnik-Neretva, SE Croatia
Métsovo *104 B4 prev.* Métsovon. Ípeiros, C Greece
Métsovon *see* Métsovo
Metz *90 D3 anc.* Divodurum Mediomatricum, Mediomatrica, Metis. Moselle, NE France
Meulaboh *138 A3* Sumatera, W Indonesia
Meuse *90 D3 cultural region* NE France
Meuse *90 D3 department* NE France
Meuse *87 C6 Dut.* Maas. *river* W Europe
Mexcala, Río *see* Balsas, Río
Mexicali *50 A1* Baja California, NW Mexico
Mexicanos, Estados Unidos *see* Mexico
México *51 E4 var.* Ciudad de México, *Eng.* Mexico City. *country capital* (Mexico) México, C Mexico

MEXICO
North America

Official name United Mexican States
Formation 1836 / 1848
Capital Mexico City
Population 107 million / 145 people per sq mile (56 people per sq km) / 74%
Total area 761,602 sq miles (1,972,550 sq km)
Languages Spanish*, Nahuatl, Mayan, Zapotec, Mixtec, Otomi, Totonac, Tzotzil, Tzeltal
Religions Roman Catholic 88%, Other 7%, Protestant 5%
Ethnic mix Mestizo 60%, Amerindian 30%, European 9%, Other 1%
Government Presidential system
Currency Mexican peso = 100 centavos
Literacy rate 90%
Calorie consumption 3145 calories

Mexico *45 G4* Missouri, C USA
Mexico *50 C3 off.* United Mexican States, *var.* Méjico, México, *Sp.* Estados Unidos Mexicanos. *country* N Central America
México *see* Mexico
Mexico City *see* México
México, Golfo de *see* Mexico, Gulf of
Mexico, Gulf of *51 F2 Sp.* Golfo de México. *gulf* W Atlantic Ocean
Meyadine *see* Al Mayādīn
Meydān Shahr *123 E4 var.* Maydān Shahr. Vardak, E Afghanistan
Meymaneh *122 D3 var.* Maimāna, Maymana. Fāryāb, NW Afghanistan
Mezen' *110 D3 river* NW Russian Federation
Mezőtúr *99 D7* Jász-Nagykun-Szolnok, E Hungary
Mġarr *102 A5* Gozo, N Malta
Miadzioł Nowy *see* Myadzyel
Miahuatlán *51 F5 var.* Miahuatlán de Porfirio Díaz. Oaxaca, SE Mexico
Miahuatlán de Porfirio Díaz *see* Miahuatlán
Miami *43 F5* Florida, SE USA
Miami *49 G1* Oklahoma, C USA
Miami Beach *43 F5* Florida, SE USA
Mīāneh *120 C2 var.* Miyāneh. Āżarbāyjān-e Sharqī, NW Iran
Mianyang *128 B5* Sichuan, C China
Miastko *98 C2 Ger.* Rummelsburg in Pommern. Pomorskie, N Poland
Mi Chai *see* Nong Khai
Michalovce *99 E5 Ger.* Grossmichel, *Hung.* Nagymihály. Košický Kraj, E Slovakia
Michigan *40 C1 off.* State of Michigan, *also known as* Great Lakes State, Lake State, Wolverine State. *state* N USA
Michigan, Lake *40 C2 lake* N USA
Michurin *see* Tsarevo
Michurinsk *111 B5* Tambovskaya Oblast', W Russian Federation
Micoud *55 F2* SE Saint Lucia
Micronesia *144 B1 off.* Federated States of Micronesia. *country* W Pacific Ocean

MICRONESIA
Australasia & Oceania

Official name Federated States of Micronesia
Formation 1986 / 1986
Capital Palikir (Pohnpei Island)
Population 108,105 / 399 people per sq mile (154 people per sq km) / 28%
Total area 271 sq miles (702 sq km)
Languages Trukese, Pohnpeian, Mortlockese, Kosraean, English
Religions Roman Catholic 50%, Protestant 48%, Other 2%
Ethnic mix Micronesian 100%
Government Nonparty system
Currency US dollar = 100 cents
Literacy rate 81%
Calorie consumption Not available

Micronesia *144 C1 island group* W Pacific Ocean
Micronesia, Federated States of *see* Micronesia
Mid-Atlantic Cordillera *see* Mid-Atlantic Ridge
Mid-Atlantic Ridge *66 C3 var.* Mid-Atlantic Cordillera, Mid-Atlantic Rise, Mid-Atlantic Swell. *undersea ridge* Atlantic Ocean
Mid-Atlantic Rise/Mid-Atlantic Swell *see* Mid-Atlantic Ridge
Middelburg *87 B5* Zeeland, SW Netherlands
Middelharnis *86 B4* Zuid-Holland, SW Netherlands
Middelkerke *87 A5* West-Vlaanderen, W Belgium
Middle America Trench *35 B7 trench* E Pacific Ocean
Middle Andaman *133 F2 island* Andaman Islands, India, NE Indian Ocean
Middle Atlas *see* Moyen Atlas
Middleburg Island *see* 'Eua
Middle Congo *see* Congo (Republic of)
Middlesboro *40 C5* Kentucky, S USA
Middlesbrough *89 D5* N England, UK
Middletown *41 F4* New Jersey, NE USA
Middletown *41 F3* New York, NE USA
Mid-Indian Basin *141 C5 undersea basin* N Indian Ocean
Mid-Indian Ridge *141 C5 var.* Central Indian Ridge. *undersea ridge* C Indian Ocean
Midland *38 D5* Ontario, S Canada
Midland *40 C3* Michigan, N USA
Midland *49 E3* Texas, SW USA
Mid-Pacific Mountains *152 C2 var.* Mid-Pacific Seamounts. *seamount range* NW Pacific Ocean
Mid-Pacific Seamounts *see* Mid-Pacific Mountains
Midway Islands *152 D2 US territory* C Pacific Ocean
Miechów *99 D5* Małopolskie, S Poland
Międzyrzec Podlaski *98 E3* Lubelskie, E Poland
Międzyrzecz *98 B3 Ger.* Meseritz. Lubuskie, W Poland
Mielec *99 D5* Podkarpackie, SE Poland
Miercurea-Ciuc *108 C4 Ger.* Szeklerburg, *Hung.* Csíkszereda. Harghita, C Romania
Mieres del Camín *see* Mieres del Camino
Mieres del Camino *108 D1 var.* Mieres del Camín. Asturias, NW Spain
Mī'ēso *73 D5 var.* Meheso, Miesso. Oromo, C Ethiopia
Miesso *see* Mī'ēso
Miguel Asua *50 D3 var.* Miguel Auza. Zacatecas, C Mexico
Miguel Auza *see* Miguel Asua
Mijdrecht *86 C3* Utrecht, C Netherlands
Mikashevichi *see* Mikashevichy
Mikashevichy *107 C7 Pol.* Mikaszewicze, *Rus.* Mikashevichi. Brestskaya Voblasts', SW Belarus
Mikaszewicze *see* Mikashevichy
Mikhaylovgrad *see* Montana
Mikhaylovka *111 B6* Volgogradskaya Oblast', SW Russian Federation
Míkonos *see* Mýkonos
Mikre *104 C2* Lovech, N Bulgaria
Mikun' *110 D4* Respublika Komi, NW Russian Federation
Mikuni-sanmyaku *131 D5 mountain range* Honshū, N Japan Asia
Mikura-jima *131 D6 island* E Japan
Milagro *60 B2* Guayas, SW Ecuador
Milan *see* Milano
Milange *79 E2* Zambézia, NE Mozambique
Milano *96 B2 Eng.* Milan, *Ger.* Mailand; *anc.* Mediolanum. Lombardia, N Italy
Milas *116 A4* Muğla, SW Turkey
Milashavichy *107 C7 Rus.* Milashevichi. Homyel'skaya Voblasts', SE Belarus
Milashevichi *see* Milashavichy
Mildura *149 C6* Victoria, SE Australia
Mile *see* Mili Atoll
Miles *149 D5* Queensland, E Australia
Miles City *44 C2* Montana, NW USA
Milford *see* Milford Haven
Milford Haven *89 C6 prev.* Milford SW Wales, UK
Milford Sound *151 A6* Southland, South Island, New Zealand
Milford Sound *151 A6 inlet* South Island, New Zealand
Milḥ, Baḥr al *see* Razāzah, Buḥayrat ar
Mili Atoll *144 D2 var.* Mile. *atoll* Ratak Chain, SE Marshall Islands
Mil'kovo *115 H3* Kamchatskaya Oblast', E Russian Federation
Milk River *37 E5* Alberta, SW Canada
Milk River *44 C1 river* Montana, NW USA
Milk, Wadi el *88 B4 var.* Wadi al Malik. *river* C Sudan
Milledgeville *43 E2* Georgia, SE USA
Mille Lacs Lake *45 F2 lake* Minnesota, N USA
Millennium Island *160 C8 prev.* Caroline Island, Thornton Island. *atoll* Line Islands, E Kiribati
Millerovo *111 B6* Rostovskaya Oblast', SW Russian Federation
Mílos *105 C6 island* Kykládes, Greece, Aegean Sea
Mílos *see* Pláka
Milton *151 B7* Otago, South Island, New Zealand
Milton Keynes *89 D6* SE England, UK
Milwaukee *40 B3* Wisconsin, N USA
Mimatum *see* Mende
Min *see* Fujian
Mīnā' Qābūs *140 B3* NE Oman
Minas Gerais *63 F3 off.* Estado de Minas Gerais. *state* E Brazil
Minas Gerais, Estado de *see* Minas Gerais
Minatitlán *51 F4* Veracruz-Llave, E Mexico
Minbu *136 A3* Magwe, W Myanmar (Burma)
Minch, The *88 B3 var.* North Minch. *strait* NW Scotland, UK
Mindanao *139 F2 island* S Philippines
Mindanao Sea *see* Bohol Sea
Mindelheim *95 C6* Bayern, S Germany
Mindello *see* Mindelo
Mindelo *74 A2 var.* Mindello; *prev.* Porto Grande. São Vicente, N Cape Verde
Minden *94 B4 anc.* Minthun. Nordrhein-Westfalen, NW Germany
Mindoro *139 E2 island* N Philippines
Mindoro Strait *139 E2 strait* W Philippines
Mineral Wells *49 F2* Texas, SW USA
Mingäçevir *117 G2 Rus.* Mingechaur, Mingechevir. C Azerbaijan
Mingāora *134 C1 var.* Mingora, Mongora. North-West Frontier Province, N Pakistan
Mingechaur/Mingechevir *see* Mingäçevir
Mingora *see* Mingāora
Minho *92 B2 former province* N Portugal
Minho, Rio *92 B2 Sp.* Miño. *river* Portugal/Spain
Minho, Rio *see* Miño
Minicoy Island *132 B3 island* SW India
Minius *see* Miño
Minna *75 G4* Niger, C Nigeria
Minneapolis *45 F2* Minnesota, N USA
Minnesota *45 F2 off.* State of Minnesota, *also known as* Gopher State, New England of the West, North Star State. *state* N USA

Miño *92 B2 var.* Mino, Minius, *Port.* Rio Minho. *river* Portugal/Spain
Miño *see* Minho, Rio
Minorca *see* Menorca
Minot *45 E1* North Dakota, N USA
Minsk *107 C6 country capital* (Belarus) Minskaya Voblasts', C Belarus
Minskaya Wzvyshsha *107 C6 mountain range* C Belarus
Mińsk Mazowiecki *98 D3 var.* Nowo-Minsk. Mazowieckie, C Poland
Minthun *see* Minden
Minto, Lac *38 D2 lake* Québec, C Canada
Minya *see* El Minya
Miraflores *50 C3* Baja California Sur, W Mexico
Miranda de Ebro *93 E1* La Rioja, N Spain
Mirgorod *see* Myrhorod
Miri *138 D3* Sarawak, East Malaysia
Mirim Lagoon *63 E5 var.* Lake Mirim, *Sp.* Laguna Merín. *lagoon* Brazil/Uruguay
Mirim, Lake *see* Mirim Lagoon
Mirina *see* Mýrina
Mirjāveh *120 E4* Sīstān va Balūchestān, SE Iran
Mirny *154 C3 Russian research station* Antarctica
Mirnyy *115 F3* Respublika Sakha (Yakutiya), NE Russian Federation
Mirpur Khās *134 B3* Sind, SE Pakistan
Mirtoan Sea *see* Mirtóo Pélagos
Mirtóo Pélagos *105 C6 Eng.* Mirtoan Sea; *anc.* Myrtoum Mare. *sea* S Greece
Misiaf *see* Maşyāf
Miskito Coast *see* La Mosquitia
Miskitos, Cayos *53 E2 island group* NE Nicaragua
Miskolc *99 D6* Borsod-Abaúj-Zemplén, NE Hungary
Misool, Pulau *139 F4 island* Maluku, E Indonesia
Mişrātah *71 F2 var.* Misurata. NW Libya
Mission *49 G5* Texas, SW USA
Mississippi *42 B2 off.* State of Mississippi, *also known as* Bayou State, Magnolia State. *state* SE USA
Mississippi River *35 C6 river* C USA
Mississippi Delta *42 B4 delta* Louisiana, S USA
Missoula *44 B1* Montana, NW USA
Missouri *45 F5 off.* State of Missouri, *also known as* Bullion State, Show Me State. *state* C USA
Missouri River *45 E3 river* C USA
Mistassini, Lac *38 D3 lake* Québec, SE Canada
Mistelbach an der Zaya *95 E6* Niederösterreich, NE Austria
Misti, Volcán *61 E4 volcano* S Peru
Misurata *see* Mişrātah
Mitau *see* Jelgava
Mitchell *149 D5* Queensland, E Australia
Mitchell *45 E3* South Dakota, N USA
Mitchell, Mount *43 E1 mountain* North Carolina, SE USA
Mitchell River *148 C2 river* Queensland, NE Australia
Mi Tho *see* My Tho
Mitilíni *see* Mytilíni
Mito *131 D5* Ibaraki, Honshū, S Japan
Mitrovica/Mitrovicë *see* Kosovska Mitrovica, Serbia
Mitrovica/Mitrowitz *see* Sremska Mitrovica, Serbia
Mits'iwa *see* Massawa
Mitspe Ramon *see* Mizpé Ramon
Mittelstadt *see* Baia Sprie
Mitú *58 C4* Vaupés, SE Colombia
Mitumba, Chaîne des/Mitumba Range *see* Mitumba, Monts
Mitumba, Monts *77 E7 var.* Chaîne des Mitumba, Mitumba Range. *mountain range* E Dem. Rep. Congo
Miueru Wantipa, Lake *77 E7 lake* N Zambia
Miyako *130 D4* Iwate, Honshū, C Japan
Miyako-jima *131 D6 island* Sakishima-shotō, SW Japan
Miyakonojō *131 B8 var.* Miyakonzyō. Miyazaki, Kyūshū, SW Japan
Miyakonzyō *see* Miyakonojō
Miyăneh *see* Miāneh

Miyazaki *131 B8* Miyazaki, Kyūshū, SW Japan
Mizil *108 C5* Prahova, SE Romania
Miziya *104 C1* Vratsa, NW Bulgaria
Mizpé Ramon *119 A7 var.* Mitspe Ramon. Southern, S Israel
Mjosa *85 B6 var.* Mjøsen. *lake* S Norway
Mjøsen *see* Mjøsa
Mladenovac *100 D4* Serbia, C Serbia
Mława *98 D3* Mazowieckie, C Poland
Mljet *101 B5 It.* Meleda; *anc.* Melita. *island* S Croatia
Mmabatho *78 C4* North-West, N South Africa
Moab *44 B5* Utah, W USA
Moa Island *148 C1 island* Queensland, NE Australia
Moanda *77 B6 var.* Mouanda. Haut-Ogooué, SE Gabon
Moba *77 E7* Katanga, E Dem. Rep. Congo
Mobay *see* Montego Bay
Mobaye *77 C5* Basse-Kotto, S Central African Republic
Moberly *45 G4* Missouri, C USA
Mobile *42 C3* Alabama, S USA
Mobutu Sese Seko, Lac *see* Albert, Lake
Moçâmedes *see* Namibe
Mochudi *78 C4* Kgatleng, SE Botswana
Mocímboa da Praia *79 F2 var.* Vila de Mocímboa da Praia. Cabo Delgado, N Mozambique
Môco *78 B2 var.* Morro de Môco. *mountain* W Angola
Mocoa *58 A4* Putumayo, SW Colombia
Môco, Morro de *see* Môco
Mocuba *79 E3* Zambézia, NE Mozambique
Modena *96 B3 anc.* Mutina. Emilia-Romagna, N Italy
Modesto *47 B6* California, W USA
Modica *97 C7 anc.* Motyca. Sicilia, Italy, C Mediterranean Sea
Modimolle *78 D4 prev.* Nylstroom. Limpopo, NE South Africa
Modohn *see* Madona
Modriča *100 C3* Republika Srpska, N Bosnia and Herzegovina
Moe *149 C7* Victoria, SE Australia
Möen *see* Møn, Denmark
Moero, Lac *see* Mweru, Lake
Moeskroen *see* Mouscron
Mogadiscio/Mogadishu *see* Muqdisho
Mogador *see* Essaouira
Mogilëv *see* Mahilyow
Mogilev-Podol'skiy *see* Mohyliv-Podil's'kyy
Mogilno *98 C3* Kujawsko-pomorskie, C Poland
Mohammedia *70 C2 prev.* Fédala. NW Morocco
Mohave, Lake *47 D7 reservoir* Arizona/ Nevada, W USA
Mohawk River *41 F3 river* New York, NE USA
Mohéli *79 F2 var.* Mwali, Mohilla, Mohila, *Fr.* Moili. *island* S Comoros
Mohila *see* Mohéli
Mohilla *see* Mohéli
Mohns Ridge *83 F3 undersea ridge* Greenland Sea/Norwegian Sea
Moho *61 E4* Puno, SE Peru
Mohoro *73 C7* Pwani, E Tanzania
Mohyliv-Podil's'kyy *108 D3 Rus.* Mogilev-Podol'skiy. Vinnyts'ka Oblast', C Ukraine
Moi *85 A6* Rogaland, S Norway
Moili *see* Mohéli
Mo i Rana *84 C3* Nordland, C Norway
Mõisaküla *106 D3 Ger.* Moiseküll. Viljandimaa, S Estonia
Moiseküll *see* Mõisaküla
Moissac *91 B6* Tarn-et-Garonne, S France
Mojácar *93 E5* Andalucía, S Spain
Mojave Desert *47 D7 plain* California, W USA
Mokrany *see* Makrany
Moktama *see* Martaban
Mol *87 C5 prev.* Moll. Antwerpen, N Belgium
Moldavia *see* Moldova
Moldavian SSR/Moldavskaya SSR *see* Moldova
Molde *85 A5* Møre og Romsdal, S Norway

Moldotau, Khrebet *see* Moldo-Too, Khrebet
Moldo-Too, Khrebet *123 G2 prev.* Khrebet Moldotau. *mountain range* C Kyrgyzstan
Moldova *108 D3 off.* Republic of Moldova, *var.* Moldavia; *prev.* Moldavian SSR, *Rus.* Moldavskaya SSR. *country* SE Europe

<table><tr><td colspan="2">**MOLDOVA**
Southeast Europe</td></tr></table>

Official name Republic of Moldova
Formation 1991 / 1991
Capital Chisinau
Population 4.2 million / 323 people per sq mile (125 people per sq km) / 46%
Total area 13,067 sq miles (33,843 sq km)
Languages Moldovan*, Ukrainian, Russian
Religions Orthodox Christian 98%, Jewish 2%
Ethnic mix Moldovan 65%, Ukrainian 14%, Russian 13%, Other 4%, Gagauz 4%
Government Parliamentary system
Currency Moldovan leu = 100 bani
Literacy rate 96%
Calorie consumption 2806 calories

Moldova Nouă *108 A4 Ger.* Neumoldowa, *Hung.* Ujmoldova. Caraş-Severin, SW Romania
Moldova, Republic of *see* Moldova
Moldoveanul *see* Vârful Moldoveanu
Molfetta *97 E5* Puglia, SE Italy
Moll *see* Mol
Mollendo *61 E4* Arequipa, SW Peru
Mölndal *85 B7* Västra Götaland, S Sweden
Molochans'k *109 G4 Rus.* Molochansk. Zaporiz'ka Oblast', SE Ukraine
Molodechno/Molodeczno *see* Maladzyechna
Molodezhnaya *154 C2 Russian research station* Antarctica
Moloka'i *47 B8 var.* Molokai. *island* Hawaiian Islands, Hawai'i, USA
Molokai Fracture Zone *153 E2 tectonic feature* NE Pacific Ocean
Molopo *78 C4 seasonal river* Botswana/ South Africa
Mólos *105 B5* Stereá Ellás, C Greece
Molotov *see* Severodvinsk, Arkhangel'skaya Oblast', Russian Federation
Molotov *see* Perm', Permskaya Oblast', Russian Federation
Moluccas *see* Maluku
Molucca Sea *139 F4 Ind.* Laut Maluku. *sea* E Indonesia
Molukken *see* Maluku
Mombasa *73 D7* Coast, SE Kenya
Mombasa *73 D7* Coast, SE Kenya
Mombetsu *see* Monbetsu
Momchilgrad *104 D3 prev.* Mastanli. Kŭrdzhali, S Bulgaria
Møn *85 B8 prev.* Möen. *island* SE Denmark
Mona, Canal de la *see* Mona Passage
Monaco *91 C7 var.* Monaco-Ville; *anc.* Monoecus. *country capital* (Monaco) S Monaco
Monaco *91 E6 off.* Principality of Monaco. *country* W Europe

<table><tr><td colspan="2">**MONACO**
Southern Europe</td></tr></table>

Official name Principality of Monaco
Formation 1861 / 1861
Capital Monaco-Ville
Population 32,409 / 43212 people per sq mile (16620 people per sq km) / 100%
Total area 0.75 sq miles (1.95 sq km)
Languages French*, Italian, Monégasque, English
Religions Roman Catholic 89%, Protestant 6%, Other 5%
Ethnic mix French 47%, Other 20%, Monégasque 17%, Italian 16%
Government Monarchy
Currency Euro = 100 cents
Literacy rate 99%
Calorie consumption Not available

Monaco *see* München
Monaco, Port de *91 C8 bay* S Monaco W Mediterranean Sea
Monaco, Principality of *see* Monaco
Monaco-Ville *see* Monaco
Monahans *49 E3* Texas, SW USA
Mona, Isla *55 E3 island* W Puerto Rico
Mona Passage *55 E3 Sp.* Canal de la Mona. *channel* Dominican Republic/ Puerto Rico
Monastir *see* Bitola
Monbetsu *130 D2 var.* Mombetsu, Monbetu. Hokkaidō, NE Japan
Monbetu *see* Monbetsu
Moncalieri *96 A2* Piemonte, NW Italy
Monchegorsk *110 C2* Murmanskaya Oblast', NW Russian Federation
Monclova *50 D2* Coahuila de Zaragoza, NE Mexico
Moncton *39 F4* New Brunswick, SE Canada
Mondovì *96 A2* Piemonte, NW Italy
Monfalcone *96 D2* Friuli-Venezia Giulia, NE Italy
Monforte de Lemos *92 C1* Galicia, NW Spain
Mongo *76 C3* Guéra, C Chad
Mongolia *126 C2 Mong.* Mongol Uls. *country* E Asia

<table><tr><td colspan="2">**MONGOLIA**
East Asia</td></tr></table>

Official name Mongolia
Formation 1924 / 1924
Capital Ulan Bator
Population 2.6 million / 4 people per sq mile (2 people per sq km) / 64%
Total area 604,247 sq miles (1,565,000 sq km)
Languages Khalkha Mongolian*, Kazakh, Chinese, Russian
Religions Tibetan Buddhist 96%, Muslim 4%
Ethnic mix Mongol 90%, Kazakh 4%, Other 2%, Chinese 2%, Russian 2%
Government Mixed presidential– parliamentary system
Currency Tugrik (tögrög) = 100 möngö
Literacy rate 98%
Calorie consumption 2249 calories

Mongolia, Plateau of *124 D1 plateau* E Mongolia
Mongol Uls *see* Mongolia
Mongora *see* Mingãora
Mongos, Chaîne des *see* Bongo, Massif des
Mongu *78 C2* Western, W Zambia
Monkchester *see* Newcastle upon Tyne
Monkey Bay *79 E2* Southern, SE Malawi
Monkey River *see* Monkey River Town
Monkey River Town *52 C2 var.* Monkey River. Toledo, SE Belize
Monoecus *see* Monaco
Mono Lake *47 C6 lake* California, W USA
Monostor *see* Beli Manastir
Monóvar *93 F4 Cat.* Monover. País Valenciano, E Spain
Monover *see* Monóvar
Monroe *42 B2* Louisiana, S USA
Monrovia *74 C5 country capital* (Liberia) W Liberia
Mons *87 B6 Dut.* Bergen. Hainaut, S Belgium
Monselice *96 C2* Veneto, NE Italy
Montana *104 C2 prev.* Ferdinand, Mikhaylovgrad. Montana, NW Bulgaria
Montana *44 B1 off.* State of Montana, *also known as* Mountain State, Treasure State. *state* NW USA
Montargis *90 C4* Loiret, C France
Montauban *91 B6* Tarn-et-Garonne, S France
Montbéliard *90 D4* Doubs, E France
Mont Cenis, Col du *91 D5 pass* E France
Mont-de-Marsan *91 B6* Landes, SW France
Monteagudo *61 G4* Chuquisaca, S Bolivia
Montecarlo *61 C8* Misiones, NE Argentina
Monte Caseros *64 D3* Corrientes, NE Argentina

Monte Cristi *54 D3 var.* San Fernando de Monte Cristi. NW Dominican Republic
Monte Croce Carnico, Passo di *see* Plöcken Pass
Montegiardino *96 E2* SE San Marino
Montego Bay *54 A4 var.* Mobay. W Jamaica
Montélimar *91 D5 anc.* Acunum Acusio, Montilium Adhemari. Drôme, E France
Montemorelos *51 E3* Nuevo León, NE Mexico
Montenegro *101 C5 Serb.* Crna Gora. *country* SW Europe

MONTENEGRO
Europe

Official name Republic of Montenegro
Formation 2006 / 2006
Capital Podgorica
Population 620,145 / 116 people per sq mile (45 people per sq km) / 62%
Total area 5,332 sq miles (13,812 sq km)
Languages Montenegrin, Serbian, Albanian
Religions Orthodox Christian 74%, Muslim 18%, Roman Catholic 4%, Other 4%
Ethnic mix Montenegrin 43%, Serb 32%, Bosniak 8%, Albanian 5%, Other 12%
Government Parliamentary system
Currency Euro = 100 cents
Literacy rate 98%
Calorie consumption Not available

Monte Patria *64 B3* Coquimbo, N Chile
Monterey *47 B6* California, W USA
Monterey *see* Monterrey
Monterey Bay *47 A6 bay* California, W USA
Montería *58 B2* Córdoba, NW Colombia
Montero *61 G4* Santa Cruz, C Bolivia
Monterrey *51 E3 var.* Monterey. Nuevo León, NE Mexico
Montes Claros *63 F3* Minas Gerais, SE Brazil
Montevideo *64 D4 country capital* (Uruguay) Montevideo, S Uruguay
Montevideo *45 F2* Minnesota, N USA
Montgenèvre, Col de *91 D5 pass* France/Italy
Montgomery *42 D2 state capital* Alabama, S USA
Montgomery *see* Sāhiwāl
Monthey *95 A7* Valais, SW Switzerland
Montilium Adhemari *see* Montélimar
Montluçon *90 C4* Allier, C France
Montoro *92 D4* Andalucía, S Spain
Montpelier *41 G2 state capital* Vermont, NE USA
Montpellier *91 C6* Hérault, S France
Montréal *39 E4 Eng.* Montreal. Québec, SE Canada
Montrose *88 D3* E Scotland, UK
Montrose *44 C5* Colorado, C USA
Montserrat *55 G3 var.* Emerald Isle. *UK dependent territory* E West Indies
Monywa *136 B3* Sagaing, C Myanmar (Burma)
Monza *96 B2* Lombardia, N Italy
Monze *78 D2* Southern, S Zambia
Monzón *93 F2* Aragón, NE Spain
Moonie *149 D5* Queensland, E Australia
Moon-Sund *see* Väinameri
Moora *147 A6* Western Australia
Moore *49 G1* Oklahoma, C USA
Moore, Lake *147 B6 lake* Western Australia
Moorhead *45 F2* Minnesota, N USA
Moose *38 C3 river* Ontario, S Canada
Moosehead Lake *41 G1 lake* Maine, NE USA
Moosonee *38 C3* Ontario, S Canada
Mopti *75 E3* Mopti, C Mali
Moquegua *61 E4* Moquegua, SE Peru
Mora *85 C5* Dalarna, C Sweden
Morales *52 C2* Izabal, E Guatemala
Morant Bay *54 B5* E Jamaica
Moratalla *93 E4* Murcia, SE Spain
Morava *99 B5* Iowa, C USA
Morava *see* Velika Morava, Serbia
Moravia *99 B5* Iowa, C USA
Moray Firth *88 C3 inlet* N Scotland, UK

Morea *see* Pelopónnisos
Moreau River *44 D2 river* South Dakota, N USA
Moree *149 D5* New South Wales, SE Australia
Morelia *51 E4* Michoacán de Ocampo, S Mexico
Morena, Sierra *92 C4 mountain range* S Spain
Moreni *108 C5* Dâmbovița, S Romania
Mórfou *see* Güzelyurt Körfezi
Morgan City *42 B3* Louisiana, S USA
Morghāb, Daryā-ye *122 D3 Rus.* Murgab, Murghab, *Turkm.* Murgap, Murgap Deryasy. *river* Afghanistan/ Turkmenistan Asia
Morghāb, Daryā-ye *see* Murgap
Morioka *130 D4* Iwate, Honshū, C Japan
Morlaix *90 A3* Finistère, NW France
Mormon State *see* Utah
Mornington Abyssal Plain *67 A7 abyssal plain* SE Pacific Ocean
Mornington Island *148 B2 island* Wellesley Islands, Queensland, N Australia
Morocco *70 B3 off.* Kingdom of Morocco, *Ar.* Al Mamlakah. *country* N Africa

MOROCCO
North Africa

Official name Kingdom of Morocco
Formation 1956 / 1956
Capital Rabat
Population 31.5 million / 183 people per sq mile (71 people per sq km) / 56%
Total area 172,316 sq miles (446,300 sq km)
Languages Arabic*, Tamazight (Berber), French, Spanish
Religions Muslim (mainly Sunni) 99%, Other (mostly Christian) 1%
Ethnic mix Arab 70%, Berber 29%, European 1%
Government Monarchy
Currency Moroccan dirham = 100 centimes
Literacy rate 51%
Calorie consumption 3052 calories

Morocco *see* Marrakech
Morocco, Kingdom of *see* Morocco
Morogoro *73 C7* Morogoro, E Tanzania
Moro Gulf *139 E3 gulf* S Philippines
Morón *54 C2* Ciego de Ávila, C Cuba
Mörön *126 D2* Hövsgöl, N Mongolia
Morondava *79 F3* Toliara, W Madagascar
Moroni *79 F2 country capital* (Comoros) Grande Comore, NW Comoros
Morotai, Pulau *139 F3 island* Maluku, E Indonesia
Morotiri *see* Marotiri
Morphou *see* Güzelyurt Körfezi
Morrinsville *150 D3* Waikato, North Island, New Zealand
Morris *45 F2* Minnesota, N USA
Morris Jesup, Kap *83 E1 headland* N Greenland
Mórtu, Kólpos *see* Güzelyurt Körfezi
Morvan *90 D4 physical region* C France
Moscow *46 C2* Idaho, NW USA
Moscow *see* Moskva
Mosel *95 A5 Fr.* Moselle. *river* W Europe
Mosel *see* Moselle
Moselle *90 D3 cultural region* NE France
Moselle *90 D3 department* NE France
Moselle *87 E8 Ger.* Mosel. *river* W Europe
Moselle *see* Mosel
Mosgiel *151 B7* Otago, South Island, New Zealand
Moshi *73 C6* Kilimanjaro, NE Tanzania
Mosjøen *84 B4* Nordland, C Norway
Moskovskiy *see* Moskva
Moskva *111 B5 Eng.* Moscow. *country capital* (Russian Federation) Gorod Moskva, W Russian Federation
Moskva *123 E3 Rus.* Moskovskiy; *prev.* Chubek. SW Tajikistan
Moson and Magyaróvár *see* Mosonmagyaróvár

Mosonmagyaróvár *99 C6 Ger.* Wieselburg-Ungarisch-Altenburg; *prev.* Moson and Magyaróvár, *Ger.* Wieselburg und Ungarisch-Altenburg. Győr-Moson-Sopron, NW Hungary
Mosquito Coast *see* La Mosquitia
Mosquito Gulf *see* Mosquitos, Golfo de los
Mosquitos, Golfo de los *53 F4 Eng.* Mosquito Gulf. *gulf* N Panama
Moss *85 B6* Østfold, S Norway
Mossâmedes *see* Namibe
Mosselbaai *78 C5 var.* Mosselbaai, Eng. Mossel Bay. Western Cape, SW South Africa
Mosselbai/Mossel Bay *see* Mosselbaai
Mossendjo *77 B6* Le Niari, SW Congo
Mossoró *63 G2* Rio Grande do Norte, NE Brazil
Most *98 A4 Ger.* Brüx. Ústecký Kraj, NW Czech Republic
Mosta *102 B5 var.* Musta. C Malta
Mostaganem *70 D2 var.* Mestghanem. NW Algeria
Mostar *100 C4* Federacija Bosna I Hercegovina, S Bosnia and Herzegovina
Mosty *see* Masty
Mosul *see* Al Mawşil
Mota del Cuervo *93 E3* Castilla-La Mancha, C Spain
Motagua, Río *52 B2 river* Guatemala/Honduras
Mother of Presidents/Mother of States *see* Virginia
Motril *92 D5* Andalucía, S Spain
Motru *108 B4* Gorj, SW Romania
Motueka *151 C5* Tasman, South Island, New Zealand
Moţul *51 H3 var.* Motul de Felipe Carrillo Puerto. Yucatán, SE Mexico
Motul de Felipe Carrillo Puerto *see* Motul
Motyca *see* Modica
Mouanda *see* Moanda
Mouhoun *see* Black Volta
Mouila *77 A6* Ngounié, C Gabon
Moukden *see* Shenyang
Mould Bay *37 E2* Northwest Territories, Prince Patrick Island, N Canada North America
Moulins *90 C4* Allier, C France
Moulmein *136 B4 var.* Maulmain, Mawlamyine. Mon State, S Myanmar (Burma)
Moundou *76 B4* Logone-Occidental, SW Chad
Moŭng Roessei *137 D5* Bătdâmbâng, W Cambodia
Moun Hou *see* Black Volta
Mountain Home *42 B1* Arkansas, C USA
Mountain State *see* Montana
Mountain State *see* West Virginia
Mount Cook *151 B6* Canterbury, South Island, New Zealand
Mount Desert Island *41 H2 island* Maine, NE USA
Mount Gambier *149 B7* South Australia
Mount Isa *148 B3* Queensland, C Australia
Mount Magnet *147 B5* Western Australia
Mount Pleasant *45 G4* Iowa, C USA
Mount Pleasant *40 C3* Michigan, N USA
Mount Vernon *40 B5* Illinois, N USA
Mount Vernon *46 B1* Washington, NW USA
Mourdi, Dépression du *76 C2 desert lowland* Chad/Sudan
Mouscron *87 A6 Dut.* Moeskroen. Hainaut, W Belgium
Mouse River *see* Souris River
Moussoro *76 B3* Kanem, W Chad
Moyen Atlas *70 C2 Eng.* Middle Atlas. *mountain range* N Morocco
Moyen-Congo *see* Congo (Republic of)
Mo'ynoq *122 C1 Rus.* Muynak. Qoraqalpog'iston Respublikasi, NW Uzbekistan
Moyobamba *60 B2* San Martín, NW Peru
Moyu *126 B3 var.* Karakax. Xinjiang Uygur Zizhiqu, NW China
Moyynkum, Peski *123 F1 Kaz.* Moyynqum. *desert* S Kazakhstan
Moyynqum, Peski *see* Moyynkum, Peski
Mozambika, Lakandranon' i *see* Mozambique Channel

MOZAMBIQUE
Southern Africa

Official name Republic of Mozambique
Formation 1975 / 1975
Capital Maputo
Population 19.8 million / 65 people per sq mile (25 people per sq km) / 40%
Total area 309,494 sq miles (801,590 sq km)
Languages Portuguese*, Makua, Xitsonga, Sena, Lomwe
Religions Traditional beliefs 56%, Christian 30%, Muslim 14%
Ethnic mix Makua Lomwe 47%, Tsonga 23%, Malawi 12%, Shona 11%, Yao 4%, Other 3%
Government Presidential system
Currency Metical = 100 centavos
Literacy rate 47%
Calorie consumption 2079 calories

Mozambique *79 E3 off.* Republic of Mozambique; *prev.* People's Republic of Mozambique, Portuguese East Africa. *country* S Africa
Mozambique Basin *see* Natal Basin
Mozambique, Canal de *see* Mozambique Channel
Mozambique Channel *79 E3 Fr.* Canal de Mozambique, *Mal.* Lakandranon' i Mozambika. *strait* W Indian Ocean
Mozambique, People's Republic of *see* Mozambique
Mozambique Plateau *69 D7 var.* Mozambique Rise. *undersea plateau* SW Indian Ocean
Mozambique, Republic of *see* Mozambique
Mozambique Rise *see* Mozambique Plateau
Mozyr' *see* Mazyr
Mpama *77 B6 river* C Congo
Mpika *78 D2* Northern, NE Zambia
Mqinvartsveri *see* Kazbek
Mragowo *98 D2 Ger.* Sensburg Warmińsko-Mazurskie, NE Poland
Mtkvari *see* Kura
Mtwara *73 D8* Mtwara, SE Tanzania
Mualo *see* Messalo, Rio
Muang Chiang Rai *see* Chiang Rai
Muang Kalasin *see* Kalasin
Muang Khammouan *see* Thakhèk
Muang Không *137 D5* Champasak, S Laos
Muang Khôngxédôn *137 D5 var.* Khong Sedone. Salavan, S Laos
Muang Khon Kaen *see* Khon Kaen
Muang Lampang *see* Lampang
Muang Loei *see* Loei
Muang Lom Sak *see* Lom Sak
Muang Nakhon Sawan *see* Nakhon Sawan
Muang Namo *136 C3* Oudômxai, N Laos
Muang Nan *see* Nan
Muang Phalan *136 D4 var.* Muang Phalane. Savannakhét, S Laos
Muang Phalane *see* Muang Phalan
Muang Phayao *see* Phayao
Muang Phitsanulok *see* Phitsanulok
Muang Phrae *see* Phrae
Muang Roi Et *see* Roi Et
Muang Sakon Nakhon *see* Sakon Nakhon
Muang Samut Prakan *see* Samut Prakan
Muang Sing *136 C3* Louang Namtha, N Laos
Muang Ubon *see* Ubon Ratchathani
Muang Xaignabouri *see* Xaignabouli
Muar *138 B3 var.* Bandar Maharani. Johor, Peninsular Malaysia
Mucojo *79 F2* Cabo Delgado, N Mozambique
Mudanjiang *129 E3 var.* Mu-tan-chiang. Heilongjiang, NE China
Mudon *137 B5* Mon State, S Myanmar (Burma)
Muenchen *see* München
Muenster *see* Münster
Mufulira *78 D2* Copperbelt, C Zambia
Mughla *see* Muğla
Muğla *116 A4 var.* Mughla. Muğla, SW Turkey
Mūh, Sabkhat al *134 C3 lake* C Syria
Muhu Väin *see* Väinameri

Muisne *60 A1* Esmeraldas, NW Ecuador
Mukacheve *108 B3 Hung.* Munkács, *Rus.* Mukachevo. Zakarpats'ka Oblast', W Ukraine
Mukachevo *see* Mukacheve
Mukalla *see* Al Mukallā
Mukden *see* Shenyang
Mula *93 E4* Murcia, SE Spain
Mulaku Atoll *132 B4 var.* Meemu Atoll. *atoll* C Maldives
Muleshoe *49 E2* Texas, SW USA
Mulhacén *93 E5 var.* Cerro de Mulhacén. *mountain* S Spain
Mulhacén, Cerro de *see* Mulhacén
Mülhausen *see* Mulhouse
Mülheim *95 A6 var.* Mulheim an der Ruhr. Nordrhein-Westfalen, W Germany
Mulheim an der Ruhr *see* Mülheim
Mulhouse *90 E4 Ger.* Mülhausen. Haut-Rhin, NE France
Müller-gerbergte *see* Muller, Pegunungan
Muller, Pegunungan *138 D4 Dut.* Müller-gerbergte. *mountain range* Borneo, C Indonesia
Mull, Isle of *88 B4 island* W Scotland, UK
Mulongo *77 D7* Katanga, SE Dem. Rep. Congo
Multān *134 C2* Punjab, E Pakistan
Mumbai *134 C5 prev.* Bombay. *state capital* Mahārāshtra, W India
Munamägi *see* Suur Munamägi
Münchberg *95 C5* Bayern, E Germany
München *80 D4 var.* Muenchen, *Eng.* Munich, *It.* Monaco. Bayern, SE Germany
Muncie *40 C4* Indiana, N USA
Mungbere *77 E5* Orientale, NE Dem. Rep. Congo
Mu Nggava *see* Rennell
Munich *see* München
Munkács *see* Mukacheve
Münster *94 A4 var.* Muenster, Münster in Westfalen. Nordrhein-Westfalen, W Germany
Munster *89 A6 Ir.* Cúige Mumhan. *cultural region* S Ireland
Münster in Westfalen *see* Münster
Muong Xiang Ngeun *136 C4 var.* Xieng Ngeun. Louangphabang, N Laos
Muonio *84 D3* Lappi, N Finland
Muonioälv/Muoniojoki *see* Muonionjoki
Muonionjoki *84 D3 var.* Muoniojoki, *Swe.* Muonioälv. *river* Finland/Sweden
Muqāṭ *119 C5* Al Mafraq, E Jordan
Muqdisho *73 D6 Eng.* Mogadishu, *It.* Mogadiscio. *country capital* (Somalia) Banaadir, S Somalia
Mur *95 E7 SCr.* Mura. *river* C Europe
Mura *see* Mur
Muradiye *117 F3* Van, E Turkey
Murapara *see* Murupara
Murata *96 E2* S San Marino
Murchison River *147 A5 river* Western Australia
Murcia *93 F4* Murcia, SE Spain
Murcia *93 E4 autonomous community* SE Spain
Mureş *108 A4 river* Hungary/Romania
Murfreesboro *42 D1* Tennessee, S USA
Murgab *see* Morghāb, Daryā-ye
Murgab *see* Morghāb, Daryā-ye
Murgab *see* Murghob
Murgap *122 D3 Rus.* Murgap. Mary Welaýaty, S Turkmenistan
Murgap *122 D3 var.* Deryasy Murgap, Murghab, *Pash.* Daryā-ye Morghāb, *Rus.* Murgab. *river* Afghanistan/Turkmenistan
Murgap *see* Morghāb, Daryā-ye
Murgap *see* Morghāb, Daryā-ye
Murgap Deryasy *see* Morghāb, Daryā-ye
Murgap Deryasy *see* Morghāb, Daryā-ye
Murghab *see* Morghāb, Daryā-ye
Murghab *see* Morghāb, Daryā-ye
Murghob *123 F3 Rus.* Murgab. SE Tajikistan
Murgon *149 E5* Queensland, E Australia
Mūrītānīyah *see* Mauritania
Müritz *94 C3 var.* Müritzee. *lake* NE Germany
Müritzee *see* Müritz
Murmansk *110 C2* Murmanskaya Oblast', NW Russian Federation
Murmashi *110 C2* Murmanskaya Oblast', NW Russian Federation
Murom *111 B5* Vladimirskaya Oblast', W Russian Federation
Muroran *130 D3* Hokkaidō, NE Japan
Muros *92 B1* Galicia, NW Spain
Murray Fracture Zone *153 E2 fracture zone* NE Pacific Ocean
Murray Range *see* Murray Ridge
Murray Ridge *112 C5 var.* Murray Range. *undersea ridge* N Arabian Sea
Murray River *149 B6 river* SE Australia
Murrumbidgee River *149 C6 river* New South Wales, SE Australia
Murska Sobota *95 E7 Ger.* Olsnitz. NE Slovenia
Murupara *150 E3 var.* Murapara. Bay of Plenty, North Island, New Zealand
Murviedro *see* Sagunto
Murwāra *135 E4* Madhya Pradesh, N India
Murwillumbah *149 E5* New South Wales, SE Australia
Murzuq, Edeyin *see* Murzuq, Idhān
Murzuq, Idhān *71 F4 var.* Edeyin Murzuq. *desert* SW Libya
Mürzzuschlag *95 E7* Steiermark, E Austria
Muş *117 F3 var.* Mush. Muş, E Turkey
Mûsa, Gebel *72 C2 mountain* NE Egypt
Musala *104 B3 mountain* W Bulgaria
Muscat *see* Masqaṭ
Muscat and Oman *see* Oman
Muscatine *45 G3* Iowa, C USA
Musgrave Ranges *147 D5 mountain range* South Australia
Musina *78 D3 prev.* Messina. Limpopo, NE South Africa
Muskegon *40 C3* Michigan, N USA
Muskogean *see* Tallahassee
Muskogee *49 G1* Oklahoma, C USA
Musoma *73 C6* Mara, N Tanzania
Musta *see* Mosta
Mustafa-Pasha *see* Svilengrad
Musters, Lago *65 B6 lake* S Argentina
Muswellbrook *149 D6* New South Wales, SE Australia
Mut *116 C4* Mersin, S Turkey
Mu-tan-chiang *see* Mudanjiang
Mutare *78 D3 var.* Mutari; *prev.* Umtali. Manicaland, E Zimbabwe
Mutari *see* Mutare
Mutina *see* Modena
Mutsu-wan *130 D3 bay* N Japan
Muttonbird Islands *151 A8 island group* SW New Zealand
Mu Us Shadi *127 E3 var.* Ordos Desert; *prev.* Mu Us Shamo. *desert* N China
Mu Us Shamo *see* Mu Us Shadi
Muy Muy *52 D3* Matagalpa, C Nicaragua
Muynak *see* Mo'ynoq
Mužlja *100 D3 Hung.* Felsőmuzslya; *prev.* Gornja Mužlja. Vojvodina, N Serbia
Mwali *see* Mohéli
Mwanza *73 B6* Mwanza, NW Tanzania
Mweka *77 C6* Kasai Occidental, C Dem. Rep. Congo
Mwene-Ditu *77 D7* Kasai Oriental, S Dem. Rep. Congo
Mweru, Lake *77 D7 var.* Lac Moero. *lake* Dem. Rep. Congo/Zambia
Myadel' *see* Myadzyel
Myadzyel *107 C5 Pol.* Miadzioł Nowy, *Rus.* Myadel'. Minskaya Voblasts', N Belarus
Myanaung *136 B4* Irrawaddy, SW Myanmar (Burma)
Myanmar *136 A3 off.* Union of Myanmar, *Eng.* Burma. *country* SE Asia

MYANMAR (BURMA)
Southeast Asia

Official name Union of Myanmar
Formation 1948 / 1948
Capital Nay Pyi Taw
Population 50.5 million / 199 people per sq mile (77 people per sq km) / 28%
Total area 261,969 sq miles (678,500 sq km)
Languages Burmese*, Shan, Karen, Rakhine, Chin, Yangbye, Kachin, Mon
Religions Buddhist 87%, Christian 6%, Muslim 4%, Other 2%, Hindu 1%
Ethnic mix Burman (Bamah) 68%, Other 13%, Shan 9%, Karen 6%, Rakhine 4%
Government Military-based regime

MYANMAR (BURMA)
Southeast Asia

Currency Kyat = 100 pyas
Literacy rate 90%
Calorie consumption 2937 calories

Myaungmya *136 A4* Irrawaddy, SW Myanmar (Burma)
Myerkulavichy *107 D7 Rus.* Merkulovichi. Homyel'skaya Voblasts', SE Belarus
Myingyan *136 B3* Mandalay, C Myanmar (Burma)
Myitkyina *136 B2* Kachin State, N Myanmar (Burma)
Mykolayiv *109 E4 Rus.* Nikolayev. Mykolayivs'ka Oblast', S Ukraine
Mýkonos *105 D6 var.* Míkonos. *island* Kykládes, Greece, Aegean Sea
Myrhorod *109 F2 Rus.* Mirgorod. Poltavs'ka Oblast', NE Ukraine
Mýrina *104 D4 var.* Mírina. Límnos, SE Greece
Myrtle Beach *43 F2* South Carolina, SE USA
Mýrtos *105 D8* Kríti, Greece, E Mediterranean Sea
Myrtoum Mare *see* Mirtóo Pélagos
Myślibórz *98 B3* Zachodnio-pomorskie, NW Poland
Mysore *132 C2 var.* Maisur. Karnātaka, W India
Mysore *see* Karnātaka
My Tho *137 E6 var.* Mi Tho. Tiên Giang, S Vietnam
Mytilene *see* Mytilíni
Mytilíni *105 D5 var.* Mitilíni; *anc.* Mytilene. Lésvos, E Greece
Mzuzu *79 E2* Northern, N Malawi

N

Naberezhnyye Chelny *111 D5 prev.* Brezhnev. Respublika Tatarstan, W Russian Federation
Nablus *119 A6 var.* Nābulus, *Heb.* Shekhem; *anc.* Neapolis, *Bibl.* Shechem. N West Bank
Nābulus *see* Nablus
Nacala *79 F2* Nampula, NE Mozambique
Na-Ch'ii *see* Nagqu
Nada *see* Danzhou
Nadi *145 E4 prev.* Nandi. Viti Levu, W Fiji
Nadur *102 A5* Gozo, N Malta
Nadvirna *108 C3 Pol.* Nadwórna, *Rus.* Nadvornaya. Ivano-Frankivs'ka Oblast', W Ukraine
Nadvoitsy *110 B3* Respublika Kareliya, NW Russian Federation
Nadvornaya/Nadwórna *see* Nadvirna
Nadym *114 C3* Yamalo-Nenetskiy Avtonomnyy Okrug, N Russian Federation
Náfpaktos *105 B5 var.* Návpaktos. Dytikí Ellás, C Greece
Náfplio *105 B6 prev.* Návplion. Pelopónnisos, S Greece
Naga *139 E2 off.* Naga City; *prev.* Nueva Caceres. Luzon, N Philippines
Naga City *see* Naga
Nagano *131 C5* Nagano, Honshū, S Japan
Nagaoka *131 D5* Niigata, Honshū, C Japan
Nagara Pathom *see* Nakhon Pathom
Nagara Sridharmaraj *see* Nakhon Si Thammarat
Nagara Svarga *see* Nakhon Sawan
Nagasaki *131 A7* Nagasaki, Kyūshū, SW Japan
Nagato *131 A7* Yamaguchi, Honshū, SW Japan
Nāgercoil *132 C3* Tamil Nādu, SE India
Nagorno-Karabakh *117 G3 var.* Nagorno- Karabakhskaya Avtonomnaya Oblast, *Arm.* Lerrnayin Gharabakh, *Az.* Dağliq Quarabağ, *Rus.* Nagornyy Karabakh. *former autonomous region* SW Azerbaijan
Nagorno- Karabakhskaya Avtonomnaya Oblast *see* Nagorno-Karabakh
Nagornyy Karabakh *see* Nagorno-Karabakh
Nagoya *131 C6* Aichi, Honshū, SW Japan
Nāgpur *134 D4* Mahārāshtra, C India
Nagqu *126 C5 Chin.* Na-Ch'ii; *prev.* Hei-ho. Xizang Zizhiqu, W China
Nagybánya *see* Baia Mare
Nagybecskerek *see* Zrenjanin
Nagydisznód *see* Cisnădie
Nagyenyed *see* Aiud
Nagykálló *99 E6* Szabolcs-Szatmár-Bereg, E Hungary
Nagykanizsa *99 C7 Ger.* Grosskanizsa. Zala, SW Hungary
Nagykároly *see* Carei
Nagykikinda *see* Kikinda
Nagykőrös *99 D7* Pest, C Hungary
Nagymihály *see* Michalovce
Nagysurány *see* Šurany
Nagyszalonta *see* Salonta
Nagyszeben *see* Sibiu
Nagyszentmiklós *see* Sânnicolau Mare
Nagyszöllös *see* Vynohradiv
Nagyszombat *see* Trnava
Nagytapolcsány *see* Topoľčany
Nagyvárad *see* Oradea
Naha *130 A3* Okinawa, Okinawa, SW Japan
Nahariya *see* Nahariyya
Nahariyya *119 A5 var.* Nahariya. Northern, N Israel
Nahuel Huapí, Lago *65 B5 lake* W Argentina
Nain *39 F2* Newfoundland and Labrador, NE Canada
Nā'īn *120 D3* Eşfahān, C Iran
Nairobi *69 E5 country capital* (Kenya) Nairobi Area, S Kenya
Nairobi *73 C6* Nairobi Area, S Kenya
Naissus *see* Niš
Najaf *see* An Najaf
Najima *see* Fukuoka
Najin *129 E3* NE North Korea
Najrān *121 B6 var.* Abā as Su'ūd. Najrān, S Saudi Arabia
Nakambé *see* White Volta
Nakamura *131 B7* Kōchi, Shikoku, SW Japan
Nakatsugawa *131 C6 var.* Nakatugawa. Gifu, Honshū, SW Japan
Nakatugawa *see* Nakatsugawa
Nakhichevan' *see* Naxçıvan
Nakhodka *115 G5* Primorskiy Kray, SE Russian Federation
Nakhon Pathom *137 C5 var.* Nagara Pathom, Nakorn Pathom. Nakhon Pathom, W Thailand
Nakhon Ratchasima *137 C5 var.* Khorat, Korat. Nakhon Ratchasima, E Thailand
Nakhon Sawan *137 C5 var.* Muang Nakhon Sawan, Nagara Svarga. Nakhon Sawan, W Thailand
Nakhon Si Thammarat *137 C7 var.* Nagara Sridharmaraj, Nakhon Sithamnaraj. Nakhon Si Thammarat, SW Thailand
Nakhon Sithamnaraj *see* Nakhon Si Thammarat
Nakorn Pathom *see* Nakhon Pathom
Nakuru *73 C6* Rift Valley, SW Kenya
Nal'chik *111 B8* Kabardino-Balkarskaya Respublika, SW Russian Federation
Nālūt *71 F2* NW Libya
Namakan Lake *40 A1 lake* Canada/USA
Namangan *123 F2* Namangan Viloyati, E Uzbekistan
Nambala *78 D2* Central, C Zambia
Nam Co *126 C5 lake* W China
Nam Đinh *136 D3* Nam Ha, N Vietnam
Namib Desert *78 B3 desert* W Namibia
Namibe *78 A2 Port.* Moçâmedes, Mossâmedes. Namibe, SW Angola
Namibia *78 B3 off.* Republic of Namibia, *var.* South West Africa, *Afr.* Suidwes-Afrika, *Ger.* Deutsch-Südwestafrika; *prev.* German Southwest Africa, South-West Africa. *country* S Africa

NAMIBIA
Southern Africa

Official name Republic of Namibia
Formation 1990 / 1994
Capital Windhoek
Population 2 million / 6 people per sq mile (2 people per sq km) / 31%
Total area 318,694 sq miles (825,418 sq km)
Languages English*, Ovambo, Kavango, Bergdama, German, Afrikaans

NAMIBIA
Southern Africa

Religions Christian 90%, Traditional beliefs 10%
Ethnic mix Ovambo 50%, Other tribes 16%, Kavango 9%, Other 9%, Damara 8%, Herero 8%
Government Presidential system
Currency Namibian dollar = 100 cents
Literacy rate 85%
Calorie consumption 2278 calories

Namibia, Republic of *see* Namibia
Namnetes *see* Nantes
Namo *see* Namu Atoll
Nam Ou *136 C3 river* N Laos
Nampa *46 D3* Idaho, NW USA
Nampula *79 E2* Nampula, NE Mozambique
Namsos *84 B4* Nord-Trøndelag, C Norway
Nam Tha *136 C4 river* N Laos
Namu Atoll *144 D2 var.* Namo. *atoll* Ralik Chain, C Marshall Islands
Namur *87 C6 Dut.* Namen. Namur, SE Belgium
Namyit Island *128 C8 island* S Spratly Islands
Nan *136 C4 var.* Muang Nan. Nan, NW Thailand
Nanaimo *36 D5* Vancouver Island, British Columbia, SW Canada
Nanchang *128 C5 var.* Nan-ch'ang, Nanch'ang-hsien. *province capital* Jiangxi, S China
Nan-ch'ang *see* Nanchang
Nanch'ang-hsien *see* Nanchang
Nan-ching *see* Nanjing
Nancy *90 D3* Meurthe-et-Moselle, NE France
Nandaime *52 D3* Granada, SW Nicaragua
Nānded *134 D5* Mahārāshtra, C India
Nandi *see* Nadi
Nándorhgy *see* Oţelu Roşu
Nandyāl *132 C1* Andhra Pradesh, E India
Nan Hai *see* South China Sea
Naniwa *see* Ōsaka
Nanjing *128 D5 var.* Nan-ching, Nanking; *prev.* Chianning, Chian-ning, Kiang-ning, Jiangsu. *province capital* Jiangsu, E China
Nanking *see* Nanjing
Nanning *128 B6 var.* Nan-ning; *prev.* Yung-ning. Guangxi Zhuangzu Zizhiqu, S China
Nan-ning *see* Nanning
Nanortalik *82 C5* Kitaa, S Greenland
Nanpan Jiang *136 D2 river* S China
Nanping *128 D6 var.* Nan-p'ing; *prev.* Yenping. Fujian, SE China
Nan-p'ing *see* Nanping
Nansei-shotō *125 E3 Eng.* Ryukyu Islands. *island group* SW Japan
Nansei Syotō Trench *see* Ryukyu Trench
Nansen Basin *155 C4 undersea basin* Arctic Ocean
Nansen Cordillera *155 B3 var.* Arctic Mid Oceanic Ridge, Nansen Ridge. *seamount range* Arctic Ocean
Nansen Ridge *see* Nansen Cordillera
Nansha Qundao *see* Spratly Islands
Nanterre *90 D1* Hauts-de-Seine, N France
Nantes *90 B4 Bret.* Naoned; *anc.* Condivincum, Namnetes. Loire-Atlantique, NW France
Nantucket Island *41 G3 island* Massachusetts, NE USA
Nanumaga *145 E3 atoll* NW Tuvalu
Nanumea Atoll *145 E3 atoll* NW Tuvalu
Nanyang *128 C5 var.* Nan-yang. Henan, C China
Nan-yang *see* Nanyang
Naoned *see* Nantes
Napa *47 B6* California, W USA
Napier *150 E4* Hawke's Bay, North Island, New Zealand
Naples *43 E5* Florida, SE USA
Naples *see* Napoli
Napo *56 A3 province* NE Ecuador
Napoléon-Vendée *see* la Roche-sur-Yon
Napoli *80 D5 Eng.* Naples, *Ger.* Neapel; *anc.* Neapolis. Campania, S Italy
Napo, Río *60 C1 river* Ecuador/Peru
Naracoorte *149 B7* South Australia
Naradhivas *see* Narathiwat
Narathiwat *137 C7 var.* Naradhivas. Narathiwat, SW Thailand
Narbada *see* Narmada
Narbo Martius *see* Narbonne
Narbonne *91 C6 anc.* Narbo Martius. Aude, S France
Narborough Island *see* Fernandina, Isla
Nares Abyssal Plain *see* Nares Plain
Nares Plain *35 E6 var.* Nares Abyssal Plain. *abyssal plain* NW Atlantic Ocean
Nares Stræde *see* Nares Strait
Nares Strait *82 D1 Dan.* Nares Stræde. *strait* Canada/Greenland
Narew *98 E3 river* E Poland
Narmada *124 B3 var.* Narbada. *river* C India
Narova *see* Narva
Narovlya *see* Narowlya
Narowlya *107 C8 Rus.* Narovlya. Homyel'skaya Voblasts', SE Belarus
Närpes *85 D5 Fin.* Närpiö. Länsi Soumi, W Finland
Närpiö *see* Närpes
Narrabri *149 D6* New South Wales, SE Australia
Narrogin *147 B6* Western Australia
Narva *106 E2* Ida-Virumaa, NE Estonia
Narva *106 E2 prev.* Narova. *river* Estonia/Russian Federation
Narva Bay *106 E2 Est.* Narva Laht, *Ger.* Narwa-Bucht, *Rus.* Narvskiy Zaliv. *bay* Estonia/Russian Federation
Narva Laht *see* Narva Bay
Narva Reservoir *106 E2 Est.* Narva Veehoidla, *Rus.* Narvskoye Vodokhranilishche. *reservoir* Estonia/Russian Federation
Narva Veehoidla *see* Narva Reservoir
Narvik *84 C3* Nordland, C Norway
Narvskiy Zaliv *see* Narva Bay
Narvskoye Vodokhranilishche *see* Narva Reservoir
Narwa-Bucht *see* Narva Bay
Nar'yan-Mar *110 D3 prev.* Beloshchel'ye, Dzerzhinskiy. Nenetskiy Avtonomnyy Okrug, NW Russian Federation
Naryn *123 G2* Narynskaya Oblast', C Kyrgyzstan
Năsăud *108 B3 Ger.* Nussdorf, *Hung.* Naszód. Bistriţa-Năsăud, N Romania
Nase *see* Naze
Nāshik *134 C5 prev.* Nāsik. Mahārāshtra, W India
Nashua *41 G3* New Hampshire, NE USA
Nashville *42 C1 state capital* Tennessee, S USA
Näsijärvi *85 D5 lake* SW Finland
Nāsik *see* Nāshik
Nāsiri *see* Ahvāz
Nasiriya *see* An Nāşirīyah
Nassau *54 C1 country capital* (Bahamas) New Providence, N Bahamas
Nasser, Lake *72 B3 lake* Egypt/Sudan
Naszód *see* Năsăud
Nata *78 C3* Central, NE Botswana
Natal *63 G2 state capital* Rio Grande do Norte, E Brazil
Natal Basin *141 A6 var.* Mozambique Basin. *undersea basin* W Indian Ocean
Natanya *see* Netanya
Natchez *42 B3* Mississippi, S USA
Natchitoches *42 A2* Louisiana, S USA
Nathanya *see* Netanya
Natitingou *75 F4* NW Benin
Natsrat *see* Nazerat
Natuna Islands *see* Natuna, Kepulauan
Natuna, Kepulauan *124 D4 var.* Natuna Islands. *island group* W Indonesia
Naturaliste Plateau *141 E6 undersea plateau* E Indian Ocean
Naugard *see* Nowogard
Naujamiestis *106 C4* Panevėžys, C Lithuania
Nauru *144 D2 off.* Republic of Nauru; *prev.* Pleasant Island. *country* W Pacific Ocean

NAURU
Australasia & Oceania

Official name Republic of Nauru
Formation 1968 / 1968
Capital None
Population 13,048 / 1611 people per sq mile (621 people per sq km) / 100%

NAURU
Australasia & Oceania

Total area 8.1 sq miles (21 sq km)
Languages Nauruan*, Kiribati, Chinese, Tuvaluan, English
Religions Nauruan Congregational Church 60%, Roman Catholic 35%, Other 5%
Ethnic mix Nauruan 62%, Other Pacific islanders 25%, Chinese and Vietnamese 8%, European 5%
Government Parliamentary system
Currency Australian dollar = 100 cents
Literacy rate 95%
Calorie consumption Not available

Nauru, Republic of *see* Nauru
Nauta *60 C2* Loreto, N Peru
Navahrudak *107 C6 Pol.* Nowogródek, *Rus.* Novogrudok. Hrodzyenskaya Voblasts', W Belarus
Navanagar *see* Jāmnagar
Navapolatsk *107 D5 Rus.* Novopolotsk. Vitsyebskaya Voblasts', N Belarus
Navarra *93 E2 Eng./Fr.* Navarre. *autonomous community* N Spain
Navarre *see* Navarra
Navassa Island *54 C3 US unincorporated territory* C West Indies
Navoi *see* Navoiy
Navoiy *123 E2 Rus.* Navoi. Navoiy Viloyati, C Uzbekistan
Navojoa *50 C2* Sonora, NW Mexico
Navolat *see* Navolato
Navolato *66 C3 var.* Navolat. Sinaloa, C Mexico
Návpaktos *see* Náfpaktos
Návplion *see* Náfplio
Nawabashah *see* Nawābshāh
Nawābshāh *134 B3 var.* Nawabashah. Sind, S Pakistan
Naxçıvan *117 G3 Rus.* Nakhichevan'. SW Azerbaijan
Náxos *105 D6 var.* Naxos. Náxos, Kykládes, Greece, Aegean Sea
Náxos *105 D6 island* Kykládes, Greece, Aegean Sea
Nayoro *130 D2* Hokkaidō, NE Japan
Nay Pyi Taw *136 B4 country capital* (Myanmar (Burma)) Mandalay, C Myanmar (Burma)
Nazareth *see* Nazerat
Nazca *60 D4* Ica, S Peru
Nazca Ridge *57 A5 undersea ridge* E Pacific Ocean
Naze *130 B3 var.* Nase. Kagoshima, Amami-ōshima, SW Japan
Nazerat *119 A5 var.* Natsrat, *Ar.* En Nazira, *Eng.* Nazareth. Northern, N Israel
Nazilli *116 A4* Aydın, SW Turkey
Nazrēt *73 C5 var.* Adama, Hadama. Oromo, C Ethiopia
N'Dalatando *78 B1 Port.* Salazar, Vila Salazar. Cuanza Norte, NW Angola
Ndélé *76 C4* Bamingui-Bangoran, N Central African Republic
Ndendé *77 B6* Ngounié, S Gabon
Ndindi *77 A6* Nyanga, S Gabon
Ndjamena *76 B3 var.* N'Djamena; *prev.* Fort-Lamy. *country capital* (Chad) Chari-Baguirmi, W Chad
N'Djamena *see* Ndjamena
Ndjolé *77 A5* Moyen-Ogooué, W Gabon
Ndola *78 D2* Copperbelt, C Zambia
Neagh, Lough *89 B5 lake* E Northern Ireland, UK
Néa Moudanía *104 C4 var.* Néa Moudhaniá. Kentrikí Makedonía, N Greece
Néa Moudhaniá *see* Néa Moudanía
Neapel *see* Napoli
Neápoli *104 B4 prev.* Neápolis. Dytikí Makedonía, N Greece
Neápoli *105 D8* Kríti, Greece, E Mediterranean Sea
Neápoli *105 C7* Pelopónnisos, S Greece
Neápolis *see* Neápoli, Greece
Neapolis *see* Napoli, Italy
Neapolis *see* Nablus, West Bank
Near Islands *36 A2 island group* Aleutian Islands, Alaska, USA
Néa Zíchni *104 C3 var.* Néa Zíkhni; *prev.* Néa Zíkhna. Kentrikí Makedonía, NE Greece
Néa Zíkhna/Néa Zíkhni *see* Néa Zíchni
Nebaj *52 B2* Quiché, W Guatemala
Nebitdag *see* Balkanabat
Neblina, Pico da *62 C1 mountain* NW Brazil
Nebraska *44 D4 off.* State of Nebraska, *also known as* Blackwater State, Cornhusker State, Tree Planters State. *state* C USA
Nebraska City *45 F4* Nebraska, C USA
Neches River *49 H3 river* Texas, SW USA
Neckar *95 B6 river* SW Germany
Necochea *65 D5* Buenos Aires, E Argentina
Nederland *see* Netherlands
Neder Rijn *86 D4 Eng.* Lower Rhine. *river* C Netherlands
Nederweert *87 D5* Limburg, SE Netherlands
Neede *86 E3* Gelderland, E Netherlands
Neerpelt *87 D5* Limburg, NE Belgium
Neftekamsk *111 D5* Respublika Bashkortostan, W Russian Federation
Neftezavodsk *see* Seýdi
Negara Brunei Darussalam *see* Brunei
Negēlē *73 D5 var.* Negelli, *It.* Neghelli. Oromo, C Ethiopia
Negelli *see* Negēlē
Negev *see* HaNegev
Neghelli *see* Negēlē
Negomane *79 E2 var.* Negomano. Cabo Delgado, N Mozambique
Negomano *see* Negomane
Negombo *132 C3* Western Province, SW Sri Lanka
Negotin *100 E4* Serbia, E Serbia
Negra, Punta *60 A3 point* NW Peru
Negreşti *see* Negreşti-Oaş
Negreşti-Oaş *108 B3 Hung.* Avasfelsőfalu; *prev.* Negreşti. Satu Mare, NE Romania
Negro, Río *65 C5 river* E Argentina
Negro, Rio *62 D1 river* N South America
Negro, Río *64 D4 river* Brazil/Uruguay
Negros *139 E2 island* C Philippines
Nehbandān *120 E3* Khorāsān, E Iran
Neijiang *128 B5* Sichuan, C China
Neiva *58 B3* Huila, S Colombia
Nellore *132 D2* Andhra Pradesh, E India
Nelson *151 C5* Nelson, South Island, New Zealand
Nelson *37 G4 river* Manitoba, C Canada
Néma *74 D3* Hodh ech Chargui, SE Mauritania
Neman *106 B4 Ger.* Ragnit. Kaliningradskaya Oblast', W Russian Federation
Neman *106 A4 Bel.* Nyoman, *Ger.* Memel, *Lith.* Nemunas, *Pol.* Niemen, *Rus.* Neman. *river* NE Europe
Nemausus *see* Nîmes
Neméa *105 B6* Pelopónnisos, S Greece
Nemetocenna *see* Arras
Nemours *90 C3* Seine-et-Marne, N France
Nemunas *see* Neman
Nemuro *130 E2* Hokkaidō, NE Japan
Neochóri *105 B5* Dytikí Ellás, C Greece
Nepal *135 E3 off.* Kingdom of Nepal. *country* S Asia

NEPAL
South Asia

Official name Kingdom of Nepal
Formation 1769 / 1769
Capital Kathmandu
Population 27.1 million / 513 people per sq mile (198 people per sq km) / 12%
Total area 54,363 sq miles (140,800 sq km)
Languages Nepali*, Maithili, Bhojpuri
Religions Hindu 90%, Buddhist 5%, Muslim 3%, Other (including Christian) 2%
Ethnic mix Nepalese 52%, Other 19%, Maithili 11%, Tibeto-Burmese 10%, Bhojpuri 8%
Government Monarchy
Currency Nepalese rupee = 100 paise
Literacy rate 49%
Calorie consumption 2453 calories

Nepal, Kingdom of *see* Nepal
Nereta *106 C4* Aizkraukle, S Latvia
Neretva *100 C4 river* Bosnia and Herzegovina/Croatia
Nerida *106 A3* Klaipėda, W Lithuania
Neris *107 C5 Bel.* Viliya, *Pol.* Wilia; *prev. Pol.* Wilja. *river* Belarus/Lithuania

Neris see Viliya
Nerva 92 C4 Andalucía, S Spain
Neryungri 115 F4 Respublika Sakha
(Yakutiya), NE Russian Federation
Neskaupstadhur 83 E5 Austurland,
E Iceland
Ness, Loch 88 C3 lake N Scotland, UK
Nesterov see Zhovkva
Néstos 104 C3 Bul. Mesta, Turk. Kara Su.
river Bulgaria/Greece
Nesvizh see Nyasvizh
Netanya 119 A6 var. Natanya, Nathanya.
Central, C Israel
Netherlands 86 C3
off. Kingdom of the Netherlands,
var. Holland, Dut. Koninkrijk der
Nederlanden, Nederland. country
NW Europe

NETHERLANDS
Northwest Europe

Official name Kingdom of the
Netherlands
Formation 1648 / 1839
Capital Amsterdam; The Hague
(administrative)
Population 16.3 million / 1245 people
per sq mile (481 people per sq km) / 89%
Total area 16,033 sq miles
(41,526 sq km)
Languages Dutch*, Frisian
Religions Roman Catholic 36%,
Other 34%, Protestant 27%, Muslim 3%
Ethnic mix Dutch 82%, Other 12%,
Surinamese 2%, Turkish 2%,
Moroccan 2%
Government Parliamentary system
Currency Euro = 100 cents
Literacy rate 99%
Calorie consumption 3362 calories

Netherlands Antilles 55 E5 prev. Dutch
West Indies. Dutch autonomous region
S Caribbean Sea
Netherlands East Indies see Indonesia
Netherlands Guiana see Surinam
Netherlands, Kingdom of the see
Netherlands
Netherlands New Guinea see Papua
Nettilling Lake 37 G3 lake Baffin Island,
Nunavut, N Canada
Netze see Noteć
Neu Amerika see Puławy
Neubrandenburg 94 D3
Mecklenburg-Vorpommern,
NE Germany
Neuchâtel 95 A7 Ger. Neuenburg.
Neuchâtel, W Switzerland
Neuchâtel, Lac de 95 A7 Ger.
Neuenburger See. lake W Switzerland
Neuenburg see Neuchâtel
Neuenburger See see Neuchâtel, Lac de
Neufchâteau 87 D8 Luxembourg,
SE Belgium
Neugradisk see Nova Gradiška
Neuhof see Zgierz
Neukuhren see Pionerskiy
Neumarkt see Târgu Secuiesc, Covasna,
Romania
Neumarkt see Târgu Mureș
Neumoldowa see Moldova Nouă
Neumünster 94 B2 Schleswig-Holstein,
N Germany
Neunkirchen 95 A5 Saarland,
SW Germany
Neuquén 65 B5 Neuquén, SE Argentina
Neuruppin 94 C3 Brandenburg,
NE Germany
Neusalz an der Oder see Nowa Sól
Neu Sandec see Nowy Sącz
Neusatz see Novi Sad
Neusiedler See 95 E6 Hung. Fertő. lake
Austria/Hungary
Neusohl see Banská Bystrica
Neustadt see Baia Mare, Maramureș,
Romania
Neustadt an der Haardt see Neustadt an
der Weinstrasse
Neustadt an der Weinstrasse
95 B5 prev. Neustadt an der Haardt,
hist. Niewenstat; anc. Nova Civitas.
Rheinland-Pfalz, SW Germany
Neustadtl see Novo mesto
Neustettin see Szczecinek
Neustrelitz 94 D3 Mecklenburg-
Vorpommern, NE Germany
Neutra see Nitra
Neu-Ulm 95 B6 Bayern, S Germany

Neuwied 95 A5 Rheinland-Pfalz,
W Germany
Neuzen see Terneuzen
Nevada 47 C5 off. State of Nevada, also
known as Battle Born State, Sagebrush
State, Silver State. state W USA
Nevers 90 C4 anc. Noviodunum. Nièvre,
C France
Neves 76 E2 São Tomé, S Sao Tome and
Principe, Africa
Nevinnomyssk 111 B7 Stavropol'skiy
Kray, SW Russian Federation
Nevşehir 116 C3 var. Nevshehr.
Nevşehir, C Turkey
Newala 73 C8 Mtwara, SE Tanzania
New Albany 40 C5 Indiana, N USA
New Amsterdam 59 G3 E Guyana
Newark 41 F4 New Jersey, NE USA
New Bedford 41 G3 Massachusetts,
NE USA
Newberg 46 B3 Oregon, NW USA
New Bern 43 F1 North Carolina, SE USA
New Braunfels 49 G4 Texas, SW USA
Newbridge 89 B6 Ir. An Droichead Nua.
Kildare, C Ireland
New Britain 144 B3 island E Papua
New Guinea
New Brunswick 39 E4 Fr. Nouveau-
Brunswick. province SE Canada
New Caledonia 144 D4 var. Kanaky, Fr.
Nouvelle-Calédonie. French overseas
territory SW Pacific Ocean
New Caledonia 144 C5 island SW Pacific
Ocean
New Caledonia Basin 142 C4 undersea
basin W Pacific Ocean
Newcastle 149 D6 New South Wales,
SE Australia
Newcastle see Newcastle upon Tyne
Newcastle upon Tyne 88 D4 var.
Newcastle, hist. Monkchester, Lat. Pons
Aelii. NE England, UK
New Delhi 134 D3 country capital
(India) Delhi, N India
New England of the West see Minnesota
Newfoundland 39 G3 Fr. Terre-Neuve.
island Newfoundland and Labrador,
SE Canada
Newfoundland and Labrador 39 F2 Fr.
Terre Neuve. province E Canada
Newfoundland Basin 66 B3 undersea
feature NW Atlantic Ocean
New Georgia Islands 144 C3 island
group NW Solomon Islands
New Glasgow 39 F4 Nova Scotia,
SE Canada
New Goa see Panaji
New Guinea 144 A3 Dut. Nieuw Guinea,
Ind. Irian. island Indonesia/Papua
New Guinea
New Hampshire 41 F2 off. State of New
Hampshire, also known as Granite
State. state NE USA
New Haven 41 G3 Connecticut, NE USA
New Hebrides see Vanuatu
New Iberia 42 B3 Louisiana, S USA
New Ireland 144 C3 island NE Papua
New Guinea
New Jersey 41 F4 off. State of New
Jersey, also known as The Garden State.
state NE USA
Newman 146 B4 Western Australia
Newmarket 89 E6 E England, UK
New Mexico 48 C2 off. State of New
Mexico, also known as Land of
Enchantment, Sunshine State. state
SW USA
New Orleans 42 B3 Louisiana, S USA
New Plymouth 150 C4 Taranaki, North
Island, New Zealand
Newport 89 D7 S England, UK
Newport 89 C7 SE Wales, UK
Newport 40 C4 Kentucky, S USA
Newport 41 G2 Vermont, NE USA
Newport News 41 F5 Virginia, NE USA
New Providence 54 C1 island
N Bahamas
Newquay 89 C7 SW England, UK
Newry 89 B5 Ir. An tIúr. SE Northern
Ireland, UK
New Sarum see Salisbury
New Siberian Islands see Novosibirskiye
Ostrova
New South Wales 149 C6 state
SE Australia
Newton 45 G3 Iowa, C USA
Newtownabbey 89 B5 Ir. Baile na
Mainistreach. E Northern Ireland, UK

New Ulm 45 F2 Minnesota, N USA
New York 41 F4 New York, NE USA
New York 41 F3 state NE USA
New Zealand 150 A4 country SW Pacific
Ocean

NEW ZEALAND
Australasia & Oceania

Official name New Zealand
Formation 1947 / 1947
Capital Wellington
Population 4 million / 39 people per
sq mile (15 people per sq km) / 86%
Total area 103,737 sq miles
(268,680 sq km)
Languages English*, Maori
Religions Anglican 24%, Other 22%,
Presbyterian 18%, Nonreligious 16%,
Roman Catholic 15%, Methodist 5%
Ethnic mix European 77%,
Maori 12%, Other immigrant 6%,
Pacific islanders 5%
Government Parliamentary system
Currency New Zealand dollar = 100 cents
Literacy rate 99%
Calorie consumption 3219 calories

Neyveli 132 C2 Tamil Nādu, SE India
Nezhin see Nizhyn
Ngangzê Co 126 B5 lake W China
Ngaoundéré 76 B4 var. N'Gaoundéré.
Adamaoua, N Cameroon
N'Gaoundéré see Ngaoundéré
N'Giva 78 B3 var. Ondjiva, Port. Vila
Pereira de Eça. Cunene, S Angola
Ngo 77 B6 Plateaux, SE Congo
Ngoko 77 B5 river Cameroon/Congo
Ngourti 75 H3 Diffa, E Niger
Nguigmi 75 H3 var. N'Guigmi. Diffa,
SE Niger
N'Guigmi see Nguigmi
N'Gunza see Sumbe
Nguru 75 G3 Yobe, NE Nigeria
Nha Trang 137 E6 Khanh Hoa,
S Vietnam
Niagara Falls 38 D5 Ontario,
S Canada
Niagara Falls 41 E3 New York,
NE USA
Niagara Falls 40 D3 waterfall
Canada/USA
Niamey 75 F3 country capital (Niger)
Niamey, SW Niger
Niangay, Lac 75 E3 lake E Mali
Nia-Nia 77 E5 Orientale, NE Dem.
Rep. Congo
Nias, Pulau 138 A3 island
W Indonesia
Nicaea see Nice
Nicaragua 52 D3 off. Republic of
Nicaragua. country Central America

NICARAGUA
Central America

Official name Republic of Nicaragua
Formation 1838 / 1838
Capital Managua
Population 5.5 million / 120 people per
sq mile (46 people per sq km) / 65%
Total area 49,998 sq miles
(129,494 sq km)
Languages Spanish*, English Creole,
Miskito
Religions Roman Catholic 80%,
Protestant Evangelical 17%, Other 3%
Ethnic mix Mestizo 69%, White 14%,
Black 8%, Amerindian 5%, Zambo 4%
Government Presidential system
Currency Córdoba oro = 100 centavos
Literacy rate 77%
Calorie consumption 2298 calories

Nicaragua, Lago de 52 D4 var.
Cocibolca, Gran Lago. Eng. Lake
Nicaragua. lake S Nicaragua
Nicaragua, Lake see Nicaragua, Lago de
Nicaragua, Republic of see Nicaragua
Nice 91 D6 It. Nizza; anc. Nicaea. Alpes-
Maritimes, SE France
Nicephorium see Ar Raqqah
Nicholas II Land see Severnaya Zemlya
Nicholls Town 54 C1 Andros Island,
NW Bahamas
Nicobar Islands 124 B4 island group
India, E Indian Ocean

Nicopolis see Nikopol, Bulgaria
Nicosia 102 C5 Gk. Lefkosía, Turk.
Lefkoşa. country capital (Cyprus)
C Cyprus
Nicoya 52 D4 Guanacaste, W Costa Rica
Nicoya, Golfo de 52 D5 gulf
W Costa Rica
Nicoya, Península de 52 D4 peninsula
NW Costa Rica
Nida 106 A3 Ger. Nidden. Klaipėda,
SW Lithuania
Nidaros see Trondheim
Nidden see Nida
Nidzica 98 D3 Ger. Niedenburg.
Warmińsko Mazurskie, NE Poland
Niedenburg see Nidzica
Niedere Tauern 99 A6 mountain range
C Austria
Niemen see Neman
Nieśwież see Nyasvizh
Nieuw Amsterdam 59 G3 Commewijne,
NE Surinam
Nieuw-Bergen 86 D4 Limburg,
SE Netherlands
Nieuwegein 86 C4 Utrecht,
C Netherlands
Nieuw Guinea see New Guinea
Nieuw Nickerie 59 G3 Nickerie,
NW Suriname
Niewenstat see Neustadt an der
Weinstrasse
Niğde 116 C4 Niğde, C Turkey
Niger 75 F3 off. Republic of Niger.
country W Africa

NIGER
West Africa

Official name Republic of Niger
Formation 1960 / 1960
Capital Niamey
Population 14 million / 29 people per
sq mile (11 people per sq km) / 21%
Total area 489,188 sq miles
(1,267,000 sq km)
Languages French*, Hausa, Djerma,
Fulani, Tuareg, Teda
Religions Muslim 85%,
Traditional beliefs 14%,
Other (including Christian) 1%
Ethnic mix Hausa 54%, Djerma and
Songhai 21%, Fulani 10%, Tuareg 9%,
Other 6%
Government Presidential system
Currency CFA franc = 100 centimes
Literacy rate 14%
Calorie consumption 2130 calories

Niger 75 F4 river W Africa
Nigeria 75 F4 off. Federal Republic of
Nigeria. country W Africa

NIGERIA
West Africa

Official name Federal Republic
of Nigeria
Formation 1960 / 1961
Capital Abuja
Population 132 million / 374 people per
sq mile (144 people per sq km) / 44%
Total area 356,667 sq miles
(923,768 sq km)
Languages English*, Hausa, Yoruba, Ibo
Religions Muslim 50%, Christian 40%,
Traditional beliefs 10%
Ethnic mix Other 29%, Hausa 21%,
Yoruba 21%, Ibo 18%, Fulani 11%
Government Presidential system
Currency Naira = 100 kobo
Literacy rate 67%
Calorie consumption 2726 calories

Nigeria, Federal Republic of see
Nigeria
Niger, Mouths of the 75 F5 delta
S Nigeria
Niger, Republic of see Niger
Nihon see Japan
Niigata 131 D5 Niigata, Honshū,
C Japan
Niihama 131 B7 Ehime, Shikoku,
SW Japan
Ni'ihau 47 A7 var. Niihau. island
Hawai'i, USA, C Pacific Ocean
Nii-jima 131 D6 island E Japan
Nijkerk 86 D3 Gelderland, C Netherlands
Nijlen 87 C5 Antwerpen, N Belgium

Nijmegen *86 D4 Ger.* Nimwegen; *anc.* Noviomagus. Gelderland, SE Netherlands

Nikaria *see* Ikaría

Nikel' *110 C2* Murmanskaya Oblast', NW Russian Federation

Nikiniki *139 E5* Timor, S Indonesia

Niklasmarkt *see* Gheorgheni

Nikolainkaupunki *see* Vaasa

Nikolayev *see* Mykolayiv

Nikol'sk *see* Ussuriysk

Nikol'sk-Ussuriyskiy *see* Ussuriysk

Nikopol *109 F3 anc.* Nicopolis. Pleven, N Bulgaria

Nikšić *101 C5* C Montenegro

Nikumaroro *145 E3* ; *prev.* Gardner Island. *atoll* Phoenix Islands, C Kiribati

Nikunau *145 E3 var.* Nukunau; *prev.* Byron Island. *atoll* Tungaru, W Kiribati

Nile *72 B2 former province* NW Uganda

Nile *68 D3 Ar.* Nahr an Nīl. *river* N Africa

Nile Delta *72 B1 delta* N Egypt

Nil, Nahr an *see* Nile

Nîmes *91 C6 anc.* Nemausus, Nismes. Gard, S France

Nimwegen *see* Nijmegen

Nine Degree Channel *132 B3 channel* India/Maldives

Ninetyeast Ridge *141 D5 undersea feature* E Indian Ocean

Ninety Mile Beach *150 C1 beach* North Island, New Zealand

Ningbo *128 D5 var.* Ning-po, Yin-hsien; *prev.* Ninghsien. Zhejiang, SE China

Ninghsia *see* Ningxia

Ninghsien *see* Ningbo

Ning-po *see* Ningbo

Ningsia/Ningsia Hui/Ningsia Hui Autonomous Region *see* Ningxia

Ningxia *128 B4 off.* Ningxia Huizu Zizhiqu, *var.* Ning-hsia, Ningsia, *Eng.* Ningsia Hui, Ningsia Hui Autonomous Region. *autonomous region* N China

Ningxia Huizu Zizhiqu *see* Ningxia

Nio *see* Íos

Nio *see* Íos

Nio *see* Íos

Niobrara River *45 F3 river* Nebraska/Wyoming, C USA

Nioro *74 D3 var.* Nioro du Sahel. Kayes, W Mali

Nioro du Sahel *see* Nioro

Niort *90 B4* Deux-Sèvres, W France

Nipigon *38 B4* Ontario, S Canada

Nipigon, Lake *38 B3 lake* Ontario, S Canada

Nippon *see* Japan

Niš *101 E5 Eng.* Nish, *Ger.* Nisch; *anc.* Naissus. Serbia, SE Serbia

Nişab *120 B4* Al Ḩudūd ash Shamāliyah, N Saudi Arabia

Nisch/Nish *see* Niš

Nisibin *see* Nusaybin

Nisíros *see* Nísyros

Nisko *98 E4* Podkarpackie, SE Poland

Nismes *see* Nîmes

Nistru *see* Dniester

Nísyros *105 E7 var.* Nisíros. *island* Dodekánisa, Greece, Aegean Sea

Nitra *99 C6 Ger.* Neutra, *Hung.* Nyitra. Nitriansky Kraj, SW Slovakia

Nitra *99 C6 Ger.* Neutra, *Hung.* Nyitra. *river* W Slovakia

Niuatobutabu *see* Niuatoputapu

Niuatoputapu *145 E4 var.* Niuatobutabu; *prev.* Keppel Island. *island* N Tonga

Niue *145 F4 self-governing territory in free association with New Zealand* S Pacific Ocean

Niulakita *145 E3 var.* Nurakita. *atoll* S Tuvalu

Niutao *145 E3 atoll* NW Tuvalu

Nivernais *90 C4 cultural region* C France

Nizāmābād *134 D5* Andhra Pradesh, C India

Nizhnegorskiy *see* Nyzhn'ohirs'kyy

Nizhnekamsk *111 C5* Respublika Tatarstan, W Russian Federation

Nizhnevartovsk *114 D3* Khanty-Mansiyskiy Avtonomnyy Okrug, C Russian Federation

Nizhniy Novgorod *111 C5 prev.* Gor'kiy. Nizhegorodskaya Oblast', W Russian Federation

Nizhniy Odes *110 D4* Respublika Komi, NW Russian Federation

Nizhnyaya Tunguska *115 E3 Eng.* Lower Tunguska. *river* N Russian Federation

Nizhyn *109 E1 Rus.* Nezhin. Chernihivs'ka Oblast', NE Ukraine

Nizza *see* Nice

Njazidja *see* Grande Comore

Njombe *73 C8* Iringa, S Tanzania

Nkayi *77 B6 prev.* Jacob. La Bouenza, S Congo

Nkongsamba *76 A4 var.* N'Kongsamba. Littoral, W Cameroon

N'Kongsamba *see* Nkongsamba

Nmai Hka *136 B2 var.* Me Hka. *river* N Myanmar (Burma)

Nobeoka *131 B7* Miyazaki, Kyūshū, SW Japan

Noboribetsu *130 D3 var.* Noboribetu. Hokkaidō, NE Japan

Noboribetu *see* Noboribetsu

Nogales *50 B1* Sonora, NW Mexico

Nogales *48 B3* Arizona, SW USA

Nogal Valley *see* Dooxo Nugaaleed

Noire, Rivi`ere *see* Black River

Nokia *85 D5* Länsi-Suomi, W Finland

Nokou *76 B3* Kanem, W Chad

Nola *77 B5* Sangha-Mbaéré, SW Central African Republic

Nolinsk *111 C5* Kirovskaya Oblast', NW Russian Federation

Nongkaya *see* Nong Khai

Nong Khai *136 C4 var.* Mi Chai, Nongkaya. Nong Khai, E Thailand

Nonouti *144 D2 prev.* Sydenham Island. *atoll* Tungaru, W Kiribati

Noord-Beveland *86 B4 var.* North Beveland. *island* SW Netherlands

Noordwijk aan Zee *86 C3* Zuid-Holland, W Netherlands

Noordzee *see* North Sea

Nora *85 C6* Örebro, C Sweden

Norak *123 E3 Rus.* Nurek. W Tajikistan

Nord *83 F1* Avannaarsua, N Greenland

Nordaustlandet *83 G1 island* NE Svalbard

Norden *94 A3* Niedersachsen, NW Germany

Norderstedt *94 B3* Schleswig-Holstein, N Germany

Nordfriesische Inseln *see* North Frisian Islands

Nordhausen *94 C4* Thüringen, C Germany

Nordhorn *94 A3* Niedersachsen, NW Germany

Nordkapp *84 D1 Eng.* North Cape. *headland* N Norway

Nord, Mer du *see* North Sea

Nord-Ouest, Territoires du *see* Northwest Territories

Nordsee/Nordsjøen/Nordsøen *see* North Sea

Norfolk *45 E3* Nebraska, C USA

Norfolk *41 F5* Virginia, NE USA

Norfolk Island *142 D4 Australian external territory* SW Pacific Ocean

Norfolk Ridge *142 D4 undersea feature* W Pacific Ocean

Norge *see* Norway

Norias *49 G5* Texas, SW USA

Noril'sk *114 D3* Taymyrskiy (Dolgano-Nenetskiy) Avtonomnyy Okrug, N Russian Federation

Norman *49 G1* Oklahoma, C USA

Normandes, Îles *see* Channel Islands

Normandie *90 B3 Eng.* Normandy. *cultural region* N France

Normandy *see* Normandie

Normanton *148 C3* Queensland, NE Australia

Norrköping *85 C6* Östergötland, S Sweden

Norrtälje *85 C6* Stockholm, C Sweden

Norseman *147 B6* Western Australia

Norske Havet *see* Norwegian Sea

North Albanian Alps *101 C5 Alb.* Bjeshkët e Namuna, *SCr.* Prokletije. *mountain range* SE Europe

Northallerton *89 D5* N England, UK

Northam *147 A6* Western Australia

North America *34 continent*

Northampton *89 D6* C England, UK

North Andaman *133 F2 island* Andaman Islands, India, NE Indian Ocean

North Australian Basin *141 E5 Fr.* Bassin Nord de l' Australie. *undersea feature* E Indian Ocean

North Bay *38 D4* Ontario, S Canada

North Beveland *see* Noord-Beveland

North Borneo *see* Sabah

North Cape *150 C1 headland* North Island, New Zealand

North Cape *66 D1 headland* New Ireland, NE Papua New Guinea

North Cape *see* Nordkapp

North Carolina *43 E1 off.* State of North Carolina, *also known as* Old North State, Tar Heel State, Turpentine State. *state* SE USA

North Channel *40 D2 lake channel* Canada/USA

North Charleston *43 F2* South Carolina, SE USA

North Dakota *44 D2 off.* State of North Dakota, *also known as* Flickertail State, Peace Garden State, Sioux State. *state* N USA

North Devon Island *see* Devon Island

North East Frontier Agency/North East Frontier Agency of Assam *see* Arunāchal Pradesh

Northeast Providence Channel *54 C1 channel* N Bahamas

Northeim *94 B4* Niedersachsen, C Germany

Northern Cook Islands *145 F4 island group* N Cook Islands

Northern Dvina *see* Severnaya Dvina

Northern Ireland *88 B4 var.* The Six Counties. *cultural region* Northern Ireland, UK

Northern Ireland *88 B4 var.* The Six Counties. *political division* Northern Ireland, UK

Northern Mariana Islands *142 B1 US commonwealth territory* W Pacific Ocean

Northern Rhodesia *see* Zambia

Northern Sporades *see* Vóreies Sporádes

Northern Territory *144 A5 territory* N Australia

North European Plain *81 E3 plain* N Europe

Northfield *45 F2* Minnesota, N USA

North Fiji Basin *142 D3 undersea feature* N Coral Sea

North Frisian Islands *94 B2 var.* Nordfriesische Inseln. *island group* N Germany

North Huvadhu Atoll *132 B5 var.* Gaafu Alifu Atoll. *atoll* S Maldives

North Island *150 B2 island* N New Zealand

North Korea *129 E3 off.* Democratic People's Republic of Korea, *Kor.* Chosŏn-minjujuŭi-inmin-kanghwaguk. *country* E Asia

NORTH KOREA
East Asia

Official name	Democratic People's Republic of Korea
Formation	1948 / 1953
Capital	Pyongyang
Population	22.5 million / 484 people per sq mile (187 people per sq km) / 60%
Total area	46,540 sq miles (120,540 sq km)
Languages	Korean*
Religions	Atheist 100%
Ethnic mix	Korean 100%
Government	One-party state
Currency	North Korean won = 100 chon
Literacy rate	99%
Calorie consumption	2142 calories

North Little Rock *42 B1* Arkansas, C USA

North Minch *see* Minch, The

North Mole *93 G4 harbour wall* NW Gibraltar Europe

North Platte *45 E4* Nebraska, C USA

North Platte River *44 D4 river* C USA

North Pole *155 B3 pole* Arctic Ocean

North Saskatchewan *37 F5 river* Alberta/Saskatchewan, S Canada

North Sea *80 Dan.* Nordsøen, *Dut.* Noordzee, *Fr.* Mer du Nord, *Ger.* Nordsee, *Nor.* Nordsjøen; *prev.* German Ocean, *Lat.* Mare Germanicum. *sea* NW Europe

North Siberian Lowland/North Siberian Plain *see* Severo-Sibirskaya Nizmennost'

North Star State *see* Minnesota

North Taranaki Bight *150 C3 gulf* North Island, New Zealand

North Uist *88 B3 island* NW Scotland, UK

Northwest Atlantic Mid-Ocean Canyon *34 E4 undersea feature* N Atlantic Ocean

North West Highlands *88 C3 mountain range* N Scotland, UK

Northwest Pacific Basin *113 G4 undersea feature* NW Pacific Ocean

Northwest Territories *37 E3 Fr.* Territoires du Nord-Ouest. *territory* NW Canada

Northwind Plain *155 B2 undersea feature* Arctic Ocean

Norton Sound *36 C2 inlet* Alaska, USA

Norway *85 A5 off.* Kingdom of Norway, *Nor.* Norge. *country* N Europe

NORWAY
Northern Europe

Official name	Kingdom of Norway
Formation	1905 / 1905
Capital	Oslo
Population	4.6 million / 39 people per sq mile (15 people per sq km) / 76%
Total area	125,181 sq miles (324,220 sq km)
Languages	Norwegian* (Bokmål "book language" and Nynorsk "new Norsk"), Sámi
Religions	Evangelical Lutheran 89%, Other and nonreligious 10%, Roman Catholic 1%
Ethnic mix	Norwegian 93%, Other 6%, Sámi 1%
Government	Parliamentary system
Currency	Norwegian krone = 100 øre
Literacy rate	99%
Calorie consumption	3484 calories

Norway, Kingdom of *see* Norway

Norwegian Basin *83 F4 undersea feature* NW Norwegian Sea

Norwegian Sea *83 F4 var.* Norske Havet. *sea* NE Atlantic Ocean

Norwich *89 E6* E England, UK

Nösen *see* Bistriţa

Noshiro *130 D4 var.* Nosiro; *prev.* Noshirominato. Akita, Honshū, C Japan

Noshirominato/Nosiro *see* Noshiro

Nosivka *109 E1 Rus.* Nosovka. Chernihivs'ka Oblast', NE Ukraine

Nosop *78 C4 river* E Namibia

Nosovka *see* Nosivka

Noşratābād *120 E3* Sīstān va Balūchestān, E Iran

Noteć *98 C3 Ger.* Netze. *river* NW Poland

Nóties Sporádes *see* Dodekánisa

Nottingham *89 D6* C England, UK

Nouâdhibou *74 B2 prev.* Port-Étienne. Dakhlet Nouâdhibou, W Mauritania

Nouakchott *74 B2 country capital* (Mauritania) Nouakchott District, SW Mauritania

Nouméa *144 C5 dependent territory capital* (New Caledonia) Province Sud, S New Caledonia

Nouveau-Brunswick *see* New Brunswick

Nouvelle-Calédonie *see* New Caledonia

Nouvelle Écosse *see* Nova Scotia

Nova Civitas *see* Neustadt an der Weinstrasse

Nova Gorica *95 D8* W Slovenia

Nova Gradiška *100 C3 Ger.* Neugradisk, *Hung.* Újgradiska. Brod-Posavina, NE Croatia

Nova Iguaçu *63 F4* Rio de Janeiro, SE Brazil

Nova Lisboa *see* Huambo

Novara *96 B2 anc.* Novaria. Piemonte, NW Italy

Novaria *see* Novara

Nova Scotia *39 F4 Fr.* Nouvelle Écosse. *province* SE Canada

Nova Scotia 35 E5 *physical region*
SE Canada
Novaya Sibir', Ostrov 115 F1 *island*
Novosibirskiye Ostrova, NE Russian
Federation
Novaya Zemlya 110 D1 *island group*
N Russian Federation
Novaya Zemlya Trough *see* East Novaya
Zemlya Trough
Novgorod *see* Velikiy Novgorod
Novi Grad *see* Bosanski Novi
Novi Iskŭr 104 C2 Sofiya-Grad,
W Bulgaria
Noviodunum *see* Nevers, Nièvre,
France
Noviomagus *see* Lisieux, Calvados,
France
Noviomagus *see* Nijmegen, Netherlands
Novi Pazar 101 D5 Shumen,
NE Bulgaria
Novi Sad 100 D3 *Ger.* Neusatz, *Hung.*
Ujvidék. Vojvodina, N Serbia
Novoazovs'k 109 G4 *Rus.* Novoazovsk.
Donets'ka Oblast', E Ukraine
Novocheboksarsk 111 C5 Chavash
Respubliki, W Russian Federation
Novocherkassk 111 B7 Rostovskaya
Oblast', SW Russian Federation
Novodvinsk 110 C3 Arkhangel'skaya
Oblast', NW Russian Federation
Novograd-Volynskiy *see*
Novohrad-Volyns'kyy
Novogrudok *see* Navahrudak
Novohrad-Volyns'kyy 108 D2 *Rus.*
Novograd-Volynskiy. Zhytomyrs'ka
Oblast', N Ukraine
Novokazalinsk *see* Ayteke Bi
Novokuznetsk 114 D4 *prev.* Stalinsk.
Kemerovskaya Oblast', S Russian
Federation
Novolazarevskaya 154 C2 Russian
research station Antarctica
Novo mesto 95 E8 *Ger.* Rudolfswert;
prev. Ger. Neustadtl. SE Slovenia
Novomoskovsk 111 B5 Tul'skaya
Oblast', W Russian Federation
Novomoskovs'k 109 F3 *Rus.*
Novomoskovsk. Dnipropetrovs'ka
Oblast', E Ukraine
Novopolotsk *see* Navapolatsk
Novoradomsk *see* Radomsko
Novo Redondo *see* Sumbe
Novorossiysk 111 A7 Krasnodarskiy
Kray, SW Russian Federation
Novoshakhtinsk 111 B6 Rostovskaya
Oblast', SW Russian Federation
Novosibirsk 114 D4 Novosibirskaya
Oblast', C Russian Federation
Novosibirskiye Ostrova 115 F1 *Eng.*
New Siberian Islands. *island group*
N Russian Federation
Novotroitsk 111 D6 Orenburgskaya
Oblast', W Russian Federation
Novotroitskoye *see* Novotroyits'ke,
Ukraine
Novotroyits'ke 109 F4 *Rus.*
Novotroitskoye. Khersons'ka Oblast',
S Ukraine
Novo-Urgench *see* Urganch
Novovolyns'k 108 C1 *Rus.* Novovolynsk.
Volyns'ka Oblast', NW Ukraine
Novy Dvor 107 B6 *Rus.* Novyy Dvor.
Hrodzyenskaya Voblasts', W Belarus
Novyy Bug *see* Novyy Buh
Novyy Buh 109 E3 *Rus.* Novyy Bug.
Mykolayivs'ka Oblast', S Ukraine
Novyy Dvor *see* Novy Dvor
Novyy Margilan *see* Farg'ona
Novyy Uzen' *see* Zhanaozen
Nowa Sól 98 B4 *var.* Nowasól, *Ger.*
Neusalz an der Oder. Lubuskie,
W Poland
Nowasól *see* Nowa Sól
Nowogard 98 B2 *var.* Nowógard,
Ger. Naugard. Zachodnio-pomorskie,
NW Poland
Nowogródek *see* Navahrudak
Nowo-Minsk *see* Mińsk Mazowiecki
Nowy Dwór Mazowiecki 98 D3
Mazowieckie, C Poland
Nowy Sącz 99 D5 *Ger.* Neu Sandec.
Małopolskie, S Poland
Nowy Tomyśl 98 B3 *var.* Nowy Tomysl.
Wielkopolskie, C Poland
Nowy Tomysl *see* Nowy Tomyśl
Noyon 90 C3 Oise, N France
Nsanje 79 E3 Southern, S Malawi
Nsawam 75 E5 SE Ghana

Ntomba, Lac 77 C6 *var.* Lac Tumba.
lake NW Dem. Rep. Congo
Nubian Desert 72 B3 *desert* NE Sudan
Nu Chiang *see* Salween
Nu'eima 119 E7 E West Bank Asia
Nueva Caceres *see* Naga
Nueva Gerona 54 B2 Isla de la Juventud,
S Cuba
Nueva Rosita 50 D2 Coahuila de
Zaragoza, NE Mexico
Nuevitas 54 C2 Camagüey, E Cuba
Nuevo, Bajo 53 G1 *island* NW Colombia
South America
Nuevo Casas Grandes 50 C1 Chihuahua,
N Mexico
Nuevo, Golfo 65 C6 *gulf* S Argentina
Nuevo Laredo 51 E2 Tamaulipas,
NE Mexico
Nui Atoll 145 E3 *atoll* W Tuvalu
Nu Jiang *see* Salween
Nûk *see* Nuuk
Nukha *see* Şäki
Nuku'alofa 145 E5 *country capital*
(Tonga) Tongatapu, S Tonga
Nukufetau Atoll 145 E3 *atoll* C Tuvalu
Nukulaelae Atoll 145 E3 *var.* Nukulailai.
atoll E Tuvalu
Nukulailai *see* Nukulaelae Atoll
Nukunau *see* Nikunau
Nukunonu Atoll 145 E3 *island*
C Tokelau
Nukus 122 C2 Qoraqalpog'iston
Respublikasi, W Uzbekistan
Nullarbor Plain 147 C6 *plateau* South
Australia/Western Australia
Nunap Isua 98 B5 *var.* Uummannarsuaq,
Dan. Kap Farvel, *Eng.* Cape Farewell.
cape S Greenland
Nunavut 37 F3 *territory* N Canada
Nuneaton 89 D6 C England, UK
Nunivak Island 36 B2 *island* Alaska,
USA
Nunspeet 86 D3 Gelderland,
E Netherlands
Nuoro 97 A5 Sardegna, Italy,
C Mediterranean Sea
Nuqui 58 A3 Chocó, W Colombia
Nurakita *see* Niulakita
Nurata *see* Nurota
Nurek *see* Norak
Nuremberg *see* Nürnberg
Nurmes 84 E4 Itä-Suomi, E Finland
Nürnberg 95 C5 *Eng.* Nuremberg.
Bayern, S Germany
Nurota 123 E2 *Rus.* Nurata. Navoiy
Viloyati, C Uzbekistan
Nusa Tenggara 139 E5 *Eng.* Lesser
Sunda Islands. *island group*
C Indonesia
Nusaybin 117 F4 *var.* Nisibin. Manisa,
SE Turkey
Nussdorf *see* Năsăud
Nutmeg State *see* Connecticut
Nuuk 82 C4 *var.* Nûk, *Dan.* Godthaab,
Godthåb. *dependent territory capital*
(Greenland) Kitaa, SW Greenland
Nyagan' 114 D3 Khanty-Mansiyskiy
Avtonomnyy Okrug, N Russian
Federation
Nyainqêntanglha Shan 126 C5
mountain range W China
Nyala 72 A4 Southern Darfur, W Sudan
Nyamapanda 78 D3 Mashonaland East,
NE Zimbabwe
Nyamtumbo 73 C8 Ruvuma, S Tanzania
Nyanda *see* Masvingo
Nyandoma 110 C4 Arkhangel'skaya
Oblast', NW Russian Federation
Nyantakara 73 B7 Kagera, NW Tanzania
Nyasa, Lake 79 E2 *var.* Lake Malawi;
prev. Lago Nyassa. *lake* E Africa
Nyasaland/Nyasaland Protectorate
see Malawi
Nyassa, Lago *see* Nyasa, Lake
Nyasvizh 107 C6 *Pol.* Nieśwież,
Rus. Nesvizh. Minskaya Voblasts',
C Belarus
Nyaunglebin 136 B4 Pegu,
SW Myanmar (Burma)
Nyeri 73 C6 Central, C Kenya
Nyima 126 C5 Xizang Zizhiqu, W China
Nyíregyháza 99 D6 Szabolcs-Szatmár-
Bereg, NE Hungary
Nyitra *see* Nitra
Nykøbing 85 B8 Storstrøm, SE Denmark
Nyköping 85 C6 Södermanland,
S Sweden
Nylstroom *see* Modimolle

Nyngan 149 D6 New South Wales,
SE Australia
Nyoman *see* Neman
Nyurba 115 F3 Respublika Sakha
(Yakutiya), NE Russian Federation
Nyzhn'ohirs'kyy 109 F4 *Rus.*
Nizhnegorskiy. Respublika Krym,
S Ukraine
NZ *see* New Zealand
Nzega 73 C7 Tabora, C Tanzania
Nzérékoré 74 D4 SE Guinea
Nzwani *see* Anjouan

O

Oa'hu 47 A7 *var.* Oahu. *island*
Hawaiian Islands, Hawai'i, USA
Oak Harbor 46 B1 Washington,
NW USA
Oakland 47 B6 California, W USA
Oamaru 151 B7 Otago, South Island,
New Zealand
Oaxaca 51 F5 *var.* Oaxaca de Juárez; *prev.*
Antequera. Oaxaca, SE Mexico
Oaxaca de Juárez *see* Oaxaca
Ob' 112 C2 *river* C Russian Federation
Obal' 107 B6 *Rus.* Obol'. Vitsyebskaya
Voblasts', N Belarus
Oban 88 C4 W Scotland, UK
Oban *see* Halfmoon Bay
Obando *see* Puerto Inírida
Obdorsk *see* Salekhard
Óbecse *see* Bečej
Obeliai 106 C4 Panevėžys, NE Lithuania
Oberhollabrunn *see* Tulln
Ob', Gulf of *see* Obskaya Guba
Obidovichi *see* Abidavichy
Obihiro 130 D2 Hokkaidō, NE Japan
Obo 76 D4 Haut-Mbomou, E Central
African Republic
Obock 72 D4 E Djibouti
Obol' *see* Obal'
Oborniki 98 C3 Wielkolpolskie,
W Poland
Obrovo *see* Abrova
Obskaya Guba 114 D3 *Eng.* Gulf of Ob.
gulf N Russian Federation
Ob' Tablemount 141 B7 *undersea*
feature S Indian Ocean
Ocala 43 E4 Florida, SE USA
Ocaña 58 B2 Norte de Santander,
N Colombia
Ocaña 92 D3 Castilla-La Mancha, C Spain
O Carballiño 92 C1 *Cast.* Carballiño.
Galicia, NW Spain
Occidental, Cordillera 61 E4 *mountain*
range Bolivia/Chile
Occidental, Cordillera 58 B2 *mountain*
range W Colombia
Ocean Falls 36 D5 British Columbia,
SW Canada
Ocean Island *see* Banaba
Oceanside 47 C8 California, W USA
Ocean State *see* Rhode Island
Ochakiv 109 E4 *Rus.* Ochakov.
Mykolayivs'ka Oblast', S Ukraine
Ochakov *see* Ochakiv
Ochamchira *see* Och'amch'ire
Och'amch'ire 117 E2 *Rus.* Ochamchira.
W Georgia
Ocho Rios 54 B4 C Jamaica
Ochrida *see* Ohrid
Ochrida, Lake *see* Ohrid, Lake
Ocotal 52 D3 Nueva Segovia,
NW Nicaragua
Ocozocuautla 51 G5 Chiapas,
SE Mexico
October Revolution Island *see*
Oktyabr'skoy Revolyutsii, Ostrov
Ocú 53 F5 Herrera, S Panama
Ōdate 130 D3 Akita, Honshū,
C Japan
Oddur *see* Xuddur
Ödemiş 116 A4 İzmir, SW Turkey
Ödenburg *see* Sopron
Odenpäh *see* Otepää
Odense 85 B7 Fyn, C Denmark
Oder 98 B3 *Cz./Pol.* Odra. *river*
C Europe
Oderhaff *see* Szczeciński, Zalew
Odesa 109 E4 *Rus.* Odessa. Odes'ka
Oblast', SW Ukraine
Odessa 49 E3 Texas, SW USA
Odessa *see* Odesa
Odessus *see* Varna
Odienné 74 D4 NW Côte d'Ivoire
(Ivory Coast)

Ŏdŏngk 137 D6 Kâmpóng Spoe,
S Cambodia
Odoorn 86 E2 Drenthe, NE Netherlands
Odra *see* Oder
Oesel *see* Saaremaa
Of 117 E2 Trabzon, NE Turkey
Ofanto 97 D5 *river* S Italy
Offenbach 95 B5 *var.* Offenbach am
Main. Hessen, W Germany
Offenbach am Main *see* Offenbach
Offenburg 95 B6 Baden-Württemberg,
SW Germany
Ogaadeen *see* Ogaden
Ogaden 73 D5 *Som.* Ogaadeen. *plateau*
Ethiopia/Somalia
Ōgaki 131 C6 Gifu, Honshū, SW Japan
Ogallala 44 D4 Nebraska, C USA
Ogbomosho 75 F4 *var.* Ogmoboso. Oyo,
W Nigeria
Ogden 44 B4 Utah, W USA
Ogdensburg 41 F2 New York, NE USA
Ogmoboso *see* Ogbomosho
Ogulin 100 A3 Karlovac, NW Croatia
Ohio 40 C4 *off.* State of Ohio,
also known as Buckeye State. *state*
N USA
Ohio River 40 C4 *river* N USA
Ohlau *see* Oława
Ohri *see* Ohrid
Ohrid 101 D6 *Turk.* Ochrida, Ohri.
SW FYR Macedonia
Ohrid, Lake 101 D6 *var.* Lake Ochrida,
Alb. Liqeni i Ohrit, *Mac.* Ohridsko
Ezero. *lake* Albania/FYR Macedonia
Ohridsko Ezero/Ohrit, Liqeni i *see*
Ohrid, Lake
Ohura 150 D3 Manawatu-Wanganui,
North Island, New Zealand
Oirschot 87 C5 Noord-Brabant,
S Netherlands
Oise 90 C3 *river* N France
Oistins 55 G2 S Barbados
Ōita 131 B7 Ōita, Kyūshū, SW Japan
Ojinaga 50 D2 Chihuahua, N Mexico
Ojos del Salado, Cerro 64 B3 *mountain*
W Argentina
Okaihau 150 C2 Northland, North
Island, New Zealand
Okanizsa *see* Kanjiža
Okāra 134 C2 Punjab, E Pakistan
Okavanggo *see* Cubango/Okavango
Okavango 78 C3 *district* NW Namibia
Okavango *see* Cubango
Okavango Delta 78 C3 *wetland*
N Botswana
Okayama 131 B6 Okayama, Honshū,
SW Japan
Okazaki 131 C6 Aichi, Honshū, C Japan
Okeechobee, Lake 43 E4 *lake* Florida,
SE USA
Okefenokee Swamp 43 E3 *wetland*
Georgia, SE USA
Okhotsk 115 G3 Khabarovskiy Kray,
E Russian Federation
Okhotsk, Sea of 113 F3 *sea* NW Pacific
Ocean
Okhtyrka 109 F2 *Rus.* Akhtyrka.
Sums'ka Oblast', NE Ukraine
Oki-guntō *see* Oki-shotō
Okinawa 130 A3 *island* SW Japan
Okinawa-shotō 130 A3 *island group*
Nansei-shotō, SW Japan Asia
Oki-shotō 131 B6 *var.* Oki-guntō. *island*
group SW Japan
Oklahoma 49 F2 *off.* State of Oklahoma,
also known as The Sooner State. *state*
C USA
Oklahoma City 49 G1 *state capital*
Oklahoma, C USA
Okmulgee 49 G1 Oklahoma, C USA
Oko, Wadi 72 C3 *river* NE Sudan
Oktyabr'skiy 111 D6 Volgogradskaya
Oblast', SW Russian Federation
Oktyabr'skiy *see* Aktsyabrski
Oktyabr'skoy Revolyutsii, Ostrov 115
E2 *Eng.* October Revolution Island.
island Severnaya Zemlya, N Russian
Federation
Okulovka *see* Uglovka
Okushiri-tō 130 C3 *var.* Okusiri Tō.
island NE Japan
Okusiri Tō *see* Okushiri-tō
Oláh-Toplicza *see* Topliţa
Öland 85 C7 *island* S Sweden
Olavarría 65 D5 Buenos Aires,
E Argentina
Oława 98 C4 *Ger.* Ohlau. Dolnośląskie,
SW Poland

Olbia 97 A5 *prev.* Terranova Pausania.
Sardegna, Italy, C Mediterranean Sea
Old Bay State/Old Colony State *see*
Massachusetts
Old Dominion *see* Virginia
Oldebroek 86 D3 Gelderland,
E Netherlands
Oldenburg 94 B3 Niedersachsen,
NW Germany
Oldenburg 94 C2 *var.* Oldenburg
in Holstein. Schleswig-Holstein,
N Germany
Oldenburg in Holstein *see* Oldenburg
Oldenzaal 86 E3 Overijssel,
E Netherlands
Old Harbour 54 B5 C Jamaica
Old Line State *see* Maryland
Old North State *see* North Carolina
Olëkma 115 F4 *river* C Russian
Federation
Olëkminsk 115 F3 Respublika Sakha
(Yakutiya), NE Russian Federation
Oleksandrivka 109 E3 *Rus.*
Aleksandrovka. Kirovohrads'ka
Oblast', C Ukraine
Oleksandriya 109 F3 *Rus.* Aleksandriya.
Kirovohrads'ka Oblast', C Ukraine
Olenegorsk 110 C2 Murmanskaya
Oblast', NW Russian Federation
Olenëk 115 E3 Respublika Sakha
(Yakutiya), NE Russian Federation
Olenëk 115 E3 *river* NE Russian
Federation
Oléron, Île d' 91 A5 *island* W France
Olevs'k 108 D1 *Rus.* Olevsk.
Zhytomyrs'ka Oblast', N Ukraine
Olevsk *see* Olevs'k
Ölgiy 126 C2 Bayan-Ölgiy, W Mongolia
Olhão 92 B5 Faro, S Portugal
Olifa 78 B3 Kunene, NW Namibia
Ólimbos *see* Ólympos
Olimpo *see* Fuerte Olimpo
Olisipo *see* Lisboa
Olita *see* Alytus
Oliva 93 F4 País Valenciano, E Spain
Olivet 90 C4 Loiret, C France
Olmaliq 123 F2 *Rus.* Almalyk. Toshkent
Viloyati, E Uzbekistan
Olmütz *see* Olomouc
Olomouc 99 C5 *Ger.* Olmütz, *Pol.*
Ołomuniec. Olomoucký Kraj,
E Czech Republic
Olomuniec *see* Olomouc
Olonets 110 B3 Respublika Kareliya,
NW Russian Federation
Olovyannaya 115 F4 Chitinskaya
Oblast', S Russian Federation
Olpe 94 B4 Nordrhein-Westfalen,
W Germany
Olshanka *see* Vil'shanka
Olsnitz *see* Murska Sobota
Olsztyn 98 D2 *Ger.* Allenstein.
Warmińsko-Mazurskie, N Poland
Olt 108 B5 *var.* Oltul, *Ger.* Alt. *river*
S Romania
Oltenița 108 C5 *prev. Eng.* Oltenitsa;
anc. Constantiola. Călăraşi,
SE Romania
Oltenitsa *see* Oltenița
Oltul *see* Olt
Olvera 92 D5 Andalucía, S Spain
Ol'viopol' *see* Pervomays'k
Olympia 46 B2 *state capital* Washington,
NW USA
Olympic Mountains 46 A2 *mountain
range* Washington, NW USA
Ólympos 104 B4 *var.* Ólimbos, *Eng.*
Mount Olympus. *mountain*
N Greece
Omagh 89 B5 *Ir.* An Ómaigh.
W Northern Ireland, UK
Omaha 45 F4 Nebraska, C USA
Oman 121 D6 *off.* Sultanate of Oman,
Ar. Salṭanat 'Umān; *prev.* Muscat and
Oman. *country* SW Asia

OMAN
Southwest Asia

Official name Sultanate of Oman
Formation 1951 / 1951
Capital Muscat
Population 2.6 million / 32 people per
sq mile (12 people per sq km) / 84%
Total area 82,031 sq miles
(212,460 sq km)
Languages Arabic*, Baluchi, Farsi,
Hindi, Punjabi

OMAN
(continued)

Religions Ibadi Muslim 75%, Other
Muslim and Hindu 25%
Ethnic mix Arab 88%, Baluchi 4%,
Persian 3%, Indian and Pakistani 3%,
African 2%
Government Monarchy
Currency Omani rial = 1000 baizas
Literacy rate 74%
Calorie consumption Not available

Oman, Gulf of 120 E4 *Ar.* Khalīj 'Umān.
gulf N Arabian Sea
Oman, Sultanate of *see* Oman
Omboué 77 A6 Ogooué-Maritime,
W Gabon
Omdurman 72 B4 *var.* Umm Durmān.
Khartoum, C Sudan
Ometepe, Isla de 52 D4 *island*
S Nicaragua
Ommen 86 E3 Overijssel, E Netherlands
Omsk 114 C4 Omskaya Oblast',
C Russian Federation
Ōmuta 131 A7 Fukuoka, Kyūshū,
SW Japan
Onda 93 F3 País Valenciano, E Spain
Ondjiva *see* N'Giva
Öndörhaan 127 E2 *var.* Undur Khan;
prev. Tsetsen Khan. Hentiy,
E Mongolia
Onega 110 C3 Arkhangel'skaya Oblast',
NW Russian Federation
Onega 110 B4 *river* NW Russian
Federation
Onega, Lake *see* Onezhskoye Ozero
Onex 95 A7 Genève, SW Switzerland
Onezhskoye Ozero 110 B4 *Eng.* Lake
Onega. *lake* NW Russian Federation
Ongole 132 D1 Andhra Pradesh,
E India
Onitsha 75 G5 Anambra, S Nigeria
Onon Gol 127 E2 *river* N Mongolia
Onslow 146 A4 Western Australia
Onslow Bay 43 F1 *bay* North Carolina,
E USA
Ontario 38 B3 *province* S Canada
Ontario, Lake 41 E3 *lake*
Canada/USA
Ontenente *see* Ontinyent
Ontinyent 93 F4 *var.* Onteniente. País
Valenciano, E Spain
Ontong Java Rise 125 H4 *undersea
feature* W Pacific Ocean
Onuba *see* Huelva
Oodeypore *see* Udaipur
Oos-Londen *see* East London
Oostakker 87 B5 Oost-Vlaanderen,
NW Belgium
Oostburg 87 B5 Zeeland,
SW Netherlands
Oostende 87 A5 *Eng.* Ostend,
Fr. Ostende. West-Vlaanderen,
NW Belgium
Oosterbeek 86 D4 Gelderland,
SE Netherlands
Oosterhout 86 C4 Noord-Brabant,
S Netherlands
Opatija 100 A2 *It.* Abbazia.
Primorje-Gorski Kotar, NW Croatia
Opava 99 C5 *Ger.* Troppau.
Moravskoslezský Kraj, E Czech
Republic
Ópazova *see* Stara Pazova
Opelika 42 D2 Alabama, S USA
Opelousas 42 B3 Louisiana, S USA
Ophiusa *see* Formentera
Opmeer 86 C2 Noord-Holland,
NW Netherlands
Opochka 110 A4 Pskovskaya Oblast',
W Russian Federation
Opole 98 C4 *Ger.* Oppeln. Opolskie,
S Poland
Oporto *see* Porto
Opotiki 150 E3 Bay of Plenty, North
Island, New Zealand
Oppeln *see* Opole
Oppidum Ubiorum *see* Köln
Oqtosh 123 E2 *Rus.* Aktash. Samarqand
Viloyati, C Uzbekistan
Oradea 108 B3 *prev.* Oradea Mare,
Ger. Grosswardein, *Hung.* Nagyvárad.
Bihor, NW Romania
Oradea Mare *see* Oradea
Orahovac 101 D5 *Alb.* Rahovec.
Kosovo, S Serbia

Oral *see* Ural'sk
Oran 70 D2 *var.* Ouahran, Wahran.
NW Algeria
Orange 149 D6 New South Wales,
SE Australia
Orange 91 D6 *anc.* Arausio. Vaucluse,
SE France
Orangeburg 43 E2 South Carolina,
SE USA
Orange Cone *see* Orange Fan
Orange Fan 69 C7 *var.* Orange Cone.
undersea feature SW Indian Ocean
Orange Mouth/Orangemund *see*
Oranjemund
Orange River 78 B4 *Afr.* Oranjerivier.
river S Africa
Orange Walk 52 C1 Orange Walk,
N Belize
Oranienburg 94 D3 Brandenburg,
NE Germany
Oranjemund 78 B4 *var.* Orangemund;
prev. Orange Mouth. Karas,
SW Namibia
Oranjerivier *see* Orange River
Oranjestad 55 E5 *dependent territory
capital* (Aruba) W Aruba
Orany *see* Varéna
Oraşul Stalin *see* Braşov
Oravicabánya *see* Oraviţa
Oraviţa 108 A4 *Ger.* Orawitza, *Hung.*
Oravicabánya. Caraş-Severin,
SW Romania
Orawitza *see* Oraviţa
Orbetello 96 B4 Toscana, C Italy
Orcadas 154 A1 *Argentinian research
station* South Orkney Islands,
Antarctica
Orchard Homes 44 B1 Montana,
NW USA
Ordino 91 A8 Ordino, NW Andorra
Europe
Ordos Desert *see* Mu Us Shadi
Ordu 116 D2 *anc.* Cotyora. Ordu,
N Turkey
Ordzhonikidze 109 F3
Dnipropetrovs'ka Oblast', E Ukraine
Ordzhonikidze *see* Vladikavkaz, Russian
Federation
Ordzhonikidze *see* Yenakiyeve, Ukraine
Orealla 59 G3 E Guyana
Örebro 85 C6 Örebro, C Sweden
Oregon 46 B3 *off.* State of Oregon, *also
known as* Beaver State, Sunset State,
Valentine State, Webfoot State. *state*
NW USA
Oregon City 46 B3 Oregon, NW USA
Oregon, State of *see* Oregon
Orekhov *see* Orikhiv
Orël 111 B5 Orlovskaya Oblast',
W Russian Federation
Orem 44 B4 Utah, W USA
Ore Mountains *see* Erzgebirge/Krušné
Hory
Orenburg 111 D6
prev. Chkalov. Orenburgskaya Oblast',
W Russian Federation
Orense *see* Ourense
Oreor *see* Koror
Orestiáda 104 D3 *prev.* Orestiás.
Anatolikí Makedonía kai Thráki,
NE Greece
Orestiás *see* Orestiáda
Organ Peak 48 D3 *mountain* New
Mexico, SW USA
Orgeyev *see* Orhei
Orhei 108 D3 *var.* Orheiu, *Rus.* Orgeyev.
N Moldova
Orheiu *see* Orhei
Oriental, Cordillera 60 D3 *mountain
range* Bolivia/Peru
Oriental, Cordillera 58 B3 *mountain
range* C Colombia
Orihuela 93 F4 País Valenciano,
E Spain
Orikhiv 109 G3 *Rus.* Orekhov.
Zaporiz'ka Oblast', SE Ukraine
Orinoco, Río 59 E2 *river*
Colombia/Venezuela
Orissa 135 F4 *cultural region* NE India
Orissa 135 F4 *state* NE India
Orissaar *see* Orissaare
Orissaare 106 C2 Ger. Orissaar.
Saaremaa, W Estonia
Oristano 97 A5 Sardegna, Italy,
C Mediterranean Sea
Orito 58 A4 Putumayo, SW Colombia
Orizaba, Volcán Pico de 35 C7 *var.*
Citlaltépetl. *mountain* S Mexico

Orkney *see* Orkney Islands
Orkney Islands 88 C2
var. Orkney, Orkneys. *island group*
N Scotland, UK
Orkneys *see* Orkney Islands
Orlando 43 E4 Florida, SE USA
Orléanais 90 C4 *cultural region*
C France
Orléans 90 C4 *anc.* Aurelianum. Loiret,
C France
Orléansville *see* Chlef
Orly 90 E2 (Paris) Essonne, N France
Orlya 107 B6 *Rus.* Orlya. Hrodzyenskaya
Voblasts', W Belarus
Ormsö *see* Vormsi
Ormuz, Strait of *see* Hormuz, Strait of
Örnsköldsvik 85 C5 Västernorrland,
C Sweden
Orolaunum *see* Arlon
Orol Dengizi *see* Aral Sea
Oromocto 39 F4 New Brunswick,
SE Canada
Orona 145 F3 *prev.* Hull Island. *atoll*
Phoenix Islands, C Kiribati
Oropeza *see* Cochabamba
Orosirá Rodhópis *see* Rhodope
Mountains
Orpington 89 B8 UK
Orschowa *see* Orşova
Orsha 107 E6 *Rus.* Orsha. Vitsyebskaya
Voblasts', NE Belarus
Orsk 114 B4 Orenburgskaya Oblast',
W Russian Federation
Orşova 108 A4 *Ger.* Orschowa, *Hung.*
Orsova. Mehedinţi, SW Romania
Ortelsburg *see* Szczytno
Orthez 91 B6 Pyrénées-Atlantiques,
SW France
Ortona 96 D4 Abruzzo, C Italy
Oruba *see* Aruba
Oruro 61 F4 Oruro, W Bolivia
Oryokko *see* Yalu
Ōsaka 131 C6 *hist.* Naniwa. Ōsaka,
Honshu, SW Japan
Osa, Península de 53 E5 *peninsula*
S Costa Rica
Osborn Plateau 141 D5 *undersea feature*
E Indian Ocean
Osca *see* Huesca
Ösel *see* Saaremaa
Osh 123 F2 Oshskaya Oblast',
SW Kyrgyzstan
Oshawa 38 D5 Ontario, SE Canada
Oshikango 78 B3 Ohangwena,
N Namibia
Ō-shima 131 D6 *island* S Japan
Oshkosh 40 B2 Wisconsin,
N USA
Oshmyany *see* Ashmyany
Osiek *see* Osijek
Osijek 100 D3 *prev.* Osiek, Osjek,
Ger. Esseg, *Hung.* Eszék. Osijek-
Baranja, E Croatia
Osipenko *see* Berdyans'k
Osipovichi *see* Asipovichy
Osjek *see* Osijek
Oskaloosa 45 G4 Iowa, C USA
Oskarshamn 85 C7 Kalmar, S Sweden
Öskemen *see* Ust'-Kamenogorsk
Oskil *see* Oskol
Oskol 109 G2 *Ukr.* Oskil. *river* Russian
Federation/Ukraine
Oslo 85 B6 *prev.* Christiania, Kristiania.
country capital (Norway) Oslo,
S Norway
Osmaniye 116 D4 Osmaniye,
S Turkey
Osnabrück 94 A3 Niedersachsen,
NW Germany
Osogov Mountains 120 B3 *var.*
Osogovske Planine, Osogovski Planina,
Mac. Osogovski Planini. *mountain
range* Bulgaria/FYR Macedonia
Osogovske Planine/Osogovski
Planina/Osogovski Planini *see*
Osogov Mountains
Oşorhei *see* Tîrgu Mureş
Osorno 65 B5 Los Lagos, C Chile
Oss 86 D4 Noord-Brabant, S Netherlands
Ossa, Serra d' 92 C4 *mountain range*
SE Portugal
Ossora 115 H2 Koryakskiy Avtonomnyy
Okrug, E Russian Federation
Ostee *see* Baltic Sea
Ostend/Ostende *see* Oostende
Oster 109 E1 Chernihivs'ka Oblast',
N Ukraine
Östermyra *see* Seinäjoki

P

Osterode/Osterode in Ostpreussen
see Ostróda
Österreich see Austria
Östersund 85 C5 Jämtland,
C Sweden
Ostfriesische Inseln 94 A3
Eng. East Frisian Islands. island group
NW Germany
Ostia Aterni see Pescara
Ostiglia 96 C2 Lombardia, N Italy
Ostrava 99 C5 Moravskoslezský Kraj,
E Czech Republic
Ostróda 98 D3 Ger. Osterode, Osterode
in Ostpreussen. Warmińsko-
Mazurskie, NE Poland
Ostrołęka 98 D3 Ger. Wiesenhof, Rus.
Ostrolenka. Mazowieckie, C Poland
Ostrolenka see Ostrołęka
Ostrov 110 A4 Ger. Schlackenwerth.
Karlovarský Kraj, W Czech Republic
Ostrovets see Ostrowiec Świętokrzyski
Ostrovnoy 110 C2 Murmanskaya
Oblast', NW Russian Federation
Ostrów see Ostrów Wielkopolski
Ostrowiec see Ostrowiec Świętokrzyski
Ostrowiec Świętokrzyski 98 D4
var. Ostrowiec, Rus. Ostrovets.
Świętokrzyskie, C Poland
Ostrów Mazowiecka 98 D3
var. Ostrów Mazowiecki. Mazowieckie,
NE Poland
Ostrów Mazowiecki see Ostrów
Mazowiecka
Ostrowo see Ostrów Wielkopolski
Ostrów Wielkopolski 98 C4 var.
Ostrów, Ger. Ostrowo. Wielkopolskie,
C Poland
Ostyako-Vogul's'k see Khanty-Mansiysk
Osum see Osumit, Lumi i
Ōsumi-shotō 131 A8 island group
Kagoshima, Nansei-shotō, SW Japan
Asia East China Sea Pacific Ocean
Osumit, Lumi i 101 C7 var. Osum. river
SE Albania
Osuna 92 D4 Andalucía, S Spain
Oswego 41 F2 New York, NE USA
Otago Peninsula 151 B7 peninsula
South Island, New Zealand
Otaki 150 D4 Wellington, North Island,
New Zealand
Otaru 130 C2 Hokkaidō, NE Japan
Otavalo 60 B1 Imbabura, N Ecuador
Otavi 78 B3 Otjozondjupa,
N Namibia
Oțelu Roșu 108 B4 Ger. Ferdinandsberg,
Hung. Nándorhgy. Caras-Severin,
SW Romania
Otepää 106 D3 Ger. Odenpäh.
Valgamaa, SE Estonia
Oti 75 E4 river N Togo
Otira 151 C6 West Coast, South Island,
New Zealand
Otjiwarongo 78 B3 Otjozondjupa,
N Namibia
Otorohanga 150 D3 Waikato, North
Island, New Zealand
Otranto, Canale d' see Otranto, Strait of
Otranto, Strait of 101 C6 It. Canale
d'Otranto. strait Albania/Italy
Otrokovice 99 C5 Ger. Otrokowitz.
Zlínský Kraj, E Czech Republic
Otrokowitz see Otrokovice
Ōtsu 131 C6 var. Ōtu. Shiga, Honshū,
SW Japan
Ottawa 38 D5 country capital (Canada)
Ontario, SE Canada
Ottawa 40 B3 Illinois, N USA
Ottawa 45 F3 Kansas, C USA
Ottawa 41 E2 Fr. Outaouais. river
Ontario/Québec, SE Canada
Ottawa Islands 38 C1 island group
Nunavut, C Canada
Ottignies 87 C6 Wallon Brabant,
C Belgium
Ottumwa 45 G4 Iowa, C USA
Ōtu see Ōtsu
Ouachita Mountains 42 A1
mountain range Arkansas/Oklahoma,
C USA
Ouachita River 42 B2 river Arkansas/
Louisiana, C USA
Ouagadougou 75 E4 var. Wagadugu.
country capital (Burkina Faso)
C Burkina Faso
Ouahigouya 75 E3 NW Burkina Faso
Ouahran see Oran
Oualâta 74 D3 var. Oualata. Hodh ech
Chargui, SE Mauritania

Ouanary 59 H3 E French Guiana
Ouanda Djallé 76 D4 Vakaga,
NE Central African Republic
Ouarâne 74 D2 desert C Mauritania
Ouargla 71 E2 var. Wargla. NE Algeria
Ouarzazate 70 C3 S Morocco
Oubangui see Ubangi
Oubangui-Chari see Central African
Republic
Oubangui-Chari, Territoire de l' see
Central African Republic
Oudjda see Oujda
Ouessant, Île d' 90 A3 Eng. Ushant.
island NW France
Ouésso 77 B5 La Sangha, NW Congo
Oujda 70 D2 Ar. Oudjda, Ujda.
NE Morocco
Oujeft 74 C2 Adrar, C Mauritania
Oulu 84 D4 Swe. Uleåborg. Oulu,
C Finland
Oulujärvi 84 D4 Swe. Uleträsk. lake
C Finland
Oulujoki 84 D4 Swe. Uleälv. river
C Finland
Ounasjoki 84 D3 river N Finland
Ounianga Kébir 76 C2
Borkou-Ennedi-Tibesti, N Chad
Oup see Auob
Oupeye 87 D6 Liège, E Belgium
Our 87 D6 river NW Europe
Ourense 92 C1 Cast. Orense, Lat.
Aurium. Galicia, NW Spain
Ourique 92 B4 Beja, S Portugal
Ours, Grand Lac de l' see
Great Bear Lake
Ourthe 87 D7 river E Belgium
Ouse 89 D5 river N England, UK
Outaouais see Ottawa
Outer Hebrides 88 B3
var. Western Isles. island group
NW Scotland, UK
Outer Islands 79 G1 island group
SW Seychelles Africa W Indian Ocean
Outes 92 B1 Galicia, NW Spain
Ouvéa 144 D5 island Îles Loyauté,
NE New Caledonia
Ouyen 149 C6 Victoria, SE Australia
Ovalle 64 B3 Coquimbo, N Chile
Ovar 92 B2 Aveiro, N Portugal
Overflakkee 86 B4 island
SW Netherlands
Overijse 87 C6 Vlaams Brabant,
C Belgium
Oviedo 92 C1 anc. Asturias. Asturias,
NW Spain
Ovilava see Wels
Ovruch 108 D1 Zhytomyrs'ka Oblast',
N Ukraine
Owando 77 B5 prev. Fort Rousset.
Cuvette, C Congo
Owase 131 C6 Mie, Honshū,
SW Japan
Owatonna 45 F3 Minnesota, N USA
Owen Fracture Zone 140 B4 tectonic
feature W Arabian Sea
Owen, Mount 151 C5 mountain South
Island, New Zealand
Owensboro 40 B5 Kentucky, S USA
Owen Stanley Range 144 B3 mountain
range S Papua New Guinea
Owerri 75 G5 Imo, S Nigeria
Owo 75 F5 Ondo, SW Nigeria
Owyhee River 46 C4 river Idaho/Oregon,
NW USA
Oxford 151 C6 Canterbury, South Island,
New Zealand
Oxford 89 D6 Lat. Oxonia.
S England, UK
Oxkutzcab 51 H4 Yucatán, SE Mexico
Oxnard 47 B7 California, W USA
Oxonia see Oxford
Oxus see Amu Darya
Oyama 131 D5 Tochigi, Honshū,
S Japan
Oyem 77 B5 Woleu-Ntem, N Gabon
Oyo 77 B6 Cuvette, C Congo
Oyo 75 F4 Oyo, W Nigeria
Ozark 42 D3 Alabama, S USA
Ozark Plateau 45 G5 plain Arkansas/
Missouri, C USA
Ozarks, Lake of the 45 F5 reservoir
Missouri, C USA
Ozbourn Seamount 152 D4 undersea
feature W Pacific Ocean
Ózd 99 D6 Borsod-Abaúj-Zemplén,
NE Hungary
Ozieri 97 A5 Sardegna, Italy,
C Mediterranean Sea

Paamiut 82 B4 var. Påmiut, Dan.
Frederikshåb. S Greenland
Pa-an 136 B4 Karen State,
S Myanmar (Burma)
Pabianice 98 C4 Łódzski, Poland
Pabna 135 G4 Rajshahi, W Bangladesh
Pacaraima, Sierra/Pacaraím, Serra see
Pakaraima Mountains
Pachuca 51 E4 var. Pachuca de Soto.
Hidalgo, C Mexico
Pachuca de Soto see Pachuca
Pacific-Antarctic Ridge 154 B5
undersea feature S Pacific Ocean
Pacific Ocean 152 D3 ocean
Padalung see Phatthalung
Padang 138 B4 Sumatera, W Indonesia
Paderborn 94 B4 Nordrhein-Westfalen,
NW Germany
Padma see Brahmaputra
Padma see Ganges
Padova 96 C2 Eng. Padua; anc. Patavium.
Veneto, NE Italy
Padre Island 49 G5 island Texas,
SW USA
Padua see Padova
Paducah 40 B5 Kentucky, S USA
Paeroa 150 D3 Waikato, North Island,
New Zealand
Páfos 102 C5 var. Paphos.
W Cyprus
Pag 100 A3 It. Pago. island Zadar,
C Croatia
Page 48 B1 Arizona, SW USA
Pago see Pag
Pago Pago 145 F4 dependent territory
capital (American Samoa) Tutuila,
W American Samoa
Pahiatua 150 D4 Manawatu-Wanganui,
North Island, New Zealand
Pahsien see Chongqing
Paide 106 D2 Ger. Weissenstein.
Järvamaa, N Estonia
Paihia 150 D2 Northland, North Island,
New Zealand
Päijänne 85 D5 lake S Finland
Paine, Cerro 65 A7 mountain
S Chile
Painted Desert 48 B1 desert Arizona,
SW USA
Paisance see Piacenza
Paisley 88 C4 W Scotland, UK
País Valenciano 93 F3 var. Valencia,
Cat. València; anc. Valentia.
autonomous community NE Spain
País Vasco 93 E1 cultural region
N Spain Europe
Paita 60 B3 Piura, NW Peru
Pakanbaru see Pekanbaru
Pakaraima Mountains 59 E3 var. Serra
Pacaraím, Sierra Pacaraima. mountain
range N South America
Pakistan 134 A2 off. Islamic Republic
of Pakistan, var. Islami Jamhuriya e
Pakistan. country S Asia

PAKISTAN
South Asia

Official name Islamic Republic of
Pakistan
Formation 1947 / 1971
Capital Islamabad
Population 158 million / 531 people per
sq mile (205 people per sq km) / 37%
Total area 310,401 sq miles
(803,940 sq km)
Languages Urdu*, Baluchi, Brahui,
Pashtu, Punjabi, Sindhi
Religions Sunni Muslim 77%, Shi'a
Muslim 20%, Hindu 2%, Christian 1%
Ethnic mix Punjabi 56%, Pathan
(Pashtun) 15%, Sindhi 14%, Mohajir 7%,
Other 4%, Baluchi 4%
Government Presidential system
Currency Pakistani rupee = 100 paisa
Literacy rate 49%
Calorie consumption 2419 calories

Pakistan, Islamic Republic of see
Pakistan
Pakistan, Islami Jamhuriya e see
Pakistan
Paknam see Samut Prakan
Pakokku 136 A3 Magwe,
C Myanmar (Burma)

Pak Phanang 137 C7 var. Ban Pak
Phanang. Nakhon Si Thammarat,
SW Thailand
Pakruojis 106 C4 Šiauliai, N Lithuania
Paks 99 C7 Tolna, S Hungary
Paksé see Pakxé
Pakxé 137 D5 var. Paksé. Champasak,
S Laos
Palafrugell 93 G2 Cataluña, NE Spain
Palagruža 101 B5 It. Pelagosa. island
SW Croatia
Palaiá Epídavros 105 C6 Pelopónnisos,
S Greece
Palaiseau 90 D2 Essonne, N France
Palamós 93 G2 Cataluña, NE Spain
Palamuse 106 E2 Ger. Sankt-
Bartholomäi. Jõgevamaa,
E Estonia
Palanka see Bačka Palanka
Pālanpur 134 C4 Gujarāt, W India
Palantia see Palencia
Palapye 78 D3 Central, SE Botswana
Palau 144 A2 var. Belau. country
W Pacific Ocean

PALAU
Australasia & Oceania

Official name Republic of Palau
Formation 1994 / 1994
Capital Koror
Population 20,303 / 104 people per
sq mile (40 people per sq km) / 70%
Total area 177 sq miles (458 sq km)
Languages Palauan, English, Japanese,
Angaur, Tobi, Sonsorolese
Religions Christian 66%,
Modekngei 34%
Ethnic mix Micronesian 87%,
Filipino 8%, Chinese and other Asian 5%
Government Nonparty system
Currency US dollar = 100 cents
Literacy rate 98%
Calorie consumption Not available

Palawan 139 E2 island W Philippines
Palawan Passage 138 D2 passage
W Philippines
Paldiski 106 D2 prev. Baltiski,
Eng Baltic Port, Ger. Baltischport.
Harjumaa, NW Estonia
Palembang 138 B4 Sumatera,
W Indonesia
Palencia 92 D2 anc. Palantia, Pallantia.
Castilla-León, NW Spain
Palerme see Palermo
Palermo 97 C7 Fr. Palerme; anc.
Panhormus, Panormus. Sicilia,
Italy, C Mediterranean Sea
Pāli 134 C3 Rājasthān, N India
Palikir 144 C2 country capital
(Micronesia) Pohnpei, E Micronesia
Palimé see Kpalimé
Palioúri, Akrotírio 104 C4
var. Akra Kanestron. headland
N Greece
Palk Strait 132 C3 strait India/Sri Lanka
Pallantia see Palencia
Palliser, Cape 151 D5 headland North
Island, New Zealand
Palma 93 G3 var. Palma de Mallorca.
Mallorca, Spain, W Mediterranean Sea
Palma del Río 92 D4 Andalucía, S Spain
Palma de Mallorca see Palma
Palmar Sur 53 E5 Puntarenas, SE Costa
Rica
Palma Soriano 54 C3 Santiago de Cuba,
E Cuba
Palm Beach 148 E1 New South Wales,
E Australia
Palmer 154 A2 US research station
Antarctica
Palmer Land 154 A3 physical region
Antarctica
Palmerston 145 F4 island S Cook Islands
Palmerston see Darwin
Palmerston North 150 D4 Manawatu-
Wanganui, North Island, New Zealand
The Palmetto State see South Carolina
Palmi 97 D7 Calabria, SW Italy
Palmira 58 B3 Valle del Cauca,
W Colombia
Palm Springs 47 D7 California, W USA
Palmyra see Tudmur
Palmyra Atoll 145 G2 US privately
owned unincorporated territory
C Pacific Ocean
Palo Alto 47 B6 California, W USA

Paloe *see* Denpasar, Bali, C Indonesia
Paloe *see* Palu
Palu *139 E4 prev.* Paloe. Sulawesi, C Indonesia
Pamiers *91 B6* Ariège, S France
Pamir *123 F3 var.* Daryā-ye Pāmīr, *Taj.* Dar"yoi Pomir. *river* Afghanistan/Tajikistan
Pāmīr, Daryā-ye *see* Pamir
Pamir/Pāmīr, Daryā-ye *see* Pamirs
Pamirs *123 F3 Pash.* Daryā-ye Pāmīr, *Rus.* Pamir. *mountain range* C Asia
Pâmiut *see* Paamiut
Pamlico Sound *43 G1 sound* North Carolina, SE USA
Pampa *49 E1* Texas, SW USA
Pampa Aullagas, Lago *see* Poopó, Lago
Pampas *64 C4 plain* C Argentina
Pampeluna *see* Pamplona
Pamplona *58 C2* Norte de Santander, N Colombia
Pamplona *93 E1 Basq.* Iruña, *prev.* Pampeluna; *anc.* Pompaelo. Navarra, N Spain
Panaji *132 B1 var.* Pangim, Panjim, New Goa. *state capital* Goa, W India
Panamá *53 G4 var.* Ciudad de Panama, *Eng.* Panama City. *country capital* (Panama) Panamá, C Panama
Panama *53 G5 off.* Republic of Panama. *country* Central America

PANAMA
Central America

Official name Republic of Panama
Formation 1903 / 1903
Capital Panama City
Population 3.2 million / 109 people per sq mile (42 people per sq km) / 56%
Total area 30,193 sq miles (78,200 sq km)
Languages Spanish*, English Creole, Amerindian languages, Chibchan languages
Religions Roman Catholic 86%, Other 8%, Protestant 6%
Ethnic mix Mestizo 60%, White 14%, Black 12%, Amerindian 8%, Asian 4%, Other 2%
Government Presidential system
Currency Balboa = 100 centesimos
Literacy rate 92%
Calorie consumption 2272 calories

Panama Basin *35 C8 undersea feature* E Pacific Ocean
Panama Canal *53 F4 shipping canal* E Panama
Panama City *42 D3* Florida, SE USA
Panama City *see* Panamá
Panamá, Golfo de *53 G5 var.* Gulf of Panama. *gulf* S Panama
Panama, Gulf of *see* Panamá, Golfo de
Panama, Isthmus of *see* Panama, Istmo de
Panama, Istmo de *53 G4 Eng.* Isthmus of Panama; *prev.* Isthmus of Darien. *isthmus* E Panama
Panama, Republic of *see* Panama
Panay Island *139 E2 island* C Philippines
Pančevo *100 D3 Ger.* Pantschowa, *Hung.* Pancsova. Vojvodina, N Serbia
Pancsova *see* Pančevo
Paneas *see* Bāniyās
Panevėžys *106 C4* Panevėžys, C Lithuania
Pangim *see* Panaji
Pangkalpinang *138 C4* Pulau Bangka, W Indonesia
Pang-Nga *see* Phang-Nga
Panhormus *see* Palermo
Panjim *see* Panaji
Panopolis *see* Akhmîm
Pánormos *105 C7* Kríti, Greece, E Mediterranean Sea
Panormus *see* Palermo
Pantanal *63 E3 var.* Pantanalmato-Grossense. *swamp* SW Brazil
Pantanalmato-Grossense *see* Pantanal
Pantelleria, Isola di *97 B7 island* SW Italy
Pantschowa *see* Pančevo
Pánuco *51 E3* Veracruz-Llave, E Mexico
Pao-chi/Paoki *see* Baoji
Paola *102 B5* E Malta
Pao-shan *see* Baoshan
Pao-t'ou/Paotow *see* Baotou
Papagayo, Golfo de *52 C4 gulf* NW Costa Rica
Papakura *150 D3* Auckland, North Island, New Zealand
Papantla *51 F4 var.* Papantla de Olarte. Veracruz-Llave, E Mexico
Papantla de Olarte *see* Papantla
Papeete *145 H4 dependent territory capital* (French Polynesia) Tahiti, W French Polynesia
Paphos *see* Páfos
Papilė *106 B3* Šiaulai, NW Lithuania
Papillion *45 F4* Nebraska, C USA
Papua *139 H4 var.* Irian Barat, West Irian, West New Guinea, West Papua; *prev.* Dutch New Guinea, Irian Jaya, Netherlands New Guinea. *province* E Indonesia
Papua and New Guinea, Territory of *see* Papua New Guinea
Papua, Gulf of *144 B3 gulf* S Papua New Guinea
Papua New Guinea *144 B3 off.* Independent State of Papua New Guinea; *prev.* Territory of Papua and New Guinea. *country* NW Melanesia

PAPUA NEW GUINEA
Australasia & Oceania

Official name Independent State of Papua New Guinea
Formation 1975 / 1975
Capital Port Moresby
Population 5.9 million / 34 people per sq mile (13 people per sq km) / 17%
Total area 178,703 sq miles (462,840 sq km)
Languages Pidgin English*, Papuan*, English, Motu, 750 (est.) native languages
Religions Protestant 60%, Roman Catholic 37%, Other 3%
Ethnic mix Melanesian and mixed race 100%
Government Parliamentary system
Currency Kina = 100 toeas
Literacy rate 57%
Calorie consumption 2193 calories

Papua New Guinea, Independent State of *see* Papua New Guinea
Papuk *100 C3 mountain range* NE Croatia
Pará *63 E2 off.* Estado do Pará. *state* NE Brazil
Pará *see* Belém
Paracel Islands *125 E3 disputed territory* SE Asia
Paraćin *100 D4* Serbia, C Serbia
Paradise of the Pacific *see* Hawai'i
Pará, Estado do *see* Pará
Paragua, Río *59 E3 river* SE Venezuela
Paraguay *64 C2 country* C South America

PARAGUAY
South America

Official name Republic of Paraguay
Formation 1811 / 1938
Capital Asunción
Population 6.2 million / 40 people per sq mile (16 people per sq km) / 56%
Total area 157,046 sq miles (406,750 sq km)
Languages Guaraní*, Spanish*, German
Religions Roman Catholic 96%, Protestant (including Mennonite) 4%
Ethnic mix Mestizo 90%, Other 8%, Amerindian 2%
Government Presidential system
Currency Guaraní = 100 centimos
Literacy rate 92%
Calorie consumption 2565 calories

Paraguay *64 D2 var.* Río Paraguay. *river* C South America
Paraguay, Río *see* Paraguay
Parahiba/Parahyba *see* Paraíba
Paraíba *63 G2 off.* Estado da Paraíba; *prev.* Parahiba, Parahyba. *state* E Brazil
Paraíba *see* João Pessoa
Paraíba, Estado da *see* Paraíba
Parakou *75 F4* C Benin
Paramaribo *59 G3 country capital* (Suriname) Paramaribo, N Surinam
Paramushir, Ostrov *115 H3 island* SE Russian Federation
Paraná *63 E4* Entre Ríos, E Argentina
Paraná *63 E5 off.* Estado do Paraná. *state* S Brazil
Paraná *57 C5 var.* Alto Paraná. *river* C South America
Paraná, Estado do *see* Paraná
Paranésti *104 C3 var* Paranestio. Anatolikí Makedonía kai Thráki, NE Greece
Paranestio *see* Paranésti
Paraparaumu *151 D5* Wellington, North Island, New Zealand
Parchim *94 C3* Mecklenburg-Vorpommern, N Germany
Parczew *98 E4* Lubelskie, E Poland
Pardubice *99 B5 Ger.* Pardubitz. Pardubický Kraj, C Czech Republic
Pardubitz *see* Pardubice
Parechcha *107 B5 Pol.* Porzecze, *Rus.* Porech'ye. Hrodzyenskaya Voblasts', W Belarus
Parecis, Chapada dos *62 D3 var.* Serra dos Parecis. *mountain range* W Brazil
Parecis, Serra dos *see* Parecis, Chapada dos
Parenzo *see* Poreč
Parepare *139 E4* Sulawesi, C Indonesia
Párga *105 A5* Ípeiros, W Greece
Paria, Golfo de *see* Paria, Gulf of
Paria, Gulf of *59 E1 var.* Golfo de Paria. *gulf* Trinidad and Tobago/Venezuela
Parika *59 F2* NE Guyana
Paris *90 D1 anc.* Lutetia, Lutetia Parisiorum, Parisii. *country capital* (France) Paris, N France
Paris *49 G2* Texas, SW USA
Parisii *see* Paris
Parkersburg *40 D4* West Virginia, NE USA
Parkes *149 D6* New South Wales, SE Australia
Parkhar *see* Farkhor
Parma *96 B2* Emilia-Romagna, N Italy
Parnahyba *see* Parnaíba
Parnaíba *63 F2 var.* Parnahyba. Piauí, E Brazil
Pärnu *106 D2 Ger.* Pernau, *Latv.* Pērnava; *prev. Rus.* Pernov. Pärnumaa, SW Estonia
Pärnu *106 D2 var.* Parnu Jõgi, *Ger.* Pernau. *river* SW Estonia
Pärnu-Jaagupi *106 D2 Ger.* Sankt-Jakobi. Pärnumaa, SW Estonia
Parnu Jõgi *see* Pärnu
Pärnu Laht *106 D2 Ger.* Pernauer Bucht. *bay* SW Estonia
Paropamisus Range *see* Safidkūh, Selseleh-ye
Paroikia *105 D6* Kykládes, Greece, Aegean Sea
Páros *105 C6 island* Kykládes, Greece, Aegean Sea
Parral *64 B4* Maule, C Chile
Parral *see* Hidalgo del Parral
Parramatta *148 D1* New South Wales, SE Australia
Parras *50 D3 var.* Parras de la Fuente. Coahuila de Zaragoza, NE Mexico
Parras de la Fuente *see* Parras
Parsons *45 F5* Kansas, C USA
Pasadena *47 C7* California, W USA
Pasadena *49 H4* Texas, SW USA
Paşcani *108 C3 Hung.* Páskán. Iaşi, NE Romania
Pasco *46 C2* Washington, NW USA
Pascua, Isla de *153 F4 var.* Rapa Nui, Easter Island. *island* E Pacific Ocean
Pasewalk *94 D3* Mecklenburg-Vorpommern, NE Germany
Pashkeni *see* Bolyarovo
Pasinler *117 F3* Erzurum, NE Turkey
Páskán *see* Paşcani
Pasłęk *98 D2 Ger.* Preußisch Holland. Warmińsko-Mazurskie, NE Poland
Pasni *134 A3* Baluchistān, SW Pakistan
Paso de Indios *65 B6* Chubut, S Argentina
Passarowitz *see* Požarevac
Passau *95 D6* Bayern, SE Germany
Passo Fundo *63 E5* Rio Grande do Sul, S Brazil
Pastavy *107 C5 Pol.* Postawy, *Rus.* Postavy. Vitsyebskaya Voblasts', NW Belarus
Pastaza, Río *60 B2 river* Ecuador/Peru
Pasto *58 A4* Nariño, SW Colombia
Pasvalys *106 C4* Panevėžys, N Lithuania
Patagonia *57 B7 semi arid region* Argentina/Chile
Patalung *see* Phatthalung
Patani *see* Pattani
Patavium *see* Padova
Patea *150 D4* Taranaki, North Island, New Zealand
Paterson *41 F3* New Jersey, NE USA
Pathein *see* Bassein
Pátmos *105 D6 island* Dodekánisa, Greece, Aegean Sea
Patna *135 F3 var.* Azimabad. *state capital* Bihār, N India
Patnos *117 F3* Ağrı, E Turkey
Patos, Lagoa dos *63 E5 lagoon* S Brazil
Pátra *105 B5 Eng.* Patras; *prev.* Pátrai. Dytikí Ellás, S Greece
Pátrai/Patras *see* Pátra
Pattani *137 C7 var.* Patani. Pattani, SW Thailand
Pattaya *137 C5* Chon Buri, S Thailand
Patuca, Río *52 D2 river* E Honduras
Pau *91 B6* Pyrénées-Atlantiques, SW France
Paulatuk *37 E3* Northwest Territories, NW Canada
Paungde *136 B4* Pegu, C Myanmar (Burma)
Pautalia *see* Kyustendil
Pavia *96 B2 anc.* Ticinum. Lombardia, N Italy
Pāvilosta *106 B3* Liepāja, W Latvia
Pavlikeni *104 D2* Veliko Tŭrnovo, N Bulgaria
Pavlodar *114 C4* Pavlodar, NE Kazakhstan
Pavlograd *see* Pavlohrad
Pavlohrad *109 G3 Rus.* Pavlograd. Dnipropetrovs'ka Oblast', E Ukraine
Pawn *136 B3 river* C Myanmar (Burma)
Pax Augusta *see* Badajoz
Pax Julia *see* Beja
Paxoí *105 A5 island* Iónia Nisiá, Greece, C Mediterranean Sea
Payo Obispo *see* Chetumal
Paysandú *64 D4* Paysandú, W Uruguay
Pazar *117 E2* Rize, NE Turkey
Pazardzhik *104 C3 prev.* Tatar Pazardzhik. Pazardzhik, SW Bulgaria
Peace Garden State *see* North Dakota
Peach State *see* Georgia
Pearl Islands *see* Perlas, Archipiélago de las
Pearl Lagoon *see* Perlas, Laguna de
Pearl River *42 B3 river* Louisiana/Mississippi, S USA
Pearsall *49 F4* Texas, SW USA
Peawanuk *38 C2* Ontario, C Canada
Peć *101 D5 Alb.* Pejë, *Turk.* Ipek. Kosovo, S Serbia
Pechora *110 D3* Respublika Komi, NW Russian Federation
Pechora *110 D3 river* NW Russian Federation
Pechora Sea *see* Pechorskoye More
Pechorskoye More *110 D2 Eng.* Pechora Sea. *sea* NW Russian Federation
Pecos *49 E3* Texas, SW USA
Pecos River *49 E3 river* New Mexico/Texas, SW USA
Pécs *99 C7 Ger.* Fünfkirchen, *Lat.* Sopianae. Baranya, SW Hungary
Pedra Lume *74 A3* Sal, NE Cape Verde
Pedro Cays *54 C3 island group* Greater Antilles, S Jamaica North America N Caribbean Sea W Atlantic Ocean
Pedro Juan Caballero *64 D2* Amambay, E Paraguay
Peer *87 D5* Limburg, NE Belgium
Pegasus Bay *151 C6 bay* South Island, New Zealand
Pegu *136 B4 var.* Bago. Pegu, SW Myanmar (Burma)
Pehuajó *64 C4* Buenos Aires, E Argentina
Pei-ching *see* Beijing/Beijing Shi
Peine *94 B3* Niedersachsen, C Germany
Pei-p'ing *see* Beijing/Beijing Shi
Peipsi Järv/Peipus-See *see* Peipus, Lake
Peipus, Lake *106 E3 Est.* Peipsi Järv, *Ger.* Peipus-See, *Rus.* Chudskoye Ozero. *lake* Estonia/Russian Federation

Peiraías *105 C6 prev.* Piraiévs, *Eng.* Piraeus. Attikí, C Greece
Pejë *see* Peć
Pèk *136 D4 var.* Xieng Khouang; *prev.* Xiangkhoang. Xiangkhoang, N Laos
Pekalongan *138 C4* Jawa, C Indonesia
Pekanbaru *138 B3 var.* Pakanbaru. Sumatera, W Indonesia
Pekin *40 B4* Illinois, N USA
Peking *see* Beijing/Beijing Shi
Pelagie, Isole *97 B8 island group* SW Italy
Pelagosa *see* Palagruža
Pelican State *see* Louisiana
Pelly Bay *37 G3* Nunavut, N Canada
Pélmonostor *see* Beli Manastir
Peloponnese/Peloponnesus *see* Pelopónnisos
Pelopónnisos *105 B6 var.* Morea, *Eng.* Peloponnese; *anc.* Peloponnesus. *peninsula* S Greece
Pematangsiantar *138 B3* Sumatera, W Indonesia
Pemba *79 F2 prev.* Port Amelia, Porto Amélia. Cabo Delgado, NE Mozambique
Pemba *73 D7 island* E Tanzania
Pembroke *38 D4* Ontario, SE Canada
Penang *see* George Town
Penang *see* Pinang, Pulau, Peninsular Malaysia
Penas, Golfo de *65 A7 gulf* S Chile
Penderma *see* Bandırma
Pendleton *46 C3* Oregon, NW USA
Pend Oreille, Lake *46 D2 lake* Idaho, NW USA
Peneius *see* Pineiós
Peng-pu *see* Bengbu
Penibético, Sistema *see* Béticos, Sistemas
Peniche *92 B3* Leiria, W Portugal
Peninsular State *see* Florida
Penninae, Alpes/Pennine, Alpi *see* Pennine Alps
Pennine Alps *95 A8 Fr.* Alpes Pennines, *It.* Alpi Pennine, *Lat.* Alpes Penninae. *mountain range* Italy/Switzerland
Pennine Chain *see* Pennines
Pennines *89 D5 var.* Pennine Chain. *mountain range* N England, UK
Pennines, Alpes *see* Pennine Alps
Pennsylvania *40 D3 off.* Commonwealth of Pennsylvania, *also known as* Keystone State. *state* NE USA
Penobscot River *41 G2 river* Maine, NE USA
Penong *149 A6* South Australia
Penonomé *53 F5* Coclé, C Panama
Penrhyn *145 G3 atoll* N Cook Islands
Penrhyn Basin *143 F3 undersea feature* C Pacific Ocean
Penrith *148 D1* New South Wales, SE Australia
Penrith *89 D5* NW England, UK
Pensacola *42 C3* Florida, SE USA
Pentecost *144 D4 Fr.* Pentecôte. *island* C Vanuatu
Pentecôte *see* Pentecost
Penza *111 C6* Penzenskaya Oblast', W Russian Federation
Penzance *89 C7* SW England, UK
Peoria *40 B4* Illinois, N USA
Perchtoldsdorf *95 E6* Niederösterreich, NE Austria
Percival Lakes *146 C4 lakes* Western Australia
Perdido, Monte *93 F1 mountain* NE Spain
Perece Vela Basin *see* West Mariana Basin
Pereira *58 B3* Risaralda, W Colombia
Peremyshl *see* Przemyśl
Pergamino *64 C4* Buenos Aires, E Argentina
Périgueux *91 C5 anc.* Vesuna. Dordogne, SW France
Perito Moreno *65 B6* Santa Cruz, S Argentina
Perlas, Archipiélago de las *53 G5 Eng.* Pearl Islands. *island group* SE Panama
Perlas, Laguna de *53 E3 Eng.* Pearl Lagoon. *lagoon* E Nicaragua
Perleberg *94 C3* Brandenburg, N Germany
Perlepe *see* Prilep
Perm' *114 C3 prev.* Molotov. Permskaya Oblast', NW Russian Federation
Pernambuco *63 G2 off.* Estado de Pernambuco. *state* E Brazil
Pernambuco *see* Recife
Pernambuco Abyssal Plain *see* Pernambuco Plain
Pernambuco, Estado de *see* Pernambuco
Pernambuco Plain *67 C5 var.* Pernambuco Abyssal Plain. *undersea feature* E Atlantic Ocean
Pernau *see* Pärnu
Pernauer Bucht *see* Pärnu Laht
Pērnava *see* Pärnu
Pernik *104 B2 prev.* Dimitrovo. Pernik, W Bulgaria
Pernov *see* Pärnu
Perote *51 F4* Veracruz-Llave, E Mexico
Pérouse *see* Perugia
Perovsk *see* Kyzylorda
Perpignan *91 C6* Pyrénées-Orientales, S France
Perryton *49 F1* Texas, SW USA
Perryville *45 H5* Missouri, C USA
Persia *see* Iran
Persian Gulf *120 C4 var.* The Gulf, *Ar.* Khalīj al 'Arabī, *Per.* Khalīj-e Fars. *Gulf* SW Asia
Perth *147 A6 state capital* Western Australia
Perth *88 C4* C Scotland, UK
Perth Basin *141 E6 undersea feature* SE Indian Ocean
Peru *60 C3 off.* Republic of Peru. *country* W South America

PERU
South America

Official name Republic of Peru
Formation 1824 / 1941
Capital Lima
Population 28 million / 57 people per sq mile (22 people per sq km) / 73%
Total area 496,223 sq miles (1,285,200 sq km)
Languages Spanish*, Quechua*, Aymara*
Religions Roman Catholic 95%, Other 5%
Ethnic mix Amerindian 50%, Mestizo 40%, White 7%, Other 3%
Government Presidential system
Currency New sol = 100 centimos
Literacy rate 88%
Calorie consumption 2571 calories

Peru *see* Beru
Peru Basin *67 A5 undersea feature* E Pacific Ocean
Peru-Chile Trench *56 A4 undersea feature* E Pacific Ocean
Perugia *96 C4 Fr.* Pérouse; *anc.* Perusia. Umbria, C Italy
Perugia, Lake of *see* Trasimeno, Lago
Peru, Republic of *see* Peru
Perusia *see* Perugia
Péruwelz *87 B6* Hainaut, SW Belgium
Pervomays'k *109 E3 prev.* Ol'viopol'. Mykolayivs'ka Oblast', S Ukraine
Pervyy Kuril'skiy Proliv *115 H3 strait* E Russian Federation
Pesaro *96 C3 anc.* Pisaurum. Marche, C Italy
Pescara *96 D4 anc.* Aternum, Ostia Aterni. Abruzzo, C Italy
Peshāwar *134 C1* North-West Frontier Province, N Pakistan
Peshkopi *101 C6 var.* Peshkopia, Peshkopija. Dibër, NE Albania
Peshkopia/Peshkopija *see* Peshkopi
Pessac *91 B5* Gironde, SW France
Petach-Tikva *see* Petah Tiqwa
Petah Tiqwa *119 A6 var.* Petach-Tikva, Petah Tiqva, Petakh Tikva. Tel Aviv, C Israel
Petakh Tikva/Petah Tiqva *see* Petah Tiqwa
Pétange *87 D8* Luxembourg, SW Luxembourg
Petchaburi *see* Phetchaburi
Peterborough *149 B6* South Australia
Peterborough *38 D5* Ontario, SE Canada
Peterborough *89 E6 prev.* Medeshamstede. E England, UK
Peterhead *88 D3* NE Scotland, UK
Peter I Island *154 A3 Norwegian dependency* Antarctica
Petermann Bjerg *83 E3 mountain* C Greenland
Petersburg *41 E5* Virginia, NE USA
Peters Mine *59 F3 var.* Peter's Mine. N Guyana
Petit St-Bernard, Col du *see* Little Saint Bernard Pass
Peto *51 H4* Yucatán, SE Mexico
Petoskey *40 C2* Michigan, N USA
Petra *see* Wādī Mūsā
Petrich *104 C3* Blagoevegrad, SW Bulgaria
Petrikau *see* Piotrków Trybunalski
Petrikov *see* Pyetrykaw
Petrinja *100 B3* Sisak-Moslavina, C Croatia
Petroaleksandrovsk *see* To'rtkok'l
Petrodvorets *110 A4 Fin.* Pietarhovi. Leningradskaya Oblast', NW Russian Federation
Petrograd *see* Sankt-Peterburg
Petrokov *see* Piotrków Trybunalski
Petropavl *see* Petropavlovsk
Petropavlovsk *114 C4 Kaz.* Petropavl. Severnyy Kazakhstan, N Kazakhstan
Petropavlovsk-Kamchatskiy *115 H3* Kamchatskaya Oblast', E Russian Federation
Petroşani *108 B4 var.* Petroşeni, *Ger.* Petroschen, *Hung.* Petrozsény. Hunedoara, W Romania
Petroschen/Petroşeni *see* Petroşani
Petroskoi *see* Petrozavodsk
Petrovgrad *see* Zrenjanin
Petrovsk-Port *see* Makhachkala
Petrozavodsk *114 B2 Fin.* Petroskoi. Respublika Kareliya, NW Russian Federation
Petrozsény *see* Petroşani
Pettau *see* Ptuj
Pevek *115 G1* Chukotskiy Avtonomnyy Okrug, NE Russian Federation
Pezinok *99 C6 Ger.* Bösing, *Hung.* Bazin. Bratislavský Kraj, W Slovakia
Pforzheim *95 B6* Baden-Württemberg, SW Germany
Pfungstadt *95 B5* Hessen, W Germany
Phangan, Ko *137 C6 island* SW Thailand
Phang-Nga *137 B7 var.* Pang-Nga, Phangnga. Phangnga, SW Thailand
Phangnga *see* Phang-Nga
Phan Rang/Phanrang *see* Phan Rang-Thap Cham
Phan Rang-Thap Cham *137 E6 var.* Phanrang, Phan Rang, Phan Rang Thap Cham. Ninh Thuân, S Vietnam
Phan Thiêt *137 E6* Binh Thuân, S Vietnam
Pharnacia *see* Giresun
Pharus *see* Hvar
Phatthalung *137 C7 var.* Padalung, Patalung. Phatthalung, SW Thailand
Phayao *136 C4 var.* Muang Phayao. Phayao, NW Thailand
Phenix City *42 D2* Alabama, S USA
Phet Buri *see* Phetchaburi
Phetchaburi *137 C5 var.* Bejraburi, Petchaburi, Phet Buri. Phetchaburi, SW Thailand
Philadelphia *41 F4* Pennsylvania, NE USA
Philadelphia *see* 'Ammān
Philippine Basin *125 F3 undersea feature* W Pacific Ocean
Philippines *139 E1 off.* Republic of the Philippines. *country* SE Asia

PHILIPPINES
Southwest Asia

Official name Republic of the Philippines
Formation 1946 / 1946
Capital Manila
Population 83.1 million / 722 people per sq mile (279 people per sq km) / 59%
Total area 115,830 sq miles (300,000 sq km)
Languages Filipino*, English*, Tagalog, Cebuano, Ilocano, Hiligaynon, many other local languages
Religions Roman Catholic 83%, Protestant 9%, Muslim 5%, Other (including Buddhist) 3%
Ethnic mix Malay 95%, Other 3%, Chinese 2%
Government Presidential system
Currency Philippine peso = 100 centavos
Literacy rate 93%
Calorie consumption 2379 calories

Philippines *139 E1 island group* W Pacific Ocean
Philippine Sea *125 F3 sea* W Pacific Ocean
Philippines, Republic of the *see* Philippines
Philippine Trench *142 A1 undersea feature* W Philippine Sea
Philippopolis *see* Plovdiv
Phitsanulok *136 C4 var.* Bisnulok, Muang Phitsanulok, Pitsanulok. Phitsanulok, C Thailand
Phlórina *see* Flórina
Phnom Penh *see* Phnum Penh
Phnum Penh *137 D6 var.* Phnom Penh. *country capital* (Cambodia) Phnum Penh, S Cambodia
Phoenix *48 B2 state capital* Arizona, SW USA
Phoenix Islands *145 E3 island group* C Kiribati
Phôngsali *136 C3 var.* Phong Saly. Phôngsali, N Laos
Phong Saly *see* Phôngsali
Phrae *136 C4 var.* Muang Phrae, Prae. Phrae, NW Thailand
Phra Nakhon Si Ayutthaya *see* Ayutthaya
Phra Thong, Ko *137 B6 island* SW Thailand
Phuket *137 B7 var.* Bhuket, Puket, *Mal.* Ujung Salang; *prev.* Junkseylon, Salang. Phuket, SW Thailand
Phuket, Ko *137 B7 island* SW Thailand
Phumĭ Kâmpóng Trâbêk *137 D5 prev.* Phum Kompong Trabek. Kâmpóng Thum, C Cambodia
Phumĭ Sâmraông *137 D5 prev.* Phum Samrong. Siĕmréab, NW Cambodia
Phum Kompong Trabek *see* Phumĭ Kâmpóng Trâbêk
Phum Samrong *see* Phumĭ Sâmraông
Phu Vinh *see* Tra Vinh
Piacenza *96 B2 Fr.* Paisance; *anc.* Placentia. Emilia-Romagna, N Italy
Piatra-Neamţ *108 C4 Hung.* Karácsonkő. Neamţ, NE Romania
Piauhy *see* Piauí
Piauí *63 F2 off.* Estado do Piauí; *prev.* Piauhy. *state* E Brazil
Piauí, Estado do *see* Piauí
Picardie *90 C3 Eng.* Picardy. *cultural region* N France
Picardie *90 C3 Eng.* Picardy. *region* N France
Picardy *see* Picardie
Piccolo San Bernardo, Colle di *see* Little Saint Bernard Pass
Pichilemu *64 B4* Libertador, C Chile
Pico *92 A5 var.* Ilha do Pico. *island* Azores, Portugal, NE Atlantic Ocean
Pico, Ilha do *see* Pico
Picos *63 F2* Piauí, E Brazil
Picton *151 C5* Marlborough, South Island, New Zealand
Piedmont *see* Piemonte
Piedras Negras *51 E2 var.* Ciudad Porfirio Díaz. Coahuila de Zaragoza, NE Mexico
Pielinen *84 E4 var.* Pielisjärvi. *lake* E Finland
Pielisjärvi *see* Pielinen
Piemonte *96 A2 Eng.* Piedmont. *region* NW Italy
Pierre *45 E3 state capital* South Dakota, N USA
Piešt'any *99 C6 Ger.* Pistyan, *Hung.* Pöstyén. Tranavský Kraj, W Slovakia
Pietarhovi *see* Petrodvorets
Pietari *see* Sankt-Peterburg
Pietarsaari *see* Jakobstad
Pietermaritzburg *78 C5 var.* Maritzburg. KwaZulu/Natal, E South Africa
Pietersburg *see* Polokwane
Pigs, Bay of *see* Cochinos, Bahía de
Pihkva Järv *see* Pskov, Lake
Pijijiapán *51 G5* Chiapas, SE Mexico
Pikes Peak *44 C5 mountain* Colorado, C USA
Pikeville *40 D5* Kentucky, S USA
Pikinni *see* Bikini Atoll
Piła *98 B3 Ger.* Schneidemühl. Wielkopolskie, C Poland
Pilar *64 D3 var.* Villa del Pilar. Ñeembucú, S Paraguay
Pilcomayo, Rio *57 C5 river* C South America

INDEX - GAZETTEER: **Pilos – Port-Francqui**

Pilos *see* Pýlos
Pilsen *see* Plzeň
Pilzno *see* Plzeň
Pinang *see* Pinang, Pulau, Peninsular Malaysia
Pinang *see* George Town
Pinang, Pulau *138 B3 var.* Penang, Pinang; *prev.* Prince of Wales Island. *island* Peninsular Malaysia
Pinar del Río *54 A2* Pinar del Río, W Cuba
Píndhos/Píndhos Óros *see* Píndos
Píndos *104 A4 var.* Píndhos Óros, *Eng.* Pindus Mountains; *prev.* Píndhos. *mountain range* C Greece
Pindus Mountains *see* Píndos
Pine Bluff *42 B2* Arkansas, C USA
Pine Creek *146 D2* Northern Territory, N Australia
Pinega *110 C3 river* NW Russian Federation
Pineiós *104 B4 var.* Piniós; *anc.* Peneius. *river* C Greece
Pineland *49 H3* Texas, SW USA
Pínes, Ákrotírio *104 C4 cape* N Greece
Pines, The Isle of the *see* Juventud, Isla de la
Pine Tree State *see* Maine
Pingdingshan *128 C4* Henan, C China
Pingkiang *see* Harbin
Ping, Mae Nam *136 B4 river* W Thailand
Piniós *see* Pineiós
Pinkiang *see* Harbin
Pinos, Isla de *see* Juventud, Isla de la
Pinotepa Nacional *51 F5 var.* Santiago Pinotepa Nacional. Oaxaca, SE Mexico
Pinsk *107 B7 Pol.* Pińsk. Brestskaya Voblasts', SW Belarus
Pinta, Isla *60 A5 var.* Abingdon. *island* Galapagos Islands, Ecuador, E Pacific Ocean
Piombino *96 B3* Toscana, C Italy
Pioneer Mountains *46 D3 mountain range* Montana, N USA North America
Pionerskiy *106 A4 Ger.* Neukuhren. Kaliningradskaya Oblast', W Russian Federation
Piotrków Trybunalski *98 D4 Ger.* Petrikau, *Rus.* Petrokov. Lodzkie, C Poland
Piraeus/Piraiévs *see* Peiraías
Pírgos *see* Pýrgos
Pirineos *see* Pyrenees
Piripiri *63 F2* Piauí, E Brazil
Pirna *94 D4* Sachsen, E Germany
Pirot *101 E5* Serbia, SE Serbia
Piryatin *see* Pyryatyn
Pisa *96 B3 var.* Pisae. Toscana, C Italy
Pisae *see* Pisa
Pisaurum *see* Pesaro
Pisco *60 D4* Ica, SW Peru
Písek *99 A5* Budějovický Kraj, S Czech Republic
Pishan *126 A3 var.* Guma. Xinjiang Uygur Zizhiqu, NW China
Pishpek *see* Bishkek
Pistoia *96 B3 anc.* Pistoria, Pistoriæ. Toscana, C Italy
Pistoria/Pistoriæ *see* Pistoia
Pistyan *see* Piešt'any
Pisz *98 D3 Ger.* Johannisburg. Warmińsko-Mazurskie, NE Poland
Pita *74 C4* NW Guinea
Pitalito *58 B4* Huila, S Colombia
Pitcairn Island *143 G4 island* S Pitcairn Islands
Pitcairn Islands *143 G4 UK dependent territory* C Pacific Ocean
Piteå *84 D4* Norrbotten, N Sweden
Pitești *108 B5* Argeș, S Romania
Pitsanulok *see* Phitsanulok
Pitt Island *see* Makin
Pittsburg *45 F5* Kansas, C USA
Pittsburgh *41 E4* Pennsylvania, NE USA
Pittsfield *41 F3* Massachusetts, NE USA
Piura *60 B2* Piura, NW Peru
Pivdennyy Buh *109 E3 Rus.* Yuzhnyy Bug. *river* S Ukraine
Placentia *see* Piacenza
Placetas *54 B2* Villa Clara, C Cuba
Plainview *49 E2* Texas, SW USA
Pláka *95 C5 prev.* Mílos. Kyládes, Greece, Aegean Sea
Planeta Rica *58 B2* Córdoba, NW Colombia
Planken *94 E1* C Liechtenstein Europe
Plano *49 G2* Texas, SW USA
Plasencia *92 C3* Extremadura, W Spain
Plata, Río de la *64 D4 var.* River Plate. *estuary* Argentina/Uruguay
Plate, River *see* Plata, Río de la
Platinum *36 C3* Alaska, USA
Plattensee *see* Balaton
Platte River *45 E4 river* Nebraska, C USA
Plattsburgh *41 F2* New York, NE USA
Plauen *95 C5 var.* Plauen im Vogtland. Sachsen, E Germany
Plauen im Vogtland *see* Plauen
Pļaviņas *106 D4 Ger.* Stockmannshof. Aizkraukle, S Latvia
Plây Cu *137 E5 var.* Pleiku. Gia Lai, C Vietnam
Pleasant Island *see* Nauru
Pleiku *see* Plây Cu
Plenty, Bay of *150 E3 bay* North Island, New Zealand
Plérin *90 A3* Côtes d'Armor, NW France
Plesetsk *110 C3* Arkhangel'skaya Oblast', NW Russian Federation
Pleshchenitsy *see* Plyeshchanitsy
Pleskau *see* Pskov
Pleskauer See *see* Pskov, Lake
Pleskava *see* Pskov
Pleszew *98 C4* Wielkopolskie, C Poland
Pleven *104 C2 prev.* Plevna. Pleven, N Bulgaria
Plevlja/Plevlje *see* Pljevlja
Plevna *see* Pleven
Pljevlja *100 C4 prev.* Plevlja, Plevlje. N Montenegro
Plocce *see* Ploče
Ploče *100 B4 It.* Plocce; *prev.* Kardeljevo. Dubrovnik-Neretva, SE Croatia
Płock *98 D3 Ger.* Plozk. Mazowieckie, C Poland
Plöcken Pass *95 C7 Ger.* Plöckenpass, *It.* Passo di Monte Croce Carnico. *pass* SW Austria
Plöckenpass *see* Plöcken Pass
Ploești *see* Ploiești
Ploiești *108 C5 prev.* Ploești. Prahova, SE Romania
Plomári *105 D5 prev.* Plomárion. Lésvos, E Greece
Plomárion *see* Plomári
Płońsk *98 D3* Mazowieckie, C Poland
Plovdiv *104 C3 prev.* Eumolpias; *anc.* Evmolpia, Philippopolis, *Lat.* Trimontium. Plovdiv, C Bulgaria
Plozk *see* Płock
Plungė *106 B3* Telšiai, W Lithuania
Plyeshchanitsy *107 D5 Rus.* Pleshchenitsy. Minskaya Voblasts', N Belarus
Plymouth *55 G3 dependent territory capital* (Montserrat) SW Montserrat
Plymouth *89 C7* SW England, UK
Plzeň *99 A5 Ger.* Pilsen, *Pol.* Pilzno. Plzeňský Kraj, W Czech Republic
Po *80 D4 river* N Italy
Pobedy, Pik *126 B3 Chin.* Tomür Feng. *mountain* China/Kyrgyzstan
Po, Bocche del *see* Po, Foci del
Pocahontas *42 B1* Arkansas, C USA
Pocatello *46 E4* Idaho, NW USA
Pochinok *111 A5* Smolenskaya Oblast', W Russian Federation
Pocking *95 D6* Bayern, SE Germany
Poděbrady *99 B5 Ger.* Podiebrad. Středočeský Kraj, C Czech Republic
Podgorica *101 C5 prev.* Titograd. *country capital* (Montenegro) S Montenegro
Podiebrad *see* Poděbrady
Podil's'ka Vysochina *108 D3 plateau* W Ukraine
Podium Anicensis *see* le Puy
Podol'sk *111 B5* Moskovskaya Oblast', W Russian Federation
Podravska Slatina *see* Slatina
Podujevo *101 D5* Kosovo, S Serbia
Podunajská Rovina *see* Little Alföld
Poetovio *see* Ptuj
Po, Foci del *96 C2 var.* Bocche del Po. *river* NE Italy
Pogradec *101 D6 var.* Pogradeci. Korçë, SE Albania
Pogradeci *see* Pogradec
Pohjanlahti *see* Bothnia, Gulf of
Pohnpei *144 C2 prev.* Ponape Ascension Island. *island* E Micronesia
Poictiers *see* Poitiers
Poinsett, Cape *154 D4 cape* Antarctica
Point de Galle *see* Galle
Pointe-à-Pitre *55 G3* Grande Terre, C Guadeloupe
Pointe-Noire *77 B6* Le Kouilou, S Congo
Point Lay *36 C2* Alaska, USA
Poitiers *90 B4 prev.* Poictiers; *anc.* Limonum. Vienne, W France
Poitou *90 B4 cultural region* W France
Pokharā *135 E3* Western, C Nepal
Pokrovka *see* Kyzyl-Suu
Pokrovs'ke *109 G3 Rus.* Pokrovskoye. Dnipropetrovs'ka Oblast', E Ukraine
Pokrovskoye *see* Pokrovs'ke
Pola *see* Pula
Pola de Lena *92 D1* Asturias, N Spain
Poland *81 E3* Kiritimati, E Kiribati
Poland *98 B4 off.* Republic of Poland, *var.* Polish Republic, *Pol.* Polska, Rzeczpospolita Polska; *prev. Pol.* Polska

POLAND
Northern Europe

Official name Republic of Poland
Formation 1918 / 1945
Capital Warsaw
Population 38.5 million / 328 people per sq mile (126 people per sq km) / 66%
Total area 120,728 sq miles (312,685 sq km)
Languages Polish*
Religions Roman Catholic 93% Other and nonreligious 5%, Orthodox Christian 2%
Ethnic mix Polish 97%, Other 2%, Silesian 1%
Government Parliamentary system
Currency Zloty = 100 groszy
Literacy rate 99%
Calorie consumption 3374 calories

Rzeczpospolita Ludowa, The Polish People's Republic. *country* C Europe
Poland, Republic of *see* Poland
Polatlı *116 C3* Ankara, C Turkey
Polatsk *107 D5 Rus.* Polotsk. Vitsyebskaya Voblasts', N Belarus
Pol-e Khomrī *123 E4 var.* Pul-i-Khumri. Baghlān, NE Afghanistan
Poli *see* Pólis
Polikastro/Políkastron *see* Polýkastro
Polikrayshte *104 D2* Veliko Tŭrnovo, N Bulgaria
Pólis *102 C5 var.* Poli. W Cyprus
Polish People's Republic, The *see* Poland
Polish Republic *see* Poland
Polkowice *98 B4 Ger.* Heerwegen. Dolnośląskie, W Poland
Pollença *93 G3* Mallorca, Spain, W Mediterranean Sea
Pologi *see* Polohy
Polohy *109 G3 Rus.* Pologi. Zaporiz'ka Oblast', SE Ukraine
Polokwane *78 D4 prev.* Pietersburg. Limpopo, NE South Africa
Polonne *108 D2 Rus.* Polonnoye. Khmel'nyts'ka Oblast', NW Ukraine
Polonnoye *see* Polonne
Polotsk *see* Polatsk
Polska/Polska, Rzeczpospolita/ Polska Rzeczpospolita Ludowa *see* Poland
Polsko Kosovo *104 D2* Ruse, N Bulgaria
Poltava *109 F2* Poltavs'ka Oblast', NE Ukraine
Poltoratsk *see* Aşgabat
Põlva *106 E3 Ger.* Pölwe. Põlvamaa, SE Estonia
Pölwe *see* Põlva
Polyarnyy *110 C2* Murmanskaya Oblast', NW Russian Federation
Polýkastro *104 B3 var.* Polikastro; *prev.* Políkastron. Kentrikí Makedonía, N Greece
Polynesia *143 F4 island group* C Pacific Ocean
Pomeranian Bay *94 D2 Ger.* Pommersche Bucht, *Pol.* Zatoka Pomorska. *bay* Germany/Poland
Pomir, Dar"yoi *see* Pamir/Pāmīr, Daryā-ye
Pommersche Bucht *see* Pomeranian Bay
Pomorska, Zatoka *see* Pomeranian Bay
Pomorskiy Proliv *110 D2 strait* NW Russian Federation
Pompaelo *see* Pamplona
Pompano Beach *43 F5* Florida, SE USA
Ponape Ascension Island *see* Pohnpei
Ponca City *49 G1* Oklahoma, C USA
Ponce *55 F3* C Puerto Rico
Pondicherry *132 C2 var.* Puduchcheri, *Fr.* Pondichéry. Pondicherry, SE India
Ponferrada *92 C1* Castilla-León, NW Spain
Poniatowa *98 E4* Lubelskie, E Poland
Pons Aelii *see* Newcastle upon Tyne
Pons Vetus *see* Pontevedra
Ponta Delgada *92 B5* São Miguel, Azores, Portugal, NE Atlantic Ocean
Ponta Grossa *63 E4* Paraná, S Brazil
Pontarlier *90 D4* Doubs, E France
Ponteareas *92 B2* Galicia, NW Spain
Ponte da Barca *92 B2* Viana do Castelo, N Portugal
Pontevedra *92 B1 anc.* Pons Vetus. Galicia, NW Spain
Pontiac *40 D3* Michigan, N USA
Pontianak *138 C4* Borneo, C Indonesia
Pontisarae *see* Pontoise
Pontivy *90 A3* Morbihan, NW France
Pontoise *90 C3 anc.* Briva Isarae, Cergy-Pontoise, Pontisarae. Val-d'Oise, N France
Ponziane, Isole *97 C5 island* C Italy
Poole *89 D7* S England, UK
Poona *see* Pune
Poopó, Lago *61 F4 var.* Lago Pampa Aullagas. *lake* W Bolivia
Popayán *58 B4* Cauca, SW Colombia
Poperinge *87 A6* West-Vlaanderen, W Belgium
Poplar Bluff *45 G5* Missouri, C USA
Popocatépetl *51 E4 volcano* S Mexico
Popper *see* Poprad
Poprad *99 D5 Ger.* Deutschendorf, *Hung.* Poprád. Prešovský Kraj, E Slovakia
Poprad *99 D5 Ger.* Popper, *Hung.* Poprád. *river* Poland/Slovakia
Porbandar *134 B4* Gujarāt, W India
Porcupine Plain *80 B3 undersea feature* E Atlantic Ocean
Pordenone *96 C2 anc.* Portenau. Friuli-Venezia Giulia, NE Italy
Poreč *100 A2 It.* Parenzo. Istra, NW Croatia
Porech'ye *see* Parechcha
Pori *85 D5 Swe.* Björneborg. Länsi-Soumi, SW Finland
Porirua *151 D5* Wellington, North Island, New Zealand
Porkhov *110 A4* Pskovskaya Oblast', W Russian Federation
Porlamar *59 E1* Nueva Esparta, NE Venezuela
Póros *105 C6* Póros, S Greece
Póros *105 A5* Kefallinía, Iónia Nisiá, Greece, C Mediterranean Sea
Pors *see* Porsangenfijorden
Porsangenfijorden *84 D2 Lapp.* Pors. *fjord* N Norway
Porsgrunn *85 B6* Telemark, S Norway
Portachuelo *61 G4* Santa Cruz, C Bolivia
Portadown *89 B5 Ir.* Port An Dúnáin. S Northern Ireland, UK
Portalegre *92 C3 anc.* Ammaia, Amoea. Portalegre, E Portugal
Port Alexander *36 D4* Baranof Island, Alaska, USA
Port Alfred *78 D5* Eastern Cape, S South Africa
Port Amelia *see* Pemba
Port An Dúnáin *see* Portadown
Port Angeles *46 B1* Washington, NW USA
Port Antonio *54 B5* NE Jamaica
Port Arthur *49 H4* Texas, SW USA
Port Augusta *149 B6* South Australia
Port-au-Prince *54 D3 country capital* (Haiti) C Haiti
Port Blair *133 F2* Andaman and Nicobar Islands, SE India
Port Charlotte *43 E4* Florida, SE USA
Port Darwin *see* Darwin
Port d'Envalira *91 B8* E Andorra Europe
Port Douglas *148 D3* Queensland, NE Australia
Port Elizabeth *78 C5* Eastern Cape, S South Africa
Portenau *see* Pordenone
Porterville *47 C7* California, W USA
Port-Étienne *see* Nouâdhibou
Port Florence *see* Kisumu
Port-Francqui *see* Ilebo

Port-Gentil *77 A6* Ogooué-Maritime, W Gabon
Port Harcourt *75 G5* Rivers, S Nigeria
Port Hardy *36 D5* Vancouver Island, British Columbia, SW Canada
Port Harrison *see* Inukjuak
Port Hedland *146 B4* Western Australia
Port Huron *40 D3* Michigan, N USA
Portimão *92 B4 var.* Vila Nova de Portimão. Faro, S Portugal
Port Jackson *148 E1 harbour* New South Wales, E Australia
Portland *149 B7* Victoria, SE Australia
Portland *41 G2* Maine, NE USA
Portland *46 B3* Oregon, NW USA
Portland *49 G4* Texas, SW USA
Portland Bight *54 B5 bay* S Jamaica
Portlaoighise *see* Port Laoise
Port Laoise *89 B6 var.* Portlaoise, *Ir.* Portlaoighise; *prev.* Maryborough. C Ireland
Portlaoise *see* Port Laoise
Port Lavaca *49 G4* Texas, SW USA
Port Lincoln *149 A6* South Australia
Port Louis *79 H3 country capital* (Mauritius) NW Mauritius
Port-Lyautey *see* Kénitra
Port Macquarie *149 E6* New South Wales, SE Australia
Port Mahon *see* Mahón
Portmore *54 B5* C Jamaica
Port Moresby *144 B3 country capital* (Papua New Guinea) Central/National Capital District, SW Papua New Guinea
Port Musgrave *149 B9 bay* Queensland, N Australia Pacific Ocean Arafua Sea Gulf of Carpentaria
Port Natal *see* Durban
Porto *92 B2 Eng.* Oporto; *anc.* Portus Cale. Porto, NW Portugal
Porto Alegre *63 E5 var.* Pôrto Alegre. *state capital* Rio Grande do Sul, S Brazil
Porto Alegre *76 E2* São Tomé, S Sao Tome and Principe, Africa
Porto Alexandre *see* Tombua
Porto Amélia *see* Pemba
Porto Bello *see* Portobelo
Portobelo *53 G4 var.* Porto Bello, Puerto Bello. Colón, N Panama
Port O'Connor *49 G4* Texas, SW USA
Porto Edda *see* Sarandë
Portoferraio *96 B4* Toscana, C Italy
Port-of-Spain *55 H5 country capital* (Trinidad and Tobago) Trinidad, Trinidad and Tobago
Porto Grande *see* Mindelo
Portogruaro *96 C2* Veneto, NE Italy
Porto-Novo *75 F5 country capital* (Benin) S Benin
Porto Rico *see* Puerto Rico
Porto Santo *70 A2 var.* Ilha do Porto Santo. *island* Madeira, Portugal, NE Atlantic Ocean
Porto Santo, Ilha do *see* Porto Santo
Porto Torres *97 A5* Sardegna, Italy, C Mediterranean Sea
Porto Velho *62 D2 var.* Velho. *state capital* Rondônia, W Brazil
Portoviejo *60 A2 var.* Puertoviejo. Manabí, W Ecuador
Port Pirie *149 B6* South Australia
Port Rex *see* East London
Port Said *72 B1 Ar.* Būr Sa'īd. N Egypt
Portsmouth *89 D7* S England, UK
Portsmouth *41 G3* New Hampshire, NE USA
Portsmouth *40 D4* Ohio, N USA
Portsmouth *41 F5* Virginia, NE USA
Port Stanley *see* Stanley
Port Sudan *72 C3* Red Sea, NE Sudan
Port Swettenham *see* Klang/Pelabuhan Klang
Port Talbot *89 C7* S Wales, UK
Portugal *92 B3 off.* Republic of Portugal. *country* SW Europe

PORTUGAL
Southwest Europe

Official name Republic of Portugal
Formation 1139 / 1640
Capital Lisbon
Population 10.5 million / 296 people per sq mile (114 people per sq km) / 64%
Total area 35,672 sq miles (92,391 sq km)
Languages Portuguese

PORTUGAL
(continued)

Religions Roman Catholic 97%, Other 2%, Protestant 1%
Ethnic mix Portuguese 98%, African and other 2%
Government Parliamentary system
Currency Euro = 100 cents
Literacy rate 93%
Calorie consumption 3741 calories

Portugal, Republic of *see* Portugal
Portuguese East Africa *see* Mozambique
Portuguese Guinea *see* Guinea-Bissau
Portuguese Timor *see* East Timor
Portuguese West Africa *see* Angola
Portus Cale *see* Porto
Portus Magnus *see* Almería
Portus Magonis *see* Mahón
Port-Vila *144 D4 var.* Vila. *country capital* (Vanuatu) Éfaté, C Vanuatu
Porvenir *61 E3* Pando, NW Bolivia
Porvenir *65 B8* Magallanes, S Chile
Porvoo *85 E6 Swe.* Borgå. Etelä-Suomi, S Finland
Porzecze *see* Parechcha
Posadas *64 D3* Misiones, NE Argentina
Poschega *see* Požega
Posen *see* Poznań
Posnania *see* Poznań
Postavy/Postawy *see* Pastavy
Posterholt *87 D5* Limburg, SE Netherlands
Postojna *95 D8 Ger.* Adelsberg, *It.* Postumia. SW Slovenia
Postumia *see* Postojna
Pöstyén *see* Piešt'any
Potamós *105 C7* Antikýthira, S Greece
Potentia *see* Potenza
Potenza *97 D5 anc.* Potentia. Basilicata, S Italy
P'ot'i *117 F2* W Georgia
Potiskum *75 G4* Yobe, NE Nigeria
Potomac River *41 E5 river* NE USA
Potosí *61 F4* Potosí, S Bolivia
Potsdam *94 D3* Brandenburg, NE Germany
Potwar Plateau *134 C2 plateau* NE Pakistan
Poŭthĭsăt *137 D6 prev.* Pursat. Poŭthĭsăt, W Cambodia
Po, Valle del *see* Po Valley
Po Valley *96 C2 It.* Valle del Po. *valley* N Italy
Považská Bystrica *99 C5 Ger.* Waagbistritz, *Hung.* Vágbeszterce. Trenčiansky Kraj, W Slovakia
Poverty Bay *150 E4 inlet* North Island, New Zealand
Póvoa de Varzim *92 B2* Porto, NW Portugal
Powder River *44 D2 river* Montana/ Wyoming, NW USA
Powell *44 C2* Wyoming, C USA
Powell, Lake *44 B5 lake* Utah, W USA
Požarevac *100 D4 Ger.* Passarowitz. Serbia, NE Serbia
Poza Rica *51 F4 var.* Poza Rica de Hidalgo. Veracruz-Llave, E Mexico
Poza Rica de Hidalgo *see* Poza Rica
Požega *100 D4 prev.* Slavonska Požega, *Ger.* Poschega, *Hung.* Pozsega. Požega-Slavonija, NE Croatia
Poznań *98 C3 Ger.* Posen, Posnania. Wielkolpolskie, C Poland
Pozoblanco *92 D4* Andalucía, S Spain
Pozsega *see* Požega
Pozsony *see* Bratislava
Pozzallo *97 C8* Sicilia, Italy, C Mediterranean Sea
Prachatice *99 A5 Ger.* Prachatitz. Jihočeský Kraj, S Czech Republic
Prachatitz *see* Prachatice
Prado del Ganso *see* Goose Green
Prae *see* Phrae
Prag/Praga/Prague *see* Praha
Prague *80 D3* Oklahoma, C USA
Praha *99 A5 Eng.* Prague, *Ger.* Prag, *Pol.* Praga. *country capital* (Czech Republic) Středočeský Kraj, NW Czech Republic
Praia *74 A3 country capital* (Cape Verde) Santiago, S Cape Verde
Prairie State *see* Illinois
Prathet Thai *see* Thailand
Prato *96 B3* Toscana, C Italy
Pratt *45 E5* Kansas, C USA
Prattville *42 D2* Alabama, S USA
Pravda *104 D1 prev.* Dogrular. Silistra, NE Bulgaria
Pravia *92 C1* Asturias, N Spain
Preny *see* Prienai
Prenzlau *94 D3* Brandenburg, NE Germany
Prerau *see* Přerov
Přerov *99 C5 Ger.* Prerau. Olomoucký Kraj, E Czech Republic
Preschau *see* Prešov
Prescott *48 B2* Arizona, SW USA
Preševo *101 D5* Serbia, SE Serbia
Presidente Epitácio *63 E4* São Paulo, S Brazil
Presidente Stroessner *see* Ciudad del Este
Prešov *99 D5 var.* Preschau, *Ger.* Eperies, *Hung.* Eperjes. Prešovský Kraj, E Slovakia
Prespa, Lake *101 D6 Alb.* Liqen i Prespës, *Gk.* Límni Megáli Préspa, Limni Prespa, *Mac.* Prespansko Ezero, *Serb.* Prespansko Jezero. *lake* SE Europe
Prespa, Limni/Prespansko Ezero/ Prespansko Jezero/Prespës, Liqen i *see* Prespa, Lake
Presque Isle *41 H1* Maine, NE USA
Pressburg *see* Bratislava
Preston *89 D5* NW England, UK
Prestwick *88 C4* W Scotland, UK
Pretoria *see* Tshwane
Preussisch Eylau *see* Bagrationovsk
Preußisch Holland *see* Pasłęk
Preussisch-Stargard *see* Starogard Gdański
Préveza *105 A5* Ípeiros, W Greece
Pribilof Islands *36 A3 island group* Alaska, USA
Priboj *100 C4* Serbia, W Serbia
Price *44 B4* Utah, W USA
Prichard *42 C3* Alabama, S USA
Priekulė *106 B3 Ger.* Prökuls. Klaipėda, W Lithuania
Prienai *107 B5 Pol.* Preny. Kaunas, S Lithuania
Prieska *78 C4* Northern Cape, C South Africa
Prijedor *100 B3* Republika Srpska, NW Bosnia and Herzegovina
Prijepolje *100 D4* Serbia, W Serbia
Prikaspiyskaya Nizmennost' *see* Caspian Depression
Prilep *101 D6 Turk.* Perlepe. S FYR Macedonia
Priluki *see* Pryluky
Primorsk *106 A4 Ger.* Fischhausen. Kaliningradskaya Oblast', W Russian Federation
Primorsko *104 E2 prev.* Keupriya. Burgas, E Bulgaria
Primorsk/Primorskoye *see* Prymors'k
Prince Albert *37 F5* Saskatchewan, S Canada
Prince Edward Island *39 F4 Fr.* Île-du Prince-Édouard. *province* SE Canada
Prince Edward Islands *69 E8 island group* S South Africa
Prince George *37 E5* British Columbia, SW Canada
Prince of Wales Island *148 B1 island* Queensland, E Australia
Prince of Wales Island *37 F2 island* Queen Elizabeth Islands, Nunavut, NW Canada
Prince of Wales Island *see* Pinang, Pulau
Prince Patrick Island *37 E2 island* Parry Islands, Northwest Territories, NW Canada
Prince Rupert *36 D4* British Columbia, SW Canada
Prince's Island *see* Príncipe
Princess Charlotte Bay *148 C2 bay* Queensland, NE Australia
Princess Elizabeth Land *154 C3 physical region* Antarctica
Príncipe *77 A5 var.* Príncipe Island, *Eng.* Prince's Island. *island* N Sao Tome and Principe
Príncipe Island *see* Príncipe
Prinzapolka *53 E3* Región Autónoma Atlántico Norte, NE Nicaragua
Pripet *107 C7 Bel.* Prypyats', *Ukr.* Pryp"yat'. *river* Belarus/Ukraine
Pripet Marshes *107 B7 forested and swampy region* Belarus/Ukraine
Prishtinë *see* Priština
Priština *101 D5 Alb.* Prishtinë. Kosovo, S Serbia
Privas *91 D5* Ardèche, E France
Privolzhskaya Vozvyshennost' *81 G3 var.* Volga Uplands. *mountain range* W Russian Federation
Prizren *101 D5 Alb.* Prizreni. Kosovo, S Serbia
Prizreni *see* Prizren
Probolinggo *138 D5* Jawa, C Indonesia
Probstberg *see* Wyszków
Progreso *51 H3* Yucatán, SE Mexico
Prokhladnyy *111 B8* Kabardino-Balkarskaya Respublika, SW Russian Federation
Prokletije *see* North Albanian Alps
Prökuls *see* Priekulė
Prokuplje *101 D5* Serbia, SE Serbia
Prome *136 B4 var.* Pyè. Pegu, C Myanmar (Burma)
Promyshlennyy *110 E3* Respublika Komi, NW Russian Federation
Prościejów *see* Prostějov
Proskurov *see* Khmel'nyts'kyy
Prossnitz *see* Prostějov
Prostějov *99 C5 Ger.* Prossnitz, *Pol.* Prościejów. Olomoucký Kraj, E Czech Republic
Provence *91 D6 cultural region* SE France
Providence *41 G3 state capital* Rhode Island, NE USA
Providence *see* Fort Providence
Providencia, Isla de *53 F3 island* NW Colombia South America
Provideniya *172 B1* Chukotskiy Avtonomnyy Okrug, NE Russian Federation
Provo *44 B4* Utah, W USA
Prudhoe Bay *36 D2* Alaska, USA
Prusa *see* Bursa
Pruszków *98 D3 Ger.* Kaltdorf. Mazowieckie, C Poland
Prut *108 D4 Ger.* Pruth. *river* E Europe
Pruth *see* Prut
Pružana *see* Pruzhany
Pruzhany *107 B6 Pol.* Prużana. Brestskaya Voblasts', SW Belarus
Prychornomor'ska Nyzovyna *see* Black Sea Lowland
Prydniprovs'ka Nyzovyna/ Prydnyaprowskaya Nizina *see* Dnieper Lowland
Prydz Bay *154 D3 bay* Antarctica
Pryluky *109 E2 Rus.* Priluki. Chernihivs'ka Oblast', NE Ukraine
Prymors'k *109 G4 Rus.* Primorsk; *prev.* Primorskoye. Zaporiz'ka Oblast', SE Ukraine
Pryp"yat'/Prypyats' *see* Pripet
Przemyśl *99 E5 Rus.* Peremyshl. Podkarpackie, C Poland
Przheval'sk *see* Karakol
Psará *105 D5 island* E Greece
Psël *109 F2 river* Russian Federation/Ukraine
Pskov *114 B2 Ger.* Pleskau, *Latv.* Pleskava. Pskovskaya Oblast', W Russian Federation
Pskov, Lake *106 E3 Est.* Pihkva Järv, *Ger.* Pleskauer See, *Rus.* Pskovskoye Ozero. *lake* Estonia/Russian Federation
Pskovskoye Ozero *see* Pskov, Lake
Ptich' *see* Ptsich
Ptsich *107 C7 Rus.* Ptich'. Homyel'skaya Voblasts', SE Belarus
Ptsich *107 C7 Rus.* Ptich'. *river* SE Belarus
Ptuj *95 E7 Ger.* Pettau; *anc.* Poetovio. NE Slovenia
Pucallpa *60 C3* Ucayali, C Peru
Puck *98 C2* Pomorskie, N Poland
Pudasjärvi *84 D4* Oulu, C Finland
Puebla *51 F4 var.* Puebla de Zaragoza. Puebla, S Mexico
Puebla de Zaragoza *see* Puebla
Pueblo *44 D5* Colorado, C USA
Puerto Acosta *61 E4* La Paz, W Bolivia
Puerto Aisén *65 B6* Aisén, S Chile
Puerto Ángel *51 F5* Oaxaca, SE Mexico
Puerto Argentino *see* Stanley
Puerto Ayacucho *58 D3* Amazonas, SW Venezuela

Puerto Baquerizo Moreno *60 B5 var.* Baquerizo Moreno. Galapagos Islands, Ecuador, E Pacific Ocean
Puerto Barrios *52 C2* Izabal, E Guatemala
Puerto Bello *see* Portobelo
Puerto Berrío *58 B2* Antioquia, C Colombia
Puerto Cabello *58 D1* Carabobo, N Venezuela
Puerto Cabezas *53 E2 var.* Bilwi. Región Autónoma Atlántico Norte, NE Nicaragua
Puerto Carreño *58 D3* Vichada, E Colombia
Puerto Cortés *52 C2* Cortés, NW Honduras
Puerto Cumarebo *58 C1* Falcón, N Venezuela
Puerto Deseado *65 C7* Santa Cruz, SE Argentina
Puerto Escondido *51 F5* Oaxaca, SE Mexico
Puerto Francisco de Orellana *60 B1 var.* Coca. Orellana, N Ecuador
Puerto Gallegos *see* Río Gallegos
Puerto Inírida *58 D3 var.* Obando. Guainía, E Colombia
Puerto La Cruz *59 E1* Anzoátegui, NE Venezuela
Puerto Lempira *53 E2* Gracias a Dios, E Honduras
Puerto Limón *see* Limón
Puertollano *92 D4* Castilla-La Mancha, C Spain
Puerto López *58 C1* La Guajira, N Colombia
Puerto Maldonado *61 E3* Madre de Dios, E Peru
Puerto México *see* Coatzacoalcos
Puerto Montt *65 B5* Los Lagos, C Chile
Puerto Natales *65 B7* Magallanes, S Chile
Puerto Obaldía *53 H5* San Blas, NE Panama
Puerto Plata *55 E3 var.* San Felipe de Puerto Plata. N Dominican Republic
Puerto Presidente Stroessner *see* Ciudad del Este
Puerto Princesa *139 E2 off.* Puerto Princesa City. Palawan, W Philippines
Puerto Princesa City *see* Puerto Princesa
Puerto Príncipe *see* Camagüey
Puerto Rico *55 F3 off.* Commonwealth of Puerto Rico; *prev.* Porto Rico. *US commonwealth territory* C West Indies
Puerto Rico *56 B1 island* C West Indies
Puerto Rico, Commonwealth of *see* Puerto Rico
Puerto Rico Trench *56 B1 trench* NE Caribbean Sea
Puerto San José *see* San José
Puerto San Julián *65 B7 var.* San Julián. Santa Cruz, SE Argentina
Puerto Suárez *61 H4* Santa Cruz, E Bolivia
Puerto Vallarta *50 D4* Jalisco, SW Mexico
Puerto Varas *65 B5* Los Lagos, C Chile
Puerto Viejo *53 E4* Heredia, NE Costa Rica
Puertoviejo *see* Portoviejo
Puget Sound *46 B1 sound* Washington, NW USA
Puglia *97 E5 var.* Le Puglie, *Eng.* Apulia. *region* SE Italy
Pukaki, Lake *151 B6 lake* South Island, New Zealand
Pukekohe *150 D3* Auckland, North Island, New Zealand
Puket *see* Phuket
Pukhavichy *107 C6 Rus.* Pukhovichi. Minskaya Voblasts', C Belarus
Pukhovichi *see* Pukhavichy
Pula *100 A3 It.* Pola; *prev.* Pulj. Istra, NW Croatia
Pulaski *40 D5* Virginia, NE USA
Puławy *98 D4 Ger.* Neu Amerika. Lubelskie, E Poland
Pul-i-Khumri *see* Pol-e Khomrī
Pulj *see* Pula
Pullman *46 C2* Washington, NW USA
Pułtusk *98 D3* Mazowieckie, C Poland
Puná, Isla *60 A2 island* SW Ecuador
Pune *134 C5 prev.* Poona. Mahārāshtra, W India
Punjab *134 C2 prev.* West Punjab, Western Punjab. *province* E Pakistan
Puno *61 E4* Puno, SE Peru
Punta Alta *65 C5* Buenos Aires, E Argentina
Punta Arenas *65 B8 prev.* Magallanes. Magallanes, S Chile
Punta Gorda *52 C2* Toledo, SE Belize
Punta Gorda *53 E4* Región Autónoma Atlántico Sur, SE Nicaragua
Puntarenas *52 D4* Puntarenas, W Costa Rica
Punto Fijo *58 C1* Falcón, N Venezuela
Pupuya, Nevado *61 E4 mountain* W Bolivia
Puri *135 F5 var.* Jagannath. Orissa, E India
Puriramya *see* Buriram
Purmerend *86 C3* Noord-Holland, C Netherlands
Pursat *see* Poŭthĭsăt, Poŭthĭsăt, W Cambodia
Purus, Rio *62 C2 var.* Río Purús. *river* Brazil/Peru
Pusan *129 E4 off.* Pusan-gwangyŏksi, *var.* Busan, *Jap.* Fusan. SE South Korea
Pusan-gwangyŏksi *see* Pusan
Pushkino *see* Biläsuvar
Püspökladány *99 D6* Hajdú-Bihar, E Hungary
Putorana, Gory/Putorana Mountains *see* Putorana, Plato
Putorana, Plato *114 D3 var.* Gory Putorana, *Eng.* Putorana Mountains. *mountain range* N Russian Federation
Putrajaya *138 B3 country capital* (Malaysia) Kuala Lumpur, Peninsular Malaysia
Puttalam *132 C3* North Western Province, W Sri Lanka
Puttgarden *94 C2* Schleswig-Holstein, N Germany
Putumayo, Río *58 B5 var.* Içá, Rio. *river* NW South America
Putumayo, Río *see* Içá, Rio
Puurmani *106 D2 Ger.* Talkhof. Jõgevamaa, E Estonia
Pyatigorsk *111 B7* Stavropol'skiy Kray, SW Russian Federation
Pyatikhatki *see* P"yatykhatky
P"yatykhatky *109 F3 Rus.* Pyatikhatki. Dnipropetrovs'ka Oblast', E Ukraine
Pyè *see* Prome
Pyetrykaw *107 C7 Rus.* Petrikov. Homyel'skaya Voblasts', SE Belarus
Pýlos *105 B6 var.* Pilos. Pelopónnisos, S Greece
P'yŏngyang *129 E3 var.* P'yŏngyang-si, *Eng.* Pyongyang. *country capital* (North Korea) SW North Korea
P'yŏngyang-si *see* P'yŏngyang
Pyramid Lake *47 C5 lake* Nevada, W USA
Pyrenaei Montes *see* Pyrenees
Pyrenees *102 B2 Fr.* Pyrénées, *Sp.* Pirineos; *anc.* Pyrenaei Montes. *mountain range* SW Europe
Pýrgos *105 B6 var.* Pírgos. Dytikí Ellás, S Greece
Pyritz *see* Pyrzyce
Pyryatyn *109 E2 Rus.* Piryatin. Poltavs'ka Oblast', NE Ukraine
Pyrzyce *98 B3 Ger.* Pyritz. Zachodnio-pomorskie, NW Poland
Pyu *136 B4* Pegu, C Myanmar (Burma)
Pyuntaza *136 B4* Pegu, SW Myanmar (Burma)

Qā' al Jafr *119 C7 lake* S Jordan
Qaanaaq *82 D1 var.* Qânâq, *Dan.* Thule. Avannaarsua, N Greenland
Qabātiya *119 E6* N West Bank Asia
Qābis *see* Gabès
Qābis, Khalīj *see* Gabès, Golfe de
Qacentina *see* Constantine
Qafṣah *see* Gafsa
Qagan Us *see* Dulan
Qahremānshahr *see* Kermānshāh
Qaidam Pendi *126 C4 basin* C China
Qal'aikhum *123 F3 Rus.* Kalaikhum. S Tajikistan
Qalāt *123 E5 Per.* Kalāt. Zābol, S Afghanistan
Qal'at Bīshah *121 B5* 'Asīr, SW Saudi Arabia
Qalqīlya *119 D6* Central, W West Bank Asia
Qamdo *126 D5* Xizang Zizhiqu, W China
Qamishly *see* Al Qāmishlī
Qânâq *see* Qaanaaq
Qaqortoq *82 C4 Dan.* Julianehåb. Kitaa, S Greenland
Qaraghandy/Qaraghandy Oblysy *see* Karaganda
Qara Qum *see* Garagum
Qarataū *see* Karatau, Zhambyl, Kazakhstan
Qarkilik *see* Ruoqiang
Qarokŭl *123 F3 Rus.* Karakul'. E Tajikistan
Qarqannah, Juzur *see* Kerkenah, Îles de
Qars *see* Kars
Qarshi *123 E3 Rus.* Karshi; *prev.* Bek-Budi. Qashqadaryo Viloyati, S Uzbekistan
Qasigianguit *see* Qasigiannguit
Qasigiannguit *82 C3 var.* Qasigianguit, *Dan.* Christianshåb. Kitaa, C Greenland
Qasr Farâfra *72 B2* W Egypt
Qaṭana *119 B5 var.* Katana. Dimashq, S Syria
Qatar *120 C4 off.* State of Qatar, *Ar.* Dawlat Qaṭar. *country* SW Asia

QATAR
Southwest Asia

Official name State of Qatar
Formation 1971 / 1971
Capital Doha
Population 813,000 / 191 people per sq mile (74 people per sq km) / 93%
Total area 4416 sq miles (11,437 sq km)
Languages Arabic*
Religions Muslim (mainly Sunni) 95%, Other 5%
Ethnic mix Arab 40%, Indian 18%, Pakistani 18%, Other 14%, Iranian 10%
Government Monarchy
Currency Qatar riyal = 100 dirhams
Literacy rate 89%
Calorie consumption Not available

Qatar, State of *see* Qatar
Qattara Depression/Qaṭṭārah, Munkhafaḍ al *see* Qaṭṭâra, Monkhafad el
Qaṭṭâra, Monkhafad el *88 A1 var.* Munkhafaḍ al Qaṭṭārah, *Eng.* Qattara Depression. *desert* NW Egypt
Qausuittuq *see* Resolute
Qazaqstan/Qazaqstan Respublikasy *see* Kazakhstan
Qazimämmäd *117 H3 Rus.* Kazi Magomed. SE Azerbaijan
Qazris *see* Cáceres
Qazvīn *120 C2 var.* Kazvin. Qazvīn, N Iran
Qena *72 B2 var.* Qinā; *anc.* Caene, Caenepolis. E Egypt
Qeqertarssuaq *see* Qeqertarsuaq
Qeqertarsuaq *82 C3 var.* Qeqertarssuaq, *Dan.* Godhavn. Kitaa, S Greenland
Qeqertarsuaq *82 C3 island* W Greenland
Qeqertarsuup Tunua *82 C3 Dan.* Disko Bugt. *inlet* W Greenland
Qerveh *see* Qorveh
Qeshm *120 D4 var.* Jazīreh-ye Qeshm, Qeshm Island. *island* S Iran
Qeshm Island/Qeshm, Jazīreh-ye *see* Qeshm
Qilian Shan *126 D3 var.* Kilien Mountains. *mountain range* N China
Qimusseriarsuaq *82 C2 Dan.* Melville Bugt, *Eng.* Melville Bay. *bay* NW Greenland
Qinā *see* Qena
Qing *see* Qinghai
Qingdao *128 D4 var.* Ching-Tao, Ch'ing-tao, Tsingtao, Tsintao, *Ger.* Tsingtau. Shandong, E China
Qinghai *126 C4 var.* Chinghai, Koko Nor, Qing, Qinghai Sheng, Tsinghai. *province* C China
Qinghai Hu *126 D4 var.* Ch'ing Hai, Tsing Hai, *Mong.* Koko Nor. *lake* C China
Qinghai Sheng *see* Qinghai
Qingzang Gaoyuan *126 B4 var.* Xizang Gaoyuan, *Eng.* Plateau of Tibet. *plateau* W China
Qinhuangdao *128 D3* Hebei, E China
Qinzhou *128 B6* Guangxi Zhuangzu Zizhiqu, S China
Qiong *see* Hainan
Qiqihar *128 D2 var.* Ch'i-ch'i-ha-erh, Tsitsihar; *prev.* Lungkiang. Heilongjiang, NE China
Qira *126 B4* Xinjiang Uygur Zizhiqu, NW China
Qita Ghazzah *see* Gaza Strip
Qitai *126 C3* Xinjiang Uygur Zizhiqu, NW China
Qīzān *see* Jīzān
Qizil Orda *see* Kyzylorda
Qizil Qum/Qizilqum *see* Kyzyl Kum
Qizilrabot *123 G3 Rus.* Kyzylrabot. SE Tajikistan
Qogir Feng *see* K2
Qom *120 C3 var.* Kum, Qum. Qom, N Iran
Qomolangma Feng *see* Everest, Mount
Qomul *see* Hami
Qo'qon *123 F2 var.* Khokand, *Rus.* Kokand. Farg'ona Viloyati, E Uzbekistan
Qorveh *120 C3 var.* Qerveh, Qurveh. Kordestān, W Iran
Qostanay/Qostanay Oblysy *see* Kostanay
Qoubaïyât *118 B4 var.* Al Qubayyāt. N Lebanon
Qoussantîna *see* Constantine
Quang Ngai *137 E5 var.* Quangngai, Quang Nghia. Quang Ngai, C Vietnam
Quangngai *see* Quang Ngai
Quang Nghia *see* Quang Ngai
Quan Long *see* Ca Mau
Quanzhou *128 D6 var.* Ch'uan-chou, Tsinkiang; *prev.* Chin-chiang. Fujian, SE China
Quanzhou *128 C6* Guangxi Zhuangzu Zizhiqu, S China
Qu'Appelle *37 F5 river* Saskatchewan, S Canada
Quarles, Pegunungan *139 E4 mountain range* Sulawesi, C Indonesia
Quarnero *see* Kvarner
Quartu Sant' Elena *97 A6* Sardegna, Italy, C Mediterranean Sea
Quba *117 H2 Rus.* Kuba. N Azerbaijan
Qubba *see* Ba'qūbah
Québec *39 E4 var.* Quebec. *province capital* Québec, SE Canada
Québec *38 D3 var.* Quebec. *province* SE Canada
Queen Charlotte Islands *36 C5 Fr.* Îles de la Reine-Charlotte. *island group* British Columbia, SW Canada
Queen Charlotte Sound *36 C5 sea area* British Columbia, W Canada
Queen Elizabeth Islands *37 E1 Fr.* Îles de la Reine-Élisabeth. *island group* Nunavut, N Canada
Queensland *148 B4 state* N Australia
Queenstown *151 B7* Otago, South Island, New Zealand
Queenstown *78 D5* Eastern Cape, S South Africa
Quelimane *79 E3 var.* Kilimane, Kilmain, Quilimane. Zambézia, NE Mozambique
Quelpart *see* Cheju-do
Quepos *53 E4* Puntarenas, S Costa Rica
Que Que *see* Kwekwe
Quera *see* Chur
Querétaro *51 E4* Querétaro de Arteaga, C Mexico
Quesada *53 E4 var.* Ciudad Quesada, San Carlos. Alajuela, N Costa Rica
Quetta *134 B2* Baluchistān, SW Pakistan
Quetzalcoalco *see* Coatzacoalcos
Quezaltenango *52 A2 var.* Quetzaltenango. Quezaltenango, W Guatemala
Quibdó *58 A3* Chocó, W Colombia
Quilimane *see* Quelimane
Quillabamba *60 D3* Cusco, C Peru
Quilon *132 C3 var.* Kolam, Kollam. Kerala, SW India
Quimper *90 A3 anc.* Quimper Corentin. Finistère, NW France
Quimper Corentin *see* Quimper
Quimperlé *90 A3* Finistère, NW France
Quincy *40 A4* Illinois, N USA
Qui Nhon/Quinhon *see* Quy Nhơn
Quissico *79 E4* Inhambane, S Mozambique

Quito *60 B1 country capital* (Ecuador) Pichincha, N Ecuador
Qulyndy Zhazyghy *see* Kulunda Steppe
Qum *see* Qom
Qurein *see* Al Kuwayt
Qŭrghonteppa *123 E3 Rus.* Kurgan-Tyube. SW Tajikistan
Qurlurtuuq *see* Kugluktuk
Qurveh *see* Qorveh
Quşayr *see* Al Quşayr
Quxar *see* Lhazê
Quy Nhơn *137 E5 var.* Quinhon, Qui Nhon. Binh Đinh, C Vietnam
Qyteti Stalin *see* Kuçovë
Qyzylorda/Qyzylorda Oblysy *see* Kyzylorda

R

Raab *100 B1 river* Austria/Hungary
Raab *see* Rába
Raab *see* Győr
Raahe *84 D4 Swe.* Brahestad. Oulu, W Finland
Raalte *86 D3* Overijssel, E Netherlands
Raamsdonksveer *86 C4* Noord-Brabant, S Netherlands
Raasiku *106 D2 Ger.* Rasik. Harjumaa, NW Estonia
Rába *99 B7 Ger.* Raab. *river* Austria/Hungary
Rabat *70 C2 var.* al Dar al Baida. *country capital* (Morocco) NW Morocco
Rabat *102 B5* W Malta
Rabat *see* Victoria
Rabbah Ammon/Rabbath Ammon *see* 'Ammān
Rabinal *52 B2* Baja Verapaz, C Guatemala
Rabka *99 D5* Małopolskie, S Poland
Râbniţa *see* Rîbniţa
Rabyānah, Ramlat *71 G4 var.* Rebiana Sand Sea, Şaḩrā' Rabyānah. *desert* SE Libya
Rabyānah, Şaḩrā' *see* Rabyānah, Ramlat
Răcari *see* Durankulak
Race, Cape *39 H3 cape* Newfoundland, Newfoundland and Labrador, E Canada
Rach Gia *137 D6* Kiên Giang, S Vietnam
Rach Gia, Vinh *137 D6 bay* S Vietnam
Racine *40 B3* Wisconsin, N USA
Rácz-Becse *see* Bečej
Rădăuţi *108 C3 Ger.* Radautz, *Hung.* Rádóc. Suceava, N Romania
Radautz *see* Rădăuţi
Rádóc *see* Rădăuţi
Radom *98 D4* Mazowieckie, C Poland
Radomsko *98 D4 Rus.* Novoradomsk. Łódzkie, C Poland
Radomyshl' *108 D2* Zhytomyrs'ka Oblast', N Ukraine
Radoviš *101 E6 prev.* Radovište. E Macedonia
Radovište *see* Radoviš
Radviliškis *106 B4* Šiaulai, N Lithuania
Radzyń Podlaski *98 E4* Lubelskie, E Poland
Rae-Edzo *see* Edzo
Raetihi *150 D4* Manawatu-Wanganui, North Island, New Zealand
Rafa *see* Rafah
Rafaela *64 C3* Santa Fe, E Argentina
Rafah *119 A7 var.* Rafa, Rafaḩ, *Heb.* Rafiaḩ, *var.* Raphiah. SW Gaza Strip
Rafḩah *120 B4* Al Ḩudūd ash Shamālīyah, N Saudi Arabia
Rafiaḩ *see* Rafah
Raga *73 A5* Western Bahr el Ghazal, SW Sudan
Ragged Island Range *54 C2 island group* S Bahamas
Ragnit *see* Neman
Ragusa *97 C7* Sicilia, Italy, C Mediterranean Sea
Ragusa *see* Dubrovnik
Rahachow *107 D7 Rus.* Rogachëv. Homyel'skaya Voblasts', SE Belarus
Rahaeng *see* Tak
Rahaţ, Ḩarrat *121 B5 lava flow* W Saudi Arabia
Rahīmyār Khān *134 C3* Punjab, SE Pakistan
Rahovec *see* Orahovac
Raiatea *145 G4 island* Îles Sous le Vent, W French Polynesia
Rāichūr *132 C1* Karnātaka, C India
Raidestos *see* Tekirdağ
Rainier, Mount *34 A4 volcano* Washington, NW USA
Rainy Lake *38 A4 lake* Canada/USA
Raipur *135 E4* Chhattīsgarh, C India
Rājahmundry *135 E5* Andhra Pradesh, E India
Rajang *see* Rajang, Batang
Rajang, Batang *138 D3 var.* Rajang. *river* East Malaysia
Rājapālaiyam *132 C3* Tamil Nādu, SE India
Rājasthān *134 C3 state* NW India
Rājasthān *134 C3 cultural region* NW India
Rājkot *134 C4* Gujarāt, W India
Rāj Nāndgaon *135 E4* Chhattīsgarh, C India
Rajshahi *135 G3 prev.* Rampur Boalia. Rajshahi, W Bangladesh
Rakahanga *145 F3 atoll* N Cook Islands
Rakaia *151 B6 river* South Island, New Zealand
Rakka *see* Ar Raqqah
Rakke *106 E2* Lääne-Virumaa, NE Estonia
Rakvere *106 E2 Ger.* Wesenberg. Lääne-Virumaa, N Estonia
Ralik Chain *144 D1 island group* Ralik Chain, W Marshall Islands
Ramadi *see* Ar Ramādī
Râmnicul-Sărat *see* Râmnicu Sărat
Râmnicu Sărat *108 C4 prev.* Râmnicul-Sărat, Rîmnicu-Sărat. Buzău, E Romania
Râmnicu Vâlcea *108 B4 prev.* Rîmnicu Vîlcea. Vâlcea, C Romania
Rampur Boalia *see* Rajshahi
Ramree Island *136 A4 island* W Myanmar (Burma)
Ramtha *see* Ar Ramthā
Rancagua *64 B4* Libertador, C Chile
Rānchi *135 F4* Jhārkhand, N India
Randers *85 B7* Århus, C Denmark
Ráneš *see* Ringvassøya
Rangiora *151 C6* Canterbury, South Island, New Zealand
Rangitikei *150 D4 river* North Island, New Zealand
Rangoon *see* Yangon
Rangpur *135 G3* Rajshahi, N Bangladesh
Rankin Inlet *37 G3* Nunavut, C Canada
Rankovićevo *see* Kraljevo
Ranong *137 B6* Ranong, SW Thailand
Rapa Nui *see* Pascua, Isla de
Raphiah *see* Rafah
Rapid City *44 D3* South Dakota, N USA
Räpina *106 E3 Ger.* Rappin. Põlvamaa, SE Estonia
Rapla *106 D2 Ger.* Rappel. Raplamaa, NW Estonia
Rappel *see* Rapla
Rappin *see* Räpina
Rarotonga *145 G5 island* S Cook Islands, C Pacific Ocean
Ras al'Ain *see* Ra's al 'Ayn
Ra's al 'Ayn *118 D1 var.* Ras al'Ain. Al Ḩasakah, N Syria
Ra's an Naqb *119 B7* Ma'ān, S Jordan
Raseiniai *106 B4* Kaunas, C Lithuania
Rasht *120 C2 var.* Resht. Gīlān, NW Iran
Rasik *see* Raasiku
Râşnov *108 C4 prev.* Rîşno, Rozsnyó, *Hung.* Barcarozsnyó. Braşov, C Romania
Rastenburg *see* Kętrzyn
Ratak Chain *144 D1 island group* Ratak Chain, E Marshall Islands
Ratan *85 C5* Jämtland, C Sweden
Rat Buri *see* Ratchaburi
Ratchaburi *137 C5 var.* Rat Buri. Ratchaburi, W Thailand
Ratisbon/Ratisbona/Ratisbonne *see* Regensburg
Rat Islands *36 A2 island group* Aleutian Islands, Alaska, USA
Ratlām *134 D4 prev.* Rutlam. Madhya Pradesh, C India
Ratnapura *132 D4* Sabaragamuwa Province, S Sri Lanka
Raton *48 D1* New Mexico, SW USA
Rättvik *85 C5* Dalarna, C Sweden
Raudhatain *see* Ar Rawḑatayn
Raufarhöfn *83 E4* Nordhurland Eystra, NE Iceland
Raukawa *see* Cook Strait
Raukumara Range *150 E3 mountain range* North Island, New Zealand
Rāurkela *151 F4 var.* Raurkela; *prev.* Rourkela. Orissa, E India
Rauma *85 D5 Swe.* Raumo. Länsi-Soumi, SW Finland
Raumo *see* Rauma
Raurkela *see* Rāurkela
Ravenna *96 C3* Emilia-Romagna, N Italy
Rāvi *134 C2 river* India/Pakistan
Rāwalpindi *134 C1* Punjab, NE Pakistan
Rawa Mazowiecka *98 D4* Łódzkie, C Poland
Rawicz *98 C4 Ger.* Rawitsch. Wielkopolskie, C Poland
Rawitsch *see* Rawicz
Rawlins *44 C3* Wyoming, C USA
Rawson *65 C6* Chubut, SE Argentina
Rayak *118 B4 var.* Rayaq, Riyāq. E Lebanon
Rayaq *see* Rayak
Rayleigh *43 F1* UK
Rayong *137 C5* Rayong, S Thailand
Razāzah, Buḩayrat ar *120 B3 var.* Baḩr al Milḩ. *lake* C Iraq
Razdolnoye *see* Rozdol'ne
Razelm, Lacul *see* Razim, Lacul
Razgrad *104 D2* Razgrad, N Bulgaria
Razim, Lacul *108 D5 prev.* Lacul Razelm. *lagoon* NW Black Sea
Reading *89 D7* S England, UK
Reading *41 F4* Pennsylvania, NE USA
Realicó *64 C4* La Pampa, C Argentina
Reăng Kesei *137 D5* Bătdâmbâng, W Cambodia
Rebecca, Lake *147 C6 lake* Western Australia
Rebiana Sand Sea *see* Rabyānah, Ramlat
Rebun-tō *130 C2 island* NE Japan
Rechitsa *see* Rechytsa
Rechytsa *107 D7 Rus.* Rechitsa. Brestskaya Voblasts', SW Belarus
Recife *63 G2 prev.* Pernambuco. *state capital* Pernambuco, E Brazil
Recklinghausen *94 A4* Nordrhein-Westfalen, W Germany
Recogne *87 C7* Luxembourg, SE Belgium
Reconquista *64 D3* Santa Fe, C Argentina
Red Deer *37 E5* Alberta, SW Canada
Redding *47 B5* California, W USA
Redon *90 B4* Ille-et-Vilaine, NW France
Red River *45 E1 river* Canada/USA
Red River *136 C2 var.* Yuan, *Chin.* Yuan Jiang, *Vtn.* Sông Hông Hà. *river* China/Vietnam
Red River *35 C6 river* S USA
Red River *42 B3 river* Louisiana, S USA
Red Sea *72 C3 var.* Sinus Arabicus. *sea* Africa/Asia
Red Wing *45 G2* Minnesota, N USA
Reefton *151 C5* West Coast, South Island, New Zealand
Reese River *47 C5 river* Nevada, W USA
Refahiye *117 E3* Erzincan, C Turkey
Regensburg *95 C6 Eng.* Ratisbon, *Fr.* Ratisbonne, *hist.* Ratisbona; *anc.* Castra Regina, Reginum. Bayern, SE Germany
Regenstauf *95 C6* Bayern, SE Germany
Reggane *70 D3* C Algeria
Reggio *see* Reggio nell'Emilia
Reggio Calabria *see* Reggio di Calabria
Reggio di Calabria *97 D7 var.* Reggio Calabria, *Gk.* Rhegion; *anc.* Regium, Rhegium. Calabria, SW Italy
Reggio Emilia *see* Reggio nell'Emilia
Reggio nell'Emilia *96 B2 var.* Reggio Emilia, *abbrev.* Reggio; *anc.* Regium Lepidum. Emilia-Romagna, N Italy
Reghin *108 C4 Ger.* Sächsisch-Reen, *Hung.* Szászrégen; *prev.* Reghinul Săsesc, *Ger.* Sächsisch-Regen. Mureş, C Romania
Reghinul Săsesc *see* Reghin
Regina *37 F5 province capital* Saskatchewan, S Canada
Reginum *see* Regensburg
Registan *see* Rīgestān
Regium *see* Reggio di Calabria
Regium Lepidum *see* Reggio nell'Emilia
Rehoboth *78 B3* Hardap, C Namibia
Rehoboth/Rehovoth *see* Reḩovot
Reḩovot *119 A6 var.* Rehoboth, Rekhovoth, Rehovoth. Central, C Israel
Reichenau *see* Bogatynia, Poland
Reichenberg *see* Liberec
Reid *147 D6* Western Australia
Reikjavik *see* Reykjavík
Ré, Île de *90 A4 island* W France
Reims *90 D3 Eng.* Rheims; *anc.* Durocortorum, Remi. Marne, N France
Reindeer Lake *37 F4 lake* Manitoba/ Saskatchewan, C Canada
Reine-Charlotte, Îles de la *see* Queen Charlotte Islands
Reine-Élisabeth, Îles de la *see* Queen Elizabeth Islands
Reinga, Cape *150 C1 headland* North Island, New Zealand
Reinosa *92 D1* Cantabria, N Spain
Reka *see* Rijeka
Rekhovoth *see* Reḩovot
Reliance *37 F4* Northwest Territories, C Canada
Remi *see* Reims
Rendina *see* Rentína
Rendsburg *94 B2* Schleswig-Holstein, N Germany
Rengat *138 B4* Sumatera, W Indonesia
Reni *108 D4* Odes'ka Oblast', SW Ukraine
Rennell *144 C4 var.* Mu Nggava. *island* S Solomon Islands
Rennes *90 B3 Bret.* Roazon; *anc.* Condate. Ille-et-Vilaine, NW France
Reno *47 C5* Nevada, W USA
Renqiu *128 C4* Hebei, E China
Rentína *105 B5 var.* Rendina. Thessalía, C Greece
Reps *see* Rupea
Republika Srpska *see* Foča
Repulse Bay *37 G3* Northwest Terretories, N Canada
Reschitza *see* Reşiţa
Resht *see* Rasht
Resicabánya *see* Reşiţa
Resistencia *64 D3* Chaco, NE Argentina
Reşiţa *108 A4 Ger.* Reschitza, *Hung.* Resicabánya. Caraş-Severin, W Romania
Resolute *37 F2 Inuit.* Qausuittuq. Cornwallis Island, Nunavut, N Canada
Resolution Island *39 E1 island* Nunavut, NE Canada
Resolution Island *151 A7 island* SW New Zealand
Réunion *79 H4 off.* La Réunion. *French overseas department* W Indian Ocean
Réunion *141 B5 island* W Indian Ocean
Reus *93 F2* Cataluña, E Spain
Reutlingen *95 B6* Baden-Württemberg, S Germany
Reuver *87 D5* Limburg, SE Netherlands
Reval/Revel *see* Tallinn
Revillagigedo Island *50 B5 island* Alexander Archipelago, Alaska, USA
Rexburg *46 E3* Idaho, NW USA
Reyes *61 F3* Beni, NW Bolivia
Rey, Isla del *53 G5 island* Archipiélago de las Perlas, SE Panama
Reykjanes Basin *82 C5 var.* Irminger Basin. *undersea basin* N Atlantic Ocean
Reykjanes Ridge *80 A1 undersea ridge* N Atlantic Ocean
Reykjavík *83 E5 var.* Reikjavik. *country capital* (Iceland) Höfudhborgarsvaedhi, W Iceland
Reynosa *51 E2* Tamaulipas, C Mexico
Rezé *90 A4* Loire-Atlantique, NW France
Rēzekne *106 D4 Ger.* Rositten; *prev. Rus.* Rezhitsa. Rēzekne, SE Latvia
Rezhitsa *see* Rēzekne
Rezovo *104 E3 Turk.* Rezve. Burgas, E Bulgaria
Rezve *see* Rezovo
Rhaedestus *see* Tekirdağ
Rhegion/Rhegium *see* Reggio di Calabria
Rheims *see* Reims
Rhein *see* Rhine
Rheine *94 A3 var.* Rheine in Westfalen. Nordrhein-Westfalen, NW Germany
Rheine in Westfalen *see* Rheine
Rheinisches Schiefergebirge *95 A5 var.* Rhine State Uplands, *Eng.* Rhenish Slate Mountains. *mountain range* W Germany
Rhenish Slate Mountains *see* Rheinisches Schiefergebirge
Rhin *see* Rhine
Rhine *80 D4 Dut.* Rijn, *Fr.* Rhin, *Ger.* Rhein. *river* W Europe
Rhinelander *40 B2* Wisconsin, N USA
Rhine State Uplands *see* Rheinisches Schiefergebirge

Rho *96 B2* Lombardia, N Italy
Rhode Island *41 G3 off.* State of Rhode Island and Providence Plantations, *also known as* Little Rhody, Ocean State. *state* NE USA
Rhodes *see* Ródos
Rhodesia *see* Zimbabwe
Rhodope Mountains *104 C3 var.* Rodhópi Óri, *Bul.* Rhodope Planina, Rodopi, *Gk.* Orosirá Rodhópis, *Turk.* Dospad Dagh. *mountain range* Bulgaria/Greece
Rhodope Planina *see* Rhodope Mountains
Rhône *91 D6 cultural region* E France
Rhône *91 D6 department* E France
Rhône *80 C4 river* France/Switzerland
Rhum *88 B3 var.* Rum. *island* W Scotland, UK
Ribble *89 D5 river* NW England, UK
Ribeira *92 B1* Galicia, NW Spain
Ribeirão Preto *63 F4* São Paulo, S Brazil
Riberalta *61 F2* Beni, N Bolivia
Rîbniţa *108 D3 var.* Râbniţa, *Rus.* Rybnitsa. NE Moldova
Rice Lake *40 A2* Wisconsin, N USA
Richard Toll *74 B3* N Senegal
Richfield *44 B4* Utah, W USA
Richland *46 C2* Washington, NW USA
Richmond *151 C5* Tasman, South Island, New Zealand
Richmond *40 C5* Kentucky, S USA
Richmond *41 E5 state capital* Virginia, NE USA
Richmond Range *151 C5 mountain range* South Island, New Zealand
Ricobayo, Embalse de *92 C2 reservoir* NW Spain
Ricomagus *see* Riom
Ridgecrest *47 C7* California, W USA
Ried *see* Ried im Innkreis
Ried im Innkreis *95 D6 var.* Ried. Oberösterreich, NW Austria
Riemst *87 D6* Limburg, NE Belgium
Riesa *94 D4* Sachsen, E Germany
Rift Valley *see* Great Rift Valley
Rīga *106 C3 Eng.* Riga. *country capital* (Latvia) Rīga, C Latvia
Rigaer Bucht *see* Riga, Gulf of
Riga, Gulf of *106 C3 Est.* Liivi Laht, *Ger.* Rigaer Bucht, *Latv.* Rigas Jūras Līcis, *Rus.* Rizhskiy Zaliv; *prev. Est.* Riia Laht. *gulf* Estonia/Latvia
Rīgān *120 E4* Kermān, SE Iran
Rīgas Jūras Līcis *see* Riga, Gulf of
Rīgestān *122 D5 var.* Registan. *desert region* S Afghanistan
Riia Laht *see* Riga, Gulf of
Riihimäki *85 D5* Etelä-Suomi, S Finland
Rijeka *100 A2 Ger.* Sankt Veit am Flaum, *It.* Fiume, *Slvn.* Reka; *anc.* Tarsatica. Primorje-Gorski Kotar, NW Croatia
Rijn *see* Rhine
Rijssel *see* Lille
Rijssen *86 E3* Overijssel, E Netherlands
Rimah, Wādī ar *120 B4 var.* Wādī ar Rummah. *dry watercourse* C Saudi Arabia
Rimini *96 C3 anc.* Ariminum. Emilia-Romagna, N Italy
Rîmnicu-Sărat *see* Râmnicu Sărat
Rîmnicu Vîlcea *see* Râmnicu Vâlcea
Rimouski *39 E4* Québec, SE Canada
Ringebu *85 B5* Oppland, S Norway
Ringen *see* Rõngu
Ringkøbing Fjord *85 A7 fjord* W Denmark
Ringvassøya *84 C2 Lapp.* Ráneš. *island* N Norway
Rio *see* Rio de Janeiro
Riobamba *60 B1* Chimborazo, C Ecuador
Rio Branco *56 B3 state capital* Acre, W Brazil
Rio Branco, Território de *see* Roraima
Río Bravo *51 E2* Tamaulipas, C Mexico
Río Cuarto *64 C4* Córdoba, C Argentina
Rio de Janeiro *63 F4 var.* Rio. *state capital* Rio de Janeiro, SE Brazil
Río Gallegos *65 B7 var.* Gallegos, Puerto Gallegos. Santa Cruz, S Argentina
Rio Grande *63 E5 var.* São Pedro do Rio Grande do Sul. Rio Grande do Sul, S Brazil
Río Grande *50 D3* Zacatecas, C Mexico
Rio Grande do Norte *63 G2 off.* Estado do Rio Grande do Norte. *state* E Brazil
Rio Grande do Norte, Estado do *see* Rio Grande do Norte
Rio Grande do Sul *63 E5 off.* Estado do Rio Grande do Sul. *state* S Brazil
Rio Grande do Sul, Estado do *see* Rio Grande do Sul
Rio Grande Plateau *see* Rio Grande Rise
Rio Grande Rise *57 E6 var.* Rio Grande Plateau. *undersea plateau* SW Atlantic Ocean
Ríohacha *58 B1* La Guajira, N Colombia
Río Lagartos *51 H3* Yucatán, SE Mexico
Riom *91 C5 anc.* Ricomagus. Puy-de-Dôme, C France
Río San Juan *53 E4 department* S Nicaragua
Río Verde *51 E4 var.* Rioverde. San Luis Potosí, C Mexico
Rioverde *see* Río Verde
Ripoll *93 G2* Cataluña, NE Spain
Rishiri-tō *130 C2 var.* Risiri Tô. *island* NE Japan
Risiri Tô *see* Rishiri-tō
Rîşno *see* Râşnov
Risti *106 D2 Ger.* Kreuz. Läänemaa, W Estonia
Rivas *52 D4* Rivas, SW Nicaragua
Rivera *64 D3* Rivera, NE Uruguay
River Falls *40 A2* Wisconsin, N USA
Riverside *47 C7* California, W USA
Riverton *151 A7* Southland, South Island, New Zealand
Riverton *44 C3* Wyoming, C USA
Rivière-du-Loup *39 E4* Québec, SE Canada
Rivne *108 C2 Pol.* Równe, *Rus.* Rovno. Rivnens'ka Oblast', NW Ukraine
Rivoli *96 A2* Piemonte, NW Italy
Riyadh/Riyāḍ, Minţaqat ar *see* Ar Riyāḍ
Riyāq *see* Rayak
Rize *117 E2* Rize, NE Turkey
Rizhao *128 D4* Shandong, E China
Rizhskiy Zaliv *see* Riga, Gulf of
Rkîz *74 C3* Trarza, W Mauritania
Road Town *55 F3 dependent territory capital* (British Virgin Islands) Tortola, C British Virgin Islands
Roanne *91 C5 anc.* Rodunma. Loire, E France
Roanoke *41 E5* Virginia, NE USA
Roanoke River *43 F1 river* North Carolina/Virginia, SE USA
Roatán *52 C2 var.* Coxen Hole, Coxin Hole. Islas de la Bahía, N Honduras
Roat Kampuchea *see* Cambodia
Roazon *see* Rennes
Robbie Ridge *143 E3 undersea ridge* W Pacific Ocean
Robert Williams *see* Caála
Robinson Range *147 B5 mountain range* Western Australia
Robson, Mount *37 E5 mountain* British Columbia, SW Canada
Robstown *49 G4* Texas, SW USA
Roca Partida, Isla *50 B5 island* W Mexico
Rocas, Atol das *63 G2 island* E Brazil
Rochefort *87 C7* Namur, SE Belgium
Rochefort *90 B4 var.* Rochefort sur Mer. Charente-Maritime, W France
Rochefort sur Mer *see* Rochefort
Rochester *45 G3* Minnesota, N USA
Rochester *41 G2* New Hampshire, NE USA
Rochester *41 E3* New York, USA
Rocheuses, Montagnes/Rockies *see* Rocky Mountains
Rockall Bank *80 B2 undersea bank* N Atlantic Ocean
Rockall Trough *80 B2 trough* N Atlantic Ocean
Rockdale *148 E2* Texas, SW USA
Rockford *40 B3* Illinois, N USA
Rockhampton *148 D4* Queensland, E Australia
Rock Hill *43 E1* South Carolina, SE USA
Rockingham *147 A6* Western Australia
Rock Island *40 B3* Illinois, N USA
Rock Sound *54 C1* Eleuthera Island, C Bahamas
Rock Springs *44 C3* Wyoming, C USA
Rockstone *59 F3* C Guyana
Rocky Mount *43 F1* North Carolina, SE USA
Rocky Mountains *34 B4 var.* Rockies, *Fr.* Montagnes Rocheuses. *mountain range* Canada/USA
Roden *86 E2* Drenthe, NE Netherlands
Rodez *91 C5 anc.* Segodunum. Aveyron, S France
Rodhópi Óri *see* Rhodope Mountains
Ródhos/Rodi *see* Ródos
Rodopi *see* Rhodope Mountains
Ródos *105 E7 var.* Ródhos, *Eng.* Rhodes, *It.* Rodi; *anc.* Rhodos. *island* Dodekánisa, Greece, Aegean Sea
Rodosto *see* Tekirdağ
Rodunma *see* Roanne
Roermond *87 D5* Limburg, SE Netherlands
Roeselare *87 A6 Fr.* Roulers; *prev.* Rousselaere. West-Vlaanderen, W Belgium
Rogachëv *see* Rahachow
Rogatica *100 C4* Republika Srpska, SE Bosnia and Herzegovina
Rogers *42 A1* Arkansas, C USA
Roger Simpson Island *see* Abemama
Roi Ed *see* Roi Et
Roi Et *137 D5 var.* Muang Roi Et, Roi Ed. Roi Et, E Thailand
Roja *106 C2* Talsi, NW Latvia
Rokiškis *106 C4* Panevėžys, NE Lithuania
Rokycany *99 A5 Ger.* Rokytzan. Plzeňský Kraj, W Czech Republic
Rokytzan *see* Rokycany
Rôlas, Ilha das *76 E2 island* S Sao Tome and Principe, Africa, E Atlantic Ocean
Rolla *45 G5* Missouri, C USA
Röm *see* Rømø
Roma *96 C4 Eng.* Rome. *country capital* (Italy) Lazio, C Italy
Roma *149 D5* Queensland, E Australia
Roman *104 C2* Vratsa, NW Bulgaria
Roman *108 C4 Hung.* Románvásár. Neamţ, NE Romania
Romania *108 B4 Bul.* Rumŭniya, *Ger.* Rumänien, *Hung.* Románia, *Rom.* România, *SCr.* Rumunjska, *Ukr.* Rumuniya, *prev.* Republica Socialistă România, Roumania, Rumania, Socialist Republic of Romania, *prev. Rom.* Romînia. *country* SE Europe

ROMANIA
Southest Europe

Official name Romania
Formation 1878 / 1947
Capital Bucharest
Population 21.7 million / 244 people per sq mile (94 people per sq km) / 56%
Total area 91,699 sq miles (237,500 sq km)
Languages Romanian*, Hungarian (Magyar), Romani, German
Religions Romanian Orthodox 87%, Roman Catholic 5%, Protestant 4%, Other 2%, Greek Orthodox 1%, Greek Catholic (Uniate) 1%
Ethnic mix Romanian 89%, Magyar 7%, Roma 3%, Other 1%
Government Presidential system
Currency Romanian leu = 100 bani
Literacy rate 97%
Calorie consumption 3455 calories

România, Republica Socialistă *see* Romania
Romania, Socialist Republic of *see* Romania
Románvásár *see* Roman
Rome *42 D2* Georgia, SE USA
Rome *see* Roma
Romînia *see* Romania
Romny *109 F2* Sums'ka Oblast', NE Ukraine
Rømø *85 A7 Ger.* Röm. *island* SW Denmark
Roncador, Serra do *56 D4 mountain range* C Brazil
Ronda *92 D5* Andalucía, S Spain
Rondônia *62 D3 off.* Estado de Rondônia; *prev.* Território de Rondônia. *state* W Brazil
Rondônia, Estado de *see* Rondônia
Rondônia, Território de *see* Rondônia
Rondonópolis *63 E3* Mato Grosso, W Brazil
Rongelap Atoll *144 D1 var.* Rōnlap. *atoll* Ralik Chain, NW Marshall Islands
Rõngu *106 D3 Ger.* Ringen. Tartumaa, SE Estonia
Rōnlap *see* Rongelap Atoll
Rønne *85 B8* Bornholm, E Denmark
Ronne Ice Shelf *154 A3 ice shelf* Antarctica
Roosendaal *87 C5* Noord-Brabant, S Netherlands
Roosevelt Island *154 B4 island* Antarctica
Roraima *62 D1 off.* Estado de Roraima; *prev.* Território de Rio Branco, Território de Roraima. *state* N Brazil
Roraima, Estado de *see* Roraima
Roraima, Mount *59 E3 mountain* N South America
Roraima, Território de *see* Roraima
Røros *85 B5* Sør-Trøndelag, S Norway
Rosa, Lake *54 D2 lake* Great Inagua, S Bahamas
Rosario *64 D4* Santa Fe, C Argentina
Rosario *64 D2* San Pedro, C Paraguay
Rosarito *50 A1* Baja California, NW Mexico
Roscianum *see* Rossano
Roscommon *40 C2* Michigan, N USA
Roseau *55 G4 prev.* Charlotte Town. *country capital* (Dominica) SW Dominica
Roseburg *46 B4* Oregon, NW USA
Rosenau *see* Rožňava
Rosenberg *49 G4* Texas, SW USA
Rosenberg *see* Ružomberok
Rosengarten *94 B3* Niedersachsen, N Germany
Rosenheim *95 C6* Bayern, S Germany
Rosia *93 H5* W Gibraltar Europe
Rosia Bay *93 H5 bay* SW Gibraltar Europe W Mediterranean Sea Atlantic Ocean
Roşiori de Vede *108 B5* Teleorman, S Romania
Rositten *see* Rēzekne
Roslavl' *111 A5* Smolenskaya Oblast', W Russian Federation
Rosmalen *86 C4* Noord-Brabant, S Netherlands
Ross *151 B6* West Coast, South Island, New Zealand
Rossano *97 E6 anc.* Roscianum. Calabria, SW Italy
Ross Ice Shelf *154 B4 ice shelf* Antarctica
Rossiyskaya Federatsiya *see* Russian Federation
Rosso *74 B3* Trarza, SW Mauritania
Rossosh' *111 B6* Voronezhskaya Oblast', W Russian Federation
Ross Sea *154 B4 sea* Antarctica
Rostak *see* Ar Rustāq
Rostock *94 C2* Mecklenburg-Vorpommern, NE Germany
Rostov *see* Rostov-na-Donu
Rostov-na-Donu *111 B7 var.* Rostov, *Eng.* Rostov-on-Don. Rostovskaya Oblast', SW Russian Federation
Rostov-on-Don *see* Rostov-na-Donu
Roswell *48 D2* New Mexico, SW USA
Rota *144 B1 island* S Northern Mariana Islands
Rotcher Island *see* Tamana
Rothera *154 A2 UK research station* Antarctica
Rotomagus *see* Rouen
Rotorua *150 D3* Bay of Plenty, North Island, New Zealand
Rotorua, Lake *150 D3 lake* North Island, New Zealand
Rotterdam *86 C4* Zuid-Holland, SW Netherlands
Rottweil *95 B6* Baden-Württemberg, S Germany
Rotuma *145 E4 island* NW Fiji Oceania S Pacific Ocean
Roubaix *90 C2* Nord, N France
Rouen *90 C3 anc.* Rotomagus. Seine-Maritime, N France
Roulers *see* Roeselare
Roumania *see* Romania
Round Rock *49 G3* Texas, SW USA
Rourkela *see* Rāurkela
Rousselaere *see* Roeselare
Roussillon *91 C6 cultural region* S France
Rouyn-Noranda *38 D4* Québec, SE Canada
Rovaniemi *84 D3* Lappi, N Finland
Rovigno *see* Rovinj
Rovigo *96 C2* Veneto, NE Italy
Rovinj *100 A3 It.* Rovigno. Istra, NW Croatia

Rovno *see* Rivne
Rovuma, Rio 79 F2 *var.* Ruvuma. *river* Mozambique/Tanzania
Rovuma, Rio *see* Ruvuma
Równe *see* Rivne
Roxas City 139 E2 Panay Island, C Philippines
Royale, Isle 40 B1 *island* Michigan, N USA
Royan 91 B5 Charente-Maritime, W France
Rozdol'ne 109 F4 *Rus.* Razdolnoye. Respublika Krym, S Ukraine
Rožňava 99 D6 *Ger.* Rosenau, *Hung.* Rozsnyó. Košický Kraj, E Slovakia
Rózsahegy *see* Ružomberok
Rozsnyó *see* Râşnov
Rozsnyó *see* Rožňava
Ruanda *see* Rwanda
Ruapehu, Mount 150 D4 *volcano* North Island, New Zealand
Ruapuke Island 151 B8 *island* SW New Zealand
Ruatoria 150 E3 Gisborne, North Island, New Zealand
Ruawai 150 D2 Northland, North Island, New Zealand
Rubezhnoye *see* Rubizhne
Rubizhne 109 H3 *Rus.* Rubezhnoye. Luhans'ka Oblast', E Ukraine
Ruby Mountains 47 D5 *mountain range* Nevada, W USA
Rucava 106 B3 Liepāja, SW Latvia
Rudensk *see* Rudzyensk
Rūdiškės 107 B5 Vilnius, S Lithuania
Rudnik 104 E2 Varna, E Bulgaria
Rudny *see* Rudnyy
Rudnyy 114 C4 *var.* Rudny. Kostanay, N Kazakhstan
Rudolf, Lake *see* Turkana, Lake
Rudolfswert *see* Novo mesto
Rudzyensk 107 C6 *Rus.* Rudensk. Minskaya Voblasts', C Belarus
Rufiji 73 C7 *river* E Tanzania
Rufino 64 C4 Santa Fe, C Argentina
Rugāji 106 D4 Balvi, E Latvia
Rügen 94 D2 *cape* NE Germany
Ruggell 94 E1 N Liechtenstein Europe
Ruhja *see* Rūjiena
Ruhnu 106 C2 *var.* Ruhnu Saar, *Swe.* Runö. *island* SW Estonia
Ruhnu Saar *see* Ruhnu
Rujen *see* Rūjiena
Rūjiena 106 D3 *Est.* Ruhja, *Ger.* Rujen. Valmiera, N Latvia
Rukwa, Lake 73 B7 *lake* SE Tanzania
Rum *see* Rhum
Ruma 100 D3 Vojvodina, N Serbia
Rumadiya *see* Ar Ramādī
Rumania/Rumänien *see* Romania
Rumbek 73 B5 El Buhayrat, S Sudan
Rum Cay 54 D2 *island* C Bahamas
Rumia 98 C2 Pomorskie, N Poland
Rummah, Wādī ar *see* Rimah, Wādī ar
Rummelsburg in Pommern *see* Miastko
Rumuniya/Rumŭniya/Rumunjska *see* Romania
Runanga 151 B5 West Coast, South Island, New Zealand
Rundu 78 C3 *var.* Runtu. Okavango, NE Namibia
Runö *see* Ruhnu
Runtu *see* Rundu
Ruoqiang 126 C3 *var.* Jo-ch'iang, *Uigh.* Charkhlik, Charkhliq, Qarkilik. Xinjiang Uygur Zizhiqu, NW China
Rupea 108 C4 *Ger.* Reps, *Hung.* Kőhalom; *prev.* Cohalm. Brașov, C Romania
Rupel 87 B5 *river* N Belgium
Rupella *see* la Rochelle
Rupert, Rivière de 38 D3 *river* Québec, C Canada
Rusaddir *see* Melilla
Ruschuk/Rusçuk *see* Ruse
Ruse 104 D1 *var.* Ruschuk, Rustchuk, *Turk.* Rusçuk. Ruse, N Bulgaria
Russadir *see* Melilla
Russellville 42 A1 Arkansas, C USA
Russia *see* Russian Federation
Russian America *see* Alaska
Russian Federation 112 D2 *off.* Russian Federation, *var.* Russia, *Latv.* Krievija, *Rus.* Rossiyskaya Federatsiya. *country* Asia/Europe

RUSSIAN FEDERATION
Europe / Asia

Official name Russian Federation
Formation 1480 / 1991
Capital Moscow
Population 143 million / 22 people per sq mile (8 people per sq km) / 78%
Total area 6,592,735 sq miles (17,075,200 sq km)
Languages Russian*, Tatar, Ukrainian, Chavash, various other national languages
Religions Orthodox Christian 75%, Other 15%, Muslim 10%
Ethnic mix Russian 82%, Other 10%, Tatar 4%, Ukrainian 3%, Chavash 1%
Government Presidential system
Currency Russian rouble = 100 kopeks
Literacy rate 99%
Calorie consumption 3072 calories

Russian Federation *see* Russian Federation
Rustaq *see* Ar Rustāq
Rust'avi 117 G2 SE Georgia
Rustchuk *see* Ruse
Ruston 42 B2 Louisiana, S USA
Rutanzige, Lake *see* Edward, Lake
Rutba *see* Ar Ruţbah
Rutlam *see* Ratlām
Rutland 41 F2 Vermont, NE USA
Rutög 126 A4 *var.* Rutog, Rutok. Xizang Zizhiqu, W China
Rutok *see* Rutög
Ruvuma 69 E5 *var.* Rio Rovuma. *river* Mozambique/Tanzania
Ruvuma *see* Rovuma, Rio
Ruwenzori 77 E5 *mountain range* Uganda/Dem. Rep. Congo
Ruzhany 107 B6 *Rus.* Ruzhany. Brestskaya Voblasts', SW Belarus
Ružomberok 99 C5 *Ger.* Rosenberg, *Hung.* Rózsahegy. Žilinský Kraj, N Slovakia
Rwanda 73 B6 *off.* Rwandese Republic; *prev.* Ruanda. *country* C Africa

RWANDA
Central Africa

Official name Republic of Rwanda
Formation 1962 / 1962
Capital Kigali
Population 9 million / 934 people per sq mile (361 people per sq km) / 6%
Total area 10,169 sq miles (26,338 sq km)
Languages Kinyarwanda*, French*, Kiswahili, English
Religions Roman Catholic 56%, Traditional beliefs 23%, Muslim 10%, Protestant 9%
Ethnic mix Hutu 90%, Tutsi 9%, Other (including Twa) 1%
Government Presidential system
Currency Rwanda franc = 100 centimes
Literacy rate 64%
Calorie consumption 2084 calories

Rwandese Republic *see* Rwanda
Ryazan' 111 B5 Ryazanskaya Oblast', W Russian Federation
Rybach'ye *see* Balykchy
Rybinsk 110 B4 *prev.* Andropov. Yaroslavskaya Oblast', W Russian Federation
Rybnik 99 C5 Śląskie, S Poland
Rybnitsa *see* Rîbniţa
Ryde 148 E1 UK
Ryki 98 D4 Lubelskie, E Poland
Rykovo *see* Yenakiyeve
Rypin 98 C3 Kujawsko-pomorskie, C Poland
Ryssel *see* Lille
Rysy 99 C5 *mountain* S Poland
Ryukyu Islands *see* Nansei-shotō
Ryukyu Islands *see* Nansei-shotō
Ryukyu Trench 125 F3 *var.* Nansei Syotō Trench. *trench* S East China Sea
Rzeszów 99 E5 Podkarpackie, SE Poland
Rzhev 110 B4 Tverskaya Oblast', W Russian Federation

S

Saale 94 C4 *river* C Germany
Saalfeld 95 C5 *var.* Saalfeld an der Saale. Thüringen, C Germany
Saalfeld an der Saale *see* Saalfeld
Saarbrücken 95 A6 *Fr.* Sarrebruck. Saarland, SW Germany
Sääre 106 C2 *var.* Sjar. Saaremaa, W Estonia
Saare *see* Saaremaa
Saaremaa 106 C2 *Ger.* Oesel, Ösel; *prev.* Saare. *island* W Estonia
Saariselkä 84 D2 *Lapp.* Suoločielgi. Lappi, N Finland
Sab' Ābār 118 C4 *var.* Sab'a Biyar, Sa'b Bi'ar. Ḥimṣ, C Syria
Sab'a Biyar *see* Sab' Ābār
Šabac 100 D3 Serbia, W Serbia
Sabadell 93 G2 Cataluña, E Spain
Sabah 138 D3 *prev.* British North Borneo, North Borneo. *state* East Malaysia
Sabanalarga 58 B1 Atlántico, N Colombia
Sabaneta 58 C1 Falcón, N Venezuela
Sabaria *see* Szombathely
Sab'atayn, Ramlat as 121 C6 *desert* C Yemen
Sabaya 61 F4 Oruro, S Bolivia
Sa'b Bi'ar *see* Sab' Ābār
Şāberī, Hāmūn-e 122 C5 *var.* Daryācheh-ye Hāmun, Daryācheh-ye Sīstān. *lake* Afghanistan/Iran
Sabhā 71 F3 C Libya
Sabi *see* Save, Rio
Sabinas 51 E2 Coahuila de Zaragoza, NE Mexico
Sabinas Hidalgo 51 E2 Nuevo León, NE Mexico
Sabine River 49 H3 *river* Louisiana/Texas, SW USA
Sabkha *see* As Sabkhah
Sable, Cape 43 E5 *headland* Florida, SE USA
Sable Island 39 G4 *island* Nova Scotia, SE Canada
Şabyā 121 B6 Jīzān, SW Saudi Arabia
Sabzawar *see* Sabzevār
Sabzevār 120 D2 *var.* Sabzawar. Khorāsān-Razavī, NE Iran
Sachsen 94 D4 *Eng.* Saxony, *Fr.* Saxe. *state* E Germany
Sachs Harbour 37 E2 Banks Island, Northwest Territories, N Canada
Sächsisch-Reen/Sächsisch-Regen *see* Reghin
Sacramento 47 B5 *state capital* California, W USA
Sacramento Mountains 48 D2 *mountain range* New Mexico, SW USA
Sacramento River 47 B5 *river* California, W USA
Sacramento Valley 47 B5 *valley* California, W USA
Sá da Bandeira *see* Lubango
Şa'dah 121 B6 NW Yemen
Sado 131 C5 *var.* Sadoga-shima. *island* C Japan
Sadoga-shima *see* Sado
Saena Julia *see* Siena
Safad *see* Zefat
Şāfāqis *see* Sfax
Safed *see* Zefat
Säffle 85 B6 Värmland, C Sweden
Safford 48 C3 Arizona, SW USA
Safi 70 B2 W Morocco
Safidkūh, Selseleh-ye 122 D4 *Eng.* Paropamisus Range. *mountain range* W Afghanistan
Sagaing 136 B3 Sagaing, C Myanmar (Burma)
Sagami-nada 131 D6 *inlet* SW Japan
Sagan *see* Żagań
Sāgar 134 D4 *prev.* Saugor. Madhya Pradesh, C India
Sagarmāthā *see* Everest, Mount
Sagebrush State *see* Nevada
Saghez *see* Saqqez
Saginaw 40 C3 Michigan, N USA
Saginaw Bay 40 D2 *lake bay* Michigan, N USA
Sagua la Grande 54 B2 Villa Clara, C Cuba

Sagunto 93 F3 *Cat.* Sagunt, *Ar.* Murviedro; *anc.* Saguntum. País Valenciano, E Spain
Sagunt/Saguntum *see* Sagunto
Sahara 68 B3 *desert* Libya/Algeria
Sahara el Gharbîya 72 B2 *var.* Aş Şaḩrā' al Gharbīyah, *Eng.* Western Desert. *desert* C Egypt
Sahara el Sharqîya 68 D3 *var.* Aş Şaḩrā' ash Sharqīyah, *Eng.* Arabian Desert, Eastern Desert. *desert* E Egypt
Saharan Atlas *see* Atlas Saharien
Sahel 74 D3 *physical region* C Africa
Sāhīliyah, Jibāl as 118 B3 *mountain range* NW Syria
Sāhīwāl 134 C2 *prev.* Montgomery. Punjab, E Pakistan
Saïda 119 A5 *var.* Şaydā, Sayida; *anc.* Sidon. W Lebanon
Sa'īdābād *see* Sīrjān
Saidpur 135 G3 *var.* Syedpur. Rajshahi, NW Bangladesh
Saigon *see* Hô Chi Minh
Saimaa 85 E5 *lake* SE Finland
St Albans 89 E6 *anc.* Verulamium. E England, UK
Saint Albans 40 D5 West Virginia, NE USA
St Andrews 88 C4 E Scotland, UK
Saint Anna Trough *see* Svyataya Anna Trough
St. Ann's Bay 54 B4 C Jamaica
St. Anthony 39 G3 Newfoundland, Newfoundland and Labrador, SE Canada
Saint Augustine 43 E3 Florida, SE USA
St Austell 89 C7 SW England, UK
St.Botolph's Town *see* Boston
St-Brieuc 90 A3 Côtes d'Armor, NW France
St. Catharines 38 D5 Ontario, S Canada
St-Chamond 91 D5 Loire, E France
Saint Christopher and Nevis, Federation of *see* Saint Kitts and Nevis
Saint Christopher-Nevis *see* Saint Kitts and Nevis
St. Clair, Lake 40 D3 *var.* Lac à L'Eau Claire. *lake* Canada/USA
St-Claude 91 D5 *anc.* Condate. Jura, E France
Saint Cloud 45 F2 Minnesota, N USA
Saint Croix 55 F3 *island* S Virgin Islands (US)
Saint Croix River 40 A2 *river* Minnesota/Wisconsin, N USA
St David's Island 42 B5 *island* E Bermuda
St-Denis 79 G4 *dependent territory capital* (Réunion) NW Réunion
St-Dié 90 E4 Vosges, NE France
St-Egrève 91 D5 Isère, E France
Sainte Marie, Cap *see* Vohimena, Tanjona
Saintes 91 B5 *anc.* Mediolanum. Charente-Maritime, W France
St-Étienne 91 D5 Loire, E France
St-Flour 91 C5 Cantal, C France
St-Gall/Saint Gall/St. Gallen *see* Sankt Gallen
St-Gaudens 91 B6 Haute-Garonne, S France
Saint George 149 D5 Queensland, E Australia
St George 42 B4 N Bermuda
Saint George 44 A5 Utah, W USA
St. George's 55 G5 *country capital* (Grenada) SW Grenada
St-Georges 39 E4 Québec, SE Canada
St-Georges 59 H3 E French Guiana
Saint George's Channel 89 B6 *channel* Ireland/Wales, UK
St George's Island 42 B4 *island* E Bermuda
Saint Helena 69 B6 *UK dependent territory* C Atlantic Ocean
St. Helena Bay 78 B5 *bay* SW South Africa
St Helier 89 D8 *dependent territory capital* (Jersey) S Jersey, Channel Islands
St.Iago de la Vega *see* Spanish Town
Saint Ignace 40 C2 Michigan, N USA
St-Jean, Lac 39 E4 *lake* Québec, SE Canada
Saint Joe River 46 D2 *river* Idaho, NW USA North America
St. John 39 F4 New Brunswick, SE Canada

INDEX - GAZETTEER: **Saint John – San Carlos**

Saint John *41 H1 Fr.* Saint-John. *river* Canada/USA
Saint-John *see* Saint John
St John's *55 G3 country capital* (Antigua and Barbuda) Antigua, Antigua and Barbuda
St. John's *39 H3 province capital* Newfoundland, Newfoundland and Labrador, E Canada
Saint Joseph *45 F4* Missouri, C USA
St Julian's *102 B5* N Malta
St Kilda *88 A3 island* NW Scotland, UK
Saint Kitts and Nevis *55 F3 off.* Federation of Saint Christopher and Nevis, *var.* Saint Christopher-Nevis. *country* E West Indies

SAINT KITTS & NEVIS
West Indies

Official name Federation of Saint Christopher and Nevis
Formation 1983 / 1983
Capital Basseterre
Population 38,958 / 280 people per sq mile (108 people per sq km) / 34%
Total area 101 sq miles (261 sq km)
Languages English*, English Creole
Religions Anglican 33%, Methodist 29%, Other 22%, Moravian 9%, Roman Catholic 7%
Ethnic mix Black 94%, Mixed race 3%, Other and Amerindian 2%, White 1%
Government Parliamentary system
Currency Eastern Caribbean dollar = 100 cents
Literacy rate 98%
Calorie consumption 2609 calories

St-Laurent *see* St-Laurent-du-Maroni
St-Laurent-du-Maroni *59 H3 var.* St-Laurent. NW French Guiana
St-Laurent, Fleuve *see* St. Lawrence
St. Lawrence *39 E4 Fr.* Fleuve St-Laurent. *river* Canada/USA
St. Lawrence, Gulf of *39 F3 gulf* NW Atlantic Ocean
Saint Lawrence Island *36 B2 island* Alaska, USA
St-Lô *90 B3 anc.* Briovera, Laudus. Manche, N France
St-Louis *90 E4* Haut-Rhin, NE France
Saint Louis *74 B3* NW Senegal
Saint Louis *45 G4* Missouri, C USA
Saint Lucia *55 E1 country* SE West Indies

SAINT LUCIA
West Indies

Official name Saint Lucia
Formation 1979 / 1979
Capital Castries
Population 166,312 / 705 people per sq mile (273 people per sq km) / 38%
Total area 239 sq miles (620 sq km)
Languages English*, French Creole
Religions Roman Catholic 90%, Other 10%
Ethnic mix Black 90%, Mulatto (mixed race) 6%, Asian 3%, White 1%
Government Parliamentary system
Currency Eastern Caribbean dollar = 100 cents
Literacy rate 90%
Calorie consumption 2988 calories

Saint Lucia Channel *55 H4 channel* Martinique/Saint Lucia
St-Malo *90 B3* Ille-et-Vilaine, NW France
St-Malo, Golfe de *90 A3 gulf* NW France
Saint Martin *see* Sint Maarten
St.Matthew's Island *see* Zadetkyi Kyun
St. Matthias Group *144 B3 island group* NE Papua New Guinea
St-Maur-des-Fossés *90 E2* Val-de-Marne, Île-de-France, N France Europe
St. Moritz *95 B7 Ger.* Sankt Moritz, *Rmsch.* San Murezzan. Graubünden, SE Switzerland
St-Nazaire *90 A4* Loire-Atlantique, NW France
Saint Nicholas *see* São Nicolau
Saint-Nicolas *see* Sint-Niklaas
St-Omer *90 C2* Pas-de-Calais, N France
Saint Paul *45 F2 state capital* Minnesota, N USA
St-Paul, Île *141 C6 island* Île St-Paul, NE French Southern and Antarctic Territories Antarctica Indian Ocea
St Peter Port *89 D8 dependent territory capital* (Guernsey) C Guernsey, Channel Islands
Saint Petersburg *43 E4* Florida, SE USA
Saint Petersburg *see* Sankt-Peterburg
St-Pierre and Miquelon *39 G4 Fr.* Îles St-Pierre et Miquelon. *French territorial collectivity* NE North America
St-Quentin *90 C3* Aisne, N France
Saint Thomas *see* São Tomé, Sao Tome and Principe
Saint Thomas *see* Charlotte Amalie, Virgin Islands (US)
Saint Ubes *see* Setúbal
Saint Vincent *55 G4 island* N Saint Vincent and the Grenadines
Saint Vincent *see* São Vicente
Saint Vincent and the Grenadines *55 H4 country* SE West Indies

SAINT VINCENT & THE GRENADINES
West Indies

Official name Saint Vincent and the Grenadines
Formation 1979 / 1979
Capital Kingstown
Population 117,534 / 897 people per sq mile (346 people per sq km) / 55%
Total area 150 sq miles (389 sq km)
Languages English*, English Creole
Religions Anglican 47%, Methodist 28%, Roman Catholic 13%, Other 12%
Ethnic mix Black 66%, Mulatto (mixed race) 19%, Asian 6%, Other 5%, White 4%
Government Parliamentary system
Currency Eastern Caribbean dollar = 100 cents
Literacy rate 88%
Calorie consumption 2599 calories

Saint Vincent, Cape *see* São Vicente, Cabo de
Saint Vincent Passage *55 H4 passage* Saint Lucia/Saint Vincent and the Grenadines
Saint Yves *see* Setúbal
Saipan *142 B1 island/country capital* (Northern Mariana Islands) S Northern Mariana Islands
Saishū *see* Cheju-do
Sajama, Nevado *61 F4 mountain* W Bolivia
Sajószentpéter *99 D6* Borsod-Abaúj-Zemplén, NE Hungary
Sakākah *120 B4* Al Jawf, NW Saudi Arabia
Sakakawea, Lake *44 D1 reservoir* North Dakota, N USA
Sak'art'velo *see* Georgia
Sakata *130 D4* Yamagata, Honshū, C Japan
Sakhalin *see* Sakhalin, Ostrov
Sakhalin, Ostrov *115 G4 var.* Sakhalin. *island* SE Russian Federation
Sakhon Nakhon *see* Sakon Nakhon
Şäki *117 G2 Rus.* Sheki; *prev.* Nukha. NW Azerbaijan
Saki *see* Saky
Sakishima-shotō *130 A3 var.* Sakisima Syotô. *island group* SW Japan
Sakisima Syotô *see* Sakishima-shotō
Sakiz *see* Saqqez
Sakiz-Adasi *see* Chíos
Sakon Nakhon *136 D4 var.* Muang Sakon Nakhon, Sakhon Nakhon. Sakon Nakhon, E Thailand
Saky *109 F5 Rus.* Saki. Respublika Krym, S Ukraine
Sal *74 A3 island* Ilhas de Barlavento, NE Cape Verde
Sala *85 C6* Västmanland, C Sweden
Salacgrīva *106 C3 Est.* Salatsi. Limbaži, N Latvia
Sala Consilina *97 D5* Campania, S Italy
Salado, Río *62 D5 river* E Argentina
Salado, Río *64 C3 river* C Argentina
Şalālah *121 D6* SW Oman
Salamá *52 B2* Baja Verapaz, C Guatemala
Salamanca *64 B4* Coquimbo, C Chile
Salamanca *92 D2 anc.* Helmantica, Salmantica. Castilla-León, NW Spain
Salamīyah *118 B3 var.* As Salamīyah. Ḩamāh, W Syria
Salang *see* Phuket
Salantai *106 B3* Klaipėda, NW Lithuania
Salatsi *see* Salacgrīva
Salavan *137 D5 var.* Saravan, Saravane. Salavan, S Laos
Salavat *111 D6* Respublika Bashkortostan, W Russian Federation
Sala y Gomez *153 F4 island* Chile, E Pacific Ocean
Sala y Gomez Fracture Zone *see* Sala y Gomez Ridge
Sala y Gomez Ridge *153 G4 var.* Sala y Gomez Fracture Zone. *fracture zone* SE Pacific Ocean
Salazar *see* N'Dalatando
Šalčininkai *107 C5* Vilnius, SE Lithuania
Salduba *see* Zaragoza
Saldus *106 B3 Ger.* Frauenburg. Saldus, W Latvia
Sale *149 C7* Victoria, SE Australia
Salé *70 C2* NW Morocco
Salekhard *114 D3 prev.* Obdorsk. Yamalo-Nenetskiy Avtonomnyy Okrug, N Russian Federation
Salem *132 C2* Tamil Nādu, SE India
Salem *46 B3 state capital* Oregon, NW USA
Salerno *97 D5 anc.* Salernum. Campania, S Italy
Salerno, Golfo di *97 C5 Eng.* Gulf of Salerno. *gulf* S Italy
Salerno, Gulf of *see* Salerno, Golfo di
Salernum *see* Salerno
Salihorsk *107 C7 Rus.* Soligorsk. Minskaya Voblasts', S Belarus
Salima *79 E2* Central, C Malawi
Salina *45 E5* Kansas, C USA
Salina Cruz *51 F5* Oaxaca, SE Mexico
Salinas *60 A2* Guayas, W Ecuador
Salinas *47 B6* California, W USA
Salisbury *89 D7 var.* New Sarum. S England, UK
Salisbury *see* Harare
Sällan *see* Sørøya
Sallyana *see* Şalyan
Salmantica *see* Salamanca
Salmon River *46 D3 river* Idaho, NW USA
Salmon River Mountains *46 D3 mountain range* Idaho, NW USA
Salo *85 D6* Länsi-Soumi, SW Finland
Salon-de-Provence *91 D6* Bouches-du-Rhône, SE France
Salonica/Salonika *see* Thessaloníki
Salonta *108 A3 Hung.* Nagyszalonta. Bihor, W Romania
Sal'sk *111 B7* Rostovskaya Oblast', SW Russian Federation
Salt *see* As Salṭ
Salta *64 C2* Salta, NW Argentina
Saltash *89 C7* SW England, UK
Saltillo *51 E3* Coahuila de Zaragoza, NE Mexico
Salt Lake City *44 B4 state capital* Utah, W USA
Salto *64 D4* Salto, N Uruguay
Salton Sea *47 D8 lake* California, W USA
Salvador *63 G3 prev.* São Salvador. *state capital* Bahia, E Brazil
Salween *124 C2 Bur.* Thanlwin, *Chin.* Nu Chiang, Nu Jiang. *river* SE Asia
Şalyan *135 E3 var.* Sallyana. Mid Western, W Nepal
Salzburg *95 D6 anc.* Juvavum. Salzburg, N Austria
Salzgitter *94 C4 prev.* Watenstedt-Salzgitter. Niedersachsen, C Germany
Salzwedel *94 C3* Sachsen-Anhalt, N Germany
Šamac *see* Bosanski Šamac
Samakhixai *137 E5 var.* Attapu, Attopeu. Attapu, S Laos
Samalayuca *50 C1* Chihuahua, N Mexico
Samar *139 F2 island* C Philippines
Samara *114 B3 prev.* Kuybyshev. Samarskaya Oblast', W Russian Federation
Samarang *see* Semarang
Samarinda *138 D4* Borneo, C Indonesia
Samarkand *see* Samarqand
Samarkandski/Samarkandskoye *see* Temirtau
Samarobriva *see* Amiens
Samarqand *123 E2 Rus.* Samarkand. Samarqand Viloyati, C Uzbekistan
Samawa *see* As Samāwah
Sambalpur *135 F4* Orissa, E India
Sambava *79 G2* Antsiranana, NE Madagascar
Sambir *108 B2 Rus.* Sambor. L'vivs'ka Oblast', NW Ukraine
Sambor *see* Sambir
Sambre *90 D2 river* Belgium/France
Samfya *78 D2* Luapula, N Zambia
Saminatal *94 E2 valley* Austria/ Liechtenstein Europe
Samnān *see* Semnān
Sam Neua *see* Xam Nua
Samoa *145 E4 off.* Independent State of Western Samoa, *var.* Sāmoa, *prev* Western Samoa. *country* W Polynesia

SAMOA
Australasia & Oceania

Official name Independent State of Samoa
Formation 1962 / 1962
Capital Apia
Population 185,000 / 169 people per sq mile (65 people per sq km) / 22%
Total area 1104 sq miles (2860 sq km)
Languages Samoan*, English*
Religions Christian 99%, Other 1%
Ethnic mix Polynesian 90%, Euronesian 9%, Other 1%
Government Parliamentary system
Currency Tala = 100 sene
Literacy rate 99%
Calorie consumption 2945 calories

Sāmoa *see* Samoa
Samoa Basin *143 E3 undersea basin* W Pacific Ocean
Samobor *100 A2* Zagreb, N Croatia
Sámos *105 E6 prev.* Límín Vathéos. Sámos, Dodekánisa, Greece, Aegean Sea
Sámos *105 D6 island* Dodekánisa, Greece, Aegean Sea
Samothrace *see* Samothráki
Samothráki *104 D4* Samothráki, NE Greece
Samothráki *104 C4 anc.* Samothrace. *island* NE Greece
Sampit *138 C4* Borneo, C Indonesia
Samsun *116 D2 anc.* Amisus. Samsun, N Turkey
Samtredia *117 F2* W Georgia
Samui, Ko *137 C6 island* SW Thailand
Samut Prakan *137 C5 var.* Muang Samut Prakan, Paknam. Samut Prakan, C Thailand
San *74 D3* Ségou, C Mali
San *99 E5 river* SE Poland
Şan'ā' *121 B6 Eng.* Sana. *country capital* (Yemen) W Yemen
Sana *100 B3 river* NW Bosnia and Herzegovina
Sanae *154 B2 South African research station* Antarctica
Sanaga *77 B5 river* C Cameroon
San Ambrosio, Isla *57 A5 Eng.* San Ambrosio Island. *island* W Chile
San Ambrosio Island *see* San Ambrosio, Isla
Sanandaj *120 C3 prev.* Sinneh. Kordestān, W Iran
San Andrés, Isla de *53 F3 island* NW Colombia South America
San Andrés Tuxtla *51 F4 var.* Tuxtla. Veracruz-Llave, E Mexico
San Angelo *49 F3* Texas, SW USA
San Antonio *52 B2* Toledo, S Belize
San Antonio *64 B4* Valparaíso, C Chile
San Antonio *49 F4* Texas, SW USA
San Antonio Oeste *65 C5* Río Negro, E Argentina
San Antonio River *49 G4 river* Texas, SW USA
Sanāw *121 C6 var.* Sanaw. NE Yemen
San Benedicto, Isla *50 B4 island* W Mexico
San Benito *52 B1* Petén, N Guatemala
San Benito *49 G5* Texas, SW USA
San Bernardino *47 C7* California, W USA
San Blas *50 C3* Sinaloa, C Mexico
San Blas, Cape *42 D3 headland* Florida, SE USA
San Blas, Cordillera de *53 G4 mountain range* NE Panama
San Carlos *52 D4* Río San Juan, S Nicaragua

San Carlos *48 B2* Arizona, SW USA
San Carlos *see* Quesada, Costa Rica
San Carlos de Ancud *see* Ancud
San Carlos de Bariloche *65 B5* Río
  Negro, SW Argentina
San Carlos del Zulia *58 C2* Zulia,
  W Venezuela
San Clemente Island *47 B8* island
  Channel Islands, California, W USA
San Cristóbal *58 C2* Táchira,
  W Venezuela
San Cristóbal *144 C4* var. Makira. island
  SE Solomon Islands
San Cristóbal *see* San Cristóbal de
  Las Casas
San Cristóbal de Las Casas *51 G5* var.
  San Cristóbal. Chiapas, SE Mexico
San Cristóbal, Isla *60 B5* var. Chatham
  Island. island Galapagos Islands,
  Ecuador, E Pacific Ocean
Sancti Spíritus *54 B2* Sancti Spíritus,
  C Cuba
Sandakan *138 D3* Sabah, East Malaysia
Sandalwood Island *see* Sumba, Pulau
Sandanski *104 C3* prev. Sveti Vrach.
  Blagoevgradt, SW Bulgaria
Sanday *88 D2* island NE Scotland, UK
Sanders *48 C2* Arizona, SW USA
Sand Hills *44 D3* mountain range
  Nebraska, C USA
San Diego *47 C8* California, W USA
Sandnes *85 A6* Rogaland, S Norway
Sandomierz *98 D4* Rus. Sandomir.
  Świętokrzyskie, C Poland
Sandomir *see* Sandomierz
Sandoway *136 A4* Arakan State,
  W Myanmar (Burma)
Sandpoint *46 C1* Idaho, NW USA
Sand Springs *49 G1* Oklahoma,
  C USA
Sandusky *40 D3* Ohio, N USA
Sandvika *85 A6* Akershus, S Norway
Sandviken *85 C6* Gävleborg, C Sweden
Sandwich Island *see* Éfaté
Sandwich Islands *see* Hawaiian Islands
Sandy Bay *33 H5* Saskatchewan,
  C Canada
Sandy City *44 B4* Utah, W USA
Sandy Lake *38 B3* lake Ontario,
  C Canada
San Esteban *52 D2* Olancho, C Honduras
San Eugenio/San Eugenio del Cuareim
  see Artigas
San Felipe *58 D1* Yaracuy,
  NW Venezuela
San Felipe de Puerto Plata *see* Puerto
  Plata
San Félix, Isla *57 A5* Eng. San Felix
  Island. island W Chile
San Felix Island *see* San Félix, Isla
San Fernando *92 C5* prev. Isla de León.
  Andalucía, S Spain
San Fernando *55 H5* Trinidad, Trinidad
  and Tobago
San Fernando *46 D1* California, W USA
San Fernando *58 D2* var. San Fernando
  de Apure. Apure, C Venezuela
San Fernando de Apure *see* San
  Fernando
San Fernando del Valle de Catamarca
  64 C3 var. Catamarca. Catamarca,
  NW Argentina
San Fernando de Monte Cristi *see*
  Monte Cristi
San Francisco *47 B6* California, W USA
San Francisco del Oro *50 C2*
  Chihuahua, N Mexico
San Francisco de Macorís *55 E3*
  C Dominican Republic
San Fructuoso *see* Tacuarembó
San Gabriel *60 B1* Carchi, N Ecuador
San Gabriel Mountains *46 E1* mountain
  range California, USA
Sangihe, Kepulauan *see* Sangir,
  Kepulauan
Sangir, Kepulauan *139 F3* var
  Kepulauan Sangihe. island group
  N Indonesia
Sāngli *132 B1* Mahārāshtra, W India
Sangmélima *77 B5* Sud, S Cameroon
Sangre de Cristo Mountains *48 D1*
  mountain range Colorado/New Mexico,
  C USA
San Ignacio *52 B1* prev. Cayo, El Cayo.
  Cayo, W Belize
San Ignacio *61 F3* Beni, N Bolivia
San Ignacio *50 B2* Baja California Sur,
  W Mexico

San Joaquin Valley *47 B7* valley
  California, W USA
San Jorge, Golfo *65 C6* var. Gulf of San
  Jorge. gulf S Argentina
San Jorge, Gulf of *see* San Jorge, Golfo
San José *53 E4* country capital (Costa
  Rica) San José, C Costa Rica
San José *61 G3* var. San José de
  Chiquitos. Santa Cruz, E Bolivia
San José *52 B3* var. Puerto San José.
  Escuintla, S Guatemala
San Jose *47 B6* California, W USA
San José *see* San José del Guaviare,
  Colombia
San José de Chiquitos *see* San José
San José de Cúcuta *see* Cúcuta
San José del Guaviare *58 C4* var. San
  José. Guaviare, S Colombia
San Juan *64 B4* San Juan, W Argentina
San Juan *55 F3* dependent territory
  capital (Puerto Rico) NE Puerto Rico
San Juan *see* San Juan de los Morros
San Juan Bautista *64 D3* Misiones,
  S Paraguay
San Juan Bautista *see* Villahermosa
San Juan Bautista Tuxtepec *see* Tuxtepec
San Juan de Alicante *93 F4* País
  Valenciano, E Spain
San Juan del Norte *53 E4* var. Greytown.
  Río San Juan, SE Nicaragua
San Juan de los Morros *58 D2* var. San
  Juan. Guárico, N Venezuela
San Juanito, Isla *50 C4* island C Mexico
San Juan Mountains *48 D1* mountain
  range Colorado, C USA
San Juan River *48 C1* river Colorado/
  Utah, W USA
San Julián *see* Puerto San Julián
Sankt-Bartholomäi *see* Palamuse
Sankt Gallen *95 B7* var. St. Gallen, Eng.
  Saint Gall, Fr. St-Gall. Sankt Gallen,
  NE Switzerland
Sankt-Georgen *see* Sfântu Gheorghe
Sankt-Jakobi *see* Pärnu-Jaagupi,
  Pärnumaa, Estonia
Sankt Martin *see* Martin
Sankt Moritz *see* St. Moritz
Sankt-Peterburg *110 B4* prev.
  Leningrad, Petrograd, Eng.
  Saint Petersburg, Fin. Pietari.
  Leningradskaya Oblast', NW Russian
  Federation
Sankt Pölten *95 E6* Niederösterreich,
  N Austria
Sankt Veit am Flaum *see* Rijeka
Sankuru *77 D6* river C Dem. Rep. Congo
Şanlıurfa *117 E4* prev. Sanli Urfa, Urfa;
  anc. Edessa. şanlıurfa, S Turkey
Sanli Urfa *see* Şanlıurfa
San Lorenzo *61 G5* Tarija, S Bolivia
San Lorenzo *60 A1* Esmeraldas,
  N Ecuador
San Lorenzo, Isla *60 C4* island W Peru
Sanlúcar de Barrameda *92 C5*
  Andalucía, S Spain
San Luis *64 C4* San Luis, C Argentina
San Luis *52 B2* Petén, NE Guatemala
San Luis *50 A1* var. San Luis Río
  Colorado. Sonora, NW Mexico
San Luis Obispo *47 B7* California,
  W USA
San Luis Potosí *51 E3* San Luis Potosí,
  C Mexico
San Luis Río Colorado *see* San Luis
San Marcos *52 A2* San Marcos,
  W Guatemala
San Marcos *49 G4* Texas, SW USA
San Marcos de Arica *see* Arica
San Marino *96 E1* country capital (San
  Marino) San Marino
San Marino *96 D1* off. Republic of San
  Marino. country S Europe

SAN MARINO
Southern Europe

Official name Republic of San Marino
Formation 1631 / 1631
Capital San Marino
Population 28,880 / 1203 people per
  sq mile (473 people per sq km) / 94%
Total area 23.6 sq miles (61 sq km)
Languages Italian*
Religions Roman Catholic 93%, Other and
  nonreligious 7%
Ethnic mix Sammarinese 80%, Italian 19%,
  Other 1%
Government Parliamentary system

SAN MARINO
(continued)

Currency Euro = 100 cents
Literacy rate 99%
Calorie consumption Not available

San Marino, Republic of *see* San Marino
San Martín *154 A2* Argentinian research
  station Antarctica
San Mateo *59 E2* Anzoátegui,
  NE Venezuela
San Matías *61 H3* Santa Cruz, E Bolivia
San Matías, Golfo *65 C5* var. Gulf of San
  Matías. gulf E Argentina
San Matías, Gulf of *see* San Matías, Golfo
Sanmenxia *128 C4* var. Shan Xian.
  Henan, C China
Sânnicláus Mare *see* Sânnicolau Mare
San Miguel *52 C3* San Miguel,
  SE El Salvador
San Miguel *50 D2* Coahuila de Zaragoza,
  N Mexico
San Miguel de Ibarra *see* Ibarra
San Miguel de Tucumán *64 C3* var.
  Tucumán. Tucumán, N Argentina
San Miguelito *53 G4* Panamá,
  C Panama
San Miguel, Río *61 G3* river E Bolivia
San Murezzan *see* St. Moritz
Sannär *see* Sennar
Sânnicolau-Mare *see* Sânnicolau Mare
Sânnicolau Mare *108 A4* var. Sânnicolaul-
  Mare, Hung. Nagyszentmiklós; prev.
  Sânmiclăuş Mare, Sínnicolau Mare.
  Timiş, W Romania
Sanok *99 E5* Podkarpackie, SE Poland
San Pablo *61 F5* Potosí, S Bolivia
San Pedro *52 C1* Corozal, NE Belize
San-Pédro *74 D5* S Côte d'Ivoire
  (Ivory Coast)
San Pedro *50 D3* var. San Pedro de
  las Colonias. Coahuila de Zaragoza,
  NE Mexico
San Pedro de la Cueva *50 C2* Sonora,
  NW Mexico
San Pedro de las Colonias *see* San Pedro
San Pedro de Lloc *60 B3* La Libertad,
  NW Peru
San Pedro Mártir, Sierra *50 A1*
  mountain range NW Mexico
San Pedro Sula *52 C2* Cortés,
  NW Honduras
San Rafael *64 B4* Mendoza, W Argentina
San Rafael Mountains *47 C7* mountain
  range California, W USA
San Ramón de la Nueva Orán *64 C2*
  Salta, N Argentina
San Remo *96 A3* Liguria, NW Italy
San Salvador *52 B3* country capital
  (El Salvador) San Salvador,
  SW El Salvador
San Salvador de Jujuy *64 C2* var. Jujuy.
  Jujuy, N Argentina
Sansanné-Mango *75 E4* var. Mango.
  N Togo
Sansepolcro *96 C3* Toscana, C Italy
San Severo *97 D5* Puglia, SE Italy
Santa Ana *61 F3* Beni, N Bolivia
Santa Ana *52 B3* Santa Ana,
  NW El Salvador
Santa Ana *46 D2* California, W USA
Santa Ana de Coro *see* Coro
Santa Ana Mountains *46 E2* mountain
  range California, W USA
Santa Barbara *50 C2* Chihuahua,
  N Mexico
Santa Barbara *47 C7* California,
  W USA
Santa Catalina Island *47 B8* island
  Channel Islands, California, W USA
Santa Catarina *63 E5* off. Estado de
  Santa Catarina. state S Brazil
Santa Catarina, Estado de *see* Santa
  Catarina
Santa Clara *54 B2* Villa Clara, C Cuba
Santa Clarita *46 D1* California, USA
Santa Comba *92 B1* Galicia, NW Spain
Santa Cruz *76 E2* São Tomé, S São Tome
  and Principe, Africa
Santa Cruz *47 B6* California, W USA
Santa Cruz *61 G4* department E Bolivia
Santa Cruz Barillas *see* Barillas
Santa Cruz del Quiché *52 B2* Quiché,
  W Guatemala
Santa Cruz de Tenerife *70 A3* Tenerife,
  Islas Canarias, Spain, NE Atlantic Ocean

Santa Cruz, Isla *60 B5* var. Indefatigable
  Island, Isla Chávez. island Galapagos
  Islands, Ecuador, E Pacific Ocean
Santa Cruz Islands *144 D3* island group
  E Solomon Islands
Santa Cruz, Río *65 B7* river S Argentina
Santa Elena *52 B1* Cayo, W Belize
Santa Fe *48 D1* state capital New Mexico,
  SW USA
Santa Fe *see* Bogotá
Santa Fe de Bogotá *see* Bogotá
Santa Genoveva *50 B3* mountain
  W Mexico
Santa Isabel *144 C3* var. Bughotu. island
  N Solomon Islands
Santa Isabel *see* Malabo
Santa Lucia Range *47 B7* mountain
  range California, W USA
Santa Margarita, Isla *50 B3* island
  W Mexico
Santa Maria *63 E5* Rio Grande do Sul,
  S Brazil
Santa Maria *47 B7* California, USA
Santa Maria *92 A5* island Azores,
  Portugal, NE Atlantic Ocean
Santa María del Buen Aire
  see Buenos Aires
Santa María, Isla *60 A5* var. Isla
  Floreana, Charles Island. island
  Galapagos Islands, Ecuador,
  E Pacific Ocean
Santa Marta *58 B1* Magdalena,
  N Colombia
Santa Maura *see* Lefkáda
Santa Monica *46 D1* California, W USA
Santana *76 E2* São Tomé, S Sao Tome
  and Principe, Africa
Santander *92 D1* Cantabria, N Spain
Santanilla, Islas *53 E1* island group
  NE Honduras North America
Santarém *63 E2* Pará, N Brazil
Santarém *92 B3* anc. Scalabis. Santarém,
  W Portugal
Santa Rosa *64 C4* La Pampa, C Argentina
Santa Rosa *see* Santa Rosa de Copán
Santa Rosa de Copán *52 C2* var. Santa
  Rosa. Copán, W Honduras
Santa Rosa Island *47 B8* island
  California, W USA
Sant Carles de la Rápida *see* Sant Carles
  de la Ràpita
Sant Carles de la Ràpita *93 F3* var. Sant
  Carles de la Rápida. Cataluña, NE Spain
Santiago *64 B4* var. Gran Santiago.
  country capital (Chile) Santiago, C Chile
Santiago *55 E3* var. Santiago de los
  Caballeros. N Dominican Republic
Santiago *53 F5* Veraguas, S Panama
Santiago *see* Santiago de
  Compostela, Eng. Compostella; anc.
  Campus Stellae. Galicia, NW Spain
Santiago *74 A3* var. São Tiago. island
  Ilhas de Sotavento, S Cape Verde
Santiago *see* Santiago de Cuba, Cuba
Santiago de Compostela *see* Santiago
Santiago de Cuba *54 C3* var. Santiago.
  Santiago de Cuba, E Cuba
Santiago de Guayaquil *see* Guayaquil
Santiago del Estero *64 C3* Santiago del
  Estero, C Argentina
Santiago de los Caballeros *see* Santiago,
  Dominican Republic
Santiago de los Caballeros *see* Ciudad de
  Guatemala, Guatemala
Santiago Pinotepa Nacional *see*
  Pinotepa Nacional
Santiago, Río *60 B2* river N Peru
Santi Quaranta *see* Sarandë
Santissima Trinidad *see* Chilung
Sant Julià de Lòria *91 A8* Sant Julià de
  Lòria, SW Andorra Europe
Santo *see* Espiritu Santo
Santo Antão *74 A2* island Ilhas de
  Barlavento, N Cape Verde
Santo António *76 E1* Príncipe,
  N Sao Tome and Principe, Africa
Santo Domingo *54 D3* prev. Ciudad
  Trujillo. country capital (Dominican
  Republic) SE Dominican Republic
Santo Domingo de los Colorados
  60 B1 Pichincha, NW Ecuador
Santo Domingo Tehuantepec *see*
  Tehuantepec
San Tomé de Guayana
  see Ciudad Guayana
Santorini *105 D7* island Kykládes,
  Greece, Aegean Sea

Santos 63 F4 São Paulo, S Brazil
Santos Plateau 57 D5 undersea plateau
SW Atlantic Ocean
Santo Tomé 64 D3 Corrientes,
NE Argentina
Santo Tomé de Guayana see Ciudad
Guayana
San Valentín, Cerro 65 A6 mountain
S Chile
San Vicente 52 C3 San Vicente,
C El Salvador
São Francisco, Rio 63 F3 river E Brazil
São Hill 73 C7 Iringa, S Tanzania
São João da Madeira 92 B2 Aveiro,
N Portugal
São Jorge 92 A5 island Azores, Portugal,
NE Atlantic Ocean
São Luís 63 F2 state capital Maranhão,
NE Brazil
São Mandol see São Manuel, Rio
São Manuel, Rio 63 E3 var. São Mandol,
Teles Pirés. river C Brazil
São Marcos, Baía de 63 F1 bay N Brazil
São Miguel 92 A5 island Azores,
Portugal, NE Atlantic Ocean
Saona, Isla 55 E3 island SE Dominican
Republic
Saône 91 D5 river E France
São Nicolau 74 A3 Eng. Saint Nicholas.
island Ilhas de Barlavento,
N Cape Verde
São Jorge 63 E4 state capital São Paulo,
S Brazil
São Paulo 63 E4 off. Estado de São
Paulo. state S Brazil
São Paulo de Loanda see Luanda
São Paulo, Estado de see São Paulo
São Pedro do Rio Grande do Sul see
Rio Grande
São Roque, Cabo de 63 G2 headland
E Brazil
São Salvador see Salvador, Brazil
São Salvador/São Salvador do Congo
see M'Banza Congo, Angola
São Tiago see Santiago
São Tomé 77 A5 country capital
(Sao Tome and Principe) São Tomé,
S Sao Tome and Principe
São Tomé 76 E2 Eng. Saint Thomas.
island S Sao Tome and Principe
Sao Tome and Principe 76 D1 off.
Democratic Republic of Sao Tome and
Principe. country E Atlantic Ocean

SÃO TOMÉ & PRÍNCIPE
West Africa

Official name Democratic Republic of
São Tomé and Príncipe
Formation 1975 / 1975
Capital São Tomé
Population 187,410 / 505 people per
sq mile (195 people per sq km) / 47%
Total area 386 sq miles (1001 sq km)
Languages Portuguese*, Portuguese
Creole
Religions Roman Catholic 84%,
Other 16%
Ethnic mix Black 90%, Portuguese and
Creole 10%
Government Presidential system
Currency Dobra = 100 centimos
Literacy rate 83%
Calorie consumption 2460 calories

**Sao Tome and Principe, Democratic
Republic of** see Sao Tome and Principe
São Tomé, Pico de 76 D2 mountain São
Tomé, C Sao Tome and Principe, Africa
São Vicente 74 A3 Eng. Saint Vincent.
island Ilhas de Barlavento, S Cape Verde
São Vicente, Cabo de 92 B5 Eng.
Cape Saint Vincent, Port. Cabode São
Vicente. cape S Portugal
São Vicente, Cabo de see São Vicente,
Cabo de
Sápai see Sápes
Sapele 75 F5 Delta, S Nigeria
Sápes 104 D4 var. Sápai. Anatolikí
Makedonía kai Thráki, NE Greece
Sapir see Sappir
Sa Pobla 93 G3 Mallorca, Spain,
W Mediterranean Sea
Sappir 119 B7 var Sapir. Southern,
S Israel
Sapporo 130 D2 Hokkaidō,
NE Japan
Sapri 97 D6 Campania, S Italy

Sapulpa 49 G1 Oklahoma, C USA
Saqqez 120 C2 var. Saghez, Sakiz,
Saqqiz. Kordestān, NW Iran
Saqqiz see Saqqez
Sara Buri 137 C5 var. Saraburi. Saraburi,
C Thailand
Saraburi see Sara Buri
Saragossa see Zaragoza
Saragt see Sarahs
Saraguro 60 B2 Loja, S Ecuador
Sarahs 122 D3 var. Saragt, Rus. Serakhs.
Ahal Welaýaty, S Turkmenistan
Sarajevo 100 C4 country capital
(Bosnia and Herzegovina) Federacija
Bosna I Hercegovina, SE Bosnia and
Herzegovina
Sarakhs 120 E2 Khorāsān-Razavī,
NE Iran
Saraktash 111 D6 Orenburgskaya
Oblast', W Russian Federation
Saran' 114 C4 Kaz. Saran. Karaganda,
C Kazakhstan
Sarandë 101 C7 var. Saranda, It. Porto
Edda; prev. Santi Quaranta. Vlorë,
S Albania
Saransk 111 C5 Respublika Mordoviya,
W Russian Federation
Sarasota 43 E4 Florida, SE USA
Saratov 114 B3 Saratovskaya Oblast',
W Russian Federation
Saravan/Saravane see Salavan
Sarawak 138 D3 state East Malaysia
Sarawak see Kuching
Sarcelles 90 D1 Val-d'Oise, Île-de-
France, N France Europe
Sardegna 97 A5 Eng. Sardinia. island
Italy, C Mediterranean Sea
Sardinia see Sardegna
Sarera, Teluk see Cenderawasih, Teluk
Sargasso Sea 66 B4 sea W Atlantic Ocean
Sargodha 134 C2 Punjab, NE Pakistan
Sarh 76 C4 prev. Fort Archambault
Moyen-Chari, S Chad
Sārī 120 D2 var. Sari, Sāri. Māzandarān,
N Iran
Saría 105 E7 island SE Greece
Sarıkamış 117 F3 Kars, NE Turkey
Sarikol Range 123 G3 Rus.
Sarykol'skiy Khrebet. mountain range
China/Tajikistan
Sark 89 D8 Fr. Sercq. island Channel
Islands
Şarkışla 116 D3 Sivas, C Turkey
Sarmiento 65 B7 Chubut, S Argentina
Sarnia 38 C5 Ontario, S Canada
Sarny 108 C1 Rivnens'ka Oblast',
NW Ukraine
Sarochyna 107 D5 Rus. Sorochino.
Vitsyebskaya Voblasts', N Belarus
Sarov 111 C5 prev. Sarova. Respublika
Mordoviya, SW Russian Federation
Sarova see Sarov
Sarpsborg 85 B6 Østfold, S Norway
Sarrebruck see Saarbrücken
Sartène 91 E7 Corse, France,
C Mediterranean Sea
Sarthe 90 B4 river N France
Sárti 104 C4 Kentrikí Makedonía,
N Greece
Saruhan see Manisa
Saryarqa see Kazakhskiy Melkosopochnik
Sarykol'skiy Khrebet see Sarikol Range
Sary-Tash 123 F2 Oshskaya Oblast',
SW Kyrgyzstan
Saryyesik-Atyrau, Peski 123 G1 desert
E Kazakhstan
Sasebo 131 A7 Nagasaki, Kyūshū,
SW Japan
Saskatchewan 37 F5 province
SW Canada
Saskatchewan 37 F5 river Manitoba/
Saskatchewan, C Canada
Saskatoon 37 F5 Saskatchewan, S Canada
Sasovo 111 B5 Ryazanskaya Oblast',
W Russian Federation
Sassandra 74 D5 S Côte d'Ivoire
(Ivory Coast)
Sassandra 74 D5 var. Ibo, Sassandra
Fleuve. river S Côte d'Ivoire
(Ivory Coast)
Sassandra Fleuve see Sassandra
Sassari 97 A5 Sardegna, Italy,
C Mediterranean Sea
Sassenheim 86 C3 Zuid-Holland,
W Netherlands
Sassnitz 94 D2 Mecklenburg-
Vorpommern, NE Germany

Sathmar see Satu Mare
Sátoraljaújhely 99 D6 Borsod-Abaúj-
Zemplén, NE Hungary
Sātpura Range 134 D4 mountain range
C India
Satsunan-shotō 130 A3 island group
Nansei-shotō, SW Japan Asia
Sattanen 84 D3 Lappi, NE Finland
Satu Mare 108 B3 Ger. Sathmar,
Hung. Szatmárrnémeti. Satu Mare,
NW Romania
Sau see Sava
Saudi Arabia 121 B5 off. Kingdom
of Saudi Arabia, Al 'Arabiyah as
Su'ūdiyah, Ar. Al Mamlakah al
'Arabiyah as Su'ūdiyah. country
SW Asia

SAUDI ARABIA
Souhwest Asia

Official name Kingdom of Saudi Arabia
Formation 1932 / 1932
Capital Riyadh
Population 24.6 million / 30 people per
sq mile (12 people per sq km) / 86%
Total area 756,981 sq miles
(1,960,582 sq km)
Languages Arabic*
Religions Sunni Muslim 85%, Shi'a
Muslim 15%
Ethnic mix Arab 90%, Afro-Asian 10%
Government Monarchy
Currency Saudi riyal = 100 halalat
Literacy rate 79%
Calorie consumption 2844 calories

Saudi Arabia, Kingdom of see Saudi
Arabia
Sauer see Sûre
Saugor see Ságar
Saulkrasti 106 C3 Riga, C Latvia
Sault Sainte Marie 40 C1 Michigan,
N USA
Sault Ste. Marie 38 C4 Ontario, S Canada
Saumur 90 B4 Maine-et-Loire,
NW France
Saurimo 78 C1 Port. Henrique de
Carvalho, Vila Henrique de Carvalho.
Lunda Sul, NE Angola
Sava 107 E6 Rus. Sava. Mahilyowskaya
Voblasts', E Belarus
Savá 52 D2 Colón, N Honduras
Sava 100 B3 Eng. Save, Ger. Sau, Hung.
Száva. river SE Europe
Savai'i 145 E4 island NW Samoa
Savannah 43 E2 Georgia, SE USA
Savannah River 43 E2 river Georgia/
South Carolina, SE USA
Savannakhét see Khanthabouli
Savanna-La-Mar 54 A5 W Jamaica
Savaria see Szombathely
Save see Sava
Save, Rio 79 E3 var. Sabi. river
Mozambique/Zimbabwe
Saverne 90 E3 var. Zabern; anc. Tres
Tabernae. Bas-Rhin, NE France
Savigliano 96 A2 Piemonte, NW Italy
Savigsivik see Savissivik
Savinski see Savinskiy
Savinskiy 110 C3 var. Savinski.
Arkhangel'skaya Oblast', NW Russian
Federation
Savissivik 82 D1 var. Savigsivik.
Avannaarsua, N Greenland
Savoie 91 D5 department E France
Savoie 91 D5 cultural region E France
Savona 96 A2 Liguria, NW Italy
Savu Sea 139 E5 Ind. Laut Sawu. sea
S Indonesia
Sawakin see Suakin
Sawdirī see Sodiri
Sawhāj see Sohâg
Şawqirah 121 D6 var. Suqrah. S Oman
Sawu, Laut see Savu Sea
Saxe see Sachsen
Saxony see Sachsen
Sayaboury see Xaignabouli
Sayanskiy Khrebet 112 D3 mountain
range S Russian Federation
Saýat 122 D3 Rus. Sayat. Lebap
Welaýaty, E Turkmenistan
Sayaxché 52 B2 Petén, N Guatemala
Saydā/Sayida see Saïda
Şaÿhūt 121 E6 E Yemen
Saynshand 127 E2 Dornogovī,
SE Mongolia
Sayre 41 E3 Pennsylvania, NE USA

Say'ūn 121 C6 var. Saywūn. C Yemen
Saywūn see Say'ūn
Scalabis see Santarém
Scandinavia 66 D2 geophysical region
NW Europe
Scarborough 89 D5 N England, UK
Scarpanto see Kárpathos
Scebeli see Shebeli
Schaan 94 E1 W Liechtenstein Europe
Schaerbeek 87 C6 Brussels, C Belgium
Schaffhausen 95 B7 Fr. Schaffhouse.
Schaffhausen, N Switzerland
Schaffhouse see Schaffhausen
Schagen 86 C2 Noord-Holland,
NW Netherlands
Schaulen see Šiauliai
Schebschi Mountains see Shebshi
Mountains
Scheessel 94 B3 Niedersachsen,
NW Germany
Schefferville 39 E2 Québec, E Canada
Schelde see Scheldt
Scheldt 87 B5 Dut. Schelde, Fr. Escaut.
river W Europe
Schell Creek Range 47 D5 mountain
range Nevada, W USA
Schenectady 41 F3 New York, NE USA
Schertz 49 G4 Texas, SW USA
Schiermonnikoog 86 D1 Fris.
Skiermûntseach. island
Waddeneilanden, N Netherlands
Schijndel 86 D4 Noord-Brabant,
S Netherlands
Schil see Jiu
Schiltigheim 90 E3 Bas-Rhin, NE France
Schivelbein see Świdwin
Schlackenwerth see Ostrov
Schleswig 94 B2 Schleswig-Holstein,
N Germany
Schleswig-Holstein 94 B2 state
N Germany
Schlettstadt see Sélestat
Schlochau see Człuchów
Schneekoppe see Sněžka
Schneidemühl see Piła
Schoden see Skuodas
Schönebeck 94 C4 Sachsen-Anhalt,
C Germany
Schönlanke see Trzcianka
Schooten see Schoten
Schoten 87 C5 var. Schooten.
Antwerpen, N Belgium
Schouwen 86 B4 island SW Netherlands
Schwabenalb see Schwäbische Alb
Schwäbische Alb 95 B6 var.
Schwabenalb, Eng. Swabian Jura.
mountain range S Germany
Schwandorf 95 C5 Bayern, SE Germany
Schwarzwald 95 B6 Eng. Black Forest.
mountain range SW Germany
Schwaz 95 C7 Tirol, W Austria
Schweidnitz see Świdnica
Schweinfurt 95 B5 Bayern, SE Germany
Schweiz see Switzerland
Schwerin 94 C3 Mecklenburg-
Vorpommern, N Germany
Schwertberg see Świecie
Schwiebus see Świebodzin
Schwyz 95 B7 var. Schwiz. Schwyz,
C Switzerland
Schyl see Jiu
Scilly, Isles of 89 B8 island group
SW England, UK
Scio see Chíos
Scoresby Sound/Scoresbysund see
Ittoqqortoormiit
Scoresby Sund see Kangertittivaq
Scotia Sea 57 C8 sea SW Atlantic Ocean
Scotland 88 C3 cultural region Scotland,
U K
Scotland 88 C3 national region
Scotland, U K
Scott Base 154 B4 NZ research station
Antarctica
Scott Island 154 B5 island Antarctica
Scottsbluff 44 D3 Nebraska, C USA
Scottsboro 42 D1 Alabama, S USA
Scottsdale 48 B2 Arizona, SW USA
Scranton 41 F3 Pennsylvania,
NE USA
Scrobesbyrig' see Shrewsbury
Scupi see Skopje
Scutari see Shkodër
Scutari, Lake 101 C5 Alb. Liqeni i
Shkodrës, SCr. Skadarsko Jezero. lake
Albania/Montenegro
Scyros see Skýros
Searcy 42 B1 Arkansas, C USA

237

Seattle *46 B2* Washington, NW USA
Sébaco *52 D3* Matagalpa, W Nicaragua
Sebaste/Sebastia *see* Sivas
Sebastían Vizcaíno, Bahía *50 A2 bay* NW Mexico
Sebastopol *see* Sevastopol'
Sebenico *see* Šibenik
Sechura, Bahía de *60 A3 bay* NW Peru
Secunderābād *134 D5 var.* Sikandarabad. Andhra Pradesh, C India
Sedan *90 D3* Ardennes, N France
Seddon *151 D5* Marlborough, South Island, New Zealand
Seddonville *151 C5* West Coast, South Island, New Zealand
Sédhiou *74 B3* SW Senegal
Sedlez *see* Siedlce
Sedona *48 B2* Arizona, SW USA
Sedunum *see* Sion
Seeland *see* Sjælland
Seesen *94 B4* Niedersachsen, C Germany
Segestica *see* Sisak
Segezha *110 B3* Respublika Kareliya, NW Russian Federation
Seghedin *see* Szeged
Segna *see* Senj
Segodunum *see* Rodez
Ségou *74 D3 var.* Segu. Ségou, C Mali
Segovia *92 D2* Castilla-León, C Spain
Segoviao Wangkí *see* Coco, Río
Segu *see* Ségou
Séguédine *75 H2* Agadez, NE Niger
Seguin *49 G4* Texas, SW USA
Segura *93 E4 river* S Spain
Seinäjoki *85 D5 Swe.* Östermyra. Länsi-Soumi, W Finland
Seine *90 D1 river* N France
Seine, Baie de la *90 B3 bay* N France
Sekondi *see* Sekondi-Takoradi
Sekondi-Takoradi *75 E5 var.* Sekondi. S Ghana
Selânik *see* Thessaloníki
Selenga *127 E1 Mong.* Selenge Mörön. *river* Mongolia/Russian Federation
Selenge Mörön *see* Selenga
Sélestat *90 E4 Ger.* Schlettstadt. Bas-Rhin, NE France
Seleucia *see* Silifke
Selfoss *83 E5* Sudhurland, SW Iceland
Sélibabi *74 C3 var.* Sélibaby. Guidimaka, S Mauritania
Sélibaby *see* Sélibabi
Selma *47 C6* California, W USA
Selway River *46 D2 river* Idaho, NW USA North America
Selwyn Range *148 B3 mountain range* Queensland, C Australia
Selzaete *see* Zelzate
Semarang *138 C5 var.* Samarang. Jawa, C Indonesia
Sembé *77 B5* La Sangha, NW Congo
Semendria *see* Smederevo
Semey *see* Semipalatinsk
Semezhevo *see* Syemyezhava
Seminole *49 E3* Texas, SW USA
Seminole, Lake *42 D3 reservoir* Florida/Georgia, SE USA
Semipalatinsk *114 D4 Kaz.* Semey. Vostochnyy Kazakhstan, E Kazakhstan
Semnān *120 D3 var.* Samnān. Semnān, N Iran
Semois *87 C8 river* SE Belgium
Sendai *131 A8* Kagoshima, Kyūshū, SW Japan
Sendai *130 D4* Miyagi, Honshū, C Japan
Sendai-wan *130 D4 bay* E Japan
Senec *99 C6 Ger.* Wartberg, *Hung.* Szenc; *prev.* Szempcz. Bratislavský Kraj, W Slovakia
Senegal *74 B3 off.* Republic of Senegal, *Fr.* Sénégal. *country* W Africa

SENEGAL
West Africa

Official name Republic of Senegal
Formation 1960 / 1960
Capital Dakar
Population 11.7 million / 157 people per sq mile (61 people per sq km) / 47%
Total area 75,749 sq miles (196,190 sq km)
Languages French*, Diola, Mandinka, Malinke, Pulaar, Serer, Soninke, Wolof
Religions Sunni Muslim 90%, Christian (mainly Roman Catholic) 5%, Traditional beliefs 5%
Ethnic mix Wolof 43%, Toucouleur 24%, Serer 15%, Other 11%, Diola 4%, Malinke 3%
Government Presidential system
Currency CFA franc = 100 centimes
Literacy rate 39%
Calorie consumption 2279 calories

Senegal *74 C3 Fr.* Sénégal. *river* W Africa
Senegal, Republic of *see* Senegal
Senftenberg *94 D4* Brandenburg, E Germany
Senia *see* Senj
Senica *99 C6 Ger.* Senitz, *Hung.* Szenice. Trnavský Kraj, W Slovakia
Seniça *see* Sjenica
Senitz *see* Senica
Senj *100 A3 Ger.* Zengg, *It.* Segna; *anc.* Senia. Lika-Senj, NW Croatia
Senja *84 C2 prev.* Senjen. *island* N Norway
Senjen *see* Senja
Senkaku-shotō *130 A3 island group* SW Japan
Senlis *90 C3* Oise, N France
Sennar *72 C4 var.* Sannār. Sinnar, C Sudan
Senones *see* Sens
Sens *90 C3 anc.* Agendicum, Senones. Yonne, C France
Sensburg *see* Mrągowo
Sên, Stœng *137 D5 river* C Cambodia
Senta *100 D3 Hung.* Zenta. Vojvodina, N Serbia
Seo de Urgel *see* La See d'Urgel
Seoul *see* Sŏul
Şepşi-Sângeorz/Sepsiszentgyőrgy *see* Sfântu Gheorghe
Sept-Îles *39 E3* Québec, SE Canada
Seraing *87 D6* Liège, E Belgium
Serakhs *see* Sarahs
Seram, Laut *see* Ceram Sea
Seram, Pulau *139 F4 var.* Serang, *Eng.* Ceram. *island* Maluku, E Indonesia
Serang *138 C5* Jawa, C Indonesia
Serang *see* Seram, Pulau
Serasan, Selat *138 C3 strait* Indonesia/Malaysia
Serbia *100 D4 off.* Federal Republic of Serbia; *prev.* Yugoslavia, *SCr.* Jugoslavija. *country* SE Europe

SERBIA
Europe

Official name Republic of Serbia
Formation 2006 / 2006
Capital Belgrade
Population 9.7 million / 290 people per sq mile (112 people per sq km) / 52%
Total area 34,116 sq miles (88,361 sq km)
Languages Serbo-Croat*, Albanian, Hungarian
Religions Orthodox Christian 85%, Muslim 6%, Other 6%, Roman Catholic 3%
Ethnic mix Serb 66%, Albanian 19%, Hungarian 4%, Bosniak 2%, Other 9%
Government Parliamentary system
Currency Dinar (Serbia) = 100 para
Literacy rate 98%
Calorie consumption Not available

Serbia, Federal Republic of *see* Serbia
Sercq *see* Sark
Serdar *122 C2 prev. Rus.* Gyzyrlabat, Kizyl-Arvat. Balkan Welaýaty, W Turkmenistan
Serdica *see* Sofiya
Serenje *78 D2* Central, E Zambia
Seres *see* Sérres
Seret/Sereth *see* Siret
Serhetabat *122 D4 prev. Rus.* Gushgy, Kushka. Mary Welaýaty, S Turkmenistan
Sérifos *105 C6 anc.* Seriphos. *island* Kykládes, Greece, Aegean Sea
Seriphos *see* Sérifos
Serov *114 C3* Sverdlovskaya Oblast', C Russian Federation
Serowe *78 D3* Central, SE Botswana
Serpa Pinto *see* Menongue
Serpent's Mouth, The *59 F2 Sp.* Boca de la Serpiente. *strait* Trinidad and Tobago/Venezuela
Serpiente, Boca de la *see* Serpent's Mouth, The
Serpukhov *111 B5* Moskovskaya Oblast', W Russian Federation
Sérrai *see* Sérres
Serrana, Cayo de *53 F2 island group* NW Colombia South America
Serranilla, Cayo de *53 F2 island group* NW Colombia South America Caribbean Sea
Serravalle *96 E1* N San Marino
Sérres *104 C3 var.* Seres; *prev.* Sérrai. Kentrikí Makedonía, NE Greece
Sesdlets *see* Siedlce
Sesto San Giovanni *96 B2* Lombardia, N Italy
Sesvete *100 B2* Zagreb, N Croatia
Setabis *see* Xátiva
Sète *91 C6 prev.* Cette. Hérault, S France
Setesdal *85 A6 valley* S Norway
Sétif *71 E2 var.* Stif. N Algeria
Setté Cama *77 A6* Ogooué-Maritime, SW Gabon
Setúbal *92 B4 Eng.* Saint Ubes, Saint Yves. Setúbal, W Portugal
Setúbal, Baía de *92 B4 bay* W Portugal
Seul, Lac *38 B3 lake* Ontario, S Canada
Sevan *117 G2* C Armenia
Sevana Lich *117 G3 Eng.* Lake Sevan, *Rus.* Ozero Sevan. *lake* E Armenia
Sevan, Lake/Sevan, Ozero *see* Sevana Lich
Sevastopol' *109 F5 Eng.* Sebastopol. Respublika Krym, S Ukraine
Severn *38 B2 river* Ontario, S Canada
Severn *89 D6 Wel.* Hafren. *river* England/Wales, UK
Severnaya Dvina *110 C4 var.* Northern Dvina. *river* NW Russian Federation
Severnaya Zemlya *115 E2 var.* Nicholas II Land. *island group* N Russian Federation
Severnyy *110 E3* Respublika Komi, NW Russian Federation
Severodonetsk *see* Syeverodonets'k
Severodvinsk *110 C3 prev.* Molotov, Sudostroy. Arkhangel'skaya Oblast', NW Russian Federation
Severomorsk *110 C2* Murmanskaya Oblast', NW Russian Federation
Severo-Sibirskaya Nizmennost' *115 E2 var.* North Siberian Plain, *Eng.* North Siberian Lowland. *lowlands* N Russian Federation
Seversk *114 D4* Tomskaya Oblast', C Russian Federation
Sevier Lake *44 A4 lake* Utah, W USA
Sevilla *92 C4 Eng.* Seville; *anc.* Hispalis. Andalucía, SW Spain
Seville *see* Sevilla
Sevlievo *104 D2* Gabrovo, N Bulgaria
Sevluš/Sevlyush *see* Vynohradiv
Seward's Folly *see* Alaska
Seychelles *79 G1 country* W Indian Ocean

SEYCHELLES
Indian Ocean

Official name Republic of Seychelles
Formation 1976 / 1976
Capital Victoria
Population 81,188 / 781 people per sq mile (301 people per sq km) / 64%
Total area 176 sq miles (455 sq km)
Languages French Creole*, English, French
Religions Anglican 8%, Roman Catholic 90%, Other (including Muslim) 2%
Ethnic mix Creole 89%, Indian 5%, Other 4%, Chinese 2%
Government Presidential system
Currency Seychelles rupee = 100 cents
Literacy rate 92%
Calorie consumption 2465 calories

Seychelles *79 G1 island group* NE Seychelles
Seydhisfjördhur *83 E5* Austurland, E Iceland
Seýdi *122 D2 Rus.* Seydi; *prev.* Neftezavodsk. Lebap Welaýaty, E Turkmenistan
Seyhan *see* Adana
Sfákia *see* Chóra Sfakíon
Sfântu Gheorghe *108 C4 Ger.* Sankt-Georgen, *Hung.* Sepsiszentgyőrgy; *prev.* Şepşi-Sângeorz, Sfîntu Gheorghe. Covasna, C Romania
Sfax *71 F2 Ar.* Şafāqis. E Tunisia
Sfîntu Gheorghe *see* Sfântu Gheorghe
's-Gravenhage *86 B4 var.* Den Haag, *Eng.* The Hague, *Fr.* La Haye. *country capital* (Netherlands-seat of government) Zuid-Holland, W Netherlands
's-Gravenzande *86 B4* Zuid-Holland, W Netherlands
Shaan/Shaanxi Sheng *see* Shaanxi
Shaanxi *128 B5 var.* Shaan, Shaanxi Sheng, Shan-hsi, Shenshi, Shensi. *province* C China
Shabani *see* Zvishavane
Shabeelle, Webi *see* Shebeli
Shache *126 A3 var.* Yarkant. Xinjiang Uygur Zizhiqu, NW China
Shacheng *see* Huailai
Shackleton Ice Shelf *154 D3 ice shelf* Antarctica
Shaddādī *see* Ash Shadādah
Shāhābād *see* Eslāmābād
Shahjahanabad *see* Delhi
Shahr-e Kord *120 C3 var.* Shahr Kord. Chahār Maḩall va Bakhtīārī, C Iran
Shahr Kord *see* Shahr-e Kord
Shāhrūd *120 D2 prev.* Emāmrūd, Emāmshahr. Semnān, N Iran
Shalkar *114 B4 var.* Chelkar. Aktyubinsk, W Kazakhstan
Shām, Bādiyat ash *see* Syrian Desert
Shandī *see* Shendi
Shandong *128 D4 var.* Lu, Shandong Sheng, Shantung. *province* E China
Shandong Sheng *see* Shandong
Shanghai *128 D5 var.* Shang-hai. Shanghai Shi, E China
Shanghi Shi *129 D5 var.* Hu, Shanghai. *municipality* E China
Shanghai *see* Shanghi Shi
Shangrao *128 D5* Jiangxi, S China
Shan-hsi *see* Shaanxi, China
Shan-hsi *see* Shanxi, China
Shannon *89 A6 Ir.* An tSionainn. *river* W Ireland
Shan Plateau *136 B3 plateau* E Myanmar (Burma)
Shansi *see* Shanxi
Shantar Islands *see* Shantarskiye Ostrova
Shantarskiye Ostrova *115 G3 Eng.* Shantar Islands. *island group* E Russian Federation
Shantou *128 D6 var.* Shan-t'ou, Swatow. Guangdong, S China
Shan-t'ou *see* Shantou
Shantung *see* Shandong
Shanxi *128 C4 var.* Jin, Shan-hsi, Shansi, Shanxi Sheng. *province* C China
Shan Xian *see* Sanmenxia
Shanxi Sheng *see* Shanxi
Shaoguan *128 C6 var.* Shao-kuan, *Cant.* Kukong; *prev.* Ch'u-chiang. Guangdong, S China
Shao-kuan *see* Shaoguan
Shaqrā' *120 B4* Ar Riyāḑ, C Saudi Arabia
Shaqrā *see* Shuqrah
Shar *130 D5 var.* Charsk. Vostochnyy Kazakhstan, E Kazakhstan
Shari *130 D2* Hokkaidō, NE Japan
Shari *see* Chari
Sharjah *see* Ash Shāriqah
Shark Bay *147 A5 bay* Western Australia
Sharqī, Al Jabal ash/Sharqi, Jebel esh *see* Anti-Lebanon
Shashe *78 D3 var.* Shashi. *river* Botswana/Zimbabwe
Shashi *see* Shashe
Shatskiy Rise *125 G1 undersea rise* N Pacific Ocean
Shawnee *49 G1* Oklahoma, C USA
Shaykh, Jabal ash *see* Hermon, Mount
Shchadryn *107 D7 Rus.* Shchedrin. Homyel'skaya Voblasts', SE Belarus
Shchedrin *see* Shchadryn
Shcheglovsk *see* Kemerovo
Shchëkino *111 B5* Tul'skaya Oblast', W Russian Federation
Shchors *109 E1* Chernihivs'ka Oblast', N Ukraine

Shchuchin see Shchuchyn
Shchuchinsk 114 C4 prev. Shchuchye.
Akmola, N Kazakhstan
Shchuchye see Shchuchinsk
Shchuchyn 107 B5 Pol. Szczuczyn
Nowogródzki, Rus. Shchuchin.
Hrodzyenskaya Voblasts', W Belarus
Shebekino 111 A6 Belgorodskaya
Oblast', W Russian Federation
Shebelē Wenz, Wabē see Shebeli
Shebeli 73 D5 Amh. Wabē Shebelē Wenz,
It. Scebeli, Som. Webi Shabeelle. river
Ethiopia/Somalia
Sheberghān 123 E3 var. Shibarghān,
Shiberghan, Shiberghān. Jowzjān,
N Afghanistan
Sheboygan 40 B2 Wisconsin, N USA
Shebshi Mountains 76 A4 var.
Schebschi Mountains. mountain range
E Nigeria
Shechem see Nablus
Shedadi see Ash Shadādah
Sheffield 89 D5 N England, UK
Shekhem see Nablus
Sheki see Şäki
Shelby 44 B1 Montana, NW USA
Sheldon 45 F3 Iowa, C USA
Shelekhov Gulf see Shelikhova, Zaliv
Shelikhova, Zaliv 115 G2
Eng. Shelekhov Gulf. gulf E Russian
Federation
Shendi 72 C4 var. Shandi. River Nile,
NE Sudan
Shengking see Liaoning
Shenking see Liaoning
Shenshi/Shensi see Shaanxi
Shenyang 128 D3 Chin. Shen-yang, Eng.
Moukden, Mukden; prev. Fengtien.
province capital Liaoning, NE China
Shen-yang see Shenyang
Shepetivka 108 D2 Rus. Shepetovka.
Khmel'nyts'ka Oblast', NW Ukraine
Shepetovka see Shepetivka
Shepparton 149 C7 Victoria,
SE Australia
Sherbrooke 39 E4 Québec, SE Canada
Shereik 72 C3 River Nile, N Sudan
Sheridan 44 C2 Wyoming, C USA
Sherman 49 G2 Texas, SW USA
's-Hertogenbosch 86 C4 Fr. Bois-le-
Duc, Ger. Herzogenbusch. Noord-
Brabant, S Netherlands
Shetland Islands 88 D1 island group
NE Scotland, UK
Shevchenko see Aktau
Shibarghān see Sheberghān
Shiberghan/Shiberghān see Sheberghān
Shibetsu 130 D2 var. Sibetu. Hokkaidō,
NE Japan
Shibh Jazīrat Sīnā see Sinai
Shibushi-wan 131 B8 bay SW Japan
Shigatse see Xigazê
Shih-chia-chuang/Shihmen see
Shijiazhuang
Shihezi 126 C2 Xinjiang Uygur Zizhiqu,
NW China
Shiichi see Shyichy
Shijiazhuang 128 C4 var. Shih-chia-
chuang; prev. Shihmen. province
capital Hebei, E China
Shikārpur 134 B3 Sind, S Pakistan
Shikoku 131 C7 var. Sikoku. island
SW Japan
Shikoku Basin 125 F2 var. Sikoku Basin.
undersea basin N Philippine Sea
Shikotan, Ostrov 130 E2 Jap. Shikotan-
tō. island NE Russian Federation
Shikotan-tō see Shikotan, Ostrov
Shilabo 73 D5 Somali, E Ethiopia
Shiliguri 135 F3 prev. Siliguri. West
Bengal, NE India
Shilka 115 F4 river S Russian Federation
Shillong 135 G3 state capital Meghālaya,
NE India
Shimbir Berris see Shimbiris
Shimbiris 72 E4 var. Shimbir Berris.
mountain N Somalia
Shimoga 132 C2 Karnātaka, W India
Shimonoseki 131 A7 var. Simonoseki,
hist. Akamagaseki, Bakan. Yamaguchi,
Honshū, SW Japan
Shinano-gawa 131 C5 var. Sinano Gawa.
river Honshū, C Japan
Shindand 122 D4 Herāt, W Afghanistan
Shingū 131 C6 var. Singû. Wakayama,
Honshū, SW Japan
Shinjō 130 D4 var. Sinzyô. Yamagata,
Honshū, C Japan

Shinyanga 73 C7 Shinyanga,
NW Tanzania
Shiprock 48 C1 New Mexico, SW USA
Shīrāz 120 D4 var. Shīrāz. Fārs, S Iran
Shishchitsy see Shyshchytsy
Shivpuri 134 D3 Madhya Pradesh,
C India
Shizugawa 130 D4 Miyagi, Honshū,
NE Japan
Shizuoka 131 D6 var. Sizuoka. Shizuoka,
Honshū, S Japan
Shklov see Shklow
Shklow 107 D6 Rus. Shklov.
Mahilyowskaya Voblasts', E Belarus
Shkodër 101 C5 var. Shkodra, It. Scutari,
SCr. Skadar. Shkodër, NW Albania
Shkodra see Shkodër
Shkodrës, Liqeni i see Scutari, Lake
Shkumbinit, Lumi i 101 C6 var.
Shkumbi, Shkumbin. river C Albania
Shkumbi/Shkumbin see Shkumbinit,
Lumi i
Sholāpur see Solāpur
Shostka 109 F1 Sums ka Oblast',
NE Ukraine
Show Low 48 B2 Arizona,
SW USA
Show Me State see Missouri
Shpola 109 E3 Cherkas'ka Oblast',
N Ukraine
Shqipëria/Shqipërisë, Republika e
see Albania
Shreveport 42 A2 Louisiana, S USA
Shrewsbury 89 D6 hist. Scrobesbyrig'.
W England, UK
Shu 114 C5 Kaz. Shū. Zhambyl,
SE Kazakhstan
Shū see Shu
Shuang-liao see Liaoyuan
Shumagin Islands 36 B3 island group
Alaska, USA
Shumen 104 D2 Shumen, NE Bulgaria
Shumilina 107 E5 Rus. Shumilino.
Vitsyebskaya Voblasts', NE Belarus
Shumilino see Shumilina
Shunsen see Ch'unch'ŏn
Shuqrah 121 B7 var. Shaqrā.
SW Yemen
Shwebo 136 B3 Sagaing,
C Myanmar (Burma)
Shyichy 107 C7 Rus. Shiichi.
Homyel'skaya Voblasts', SE Belarus
Shymkent 114 B5 prev. Chimkent.
Yuzhnyy Kazakhstan, S Kazakhstan
Shyshchytsy 107 C6 Rus. Shishchitsy.
Minskaya Voblasts', C Belarus
Siam see Thailand
Siam, Gulf of see Thailand, Gulf of
Sian see Xi'an
Siang see Brahmaputra
Siangtan see Xiangtan
Šiauliai 106 B4 Ger. Schaulen. Šiauliai,
N Lithuania
Siazan' see Siyäzän
Sibay 111 D6 Respublika Bashkortostan,
W Russian Federation
Šibenik 116 B4 It. Sebenico. Šibenik-
Knin, S Croatia
Siberia see Sibir'
Siberoet see Siberut, Pulau
Siberut, Pulau 138 A4 prev. Siberoet.
island Kepulauan Mentawai,
W Indonesia
Sibi 134 B2 Baluchistān, SW Pakistan
Sibir' 115 E3 var. Siberia. physical region
NE Russian Federation
Sibiti 77 B6 La Lékoumou, S Congo
Sibiu 108 B4 Ger. Hermannstadt, Hung.
Nagyszeben. Sibiu, C Romania
Sibolga 138 B3 Sumatera, W Indonesia
Sibu 138 D3 Sarawak, East Malaysia
Sibut 76 C4 prev. Fort-Sibut. Kémo,
S Central African Republic
Sibuyan Sea 139 E2 sea W Pacific Ocean
Sichon 137 C6 var. Ban Sichon, Si Chon.
Nakhon Si Thammarat, SW Thailand
Si Chon see Sichon
Sichuan 128 B5 var. Chuan, Sichuan
Sheng, Ssu-ch'uan, Szechuan,
Szechwan. province C China
Sichuan Pendi 128 B5 basin C China
Sichuan Sheng see Sichuan
Sicilia 97 C7 Eng. Sicily; anc. Trinacria.
island Italy, C Mediterranean Sea
Sicilian Channel see Sicily, Strait of
Sicily, Strait of 97 B7 var. Sicilian
Channel. strait C Mediterranean Sea
Sicuani 61 E4 Cusco, S Peru

Sidári 104 A4 Kérkyra, Iónia Nisiá,
Greece, C Mediterranean Sea
Sidas 138 C4 Borneo, C Indonesia
Siderno 97 D7 Calabria, SW Italy
Sidhirókastron see Sidirókastro
Sīdī Barrānī 72 A1 NW Egypt
Sidi Bel Abbès 70 D2 var. Sīdī bel Abbès,
Sidi-Bel-Abbès. NW Algeria
Sidirókastro 104 C3 prev.
Sidhirókastron. Kentrikí Makedonía,
NE Greece
Sidley, Mount 154 B4 mountain
Antarctica
Sidney 44 D1 Montana, NW USA
Sidney 44 D4 Nebraska, C USA
Sidney 40 C4 Ohio, N USA
Sidon see Saïda
Sidra see Surt
Sidra/Sidra, Gulf of see Surt, Khalīj,
N Libya
Siebenbürgen see Transylvania
Siedlce 98 E3 Ger. Sedlez, Rus. Sesdlets.
Mazowieckie, C Poland
Siegen 94 B3 Nordrhein-Westfalen,
W Germany
Siemiatycze 98 E3 Podlaskie, NE Poland
Siena 96 B3 Fr. Sienne; anc. Saena Julia.
Toscana, C Italy
Sienne see Siena
Sieradz 98 C4 Sieradz, C Poland
Sierpc 98 D3 Mazowieckie, C Poland
Sierra Leone 74 C4 off. Republic of Sierra
Leone. country W Africa

SIERRA LEONE
West Africa

Official name Republic of
Sierra Leone
Formation 1961 / 1961
Capital Freetown
Population 5.5 million / 199 people per
sq mile (77 people per sq km) / 37%
Total area 27,698 sq miles
(71,740 sq km)
Languages English*, Mende, Temne, Krio
Religions Muslim 30%, Traditional
beliefs 30%, Other 30%, Christian 10%
Ethnic mix Mende 35%, Temne 32%,
Other 21%, Limba 8%, Kuranko 4%
Government Presidential system
Currency Leone = 100 cents
Literacy rate 30%
Calorie consumption 1936 calories

Sierra Leone Basin 66 C4 undersea basin
E Atlantic Ocean
Sierra Leone, Republic of see Sierra
Leone
Sierra Leone Ridge see Sierra Leone Rise
Sierra Leone Rise 66 C4 var. Sierra
Leone Ridge, Sierra Leone Schwelle.
undersea rise E Atlantic Ocean
Sierra Leone Schwelle see Sierra
Leone Rise
Sierra Madre 52 B2 var. Sierra
de Soconusco. mountain range
Guatemala/Mexico
Sierra Madre del Sur 51 E5 mountain
range S Mexico
Sierra Madre Occidental 50 C3 var.
Western Sierra Madre. mountain range
C Mexico
Sierra Madre Oriental 51 E3 var.
Eastern Sierra Madre. mountain range
C Mexico
Sierra Nevada 52 D5 mountain range
S Spain
Sierra Nevada 47 C6 mountain range
W USA
Sierra Vieja 48 D3 mountain range
Texas, SW USA
Sierra Vista 48 B3 Arizona, SW USA
Sífnos 105 C6 anc. Siphnos. island
Kykládes, Greece, Aegean Sea
Sigli 138 A3 Sumatera, W Indonesia
Siglufjördhur 83 E4 Nordhurland
Vestra, N Iceland
Signal Peak 48 A2 mountain Arizona,
SW USA
Signan see Xi'an
Signy 154 A2 UK research station South
Orkney Islands, Antarctica
Siguatepeque 52 C2 Comayagua,
W Honduras
Siguiri 74 D4 NE Guinea
Sihanoukville see Kâmpóng Saôm
Siilinjärvi 84 E4 Itä-Suomi, C Finland

Siirt 117 F4 var. Sert; anc. Tigranocerta.
Siirt, SE Turkey
Sikandarabad see Secunderābād
Sikasso 74 D4 Sikasso, S Mali
Sikeston 45 H5 Missouri, C USA
Sikhote-Alin', Khrebet 115 G4
mountain range SE Russian Federation
Sikinos see Xi'an
Siklós 99 C7 Baranya, SW Hungary
Sikoku see Shikoku
Sikoku Basin see Shikoku Basin
Šilalė 106 B4 Tauragė, W Lithuania
Silchar 135 G3 Assam, NE India
Silesia 98 B4 physical region
SW Poland
Silifke 116 C4 anc. Seleucia. Mersin,
S Turkey
Siliguri see Shiliguri
Siling Co 126 C5 lake W China
Silinhot see Xilinhot
Silistra 104 E1 var. Silistria; anc.
Durostorum. Silistra, NE Bulgaria
Silistria see Silistra
Sillamäe 106 E2 Ger. Sillamäggi. Ida-
Virumaa, NE Estonia
Sillamäggi see Sillamäe
Sillein see Žilina
Šilutė 106 B4 Ger. Heydekrug. Klaipėda,
W Lithuania
Sılvan 117 E4 Diyarbakır, SE Turkey
Silva Porto see Kuito
Silver State see Colorado
Silver State see Nevada
Simanichy 107 C7 Rus. Simonichi.
Homyel'skaya Voblasts', SE Belarus
Simav 116 B3 Kütahya, W Turkey
Simav Çayı 116 A3 river NW Turkey
Simbirsk see Ul'yanovsk
Simeto 97 C7 river Sicilia, Italy,
C Mediterranean Sea
Simeulue, Pulau 138 A3 island
NW Indonesia
Simferopol' 109 F5 Respublika Krym,
S Ukraine
Simitla 104 C3 Blagoevgrad, SW Bulgaria
Şimläul Silvaniei/Şimleul Silvaniei see
Şimleu Silvaniei
Şimleu Silvaniei 108 B3 Hung.
Szilágysomlyó; prev. Simläul Silvaniei,
Şimleul Silvaniei. Sälaj, NW Romania
Simonichi see Simanichy
Simonoseki see Shimonoseki
Simpelveld 87 D6 Limburg,
SE Netherlands
Simplon Pass 95 B8 pass S Switzerland
Simpson see Fort Simpson
Simpson Desert 148 B4 desert Northern
Territory/South Australia
Sinai 72 C2 var. Sinai Peninsula, Ar.
Shibh Jazīrat Sīnā, Sīnā'. physical
region NE Egypt
Sinaia 108 C4 Prahova, SE Romania
Sinano Gawa see Shinano-gawa
Sīnā'/Sinai Peninsula see Sinai
Sincelejo 58 B2 Sucre, NW Colombia
Sind 134 B3 var. Sindh. province
SE Pakistan
Sindelfingen 95 B6 Baden-Württemberg,
SW Germany
Sindh see Sind
Sindi 106 D2 Ger. Zintenhof. Pärnumaa,
SW Estonia
Sines 92 B4 Setúbal, S Portugal
Singan see Xi'an
Singapore 138 A1 off. Republic of
Singapore. country SE Asia

SINGAPORE
Southeast Asia

Official name Republic of Singapore
Formation 1965 / 1965
Capital Singapore
Population 4.3 million / 18220 people
per sq mile (7049 people per sq km)
/ 100%
Total area 250 sq miles (648 sq km)
Languages English*, Malay*, Mandarin*,
Tamil*
Religions Buddhist 55%, Taoist 22%,
Muslim 16%, Hindu, Christian,
and Sikh 7%
Ethnic mix Chinese 77%, Malay 14%,
Indian 8%, Other 1%
Government Parliamentary system
Currency Singapore dollar = 100 cents
Literacy rate 93%
Calorie consumption Not available

Singapore *138 B3 country capital* (Singapore) S Singapore
Singapore, Republic of *see* Singapore
Singen *95 B6* Baden-Württemberg, S Germany
Singida *73 C7* Singida, C Tanzania
Singkang *139 E4* Sulawesi, C Indonesia
Singkawang *138 C3* Borneo, C Indonesia
Singora *see* Songkhla
Singû *see* Shingū
Sining *see* Xining
Siniscola *97 A5* Sardegna, Italy, C Mediterranean Sea
Sinj *100 B4* Split-Dalmacija, SE Croatia
Sinkiang/Sinkiang Uighur Autonomous Region *see* Xinjiang Uygur Zizhiqu
Sinnamarie *see* Sinnamary
Sinnamary *59 H3 var.* Sinnamarie. N French Guiana
Sinneh *see* Sanandaj
Sinnicolau Mare *see* Sânnicolau Mare
Sinoe, Lacul *see* Sinoie, Lacul
Sinoie, Lacul *108 D5 prev.* Lacul Sinoe. *lagoon* SE Romania
Sinop *116 D2 anc.* Sinope. Sinop, N Turkey
Sinope *see* Sinop
Sinsheim *95 B6* Baden-Württemberg, SW Germany
Sint Maarten *55 G3 Eng.* Saint Martin. *island* N Netherlands Antilles
Sint-Michielsgestel *86 C4* Noord-Brabant, S Netherlands
Sîn-Miclăuş *see* Gheorgheni
Sint-Niklaas *87 B5 Fr.* Saint-Nicolas. Oost-Vlaanderen, N Belgium
Sint-Pieters-Leeuw *87 B6* Vlaams Brabant, C Belgium
Sintra *92 B3 prev.* Cintra. Lisboa, W Portugal
Sinujiif *73 E5* Nugaal, NE Somalia
Sinus Aelaniticus *see* Aqaba, Gulf of
Sinus Gallicus *see* Lion, Golfe du
Sinyang *see* Xinyang
Sinzyô *see* Shinjō
Sion *95 A7 Ger.* Sitten; *anc.* Sedunum. Valais, SW Switzerland
Sioux City *45 F3* Iowa, C USA
Sioux Falls *45 F3* South Dakota, N USA
Sioux State *see* North Dakota
Siphnos *see* Sífnos
Siping *128 D3 var.* Ssu-p'ing, Szeping; *prev.* Ssu-p'ing-chieh. Jilin, NE China
Siple, Mount *154 A4 mountain* Siple Island, Antarctica
Siquirres *53 E4* Limón, E Costa Rica
Siracusa *97 D7 Eng.* Syracuse. Sicilia, Italy, C Mediterranean Sea
Sir Edward Pellew Group *148 B2 island group* Northern Territory, NE Australia
Siret *108 C3 var.* Siretul, *Ger.* Sereth, *Rus.* Seret, *Ukr.* Siret. *river* Romania/Ukraine
Siretul *see* Siret
Siria *see* Syria
Sirikit Reservoir *136 C4 lake* N Thailand
Sīrjān *120 D4 prev.* Sa'īdābād. Kermān, S Iran
Sirna *see* Sýrna
Şırnak *117 F4* Şırnak, SE Turkey
Síros *see* Sýros
Sirte *see* Surt
Sirti, Gulf of *see* Surt, Khalīj
Sisak *100 B3 var.* Siscia, *Ger.* Sissek, *Hung.* Sziszek; *anc.* Segestica. Sisak-Moslavina, C Croatia
Siscia *see* Sisak
Sisimiut *82 C3 var.* Holsteinborg, Holsteinsborg, Holstenborg, Holstensborg. Kitaa, S Greenland
Sissek *see* Sisak
Sīstān, Daryācheh-ye *see* Şāberī, Hāmūn-e
Sitaş Cristuru *see* Cristuru Secuiesc
Siteía *105 D8 var.* Sitía. Kríti, Greece, E Mediterranean Sea
Sitges *93 G2* Cataluña, NE Spain
Sitía *see* Siteía
Sittang *136 B4 var.* Sittoung. *river* S Myanmar (Burma)
Sittard *87 D5* Limburg, SE Netherlands
Sitten *see* Sion
Sittoung *see* Sittang
Sittwe *136 A3 var.* Akyab. Arakan State, W Myanmar (Burma)
Siuna *52 D3* Región Autónoma Atlántico Norte, NE Nicaragua
Siut *see* Asyût
Sivas *116 D3 anc.* Sebastia, Sebaste. Sivas, C Turkey
Siverek *117 E4* Şanlıurfa, S Turkey
Siwa *72 A2 var.* Sīwah. NW Egypt
Sīwah *see* Siwa
Six Counties, The *see* Northern Ireland
Six-Fours-les-Plages *91 D6* Var, SE France
Siyäzän *117 H2 Rus.* Siazan'. NE Azerbaijan
Sjælland *85 B8 Eng.* Zealand, *Ger.* Seeland. *island* E Denmark
Sjar *see* Säärе
Sjenica *101 D5 Turk.* Seniça. Serbia, SW Serbia
Skadar *see* Shkodër
Skadarsko Jezero *see* Scutari, Lake
Skagerak *see* Skagerrak
Skagerrak *85 A6 var.* Skagerak. *channel* N Europe
Skagit River *46 B1 river* Washington, NW USA
Skalka *84 C3 lake* N Sweden
Skarżysko-Kamienna *98 D4* Świętokrzyskie, C Poland
Skaudvilė *106 B4* Tauragė, SW Lithuania
Skegness *89 E6* E England, UK
Skellefteå *84 D4* Västerbotten, N Sweden
Skellefteälven *84 C4 river* N Sweden
Ski *85 B6* Akershus, S Norway
Skíathos *105 C5* Skíathos, Vóreies Sporádes, Greece, Aegean Sea
Skidal' *107 B5 Rus.* Skidel'. Hrodzyenskaya Voblasts', W Belarus
Skidel' *see* Skidal'
Skiermûntseach *see* Schiermonnikoog
Skierniewice *98 D3* Łódzkie, C Poland
Skiftet *106 C1 strait* Finland Atlantic Ocean Baltic Sea Gulf of Bothnia/Gulf of Finland
Skíros *see* Skýros
Skópelos *105 C5* Skópelos, Vóreies Sporádes, Greece, Aegean Sea
Skopje *101 D6 var.* Üsküb, *Turk.* Üsküp, *prev.* Skoplje; *anc.* Scupi. *country capital* (FYR Macedonia) N FYR Macedonia
Skoplje *see* Skopje
Skovorodino *115 F4* Amurskaya Oblast', SE Russian Federation
Skuodas *106 B3 Ger.* Schoden, *Pol.* Szkudy. Klaipėda, NW Lithuania
Skye, Isle of *88 B3 island* NW Scotland, UK
Skylge *see* Terschelling
Skýros *105 C5 var.* Skíros. Skńyros, Vóreies Sporádes, Greece, Aegean Sea
Skýros *105 C5 var.* Skíros; *anc.* Scyros. *island* Vóreies Sporádes, Greece, Aegean Sea
Slagelse *85 B7* Vestsjælland, E Denmark
Slatina *100 C3 Hung.* Szlatina; *prev.* Podravska Slatina. Virovitica-Podravina, NE Croatia
Slatina *108 B5* Olt, S Romania
Slavgorod *see* Slawharad
Slavonska Požega *see* Požega
Slavonski Brod *100 C3 Ger.* Brod, *Hung.* Bród; *prev.* Brod, Brod na Savi. Brod-Posavina, NE Croatia
Slavuta *108 C2* Khmel'nyts'ka Oblast', NW Ukraine
Slavyansk *see* Slov"yans'k
Slawharad *107 E7 Rus.* Slavgorod. Mahilyowskaya Voblasts', E Belarus
Sławno *98 C2* Zachodnio-pomorskie, NW Poland
Slēmānī *see* As Sulaymānīyah
Sliema *102 B5* N Malta
Sligo *89 A5 Ir.* Sligeach. Sligo, NW Ireland
Sliven *104 D2 var.* Slivno. Sliven, C Bulgaria
Slivnitsa *104 B2* Sofiya, W Bulgaria
Slivno *see* Sliven
Slobozia *108 C5* Ialomiţa, SE Romania
Slonim *107 B6 Pol.* Słonim, *Rus.* Slonim. Hrodzyenskaya Voblasts', W Belarus
Słonim *see* Slonim
Slovakia *99 C6 off.* Slovenská Republika, *Ger.* Slowakei, *Hung.* Szlovákia, *Slvk.* Slovensko. *country* C Europe

SLOVAKIA
Central Europe

Official name Slovak Republic
Formation 1993 / 1993
Capital Bratislava
Population 5.4 million / 285 people per sq mile (110 people per sq km) / 57%
Total area 18,859 sq miles (48,845 sq km)
Languages Slovak*, Hungarian (Magyar), Czech
Religions Roman Catholic 60%, Other 18%, Atheist 10%, Protestant 8%, Orthodox Christian 4%
Ethnic mix Slovak 85%, Magyar 11%, Other 2%, Roma 1%, Czech 1%
Government Parliamentary system
Currency Slovak koruna = 100 halierov
Literacy rate 99%
Calorie consumption 2889 calories

Slovak Ore Mountains *see* Slovenské rudohorie
Slovenia *95 D8 off.* Republic of Slovenia, *Ger.* Slowenien, *Slvn.* Slovenija. *country* SE Europe

SLOVENIA
Central Europe

Official name Republic of Slovenia
Formation 1991 / 1991
Capital Ljubljana
Population 2 million / 256 people per sq mile (99 people per sq km) / 50%
Total area 7820 sq miles (20,253 sq km)
Languages Slovene*, Serbo-Croat
Religions Roman Catholic 96%, Other 3%, Muslim 1%
Ethnic mix Slovene 83%, Other 12%, Serb 2%, Croat 2%, Bosniak 1%
Government Parliamentary system
Currency Tolar = 100 stotinov
Literacy rate 99%
Calorie consumption 3001 calories

Slovenia, Republic of *see* Slovenia
Slovenija *see* Slovenia
Slovenská Republika *see* Slovakia
Slovenské rudohorie *99 D6 Eng.* Slovak Ore Mountains, *Ger.* Slowakisches Erzgebirge, Ungarisches Erzgebirge. *mountain range* C Slovakia
Slovensko *see* Slovakia
Slov"yans'k *109 G3 Rus.* Slavyansk. Donets'ka Oblast', E Ukraine
Slowakei *see* Slovakia
Slowakisches Erzgebirge *see* Slovenské rudohorie
Slowenien *see* Slovenia
Słubice *98 B3 Ger.* Frankfurt. Lubuskie, W Poland
Sluch *108 D1 river* NW Ukraine
Słupsk *98 C2 Ger.* Stolp. Pomorskie, N Poland
Slutsk *107 C6 Rus.* Slutsk. Minskaya Voblasts', S Belarus
Smallwood Reservoir *39 F2 lake* Newfoundland and Labrador, S Canada
Smara *70 B3 var.* Es Semara. N Western Sahara
Smarhon' *107 C5 Pol.* Smorgonie, *Rus.* Smorgon'. Hrodzyenskaya Voblasts', W Belarus
Smederevo *100 D4 Ger.* Semendria. Serbia, N Serbia
Smederevska Palanka *100 D4* Serbia, C Serbia
Smela *see* Smila
Smila *109 E2 Rus.* Smela. Cherkas'ka Oblast', C Ukraine
Smilten *see* Smiltene
Smiltene *106 D3 Ger.* Smilten. Valka, N Latvia
Smøla *84 A4 island* W Norway
Smolensk *111 A5* Smolenskaya Oblast', W Russian Federation
Smorgon'/Smorgonie *see* Smarhon'
Smyrna *see* İzmir
Snake *34 B4 river* Yukon Territory, NW Canada
Snake River *46 C3 river* NW USA
Snake River Plain *46 D4 plain* Idaho, NW USA
Sneek *86 D2* Friesland, N Netherlands
Sneeuw-gebergte *see* Maoke, Pegunungan
Sněžka *98 B4 Ger.* Schneekoppe, *Pol.* Śnieżka. *mountain* N Czech Republic/Poland
Śniardwy, Jezioro *114 D2 Ger.* Spirdingsee. *lake* NE Poland
Sniečkus *see* Visaginas
Śnieżka *see* Sněžka
Snina *99 E5 Hung.* Szinna. Prešovský Kraj, E Slovakia
Snowdonia *89 C6 mountain range* NW Wales, UK
Snowdrift *see* Łutselk'e
Snow Mountains *see* Maoke, Pegunungan
Snyder *49 F3* Texas, SW USA
Sobradinho, Barragem de *see* Sobradinho, Represa de
Sobradinho, Represa de *63 F2 var.* Barragem de Sobradinho. *reservoir* E Brazil
Sochi *111 A7* Krasnodarskiy Kray, SW Russian Federation
Socialist People's Libyan Arab Jamahiriya *see* Libya
Société, Archipel de la *145 G4 var.* Archipel de Tahiti, Îles de la Société, *Eng.* Society Islands. *island group* W French Polynesia
Société, Îles de la/Society Islands *see* Société, Archipel de la
Society Islands *see* Société, Archipel de la
Soconusco, Sierra de *see* Sierra Madre
Socorro *48 D2* New Mexico, SW USA
Socorro, Isla *50 B5 island* W Mexico
Socotra *see* Suquţrā
Soc Trăng *137 D6 var.* Khanh Hung. Soc Trăng, S Vietnam
Socuéllamos *93 E3* Castilla-La Mancha, C Spain
Sodankylä *84 D3* Lappi, N Finland
Sodari *see* Sodiri
Söderhamn *85 C5* Gävleborg, C Sweden
Södertälje *85 C6* Stockholm, C Sweden
Sodiri *72 B4 var.* Sawdirī, Sodari. Northern Kordofan, C Sudan
Soekaboemi *see* Sukabumi
Soemba *see* Sumba, Pulau
Soengaipenoeh *see* Sungaipenuh
Soerabaja *see* Surabaya
Soerakarta *see* Surakarta
Sofia *see* Sofiya
Sofiya *104 C2 var.* Sophia, *Eng.* Sofia, *Lat.* Serdica. *country capital* (Bulgaria) (Bulgaria) Sofiya-Grad, W Bulgaria
Sogamoso *58 B3* Boyacá, C Colombia
Sognefjorden *85 A5 fjord* NE North Sea
Sohâg *72 B2 var.* Sawhāj, Suliag. C Egypt
Sohar *see* Şuḩār
Sohm Plain *66 B3 abyssal plain* NW Atlantic Ocean
Sohrau *see* Żory
Sokal' *108 C2 Rus.* Sokal. L'vivs'ka Oblast', NW Ukraine
Söke *116 A4* Aydın, SW Turkey
Sokhumi *117 E1 Rus.* Sukhumi. NW Georgia
Sokodé *75 F4* C Togo
Sokol *110 C4* Vologodskaya Oblast', NW Russian Federation
Sokółka *98 E3* Podlaskie, NE Poland
Sokolov *99 A5 Ger.* Falkenau an der Eger; *prev.* Falknov nad Ohří. Karlovarský Kraj, W Czech Republic
Sokone *74 B3* W Senegal
Sokoto *75 F3* Sokoto, NW Nigeria
Sokoto *75 F4 river* NW Nigeria
Sokotra *see* Suquţrā
Solāpur *124 B3 var.* Sholāpur. Mahārāshtra, W India
Solca *108 C3 Ger.* Solka. Suceava, N Romania
Sol, Costa del *92 D5 coastal region* S Spain
Soldeu *91 B7* NE Andorra Europe
Solec Kujawski *98 C3* Kujawsko-pomorskie, C Poland
Soledad *58 B1* Anzoátegui, NE Venezuela
Isla Soledad *see* East Falkland
Soligorsk *see* Salihorsk

Solikamsk 114 C3 Permskaya Oblast', NW Russian Federation
Sol'-Iletsk 111 D6 Orenburgskaya Oblast', W Russian Federation
Solingen 94 A4 Nordrhein-Westfalen, W Germany
Solka see Solca
Sollentuna 85 C6 Stockholm, C Sweden
Solo see Surakarta
Solok 138 B4 Sumatera, W Indonesia
Solomon Islands 144 C3 prev. British Solomon Islands Protectorate. country W Solomon Islands N Melanesia W Pacific Ocean

SOLOMON ISLANDS
Australasia & Oceania

Official name Solomon Islands
Formation 1978 /1978
Capital Honiara
Population 478,000 / 44 people per sq mile (17 people per sq km) / 20%
Total area 10,985 sq miles (28,450 sq km)
Languages English*, Melanesian Pidgin, Pidgin English
Religions Anglican 34%, Roman Catholic 19%, Methodist 11%, Seventh-day Adventist 10%, South Seas Evangelical Church 17%, Other 9%
Ethnic mix Melanesian 94%, Polynesian 4%, Other 2%
Government Parliamentary system
Currency Solomon Islands dollar = 100 cents
Literacy rate 77%
Calorie consumption 2265 calories

Solomon Islands 144 C3 island group Papua New Guinea/Solomon Islands
Solomon Sea 144 B3 sea W Pacific Ocean
Soltau 94 B3 Niedersachsen, NW Germany
Sol'tsy 110 A4 Novgorodskaya Oblast', W Russian Federation
Solun see Thessaloníki
Solwezi 78 D2 North Western, NW Zambia
Sôma 130 D4 Fukushima, Honshū, C Japan
Somalia 73 D5 off. Somali Democratic Republic, Som. Jamuuriyada Demuqraadiga Soomaaliyeed, Soomaaliya; prev. Italian Somaliland, Somaliland Protectorate. country E Africa

SOMALIA
East Africa

Official name Somalia
Formation 1960 / 1960
Capital Mogadishu
Population 8.2 million / 34 people per sq mile (13 people per sq km) / 28%
Total area 246,199 sq miles (637,657 sq km)
Languages Somali*, Arabic*, English, Italian
Religions Sunni Muslim 98%, Christian 2%
Ethnic mix Somali 85%, Other 15%
Government Transitional regime
Currency Somali shilling = 100 centesimi
Literacy rate 24%
Calorie consumption 1628 calories

Somali Basin 69 E5 undersea basin N Indian Ocean
Somali Democratic Republic see Somalia
Somaliland 73 D5 disputed territory N Somalia
Somaliland Protectorate see Somalia
Sombor 100 C3 Hung. Zombor. Vojvodina, NW Serbia
Someren 87 D5 Noord-Brabant, SE Netherlands
Somerset 42 A5 var. Somerset Village. W Bermuda
Somerset 40 C5 Kentucky, S USA
Somerset Island 42 A5 island W Bermuda
Somerset Island 37 F2 island Queen Elizabeth Islands, Nunavut, NW Canada

Somerset Village see Somerset
Somers Islands see Bermuda
Somerton 48 A2 Arizona, SW USA
Someş 108 B3 river Hungary/Romania Europe
Somme 90 C2 river N France
Sommerfeld see Lubsko
Somotillo 52 C3 Chinandega, NW Nicaragua
Somoto 52 D3 Madriz, NW Nicaragua
Songea 73 C8 Ruvuma, S Tanzania
Sŏngjin see Kimch'aek
Songkhla 137 C7 var. Songkla, Mal. Singora. Songkhla, SW Thailand
Songkla see Songkhla
Sonoran Desert 48 A3 var. Desierto de Altar. desert Mexico/USA
Sonoran Desert see Altar, Desierto de
Sonsonate 52 B3 Sonsonate, W El Salvador
Soochow see Suzhou
Soomaaliya/Soomaaliyeed, Jamuuriyada Demuqraadiga see Somalia
Soome Laht see Finland, Gulf of
Sop Hao 136 D3 Houaphan, N Laos
Sophia see Sofiya
Šopianae see Pécs
Sopot 98 C2 Plovdiv, C Bulgaria
Sopron 99 B6 Ger. Ödenburg. Győr-Moson-Sopron, NW Hungary
Sorau/Sorau in der Niederlausitz see Żary
Sorgues 91 D6 Vaucluse, SE France
Sorgun 116 D3 Yozgat, C Turkey
Soria 93 E2 Castilla-León, N Spain
Soroca 108 D3 Rus. Soroki. N Moldova
Sorochino see Sarochyna
Soroki see Soroca
Sorong 139 F4 Papua, E Indonesia
Sørøy see Sørøya
Sørøya 84 C2 var. Sørøy, Lapp. Sállan. island N Norway
Sortavala 110 B3 Respublika Kareliya, NW Russian Federation
Sotavento, Ilhas de 74 A3 var. Leeward Islands. island group S Cape Verde
Sotkamo 84 E4 Oulu, C Finland
Souanké 77 B5 La Sangha, NW Congo
Soueida see As Suwaydā'
Souflí 104 D3 prev. Souflion. Anatolikí Makedonía kai Thráki, NE Greece
Souflion see Souflí
Soufrière 55 F2 W Saint Lucia
Soukhné see As Sukhnah
Sŏul 129 E4 off. Sŏul-t'ükpyŏlsi, Eng. Seoul, Jap. Keijō; prev. Kyŏngsŏng. country capital (South Korea) NW South Korea
Sŏul-t'ükpyŏlsi see Sŏul
Soûr 119 A5 var. Şūr; anc. Tyre. SW Lebanon
Souris River 45 E1 var. Mouse River. river Canada/USA
Soúrpi 105 B5 Thessalía, C Greece
Sousse 71 F2 var. Sūsah. NE Tunisia
South Africa 78 C4 off. Republic of South Africa, Afr. Suid-Afrika. country S Africa

SOUTH AFRICA
Southern Africa

Official name Republic of South Africa
Formation 1934 / 1994
Capital Pretoria; Cape Town; Bloemfontein
Population 47.4 million / 101 people per sq mile (39 people per sq km) / 55%
Total area 471,008 sq miles (1,219,912 sq km)
Languages English, isiZulu, isiXhosa, Afrikaans, Sepedi, Setswana, Sesotho, Xitsonga, siSwati, Tshivenda, isiNdebele
Religions Christian 68%, Traditional beliefs and animist 29%, Muslim 2%, Hindu 1%
Ethnic mix Black 79%, White 10%, Colored 9%, Asian 2%
Government Presidential system
Currency Rand = 100 cents
Literacy rate 82%
Calorie consumption 2956 calories

South Africa, Republic of see South Africa
South America 56 continent
Southampton 89 D7 hist. Hamwih, Lat. Clausentum. S England, UK
Southampton Island 37 G3 island Nunavut, NE Canada
South Andaman 133 F2 island Andaman Islands, India, NE Indian Ocean
South Australia 147 A5 state S Australia
South Australian Basin 142 B5 undersea basin SW Indian Ocean
South Bend 40 C3 Indiana, N USA
South Beveland see Zuid-Beveland
South Bruny Island 149 C8 island Tasmania, SE Australia
South Carolina 43 E2 off. State of South Carolina, also known as The Palmetto State. state SE USA
South Carpathians see Carpaţii Meridionali
South China Basin 125 E4 undersea basin SE South China Sea
South China Sea 124 D4 Chin. Nan Hai, Ind. Laut Cina Selatan, Vtn. Biển Đông. sea SE Asia
South Dakota 44 D2 off. State of South Dakota, also known as The Coyote State, Sunshine State. state N USA
Southeast Indian Ridge 141 D7 undersea ridge Indian Ocean/Pacific Ocean
Southeast Pacific Basin 153 E5 var. Belling Hausen Mulde. undersea basin SE Pacific Ocean
South East Point 149 C7 headland Victoria, S Australia
Southend-on-Sea 89 E6 E England, UK
Southern Alps 151 B6 mountain range South Island, New Zealand
Southern Cook Islands 145 F4 island group S Cook Islands
Southern Cross 147 B6 Western Australia
Southern Indian Lake 37 F4 lake Manitoba, C Canada
Southern Ocean 67 B7 ocean Atlantic Ocean/Indian Ocean/Pacific Ocean
Southern Uplands 88 C4 mountain range S Scotland, UK
South Fiji Basin 142 D4 undersea basin S Pacific Ocean
South Geomagnetic Pole 154 B3 pole Antarctica
South Georgia 57 D8 island South Georgia and the South Sandwich Islands, SW Atlantic Ocean
South Goulburn Island 146 E2 island Northern Territory, N Australia
South Huvadhu Atoll 132 A5 atoll S Maldives
South Indian Basin 141 D7 undersea basin Indian Ocean/Pacific Ocean
South Island 151 C6 island S New Zealand
South Korea 129 E4 off. Republic of Korea, Kor. Taehan Min'guk. country E Asia

SOUTH KOREA
East Asia

Official name Republic of Korea
Formation 1948 / 1953
Capital Seoul
Population 47.8 million / 1254 people per sq mile (484 people per sq km) / 82%
Total area 38,023 sq miles (98,480 sq km)
Languages Korean*
Religions Mahayana Buddhist 47%, Protestant 38%, Roman Catholic 11%, Confucianist 3%, Other 1%
Ethnic mix Korean 100%
Government Presidential system
Currency South Korean won = 100 chon
Literacy rate 98%
Calorie consumption 3058 calories

South Lake Tahoe 47 C5 California, W USA
South Orkney Islands 154 A2 island group Antarctica
South Ossetia 117 F2 former autonomous region SW Georgia
South Pacific Basin see Southwest Pacific Basin

South Platte River 44 D4 river Colorado/Nebraska, C USA
South Pole 154 B3 pole Antarctica
South Sandwich Islands 57 D8 island group SE South Georgia and South Sandwich Islands
South Sandwich Trench 57 E8 trench SW Atlantic Ocean
South Shetland Islands 154 A2 island group Antarctica
South Shields 88 D4 NE England, UK
South Sioux City 45 F3 Nebraska, C USA
South Taranaki Bight 150 C4 bight SE Tasman Sea
South Tasmania Plateau see Tasman Plateau
South Uist 88 B3 island NW Scotland, UK
South-West Africa/South West Africa see Namibia
South West Cape 151 A8 headland Stewart Island, New Zealand
Southwest Indian Ocean Ridge see Southwest Indian Ridge
Southwest Indian Ridge 141 B6 var. Southwest Indian Ocean Ridge. undersea ridge SW Indian Ocean
Southwest Pacific Basin 143 E4 var. South Pacific Basin. undersea basin SE Pacific Ocean
Sovereign Base Area 102 C5 UK military installation S Cyprus
Soweto 78 D4 Gauteng, NE South Africa
Sŏya-kaikyŏ see La Perouse Strait
Spain 92 D3 off. Kingdom of Spain, Sp. España; anc. Hispania, Iberia, Lat. Hispana. country SW Europe

SPAIN
Southeast Europe

Official name Kingdom of Spain
Formation 1492 / 1713
Capital Madrid
Population 43.1 million / 224 people per sq mile (86 people per sq km) / 78%
Total area 194,896 sq miles (504,782 sq km)
Languages Spanish*, Catalan*, Galician*, Basque*
Religions Roman Catholic 96%, Other 4%
Ethnic mix Castilian Spanish 72%, Catalan 17%, Galician 6%, Basque 2%, Other 2%, Roma 1%
Government Parliamentary system
Currency Euro = 100 cents
Literacy rate 98%
Calorie consumption 3371 calories

Spain, Kingdom of see Spain
Spalato see Split
Spanish Town 54 B5 hist. St.Iago de la Vega. C Jamaica
Sparks 47 C5 Nevada, W USA
Sparta see Spárti
Spartanburg 43 E1 South Carolina, SE USA
Spárti 105 B6 Eng. Sparta. Pelopónnisos, S Greece
Spearfish 44 D2 South Dakota, N USA
Speightstown 55 G1 NW Barbados
Spencer 45 F3 Iowa, C USA
Spencer Gulf 149 B6 gulf South Australia
Spey 88 C3 river NE Scotland, UK
Spice Islands see Maluku
Spiess Seamount 67 C7 seamount S Atlantic Ocean
Spijkenisse 86 B4 Zuid-Holland, SW Netherlands
Spili 105 C8 Kríti, Greece, E Mediterranean Sea
Spīn Būldak 123 E5 Kandahār, S Afghanistan
Spirdingsee see Śniardwy, Jezioro
Spitsbergen 83 F2 island NW Svalbard
Split 100 B4 It. Spalato. Split-Dalmacija, S Croatia
Spogi 106 D4 Daugvapils, SE Latvia
Spokane 46 C2 Washington, NW USA
Spratly Islands 138 B2 Chin. Nansha Qundao. disputed territory SE Asia
Spree 94 D4 river E Germany
Springfield 40 B4 state capital Illinois, N USA
Springfield 41 G3 Massachusetts, NE USA

Springfield *45 G5* Missouri, C USA
Springfield *40 C4* Ohio, N USA
Springfield *46 B3* Oregon, NW USA
Spring Garden *59 F2* NE Guyana
Spring Hill *43 E4* Florida, SE USA
Springs Junction *151 C5* West Coast, South Island, New Zealand
Springsure *148 D4* Queensland, E Australia
Sprottau *see* Szprotawa
Spruce Knob *41 E4 mountain* West Virginia, NE USA
Srbinje *see* Foča
Srebrenica *100 C4* Republika Srpska, E Bosnia and Herzegovina
Sredets *104 D2 prev.* Syulemeshlii. Stara Zagora, C Bulgaria
Sredets *104 E2 prev.* Grudovo. Burgas, E Bulgaria
Srednerusskaya Vozvyshennost' *109 G1 Eng.* Central Russian Upland. *mountain range* W Russian Federation
Srednesibirskoye Ploskogor'ye *114 D3 var.* Central Siberian Uplands, *Eng.* Central Siberian Plateau. *mountain range* N Russian Federation
Sremska Mitrovica *100 C3 prev.* Mitrovica, *Ger.* Mitrowitz. Vojvodina, NW Serbia
Srepok, Sông *see* Srêpôk, Tônle
Srêpôk, Tônle *137 E5 var.* Sông Srepok. *river* Cambodia/Vietnam
Sri Aman *138 C3* Sarawak, East Malaysia
Sri Jayawardanapura *132 D3 var.* Sri Jayawardenapura; *prev.* Kotte. Western Province, W Sri Lanka
Sri Jayawardenepura *see* Sri Jayawardanapura
Srīkākulam *135 F5* Andhra Pradesh, E India
Sri Lanka *132 D3 off.* Democratic Socialist Republic of Sri Lanka; *prev.* Ceylon. *country* S Asia

SRI LANKA
South Asia

Official name	Democratic Socialist Republic of Sri Lanka
Formation	1948 / 1948
Capital	Colombo
Population	20.7 million / 828 people per sq mile (320 people per sq km) / 24%
Total area	25,332 sq miles (65,610 sq km)
Languages	Sinhala, Tamil, Sinhala-Tamil, English
Religions	Buddhist 69%, Hindu 15%, Muslim 8%, Christian 8%
Ethnic mix	Sinhalese 74%, Tamil 18%, Moor 7%, Burgher, Malay, and Veddha 1%
Government	Mixed presidential–parliamentary system
Currency	Sri Lanka rupee = 100 cents
Literacy rate	90%
Calorie consumption	2385 calories

Sri Lanka, Democratic Socialist Republic of *see* Sri Lanka
Srinagarind Reservoir *137 C5 lake* W Thailand
Srpska, Respublika *100 B3 republic* Bosnia and Herzegovina
Ssu-ch'uan *see* Sichuan
Ssu-p'ing/Ssu-p'ing-chieh *see* Siping
Stabroek *87 B5* Antwerpen, N Belgium
Stade *94 B3* Niedersachsen, NW Germany
Stadskanaal *86 E2* Groningen, NE Netherlands
Stafford *89 D6* C England, UK
Staicele *106 D3* Limbaži, N Latvia
Ştaierdorf-Anina *see* Anina
Stájerlakanina *see* Anina
Stakhanov *109 H3* Luhans'ka Oblast', E Ukraine
Stalin *see* Varna
Stalinabad *see* Dushanbe
Stalingrad *see* Volgograd
Stalino *see* Donets'k
Stalinobod *see* Dushanbe
Stalinsk *see* Novokuznetsk
Stalinski Zaliv *see* Varnenski Zaliv
Stalin, Yazovir *see* Iskŭr, Yazovir
Stalowa Wola *98 E4* Podkarpackie, SE Poland
Stalstom *41 F3* Connecticut, NE USA
Stampalia *see* Astypálaia
Stanislau *see* Ivano-Frankivs'k
Stanislav *see* Ivano-Frankivs'k
Stanisławów *see* Ivano-Frankivs'k
Stanke Dimitrov *see* Dupnitsa
Stanley *65 D7 var.* Port Stanley, Puerto Argentino. *dependent territory capital* (Falkland Islands) East Falkland, Falkland Islands
Stanleyville *see* Kisangani
Stann Creek *see* Dangriga
Stanovoy Khrebet *113 E3 mountain range* SE Russian Federation
Stanthorpe *149 D5* Queensland, E Australia
Staphorst *86 D2* Overijssel, E Netherlands
Starachowice *98 D4* Świętokrzyskie, C Poland
Stara Kanjiža *see* Kanjiža
Stara Pazova *100 D3 Ger.* Altpasua, *Hung.* Ópazova. Vojvodina, N Serbia
Stara Planina *see* Balkan Mountains
Stara Zagora *104 D2 Lat.* Augusta Trajana. Stara Zagora, C Bulgaria
Starbuck Island *145 G3 prev.* Volunteer Island. *island* E Kiribati
Stargard in Pommern *see* Stargard Szczeciński
Stargard Szczeciński *98 B3 Ger.* Stargard in Pommern. Zachodnio-pomorskie, NW Poland
Stari Bečej *see* Bečej
Starobel'sk *see* Starobil's'k
Starobil's'k *109 H2 Rus.* Starobel'sk. Luhans'ka Oblast', E Ukraine
Starobin *107 C7 var.* Starobyn. Minskaya Voblasts', S Belarus
Starobyn *see* Starobin
Starogard Gdański *98 C2 Ger.* Preussisch-Stargard. Pomorskie, N Poland
Starokonstantinov *see* Starokostyantyniv
Starokostyantyniv *108 D2 Rus.* Starokonstantinov. Khmel'nyts'ka Oblast', NW Ukraine
Starominskaya *111 A7* Krasnodarskiy Kray, SW Russian Federation
Staryya Darohi *107 C6 Rus.* Staryye Dorogi. Minskaya Voblasts', S Belarus
Staryye Dorogi *see* Staryya Darohi
Staryy Oskol *111 B6* Belgorodskaya Oblast', W Russian Federation
State College *41 E4* Pennsylvania, NE USA
Staten Island *see* Estados, Isla de los
Statesboro *43 E2* Georgia, SE USA
States, The *see* United States of America
Staunton *41 E5* Virginia, NE USA
Stavanger *85 A6* Rogaland, S Norway
Stavers Island *see* Vostok Island
Stavropol' *111 B7 prev.* Voroshilovsk. Stavropol'skiy Kray, SW Russian Federation
Stavropol' *see* Tol'yatti
Steamboat Springs *44 C4* Colorado, C USA
Steenwijk *86 D2* Overijssel, N Netherlands
Steier *see* Steyr
Steierdorf/Steierdorf-Anina *see* Anina
Steinamanger *see* Szombathely
Steinkjer *84 B4* Nord-Trøndelag, C Norway
Stejarul *see* Karapelit
Stendal *94 C3* Sachsen-Anhalt, C Germany
Stepanakert *see* Xankändi
Stephenville *49 F3* Texas, SW USA
Sterling *44 D4* Colorado, C USA
Sterling *40 B3* Illinois, N USA
Sterlitamak *114 B3* Respublika Bashkortostan, W Russian Federation
Stettin *see* Szczecin
Stettiner Haff *see* Szczeciński, Zalew
Stevenage *89 E6* E England, UK
Stevens Point *40 B2* Wisconsin, N USA
Stewart Island *151 A8 island* S New Zealand
Steyerlak-Anina *see* Anina
Steyr *95 D6 var.* Steier. Oberösterreich, N Austria
Stif *see* Sétif
Stillwater *49 G1* Oklahoma, C USA
Stirling *88 C4* C Scotland, UK
Stjørdalshalsen *84 B4* Nord-Trøndelag, C Norway
Stockach *95 B6* Baden-Württemberg, S Germany
Stockholm *85 C6 country capital* (Sweden) Stockholm, C Sweden
Stockmannshof *see* Pļaviņas
Stockton *47 B6* California, W USA
Stockton Plateau *49 E4 plain* Texas, SW USA
Stœng Trêng *137 D5 prev.* Stung Treng. Stœng Trêng, NE Cambodia
Stoke *see* Stoke-on-Trent
Stoke-on-Trent *89 D6 var.* Stoke. C England, UK
Stolbce *see* Stowbtsy
Stolbtsy *see* Stowbtsy
Stolp *see* Słupsk
Stolpmünde *see* Ustka
Stómio *104 B4* Thessalía, C Greece
Storebælt *85 B8 var.* Store Bælt, *Eng.* Great Belt, Storebelt. *channel* Baltic Sea/Kattegat
Store Bælt *see* Storebælt
Storebelt *see* Storebælt
Støren *85 B5* Sør-Trøndelag, S Norway
Storfjorden *83 G2 fjord* S Norway
Storhammer *see* Hamar
Stornoway *88 B2* NW Scotland, UK
Storsjön *85 B5 lake* C Sweden
Storuman *84 C4* Västerbotten, N Sweden
Storuman *84 C4 lake* N Sweden
Stowbtsy *107 C6 Pol.* Stołbce, *Rus.* Stolbtsy. Minskaya Voblasts', C Belarus
Strabane *89 B5 Ir.* An Srath Bán. W Northern Ireland, UK
Strakonice *99 A5 Ger.* Strakonitz. Jihočeský Kraj, S Czech Republic
Strakonitz *see* Strakonice
Stralsund *94 D2* Mecklenburg-Vorpommern, NE Germany
Stranraer *89 C5* S Scotland, UK
Strasbourg *90 E3 Ger.* Strassburg; *anc.* Argentoratum. Bas-Rhin, NE France
Strasheny *see* Strǎșeni
Strassburg *see* Strasbourg, France
Strassburg *see* Aiud, Romania
Stratford *150 D4* Taranaki, North Island, New Zealand
Strathfield *148 E2* New South Wales, E Australia
Straubing *95 C6* Bayern, SE Germany
Strehaia *108 B5* Mehedinți, SW Romania
Strelka *114 D4* Krasnoyarskiy Kray, C Russian Federation
Strigonium *see* Esztergom
Strofília *see* Strofyliá
Strofyliá *105 C5 var.* Strofilia. Évvoia, C Greece
Stromboli, Isola *97 D6 island* Isole Eolie, S Italy
Stromeferry *88 C3* N Scotland, UK
Strömstad *85 B6* Västra Götaland, S Sweden
Strömsund *84 C4* Jämtland, C Sweden
Struga *101 D6* SW FYR Macedonia
Struma *see* Strymónas
Strumica *101 E6* E FYR Macedonia
Strumyani *104 C3* Blagoevgrad, SW Bulgaria
Strymónas *104 C3 Bul.* Struma. *river* Bulgaria/Greece
Stryy *108 B2* L'vivs'ka Oblast', NW Ukraine
Studholme *151 B6* Canterbury, South Island, New Zealand
Stuhlweissenberg *see* Székesfehérvár
Stung Treng *see* Stœng Trêng
Sturgis *44 D3* South Dakota, N USA
Stuttgart *95 B6* Baden-Württemberg, SW Germany
Stykkishólmur *83 E4* Vesturland, W Iceland
Styr *108 C1 Rus.* Styr'. *river* Belarus/Ukraine
Su *see* Jiangsu
Suakin *72 C3 var.* Sawakin. Red Sea, NE Sudan
Subačius *106 C4* Panevėžys, NE Lithuania
Subaykhān *118 E3* Dayr az Zawr, E Syria
Subotica *100 D2 Ger.* Maria-Theresiopel, *Hung.* Szabadka. Vojvodina, N Serbia
Suceava *108 C3 Ger.* Suczawa, *Hung.* Szucsava. Suceava, NE Romania
Su-chou *see* Suzhou
Suchow *see* Xuzhou, Jiangsu, China
Suchow *see* Suzhou, Jiangsu, China
Sucker State *see* Illinois
Sucre *61 F4 hist.* Chuquisaca, La Plata. *country capital* (Bolivia-legal capital) Chuquisaca, S Bolivia
Suczawa *see* Suceava
Sudan *72 A4 off.* Republic of Sudan, *Ar.* Jumhuriyat as-Sudan; *prev.* Anglo-Egyptian Sudan. *country* N Africa

SUDAN
East Africa

Official name	Republic of the Sudan
Formation	1956 / 1956
Capital	Khartoum
Population	36.2 million / 37 people per sq mile (14 people per sq km) / 36%
Total area	967,493 sq miles (2,505,810 sq km)
Languages	Arabic*, Dinka, Nuer, Nubian, Beja, Zande, Bari, Fur, Shilluk, Lotuko
Religions	Muslim (mainly Sunni) 70%, Traditional beliefs 20%, Christian 9%, Other 1%
Ethnic mix	Other Black 52%, Arab 40%, Dinka and Beja 7%, Other 1%
Government	Presidential system
Currency	Sudanese pound or dinar = 100 piastres
Literacy rate	59%
Calorie consumption	2228 calories

Sudanese Republic *see* Mali
Sudan, Jumhuriyat as- *see* Sudan
Sudan, Republic of *see* Sudan
Sudbury *38 C4* Ontario, S Canada
Sudd *73 B5 swamp region* S Sudan
Sudeten *98 B4 var.* Sudetes, Sudetic Mountains, *Cz./Pol.* Sudety. *mountain range* Czech Republic/Poland
Sudetes/Sudetic Mountains/Sudety *see* Sudeten
Südkarpaten *see* Carpații Meridionali
Südliche Morava *see* Južna Morava
Sudostroy *see* Severodvinsk
Sue *73 B5 river* S Sudan
Sueca *93 F3* País Valenciano, E Spain
Sue Wood Bay *42 B5* W Bermuda
Suez *72 B1 Ar.* As Suways, *Fr.* El Suweis. NE Egypt
Suez Canal *72 B1 Ar.* Qanāt as Suways. *canal* NE Egypt
Suez, Gulf of *72 B2 Ar.* Khalīj as Suways. *gulf* NE Egypt
Sŭğla Gölü *116 C4 lake* SW Turkey
Şuḩār *121 D5 var.* Sohar. N Oman
Sühbaatar *127 E1* Selenge, N Mongolia
Suhl *95 C5* Thüringen, C Germany
Suicheng *see* Suixi
Suid-Afrika *see* South Africa
Suidwes-Afrika *see* Namibia
Suixi *128 C6 var.* Suicheng. Guangdong, S China
Sujāwal *134 B3* Sind, SE Pakistan
Sukabumi *138 C5 prev.* Soekaboemi. Jawa, C Indonesia
Sukagawa *131 D5* Fukushima, Honshū, C Japan
Sukarnapura *see* Jayapura
Sukarno, Puntjak *see* Jaya, Puncak
Sukhne *see* As Sukhnah
Sukhona *110 C4 var.* Tot'ma. *river* NW Russian Federation
Sukhumi *see* Sokhumi
Sukkertoppen *see* Maniitsoq
Sukkur *134 B3* Sind, SE Pakistan
Sukumo *131 B7* Kōchi, Shikoku, SW Japan
Sulaimaniya *see* As Sulaymānīyah
Sulaimān Range *134 C2 mountain range* C Pakistan
Sula, Kepulauan *139 E4 island group* C Indonesia
Sulawesi *139 E4 Eng.* Celebes. *island* C Indonesia
Sulawesi, Laut *see* Celebes Sea
Sulechów *98 B3 Ger.* Züllichau. Lubuskie, W Poland
Suliag *see* Sohâg

Sullana *60 B2* Piura, NW Peru
Sullivan Island *see* Lanbi Kyun
Sulphur Springs *49 G2* Texas, SW USA
Sultānābād *see* Arāk
Sulu Archipelago *139 E3 island group* SW Philippines
Sülüktü *see* Sulyukta
Sulu, Laut *see* Sulu Sea
Sulu Sea *139 E2 var.* Laut Sulu. *sea* SW Philippines
Sulyukta *123 E2 Kir.* Sülüktü. Batkenskaya Oblast', SW Kyrgyzstan
Sumatera *137 B8 Eng.* Sumatra. *island* W Indonesia
Sumatra *see* Sumatera
Šumava *see* Bohemian Forest
Sumba, Pulau *139 E5 Eng.* Sandalwood Island; *prev.* Soemba. *island* Nusa Tenggara, C Indonesia
Sumba, Selat *139 E5 strait* Nusa Tenggara, S Indonesia
Sumbawanga *73 B7* Rukwa, W Tanzania
Sumbe *78 B2 var.* N'Gunza, *Port.* Novo Redondo. Cuanza Sul, W Angola
Sumeih *73 B5* Southern Darfur, S Sudan
Sumgait *see* Sumqayıt, Azerbaijan
Summer Lake *46 B4 lake* Oregon, NW USA
Summit *93 H5* Alaska, USA
Sumqayıt *117 H2 Rus.* Sumgait. E Azerbaijan
Sumy *109 F2* Sums'ka Oblast', NE Ukraine
Sunbury *149 C7* Victoria, SE Australia
Sunda Islands *see* Greater Sunda Islands
Sunda, Selat *138 B5 strait* Jawa/ Sumatera, SW Indonesia
Sunda Trench *see* Java Trench
Sunderland *88 D4 var.* Wearmouth. NE England, UK
Sundsvall *85 C5* Västernorrland, C Sweden
Sunflower State *see* Kansas
Sungaipenuh *138 B4 prev.* Soengaipenoeh. Sumatera, W Indonesia
Sunnyvale *47 A6* California, W USA
Sunset State *see* Oregon
Sunshine State *see* Florida
Sunshine State *see* New Mexico
Sunshine State *see* South Dakota
Suntar *115 F3* Respublika Sakha (Yakutiya), NE Russian Federation
Sunyani *75 E5* W Ghana
Suoločielgi *see* Saariselkä
Suomenlahti *see* Finland, Gulf of
Suomen Tasavalta/Suomi *see* Finland
Suomussalmi *84 E4* Oulu, E Finland
Suŏng *137 D6* Kâmpóng Cham, C Cambodia
Suoyarvi *110 B3* Respublika Kareliya, NW Russian Federation
Supe *60 C3* Lima, W Peru
Supérieur, Lac *see* Superior, Lake
Superior *40 A1* Wisconsin, N USA
Superior, Lake *40 B1 Fr.* Lac Supérieur. *lake* Canada/USA
Suqrah *see* Şawqirah
Suquṭrā *121 C7 var.* Sokotra, *Eng.* Socotra. *island* SE Yemen
Şūr *121 E5* NE Oman
Şūr *see* Soûr
Surabaja *see* Surabaya
Surabaya *138 D5 prev.* Surabaja, Soerabaja. Jawa, C Indonesia
Surakarta *138 C5 Eng.* Solo; *prev.* Soerakarta. Jawa, S Indonesia
Šurany *99 C6 Hung.* Nagysurány. Nitriansky Kraj, SW Slovakia
Sūrat *134 C4* Gujarāt, W India
Suratdhani *see* Surat Thani
Surat Thani *137 C6 var.* Suratdhani. Surat Thani, SW Thailand
Surazh *107 E5 Rus.* Surazh. Vitsyebskaya Voblasts', NE Belarus
Surdulica *101 E5* Serbia, SE Serbia
Sûre *87 D7 var.* Sauer. *river* W Europe
Surendranagar *134 C4* Gujarāt, W India
Surfers Paradise *149 E5* Queensland, E Australia
Surgut *114 D3* Khanty-Mansiyskiy Avtonomnyy Okrug, C Russian Federation
Surin *137 D5* Surin, E Thailand
Surinam *see* Surinam
Suriname *59 G3 off.* Republic of Suriname, *var.* Suriname; *prev.* Dutch Guiana, Netherlands Guiana. *country* N South America

SURINAME
South America

Official name Republic of Suriname
Formation 1975 / 1975
Capital Paramaribo
Population 499,000 / 8 people per sq mile (3 people per sq km) / 74%
Total area 63,039 sq miles (163,270 sq km)
Languages Dutch*, Sranan (Creole), Javanese, Sarnami Hindi, Saramaccan, Chinese, Carib
Religions Hindu 27%, Protestant 25%, Roman Catholic 23%, Muslim 20%, Traditional beliefs 5%
Ethnic mix Creole 34%, South Asian 34%, Javanese 18%, Black 9%, Other 5%
Government Parliamentary system
Currency Suriname dollar (guilder until 2004) = 100 cents
Literacy rate 88%
Calorie consumption 2652 calories

Suriname, Republic of *see* Surinam
Sūrīya/Sūrīyah, Al-Jumhūrīyah al-'Arabīyah as- *see* Syria
Surkhab, Darya-i- *see* Kahmard, Daryā-ye
Surkhob *123 F3 river* C Tajikistan
Surt *71 G2 var.* Sidra, Sirte. N Libya
Surt, Khalīj *71 F2 Eng.* Gulf of Sidra, Gulf of Sirti, Sidra. *gulf* N Libya
Surtsey *83 E5 island* S Iceland
Suruga-wan *131 D6 bay* SE Japan
Susa *96 A2* Piemonte, NE Italy
Sūsah *see* Sousse
Susanville *47 B5* California, W USA
Susitna *36 C3* Alaska, USA
Susteren *87 D5* Limburg, SE Netherlands
Susuman *115 G3* Magadanskaya Oblast', E Russian Federation
Sutlej *134 C2 river* India/Pakistan
Suur Munamägi *106 D3 var.* Munamägi, *Ger.* Eier-Berg. *mountain* SE Estonia
Suur Väin *106 C2 Ger.* Grosser Sund. *strait* W Estonia
Suva *145 E4 country capital* (Fiji) Viti Levu, W Fiji
Suvalkai/Suvalki *see* Suwałki
Suwałki *98 E2 Lith.* Suvalkai, *Rus.* Suvalki. Podlaskie, NE Poland
Şuwār *see* Aş Şuwār
Suways, Khalīj as *see* Suez, Gulf of
Suways, Qanāt as *see* Suez Canal
Suweida *see* As Suwaydā'
Suzhou *128 D5 var.* Soochow, Su-chou, Suchow; *prev.* Wuhsien. Jiangsu, E China
Svalbard *83 E1 Norwegian dependency* Arctic Ocean
Svartisen *84 C3 glacier* C Norway
Svay Riĕng *137 D6* Svay Riĕng, S Cambodia
Sveg *85 B5* Jämtland, C Sweden
Svenstavik *85 C5* Jämtland, C Sweden
Sverdlovsk *see* Yekaterinburg
Sverige *see* Sweden
Sveti Vrach *see* Sandanski
Svetlogorsk *see* Svyetlahorsk
Svetlograd *111 B7* Stavropol'skiy Kray, SW Russian Federation
Svetlovodsk *see* Svitlovods'k
Svetozarevo *see* Jagodina
Svilengrad *104 D3 prev.* Mustafa-Pasha. Khaskovo, S Bulgaria
Svitlovods'k *109 F3 Rus.* Svetlovodsk. Kirovohrads'ka Oblast', C Ukraine
Svizzera *see* Switzerland
Svobodnyy *115 G4* Amurskaya Oblast', SE Russian Federation
Svyataya Anna Trough *172 C4 var.* Saint Anna Trough. *trough* N Kara Sea
Svyetlahorsk *107 D7 Rus.* Svetlogorsk. Homyel'skaya Voblasts', SE Belarus
Swabian Jura *see* Schwäbische Alb
Swakopmund *78 B3* Erongo, W Namibia
Swansea *89 C7 Wel.* Abertawe. S Wales, UK
Swarzędz *98 C3* Poznań, W Poland
Swatow *see* Shantou
Swaziland *78 D4 off.* Kingdom of Swaziland. *country* S Africa

SWAZILAND
Southern Africa

Official name Kingdom of Swaziland
Formation 1968 / 1968
Capital Mbabane
Population 1 million / 151 people per sq mile (58 people per sq km) / 26%
Total area 6704 sq miles (17,363 sq km)
Languages English*, siSwati*, isiZulu, Xitsonga
Religions Christian 60%, Traditional beliefs 40%
Ethnic mix Swazi 97%, Other 3%
Government Monarchy
Currency Lilangeni = 100 cents
Literacy rate 79%
Calorie consumption 2322 calories

Swaziland, Kingdom of *see* Swaziland
Sweden *84 B4 off.* Kingdom of Sweden, *Swe.* Sverige. *country* N Europe

SWEDEN
Northern Europe

Official name Kingdom of Sweden
Formation 1523 / 1905
Capital Stockholm
Population 9 million / 57 people per sq mile (22 people per sq km) / 83%
Total area 173,731 sq miles (449,964 sq km)
Languages Swedish*, Finnish, Sámi
Religions Evangelical Lutheran 82%, Other 13%, Roman Catholic 2%, Muslim 2%, Orthodox Christian 1%
Ethnic mix Swedish 88%, Foreign-born or first-generation immigrant 10%, Finnish and Sámi 2%
Government Parliamentary system
Currency Swedish krona = 100 öre
Literacy rate 99%
Calorie consumption 3185 calories

Sweden, Kingdom of *see* Sweden
Sweetwater *49 F3* Texas, SW USA
Świdnica *98 B4 Ger.* Schweidnitz. Wałbrzych, SW Poland
Świdwin *98 B2 Ger.* Schivelbein. Zachodnio-pomorskie, NW Poland
Świebodzice *98 B4 Ger.* Freiburg in Schlesien, Swiebodzice. Walbrzych, SW Poland
Świebodzin *98 B3 Ger.* Schwiebus. Lubuskie, W Poland
Świecie *98 C3 Ger.* Schwertberg. Kujawsko-pomorskie, C Poland
Swindon *89 D7* S England, UK
Swinemünde *see* Świnoujście
Świnoujście *98 B2 Ger.* Swinemünde. Zachodnio-pomorskie, NW Poland
Swiss Confederation *see* Switzerland
Switzerland *95 A7 off.* Swiss Confederation, *Fr.* La Suisse, *Ger.* Schweiz, *It.* Svizzera; *anc.* Helvetia. *country* C Europe

SWITZERLAND
Central Europe

Official name Swiss Confederation
Formation 1291 / 1857
Capital Bern
Population 7.3 million / 475 people per sq mile (184 people per sq km) / 68%
Total area 15,942 sq miles (41,290 sq km)
Languages German*, French*, Italian*, Romansch*, Swiss-German
Religions Roman Catholic 46%, Protestant 40%, Other and nonreligious 12%, Muslim 2%
Ethnic mix German 65%, French 18%, Italian 10%, Other 6%, Romansch 1%
Government Parliamentary system
Currency Swiss franc = 100 rappen/ centimes
Literacy rate 99%
Calorie consumption 3526 calories

Sycaminum *see* Ḩefa
Sydenham Island *see* Nonouti
Sydney *148 D1 state capital* New South Wales, SE Australia
Sydney *39 G4* Cape Breton Island, Nova Scotia, SE Canada
Sydney Island *see* Manra
Syedpur *see* Saidpur
Syemyezhava *107 C6 Rus.* Semezhevo. Minskaya Voblasts', C Belarus
Syene *see* Aswân
Syeverodonets'k *109 H3 Rus.* Severodonetsk. Luhans'ka Oblast', E Ukraine
Syktyvkar *110 D4 prev.* Ust'-Sysol'sk. Respublika Komi, NW Russian Federation
Sylhet *135 G3* Sylhet, NE Bangladesh
Synel'nykove *109 G3* Dnipropetrovs'ka Oblast', E Ukraine
Syowa *154 C2 Japanese research station* Antarctica
Syracuse *41 E3* New York, NE USA
Syracuse *see* Siracusa
Syrdar'ya *114 B4* Sirdaryo Viloyati, E Uzbekistan
Syria *118 B3 off.* Syrian Arab Republic, *var.* Siria, Syrie, *Ar.* Al-Jumhūrīyah al-'Arabīyah as-Sūrīyah, Sūrīya. *country* SW Asia

SYRIA
Southwest Asia

Official name Syrian Arab Republic
Formation 1941 / 1967
Capital Damascus
Population 19 million / 267 people per sq mile (103 people per sq km) / 55%
Total area 71,498 sq miles (184,180 sq km)
Languages Arabic*, French, Kurdish, Armenian, Circassian, Turkic languages, Assyrian, Aramaic
Religions Sunni Muslim 74%, Other Muslim 16%, Christian 10%
Ethnic mix Arab 89%, Kurdish 6%, Other 3%, Armenian, Turkmen, and Circassian 2%
Government One-party state
Currency Syrian pound = 100 piasters
Literacy rate 83%
Calorie consumption 3038 calories

Syrian Arab Republic *see* Syria
Syrian Desert *119 D5 Ar.* Al Hamad, Bādiyat ash Shām. *desert* SW Asia
Syrie *see* Syria
Sýrna *105 E7 var.* Sirna. *island* Kykládes, Greece, Aegean Sea
Sýros *105 C6 var.* Síros. *island* Kykládes, Greece, Aegean Sea
Syulemeshlii *see* Sredets
Syvash, Zaliv *see* Syvash, Zatoka
Syvash, Zatoka *109 F4 Rus.* Zaliv Syvash. *inlet* S Ukraine
Syzran' *111 C6* Samarskaya Oblast', W Russian Federation
Szabadka *see* Subotica
Szamotuły *98 B3* Poznań, W Poland
Szászrégen *see* Reghin
Szatmárnémeti *see* Satu Mare
Száva *see* Sava
Szczecin *98 B3 Eng./Ger.* Stettin. Zachodnio-pomorskie, NW Poland
Szczecinek *98 B2 Ger.* Neustettin. Zachodnio-pomorskie, NW Poland
Szczeciński, Zalew *98 A2 var.* Stettiner Haff, *Ger.* Oderhaff. *bay* Germany/Poland
Szczuczyn Nowogródzki *see* Shchuchyn
Szczytno *98 D3 Ger.* Ortelsburg. Warmińsko-Mazurskie, NE Poland
Szechuan/Szechwan *see* Sichuan
Szeged *99 D7 Ger.* Szegedin, *Rom.* Seghedin. Csongrád, SE Hungary
Szegedin *see* Szeged
Székelykeresztúr *see* Cristuru Secuiesc
Székesfehérvár *99 C6 Ger.* Stuhlweissenberg; *anc.* Alba Regia. Fejér, W Hungary
Szeklerburg *see* Miercurea-Ciuc
Szekler Neumarkt *see* Târgu Secuiesc
Szekszárd *99 C7* Tolna, S Hungary
Szempcz/Szenc *see* Senec

Szenice see Senica
Szeping see Siping
Szilágysomlyó see Şimleu Silvaniei
Szinna see Snina
Sziszek see Sisak
Szitás-Keresztúr see Cristuru Secuiesc
Szkudy see Skuodas
Szlatina see Slatina
Szlovákia see Slovakia
Szolnok 99 D6 Jász-Nagykun-Szolnok, C Hungary
Szombathely 99 B6 Ger. Steinamanger; anc. Sabaria, Savaria. Vas, W Hungary
Szprotawa 98 B4 Ger. Sprottau. Lubuskie, W Poland
Sztálinváros see Dunaújváros
Szucsava see Suceava

T

Tabariya, Bahrat see Tiberias, Lake
Table Rock Lake 49 G1 reservoir Arkansas/Missouri, C USA
Tábor 99 B5 Jihočeský Kraj, S Czech Republic
Tabora 73 B7 Tabora, W Tanzania
Tabrīz 120 C2 var. Tebriz; anc. Tauris. Āźarbāyjān-e Sharqī, NW Iran
Tabuaeran 145 G2 prev. Fanning Island. atoll Line Islands, E Kiribati
Tabūk 120 A4 Tabūk, NW Saudi Arabia
Täby 85 C6 Stockholm, C Sweden
Tachau see Tachov
Tachov 99 A5 Ger. Tachau. Plveňský Kraj, W Czech Republic
Tacloban 139 F2 off. Tacloban City. Leyte, C Philippines
Tacloban City see Tacloban
Tacna 61 E4 Tacna, SE Peru
Tacoma 46 B2 Washington, NW USA
Tacuarembó 64 D4 prev. San Fructuoso. Tacuarembó, C Uruguay
Tademaït, Plateau du 70 D3 plateau C Algeria
Tadmor/Tadmur see Tudmur
Tādpatri 132 C2 Andhra Pradesh, E India
Tadzhikistan see Tajikistan
Taegu 129 E4 off. Taegu-gwangyŏksi, var. Daegu, Jap. Taikyū. SE South Korea
Taegu-gwangyŏksi see Taegu
Taehan-haehyŏp see Korea Strait
Taehan Min'guk see South Korea
Taejŏn 129 E4 off. Taejŏn-gwangyŏksi, Jap. Taiden. C South Korea
Taejŏn-gwangyŏksi see Taejŏn
Tafassâsset, Ténéré du 75 G2 desert N Niger
Tafila/Tafilah, Muḩāfaẓat aṭ see Aṭ Ţafilah
Taganrog 111 A7 Rostovskaya Oblast', SW Russian Federation
Taganrog, Gulf of 109 G4 Rus. Taganrogskiy Zaliv, Ukr. Tahanroz'ka Zatoka. gulf Russian Federation/Ukraine
Taganrogskiy Zaliv see Taganrog, Gulf of
Taguatinga 63 F3 Tocantins, C Brazil
Tagus 92 C3 Port. Rio Tejo, Sp. Río Tajo. river Portugal/Spain
Tagus Plain 80 A4 abyssal plain E Atlantic Ocean
Tahanroz'ka Zatoka see Taganrog, Gulf of
Tahat 71 A7 mountain SE Algeria
Tahiti 145 H4 island Îles du Vent, W French Polynesia
Tahiti, Archipel de see Société, Archipel de la
Tahlequah 49 G1 Oklahoma, C USA
Tahoe, Lake 47 B5 lake California/ Nevada, W USA
Tahoua 75 F3 Tahoua, W Niger
Taichū see T'aichung
T'aichung 128 D6 Jap. Taichū; prev. Taiwan. C Taiwan
Taiden see Taejŏn
Taieri 151 B7 river South Island, New Zealand
Taihape 150 D4 Manawatu-Wanganui, North Island, New Zealand
Taihoku see T'aipei
Taikyū see Taegu
Tailem Bend 149 B7 South Australia

T'ainan 128 D6 Jap. Tainan; prev. Dainan. S Taiwan
T'aipei 128 D6 Jap. Taihoku; prev. Daihoku. country capital (Taiwan) N Taiwan
Taiping 138 B3 Perak, Peninsular Malaysia
Taiwan 128 D6 off. Republic of China, var. Formosa, Formo'sa. country E Asia

TAIWAN
East Asia

Official name Republic of China (ROC)
Formation 1949 / 1949
Capital Taipei
Population 22.9 million / 1838 people per sq mile (710 people per sq km) / 69%
Total area 13,892 sq miles (35,980 sq km)
Languages Amoy Chinese, Mandarin Chinese, Hakka Chinese
Religions Buddhist, Confucianist, and Taoist 93%, Christian 5%, Other 2%
Ethnic mix Han (pre-20th-century migration) 84%, Han (20th-century migration) 14%, Aboriginal 2%
Government Presidential system
Currency Taiwan dollar = 100 cents
Literacy rate 97%
Calorie consumption Not available

Taiwan see T'aichung
Taiwan Haihsia/Taiwan Haixia see Taiwan Strait
Taiwan Strait 128 D6 var. Formosa Strait, Chin. T'aiwan Haihsia, Taiwan Haixia. strait China/Taiwan
Taiyuan 128 C4 var. T'ai-yuan, T'ai-yüan; prev. Yangku. province capital Shanxi, C China
T'ai-yuan/T'ai-yüan see Taiyuan
Ta'izz 121 B7 SW Yemen
Tajikistan 123 E3 off. Republic of Tajikistan, Rus. Tadzhikistan, Taj. Jumhurii Tojikiston; prev. Tajik S.S.R. country C Asia

TAJIKISTAN
Central Asia

Official name Republic of Tajikistan
Formation 1991 / 1991
Capital Dushanbe
Population 6.5 million / 118 people per sq mile (45 people per sq km) / 28%
Total area 55,251 sq miles (143,100 sq km)
Languages Tajik*, Uzbek, Russian
Religions Sunni Muslim 80%, Other 15%, Shi'a Muslim 5%
Ethnic mix Tajik 62%, Uzbek 24%, Russian 8%, Other 4%, Tatar 1%, Kyrgyz 1%
Government Presidential system
Currency Somoni = 100 diram
Literacy rate 99%
Calorie consumption 1828 calories

Tajikistan, Republic of see Tajikistan
Tajik S.S.R see Tajikistan
Tajo, Río see Tagus
Tak 136 C4 var. Rahaeng. Tak, W Thailand
Takao see Kaohsiung
Takaoka 131 C5 Toyama, Honshū, SW Japan
Takapuna 150 D2 Auckland, North Island, New Zealand
Takhiatash see Takhiatosh
Takhtakupyr see Taxtako'pir
Takikawa 130 D2 Hokkaidō, NE Japan
Takla Makan Desert see Taklimakan Shamo
Taklimakan Shamo 126 B3 Eng. Takla Makan Desert. desert NW China
Takow see Kaohsiung
Takutea 145 G4 island S Cook Islands
Talabriga see Aveiro
Talabriga see Talavera de la Reina
Talachyn 107 D6 Rus. Tolochin. Vitsyebskaya Voblasts', NE Belarus
Talamanca, Cordillera de 53 E5 mountain range S Costa Rica
Talara 60 B2 Piura, NW Peru
Talas 123 F2 Talasskaya Oblast', NW Kyrgyzstan
Talaud, Kepulauan 139 F3 island group E Indonesia

Talavera de la Reina 92 D3 anc. Caesarobriga, Talabriga. Castilla-La Mancha, C Spain
Talca 64 B4 Maule, C Chile
Talcahuano 65 B5 Bío Bío, C Chile
Taldykorgan 114 C5 Kaz. Taldyqorghan; prev. Taldy-Kurgan. Taldykorgan, SE Kazakhstan
Taldy-Kurgan/Taldyqorghan see Taldykorgan
Ta-lien see Dalian
Taliq-an see Tāloqān
Tal'ka 107 C6 Rus. Tal'ka. Minskaya Voblasts', C Belarus
Talkhof see Puurmani
Tallahassee 42 D3 prev. Muskogean. state capital Florida, SE USA
Tall al Abyaḑ see At Tall al Abyaḑ
Tallin see Tallinn
Tallinn 106 D2 Ger. Reval, Rus. Tallin; prev. Revel. country capital (Estonia) Harjumaa, NW Estonia
Tall Kalakh 118 B4 var. Tell Kalakh. Ḩimş, C Syria
Tallulah 42 B2 Louisiana, S USA
Talnakh 114 D3 Taymyrskiy (Dolgano-Nenetskiy) Avtonomnyy Okrug, N Russian Federation
Tal'ne 109 E3 Rus. Tal'noye. Cherkas'ka Oblast', C Ukraine
Tal'noye see Tal'ne
Taloga 49 F1 Oklahoma, C USA
Tāloqān 123 E3 var. Taliq-an. Takhār, NE Afghanistan
Talsen see Talsi
Talsi 106 C3 Ger. Talsen. Talsi, NW Latvia
Taltal 64 B2 Antofagasta, N Chile
Talvik 84 D2 Finnmark, N Norway
Tamabo, Banjaran 138 D3 mountain range East Malaysia
Tamale 75 E4 C Ghana
Tamana 145 E3 prev. Rotcher Island. atoll Tungaru, W Kiribati
Tamanrasset 71 F4 var. Tamenghest. S Algeria
Tamar 89 C7 river SW England, UK
Tamar see Tudmur
Tamatave see Toamasina
Tamazunchale 51 E4 San Luis Potosí, C Mexico
Tambacounda 74 C3 SE Senegal
Tambov 111 B6 Tambovskaya Oblast', W Russian Federation
Tambura 73 B5 Western Equatoria, SW Sudan
Tamchaket see Tâmchekkeţ
Tâmchekkeţ 74 C3 var. Tamchaket. Hodh el Gharbi, S Mauritania
Tamenghest see Tamanrasset
Tamiahua, Laguna de 51 F4 lagoon Veracruz-Llave, Mexico
Tamil Nādu 132 C3 prev. Madras. cultural region SE India
Tamil Nādu 132 C2 prev. Madras. state SE India
Tam Ky 137 E5 Quang Nam-ƒa Năng, C Vietnam
Tammerfors see Tampere
Tampa 43 E4 Florida, SE USA
Tampa Bay 43 E4 bay Florida, SE USA
Tampere 85 D5 Swe. Tammerfors. Länsi-Suomi, W Finland
Tampico 51 E3 Tamaulipas, C Mexico
Tamworth 149 D6 New South Wales, SE Australia
Tanabe 131 C7 Wakayama, Honshū, SW Japan
Tana Bru 84 D2 Finnmark, N Norway
T'ana Hāyk' 72 C4 var. Lake Tana. lake NW Ethiopia
Tanais see Don
Tana, Lake see T'ana Hāyk'
Tanami Desert 146 D3 desert Northern Territory, N Australia
Tananarive see Antananarivo
Ţăndărei 108 D5 Ialomiţa, SE Romania
Tandil 65 D5 Buenos Aires, E Argentina
Tandjoengkarang see Bandar Lampung
Tanega-shima 131 B8 island Nansei-shotō, SW Japan
Tanen Taunggyi see Tane Range
Tane Range 136 B4 Bur. Tanen Taunggyi. mountain range W Thailand

Tanezrouft 70 D4 desert Algeria/Mali
Ţanf, Jabal aṭ 118 D4 mountain SE Syria
Tanga 69 E5 Tanga, E Tanzania
Tanga 73 C7 region E Tanzania
Tanganyika and Zanzibar see Tanzania
Tanger 70 C2 var. Tangiers, Tangier, Fr./Ger. Tangerk, Sp. Tánger; anc. Tingis. NW Morocco
Tangerk see Tanger
Tanggula Shan 126 C4 mountain W China
Tangier see Tanger
Tangiers see Tanger
Tangra Yumco 126 B5 var. Tangro Tso. lake W China
Tangro Tso see Tangra Yumco
Tangshan 128 D3 var. T'ang-shan. Hebei, E China
T'ang-shan see Tangshan
Tanimbar, Kepulauan 139 F5 island group Maluku, E Indonesia
Tanjungkarang/Tanjungkarang-Telukbetung see Bandar Lampung
Tanna 144 D4 island S Vanuatu
Tannenhof see Krynica
Tan-Tan 70 B3 SW Morocco
Tan-tung see Dandong
Tanzania 73 C7 off. United Republic of Tanzania, Swa. Jamhuri ya Muungano wa Tanzania; prev. German East Africa, Tanganyika and Zanzibar. country E Africa

TANZANIA
East Africa

Official name United Republic of Tanzania
Formation 1964 / 1964
Capital Dodoma
Population 38.3 million / 112 people per sq mile (43 people per sq km) / 33%
Total area 364,898 sq miles (945,087 sq km)
Languages English*, Kiswahili*, Sukuma, Chagga, Nyamwezi, Hehe, Makonde, Yao, Sandawe
Religions Muslim 33%, Christian 33%, Traditional beliefs 30%, Other 4%
Ethnic mix Native African (over 120 tribes) 99%, European and Asian 1%
Government Presidential system
Currency Tanzanian shilling = 100 cents
Literacy rate 69%
Calorie consumption 1975 calories

Tanzania, Jamhuri ya Muungano wa see Tanzania
Tanzania, United Republic of see Tanzania
Taoudenit see Taoudenni
Taoudenni 75 E2 var. Taoudenit. Tombouctou, N Mali
Tapa 106 E2 Ger. Taps. Lääne-Virumaa, NE Estonia
Tapachula 51 G5 Chiapas, SE Mexico
Tapaiu see Gvardeysk
Tapajós, Rio 63 E2 var. Tapajóz. river NW Brazil
Tapajóz see Tapajós, Rio
Taps see Tapa
Ţarābulus 71 F2 var. Ţarābulus al Gharb, Eng. Tripoli. country capital (Libya) NW Libya
Ţarābulus al Gharb see Ţarābulus
Ţarābulus/Ţarābulus ash Shām see Tripoli
Taraclia 108 D4 Rus. Tarakilya. S Moldova
Tarakilya see Taraclia
Taranaki, Mount 150 C4 var. Egmont. volcano North Island, New Zealand
Tarancón 93 E3 Castilla-La Mancha, C Spain
Taranto 97 E5 var. Tarentum. Puglia, SE Italy
Taranto, Golfo di 97 E6 Eng. Gulf of Taranto. gulf S Italy
Taranto, Gulf of see Taranto, Golfo di
Tarapoto 60 C2 San Martín, N Peru
Tarare 91 D5 Rhône, E France
Tarascon 91 D6 Bouches-du-Rhône, SE France
Tarawa 144 D2 atoll Tungaru, W Kiribati

INDEX - GAZETTEER: **Taraz – Thamarīt**

Taraz *114 C5 prev.* Aulie Ata, Auliye-Ata, Dzhambul, Zhambyl. Zhambyl, S Kazakhstan
Tarazona *93 E2* Aragón, NE Spain
Tarbes *91 B6 anc.* Bigorra. Hautes-Pyrénées, S France
Tarcoola *149 A6* South Australia
Taree *149 D6* New South Wales, SE Australia
Tarentum *see* Taranto
Târgovişte *108 C5 prev.* Tîrgovişte. Dâmboviţa, S Romania
Târgu Jiu *108 B4 prev.* Tîrgu Jiu. Gorj, W Romania
Târgul-Neamţ *see* Târgu-Neamţ
Târgul-Săcuiesc *see* Târgu Secuiesc
Târgu Mureş *108 B4 prev.* Oşorhei, Tîrgu Mures, *Ger.* Neumarkt, *Hung.* Marosvásárhely. Mureş, C Romania
Târgu-Neamţ *108 C3 var.* Târgul-Neamţ; *prev.* Tîrgu-Neamţ. Neamţ, NE Romania
Târgu Ocna *108 C4 Hung.* Aknavásár; *prev.* Tîrgu Ocna. Bacău, E Romania
Târgu Secuiesc *108 C4 Ger.* Neumarkt, Szekler Neumarkt, *Hung.* Kezdivásárhely; *prev.* Chezdi-Oşorheiu, Târgul-Săcuiesc, Tîrgu Secuiesc. Covasna, E Romania
Tar Heel State *see* North Carolina
Tarija *61 G5* Tarija, S Bolivia
Tarīm *121 C6* C Yemen
Tarim Basin *see* Tarim Pendi
Tarim He *126 B3 river* NW China
Tarim Pendi *124 C2 Eng.* Tarim Basin. *basin* NW China
Tarma *60 C3* Junín, C Peru
Tarn *91 C6 cultural region* S France
Tarn *91 C6 department* S France
Tarn *91 C6 river* S France
Tarnobrzeg *98 D4* Podkarpackie, SE Poland
Tarnopol *see* Ternopil'
Tarnów *99 D5* Małopolskie, S Poland
Tarraco *see* Tarragona
Tarragona *93 G2 anc.* Tarraco. Cataluña, E Spain
Tarrasa *see* Terrassa
Tàrrega *93 F2 var.* Tarrega. Cataluña, NE Spain
Tarsatica *see* Rijeka
Tarsus *116 C4* Mersin, S Turkey
Tartous/Tartouss *see* Ţarţūs
Tartu *106 D3 Ger.* Dorpat; *prev. Rus* Yurev, Yury'ev. Tartumaa, SE Estonia
Ţarţūs *118 A3 off.* Muḩāfaz̧at Ţarţūs, *var.* Tartous, Tartus. *governorate* W Syria
Ţarţūs, Muḩāfaz̧at *see* Ţarţūs
Ta Ru Tao, Ko *137 B7 island* S Thailand Asia
Tarvisio *96 D2* Friuli-Venezia Giulia, NE Italy
Tarvisium *see* Treviso
Tashauz *see* Daşoguz
Tashi Chho Dzong *see* Thimphu
Tashkent *see* Toshkent
Tash-Kömür *see* Tash-Kumyr
Tash-Kumyr *123 F2 Kir.* Tash-Kömür. Dzhalal-Abadskaya Oblast', W Kyrgyzstan
Tashqurghan *see* Kholm
Tasikmalaja *see* Tasikmalaya
Tasikmalaya *138 C5 prev.* Tasikmalaja. Jawa, C Indonesia
Tasman Basin *142 C5 var.* East Australian Basin. *undersea basin* S Tasman Sea
Tasman Bay *151 C5 inlet* South Island, New Zealand
Tasmania *149 B8 prev.* Van Diemen's Land. *state* SE Australia
Tasmania *152 B4 island* SE Australia
Tasman Plateau *142 C5 var.* South Tasmania Plateau. *undersea plateau* SW Tasman Sea
Tasman Sea *142 C5 sea* SW Pacific Ocean
Tassili-n-Ajjer *71 E4 plateau* E Algeria
Tatabánya *99 C6* Komárom-Esztergom, NW Hungary
Tatar Pazardzhik *see* Pazardzhik
Tathlīth *121 B5* 'Asīr, S Saudi Arabia
Tatra Mountains *99 D5 Ger.* Tatra, *Hung.* Tátra, *Pol./Slvk.* Tatry. *mountain range* Poland/Slovakia
Tatra/Tátra *see* Tatra Mountains
Tatry *see* Tatra Mountains
Ta-t'ung/Tatung *see* Datong
Tatvan *117 F3* Bitlis, SE Turkey
Ta'ū *145 F4 island* Manua Islands, E American Samoa
Taukum, Peski *123 G1 desert* SE Kazakhstan
Taumarunui *150 D4* Manawatu-Wanganui, North Island, New Zealand
Taungdwingyi *136 B3* Magwe, C Myanmar (Burma)
Taunggyi *136 B3* Shan State, C Myanmar (Burma)
Taunton *89 C7* SW England, UK
Taupo *150 D3* Waikato, North Island, New Zealand
Taupo, Lake *150 D3 lake* North Island, New Zealand
Tauragė *106 B4 Ger.* Tauroggen. Tauragė, SW Lithuania
Tauranga *150 D3* Bay of Plenty, North Island, New Zealand
Tauris *see* Tabrīz
Tauroggen *see* Tauragė
Taurus Mountains *see* Toros Dağları
Tavas *116 B4* Denizli, SW Turkey
Tavastehus *see* Hämeenlinna
Tavira *92 C5* Faro, S Portugal
Tavoy *137 B5 var.* Dawei. Tenasserim, S Myanmar (Burma)
Tavoy Island *see* Mali Kyun
Tawakoni, Lake *49 G2 reservoir* Texas, SW USA
Tawau *138 D3* Sabah, East Malaysia
Ţawkar *see* Tokar
Tawzar *see* Tozeur
Taxco *51 E4 var.* Taxco de Alarcón. Guerrero, S Mexico
Taxco de Alarcón *see* Taxco
Takhiatosh *122 C2 Rus.* Takhiatash. Qoraqalpoghiston Respublikasi, W Uzbekistan
Taxtako'pir *122 D1 Rus.* Takhtakupyr. Qoraqalpog'iston Respublikasi, NW Uzbekistan
Tay *88 C3 river* C Scotland, UK
Taylor *49 G3* Texas, SW USA
Taymā' *120 A4* Tabūk, NW Saudi Arabia
Taymyr, Ozero *115 E2 lake* N Russian Federation
Taymyr, Poluostrov *115 E2 peninsula* N Russian Federation
Taz *114 D3 river* N Russian Federation
T'bilisi *117 G2 Eng.* Tiflis. *country capital* (Georgia) SE Georgia
Tchad *see* Chad
Tchad, Lac *see* Chad, Lake
Tchien *see* Zwedru
Tchongking *see* Chongqing
Tczew *98 C2 Ger.* Dirschau. Pomorskie, N Poland
Te Anau *151 A7* Southland, South Island, New Zealand
Te Anau, Lake *151 A7 lake* South Island, New Zealand
Teapa *51 G4* Tabasco, SE Mexico
Teate *see* Chieti
Tebingtinggi *138 B3* Sumatera, N Indonesia
Tebriz *see* Tabrīz
Techirghiol *108 D5* Constanţa, SE Romania
Tecomán *50 D4* Colima, SW Mexico
Tecpan *51 E5 var.* Tecpan de Galeana. Guerrero, S Mexico
Tecpan de Galeana *see* Tecpan
Tecuci *108 C4* Galaţi, E Romania
Tedzhen *see* Harīrūd/Tejen
Tedzhen *see* Tejen
Tees *89 D5 river* N England, UK
Tefé *62 D2* Amazonas, N Brazil
Tegal *138 C4* Jawa, C Indonesia
Tegelen *87 D5* Limburg, SE Netherlands
Tegucigalpa *52 C3 country capital* (Honduras) Francisco Morazán, SW Honduras
Teheran *see* Tehrān
Tehrān *120 C3 var.* Teheran. *country capital* (Iran) Tehrān, N Iran
Tehuacán *51 F4* Puebla, S Mexico
Tehuantepec *51 F5 var.* Santo Domingo Tehuantepec. Oaxaca, SE Mexico
Tehuantepec, Golfo de *51 F5 var.* Gulf of Tehuantepec. *gulf* S Mexico
Tehuantepec, Gulf of *see* Tehuantepec, Golfo de
Tehuantepec, Isthmus of *see* Tehuantepec, Istmo de
Tehuantepec, Istmo de *51 F5 var.* Isthmus of Tehuantepec. *isthmus* SE Mexico
Tejen *122 C3 Rus.* Tedzhen. Ahal Welaýaty, S Turkmenistan
Tejen *see* Harīrūd
Tejo, Rio *see* Tagus
Te Kao *150 C1* Northland, North Island, New Zealand
Tekax *51 H4 var.* Tekax de Álvaro Obregón. Yucatán, SE Mexico
Tekax de Álvaro Obregón *see* Tekax
Tekeli *114 C5* Almaty, SE Kazakhstan
Tekirdağ *116 A2 It.* Rodosto; *anc.* Bisanthe, Raidestos, Rhaedestus. Tekirdağ, NW Turkey
Te Kuiti *150 D3* Waikato, North Island, New Zealand
Tela *52 C2* Atlántida, NW Honduras
Telanaipura *see* Jambi
Tel Aviv-Jaffa *see* Tel Aviv-Yafo
Tel Aviv-Yafo *119 A6 var.* Tel Aviv-Jaffa. Tel Aviv, C Israel
Teles Pirés *see* São Manuel, Rio
Telish *104 C2 prev.* Azizie. Pleven, N Bulgaria
Tell Abiad/Tell Abyad *see* At Tall al Abyaḑ
Tell Kalakh *see* Tall Kalakh
Tell Shedadi *see* Ash Shadādah
Tel'man/Tel'mansk *see* Gubadag
Teloekbetoeng *see* Bandar Lampung
Telo Martius *see* Toulon
Telschen *see* Telšiai
Telšiai *106 B3 Ger.* Telschen. Telšiai, NW Lithuania
Telukbetung *see* Bandar Lampung
Temerin *100 D3* Vojvodina, N Serbia
Temeschburg/Temeschwar *see* Timişoara
Temesvár/Temeswar *see* Timişoara
Temirtau *114 C4 prev.* Samarkandski, Samarkandskoye. Karaganda, C Kazakhstan
Tempio Pausania *97 A5* Sardegna, Italy, C Mediterranean Sea
Temple *49 G3* Texas, SW USA
Temuco *65 B5* Araucanía, C Chile
Temuka *151 B6* Canterbury, South Island, New Zealand
Tenasserim *137 B6* Tenasserim, S Myanmar (Burma)
Ténenkou *74 D3* Mopti, C Mali
Ténéré *75 G3 physical region* C Niger
Tenerife *70 A3 island* Islas Canarias, Spain, NE Atlantic Ocean
Tengger Shamo *127 E3 desert* N China
Tengréla *74 D4 var.* Tingréla. N Côte d'Ivoire (Ivory Coast)
Tenkodogo *75 E4* S Burkina Faso
Tennant Creek *148 A3* Northern Territory, C Australia
Tennessee *42 C1 off.* State of Tennessee, *also known as* The Volunteer State. *state* SE USA
Tennessee River *42 C1 river* S USA
Tenojoki *see* Deatnu
Tenos *see* Tínos
Tepelena *see* Tepelenë
Tepelenë *101 C7 var.* Tepelena, *It.* Tepeleni. Gjirokastër, S Albania
Tepeleni *see* Tepelenë
Tepic *50 D4* Nayarit, C Mexico
Teplice *98 A4 Ger.* Teplitz; *prev.* Teplice-Šanov, Teplitz-Schönau. Ústecký Kraj, NW Czech Republic
Teplice-Šanov/Teplitz/Teplitz-Schönau *see* Teplice
Tequila *50 D4* Jalisco, SW Mexico
Teraina *145 G2 prev.* Washington Island. *atoll* Line Islands, E Kiribati
Teramo *96 C4 anc.* Interamna. Abruzzi, C Italy
Tercan *117 E3* Erzincan, NE Turkey
Terceira *92 A5 var.* Ilha Terceira. *island* Azores, Portugal, NE Atlantic Ocean
Terceira, Ilha *see* Terceira
Terekhovka *see* Tsyerakhowka
Teresina *63 F2 var.* Therezina. *state capital* Piauí, NE Brazil
Termez *see* Termiz
Termia *see* Kýthnos
Términos, Laguna de *51 G4 lagoon* SE Mexico
Termiz *123 E3 Rus.* Termez. Surkhondaryo Viloyati, S Uzbekistan
Termoli *96 D4* Molise, C Italy
Terneuzen *87 B5 var.* Neuzen. Zeeland, SW Netherlands
Terni *96 C4 anc.* Interamna Nahars. Umbria, C Italy
Ternopil' *108 C2 Pol.* Tarnopol, *Rus.* Ternopol'. Ternopil's'ka Oblast', W Ukraine
Ternopol' *see* Ternopil'
Terracina *97 C5* Lazio, C Italy
Terranova di Sicilia *see* Gela
Terranova Pausania *see* Olbia
Terrassa *93 G2 Cast.* Tarrasa. Cataluña, E Spain
Terre Adélie *154 C4 physical region* SE Antarctica Antarctica
Terre Haute *40 B4* Indiana, N USA
Terre Neuve *see* Newfoundland and Labrador
Terschelling *86 C1 Fris.* Skylge. *island* Waddeneilanden, N Netherlands
Teruel *93 F3 anc.* Turba. Aragón, E Spain
Tervel *101 E1 prev.* Kurtbunar, *Rom.* Curtbunar. Dobrich, NE Bulgaria
Tervueren *see* Tervuren
Tervuren *87 C6 var.* Tervueren. Vlaams Brabant, C Belgium
Teseney *72 C4 var.* Tessenei. W Eritrea
Tessalit *75 E2* Kidal, NE Mali
Tessaoua *75 G3* Maradi, S Niger
Tessenderlo *87 C5* Limburg, NE Belgium
Tessenei *see* Teseney
Testigos, Islas los *59 E1 island group* N Venezuela
Tete *79 E2* Tete, NW Mozambique
Teterow *94 C3* Mecklenburg-Vorpommern, NE Germany
Tétouan *70 C2 var.* Tetouan, Tetuán. N Morocco
Tetovo *101 D5* Razgrad, N Bulgaria
Tetschen *see* Děčín
Tetuán *see* Tétouan
Tevere *96 C4 Eng.* Tiber. *river* C Italy
Teverya *119 B5 var.* Tiberias, Tverya. Northern, N Israel
Te Waewae Bay *151 A7 bay* South Island, New Zealand
Texarkana *42 A2* Arkansas, C USA
Texarkana *49 H2* Texas, SW USA
Texas *49 F3 off.* State of Texas, *also known as* Lone Star State. *state* S USA
Texas City *49 H4* Texas, SW USA
Texel *86 C2 island* Waddeneilanden, NW Netherlands
Texoma, Lake *49 G2 reservoir* Oklahoma/Texas, C USA
Teziutlán *51 F4* Puebla, S Mexico
Thai, Ao *see* Thailand, Gulf of
Thai Binh *136 D3* Thai Binh, N Vietnam
Thailand *137 C5 off.* Kingdom of Thailand, *Th.* Prathet Thai; *prev.* Siam. *country* SE Asia

THAILAND
Southeastern Asia

Official name Kingdom of Thailand
Formation 1238 / 1907
Capital Bangkok
Population 64.2 million / 325 people per sq mile (126 people per sq km) / 22%
Total area 198,455 sq miles (514,000 sq km)
Languages Thai*, Chinese, Malay, Khmer, Mon, Karen, Miao
Religions Buddhist 95%, Muslim 4%, Other (including Christian) 1%
Ethnic mix Thai 83%, Chinese 12%, Malay 3%, Khmer and Other 2%
Government Parliamentary system
Currency Baht = 100 stang
Literacy rate 93%
Calorie consumption 2467 calories

Thailand, Gulf of *137 C6 var.* Gulf of Siam, *Th.* Ao Thai, *Vtn.* Vinh Thai Lan. *gulf* SE Asia
Thailand, Kingdom of *see* Thailand
Thai Lan, Vinh *see* Thailand, Gulf of
Thai Nguyên *136 D3* Bắc Thai, N Vietnam
Thakhèk *136 D4 var.* Muang Khammouan. Khammouan, C Laos
Thamarīd *see* Thamarīt
Thamarīt *121 D6 var.* Thamarīd, Thumrayt. SW Oman

Thames *150 D3* Waikato, North Island, New Zealand
Thames *89 B8* *river* S England, UK
Thanh Hoa *136 D3* Thanh Hoa, N Vietnam
Thanintari Taungdan *see* Bilauktaung Range
Thanlwin *see* Salween
Thar Desert *134 C3* *var.* Great Indian Desert, Indian Desert. *desert* India/Pakistan
Tharthār, Buḥayrat ath *120 B3* *lake* C Iraq
Thásos *104 C4* Thásos, E Greece
Thásos *104 C4* *island* E Greece
Thaton *136 B4* Mon State, S Myanmar (Burma)
Thayetmyo *136 A4* Magwe, C Myanmar (Burma)
The Crane *55 H2* *var.* Crane. S Barbados
The Dalles *46 B3* Oregon, NW USA
The Flatts Village *see* Flatts Village
The Hague *see* 's-Gravenhage
Theodosia *see* Feodosiya
The Pas *37 F5* Manitoba, C Canada
Therezina *see* Teresina
Thérma *105 D6* Ikaría, Dodekánisa, Greece, Aegean Sea
Thermaic Gulf/Thermaicus Sinus *see* Thermaïkós Kólpos
Thermaïkós Kólpos *104 B4* *Eng.* Thermaic Gulf; *anc.* Thermaicus Sinus. *gulf* N Greece
Thérmia *see* Kýthnos
Thérmo *105 B5* Dytikí Ellás, C Greece
The Rock *93 H4* New South Wales, SE Australia
The Sooner State *see* Oklahoma
Thessaloníki *104 C3* *Eng.* Salonica, Salonika, *SCr.* Solun, *Turk.* Selânik. Kentrikí Makedonía, N Greece
The Valley *55 G3* *dependent territory capital* (Anguilla) E Anguilla
The Village *49 G1* Oklahoma, C USA
The Volunteer State *see* Tennessee
Thiamis *see* Kalamás
Thian Shan *see* Tien Shan
Thibet *see* Xizang Zizhiqu
Thief River Falls *45 F1* Minnesota, N USA
Thienen *see* Tienen
Thiers *91 C5* Puy-de-Dôme, C France
Thiès *74 B3* W Senegal
Thikombia *see* Cikobia
Thimbu *see* Thimphu
Thimphu *135 G3* *var.* Thimbu; *prev.* Tashi Chho Dzong. *country capital* (Bhutan) W Bhutan
Thionville *90 D3* *Ger.* Diedenhofen. Moselle, NE France
Thíra *105 D7* Santorini, Kykládes, Greece, Aegean Sea
Thíra *see* Santorini
Thiruvanathapuram *see* Trivandrum
Thitu Island *128 C8* *island* NW Spratly Islands
Tholen *86 B4* *island* SW Netherlands
Thomasville *42 D3* Georgia, SE USA
Thompson *37 F4* Manitoba, C Canada
Thonon-les-Bains *91 D5* Haute-Savoie, E France
Thorenburg *see* Turda
Thorlákshöfn *83 E5* Sudhurland, SW Iceland
Thorn *see* Toruń
Thornton Island *see* Millennium Island
Thorshavn *see* Tórshavn
Thospitis *see* Van Gölü
Thouars *90 B4* Deux-Sèvres, W France
Thoune *see* Thun
Thracian Sea *104 D4* *Gk.* Thrakikó Pélagos; *anc.* Thracium Mare. *sea* Greece/Turkey
Thracium Mare/Thrakikó Pélagos *see* Thracian Sea
Three Kings Islands *150 C1* *island group* N New Zealand
Thrissur *see* Kýthnos
Thuin *87 B7* Hainaut, S Belgium
Thule *see* Qaanaaq

Thumrayt *see* Thamarīt
Thun *95 A7* *Fr.* Thoune. Bern, W Switzerland
Thunder Bay *38 B4* Ontario, S Canada
Thuner See *95 A7* *lake* C Switzerland
Thung Song *137 C7* *var.* Cha Mai. Nakhon Si Thammarat, SW Thailand
Thurso *88 C2* N Scotland, UK
Thýamis *see* Kalamás
Tianjin *128 D4* *var.* Tientsin. Tianjin Shi, E China
Tianjin *see* Tianjin Shi
Tianjin Shi *128 D4* *var.* Jīn, Tianjin, T'ien-ching, Tientsin. *municipality* E China
Tian Shan *see* Tien Shan
Tianshui *128 B4* Gansu, C China
Tiba *see* Chiba
Tiber *see* Tevere, Italy
Tiber *see* Tivoli, Italy
Tiberias *see* Teverya
Tiberias, Lake *119 B5* *var.* Chinnereth, Sea of Bahr Tabariya, Sea of Galilee, *Ar.* Bahrat Tabariya, *Heb.* Yam Kinneret. *lake* N Israel
Tibesti *76 C2* *var.* Tibesti Massif, *Ar.* Tibīstī. *mountain range* N Africa
Tibesti Massif *see* Tibesti
Tibet *see* Xizang Zizhiqu
Tibetan Autonomous Region *see* Xizang Zizhiqu
Tibet, Plateau of *see* Qingzang Gaoyuan
Tibistī *see* Tibesti
Tibni *see* At Tibnī
Tiburón, Isla *50 B2* *var.* Isla del Tiburón. *island* NW Mexico
Tiburón, Isla del *see* Tiburón, Isla
Tichau *see* Tychy
Tichît *74 D2* *var.* Tichitt. Tagant, C Mauritania
Tichitt *see* Tichît
Ticinum *see* Pavia
Ticul *51 H3* Yucatán, SE Mexico
Tidjikdja *see* Tidjikja
Tidjikja *74 C2* *var.* Tidjikdja; *prev.* Fort-Cappolani. Tagant, C Mauritania
T'ien-ching *see* Tianjin Shi
Tienen *87 C6* *var.* Thienen, *Fr.* Tirlemont. Vlaams Brabant, C Belgium
Tiên Giang, Sông *see* Mekong
Tien Shan *126 B3* *Chin.* Thian Shan, Tian Shan, T'ien Shan, *Rus.* Tyan'-Shan'. *mountain range* C Asia
Tientsin *see* Tianjin
Tierp *85 C6* Uppsala, C Sweden
Tierra del Fuego *65 B8* *island* Argentina/Chile
Tiflis *see* T'bilisi
Tifton *42 D3* Georgia, SE USA
Tifu *139 F4* Pulau Buru, E Indonesia
Tighina *108 D4* *Rus.* Bendery; *prev.* Bender. E Moldova
Tigranocerta *see* Siirt
Tigris *120 B2* *Ar.* Dijlah, *Turk.* Dicle. *river* Iraq/Turkey
Tiguentourine *71 E3* E Algeria
Ti-hua/Tihwa *see* Ürümqi
Tijuana *50 A1* Baja California, NW Mexico
Tikhoretsk *111 A7* Krasnodarskiy Kray, SW Russian Federation
Tikhvin *110 B4* Leningradskaya Oblast', NW Russian Federation
Tiki Basin *143 G3* *undersea basin* S Pacific Ocean
Tikinsso *43 G3* *river* E Guinea
Tiksi *115 F2* Respublika Sakha (Yakutiya), NE Russian Federation
Tilburg *86 C4* Noord-Brabant, S Netherlands
Tilimsen *see* Tlemcen
Tilio Martius *see* Toulon
Tillabéri *75 F3* *var.* Tillabéry. Tillabéri, W Niger
Tillabéry *see* Tillabéri
Tílos *105 E7* *island* Dodekánisa, Greece, Aegean Sea
Timan Ridge *see* Timanskiy Kryazh
Timanskiy Kryazh *110 D3* *Eng.* Timan Ridge. *ridge* NW Russian Federation
Timaru *151 B6* Canterbury, South Island, New Zealand
Timbaki/Timbákion *see* Tympáki
Timbedgha *74 D3* *var.* Timbédra. Hodh ech Chargui, SE Mauritania

Timbédra *see* Timbedgha
Timbuktu *see* Tombouctou
Timiş *108 A4* *county* SW Romania
Timişoara *108 A4* *Ger.* Temeschwar, Temeswar, *Hung.* Temesvár; *prev.* Temeschburg. Timiş, W Romania
Timmins *38 C4* Ontario, S Canada
Timor *125 F5* *island* Nusa Tenggara, C Indonesia
Timor Sea *125 F5* *sea* E Indian Ocean
Timor Timur *see* East Timor
Timor Trench *see* Timor Trough
Timor Trough *125 F5* *var.* Timor Trench. *trough* NE Timor Sea
Timrå *85 C5* Västernorrland, C Sweden
Tindouf *70 C3* W Algeria
Tineo *92 C1* Asturias, N Spain
Tingis *see* Tanger
Tingo María *60 C3* Huánuco, C Peru
Tingréla *see* Tengréla
Tinhosa Grande *76 E2* *island* N Sao Tome and Principe, Africa, E Atlantic Ocean
Tinhosa Pequena *76 E1* *island* N Sao Tome and Principe, Africa, E Atlantic Ocean
Tinian *144 B1* *island* S Northern Mariana Islands
Tínos *105 D6* Tínos, Kykládes, Greece, Aegean Sea
Tínos *105 D6* *anc.* Tenos. *island* Kykládes, Greece, Aegean Sea
Tip *101 E6* Papua, E Indonesia
Tipitapa *52 D3* Managua, W Nicaragua
Tip Top Mountain *38 C4* *mountain* Ontario, S Canada
Tirana *see* Tiranë
Tiranë *101 C6* *var.* Tirana. *country capital* (Albania) Tiranë, C Albania
Tiraspol *108 D4* *Rus.* Tiraspol'. E Moldova
Tiraspol *see* Tiraspol
Tiree *88 B3* *island* W Scotland, UK
Tîrgovişte *see* Târgovişte
Tîrgu Jiu *see* Târgu Jiu
Tîrgu Mures *see* Târgu Mureş
Tîrgu-Neamţ *see* Târgu-Neamţ
Tîrgu Ocna *see* Târgu Ocna
Tîrgu Secuiesc *see* Târgu Secuiesc
Tirlemont *see* Tienen
Tírnavos *see* Týrnavos
Tirnovo *see* Veliko Tŭrnovo
Tirol *95 C7* *off.* Land Tirol, *var.* Tyrol, *It.* Tirolo. *state* W Austria
Tirol, Land *see* Tirol
Tirolo *see* Tirol
Tirreno, Mare *see* Tyrrhenian Sea
Tiruchchirāppalli *132 C3* *prev.* Trichinopoly. Tamil Nādu, SE India
Tiruppattūr *132 C2* Tamil Nādu, SE India
Tisa *see* Tisza
Tisza *103 F1* *Ger.* Theiss, *Rom./Slvn./SCr.* Tisa, *Rus.* Tissa, *Ukr.* Tysa. *river* SE Europe
Tiszakécske *99 D7* Bács-Kiskun, C Hungary
Titano, Monte *96 E1* *mountain* C San Marino
Titicaca, Lake *61 E4* *lake* Bolivia/Peru
Titograd *see* Podgorica
Titose *see* Chitose
Titova Mitrovica *see* Kosovska Mitrovica
Titovo Užice *see* Užice
Titu *108 C5* Dâmbovíţa, S Romania
Titule *77 D5* Orientale, N Dem. Rep. Congo
Tiverton *89 C7* SW England, UK
Tivoli *96 C4* *anc.* Tiber. Lazio, C Italy
Tizimín *51 H3* Yucatán, SE Mexico
Tizi-Ouzou *71 E1* *var.* Tizi-Ouzou. N Algeria
Tizi-Ouzou *see* Tizi Ouzou
Tiznit *70 B3* SW Morocco
Tjilatjap *see* Cilacap
Tjirebon *see* Cirebon
Tlaquepaque *50 D4* Jalisco, C Mexico
Tlascala *see* Tlaxcala
Tlaxcala *51 F4* *var.* Tlascala, Tlaxcala de Xicohténcatl. Tlaxcala, C Mexico
Tlaxcala de Xicohténcatl *see* Tlaxcala
Tlemcen *70 D2* *var.* Tilimsen, Tlemsen. NW Algeria
Tlemsen *see* Tlemcen
Toamasina *79 G3* *var.* Tamatave. Toamasina, E Madagascar

Toba, Danau *138 B3* *lake* Sumatera, W Indonesia
Tobago *55 H5* *island* NE Trinidad and Tobago
Tobol *114 C4* *Kaz.* Tobyl. *river* Kazakhstan/Russian Federation
Tobol'sk *114 C3* Tyumenskaya Oblast', C Russian Federation
Tobruch/Tobruk *see* Ţubruq
Tobyl *see* Tobol
Tocantins *63 E3* *off.* Estado do Tocantins. *state* C Brazil
Tocantins, Estado do *see* Tocantins
Tocantins, Rio *63 F2* *river* N Brazil
Tocoa *52 D2* Colón, N Honduras
Tocopilla *64 B2* Antofagasta, N Chile
Todi *96 C4* Umbria, C Italy
Todos os Santos, Baía de *63 G3* *bay* E Brazil
Toetoes Bay *151 B8* *bay* South Island, New Zealand
Tofua *145 E4* *island* Ha'apai Group, C Tonga
Togo *75 E4* *off.* Togolese Republic; *prev.* French Togoland. *country* W Africa

TOGO
Western Africa

Official name Republic of Togo
Formation 1960 / 1960
Capital Lomé
Population 6.1 million / 290 people per sq mile (112 people per sq km) / 33%
Total area 21,924 sq miles (56,785 sq km)
Languages French*, Ewe, Kabye, Gurma
Religions Traditional beliefs 50%, Christian 35%, Muslim 15%
Ethnic mix Ewe 46%, Kabye 27%, Other African 26%, European 1%
Government Presidential system
Currency CFA franc = 100 centimes
Literacy rate 53%
Calorie consumption 2345 calories

Togolese Republic *see* Togo
Tojikiston, Jumhurii *see* Tajikistan
Tokanui *151 B7* Southland, South Island, New Zealand
Tokar *72 C3* *var.* Ţawkar. Red Sea, NE Sudan
Tokat *116 D3* Tokat, N Turkey
Tokelau *145 E3* *NZ overseas territory* W Polynesia
Tōketerebes *see* Trebišov
Tokio *see* Tōkyō
Tokmak *123 G2* *Kir.* Tokmok. Chuyskaya Oblast', N Kyrgyzstan
Tokmak *109 G4* *var.* Velykyy Tokmak. Zaporiz'ka Oblast', SE Ukraine
Tokmok *see* Tokmak
Tokoroa *150 D3* Waikato, North Island, New Zealand
Tokounou *74 C4* C Guinea
Tokushima *131 C6* *var.* Tokusima. Tokushima, Shikoku, SW Japan
Tōkyō *130 A1* *var.* Tokio. *country capital* (Japan) Tōkyō, Honshū, S Japan
Tōkyō-wan *130 A2* *bay* S Japan
Tolbukhin *see* Dobrich
Toledo *92 D3* *anc.* Toletum. Castilla-La Mancha, C Spain
Toledo *40 D3* Ohio, N USA
Toledo Bend Reservoir *49 G3* *reservoir* Louisiana/Texas, SW USA
Toletum *see* Toledo
Toliara *79 F4* *var.* Toliary; *prev.* Tuléar. Toliara, SW Madagascar
Toliary *see* Toliara
Tolmein *see* Tolmin
Tolmin *95 D7* *Ger.* Tolmein, *It.* Tolmino. W Slovenia
Tolmino *see* Tolmin
Tolna *99 C7* *Ger.* Tolnau. Tolna, S Hungary
Tolnau *see* Tolna
Tolochin *see* Talachyn
Tolosa *93 E1* País Vasco, N Spain
Tolosa *see* Toulouse
Toluca *51 E4* *var.* Toluca de Lerdo. México, S Mexico
Toluca de Lerdo *see* Toluca
Tol'yatti *111 C6* *prev.* Stavropol'. Samarskaya Oblast', W Russian Federation

Tomah *40 B2* Wisconsin, N USA
Tomakomai *130 D2* Hokkaidō, NE Japan
Tomar *92 B3* Santarém, W Portugal
Tomaschow *see* Tomaszów Mazowiecki
Tomaschow *see* Tomaszów Lubelski
Tomaszów *see* Tomaszów Mazowiecki
Tomaszów Lubelski *98 E4 Ger.* Tomaschow. Lubelskie, E Poland
Tomaszów Mazowiecka *see* Tomaszów Mazowiecki
Tomaszów Mazowiecki *98 D4 var.* Tomaszów Mazowiecka; *prev.* Tomaszów, *Ger.* Tomaschow. Łódzkie, C Poland
Tombigbee River *42 C3 river* Alabama/Mississippi, S USA
Tombouctou *75 E3 Eng.* Timbuktu. Tombouctou, N Mali
Tombua *78 A2 Port.* Porto Alexandre. Namibe, SW Angola
Tomelloso *93 E3* Castilla-La Mancha, C Spain
Tomini, Gulf of *139 E4 var.* Teluk Tomini; *prev.* Teluk Gorontalo. *bay* Sulawesi, C Indonesia
Tomini, Teluk *see* Tomini, Gulf of
Tomsk *114 D4* Tomskaya Oblast', C Russian Federation
Tomür Feng *see* Pobedy, Pik
Tonezh *see* Tonyezh
Tonga *145 E4 off.* Kingdom of Tonga, *var.* Friendly Islands. *country* SW Pacific Ocean

TONGA
Australasia & Oceania

Official name Kingdom of Tonga
Formation 1970 / 1970
Capital Nuku'alofa
Population 112,422 / 404 people per sq mile (156 people per sq km) / 43%
Total area 289 sq miles (748 sq km)
Languages Tongan*, English
Religions Free Wesleyan 41%, Roman Catholic 16%, Church of Jesus Christ of Latter-day Saints 14%, Free Church of Tonga 12%, Other 17%
Ethnic mix Polynesian 99%, Other 1%
Government Monarchy
Currency Pa'anga (Tongan dollar) = 100 seniti
Literacy rate 99%
Calorie consumption Not available

Tonga, Kingdom of *see* Tonga
Tongatapu *145 E5 island* Tongatapu Group, S Tonga
Tonga Trench *143 E3 trench* S Pacific Ocean
Tongchuan *128 C4* Shaanxi, C China
Tongeren *87 D6 Fr.* Tongres. Limburg, NE Belgium
Tongking, Gulf of *128 B7 Chin.* Beibu Wan, *Vtn.* Vinh Băc Bô. *gulf* China/Vietnam
Tongliao *127 G2* Nei Mongol Zizhiqu, N China
Tongres *see* Tongeren
Tongshan *see* Xuzhou, Jiangsu, China
Tongtian He *126 C4 river* C China
Tonj *73 B5* Warab, SW Sudan
Tônlé Sap *137 D5 Eng.* Great Lake. *lake* W Cambodia
Tonopah *47 C6* Nevada, W USA
Tonyezh *107 C7 Rus.* Tonezh. Homyel'skaya Voblasts', SE Belarus
Tooele *44 B4* Utah, W USA
Toowoomba *149 E5* Queensland, E Australia
Topeka *45 F4 state capital* Kansas, C USA
Toplicza *see* Toplița
Toplița *108 C3 Ger.* Töplitz, *Hung.* Maroshevíz; *prev.* Toplița Română, *Hung.* Oláh-Toplicza, Toplicza. Harghita, C Romania
Toplița Română/Töplitz *see* Toplița
Topoľčany *99 C6 Hung.* Nagytapolcsány. Nitriansky Kraj, W Slovakia
Topolovgrad *104 D3 prev.* Kavakli. Khaskovo, S Bulgaria
Topolya *see* Bačka Topola
Top Springs Roadhouse *146 D3* Northern Territory, N Australia
Torda *see* Turda
Torez *109 H3* Donets'ka Oblast', SE Ukraine
Torgau *94 D4* Sachsen, E Germany
Torhout *87 A5* West-Vlaanderen, W Belgium
Torino *96 A2 Eng.* Turin. Piemonte, NW Italy
Tornacum *see* Tournai
Torneå *see* Tornio
Torneträsk *84 C3 lake* N Sweden
Tornio *84 D4 Swe.* Torneå. Lappi, NW Finland
Tornionjoki *84 D3 river* Lappi/Norrbotten, Finland/Sweden
Toro *92 D2* Castilla-León, N Spain
Toronto *38 D5 province capital* Ontario, S Canada
Toros Dağları *116 C4 Eng.* Taurus Mountains. *mountain range* S Turkey
Torquay *89 C7* SW England, UK
Torrance *46 D2* California, W USA
Torre, Alto da *92 B3 mountain* C Portugal
Torre del Greco *97 D5* Campania, S Italy
Torrejón de Ardoz *93 E3* Madrid, C Spain
Torrelavega *92 D1* Cantabria, N Spain
Torrens, Lake *149 A6 salt lake* South Australia
Torrent *93 F3 Cas.* Torrente, *var.* Torrent de l'Horta. País Valenciano, E Spain
Torrent de l'Horta/Torrente *see* Torrent
Torreón *50 D3* Coahuila de Zaragoza, NE Mexico
Torres Strait *148 C1 strait* Australia/Papua New Guinea
Torres Vedras *92 B3* Lisboa, C Portugal
Torrington *44 D3* Wyoming, C USA
Tórshavn *83 F5 Dan.* Thorshavn. *Dependent territory capital* Streymoy, N Faeroe Islands Europe
To'rtkok'l *122 D2 var* Tŭrtkŭl, *Rus.* Turtkul'; *prev.* Petroaleksandrovsk. Qoraqalpog'iston Respublikasi, W Uzbekistan
Tortoise Islands *see* Colón, Archipiélago de
Tortosa *93 F2 anc.* Dertosa. Cataluña, E Spain
Tortue, Montagne *59 H3 mountain range* C French Guiana
Tortuga, Isla *see* La Tortuga, Isla
Toruń *98 C3 Ger.* Thorn. Toruń, Kujawsko-pomorskie, C Poland
Tõrva *106 D3 Ger.* Törwa. Valgamaa, S Estonia
Törwa *see* Tõrva
Torzhok *110 B4* Tverskaya Oblast', W Russian Federation
Tosa-wan *131 B7 bay* SW Japan
Toscana *96 B3 Eng.* Tuscany. *region* C Italy
Toscano, Arcipelago *96 B4 Eng.* Tuscan Archipelago. *island group* C Italy
Toshkent *123 E2 Eng./Rus.* Tashkent. *country capital* (Uzbekistan) Toshkent Viloyati, E Uzbekistan
Totana *93 E4* Murcia, SE Spain
Tot'ma *see* Sukhona
Totness *59 G3* Coronie, N Suriname
Tottori *131 B6* Tottori, Honshū, SW Japan
Touâjîl *74 C2* Tiris Zemmour, N Mauritania
Touggourt *71 E2* NE Algeria
Toukoto *74 C3* Kayes, W Mali
Toul *90 D3* Meurthe-et-Moselle, NE France
Toulon *91 D6 anc.* Telo Martius, Tilio Martius. Var, SE France
Toulouse *91 B6 anc.* Tolosa. Haute-Garonne, S France
Toungoo *136 B4* Pegu, C Myanmar (Burma)
Touraine *90 B4 cultural region* C France
Tourane *see* Đă Năng
Tourcoing *90 C2* Nord, N France
Tournai *87 A6 var.* Tournay, *Dut.* Doornik; *anc.* Tornacum. Hainaut, SW Belgium
Tournay *see* Tournai
Tours *90 B4 anc.* Caesarodunum, Turoni. Indre-et-Loire, C France
Tovarkovskiy *111 B5* Tul'skaya Oblast', W Russian Federation
Tower Island *see* Genovesa, Isla
Townsville *148 D3* Queensland, NE Australia
Towoeti Meer *see* Towuti, Danau
Towraghoudī *122 D4* Herāt, NW Afghanistan
Towson *41 F4* Maryland, NE USA
Towuti, Danau *139 E4 Dut.* Towoeti Meer. *lake* Sulawesi, C Indonesia
Toyama *131 C5* Toyama, Honshū, SW Japan
Toyama-wan *131 B5 bay* W Japan
Toyohara *see* Yuzhno-Sakhalinsk
Toyota *131 C6* Aichi, Honshū, SW Japan
Tozeur *71 E2 var.* Tawzar. W Tunisia
Trâblous *see* Tripoli
Trabzon *117 E2 Eng.* Trebizond; *anc.* Trapezus. Trabzon, NE Turkey
Traiectum ad Mosam/Traiectum Tungorum *see* Maastricht
Traiskirchen *95 E6* Niederösterreich, NE Austria
Trajani Portus *see* Civitavecchia
Trajectum ad Rhenum *see* Utrecht
Trakai *107 C5 Ger.* Traken, *Pol.* Troki. Vilnius, SE Lithuania
Traken *see* Trakai
Tralee *89 A6 Ir.* Trá Lí. SW Ireland
Trá Lí *see* Tralee
Tralles Aydın *see* Aydın
Trang *137 C7* Trang, S Thailand
Transantarctic Mountains *154 B3 mountain range* Antarctica
Transilvania *see* Transylvania
Transilvaniei, Alpi *see* Carpații Meridionali
Transjordan *see* Jordan
Transsylvanische Alpen/Transylvanian Alps *see* Carpații Meridionali
Transylvania *108 B4 Eng.* Ardeal, Transilvania, *Ger.* Siebenbürgen, *Hung.* Erdély. *cultural region* NW Romania
Trapani *97 B7 anc.* Drepanum. Sicilia, Italy, C Mediterranean Sea
Trâpeăng Vêng *137 D5* Kâmpóng Thum, C Cambodia
Trapezus *see* Trabzon
Traralgon *149 C7* Victoria, SE Australia
Trasimenischersee *see* Trasimeno, Lago
Trasimeno, Lago *96 C4 Eng.* Lake of Perugia, *Ger.* Trasimenischersee. *lake* C Italy
Traù *see* Trogir
Traverse City *40 C2* Michigan, N USA
Tra Vinh *137 D6 var.* Phu Vinh. Tra Vinh, S Vietnam
Travis, Lake *49 F3 reservoir* Texas, SW USA
Travnik *100 C4* Federacija Bosna I Hercegovina, C Bosnia and Herzegovina
Trbovlje *95 E7 Ger.* Trifail. C Slovenia
Treasure State *see* Montana
Třebíč *99 B5 Ger.* Trebitsch. Vysočina, C Czech Republic
Trebinje *101 C5* Republika Srpska, S Bosnia and Herzegovina
Trebišov *99 D6 Hung.* Tőketerebes. Košický Kraj, E Slovakia
Trebitsch *see* Třebíč
Trebnitz *see* Trzebnica
Tree Planters State *see* Nebraska
Trélazé *90 B4* Maine-et-Loire, NW France
Trelew *65 C6* Chubut, SE Argentina
Tremelo *87 C5* Vlaams Brabant, C Belgium
Trenčín *99 C5 Ger.* Trentschin, *Hung.* Trencsén. Trenčiansky Kraj, W Slovakia
Trencsén *see* Trenčín
Trengganu, Kuala *see* Kuala Terengganu
Trenque Lauquen *64 C4* Buenos Aires, E Argentina
Trent *see* Trento
Trento *96 C2 Eng.* Trent, *Ger.* Trient; *anc.* Tridentum. Trentino-Alto Adige, N Italy
Trenton *41 F4 state capital* New Jersey, NE USA
Trentschin *see* Trenčín
Tres Arroyos *65 D5* Buenos Aires, E Argentina
Treskavica *100 C4 mountain range* SE Bosnia and Herzegovina
Tres Tabernae *see* Saverne
Treves/Trèves *see* Trier
Treviso *96 C2 anc.* Tarvisium. Veneto, NE Italy
Trichinopoly *see* Tiruchchirāppalli
Trichūr *132 C3 var.* Thrissur. Kerala, SW India
Tridentum/Trient *see* Trento
Trier *95 A5 Eng.* Treves, *Fr.* Trèves; *anc.* Augusta Treverorum. Rheinland-Pfalz, SW Germany
Triesen *94 E2* SW Liechtenstein Europe
Triesenberg *94 E2* SW Liechtenstein
Trieste *96 D2 Slvn.* Trst. Friuli-Venezia Giulia, NE Italy
Trifail *see* Trbovlje
Tríkala *101 B4 prev.* Trikkala. Thessalía, C Greece
Trikkala *see* Tríkala
Trimontium *see* Plovdiv
Trinacria *see* Sicilia
Trincomalee *132 D3 var.* Trinkomali. Eastern Province, NE Sri Lanka
Trindade, Ilha da *67 C5 island* Brazil, W Atlantic Ocean
Trinidad *61 F3* Beni, N Bolivia
Trinidad *64 D4* Flores, S Uruguay
Trinidad *44 D5* Colorado, C USA
Trinidad *55 H5 island* C Trinidad and Tobago
Trinidad and Tobago *55 H5 off.* Republic of Trinidad and Tobago. *country* SE West Indies

TRINIDAD & TOBAGO
West Indies

Official name Republic of Trinidad and Tobago
Formation 1962 / 1962
Capital Port-of-Spain
Population 1.3 million / 656 people per sq mile (253 people per sq km) / 74%
Total area 1980 sq miles (5128 sq km)
Languages English*, English Creole, Hindi, French, Spanish
Religions Christian 60%, Hindu 24%, Other and nonreligious 9%, Muslim 7%
Ethnic mix East Indian 40%, Black 40%, Mixed race 19%, White and Chinese 1%
Government Parliamentary system
Currency Trinidad and Tobago dollar = 100 cents
Literacy rate 99%
Calorie consumption 2732 calories

Trinidad and Tobago, Republic of *see* Trinidad and Tobago
Trinité, Montagnes de la *59 H3 mountain range* C French Guiana
Trinity River *49 G3 river* Texas, SW USA
Trinkomali *see* Trincomalee
Trípoli *105 B6 prev.* Trípolis. Pelopónnisos, S Greece
Tripoli *118 B4 var.* Tarābulus, Ţarābulus ash Shām, Trâblous; *anc.* Tripolis. N Lebanon
Tripoli *see* Ţarābulus
Trípolis *see* Trípoli, Greece
Tripolis *see* Tripoli, Lebanon
Tristan da Cunha *69 B7 dependency of Saint Helena* SE Atlantic Ocean
Triton Island *128 B7 island* S Paracel Islands
Trivandrum *132 C3 var.* Thiruvanathapuram. *state capital* Kerala, SW India
Trnava *99 C6 Ger.* Tyrnau, *Hung.* Nagyszombat. Trnavský Kraj, W Slovakia
Trnovo *see* Veliko Tŭrnovo
Trogir *100 B4 It.* Traù. Split-Dalmacija, S Croatia
Troglav *100 B4 mountain* Bosnia and Herzegovina/Croatia
Trois-Rivières *39 E4* Québec, SE Canada
Troki *see* Trakai
Trollhättan *85 B6* Västra Götaland, S Sweden

Tromsø *84 C2 Fin.* Tromssa. Troms, N Norway
Tromssa *see* Tromsø
Trondheim *84 B4 Ger.* Drontheim; *prev.* Nidaros, Trondhjem. Sør-Trøndelag, S Norway
Trondheimsfjorden *84 B4 fjord* S Norway
Trondhjem *see* Trondheim
Troódos *102 C5 var.* Troodos Mountains. *mountain range* C Cyprus
Troodos Mountains *see* Troódos
Troppau *see* Opava
Troy *42 D3* Alabama, S USA
Troy *41 F3* New York, NE USA
Troyan *104 C2* Lovech, N Bulgaria
Troyes *90 D3 anc.* Augustobona Tricassium. Aube, N France
Trst *see* Trieste
Trstenik *100 E4* Serbia, C Serbia
Trucial States *see* United Arab Emirates
Trujillo *52 D2* Colón, NE Honduras
Trujillo *60 B3* La Libertad, NW Peru
Trujillo *92 C3* Extremadura, W Spain
Truk Islands *see* Chuuk Islands
Trün *104 B2* Pernik, W Bulgaria
Truro *39 F4* Nova Scotia, SE Canada
Truro *89 C7* SW England, UK
Trzcianka *98 B3 Ger.* Schönlanke. Pila, Wielkopolskie, C Poland
Trzebnica *98 C4 Ger.* Trebnitz. Dolnośląskie, SW Poland
Tsalka *117 F2* S Georgia Asia
Tsamkong *see* Zhanjiang
Tsangpo *see* Brahmaputra
Tsarevo *104 E2 prev.* Michurin. Burgas, E Bulgaria
Tsarigrad *see* Istanbul
Tsaritsyn *see* Volgograd
Tschakathurn *see* Čakovec
Tschaslau *see* Čáslav
Tschenstochau *see* Częstochowa
Tsefat *see* Zefat
Tselinograd *see* Astana
Tsetsen Khan *see* Öndörhaan
Tsetserleg *126 D2* Arhangay, C Mongolia
Tshela *77 B6* Bas-Congo, W Dem. Rep. Congo
Tshikapa *77 C7* Kasai Occidental, SW Dem. Rep. Congo
Tshuapa *77 D6 river* C Dem. Rep. Congo
Tshwane *78 D4 var.* Epitoli; *prev.* Pretoria. *country capital* (South Africa-administrative capital) Gauteng, NE South Africa
Tsinan *see* Jinan
Tsinghai *see* Qinghai, China
Tsing Hai *see* Qinghai Hu, China
Tsingtao/Tsingtau *see* Qingdao
Tsinkiang *see* Quanzhou
Tsintao *see* Qingdao
Tsitsihar *see* Qiqihar
Tsu *131 C6 var.* Tu. Mie, Honshū, SW Japan
Tsugaru-kaikyō *130 C3 strait* N Japan
Tsumeb *78 B3* Otjikoto, N Namibia
Tsuruga *131 C6 var.* Turuga. Fukui, Honshū, SW Japan
Tsuruoka *130 D4 var.* Turuoka. Yamagata, Honshū, C Japan
Tsushima *131 A7 var.* Tsushima-tō, Tusima. *island group* SW Japan
Tsushima-tō *see* Tsushima
Tsyerakhowka *107 D8 Rus.* Terekhovka. Homyel'skaya Voblasts', SE Belarus
Tsyurupinsk *see* Tsyurupyns'k
Tsyurupyns'k *109 E4 Rus.* Tsyurupinsk. Khersons'ka Oblast', S Ukraine
Tu *see* Tsu
Tuamotu, Archipel des *see* Tuamotu, Îles
Tuamotu Fracture Zone *143 H3 fracture zone* E Pacific Ocean
Tuamotu, Îles *145 H4 var.* Archipel des Tuamotu, Dangerous Archipelago, Tuamotu Islands. *island group* N French Polynesia
Tuamotu Islands *see* Tuamotu, Îles
Tuapi *53 E2* Región Autónoma Atlántico Norte, NE Nicaragua
Tuapse *111 A7* Krasnodarskiy Kray, SW Russian Federation
Tuba City *48 B1* Arizona, SW USA
Tubbergen *86 E3* Overijssel, E Netherlands
Tubeke *see* Tubize
Tubize *87 B6 Dut.* Tubeke. Walloon Brabant, C Belgium

Tubmanburg *74 C5* NW Liberia
Ṭubruq *71 H2 Eng.* Tobruk, *It.* Tobruch. NE Libya
Tubuai, Îles/Tubuai Islands *see* Australes, Îles
Tucker's Town *42 B5* E Bermuda
Tuckum *see* Tukums
Tucson *48 B3* Arizona, SW USA
Tucumán *see* San Miguel de Tucumán
Tucumcari *49 E2* New Mexico, SW USA
Tucupita *59 E2* Delta Amacuro, NE Venezuela
Tucuruí, Represa de *63 F2 reservoir* NE Brazil
Tudela *93 E2 Basq.* Tutera; *anc.* Tutela. Navarra, N Spain
Tudmur *118 C3 var.* Tadmur, Tamar, *Gk.* Palmyra, *Bibl.* Tadmor. Ḥimṣ, C Syria
Tuguegarao *139 E1* Luzon, N Philippines
Tuktoyaktuk *37 E3* Northwest Territories, NW Canada
Tukums *106 C3 Ger.* Tuckum. Tukums, W Latvia
Tula *111 B5* Tul'skaya Oblast', W Russian Federation
Tulancingo *51 E4* Hidalgo, C Mexico
Tulare Lake Bed *47 C7 salt flat* California, W USA
Tulcán *60 B1* Carchi, N Ecuador
Tulcea *108 D5* Tulcea, E Romania
Tul'chin *see* Tul'chyn
Tul'chyn *108 D3 Rus.* Tul'chin. Vinnyts'ka Oblast', C Ukraine
Tuléar *see* Toliara
Tulia *49 E2* Texas, SW USA
Tulle *91 C5 anc.* Tutela. Corrèze, C France
Tulln *95 E6 var.* Oberhollabrunn. Niederösterreich, NE Austria
Tully *148 D3* Queensland, NE Australia
Tulsa *49 G1* Oklahoma, C USA
Tuluá *58 B3* Valle del Cauca, W Colombia
Tulun *114 E4* Irkutskaya Oblast', S Russian Federation
Tumaco *58 A4* Nariño, SW Colombia
Tumba, Lac *see* Ntomba, Lac
Tumbes *60 A2* Tumbes, NW Peru
Tumkūr *132 C2* Karnātaka, W India
Tumuc-Humac Mountains *63 E1 var.* Serra Tumucumaque. *mountain range* N South America
Tumucumaque, Serra *see* Tumuc Humac Mountains
Tunca Nehri *see* Tundzha
Tunduru *73 C8* Ruvuma, S Tanzania
Tundzha *104 D3 Turk.* Tunca Nehri. *river* Bulgaria/Turkey
Tungabhadra Reservoir *132 C2 lake* S India
Tungaru *145 E2 prev.* Gilbert Islands. *island group* W Kiribati
T'ung-shan *see* Xuzhou
Tungsten *36 D4* Northwest Territories, W Canada
Tung-t'ing Hu *see* Dongting Hu
Tunis *71 E2 var.* Tūnis. *country capital* (Tunisia) NE Tunisia
Tunis, Golfe de *102 D3 Ar.* Khalīj Tūnis. *gulf* NE Tunisia
Tunisia *71 F2 off.* Republic of Tunisia, *Ar.* Al Jumhūrīyah at Tūnisīyah, *Fr.* République Tunisienne. *country* N Africa

TUNISIA
North Africa

Official name Republic of Tunisia
Formation 1956 / 1956
Capital Tunis
Population 10.1 million / 168 people per sq mile (65 people per sq km) / 75%
Total area 63,169 sq miles (163,610 sq km)
Languages Arabic*, French
Religions Muslim (mainly Sunni) 98%, Christian 1%, Jewish 1%
Ethnic mix Arab and Berber 98%, Jewish 1%, European 1%
Government Presidential system
Currency Tunisian dinar = 1000 millimes
Literacy rate 74%
Calorie consumption 3238 calories

Tunisia, Republic of *see* Tunisia
Tunisienne, République *see* Tunisia

Tūnisīyah, Al Jumhūrīyah at *see* Tunisia
Tūnis, Khalīj *see* Tunis, Golfe de
Tunja *58 B3* Boyacá, C Colombia
Tuong Buong *see* Tương Đương
Tương Đương *136 D4 var.* Tuong Buong. Nghệ An, N Vietnam
Tüp *see* Tyup
Tupelo *42 C2* Mississippi, S USA
Tupiza *61 G5* Potosí, S Bolivia
Turabah *121 B5* Makkah, W Saudi Arabia
Turangi *150 D4* Waikato, North Island, New Zealand
Turan Lowland *122 C2 var.* Turan Plain, *Kaz.* Turan Oypaty, *Rus.* Turanskaya Nizmennost', *Turk.* Turan Pesligi, *Uzb.* Turan Pasttekisligi. *plain* C Asia
Turan Oypaty/Turan Pesligi/Turan Plain/Turanskaya Nizmennost' *see* Turan Lowland
Turan Pasttekisligi *see* Turan Lowland
Ṭurayf *120 A3* Al Ḥudūd ash Shamālīyah, NW Saudi Arabia
Turba *see* Teruel
Turbat *134 A3* Baluchistān, SW Pakistan
Turčiansky Svätý Martin *see* Martin
Turda *108 B4 Ger.* Thorenburg, *Hung.* Torda. Cluj, NW Romania
Turek *98 C3* Wielkopolskie, C Poland
Turfan *see* Turpan
Turin *see* Torino
Turkana, Lake *89 C6 var.* Lake Rudolf. *lake* N Kenya
Turkestan *114 B5 Kaz.* Türkistan. Yuzhnyy Kazakhstan, S Kazakhstan
Turkey *116 B3 off.* Republic of Turkey, *Turk.* Türkiye Cumhuriyeti. *country* SW Asia

TURKEY
Asia / Europe

Official name Republic of Turkey
Formation 1923 / 1939
Capital Ankara
Population 73.2 million / 246 people per sq mile (95 people per sq km) / 75%
Total area 301,382 sq miles (780,580 sq km)
Languages Turkish*, Kurdish, Arabic, Circassian, Armenian, Greek, Georgian, Ladino
Religions Muslim (mainly Sunni) 99%, Other 1%
Ethnic mix Turkish 70%, Kurdish 20%, Other 8%, Arab 2%
Government Parliamentary system
Currency new Turkish lira = 100 kurus
Literacy rate 88%
Calorie consumption 3357 calories

Turkey, Republic of *see* Turkey
Turkish Republic of Northern Cyprus *102 D5 disputed territory* Cyprus
Türkistan *see* Turkestan
Türkiye Cumhuriyeti *see* Turkey
Türkmenabat *122 D3 prev. Rus.* Chardzhev, Chardzhou, Chardzhui, Lenin-Turkmenski, *Turkm.* Chärjew. Lebap Welaýaty, E Turkmenistan
Turkmen Aylagy *122 B2 Rus.* Turkmenskiy Zaliv. *lake gulf* W Turkmenistan
Turkmenbashi *see* Türkmenbaşy
Türkmenbaşy *122 B2 Rus.* Turkmenbashi; *prev.* Krasnovodsk. Balkan Welaýaty, W Turkmenistan
Türkmenbaşy Aylagy *122 A2 prev. Rus.* Krasnovodskiy Zaliv, *Turkm.* Krasnowodsk Aylagy. *lake Gulf* W Turkmenistan
Turkmenistan *122 B2* ; *prev.* Turkmenskaya Soviet Socialist Republic. *country* C Asia

TURKMENISTAN
Central Asia

Official name Turkmenistan
Formation 1991 / 1991
Capital Ashgabat
Population 4.8 million / 25 people per sq mile (10 people per sq km) / 45%
Total area 188,455 sq miles (488,100 sq km)
Languages Turkmen*, Uzbek, Russian, Kazakh, Tatar

TURKMENISTAN
Central Asia

OReligions Sunni Muslim 87%, Orthodox Christian 11%, Other 2%
Ethnic mix Turkmen 77%, Uzbek 9%, Russian 7%, Other 4%, Kazakh 2%, Tatar 1%
Government One-party state
Currency Manat = 100 tenga
Literacy rate 99%
Calorie consumption 2742 calories

Turkmenskaya Soviet Socialist Republic *see* Turkmenistan
Turkmenskiy Zaliv *see* Turkmen Aylagy
Turks and Caicos Islands *55 E2 UK dependent territory* N West Indies
Turlock *47 B6* California, W USA
Turnagain, Cape *150 D4 headland* North Island, New Zealand
Turnau *see* Turnov
Turnhout *87 C5* Antwerpen, N Belgium
Turnov *98 B4 Ger.* Turnau. Liberecký Kraj, N Czech Republic
Tŭrnovo *see* Veliko Tŭrnovo
Turnu Măgurele *108 B5 var.* Turnu-Măgurele. Teleorman, S Romania
Turnu Severin *see* Drobeta-Turnu Severin
Turócszentmárton *see* Martin
Turoni *see* Tours
Turpan *126 C3 var.* Turfan. Xinjiang Uygur Zizhiqu, NW China
Turpan Depression *see* Turpan Pendi
Turpan Pendi *126 C3 Eng.* Turpan Depression. *depression* NW China
Turpentine State *see* North Carolina
Türtkül/Turtkul' *see* To'rtkok'l
Turuga *see* Tsuruga
Turuoka *see* Tsuruoka
Tuscaloosa *42 C2* Alabama, S USA
Tuscan Archipelago *see* Toscano, Arcipelago
Tuscany *see* Toscana
Tusima *see* Tsushima
Tutela *see* Tulle, France
Tutela *see* Tudela, Spain
Tutera *see* Tudela
Tuticorin *132 C3* Tamil Nādu, SE India
Tutrakan *104 D1* Silistra, NE Bulgaria
Tutuila *145 F4 island* W American Samoa
Tuvalu *145 E3 prev.* Ellice Islands. *country* SW Pacific Ocean

TUVALU
Australasia & Oceania

Official name Tuvalu
Formation 1978 / 1978
Capital Fongafale, on Funafuti Atoll
Population 11,636 / 1164 people per sq mile (448 people per sq km) / 45%
Total area 10 sq miles (26 sq km)
Languages Tuvaluan, Kiribati, English
Religions Church of Tuvalu 97%, Other 1%, Baha'i 1%, Seventh-day Adventist 1%
Ethnic mix Polynesian 96%, Other 4%
Government Nonparty system
Currency Australian dollar and Tuvaluan dollar = 100 cents
Literacy rate 98%
Calorie consumption Not available

Ṭuwayq, Jabal *121 C5 mountain range* C Saudi Arabia
Tuxpan *50 D4* Jalisco, C Mexico
Tuxpan *50 D4* Nayarit, C Mexico
Tuxpán *51 F4 var.* Tuxpán de Rodríguez Cano. Veracruz-Llave, E Mexico
Tuxpán de Rodríguez Cano *see* Tuxpán
Tuxtepec *51 F4 var.* San Juan Bautista Tuxtepec. Oaxaca, S Mexico
Tuxtla *51 G5 var.* Tuxtla Gutiérrez. Chiapas, SE Mexico
Tuxtla *see* San Andrés Tuxtla
Tuxtla Gutiérrez *see* Tuxtla
Tuy Hoa *137 E5* Phu Yên, S Vietnam
Tuz Gölü *116 C3 lake* C Turkey

Tver' *110 B4 prev.* Kalinin. Tverskaya Oblast', W Russian Federation
Tverya *see* Teverya
Twin Falls *46 D4* Idaho, NW USA
Tyan'-Shan' *see* Tien Shan
Tychy *99 D5 Ger.* Tichau. Śląskie, S Poland
Tyler *49 G3* Texas, SW USA
Tylos *see* Bahrain
Tympáki *105 C8 var.* Timbaki; *prev.* Timbákion. Kríti, Greece, E Mediterranean Sea
Tynda *115 F4* Amurskaya Oblast', SE Russian Federation
Tyne *88 D4 river* N England, UK
Tyôsi *see* Chōshi
Tyras *see* Dniester
Tyre *see* Soûr
Tyrnau *see* Trnava
Týrnavos *104 B4 var.* Tírnavos. Thessalía, C Greece
Tyrol *see* Tirol
Tyros *see* Bahrain
Tyrrhenian Sea *97 B6 It.* Mare Tirreno. *sea* N Mediterranean Sea
Tyumen' *114 C3* Tyumenskaya Oblast', C Russian Federation
Tyup *123 G2 Kir.* Tüp. Issyk-Kul'skaya Oblast', NE Kyrgyzstan
Tywyn *80 C6* W Wales, UK
Tzekung *see* Zigong
Tziá *105 C6 prev.* Kéa, Kéos; *anc.* Ceos. *island* Kykládes, Greece, Aegean Sea

U

Uaco Cungo *78 B2* C Angola
UAE *see* United Arab Emirates
Uanle Uen *see* Wanlaweyn
Uaupés, Rio *see* Vaupés, Río
Ubangi *77 C5 Fr.* Oubangui. *river* C Africa
Ubangi-Shari *see* Central African Republic
Ube *131 B7* Yamaguchi, Honshū, SW Japan
Ubeda *93 E4* Andalucía, S Spain
Uberaba *63 F4* Minas Gerais, SE Brazil
Uberlândia *63 F4* Minas Gerais, SE Brazil
Ubol Rajadhani/Ubol Ratchathani *see* Ubon Ratchathani
Ubon Ratchathani *137 D5 var.* Muang Ubon, Ubol Rajadhani, Ubol Ratchathani, Udon Ratchathani. Ubon Ratchathani, E Thailand
Ubrique *92 D5* Andalucía, S Spain
Ubsu-Nur, Ozero *see* Uvs Nuur
Ucayali, Río *60 D3 river* C Peru
Uchiura-wan *130 D3 bay* NW Pacific Ocean
Uchkuduk *see* Uchquduq
Uchquduq *122 D2 Rus.* Uchkuduk. Navoiy Viloyati, N Uzbekistan
Uchtagan Gumy/Uchtagan, Peski *see* Uçtagan Gumy
Uçtagan Gumy *122 C2 var.* Uchtagan Gumy, *Rus.* Peski Uchtagan. *desert* NW Turkmenistan
Udaipur *134 C3 prev.* Oodeypore. Rājasthān, N India
Uddevalla *85 B6* Västra Götaland, S Sweden
Udine *96 D2 anc.* Utina. Friuli-Venezia Giulia, NE Italy
Udintsev Fracture Zone *154 A5 tectonic feature* S Pacific Ocean
Udipi *see* Udupi
Udon Ratchathani *see* Ubon Ratchathani
Udon Thani *136 C4 var.* Ban Mak Khaeng, Udorndhani. Udon Thani, N Thailand
Udorndhani *see* Udon Thani
Udupi *132 B2 var.* Udipi. Karnātaka, SW India
Uele *77 D5 var.* Welle. *river* NE Dem. Rep. Congo
Uelzen *94 C3* Niedersachsen, N Germany
Ufa *111 D6* Respublika Bashkortostan, W Russian Federation
Ugāle *106 C2* Ventspils, NW Latvia
Uganda *73 B6 off.* Republic of Uganda. *country* E Africa

UGANDA
East Africa

Official name Republic of Uganda
Formation 1962 / 1962
Capital Kampala
Population 28.8 million / 374 people per sq mile (144 people per sq km) / 14%
Total area 91,135 sq miles (236,040 sq km)
Languages English*, Luganda, Nkole, Chiga, Lango, Acholi, Teso, Lugbara
Religions Roman Catholic 38%, Protestant 33%, Traditional beliefs 13%, Muslim (mainly Sunni) 8%, Other 8%
Ethnic mix Bantu tribes 50%, Other 45%, Sudanese 5%
Government Nonparty system
Currency New Uganda shilling = 100 cents
Literacy rate 69%
Calorie consumption 2410 calories

Uganda, Republic of *see* Uganda
Uglovka *110 B4 var.* Okulovka. Novgorodskaya Oblast', W Russian Federation
Uhorshchyna *see* Hungary
Uhuru Peak *see* Kilimanjaro
Uíge *78 B1 Port.* Carmona, Vila Marechal Carmona. Uíge, NW Angola
Uinta Mountains *44 B4 mountain range* Utah, W USA
Uitenhage *78 C5* Eastern Cape, S South Africa
Uithoorn *86 C3* Noord-Holland, C Netherlands
Ujda *see* Oujda
Ujelang Atoll *144 C1 var.* Wujlān. *atoll* Ralik Chain, W Marshall Islands
Újgradiska *see* Nova Gradiška
Újmoldova *see* Moldova Nouă
Ujungpandang *see* Makassar
Ujung Salang *see* Phuket
Újvidék *see* Novi Sad
UK *see* United Kingdom
Ukhta *114 C3* Respublika Komi, NW Russian Federation
Ukiah *47 B5* California, W USA
Ukmergė *106 C4 Pol.* Wiłkomierz. Vilnius, C Lithuania
Ukraina *see* Ukraine
Ukraine *108 C2 off.* Ukraine, *Rus.* Ukraina, *Ukr.* Ukrayina; *prev.* Ukrainian Soviet Socialist Republic, Ukrainskay S.S.R. *country* SE Europe

UKRAINE
Eastern Europe

Official name Ukraine
Formation 1991 / 1991
Capital Kiev
Population 46.5 million / 199 people per sq mile (77 people per sq km) / 68%
Total area 223,089 sq miles (603,700 sq km)
Languages Ukrainian*, Russian, Tatar
Religions Christian (mainly Orthodox) 95%, Other 4%, Jewish 1%
Ethnic mix Ukrainian 73%, Russian 22%, Other 4%, Jewish 1%
Government Presidential system
Currency Hryvna = 100 kopiykas
Literacy rate 99%
Calorie consumption 3054 calories

Ukraine *see* Ukraine
Ukrainian Soviet Socialist Republic *see* Ukraine
Ukrainskay S.S.R/Ukrayina *see* Ukraine
Ulaanbaatar *127 E2 Eng.* Ulan Bator; *prev.* Urga. *country capital* (Mongolia) Töv, C Mongolia
Ulaangom *126 C2* Uvs, NW Mongolia
Ulan Bator *see* Ulaanbaatar
Ulanhad *see* Chifeng
Ulan-Ude *115 E4 prev.* Verkhneudinsk. Respublika Buryatiya, S Russian Federation
Uleälv *see* Oulujoki
Uleträsk *see* Oulujärvi
Ulft *86 E4* Gelderland, E Netherlands
Ullapool *88 C3* N Scotland, UK
Ulm *95 B6* Baden-Württemberg, S Germany
Ulsan *129 E4 Jap.* Urusan. SE South Korea
Ulster *89 B5 province* Northern Ireland, UK/Ireland
Ulungur Hu *126 B2 lake* NW China
Uluru *147 D5 var.* Ayers Rock. *rocky outcrop* Northern Territory, C Australia
Ulyanivka *109 E3 Rus.* Ul'yanovka. Kirovohrads'ka Oblast', C Ukraine
Ul'yanovka *see* Ulyanivka
Ul'yanovsk *111 C5 prev.* Simbirsk. Ul'yanovskaya Oblast', W Russian Federation
Umán *51 H3* Yucatán, SE Mexico
Uman' *109 E3 Rus.* Uman. Cherkas'ka Oblast', C Ukraine
Uman *see* Uman'
Umanak/Umanaq *see* Uummannaq
'Umān, Khalīj *see* Oman, Gulf of
'Umān, Salṭanat *see* Oman
Umbrian-Machigian Mountains *see* Umbro-Marchigiano, Appennino
Umbro-Marchigiano, Appennino *96 C3 Eng.* Umbrian-Machigian Mountains. *mountain range* C Italy
Umeå *84 C4* Västerbotten, N Sweden
Umeälven *84 C4 river* N Sweden
Umiat *36 D2* Alaska, USA
Umm Buru *72 A4* Western Darfur, W Sudan
Umm Durmān *see* Omdurman
Umm Ruwaba *72 C4 var.* Umm Ruwābah, Um Ruwāba. Northern Kordofan, C Sudan
Umm Ruwābah *see* Umm Ruwaba
Umnak Island *36 A3 island* Aleutian Islands, Alaska, USA
Um Ruwāba *see* Umm Ruwaba
Umtali *see* Mutare
Umtata *78 D5* Eastern Cape, SE South Africa
Una *100 B3 river* Bosnia and Herzegovina/Croatia
Unac *100 B3 river* W Bosnia and Herzegovina
Unalaska Island *36 A3 island* Aleutian Islands, Alaska, USA
'Unayzah *120 B4 var.* Anaiza. Al Qaṣīm, C Saudi Arabia
Unci *see* Almería
Uncía *61 F4* Potosí, C Bolivia
Uncompahgre Peak *44 B5 mountain* Colorado, C USA
Undur Khan *see* Öndörhaan
Ungaria *see* Hungary
Ungarisches Erzgebirge *see* Slovenské rudohorie
Ungarn *see* Hungary
Ungava Bay *39 E1 bay* Québec, E Canada
Ungava, Péninsule d' *38 D1 peninsula* Québec, SE Canada
Ungeny *see* Ungheni
Ungheni *108 D3 Rus.* Ungeny. W Moldova
Unguja *see* Zanzibar
Üngüz Angyrsyndaky Garagum *122 C2 Rus.* Zaunguzskiye Garagumy. *desert* N Turkmenistan
Ungvár *see* Uzhhorod
Unimak Island *36 B3 island* Aleutian Islands, Alaska, USA
Union *43 E1* South Carolina, SE USA
Union City *42 C1* Tennessee, S USA
Union of Myanmar *see* Burma
United Arab Emirates *121 C5 Ar.* Al Imārāt al 'Arabīyah al Muttaḥidah, *abbrev.* UAE; *prev.* Trucial States. *country* SW Asia

UNITED ARAB EMIRATES
Southwest Asia

Official name United Arab Emirates
Formation 1971 / 1972
Capital Abu Dhabi
Population 4.5 million / 139 people per sq mile (54 people per sq km) / 86%
Total area 32,000 sq miles (82,880 sq km)
Languages Arabic*, Farsi, Indian and Pakistani languages, English
Religions Muslim (mainly Sunni) 96%, Christian, Hindu, and other 4%

UNITED ARAB EMIRATES
(continued)

Ethnic mix Asian 60%, Emirian 25%, Other Arab 12%, European 3%
Government Monarchy
Currency UAE dirham = 100 fils
Literacy rate 77%
Calorie consumption 3225 calories

United Arab Republic *see* Egypt
United Kingdom *89 B5 off.* United Kingdom of Great Britain and Northern Ireland, *abbrev.* UK. *country* NW Europe

UNITED KINGDOM
Northwest Europe

Official name United Kingdom of Great Britain and Northern Ireland
Formation 1707 / 1922
Capital London
Population 59.7 million / 640 people per sq mile (247 people per sq km) / 90%
Total area 94,525 sq miles (244,820 sq km)
Languages English*, Welsh, Scottish Gaelic
Religions Anglican 45%, Roman Catholic 9%, Presbyterian 4%, Other 42%
Ethnic mix English 80%, Scottish 9%, West Indian, Asian, and other 5%, Northern Irish 3%, Welsh 3%
Government Parliamentary system
Currency Pound sterling = 100 pence
Literacy rate 99%
Calorie consumption 3412 calories

United Kingdom of Great Britain and Northern Ireland *see* United Kingdom
United Mexican States *see* Mexico
United Provinces *see* Uttar Pradesh
United States of America *35 B5 off.* United States of America, *var.* America, The States, *abbrev.* U.S., USA. *country*

UNITED STATES
North America

Official name United States of America
Formation 1776 / 1959
Capital Washington D.C.
Population 298 million / 84 people per sq mile (33 people per sq km) / 77%
Total area 3,717,792 sq miles (9,626,091 sq km)
Languages English*, Spanish, Chinese, French, German, Tagalog, Vietnamese, Italian, Korean, Russian, Polish
Religions Protestant 52%, Roman Catholic 25%, Muslim 2%, Jewish 2%, Other 19%
Ethnic mix White 69%, Hispanic 13%, Black American/African 13%, Asian 4%, Native American 1%
Government Presidential system
Currency US dollar = 100 cents
Literacy rate 99%
Calorie consumption 3774 calories

United States of America *see* United States of America
Unst *88 D1 island* NE Scotland, UK
Ünye *116 D2* Ordu, W Turkey
Upala *52 D4* Alajuela, NW Costa Rica
Upata *59 E2* Bolívar, E Venezuela
Upemba, Lac *77 D7 lake* SE Dem. Rep. Congo
Upernavik *82 C2 var.* Upernivik. Kitaa, C Greenland
Upernivik *see* Upernavik
Upington *78 C4* Northern Cape, W South Africa
Upolu *145 F4 island* SE Samoa
Upper Klamath Lake *46 A4 lake* Oregon, NW USA
Upper Lough Erne *89 A5 lake* SW Northern Ireland, UK
Upper Red Lake *45 F1 lake* Minnesota, N USA
Upper Volta *see* Burkina Faso
Uppsala *85 C6* Uppsala, C Sweden
Ural *112 B3 Kaz.* Zayyq. *river* Kazakhstan/Russian Federation
Ural Mountains *see* Ural'skiye Gory

Ural'sk 114 B3 Kaz. Oral. Zapadnyy Kazakhstan, NW Kazakhstan
Ural'skiye Gory 114 C3 var. Ural'skiy Khrebet, Eng. Ural Mountains. *mountain range* Kazakhstan/Russian Federation
Ural'skiy Khrebet see Ural'skiye Gory
Ura-Tyube see Ŭroteppa
Uraricoera 62 D1 Roraima, N Brazil
Urbandale 45 F3 Iowa, C USA
Urdunn see Jordan
Uren' 111 C5 Nizhegorodskaya Oblast', W Russian Federation
Urga see Ulaanbaatar
Urganch 122 D2 Rus. Urgench; prev. Novo-Urgench. Xorazm Viloyati, W Uzbekistan
Urgench see Urganch
Urgut 123 E3 Samarqand Viloyati, C Uzbekistan
Uroševac 101 D5 Alb. Ferizaj. Kosovo, S Serbia
Ŭroteppa 123 E2 Rus. Ura-Tyube. NW Tajikistan
Uruapan 51 E4 var. Uruapan del Progreso. Michoacán de Ocampo, SW Mexico
Uruapan del Progreso see Uruapan
Uruguai, Rio see Uruguay
Uruguay 64 D4 off. Oriental Republic of Uruguay; prev. La Banda Oriental. *country* E South America

URUGUAY
South America

Official name Eastern Republic of Uruguay
Formation 1828 / 1828
Capital Montevideo
Population 3.5 million / 52 people per sq mile (20 people per sq km) / 91%
Total area 68,039 sq miles (176,220 sq km)
Languages Spanish*
Religions Roman Catholic 66%, Other and nonreligious 30%, Jewish 2%, Protestant 2%
Ethnic mix White 90%, Mestizo 6%, Black 4%
Government Presidential system
Currency Uruguayan peso = 100 centésimos
Literacy rate 98%
Calorie consumption 2828 calories

Uruguay 64 D3 var. Rio Uruguai, Río Uruguay. *river* E South America
Uruguay, Oriental Republic of see Uruguay
Uruguay, Río see Uruguay
Urumchi see Ürümqi
Ürümqi 126 C3 var. Tihwa, Urumchi, Urumqi, Urumtsi, Wu-lu-k'o-mu-shi, Wu-lu-mu-ch'i; prev. Ti-hua. Xinjiang Uygur Zizhiqu, NW China
Urumtsi see Ürümqi
Urundi see Burundi
Urup, Ostrov 115 H4 island Kuril'skiye Ostrova, SE Russian Federation
Urusan see Ulsan
Urziceni 108 C5 Ialomiţa, SE Romania
Usa 110 E3 river NW Russian Federation
Uşak 116 B3 prev. Ushak. Uşak, W Turkey
Ushak see Uşak
Ushant see Ouessant, Île d'
Ushuaia 65 B8 Tierra del Fuego, S Argentina
Usinsk 110 E3 Respublika Komi, NW Russian Federation
Üsküb/Üsküp see Skopje
Usmas Ezers 106 B3 lake NW Latvia
Usol'ye-Sibirskoye 115 E4 Irkutskaya Oblast', C Russian Federation
Ussel 91 C5 Corrèze, C France
Ussuriysk 115 G5 prev. Nikol'sk, Nikol'sk-Ussuriyskiy, Voroshilov. Primorskiy Kray, SE Russian Federation
Ustica, Isola d' 97 B6 island S Italy
Ust'-Ilimsk 115 E4 Irkutskaya Oblast', C Russian Federation
Ústí nad Labem 98 A4 Ger. Aussig. Ústecký Kraj, NW Czech Republic

Ustinov see Izhevsk
Ustka 98 C2 Ger. Stolpmünde. Pomorskie, N Poland
Ust'-Kamchatsk 115 H2 Kamchatskaya Oblast', E Russian Federation
Ust'-Kamenogorsk 114 D5 Kaz. Öskemen. Vostochnyy Kazakhstan, E Kazakhstan
Ust'-Kut 115 E4 Irkutskaya Oblast', C Russian Federation
Ust'-Olenëk 115 E3 Respublika Sakha (Yakutiya), NE Russian Federation
Ustrzyki Dolne 99 E5 Podkarpackie, SE Poland
Ust'-Sysol'sk see Syktyvkar
Ust Urt see Ustyurt Plateau
Ustyurt Plateau 122 B1 var. Ust Urt, Uzb. Ustyurt Platosi. *plateau* Kazakhstan/Uzbekistan
Ustyurt Platosi see Ustyurt Plateau
Usulután 52 C3 Usulután, SE El Salvador
Usumacinta, Río 52 B1 river Guatemala/Mexico
Usumbura see Bujumbura
U.S./USA see United States of America
Utah 48 A1 off. State of Utah, also known as Beehive State, Mormon State. *state* W USA
Utah Lake 44 B4 lake Utah, W USA
Utena 106 C4 Utena, E Lithuania
Utica 41 F3 New York, NE USA
Utina see Udine
Utrecht 86 C3 Lat. Trajectum ad Rhenum. Utrecht, C Netherlands
Utsunomiya 131 D5 var. Utunomiya. Tochigi, Honshū, S Japan
Uttaranchal 135 E2 state N India
Uttaranchal 135 E2 cultural region N India
Uttar Pradesh 135 E3 prev. United Provinces, United Provinces of Agra and Oudh. *cultural region* N India
Uttar Pradesh 135 E3 prev. United Provinces, United Provinces of Agra and Oudh. *state* N India
Utunomiya see Utsunomiya
Uulu 82 C3 Pärnumaa, SW Estonia
Uummannaq 82 C3 var. Umanak, Umanaq. Kitaa, C Greenland
Uummannarsuaq see Nunap Isua
Uvalde 49 F4 Texas, SW USA
Uvarovichy 107 D7 Rus. Uvarovichi. Homyel'skaya Voblasts', SE Belarus
Uvarovichi see Uvarovichy
Uvea, Île 145 E4 island N Wallis and Futuna
Uvs Nuur 126 C1 var. Ozero Ubsu-Nur. lake Mongolia/Russian Federation
'Uwaynāt, Jabal al 88 A3 var. Jebel Uweinat. *mountain* Libya/Sudan
Uweinat, Jebel see 'Uwaynāt, Jabal al
Uyo 75 G5 Akwa Ibom, S Nigeria
Uyuni 61 F5 Potosí, W Bolivia
Uzbekistan 122 D2 off. Republic of Uzbekistan. *country* C Asia

UZBEKISTAN
Central Asia

Official name Republic of Uzbekistan
Formation 1991 / 1991
Capital Tashkent
Population 26.6 million / 154 people per sq mile (59 people per sq km) / 37%
Total area 172,741 sq miles (447,400 sq km)
Languages Uzbek*, Russian, Tajik, Kazakh
Religions Sunni Muslim 88%, Orthodox Christian 9%, Other 3%
Ethnic mix Uzbek 71%, Other 12%, Russian 8%, Tajik 5%, Kazakh 4%
Government Presidential system
Currency Som = 100 tiyin
Literacy rate 99%
Calorie consumption 2241 calories

Uzbekistan, Republic of see Uzbekistan
Uzhgorod see Uzhhorod
Uzhhorod 108 B2 Rus. Uzhgorod; prev. Ungvár. Zakarpats'ka Oblast', W Ukraine
Užice 100 D4 prev. Titovo Užice. Serbia, W Serbia

V

Vaal 78 D4 river C South Africa
Vaals 87 D6 Limburg, SE Netherlands
Vaasa 85 D5 Swe. Vasa; prev. Nikolainkaupunki. Länsi-Suomi, W Finland
Vaassen 86 D3 Gelderland, E Netherlands
Vác 99 C6 Ger. Waitzen. Pest, N Hungary
Vadodara 134 C4 prev. Baroda. Gujarāt, W India
Vaduz 94 E2 country capital (Liechtenstein) W Liechtenstein
Vág see Váh
Vágbeszterce see Považská Bystrica
Váh 99 C5 Ger. Waag, Hung. Vág. river W Slovakia
Váhtjer see Gällivare
Väinameri 106 C2 prev. Muhu Väin, Ger. Moon-Sund. sea E Baltic Sea
Vajdahunyad see Hunedoara
Valachia see Wallachia
Valday 110 B4 Novgorodskaya Oblast', W Russian Federation
Valdecañas, Embalse de 92 D3 reservoir W Spain
Valdepeñas 93 E4 Castilla-La Mancha, C Spain
Valdés, Península 65 C6 peninsula SE Argentina
Valdez 36 C3 Alaska, USA
Valdia see Weldiya
Valdivia 65 B5 Los Lagos, C Chile
Val-d'Or 38 D4 Québec, SE Canada
Valdosta 43 E3 Georgia, SE USA
Valence 91 D5 anc. Valentia, Valentia Julia, Ventia. Drôme, E France
Valencia 93 F3 País Valenciano, E Spain
Valencia 46 D1 California, USA
Valencia 58 D1 Carabobo, N Venezuela
Valencia, Golfo de 93 F3 var. Gulf of Valencia. *gulf* E Spain
Valencia, Gulf of see Valencia, Golfo de
Valencia/València see País Valenciano
Valenciennes 90 D2 Nord, N France
Valentia see Valence, France
Valentia see País Valenciano
Valentia Julia see Valence
Valentine State see Oregon
Valera 58 C2 Trujillo, NW Venezuela
Valetta see Valletta
Valga 106 D3 Ger. Walk, Latv. Valka. Valgamaa, S Estonia
Valira 91 A8 river Andorra/Spain Europe
Valjevo 100 C4 Serbia, W Serbia
Valjok see Válljohka
Valka 106 D3 Ger. Walk. Valka, N Latvia
Valka see Valga
Valkenswaard 87 D5 Noord-Brabant, S Netherlands
Valladolid 51 H3 Yucatán, SE Mexico
Valladolid 92 D2 Castilla-León, NW Spain
Vall D'Uxó see La Vall D'Uixó
Valle de La Pascua 58 D2 Guárico, N Venezuela
Valledupar 58 B1 Cesar, N Colombia
Vallejo 47 B6 California, W USA
Vallenar 64 B3 Atacama, N Chile
Valletta 97 C8 prev. Valetta. *country capital* (Malta) E Malta
Valley City 45 E2 North Dakota, N USA
Válljohka 84 D2 var. Valjok. Finnmark, N Norway
Valls 93 G2 Cataluña, NE Spain
Valmiera 106 D3 Est. Volmari, Ger. Wolmar. Valmiera, N Latvia
Valona see Vlorë
Valozhyn 107 C5 Pol. Wołożyn, Rus. Volozhin. Minskaya Voblasts', C Belarus
Valparaíso 64 B4 Valparaíso, C Chile
Valparaiso 40 C3 Indiana, N USA
Valverde del Camino 92 C4 Andalucía, S Spain
Van 117 F3 Van, E Turkey
Vanadzor 117 F2 prev. Kirovakan. N Armenia
Vancouver 36 D5 British Columbia, SW Canada
Vancouver 46 B3 Washington, NW USA

Vancouver Island 36 D5 island British Columbia, SW Canada
Vanda see Vantaa
Van Diemen Gulf 146 D2 gulf Northern Territory, N Australia
Van Diemen's Land see Tasmania
Vaner, Lake see Vänern
Vänern 85 B6 Eng. Lake Vaner; prev. Lake Vener. *lake* S Sweden
Vangaindrano 79 G4 Fianarantsoa, SE Madagascar
Van Gölü 117 F3 Eng. Lake Van; anc. Thospitis. *salt lake* E Turkey
Van Horn 48 D3 Texas, SW USA
Van, Lake see Van Gölü
Vannes 90 A3 anc. Dariorigum. Morbihan, NW France
Vantaa 85 D6 Swe. Vanda. Etelä-Suomi, S Finland
Vanua Levu 145 E4 island N Fiji
Vanuatu 144 C4 off. Republic of Vanuatu; prev. New Hebrides. *country* SW Pacific Ocean

VANUATU
Australasia & Oceania

Official name Republic of Vanuatu
Formation 1980 / 1980
Capital Port Vila
Population 211,000 / 45 people per sq mile (17 people per sq km) / 20%
Total area 4710 sq miles (12,200 sq km)
Languages Bislama* (Melanesian pidgin), English*, French*, other indigenous languages
Religions Presbyterian 37%, Other 19%, Anglican 15%, Roman Catholic 15%, Traditional beliefs 8%, Seventh-day Adventist 6%
Ethnic mix Melanesian 94%, Other 3%, Polynesian 3%
Government Parliamentary system
Currency Vatu = 100 centimes
Literacy rate 74%
Calorie consumption 2587 calories

Vanuatu, Republic of see Vanuatu
Van Wert 40 C4 Ohio, N USA
Vapincum see Gap
Varaklani 106 D4 Madona, C Latvia
Vārānasi 135 E3 prev. Banaras, Benares, hist. Kasi. Uttar Pradesh, N India
Varangerfjorden 84 E2 Lapp. Várjjatvuotna. *fjord* N Norway
Varangerhalvøya 84 D2 Lapp. Várnjárga. *peninsula* N Norway
Varannó see Vranov nad Topl'ou
Varasd see Varaždin
Varaždin 100 B2 Ger. Warasdin, Hung. Varasd. Varaždin, N Croatia
Varberg 85 B7 Halland, S Sweden
Vardar 101 E6 Gk. Axiós. *river* FYR Macedonia/Greece
Varde 85 A7 Ribe, W Denmark
Vareia see Logroño
Varéna 107 B5 Pol. Orany. Alytus, S Lithuania
Varese 96 B2 Lombardia, N Italy
Vârful Moldoveanu 108 B4 var. Moldoveanul; prev. Vîrful Moldoveanu. *mountain* C Romania
Várjjatvuotna see Varangerfjorden
Varkaus 85 E5 Itä-Suomi, C Finland
Varna 104 E2 prev. Stalin; anc. Odessus. Varna, E Bulgaria
Varnenski Zaliv 104 E2 prev. Stalinski Zaliv. *bay* E Bulgaria
Várnjárga see Varangerhalvøya
Varshava see Warszawa
Vasa see Vaasa
Vasiliki 105 A5 Lefkáda, Iónioi Nísoi, Greece, C Mediterranean Sea
Vasilishki 107 B5 Pol. Wasiliszki, Rus. Vasilishki. Hrodzyenskaya Voblasts', W Belarus
Vasil'kov see Vasyl'kiv
Vaslui 108 D4 Vaslui, C Romania
Västerås 85 C6 Västmanland, C Sweden
Vasyl'kiv 109 E2 var. Vasil'kov. Kyyivs'ka Oblast', N Ukraine
Vaté see Éfaté
Vatican City 97 A7 off. Vatican City State. *country* S Europe

VATICAN CITY
Southern Europe

Official name State of the Vatican City
Formation 1929 / 1929
Capital Vatican City
Population 921 / 5418 people per sq mile
(2093 people per sq km) / 100%
Total area 0.17 sq miles (0.44 sq km)
Languages Italian*, Latin*
Religions Roman Catholic 100%
Ethnic mix The current pope is
German. Cardinals are from many
nationalities, but Italians form the
largest group. Most of the resident lay
persons are Italian.
Government Papal state
Currency Euro = 100 cents
Literacy rate 99%
Calorie consumption Not available

Vatican City State *see* Vatican City
Vatnajökull *83 E5 glacier* SE Iceland
Vatter, Lake *see* Vättern
Vättern *85 B6 Eng.* Lake Vatter; *prev.*
Lake Vetter. *lake* S Sweden
Vaughn *48 D2* New Mexico, SW USA
Vaupés, Río *58 C4 var.* Rio Uaupés.
river Brazil/Colombia
Vava'u Group *145 E4 island group*
N Tonga
Vavuniya *132 D3* Northern Province,
N Sri Lanka
Vawkavysk *107 B6 Pol.* Wołkowysk,
Rus. Volkovysk. Hrodzyenskaya
Voblasts', W Belarus
Växjö *85 C7 var.* Vexiö. Kronoberg,
S Sweden
Vaygach, Ostrov *110 E2 island*
NW Russian Federation
Veendam *86 E2* Groningen,
NE Netherlands
Veenendaal *86 D4* Utrecht,
C Netherlands
Vega *84 B4 island* C Norway
Veglia *see* Krk
Veisiejai *107 B5* Alytus, S Lithuania
Vejer de la Frontera *92 C5* Andalucía,
S Spain
Veldhoven *87 D5* Noord-Brabant,
S Netherlands
Velebit *100 A3 mountain range*
C Croatia
Velenje *95 E7 Ger.* Wöllan. N Slovenia
Veles *101 E6 Turk.* Köprülü.
C FYR Macedonia
Velho *see* Porto Velho
Velika Kladuša *see* Kikinda
Velika Morava *100 D4 var.* Glavn'a
Morava, Morava, *Ger.* Grosse Morava.
river C Serbia
Velikaya *113 G2 river* NW Russian
Federation
Veliki Bečkerek *see* Zrenjanin
Velikiye Luki *110 A4* Pskovskaya
Oblast', W Russian Federation
Velikiy Novgorod *110 B4 prev.*
Novgorod. Novgorodskaya Oblast',
W Russian Federation
Veliko Tŭrnovo *see* Veliko Tŭrnovo
Veliko Tŭrnovo *104 D2 prev.* Tirnovo,
Trnovo, Tŭrnovo, Veliko Tărnovo.
Veliko Tŭrnovo, N Bulgaria
Velingrad *104 C3* Pazardzhik, C Bulgaria
Vel'ký Krtíš *99 D6* Banskobystrický
Kraj, C Slovakia
Vellore *132 C2* Tamil Nādu, SE India
Velobriga *see* Viana do Castelo
Velsen *see* Velsen-Noord
Velsen-Noord *86 C3 var.* Velsen.
Noord-Holland, W Netherlands
Vel'sk *110 C4 var.* Velsk.
Arkhangel'skaya Oblast',
NW Russian Federation
Velvendós *see* Velvéntos
Velvéntos *104 B4 var.* Velvendós.
Dytiki Makedonía, N Greece
Velykyy Tokmak *see* Tokmak
Vendôme *90 C4* Loir-et-Cher,
C France
Venedig *see* Venezia
Vener, Lake *see* Vänern
Venetia *see* Venezia
Venezia *96 C2 Eng.* Venice, *Fr.* Venise,
Ger. Venedig; *anc.* Venetia. Veneto,
NE Italy
Venezia, Golfo di *see* Venice, Gulf of

Venezuela *58 D2 off.* Republic of
Venezuela; *prev.* Estados Unidos de
Venezuela, United States of Venezuela.
country N South America

VENEZUELA
South America

Official name Bolivarian Republic of
Venezuela
Formation 1830 / 1830
Capital Caracas
Population 26.7 million / 78 people per
sq mile (30 people per sq km) / 87%
Total area 352,143 sq miles
(912,050 sq km)
Languages Spanish*, Amerindian
languages
Religions Roman Catholic 89%,
Protestant and other 11%
Ethnic mix Mestizo 69%, White 20%,
Black 9%, Amerindian 2%
Government Presidential system
Currency Bolívar = 100 centimos
Literacy rate 93%
Calorie consumption 2336 calories

Venezuela, Estados Unidos de *see*
Venezuela
Venezuela, Golfo de *58 C1 Eng.* Gulf
of Maracaibo, Gulf of Venezuela. *gulf*
NW Venezuela
Venezuela, Gulf of *see* Venezuela,
Golfo de
Venezuelan Basin *56 B1 undersea basin*
E Caribbean Sea
Venezuela, Republic of *see* Venezuela
Venezuela, United States of *see*
Venezuela
Venice *42 C4* Louisiana, S USA
Venice *see* Venezia
Venice, Gulf of *96 C2 It.* Golfo di
Venezia, *Slvn.* Beneški Zaliv. *gulf*
N Adriatic Sea
Venise *see* Venezia
Venlo *87 D5 prev.* Venloo. Limburg,
SE Netherlands
Venloo *see* Venlo
Venta *106 B3 Ger.* Windau. *river*
Latvia/Lithuania
Venta Belgarum *see* Winchester
Ventia *see* Valence
Ventimiglia *96 A3* Liguria,
NW Italy
Ventspils *106 B2 Ger.* Windau.
Ventspils, NW Latvia
Vera *64 D3* Santa Fe, C Argentina
Veracruz *51 F4 var.* Veracruz Llave.
Veracruz-Llave, E Mexico
Veracruz Llave *see* Veracruz
Vercellae *see* Vercelli
Vercelli *96 A2 anc.* Vercellae.
Piemonte, NW Italy
Verdal *see* Verdalsøra
Verdalsøra *84 B4 var.* Verdal. Nord-
Trøndelag, C Norway
Verde, Cabo *see* Cape Verde
Verde, Costa *92 D1 coastal region*
N Spain
Verden *94 B3* Niedersachsen,
NW Germany
Veria *see* Véroia
Verkhnedvinsk *see* Vyerkhnyadzvinsk
Verkhneudinsk *see* Ulan-Ude
Verkhoyanskiy Khrebet *133 F3*
mountain range NE Russian Federation
Vermillion *45 F3* South Dakota,
N USA
Vermont *41 F2 off.* State of Vermont,
also known as Green Mountain State.
state NE USA
Vernal *44 B4* Utah, W USA
Vernon *49 F2* Texas, SW USA
Verőcze *see* Virovitica
Véroia *104 B4 var.* Veria,
Vérroia, *Turk.* Karaferiye. Kentrikí
Makedonía, N Greece
Verona *96 C2* Veneto, NE Italy
Vérroia *see* Véroia
Versailles *90 D1* Yvelines, N France
Verulamium *see* St Albans
Verviers *87 D6* Liège, E Belgium
Vesdre *87 D6 river* E Belgium
Veselinovo *104 D2* Shumen,
NE Bulgaria
Vesontio *see* Besançon
Vesoul *90 D4 anc.* Vesulium, Vesulum.
Haute-Saône, E France

Vesterålen *84 B2 island group*
N Norway
Vestfjorden *84 C3 fjord* C Norway
Vestmannaeyjar *83 E5* Sudhurland,
S Iceland
Vesulium/Vesulum *see* Vesoul
Vesuna *see* Périgueux
Vesuvio *97 D5 Eng.* Vesuvius. *volcano*
S Italy
Vesuvius *see* Vesuvio
Veszprém *99 C7 Ger.* Veszprim.
Veszprém, W Hungary
Veszprim *see* Veszprém
Vetrino *104 E2* Varna, E Bulgaria
Vetrino *see* Vyetryna
Vetter, Lake *see* Vättern
Veurne *87 A5 var.* Furnes. West-
Vlaanderen, W Belgium
Vexiö *see* Växjö
Viacha *61 F4* La Paz, W Bolivia
Viana de Castelo *see* Viana do Castelo
Viana do Castelo *92 B2 var.* Viana de
Castelo; *anc.* Velobriga. Viana do
Castelo, NW Portugal
Vianen *86 C4* Utrecht, C Netherlands
Viangchan *136 C4 Eng./Fr.* Vientiane.
country capital (Laos) C Laos
Viangphoukha *136 C3*
var. Vieng Pou Kha. Louang Namtha,
N Laos
Viareggio *96 B3* Toscana,
C Italy
Viborg *85 A7* Viborg, NW Denmark
Vic *93 G2 var.* Vich; *anc.* Ausa, Vicus
Ausonensis. Cataluña, NE Spain
Vicentia *see* Vicenza
Vicenza *96 C2 anc.* Vicentia. Veneto,
NE Italy
Vich *see* Vic
Vichy *101 C5 Allier, C France
Vicksburg *42 B2* Mississippi,
S USA
Victoria *79 H1 country capital*
(Seychelles) Mahé, SW Seychelles
Victoria *36 D3 province capital*
Vancouver Island, British Columbia,
SW Canada
Victoria *102 A5 var.* Rabat. Gozo,
NW Malta
Victoria *49 G4* Texas, SW USA
Victoria *149 C7 state* SE Australia
Victoria *see* Masvingo, Zimbabwe
Victoria Bank *see* Vitória Seamount
Victoria de Durango *see* Durango
Victoria de las Tunas *see* Las Tunas
Victoria Falls *78 C3* Matabeleland
North, W Zimbabwe
Victoria Falls *78 C2 waterfall*
Zambia/Zimbabwe
Victoria Falls *see* Iguaçu, Saltos do
Victoria Island *73 F3 island* Northwest
Territories, NW Canada
Victoria, Lake *73 B6 var.* Victoria
Nyanza. *lake* E Africa
Victoria Land *154 C4 physical region*
Antarctica
Victoria Nyanza *see* Victoria, Lake
Victoria River *146 D3 river* Northern
Territory, N Australia
Victorville *47 C7* California,
W USA
Vicus Ausonensis *see* Vic
Vicus Elbii *see* Viterbo
Vidalia *43 E2* Georgia,
SE USA
Videm-Krško *see* Krško
Viden *see* Wien
Vidin *104 B1 anc.* Bononia. Vidin,
NW Bulgaria
Vidzy *107 C5 Rus.* Vidzy. Vitsyebskaya
Voblasts', NW Belarus
Viedma *65 C5* Río Negro,
E Argentina
Vieng Pou Kha *see* Viangphoukha
Vienna *see* Wien, Austria
Vienna *90 B4 river* W France
Vienne *91 D5 anc.* Vienna. *Isère*,
E France
Vienne *90 B4 river* W France
Vientiane *see* Viangchan
Vientos, Paso de los *see* Windward
Passage
Vierzon *90 C4* Cher, C France
Viesite *106 C4 Ger.* Eckengraf.
Jēkabpils, S Latvia
Vietnam *136 D4 off.* Socialist Republic of
Vietnam, *Vtn.* Công Hoa Xa Hôi Chu
Nghia Viêt Nam. *country* SE Asia

VIETNAM
Southeast Asia

Official name Socialist Republic of
Vietnam
Formation 1976 / 1976
Capital Hanoi
Population 84.2 million / 670 people per
sq mile (259 people per sq km) / 20%
Total area 127,243 sq miles
(329,560 sq km)
Languages Vietnamese*, Chinese, Thai,
Khmer, Muong, Nung, Miao, Yao, Jarai
Religions Buddhist 55%, Other and
nonreligious 38%, Christian (mainly
Roman Catholic) 7%
Ethnic mix Vietnamese 88%, Other 6%,
Chinese 4%, Thai 2%
Government One-party state
Currency Dông = 10 hao = 100 xu
Literacy rate 90%
Calorie consumption 2566 calories

Vietnam, Socialist Republic of *see*
Vietnam
Vietri *see* Viêt Tri
Viêt Tri *136 D3 var.* Vietri. Vinh Phu,
N Vietnam
Vieux Fort *55 F2* S Saint Lucia
Vigo *92 B2* Galicia, NW Spain
Viipuri *see* Vyborg
Vijayawāda *132 D1 prev.* Bezwada.
Andhra Pradesh, SE India
Vila *see* Port-Vila
Vila Artur de Paiva *see* Cubango
Vila Bela da Santissima Trindade *see*
Mato Grosso
Vila da Ponte *see* Cubango
Vila de João Belo *see* Xai-Xai
Vila de Mocímboa da Praia *see*
Mocímboa da Praia
Vila do Conde *92 B2* Porto,
NW Portugal
Vila do Zumbo *78 D2 prev.*
Vila do Zumbo, Zumbo. Tete,
NW Mozambique
Vila do Zumbo *see* Vila do Zumbo
Vilafranca del Penedès *93 G2 var.*
Villafranca del Panadés. Cataluña,
NE Spain
Vila General Machado *see* Camacupa
Vila Henrique de Carvalho *see* Saurimo
Vîlaka *106 D4 Ger.* Marienhausen.
Balvi, NE Latvia
Vilalba *92 C1* Galicia, NW Spain
Vila Marechal Carmona *see* Uíge
Vila Nova de Gaia *92 B2* Porto,
NW Portugal
Vila Nova de Portimão *see* Portimão
Vila Pereira de Eça *see* N'Giva
Vila Real *92 C2 var.* Vila Rial.
Vila Real, N Portugal
Vila Rial *see* Vila Real
Vila Robert Williams *see* Caála
Vila Salazar *see* N'Dalatando
Vila Serpa Pinto *see* Menongue
Vileyka *see* Vilyeyka
Vilhelmina *84 C4* Västerbotten,
N Sweden
Vilhena *62 D3* Rondônia,
W Brazil
Vília *105 C5* Attikí, C Greece
Viliya *107 C5 Lith.* Neris,
Rus. Viliya. *river* W Belarus
Viliya *see* Neris
Viljandi *106 D2 Ger.* Fellin.
Viljandimaa, S Estonia
Vilkaviškis *106 B4 Pol.* Wyłkowyszki.
Marijampolė, SW Lithuania
Villa Acuña *50 D2 var.* Ciudad Acuña.
Coahuila de Zaragoza, NE Mexico
Villa Bella *61 F2* Beni, N Bolivia
Villacarrillo *93 E4* Andalucía,
S Spain
Villa Cecilia *see* Ciudad Madero
Villach *95 D7 Slvn.* Beljak. Kärnten,
S Austria
Villacidro *97 A5* Sardegna, Italy,
C Mediterranean Sea
Villa Concepción *see* Concepción
Villa del Pilar *see* Pilar
Villafranca de los Barros *92 C4*
Extremadura, W Spain
Villafranca del Panadés *see* Vilafranca
del Penedès
Villahermosa *51 G4 prev.* San Juan
Bautista. Tabasco, SE Mexico

Villajoyosa *93 F4 Cat.* La Vila Joíosa. País Valenciano, E Spain

Villa María *64 C4* Córdoba, C Argentina

Villa Martín *61 F5* Potosí, SW Bolivia

Villa Mercedes *64 C4* San Juan, Argentina

Villanueva *50 D3* Zacatecas, C Mexico

Villanueva de la Serena *92 C3* Extremadura, W Spain

Villanueva de los Infantes *93 E4* Castilla-La Mancha, C Spain

Villarrica *64 D2* Guairá, SE Paraguay

Villavicencio *58 B3* Meta, C Colombia

Villaviciosa *92 D1* Asturias, N Spain

Villazón *61 G5* Potosí, S Bolivia

Villena *93 F4* País Valenciano, E Spain

Villeurbanne *91 D5* Rhône, E France

Villingen-Schwenningen *95 B6* Baden-Württemberg, S Germany

Villmanstrand *see* Lappeenranta

Vilna *see* Vilnius

Vilnius *107 C5 Pol.* Wilno, *Ger.* Wilna; *prev. Rus.* Vilna. *country capital* (Lithuania) Vilnius, SE Lithuania

Vil'shanka *109 E3 Rus.* Olshanka. Kirovohrads'ka Oblast', C Ukraine

Vilvoorde *87 C6 Fr.* Vilvorde. Vlaams Brabant, C Belgium

Vilvorde *see* Vilvoorde

Vilyeyka *107 C5 Pol.* Wilejka, *Rus.* Vileyka. Minskaya Voblasts', NW Belarus

Vilyuy *115 F3 river* NE Russian Federation

Viña del Mar *64 B4* Valparaíso, C Chile

Vinaròs *93 F3* País Valenciano, E Spain

Vincennes *40 B4* Indiana, N USA

Vindhya Mountains *see* Vindhya Range

Vindhya Range *134 D4 var.* Vindhya Mountains. *mountain range* N India

Vindobona *see* Wien

Vineland *41 F4* New Jersey, NE USA

Vinh *136 D4* Nghê An, N Vietnam

Vinh Loi *see* Bac Liêu

Vinishte *104 C2* Montana, NW Bulgaria

Vinita *49 G1* Oklahoma, C USA

Vinkovci *100 C3 Ger.* Winkowitz, *Hung.* Vinkovcze. Vukovar-Srijem, E Croatia

Vinkovcze *see* Vinkovci

Vinnitsa *see* Vinnytsya

Vinnytsya *108 D2 Rus.* Vinnitsa. Vinnyts'ka Oblast', C Ukraine

Vinogradov *see* Vynohradiv

Vinson Massif *154 A3 mountain* Antarctica

Vinson *117 E4* Şanlıurfa, W Turkey

Virful Moldoveanu *see* Vârful Moldoveanu

Virginia *45 G1* Minnesota, N USA

Virginia *41 E5 off.* Commonwealth of Virginia, *also known as* Mother of Presidents, Mother of States, Old Dominion. *state* NE USA

Virginia Beach *41 F5* Virginia, NE USA

Virgin Islands *see* British Virgin Islands

Virgin Islands (US) *55 F3 var.* Virgin Islands of the United States; *prev.* Danish West Indies. *US unincorporated territory* E West Indies

Virgin Islands of the United States *see* Virgin Islands (US)

Viróchey *137 E5* Rôtânôkiri, NE Cambodia

Virovitica *100 C2 Ger.* Virovititz, *Hung.* Verőcze; *prev. Ger.* Werowitz. Virovitica-Podravina, NE Croatia

Virovititz *see* Virovitica

Virton *87 D8* Luxembourg, SE Belgium

Virtsu *106 D2 Ger.* Werder. Läänemaa, W Estonia

Vis *100 B4 It.* Lissa; *anc.* Issa. *island* S Croatia

Vis *see* Fish

Visaginas *106 C4 prev.* Sniečkus. Utena, E Lithuania

Visākhapatnam *135 E5* Andhra Pradesh, SE India

Visalia *47 C6* California, W USA

Visby *85 C7 Ger.* Wisby. Gotland, SE Sweden

Viscount Melville Sound *37 F2 prev.* Melville Sound. *sound* Northwest Territories, N Canada

Visé *87 D6* Liège, E Belgium

Viseu *92 C2 prev.* Vizeu. Viseu, N Portugal

Vislinskiy Zaliv *see* Vistula Lagoon

Visoko *100 C4* Federacija Bosna I Hercegovina, C Bosnia and Herzegovina

Visttasjohka *84 D3 River* N Sweden

Vistula *see* Wisła

Vistula Lagoon *98 C2 Ger.* Frisches Haff, *Pol.* Zalew Wiślany, *Rus.* Vislinskiy Zaliv. *lagoon* Poland/Russian Federation

Vitebsk *see* Vitsyebsk

Viterbo *96 C4 anc.* Vicus Elbii. Lazio, C Italy

Viti *see* Fiji

Viti Levu *145 E4 island* W Fiji

Vitim *115 F4 river* C Russian Federation

Vitória *63 F4 state capital* Espírito Santo, SE Brazil

Vitoria *see* Vitoria-Gasteiz

Vitoria Bank *see* Vitória Seamount

Vitória da Conquista *63 F3* Bahia, E Brazil

Vitoria-Gasteiz *93 E1 var.* Vitoria, *Eng.* Vittoria. País Vasco, N Spain

Vitória Seamount *67 B5 var.* Victoria Bank, Vitoria Bank. *seamount* C Atlantic Ocean

Vitré *90 B3* Ille-et-Vilaine, NW France

Vitsyebsk *107 E5 Rus.* Vitebsk. Vitsyebskaya Voblasts', NE Belarus

Vittoria *97 C7* Sicilia, Italy, C Mediterranean Sea

Vittoria *see* Vitoria-Gasteiz

Vizcaya, Golfo de *see* Biscay, Bay of

Vizianagaram *135 E5 var.* Vizianagram. Andhra Pradesh, E India

Vizianagram *see* Vizianagaram

Vjosës, Lumi i *101 C7 var.* Vijosa, Vijosë, *Gk.* Aóos. *river* Albania/Greece

Vlaanderen *see* Flanders

Vlaardingen *86 B4* Zuid-Holland, SW Netherlands

Vladikavkaz *111 B8 prev.* Dzaudzhikau, Ordzhonikidze. Respublika Severnaya Osetiya, SW Russian Federation

Vladimir *111 B5* Vladimirskaya Oblast', W Russian Federation

Vladimirovka *see* Yuzhno-Sakhalinsk

Vladimir-Volynskiy *see* Volodymyr-Volyns'kyy

Vladivostok *115 G5* Primorskiy Kray, SE Russian Federation

Vlagtwedde *86 E2* Groningen, NE Netherlands

Vlasotince *101 E5* Serbia, SE Serbia

Vlieland *86 C1 Fris.* Flylân. *island* Waddeneilanden, N Netherlands

Vlijmen *86 C4* Noord-Brabant, S Netherlands

Vlissingen *87 B5 Eng.* Flushing, *Fr.* Flessingue. Zeeland, SW Netherlands

Vlodava *see* Włodawa

Vlonë/Vlora *see* Vlorë

Vlorë *101 C7 prev.* Vlonë, *It.* Valona, Vlora. Vlorë, SW Albania

Vlotslavsk *see* Włocławek

Vöcklabruck *95 D6* Oberösterreich, NW Austria

Vogelpoot *see* Doberai, Jazirah

Vohimena, Tanjona *79 F4 Fr.* Cap Sainte Marie. *headland* S Madagascar

Voiron *91 D5* Isère, E France

Vojvodina *100 D3* Ger. Wojwodina. Vojvodina, N Serbia

Volga *111 B7 river* NW Russian Federation

Volga Uplands *see* Privolzhskaya Vozvyshennost'

Volgodonsk *111 B7* Rostovskaya Oblast', SW Russian Federation

Volgograd *111 B7 prev.* Stalingrad, Tsaritsyn. Volgogradskaya Oblast', SW Russian Federation

Volkhov *110 B4* Leningradskaya Oblast', NW Russian Federation

Volkovysk *see* Vawkavysk

Volmari *see* Valmiera

Volnovakha *109 G3* Donets'ka Oblast', SE Ukraine

Volodymyr-Volyns'kyy *108 C1 Pol.* Włodzimierz, *Rus.* Vladimir-Volynskiy. Volyns'ka Oblast', NW Ukraine

Vologda *110 B4* Vologodskaya Oblast', W Russian Federation

Vólos *105 B5* Thessalía, C Greece

Volozhin *see* Valozhyn

Vol'sk *111 C6* Saratovskaya Oblast', W Russian Federation

Volta *75 E5 river* SE Ghana

Volta Blanche *see* White Volta

Volta, Lake *75 E5 reservoir* SE Ghana

Volta Noire *see* Black Volta

Volturno *97 D5 river* S Italy

Volunteer Island *see* Starbuck Island

Volzhskiy *111 B6* Volgogradskaya Oblast', SW Russian Federation

Võnnu *106 E3 Ger.* Wendau. Tartumaa, SE Estonia

Voorst *86 D3* Gelderland, E Netherlands

Voranava *107 C5 Pol.* Werenów, *Rus.* Voronovo. Hrodzyenskaya Voblasts', W Belarus

Vorderrhein *95 B7 river* SE Switzerland

Vóreies Sporádes *105 C5 var.* Vóreioi Sporádes, Vórioi Sporádhes, *Eng.* Northern Sporades. *island group* E Greece

Vóreioi Sporádes *see* Vóreies Sporádes

Vórioi Sporádhes *see* Vóreies Sporádes

Vorkuta *114 C2* Respublika Komi, NW Russian Federation

Vormsi *106 C2 var.* Vormsi Saar, *Ger.* Worms, *Swed.* Ormsö. *island* W Estonia

Vormsi Saar *see* Vormsi

Voronezh *111 B6* Voronezhskaya Oblast', W Russian Federation

Voronovo *see* Voranava

Voroshilov *see* Ussuriysk

Voroshilovgrad *see* Luhans'k, Ukraine

Voroshilovsk *see* Stavropol', Russian Federation

Võru *106 D3 Ger.* Werro. Võrumaa, SE Estonia

Vosges *90 E4 mountain range* NE France

Vostochno-Sibirskoye More *115 F1 Eng.* East Siberian Sea. *sea* Arctic Ocean

Vostochnyy Sayan *see* Eastern Sayans

Vostock Island *see* Vostok Island

Vostok *154 C3 Russian research station* Antarctica

Vostok Island *145 G3 var.* Vostock Island; *prev.* Stavers Island. *island* Line Islands, SE Kiribati

Voznesens'k *109 E3 Rus.* Voznesensk. Mykolayivs'ka Oblast', S Ukraine

Vrangelya, Ostrov *115 F1 Eng.* Wrangel Island. *island* NE Russian Federation

Vranje *101 E5* Serbia, SE Serbia

Vranov *see* Vranov nad Topl'ou

Vranov nad Topl'ou *99 D5 var.* Vranov, *Hung.* Varannó. Prešovský Kraj, E Slovakia

Vratsa *104 C2* Vratsa, NW Bulgaria

Vrbas *100 C3* Vojvodina, NW Serbia

Vrbas *100 C3 river* N Bosnia and Herzegovina

Vsetín *99 C5 Ger.* Wsetin. Zlínský Kraj, E Czech Republic

Vučitrn *101 D5* Kosovo, S Serbia

Vukovar *100 C3 Hung.* Vukovár. Vukovar-Srijem, E Croatia

Vulcano, Isola *97 C7 island* Isole Eolie, S Italy

Vung Tau *137 E6 prev. Fr.* Cape Saint Jacques, Cap Saint-Jacques. Ba Ria-Vung Tau, S Vietnam

Vyatka *111 C5 river* NW Russian Federation

Vyatka *see* Kirov

Vyborg *110 B3 Fin.* Viipuri. Leningradskaya Oblast', NW Russian Federation

Vyerkhnyadzvinsk *107 D5 Rus.* Verkhnedvinsk. Vitsyebskaya Voblasts', N Belarus

Vyetryna *107 D5 Rus.* Vetrino. Vitsyebskaya Voblasts', N Belarus

Vynohradiv *108 B3 Cz.* Sevluš, *Hung.* Nagyszöllös, *Rus.* Vinogradov; *prev.* Sevlyush. Zakarpats'ka Oblast', W Ukraine

W

Wa *75 E4* NW Ghana

Waag *see* Váh

Waagbistritz *see* Považská Bystrica

Waal *86 C4 river* S Netherlands

Wabash *40 C4* Indiana, N USA

Wabash River *40 B5 river* N USA

Waco *49 G3* Texas, SW USA

Wad Al-Hajarah *see* Guadalajara

Waddän *71 F3* NW Libya

Waddeneilanden *86 C1 Eng.* West Frisian Islands. *island group* N Netherlands

Waddenzee *86 C1 var.* Wadden Zee. *sea* SE North Sea

Wadden Zee *see* Waddenzee

Waddington, Mount *36 D5 mountain* British Columbia, SW Canada

Wādī as Sir *119 B6 var.* Wadi es Sir. 'Ammān, NW Jordan

Wadi es Sir *see* Wādī as Sir

Wadi Halfa *72 B3 var.* Wādī Ḥalfa'. Northern, N Sudan

Wādī Mūsā *119 B7 var.* Petra. Ma'ān, S Jordan

Wad Madani *see* Wad Medani

Wad Medani *72 C4 var.* Wad Madanī. Gezira, C Sudan

Waflia *139 F4* Pulau Buru, E Indonesia

Wagadugu *see* Ouagadougou

Wagga Wagga *149 C7* New South Wales, SE Australia

Wagin *147 B7* Western Australia

Wāh *134 C1* Punjab, NE Pakistan

Wahai *139 F4* Pulau Seram, E Indonesia

Wahaybah, Ramlat Al *see* Wahībah, Ramlat Āl

Wahiawā *47 A8 var.* Wahiawa. O'ahu, Hawai'i, USA

Wahībah, Ramlat Ahl *see* Wahībah, Ramlat Āl

Wahībah, Ramlat Āl *121 E5 var.* Ramlat Ahl Wahībah, Ramlat Al Wahaybah, *Eng.* Wahībah Sands. *desert* N Oman

Wahībah Sands *see* Wahībah, Ramlat Āl

Wahpeton *45 F2* North Dakota, N USA

Wahran *see* Oran

Waiau *151 A7 river* South Island, New Zealand

Waigeo, Pulau *139 G4 island* Maluku, E Indonesia

Waikaremoana, Lake *150 E4 lake* North Island, New Zealand

Wailuku *47 B8* Maui, Hawai'i, USA

Waimate *151 B6* Canterbury, South Island, New Zealand

Waiouru *150 D4* Manawatu-Wanganui, North Island, New Zealand

Waipara *151 C6* Canterbury, South Island, New Zealand

Waipawa *150 E4* Hawke's Bay, North Island, New Zealand

Waipukurau *150 D4* Hawke's Bay, North Island, New Zealand

Wairau *151 C5 river* South Island, New Zealand

Wairoa *150 E4* Hawke's Bay, North Island, New Zealand

Wairoa *150 D2 river* North Island, New Zealand

Waitaki *151 B6 river* South Island, New Zealand

Waitara *150 D4* Taranaki, North Island, New Zealand

Waitzen *see* Vác

Waiuku *150 D3* Auckland, North Island, New Zealand

Wakasa-wan *131 C6 bay* C Japan

Wakatipu, Lake *151 A7 lake* South Island, New Zealand

Wakayama *131 C6* Wakayama, Honshū, SW Japan

Wake Island *152 C2 US unincorporated territory* NW Pacific Ocean

Wake Island *142 D1 atoll* NW Pacific Ocean

Wakkanai *130 C1* Hokkaidō, NE Japan

Walachei/Walachia *see* Wallachia

Wałbrzych *98 B4 Ger.* Waldenburg, Waldenburg in Schlesien. Dolnośląskie, SW Poland

Walcourt *87 C7* Namur, S Belgium

Wałcz *98 B3 Ger.* Deutsch Krone. Zachodnio-pomorskie, NW Poland

Waldenburg/Waldenburg in Schlesien
see Wałbrzych
Waldia *see* Weldiya
Wales 36 C2 Alaska, USA
Wales 89 C6 *Wel. Cymru. cultural region*
Wales, UK
Wales 89 C6 *Wel. Cymru. national region* Wales, UK
Walgett 149 D5 New South Wales,
SE Australia
Walk *see* Valga, Estonia
Walk *see* Valka, Latvia
Walker Lake 47 C5 *lake* Nevada,
W USA
Wallachia 108 B5 *var.* Walachia, *Ger.*
Walachei, *Rom.* Valachia. *cultural region* S Romania
Walla Walla 46 C2 Washington,
NW USA
Wallenthal *see* Haţeg
Wallis and Futuna 145 E4 Fr. Territoire
de Wallis et Futuna. *French overseas territory* C Pacific Ocean
Wallis et Futuna, Territoire de *see*
Wallis and Futuna
Walnut Ridge 42 B1 Arkansas, C USA
Waltenberg *see* Zalău
Walthamstow 89 B7 Waltham Forest,
SE England, UK
Walvisbaai *see* Walvis Bay
Walvis Bay 78 A4 *Afr.* Walvisbaai.
Erongo, NW Namibia
Walvis Ridge 69 B7 *var.* Walvish Ridge.
undersea ridge E Atlantic Ocean
Wan *see* Anhui
Wanaka 151 B6 Otago, South Island,
New Zealand
Wanaka, Lake 151 A6 *lake* South Island,
New Zealand
Wanchuan *see* Zhangjiakou
Wandel Sea 83 F1 *sea* Arctic Ocean
Wandsworth 89 A8 Wandsworth,
SE England, UK
Wanganui 150 D4 Manawatu-
Wanganui, North Island, New Zealand
Wangaratta 149 C7 Victoria,
SE Australia
Wankie *see* Hwange
Wanki, Río *see* Coco, Río
Wanlaweyn 73 D6 *var.* Wanle Weyn,
It. Uanle Uen. Shabeellaha Hoose,
SW Somalia
Wanle Weyn *see* Wanlaweyn
Wanxian *see* Wanzhou
Wanzhou 128 B5 *var.* Wanxian.
Chongqing Shi, C China
Warangal 135 E5 Andhra Pradesh,
C India
Warasdin *see* Varaždin
Warburg 94 B4 Nordrhein-Westfalen,
W Germany
Ware 37 E4 British Columbia,
W Canada
Waremme 87 C6 Liège, E Belgium
Waren 94 C3 Mecklenburg-
Vorpommern, NE Germany
Wargla *see* Ouargla
Warkworth 150 D2 Auckland, North
Island, New Zealand
Warnemünde 94 C2 Mecklenburg-
Vorpommern, NE Germany
Warner 49 G1 Oklahoma, C USA
Warnes 61 G4 Santa Cruz, C Bolivia
Warrego River 149 C5 *seasonal river*
New South Wales/Queensland,
E Australia
Warren 40 D3 Michigan, N USA
Warren 40 D3 Ohio, N USA
Warren 41 E3 Pennsylvania, NE USA
Warri 75 F5 Delta, S Nigeria
Warrnambool 149 B7 Victoria,
SE Australia
Warsaw/Warschau *see* Warszawa
Warszawa 98 D3 *Eng.* Warsaw,
Ger. Warschau, *Rus.* Varshava. *c ountry capital* (Poland) Mazowieckie,
C Poland
Warta 98 B3 *Ger.* Warthe. *river*
W Poland
Wartberg *see* Senec
Warthe *see* Warta
Warwick 149 E5 Queensland,
E Australia
Washington 44 A2 NE England, UK
Washington DC 41 E4 *country capital*
(USA) District of Columbia,
NE USA

Washington Island *see* Teraina
Washington, Mount 41 G2 *mountain*
New Hampshire, NE USA
Wash, The 89 E6 *inlet* E England, UK
Wasiliszki *see* Vasilishki
Waspam 53 E2 *var.* Waspán. Región
Autónoma Atlántico Norte,
NE Nicaragua
Waspán *see* Waspam
Watampone 139 E4 *var.* Bone. Sulawesi,
C Indonesia
Watenstedt-Salzgitter *see* Salzgitter
Waterbury 41 F3 Connecticut,
NE USA
Waterford 89 B6 *Ir.* Port Láirge.
Waterford, S Ireland
Waterloo 45 G3 Iowa, C USA
Watertown 41 F2 New York, NE USA
Watertown 45 F2 South Dakota,
N USA
Waterville 41 G2 Maine, NE USA
Watford 89 A7 E England, UK
Watsa 77 E5 Orientale, NE Dem. Rep.
Congo
Watts Bar Lake 42 D1 *reservoir*
Tennessee, S USA
Wau 73 B5 *var.* Wāw. Western Bahr el
Ghazal, S Sudan
Waukegan 40 B3 Illinois, N USA
Waukesha 40 B3 Wisconsin, N USA
Wausau 40 B2 Wisconsin, N USA
Waverly 45 G3 Iowa, C USA
Wavre 87 C6 Walloon Brabant,
C Belgium
Wāw *see* Wau
Wawa 38 C4 Ontario, S Canada
Waycross 43 E3 Georgia, SE USA
Wearmouth *see* Sunderland
Webfoot State *see* Oregon
Webster City 45 F3 Iowa, C USA
Weddell Plain 154 A2 *abyssal plain*
SW Atlantic Ocean
Weddell Sea 154 A2 *sea* SW Atlantic
Ocean
Weener 94 A3 Niedersachsen,
NW Germany
Weert 87 D5 Limburg, SE Netherlands
Weesp 86 C3 Noord-Holland,
C Netherlands
Węgorzewo 98 D2 *Ger.* Angerburg.
Warmińsko-Mazurskie, NE Poland
Weichsel *see* Wisła
Weimar 94 C4 Thüringen, C Germany
Weissenburg *see* Alba Iulia
Weissenburg in Bayern 95 C6 Bayern,
SE Germany
Weissenstein *see* Paide
Weisskirchen *see* Bela Crkva
Weiswampach 87 D7 Diekirch,
N Luxembourg
Wejherowo 98 C2 Pomorskie,
NW Poland
Welchman Hall 55 G1 C Barbados
Weldiya 72 C4 *var.* Waldia, *It.* Valdia.
Amhara, N Ethiopia
Welkom 78 D4 Free State,
C South Africa
Welle *see* Uele
Wellesley Islands 148 B2 *island group*
Queensland, N Australia
Wellington 151 D5 *country capital*
(New Zealand) Wellington, North
Island, New Zealand
Wellington 45 F5 Kansas, C USA
Wellington *see* Wellington, Isla
Wellington, Isla 65 A7 *var.* Wellington.
island S Chile
Wells 46 D1 Nevada, W USA
Wellsford 150 D2 Auckland, North
Island, New Zealand
Wells, Lake 147 C5 *lake* Western
Australia
Wels 95 D6 *anc.* Ovilava. Oberösterreich,
N Austria
Wembley 89 A8 Alberta, W Canada
Wemmel 87 B6 Vlaams Brabant,
C Belgium
Wenatchee 46 B2 Washington,
NW USA
Wenchi 75 E4 W Ghana
Wen-chou/Wenchow *see* Wenzhou
Wendau *see* Võnnu
Wenden *see* Cēsis
Wenzhou 128 D5 *var.* Wen-chou,
Wenchow. Zhejiang, SE China
Werda 78 C4 Kgalagadi, S Botswana
Werder *see* Virtsu
Werenów *see* Voranava

Werkendam 86 C4 Noord-Brabant,
S Netherlands
Werowitz *see* Virovitica
Werro *see* Võru
Wesenberg *see* Rakvere
Weser 94 B3 *river* NW Germany
Wessel Islands 148 B1 *island group*
Northern Territory, N Australia
West Antarctica *see* Lesser Antarctica
West Australian Basin *see* Wharton
Basin
West Bank 119 A6 *disputed region*
SW Asia
West Bend 40 B3 Wisconsin, N USA
West Bengal 135 F4 *cultural region*
NE India
West Bengal 135 F4 *state* NE India
West Cape 151 A7 *headland* South
Island, New Zealand
West Des Moines 45 F3 Iowa,
C USA
Westerland 94 B2 Schleswig-Holstein,
N Germany
Western Australia 146 B4 *state*
W Australia
Western Bug *see* Bug
Western Desert *see* Sahara el Gharbîya
Western Dvina 85 E7 *Bel.* Dzvina, *Ger.*
Düna, *Latv.* Daugava, *Rus.* Zapadnaya
Dvina. *river* W Europe
Western Ghats 114 C5 *mountain range*
SW India
Western Isles *see* Outer Hebrides
Western Punjab *see* Punjab
Western Sahara 70 B3 *disputed territory*
N Africa
Western Samoa *see* Samoa
**Western Samoa, Independent State
of** *see* Samoa
Western Sayans *see* Zapadnyy Sayan
Western Scheldt *see* Westerschelde
Western Sierra Madre *see* Sierra Madre
Occidental
Westerschelde 87 B5 *Eng.* Western
Scheldt; *prev.* Honte. *inlet* S North Sea
West Falkland 65 C7 *var.* Gran Malvina.
island W Falkland Islands
West Fargo 45 F2 North Dakota,
N USA
West Frisian Islands *see*
Waddeneilanden
West Irian *see* Papua
Westliche Morava *see* Zapadna Morava
West Mariana Basin 142 B1 *var.* Perece
Vela Basin. *undersea feature* W Pacific
Ocean
West Memphis 42 B1 Arkansas,
C USA
West New Guinea *see* Papua
Weston-super-Mare 89 D7
SW England, UK
West Palm Beach 43 F4 Florida,
SE USA
West Papua *see* Papua
Westport 151 C5 West Coast, South
Island, New Zealand
West Punjab *see* Punjab
West River *see* Xi Jiang
West Siberian Plain *see* Zapadno-
Sibirskaya Ravnina
West Virginia 10 D4 *off.* State of West
Virginia, *also known as* Mountain State.
state NE USA
Wetar, Pulau 139 F5 *island* Kepulauan
Damar, E Indonesia
Wetzlar 95 B5 Hessen, W Germany
Wevok 36 C2 *var.* Wewuk. Alaska, USA
Wewuk *see* Wevok
Wexford 89 B6 *Ir.* Loch Garman.
SE Ireland
Weyburn 37 F5 Saskatchewan, S Canada
Weymouth 89 D7 S England, UK
Wezep 86 D3 Gelderland, E Netherlands
Whakatane 150 E3 Bay of Plenty, North
Island, New Zealand
Whale Cove 37 G3 Nunavut, C Canada
Whangarei 150 D2 Northland, North
Island, New Zealand
Wharton Basin 141 D5 *var.* West
Australian Basin. *undersea feature*
E Indian Ocean
Whataroa 151 B6 West Coast, South
Island, New Zealand
Wheatland 44 D3 Wyoming, C USA
Wheeler Peak 48 D1 *mountain* New
Mexico, SW USA
Wheeling 40 D4 West Virginia,
NE USA

Whitby 89 D5 N England, UK
Whitefish 44 B1 Montana, NW USA
Whitehaven 89 C5 NW England, UK
Whitehorse 36 D4 *territory capital*
Yukon Territory, W Canada
White Nile 72 B4 *var.* Bahr el Jebel.
river S Sudan
White Nile 72 B4 *Ar.* Al Baḥr al Abyaḍ,
An Nīl al Abyaḍ, Bahr el Jebel. *river*
SE Sudan
White River 44 D3 *river* South Dakota,
N USA
White Sea *see* Beloye More
White Volta 75 E4 *var.* Nakambé,
Fr. Volta Blanche. *river* Burkina
Faso/Ghana
Whitianga 150 D2 Waikato, North
Island, New Zealand
Whitney, Mount 47 C6 *mountain*
California, W USA
Whitsunday Group 148 D3 *island group*
Queensland, E Australia
Whyalla 149 B6 South Australia
Wichita 45 F5 Kansas, C USA
Wichita Falls 49 F2 Texas, SW USA
Wichita River 49 F2 *river* Texas, SW USA
Wickenburg 48 B2 Arizona, SW USA
Wicklow 89 B6 *Ir.* Cill Mhantáin. *county*
E Ireland
Wicklow Mountains 89 B6 *Ir.* Sléibhte
Chill Mhantáin. *mountain range*
E Ireland
Wieliczka 99 D5 Małopolskie, S Poland
Wieluń 98 C4 Sieradz, C Poland
Wien 95 E6 *Eng.* Vienna, *Hung.*
Bécs, *Slvk.* Videň, *Slvn.* Dunaj; *anc.*
Vindobona. *country capital* (Austria)
Wien, NE Austria
Wiener Neustadt 95 E6
Niederösterreich, E Austria
Wierden 86 E3 Overijssel, E Netherlands
Wiesbaden 95 B5 Hessen, W Germany
**Wieselburg and Ungarisch-Altenburg/
Wieselburg-Ungarisch-Altenburg**
see Mosonmagyaróvár
Wiesenhof *see* Ostrołęka
Wight, Isle of 89 D7 *island* UK
Wigorna Ceaster *see* Worcester
Wijchen 86 D4 Gelderland,
SE Netherlands
Wijk bij Duurstede 86 D4 Utrecht,
C Netherlands
Wilcannia 149 C6 New South Wales,
SE Australia
Wilejka *see* Vilyeyka
Wilhelm, Mount 144 B3 *mountain*
C Papua New Guinea
Wilhelm-Pieck-Stadt *see* Guben
Wilhelmshaven 94 B3 Niedersachsen,
NW Germany
Wilia/Wilja *see* Neris
Wilkes Barre 41 F3 Pennsylvania,
NE USA
Wilkes Land 154 C4 *physical region*
Antarctica
Wilkomierz *see* Ukmergė
Willard 48 D2 New Mexico,
SW USA
Willcox 48 C3 Arizona, SW USA
Willebroek 87 B5 Antwerpen,
C Belgium
Willemstad 55 E5 *dependent territory
capital* (Netherlands Antilles) Curaçao,
Netherlands Antilles
Williston 44 D1 North Dakota,
N USA
Wilmington 41 F4 Delaware,
NE USA
Wilmington 43 F2 North Carolina,
SE USA
Wilmington 40 C4 Ohio, N USA
Wilna/Wilno *see* Vilnius
Wilrijk 87 C5 Antwerpen, N Belgium
Winchester 89 D7 *hist.* Wintanceaster,
Lat. Venta Belgarum. S England, UK
Winchester 41 E4 Virginia, NE USA
Windau *see* Ventspils
Windau *see* Venta
Windhoek 78 B3 *Ger.* Windhuk.
country capital (Namibia) Khomas,
C Namibia
Windhuk *see* Windhoek
Windorah 148 C4 Queensland,
C Australia
Windsor 38 C5 Ontario, S Canada
Windsor 89 D7 S England, UK
Windsor 41 G3 Connecticut,
NE USA

Windward Islands *55 H4 island group* E West Indies
Windward Islands *see* Barlavento, Ilhas de, Cape Verde
Windward Passage *54 D3 Sp.* Paso de los Vientos. *channel* Cuba/Haiti
Winisk *38 C2 river* Ontario, S Canada
Winkowitz *see* Vinkovci
Winnebago, Lake *40 B2 lake* Wisconsin, N USA
Winnemucca *47 C5* Nevada, W USA
Winnipeg *37 G5 province capital* Manitoba, S Canada
Winnipeg, Lake *37 G5 lake* Manitoba, C Canada
Winnipegosis, Lake *38 A3 lake* Manitoba, C Canada
Winona *45 G3* Minnesota, N USA
Winschoten *86 E2* Groningen, NE Netherlands
Winsen *94 B3* Niedersachsen, N Germany
Winston Salem *43 E1* North Carolina, SE USA
Winsum *86 D1* Groningen, NE Netherlands
Wintanceaster *see* Winchester
Winterswijk *86 E4* Gelderland, E Netherlands
Winterthur *95 B7* Zürich, NE Switzerland
Winton *148 C4* Queensland, E Australia
Winton *151 A7* Southland, South Island, New Zealand
Wisby *see* Visby
Wisconsin *40 A2 off.* State of Wisconsin, *also known as* Badger State. *state* N USA
Wisconsin Rapids *40 B2* Wisconsin, N USA
Wisconsin River *40 B3 river* Wisconsin, N USA
Wisła *98 C2 Eng.* Vistula, *Ger.* Weichsel. *river* C Poland
Wiślany, Zalew *see* Vistula Lagoon
Wismar *94 C2* Mecklenburg-Vorpommern, N Germany
Wittenberge *94 C3* Brandenburg, N Germany
Wittlich *95 A5* Rheinland-Pfalz, SW Germany
Wittstock *94 C3* Brandenburg, NE Germany
W. J. van Blommesteinmeer *59 G3 reservoir* E Suriname
Władysławowo *98 C2* Pomorskie, N Poland
Włocławek *98 C3 Ger./Rus.* Vlotslavsk. Kujawsko-pomorskie, C Poland
Włodawa *98 E4 Rus.* Vlodava. Lubelskie, SE Poland
Włodzimierz *see* Volodymyr-Volyns'kyy
Wlotzkasbaken *78 B3* Erongo, W Namibia
Wodonga *149 C7* Victoria, SE Australia
Wodzisław Śląski *99 C5 Ger.* Loslau. Śląskie, S Poland
Wojerecy *see* Hoyerswerda
Wōjjā *see* Wotje Atoll
Wojwodina *see* Vojvodina
Woking *89 D7* SE England, UK
Wolf, Isla *60 A4 island* Galápagos, Galapagos Islands, W Ecuador South America
Wolfsberg *95 D7* Kärnten, SE Austria
Wolfsburg *94 C3* Niedersachsen, N Germany
Wolgast *94 D2* Mecklenburg-Vorpommern, NE Germany
Wołkowysk *see* Vawkavysk
Wöllan *see* Velenje
Wollaston Lake *37 F4* Saskatchewan, C Canada
Wollongong *149 D6* New South Wales, SE Australia
Wolmar *see* Valmiera
Wołożyn *see* Valozhyn
Wolvega *86 D2 Fris.* Wolvegea. Friesland, N Netherlands
Wolvegea *see* Wolvega
Wolverhampton *89 D6* C England, UK
Wolverine State *see* Michigan
Wŏnsan *129 E3* SE North Korea
Woodburn *46 B3* Oregon, NW USA
Woodland *47 B5* California, W USA
Woodruff *40 B2* Wisconsin, N USA
Woods, Lake of the *38 A3 Fr.* Lac des Bois. *lake* Canada/USA
Woodville *150 D4* Manawatu-Wanganui, North Island, New Zealand
Woodward *49 F1* Oklahoma, C USA
Worcester *78 C5* Western Cape, SW South Africa
Worcester *89 D6 hist.* Wigorna Ceaster. W England, UK
Worcester *41 G3* Massachusetts, NE USA
Workington *89 C5* NW England, UK
Worland *44 C3* Wyoming, C USA
Wormatia *see* Worms
Worms *95 B5 anc.* Augusta Vangionum, Borbetomagus, Wormatia. Rheinland-Pfalz, SW Germany
Worms *see* Vormsi
Worthington *45 F3* Minnesota, N USA
Wotje Atoll *144 D1 var.* Wōjjā. *atoll* Ratak Chain, E Marshall Islands
Woudrichem *86 C4* Noord-Brabant, S Netherlands
Wrangel Island *see* Vrangelya, Ostrov
Wrangel Plain *155 B2 undersea feature* Arctic Ocean
Wrocław *98 C4 Eng./Ger.* Breslau. Dolnośląskie, SW Poland
Września *98 C3* Wielkopolskie, C Poland
Wsetin *see* Vsetín
Wuchang *see* Wuhan
Wuday'ah *121 C6 spring/well* S Saudi Arabia
Wuhai *127 E3 var.* Haibowan. Nei Mongol Zizhiqu, N China
Wuhan *128 C5 var.* Han-kou, Han-k'ou, Hanyang, Wuchang, Wu-han; *prev.* Hankow. *province capital* Hubei, C China
Wu-han *see* Wuhan
Wuhsien *see* Suzhou
Wuhsi/Wu-his *see* Wuxi
Wuhu *128 D5 var.* Wu-na-mu. Anhui, E China
Wujlān *see* Ujelang Atoll
Wukari *75 G4* Taraba, E Nigeria
Wuliang Shan *128 A6 mountain range* SW China
Wu-lu-k'o-mu-shi/Wu-lu-mu-ch'i *see* Ürümqi
Wu-na-mu *see* Wuhu
Wuppertal *94 A4 prev.* Barmen-Elberfeld. Nordrhein-Westfalen, W Germany
Würzburg *95 B5* Bayern, SW Germany
Wusih *see* Wuxi
Wuxi *128 D5 var.* Wuhsi, Wu-hsi, Wusih. Jiangsu, E China
Wuyi Shan *125 E3 mountain range* SE China
Wye *89 C6 Wel.* Gwy. *river* England/Wales, UK
Wyłkowyszki *see* Vilkaviškis
Wyndham *146 D3* Western Australia
Wyoming *40 C3* Michigan, N USA
Wyoming *44 B3 off.* State of Wyoming, *also known as* Equality State. *state* C USA
Wyszków *98 D3 Ger.* Probstberg. Mazowieckie, NE Poland

X

Xaafuun, Raas *72 E4 var.* Ras Hafun. *cape* NE Somalia
Xaçmaz *117 H2 Rus.* Khachmas. N Azerbaijan
Xaignabouli *136 C4 prev* Muang Xaignabouri, *Fr.* Sayaboury. Xaignabouli, N Laos
Xai-Xai *79 E4 prev.* João Belo, Vila de João Belo. Gaza, S Mozambique
Xalapa *51 F4* Veracruz-Llave, Mexico
Xam Nua *136 D3 var.* Sam Neua. Houaphan, N Laos
Xankändi *117 G3 Rus.* Khankendi; *prev.* Stepanakert. SW Azerbaijan
Xánthi *104 C3* Anatolikí Makedonía kai Thráki, NE Greece
Xátiva *93 F3 var.* Jativa; *anc.* Setabis. País Valenciano, E Spain
Xauen *see* Chefchaouen
Xäzär Dänizi *see* Caspian Sea
Xeres *see* Jeréz de la Frontera
Xiaguan *see* Dali
Xiamen *128 D6 var.* Hsia-men; *prev.* Amoy. Fujian, SE China
Xi'an *128 C4 var.* Changan, Sian, Signan, Siking, Singan, Xian. *province capital* Shaanxi, C China
Xiang *see* Hunan
Xianggang *see* Hong Kong
Xiangkhoang *see* Pèk
Xiangtan *128 C5 var.* Hsiang-t'an, Siangtan. Hunan, S China
Xiao Hinggan Ling *128 D2 Eng.* Lesser Khingan Range. *mountain range* NE China
Xichang *128 B5* Sichuan, C China
Xieng Khouang *see* Pèk
Xieng Ngeun *see* Muong Xiang Ngeun
Xigazê *126 C5 var.* Jih-k'a-tse, Shigatse, Xigaze. Xizang Zizhiqu, W China
Xi Jiang *124 D3 var.* Hsi Chiang, *Eng.* West River. *river* S China
Xilinhot *127 F2 var.* Silinhot. Nei Mongol Zizhiqu, N China
Xilokastro *see* Xylókastro
Xin *see* Xinjiang Uygur Zizhiqu
Xingkai Hu *see* Khanka, Lake
Xingu, Rio *63 E2 river* C Brazil
Xingxingxia *126 D3* Xinjiang Uygur Zizhiqu, NW China
Xining *127 E4 var.* Hsining, Hsi-ning, Sining. *province capital* Qinghai, C China
Xinjiang *see* Xinjiang Uygur Zizhiqu
Xinjiang Uygur Zizhiqu *126 B3 var.* Sinkiang, Sinkiang Uighur Autonomous Region, Xin, Xinjiang. *autonomous region* NW China
Xinpu *see* Lianyungang
Xinxiang *128 C4* Henan, C China
Xinyang *128 C5 var.* Hsin-yang, Sinyang. Henan, C China
Xinzo de Limia *92 C2* Galicia, NW Spain
Xiqing Shan *124 D2 mountain range* C China
Xiva *122 D2 Rus.* Khiva, Khiwa. Xorazm Viloyati, W Uzbekistan
Xixón *see* Gijón
Xizang *see* Xizang Zizhiqu
Xizang Gaoyuan *see* Qingzang Gaoyuan
Xizang Zizhiqu *126 B4 var.* Thibet, Tibetan Autonomous Region, Xizang, *Eng.* Tibet. *autonomous region* W China
Xolotlán *see* Managua, Lago de
Xuddur *73 D5 var.* Hudur, *It.* Oddur. Bakool, SW Somalia
Xuwen *128 C7* Guangdong, S China
Xuzhou *128 D4 var.* Hsu-chou, Suchow, Tongshan; *prev.* T'ung-shan. Jiangsu, E China
Xylókastro *105 B5 var.* Xilokastro. Pelopónnisos, S Greece

Y

Ya'an *128 B5 var.* Yaan. Sichuan, C China
Yabēlo *73 C5* Oromo, C Ethiopia
Yablis *53 E2* Región Autónoma Atlántico Norte, NE Nicaragua
Yablonovyy Khrebet *115 F4 mountain range* S Russian Federation
Yabrai Shan *127 E3 mountain range* NE China
Yafran *71 F2* NW Libya
Yaghan Basin *67 B7 undersea feature* SE Pacific Ocean
Yagotin *see* Yahotyn
Yahotyn *109 E2 Rus.* Yagotin. Kyyivs'ka Oblast', N Ukraine
Yahualica *50 D4* Jalisco, SW Mexico
Yakima *46 B2* Washington, NW USA
Yakima River *46 B2 river* Washington, NW USA
Yakoruda *104 C3* Blagoevgrad, SW Bulgaria
Yaku-shima *131 B8 island* Nansei-shotō, SW Japan
Yakutat *36 D4* Alaska, USA
Yakutsk *115 F3* Respublika Sakha (Yakutiya), NE Russian Federation
Yala *137 C7* Yala, SW Thailand
Yalizava *107 D6 Rus.* Yelizovo. Mahilyowskaya Voblasts', E Belarus
Yalong Jiang *128 A5 river* C China
Yalova *116 B3* Yalova, NW Turkey
Yalpug, Ozero *see* Yalpuh, Ozero
Yalpuh, Ozero *108 D4 Rus.* Ozero Yalpug. *lake* SW Ukraine
Yalta *109 F5* Respublika Krym, S Ukraine
Yalu *125 E2 Chin.* Yalu Jiang, *Jap.* Oryokko, *Kor.* Amnok-kang. *river* China/North Korea
Yalu Jiang *see* Yalu
Yamaguchi *131 B7 var.* Yamaguti. Yamaguchi, Honshū, SW Japan
Yamal, Poluostrov *114 D2 peninsula* N Russian Federation
Yamanīyah, Al Jumhūrīyah al *see* Yemen
Yambio *73 B5 var.* Yambiyo. Western Equatoria, S Sudan
Yambiyo *see* Yambio
Yambol *104 D2 Turk.* Yanboli. Yambol, E Bulgaria
Yamdena, Pulau *139 G5 prev.* Jamdena. *island* Kepulauan Tanimbar, E Indonesia
Yamoussoukro *74 D5 country capital* (Côte d'Ivoire (Ivory Coast)) C Côte d'Ivoire (Ivory Coast)
Yamuna *134 D3 prev.* Jumna. *river* N India
Yana *115 F2 river* NE Russian Federation
Yanboli *see* Yambol
Yanbu 'al Baḥr *121 A5* Al Madīnah, W Saudi Arabia
Yangambi *77 D5* Orientale, N Dem. Rep. Congo
Yangchow *see* Yangzhou
Yangiyo'l *123 E2 Rus.* Yangiyul'. Toshkent Viloyati, E Uzbekistan
Yangiyul' *see* Yangiyo'l
Yangku *see* Taiyuan
Yangon *136 B4 Eng.* Rangoon. Yangon, S Myanmar (Burma)
Yangtze *see* Chang Jiang/Jinsha Jiang
Yangtze *see* Jinsha Jiang
Yangtze Kiang *see* Chang Jiang
Yangzhou *128 D5 var.* Yangchow. Jiangsu, E China
Yankton *45 E3* South Dakota, N USA
Yannina *see* Ioánnina
Yanskiy Zaliv *113 F2 bay* N Russian Federation
Yantai *128 D4 var.* Yan-t'ai; *prev.* Chefoo, Chih-fu. Shandong, E China
Yaoundé *77 B5 var.* Yaunde. *country capital* (Cameroon) Centre, S Cameroon
Yap *144 A1 island* Caroline Islands, W Micronesia
Yapanskoye More East Sea/Japan, Sea of
Yapen, Pulau *139 G4 prev.* Japen. *island* E Indonesia
Yap Trench *142 B2 var.* Yap Trough. *undersea feature* SE Philippine Sea
Yap Trough *see* Yap Trench
Yapurá *see* Caquetá, Río, Brazil/Colombia
Yapurá *see* Japurá, Rio, Brazil/Colombia
Yaqui, Río *50 C2 river* NW Mexico
Yaransk *111 C5* Kirovskaya Oblast', NW Russian Federation
Yarega *110 D4* Respublika Komi, NW Russian Federation
Yarkant *see* Shache
Yarlung Zangbo Jiang *see* Brahmaputra
Yarmouth *39 F5* Nova Scotia, SE Canada
Yarmouth *see* Great Yarmouth
Yaroslav *see* Jarosław
Yaroslavl' *110 B4* Yaroslavskaya Oblast', W Russian Federation
Yarumal *58 B2* Antioquia, NW Colombia
Yasyel'da *107 B7 river* Brestskaya Voblasts', SW Belorussia Europe
Yatsushiro *131 A7 var.* Yatusiro. Kumamoto, Kyūshū, SW Japan
Yatusiro *see* Yatsushiro
Yaunde *see* Yaoundé
Yavarí *see* Javari, Rio
Yaviza *53 H5* Darién, SE Panama
Yavoriv *108 B2 Pol.* Jaworów, *Rus.* Yavorov. L'vivs'ka Oblast', NW Ukraine
Yavorov *see* Yavoriv
Yazd *120 D3 var.* Yezd. Yazd, C Iran
Yazoo City *42 B2* Mississippi, S USA
Yding Skovhøj *85 A7 hill* C Denmark
Ýdra *105 C6 var.* Ídhra. *island* Ýdra, S Greece

Ye *137 B5* Mon State, S Myanmar (Burma)
Yecheng *126 A3* *var.* Kargilik. Xinjiang Uygur Zizhiqu, NW China
Yefremov *111 B5* Tul'skaya Oblast', W Russian Federation
Yekaterinburg *114 C3* *prev.* Sverdlovsk. Sverdlovskaya Oblast', C Russian Federation
Yekaterinodar *see* Krasnodar
Yekaterinoslav *see* Dnipropetrovs'k
Yelets *111 B5* Lipetskaya Oblast', W Russian Federation
Yelisavetpol *see* Gäncä
Yelizavetgrad *see* Kirovohrad
Yelizovo *see* Yalizava
Yell *88 D1* *island* NE Scotland, UK
Yellowhammer State *see* Alabama
Yellowknife *37 E4* *territory capital* Northwest Territories, W Canada
Yellow River *see* Huang He
Yellow Sea *128 D4* *Chin.* Huang Hai, *Kor.* Hwang Hae. *sea* E Asia
Yellowstone River *44 C2* *river* Montana/ Wyoming, NW USA
Yel'sk *107 C7* *Rus.* Yel'sk. Homyel'skaya Voblasts', SE Belarus
Yelwa *75 F4* Kebbi, W Nigeria
Yemen *121 C7* *off.* Republic of Yemen, *Ar.* Al Jumhuriyah al Yamaniyah, Al Yaman. *country* SW Asia

YEMEN
Southwest Asia

Official name Republic of Yemen
Formation 1990 / 1990
Capital Sana
Population 21 million / 97 people per sq mile (37 people per sq km) / 25%
Total area 203,849 sq miles (527,970 sq km)
Languages Arabic*
Religions Sunni Muslim 55%, Shi'a Muslim 42%, Christian, Hindu, and Jewish 3%
Ethnic mix Arab 95%, Afro-Arab 3%, Indian, Somali, and European 2%
Government Presidential system
Currency Yemeni rial = 100 sene
Literacy rate 49%
Calorie consumption 2038 calories

Yemen, Republic of *see* Yemen
Yemva *110 D4* *prev.* Zheleznodorozhnyy. Respublika Komi, NW Russian Federation
Yenakiyeve *109 G3* *Rus.* Yenakiyevo; *prev.* Ordzhonikidze, Rykovo. Donets'ka Oblast', E Ukraine
Yenakiyevo *see* Yenakiyeve
Yenangyaung *136 A3* Magwe, W Myanmar (Burma)
Yendi *75 E4* NE Ghana
Yengisar *126 A3* Xinjiang Uygur Zizhiqu, NW China
Yenierenköy *102 D4* *var.* Yialousa, *Gk.* Agialoúsa. NE Cyprus
Yenisey *114 D3* *river* Mongolia/Russian Federation
Yenping *see* Nanping
Yeovil *89 D7* SW England, UK
Yeppoon *148 D4* Queensland, E Australia
Yerevan *117 F3* *Eng.* Erivan. *country capital* (Armenia) C Armenia
Yeriho *see* Jericho
Yerushalayim *see* Jerusalem
Yeso *see* Hokkaidō
Yeu, Île d' *90 A4* *island* NW France
Yevlakh *see* Yevlax
Yevlax *117 G2* *Rus.* Yevlakh. C Azerbaijan
Yevpatoriya *109 F5* Respublika Krym, S Ukraine
Yeya *109 H4* *river* SW Russian Federation
Yezerishche *see* Yezyaryshcha
Yezo *see* Hokkaidō
Yezyaryshcha *107 E5* *Rus.* Yezerishche. Vitsyebskaya Voblasts', NE Belarus
Yialousa *see* Yenierenköy
Yiannitsá *see* Giannitsá
Yichang *128 C5* Hubei, C China
Yıldızeli *116 D3* Sivas, N Turkey
Yinchuan *128 B4* *var.* Yinch'uan, Yin-ch'uan, Yinchwan. *province capital* Ningxia, N China
Yin-ch'uan/Yinch'uan *see* Yinchuan
Yinchwan *see* Yinchuan
Yindu He *see* Indus
Yin-hsien *see* Ningbo
Yining *126 B2* *var.* I-ning, *Uigh.* Gulja, Kuldja. Xinjiang Uygur Zizhiqu, NW China
Yin-tu Ho *see* Indus
Yisrael/Yisra'el *see* Israel
Yíthion *see* Gýtheio
Yogyakarta *138 C5* *prev.* Djokjakarta, Jogjakarta, Jokyakarta. Jawa, C Indonesia
Yokohama *131 D5* Aomori, Honshū, C Japan
Yokohama *130 A2* Kanagawa, Honshū, S Japan
Yokote *130 D4* Akita, Honshū, C Japan
Yola *75 H4* Adamawa, E Nigeria
Yonago *131 B6* Tottori, Honshū, SW Japan
Yong'an *120 D6* *var.* Yongan. Fujian, SE China
Yongzhou *129 C6* *var.* Lengshuitan. Hunan, S China
Yonkers *41 F3* New York, NE USA
Yonne *90 C4* *river* C France
Yopal *58 C3* *var.* El Yopal. Casanare, C Colombia
York *89 D5* *anc.* Eboracum, Eburacum. N England, UK
York *45 E4* Nebraska, C USA
York, Cape *148 C1* *headland* Queensland, NE Australia
York, Kap *see* Innaanganeq
Yorkton *37 F5* Saskatchewan, S Canada
Yoro *52 C2* Yoro, C Honduras
Yoshkar-Ola *111 C3* Respublika Mariy El, W Russian Federation
Yösönbulag *see* Altay
Youngstown *40 D4* Ohio, N USA
Youth, Isle of *see* Juventud, Isla de la
Ypres *see* Ieper
Yreka *46 B4* California, W USA
Yrendagüé *see* General Eugenio A. Garay
Yssel *see* IJssel
Ysyk-Köl *see* Issyk-Kul', Ozero
Ysyk-Köl *see* Balykchy
Yu *see* Henan
Yuan *see* Red River
Yuan Jiang *see* Red River
Yuba City *47 B5* California, W USA
Yucatán, Canal de *see* Yucatan Channel
Yucatan Channel *51 H3* *Sp.* Canal de Yucatán. *channel* Cuba/Mexico
Yucatan Peninsula *see* Yucatán, Península de
Yucatán, Península de *35 C7* *Eng.* Yucatan Peninsula. *peninsula* Guatemala/Mexico
Yuci *see* Jinzhong
Yue *see* Guangdong
Yue Shan, Tai *see* Lantau Island
Yueyang *128 C5* Hunan, S China
Yugoslavia *see* Serbia
Yukhavichy *107 D5* *Rus.* Yukhovichi. Vitsyebskaya Voblasts', N Belarus
Yukhovichi *see* Yukhavichy
Yukon *36 C2* *river* Canada/USA
Yukon *see* Yukon Territory
Yukon, Territoire du *see* Yukon Territory
Yukon Territory *36 D3* *var.* Yukon, *Fr.* Territoire du Yukon. *territory* NW Canada
Yulin *128 C6* Guangxi Zhuangzu Zizhiqu, S China
Yuma *48 A2* Arizona, SW USA
Yumen *128 A3* *var.* Laojunmiao, Yümen. Gansu, N China
Yun *see* Yunnan
Yungki *see* Jilin
Yung-ning *see* Nanning
Yunjinghong *see* Jinghong
Yunki *see* Jilin
Yunnan *128 A6* *var.* Yun, Yunnan Sheng, Yünnan, Yun-nan. *province* SW China
Yunnan *see* Kunming
Yunnan Sheng *see* Yunnan
Yünnan/Yun-nan *see* Yunnan
Yurev *see* Tartu
Yuruá, Río *see* Juruá, Rio
Yury'ev *see* Tartu
Yushu *126 D4* *var.* Gyêgu. Qinghai, C China
Yuty *64 D3* Caazapá, S Paraguay
Yuzhno-Sakhalinsk *115 H4* *Jap.* Toyohara; *prev.* Vladimirovka. Ostrov Sakhalin, Sakhalinskaya Oblast', SE Russian Federation
Yuzhnyy Bug *see* Pivdennyy Buh
Yuzhou *see* Chongqing
Ýylanly *see* Gurbansoltan Eje

Z

Zaandam *see* Zaanstad
Zaanstad *86 C3* *prev.* Zaandam. Noord-Holland, C Netherlands
Zabaykal'sk *115 F5* Chitinskaya Oblast', S Russian Federation
Zabern *see* Saverne
Zabīd *121 B7* W Yemen
Żabinka *see* Zhabinka
Ząbkowice *see* Ząbkowice Śląskie
Ząbkowice Śląskie *98 B4* *var.* Ząbkowice, *Ger.* Frankenstein, Frankenstein in Schlesien. Dolnośląskie, SW Poland
Zábřeh *99 C5* *Ger.* Hohenstadt. Olomoucký Kraj, E Czech Republic
Zacapa *52 B2* Zacapa, E Guatemala
Zacatecas *50 D3* Zacatecas, C Mexico
Zacatepec *51 E4* Morelos, S Mexico
Zacháro *105 B6* *var.* Zaharo, Zakháro. Dytikí Ellás, S Greece
Zadar *100 A3* *It.* Zara; *anc.* Iader. Zadar, SW Croatia
Zadetkyi Kyun *137 B6* *var.* St.Matthew's Island. *island* Mergui Archipelago, S Myanmar (Burma)
Zafra *92 C4* Extremadura, W Spain
Żagań *98 B4* *var.* Żagan, Żegań, *Ger.* Sagan. Lubuskie, W Poland
Zagazig *72 B1* *var.* Az Zaqāzīq. N Egypt
Zágráb *see* Zagreb
Zagreb *100 B2* *Ger.* Agram, *Hung.* Zágráb. *country capital* (Croatia) Zagreb, N Croatia
Zāgros, Kūhhā-ye *120 C3* *Eng.* Zagros Mountains. *mountain range* W Iran
Zagros Mountains *see* Zāgros, Kūhhā-ye
Zaharo *see* Zacháro
Zāhedān *120 E4* *var.* Zahidan; *prev.* Duzdab. Sīstān va Balūchestān, SE Iran
Zahidan *see* Zāhedān
Zaḩlah *see* Zahlé
Zahlé *118 B4* *var.* Zaḩlah. C Lebanon
Záhony *99 E6* Szabolcs-Szatmár-Bereg, NE Hungary
Zaire *see* Congo (river)
Zaire *see* Congo (Democratic Republic of)
Zaječar *100 E4* Serbia, E Serbia
Zakataly *see* Zaqatala
Zakháro *see* Zacháro
Zakhidnyy Buh/Zakhodni Buh *see* Bug
Zākhō *120 B2* *var.* Zākhū. N Iraq
Zākhū *see* Zākhō
Zakopane *99 D5* Małopolskie, S Poland
Zákynthos *105 A6* *var.* Zákinthos, *It.* Zante. *island* Iónia Nísoi, Greece, C Mediterranean Sea
Zalaegerszeg *99 B7* Zala, W Hungary
Zalău *108 B3* *Ger.* Waltenberg, *Hung.* Zilah; *prev.* *Ger.* Zillenmarkt. Sălaj, NW Romania
Ẕalim *121 B5* Makkah, W Saudi Arabia
Zambesi/Zambeze *see* Zambezi
Zambezi *78 C2* North Western, W Zambia
Zambezi *78 D2* *var.* Zambesi, *Port.* Zambeze. *river* S Africa
Zambia *78 C2* *off.* Republic of Zambia; *prev.* Northern Rhodesia. *country* S Africa

ZAMBIA
Southern Africa

Official name Republic of Zambia
Formation 1964 / 1964
Capital Lusaka
Population 11.7 million / 41 people per sq mile (16 people per sq km) / 45%
Total area 290,584 sq miles (752,614 sq km)
Languages English*, Bemba, Tonga, Nyanja, Lozi, Lala-Bisa, Nsenga
Religions Christian 63%, Traditional beliefs 36%, Muslim and Hindu 1%
Ethnic mix Bemba 34%, Other

ZAMBIA
(continued)

OAfrican 26%, Tonga 16%, Nyanja 14%, Lozi 9%, European 1%
Government Presidential system
Currency Zambian kwacha = 100 ngwee
Literacy rate 68%
Calorie consumption 1927 calories

Zambia, Republic of *see* Zambia
Zamboanga *139 E3* *off.* Zamboanga City. Mindanao, S Philippines
Zamboanga City *see* Zamboanga
Zambrów *98 E3* Łomża, E Poland
Zamora *92 D2* Castilla-León, NW Spain
Zamora de Hidalgo *50 D4* Michoacán de Ocampo, SW Mexico
Zamość *98 E4* *Rus.* Zamoste. Lubelskie, E Poland
Zamoste *see* Zamość
Zancle *see* Messina
Zanda *126 A4* Xizang Zizhiqu, W China
Zanesville *40 D4* Ohio, N USA
Zanjān *120 C2* *var.* Zenjan, Zinjan. Zanjān, NW Iran
Zante *see* Zákynthos
Zanthus *147 C6* Western Australia, S Australia Oceania
Zanzibar *73 D7* Zanzibar, E Tanzania
Zanzibar *73 C7* *Swa.* Unguja. *island* E Tanzania
Zaozhuang *128 D4* Shandong, E China
Zapadna Morava *100 D4* *Ger.* Westliche Morava. *river* C Serbia
Zapadnaya Dvina *110 A4* Tverskaya Oblast', W Russian Federation
Zapadnaya Dvina *see* Western Dvina
Zapadno-Sibirskaya Ravnina *114 C3* *Eng.* West Siberian Plain. *plain* C Russian Federation
Zapadnyy Bug *see* Bug
Zapadnyy Sayan *114 D4* *Eng.* Western Sayans. *mountain range* S Russian Federation
Zapala *65 B5* Neuquén, W Argentina
Zapiola Ridge *67 B6* *undersea feature* SW Atlantic Ocean
Zapolyarnyy *110 C2* Murmanskaya Oblast', NW Russian Federation
Zaporizhzhya *109 F3* *Rus.* Zaporozh'ye; *prev.* Aleksandrovsk. Zaporiz'ka Oblast', SE Ukraine
Zaporozh'ye *see* Zaporizhzhya
Zapotiltic *50 D4* Jalisco, SW Mexico
Zaqatala *117 G2* *Rus.* Zakataly. NW Azerbaijan
Zara *116 D3* Sivas, C Turkey
Zara *see* Zadar
Zarafshan *see* Zarafshon
Zarafshon *122 D2* *Rus.* Zarafshan. Navoiy Viloyati, N Uzbekistan
Zarafshon *see* Zeravshan
Zaragoza *93 F2* *Eng.* Saragossa; *anc.* Caesaraugusta, Salduba. Aragón, NE Spain
Zarand *120 D3* Kermān, C Iran
Zaranj *122 D5* Nīmrūz, SW Afghanistan
Zarasai *106 C4* Utena, E Lithuania
Zárate *64 D4* *prev.* General José F.Uriburu. Buenos Aires, E Argentina
Zarautz *93 E1* *var.* Zarauz. País Vasco, N Spain
Zarauz *see* Zarautz
Zaraza *59 E2* Guárico, N Venezuela
Zarghūn Shahr *123 E4* *var.* Katawaz. Paktīkā, SE Afghanistan
Zaria *75 G4* Kaduna, C Nigeria
Zarós *105 D8* Kríti, Greece, E Mediterranean Sea
Zarqa *see* Az Zarqā'
Żary *98 B4* *Ger.* Sorau, Sorau in der Niederlausitz. Lubuskie, W Poland
Zaunguzskiye Garagumy *see* Üngüz Angyrsyndaky Garagum
Zavertse *see* Zawiercie
Zavet *104 D1* Razgrad, NE Bulgaria
Zavidovići *100 C3* Federacija Bosna I Hercegovina, N Bosnia and Herzegovina
Zawia *see* Az Zāwiyah

Zawiercie *98 D4 Rus.* Zavertse. Śląskie, S Poland
Zawīlah *71 F3 var.* Zuwaylah, *It.* Zueila. C Libya
Zaysan Köl *see* Zaysan, Ozero
Zaysan, Ozero *114 D5 Kaz.* Zaysan Köl. *lake* E Kazakhstan
Zayyq *see* Ural
Zbarazh *108 C2* Ternopil's'ka Oblast', W Ukraine
Zduńska Wola *98 C4* Sieradz, C Poland
Zealand *see* Sjælland
Zeebrugge *87 A5* West-Vlaanderen, NW Belgium
Zeewolde *86 D3* Flevoland, C Netherlands
Zefat *119 B5 var.* Safed, Tsefat, *Ar.* Safad. Northern, N Israel
Żegań *see* Żagań
Zeiden *see* Codlea
Zeist *86 C4* Utrecht, C Netherlands
Zele *87 B5* Oost-Vlaanderen, NW Belgium
Zelenoborskiy *110 B2* Murmanskaya Oblast', NW Russian Federation
Zelenograd *111 B5* Moskovskaya Oblast', W Russian Federation
Zelenogradsk *106 A4 Ger.* Cranz, Kranz. Kaliningradskaya Oblast', W Russian Federation
Zelle *see* Celle
Zel'va *107 B6 Pol.* Zelwa. Hrodzyenskaya Voblasts', W Belarus
Zelwa *see* Zel'va
Zelzate *87 B5 var.* Selzaete. Oost-Vlaanderen, NW Belgium
Žemaičių Aukštumas *106 B4 physical region* W Lithuania
Zemst *87 C5* Vlaams Brabant, C Belgium
Zemun *100 D3* Serbia, N Serbia
Zengg *see* Senj
Zenica *100 C4* Federacija Bosna I Hercegovina, C Bosnia and Herzegovina
Zenta *see* Senta
Zeravshan *123 E3 Taj./Uzb.* Zarafshon. *river* Tajikistan/Uzbekistan
Zevenaar *86 D4* Gelderland, SE Netherlands
Zevenbergen *86 C4* Noord-Brabant, S Netherlands
Zeya *113 E3 river* SE Russian Federation
Zgerzh *see* Zgierz
Zgierz *98 C4 Ger.* Neuhof, *Rus.* Zgerzh. Łódź, C Poland
Zgorzelec *98 B4 Ger.* Görlitz. Dolnośląskie, SW Poland
Zhabinka *107 A6 Pol.* Żabinka, *Rus.* Zhabinka. Brestskaya Voblasts', SW Belarus
Zhambyl *see* Taraz
Zhanaozen *114 A4 Kaz.* Zhangaözen; *prev.* Novyy Uzen'. Mangistau, W Kazakhstan
Zhangaözen *see* Zhanaozen
Zhangaqazaly *see* Ayteke Bi
Zhang-chia-k'ou *see* Zhangjiakou
Zhangdian *see* Zibo
Zhangjiakou *128 C3 var.* Changkiakow, Zhang-chia-k'ou, *Eng.* Kalgan; *prev.* Wanchuan. Hebei, E China
Zhangzhou *128 D6* Fujian, SE China
Zhanjiang *128 C7 var.* Chanchiang, Chan-chiang, *Cant.* Tsamkong, *Fr.* Fort-Bayard. Guangdong, S China
Zhaoqing *128 C6* Guangdong, S China
Zhdanov *see* Mariupol'
Zhe *see* Zhejiang
Zhejiang *128 D5 var.* Che-chiang, Chekiang, Zhe, Zhejiang Sheng. *province* SE China
Zhejiang Sheng *see* Zhejiang
Zheleznodorozhnyy *106 A4* Irkutskaya Oblast', C Russian Federation
Zheleznodorozhnyy *see* Yemva
Zheleznogorsk *111 A5* Kurskaya Oblast', W Russian Federation
Zhëltyye Vody *see* Zhovti Vody
Zhengzhou *128 C4 var.* Ch'eng-chou, Chengchow; *prev.* Chenghsien. *province capital* Henan, C China
Zhezkazgan *114 C4 Kaz.* Zhezqazghan; *prev.* Dzhezkazgan. Karaganda, C Kazakhstan
Zhezqazghan *see* Zhezkazgan
Zhidachov *see* Zhydachiv
Zhitkovichi *see* Zhytkavichy
Zhitomir *see* Zhytomyr
Zhlobin *107 D7* Homyel'skaya Voblasts', SE Belarus
Zhmerinka *see* Zhmerynka
Zhmerynka *108 D2 Rus.* Zhmerinka. Vinnyts'ka Oblast', C Ukraine
Zhodino *see* Zhodzina
Zhodzina *107 D6 Rus.* Zhodino. Minskaya Voblasts', C Belarus
Zholkev/Zholkva *see* Zhovkva
Zholsaly *see* Dzhusaly
Zhonghua Renmin Gongheguo *see* China
Zhovkva *108 B2 Pol.* Zółkiew, *Rus.* Zholkev, Zholkva; *prev.* Nesterov. L'vivs'ka Oblast', NW Ukraine
Zhovti Vody *109 F3 Rus.* Zhëltyye Vody. Dnipropetrovs'ka Oblast', E Ukraine
Zhovtneve *109 E4 Rus.* Zhovtnevoye. Mykolayivs'ka Oblast', S Ukraine
Zhovtnevoye *see* Zhovtneve
Zhydachiv *108 B2 Pol.* Żydaczów, *Rus.* Zhidachov. L'vivs'ka Oblast', NW Ukraine
Zhytkavichy *107 C7 Rus.* Zhitkovichi. Homyel'skaya Voblasts', SE Belarus
Zhytomyr *108 D2 Rus.* Zhitomir. Zhytomyrs'ka Oblast', NW Ukraine
Zibo *128 D4 var.* Zhangdian. Shandong, E China
Zichenau *see* Ciechanów
Zielona Góra *98 B4 Ger.* Grünberg, Grünberg in Schlesien, Grüneberg. Lubuskie, W Poland
Zierikzee *86 B4* Zeeland, SW Netherlands
Zigong *128 B5 var.* Tzekung. Sichuan, C China
Ziguinchor *74 B3* SW Senegal
Zilah *see* Zalău
Žilina *99 C5 Ger.* Sillein, *Hung.* Zsolna. Zlínský Kraj, N Slovakia
Zillenmarkt *see* Zalău
Zimbabwe *78 D3 off.* Republic of Zimbabwe; *prev.* Rhodesia. *country* S Africa

ZIMBABWE
Southern Africa

Official name Republic of Zimbabwe
Formation 1980 / 1980
Capital Harare
Population 13 million / 87 people per sq mile (34 people per sq km) / 35%
Total area 150,803 sq miles (390,580 sq km)
Languages English*, Shona, isiNdebele
Religions Syncretic (Christian/traditional beliefs) 50%, Christian 25%, Traditional beliefs 24%, Other (including Muslim) 1%
Ethnic mix Shona 71%, Ndebele 16%, Other African 11%, White 1%, Asian 1%
Government Presidential system
Currency Zimbabwe dollar = 100 cents
Literacy rate 90%
Calorie consumption 1943 calories

Zimbabwe, Republic of *see* Zimbabwe
Zimnicea *108 C5* Teleorman, S Romania
Zimovniki *111 B7* Rostovskaya Oblast', SW Russian Federation
Zinder *75 G3* Zinder, S Niger
Zinov'yevsk *see* Kirovohrad
Zintenhof *see* Sindi
Zipaquirá *58 B3* Cundinamarca, C Colombia
Zittau *94 D4* Sachsen, E Germany
Zlatni Pyasŭtsi *104 E2* Dobrich, NE Bulgaria
Zlín *99 C5 prev.* Gottwaldov. Zlínský Kraj, E Czech Republic
Złoczów *see* Zolochiv
Złotów *98 C3* Wielkopolskie, C Poland
Znamenka *see* Znam"yanka
Znam"yanka *109 F3 Rus.* Znamenka. Kirovohrads'ka Oblast', C Ukraine
Żnin *98 C3* Kujawsko-pomorskie, C Poland
Zoetermeer *86 C4* Zuid-Holland, W Netherlands
Zółkiew *see* Zhovkva
Zolochev *see* Zolochiv
Zolochiv *109 G2 Rus.* Zolochev. Kharkivs'ka Oblast', E Ukraine
Zolochiv *108 C2 Pol.* Złoczów, *Rus.* Zolochev. L'vivs'ka Oblast', W Ukraine
Zolote *109 H3 Rus.* Zolotoye. Luhans'ka Oblast', E Ukraine
Zolotonosha *109 E2* Cherkas'ka Oblast', C Ukraine
Zolotoye *see* Zolote
Zólyom *see* Zvolen
Zomba *79 E2* Southern, S Malawi
Zombor *see* Sombor
Zongo *77 C5* Equateur, N Dem. Rep. Congo
Zonguldak *116 C2* Zonguldak, NW Turkey
Zonhoven *87 D6* Limburg, NE Belgium
Żory *99 C5 var.* Zory, *Ger.* Sohrau. Śląskie, S Poland
Zouar *76 C2* Borkou-Ennedi-Tibesti, N Chad
Zouérat *74 C2 var.* Zouérate, Zouîrât. Tiris Zemmour, N Mauritania
Zouérate *see* Zouérat
Zouîrât *see* Zouérat
Zrenjanin *100 D3 prev.* Petrovgrad, Veliki Bečkerek, *Ger.* Grossbetschkerek, *Hung.* Nagybecskerek. Vojvodina, N Serbia
Zsil/Zsily *see* Jiu
Zsolna *see* Žilina
Zsombolya *see* Jimbolia
Zsupanya *see* Županja
Zubov Seamount *67 D5 undersea feature* E Atlantic Ocean
Zueila *see* Zawīlah
Zug *95 B7 Fr.* Zoug. Zug, C Switzerland
Zugspitze *95 C7 mountain* S Germany
Zuid-Beveland *87 B5 var.* South Beveland. *island* SW Netherlands
Zuider Zee *see* IJsselmeer
Zuidhorn *86 E1* Groningen, NE Netherlands
Zuidlaren *86 E2* Drenthe, NE Netherlands
Zula *72 C4* E Eritrea
Züllichau *see* Sulechów
Zumbo *see* Vila do Zumbo
Zundert *87 C5* Noord-Brabant, S Netherlands
Zunyi *128 B5* Guizhou, S China
Županja *100 C3 Hung.* Zsupanya. Vukovar-Srijem, E Croatia
Zürich *95 B7 Eng./Fr.* Zurich, *It.* Zurigo. Zürich, N Switzerland
Zurich, Lake *see* Zürichsee
Zürichsee *95 B7 Eng.* Lake Zurich. *lake* NE Switzerland
Zurigo *see* Zürich
Zutphen *86 D3* Gelderland, E Netherlands
Zuwārah *71 F2* NW Libya
Zuwaylah *see* Zawīlah
Zuyevka *111 D5* Kirovskaya Oblast', NW Russian Federation
Zvenigorodka *see* Zvenyhorodka
Zvenyhorodka *109 E2 Rus.* Zvenigorodka. Cherkas'ka Oblast', C Ukraine
Zvishavane *78 D3 prev.* Shabani. Matabeleland South, S Zimbabwe
Zvolen *99 C6 Ger.* Altsohl, *Hung.* Zólyom. Banskobystrický Kraj, C Slovakia
Zvornik *100 C4* E Bosnia and Herzegovina
Zwedru *74 D5 var.* Tchien. E Liberia
Zwettl *95 E6* Wien, NE Austria
Zwevegem *87 A6* West-Vlaanderen, W Belgium
Zwickau *95 C5* Sachsen, E Germany
Zwolle *86 D3* Overijssel, E Netherlands
Żydaczów *see* Zhydachiv
Zyôetu *see* Jōetsu
Żyrardów *98 D3* Mazowieckie, C Poland
Zyryanovsk *114 D5* Vostochnyy Kazakhstan, E Kazakhstan